South University Library
Richmond Campus
2151 Old Brick Road
Glen Allen, Va 23060

JUN 1 2 2017

A Select Library of the Christian Church

NICENE AND POST-NICENE FATHERS

VOLUME 9

CHRYSOSTOM: ON THE PRIESTHOOD, ASCETIC TREATISES, SELECT HOMILIES AND LETTERS, HOMILIES ON THE STATUES

FIRST SERIES

Edited by

PHILIP SCHAFF, D.D., LL.D.

The Church Fathers—Nicene and Post-Nicene Fathers
First Series
Philip Schaff, D.D., LL.D., editor

Hendrickson Publishers Marketing, LLC
P. O. Box 3473
Peabody, Massachusetts 01961-3473

Volume 9 of 14 volumes
ISBN for set: 978-1-56563-094-9

This is a reprint edition of the American Edition of the *Nicene and Post-Nicene Fathers, First Series, Volume 9, Chrysostom: On the Priesthood, Ascetic Treatises, Select Homilies and Letters, Homilies on the Statues*, originally published in the United States by the Christian Literature Publishing Company, 1889.

Volume 10 of the *Ante-Nicene Fathers, Bibliography and General Index*, contains a newly prepared *Annotated Index of Authors and Works of the Ante-Nicene, Nicene, and Post-Nicene Fathers, First and Second Series* ©1994 Hendrickson Publishers, Inc. All rights reserved. No part of this work may be used or reproduced in any manner without written permission of the publisher.

Printed in the United States of America

Fifth printing—January 2012

PREFACE.

WITH this volume, we begin the Works of St. Chrysostom. It contains a sketch of his life and labors, the book on the priesthood, the letters to Theodore, the catechetical instructions, and a selection of ascetic treatises, special homilies, letters to Olympias and Innocent, and the twenty-one Homilies on the Statues.

The translations are entirely new, or thoroughly revised, by the Rev. W. R. W. Stephens, whose services I was so fortunate as to secure. He has written the best biography of St. Chrysostom and is thoroughly at home in his writings. He has taken great pains, with the aid of two friends, the Rev. T. P. Brandram and Rev. R. Blackburn, and is responsible for the whole volume, with the exception of the Prolegomena, which I wrote myself, to correspond with the Prolegomena to the works of St. Augustin.

The other volumes of St. Chrysostom in this series will be devoted to his exegetical Homilies on the greater part of the New Testament.

PHILIP SCHAFF.

NEW YORK, March, 1889.

CONTENTS.

	PAGE
PROLEGOMENA BY THE GENERAL EDITOR	3–23
INTRODUCTION TO THE TREATISE ON THE PRIESTHOOD.	27–29
By the REV. W. R. W. STEPHENS, M.A., Prebendary of Chichester and Rector of Woolbeding, Sussex.	
SIX BOOKS ON THE PRIESTHOOD	33–83
Translated with notes by the REV. W. R. W. STEPHENS, assisted by the REV. T. P. BRANDRAM, M.A., Rector of Rumboldswhyke, Chichester.	
TWO LETTERS TO THEODORE AFTER HIS FALL	87–116
Translated with introduction and notes by REV. W. R. W. STEPHENS.	
LETTER TO A YOUNG WIDOW.	119–128
Translated with introduction and notes by the REV. W. R. W. STEPHENS.	
TWO HOMILIES. (I.) ON ST. BABYLAS: (II.) ON ST. IGNATIUS . . .	131–143
Introduction by the REV. W. R. W. STEPHENS; translation and notes by REV. T. P. BRANDRAM.	
HOMILY CONCERNING "LOWLINESS OF MIND"	147–155
Translated with notes by the REV. R. BLACKBURN, M.A., Rector of Selham, Sussex, late Fellow of Brasenose College, Oxford.	
TWO INSTRUCTIONS TO CANDIDATES FOR BAPTISM	159–171
Translation and notes by REV. T. P. BRANDRAM.	
THREE HOMILIES. (I.) THAT DEMONS DO NOT GOVERN THE WORLD: (II. and III.) CONCERNING THE POWER OF THE TEMPTER . . .	177–197
Introduction by REV. W. R. W. STEPHENS; translation and notes by REV. T. P. BRANDRAM.	
THREE HOMILIES. (I.) AGAINST MARCIONISTS AND MANICHÆANS, ON THE PASSAGE "FATHER, IF IT BE POSSIBLE," ETC.: (II.) ON THE PARALYTIC LET DOWN THROUGH THE ROOF: (III.) TO THOSE WHO HAD NOT ATTENDED THE ASSEMBLY; ON THE PASSAGE, "IF THINE ENEMY HUNGER FEED HIM"	201–232
Translated with notes by REV. W. R. W. STEPHENS.	

CONTENTS.

	PAGE
HOMILY AGAINST PUBLISHING THE ERRORS OF THE BRETHREN	235–242
Translated with notes by REV. R. BLACKBURN, M.A.	
TWO HOMILIES ON EUTROPIUS	245–265
Translated with introduction and notes by REV. W. R. W. STEPHENS.	
TREATISE TO PROVE THAT NO ONE CAN HARM THE MAN WHO DOES NOT INJURE HIMSELF	269–284
Translated with introduction and notes by REV. W. R. W. STEPHENS.	
FOUR LETTERS TO OLYMPIAS AND ONE TO PRESBYTERS AT ANTIOCH	287–304
Translated with introduction and notes by REV. W. R. W. STEPHENS.	
CORRESPONDENCE OF INNOCENT, BISHOP OF ROME, WITH ST. CHRYSOSTOM AND THE CHURCH OF CONSTANTINOPLE	307–314
Translated with introduction and notes by REV. W. R. W. STEPHENS.	
TWENTY-ONE HOMILIES ON THE STATUES.	317–489
Translation adopted from "Oxford Library of the Fathers," carefully revised with introduction and notes by REV. W. R. W. STEPHENS.	

CONTENTS OF PROLEGOMENA.

	PAGE
CHAPTER I.—LITERATURE	3
CHAPTER II.—CHRYSOSTOM'S YOUTH AND TRAINING, A.D. 347–370	5
CHAPTER III.—HIS CONVERSION AND ASCETIC LIFE, A.D. 370–374	6
CHAPTER IV.—HE EVADES ELECTION TO A BISHOPRIC, AND WRITES HIS WORK ON THE PRIESTHOOD	7
CHAPTER V.—CHRYSOSTOM AS A MONK, A.D. 374–381	9
CHAPTER VI.—CHRYSOSTOM AS DEACON, PRIEST AND PREACHER AT ANTIOCH, A.D. 381–398	10
CHAPTER VII.—CHRYSOSTOM AS PATRIARCH OF CONSTANTINOPLE, A.D. 398–403	12
CHAPTER VIII.—CHRYSOSTOM AND THEOPHILUS. HIS FIRST DEPOSITION AND BANISHMENT	13
CHAPTER IX.—CHRYSOSTOM AND EUDOXIA. HIS SECOND BANISHMENT, A.D. 403	14
CHAPTER X.—CHRYSOSTOM IN EXILE. HIS DEATH, A.D. 404–407	15
CHAPTER XI.—HIS CHARACTER	16
CHAPTER XII.—HIS WRITINGS	17
CHAPTER XIII.—HIS THEOLOGY AND EXEGESIS	18
CHAPTER XIV.—CHRYSOSTOM AS A PREACHER	22

PROLEGOMENA.

THE LIFE AND WORK OF

ST. JOHN CHRYSOSTOM.

BY PHILIP SCHAFF.

CHAPTER I.—*Literature.*

1. EDITIONS OF CHRYSOSTOM'S WORKS.

S. JOANNIS CHRYSOSTOMI, *archiepiscopi Constantinopolitani, Opera omnia quæ exstant vel quæ ejus nomine circumferuntur, ad MSS. codices Gallicos, Vaticanos, Anglicos, Germanicosque castigata, etc. Opera et studio D.* BERNARDI DE MONTFAUCON, *monachi ordinis S. Benedicti e congregatione S. Mauri, opem ferentibus aliis ex eodem sodalitio, monachis.* Greek and Latin, Paris, 1718–'38, in 13 vols., fol. This is the best edition, and the result of about twenty years of the patient labor of Montfaucon (d. Dec. 21, 1741, 86 years old), and several assistants of the brotherhood of St. Maur. More than three hundred MSS. were made use of, but the eight principal MSS., as Field has shown, were not very carefully collated. Montfaucon, who at the date of the completion of his edition was 83 years old, prepared valuable prefaces to every treatise and set of homilies, arranged the works in chronological order, and added in vol. XIII. learned dissertations on the life, doctrine, discipline and heresies of the age of Chrysostom.

The Benedictine edition was reprinted at Venice, 1734–'41, in 13 vols. fol.; at Paris, ed. by F. DE SINNER (GAUME), 1834–'39, in 13 vols. (an elegant edition, with some additions); and, with various improvements and corrections, by J. P. MIGNE, Petit-Montrouge, 1859–'63, in 13 vols. The last is the most complete edition, but inferior in paper and type to that of Gaume. Migne uses the critical text of Field in Matthew and the Pauline Epp. He had previously edited a Latin Version, 1842, in 9 vols.

The edition of Sir HENRY SAVILE (Provost of Eton), Etonæ, 1612, in 8 vols. fol., is less complete than the Benedictine edition, but gives a more correct Greek text (as was shown by F. Dübner from a collation of manuscripts) and valuable notes. Savile personally examined the libraries of Europe and spent £8,000 on his edition. His wife was so jealous of his devotion to Chrysostom that she threatened to burn his manuscripts.

The edition of FRONTON LE DUC, a French Jesuit, and the two brothers, FREDERICK and CLAUDE MOREL, was published at Paris, 1636, in 12 vols. fol., Greek and Latin.

A selection of Chrysostom's works (*Opera præstantissima*) in Greek and Latin, was edited by T. G. LOMLER, Rudolphopoli (Rudolstadt), 1840 (unfinished).

The best edition of the *Greek* text of the *Homilies* on *Matthew*, and all the *Pauline Epistles* is by Dr. FREDERICK FIELD, of the Church of England (d. 1883), in the "*Bibliotheca Patrum Ecclesiæ Orientalis qui ante Orientis et Occidentis schisma floruerunt.*" The Homilies on Matthew appeared at Cambridge, 1839, 3 vols.; the Homilies on the Epistles of Paul and the Hebrews, Oxford, 1839–'62, in 7 vols.

The treatise *De Sacerdotio* (περὶ ἱερωσύνης) was separately edited by ERASMUS in Greek (Basel, 1525, from the press of Frobenius), by J. HUGHES, in Greek and Latin (Cambridge, 1710), and by J. A. BENGEL, the commentator, in Greek (Stuttgart, 1725, and repeatedly reprinted since at Leipzig, 1825, 1834, 1872, by C. Tauchnitz). LOMLER (*Chrys. Opera*, pp. viii. and ix.) enumerates twenty-three separate editions and translations of the treatise on the Priesthood.

II. TRANSLATIONS.—(*a*) GERMAN TRANSLATIONS.

The treatise on the Priesthood has been translated by HASSELBACH, 1820; RITTER, 1821, and others. The *Bibliothek der Kirchenväter* (Rom. Cath.), published at Kempten in Bavaria, devotes ten small volumes to St. Chrysostom, including the *Priesthood*, ascetic *Treatises*, and *Homilies*, translated by JOH. CHRYSOSTOMUS MITTERRUTZNER, 1869–'84. German translations of selected *Homilies* by J. A. CRAMER (Leipzig, 1748–'51, 10 vols.); FEDER (Augsburg, 1786); PH. MAYER (Nürnberg, 1830); W. ARNOLDI (Trier, 1835); AUGUSTI (*Predigten der Kirchenväter*, vols. I. and II., Leipzig, 1839); Jos. LUTZ (Tübingen, 2d ed. 1859); GUST. LEONHARDI (Leipzig, 1888, selected sermons and orations, in vol I. of *Klassikerbibliothek der Christl. Predigtliteratur*).

(*b*) ENGLISH TRANSLATIONS.

The work on the *Priesthood* was translated by HOLLIER (London, 1728); BUNCE (London, 1759); HOHLER (Cambridge, 1837); MARSH (London, 1844); HARRIS COWPER (London, 1866); and STEPHENS (N. York, 1888, prepared for this "Library").

The *Homilies on the Statues* and on the *New Testament* were translated by several scholars for the "Oxford Library of the Fathers," 1839–'77, 16 vols. The earlier parts (on the First Epistle to the Corinthians, and on the Statues) are based on the text of Montfaucon and Savile, the later parts on the improved text of Field. The Oxford translation has been revised and annotated by American scholars for this "Library," and new translations of other works of St. Chrysostom have been added, namely, the treatise on the Priesthood, the Exhortation to the fallen Theodore, Letters, Tracts, and Special Homilies (in this first volume).

III. BIOGRAPHIES AND ESSAYS.

PALLADIUS (a friend of Chrysostom and bishop of Helenopolis in Bithynia, author of the *Historia Lausiaca;* according to others a different person): *Dialogus historicus de vita et conversatione beati Joannis Chrysostomi cum Theodoro ecclesiæ Romanæ diacono* (in the Bened. edition of the *Opera*, tom. xiii. pp. 1–89; in MIGNE's ed., tom. i., Pars prior, 5–84, in Greek and Latin). HIERONYMUS: *De viris illustribus*, c. 129 (a very brief notice, mentioning only the work *De Sacerdotio*). SOCRATES: *Hist. Eccl.* VI., 3–21. SOZOMEN: *Hist. Eccl.* VIII. 2–23. THEODORET: *Hist. Eccl.* V. 27–36. B. DE MONTFAUCON: *Vita Joannis Chrysost.* (in his edition of the *Opera*, tom. xiii. 91–178; in MIGNE, I.I. 84–264): *Testimonia Veterum de S. Joann. Chrys. scriptis, ibid.* tom. xiii. 256–292. TILLEMONT: *Mémoires*, vol. XI. pp. 1–405, 547–626 (exceedingly minute and accurate from the works of Chrys.). F. STILTING: *Acta Sanctorum*, Sept. 14 (the day of Chrysostom's death), tom. iv. pp. 401–709; comp. STILTING'S *Compendium chronologicum gestorum et scriptorum S. Joh. Chrys.*, in MIGNE, tom. i. 264–272. ALBAN BUTLER: *Lives of Saints*, sub. Jan. 27 (the day of the translation of the remains of Chrys.). W. CAVE: *Lives of the Fathers*, vol. III. p. 237 sqq. J. A. FABRICIUS: *Biblioth Gr.*, tom. viii. 454 sqq. SCHRÖCKH: *Kirchengeschichte*, vol. X. p. 309 sqq. GIBBON: *Decline and Fall*, ch. xxxii. (a brilliant and appreciative sketch). NEANDER: *Der heilige Chrysostomus*, 1821–'22, in 3 vols., second ed. 1832, third ed. Berlin, 1848, in 2 vols. (English translation of the same by J. C. STAPLETON, vol. I., London, 1838, unfinished). The best monograph in the German language. Neander represents Chrysostom as a type of the Johannean tendency among the Fathers, as distinct from Augustin, the strongest type of the Pauline tendency. He gives a full account of the opinions and religious life of Chrysostom, but without a clear picture of his personality. (HASE says: "*Neander hat uns das Lebensbild des Chrys. aufgestellt als ein Herzensverwandter, doch nicht ohne einige Abschwächung seiner Kraft und seines Gegensatzes zur Regierung.*" *K. Gesch.* I. 511.) J. PETTERSSON: *Chrys. homileta*, Lund, 1833. C. DATT: *S. Jean Chrys. comme prédicateur*, Strassb., 1837. A. F. VILLEMAIN: *Tableau de l'éloquence chrétienne au quatrième siècle*, Paris, 1849, new ed. 1857. PERTHES: *Life of Chrysostom*, Boston, 1854. P. ALBERT: *St. Jean Chrysostome considéré comme orateur populaire*, Paris, 1858. Abbé E. MARTIN: *Saint Jean Chrysostome, ses œuvres et son siècle*, Montpellier and Paris, 1861, 3 vols. Abbé ROCHET: *Histoire de S. Jean Chrysostome*, Paris, 1866, 2 vols. AMÉDÉE THIERRY: *St. Chrysostome et l'imperatrice Eudoxie*, 2d ed., Paris, 1874 (originally in the "*Revue des deux Mondes*"). BÖHRINGER: *Johann Chrysostomus und Olympias*, in "*Kirchengesch. in Biogr.*," vol. IX. new ed. 1876. TH. FÖRSTER: *Chrysostomus in seinem Verhältniss zur Antiochenischen Schule*, Gotha, 1869. W. MAGGILORY: *John of the Golden Mouth*, Lond. 1871. W. R. W. STEPHENS: *St. John Chrysostom, his Life and Times*, London, 1872, 2d ed. 1880, 3rd ed. 1883 (the best biography of Chr.). R. W. BUSH, *Life and Times of Chrysostom*, London, Rel. Tract Soc., 1885.

Canon E. VENABLES: in "*Smith and Wace*," I. 518–535 (a very good sketch). C. BURK: in *Herzog*, 2d ed.,

III. 225–231. E. Dandiran: in Lightenberger's "*Encyclopédie*," etc., III. 165–176. Schaff: *Church Hist.* III. 702 sqq., 933 sqq., 1036 sq. Hase: *Kirchengesch.* (*Vorlesungen*, 1885), I. 510 sqq. F. W. Farrar: *Lives of the Fathers*, London, 1889. Vol. II. 460–527.

CHAPTER II.—*Chrysostom's Youth and Training*, A.D. 347–370.

"Almighty God, who hast given us grace at this time with one accord to make our common supplications unto Thee; and doest promise, that when two or three are gathered together in Thy name Thou wilt grant their requests : fulfil now, O Lord, the desires and petitions of Thy servants, as may be most expedient for them ; granting us in this world knowledge of Thy truth, and in the world to come life everlasting, Amen."[1]

This beautiful and comprehensive prayer, which is translated from the Liturgy of St. Chrysostom, has made his name a household word wherever the Anglican Liturgy is known and used.

John, surnamed Chrysostom (Ἰωάννης Χρυσόστομος) is the greatest pulpit orator and commentator of the Greek Church, and still deservedly enjoys the highest honor in the whole Christian world. No one of the Oriental Fathers has left a more spotless reputation; no one is so much read and so often quoted by modern preachers and commentators. An admiring posterity, since the close of the fifth century, has given him the surname Chrysostom (The Golden Mouth), which has entirely superseded his personal name John, and which best expresses the general estimate of his merits.

His life may be divided into five periods: (1) His youth and training till his conversion and baptism, A.D. 347-370. (2) His ascetic and monastic life, 370-381. (3) His public life as priest and preacher at Antioch, 381-398. (4) His episcopate at Constantinople, 398-404. (5) His exile to his death, 404-407.

John (the name by which alone he is known among contemporary writers and his first biographers) was born in 347,[2] at Antioch, the capital of Syria, and the home of the mother church of Gentile Christianity, where the disciples of Jesus were first called "Christians."

His father, Secundus, was a distinguished military officer (*magister militum*) in the imperial army of Syria, and died during the infancy of John, without professing Christianity, as far as we know. His mother, Anthusa, was a rare woman. Left a widow at the age of twenty, she refused all offers of marriage, and devoted herself exclusively to the education of her only son and his older sister. She was probably from principle averse to a second marriage, according to a prevailing view of the Fathers. She shines, with Nonna and Monica, among the most pious mothers of the fourth century, who prove the ennobling influence of Christianity on the character of woman, and through her on all the family relations. Anthusa gained general esteem by her exemplary life. The famous advocate of heathenism, Libanius, on hearing of her consistency and devotion, felt constrained to exclaim: "Bless me! what wonderful women there are among the Christians."[3]

She gave her son an admirable education, and early planted in his soul the germs of piety, which afterwards bore the richest fruits for himself and the church. By her admonitions and the teachings of the Bible, he was secured against the seductions of heathenism.

---

[1] See the Greek original of this collect in Chrysostom's Liturgy, in Migne's edition, Tom. xii. 908; Daniel's *Codex Liturgicus*, tom. iv.; Fasc. II. p. 343 (comp. the foot-note in tom. iii. 358); and Fr. Procter's *History of the Book of Common Prayer* (11th ed. 1874), p. 245 sq. The precise origin of this prayer is uncertain. It does not occur in the oldest MSS. of Chrysostom's Liturgy, but in those of the Liturgy of St. Basil. It precedes the third anthem in the communion service, and was used since the ninth century or earlier in the exarchate of Cæsarea and the patriarchate of Constantinople. In the Oriental churches the prayer is said silently by the priest. See Bjerring, *The Offices of the Oriental Church*, p. 43. In the Anglican Church, it was placed at the end of the Litany (by Cranmer), in 1544, and at the close of the daily Morning and Evening Prayer in 1661. In the English Homilies (*Hom.* I.), Chrysostom is called " that godly clerk and great preacher."

[2] So Montfaucon, Tillemont, Neander, Stephens, Venables, and others. Baur (*Vorlesungen über die Dogmengeschichte*, Bd. I. Abthlg. II., p. 50) and others erroneously state the year 354 or 355, Villemain assigns the year 344 as that of his birth.

[3] Βαβαί, οἷαι παρὰ χριστιανοῖς γυναῖκές εἰσι. Chrysostom himself relates this of his heathen teacher (by whom, undoubtedly, we are to understand Libanius), though, it is true, with immediate reference only to the twenty years' widowhood of his mother, and adds: " Such is the praise and admiration of widowhood not only with us, but even with the heathen." *Ad viduam juniorem* (*Opera*, Bened. ed. Tom. i. 340; in Migne's ed. Tom. i., P. II., 601).

Yet he was not baptized till he had reached the age of maturity. In that age of transition from heathenism to Christianity, the number of adult baptisms far exceeded that of infant baptisms. Hence the large baptisteries for the baptism of crowds of converts; hence the many sermons and lectures of Chrysostom, Cyril of Jerusalem and other preachers to catechumens, and their careful instruction before baptism and admission to the Missa Fidelium or the holy communion. Even Christian parents, as the father and mother of Gregory Nazianzen, the mother of Chrysostom, and the mother of Augustin, put off the baptism of their offspring, partly no doubt from a very high conception of baptism as the sacrament of regeneration, and the superstitious fear that early baptism involved the risk of a forfeiture of baptismal grace. This was the argument which Tertullian in the second century urged against infant baptism, and this was the reason why many professing Christians put off their baptism till the latest hour; just as now so many from the same motive delay repentance and conversion to their death-bed. Chrysostom often rebukes that custom. The Emperor Constantine who favored Christianity as early as 312, and convened the Council of Nicæa in 325, postponed baptism till 337, shortly before his death. The orthodox Emperor Theodosius the Great was not baptized till the first year of his reign (380), when attacked by a serious illness.

Chrysostom received his literary training chiefly from Libanius, the admirer and friend of Julian the Apostate, and the first classical scholar and rhetorician of his age, who after a long career as public teacher at Athens and Constantinople, returned to his native Antioch and had the misfortune to outlive the revival of heathenism under Julian and to lament the triumph of Christianity under his successors. He was introduced by him into a knowledge of the Greek classics and the arts of rhetoric, which served him a good purpose for his future labors in the church. He was his best scholar, and when Libanius, shortly before his death (about 393), was asked whom he wished for his successor, he replied: "John, if only the Christians had not stolen him from us."[1]

After the completion of his studies Chrysostom became a rhetorician, and began the profitable practice of law, which opened to him a brilliant political career. The amount of litigation was enormous. The display of talent in the law-courts was the high-road to the dignities of vice-prefect, prefect, and consul. Some of his speeches at the bar excited admiration and were highly commended by Libanius. For some time, as he says, he was "a never-failing attendant at the courts of law, and passionately fond of the theatre." But he was not satisfied. The temptations of a secular profession in a corrupt state of society discouraged him. To accept a fee for making the worse cause appear the better cause, seemed to him to be taking Satan's wages.

CHAPTER III.—*His Conversion and Ascetic Life.*

The quiet study of the Scriptures, the example of his pious mother, the acquaintance with Bishop Meletius, and the influence of his intimate friend Basil, who was of the same age and devoted to ascetic life, combined to produce a gradual change in his character.[2]

He entered the class of catechumens, and after the usual period of three years of instruction and probation, he was baptized by Meletius in his twenty-third year (369 or 370). From this time on, says Palladius, "he neither swore, nor defamed any one, nor spoke falsely, nor cursed, nor even tolerated facetious jokes." His baptism was, as in the case of St. Augustin, the turning point in his life, an entire renunciation of this world and dedication to the service of Christ. The change was radical and permanent.

Meletius, who foresaw the future greatness of the young lawyer, wished to secure him for

---

[1] Sozomen, *Ch. Hist.*, VIII. 2.

[2] Socrates and Kurtz (in the 10th edition of his *Kirchengeschichte*, I. 223), confound this Basil with Basil the Great of Cappadocia, who was eighteen years older than Chrysostom and died in 379. Chrysostom's friend was probably (as Baronius and Montfaucon conjecture) identical with Basil, bishop of Raphanea in Syria, near Antioch, who attended the Council of Constantinople in 381. Comp. Stephens, *l. c.* p. 14; and Venables in *Smith & Wace*, I. 297.

the active service of the church, and ordained him to the subordinate office of lector (anagnostes, reader), about A.D. 370. The lectors had to read the Scripture lessons in the first part of divine service (the "Missa Catechumenorum"), and to call upon the people to pray, but could not preach nor distribute the sacraments.

The first inclination of Chrysostom after baptism was to adopt the monastic life as the safest mode, according to the prevailing notions of the church in that age, to escape the temptations and corruptions of the world, to cultivate holiness and to secure the salvation of the soul. But the earnest entreaties of his mother prevailed on him to delay the gratification of his desire. He relates the scene with dramatic power. She took him to her chamber, and by the bed where she had given him birth, she adjured him with tears not to forsake her. "My son," she said in substance, "my only comfort in the midst of the miseries of this earthly life is to see thee constantly, and to behold in thy features the faithful image of my beloved husband who is no more. This comfort commenced with your infancy before you could speak. I ask only one favor from you: do not make me a widow a second time; wait at least till I die; perhaps I shall soon leave this world. When you have buried me and joined my ashes with those of your father, nothing will then prevent you from retiring into monastic life. But as long as I breathe, support me by your presence, and do not draw down upon you the wrath of God by bringing such evils upon me who have given you no offence."[1]

These tender, simple and impressive words suggest many heart-rending scenes caused by the ascetic enthusiasm for separation from the sacred ties of the family. It is honorable to Chrysostom that he yielded to the reasonable wishes of his devoted mother. He remained at home, but turned his home into a monastery. He secluded himself from the world and practised a rigid asceticism. He ate little and seldom, and only the plainest food, slept on the bare floor and frequently rose to prayer. He kept almost unbroken silence to prevent a relapse into the habit of slander.

His former associates at the bar called him unsociable and morose. But two of his fellow-pupils under Libanius joined him in his ascetic life, Maximus (afterwards bishop of Seleucia), and Theodore of Mopsuestia. They studied the Scriptures under the direction of Diodorus (afterwards bishop of Tarsus), the founder of the Antiochian school of theology, of which Chrysostom and Theodore became the chief ornaments.[2]

Theodore was warmly attached to a young lady named Hermione, and resolved to marry and to leave the ascetic brotherhood. This gave rise to the earliest treatise of Chrysostom—namely, an exhortation to Theodore, in two letters.[3] He plied all his oratorical arts of sad sympathy, tender entreaty, bitter reproach, and terrible warning, to reclaim his friend to what he thought the surest and safest way to heaven. To sin, he says, is human, but to persist in sin is devilish; to fall is not ruinous to the soul, but to remain on the ground is. The appeal had its desired effect; Theodore resumed his monastic life and became afterwards bishop of Mopsuestia in Cilicia and one of the first biblical scholars. The arguments which Chrysostom used, would condemn all who broke their monastic vows. They retain moral force only if we substitute apostasy from faith for apostasy from monasticism, which must be regarded as a temporary and abnormal or exceptional form of Christian life.

CHAPTER IV.—*Chrysostom evades Election to a Bishopric, and writes his Work on the Priesthood.*

About this time several bishoprics were vacant in Syria, and frequent depositions took

---
[1] *De Sacerd.* I. 5.
[2] Socrates and Sozomenus represent Diodor and Karterius as abbots under whom Chrysostom lived as monk, but NEANDER (in the 3d ed. I. 29) thinks it more likely that Chrysostom was previously instructed by Diodor at Antioch.
[3] *Parænesis ad Theodorum Lapsum*, in MIGNE's ed. I., Pars I. 277-319. The second letter is milder than the first, and was written earlier. It is somewhat doubtful whether the first refers to the same case. NEANDER (I. 38 sq.) conjectures that the second only is addressed to Theodore.

place with the changing fortunes of orthodoxy and Arianism, and the interference of the court. The attention of the clergy and the people turned to Chrysostom and his friend Basil as suitable candidates for the episcopal office, although they had not the canonical age of thirty. Chrysostom shrunk from the responsibilities and avoided an election by a pious fraud. He apparently assented to an agreement with Basil that both should either accept, or resist the burden of the episcopate, but instead of that he concealed himself and put forward his friend whom he accounted much more worthy of the honor. Basil, under the impression that Chrysostom had already been consecrated, reluctantly submitted to the election. When he discovered the cheat, he upbraided his friend with the breach of compact, but Chrysostom laughed and rejoiced at the success of his plot. This conduct, which every sound Christian conscience must condemn, caused no offense among the Christians of that age, still less among the heathen, and was regarded as good management or "economy." The moral character of the deception was supposed to depend altogether on the motive, which made it good or bad. Chrysostom appealed in justification of laudable deception to the stratagems of war, the conduct of physicians in dealing with refractory patients, to several examples of the Old Testament (Abraham, Jacob, David), and to the conduct of the Apostle Paul in circumcising Timothy for the sake of the Jews (Acts xvi. 3) and in observing the ceremonial law in Jerusalem at the advice of James (Acts xxi. 26).

The Jesuitical maxim, "the end justifies the means," is much older than Jesuitism, and runs through the whole apocryphal, pseudo-prophetic, pseudo-apostolic, pseudo-Clementine and pseudo-Isidorian literature of the early centuries. Several of the best Fathers show a surprising want of a strict sense of veracity. They introduce a sort of cheat even into their strange theory of redemption, by supposing that the Devil caused the crucifixion under the delusion that Christ was a mere man, and thus lost his claim upon the fallen race. Origen, Chrysostom, and Jerome explain the offense of the collision between Paul and Peter at Antioch (Gal. ii. 11 sqq.) away by turning it into a theatrical and hypocritical farce, which was shrewdly arranged by the two apostles for the purpose of convincing the Jewish Christians that circumcision was not necessary. Against such wretched exegesis the superior moral sense of Augustin rightly protested, and Jerome changed his view on this particular passage. Here is a point where the modern standard of ethics is far superior to that of the Fathers, and more fully accords with the spirit of the New Testament, which inculcates the strictest veracity as a fundamental virtue.[1]

The escape from the episcopate was the occasion for one of the best and most popular works of Chrysostom, the Six Books *On the Priesthood*, which he wrote probably before his ordination (between 375 and 381), or during his diaconate (between 381 and 386). It is composed in the form of a Platonic dialogue between Chrysostom and Basil. He first vindicates by argument and examples his well-meant but untruthful conduct towards his friend, and the advantages of timely fraud; and then describes with youthful fervor and eloquence the importance, duties and trials of the Christian ministry, without distinguishing between the priestly and the episcopal office. He elevates it above all other offices. He requires wholesouled consecration to Christ and love to his flock. He points to the Scriptures (quoting also from the Apocrypha) as the great weapon of the minister. He assumes, as may be expected, the then prevailing conception of a real priesthood and sacrifice, baptismal regeneration, the corporal presence, the virtue of absolution, prayers for the dead, but is silent about pope and councils, the orders of the clergy, prayers to saints, forms of prayer, priestly vestments, incense, crosses and other doctrines and ceremonies of the Greek and Roman churches.

---

[1] Comp. on the patristic views of accommodation, NEANDER, *Geschichte der Christl. Ethik.*, p. 156 sqq.; and WUTTKE, *Christl. Sittenlehre*, 3d ed. vol. II., 325 sq. Canon VENABLES of Lincoln (in *Smith & Wace*, I. 519 sq.) justly condemns Chrysostom's conduct on this occasion " as utterly at variance with the principles of truth and honor."

He holds up St. Paul as a model for imitation. The sole object of the preacher must be to please God rather than men (Gal. i. 10). "He must not indeed despise approving demonstrations, but as little must he court them, nor trouble himself when they are withheld." He should combine the qualities of dignity and humility, authority and sociability, impartiality and courtesy, independence and lowliness, strength and gentleness, and keep a single eye to the glory of Christ and the welfare of the church.

This book is the most useful or at least the best known among the works of Chrysostom, and is well calculated to inspire a profound sense of the tremendous responsibilities of the ministry. But it has serious defects, besides the objectionable justification of pious fraud, and cannot satisfy the demands of an evangelical minister. In all that pertains to the proper care of souls it is inferior to the "Reformed Pastor" of Richard Baxter.

CHAPTER V.—*Chrysostom as a Monk.* A.D. 374-381.

After the death of his mother, Chrysostom fled from the seductions and tumults of city life to the monastic solitude of the mountains south of Antioch, and there spent six happy years in theological study and sacred meditation and prayer. Monasticism was to him (as to many other great teachers of the church, and even to Luther) a profitable school of spiritual experience and self-government. He embraced this mode of life as "the true philosophy" from the purest motives, and brought into it intellect and cultivation enough to make the seclusion available for moral and spiritual growth.[1]

He gives us a lively description of the bright side of this monastic life. The monks lived in separate cells or huts ($καλύβαι$), but according to a common rule and under the authority of an abbot. They wore coarse garments of camel's hair or goat's hair over their linen tunics. They rose before sunrise, and began the day by singing a hymn of praise and common prayer under the leadership of the abbot. Then they went to their allotted task, some to read, others to write, others to manual labor for the support of the poor. Four hours in each day were devoted to prayer and singing. Their only food was bread and water, except in case of sickness. They slept on straw couches, free from care and anxiety. There was no need of bolts and bars. They held all things in common, and the words of "mine and thine," which cause innumerable strifes in the world, were unknown among the brethren. If one died, he caused no lamentation, but thanksgiving, and was carried to the grave amidst hymns of praise; for he was not dead, but "perfected," and permitted to behold the face of Christ. For them to live was Christ, and to die was gain.

Chrysostom was an admirer of active and useful monasticism, and warns against the dangers of idle contemplation. He shows that the words of our Lord, "One thing is needful;" "Take no anxious thought for the morrow;" "Labor not for the meat that perisheth," do not inculcate total abstinence from work, but only undue anxiety about worldly things, and must be harmonized with the apostolic exhortation to labor and to do good. He defends monastic seclusion on account of the prevailing immorality in the cities, which made it almost impossible to cultivate there a higher Christian life.

In this period, from 374 to 381, Chrysostom composed his earliest writings in praise of monasticism and celibacy.[2] The letters "to the fallen Theodore," have already been mentioned. The three books against the Opponents of Monasticism were occasioned by a decree of the Arian Emperor Valens in 373, which aimed at the destruction of that system and compelled the monks to discharge their duties to the state by military or civil service. Chrysostom regarded this decree as a sacrilege, and the worst kind of persecution.

---

[1] On the origin and character of early monasticism, see SCHAFF, *Ch. Hist.* vol. III., 147 sqq.
[2] In the first volume, first part, of MIGNE's edition, col. 277-532.

CHAPTER VI.—*Chrysostom as Deacon, Priest and Preacher at Antioch.* A.D. 381-398.

By excessive self-mortifications John undermined his health, and returned to Antioch. There he was immediately ordained deacon by Meletius in 380 or 381, and a few years afterwards presbyter by Flavian (386).

As deacon he had the best opportunity to become acquainted with the practical needs of the population, the care of the poor and the sick. After his ordination to the priesthood he preached in the presence of the bishop his first sermon to a vast crowd. It abounds in flowery Asiatic eloquence, in humble confession of his own unworthiness, and exaggerated praise of Meletius and Flavian.[1]

He now entered upon a large field of usefulness, the real work of his life. The pulpit was his throne, and he adorned it as much as any preacher of ancient or modern times.

Antioch was one of the great capitals of the Roman empire along with Alexandria, Constantinople, and Rome. Nature and art combined to make it a delightful residence, though it was often visited by inundations and earthquakes. An abundance of pure water from the river Orontes, a large lake and the surrounding hills, fertile plains, the commerce of the sea, imposing buildings of Asiatic, Greek, and Roman architecture, rich gardens, baths, and colonnaded streets, were among its chief attractions. A broad street of four miles, built by Antiochus Epiphanes, traversed the city from east to west; the spacious colonnades on either side were paved with red granite. Innumerable lanterns illuminated the main thoroughfares at night. The city was supplied with good schools and several churches; the greatest of them, in which Chrysostom preached, was begun by the Emperor Constantine and finished by Constantius. The inhabitants were Syrians, Greeks, Jews, and Romans. The Asiatic element prevailed. The whole population amounted, as Chrysostom states, to 200,000, of whom one half were nominally Christians. Heathenism was therefore still powerful as to numbers, but as a religion it had lost all vitality. This was shown by the failure of the attempt of the Emperor Julian the Apostate to revive the sacrifices to the gods. When he endeavored in 362 to restore the oracle of Apollo Daphneus in the famous cypress grove at Antioch and arranged for a magnificent procession, with libation, dances, and incense, he found in the temple one solitary old priest, and this priest ominously offered in sacrifice—a goose! Julian himself relates this ludicrous farce, and vents his anger at the Antiochians for squandering the rich incomes of the temple upon Christianity and worldly amusements.

Chrysostom gives us in his sermons lively pictures of the character of the people and the condition of the church. The prevailing vices even among Christians were avarice, luxury, sensuality, and excessive love of the circus and the theatre. "So great," he says, "is the depravity of the times, that if a stranger were to compare the precepts of the gospel with the actual practice of society, he would infer that men were not the disciples, but the enemies of Christ." Gibbon thus describes the morals of Antioch:[2] "The warmth of the climate disposed the natives to the most intemperate enjoyment of tranquility and opulence, and the lively licentiousness of the Greeks was blended with the hereditary softness of the Syrians. Fashion was the only law, pleasure the only pursuit, and the splendor of dress and furniture was the only distinction of the citizens of Antioch. The arts of luxury were honored, the serious and manly virtues were the subject of ridicule, and the contempt for female modesty and reverent age announced the universal corruption of the capital of the East. The love of spectacles was the taste, or rather passion of the Syrians; the most skilful artists were procured from the adjacent cities. A considerable share of the revenue was devoted to the public amusements, and the magnificence of the games of the theatre and circus was considered as the happiness and as the glory of Antioch."

---

[1] MIGNE, III. 693 sqq.   [2] *Decline and Fall*, ch. xxiv.

The church of Antioch was rent for eighty-five years (330-415) by heresy and schism. There were three parties and as many rival bishops. The Meletians, under the lead of Meletius, were the party of moderate orthodoxy holding the Nicene Creed; the Arians, headed by Eudoxius, and supported by the Emperor Valens, denied the eternal divinity of Christ; the Eustathians, under the venerated priest Paulinus, were in communion with Athanasius, but were accused of Sabellianism, which maintained the Divine unity and strict deity of Christ and the Holy Spirit, but denied the tri-personality except in the form of three modes of self-revelation. Pope Damasus declared for Paulinus and condemned Meletius as a heretic. Alexandria likewise sided against him. Meletius was more than once banished from his see, and recalled. He died during the sessions of the Council of Constantinople, 381, over which he presided for a while. His remains were carried with great solemnities to Antioch and buried by the side of Babylas the Martyr. Chrysostom reconciled Flavian, the successor of Meletius, with Alexandria and Rome in 398. Alexander, the successor of Flavian, led the Eustathians back into the orthodox church in 415, and thus unity was restored.

Chrysostom preached Sunday after Sunday and during Lent, sometimes twice or oftener during the week, even five days in succession, on the duties and responsibilities of Christians, and fearlessly attacked the immorality of the city. He declaimed with special severity against the theatre and the chariot-races; and yet many of his hearers would run from his sermons to the circus to witness those exciting spectacles with the same eagerness as Jews and Gentiles. He exemplified his preaching by a blameless life, and soon acquired great reputation and won the love of the whole congregation. Whenever he preached the church was crowded. He had to warn his hearers against pickpockets, who found an inviting harvest in these dense audiences.

A serious disturbance which took place during his career at Antioch, called forth a remarkable effort of his oratorical powers. The populace of the city, provoked by excessive taxes, rose in revolt against the Emperor Theodosius the Great, broke down his statues and those of his deceased excellent wife Flacilla (d. 385) and his son Arcadius, dragged the fragments through the streets, and committed other acts of violence. The Emperor threatened to destroy the whole city. This caused general consternation and agony, but the city was saved by the intercession of Bishop Flavian, who in his old age proceeded to Constantinople and secured free pardon from the Emperor. Although a man of violent temper, Theodosius had profound reverence for bishops, and on another occasion he submitted to the rebuke of St. Ambrose for the wholesale massacre of the Thessalonians (390).

In this period of public anxiety, which lasted several months, Chrysostom delivered a series of extempore orations, in which he comforted the people and exhorted them to correct their vices. These are his twenty-one *Homilies on the Statues*, so-called from the overthrow of the imperial statues which gave rise to them. They were preached during Lent 387.[1] In the same year St. Augustin submitted to baptism at the hands of St. Ambrose in Milan. One of the results of those sermons was the conversion of a large number of heathens. Thus the calamity was turned into a blessing to the church.

During the sixteen or seventeen years of his labors in Antioch Chrysostom wrote the greater part of his Homilies and Commentaries; a consolatory Epistle to the despondent Stagirius; the excellent book on the martyr Babylas, which illustrates by a striking example the divine power of Christianity; a treatise on Virginity, which he puts above marriage; and an admonition to a young widow on the glory of widowhood, and the duty of continuing in it.

---

[1] Montfaucon goes with tedious minuteness into the chronology of these sermons. The twentieth was delivered ten days before Easter, the twenty-first on Easter, after the return of Flavian from Rome with the Emperor's pardon. The first sermon was preached shortly before the sedition and has nothing to do with it, but is alluded to in the second. It is a temperance sermon, based on Paul's advice to Timothy, 1 Tim. v. 23, where he emphasizes the word "*little*" and the "often *infirmities*."

He disapproved of second marriage, not as sinful or illegal, but as inconsistent with an ideal conception of marriage and a high order of piety.[1]

CHAPTER VII.—*Chrysostom as Patriarch of Constantinople.* A.D. 398-404.

After the death of Nectarius (successor to Gregory Nazianzen), towards the end of the year 397, Chrysostom was chosen, entirely without his own agency and even against his remonstrance, archbishop of Constantinople. He was hurried away from Antioch by a military escort, to avoid a commotion in the congregation and to make resistance useless. He was consecrated Feb. 26, 398, by his enemy Theophilus, patriarch of Alexandria, who reluctantly yielded to the command of the Emperor Arcadius or rather his prime minister, the eunuch Eutropius, and nursed his revenge for a more convenient season.

Constantinople, built by Constantine the Great in 330, on the site of Byzantium, assumed as the Eastern capital of the Roman empire the first position among the episcopal sees of the East, and became the centre of court theology, court intrigues, and theological controversies. The second œcumenical council, which was held there in 381, under Theodosius the Great, the last Roman emperor worthy of the name (d. 395), decided the victory of Nicene orthodoxy over the Arian heresy, and gave the bishop of Constantinople a primacy of honor, next in rank to the bishop of old Rome—a position which was afterwards confirmed by the Council of Chalcedon in 451, but disputed by Pope Leo and his successors.

Chrysostom soon gained by his eloquent sermons the admiration of the people, of the weak Emperor Arcadius, and, at first, even of his wife Eudoxia, with whom he afterwards waged a deadly war. He extended his pastoral care to the Goths who were becoming numerous in Constantinople, had a part of the Bible translated for them, often preached to them himself through an interpreter, and sent missionaries to the Gothic and Scythian tribes on the Danube. He continued to direct by correspondence those missionary operations even during his exile. For a short time he enjoyed the height of power and popularity.

But he also made enemies by his denunciations of the vices and follies of the clergy and aristocracy. He emptied the episcopal palace of its costly plate and furniture and sold it for the benefit of the poor and the hospitals. He introduced his strict ascetic habits and reduced the luxurious household of his predecessors to the strictest simplicity. He devoted his large income to benevolence. He refused invitations to banquets, gave no dinner parties, and ate the simplest fare in his solitary chamber.[2] He denounced unsparingly luxurious habits in eating and dressing, and enjoined upon the rich the duty of almsgiving to an extent that tended to increase rather than diminish the number of beggars who swarmed in the streets and around the churches and public baths. He disciplined the vicious clergy and opposed the perilous and immoral habit of unmarried priests of living under the same roof with "spiritual sisters" (συνείσακται). This habit dated from an earlier age, and was a reaction against celibacy. Cyprian had raised his protest against it, and the Council of Nicæa forbade unmarried priests to live with any females except close relations. Chrysostom's unpopularity was increased by his irritability and obstinacy, and his subservience to a proud and violent archdeacon, Serapion. The Empress Eudoxia was jealous of his influence over Arcadius and angry at his uncompromising severity against sin and vice. She became the chief instrument of his downfall.

The occasion was furnished by an unauthorized use of his episcopal power beyond the lines of his diocese, which was confined to the city. At the request of the clergy of Ephesus and the neighboring bishops, he visited that city in January, 401, held a synod and deposed six bishops convicted of shameful simony. During his absence of several months he left the

---

[1] NEANDER (vol. I.) gives large extracts from these ascetic treatises with many judicious and discriminating observations.

[2] SOCRATES (VI. 5) says that some justified this habit by his delicate stomach and weak digestion, others attributed it to his rigid abstinence. His enemies construed it as pride, and based upon it a serious accusation.

episcopate of Constantinople in the hands of Severian, bishop of Gabala, an unworthy and adroit flatterer, who basely betrayed his trust and formed a cabal headed by the empress and her licentious court ladies, for the ruin of Chrysostom. On his return he used unguarded language in the pulpit, and spoke on Elijah's relation to Jezebel in such a manner that Eudoxia understood it as a personal insult. The clergy were anxious to get rid of a bishop who was too severe for their lax morals.

CHAPTER VIII.—*Chrysostom and Theophilus. His first Deposition and Banishment.*

At this time Chrysostom became involved in the Origenistic controversies which are among the most violent and most useless in ancient church history, and full of personal invective and calumny.[1] The object in dispute was the orthodoxy of the great Origen, which long after his death was violently defended and as violently assailed.

Theophilus of Alexandria, an able and vigorous but domineering, contentious and unscrupulous prelate, was at first an admirer of Origen, but afterwards in consequence of a personal quarrel joined the opponents, condemned his memory and banished the Origenistic monks from Egypt. Some fifty of them, including the four "Tall Brethren," so-called on account of their extraordinary stature, fled to Constantinople and were hospitably received by Chrysostom (401). He had no sympathy with the philosophical speculations of Origen, but appreciated his great merits, and felt that injustice was done to the persecuted monks. He interceded in their behalf with Theophilus, who replied with indignant remonstrance against protecting heretics and interfering in another diocese.

Theophilus, long desirous of overthrowing Chrysostom, whom he had reluctantly consecrated, set every instrument in motion to take revenge. He sent the octogenarian bishop Epiphanius of Salamis, a well-meaning and learned but bigoted zealot for orthodoxy, to Constantinople, as a tool of his hierarchical plans (402); but Epiphanius soon returned and died on the ship (403). Theophilus now traveled himself to Constantinople, accompanied by a body-guard of rough sailors and provided with splendid presents. He appeared at once as accuser and judge, aided by Eudoxia and the disaffected clergy. He held a secret council of thirty-six bishops, all of them Egyptians except seven, in a suburb of Chalcedon on the Asiatic side of the Bosphorus, and procured in this so-called synod at the Oak, the deposition and banishment of Chrysostom, on false charges of immorality and high treason (403). Among the twenty-nine charges were these: that Chrysostom had called the saintly Epiphanius a fool and a demon, that he abused the clergy, that he received females without witnesses, that he ate sumptuously alone and bathed alone, that he had compared the empress to Jezebel.

The innocent bishop refused to appear before a packed synod of his enemies, and appealed to a general council. As the sentence of banishment for life became known, the indignation of the people was immense. A single word from him would have raised an insurrection; but he surrendered himself freely to the imperial officers, who conveyed him in the dark to the harbor and put him on board a ship destined for Hieron at the mouth of the Pontus. Theophilus entered the city in triumph and took vengeance on Chrysostom's friends.

The people besieged the palace and demanded the restoration of their bishop. Constantinople was almost in a state of insurrection. The following night the city was convulsed by an earthquake, which was felt with peculiar violence in the bedroom of Eudoxia and frightened her into submission. She implored the emperor to avert the wrath of God by recalling Chrysostom. Messengers were despatched with abject apologies to bring him back. A whole fleet of barks put forth to greet him, the Bosphorus blazed with torches and resounded with songs of rejoicing. On passing the gates he was borne aloft by the people to the church, seated in the episcopal chair and forced to make an address. His triumph was complete,

---

[1] SCHAFF, *Church History*, III. 698 sqq.

but of short duration. Theophilus felt unsafe in Constantinople and abruptly sailed in the night for Alexandria.

The feelings with which Chrysostom went into his first and second exile, he well describes in a letter to Bishop Cyriacus: "When I was driven from the city, I felt no anxiety, but said to myself: If the empress wishes to banish me, let her do so; 'the earth is the Lord's.' If she wants to have me sawn asunder, I have Isaiah for an example. If she wants me to be drowned in the ocean, I think of Jonah. If I am to be thrown into the fire, the three men in the furnace suffered the same. If cast before wild beasts, I remember Daniel in the lion's den. If she wants me to be stoned, I have before me Stephen, the first martyr. If she demands my head, let her do so; John the Baptist shines before me. Naked I came from my mother's womb, naked shall I leave this world. Paul reminds me, 'If I still pleased men, I would not be the servant of Christ.'"

CHAPTER IX.—*Chrysostom and Eudoxia. His second Banishment*, A.D. 403.

The restored patriarch and the repentant empress seemed reconciled, and vied with one another in extravagant laudations for two months, when the feud broke out afresh and ended in perpetual exile and death.

Eudoxia was a beautiful, imperious, intriguing and revengeful woman, who despised her husband and indulged her passions. Not content with the virtual rule of the Roman empire, she aspired to semi-divine honors, which used to be paid to the heathen Cæsars. A column of porphyry with her silver statue for public adoration was erected in September, 403, on the forum before the church of St. Sophia, and dedicated amid boisterous and licentious revelry, which disturbed the sacred services.

Chrysostom ascended the pulpit on the commemoration day of the martyrdom of John the Baptist, and thundered his righteous indignation against all who shared in these profane amusements, the people, the prefect, and the haughty woman on the throne. In the heat of his zeal the imprudent words are said to have escaped his lips: "Again Herodias is raging, again she is dancing, again she demands the head of John on a platter."[1] The comparison of Eudoxia with Herodias, and himself (John) with John the Baptist was even more directly personal than his former allusion to the relation of Jezebel and Elijah. Whether he really spoke these or similar words is at least doubtful, but they were reported to Eudoxia, who as a woman and an empress could never forgive such an insult. She demanded from the emperor signal redress. In the conflict of imperial and episcopal authority the former achieved a physical and temporary, the latter a moral and enduring victory.

The enemies of Chrysostom flocked like vultures down to their prey. Theophilus directed the plot from a safe distance. Arcadius was persuaded to issue an order for the removal of Chrysostom. He continued to preach and refused to leave the church over which God had placed him, but had to yield to armed force. He was dragged by imperial guards from the cathedral on the vigil of the resurrection in 404, while the sacrament of baptism was being administered to hundreds of catechumens. "The waters of regeneration," says Palladius, "were stained with blood." The female candidates, half dressed, were driven by licentious soldiers into the dark streets. The eucharistic elements were profaned by pagan hands. The clergy in their priestly robes were ejected and chased through the city. The horrors of that night were long afterwards remembered with a shudder. During the greater part of the Easter week the city was kept in a state of consternation. Private dwellings were invaded, and

---

[1] According to the report of SOCRATES, VI. 18, and SOZOMENUS, VIII. 20. A homily which begins with this exordium: πάλιν Ἡρωδίας μαίνεται, πάλιν ταράσσεται, πάλιν ὀρχεῖται, πάλιν ἐπὶ πίνακι τὴν κεφαλὴν τοῦ Ἰωάννου ζητεῖ λαβεῖν (comp. Mark vi. 25), is unworthy of his pen and rejected as spurious by Tillemont, Savile and Montfaucon. But it is quite probable that Chrysostom made some allusion to Eudoxia which might be construed by his enemies in that way. See NEANDER, II. 177 sq.

suspected Joannites—the partisans of Chrysostom—thrown into prison, scourged and tortured. Chrysostom, who was shut up in his episcopal palace, twice narrowly escaped assassination.

At last on June 5, 404, the timid and long hesitating Arcadius signed the edict of banishment. Chrysostom received it with calm submission, and after a final prayer in the cathedral with some of his faithful bishops, and a tender farewell to his beloved Olympias and her attendant deaconesses, he surrendered himself to the guards and was conveyed at night to the Asiatic shore. He had scarcely left the city, when the cathedral was consumed by fire. The charge of incendiarism was raised against his friends, but neither threats, nor torture and mutilation could elicit a confession of guilt. He refused to acknowledge Arsacius and Atticus as his successors; and this was made a crime punishable with degradation, fine and imprisonment. The clergy who continued faithful to him were deposed and banished. Pope Innocent of Rome was appealed to, pronounced the synod which had condemned Chrysostom irregular, annulled the deposition, and wrote him a letter of sympathy, and urged upon Arcadius the convocation of a general council, but without effect.

CHAPTER X.—*Chrysostom in Exile. His Death.* A.D. 404-407.

Chrysostom was conveyed under the scorching heat of July and August over Galatia and Cappadocia, to the lonely mountain village Cucusus, on the borders of Cilicia and Armenia, which the wrath of Eudoxia had selected for his exile. The climate was inclement and variable, the winter severe, the place was exposed to Isaurian brigands. He suffered much from fever and headache, and was more than once brought to the brink of the grave. Nevertheless the bracing mountain air invigorated his feeble constitution, and he was hopeful of returning to his diocese. He was kindly treated by the bishop of Cucusus. He received visits, letters and presents from faithful friends, and by his correspondence exerted a wider influence from that solitude than from the episcopal throne.

His 242 extant letters are nearly all from the three years of his exile, and breathe a noble Christian spirit, in a clear, brilliant and persuasive style. They exhibit his faithful care for all the interests of the church and look calmly and hopefully to the glories of heaven. They are addressed to Eastern and Western bishops, presbyters, deacons, deaconesses, monks and missionaries; they describe the fatigues of his journey, give advice on a variety of subjects, strengthen and comfort his distant flock, urge the destruction of heathen temples in Phœnicia, the extirpation of heresy in Cyprus, and encourage the missions in Persia and Scythia.[1] Two letters are addressed to the Roman bishop Innocent I., whose sympathy and assistance he courted. Seventeen letters—the most important of all—are addressed to Olympias, the deaconess, a widow of noble birth, personal beauty and high accomplishments, who devoted her fortune and time to the poor and the sick. She died between 408 and 420. To her he revealed his inner life, upon her virtues he lavished extravagant praise, which offends modern taste as fulsome flattery. For her consolation he wrote a special treatise on the theme that "No one is really injured except by himself."[2]

The cruel empress, stung by disappointment at the continued power of the banished bishop, forbade all correspondence and ordered his transfer by two brutal guards, first to Arabissus, then to Pityus on the Caucasus, the most inhospitable spots in the empire.

The journey of three months on foot was a slow martyrdom to the feeble and sickly old man. He did not reach his destination, but ended his pilgrimage five or six miles from Comana in Pontus in the chapel of the martyr Basiliscus on the 14th of September, 407, in his sixtieth year, the tenth of his episcopate. Clothed in his white baptismal robes, he partook of the

---

[1] See Tom. iii. of the Bened. ed. (in Migne, III. 529 sqq.)

[2] Comp. on Olympias the *Mémoirs* of TILLEMONT, XI. 416-440; STEPHENS, *l. c.*, 280, 367-373; and VENABLES in *Smith & Wace*, IV. 73-75. The letters to Olympias and Innocent are also published in LOMLER's selection (pp. 165-252).

eucharist and commended his soul to God. His last words were his accustomed doxology, the motto of his life: "Glory be to God for all things, Amen."[1]

He was buried by the side of Basiliscus in the presence of monks and nuns.

He was revered as a saint by the people. Thirty-one years afterwards, January 27, 438, his body was translated with great pomp to Constantinople and deposited with the emperors and patriarchs beneath the altar of the church of the Holy Apostles. The young Emperor Theodosius II. and his sister Pulcheria met the procession at Chalcedon, kneeled down before the coffin, and in the name of their guilty parents implored the forgiveness of heaven for the grievous injustice done to the greatest and saintliest man that ever graced the pulpit and episcopal chair of Constantinople. The Eastern church of that age shrunk from the bold speculations of Origen, but revered the narrow orthodoxy of Epiphanius and the ascetic piety of Chrysostom.

The personal appearance of the golden-mouthed orator was not imposing, but dignified and winning. He was of small stature (like David, Paul, Athanasius, Melanchthon, John Wesley, Schleiermacher). He had an emaciated frame, a large, bald head, a lofty, wrinkled forehead, deep-set, bright, piercing eyes, pallid, hollow cheeks, and a short, gray beard.[2]

CHAPTER XI.—*His Character.*

Chrysostom was one of those rare men who combine greatness and goodness, genius and piety, and continue to exercise by their writings and example a happy influence upon the Christian church. He was a man for his time and for all times. But we must look at the spirit rather than the form of his piety, which bore the stamp of his age.

He took Paul for his model, but had a good deal of the practical spirit of James, and of the fervor and loveliness of John. The Scriptures were his daily food, and he again and again recommended their study to laymen as well as ministers. He was not an ecclesiastical statesman, like St. Ambrose, not a profound divine like St. Augustin, but a pure man, a practical Christian, and a king of preachers. "He carried out in his own life," says Hase, "as far as mortal man can do it, the ideal of the priesthood which he once described in youthful enthusiasm." He considered it the duty of every Christian to promote the spiritual welfare of his fellowmen. "Nothing can be more chilling," he says in the 20th Homily on Acts, "than the sight of a Christian who makes no effort to save others. Neither poverty, nor humble station, nor bodily infirmity can exempt men and women from the obligation of this great duty. To hide our light under pretense of weakness is as great an insult to God as if we were to say that He could not make His sun to shine."

It is very much to his praise that in an age of narrow orthodoxy and doctrinal intolerance he cherished a catholic and irenical spirit. He by no means disregarded the value of theological soundness, and was in hearty agreement with the Nicene creed, which triumphed over the Arians during his ministry in Antioch; he even refused a church in Constantinople which the Arian Goths claimed. But he took no share in the persecution of heretics, and even sheltered the Origenistic monks against the violence of Theophilus of Alexandria. He hated sin more than error, and placed charity above orthodoxy.

Like all the Nicene Fathers, he was an enthusiast for ascetic and monastic virtue, which shows itself in seclusion rather than in transformation of the world and the natural ordinances of God. He retained as priest and bishop his cloister habits of simplicity, abstemiousness and unworldliness. He presents the most favorable aspect of that mode of life, which must be regarded as a wholesome reaction against the hopeless corruption of pagan society. He

---

[1] Δόξα τῷ θεῷ πάντων ἕνεκεν.
[2] See the frontispiece in the edition of FRONTO DUCÆUS, and in the monograph of STEPHENS.

thought with St. Paul that he could best serve the Lord in single life, and no one can deny that he was unreservedly devoted to the cause of religion.[1]

He was not a man of affairs, and knew little of the world. He had the harmlessness of the dove without the wisdom of the serpent. He knew human nature better than individual men. In this respect he resembles Neander, his best biographer. Besides, he was irritable of temper, suspicious of his enemies, and easily deceived and misled by such men as Serapion. He showed these defects in his quarrel with the court and the aristocracy of Constantinople. With a little more worldly wisdom and less ascetic severity he might perhaps have conciliated and converted those whom he repelled by his pulpit fulminations. Fearless denunciation of immorality and vice in high places always commands admiration and respect, especially in a bishop and court preacher who is exposed to the temptations of flattery. But it is unwise to introduce personalities into the pulpit and does more harm than good. His relation to Eudoxia reminds one of the attitude of John Knox to Mary Stuart. The contrast between the pure and holy zeal of the preacher and the reformer and the ambition and vanity of a woman on the throne is very striking and must be judged by higher rules than those of gallantry and courtesy. But after all, the conduct of Christ, the purest of the pure, towards Mary Magdalene and the woman taken in adultery is far more sublime.

The conflict of Chrysostom with Eudoxia imparts to his latter life the interest of a romance, and was over-ruled for his benefit. In his exile his character shines brighter than even in the pulpit of Antioch and Constantinople. His character was perfected by suffering. The gentleness, meekness, patience, endurance and devotion to his friends and his work which he showed during the last three years of his life are the crowning glory of his career. Though he did not die a violent death, he deserves to be numbered among the true martyrs, who are ready for any sacrifice to the cause of virtue and piety.

CHAPTER XII.—*The Writings of Chrysostom.*

Chrysostom was the most fruitful author among the Greek Fathers. Suidas makes the extravagant remark that only the omniscient God could recount all his writings. The best have been preserved and have already been noticed in chronological order. They may be divided into five classes: (1) Moral and ascetic treatises, including the work on the Priesthood; (2) About six hundred Homilies and Commentaries; (3) Occasional, festal and panegyrical orations; (4) Letters; (5) Liturgy.

His most important and permanently useful works are his Homilies and Commentaries, which fill eleven of the thirteen folio volumes of the Benedictine edition. They go together; his homilies are expository, and his commentaries are homiletical and practical. Continuous expositions, according to chapter and verse, he wrote only on the first eight chapters of Isaiah, and on the Epistle to the Galatians. All others are arranged in sermons with a moral application at the close. Suidas and Cassiodorus state that he wrote commentaries on the whole Bible. We have from him Homilies on Genesis, the Psalms, the Gospel of Matthew, the Gospel of John, the Acts, the Pauline Epistles including the Hebrews, which he considered Pauline. Besides, he delivered discourses on separate texts of Scripture, on church festivals, eulogies on apostles and martyrs, sermons against the Pagans, against the Jews and Judaizing Christians, against the Arians, and the famous twenty-one orations on the Statues.

He published some of his sermons himself, but most of them were taken down by short-

---

[1] Luther's intense aversion to monkery, although he himself passed through its discipline, must be taken into account in his unfavorable judgments of Chrysostom, Jerome and other Fathers except St. Augustin, whom he esteemed very highly. Of Chrysostom he must have read very little, or he could not have called him a "rhetorician full of words and empty of matter." He spoke well, however, of Theodoret's commentaries on the Pauline Epistles, which is an indirect testimony in favor of Chrysostom's exegesis. See SCHAFF, *Church Hist.* vol. VI. 536.

hand writers.[1] Written sermons were the exceptions in those days. The preacher usually was seated, the people were standing.

Of the letters of Chrysostom we have already spoken.

The Liturgy of Chrysostom so-called is an abridgment and improvement of the Liturgy of St. Basil (d. 379), and both are descended from the Liturgy of James, which they superseded. They have undergone gradual changes. It is impossible to determine the original text, as no two copies precisely agree. Chrysostom frequently refers to different parts of the divine service customary in his day, but there is no evidence that he composed a liturgy, nor is it probable.[2] The Liturgy which bears his name is still used in the orthodox Greek and Russian church on all Sundays, except those during Lent, and on the eve of Epiphany, Easter and Christmas, when the Liturgy of Basil takes its place.

CHAPTER XIII.—*His Theology and Exegesis.*

Chrysostom belonged to the Antiochian school of theology and exegesis, and is its soundest and most popular representative. It was founded by his teacher Diodor of Tarsus (d. 393), developed by himself and his fellow-student Theodore of Mopsuestia (d. 429), and followed by Theodoret and the Syrian and Nestorian divines. Theodore was the exegete, Chrysostom the homilist, Theodoret the annotator. The school was afterwards condemned for its alleged connection with the Nestorian heresy; but that connection was accidental, not necessary. Chrysostom's mind was not given to dogmatizing, and too well balanced to run into heresy.

The Antiochian school agreed with the Alexandrian school founded by Origen, in maintaining the divine inspiration and authority of the Scriptures, but differed from it in the method of interpretation, and in a sharper distinction between the Old and the New Testaments, and the divine and human elements in the same.

To Origen belongs the great merit of having opened the path of biblical science and criticism, but he gave the widest scope to the allegorizing and mystical method by which the Bible may be made to say anything that is pious and edifying.[3] Philo of Alexandria had used that method for introducing the Platonic philosophy into the Mosaic writings. Origen was likewise a Platonist, but his chief object was to remove all that was offensive in the literal sense. The allegorical method is imposition rather than exposition. Christ sanctions parabolic teaching and typical, but not allegorical, interpretation. Paul uses it once or twice, but only incidentally, when arguing from the rabbinical standpoint.

The Antiochian school seeks to explain the obvious grammatical and historical sense, which is rich enough for all purposes of instruction and edification. It takes out of the Word what is actually in it, instead of putting into it all sorts of foreign notions and fancies.

Chrysostom recognizes allegorizing in theory, but seldom uses it in practice, and then more by way of rhetorical ornament and in deference to custom. He was generally guided by sound common sense and practical wisdom. He was more free from arbitrary and absurd interpretations than almost any other patristic commentator. He pays proper attention to the connection, and puts himself into the psychological state and historical situation of the writer. In one word, he comes very near to what we now call the grammatico-historical exegesis. This is the only solid and sound foundation for any legitimate use of the Scriptures. The sacred writers had one definite object in view; they wished to convey one particular sense by the ordinary use of language, and to be clearly understood by their readers. At the

---

[1] ὀξυγράφοι, SOCRATES, VI. 5. The term occurs also in the Septuagint (Ps. xlv. 2) and in Philo. The Byzantine writers use the verb ὀξυγραφέω, *to write fast*, and the noun ὀξυγραφία, *the art of writing fast*.

[2] The liturgical references in Chrysostom's works are carefully collected by BINGHAM, in Bk. XV. of his *Antiquities*. Comp. STEPHENS, p. 419 sqq.

[3] Allegorical interpretation makes the writer say something else than what he meant, ἄλλο μὲν ἀγορεύει, ἄλλο δὲ νοεῖ.

same time the truths of revelation are so deep and so rich that they can be indefinitely expanded and applied to all circumstances and conditions. Interpretation is one thing, application is another thing. Chrysostom knew as well as any allegorist how to derive spiritual nourishment from the Scriptures and to make them "profitable for teaching, for reproof, for correction, for instruction in righteousness; that the man of God may be complete, thoroughly furnished unto every good work."[1] As to the text of the Greek Testament, he is the chief witness of the Syro-Constantinopolitan recension, which was followed by the later Greek Fathers.[2] He accepts the Syrian canon of the Peshito, which includes the Old Testament with the Apocrypha, but omits from the New Testament the Apocalypse and four Catholic Epistles (2 Peter, 2 and 3 John, and Jude); at least in the *Synopsis Veteris et novi Testamenti* which is found in his works, those five books are wanting, but this does not prove that he did not know them.[3]

The commentaries of Chrysostom are of unequal merit. We must always remember that he is a *homiletical* commentator who aimed at the conversion and edification of his hearers. He makes frequent digressions and neglects to explain the difficulties of important texts. Grammatical remarks are rare, but noteworthy on account of his familiarity with the Greek as his mother tongue, though by no means coming up to the accuracy of a modern expert in philology. In the Old Testament he depended altogether on the Septuagint, being ignorant of Hebrew, and often missed the mark. The Homilies on the Pauline Epistles are considered his best, especially those to the Corinthians, where he had to deal with moral and pastoral questions. The doctrinal topics of Romans and Galatians were less to his taste, and it cannot be said that he entered into the depths of Paul's doctrines of sin and grace, or ascended the height of his conception of freedom in Christ. His Homilies on Romans are argumentative; his continuous notes on Galatians somewhat hasty and superficial. The eighty Homilies on Matthew from his Antiochian period are very valuable. Thomas Aquinas declared he would rather possess them than be the master of all Paris. The eighty-eight Homilies on John, also preached at Antioch, but to a select audience early in the morning, are more doctrinal and controversial, being directed against the Anomœans (Arians).[4] We have no commentaries from him on Mark and Luke, nor on the Catholic Epistles and the Apocalypse. The fifty-five homilies on the Acts, delivered at Constantinople between Easter and Whitsuntide, when that book was read in the public lessons, contain much interesting information about the manners and customs of the age, but are the least polished of his productions. Erasmus, who translated them into Latin, doubted their genuineness. His life in Constantinople was too much disturbed to leave him quiet leisure for preparation. The Homilies on the Hebrews, likewise preached in Constantinople, were published after his death from notes of his friend, the presbyter Constantine, and the text is in a confused state.

The Homilies of Chrysostom were a rich storehouse for the Greek commentators, compilers and epitomizers, such as Theodoret, Oecumenius, Theophylact, and Euthymius Zigabenus, and they are worth consulting to this day for their exegetical as well as their practical value.

The theology of Chrysostom must be gathered chiefly from his commentaries. He differs from the metaphysical divines of the Nicene age by his predominantly practical ten-

---

[1] On the school of Antioch, see SCHAFF, *Church Hist.* II. 816-818 ; III. 612, 707, 937; NEANDER, *Chrysost.* I. 35 sqq.; FÖRSTER, *Chrysostomus in seinem Verhältniss zur Antioch. Schule* (1869); REUSS, *Geschichte des N. T.*, 6th ed. (1887), secs. 320, 518, 521; FARRAR, *History of Interpretation* (1886), pp. 210 sqq., 220 sqq. Reuss pays this tribute to Chrysostom (p. 593): "The Christian people of ancient times never enjoyed richer instruction out of the Bible than from the golden mouth of a genuine and thoroughly equipped biblical preacher." Farrar calls Chrysostom "the ablest of Christian homilists and one of the best Christian men," and "the bright consummate flower of the school of Antioch."

[2] WESTCOTT & HORT, *Gr. Test.*, II. 141 sqq.; SCHAFF, *Companion to the Greek Test.* (3rd ed.), p. 206.

[3] REUSS, *l. c.* sec. 320 (p. 359); HOLTZMANN, *Einleitung ins N. T.*, ed. II. (1886), p. 171.

[4] So called because they taught that the Son is *unlike* or *dissimilar* (ἀνόμοιος) to the Father and of a *different* substance, in opposition to the Nicene doctrine of *equal* substance (ὁμοουσία), and the semi-Arian doctrine of *like*, or *similar* substance (ὁμοιουσία).

dency, and in this respect he approaches the genius of the Western church. He lived between the great trinitarian and christological controversies and was only involved incidentally in the subordinate Origenistic controversy, in which he showed a charitable and liberal spirit. He accepted the Nicene Creed, but he died before the rise of the Nestorian and Eutychian heresies. Speculation was not his forte, and as a thinker he is behind Athanasius, Gregory of Nyssa, and John of Damascus. He was a rhetorician rather than a logician.

Like all the Greek fathers, he laid great stress on free-will and the co-operation of the human will with divine grace in the work of conversion. Cassian, the founder of Semi-Pelagianism, was his pupil and appealed to his authority. Julian of Eclanum, the ablest opponent of Augustin, quoted Chrysostom against original sin; Augustin tried from several passages to prove the reverse, but could only show that Chrysostom was no Pelagian. We may say that in tendency and spirit he was a catholic Semi-Pelagian or Synergist before Semi-Pelagianism was brought into a system.

His anthropology forms a wholesome contrast and supplement to the anthropology of his younger contemporary, the great bishop of Hippo, the champion of the slavery of the human will and the sovereignty of divine grace.

We look in vain in Chrysostom's writings for the Augustinian and Calvinistic doctrines of absolute predestination, total depravity, hereditary guilt, irresistible grace, perseverance of saints, or for the Lutheran theory of forensic and solifidian justification. He teaches that God foreordained all men to holiness and salvation, and that Christ died for all and is both willing and able to save all, but not against their will and without their free consent. The vessels of mercy were prepared by God unto glory, the vessels of wrath were not intended by God, but fitted by their own sin, for destruction. The will of man, though injured by the Fall, has still the power to accept or to reject the offer of salvation. It must first obey the divine call. "When we have begun," he says, in commenting on John i. 38, "when we have sent our will before, then God gives us abundant opportunities of salvation." God helps those who help themselves. "When God," he says, "sees us eagerly prepare for the contest of virtue, he instantly supplies us with his assistance, lightens our labors and strengthens the weakness of our nature." Faith and good works are necessary conditions of justification and salvation, though Christ's merits alone are the efficient cause. He remarks on John vi. 44, that while no man can come to Christ unless drawn and taught by the Father, there is no excuse for those who are unwilling to be thus drawn and taught. Yet on the other hand he fully admits the necessity of divine grace at the very beginning of every good action. "We can do no good thing at all," he says, "except we are aided from above." And in his dying hour he gave glory to God "for all things."

Thus Augustinians and Semi-Pelagians, Calvinists and Arminians, widely as they differ in theory about human freedom and divine sovereignty, meet in the common feeling of personal responsibility and absolute dependence on God. With one voice they disclaim all merit of their own and give all glory to Him who is the giver of every good and perfect gift and works in us "both to will and to work, for his good pleasure" (Phil. ii. 12).[1]

---

[1] I add the remarks of STEPHENS on the difference between Chrysostom and Augustin (p. 430): "Unquestionably as the intellectual genius of Chrysostom was, yet it is rather in the purity of his moral character, his single-minded boldness of purpose, and the glowing piety which burns through all his writings, that we find the secret of his influence. If it was rather the mission of Augustin to mould the minds of men so as to take a firm grasp of certain great doctrines, it was the mission of Chrysostom to inflame the whole heart with a fervent love of God. Rightly has he been called the great teacher of consummate holiness, as Augustin was the great teacher of efficient grace; rightly has it been remarked that, like Fénelon, he is to be ranked among those who may be termed disciples of St. John, men who seem to have been pious without intermission from their childhood upwards, and of whose piety the leading characteristics are ease, cheerfulness and elevation; while Augustin belongs to the disciples of St. Paul, those who have been converted from error to truth, or from sin to holiness, and whose characteristics are gravity, earnestness, depth. If Augustin has done more valuable service in building up the church at large, Chrysostom is the more lovable to the individual, and speaks out of a heart overflowing to God and man, unconstrained by the fetters of a severe and rigid system. Yet it is precisely on this account that he has not been so generally appreciated as he deserves. His tone is too catholic for the Romanist, or for the sectarian partisan of any denomination. 'It would be easy to produce abundant instances of his oratorical abilities; I wish it were in my power to record as

As to the doctrines which separate the Greek, Roman and Protestant churches, Chrysostom faithfully represents the Greek Catholic church prior to the separation from Rome. In addition to the œcumenical doctrines of the Nicene Creed, he expresses strong views on baptismal regeneration, the real presence, and the eucharistic sacrifice, yet without a clearly defined theory, which was the result of later controversies; hence it would be unjust to press his devotional and rhetorical language into the service of transubstantiation, or consubstantiation, or the Roman view of the mass.[1]

His extravagant laudations of saints and martyrs promoted that refined form of idolatry which in the Nicene age began to take the place of the heathen hero-worship. But it is all the more remarkable that he furnishes no support to Mariolatry, which soon after his death triumphed in the Greek as well as the Latin church. He was far from the idea of the sinless perfection and immaculate conception of the Virgin Mary. He attributes her conduct at the wedding of Cana (John ii. 3, 4) to undue haste, a sort of unholy ambition for the premature display of the miraculous power of her Son; and in commenting on Matthew xii. 46–49, he charges her and his brethren with vanity and a carnal mind.[2] He does not use the term *theotokos*, which twenty years after his death gave rise to the Nestorian controversy, and which was endorsed by the third and fourth œcumenical councils.

As to the question of the papacy he considered the bishop of Rome as the successor of Peter, the prince of the Apostles, and appealed to him in his exile against the unjust condemnation of the Council at the Oak. Such appeals furnished the popes with a welcome opportunity to act as judges in the controversies of the Eastern church, and greatly strengthened their claims. But his Epistle to Innocent was addressed also to the bishops of Milan and Aquileia, and falls far short of the language of submission to an infallible authority. He conceded to the pope merely a primacy of honor ($\pi\rho o\sigma\tau\alpha\sigma\iota\alpha$, $\dot{\alpha}\rho\chi\eta$), not a supremacy of jurisdiction. He calls the bishop of Antioch (Ignatius and Flavian) likewise a successor of Peter, who labored there according to the express testimony of Paul. In commenting on Gal. i. 18, he represents Paul as equal in dignity ($\iota\sigma\acute{o}\tau\iota\mu o\varsigma$) to Peter.[3] He was free from jealousy of Rome, but had he lived during the violent controversies between the patriarch of new Rome and the pope of old Rome, it is not doubtful on which side he would have stood.

In one important point Chrysostom approaches the evangelical theology of the Reformation, his devotion to the Holy Scriptures as the only rule of faith. "There is no topic on which he dwells more frequently and earnestly than on the duty of every Christian man and woman to study the Bible; and what he bade others do, that he did pre-eminently him-

---

many of his evangelical excellencies.' Such is the verdict of a narrow-minded historian [Milner], and the comparative estimation in which he held St. Augustin and St. Chrysostom may be inferred from the number of pages in his History given to each: St. Augustin is favored with 187, Chrysostom with 20. But he whose judgment is not cramped by the shackles of some harsh and stiff theory of gospel truth will surely allow that Chrysostom not only preached the gospel, but lived it. To the last moment of his life he exhibited that calm, cheerful faith, that patient resignation under affliction, and untiring perseverance for the good of others, which are pre-eminently the marks of a Christian saint. The cause for which he fought and died in a corrupt age was the cause of Christian holiness."

[1] In his comments on Heb. ix. 26 (Hom. XVII. on Hebrews, in the Bened. ed. XII. 241 sq.; in the Oxford translation, p. 213), he expresses himself on the sacrificial aspect of the eucharist in these words: "Christ is our High Priest, who offered the sacrifice that cleanses us. That sacrifice we offer now also, which was then offered, which cannot be exhausted. This is done in remembrance of what was then done. For, saith He, 'Do this in remembrance of Me.' It is not another sacrifice that we make ($\pi o\iota o\tilde{\upsilon}\mu\epsilon\nu$), as the High Priest of old, but always the same, or rather we perform a remembrance of a sacrifice ($\mu\tilde{\alpha}\lambda\lambda o\nu$ $\delta\grave{\epsilon}$ $\dot{\alpha}\nu\acute{\alpha}\mu\nu\eta\sigma\iota\nu$ $\dot{\epsilon}\rho\gamma\alpha\zeta\acute{o}\mu\epsilon\theta\alpha$ $\vartheta\upsilon\sigma\acute{\iota}\alpha\varsigma$)." The word *remembrance* would favor the Protestant rather than the Roman view, which demands an actual, though unbloody, repetition of the sacrifice of the cross in the mass. Other passages, however, are much stronger, though highly rhetorical, e. g., *De Sacerd*. III. 4: "When you behold the Lord slain, and lying there, and the priest standing over the sacrifice and praying, and all stained with that precious blood, do you then suppose you are among men, and standing upon earth? Are you not immediately transported to Heaven?" In another place he says, "Christ lies slain ($\tau\epsilon\vartheta\upsilon\mu\acute{\epsilon}\nu o\varsigma$) upon the altar." And yet the people were so indifferent that Chrysostom laments: "In vain is the daily sacrifice, in vain stand we at the altar; there is no one to take part" (Third Hom. on Ephesians).

[2] See his 21st Homily on John, and his 44th Homily on Matthew. Comp. STEPHENS, p. 417 sqq.

[3] See his letter to Innocent I. and his comments on Gal. i. and ii. The passages of Chrysostom on Peter and his successors are collected in BERINGTON & KIRK, *The Faith of Catholics*, ed. 3, vol. II. 32–35, 80, but the important passage from his Commentary on Galatians is omitted. See TREAT, *The Catholic Faith* (1888), p. 396.

self."[1] He deemed the reading of the Bible the best means for the promotion of Christian life. A Christian without the knowledge of the Scriptures is to him a workman without tools. Even the sight of the Bible deters from sin, how much more the reading. It purifies and consecrates the soul, it introduces it into the holy of holies and brings it into direct communion with God.[2]

CHAPTER XIV.—*Chrysostom as a Preacher.*

The crowning merit of Chrysostom is his excellency as a preacher. He is generally and justly regarded as the greatest pulpit orator of the Greek church. Nor has he any superior or equal among the Latin Fathers. He remains to this day a model for preachers in large cities.

He was trained in the school of Demosthenes and Libanius, and owed much of his literary culture to the classics. He praises "the polish of Isocrates, the gravity of Demosthenes, the dignity of Thucydides, and the sublimity of Plato." He assigns to Plato the first rank among the philosophers, but he places St. Paul far above him, and glories in the victory of the tent-maker and fishermen over the wisdom of the Greeks.[3]

He was not free from the defects of the degenerate rhetoric of his age, especially a flowery exuberance of style and fulsome extravagance in eulogy of dead martyrs and living men. But the defects are overborne by the virtues: the fulness of Scripture knowledge, the intense earnestness, the fruitfulness of illustration and application, the variation of topics, the command of language, the elegance and rhythmic flow of his Greek style, the dramatic vivacity, the quickness and ingenuity of his turns, and the magnetism of sympathy with his hearers. He knew how to draw in the easiest manner spiritual nourishment and lessons of practical wisdom from the Word of God, and to make it a divine voice of warning and comfort to every hearer. He was a faithful preacher of truth and righteousness and fearlessly told the whole duty of man. If he was too severe at times, he erred on virtue's side. He preached morals rather than dogmas, Christianity rather than theology, active, practical Christianity that proves itself in holy living and dying. He was a martyr of the pulpit, for it was chiefly his faithful preaching that caused his exile. The effect of his oratory was enhanced by the magnetism of his personality, and is weakened to the reader of a translation or even the Greek original. The living voice and glowing manner are far more powerful than the written and printed letter.

Chrysostom attracted large audiences, and among them many who would rather have gone to the theatre than hear any ordinary preacher. He held them spell-bound to the close. Sometimes they manifested their admiration by noisy applause, and when he rebuked them for it, they would applaud his rebuke. "You praise," he would tell them, "what I have said, and receive my exhortation with tumults of applause; but show your approbation by obedience; that is the only praise I seek."

The great mediæval poet assigns to Chrysostom a place in Paradise between Nathan the prophet and Anselm the theologian, probably because, like Nathan, he rebuked the sins of the court, and, like Anselm, he suffered exile for his conviction.[4] The best French pulpit orators—Bossuet, Massilon, Bourdaloue—have taken him for their model, even in his faults, the flattery of living persons. Villemain praises him as the greatest orator who combined all the attributes of eloquence.[5] Hase calls his eloquence "Asiatic, flowery, full of spirit

---

[1] STEPHENS, p. 422.
[2] Comp. the rich extracts from his writings bearing on the Bible, in NEANDER, I. 211-226.
[3] *De Sacerd.*, IV. 6.
[4] *Paradiso*, XII. 136-139:
"*Natan profeta e il metropolitano
Chrisostomo, ed Anselmo, e quel Donato,
Che alla prim' arte degnò poner mano.*"

[5] *Tableau*, etc., p. 154: "*Ce sont ces qualités plus hautes, ou plutot c'est la réunion de tous les attributs oratoires, le naturel, le pathétique et la grandeur, qui' ont fait de saint Jean Chrysostome le plus grande orateur de l'église primitive, le plus éclatant interprète de cette mémorable époque.*"

and of the Holy Spirit, based on sound exegesis, and with steady application to life."[1] English writers compare him to Jeremy Taylor. Gibbon (who confesses, however, to have read very few of his Homilies) attributes to him "the happy art of engaging the passions in the service of virtue, and of exposing the folly as well as the turpitude of vice, almost with the truth and spirit of a dramatic representation." Dean Milman describes him as an "unrivalled master in that rapid and forcible application of incidental occurrences which gives such life and reality to eloquence. He is at times, in the highest sense, dramatic in manner." Stephens thus characterizes his sermons:[2]

"A power of exposition which unfolded in lucid order, passage by passage, the meaning of the book in hand; a rapid transition from clear exposition, or keen logical argument, to fervid exhortation, or pathetic appeal, or indignant denunciation; the versatile ease with which he could lay hold of any little incident of the moment, such as the lighting of the lamps in the church, and use it to illustrate his discourse; the mixture of plain common sense, simple boldness, and tender affection, with which he would strike home to the hearts and consciences of his hearers—all these are not only general characteristics of the man, but are usually to be found manifested more or less in the compass of each discourse. It is this rare union of powers which constitutes his superiority to almost all other Christian preachers with whom he might be, or has been, compared. Savonarola had all, and more than all, his fire and vehemence, but untempered by his sober, calm good sense, and wanting his rational method of interpretation. Chrysostom was eager and impetuous at times in speech as well as in action, but never fanatical. Jeremy Taylor combines, like Chrysostom, real earnestness of purpose with rhetorical forms of expression and florid imagery; but, on the whole, his style is far more artificial, and is overlaid with a multifarious learning, from which Chrysostom's was entirely free. Wesley is almost his match in simple, straightforward, practical exhortation, but does not rise into flights of eloquence like his. The great French preachers, again, resemble him in his more ornate and declamatory vein, but they lack that simpler common-sense style of address which equally distinguished him."

---

[1] "*Seine Beredtsamkeit ist asiatisch, bilderreich, geistvoll und H. Geistes voll, auf gesunder Schriftauslegung, mit steter Anwendung auf's Leben, in seinen Forderungen an Andere sittlich ernst ohne asketische Ueberspannung.*"—*Kirchengeschichte*, I. 511.

[2] *St. Chrysostom*, p. 426 sq.

ST. CHRYSOSTOM:

TREATISE CONCERNING THE CHRISTIAN PRIESTHOOD.

TRANSLATED WITH INTRODUCTION AND NOTES BY

REV. W. R. W. STEPHENS, M.A.,

PREBENDARY OF CHICHESTER CATHEDRAL, AND RECTOR OF WOOLBEDING, SUSSEX.

INTRODUCTION TO THE TREATISE ON THE PRIESTHOOD.

The events recorded in this celebrated treatise on the Priesthood must have occurred when St. John Chrysostom was about twenty-eight years of age. His father had died when he was a young child; his mother was a devout Christian, but had not destined him for the clerical vocation. The great ability which he showed in early youth seemed to mark him out for distinction in one of the learned professions, and at the age of eighteen he began to attend the school of Libanius, the most celebrated sophist of the day, who had won a great reputation as a professor of philosophy and rhetoric, and as an eloquent opponent of Christianity, not only in his native city, Antioch, but also in Athens, Nicomedia, and Constantinople. The artificial character however of his writings indicates the decadence of literary power; he could skillfully imitate the style of ancient writers but he could not inform himself with their spirit; "his productions" says Gibbon [ch. xxiv], "are for the most part the vain and idle composition of an orator who cultivated the science of words."

In the school of Libanius Chrysostom no doubt studied the best classical Greek authors, and although he retained little admiration for them in later life and probably read them but rarely, his tenacious memory enabled him to the last to adorn his homilies with quotations from Homer, Plato and the Tragedians. In the school of Libanius also he began to practise his nascent power of eloquence, and a speech which he made in honor of the Emperors is highly commended in an extant letter of his master. Thus the Pagan sophist helped to forge the weapons which were destined to be turned against his own cause. When he was on his death-bed being asked by his friends who was most worthy to succeed him, "it would have been John" he replied, "if the Christians had not stolen him from us."

In due time Chrysostom began to practise as a lawyer; and as the profession of the law was reckoned one of the surest avenues to political distinction for a man of talent, and the speeches of Chrysostom excited great admiration, a brilliant and prosperous career seemed to lie before him. But the soul of the young advocate had drunk draughts from a purer well-spring than the school of Libanius could supply, and like many other Christians in that age when society, even Christian society, was deeply tainted by Pagan sentiments and habits of life, especially in a profligate city like Antioch, he recoiled from the contrast between the morality of the world in which he lived, and the standard of holiness which was presented in the Gospel. The chicanery and rapacity also prevalent in the profession which he had adopted became especially repugnant to his conscience. And these feelings were strengthened by the influence of his intimate friend Basil who had been a fellow pupil with him at the school of Libanius.

The first book of the treatise on the Priesthood opens with a description of his friendship with Basil; how they studied the same subjects together under the same teachers, and how entirely harmonious they were in all their tastes, and inclinations [ci and ii.] Nevertheless when Basil decided to follow what Chrysostom calls the "true philosophy," by which he means a life of religious seclusion and study, Chrysostom could not immediately make up his mind to follow his example. The balance he says was no longer even between them; the scale of Basil mounted heavenward, while his own was depressed by the weight of earthly interests, and youthful ambitions. For a time he continued to practise in the law courts and to frequent the theatre, and other places of amusement. But gradually the study of Scripture, the longing for renewed intercourse with his friend, and the influence of Meletius the amiable and saintly Bishop of Antioch so wrought upon his mind that he resolved to abandon his secular calling. And in the first place after the usual course of probation he was baptized. It may seem surprising that he had not been baptized in childhood; but a corrupt practice of delaying baptism (which Chrysostom himself often reprobates in his Homilies) was prevalent at that time. It was due in some persons to a notion that sin before Baptism was comparatively venial, in others to a dread of binding themselves or their children to the purity of life which was demanded by the Baptismal vows. In the case of Chrysostom it is possible, I think, that the distracted condition of the church in Antioch may have operated as a reason, perhaps the chief reason for the delay. At the date of his birth (about A.D. 345) and for sixteen years afterwards the See was occupied by Arian Bishops of the most worldly time-serving type. The good Catholic Bishop Meletius was appointed in 361 and it was probably some seven or eight years later that Chrysostom was baptized by him, and ordained to the office of Reader in the Church.

There can be no doubt that Baptism, from whatever cause delayed, must have come home to the recipient at last with all the more solemnity of meaning. It was often a decisive turning point in the life, the beginning of a definite renunciation of the world, and dedication of the whole man to God. To Chrysostom it evidently was this. For a time he became an enthusiastic ascetic; and then settled down into that more tranquil, but intense glow of piety which burned with unabated force to the close of his life. His baptism and the relinquishment of his secular calling are probably alluded to in the following treatise c. 3. where he speaks of "emerging a little from the flood of worldliness" in which he had been involved. His friend Basil who received him with open arms does not seem to have joined any monastic community, but merely to have been living in retirement and practising some of the usual monastic austerities. The two friends now formed a plan for withdrawing together to some quiet retreat, there to support one another in habits of study, meditation, and prayer. c. 4. The execution of the project was delayed for a time l y the passionate entreaties of Chrysostom's mother that he would not deprive her of his companionship and protection. c. 5. He must have been a poor companion however, for we learn (vi. c. 12) that he rarely went outside the house, maintained an almost perpetual silence, and was constantly absorbed in study and prayer. He and Basil in fact formed with a few other friends a voluntary association of youthful ascetics who lived under a strict rule. We might compare it with the association or club formed by John Wesley and his brother at Oxford which first earned for them the nickname of "Methodists." Chrysostom and his friends placed the general regulation of their studies and religious life under Diodorus and Carterius the presidents of the two principal monastic communities in the neighborhood of Antioch. Diodorus was a man of learning and ability, opposed to those mystical and allegorical interpretations of Holy Scripture which often disguised rather than elucidated the real meaning of the sacred text, so that to his training probably we are largely indebted for that clear, sensible practical method of exposition in which Chrysostom so remarkably excels nearly all the ancient fathers of the Church.

Not long after the two friends had adopted this course of life, probably about the year 374, they were agitated by a report that they were likely to be advanced to the Episcopate (c. 6.) By a custom which was then common in the Church they were liable if elected by the clergy and people to be forcibly seized and ordained however unwilling they might be to accept the dignity [see notes to chapters 6 and 7]. Basil entreated his friend that in this crisis of their lives they might act as in former times in concert, and together accept, or evade if possible the expected but unwelcome honor. Chrysostom affected assent to this proposal, but secretly resolved to entrap Basil into the sacred office for which he considered him to be as eminently fitted, as he deemed himself to be unworthy. The Church should not on account of his own feebleness be deprived if he could help it, of the able ministrations of such a man as Basil. Accordingly when some agents of the electing body [as to the composition of this body, see note 3, p. 21] were sent to seize the two young men, Chrysostom contrived to hide himself. His language c. 6. seems to imply that he had some intimation of their coming which he purposely withheld from Basil who consequently was caught. He made at first a violent resistance, but the officials led him to suppose that Chrysostom had already submitted, and under this delusion he acquiesced. When he discovered the trick which had been played upon him he naturally reproached Chrysostom bitterly for his unkind treachery. But the conscience of Chrysostom seems to have been quite at ease throughout the transaction. He regarded it as a pious fraud and when he saw the mingled distress and anger of his friend he could not refrain, he says, from laughing aloud for joy, and thanking God for the success of his stratagem. The remainder of the 1st Book [chs. 8, 9] is occupied by Chrysostom's vindication of his conduct, the principle that deceit for a righteous end is often salutary and justifiable being maintained with an ingenuity and skill which bespeaks a man who had recently practised in the law-courts. His arguments indeed savor somewhat unpleasantly of casuistry, and it must be confessed that in his conduct on this occasion there is a tinge of something like oriental duplicity which is repugnant to our moral sense. On the other hand it must be borne in mind that neither in the East nor in the West, for many ages were "pious frauds" absolutely condemned by the conscience of Christendom; there was always an inclination to judge each case on its own merits, and to condone if not to approve those in which the balance of evidence was in favor of a righteous or holy purpose, and a beneficial result. And it must also be owned, in justice to Chrysostom, that one of the qualities most conspicuous in him throughout the whole of his subsequent career is fearless, straightforward honesty alike in act and in speech; and this under the pressure very often of strong temptation to dissemble and temporize.

The remaining books on the Priesthood treat of the pre-eminent dignity, and sanctity of the priestly office and the peculiar difficulties and perils which beset it. They abound with wise and weighty observations instructive for all times, but they are also interesting from the light which they throw upon the condition of the Church and of society in the age when Chrysostom lived. It is to be noted that he is speaking of the priesthood generally and that it is not always easy to say in any given passage which of the first two orders in the ministry he has in his mind. In many instances perhaps he was not thinking of one more than the other. Where, as was very commonly the case, the jurisdiction of a bishop did not extend very far beyond the limits of the city in which his See was placed, his functions would more nearly resemble those which in our day are discharged by the incumbent of a large town parish than those which are performed by the modern Bishop of a large diocese. He was the chief pastor of the people, as well as the overseer of the clergy. Chrysostom's friend Basil has been confused by some with the great Basil, Bishop of Cæsarea in Cappadocia, who was fifteen years older than Chrysostom, by others with Basil Bishop of Seleucia, who was many years younger. Nothing in fact is known about him beyond what is recorded in this treatise, but he has been conjecturally identified with Basil Bishop of Raphnea in Syria, not far from Antioch, who attended the Council of Constantinople in 381.

CONTENTS.

BOOK I.
                                                          PAGE

1. How Basil excelled all the friends of Chrysostom 33
2. The unanimity of Basil and Chrysostom, and their joint study of all subjects 33
3. The balance upset in the pursuit of the monastic life 33
4. The proposal to occupy a common home 33
5. The fond entreaties of Chrysostom's mother 34
6. The deceit employed by Chrysostom in the matter of ordination 34
7. Chrysostom's defence in reply to objections 35
8. The great advantage of deceit when well timed; conclusion and general remarks 37

BOOK II.

1. The priesthood the greatest evidence of love to Christ 39
2. The service of the priesthood greater than all other services 40
3. The priesthood has need of a large and excellent spirit 41
4. It is full of great difficulty and danger 41
5. The office avoided by Chrysostom out of his love to Christ 43
6. A demonstration of the virtue of Basil, and of his ardent love 43
7. In avoiding ordination Chrysostom had no intention of insulting the electors 43
8. By his flight he saved them from blame 44

BOOK III.

1. Those who suspected me of declining this office through arrogance injured their own reputation . . . 45
2. I did not avoid it through vainglory 46
3. If I had desired glory I should rather have chosen the work 46
4. The priesthood is an awful thing, and the service thereof under the new dispensation far more awful than under the old 46
5. The great authority and dignity of the priesthood 47
6. Sacred ministries are amongst the greatest of God's gifts. 47
7. Even Paul was filled with fear when he considered the magnitude of the office. 48
8. He who enters upon it is often snared into sin, unless he is very noble-minded 49
9. He is caught by vainglory and its attendant evils 49
10. The priesthood is not the cause of these things, but our own indolence 49
11. The lust of domination should be cast out of the soul of a priest 50

(See note 1, p. 45)

BOOK IV.

1. Those who allow themselves to be forced into the clerical office, no less than they who enter upon it from ambitious motives, are sorely punished hereafter for their sin. 60

		PAGE
2.	They who ordain unworthy men, even where they do not know their character, will share their punishment.	63
3.	The priest ought to have great powers of speaking	64
4.	He should be fully prepared for controversy with all adversaries—Greeks, Jews, and heretics	65
5.	He should be very skillful in argument	66
6.	In which Saint Paul especially excelled	66
7.	So that he became illustrious not so much for his miracles as for his words	67
8.	Herein he would have us excel also	68
9.	For the lack of this in the priest must injuriously affect those over whom he is set	69

BOOK V.

1.	Public preaching needs much labor and study	70
2.	He who is appointed to this work must be indifferent to praise, and able in speaking	70
3.	Unless he have both these qualifications he will be unserviceable to the multitude	71
4.	He should above all take no notice of slander	71
5.	The skillful in preaching need more study than the unlearned	71
6.	He must not think too little or too much of the unreasoned verdict of the multitude	72
7.	He must order his words with a view to pleasing God alone	72
8.	He who is not indifferent to praise will undergo many sufferings	73

BOOK VI.

1.	Priests are liable to render account for the sins committed by others	74
2.	They need more circumspection than the recluses	75
3.	The recluse enjoys more ease of mind than he who is set over the church	75
4.	The priest has been entrusted with the government of the world and with other formidable duties	76
5.	The priest must be adapted to all circumstances.	77
6.	To live the life of a recluse is not such a mark of endurance as to govern the multitude well	77
7.	The habits of him who lives alone, and of him who has his conversation in the world are not for the same ends	77
8.	They who live alone become proficient in virtue more easily than they who have the care of many	78
9.	One ought not to think lightly of popular suspicion, even though it happen to be false	79
10.	It is no very great matter to save oneself.	79
11.	Much sorer punishment awaits the sins of the priests than those of the laity	80
12.	A representation by way of example both of the pain and of the fear which arises from the expectation of the priesthood.	80
13.	The warfare of the devil against us is more severe than any other	82

TREATISE ON THE PRIESTHOOD.

BOOK I.

CONTENTS.

I. HOW BASIL EXCELLED ALL THE FRIENDS OF CHRYSOSTOM.
II. THE UNANIMITY OF BASIL AND CHRYSOSTOM, AND THEIR JOINT STUDY OF ALL SUBJECTS.
III. THE BALANCE UPSET IN THE PURSUIT OF THE MONASTIC LIFE.
IV. THE PROPOSAL TO OCCUPY A COMMON HOME.
V. THE FOND ENTREATIES OF CHRYSOSTOM'S MOTHER.
VI. THE DECEIT EMPLOYED BY CHRYSOSTOM IN THE MATTER OF ORDINATION.
VII. CHRYSOSTOM'S DEFENCE IN REPLY TO OBJECTIONS.
VIII. THE GREAT ADVANTAGE OF DECEIT WHEN WELL-TIMED; CONCLUSION AND GENERAL REMARKS.

1. I HAD many genuine and true friends, men who understood the laws of friendship, and faithfully observed them; but out of this large number there was one who excelled all the rest in his attachment to me, striving to outstrip them as much as they themselves outstripped ordinary acquaintance. He was one of those who were constantly at my side; for we were engaged in the same studies, and employed the same teachers.[1] We had the same eagerness and zeal about the studies at which we worked, and a passionate desire produced by the same circumstances was equally strong in both of us. For not only when we were attending school, but after we had left it, when it became necessary to consider what course of life it would be best for us to adopt, we found ourselves to be of the same mind.

2. And in addition to these, there were other things also which preserved and maintained this concord unbroken and secure. For as regarded the greatness of our fatherland neither had one cause to vaunt himself over the other, nor was I burdened with riches, and he pinched by poverty, but our means corresponded as closely as our tastes. Our families also were of equal rank, and thus everything concurred with our disposition.

3. But when it became our duty to pursue the blessed life of monks, and the true philosophy,[2] our balance was no longer even, but his scale mounted high, while I, still entangled in the lusts of this world, dragged mine down and kept it low, weighting it with those fancies in which youths are apt to indulge. For the future our friendship indeed remained as firm as it was before, but our intercourse was interrupted; for it was impossible for persons who were not interested about the same things to spend much time together. But as soon as I also began to emerge a little from the flood of worldliness, he received me with open arms; yet not even thus could we maintain our former equality: for having got the start of me in time, and having displayed great earnestness, he rose again above my level, and soared to a great height.

4. Being a good man, however, and placing a high value on my friendship, he separated himself from all the rest (of the brethren), and spent the whole of his time with me, which he had desired to do before, but had been prevented as I was saying by my frivolity. For it was impossible for a man who attended the law-courts, and was in a flutter of excitement

---

[1] Androgathius in philosophy, Libanius in rhetoric.
[2] An expression frequently employed by St. Chrysostom in the sense of a life of religious contemplation and study.

about the pleasures of the stage, to be often in the company of one who was nailed to his books, and never set foot in the market place. Consequently when the hindrances were removed, and he had brought me into the same condition of life as himself, he gave free vent to the desire with which he had long been laboring. He could not bear leaving me even for a moment, and he persistently urged that we should each of us abandon our own home and share a common dwelling:—in fact he persuaded me, and the affair was taken in hand.

5. But the continual lamentations of my mother hindered me from granting him the favor, or rather from receiving this boon at his hands. For when she perceived that I was meditating this step, she took me into her own private chamber, and, sitting near me on the bed where she had given birth to me, she shed torrents of tears, to which she added words yet more pitiable than her weeping, in the following lamentable strain: My child, it was not the will of Heaven that I should long enjoy the benefit of thy father's virtue. For his death soon followed the pangs which I endured at thy birth, leaving thee an orphan and me a widow before my time to face all the horrors of widowhood, which only those who have experienced them can fairly understand. For no words are adequate to describe the tempest-tossed condition of a young woman who, having but lately left her paternal home, and being inexperienced in business, is suddenly racked by an overwhelming sorrow, and compelled to support a load of care too great for her age and sex. For she has to correct the laziness of servants, and to be on the watch for their rogueries, to repel the designs of relations, to bear bravely the threats of those who collect the public taxes,[1] and harshness in the imposition of rates. And if the departed one should have left a child, even if it be a girl, great anxiety will be caused to the mother, although free from much expense and fear: but a boy fills her with ten thousand alarms and many anxieties every day, to say nothing of the great expense which one is compelled to incur if she wishes to bring him up in a liberal way. None of these things, however, induced me to enter into a second marriage, or introduce a second husband into thy father's house: but I held on as I was, in the midst of the storm and uproar, and did not shun the iron furnace[2] of widowhood. My foremost help indeed was the grace from above; but it was no small consolation to me under those terrible trials to look continually on thy face and to preserve in thee a living image of him who had gone, an image indeed which was a fairly exact likeness.

On this account, even when thou wast an infant, and hadst not yet learned to speak, a time when children are the greatest delight to their parents, thou didst afford me much comfort. Nor indeed can you complain that, although I bore my widowhood bravely, I diminished thy patrimony, which I know has been the fate of many who have had the misfortune to be orphans. For, besides keeping the whole of it intact, I spared no expense which was needful to give you an honorable position, spending for this purpose some of my own fortune, and of my marriage dowry. Yet do not think that I say these things by way of reproaching you; only in return for all these benefits I beg one favor: do not plunge me into a second widowhood; nor revive the grief which is now laid to rest: wait for my death: it may be in a little while I shall depart. The young indeed look forward to a distant old age; but we who have grown old[3] have nothing but death to wait for. When, then, you shall have committed my body to the ground, and mingled my bones with thy father's, embark for a long voyage, and set sail on any sea thou wilt: then there will be no one to hinder thee: but as long as my life lasts, be content to live with me. Do not, I pray you, oppose God in vain, involving me without cause, who have done you no wrong, in these great calamities. For if you have any reason to complain that I drag you into worldly cares, and force you to attend to business, do not be restrained by any reverence for the laws of nature, for training or custom, but fly from me as an enemy; but if, on the contrary, I do everything to provide leisure for thy journey through this life, let this bond at least if nothing else keep thee by me. For couldst thou say that ten thousand loved thee, yet no one will afford thee the enjoyment of so much liberty, seeing there is no one who is equally anxious for thy welfare.

6. These words, and more, my mother spake to me, and I related them to that noble youth. But he, so far from being disheartened by these speeches, was the more urgent in making the same request as before. Now while we were thus situated, he continually entreating, and I refusing my assent, we were both of us disturbed by a report suddenly reaching us that we were about to be advanced to the dignity of

---

[1] For an account of the oppressive way in which the public taxes were collected, see Gibbon's History (Milman's edition), vol. iii. 78.
[2] The iron furnace was a Hebrew proverbial expression signifying "a furnace hot enough to melt iron," and so a condition of peculiar trial. See Deut. iv. 20, and Jer. xi. 4.

[3] This must be regarded as a kind of rhetorical expression, as we learn from Chrysostom's "Letter to a young widow" (see page   ), that his mother was not much past 40 at this time.

the episcopate.[1] As soon as I heard this rumor I was seized with alarm and perplexity: with alarm lest I should be made captive against my will, and perplexity, inquiring as I often did whence any such idea concerning us could have entered the minds of these men; for looking to myself I found nothing worthy of such an honor. But that noble youth having come to me privately, and having conferred with me about these things as if with one who was ignorant of the rumor, begged that we might in this instance also as formerly shape our action and our counsels the same way: for he would readily follow me whichever course I might pursue, whether I attempted flight or submitted to be captured. Perceiving then his eagerness, and considering that I should inflict a loss upon the whole body of the Church if, owing to my own weakness, I were to deprive the flock of Christ of a young man who was so good and so well qualified for the supervision of large numbers, I abstained from disclosing to him the purpose which I had formed, although I had never before allowed any of my plans to be concealed from him. I now told him that it would be best to postpone our decision concerning this matter to another season, as it was not immediately pressing, and by so doing persuaded him to dismiss it from his thoughts, and at the same time encouraged him to hope that, if such a thing should ever happen to us, I should be of the same mind with him. But after a short time, when one who was to ordain us arrived, I kept myself concealed, but Basil, ignorant of this, was taken away on another pretext, and made to take the yoke, hoping from the promises which I had made to him that I should certainly follow, or rather supposing that he was following me. For some of those who were present, seeing that he resented being seized, deceived him by exclaiming how strange it was that one who was generally reputed to be the more hot tempered (meaning me), had yielded very mildly to the judgment of the Fathers, whereas he, who was reckoned a much wiser and milder kind of man, had shown himself hotheaded and conceited, being unruly, restive, and contradictory.[2] Having yielded to these remonstrances, and afterwards having learned that I had escaped capture, he came to me in deep dejection, sat down near me and tried to speak, but was hindered by distress of mind and inability to express in words the violence to which he had been subjected. No sooner had he opened his mouth than he was prevented from utterance by grief cutting short his words before they could pass his lips. Seeing, then, his tearful and agitated condition, and knowing as I did the cause, I laughed for joy, and, seizing his right hand, I forced a kiss on him, and praised God that my plan had ended so successfully, as I had always prayed it might. But when he saw that I was delighted and beaming with joy, and understood that he had been deceived by me, he was yet more vexed and distressed.

7. And when he had a little recovered from this agitation of mind, he began: If you have rejected the part allotted to you, and have no further regard for me (I know not indeed for what cause), you ought at least to consider your own reputation; but as it is you have opened the mouths of all, and the world is saying that you have declined this ministry through love of vainglory, and there is no one who will deliver you from this accusation. As for me, I cannot bear to go into the market place; there are so many who come up to me and reproach me every day. For, when they see me anywhere in the city, all my intimate friends take me aside, and cast the greater part of the blame upon me. Knowing his intention, they say, for none of his affairs could be kept secret from you, you should not have concealed it, but ought to have communicated it to us, and we should have been at no loss to devise some plan for capturing him. But I am too much ashamed and abashed to tell them that I did not know you had long been plotting this trick, lest they should say that our friendship was a mere pretence. For even if it is so, as indeed it is—nor would you yourself deny it after what you have done to me—yet it is well to hide our misfortune from the outside world, and persons who entertain but a moderate opinion of us. I shrink from telling them the truth, and how things really stand with us, and I am compelled in future to keep silence, and look down on the ground, and turn away to avoid those whom I meet. For if I escape the condemnation on the former charge, I am forced to undergo judgment for speaking falsehood. For they will never believe me when I say that you ranged Basil amongst those who are not permitted to know your secret affairs. Of this, however, I will not take much account, since it has seemed agreeable to you, but how shall we endure the future disgrace? for some accuse you of arrogance, others of vainglory: while those

---

[1] ἐπισκοπῆς is the reading of most MSS., but four have ἱερωσύνης "the priesthood," which Bengel adopts, thinking that neither Basil nor Chrysostom could have been elected for the higher order at so early an age, but see below, p. 4, note 1.

[2] Forcible ordinations were not uncommon in the Church at this time. St. Augustin was dragged weeping by the people before the Bishop, and his ordination demanded. St. Martin of Tours was torn from his cell, and conveyed to ordination under a guard. Possid. Vita Aug. 4; Sulp. Severus, Vit. St. Martin, i. 224. The affectation of reluctance to be consecrated became a fashion in the Coptic Church. The patriarch elect of Alexandria is still brought to Cairo loaded with chains, as if to prevent his escape. Stanley, Eastern Church, vii. p. 226.

who are our more merciful accusers, lay both these offences to our charge, and add that we have insulted those who did us honor, although had they experienced even greater indignity it would only have served them right for passing over so many and such distinguished men and advancing mere youths,[1] who were but yesterday immersed in the interests of this world, to such a dignity as they never have dreamed of obtaining, in order that they may for a brief season knit the eyebrows, wear dusky garments, and put on a grave face. Those who from the dawn of manhood to extreme old age have diligently practised self-discipline, are now to be placed under the government of youths who have not even heard the laws which should regulate their administration of this office. I am perpetually assailed by persons who say such things and worse, and am at a loss how to reply to them; but I pray you tell me: for I do not suppose that you took to flight and incurred such hatred from such distinguished men without cause or consideration, but that your decision was made with reasoning and circumspection: whence also I conjecture that you have some argument ready for your defence. Tell me, then, whether there is any fair excuse which I can make to those who accuse us.

For I do not demand any account for the wrongs which I have sustained at your hands, nor for the deceit or treachery you have practised, nor for the advantage which you have derived from me in the past. For I placed my very life, so to say, in your hands, yet you have treated me with as much guile as if it had been your business to guard yourself against an enemy. Yet if you knew this decision of ours to be profitable, you ought not to have avoided the gain: if on the contrary injurious, you should have saved me also from the loss, as you always said that you esteemed me before every one else. But you have done everything to make me fall into the snare: and you had no need of guile and hypocrisy in dealing with one who was wont to display the utmost sincerity and candor in speech and action towards thee. Nevertheless, as I said, I do not now accuse you of any of these things, or reproach you for the lonely position in which you have placed me by breaking off those conferences from which we often derived no small pleasure and profit; but all these things I pass by, and bear in silence and meekness, not that thou hast acted meekly in transgressing against me, but because from the day that I cherished thy friendship I laid it down as a rule for myself, that whatever sorrow you might cause me I would never force you to the necessity of an apology. For you know yourself that you have inflicted no small loss on me if at least you remember what we were always saying ourselves, and the outside world also said concerning us, that it was a great gain for us to be of one mind and be guarded by each other's friendship. Every one said, indeed, that our concord would bring no small advantage to many besides ourselves; I never perceived, however, so far as I am concerned, how it could be of advantage to others: but I did say that we should at least derive this benefit from it: that those who wished to contend with us would find us difficult to master. And I never ceased reminding you of these things: saying the age is a cruel one, and designing men are many, genuine love is no more, and the deadly pest of envy has crept into its place: we walk in the midst of snares, and on the edge of battlements;[2] those who are ready to rejoice in our misfortunes, if any should befall us, are many and beset us from many quarters: whereas there is no one to condole with us, or at least the number of such may be easily counted. Beware that we do not by separation incur much ridicule, and damage worse than ridicule. Brother aided by brother is like a strong city, and well fortified kingdom.[3] Do not dissolve this genuine intimacy, nor break down the fortress. Such things and more I was continually saying, not indeed that I ever suspected anything of this kind, but supposing you to be entirely sound in your relation towards me, I did it as a superfluous precaution, wishing to preserve in health one who was already sound; but unwittingly, as it seems, I was administering medicines to a sick man: and even so I have not been fortunate enough to do any good, and have gained nothing by my excess of forethought. For having totally cast away all these considerations, without giving them a thought, you have turned me adrift like an unballasted vessel on an untried ocean, taking no heed of those fierce billows which I must encounter. For if it should ever be my lot to undergo calumny, or mockery, or any other kind of insult or menace (and such things must frequently occur), to whom shall I fly for refuge: to whom shall I impart my distress, who will be willing to succour me and drive back my assailants and put a stop to their assaults? who

---

[1] Chrysostom was about 28 at this time. The Council of Neo Cæsarea (about 320) fixed 30 as the age at which men were eligible for the priesthood, and the same age at least must have been required for a bishop, yet Remigius was consecrated to the See of Reims at the age of 22, A.D. 457; and there are many other instances of bishops, under the prescribed age.

[2] A metaphorical expression to denote a perilous position, as those who walked on the edge of the walls would be exposed to the missiles of the enemy.
[3] Proverbs xviii. 19. LXX. version.

will solace me and prepare me to bear the coarse ribaldry which may yet be in store for me. There is no one since you stand aloof from this terrible strife, and cannot even hear my cry. Seest thou then what mischief thou hast wrought? now that thou hast dealt the blow, dost thou perceive what a deadly wound thou hast inflicted? But let all this pass: for it is impossible to undo the past, or to find a path through pathless difficulties. What shall I say to the outside world? what defence shall I make to their accusations.

8. CHRYSOSTOM: Be of good cheer, I replied, for I am not only ready to answer for myself in these matters, but I will also endeavor as well as I am able to render an account of those for which you have not held me answerable. Indeed, if you wish it, I will make them the starting-point of my defence. For it would be a strange piece of stupidity on my part if, thinking only of praise from the outside public, and doing my best to silence their accusations, I were unable to convince my dearest of all friends that I am not wronging him, and were to treat him with indifference greater than the zeal which he has displayed on my behalf, treating me with such forbearance as even to refrain from accusing me of the wrongs which he says he has suffered from me, and putting his own interests out of the question in consideration for mine.

What is the wrong that I have done thee, since I have determined to embark from this point upon the sea of apology? Is it that I misled you and concealed my purpose? Yet I did it for the benefit of thyself who wast deceived, and of those to whom I surrendered you by means of this deceit. For if the evil of deception is absolute, and it is never right to make use of it, I am prepared to pay any penalty you please: or rather, as you will never endure to inflict punishment upon me, I shall subject myself to the same condemnation which is pronounced by judges on evil-doers when their accusers have convicted them. But if the thing is not always harmful, but becomes good or bad according to the intention of those who practise it, you must desist from complaining of deceit, and prove that it has been devised against you for a bad purpose; and as long as this proof is wanting it would only be fair for those who wish to conduct themselves prudently, not only to abstain from reproaches and accusation, but even to give a friendly reception to the deceiver. For a well-timed deception, undertaken with an upright intention, has such advantages, that many persons have often had to undergo punishment for abstaining from fraud. And if you investigate the history of generals who have enjoyed the highest reputation from the earliest ages, you will find that most of their triumphs were achieved by stratagem, and that such are more highly commended than those who conquer in open fight. For the latter conduct their campaigns with greater expenditure of money and men, so that they gain nothing by the victory, but suffer just as much distress as those who have been defeated, both in the sacrifice of troops and the exhaustion of funds. But, besides this, they are not even permitted to enjoy all the glory which pertains to the victory; for no small part of it is reaped by those who have fallen, because in spirit they were victorious, their defeat was only a bodily one: so that had it been possible for them not to fall when they were wounded, and death had not come and put the finishing stroke to their labors, there would have been no end of their prowess. But one who has been able to gain the victory by stratagem involves the enemy in ridicule as well as disaster. Again, in the other case both sides equally carry off the honors bestowed upon valor, whereas in this case they do not equally obtain those which are bestowed on wisdom, but the prize falls entirely to the victors, and, another point no less important is that they preserve the joy of the victory for the state unalloyed; for abundance of resources and multitudes of men are not like mental powers: the former indeed if continually used in war necessarily become exhausted, and fail those who possess them, whereas it is the nature of wisdom to increase the more it is exercised. And not in war only, but also in peace the need of deceit may be found, not merely in reference to the affairs of the state, but also in private life, in the dealings of husband with wife and wife with husband, son with father, friend with friend, and also children with a parent. For the daughter of Saul would not have been able to rescue her husband out of Saul's hands [1] except by deceiving her father. And her brother, wishing to save him whom she had rescued when he was again in danger, made use of the same weapon as the wife.[2]

BASIL: But none of these cases apply to me: for I am not an enemy, nor one of those who are striving to injure thee, but quite the contrary. For I entrusted all my interests to your judgment, and always followed it whenever you bid me.

CHRYSOSTOM: But, my admirable and excellent Sir, this is the very reason why I took the precaution of saying that it was a good thing to employ this kind of deceit, not only in war, and in dealing with enemies, but also

---

[1] 1 Sam. xix. 12-18. [2] 1 Sam. xx. 11.

in peace, and in dealing with our dearest friends. For as a proof that it is beneficial not only to the deceivers, but also to those who are deceived; if you go to any of the physicians and ask them how they relieve their patients from disease, they will tell you that they do not depend upon their professional skill alone, but sometimes conduct the sick to health by availing themselves of deceit, and blending the assistance which they derive from it with their art. For when the waywardness of the patient and the obstinacy of the complaint baffle the counsels of the physicians, it is then necessary to put on the mask of deceit in order that, as on the stage, they may be able to hide what really takes place. But, if you please, I will relate to you one instance of stratagem out of many which I have heard of being contrived by the sons of the healing art.[1] A man was once suddenly attacked by a fever of great severity; the burning heat increased, and the patient rejected the remedies which could have reduced it and craved for a draught of pure wine, passionately entreating all who approached to give it him and enable him to satiate this deadly craving—I say deadly, for if any one had gratified this request he would not only have exasperated the fever, but also have driven the unhappy man frantic. Thereupon, professional skill being baffled, and at the end of its resources and utterly thrown away, stratagem stepped in and displayed its power in the way which I will now relate. For the physician took an earthen cup brought straight out of the furnace, and having steeped it in wine, then drew it out empty, filled it with water, and, having ordered the chamber where the sick man lay to be darkened with curtains that the light might not reveal the trick, he gave it him to drink, pretending that it was filled with undiluted wine. And the man, before he had taken it in his hands, being deceived by the smell, did not wait to examine what was given him, but convinced by the odor, and deceived by the darkness, eagerly gulped down the draught, and being satiated with it immediately shook off the feeling of suffocation and escaped the imminent peril.[2] Do you see the advantage of deceit? And if any one were to reckon up all the tricks of physicians the list would run on to an indefinite length. And not only those who heal the body but those also who attend to the diseases of the soul may be found continually making use of this remedy. Thus the blessed Paul attracted those multitudes of Jews:[3] with this purpose he circumcised Timothy,[4] although he warned the Galatians in his letter[5] that Christ would not profit those who were circumcised. For this cause he submitted to the law, although he reckoned the righteousness which came from the law but loss after receiving the faith in Christ.[6] For great is the value of deceit, provided it be not introduced with a mischievous intention. In fact action of this kind ought not to be called deceit, but rather a kind of good management, cleverness and skill, capable of finding out ways where resources fail, and making up for the defects of the mind. For I would not call Phinees a murderer, although he slew two human beings with one stroke:[7] nor yet Elias after the slaughter of the 100 soldiers, and the captain,[8] and the torrents of blood which he caused to be shed by the destruction of those who sacrificed to devils.[9] For if we were to concede this, and to examine the bare deeds in themselves apart from the intention of the doers, one might if he pleased judge Abraham guilty of child-murder[10] and accuse his grandson[11] and descendant[12] of wickedness and guile. For the one got possession of the birthright, and the other transferred the wealth of the Egyptians to the host of the Israelites. But this is not the case: away with the audacious thought! For we not only acquit them of blame, but also admire them because of these things, since even God commended them for the same. For that man would fairly deserve to be called a deceiver who made an unrighteous use of the practice, not one who did so with a salutary purpose. And often it is necessary to deceive, and to do the greatest benefits by means of this device, whereas he who has gone by a straight course has done great mischief to the person whom he has not deceived.

---

[1] Literally, "sons of physicians." Compare the expression "sons of the prophets" in the Old Testament.
[2] Clement of Alexandria (Stromata vii.) illustrates the same doctrine of allowable deceit for a useful purpose by a similar reference to the practice of physicians.
[3] Acts xxi. 26.
[4] Ib. xvi. 3.
[5] Gal. v. 2.
[6] Philipp. iii. 7.
[7] Numb. xxv. 7.
[8] 2 Kings i. 9-12.
[9] 1 Kings xviii. 34.
[10] Gen. xxii. 3.
[11] Ib. xxvii. 19.
[12] Exod. xi. 2.

BOOK II.

Contents.

I. THE PRIESTHOOD THE GREATEST EVIDENCE OF LOVE TO CHRIST.
II. THE SERVICE OF THE PRIESTHOOD GREATER THAN ALL OTHER SERVICES.
III. THE PRIESTHOOD HAS NEED OF A LARGE AND EXCELLENT SPIRIT.
IV. IT IS FULL OF GREAT DIFFICULTY AND DANGER.
V. THE OFFICE AVOIDED BY CHRYSOSTOM OUT OF HIS LOVE TO CHRIST.
VI. A DEMONSTRATION OF THE VIRTUE OF BASIL, AND OF HIS ARDENT LOVE.
VII. IN AVOIDING ORDINATION CHRYSOSTOM HAD NO INTENTION OF INSULTING THE ELECTORS.
VIII. BY HIS FLIGHT HE SAVED THEM FROM BLAME.

1. THAT it is possible then to make use of deceit for a good purpose, or rather that in such a case it ought not to be called deceit, but a kind of good management worthy of all admiration, might be proved at greater length; but since what has already been said suffices for demonstration, it would be irksome and tedious to lengthen out my discourse upon the subject. And now it will remain for you to prove whether I have not employed this art to your advantage.

BASIL: And what kind of advantage have I derived from this piece of good management, or wise policy, or whatever you may please to call it, so as to persuade me that I have not been deceived by you?

CHRYSOSTOM: What advantage, pray, could be greater than to be seen doing those things which Christ with his own lips declared to be proofs of love to Himself?[1] For addressing the leader of the apostles He said, "Peter, lovest thou me?" and when he confessed that he did, the Lord added, "if thou lovest me tend my sheep." The Master asked the disciple if He was loved by him, not in order to get information (how should He who penetrates the hearts of all men?), but in order to teach us how great an interest He takes in the superintendence of these sheep. This being plain, it will likewise be manifest that a great and unspeakable reward will be reserved for him whose labors are concerned with these sheep, upon which Christ places such a high value. For when we see any one bestowing care upon members of our household, or upon our flocks, we count his zeal for them as a sign of love towards ourselves: yet all these things are to be bought for money:—with how great a gift then will He requite those who tend the flock which He purchased, not with money, nor anything of that kind, but by His own death, giving his own blood as the price of the herd. Wherefore when the disciple said, "Thou knowest Lord that I love Thee," and invoked the beloved one Himself as a witness of his love, the Saviour did not stop there, but added that which was the token of love. For He did not at that time wish to show how much Peter loved Him, but how much He Himself loved His own Church, and he desired to teach Peter and all of us that we also should bestow much zeal upon the same. For why did God not spare His only-begotten Son, but delivered Him up, although the only one He had?[2] It was that He might reconcile to Himself those who were disposed towards Him as enemies, and make them His peculiar people. For what purpose did He shed His blood? It was that He might win these sheep which He entrusted to Peter and his successors. Naturally then did Christ say, "Who then is the faithful and wise servant, whom his lord shall make ruler over His household."[3] Again, the

---
[1] John xxi. 15-17.
[2] Rom. viii. 32; John iii. 16.
[3] Matt. xxiv. 45. Some MSS. of Chrysostom have the future καταστήσει, *shall* make ruler, but all MSS. of the New Testament have the aorist κατέστησε, made ruler.

words are those of one who is in doubt, yet the speaker did not utter them in doubt, but just as He asked Peter whether he loved Him, not from any need to learn the affection of the disciple, but from a desire to show the exceeding depth of his own love: so now also when He says, "Who then is the faithful and wise servant?" he speaks not as being ignorant who is faithful and wise, but as desiring to set forth the rarity of such a character, and the greatness of this office. Observe at any rate how great the reward is—" He will appoint him," he says, " ruler over all his goods."[1]

2. Will you, then, still contend that you were not rightly deceived, when you are about to superintend the things which belong to God, and are doing that which when Peter did the Lord said he should be able to surpass the rest of the apostles, for His words were, "Peter, lovest thou me more than these?"[2] Yet He might have said to him, "If thou lovest me practise fasting, sleeping on the ground, and prolonged vigils, defend the wronged, be as a father to orphans, and supply the place of a husband to their mother." But as a matter of fact, setting aside all these things, what does He say? "Tend my sheep." For those things which I have already mentioned might easily be performed by many even of those who are under authority, women as well as men; but when one is required to preside over the Church, and to be entrusted with the care of so many souls, the whole female sex must retire before the magnitude of the task, and the majority of men also; and we must bring forward those who to a large extent surpass all others, and soar as much above them in excellence of spirit as Saul overtopped the whole Hebrew nation in bodily stature: or rather far more.[3] For in this case let me not take the height of shoulders as the standard of inquiry; but let the distinction between the pastor and his charge be as great as that between rational man and irrational creatures, not to say even greater, inasmuch as the risk is concerned with things of far greater importance. He indeed who has lost sheep, either through the ravages of wolves, or the attacks of robbers, or through murrain, or any other disaster befalling them, might perhaps obtain some indulgence from the owner of the flock; and even if the latter should demand satisfaction the penalty would be only a matter of money: but he who has human beings entrusted to him, the rational flock of Christ, incurs a penalty in the first place for the loss of the sheep, which goes beyond material things and touches his own life: and in the second place he has to carry on a far greater and more difficult contest. For he has not to contend with wolves, nor to dread robbers, nor to consider how he may avert pestilence from the flock. With whom then has he to fight? with whom has he to wrestle? Listen to the words of St. Paul. "We wrestle not against flesh and blood, but against principalities, against powers, against the rulers of the darkness of this world, against spiritual wickedness in high places."[4] Do you see the terrible multitude of enemies, and their fierce squadrons, not steel clad, but endued with a nature which is of itself an equivalent for a complete suit of armor. Would you see yet another host, stern and cruel, beleaguering this flock? This also you shall behold from the same post of observation. For he who has discoursed to us concerning the others, points out these enemies also to us, speaking in a certain place on this wise: " The works of the flesh are manifest, which are these, fornication, adultery, uncleanness, lasciviousness, idolatry, witchcraft, hatred, variance, emulation, wrath, strife,[5] backbitings, whisperings, swellings, tumults,"[6] and many more besides; for he did not make a complete list, but left us to understand the rest from these. Moreover, in the case of the shepherd of irrational creatures, those who wish to destroy the flock, when they see the guardian take to flight, cease making war upon him, and are contented with the seizure of the cattle: but in this case, even should they capture the whole flock, they do not leave the shepherd unmolested, but attack him all the more, and wax bolder, ceasing not until they have either overthrown him, or have themselves been vanquished. Again, the afflictions of sheep are manifest, whether it be famine, or pestilence, or wounds, or whatsoever else it may be which distresses them, and this might help not a little towards the relief of those who are oppressed in these ways. And there is yet another fact greater than this which facilitates release from this kind of infirmity. And what is that? The shepherds with great authority compel the sheep to receive the remedy when they do not willingly submit to it. For it is easy to bind them when cautery or cutting is required, and to keep them inside the fold for a long time, whenever it is expedient, and to bring them one kind of food instead of another, and to cut them off from their supplies of water, and all other things which the shepherds may decide to be conducive to their health they perform with great ease.

---

[1] Matt. xxiv. 47.
[2] In some editions the words "tend my sheep" are added here.
[3] 1 Sam. x. 23.
[4] Ephes. vi. 12.　[5] Gal. v. 19, 20, 21.　[6] 2 Cor. xii. 20.

3. But in the case of human infirmities, it is not easy in the first place for a man to discern them, for no man "knoweth the things of a man, save the spirit of man which is in him."[1] How then can any one apply the remedy for the disease of which he does not know the character, often indeed being unable to understand it even should he happen to sicken with it himself? And even when it becomes manifest, it causes him yet more trouble: for it is not possible to doctor all men with the same authority with which the shepherd treats his sheep. For in this case also it is necessary to bind and to restrain from food, and to use cautery or the knife: but the reception of the treatment depends on the will of the patient, not of him who applies the remedy. For this also was perceived by that wonderful man (St. Paul) when he said to the Corinthians—"Not for that we have dominion over your faith, but are helpers of your joy."[2] For Christians above all men are not permitted forcibly to correct the failings of those who sin. Secular judges indeed, when they have captured malefactors under the law, show their authority to be great, and prevent them even against their will from following their own devices: but in our case the wrong-doer must be made better, not by force, but by persuasion. For neither has authority of this kind for the restraint of sinners been given us by law, nor, if it had been given, should we have any field for the exercise of our power, inasmuch as God rewards those who abstain from evil by their own choice, not of necessity. Consequently much skill is required that our patients may be induced to submit willingly to the treatment prescribed by the physicians, and not only this, but that they may be grateful also for the cure. For if any one when he is bound becomes restive (which it is in his power to be), he makes the mischief worse; and if he should pay no heed to the words which cut like steel, he inflicts another wound by means of this contempt, and the intention to heal only becomes the occasion of a worse disorder. For it is not possible for any one to cure a man by compulsion against his will.

4. What then is one to do? For if you deal too gently with him who needs a severe application of the knife, and do not strike deep into one who requires such treatment, you remove one part of the sore but leave the other: and if on the other hand you make the requisite incision unsparingly, the patient, driven to desperation by his sufferings, will often fling everything away at once, both the remedy and the bandage, and throw himself down headlong, "breaking the yoke and bursting the band."[3] I could tell of many who have run into extreme evils because the due penalty of their sins was exacted. For we ought not, in applying punishment, merely to proportion it to the scale of the offence, but rather to keep in view the disposition of the sinner, lest whilst wishing to mend what is torn, you make the rent worse, and in your zealous endeavors to restore what is fallen, you make the ruin greater. For weak and careless characters, addicted for the most part to the pleasures of the world, and having occasion to be proud on account of birth and position, may yet, if gently and gradually brought to repent of their errors, be delivered, partially at least, if not perfectly, from the evils by which they are possessed: but if any one were to inflict the discipline all at once, he would deprive them of this slight chance of amendment. For when once the soul has been forced to put off shame it lapses into a callous condition, and neither yields to kindly words nor bends to threats, nor is susceptible of gratitude, but becomes far worse than that city which the prophet reproached, saying, "thou hadst the face of a harlot, refusing to be ashamed before all men."[4] Therefore the pastor has need of much discretion, and of a myriad eyes to observe on every side the habit of the soul. For as many are uplifted to pride, and then sink into despair of their salvation, from inability to endure severe remedies, so are there some, who from paying no penalty equivalent to their sins, fall into negligence, and become far worse, and are impelled to greater sins. It behoves the priest therefore to leave none of these things unexamined, but, after a thorough inquiry into all of them, to apply such remedies as he has appositely to each case, lest his zeal prove to be in vain. And not in this matter only, but also in the work of knitting together the severed members of the Church, one can see that he has much to do. For the pastor of sheep has his flock following him, wherever he may lead them: and if any should stray out of the straight path, and, deserting the good pasture, feed in unproductive or rugged places, a loud shout suffices to collect them and bring back to the fold those who have been parted from it: but if a human being wanders away from the right faith, great exertion, perseverance and patience are required; for he cannot be dragged back by force, nor constrained by fear, but must be led back by persuasion to the truth from which be originally swerved. The pastor therefore ought to be of a noble spirit, so as not to despond, or to despair of the salvation of wan-

---

[1] 1 Cor. ii. 11. [2] 2 Cor. i. 24. [3] Conf. Jer. v. 5. [4] Jer. iii. 3.

derers from the fold, but continually to reason with himself and say, "Peradventure God will give them repentance to the acknowledging of the truth, and that they may recover themselves out of the snare of the devil."[1] Therefore the Lord, when addressing His disciples, said, "Who then is the faithful and wise servant?"[2] For he indeed who disciplines himself compasses only his own advantage, but the benefit of the pastoral function extends to the whole people. And one who dispenses money to the needy, or otherwise succors the oppressed, benefits his neighbors to some extent, but so much less than the priest in proportion as the body is inferior to the soul. Rightly therefore did the Lord say that zeal for the flock was a token of love for Himself.

BASIL: But thou thyself—dost thou not love Christ?

CHRYSOSTOM: Yea, I love Him, and shall never cease loving Him; but I fear lest I should provoke Him whom I love.

BASIL: But what riddle can there be more obscure than this—Christ has commanded him who loves Him to tend His sheep, and yet you say that you decline to tend them because you love Him who gave this command?

CHRYSOSTOM: My saying is no riddle, but very intelligible and simple, for if I were well qualified to administer this office, as Christ desired it, and then shunned it, my remark might be open to doubt, but since the infirmity of my spirit renders me useless for this ministry, why does my saying deserve to be called in question? For I fear lest if I took the flock in hand when it was in good condition and well nourished, and then wasted it through my unskilfulness, I should provoke against myself the God who so loved the flock as to give Himself up for their salvation and ransom.

BASIL: You speak in jest: for if you were in earnest I know not how you would have proved me to be justly grieved otherwise than by means of these very words whereby you have endeavored to dispel my dejection. I knew indeed before that you had deceived and betrayed me, but much more now, when you have undertaken to clear yourself of my accusations, do I plainly perceive and understand the extent of the evils into which you have led me. For if you withdrew yourself from this ministry because you were conscious that your spirit was not equal to the burden of the task, I ought to have been rescued from it before you, even if I had chanced to have a great desire for it, to say nothing of having confided to you the entire decision of these matters: but as it is, you have looked solely to your own interest and neglected mine. Would indeed you had entirely neglected them; then I should have been well content: but you plotted to facilitate my capture by those who wished to seize me. For you cannot take shelter in the argument that public opinion deceived you and induced you to imagine great and wonderful things concerning me. For I was none of your wonderful and distinguished men, nor, had this been the case, ought you to have preferred public opinion to truth. For if I had never permitted you to enjoy my society, you might have seemed to have a reasonable pretext for being guided in your vote by public report; but if there is no one who has such thorough knowledge of my affairs, if you are acquainted with my character better than my parents and those who brought me up, what argument can you employ which will be convincing enough to persuade your hearers that you did not purposely thrust me into this danger: say, what answer shall I make to your accusers?

CHRYSOSTOM: Nay! I will not proceed to those questions until I have resolved such as concern yourself alone, if you were to ask me ten thousand times to dispose of these charges. You said indeed that ignorance would bring me forgiveness, and that I should have been free from all accusation if I had brought you into your present position not knowing anything about you, but that as I did not betray you in ignorance, but was intimately acquainted with your affairs, I was deprived of all reasonable pretext and excuse. But I say precisely the reverse: for in such matters there is need of careful scrutiny, and he who is going to present any one as qualified for the priesthood ought not to be content with public report only, but should also himself, above all and before all, investigate the man's character. For when the blessed Paul says, "He must also have a good report of them which are without,"[3] he does not dispense with an exact and rigorous inquiry, nor does he assign to such testimony precedence over the scrutiny required in such cases. For after much previous discourse, he mentioned this additional testimony, proving that one must not be contented with it alone for elections of this kind, but take it into consideration along with the rest. For public report often speaks false; but when careful investigation precedes, no further danger need be apprehended from it. On this account, after the other kinds of evidence he places that which comes from those who are without. For he did not simply say, "he must have a good report," but added the

---

[1] 2 Tim. ii. 25.   [2] Matt. xxiv. 45.   [3] 1 Tim. iii. 7.

words, "from them which are without," wishing to show that before the report of those without he must be carefully examined. Inasmuch, then, as I myself knew your affairs better than your parents, as you also yourself acknowledged, I might deserve to be released from all blame.

BASIL: Nay this is the very reason why you could not escape, if any one chose to indite you. Do you not remember hearing from me, and often learning from my actual conduct, the feebleness of my character? Were you not perpetually taunting me for my pusillanimity, because I was so easily dejected by ordinary cares?

5. CHRYSOSTOM: I do indeed remember often hearing such things said by you; I would not deny it. But if I ever taunted you, I did it in sport and not in serious truth. However, I do not now dispute about these matters, and I claim the same degree of forbearance from you while I wish to make mention of some of the good qualities which you possess. For if you attempt to convict me of saying what is untrue, I shall not spare you, but shall prove that you say these things rather by way of self-depreciation than with a view to truth, and I will employ no evidence but your own words and deeds to demonstrate the truth of my assertion. And now the first question I wish to ask of you is this: do you know how great the power of love is? For omitting all the miracles which were to be wrought by the apostles, Christ said, "Hereby shall men know that ye are my disciples if ye love one another,"[1] and Paul said that it was the fulfilling of the law,[2] and that in default of it no spiritual gift had any profit. Well, this choice good, the distinguishing mark of Christ's disciples, the gift which is higher than all other gifts, I perceived to be deeply implanted in your soul, and teeming with much fruit.

BASIL: I acknowledge indeed that the matter is one of deep concern to me, and that I endeavor most earnestly to keep this commandment, but that I have not even half succeeded in so doing, even you yourself would bear me witness if you would leave off talking out of partiality, and simply respect the truth.

6. CHRYSOSTOM: Well, then, I shall betake myself to my evidences, and shall now do what I threatened, proving that you wish to disparage yourself rather than to speak the truth. But I will mention a fact which has only just occurred, that no one may suspect me of attempting to obscure the truth by the great lapse of time in relating events long past, as oblivion would then prevent any objection being made to the things which I might say with a view to gratification.[3] For when one of our intimate friends, having been falsely accused of insult and folly, was in extreme peril, you then flung yourself into the midst of the danger, although you were not summoned by any one, or appealed to by the person who was about to be involved in danger. Such was the fact: but that I may convict you out of your own mouth, I will remind you of the words you uttered: for when some did not approve of this zeal, while others commended and admired it, "How can I help myself?" you said to those who accused you, "for I do not know how otherwise to love than by giving up my life when it is necessary to save any of my friends who is in danger:" thus repeating, in different words, indeed, but with the same meaning, what Christ said to his disciples when he laid down the definition of perfect love. "Greater love," He said, "hath no man than this that a man lay down his life for his friends." If then it is impossible to find greater love than this, you have attained its limit, and both by your deeds and words have crowned the summit. This is why I betrayed you, this is why I contrived that plot. Do I now convince you that it was not from any malicious intent, nor from any desire to thrust you into danger, but from a persuasion of your future usefulness that I dragged you into this course?

BASIL: Do you then suppose that love is sufficient for the correction of one's fellow-men?

CHRYSOSTOM: Certainly it would contribute in a great measure to this end. But if you wish me to produce evidence of your practical wisdom also, I will proceed to do so, and will prove that your understanding exceeds your lovingkindness.

At these remarks he blushed scarlet and said, "Let my character be now dismissed: for it was not about this that I originally demanded an explanation; but if you have any just answer to make to those who are without, I would gladly hear what you have to say. Wherefore, abandoning this vain contest, tell me what defence I shall make, both to those who have honored you and to those who are distressed on their account, considering them to be insulted.

7. CHRYSOSTOM: This is just the point to which I am finally hastening, for as my ex-

---

[1] John xiii. 35. [2] Rom. xiii. 10.

[3] The passage is awkwardly expressed in the original. What Chrysostom says is that he will mention an event which has recently occurred as an evidence of Basil's character, because if he referred to events which were no longer fresh in people's recollection, the accuracy of his statements could not be tested, and he might be suspected of partiality.

planation to you has been completed I shall easily turn to this part of my defence. What then is the accusation made by these persons, and what are their charges? They say that they have been insulted and grievously wronged by me because I have not accepted the honor which they wished to confer upon me. Now in the first place I say that no account should be taken of the insult shown to men, seeing that by paying honor to them I should be compelled to offend God. And I should say to those who are displeased that it is not safe to take offence at these things, but does them much harm. For I think that those who stay themselves on God and look to Him alone, ought to be so religiously disposed as not to account such a thing an insult, even if they happened to be a thousand times dishonored. But that I have not gone so far as even to think of daring anything of this kind is manifest from what I am about to say. For if indeed I had been induced by arrogance and vainglory, as you have often said some slanderously affirm, to assent to my accusers, I should have been one of the most iniquitous of mankind, having treated great and excellent men, my benefactors moreover, with contempt. For if men ought to be punished for wronging those who have never wronged them, how ought we to honor those who have spontaneously preferred to honor us? For no one could possibly say that they were requiting me for any benefits small or great which they had received at my hands. How great a punishment then would one deserve if one requited them in the contrary manner. But if such a thing never entered my mind, and I declined the heavy burden with quite a different intention, why do they refuse to pardon me (even if they do not consent to approve), but accuse me of having selfishly spared my own soul? For so far from having insulted the men in question I should say that I had even honored them by my refusal.

And do not be surprised at the paradoxical nature of my remark, for I shall supply a speedy solution of it.

8. For had I accepted the office, I do not say all men, but those who take pleasure in speaking evil, might have suspected and said many things concerning myself who had been elected and concerning them, the electors: for instance, that they regarded wealth, and admired splendor of rank, or had been induced by flattery to promote me to this honor: indeed I cannot say whether some one might not have suspected that they were bribed by money. Moreover, they would have said, "Christ called fishermen, tentmakers, and publicans to this dignity, whereas these men reject those who support themselves by daily labor: but if there be any one who devotes himself to secular learning, and is brought up in idleness, him they receive and admire. For why, pray, have they passed by men who have undergone innumerable toils in the service of the Church, and suddenly dragged into this dignity one who has never experienced any labors of this kind, but has spent all his youth in the vain study of secular learning." These things and more they might have said had I accepted the office: but not so now. For every pretext for maligning is now cut away from them, and they can neither accuse me of flattery, nor the others of receiving bribes, unless some choose to act like mere madmen. For how could one who used flattery and expended money in order to obtain the dignity, have abandoned it to others when he might have obtained it? For this would be just as if a man who had bestowed much labor upon the ground in order that the corn field might be laden with abundant produce, and the presses overflow with wine, after innumerable toils and great expenditure of money were to surrender the fruits to others just when it was time to reap his corn and gather in his vintage. Do you see that although what was said might be far from the truth, nevertheless those who wished to calumniate the electors would then have had a pretext for alleging that the choice was made without fair judgment and consideration. But as it is I have prevented them from being open mouthed, or even uttering a single word on the subject. Such then and more would have been their remarks at the outset. But after undertaking the ministry I should not have been able day by day to defend myself against accusers, even if I had done everything faultlessly, to say nothing of the many mistakes which I must have made owing to my youth and inexperience. But now I have saved the electors from this kind of accusation also, whereas in the other case I should have involved them in innumerable reproaches. For what would not the world have said? "They have committed affairs of such vast interest and importance to thoughtless youths, they have defiled the flock of God, and Christian affairs have become a jest and a laughingstock." But now "all iniquity shall stop her mouth."[1] For although they may say these things on your account, you will speedily teach them by your acts that understanding is not to be estimated by age, and the grey head is not to be the test of an elder—that the young man ought not to be absolutely excluded from the ministry, but only the novice: and the difference between the two is great.

---

[1] Ps. cvii. 42.

BOOK III.

CONTENTS.

I. THOSE WHO SUSPECTED ME OF DECLINING THIS OFFICE THROUGH ARROGANCE INJURED THEIR OWN REPUTATION.
II. I DID NOT AVOID IT THROUGH VAINGLORY.
III. IF I HAD DESIRED GLORY I SHOULD RATHER HAVE CHOSEN THE WORK.
IV. THE PRIESTHOOD IS AN AWFUL THING, AND THE SERVICE THEREOF UNDER THE NEW DISPENSATION FAR MORE AWFUL THAN UNDER THE OLD.
V. THE GREAT AUTHORITY AND DIGNITY OF THE PRIESTHOOD.
VI. SACRED MINISTRIES ARE AMONGST THE GREATEST OF GOD'S GIFTS.
VII. EVEN PAUL WAS FILLED WITH FEAR WHEN HE CONSIDERED THE MAGNITUDE OF THE OFFICE.
VIII. HE WHO ENTERS UPON IT IS OFTEN SNARED INTO SIN, UNLESS HE IS VERY NOBLE-MINDED.
IX. HE IS CAUGHT BY VAINGLORY AND ITS ATTENDANT EVILS.
X. THE PRIESTHOOD IS NOT THE CAUSE OF THESE THINGS, BUT OUR OWN INDOLENCE.
XI. THE LUST OF DOMINATION SHOULD BE CAST OUT OF THE SOUL OF A PRIEST.[1]

1. CHRYSOSTOM: As regards the insult to those who have done me honor, what I have already said might be sufficient to prove that in avoiding this office I had no desire to put them to shame; but I will now endeavor to make it evident, to the best of my ability, that I was not puffed up by arrogance of any kind. For if the choice of a generalship or a kingdom had been submitted to me, and I had then formed this resolution, any one might naturally have suspected me of this fault, or rather I should have been found guilty by all men, not of arrogance, but of senseless folly. But when the priesthood is offered to me, which exceeds a kingdom as much as the spirit differs from the flesh, will any one dare to accuse me of disdain? And is it not preposterous to charge with folly those who reject small things, but when any do this in matters of pre-eminent importance, to exempt such persons from accusations of mental derangement, and yet subject them to the charge of pride? It is just as if one were to accuse, not of pride, but of insanity, a man who looked with contempt on a herd of oxen and refused to be a herdsman, and yet were to say that a man who declined the empire of the world, and the command of all the armies of the earth, was not mad, but inflated with pride. But this assuredly is not the case; and they who say such things do not injure me more than they injure themselves. For merely to imagine it possible for human nature to despise this dignity is an evidence against those who bring this charge of the estimate which they have formed of the office. For if they did not consider it to be an ordinary thing of no great account, such a suspicion as this would never have entered their heads. For why is it that no one has ever dared to entertain such a suspicion with reference to the dignity of the angels, and to say that arrogance is the reason why human nature would not aspire to the rank of the angelic nature? It is because we imagine great things concerning those powers, and this does not suffer us to believe that a man can conceive anything greater than that honor. Wherefore one might with more justice indite those persons of arrogance who accuse me of it. For they would never have suspected this of others if they had not previously depreciated the matter as being of no account. But if they say that I have done this with a view to glory, they will be convicted of fighting openly against themselves and falling into their own snare; for I do not know

---

[1] There are six chapters more, but the headings are wanting in the Greek copies. They have been added by one of the Latin translators, and are as follows:
XII. That the priest ought to be very wise.
XIII. Besides the greatest forbearance other things also are needed in the soul of a priest.
XIV. Nothing blunts the purity and keenness of the mind so much as unregulated anger.
XV. Chrysostom points out another form of strife full of perils.
XVI. How great he ought to be, who has to confront such storms.
XVII. How much there is to dread in the management of virgins.

what kind of arguments they could have sought in preference to these if they had wished to release me from the charge of vainglory.

2. For if this desire had ever entered my mind, I ought to have accepted the office rather than avoided it. Why? because it would have brought me much glory. For the fact that one of my age, who had so recently abandoned secular pursuits, should suddenly be deemed by all worthy of such admiration as to be advanced to honor before those who have spent all their life in labors of this kind, and to obtain more votes than all of them, might have persuaded all men to anticipate great and marvellous things of me. But, as it is, the greater part of the Church does not know me even by name: so that even my refusal of the office will not be manifest to all, but only to a few, and I am not sure that all even of these know it for certain; but probably many of them either imagine that I was not elected at all, or that I was rejected after the election, being considered unsuitable, not that I avoided the office of my own accord.

3. BASIL: But those who do know the truth will be surprised.

CHRYSOSTOM: And lo! these are they who, according to you, falsely accuse me of vainglory and pride. Whence then am I to hope for praise? From the many? They do not know the actual fact. From the few? Here again the matter is perverted to my disadvantage. For the only reason why you have come here now is to learn what answer ought to be given to them. And what shall I now certainly say on account of these things? For wait a little, and you will clearly perceive that even if all know the truth they ought not to condemn me for pride and love of glory. And in addition to this there is another consideration: that not only those who make this venture, if there be any such (which for my part I do not believe), but also those who suspect it of others, will be involved in no small danger.

4. For the priestly office is indeed discharged on earth, but it ranks amongst heavenly ordinances; and very naturally so: for neither man, nor angel, nor archangel, nor any other created power, but the Paraclete Himself, instituted this vocation, and persuaded men while still abiding in the flesh to represent the ministry of angels. Wherefore the consecrated priest ought to be as pure as if he were standing in the heavens themselves in the midst of those powers. Fearful, indeed, and of most awful import, were the things which were used before the dispensation of grace, as the bells, the pomegranates, the stones on the breastplate and on the ephod, the girdle, the mitre, the long robe, the plate of gold, the holy of holies,

the deep silence within.[1] But if any one should examine the things which belong to the dispensation of grace, he will find that, small as they are, yet are they fearful and full of awe, and that what was spoken concerning the law is true in this case also, that "what has been made glorious hath no glory in this respect by reason of the glory which excelleth."[2] For when thou seest the Lord sacrificed, and laid upon the altar,[3] and the priest standing and praying over the victim, and all the worshippers empurpled with that precious blood,[4] canst thou then think that thou art still amongst men, and standing upon the earth? Art thou not, on the contrary, straightway translated to Heaven, and casting out every carnal thought from the soul, dost thou not with disembodied spirit and pure reason contemplate the things which are in Heaven? Oh! what a marvel! what love of God to man! He who sitteth on high with the Father is at that hour held in the hands of all,[5] and gives Himself to those who are willing to embrace and grasp Him. And this all do through

---

[1] Exod. xxviii. 4 sq.   [2] 2 Cor. iii. 10.

[3] The Holy Eucharist is frequently called by St. chrysostom and other Greek Fathers the Sacrifice, sometimes the "unbloody Sacrifice," partly as being an offering of praise and thanksgiving, partly as being a commemoration or representation of the sacrifice of Christ. We must bear in mind that no controversy had then arisen about this Sacrament, and that writers could freely use expressions which in later times would have been liable to objection or misconstruction.

The passage before us must be read in the light of other passages in Chrysostom's works; but one of these is sufficient to indicate the sense in which it is to be understood. In Homily xvii. *c.* 3. on the Epistle to the Hebrews, after contrasting the many and ineffectual sacrifices of the Jews with the one perfect and efficient sacrifice of Christ, he proceeds, "What then? do we not make an offering every day? We do, certainly, but by making a memorial of His death; and this memorial is one, not many. How one, not many? Because the sacrifice was offered once for all, as that great sacrifice was in the Holy of Holies. This is a figure of that great sacrifice, as that was of this: for we do not offer one victim to-day and another to-morrow, but always the same: wherefore the sacrifice is one. Well, then, as He is offered in many places, are there many Christs? No, by no means, but everywhere one Christ, complete both in this world and in the other, one body. As then, though offered in many places, He is but one body, so is there but one sacrifice. Our High Priest is He who offers the sacrifice which cleanses us. We offer that now which was offered then: which is indeed inconsumable. This takes place now, for a memorial of what took place then. 'Do this,' said He, 'for my memorial.' We do not then offer a different sacrifice, as the high priest formerly did, but always the same; or rather we celebrate a memorial of a sacrifice."

[4] This may be only a rhetorical expression, but perhaps there is an allusion to a custom which prevailed in some churches, that the worshippers, after receiving the cup, applied the finger to the moistened lip, and then touched their breast, eyes and ears.

[5] The caution mentioned just now in note 3 must be repeated here. A comparison of passages in the writings of Chrysostom and his contemporaries proves clearly enough that they did not hold that the elements of bread and wine were transmuted into the body and blood of Christ in such a sense as to cease to be bread and wine. The authenticity of the letter of Chrysostom to Cæsarius is doubtful, but whoever the writer may have been, he is clearly representing the current orthodox belief of the Church in his day. He maintains, in opposition to the Apollinarian, or perhaps the Eutychian heresy, that there are two complete natures in the one person of God the Son Incarnate, and he illustrates it by the following reference to the holy elements in the Eucharist: "Just as the bread before consecration is called bread, but when the Divine Grace sanctifies it through the agency of the priest is released from the appellation of bread, and is deemed worthy of the appellation of the 'Lord's Body,' *although the nature of bread remains in it*, and we speak not of two bodies, but one body of the Son: so here the Divine nature, being seated in the human body, the two together make up but one Son—one Person."

the eyes of faith![1] Do these things seem to you fit to be despised, or such as to make it possible for any one to be uplifted against them?

Would you also learn from another miracle the exceeding sanctity of this office? Picture Elijah and the vast multitude standing around him, and the sacrifice laid upon the altar of stones, and all the rest of the people hushed into a deep silence while the prophet alone offers up prayer: then the sudden rush of fire from Heaven upon the sacrifice:—these are marvellous things, charged with terror. Now then pass from this scene to the rites which are celebrated in the present day; they are not only marvellous to behold, but transcendent in terror. There stands the priest, not bringing down fire from Heaven, but the Holy Spirit: and he makes prolonged supplication,[2] not that some flame sent down from on high may consume the offerings, but that grace descending on the sacrifice may thereby enlighten the souls of all, and render them more refulgent than silver purified by fire. Who can despise this most awful mystery, unless he is stark mad and senseless? Or do you not know that no human soul could have endured that fire in the sacrifice, but all would have been utterly consumed, had not the assistance of God's grace been great.

5. For if any one will consider how great a thing it is for one, being a man, and compassed with flesh and blood, to be enabled to draw nigh to that blessed and pure nature, he will then clearly see what great honor the grace of the Spirit has vouchsafed to priests; since by their agency these rites are celebrated, and others nowise inferior to these both in respect of our dignity and our salvation. For they who inhabit the earth and make their abode there are entrusted with the administration of things which are in Heaven, and have received an authority which God has not given to angels or archangels. For it has not been said to them, "Whatsoever ye shall bind on earth shall be bound in Heaven, and whatsoever ye shall loose on earth shall be loosed in Heaven."[3] They who rule on earth have indeed authority to bind, but only the body: whereas this binding lays hold of the soul and penetrates the heavens; and what priests do here below God ratifies above, and the Master confirms the sentence of his servants. For indeed what is it but all manner of heavenly authority which He has given them when He says, "Whose sins ye remit they are remitted, and whose sins ye retain they are retained?"[4] What authority could be greater than this? "The Father hath committed all judgment to the Son?"[5] But I see it all put into the hands of these men by the Son. For they have been conducted to this dignity as if they were already translated to Heaven, and had transcended human nature, and were released from the passions to which we are liable. Moreover, if a king should bestow this honor upon any of his subjects, authorizing him to cast into prison whom he pleased and to release them again, he becomes an object of envy and respect to all men; but he who has received from God an authority as much greater as heaven is more precious than earth, and souls more precious than bodies, seems to some to have received so small an honor that they are actually able to imagine that one of those who have been entrusted with these things will despise the gift. Away with such madness! For transparent madness it is to despise so great a dignity, without which it is not possible to obtain either our own salvation, or the good things which have been promised to us. For if no one can enter into the kingdom of Heaven except he be regenerate through water and the Spirit, and he who does not eat the flesh of the Lord and drink His blood is excluded from eternal life, and if all these things are accomplished only by means of those holy hands, I mean the hands of the priest, how will any one, without these, be able to escape the fire of hell, or to win those crowns which are reserved for the victorious?

6. These verily are they who are entrusted with the pangs of spiritual travail and the birth which comes through baptism: by their means we put on Christ, and are buried with the Son of God, and become members of that blessed Head. Wherefore they might not only be more justly feared by us than rulers and kings, but also be more honored than parents; since these begat us of blood and the will of the flesh, but the others are the authors of our birth from God, even that blessed regeneration which is the true freedom and the sonship according to grace. The Jewish priests had authority to release the body from leprosy, or, rather, not to release it but only to examine those who were already released, and you know how much the office of priest

---

[1] Some mss. omit the word πίστεως "of faith," having in its place τότε "at that time."
[2] In the Liturgy which bears the name of St. Chrysostom, the following invocation of the Holy Spirit occurs: "Grant that we may find grace in thy sight, that our sacrifice may become acceptable to Thee, and that the Good Spirit of thy grace may rest upon us, and upon these gifts spread before Thee, and upon all Thy people," and presently the deacon bids the people, "Let us pray on behalf of the precious gifts (i. e., the bread and wine) which have been provided, that the merciful God who has received them upon His holy spiritual altar beyond the heavens may in return send down upon us the divine grace and the fellowship of the Holy Ghost."
[3] Matt. xviii. 18.
[4] John xx. 23.
[5] John v. 22.

was contended for at that time. But our priests have received authority to deal, not with bodily leprosy, but spiritual uncleanness—not to pronounce it removed after examination, but actually and absolutely to take it away. Wherefore they who despise these priests would be far more accursed than Dathan and his company, and deserve more severe punishment. For the latter, although they laid claim to the dignity which did not belong to them, nevertheless had an excellent opinion concerning it, and this they evinced by the great eagerness with which they pursued it; but these men, when the office has been better regulated, and has received so great a development, have displayed an audacity which exceeds that of the others, although manifested in a contrary way. For there is not an equal amount of contempt involved in aiming at an honor which does not pertain to one, and in despising such great advantages, but the latter exceeds the former as much as scorn differs from admiration. What soul then is so sordid as to despise such great advantages? None whatever, I should say, unless it were one subject to some demoniacal impulse. For I return once more to the point from which I started: not in the way of chastising only, but also in the way of benefiting, God has bestowed a power on priests greater than that of our natural parents. The two indeed differ as much as the present and the future life. For our natural parents generate us unto this life only, but the others unto that which is to come. And the former would not be able to avert death from their offspring, or to repel the assaults of disease; but these others have often saved a sick soul, or one which was on the point of perishing, procuring for some a milder chastisement, and preventing others from falling altogether, not only by instruction and admonition, but also by the assistance wrought through prayers. For not only at the time of regeneration, but afterwards also, they have authority to forgive sins. "Is any sick among you?" it is said, "let him call for the elders of the Church and let them pray over him, anointing him with oil in the name of the Lord. And the prayer of faith shall save the sick, and the Lord will raise him up: and if he have committed sins they shall be forgiven him."[1] Again: our natural parents, should their children come into conflict with any men of high rank and great power in the world, are unable to profit them: but priests have reconciled, not rulers and kings, but God Himself when His wrath has often been provoked against them.

Well! after this will any one venture to condemn me for arrogance? For my part, after what has been said, I imagine such religious fear will possess the souls of the hearers that they will no longer condemn those who avoid the office for arrogance and temerity, but rather those who voluntarily come forward and are eager to obtain this dignity for themselves. For if they who have been entrusted with the command of cities, should they chance to be wanting in discretion and vigilance, have sometimes destroyed the cities and ruined themselves in addition, how much power think you both in himself and from above must he need, to avoid sinning, whose business it is to beautify the Bride of Christ?

7. No man loved Christ more than Paul: no man exhibited greater zeal, no man was counted worthy of more grace: nevertheless, after all these great advantages, he still has fears and tremblings concerning this government and those who were governed by him. "I fear," he says, "lest by any means, as the serpent beguiled Eve through his subtlety, so your minds should be corrupted from the simplicity which is in Christ."[2] And again, "I was with you in fear and in much trembling;"[3] and this was a man who had been caught up to the third Heaven, and made partaker of the unspeakable mysteries of God,[4] and had endured as many deaths as he had lived days after he became a believer—a man, moreover, who would not use the authority given him from Christ lest any of his converts should be offended.[5] If, then, he who went beyond the ordinances of God, and nowhere sought his own advantage, but that of those whom he governed, was always so full of fear when he considered the greatness of his government, what shall our condition be who in many ways seek our own, who not only fail to go beyond the commandments of Christ, but for the most part transgress them? "Who is weak," he says, "and I am not weak? who is offended and I burn not?"[6] Such an one ought the priest to be, or, rather, not such only: for these are small things, and as nothing compared with what I am about to say. And what is this? "I could wish," he says, "that myself were accursed from Christ for my brethren, my kinsmen according to the flesh."[7] If any one can utter such a speech, if any one has the soul which attains to such a prayer, he might justly be blamed if he took to flight: but if any one should lack such excellence as much as I do, he would deserve to be hated, not if he avoided the office, but if he accepted

---

[1] James v. 14, 15.
[2] 2 Cor. xi. 3. [3] 1 Cor. ii. 3. [4] 2 Cor. xii. 4.
[5] 2 Cor. xi. 9; 1 Thess. ii. 9. [6] 2 Cor. xi. 29.
[7] Rom. ix. 3.

it. For if an election to a military dignity was the business in hand, and they who had the right of conferring the honor were to drag forward a brazier, or a shoemaker, or some such artisan, and entrust the army to his hands, I should not praise the wretched man if he did not take to flight, and do all in his power to avoid plunging into such manifest trouble. If, indeed, it be sufficient to bear the name of pastor, and to take the work in hand hap-hazard, and there be no danger in this, then let whoso pleases accuse me of vainglory; but if it behoves one who undertakes this care to have much understanding, and, before understanding, great grace from God, and uprightness of conduct, and purity of life and superhuman virtue, do not deprive me of forgiveness if I am unwilling to perish in vain without a cause.

Moreover, if any one in charge of a full-sized merchant ship, full of rowers, and laden with a costly freight, were to station me at the helm and bid me cross the Ægean or the Tyrrhene sea, I should recoil from the proposal at once: and if any one asked me why? I should say, "Lest I should sink the ship." Well, where the loss concerns material wealth, and the danger extends only to bodily death, no one will blame those who exercise great prudence; but where the shipwrecked are destined to fall, not into the ocean, but into the abyss of fire, and the death which awaits them is not that which severs the soul from the body, but one which together with this dismisses it to eternal punishment, shall I incur your wrath and hate because I did not plunge headlong into so great an evil?

8. Do not thus, I pray and beseech you. I know my own soul, how feeble and puny it is: I know the magnitude of this ministry, and the great difficulty of the work; for more stormy billows vex the soul of the priest than the gales which disturb the sea.

9. And first of all is that most terrible rock of vainglory, more dangerous than that of the Sirens, of which the fable-mongers tell such marvellous tales: for many were able to sail past that and escape unscathed; but this is to me so dangerous that even now, when no necessity of any kind impels me into that abyss, I am unable to keep clear of the snare: but if any one were to commit this charge to me, it would be all the same as if he tied my hands behind my back, and delivered me to the wild beasts dwelling on that rock to rend me in pieces day by day. Do you ask what those wild beasts are? They are wrath, despondency, envy, strife, slanders, accusations, falsehood, hypocrisy, intrigues, anger against those who have done no harm, pleasure at the indecorous acts of fellow ministers, sorrow at their prosperity, love of praise, desire of honor (which indeed most of all drives the human soul headlong to perdition), doctrines devised to please, servile flatteries, ignoble fawning, contempt of the poor, paying court to the rich, senseless and mischievous honors, favors attended with danger both to those who offer and those who accept them, sordid fear suited only to the basest of slaves, the abolition of plain speaking, a great affectation of humility, but banishment of truth, the suppression of convictions and reproofs, or rather the excessive use of them against the poor, while against those who are invested with power no one dare open his lips.

For all these wild beasts, and more than these, are bred upon that rock of which I have spoken, and those whom they have once captured are inevitably dragged down into such a depth of servitude that even to please women they often do many things which it is well not to mention. The divine law indeed has excluded women from the ministry, but they endeavor to thrust themselves into it; and since they can effect nothing of themselves, they do all through the agency of others; and they have become invested with so much power that they can appoint or eject priests at their will:[1] things in fact are turned upside down, and the proverbial saying may be seen realized —"The ruled lead the rulers:" and would that it were men who do this instead of women, who have not received a commission to teach. Why do I say teach? for the blessed Paul did not suffer them even to speak in the Church.[2] But I have heard some one say that they have obtained such a large privilege of free speech, as even to rebuke the prelates of the Churches, and censure them more severely than masters do their own domestics.

10. And let not any one suppose that I subject all to the aforesaid charges: for there are some, yea many, who are superior to these entanglements, and exceed in number those who have been caught by them. Nor would I indeed make the priesthood responsible for these evils: far be such madness from me. For men of understanding do not say that the sword is to blame for murder, nor wine for drunkenness, nor strength for outrage, nor courage for foolhardiness, but they lay the blame on those who make an improper use of the gifts which have been bestowed upon them by God, and punish them accordingly. Certainly, at least, the priesthood may justly accuse us

---

[1] Chrysostom himself experienced the truth of this, for it was through the influence of Eudoxia, the wife of the Emperor Arcadius, that he was deposed from the See of Constantinople and banished.
[2] 1 Cor. xiv. 34; 1 Tim. ii. 12.

if we do not rightly handle it. For it is not itself a cause of the evils already mentioned, but we, who as far as lies in our power have defiled it with so many pollutions, by entrusting it to commonplace men who readily accept what is offered them, without having first acquired a knowledge of their own souls, or considered the gravity of the office, and when they have entered on the work, being blinded by inexperience, overwhelm with innumerable evils the people who have been committed to their care. This is the very thing which was very nearly happening in my case, had not God speedily delivered me from those dangers, mercifully sparing his Church and my own soul. For, tell me, whence do you think such great troubles are generated in the Churches? I, for my part, believe the only source of them to be the inconsiderate and random way in which prelates are chosen and appointed. For the head ought to be the strongest part, that it may be able to regulate and control the evil exhalations which arise from the rest of the body below; but when it happens to be weak in itself, and unable to repel those pestiferous attacks, it becomes feebler itself than it really is, and ruins the rest of the body as well. And to prevent this now coming to pass, God kept me in the position of the feet, which was the rank originally assigned to me. For there are very many other qualities, Basil, besides those already mentioned, which the priest ought to have, but which I do not possess; and, above all, this one:—his soul ought to be thoroughly purged from any lust after the office: for if he happens to have a natural inclination for this dignity, as soon as he attains it a stronger flame is kindled, and the man being taken completely captive will endure innumerable evils in order to keep a secure hold upon it, even to the extent of using flattery, or submitting to something base and ignoble, or expending large sums of money. For I will not now speak of the murders with which some have filled the Churches,[1] or the desolation which they have brought upon cities in contending for the dignity, lest some persons should think what I say incredible. But I am of opinion one ought to exercise so much caution in the matter, as to shun the burden of the office,[2] and when one has entered upon it, not to wait for the judgment of others should any fault be committed which warrants deposition, but to anticipate it by ejecting oneself from the dignity; for thus one might probably win mercy for himself from God: but to cling to it in defiance of propriety is to deprive oneself of all forgiveness, or rather to kindle the wrath of God, by adding a second error more offensive than the first.

11. But no one will always endure the strain; for fearful, truly fearful is the eager desire after this honor. And in saying this I am not in opposition to the blessed Paul, but in complete harmony with his words. For what says he? "If any man desireth the office of a bishop, he desireth a good work."[3] Now I have not said that it is a terrible thing to desire the *work*, but only the authority and power. And this desire I think one ought to expel from the soul with all possible earnestness, not permitting it at the outset to be possessed by such a feeling, so that one may be able to do everything with freedom. For he who does not desire to be exhibited in possession of this authority, does not fear to be deposed from it, and not fearing this will be able to do everything with the freedom which becomes Christian men: whereas they who fear and tremble lest they should be deposed undergo a bitter servitude, filled with all kinds of evils, and are often compelled to offend against both God and man. Now the soul ought not to be affected in this way; but as in warfare we see those soldiers who are noble-spirited fight willingly and fall bravely, so they who have attained to this stewardship should be contented to be consecrated to the dignity or removed from it, as becomes Christian men, knowing that deposition of this kind brings its reward no less than the discharge of the office. For when any one suffers anything of this kind, in order to avoid submitting to something which is unbecoming or unworthy of this dignity, he procures punishment for those who wrongfully depose him, and a greater reward for himself. "Blessed," says our Lord, "are ye when men shall revile you and persecute you, and shall say all manner of evil against you falsely for my sake; rejoice and be exceeding glad, for great is your reward in Heaven."[4] And this, indeed, is the case when any one is expelled by those of his own rank either on account of envy, with a view to the favor of others, or through hatred, or from any other wrong motive: but when it is the lot of any one to experience this treatment at the hand of opponents, I do not think a word is needed to prove what great gain they confer upon him by their wickedness.

It behoves us, then, to be on the watch on all sides, and to make a careful search lest any

---

[1] Possibly the building, not the body of Christians is here signified; for in the contest between Damasus and Ursicinus for the See of Rome, A.D. 367, which Chrysostom probably had in his mind, 137 persons are said to have been slain in one of the Churches in a single day.
[2] According to another reading the passage must be rendered, "shun the burden at the outset."
[3] 1 Tim. iii. 1.
[4] Matt. v. 1

spark of this desire should be secretly smouldering somewhere. For it is much to be wished that those who are originally free from this passion, should also be able to avoid it when they have lighted upon this office. But if any one, before he obtains the honor, cherishes in himself this terrible and savage monster, it is impossible to say into what a furnace he will fling himself after he has attained it. Now I possessed this desire in a high degree (and do not suppose that I would ever tell you what was untrue in self-disparagement): and this, combined with other reasons, alarmed me not a little, and induced me to take flight. For just as lovers of the human person, as long as they are permitted to be near the objects of their affection, suffer more severe torment from their passion, but when they remove as far as possible from these objects of desire, they drive away the frenzy: even so when those who desire this dignity are near it, the evil becomes intolerable: but when they cease to hope for it, the desire is extinguished together with the expectation.

12. This single motive then is no slight one: and even taken by itself it would have sufficed to deter me from this dignity: but, as it is, another must be added not less than the former. And what is this? A priest ought to be sober minded, and penetrating in discernment, and possessed of innumerable eyes in every direction, as one who lives not for himself alone but for so great a multitude. But that I am sluggish and slack, and scarcely able to bring about my own salvation, even you yourself would admit, who out of love to me art especially eager to conceal my faults. Talk not to me in this connexion of fasting, and watching, or sleeping on the ground, and other hard discipline of the body: for you know how defective I am in these matters: and even if they had been carefully practised by me they could not with my present sluggishness have been of any service to me with a view to this post of authority. Such things might be of great service to a man who was shut up in a cell, and caring only for his own concerns: but when a man is divided among so great a multitude, and enters separately into the private cares of those who are under his direction, what appreciable help can be given to their improvement unless he possesses a robust and exceedingly vigorous character?

13. And do not be surprised if, in connexion with such endurance, I seek another test of fortitude in the soul. For to be indifferent to food and drink and a soft bed, we see is to many no hard task, especially at least to such as are of a rough habit of life and have been brought up in this way from early youth, and to many others also; bodily discipline and custom softening the severity of these laborious practices: but insult, and abuse, and coarse language, and gibes from inferiors, whether wantonly or justly uttered, and rebukes vainly and idly spoken both by rulers and the ruled—this is what few can bear, in fact only one or two here and there; and one may see men, who are strong in the former exercises, so completely upset by these things, as to become more furious than the most savage beasts. Now such men especially we should exclude from the precincts of the priesthood. For if a prelate did not loathe food, or go barefoot, no harm would be done to the common interests of the Church; but a furious temper causes great disasters both to him who possesses it, and to his neighbours. And there is no divine threat against those who fail to do the things referred to, but hell and hell-fire are threatened against those who are angry without a cause.[1] As then the lover of vainglory, when he takes upon him the government of numbers, supplies additional fuel to the fire, so he who by himself, or in the company of a few, is unable to control his anger, but readily carried away by it, should he be entrusted with the direction of a whole multitude, like some wild beast goaded on all sides by countless tormentors, would never be able to live in tranquillity himself, and would cause incalculable mischief to those who have been committed to his charge.

14. For nothing clouds the purity of the reason, and the perspicuity of the mental vision so much as undisciplined wrath, rushing along with violent impetuosity. "For wrath," says one, "destroys even the prudent."[2] For the eye of the soul being darkened as in some nocturnal battle is not able to distinguish friends from foes, nor the honorable from the unworthy, but handles them all in turn in the same way; even if some harm must be suffered, readily enduring everything, in order to satisfy the pleasure of the soul. For the fire of wrath is a kind of pleasure, and tyrannizes over the soul more harshly than pleasure, completely upsetting its healthy organization. For it easily impels men to arrogance, and unseasonable enmities, and unreasonable hatred, and it continually makes them ready to commit wanton and vain offences; and forces them to say and do many other things of that kind, the soul being swept along by the rush of passion, and having nothing on which to fasten its strength and resist so great an impulse.

BASIL: I will not endure this irony of yours any longer: for who knows not how far removed you are from this infirmity?

---

[1] Matt. v. 22. [2] Prov. xv. 1, the Septuagint version.

CHRYSOSTOM: Why then, my good friend, do you wish to bring me near the pyre, and to provoke the wild beast when he is tranquil? Are you not aware that I have achieved this condition, not by any innate virtue, but by my love of retirement? and that when one who is so constituted remains contented by himself, or only associates with one or two friends, he is able to escape the fire which arises from this passion, but not if he has plunged into the abyss of all these cares? for then he drags not only himself but many others with him to the brink of destruction, and renders them more indifferent to all consideration for mildness. For the mass of people under government are generally inclined to regard the manners of those who govern as a kind of model type, and to assimilate themselves to them. How then could any one put a stop to their fury when he is swelling himself with rage? And who amongst the multitude would straightway desire to become moderate when he sees the ruler irritable? For it is quite impossible for the defects of priests to be concealed, but even trifling ones speedily become manifest. So an athlete, as long as he remains at home, and contends with no one, can dissemble his weakness even if it be very great, but when he strips for the contest he is easily detected. And thus for some who live this private and inactive life, their isolation serves as a veil to hide their defects; but when they have been brought into public they are compelled to divest themselves of this mantle of seclusion, and to lay bare their souls to all through their visible movements. As therefore their right deeds profit many, by provoking them to equal zeal, so their shortcomings make men more indifferent to the practice of virtue, and encourage them to indolence in their endeavours after what is excellent. Wherefore his soul ought to gleam with beauty on every side, that it may be able to gladden and to enlighten the souls of those who behold it. For the faults of ordinary men, being committed as it were in the dark, ruin only those who practise them: but the errors of a man in a conspicuous position, and known to many, inflicts a common injury upon all, rendering those who have fallen more supine in their efforts for good, and driving to desperation those who wish to take heed to themselves. And apart from these things, the faults of insignificant men, even if they are exposed, inflict no injury worth speaking of upon any one: but they who occupy the highest seat of honor are in the first place plainly visible to all, and if they err in the smallest matters these trifles seem great to others: for all men measure the sin, not by the magnitude of the offence, but by the rank of the offender.

Thus the priest ought to be protected on all sides by a kind of adamantine armour, by intense earnestness, and perpetual watchfulness concerning his manner of life, lest some one discovering an exposed and neglected spot should inflict a deadly wound: for all who surround him are ready to smite and overthrow him: not enemies only and adversaries, but many even of those who profess friendship.

The souls therefore of men elected to the priesthood ought to be endued with such power as the grace of God bestowed on the bodies of those saints who were cast into the Babylonian furnace.[1] Faggot and pitch and tow are not the fuel of this fire, but things far more dreadful: for it is no material fire to which they are subjected, but the all-devouring flame of envy encompasses them, rising up on every side, and assailing them, and putting their life to a more searching test than the fire then was to the bodies of those young men. When then it finds a little trace of stubble, it speedily fastens upon it; and this unsound part it entirely consumes, but all the rest of the fabric, even if it be brighter than the sunbeams, is scorched and blackened by the smoke. For as long as the life of the priest is well regulated in every direction, it is invulnerable to plots; but if he happens to overlook some trifle, as is natural in a human being, traversing the treacherous ocean of this life, none of his other good deeds are of any avail in enabling him to escape the mouths of his accusers; but that little blunder overshadows all the rest. And all men are ready to pass judgment on the priest as if he was not a being clothed with flesh, or one who inherited a human nature, but like an angel, and emancipated from every species of infirmity. And just as all men fear and flatter a tyrant as long as he is strong, because they cannot put him down, but when they see his affairs going adversely, those who were his friends a short time before abandon their hypocritical respect, and suddenly become his enemies and antagonists, and having discovered all his weak points, make an attack upon him, and depose him from the government; so is it also in the case of priests. Those who honored him and paid court to him a short time before, while he was strong, as soon as they have found some little handle eagerly prepare to depose him, not as a tyrant only, but something far more dreadful than that. And as the tyrant fears his body guards, so also does the priest dread most of all his neighbours and fellow-ministers. For no others covet his dignity so much, or know his affairs so well as these; and if anything occurs, be-

---

[1] Dan. iii.

ing near at hand, they perceive it before others, and even if they slander him, can easily command belief, and, by magnifying trifles, take their victim captive. For the apostolic saying is reversed, "whether one member suffer, all the members suffer with it; or one member be honored, all the members rejoice with it;"[1] unless indeed a man should be able by his great discretion to stand his ground against everything.

Are you then for sending me forth into so great a warfare? and did you think that my soul would be equal to a contest so various in character and shape? Whence did you learn this, and from whom? If God certified this to you, show me the oracle, and I obey; but if you cannot, and form your judgment from human opinion only, please to set yourself free from this delusion. For in what concerns my own affairs it is fairer to trust me than others; inasmuch as "no man knoweth the things of a man, save the spirit of man which is in him."[2] That I should have made myself and my electors ridiculous, had I accepted this office, and should with great loss have returned to this condition of life in which I now am, I trust I have now convinced you by these remarks, if not before. For not malice only, but something much stronger—the lust after this dignity—is wont to arm many against one who possesses it. And just as avaricious children are oppressed by the old age of their parents, so some of these, when they see the priestly office held by any one for a protracted time—since it would be wickedness to destroy him—hasten to depose him from it, being all desirous to take his place, and each expecting that the dignity will be transferred to himself.

15. Would you like me to show you yet another phase of this strife, charged with innumerable dangers? Come, then, and take a peep at the public festivals when it is generally the custom for elections to be made to ecclesiastical dignities, and you will then see the priest assailed with accusations as numerous as the people whom he rules. For all who have the privilege of conferring the honor are then split into many parties; and one can never find the council of elders[3] of one mind with each other, or about the man who has won the prelacy; but each stands apart from the others, one preferring this man, another that. Now the reason is that they do not all look to one thing, which ought to be the only object kept in view, the excellence of the character; but other qualifications are alleged as recommending to this honor; for instance, of one it is said, "let him be elected because he belongs to an illustrious family," of another "because he is possessed of great wealth, and would not need to be supported out of the revenues of the Church," of a third "because he has come over from the camp of the adversary;" one is eager to give the preference to a man who is on terms of intimacy with himself, another to the man who is related to him by birth, a third to the flatterer, but no one will look to the man who is really qualified, or make some test of his character. Now I am so far from thinking these things trustworthy criteria of a man's fitness for the priesthood, that even if any one manifested great piety, which is no small help in the discharge of that office, I should not venture to approve him on that account alone, unless he happened to combine good abilities with his piety. For I know many men who have exercised perpetual restraint upon themselves, and consumed themselves with fastings, who, as long as they were suffered to be alone, and attend to their own concerns, have been acceptable to God, and day by day have made no small addition to this kind of learning; but as soon as they entered public life, and were compelled to correct the ignorance of the multitude, have, some of them, proved from the outset incompetent for so great a task, and others when forced to persevere in it, have abandoned their former strict way of living, and thus inflicted great injury on themselves without profiting others at all. And if any one spent his whole time in the lowest rank of the ministry, and reached extreme old age, I would not, merely out of reverence for his years, promote him to the higher dignity; for what if, after arriving at that time of life, he should still remain unfit for the office? And I say this now, not as wishing to dishonor the grey head, nor as laying down a law absolutely to exclude from this authority those who come from the monastic circle (for there are instances of many who issued from that body, having shone conspicuously in this dignity); but the point which I am anxious to prove is, that if neither piety of itself, nor advanced age, would suffice to show that a man who had obtained the priesthood really deserved it, the reasons formerly alleged would scarcely effect this. There are also men who bring forward other pretexts yet more

---

[1] 1 Cor. xii. 26.   [2] 1 Cor. ii. 11.

[3] It is not possible to say precisely who the electors to bishoprics were at this time, but probably a mixed body of the clergy and leading laymen of the diocese. Chrysostom calls the electors "fathers," i. ch. 6, and "great men," ch. 7, and here he speaks of a "council of elders," which may mean the whole body of clergy of the second order, or a select body of laymen, or possibly the two combined. In one way or other, during the first five centuries, the people certainly had a considerable voice in the election of bishops. Socrates, the historian, vi. c. 2, says that Chrysostom himself was chosen for the See of Constantinople "by the common vote of all, clergy and people." Pope Leo (A.D. 440-461) lays down the rule that "when the election of a bishop is handled he is to be preferred who is demanded by the unanimous consent of clergy and people," Epist. 84. A law of the Emperor Justinian restricted the right of election to the clergy and the "optimates" or people of chief rank.

absurd; for some are enrolled in the ranks of the clergy, that they may not range themselves among opponents, and others on account of their evil disposition, lest they should do great mischief if they are overlooked. Could anything be more contrary to right rule than this? that bad men, laden with iniquity, should be courted on account of those things for which they ought to be punished, and ascend to the priestly dignity on account of things for which they ought to be debarred from the very threshold of the Church. Tell me, then, shall we seek any further the cause of God's wrath, when we expose things so holy and awful to be defiled by men who are either wicked or worthless? for when some men are entrusted with the administration of things which are not at all suitable to them, and others of things which exceed their natural power, they make the condition of the Church like that of Euripus.[1]

Now formerly I used to deride secular rulers, because in the distribution of their honors they are not guided by considerations of moral excellence, but of wealth, and seniority, and human distinction; but when I heard that this kind of folly had forced its way into our affairs also, I no longer regarded their conduct as so atrocious. For what wonder is it that worldly men, who love the praise of the multitude, and do everything for the sake of gain, should commit these sins, when those who affect at least to be free from all these influences are in no wise better disposed than they, but although engaged in a contest for heavenly things, act as if the question submitted for decision was one which concerned acres of land, or something else of that kind? for they take commonplace men off-hand, and set them to preside over those things, for the sake of which the only begotten Son of God did not refuse to empty Himself of His glory and become man, and take the form of a servant, and be spat upon, and buffeted, and die a death of reproach in the flesh. Nor do they stop even here, but add to these offences others still more monstrous; for not only do they elect unworthy men, but actually expel those who are well qualified. As if it were necessary to ruin the safety of the Church on both sides, or as if the former provocation were not sufficient to kindle the wrath of God, they have contrived yet another not less pernicious. For I consider it as atrocious to expel the useful men as to force in the useless. And this in fact takes place, so that the flock of Christ is unable to find consolation in any direction, or draw its breath freely. Now do not such deeds deserve to be punished by ten thousand thunder-bolts, and a hell-fire hotter than that with which we are threatened [in Holy Scripture]? Yet these monstrous evils are borne with by Him who willeth not the death of a sinner, that he may be converted and live. And how can one sufficiently marvel at His lovingkindness, and be amazed at His mercy? They who belong to Christ destroy the property of Christ more than enemies and adversaries, yet the good Lord still deals gently with them, and calls them to repentance. Glory be to Thee, O Lord! Glory to Thee! How vast is the depth of Thy lovingkindness! how great the riches of Thy forbearance! Men who on account of Thy name have risen from insignificance and obscurity to positions of honor and distinction, use the honor they enjoy against Him who has bestowed it, do deeds of outrageous audacity, and insult holy things, rejecting and expelling men of zeal in order that the wicked may ruin everything at their pleasure in much security, and with the utmost fearlessness. And if you would know the causes of this dreadful evil, you will find that they are similar to those which were mentioned before; for they have one root and mother, so to say—namely, envy; but this is manifested in several different forms. For one we are told is to be struck out of the list of candidates, because he is young; another because he does not know how to flatter; a third because he has offended such and such a person; a fourth lest such and such a man should be pained at seeing one whom he has presented rejected, and this man elected; a fifth because he is kind and gentle; a sixth because he is formidable to the sinful; a seventh for some other like reason; for they are at no loss to find as many pretexts as they want, and can even make the abundance of a man's wealth an objection when they have no other. Indeed they would be capable of discovering other reasons, as many as they wish, why a man ought not to be brought suddenly to this honor, but gently and gradually. And here I should like to ask the question, "What, then, is the prelate to do, who has to contend with such blasts? How shall he hold his ground against such billows? How shall he repel all these assaults?"

For if he manages the business[2] upon upright principles, all those who are enemies and adversaries both to him and to the candidates do everything with a view to contention, provoking daily strife, and heaping infinite

---

[1] A narrow strait between the island of Eubœa and the mainland of Greece, in which the tide was very rapid. Hence the "condition of Euripus" became a proverbial expression indicative of agitation and fluctuation.

[2] *i. e.*, the business of elections. Chrysostom seems to have passed on from the elections of bishops to the consideration of elections to clerical offices over which the bishop had to preside.

scorn upon the candidates, until they have got them struck off the list, or have introduced their own favorites. In fact it is just as if some pilot had pirates sailing with him in his ship, perpetually plotting every hour against him, and the sailors, and marines. And if he should prefer favor with such men to his own salvation, accepting unworthy candidates, he will have God for his enemy in their stead; and what could be more dreadful than that? And yet his relations with them will be more embarrassing than formerly, as they will all combine with each other, and thereby become more powerful than before. For as when fierce winds coming from opposite directions clash with one another, the ocean, hitherto calm, becomes suddenly furious and raises its crested waves, destroying those who are sailing over it, so also when the Church has admitted corrupt men, its once tranquil surface is covered with rough surf and strewn with shipwrecks.

16. Consider, then, what kind of man he ought to be who is to hold out against such a tempest, and to manage skillfully such great hindrances to the common welfare; for he ought to be dignified yet free from arrogance, formidable yet kind, apt to command yet sociable, impartial yet courteous, humble yet not servile, strong yet gentle, in order that he may contend successfully against all these difficulties. And he ought to bring forward with great authority the man who is properly qualified for the office, even if all should oppose him, and with the same authority to reject the man who is not so qualified, even if all should conspire in his favor, and to keep one aim only in view, the building up of the Church, in nothing actuated either by enmity or favor. Well, do you now think that I acted reasonably in declining the ministry of this office? But I have not even yet gone through all my reasons with you; for I have some others still to mention. And do not grow impatient of listening to a friendly and sincere man, who wishes to clear himself from your accusations; for these statements are not only serviceable for the defence which you have to make on my behalf, but they will also prove of no small help for the due administration of the office. For it is necessary for one who is going to enter upon this path of life to investigate all matters thoroughly well, before he sets his hand to the ministry. Do you ask why? Because one who knows all things clearly will have this advantage, if no other, that he will not feel strange when these things befall him. Would you like me then to approach the question of superintending widows, first of all, or of the care of virgins, or the difficulty of the judicial function. For in each of these cases there is a different kind of anxiety, and the fear is greater than the anxiety.

Now in the first place, to start from that subject which seems to be simpler than the others, the charge of widows appears to cause anxiety to those who take care of them only so far as the expenditure of money is concerned; but the case is otherwise, and here also a careful scrutiny is needed, when they have to be enrolled,[1] for infinite mischief has been caused by putting them on the list without due discrimination. For they have ruined households, and severed marriages, and have often been detected in thieving and pilfering and unseemly deeds of that kind. Now that such women should be supported out of the Church's revenues provokes punishment from God, and extreme condemnation among men, and abates the zeal of those who wish to do good. For who would ever choose to expend the wealth which he was commanded to give to Christ upon those who defame the name of Christ? For these reasons a strict and accurate scrutiny ought to be made so as to prevent the supply of the indigent being wasted, not only by the women already mentioned, but also by those who are able to provide for themselves. And this scrutiny is succeeded by no small anxiety of another kind, to ensure an abundant and unfailing stream of supply as from a fountain; for compulsory poverty is an insatiable kind of evil, querulous and ungrateful. And great discretion and great zeal is required so as to stop the mouths of complainers, depriving them of every excuse. Now most men, when they see any one superior to the love of money, forthwith represent him as well qualified for this stewardship. But I do not think that this greatness of soul is ever sufficient of itself, although it ought to be possessed prior to all other qualities; for without this a man would be a destroyer rather than a protector, a wolf instead of a shepherd; nevertheless, combined with this, the possession of another quality also should be demanded. And this quality is forbearance, the cause of all good things in men, impelling as it were and conducting the soul into a serene haven. For widows are a class who, both on account of their poverty, their age and natural dispo-

---

[1] That is, ' put upon the Church-roll." From apostolic times, as we know from 1 Tim. v. 9, 10, the Church had recognized the care of widows as a duty; but one to be exercised with caution, lest unworthy persons should take advantage of it. In Chrysostom's time there was an "order of widows, which had departed very much from the primitive simplicity and devotion to religious works which distinguished the order of earlier days. The Church strongly encouraged abstinence from a second marriage: and many women seem to have taken a vow of widowhood, and secured a place in the Church-roll, only in the hope of throwing a decent veil over an irreligious, if not immoral life.

sition, indulge in unlimited freedom of speech (so I had best call it); and they make an unseasonable clamor and idle complaints and lamentations about matters for which they ought to be grateful, and bring accusations concerning things which they ought contentedly to accept. Now the superintendent should endure all these things in a generous spirit, and not be provoked either by their unreasonable annoyance or their unreasonable complaints. For this class of persons deserve to be pitied for their misfortunes, not to be insulted; and to trample upon their calamities, and add the pain of insult to that which poverty brings, would be an act of extreme brutality. On this account one of the wisest of men, having regard to the avarice and pride of human nature, and considering the nature of poverty and its terrible power to depress even the noblest character, and induce it often to act in these same respects without shame, in order that a man should not be irritated when accused, nor be provoked by continual importunity to become an enemy where he ought to bring aid, he instructs him to be affable and accessible to the suppliant, saying, "Incline thine ear to a poor man and give him a friendly answer with meekness."[1] And passing by the case of one who succeeds in exasperating (for what can one say to him who is overcome?), he addresses the man who is able to bear the other's infirmity, exhorting him before he bestows his gift to correct the suppliant by the gentleness of his countenance and the mildness of his words. But if any one, although he does not take the property (of these widows), nevertheless loads them with innumerable reproaches, and insults them, and is exasperated against them, he not only fails through his gift to alleviate the despondency produced by poverty, but aggravates the distress by his abuse. For although they may be compelled to act very shamelessly through the necessity of hunger, they are nevertheless distressed at this compulsion. When, then, owing to the dread of famine, they are constrained to beg, and owing to their begging are constrained to put off shame, and then again on account of their shamelessness are insulted, the power of despondency becoming of a complex kind, and accompanied by much gloom, settles down upon the soul. And one who has the charge of these persons ought to be so long-suffering, as not only not to increase their despondency by his fits of anger, but also to remove the greater part of it by his exhortation. For as the man who has been insulted, although he is in the enjoyment of great abundance, does not feel the advantage of his wealth, on account of the blow which he has received from the insult; so on the other hand, the man who has been addressed with kindly words, and for whom the gift has been accompanied with encouragement, exults and rejoices all the more, and the thing given becomes doubled in value through the manner in which it is offered. And this I say not of myself, but borrow from him whose precept I quoted just now: "My son, blemish not thy good deeds, neither use uncomfortable words when thou givest anything. Shall not the dew assuage the heat? So is a word better than a gift. Lo! is not a word better than a gift? but both are with a gracious man."[2]

But the superintendent of these persons ought not only to be gentle and forbearing, but also skillful in the management of property; for if this qualification is wanting, the affairs of the poor are again involved in the same distress. One who was entrusted not long ago with this ministry, and got together a large hoard of money, neither consumed it himself, nor expended it with a few exceptions upon those who needed it, but kept the greater part of it buried in the earth until a season of distress occurred, when it was all surrendered into the hands of the enemy. Much forethought, therefore, is needed, that the resources of the Church should be neither over abundant, nor deficient, but that all the supplies which are provided should be quickly distributed among those who require them, and the treasures of the Church stored up in the hearts of those who are under her rule.

Moreover, in the reception of strangers, and the care of the sick, consider how great an expenditure of money is needed, and how much exactness and discernment on the part of those who preside over these matters. For it is often necessary that this expenditure should be even larger than that of which I spoke just now, and that he who presides over it should combine prudence and wisdom with skill in the art of supply, so as to dispose the affluent to be emulous and ungrudging in their gifts, lest while providing for the relief of the sick, he should vex the souls of those who supply their wants. But earnestness and zeal need to be displayed here in a far higher degree; for the sick are difficult creatures to please, and prone to languor; and unless great accuracy and care are used, even a slight oversight is enough to do the patient great mischief.

17. But in the care of virgins, the fear is greater in proportion as the possession is more precious, and this flock is of a nobler character

---

[1] Ecclus. iv. 8.

[2] Ecclus. xviii. 15-17.

than the others. Already, indeed, even into the band of these holy ones, an infinite number of women have rushed full of innumerable bad qualities; and in this case our grief is greater than in the other; for there is just the same difference between a virgin and a widow going astray, as between a free-born damsel and her handmaid. With widows, indeed, it has become a common practice to trifle, and to rail at one another, to flatter or to be impudent, to appear everywhere in public, and to perambulate the market-place. But the virgin has striven for nobler aims, and eagerly sought the highest kind of philosophy,[1] and professes to exhibit upon earth the life which angels lead, and while yet in the flesh proposes to do deeds which belong to the incorporeal powers. Moreover, she ought not to make numerous or unnecessary journeys, neither is it permissible for her to utter idle and random words; and as for abuse and flattery, she should not even know them by name. On this account she needs the most careful guardianship, and the greater assistance. For the enemy of holiness is always surprising and lying in wait for these persons, ready to devour any one of them if she should slip and fall; many men also there are who lay snares for them; and besides all these things there is the passionateness of their own human nature, so that, speaking generally, the virgin has to equip herself for a twofold war, one which attacks her from without, and the other which presses upon her from within. For these reasons he who has the superintendence of virgins suffers great alarm, and the danger and distress is yet greater, should any of the things which are contrary to his wishes occur, which God forbid. For if a daughter kept in seclusion is a cause of sleeplessness to her father, his anxiety about her depriving him of sleep, where the fear is so great lest she should be childless, or pass the flower of her age (unmarried), or be hated (by her husband),[2] what will he suffer whose anxiety is not concerned with any of these things, but others far greater? For in this case it is not a man who is rejected, but Christ Himself, nor is this barrenness the subject merely of reproach, but the evil ends in the destruction of the soul; "for every tree," it is said, "which bringeth not forth good fruit, is hewn down and cast into the fire."[3] And for one who has been repudiated by the divine Bridegroom, it is not sufficient to receive a certificate of divorce and so to depart, but she has to pay the penalty of everlasting punishment. Moreover, a father according to the flesh has many things which make the custody of his daughter easy; for the mother, and nurse, and a multitude of handmaids share in helping the parent to keep the maiden safe. For neither is she permitted to be perpetually hurrying into the market-place, nor when she does go there is she compelled to show herself to any of the passers-by, the evening darkness concealing one who does not wish to be seen no less than the walls of the house. And apart from these things, she is relieved from every cause which might otherwise compel her to meet the gaze of men; for no anxiety about the necessaries of life, no menaces of oppressors, nor anything of that kind reduces her to this unfortunate necessity, her father acting in her stead in all these matters; while she herself has only one anxiety, which is to avoid doing or saying anything unworthy the modest conduct which becomes her. But in the other case there are many things which make the custody of the virgin difficult, or rather impossible for the father; for he could not have her in his house with himself, as dwelling together in that way would be neither seemly nor safe. For even if they themselves should suffer no loss, but continue to preserve their innocence unsullied, they would have to give an account for the souls which they have offended, just as much as if they happened to sin with one another. And it being impossible for them to live together, it is not easy to understand the movements of the character, and to suppress the impulses which are ill regulated, or train and improve those which are better ordered and tuned. Nor is it an easy thing to interfere in her habits of walking out; for her poverty and want of a guardian does not permit him to become an exact investigator of the propriety of her conduct. For as she is compelled to manage all her affairs she has many pretexts for going out, if at least she is not inclined to be self-controlled. Now he who commands her to stay always at home ought to cut off these pretexts, providing for her independence in the necessaries of life, and giving her some woman who will see to the management of these things. He must also keep her away from funeral obsequies, and nocturnal festivals; for that artful serpent knows only too well how to scatter his poison through the medium even of good deeds. And the maiden must be fenced on every side, and rarely go out of the house during the whole year, except when she is constrained by inexorable necessity. Now if any one should say

---

[1] *i.e.*, a life of religious contemplation, not, however, as a member of a monastic community, for Chrysostom, throughout this section, appears to be speaking of the canonical or ecclesiastical virgins who were consecrated to a religious life, yet remained at home under the care of their parents (if living) or of the Church. The first notices of separate houses for women who had taken the vow of virginity occur in the middle of the 4th century. St. Ambrose mentions one at Bologna. De Virg. i. 10. St. Basil is said to have founded some (See St. Greg. Naz. Orat. 47).
[2] Ecclus. xlii. 9.   [3] Matt. iii. 10.

that none of these things is the proper work of a bishop to take in hand, let him be assured that the anxieties and the reasons concerning what takes place in every case have to be referred to him. And it is far more expedient that he should manage everything, and so be delivered from the complaints which he must otherwise undergo on account of the faults of others, than that he should abstain from the management, and then have to dread being called to account for things which other men have done. Moreover, he who does these things by himself, gets through them all with great ease; but he who is compelled to do it by converting every one's opinion does not get relief by being saved from working single-handed, equivalent to the trouble and turmoil which he experiences through those who oppose him and combat his decisions. However, I could not enumerate all the anxieties concerned with the care of virgins; for when they have to be entered on the list, they occasion no small trouble to him who is entrusted with this business.

Again, the judicial department of the bishop's office involves innumerable vexations, great consumption of time, and difficulties exceeding those experienced by men who sit to judge secular affairs; for it is a labor to discover exact justice, and when it is found, it is difficult to avoid destroying it. And not only loss of time and difficulty are incurred, but also no small danger. For ere now, some of the weaker brethren having plunged into business, because they have not obtained patronage have made shipwreck concerning the faith. For many of those who have suffered wrong, no less than those who have inflicted wrong, hate those who do not assist them, and they will not take into account either the intricacy of the matters in question, or the difficulty of the times, or the limits of sacerdotal authority, or anything of that kind; but they are merciless judges, recognizing only one kind of defence—release from the evils which oppress them. And he who is unable to furnish this, although he may allege innumerable excuses, will never escape their condemnation.

And talking of patronage, let me disclose another pretext for fault-finding. For if the bishop does not pay a round of visits every day, more even than the idle men about town, unspeakable offence ensues. For not only the sick, but also the whole, desire to be looked after, not that piety prompts them to this, but rather that in most cases they pretend claims to honor and distinction. And if he should ever happen to visit more constantly one of the richer and more powerful men, under the pressure of some necessity, with a view to the common benefit of the Church, he is immediately stigmatized with a character for fawning and flattery. But why do I speak of patronage and visiting? For merely from their mode of accosting persons, bishops have to endure such a load of reproaches as to be often oppressed and overwhelmed by despondency; in fact, they have also to undergo a scrutiny of the way in which they use their eyes. For the public rigorously criticize their simplest actions, taking note of the tone of their voice, the cast of their countenance, and the degree of their laughter. He laughed heartily to such a man, one will say, and accosted him with a beaming face, and a clear voice, whereas to me he addressed only a slight and passing remark. And in a large assembly, if he does not turn his eyes in every direction when he is conversing, the majority declare that his conduct is insulting.

Who, then, unless he is exceedingly strong, could cope with so many accusers, so as either to avoid being indited altogether, or, if he is indited, to escape? For he must either be without any accusers, or, if this is impossible, purge himself of the accusations which are brought against him; and if this again is not an easy matter, as some men delight in making vain and wanton charges, he must make a brave stand against the dejection produced by these complaints. He, indeed, who is justly accused, may easily tolerate the accuser, for there is no bitterer accuser than conscience; wherefore, if we are caught first by this most terrible adversary, we can readily endure the milder ones who are external to us. But he who has no evil thing upon his conscience, when he is subjected to an empty charge, is speedily excited to wrath, and easily sinks into dejection, unless he happens to have practised beforehand how to put up with the follies of the multitude. For it is utterly impossible for one who is falsely accused without cause, and condemned, to avoid feeling some vexation and annoyance at such great injustice.

And how can one speak of the distress which bishops undergo, whenever it is necessary to cut some one off from the full communion of the Church? Would indeed that the evil went no further than distress! but in fact the mischief is not trifling. For there is a fear lest the man, if he has been punished beyond what he deserves, should experience that which was spoken of by the blessed Paul and "be swallowed up by overmuch sorrow."[1] The nicest accuracy, therefore, is required in this matter also, lest what is intended to be

---

[1] 2 Cor. ii. 7.

profitable should become to him an occasion of greater damage. For whatever sins he may commit after such a method of treatment, the wrath caused by each of them must be shared by the physician who so unskillfully applied his knife to the wound. What severe punishment, then, must be expected by one who has not only to render an account of the offences which he himself has separately committed, but also incurs extreme danger on account of the sins committed by others? For if we shudder at undergoing judgment for our own misdeeds, believing that we shall not be able to escape the fire of the other world, what must one expect to suffer who has to answer for so many others? To prove the truth of this, listen to the blessed Paul, or rather not to him, but to Christ speaking in him, when he says: "Obey them that have the rule over you, and submit, for they watch for your souls as they that shall give account."[1] Can the dread of this threat be slight? It is impossible to say: but these considerations are sufficient to convince even the most incredulous and obdurate that I did not make this escape under the influence of pride or vainglory, but merely out of fear for my own safety, and consideration of the gravity of the office.

---

[1] Hebrews xiii. 17.

BOOK IV.

Contents.

I. THOSE WHO ALLOW THEMSELVES TO BE FORCED INTO THE CLERICAL OFFICE, NO LESS THAN THEY WHO ENTER UPON IT FROM AMBITIOUS MOTIVES, ARE SORELY PUNISHED HEREAFTER FOR THEIR SIN.
II. THEY WHO ORDAIN UNWORTHY MEN, EVEN WHERE THEY DO NOT KNOW THEIR CHARACTER, WILL SHARE THEIR PUNISHMENT.
III. THE PRIEST OUGHT TO HAVE GREAT POWERS OF SPEAKING.
IV. HE SHOULD BE FULLY PREPARED FOR CONTROVERSY WITH ALL ADVERSARIES—GREEKS, JEWS, AND HERETICS.
V. HE SHOULD BE VERY SKILFUL IN ARGUMENT.
VI. IN WHICH SAINT PAUL ESPECIALLY EXCELLED.
VII. SO THAT HE BECAME ILLUSTRIOUS NOT SO MUCH FOR HIS MIRACLES AS FOR HIS WORDS.
VIII. HEREIN HE WOULD HAVE US EXCEL ALSO.
IX. FOR THE LACK OF THIS IN THE PRIEST MUST INJURIOUSLY AFFECT THOSE OVER WHOM HE IS SET.

BASIL heard this, and after a little pause thus replied:

If thou wert thyself ambitious of obtaining this office, thy fear would have been reasonable; for in being ambitious of undertaking it, a man confesses himself to be qualified for its administration, and if he fail therein, after it has been entrusted to him, he cannot take refuge in the plea of inexperience, for he has deprived himself of this excuse beforehand,[a] by having hurriedly seized upon the ministry, and whoever willingly and deliberately enters upon it, can no longer say, "I have sinned in this matter against my will— and against my will I have ruined such and such a soul;" for He who will one day judge him, will say to him, "Since then thou wert conscious of such inexperience, and hadst not ability for undertaking this matter without incurring reproach, why wert thou so eager and presumptuous as to take in hand what was so far beyond thy power? Who compelled thee to do so? Didst thou shrink or fly, and did any one drag thee on by force?" But thou wilt hear nothing like this, for thou canst have nothing of this kind to condemn thyself for; and it is evident to all that thou wert in no degree ambitious of this dignity, for the accomplishment of the matter was due to the action of others. Hence, circumstances which leave those who are ambitious of this office no chance of pardon when they err therein, afford thee ample ground for excuse.

CHRYSOSTOM: At this I shook my head and smiled a little, admiring the simple-mindedness of the man, and thus addressed him: I could wish indeed that matters were as thou sayest, most excellent of men, but not in order that I might be able to accept that office from which I lately fled. For if, indeed, no chastisement were to await me for undertaking the care of the flock of Christ without consideration and experience, yet to me it would be worse than all punishment, after being entrusted with so great a charge, to have seemed so base towards Him who entrusted me with it. For what reason, then, did I wish that thou wert not mistaken in this opinion of thine? truly for the sake of those wretched and unhappy beings (for so must I call them, who have not found out how to discharge the duties of this office well, though thou wert to say ten thousand times

---
[a] προλαβὼν γὰρ αὐτὸς ἑαυτοῦ ταύτην ἀφείλετο τὴν ἀπολογίαν.

over that they had been driven to undertake it, and that, therefore, their errors therein are sins of ignorance)—for the sake, I say, of such that they might succeed in escaping that unquenchable fire, and the outer darkness[1] and the worm that dieth not[2] and the punishment of being cut asunder,[3] and perishing together with the hypocrites.

But what am I to do for thee? It is not as thou sayest; no, by no means. And if thou wilt, I will give thee a proof of what I maintain, from the case of a kingdom, which is not of such account with God as the priesthood. Saul, that son of Kish, was not himself at all ambitious of becoming a king, but was going in quest of his asses, and came to ask the prophet about them. The prophet, however, proceeded to speak to him of the kingdom, but not even then did he run greedily after it, though he heard about it from a prophet, but drew back and deprecated it, saying, "Who am I, and what is my father's house."[4] What then? When he made a bad use of the honor which had been given him by God, were those words of his able to rescue him from the wrath of Him who had made him king? And was he able to say to Samuel, when rebuked by him: "Did I greedily run and rush after the kingdom and sovereign power? I wished to lead the undisturbed and peaceful life of ordinary men, but *thou* didst drag me to this post of honor. Had I remained in my low estate I should easily have escaped all these stumbling blocks, for were I one of the obscure multitude, I should never have been sent forth on this expedition, nor would God have committed to my hands the war against the Amalekites, and if I had not had it committed to me, I should not have sinned this sin." But all such arguments are weak as excuses, and not only weak, but perilous, inasmuch as they rather kindle the wrath of God. For he who has been promoted to great honor by God, must not advance the greatness of his honor as an excuse for his errors, but should make God's special favor towards him the motive for further improvement; whereas he who thinks himself at liberty to sin because he has obtained some uncommon dignity, what does he but study to show that the lovingkindness of God is the cause of his personal transgression, which is always the argument of those who lead godless and careless lives. But *we* ought to be on no account thus minded, nor to fall away into the insane folly of such people, but be ambitious at all times to make the most of such powers as we have, and to be reverent both in speech and thought.

For (to leave the kingdom and to come to the priesthood, which is the more immediate subject of our discourse) neither was Eli ambitious of obtaining his high office, yet what advantage was this to him when he sinned therein? But why do I say obtain it? not even had he wished could he have avoided it, because he was under a legal necessity to accept it. For he was of the tribe of Levi, and was bound to undertake that high office which descended to him from his forefathers, notwithstanding which even he paid no small penalty for the lawlessness[5] of his sons. And the very first High Priest of the Jews,[6] concerning whom God spake so many words to Moses, when he was unable to withstand alone the frenzy of so great a multitude, was he not very nearly being destroyed, but for the intercession of his brother, which averted the wrath of God?[7] And since we have mentioned Moses, it will be well to show the truth of what we are saying from what happened to him. For this same saintly Moses was so far from grasping at the leadership of the Jews as to deprecate the offer,[8] and to decline it when God commanded him to take it, and so to provoke the wrath of Him who appointed him; and not only then, but afterwards when he entered upon his rule, he would gladly have died to have been set free from it: "Kill me," saith he, "if thou art going to deal thus with me."[9] But what then? when he sinned at the waters of strife,[10] could these repeated refusals be pleaded in excuse for him? Could they prevail with God to grant him pardon? And wherefore was he deprived of the promised land? for no other reason, as we all know, than for this sin of his, for which that wondrous man was debarred from enjoying the same blessings which those over whom he ruled obtained; but after many labors and sufferings, after that unspeakable wandering, after so many battles fought and victories won, he died outside the land to reach which he had undergone so much toil and trial; and though he had weathered the storms of the deep, he failed to enjoy the blessings of the haven after all. From hence then thou seest that not only they who grasp at this office are left without excuse for the sins they commit in the dis-

---

[1] Matt. xxv. 30.   [2] Mark ix. 44.
[3] Matt. xxiv. 51; Luke xii. 46. Διχοτομηθῆναι. Some take this word to express the severance of the unrighteous from the godly priest, but others seek its meaning rather in the "dividing asunder" of sacrificial victims (Heb. iv. 12), or in the punishment of "sawing asunder" (Dan. iii. 29; Heb. xi. 37): so that its use by SS. Matthew and Luke would point to the distress caused by the severance between conscience and practice, which will be the reflective torment of lost souls.
[4] 1 Sam. ix. 21.
[5] παρανομίας. If παροινίας be read, then "excesses" must be understood:—the word meaning, 1st, excess in drink; and 2d, excess of any kind.
[6] Aaron.   [7] Ex. xxxii. 10, 11.   [8] Ex. iv. 13.
[9] Numb. xi. 15. Εἰ δ'οὕτω σὺ ποιεῖς μοι ἀπόκτεινόν με, LXX.
[10] Numb. xx. 12.

charge thereof, but they too who come to it through the ambitious desire of others; for truly if those persons who have been chosen for this high office by God himself, though they have never so often refused it, have paid such heavy penalties, and if nothing has availed to deliver any of them from this danger, neither Aaron nor Eli, nor that holy man the Saint, the prophet, the wonder-worker, the meek above all the men which were upon the face of the earth,[1] who spake with God, as a man speaketh unto his friend,[2] hardly shall we who fall so infinitely short of the excellence of that great man, be able to plead as a sufficient excuse the consciousness that we have never been ambitious of the dignity, more especially when many of the ordinations now-a-days do not proceed from the grace of God, but are due to human ambition. God chose Judas, and counted him one of the sacred band, and committed to him, as to the rest, the dignity of the apostolic office; yea he gave him somewhat beyond the others, the stewardship of the money.[3] But what of that? when he afterwards abused both these trusts, betraying Him whom he was commissioned to preach, and misapplying the money which he should have laid out well; did he escape punishment?[4] nay for this very reason he even brought upon himself greater punishment, and very reasonably too. For we must not use the high honors given to us by God so as to offend Him, but so as to please Him better. But he who claims exemption from punishment where it is due, because he has been exalted to higher honor than others, acts very much like one of those unbelieving Jews, who after hearing Christ say, "If I had not come and spoken unto them, they had not had sin," "If I had not done among them the works which none other did, they had not had sin,"[5] should reproach the Saviour and benefactor of mankind by replying, "Why, then, didst thou come and speak? why didst thou work miracles? was it that thou mightest punish us the more?" But these are the words of madness and of utter senselessness. For the Great Physician came not to give thee over, but to heal thee—not to pass thee by when thou wert sick, but to rid thee entirely of disease. But thou hast of thine own accord withdrawn thyself from his hands; receive therefore the sorer punishment. For as thou wouldest have been freed from thy former maladies if thou hadst yielded to his treatment, so if, when thou sawest him coming to thine aid thou fleddest from him, thou wilt no longer be able to cleanse thyself of these infirmities, and as thou art unable, thou wilt both suffer punishment for them, and also because for thy part thou madest God's solicitude for thy good of none effect. Therefore we who act like this are not subjected to the same torment after as before we received honor at God's hands, but far severer torment after than before. For he who has not become good even by being well treated, deserves all the bitterer punishment. Since, then, this excuse of thine has been shown to be weak, and not only fails to save those who take refuge in it, but exposes them so much the more, we must provide ourselves with some other means of safety.

BASIL: Tell me of what nature is that? since, as for me, I am at present scarce master of myself, thou hast reduced me to such a state of fear and trembling by what thou hast said.

CHRYSOSTOM: Do not, I beseech and implore thee, do not be so downcast. For while there is safety for us who are weak, namely, in not undertaking this office at all, there is safety for you too who are strong, and this consists in making your hopes of salvation depend, next to the grace of God, on avoiding every act unworthy of this gift, and of God who gave it. For they certainly would be deserving of the greatest punishment who, after obtaining this dignity through their own ambition, should then either on account of sloth, or wickedness, or even inexperience, abuse the office. Not that we are to gather from this that there is pardon in store for those who have not been thus ambitious. Yea, even they too are deprived of all excuse. For in my judgment, if ten thousand were to entreat and urge, a man should pay them no attention, but should first of all search his own heart, and examine the whole matter carefully before yielding to their importunities. Now no one would venture to undertake the building of a house were he not an architect, nor will any one attempt the cure of sick bodies who is not a skilled physician; but even though many urge him, will beg off, and will not be ashamed to own his ignorance; and shall he who is going to have the care of so many souls entrusted to him, not examine himself beforehand? will he accept this ministry even though he be the most inexperienced of men, because this one commands him, or that man constrains him, or for fear of offending a third? And if so, how will he escape casting himself together with them into manifest misery. Had he continued as he was, it were possible for him to be saved, but now he involves others in his own destruction. For whence can he hope for salvation? whence

---

[1] Numb. xii. 3. [2] Ex. xxxiii. 11. [3] John xii. 6.
[4] i. e., because he had been chosen an apostle.
[5] John xv. 22-24.

to obtain pardon? Who will then successfully intercede for us? they who are now perhaps urging us and forcibly dragging us on? But who will save these same at such a moment? For even they too will stand in need in their turn of intercession, that they may escape the fire. Now, that I say not these things to frighten thee, but as representing the matter as in truth it is, hear what the holy Apostle Paul saith to Timothy his disciple, his own and beloved son, "Lay hands suddenly on no man, neither be partaker of other men's sins."[1] Dost thou not see from what great blame, yea and vengeance, we, so far as in us lies, have delivered those who were ready to put us forward for this office.

2. For as it is not enough for those who are chosen to say in excuse for themselves, "I did not summon myself to this office, nor could I avoid what I did not see beforehand;" so neither will it be a sufficient plea for those who ordain them to say that they did not know him who was ordained. The charge against them becomes greater on account of their ignorance of him whom they brought forward, and what seems to excuse them only serves to accuse them the more. For how absurd a thing, is it not? that they who want to buy a slave, show him to the physician, and require sureties for the sale, and information about him from their neighbours, and after all this do not yet venture on his purchase without asking for some time for a trial of him; while they who are going to admit any one to so great an office as this, give their testimonial and their sanction loosely and carelessly, without further investigation, just because some one wishes it, or to court the favor, or to avoid the displeasure of some one else. Who shall then successfully intercede for us in that day, when they who ought to defend us stand themselves in need of defenders? He who is going to ordain, therefore, ought to make diligent inquiry, and much more he who is to be ordained. For though they who ordain him share his punishment, for any sins which he may commit in his office, yet so far from escaping vengeance he will even pay a greater penalty than they—save only if they who chose him acted from some worldly motive contrary to what seemed justifiable to themselves. For if they should be detected so doing, and knowing a man to be unworthy have brought him forward on some pretext or other, the amount of their punishment shall be equivalent to his, nay perhaps the punishment shall be even greater for them who appointed the unfit man. For he who gives authority to any one who is minded to destroy the Church, would be certainly to blame for the outrages which that person commits. But if he is guilty of no such thing, and says that he has been misled by the opinions of others, even then he shall not altogether remain unpunished, but his punishment shall be a little lighter than his who has been ordained. What then? It is possible that they who elect may come to the election deceived by a false report. But he who is elected could not say, "I am ignorant of myself," as others were of him. As one who will receive therefore a sorer punishment than they who put him forward, so should he make his scrutiny of himself more careful than that which they make of him; and if they in ignorance drag him on, he ought to come forward and instruct them carefully about any matters whereby he may stop their being misled; and so having shown himself unworthy of trial may escape the burden of so high an office.

For what is the reason why, in the arts of war, and merchandize,[2] and husbandry, and other departments of this life, when some plan is proposed, the husbandman will not undertake to navigate the ship, nor the soldier to till the ground, nor the pilot to lead an army, under pain of ten thousand deaths? Is it not plainly this? that each foresees the danger which would attend his incompetence? Well, where the loss is concerned with trifles shall we use so much forethought, and refuse to yield to the pressure of compulsion, but where the punishment is eternal, as it is for those who know not how to handle the Priesthood, shall we wantonly and inconsiderately run into so great danger, and then advance, as our excuse, the pressing entreaties of others? But He who one day will judge us will entertain no such plea as this. For we ought to show far more caution in spiritual matters than in carnal. But now we are not found exhibiting as much caution. For tell me: if supposing a man to be an artificer, when he is not so, we invited him to do a piece of work, and he were to respond to the call, and then having set his hand to the material prepared for the building, were to spoil the wood and spoil the stone, and so to build the house that it straightway fell to pieces, would it be sufficient excuse for him to allege that he had been urged by others and did not come of his own accord? in no wise; and very reasonably and justly so. For he ought to have refused even at the call of others. So for the man who only spoils wood and stone, there will be no escape from paying the penalty, and is he who de-

---

[1] 1 Tim. v. 22.

[2] Ἐμπορίας, restricted here to commerce carried on by sea, as the context shows.

stroys souls, and builds the temple of God carelessly, to think that the compulsion of others is his warrant for escaping punishment? Is not this very absurd? For I omit the fact as yet that no one is able to compel the man who is unwilling. But be it that he was subjected to excessive pressure and divers artful devices, and then fell into a snare; will this therefore rescue him from punishment? I beseech thee, let us not deceive ourselves, and pretend that we know not what is obvious to a mere child. For surely this pretence of ignorance will not be able to profit in the day of reckoning. Thou wert not ambitious, thou sayest, of receiving this high office, conscious of thine own weakness. Well and good. Then thou oughtest, with the same mind, to have declined the solicitation of others; or, when no one called thee, wast thou weak and incapable, but when those were found ready to offer thee this dignity, didst thou suddenly become competent? What ludicrous nonsense! worthy of the extremest punishment. For this reason also the Lord counsels the man who wishes to build a tower, not to lay the foundation before he has taken his own ability to build into account, lest he should give the passers by innumerable opportunities of mocking at him.[1] But in his case the penalty only consists in becoming a laughing-stock; while in that before us the punishment is that of fire unquenchable, and of an undying worm,[2] gnashing of teeth, outer darkness, and being cut asunder,[3] and having a portion with the hypocrites.

But my accusers are unwilling to consider any of these things. For otherwise they would cease to blame a person who is unwilling to perish without cause. It is not the management of corn and barley, oxen or sheep, that is now under our consideration, nor any such like matters, but the very Body of Jesus. For the Church of Christ, according to St. Paul, is Christ's Body,[4] and he who is entrusted with its care ought to train it up to a state of healthiness, and beauty unspeakable, and to look everywhere, lest any spot or wrinkle,[5] or other like blemish should mar its vigor and comeliness. For what is this but to make it appear worthy, so far as human power can, of the incorruptible and ever-blessed Head which is set over it? If they who are ambitious of reaching an athletic condition of body need the help of physicians and trainers,[6] and exact diet, and constant exercise, and a thousand other rules (for the omission of the merest trifle upsets and spoils the whole), how shall they to whose lot falls the care of the body, which has its conflict not against flesh and blood, but against powers unseen, be able to keep it sound and healthy, unless they far surpass ordinary human virtue, and are versed in all healing proper for the soul?

3. Pray, art thou not aware that that body is subject to more diseases and assaults than this flesh of ours, is more quickly corrupted, and more slow to recover? and by those who have the healing of these bodies, divers medicines have been discovered, and an apparatus of different instruments, and diet suitable for the sick; and often the condition of the atmosphere is of itself enough for the recovery of a sick man; and there are instances of seasonable sleep having saved the physician all further labor. But in the case before us, it is impossible to take any of these things into consideration; nay there is but one method and way of healing appointed, after we have gone wrong, and that is, the powerful application of the Word. This is the one instrument, the only diet, the finest atmosphere. This takes the place of physic, cautery and cutting, and if it be needful to sear and amputate, this is the means which we must use, and if this be of no avail, all else is wasted; with this we both rouse the soul when it sleeps, and reduce it when it is inflamed; with this we cut off excesses, and fill up defects, and perform all manner of other operations which are requisite for the soul's health. Now as regards the ordering of our daily life for the best, it is true that the life of another may provoke us to emulation. But in the matter of spurious doctrine, when any soul is diseased thereby, then there is great need of the Word, not only in view of the safety of our own people, but in view of the enemy without. If, indeed, one had the sword of the spirit, and the shield of faith,[7] so as to be able to work miracles, and by means of these marvels to stop the mouths of impudent gainsayers, one would have little need of the assistance of the Word; still in the days of miracles the Word was by no means useless, but essentially necessary. For St. Paul made use of it himself, although he was everywhere so great an object of wonder for his miracles; and another[8] of those who belonged to the "glorious company of the Apostles" exhorts us to apply ourselves to acquiring this power, when he says: "Be ready always to give an answer to every man that asketh you a reason concerning the hope that

---

[1] See Luke xiv. 28, 29. [2] Is. lxvi. 24.
[3] Matt. xxiv. 51. The Revised Version in the margin renders, the lord of that servant shall severely scourge him. See above, p. 61, note. [4] Col. i. 18, 24. [5] Eph. v. 27.
[6] Παιδοτριβῶν, literally, those who teach boys wrestling.

[7] Eph. vi. 16, 17.
[8] 1 Pet. iii. 15. *Haud seio an ita loqui possit primatus Romani defensor.*" Bengel's Edition of this Treatise, Leipzig, 1834. p. 145, note 17.

is in you," and they all, with one accord, committed the care of the poor widows to Stephen, for no other reason than that they themselves might have leisure "for the ministry of the Word."[1] To this we ought equally to apply ourselves, unless indeed we are endued with a power of working miracles. But if there is not the least sign of such a power being left us, while on every side many enemies are constantly attacking us, why then it necessarily follows that we should arm ourselves with this weapon, both in order that we may not be wounded ourselves with the darts of the enemy, and in order that we may wound him.

4. Wherefore it should be our ambition that the Word of Christ dwell in us richly.[2] For it is not for one kind of battle only that we have to be prepared. This warfare is manifold, and is engaged with a great variety of enemies; neither do all these use the same weapons, nor do they practice the same method of attack; and he who has to join battle with all, must needs know the artifices of all, and be at once both archer and slinger, captain and general, in the ranks and in command, on foot and on horseback, in sea-fight and in siege. In common warfare, indeed, each man repels the enemy by discharging the particular duty which he has undertaken. But here it is otherwise; and if any one wishes to come off conqueror in this warfare, he must understand all forms of the art, as the devil knows well how to introduce his own assailants through any one spot which may happen to be unguarded, and to carry off the sheep. But not so where he perceives the shepherd coming equipped with accurate knowledge at all points, and well acquainted with his plottings. Wherefore we ought to be well-guarded in all parts; for a city, so long as it happens to be surrounded with a wall, laughs to scorn the besiegers, abiding in great security; but if any one makes a breach in the wall, though but of the size of a gate, the rest of the circuit is of no use, although the whole of it stand quite securely; so it is with the city of God: so long as the presence of mind and wisdom of the shepherd, which answers to the wall, protect it on all sides, all the enemy's devices end in his confusion and ridicule, and they who dwell within the wall abide unmolested, but wherever any one has been able to demolish a single part, though the rest stand never so fast, through that breach ruin will enter upon the whole. For to what purpose does a man contend earnestly with the Greeks, if at the same time he becomes a prey to the Jews? or get the better of both these and then fall into the clutches of the Manichæans?[3] or after he has proved himself superior to them even, if they who introduce fatalism[4] enter in, and make havoc of the flock? But not to enumerate all the heresies of the devil, it will be enough to say that unless the shepherd is well skilled in refuting them all, the wolf, by means of any one of them, can enter, and devour the greater part of the flock. In ordinary warfare we must always look for victory being won or defeat sustained by the soldiers who are on the field of battle. But in the spiritual warfare the case is quite different. For there it often happens that the combat with one set of enemies secures a victory for others who never engaged in battle at all, nor took any trouble, but were sitting still all the while; and he who has not much experience in such occurrences will get pierced, so to say, with his own sword, and become the laughing-stock of friends and foes alike. I will try by an example to make clear what I am saying. They who receive the wild doctrines of Valentinus and Marcion,[5] and of all whose minds are similarly diseased, exclude the Law given by God to Moses from the catalogue of the Divine Scriptures. But Jews so revere the Law, that although the time has come which annuls it, they still contend for the observance of all its contents, contrary to the purpose of God. But the Church of God, avoiding either extreme, has trodden a middle path, and is neither induced on the one hand to place herself under its yoke, nor on the other does she tolerate its being slandered, but commends it, though its day is over, because of its profitableness while its season lasted. Now it is necessary for him who is going to fight with both these enemies,[6] to be fully conversant with this middle course. For if in wishing to teach the Jews that they are out of date in clinging to the old law, he begins to find fault with it unsparingly, he gives no little handle to those heretics who wish to pull it to pieces; and if in his ambition to stop their mouths he extols it immoderately, and speaks of it with admiration, as

---

[1] Acts vi. 4.   [2] Col. iii. 16.

[3] The followers of Manes, or Manichæus, who was born about 240 A.D. He taught that God was the cause of good, and matter the cause of evil. This theory about matter led him to hold that the body of Jesus was an incorporeal phantom. He eliminated the Old Testament from the Scriptures, and held himself at liberty also to reject such passages in the New Testament as were opposed to his own opinions. See Robertson: Hist. of the Christian Church, vol. i. 139-145.

[4] "οἱ τὴν εἱμαρμένην εἰσάγοντες," sc. The Stoics. They were still a numerous body, and St. Chrysostom himself wrote six Homilies against them.

[5] Marcion and Valentinus (A.D. 140) were each founders of a form of Gnosticism. Each held that the God of the Old Testament was morally contrary to the God of the New: while the system of Valentinus represented the imaginative and speculative side of Gnosticism, that of Marcion represented its practical side, and was rather religious than theological. The sect of the Valentinians lasted as late as the 5th century; and Marcionism was not extinct till the 6th.

[6] Sc. Jews and Marcionites.

necessary for this present time, he unseals the lips of the Jews. Again they who labor under the frenzy of Sabellius and the craze of Arius,[1] have both fallen from a sound faith for want of observing a middle course. The name of Christian is applied to both these heretics; but if any one examines their doctrines, he will find the one sect not much better than the Jews, and differing from them only in name, and the other[2] very nearly holding the heresy of Paul of Samosata,[3] and that both are very wide of the truth. Great, therefore, is the danger in such cases, and the way of orthodoxy is narrow and hemmed in by threatening crags on either side, and there is no little fear lest when intending to strike at one enemy we should be wounded by the other. For if any one assert the unity of the Godhead, Sabellius straightway turns that expression to the advantage of his own mental vagary,[4] and if he distinguish the Persons, and say that the Father is one, and the Son another, and the Holy Spirit a third, up gets Arius, ready to wrest that distinction of Persons into a difference of substance;[5] so we must turn and flee both from the impious confounding of the Persons by the one, and the senseless division of the substance by the other, confessing, indeed, that the Godhead of the Father and of the Son and of the Holy Ghost, is all one, while we add thereunto a Trinity of Persons. For then we shall be able to fortify ourselves against the attacks of both heretics. I might tell thee besides these, of several other adversaries against which, except we contend bravely and carefully, we shall leave the field covered with wounds.

5. Why should any one describe the silly chatter of our own people? For these are not less than the attacks upon us from without, while they give the teacher even more trouble. Some out of an idle curiosity are rashly bent upon busying themselves about matters which are neither possible for them to know, nor of any advantage to them if they could know them. Others again demand from God an account of his judgments, and force themselves to sound the depth of that abyss which is unfathomable. "For thy judgments," saith the Scriptures, "are a great deep,"[6] and about their faith and practice thou wouldest find few of them anxious, but the majority curiously inquiring into matters which it is not possible to discover, and the mere inquiry into which provokes God. For when we make a determined effort to learn what *He* does not wish us to know, we fail to succeed (for how should we succeed against the will of God?); and there only remains for us the danger arising from our inquiry. Now, though this be the case, whenever any one authoritatively stops the search, into such fathomless depths, he gets himself the reputation of being proud and ignorant; so that at such times much tact is needed on the Bishop's part, so as to lead his people away from these unprofitable questions, and himself escape the above-named censures. In short, to meet all these difficulties, there is no help given but that of speech, and if any be destitute of this power, the souls of those who are put under his charge (I mean of the weaker and more meddlesome kind) are no better off than ships continually storm-tossed. So that the Priest should do all that in him lies, to gain this means of strength.

6. BASIL: "Why, then, was not St. Paul ambitious of becoming perfect in this art? He makes no secret of his poverty of speech, but distinctly confesses himself to be unskilled, even telling the Corinthians so,[7] who were admired for their eloquence, and prided themselves upon it."

CHRYSOSTOM: This is the very thing which has ruined many and made them remiss in the study of true doctrine. For while they failed to fathom the depths of the apostle's mind, and to understand the meaning of his words, they passed all their time slumbering and yawning, and paying respect not to that ignorance which St. Paul acknowledges, but to a kind from which he was as free as any man ever was in the world.

But leaving this subject to await our consideration, I say this much in the meantime. Granting that St. Paul was in this respect as unskilled as they would have him to be, what has that to do with the men of to-day? For he had a greater power by far than power of speech, power which brought about greater results too; which was that his bare presence, even though he was silent, was terrible to the

---

[1] Sabellius was condemned in a Council held in Rome, A.D. 263, for holding that there is but one person in the Godhead, and that the Word and Holy Spirit are only virtues or emanations of the Deity. Arius held that our Lord Jesus Christ existed before His Incarnation, that by Him as by an instrument the Supreme God made the worlds, and that as being the most ancient and the highest of created beings, He is to be worshipped; but that He had a beginning of existence, and so is not God's co-eternally begotten Son, nor of the very substance of the Supreme God. See Liddon, Bampton Lectures, i. p. 25. The heresy of Arius was condemned at the Council of Nicæa, A.D. 325.
[2] Sc. The Arians.
[3] Paul of Samosata was appointed Bishop of Antioch about 260 A.D. The Humanitarian movement culminated in his teaching, which maintained that the Word was only in the Father, as reason is in man; that Jesus was a mere man, and that he is called Son of God as having, in a certain sense, become such through the influence of the Divine Word which dwelt in him, but without any personal union.
[4] *i. e.*, while he maintained the Unity of the Godhead against the Arians there was danger of slipping into the Sabellian error of "confounding the Persons."
[5] *i. e.*, while he divided the Persons against the Sabellians he had to guard against the Arian error of "dividing the substance" also.

[6] Ps. xxxvi. 6.   [7] 2 Cor. xi. 6. See also, 2 Cor. x. 10.

demons. But the men of the present day, if they were all collected in one place, would not be able, with infinite prayers and tears, to do the wonders that once were done by the handkerchief of St. Paul. He too by his prayers raised the dead,[1] and wrought such other miracles, that he was held to be a god by heathen;[2] and before he was removed from this life, he was thought worthy to be caught up as far as the third heaven, and to share in such converse as it is not lawful for mortal ears to hear.[3] But the men of to-day—not that I would say anything harsh or severe, for indeed I do not speak by way of insult to them, but only in wonder—how is it that they do not shudder when they measure themselves with so great a man as this? For if we leave the miracles and turn to the life of this blessed saint, and look into his angelic conversation, it is in this rather than in his miracles that thou wilt find this Christian athlete a conqueror. For how can one describe his zeal and forbearance, his constant perils, his continual cares, and incessant anxiety for the Churches; his sympathy with the weak, his many afflictions, his unwonted persecutions, his deaths daily? Where is the spot in the world, where is the continent or sea, that is a stranger to the labours of this righteous man? Even the desert has known his presence, for it often sheltered him in time of danger. For he underwent every species of attack, and achieved every kind of victory, and there was never any end to his contests and his triumphs.

Yet, all unawares, I have been led to do this man an injury. For his exploits are beyond all powers of description, and beyond mine in particular, just as the masters of eloquence surpass me. Nevertheless, since that holy apostle will judge us, not by the issue, but by the motive, I shall not forbear till I have stated one more circumstance which surpasses anything yet mentioned, as much as he himself surpasses all his fellow men. And what is this? After so many exploits, after such a multitude of victories, he prayed that he might go into hell, and be handed over to eternal punishment, if so be that those Jews, who had often stoned him, and done what they could to make away with him, might be saved, and come over to Christ.[4] Now who so longed for Christ? If, indeed, his feelings towards him ought not to be described as something nobler than longing; shall we then any more compare ourselves with this saint, after so great grace was imparted to him from above, after so great virtue was manifested in himself? What could be more presumptuous?

Now, that he was not so unskilled, as some count him to be, I shall try to show in what follows. The unskilled person in men's estimation is not only one who is unpracticed in the tricks of profane oratory,[5] but the man who is incapable of contending for the defence of the right faith, and they are right. But St. Paul did not say that he was unskilled in both these respects, but in one only; and in support of this he makes a careful distinction, saying that he was "rude in speech, but not in knowledge."[6] Now were I to insist upon the polish of Isocrates, the weight of Demosthenes, the dignity of Thucydides, and the sublimity of Plato, in any one bishop, St. Paul would be a strong evidence against me. But I pass by all such matters and the elaborate ornaments of profane oratory; and I take no account of style or of delivery; yea let a man's diction be poor and his composition simple and unadorned, but let him not be unskilled in the knowledge and accurate statement of doctrine; nor in order to screen his own sloth, deprive that holy apostle of the greatest of his gifts, and the sum of his praises.

7. For how was it, tell me, that he confounded the Jews which dwelt at Damascus,[7] though he had not yet begun to work miracles? How was it that he wrestled with the Grecians and threw them?[8] and why was he sent to Tarsus? Was it not because he was so mighty and victorious in the word, and brought his adversaries to such a pass that they, unable to brook their defeat, were provoked to seek his life? At that time, as I said, he had not begun to work miracles, nor could any one say that the masses looked upon him with astonishment on account of any glory belonging to his mighty works, or that they who contended with him were overpowered by the force of public opinion concerning him. For at this time he conquered by dint of argument only. How was it, moreover, that he contended and disputed successfully with those who tried to Judaize in Antioch? and how was it that that Areopagite,[9] an inhabitant of Athens, that most devoted of all cities to the gods, followed the apostle, he and his wife? was it not owing to the discourse which they heard? And when Eutychus[10] fell from the lattice, was it not owing to his long attendance even until midnight to St. Paul's preaching? How do we find him employed at Thessalonica and Corinth, in Ephesus and in Rome itself? Did he not spend whole nights and days in interpreting the Scriptures in their order? and

---

[1] Acts xx. 10.   [2] Acts xiv 11.
[3] 2 Cor. xii. 2-4.   [4] Rom. ix. 3.

[5] τερθρείαν, from τέρθρον, literally, a sail-rope. The man who condescends to catching the ear by mere rhetorical artifice being like the mountebank on the trapeze, fascinating the spectators in a circus by his performances.   [6] 2 Cor. xi. 6.
[7] Acts ix. 22.   [8] See Acts ix. 29.   [9] Acts xvii. 34.   [10] Acts xx. 9.

why should any one recount his disputes with the Epicureans and Stoics.[1] For were we resolved to enter into every particular, our story would grow to an unreasonable length.

When, therefore, both before working miracles, and after, St. Paul appears to have made much use of argument, how can any one dare to pronounce him unskillful whose sermons and disputations were so exceedingly admired by all who heard them? Why did the Lycaonians[2] imagine that he was Hermes? The opinion that he and Barnabas were gods indeed, arose out of the sight of their miracles; but the notion that he was Hermes did not arise from this, but was a consequence of his speech. In what else did this blessed saint excel the rest of the apostles? and how comes it that up and down the world he is so much on every one's tongue? How comes it that not merely among ourselves, but also among Jews and Greeks, he is the wonder of wonders? Is it not from the power of his epistles? whereby not only to the faithful of to-day, but from his time to this, yea and up to the end, even the appearing of Christ, he has been and will be profitable, and will continue to be so as long as the human race shall last. For as a wall built of adamant, so his writings fortify all the Churches of the known world, and he as a most noble champion stands in the midst, bringing into captivity every thought to the obedience of Christ, casting down imaginations, and every high thing which exalts itself against the knowledge of God,[3] and all this he does by those epistles which he has left to us full of wonders and of Divine wisdom. For his writings are not only useful to us, for the overthrow of false doctrine and the confirmation of the true, but they help not a little towards living a good life. For by the use of these, the bishops of the present day fit and fashion the chaste virgin, which St. Paul himself espoused to Christ,[4] and conduct her to the state of spiritual beauty; with these, too, they drive away from her the noisome pestilences which beset her, and preserve the good health thus obtained. Such are the medicines and such their efficacy left us by this so-called unskillful man, and they know them and their power best who constantly use them. From all this it is evident that St. Paul had given himself to the study of which we have been speaking with great diligence and zeal.

8. Hear also what he says in his charge to his disciple:[5] "Give heed to reading, to exhortation, to teaching," and he goes on to show the usefulness of this by adding, "For in doing this thou shalt save both thyself and them that hear thee."[6] And again he says, "The Lord's servant must not strive, but be gentle towards all, apt to teach, forbearing;"[7] and he proceeds to say, "But abide thou in the things which thou hast learned, and hast been assured of, knowing of whom thou hast learned them, and that from a babe thou hast known the sacred writings which are able to make thee wise unto salvation,"[8] and again, "Every Scripture is inspired of God, and also profitable for teaching, for reproof, for correction, for instruction which is in righteousness, that the man of God may be complete."[9] Hear what he adds further in his directions to Titus about the appointment of bishops. "The bishop," he says, "must be holding to the faithful word which is according to the teaching, that he may be able to convict the gainsayers."[10] But how shall any one who is unskillful as these men pretend, be able to convict the gainsayers and stop their mouths? or what need is there to give attention to reading and to the Holy Scriptures, if such a state of unskillfulness is to be welcome among us? Such arguments are mere makeshifts and pretexts, the marks of idleness and sloth. But some one will say, "it is to the priests that these charges are given:"—certainly, for they are the subjects of our discourse. But that the apostle gives the same charge to the laity, hear what he says in another epistle to other than the priesthood: "Let the word of Christ dwell in you richly in all wisdom,"[11] and again, "Let your speech be always with grace seasoned with salt, that ye may know how ye ought to answer each one,"[12] and there is a general charge to all that they "be ready to"[13] render an account of their faith, and to the Thessalonians, he gives the following command: "Build each other up, even as also ye do."[14] But when he speaks of priests he says, "Let the elders that rule well be counted worthy of double honor, especially those who labor in the word, and in teaching."[15] For this is the perfection of teaching when the teachers both by what they do, and by what they say as well, bring their disciples to that blessed state of life which Christ appointed for them. For example alone is not enough to instruct others. Nor do I say this of myself; it is our Saviour's own word. "For whosoever shall do and teach them, he shall be called great.[16] Now if doing were the same as teaching, the second word here would be superfluous; and it had been enough to have said "whosoever shall

---

[1] Acts xvii. 18.   [2] Acts xiv. 11.   [3] 2 Cor. x. 5.
[4] 2 Cor. xi. 2.   [5] 1 Tim. iv. 13.
[6] 1 Tim. iv. 16.   [7] 2 Tim. ii. 24.   [8] 2 Tim. iii. 14, 15.
[9] 2 Tim. iii. 16, 17, or "every Scripture inspired of God is also profitable," etc., so rendered in the Revised Version.
[10] Titus i. 7, 9. Revised Version.   [11] Col. iii. 16.
[12] Col. iv. 6.   [13] 1 Peter iii. 15.   [14] 1 Thess. v. 11.
[15] 1 Tim. v. 17.   [16] Matt. v. 19.

do" simply. But now by distinguishing the two, he shows that practice is one thing, and doctrine another, and that each needs the help of the others in order to complete edification. Thou hearest too what the chosen vessel of Christ says to the Ephesian elders: "Wherefore watch ye, remembering that for the space of three years, I ceased not to admonish every one, night and day, with tears."[1] But what need was there for his tears or for admonition by word of mouth, while his life as an apostle was so illustrious? His holy life might be a great inducement to men to keep the commandments, yet I dare not say that it alone could accomplish everything.

9. But when a dispute arises concerning matters of doctrine, and all take their weapons from the same Scriptures, of what weight will any one's life be able to prove? What then will be the good of his many austerities, when after such painful exercises, any one from the Priest's great unskillfulness in argument fall into heresy, and be cut off from the body of the Church, a misfortune which I have myself seen many suffering. Of what profit then will his patience be to to him? None; no more than there will be in a sound faith if the life is corrupt. Wherefore, for this reason more than for all others, it concerns him whose office it is to teach others, to be experienced in disputations of this kind. For though he himself stands safely, and is unhurt by the gainsayers, yet the simple multitude under his direction, when they see their leader defeated, and without any answer for the gainsayers, will be apt to lay the blame of his discomfiture not on his own weakness, but on the doctrines themselves, as though they were faulty; and so by reason of the inexperience of one, great numbers are brought to extreme ruin; for though they do not entirely go over to the adversary, yet they are forced to doubt about matters in which formerly they firmly believed, and those whom they used to approach with unswerving confidence, they are unable to hold to any longer steadfastly, but in consequence of their leader's defeat, so great a storm settles down upon their souls, that the mischief ends in their shipwreck altogether. But how dire is the destruction, and how terrible the fire which such a leader brings upon his own wretched head for every soul which is thus lost, thou wilt not need to learn from me, as thou knowest all this perfectly. Is this then pride, is this vainglory in me, to be unwilling to be the cause of the destruction of so many souls? and of procuring for myself greater punishment in the world to come, than that which now awaits me there? Who would say so? surely no one, unless he should wish to find fault where there is none, and to moralize over other men's calamities.

---

[1] Acts xx. 31.

BOOK V.

Contents.

I. PUBLIC PREACHING NEEDS MUCH LABOR AND STUDY.
II. HE WHO IS APPOINTED TO THIS WORK MUST BE INDIFFERENT TO PRAISE, AND ABLE IN SPEAKING.
III. UNLESS HE HAVE BOTH THESE QUALIFICATIONS HE WILL BE UNSERVICEABLE TO THE MULTITUDE.
IV. HE SHOULD ABOVE ALL TAKE NO NOTICE OF SLANDER.
V. THE SKILLFUL IN PREACHING NEED MORE STUDY THAN THE UNLEARNED.
VI. HE MUST NOT THINK TOO LITTLE, OR TOO MUCH OF THE UNREASONED VERDICT OF THE MULTITUDE.
VII. HE MUST ORDER HIS WORDS WITH A VIEW TO PLEASING GOD ALONE.
VIII. HE WHO IS NOT INDIFFERENT TO PRAISE WILL UNDERGO MANY SUFFERINGS.

1. How great is the skill required for the teacher in contending earnestly for the truth, has been sufficiently set forth by us. But I have to mention one more matter beside this, which is a cause of numberless dangers, though for my own part I should rather say that the thing itself is not the cause, but they who know not how to use it rightly, since it is of itself a help to salvation and to much good besides, whenever thou findest that earnest and good men have the management of it. What then, do I mean by this? The expenditure of great labor upon the preparation of discourses to be delivered in public. For to begin with, the majority of those who are under the preachers' charge are not minded to behave towards them as towards teachers, but disdaining the part of learners, they assume instead the attitude of those who sit and look on at the public games; and just as the multitude there is separated into parties, and some attach themselves to one, and some to another, so here also men are divided, and become the partisans now of this teacher, now of that, listening to them with a view to favor or spite. And not only is there this hardship, but another quite as great. For if it has occurred to any preacher to weave into his sermons any part of other men's works, he is exposed to greater disgrace than those who steal money. Nay, often where he has not even borrowed anything from any one, but is only suspected, he has suffered the fate of a thief. And why do I speak of the works of others when it is not permitted to him to use his own resources without variety? For the public are accustomed to listen not for profit, but for pleasure, sitting like critics of tragedies, and of musical entertainments, and that facility of speech against which we declaimed just now, in this case becomes desirable, even more than in the case of barristers, where they are obliged to contend one against the other. A preacher then should have loftiness of mind, far exceeding my own littleness of spirit, that he may correct this disorderly and unprofitable pleasure on the part of the multitude, and be able to lead them over to a more useful way of hearing, that his people may follow and yield to him, and that he may not be led away by their own humors, and this it is not possible to arrive at, except by two means: indifference to their praise, and the power of preaching well.[1]

2. For if either of these be lacking, the remaining one becomes useless, owing to its divorce from the other, for if a preacher be indifferent to praise, and yet cannot produce the doctrine

---
[1] Chrysostom's own sermons were often interrupted by applause, which he always severely reprimanded.

"which is with grace seasoned with salt,"[1] he becomes despised by the multitude, while he gains nothing from his own nobleness of mind; and if on the other hand he is successful as a preacher, and is overcome by the thought of applause, harm is equally done in turn, both to himself and the multitude, because in his desire for praise he is careful to speak rather with a view to please than to profit. And as he who neither lets good opinion influence him, nor is skillful in speaking, does not yield to the pleasure of the multitude, and is unable to do them any good worth mentioning, because he has nothing to say, so he who is carried away with desire for praise, though he is able to render the multitude better service, rather provides in place of this such food as will suit their taste, because he purchases thereby the tumult of acclamation.

3. The best kind of Bishop must, therefore, be strong in both these points, so that neither may supplant the other. For if when he stands up in the congregation and speaks words calculated to make the careless wince,[2] he then stumbles, and stops short, and is forced to blush at his failure, the good of what he has spoken is immediately wasted. For they who are rebuked, being galled by what has been told them, and unable to avenge themselves on him otherwise, taunt him, with jeers at this ignorance of his, thinking to screen their own reproach thereby. Wherefore he ought, like some very good charioteer, to come to an accurate judgment about both these good things, in order that he may be able to deal with both as he may have need; for when he is irreproachable in the eyes of all, then he will be able, with just so much authority as he wishes, both to correct and to remit from correction all those who are under his rule. But without this it will not be easy for him to do so. But this nobleness of soul should be shown not only up to the limit of indifference to praise, but should go further in order that the gain thus gotten may not in its turn be fruitless.

4. To what else ought he then to be indifferent? Slander and envy. Unseasonable evil speaking,[3] however (for of course the Bishop undergoes some groundless censure), it is well that he should neither fear nor tremble at excessively, nor entirely pass over; but we ought, though it happen to be false, or to be brought against us by the common herd, to try and extinguish it immediately. For nothing so magnifies both an evil and a good report as the undisciplined mob. For accustomed to hear and to speak without stopping to make inquiry, they repeat at random everything which comes in their way, without any regard to the truth of it. Therefore the Bishop ought not to be unconcerned about the multitude, but straightway to nip their evil surmisings in the bud; persuading his accusers, even if they be the most unreasonable of all men, and to omit nothing which is able to dispel an ill-favored report. But if, when we do all this, they who blame us will not be persuaded, thenceforward we should give them no concern. Since if any one be too quick to be dejected by these accidents, he will not be able at any time to produce anything noble and admirable. For despondency and constant cares are mighty for destroying the powers of the mind, and for reducing it to extreme weakness. Thus then must the Priest behave towards those in his charge, as a father would behave to his very young children; and as such are not disturbed either by their insults or their blows, or their lamentations, nor even if they laugh and rejoice with us, do we take much account of it; so should we neither be puffed up by the promises of these persons nor cast down at their censure, when it comes from them unseasonably. But this is hard, my good friend; and perhaps, methinks, even impossible. For I know not whether any man ever succeeded in the effort not to be pleased when he is praised, and the man who is pleased at this is likely also to desire to enjoy it, and the man who desires to enjoy it will, of necessity, be altogether vexed and beside himself whenever he misses it. For as they who revel in being rich, when they fall into poverty are grieved, and they who have been used to live luxuriously cannot bear to live shabbily; so, too, they who long for applause, not only when they are blamed without a cause, but when they are not constantly being praised, become, as by some famine, wasted in soul, particularly when they happen themselves to have been used to praise, or if they hear others being praised. He who enters upon the trial of preaching with desires of this kind, how many annoyances and how many pangs dost thou think that he has? It is no more possible for the sea to be without waves than that man to be without cares and grief.

5. For though the preacher may have great ability (and this one would only find in a few), not even in this case is he released from perpetual toil. For since preaching does not come by nature, but by study, suppose a man to reach a high standard of it, this will then forsake him if he does not cultivate his power by constant application and exercise. So that there is greater labor for the wiser than for the

---

[1] Col. iv. 6.
[2] ἐπιστύψαι, literally, to purse up the mouth, as at the taste of what is tart and sour.
[3] κακηγορία—if κατηγορία be read, "accusation" will be the meaning.

unlearned. For there is not the same degree of loss attending negligence on the part of the one and the other, but the loss is in exact proportion to the difference between the two possessions. For the latter[1] no one would blame, as they furnish nothing worth regarding. But the former, unless they are constantly producing matter beyond the reputation in which all hold them, great censure attends on all hands; and besides these things, the latter would meet with considerable praise, even for small performances, while the efforts of the former, unless they be specially wonderful and startling, not only fail to win applause, but meet with many fault-finders. For the audience set themselves to be critics, not so much in judgment of what is said as of the reputation of the speaker, so that whenever any one excels all others in oratorical powers, then especially of all others does he need laborious study. For this man is not allowed to avail himself of the usual plea which human nature urges, that one cannot succeed in everything; but if his sermons do not throughout correspond to the greatness of the expectations formed, he will go away without having gained anything but countless jeers and censures; and no one takes this into consideration about him, that dejection and pain, and anxiety, and often anger, may step in, and dim the clearness of his thoughts and prevent his productions from coming from him unalloyed,[2] and that on the whole, being but a man, he cannot be constantly the same, nor at all times acquit himself successfully, but naturally must sometimes fall short of the mark, and appear on a lower level of ability than usual. None of these things, as I said, are they willing to take into consideration, but charge him with faults as if they were sitting in judgment on an angel; though in other cases, too, a man is apt to overlook the good performances of his neighbor, though they be many and great, and if anywhere a defect appears, even if it be accidental, even if it only occur at long intervals, it is quickly perceived, and always remembered, and thus small and trifling matters have often lessened the glory of many and great doings.

6. Thou seest, my excellent friend, that the man who is powerful in preaching has peculiar need of greater study than others; and besides study, of forbearance also greater than what is needed by all those whom I have already mentioned. For thus are many constantly springing up against him, in a vain and senseless spirit, and having no fault to find with him, but that he is generally approved of, hate him; and he must bear their bitter malice nobly, for as they are not able to hide this cursed hatred, which they so unreasonably entertain, they both revile, and censure, and slander in private, and defame in public, and the mind which has begun to be pained and exasperated, on every one of these occasions, will not escape being corrupted by grief. For they will not only revenge themselves upon him by their own acts, but will try to do so by means of others, and often having chosen some one of those who are unable to speak a word, will extol him with their praises and admire him beyond his worth. Some do this through ignorance alone,[3] some through ignorance and envy, in order that they may ruin the reputation of the other, not that they may prove the man to be wonderful who is not so, and the noble-minded man has not only to struggle against these, but often against the ignorance of the whole multitude; for since it is not possible that all those who come together should consist of learned men, but the chances are that the larger part of the congregation is composed of unlearned people, and that even the rest, who are clearer headed than they, fall as far short of being able to criticize sermons as the remainder again fall short of them; so that only one or two are seated there who possess this power; it follows, of necessity, that he who preaches better than others carries away less applause, and possibly goes home without being praised at all, and he must be prepared to meet such anomalies nobly, and to pardon those who commit them in ignorance, and to weep for those who acquiesce in them on account of envy as wretched and pitiable creatures, and not to consider that his powers have become less on either of these accounts. For if a man, being a pre-eminently good painter, and superior to all in his art, sees the portrait which he has drawn with great accuracy held up to ridicule, he ought not to be dejected, and to consider the picture poor, because of the judgment of the ignorant; as he would not consider the drawing that is really poor to be something wonderful and lovely, because of the astonishment of the inartistic.

7. For let the best artificer be himself the critic of his own designs, and let his performances be determined to be good or poor, according as the mind which designed them gives sentence upon them. But let him not even consider the opinion, so erroneous and inartistic, of the outside world. Let, therefore, the man who undertakes the strain of

---

[1] Sc. The unlearned.
[2] εἰλικρινῆ—literally, so that the sunlight fails to discern a flaw in them.
[3] Another reading is μανίᾳ, infatuation.

teaching never give heed to the good opinion of the outside world, nor be dejected in soul on account of such persons; but laboring at his sermons so that he may please God, (For let this alone be his rule and determination, in discharging this best kind of workmanship, not acclamation, nor good opinions,) if, indeed, he be praised by men, let him not repudiate their applause, and when his hearers do not offer this, let him not seek it, let him not be grieved. For a sufficient consolation in his labors, and one greater than all, is when he is able to be conscious of arranging and ordering his teaching with a view to pleasing God.

8. For if he be first carried away with the desire for indiscriminate praise, he will reap no advantage from his labors, or from his power in preaching, for the mind being unable to bear the senseless censures of the multitude is dispirited, and casts aside all earnestness about preaching. Therefore it is especially necessary to be trained to be indifferent to all kinds of praise. For to know how to preach is not enough for the preservation of that power, if this be not added: and if any one would examine accurately the man who is destitute of this art, he will find that he needs to be indifferent to praise no less than the other,[1] for he will be forced to do many wrong things in placing himself under the control of popular opinion. For not having the energy to equal those who are in repute for the quality of their preaching, he will not refrain from forming ill designs against them, from envying them, and from blaming them without reason, and from many such discreditable practices, but will venture everything, even if it be needful to ruin his own soul, for the sake of bringing down their fame to the level of his own insignificance. And in addition to this, he will leave off his exertions about his work; a kind of numbness, as it were, spreading itself over his mind. For much toil, rewarded by scanty praise, is sufficient to cast down a man who cannot despise praise, and put him into a deep lethargy, since the husbandman even when he spends time over some sorry piece of land, and is forced to till a rock, quickly desists from his work, unless he is possessed of much earnestness about the matter, or has a fear of famine impending over him. For if they who are able to speak with considerable power, need such constant exercise for the preservation of their talent, he who collects no materials at all, but is forced in the midst of his efforts to meditate; what difficulty, what confusion, what trouble will he experience, in order that he may be able at great labor to collect a few ideas! and if any of those clergy who are under his authority, and who are placed in the inferior order, be able in that position to appear to better advantage than he; what a divine mind must he have, so as not to be seized with envy or cast down by despondency. For, for one to be placed in a station of higher dignity, and to be surpassed by his inferior in rank, and to bear this nobly, would not be the part of any ordinary mind, nor of such as my own, but of one as hard as adamant; and if, indeed, the man who is in greater repute be very forbearing and modest, the suffering becomes so much the more easily borne. But if he is bold and boastful and vainglorious, a daily death would be desirable for the other; he will so embitter his life, insulting him to his face, and laughing at him behind his back, wresting much of his authority from him, and wishing to be everything himself. But he is possessed of the greatest security, in all these circumstances, who has fluency in preaching, and the earnest attention of the multitude about him, and the affection of all those who are under his charge. Dost not thou know what a passion for sermons has burst in upon the minds of Christians now-a-days? and that they who practice themselves in preaching are in especial honor, not only among the heathen, but among them of the household of the faith? How then could any one bear such disgrace as to find that all are mute when he is preaching, and think that they are oppressed, and wait for the end of the sermon, as for some release from work; while they listen to another with eagerness though he preach long, and are sorry when he is about to conclude; and almost angry when it is his purpose to be silent. If these matters seem to thee to be small, and easily to be despised, it is because of thine inexperience. They are truly enough to quench zeal, and to paralyze the powers of the mind, unless a man withdraw himself from all human passions, and study to frame his conduct after the pattern of those incorporeal powers, who are neither pursued by envy, nor by longing for fame, nor by any other morbid feeling. If then there be any man so constituted as to be able to subdue this wild beast, so difficult to capture, so unconquerable, so fierce; that is to say, public fame, and to cut off its many heads, or rather to forbid their growth altogether; he will easily be able to repel these many violent assaults, and to enjoy a kind of quiet haven of rest. But he who has not freed himself from this monster, involves his soul in struggles of various kinds, and perpetual agitation, and the burden both of despondency and of other passions. But why need I detail the rest of these difficulties, which no one will be able to describe, or to learn unless he has had actual experience of them.

---

[1] *i. e.*, The skillful preacher.

BOOK VI.

Contents.

I. PRIESTS ARE LIABLE TO RENDER ACCOUNT FOR THE SINS COMMITTED BY OTHERS.
II. THEY NEED MORE CIRCUMSPECTION THAN THE RECLUSES.
III. THE RECLUSE ENJOYS MORE EASE OF MIND THAN HE WHO IS SET OVER THE CHURCH.
IV. THE PRIEST HAS BEEN ENTRUSTED WITH THE GOVERNMENT OF THE WORLD AND WITH OTHER FORMIDABLE DUTIES.
V. THE PRIEST MUST BE ADAPTED TO ALL CIRCUMSTANCES.
VI. TO LIVE THE LIFE OF A RECLUSE IS NOT SUCH A MARK OF ENDURANCE AS TO GOVERN THE MULTITUDE WELL.
VII. THE HABITS OF HIM WHO LIVES ALONE, AND OF HIM WHO HAS HIS CONVERSATION IN THE WORLD ARE NOT FOR THE SAME ENDS.
VIII. THEY WHO LIVE ALONE BECOME PROFICIENT IN VIRTUE MORE EASILY THAN THEY WHO HAVE THE CARE OF MANY.
IX. ONE OUGHT NOT TO THINK LIGHTLY OF POPULAR SUSPICION, EVEN THOUGH IT HAPPEN TO BE FALSE.
X. IT IS NO VERY GREAT MATTER TO SAVE ONESELF.
XI. MUCH SORER PUNISHMENT AWAITS THE SINS OF THE PRIESTS THAN THOSE OF THE LAITY.
XII. A REPRESENTATION BY WAY OF EXAMPLE BOTH OF THE PAIN AND OF THE FEAR WHICH ARISES FROM THE EXPECTATION OF THE PRIESTHOOD.
XIII. THE WARFARE OF THE DEVIL AGAINST US IS MORE SEVERE THAN ANY OTHER.

1. Our condition here, indeed, is such as thou hast heard. But our condition hereafter how shall we endure, when we are compelled to give our account for each of those who have been entrusted to us? For our penalty is not limited to shame, but everlasting chastisement awaits us as well. As for the passage, "Obey them that have the rule over you, and submit to them, for they watch in behalf of your souls as they that shall give account;"[1] though I have mentioned it once already, yet I will break silence about it now, for the fear of its warning is continually agitating my soul. For if for him who causes one only, and that the least, to stumble, it is profitable that "a great millstone should be hanged about his neck, and that he should be sunk in the depth of the sea;"[2] and if they who wound the consciences of the brethren, sin against Christ Himself,[3] what then will they one day suffer, what kind of penalty will they pay, who destroy not one only, or two, or three, but so many multitudes? For it is not possible for inexperience to be urged as an excuse, nor to take refuge in ignorance, nor for the plea of necessity or force to be put forward. Yea, if it were possible, one of those under their charge could more easily make use of this refuge for his own sins than bishops in the case of the sins of others. Dost thou ask why? Because he who has been appointed to rectify the ignorance of others, and to warn them beforehand of the conflict with the devil which is coming upon them, will not be able to put forward ignorance as his excuse, or to say, "I have never heard the trumpet sound, I did not foresee the conflict." For he is set for that very purpose, says Ezekiel, that he may sound the trumpet for others, and warn them of the dangers at hand. And therefore his chastisement is inevitable, though he that perishes happen to be but one. "For if when the sword comes, the

---

[1] Heb. xiii. 17.   [2] Matt. xviii. 6.   [3] 1 Cor. viii. 12.

watchman does not sound the trumpet to the people, nor give them a sign, and the sword come and take any man away, he indeed is taken away on account of his iniquity, but his blood will I require at the watchman's hands."[1]

2. Cease then to urge us on to a penalty so inevitable; for our discourse is not about an army, or a kingdom; but about an office which needs the virtues of an angel. For the soul of the Priest ought to be purer than the very sunbeams, in order that the Holy Spirit may not leave him desolate, in order that he may be able to say, "Now I live; and yet no longer I, but Christ liveth in me."[2] For if they who dwell in the desert, and are removed far from the city and the market-place, and the tumult therein, and who enjoy all their time a haven of rest, and of peacefulness, are not willing to rely on the security of that manner of life, but add to it numberless other safeguards, hedging themselves round on every side, and studying both to speak and to act with great circumspection, so that to the utmost extent of human power they may draw near to God with assurance, and with unstained purity, what power and strength, thinkest thou, does the ordained Priest need so as to be able to tear his soul away from every defilement, and to keep its spiritual beauty unsullied? For he has need of far greater purity than they; and whoever has need of greater purity, he too is subject to more pressing temptations than they, which are able to defile him, unless by using constant self-denial and much labor, he renders his soul inaccessible to them. For beauty of face, elegance of movement, an affected gait and lisping voice, pencilled eyebrows and enamelled cheeks, elaborate braiding and dyeing of hair, costliness of dress, variety of golden ornaments, and the glory of precious stones, the scent of perfumes, and all those other matters to which womankind devote themselves, are enough to disorder the mind, unless it happen to be hardened against them, through much austerity of self restraint. Now to be disturbed indeed by such things is nothing wonderful. But on the other hand, that the devil should be able to hit and shoot down the souls of men by the opposite of these—this is a matter which fills us with astonishment and perplexity.

3. For ere now some men who have escaped these snares, have been caught by others widely differing from these. For even a neglected appearance, unkempt hair, squalid dress, and an unpainted face, simple behavior, and homely language, unstudied gait, and unaffected voice, a life of poverty, a despised, unpatronized and lonely condition, have first drawn on the beholder to pity, and next to utter ruin; and many who have escaped the former nets, in the way of gold ornaments and perfumes, and apparel, and all the rest, of which I have spoken as connected with them, have easily fallen into these so widely differing from them, and have perished. When then both by poverty and by riches, both by the adornment and the neglect of the personal appearance, both by studied and unaffected manners, in short by all those means which I have enumerated, war is kindled in the soul of the beholder, and its artifices surround him on every side, how will he be able to breathe freely while so many snares encompass him? and what hiding-place will he be able to find —I do not say so as to avoid being forcibly seized by them (for this is not altogether difficult)—but so as to keep his own soul undisturbed by polluting thoughts?

And I pass by honors, which are the cause of countless evils. For those which come from the hands of women are ruinous to the vigor of self-restraint, and often overthrow it when a man does not know how to watch constantly against such designs; while those which come from the hands of men, unless a man receive them with much nobleness of mind, he is seized with two contrary emotions, servile flattery and senseless pride. To those who patronize him, he is obliged to cringe; and towards his inferiors he is puffed up, on account of the honors which the others confer, and is driven into the gulf of arrogance. We have mentioned these matters indeed, but how harmful they actually are, no one could well learn without experience. For not only these snares, but greater and more delusive than these, he must needs encounter, who has his conversation in the world. But he who is content with solitude, has freedom from all this, and if at any time a strange thought creates a representation of this kind, the image is weak, and capable of being speedily subdued, because there is no fuel added to the flame from without, arising from actual sight. For the recluse has but himself to fear for; or should he be forced to have the care of others they are easily counted: and if they be many, yet they are less than those in our Churches, and they give him who is set over them much lighter anxiety about them, not only on account of their fewness, but because they are all free from worldly concerns, and have neither wife nor children, nor any such thing to care about; and this makes them very deferential to their rulers, and allows them to share the same abode with them, so that they are able to take in their failings accurately at a glance and correct them, seeing that the constant

---

[1] Ezek. xxxiii. 6. Gal. ii. 20.

supervision of a teacher is no little help towards advance in virtue.

4. But of those who are subject to the Priest, the greater number are hampered with the cares of this life, and this makes them the slower in the performance of spiritual duties. Whence it is necessary for the teacher to sow every day (so to speak), in order that by its frequency at least, the word of doctrine may be able to be grasped by those who hear. For excessive wealth, and an abundance of power, and sloth the offspring of luxury, and many other things beside these, choke the seeds which have been let fall. Often too the thick growth of thorns does not suffer the seed to drop even upon the surface of the soil. Again, excess of trouble, stress of poverty, constant insults, and other such things, the reverse of the foregoing, take the mind away from anxiety about things divine; and of their people's sins, not even the smallest part can become apparent; for how should it, in the case of those the majority of whom they do not know even by sight?

The Priest's relations with his people involve thus much difficulty. But if any inquire about his relations with God, he will find the others to be as nothing, since these require a greater and more thorough earnestness. For he who acts as an ambassador on behalf of the whole city—but why do I say the city? on behalf of the whole world indeed—prays that God would be merciful to the sins of all, not only of the living, but also of the departed.[1] What manner of man ought he to be? For my part I think that the boldness of speech of Moses and Elias, is insufficient for such supplication. For as though he were entrusted with the whole world and were himself the father of all men, he draws near to God, beseeching that wars may be extinguished everywhere, that tumults may be quelled; asking for peace and plenty, and a swift deliverance from all the ills that beset each one, publicly and privately; and he ought as much to excel in every respect all those on whose behalf he prays, as rulers should excel their subjects.

And whenever he invokes the Holy Spirit, and offers the most dread sacrifice, and constantly handles the common Lord of all, tell me what rank shall we give him? What great purity and what real piety must we demand of him? For consider what manner of hands they ought to be which minister in these things, and of what kind his tongue which utters such words,[2] and ought not the soul which receives so great a spirit to be purer and holier than anything in the world? At such a time angels stand by the Priest; and the whole sanctuary, and the space round about the altar, is filled with the powers of heaven, in honor of Him who lieth thereon. For this, indeed, is capable of being proved from the very rites which are being then celebrated. I myself, moreover, have heard some one once relate, that a certain aged, venerable man, accustomed to see revelations, used to tell him, that he being thought worthy of a vision of this kind, at such a time, saw, on a sudden, so far as was possible for him, a multitude of angels, clothed in shining robes, and encircling the altar, and bending down, as one might see soldiers in the presence of their King, and for my part I believe it. Moreover another told me, without learning it from some one else, but as being himself thought worthy to be both an ear and eye witness of it, that, in the case of those who are about to depart hence, if they happen to be partakers of the mysteries, with a pure conscience, when they are about to breathe their last, angels keep guard over them for the sake of what they have received, and bear them hence. And dost thou not yet tremble to introduce a soul into so sacred a mystery of this kind, and to advance to the dignity of the Priesthood, one robed in filthy raiment, whom Christ has shut out from the rest of the band of guests?[3] The soul of the Priest should shine like a light beaming over the whole world. But mine has so great darkness overhanging it, because of my evil conscience, as to be always cast down and never able to look up with confidence to its Lord. Priests are the salt of the earth.[4] But who would easily put up with my lack of understanding, and my inexperience in all things, but thou, who hast been wont to love me beyond measure. For the Priest ought not only to be thus pure as one who has been dignified with so high a ministry, but very discreet, and skilled in many matters, and to be as well versed in the affairs of this life as they who are engaged in the world, and yet to be free from them all more than the recluses who occupy the mountains. For since he must mix with men who have wives, and who bring up children, who possess servants, and are surrounded with

---

[1] All the ancient Liturgies contained prayers for the departed. St. Cyril of Jerusalem (Catech. Mystag., v. n. vi.), speaking of the prayer after consecration, says: "and then we pray for our holy fathers and bishops, and for all that have fallen asleep before us, believing that it will be a very great benefit to their souls to have supplication offered for them whilst the holy and most awful sacrifice is lying upon the altar," but the practice was not based upon anything like the later Roman doctrine of purgatory. It was the natural expression of a devout belief in the "communion of saints." See Bingham's Antiquities, Book xv.

[2] "And we pray and beseech Thee, send down thy Holy Ghost upon us and upon these gifts here outspread, and make this bread to be the precious body of thy Christ, and that which is in the cup the precious blood of Christ, having so changed them by thy Holy Spirit that to us who partake of them may be for the cleansing of our souls, the remission of sins, the communion of the Holy Spirit." (Liturgy of St. Chrysostom.)

[3] Matt. xxii. 13.

[4] Matt. v. 13.

wealth, and fill public positions, and are persons of influence, he too should be a many-sided man—I say many-sided, not unreal, nor yet fawning and hypocritical, but full of much freedom and assurance, and knowing how to adapt himself profitably, where the circumstances of the case require it, and to be both kind and severe, for it is not possible to treat all those under one's charge on one plan, since neither is it well for physicians to apply one course of treatment to all their sick, nor for a pilot to know but one way of contending with the winds. For, indeed, continual storms beset this ship of ours, and these storms do not assail from without only, but take their rise from within, and there is need of much condescension, and circumspection, and all these different matters have one end in view, the glory of God, and the edifying of the Church.

5. Great is the conflict which recluses undergo, and much their toil. But if any one compare their exertions with those which the right exercise of the Priesthood involves, he will find the difference as great as the distance between a king and a commoner. For there, if the labor is great indeed, yet the conflict is common to body and soul, or rather the greater part of it is accomplished by the condition of the body, and if this be not strong, the inclination remains undeveloped, and is unable to come out into action. For the habit of intense fasting, and sleeping on the ground, and keeping vigil, and refraining from the bath, and great toil, and all other means which they use for the affliction of the body are given up, when the body to be thus disciplined is not strong. But in this case purity of soul is the business in hand, and no bodily vigor is required to show its excellence. For what does strength of body contribute towards our being not self-willed, or proud, or headstrong, but sober and prudent, and orderly, and all else, wherein St. Paul filled up the picture of the perfect Priest? But no one could say this of the virtues of the recluse.

6. But as in the case of wonder-workers, a large apparatus is required, both wheels and ropes and daggers; while the philosopher has the whole of his art stored up in his mind, not requiring any external appliances: So accordingly in the case before us. The recluse requires both a good condition of body, and a place suitable for his course of life, in order that such may not be settled too far from intercourse with their fellow men, and may have the tranquillity which belongs to desert places, and yet further, may not fail to enjoy the most favorable climate. For nothing is so unbearable to a body worn with fastings as a climate which is not equable. And what trouble they are compelled to take in the preparation of their clothing and daily food, as they are themselves ambitious of doing all with their own hands, I need not speak of now. But the Priest will require none of these things to supply his wants, but is unconcerned about them, and participates in all things which are harmless, while he has all his skill stored up in the treasure-house of his mind. But if any one admire a solitary life, and retirement from the society of the multitude, I should say myself that such a life was a token of patience, but not a sufficient proof of entire fortitude of soul. For the man who sits at the helm in harbor, does not yet give any certain proof of his art. But if one is able to guide his ship safely in the midst of the sea, no one would deny him to be an excellent steersman.

7. It would be, therefore, in no wise excessively surprising to us, that the recluse, living as he does by himself, is undisturbed and does not commit many and great sins. For he does not meet with things which irritate and excite his mind. But if any one who has devoted himself to whole multitudes, and has been compelled to bear the sins of many, has remained steadfast and firm, guiding his soul in the midst of the storm as if he were in a calm, he is the man to be justly applauded and admired of all, for he has shown sufficient proof of personal manliness. Do not thou, therefore, for thy part wonder if I, who avoid the market-place and the haunts of the multitude, have not many to accuse me. For I ought not to wonder, if I sinned not when asleep, nor fell when I did not wrestle, nor was hit if I did not fight. For who, tell me, who will be able to speak against me, and reveal my depravity? Can this roof or cell? Nay, they would not be able to give tongue? Would my mother, who best of all knows my affairs? Well, certainly with her I am neither in communication, nor have we ever come to a quarrel, and if this had happened, no mother is so heartless and wanting in affection for her child as to revile and accuse before all him whom she travailed with, and brought forth, and reared, if there were no reason to constrain her, nor any person to urge her to such an act. Nevertheless, if any one desires to make a careful inspection of my mind, he will discover much which is corrupt there. Nor art thou unaware of this who art specially wont to extol me with

---

[1] The following descriptions of monastic life were no doubt drawn from the habits of the monks in the neighbourhood of Antioch, who dwelt on the mountainous heights of Silpius and Casius, south of the city. They lived in separate huts or cabins, but were subject to an abbot and a common rule, probably very similar to that which Pachomius had recently established in Egypt, and which became very generally adopted in the East. There are frequent allusions to the habits of these monks in Chrysostom's Homilies. See especially St. Matt. Hom. LXVIII. c. 3, and LXIX. c. 3 ; also Life of St. Chrysostom by the translator, pp. 59–68, 3d ed.

praises before all. Now that I do not say these things out of mere modesty, recollect how often I said to thee, when this subject was being discussed between us, "If any one were to give me my choice whether I would rather gain distinction in the oversight of the Church, or in the life of the recluse, I would vote a thousand times over for accepting the former. For I have never failed to congratulate those who have been able to discharge this office well, and no one will gainsay that what I counted blessed I would not have shunned were I able to take part in it fitly. But what am I to do? There is nothing so prejudicial to the oversight of the Church as this inactivity and negligence of mine, which others think to be a sort of self-discipline, but which I hold to be a veil as it were of my personal infirmity, covering the greater number of my defects and not suffering them to appear. For he who is accustomed to enjoy such great freedom from business, and to pass his time in much repose, even if he be of a noble nature, is confused by his inexperience, and is disturbed, and his inactivity deprives him of no small part of his natural ability. But when, besides, he is of slow intellect, and ignorant also of these severe trials, which I take it is my case, he will carry on this ministry which he has received no better than a statue. Wherefore of those who have come to such great trial, out of that school, few shine; and the greater part betray themselves, and fall, and undergo much hardship and sufferings; and no wonder. For the trials and the discipline are not concerned with the same things. The man who is contending in no wise differs from those who are untrained. He who thus enters this list should despise glory, be superior to anger, full of great discretion. But for the exercise of these qualities there is no scope in his case who affects a secluded life. For he does not have many to provoke him in order that he may practise chastising, the force of his anger: nor admirers and applauders in order that he may be trained to despise the praises of the multitudes. And of the discretion which is required in the Church, there is no taking account in their case. Whenever, therefore, they come to the trials of which they have never had practical experience, they get bewildered, their heads are turned, they fall into a state of helplessness, and besides adding nothing to their excellence, may have often lost that which they brought with them.

8. BASIL: What then? shall we set over the administration of the Church those who move in society, and who are careful about the concerns of this world, who are adepts at wrangling and vituperation, who are full of countless artifices, and versed in luxurious ways?

CHRYSOSTOM: Hush, dear friend that thou art! Thou shouldest never entertain in thy thoughts such men as these, when the Priesthood is under discussion, but only such as are able after mixing and associating with all, to keep their purity undefiled, and their unworldliness, their holiness, constancy and sobriety unshaken, and to possess all other virtues which belong to recluses, in a greater degree than they. He who has many defects, but is able to hide them, by means of his seclusion, and to make them ineffectual, because he does not associate with any one, when *he* comes into society will gain nothing, but the position of a laughing-stock, and will run greater risks still, which I was very nearly experiencing myself, had not the providence of God quickly warded off such fire from my head. For it is not possible for one in such a position to escape notice when he is so conspicuously placed, but everything then is detected, and as the fire tests the material of metals, so too the trial of the clerical office searches the souls of mortal men; and if any one be passionate or mean, or ambitious of fame, if he be boastful, or anything else of the kind, it unveils all; and speedily lays bare his defects, and not only lays them bare, but increases their painfulness and strength. For the wounds of the body, if they are galled, become harder to heal, and the emotions of the mind when chafed and irritated, are naturally more exasperated, and those who possess them are driven to commit greater sins. For they excite him who does not restrain them, to love of glory, and to boastfulness, and to desire for this world's goods, and draw him downwards, both to luxury and laxity of life, and to laziness, and, little by little, to evils worse than these which result from them. For many are the circumstances in society which have the power to upset the balance of the mind, and to hinder its straightforward course;[1] and first of all is his social intercourse with women. For it is not possible for the Bishop, and one who is concerned with the whole flock, to have a care for the male portion of it, but to pass over the female, which needs more particular forethought, because of its propensity to sins. But the man who is appointed to the administration of a Bishopric must have a care for the moral health of these, if not in a greater, at least in no less a degree than the others. For it is necessary to visit them when they are sick, to comfort them when they are sorrowful, and to reprove them when they are idle,

---

[1] Another reading gives its "career towards God."

and to help them when they are distressed; and in such cases the evil one would find many opportunities of approach, if a man did not fortify himself with a very strict guard. For the eye, not only of the unchaste, but of the modest woman pierces and disturbs the mind. Flatteries enervate it, and favors enslave it, and fervent love—the spring one may say of all good—becomes the cause of countless evils to those who do not make a right use of it. Constant cares too have ere now blunted the edge of the understanding, and have made that which was buoyant heavier than lead, while anger has burst in like smoke, and taken possession of all the inner man.

9. Why should any one speak of the injuries that result from grief,[1] the insults, the abuse, the censure from superiors, from inferiors, from the wise, and from fools; for the class who are wanting in right judgment are particularly fond of censuring, and will never readily allow any excuse. But the truly excellent Bishop ought neither to think lightly of these, but to clear himself with all men of the charges which they bring against him, with great forbearance and meekness, pardoning their unreasonable fault-finding, rather than being indignant and angry about it. For if St. Paul feared lest he should incur a suspicion of theft, among his disciples, and therefore procured others for the management of the money, that "no one" he says, "should blame us in this abundance which is administered by us,[2] how ought we not to do all so as to remove evil suspicions, even if they happen to be false, and most unreasonable, and very foreign to our thought? For we are not so utterly removed from any sin as St. Paul from theft; notwithstanding, though so far from this evil practice, he did not, therefore, slight the suspicion of the world, although it was very absurd, and even insane. For it was madness to have any such suspicion about that blessed and admirable character. But none the less does he remove far off the causes of this suspicion, unreasonable though it was, and such as no one who was in his senses would entertain, and he neither disdained the folly of the multitudes, nor did he say, "To whose mind did it ever occur to suspect such things of us, after the signs which I have wrought, and the forbearance which has marked my life, and when you all revered and admired us?" Quite the contrary: he foresaw and expected this base suspicion, and pulled it up by the roots, or rather did not suffer it to grow at all. Why? "Because," saith he, "we provide things honest not only before the Lord, but before all men."[3] So great, yea and far greater zeal must we use, to uproot and prevent floating reports which are not good, but to see beforehand from afar whence they come, and to remove beforehand the causes from which they are produced, not to wait till they are established and are the common topics in every one's mouth. For then it is not easy in the future to destroy them, but very difficult, perhaps impossible, and not without mischief, because this is done after many have been injured. But how far shall I continue pursuing the unattainable? For to enumerate all the difficulties in this direction, is nothing more nor less than measuring the ocean. Even when any one should clear himself from every passion (which is a thing impossible) in order to correct the failings of others, he is forced to undergo countless trials, and when his own infirmities are added, behold, an abyss of toil and care, and all that he must suffer, who wishes to subdue the evils in himself and in those around him.

10. BASIL: And now, art *thou* free from toils? hast thou no cares while thou livest by thyself?

CHRYSOSTOM: I have indeed even now. For how is it possible for one who is a man, and who is living this toilsome life of ours, to be free from cares and conflict? But it is not quite the same thing for man to plunge into a boundless ocean and to cross a river, so great is the difference between these cares and those. For now, indeed, if I were able to become serviceable to others, I should wish it myself, and this would be a matter of prayer with me. But if it is not possible to help another, yet if it be practicable to save and rescue myself from the waves, I shall be contented.

BASIL: Dost thou then think this to be a great thing? and dost thou fancy that thou wilt be saved when thou art not profitable to any other?

CHRYSOSTOM: Thou hast spoken well and nobly, for I am not myself able to believe that it is possible for one who has not labored for the salvation of his fellow to be saved, nor did it at all profit the wretched man in the Gospel that he had not diminished his talent; but he perished through not increasing it and bringing it doubled to his master.[4] Nevertheless, I think that my punishment will be milder when I am called to account, because I have not saved others, than it would be if I should destroy myself and others too by becoming far worse after so great an honor. For now I trust that my chastisement will be proportioned

---

[1] According to a different reading, τὰς λοιπὰς βχάβας, "The injuries which remain."
[2] 2 Cor. viii. 20.
[3] 2 Cor. viii. 21; Rom. xii. 17.
[4] Matt. xxv. 24.

to the amount of my sins, but after receiving this office, I fear it would be not double, or threefold, but manifold, because I should have caused very many to stumble, and after additional honor should have offended the God who honored me.

11. For this very cause God accuses the Israelites more vehemently, and shows that they were worthy of greater chastisement, because they sinned after so many honors had come to them from Him, saying in one place: "But you only have I known of all the families of the earth, therefore will I punish you for your iniquities,"[1] and again, "and I raised up of your sons for prophets, and of your young men for Nazarites;[2] and before the times of the prophets, wishing to show that sins receive sorer punishment by far when they occur in the case of the Priest than in the case of the laity, He enjoins as great a sacrifice to be offered for the Priest as for the whole people,[3] and this amounts to a proof on his part, that the wounds of the Priesthood need more assistance—that is, as great as those of all the people together, and they would not have needed a greater, except they were worse; and they are not worse in their nature, but are aggravated through the dignity of the Priest, who dares to commit them. And why do I speak of the *men* who follow this ministration. For the daughters of the Priests,[4] who have no part in the Priestly office, yet on account of their father's dignity undergo a far bitterer punishment for the same sins as others, and the offense is the same in their case and in the daughters of the laity; namely, fornication in both; yet the penalty is far severer for the former. Dost thou see with what abundant proof God shows thee that he demands much greater punishment for the ruler than for the ruled? For no doubt he who punishes to a greater degree than others the daughter of a certain man for that man's sake, will not exact the same penalty from the man who is the cause of her additional chastisement as from others, but a much heavier one; and very reasonably; for the mischief does not merely involve himself, but it destroys the souls of the weaker brethren and of them who look up to him, and Ezekiel, writing to show this, distinguishes from one another the judgment of the rams and of the sheep.[5]

12. Do we then seem to thee to entertain a reasonable fear? for in addition to what has been said, although much toil is needful on my part, so that I should not be completely overwhelmed by the passions of my soul, yet I endure the toil, and I do not shun the conflict. For even now I am taken captive by vainglory, but I often recover myself, and I see at a glance that I have been taken, and there are times when I rebuke my soul, which has been enslaved; outrageous desires even now come over me, but they kindle only a languid flame, since my bodily eyes cannot fasten upon any fuel to feed the fire. From speaking ill of any, or from hearing any one evil spoken of, I am utterly removed, since I have no one to talk with; for surely these walls would never give tongue; yet it is not altogether in like manner possible to avoid anger, although there be none to provoke it. For often when the recollection of outrageous men has come over me, and of the deeds done by them, it makes my heart swell. But not permanently, for I quickly subdue its kindling, and persuade it to be quiet, saying that it is very inexpedient and extremely despicable to leave one's own fault alone, and to busy one's self about the faults of one's neighbors. But were I to come among the multitude, and to be involved in countless excitements, I should not be able to have the benefit of this warning, nor to experience reflections which take me thus to task. But just as they who are driven over precipices by a torrent, or in some other way, are able to foresee the destruction to which they are finally going, and are unable to think of any means of help, so I, when I have fallen into the great tumult of my passions, shall be able to see at a glance my chastisement daily increasing. But to be master of myself as I am now, and to rebuke diseases of this sort raging on every side, would not be equally easy for me as it was before. For my soul is weak and puny, and easily mastered, not only by these passions, but by envy, which is bitterer than all of them. Neither does it know how to bear insults or honors temperately. But these do exceedingly elate it, while those depress it. As, then, savage wild beasts, when they are in good condition, and in full vigor, overcome those that fight with them, particularly, too, if they be feeble and unskillful; but if any one were to weaken them by starvation, he will put their rage to sleep, and will extinguish most of their strength; so that one, not over valiant, might take up the conflict and battle with them: so also with the passions of the soul. He who makes them weak, places them in subjection to right reason; but he who nourishes them carefully, makes his battle with them harder, and renders them so formidable that he passes all his time in bondage and fear.

What then is the food of these wild beasts? Of vainglory, indeed, it is honors and applause; of pride, abundance of authority and power;

---
[1] Amos iii. 2.   [2] Amos ii. 11.   [3] Lev. iv. 3, 14.
[4] Lev. xxi. 9.   [5] Ez. xxxiv. 17.

of envy, the reputation of one's neighbors; of avarice, the munificence of the generous; of incontinence, luxury and the constant society of women; and other passions have their proper nutriment? And all these things will sorely attack me if I come forth into the world, and will tear my soul to pieces, will be the more formidable and will make my battle with them the harder. Whereas, while I am established here they will be subdued; and then, indeed, only with great exertion; yet at the same time, by the Grace of God, they *will* be subdued, and there will not be anything worse then than their bark. For these reasons I keep to this cell, and am inaccessible, self-contained, and unsociable, and I put up with hearing countless complaints of this kind, although I would gladly efface them, and have been vexed and grieved because I cannot; for it is not easy for me to become sociable, and at the same time to remain in my present security. Therefore I beseech thee, too, to pity rather than to censure one beset with such great difficulty.

But we cannot yet persuade thee. Accordingly the time is now come that I should utter to thee the only thing which I have left unspoken. Perhaps it may seem to many to be incredible, but even so I shall not be ashamed to bring it before the world, for though what is said is proof of an evil conscience and of many sins, yet, since God, who is about to judge us, knows all accurately, what gain will result to us from the ignorance of men? What then is this, which is yet unspoken? From that day on which thou didst impart to me the suspicion of the bishopric, my whole system has often been in danger of being completely unhinged, such was the fear, such the despondency which seized my soul; for on considering the glory of the Bride of Christ, the holiness, the spiritual beauty and wisdom, and comeliness, and then reckoning up my own faults, I used not to cease bewailing both her and myself, and amidst continual distress and perplexity, I kept saying—who then made such a suggestion as this? why has the Church of God made so great a mistake? why has she so provoked her Master, as to be delivered over to me, the unworthiest of all men, and to undergo such great disgrace? Considering these things often by myself, and being unable to bear the thought of so monstrous a thing, I used to be like thunderstruck people, speechless, and unable either to see or hear. And when this condition of great helplessness left me, for there were times when it passed off, tears and despondency succeeded to it, and after the flood of tears, then fear again, entered in their stead, disturbing, confusing and agitating my mind. In such a tempest I used to pass the time that is gone; but thou wast ignorant of it, and thoughtest that I was spending my time in a perfect tranquillity, but I will now try and unveil to thee the storm of my soul, for it may be thou wilt henceforth pardon me, abandoning your accusations. How then shall I unveil this to thee? For if thou wouldest see this clearly, it is not otherwise possible than by laying bare my own heart; but as this is impossible, I will try and show you as well as I can, by a certain faint illustration, the gloom of my despondency, and from this image please to infer my condition.

Let us suppose that the daughter of the King of all the earth under the sun is the betrothed of a certain man, and that this damsel has matchless beauty, transcending that of human nature, and that in this respect she outstrips by a long distance the whole race of women; also that she has virtues of the soul, so great as to distance by a long way the whole generation of men that have been, or that shall be; and that the grace of her manners transcends all standards of art, and that the loveliness of her person is eclipsed by the beauty of her countenance; and that her betrothed, not only for the sake of these things, is enamored of the maiden, but apart from these things has an affection for her, and by his ardor throws into the shade the most passionate of lovers that ever were. Then let us suppose, whilst he is burning with love, he hears from some quarter that some mean, abject man, low born, and crippled in body, in fact a thoroughly bad fellow, was about to wed this wondrous, well-beloved maiden. Have we then presented to thee some small portion of our grief? and is it enough to stay my illustration at this point? So far as my despondency is concerned, I think it is enough; for this was the only purpose for which I introduced the comparison, but that I may show you the measure of my fear, and my terror, let me proceed to another description.

Let there be an armament composed of infantry, cavalry, and marines, and let a number of triremes cover the sea, and phalanxes of foot and horse cover most of the plains, and the ridges of the mountains, and let the metal of their armor reflect the sunshine, and the glitter of the helmets and shields be reflected by the beams which are emitted from them; let the clashing of spears and the neighing of horses be borne up to the very heavens, and let neither sea nor land appear, but only brass and iron in every direction. Let the enemy be drawn up in battle array opposite to these, fierce and savage men, and let the time of the engagement be now at hand. Then let some one suddenly seize some young lad, one of those brought up in the country, knowing nothing but the use of the shepherd's pipe and crook; let him be clad in brazen armor, and let him be led round the whole camp and be shown the squadrons and their officers, the archers, slingers, captains, generals, the foot and horse, the spearmen, the triremes and their commanders, the dense mass of soldiers in the ships, and the multitude of engines of war lying ready on board. Let him be shown, moreover, the whole array of the enemy, their repulsive aspect, and the varied stores and unusual quantity of their arms; the ravines also and precipices of the mountains, deep and difficult. Let him be shown further on the enemies' side, horses flying by some enchantment and infantry borne through the air, and sorcery of every power and form; and let him consider the calamities of war, the cloud of spears, the hailstorm of arrows, that great mist and obscurity, that gloomiest night which the multitude of weapons occasions, eclipsing the sunbeams with their cloud, the dust no less than the darkness baffling the eyesight. The torrents of blood, the groanings of the falling, the shouts of the surviving, the heaps of slain, wheels bathed in blood, horses with their riders thrown headlong down, owing to the number of corpses, the ground a scene of general confusion, blood, and bows, and arrows, hoofs of horses and heads of men lying together, a human arm and a chariot wheel and a helmet, a breast pierced through, brains sticking to swords, the point of a dart broken off with an eye transfixed upon it. Then let him reckon up the sufferings of the naval force, the triremes burning in the midst of the waves, and sinking with their armed crews, the roaring of the sea, the tumult of the sailors, the shout of the soldiers, the foam of the waves mixed with blood, and dashing over into all the ships; the corpses on the decks, some sinking, some floating, some cast upon the beach, overwhelmed by the waves, and obstructing the passage of the ships. And when he has been carefully instructed in all the tragedy of warfare, let the horrors of captivity and of slavery be added to it, worse than any kind of death; and having told him all this, bid him mount his horse straightway, and take command of all that armament.

Dost thou really think that this lad would be equal to more than the mere description, and would not, at the very first glance, lose heart?

13. Do not think that I have exaggerated the matter by my account, nor suppose that because we are shut up in this body, as in some prison house, and are unable to see anything of the invisible world, that what has been said is overstated. For thou wouldest see a far greater and more formidabl econflict than this, couldest thou ever behold, with these eyes of thine, the devil's most gloomy battle array, and his frantic onset. For there is no brass or iron there. No horses, or chariots or wheels, no fire and darts. These are visible things. But there are other much more fearful engines than these. One does not need against these enemies breastplate or shield, sword and spear, yet the sight only of this accursed array is enough to paralyze the soul, unless it happen to be very noble, and to enjoy in a high degree as a protection to its own courage the providential care of God. And if it were possible by putting off this body, or still keeping it, to see clearly and fearlessly with the naked eye the whole of his battle array, and his warfare against us, thou wouldest see no torrents of blood, nor dead bodies, but so many fallen souls, and such disastrous wounds that the whole of that description of warfare which I just now detailed to thee thou wouldest think to be mere child's sport and pastime rather than war: so many are there smitten every day, and the wounds in the two cases do not bring about the same death, but as great as is the difference between the soul from the body, so great is the difference between that death and this. For when the soul receives a wound, and falls, it does not lie as a lifeless body, but it is thenceforth tormented, being gnawed by an evil conscience; and after its removal hence, at the time of judgment, it is delivered over to eternal punishment; and if any one be without grief in regard to the wounds given by the devil, his danger becomes the greater for his insensibility. For whoever is not pained by the first wound, will readily receive a second, and after that a third. For the unclean spirit will not cease assaulting to the last breath, whenever he finds a soul supine and indifferent to his first wounds; and if thou wouldest inquire into the method of attack, thou wouldest find this much more severe and varied. For no one ever knew so many forms of craft and deceit as that unclean spirit. By this indeed, he has acquired the greater part of his power, nor can any one have so implacable a hatred against his worst enemies as the evil one against the human race. And if any one inquire into the vehemence with which he fights, here again it would be ludicrous to bring men into comparison with him. But if any one choose out the fiercest and most savage of beasts, and is minded to set their fury against his, he will find that they were meek and quiet in comparison, such rage does he breathe forth when he attacks our souls; and the period of the war-

fare indeed in the former case is brief, and in this brief space there are respites; for the approach of the night and the fatigue of slaughter, meal-times also, and many other things, afford a respite to the soldier, so that he can doff his armor and breathe a little, and refresh himself with food and drink, and in many other ways recover his former strength. But in the case of the evil one it is not possible ever to lay aside one's armor, it is not possible even to take sleep, for one who would remain always unscathed. For one of two things must be: either to fall and perish unarmed, or to stand equipped and ever watchful. For he ever stands with his own battle array, watching for our indolence, and laboring more zealously for our destruction, than we for our salvation.

And that he is not seen by us, and suddenly assails us, which things are a source of countless evils to those who are not always on the watch, proves this kind of war to be harder than the other. Couldest thou wish us, then, in such a case to command the soldiers of Christ? yea, this were to command them for the devil's service, for whenever he who ought to marshal and order others is the most inexperienced and feeble of all men, by betraying through this inexperience those who have been entrusted to his charge, he commands them in the devil's interests rather than in Christ's.

But why dost thou sigh? why weep? For my ease does not now call for wailing, but for joy and gladness.

BASIL: But not my case, yea this calls for countless lamentations. For I am hardly able yet to understand to what degree of evil thou hast brought me. For I came to thee wanting to learn what excuse I should make on thy behalf to those who find fault with thee; but thou sendest me back after putting another case in the place of that I had. For I am no longer concerned about the excuses I shall give them on thy behalf, but what excuse I shall make to God for myself and my own faults. But I beseech thee, and implore thee, if my welfare is at all regarded by thee, if there be any consolation in Christ, if any comfort of love, if any bowels, and mercies,[1] for thou knowest that thyself above all hast brought me into this danger, stretch forth thine hand, both saying and doing what is able to restore me, do not have the heart to leave me for the briefest moment, but now rather than before let me pass my life with thee.

CHRYSOSTOM: But I smiled, and said, how shall I be able to help, how to profit thee under so great a burden of office? But since this is pleasant to thee, take courage, dear soul, for at any time at which it is possible for thee to have leisure amid thine own cares, I will come and will comfort thee, and nothing shall be wanting of what is in my power.

On this, he weeping yet more, rose up. But I, having embraced him and kissed his head, led him forth, exhorting him to bear his lot bravely. For I believe, said I, that through Christ who has called thee, and set thee over his own sheep, thou wilt obtain such assurance from this ministry as to receive me also, if I am in danger at the last day, into thine everlasting tabernacle.

[1] Phil. ii. 1.

ST. CHRYSOSTOM:

AN EXHORTATION TO THEODORE AFTER HIS FALL.

TRANSLATED WITH INTRODUCTION AND NOTES BY

REV. W. R. W. STEPHENS, M.A.,

PREBENDARY OF CHICHESTER, AND RECTOR OF WOOLBEDING, SUSSEX.

INTRODUCTION TO THE LETTERS TO THEODORE.

THESE two letters, which are the earliest of Chrysostom's extant works, are addressed to a friend who had been a member of the little ascetic brotherhood which Chrysostom and Basil formed, soon after they had abandoned secular life, as described in the first book of the Treatise on the Priesthood. Theodore, like Maximus, afterwards Bishop of Isaurian Seleucia, who was another member of the same fraternity, had been a fellow student with Chrysostom and Basil in the school of Libanius,[1] but was a few years younger than either of them. The strain upon his powers of religious devotion had proved too much for him; he had withdrawn from the ascetic brotherhood, and relapsed for a season into worldly habits, being fascinated by the beauty of a young lady named Hermione, whom he was anxious to marry. His fall was regarded with almost as much sorrow and dismay by his austere friends as if he had plunged into deadly vice. Prayers were continually offered, and great efforts made for his restoration, amongst which must be reckoned the two letters which are here translated. They are the productions of a youthful enthusiast, and as such allowances must be made for them; but they abound in passages of great beauty and power, especially upon the infinite love and forbearance of God, as encouraging to repentance and withholding from despair and recklessness into which Theodore seems to have been inclined to sink. The appeal of Chrysostom, combined with the efforts of his other friends, was not in vain. Theodore once more renounced the world and his matrimonial intentions, and retired into the seclusion of the fraternity. In A.D. 383, when he was about thirty-three years of age, he was ordained priest, and in 392 he became Bishop of Mopsuestia, where he died in A.D. 428 at the age of seventy-eight. Chrysostom seems to have retained his affection to him to the last, and during his own exile at Cucusus, A.D. 404-7, wrote a letter to him which is full of expressions of fervent admiration and regard. He was a most voluminous writer, and may be regarded as the ablest representative of the school of Biblical interpretation founded by Diodorus of Tarsus, under whom he had studied, together with Chrysostom and Basil. A fierce controversy raged during the fifth and sixth centuries respecting the orthodoxy of some of his writings which some accused of preparing the way for Nestorianism. When this had died down his name was comparatively forgotten, and it is only in modern times that his great merits as a commentator, who boldly applied the historical and grammatical methods of examination to the books of Holy Scripture, have been fully recognized.

Tillemont was of opinion that of the two letters of Chrysostom the second only was addressed to Theodore, who was afterwards Bishop of Mopsuestia. Montfaucon, however, Dupin, and Savile, maintain that both were addressed to him, and their view is confirmed by the fact that Leontius of Byzantium (in Nest. et. Eutych. lib. iii. c. 7) and Isidore of Seville (de Script. Eccl. c. 6.) mention two letters of Chrysostom to Theodore of Mopsuestia.

---

[1] See introduction to the "Treatise on the Priesthood."

CONTENTS.

	PAGE
LETTER I.	91
LETTER II.	111

AN EXHORTATION TO THEODORE AFTER HIS FALL.

LETTER I.

"OH! that my head were water, and mine eyes a fountain of tears!"[1] it is seasonable for me to utter these words now, yea much more than for the prophet in his time. For although I am not about to mourn over many cities, or whole nations, yet shall I mourn over a soul which is of equal value with many such nations, yea even more precious. For if one man who does the will of God is better than ten thousand transgressors, then thou wast formerly better than ten thousand Jews. Wherefore no one would now blame me if I were to compose more lamentations than those which are contained in the prophet, and to utter complaints yet more vehement. For it is not the overthrow of a city which I mourn, nor the captivity of wicked men, but the desolation of a sacred soul, the destruction and effacement of a Christ-bearing temple.[2] For would not any one who knew in the days of its glory that well-ordered mind of thine which the devil has now set on fire, groan, imitating the lamentation of the prophet; when he hears that barbarian hands have defiled the holy of holies, and have set fire to all things and burned them up, the cherubim, the ark, the mercy seat, the tables of stone, the golden pot? For this calamity is bitterer, yea bitterer than that, in proportion as the pledges deposited in thy soul were far more precious than those. This temple is holier than that; for it glistened not with gold and silver, but with the grace of the Spirit, and in place of the ark and the cherubim, it had Christ, and His Father, and the Paraclete seated within. But now all is changed, and the temple is desolate, and bare of its former beauty and comeliness, unadorned with its divine and unspeakable adornments, destitute of all security and protection; it has neither door nor bolt, and is laid open to all manner of soul-destroying and shameful thoughts; and if the thought of arrogance or fornication, or avarice, or any more accursed than these, wish to enter in there is no one to hinder them; whereas formerly, even as the Heaven is inaccessible to all these, so also was the purity of thy soul. Now perhaps I shall seem to say what is incredible to some who now witness thy desolation and overthrow; for on this account I wail and mourn, and shall not cease doing so, until I see thee again established in thy former lustre. For although this seems to be impossible to men, yet to God all things are possible. For it is He "who raiseth the poor from the earth, and lifteth up the beggar from the dunghill, to set him with the princes, even with the princes of his people." It is He "who makes the barren woman to dwell at home, a mother rejoicing over her children."[3] Do not then despair of the most perfect change. For if the devil had such great power as to cast thee down from that pinnacle and height of virtue into the extremity of evil doing, much more will God be able to draw thee up again to thy former confidence; and not only indeed to make you what you were before, but even much happier. Only be not downcast, nor fling away good hopes, nor fall into the condition of the ungodly. For it is not the multitude of sins which is wont to plunge men into despair, but impiety of soul. Therefore Solomon did not make the unqualified statement "*every one* who has entered into the den of the wicked, despiseth;" but only "he who is ungodly."[4] For

---

[1] Jer. ix. 1.
[2] See 1 Cor. iii. 16, 17; and vi. 19. Ignatius the martyr had the name Θεοφόρος, "the God-bearer," which was probably given at the time of his conversion, or of baptism, to remind him continually of his Christian privileges and duties. See note, p. 73.
[3] Ps. cxiii. 7–9.
[4] Prov. xviii. 3, LXX.

it is such persons only who are affected in this way when they have entered the den of the wicked. And this it is which does not suffer them to look up, and re-ascend to the position from which they fell. For this accursed thought pressing down like some yoke upon the neck of the soul, and so forcing it to stoop, hinders it from looking up to the Master. Now it is the part of a brave and excellent man to break this yoke in pieces, to shake off the tormentor fastened upon him; and to utter the words of the prophet, "As the eyes of a maiden look unto the hands of her mistress, even so our eyes look unto the Lord our God until He have mercy upon us. Have pity upon us, O Lord, have pity upon us, for we have been utterly filled with contempt."[1] Truly divine are these precepts, and decrees of the highest form of spiritual wisdom. We have been filled, it is said, with contempt, and have undergone countless distresses; nevertheless we shall not desist from looking up to God, neither shall we cease praying to him until He has received our petition. For this is the mark of a noble soul, not to be cast down, nor be dismayed at the multitude of the calamities which oppress it, nor to withdraw, after praying many times without success, but to persevere, until He have mercy upon us, even as the blessed David saith.

2. For the reason why the devil plunges us into thoughts of despair is that he may cut off the hope which is towards God, the safe anchor, the foundation of our life, the guide of the way which leads to heaven, the salvation of perishing souls. "For by hope" it is said, "we are saved."[2] For this assuredly it is which, like some strong cord suspended from the heavens, supports our souls, gradually drawing towards that world on high those who cling firmly to it, and lifting them above the tempest of the evils of this life. If any one then becomes enervated, and lets go this sacred anchor, straightway he falls down, and is suffocated, having entered into the abyss of wickedness. And the Evil One knowing this, when he perceives that we are ourselves oppressed by the consciousness of evil deeds, steps in himself and lays upon us the additional burden, heavier than lead, of anxiety arising from despair; and if we accept it, it follows of necessity that we are forthwith dragged down by the weight, and having been parted from that cord, descend into the depth of misery where thou thyself art now, having forsaken the commandments of the meek and lowly Master and executing all the injunctions of the cruel tyrant, and implacable enemy of our salvation; having broken in pieces the easy yoke, and cast away the light burden, and having put on the iron collar instead of these things, yea, having hung the ponderous millstone[3] from thy neck. Where then canst thou find a footing henceforth when thou art submerging thy unhappy soul, imposing on thyself this necessity of continually sinking downwards? Now the woman who had found the one coin called her neighbors to share her joy; saying, "Rejoice with me;" but I shall now invoke all friends, both mine and thine, for the contrary purpose, saying not "Rejoice with me" but "Mourn with me," and take up the same strain of mourning, and utter the same cry of distress with me. For the worst possible loss has befallen me, not that some given number of talents of gold, or some large quantity of precious stones have dropped out of my hand, but that he who was more precious than all these things, who was sailing over this same sea, this great and broad sea with me, has, I know not how, slipped overboard, and fallen into the very pit of destruction.

3. Now if any should attempt to divert me from mourning, I shall reply to them in the words of the prophet, saying "Let me alone, I will weep bitterly; labour not to comfort me."[4] For the mourning with which I mourn now is not of a kind to subject me to condemnation for excess in lamentation, but the cause is one for which even Paul, or Peter, had they been here, would not have been ashamed to weep and mourn, and reject all kinds of consolation. For those who bewail that death which is common to all one might reasonably accuse of much feebleness of spirit; but when in place of a corpse a dead soul lies before us, pierced with innumerable wounds, and yet even in its death manifesting its former natural comeliness, and health, and beauty now extinguished, who can be so harsh and unsympathetic as to utter words of encouragement in place of wailing and lamentation? For as in the other world the absence of mourning is a mark of divine wisdom, so in this world the act of mourning is a mark of the same. He who had already mounted to the sky, who was laughing to scorn the vanity of this life, who regarded bodily beauty no more than if it had been in forms of stone, who despised gold as it had been mud, and every kind of luxury as mire, even he, having been suddenly overwhelmed with the feverish longing of a preposterous passion, has ruined his health, and manly strength, and the bloom of his youth, and

---

[1] Ps. cxxiii. 2, 3. [2] Rom. viii. 24.
[3] μύλος ὀνικός, lit. the mill-stone turned by an ass, as being heavier than the common hand-mill. So in Matt. xviii. 6.
[4] Is. xxii. 4.

become a slave of pleasure. Shall we not weep then, I pray you, for such a man and bewail him, until we have got him back again? And where do these things concern the human soul? It is not possible indeed to discover in this world the means of release from the death of the body, and yet even this does not stay the mourners from lamenting; but only in this world is it possible to bring to naught the death of the soul. "For in Hades" we read, "who will confess thee?"[1] Is it not then the height of stupidity that they who mourn the death of the body should do this so earnestly, although they know that they will not raise the dead man to life by their lamentation; but that we should not manifest anything of the kind, and this when we know that often there is hope of conducting the lost soul back to its former life? For many both now and in the days of our forefathers, having been perverted from the right position, and fallen headlong out of the straight path, have been so completely restored as to eclipse their former deeds by the latter, and to receive the prize, and be wreathed with the garland of victory, and be proclaimed among the conquerors, and be numbered in the company of the saints. For as long as any one stands in the furnace of pleasures, even if he has countless examples of this kind before him, the thing seems to him to be impossible; but if he once gets a short start upon the way out from thence, by continually advancing he leaves the fiercer part of the fire behind him and will see the parts which are in front of him, and before his footsteps full of dew and much refreshment; only let us not despair or grow weary of the return; for he who is so affected, even if he has acquired boundless power and zeal, has acquired it to no purpose. For when he has once shut the door of repentance against himself, and has blocked the entrance into the race-course, how will he be able while he abides outside to accomplish any good thing, either small or great? On this account the Evil One uses all kinds of devices in order to plant in us this thought (of despair); for (if he succeeds) he will no longer have to sweat and toil in contending with us; how should he, when we are prostrate and fallen, and unwilling to resist him? For he who has been able to slip out of this chain, will recover his own strength and will not cease struggling against the devil to his last gasp, and even if he had countless other falls, he will get up again, and will smite his enemy; but he who is in bondage to the cogitations of despair, and has unstrung his own strength, how will he be able to prevail, and to resist, having on the contrary taken to flight?

4. And speak not to me of those who have committed small sins, but suppose the case of one who is filled full of all wickedness, and let him practice everything which excludes him from the kingdom, and let us suppose that this man is not one of those who were unbelievers from the beginning, but formerly belonged to the believers, and such as were well pleasing to God, but afterwards has become a fornicator, adulterer, effeminate, a thief, a drunkard, a sodomite, a reviler, and everything else of this kind; I will not approve even of this man despairing of himself, although he may have gone on to extreme old age in the practice of this great and unspeakable wickedness. For if the wrath of God were a passion, one might well despair as being unable to quench the flame which he had kindled by so many evil doings; but since the Divine nature is passionless, even if He punishes, even if He takes vengeance, he does this not with wrath, but with tender care, and much lovingkindness; wherefore it behoves us to be of much good courage, and to trust in the power of repentance. For even those who have sinned against Him He is not wont to visit with punishment for His own sake; for no harm can traverse that divine nature; but He acts with a view to our advantage, and to prevent our perverseness becoming worse by our making a practice of despising and neglecting Him. For even as one who places himself outside the light inflicts no loss on the light, but the greatest upon himself being shut up in darkness; even so he who has become accustomed to despise that almighty power, does no injury to the power, but inflicts the greatest possible injury upon himself. And for this reason God threatens us with punishments, and often inflicts them, not as avenging Himself, but by way of attracting us to Himself. For a physician also is not distressed or vexed at the insults of those who are out of their minds, but yet does and contrives everything for the purpose of stopping those who do such unseemly acts, not looking to his own interests but to their profit; and if they manifest some small degree of self-control and sobriety he rejoices and is glad, and applies his remedies much more earnestly, not as revenging himself upon them for their former conduct, but as wishing to increase their advantage, and to bring them back to a purely sound state of health. Even so God when we fall into the very extremity of madness, says and does everything, not by way of avenging Himself on account of our former deeds; but because He wishes to release us from our disorder; and by means of

---

[1] Ps. vi. 5.

right reason it is quite possible to be convinced of this.

5. Now if any one should dispute with us concerning these things we will confirm them out of the divine oracles. For who, I ask, became more depraved than the king of the Babylonians, who after having received such great experience of God's power as to make obeisance to His prophet, and command offerings and incense to be sacrificed to Him was again carried away to his former pride, and cast bound into the furnace those who did not honour himself before God. Nevertheless this man who was so cruel and impious, and rather a beast than a human being, God invited to repentance, and granted him several opportunities of conversion, first of all the miracle which took place in the furnace, and after that the vision which the king saw but which Daniel interpreted, a vision sufficient to bend even a heart of stone; and in addition to these things after the exhortation derived from events the prophet also himself advised him, saying "Therefore, O king, let my counsel please thee, and redeem thy sins by alms, and thy iniquities by showing mercy to the poor; it may be that long suffering will be shown to thy offence."[1] What sayest thou O wise and blessed man? After so great a fall is there again a way of return? and after so great a disease is health possible? and after so great a madness is there again a hope of soundness of mind? The king has deprived himself beforehand of all hope, first of all by having ignored Him who created him; and conducted him to this honour, although he had many evidences of His power and forethought to recount which occurred both in his own case and in the case of his forefathers; but after this again when he had received distinct tokens of God's wisdom and foreknowledge, and had seen magic, and astronomy and the theatre of the whole satanic system of jugglery overthrown, he exhibited deeds yet worse than the former. For things which the wise magi, the Gazarenes, could not explain, but confessed that they were beyond human nature, these a captive youth having caused to be solved for him, so moved him by that miracle that he not only himself believed, but also became to the whole world a clear herald and teacher of this doctrine.[2] Wherefore if even before having received such a token it was unpardonable in him to ignore God, much more so was it after that miracle; and his confession, and the teaching which was extended to others. For if he had not honestly believed that He was the only true God he would not have shown such honour to His servant, or have laid down such laws for others. But yet after making this kind of confession, he again lapsed into idolatry, and he who once fell on his face and made obeisance to the servant of God, broke out into such a pitch of madness, as to cast into the furnace the servants of God who did not make obeisance to himself. What then? did God visit the apostate, as he deserved to be visited? No! He supplied him with greater tokens of His own power, drawing him back again after so great a display of arrogance to his former condition; and, what is yet more wonderful, that owing to the abundance of the miracles he might not again disbelieve what was done, the subject upon which He wrought the sign was none other than the furnace which the king himself kindled for the children whom he bound, and cast therein. Even to extinguish the flame would have been a wonderful and strange thing; but the benign Deity in order to inspire him with greater fear, and increase his dismay, and undo all his hardness of heart, did what was greater and stranger than this. For, permitting the furnace to be kindled to as high a pitch as he desired, He then exhibited his own peculiar power, not by putting down the devices of his enemies, but by frustrating them when they were set on foot. And, to prevent any one who saw them survive the flame from supposing that it was a vision, He suffered those who cast them in to be burned, thus proving that the thing seen was really fire; for otherwise it would not have devoured naphtha and tow, and fagots and such a large number of bodies; but nothing is stronger than His command; but the nature of all existing things obeys Him who brought them into being out of nothing; which was just what He manifested at that time; for the flame having received perishable bodies, held aloof from them as if they had been imperishable, and restored in safety, with the addition of much lustre, the deposit entrusted to it. For like kings from some royal court, even so did those children come forth from the furnace, no one having the patience to look any longer at the king, but all transferring their eyes from him to the strange spectacle, and neither the diadem nor the purple robe, nor any other feature of royal pomp, attracted the multitudes of unbelievers so much as the sight of those faithful ones, who tarried long in the fire, and then came out of it as men might have done who had undergone this in a dream. For the most fragile of all our features, I mean the hair, prevailed more mightily than adamant against the all-devouring flame. And the fact that when they were cast into the midst of the fire they suffered no harm was not the only

---

[1] Dan. iv. 27. [2] Dan. ii.

wonder, but the further fact that they were speaking the whole time. Now all who have witnessed persons burning are aware, that if they keep their lips fast closed, they can hold out for a short time at least against the conflagration; but if any one chances to open his mouth, the soul instantly takes its flight from the body. Nevertheless after such great miracles had taken place, and all who were present and beheld were amazed, and those who were absent had been informed of the fact by means of letters, the king who instructed others remained himself without amendment, and went back again to his former wickedness. And yet even then God did not punish him, but was still long-suffering, counselling him both by means of visions and by His prophet. But when he was not made anywise better by any of these things, then at last God inflicted punishment upon him, not by way of avenging himself on account of his former deeds, but as cutting off the occasion of future evils, and checking the advance of wickedness, and He did not inflict even this permanently, but after having chastised him for a few years, He restored him again to his former honour, without having suffered any loss from his punishment, but on the contrary having gained the greatest possible good; a firm hold upon faith in God, and repentance on account of his former misdeeds.[1]

6. For such is the loving-kindness of God; He never turns his face away from a sincere repentance, but if any one has pushed on to the very extremity of wickedness, and chooses to return thence towards the path of virtue, God accepts and welcomes, and does everything so as to restore him to his former position. And He does what is yet more merciful; for even should any one not manifest complete repentance, he does not pass by one which is small and insignificant, but assigns a great reward even to this; which is evident from what Esaias the prophet says concerning the people of the Jews, speaking on this wise: "On account of his sin I put him to pain for a little while, and smote him, and turned my face away from him, and he was pained, and walked sorrowfully, and then I healed him, and comforted him."[2] And we might cite as another witness that most ungodly king, who was given over to sin by the influence of his wife: yet when he only sorrowed, and put on sackcloth, and condemned his offences, he so won for himself the mercy of God, as to be released from all the evils which were impending over him. For God said to Elias "Seest thou how Ahab is pricked in the heart before my face? I will not bring the evil upon him in his own days, because he hath wept before me."[3] And after this again, Manasses, having exceeded all in fury and tyranny, and having subverted the legal form of worship, and shut up the temple, and caused the deceit of idolatry to flourish, and having become more ungodly than all who were before him, when he afterwards repented, was ranked amongst the friends of God. Now if, looking to the magnitude of his own iniquities, he had despaired of restoration and repentance, he would have missed all which he afterwards obtained: but as it was, looking to the boundlessness of God's tender mercy instead of the enormity of his transgressions, and having broken in sunder the bonds of the devil, he rose up and contended with him, and finished the good course.[4] And not only by what was done to these men, but also by the words of the prophet does God destroy the counsels of despair, speaking on this wise: "To-day, if ye will hear His voice, harden not your hearts, as in the provocation."[5] Now that expression "to-day," may be uttered at every time of life, even on the verge of old age, if you desire it: for repentance is judged not by quantity of time, but by disposition of the soul. For the Ninevites did not need many days to blot out their sin, but the short space of one day availed to efface all their iniquity: and the robber also did not take a long time to effect his entrance into Paradise, but in such a brief moment as one might occupy in uttering a single word, did he wash off all the sins which he had committed in his whole life, and received the prize bestowed by the divine approval even before the Apostles. And we also see the martyrs obtain glorious crowns for themselves in the course, not of many years, but of a few days, and often in a single day only.

7. Wherefore we have need of zeal in every direction, and much preparation of mind: and if we so order our conscience as to hate our former wickedness, and choose the contrary path with as much energy as God desires and commands, we shall not have anything less on account of the short space of time: many at least who were last have far outstripped those who were first. For to have fallen is not a grievous thing, but to remain prostrate after falling, and not to get up again; and, playing the coward and the sluggard, to conceal feebleness of moral purpose under the reasoning of despair. To whom also the prophet spoke in perplexity saying "Doth he who falleth not rise

---

[1] Dan. iv.
[2] Isa. lvii. 17, 18. LXX., which has after "sorrowfully" the words "in his ways." I beheld his ways and healed him, etc.
[3] 1 Kings xxi. 29. The words "because he hath wept before me," are not in the LXX.
[4] 2 Chron. xxxiii. 10–19.
[5] Ps. xcv. 9.

up, or he who turneth away not turn back?"[1] But if you inquire of me for instances of persons who have fallen away after having believed, all these things have been said with reference to such persons, for he who has fallen belonged formerly to those who were standing, not to those who were prostrate; for how should one in that condition fall? But other things also shall be said, partly by means of parables, partly by plainer deeds and words. Now that sheep which had got separated from the ninety and nine,[2] and then was brought back again, represents to us nothing else than the fall and return of the faithful; for it was a sheep not of some alien flock, but belonging to the same number as the rest, and was formerly pastured by the same shepherd, and it strayed on no common straying, but wandered away to the mountains and in valleys, that is to say some long journey, far distant from the right path. Did he then suffer it to stray? By no means, but brought it back neither driving it, nor beating it, but taking it upon his shoulders. For as the best physicians bring back those who are far gone in sickness with careful treatment to a state of health, not only treating them according to the laws of the medical art, but sometimes also giving them gratification: even so God conducts to virtue those who are much depraved, not with great severity, but gently and gradually, and supporting them on every side, so that the separation may not become greater, nor the error more prolonged. And the same truth is implied in the parable of the prodigal son as well as in this. For he also was no stranger, but a son, and a brother of the child who had been well pleasing to the father, and he plunged into no ordinary vice, but went to the very extremity, so to say, of evil, he the rich and free and well-bred son being reduced to a more miserable condition than that of household slaves, strangers, and hirelings. Nevertheless he returned again to his original condition, and had his former honour restored to him. But if he had despaired of his life, and, dejected by what had befallen him, had remained in the foreign land, he would not have obtained what he did obtain, but would have been consumed with hunger, and so have undergone the most pitiable death: but since he repented, and did not despair, he was restored, even after such great corruption, to the same splendour as before, and was arrayed in the most beautiful robe, and enjoyed greater honours than his brother who had not fallen. For "these many years," saith he "do I serve thee, neither transgressed I thy commandment at any time, and yet thou never gavest me a kid, that I might make merry with my friends; but when this thy son is come who hath devoured thy living with harlots, thou hast killed for him the fatted calf."[3] So great is the power of repentance.

8. Having then such great examples, let us not continue in evil, nor despair of reconciliation, but let us say also ourselves "I will go to my Father," and let us draw nigh to God. For He Himself never turns away from us, but it is we who put ourselves far off: for "I am a God" we read "at hand and not a God afar off."[4] And again, when He was rebuking them by the mouth of this prophet He said "Do not your sins separate between you and me?"[5] Inasmuch then as this is the cause which puts us far from God, let us remove this obnoxious barrier, which prevents any near approach being made.

But now hear how this has actually occurred in real instances. Amongst the Corinthians some man of mark committed a sin such as was not named even among the Gentiles. This man was a believer and belonged to the household of Christ; and some say that he was actually a member of the priesthood. What then? Did Paul cut him off from the communion of those who were in the way of salvation. By no means: for he himself it is who rebukes the Corinthians countless times, backwards and forwards, because they did not bring the man to a state of repentance: but, desiring to prove to us that there is no sin which cannot be healed, he said again concerning the man who had transgressed more grievously than the Gentiles: "Deliver such an one to Satan for destruction of the flesh that his spirit may be saved in the day of the Lord Jesus Christ."[6] Now this was prior to repentance: but after he had repented "Sufficient," said he, "for such an one is this punishment which was inflicted by the many[7]" and he charged them by a letter to console the man again, and to welcome his repentance, so that he should not be got the better of by Satan. Moreover when the whole Galatian people fell after having believed, and wrought miracles, and endured many trials for the sake of their faith in Christ he sets them up again. For that they had done miracles he testified when he said: "He therefore that supplieth to you the Spirit and worketh miracles among you:"[8] and that they endured many contests for the sake of the faith, he also testified when he says:

---

[1] Jer. viii. 4.
[2] Luke xv. 4, 5.
[3] Luke xv. 29, 30.
[4] Jer. xxiii. 23, where the passage is interrogatory, "Am I a God at hand and not?" etc., being a warning addressed to those who hoped to elude the vigilance of God, so that it is not quite appropriate here.
[5] Isa. lix. 2. Chrysostom by mistake attributes the quotation to Jeremiah.
[6] 1 Cor. v. 5.
[7] 2 Cor. ii. 6.
[8] Gal. iii. 5.

"Have ye suffered so many things in vain if it be indeed in vain."[1] Nevertheless after making so great an advance they committed sin sufficient to estrange them from Christ concerning which he declares saying: "Behold, I Paul tell you, that if ye be circumcised, Christ will profit you nothing:" and again "ye who would be justified by the law are fallen away from grace:"[2] and yet even after so great a lapse he welcomes them saying "my little children of whom I am in travail again until Christ be formed in you[3]" showing that after extreme perversion it is possible for Christ to be formed again in us: for He doth not desire the death of a sinner, but rather that he should be converted and live.

9. Let us then turn to Him, my beloved friend, and execute the will of God. For He created us and brought us into being, that He might make us partakers of eternal blessings, that He might offer us the kingdom of Heaven, not that He might cast us into Hell and deliver us to the fire; for this was made not for us, but for the devil: but for us the kingdom has been destined and made ready of old time. And by way of indicating both these truths He saith to those on the right hand, "Come ye blessed of my Father inherit the kingdom prepared for you from the foundation of the world:" but to those on the left "Depart from me, ye cursed, into fire everlasting prepared" (he no longer says "for you" but) "for the devil and his angels."[4] Thus hell has not been made for us but for him and his angels: but the kingdom has been prepared for us before the foundation of the world. Let us not then make ourselves unworthy of entrance into the bride-chamber: for as long as we are in this world, even if we commit countless sins, it is possible to wash them all away by manifesting repentance for our offences: but when once we have departed to the other world, even if we display the most earnest repentance it will be of no avail, not even if we gnash our teeth, beat our breasts, and utter innumerable calls for succour, no one with the tip of his finger will apply a drop to our burning bodies, but we shall only hear those words which the rich man heard in the parable "Between us and you a great gulf has been fixed."[5] Let us then, I beseech you, recover our senses here and let us recognize our Master as He ought to be recognized. For only when we are in Hades should we abandon the hope derived from repentance: for there only is this remedy weak and unprofitable: but while we are here, even if it is applied in old age itself it exhibits much strength. Wherefore also the devil sets everything in motion in order to root in us the reasoning which comes of despair: for he knows that if we repent even a little we shall not do this without some reward. But just as he who gives a cup of cold water has his recompense reserved for him, so also the man who has repented of the evils which he has done, even if he cannot exhibit the repentance which his offences deserve, will have a commensurate reward. For not a single item of good, however small it may be, will be overlooked by the righteous judge. For if He makes such an exact scrutiny of our sins, as to require punishment for both our words and thoughts, much more will our good deeds, whether they be great or small, be reckoned to our credit at that day. Wherefore, even if thou art not able to return again to the most exact state of discipline, yet if thou withdraw thyself in a slight degree at least from thy present disorder and excess, even this will not be impossible: only set thyself to the task at once, and open the entrance into the place of contest; but as long as thou tarriest outside this naturally seems difficult and impracticable to thee. For before making the trial even if things are easy and manageable they are wont to present an appearance of much difficulty to us: but when we are actually engaged in the trial, and making the venture the greater part of our distress is removed, and confidence taking the place of tremor and despair, lessens the fear and increases the facility of operation, and makes our good hopes stronger. For this reason also the wicked one dragged Judas out of this world, lest he should make a fair beginning, and so return by means of repentance to the point from which he fell. For although it may seem a strange thing to say, I will not admit even that sin to be too great for the succour which is brought to us from repentance. Wherefore I pray and beseech you to banish all this Satanic mode of thinking from your soul, and to return to this state of salvation. For if indeed I were commanding you to ascend to your former altitude all at once, you would naturally complain of there being much difficulty in doing this: but if all which I now ask you to do is to get up and return thence in the opposite direction, why do you hesitate, and shrink, and make a retrograde movement? Have you not seen those who have died in the midst of luxury and drunkenness, and sport and all the other folly of this life? Where are they now who used to strut through the market place with much pomp, and a crowd of attendants? who were clothed in silk and redolent with perfumes, and kept a table for their parasites, and were in constant attendance at the theatre? What has now become of all that

---

[1] Gal. iii. 4.   [2] Gal. v. 2, 4.   [3] Gal. iv. 19.
[4] Matt. xxv. 34.   [5] Luke xvi. 26.

parade of theirs? It is all gone;—the costly splendour of their banquets, the throng of musicians, the attentions of flatterers, the loud laughter, the relaxation of spirit, the enervation of mind, the voluptuous, abandoned, extravagant manner of life—it has all come to an end. Where now have all these things taken their flight? What has become of the body which enjoyed so much attention, and cleanliness. Go thy way to the coffin, behold the dust, the ashes, the worms, behold the loathsomeness of the place, and groan bitterly. And would that the penalty were limited to the ashes! but now transfer thy thought from the coffin and these worms to that undying worm, to the fire unquenchable, to the gnashing of teeth, to the outer darkness, to affliction and straitness, to the parable of Lazarus and the rich man, who although the owner of so much wealth, and clothed in purple could not become the owner of even a drop of water; and this when he was placed in a condition of such great necessity. The things of this world are in their nature no-wise better than dreams. For just as those who work in the mines or suffer some other kind of punishment more severe than this, when they have fallen asleep owing to their many weary toils and the extreme bitterness of their life, and in their dreams see themselves living in luxury and prosperity, are in no wise grateful to their dreams after they have awaked, even so that rich man having become rich in this present life, as it were in a dream, after his departure hence was punished with that bitter punishment. Consider these things, and having contrasted that fire with the conflagration of desires which now possesses thee, release thyself from the furnace. For he who has thoroughly quenched this furnace here, will have no experience of that in the other world: but if a man does not get the better of this furnace here, the other will lay hold of him more vehemently when he has departed hence. How long a time dost thou wish the enjoyment of the present life to be extended? For I do not suppose indeed that more than fifty years remain to thee so as to reach extreme old age, nor indeed is even this at all assured to us: for how should they who cannot be confident about living even to the evening rely upon so many years as these? And not only is this uncertain, but there is the uncertainty also of a change in our affairs, for often when life has been extended for a long period, the conditions of luxury have not been extended with it, but have come, and at the same time hastily departed. However, if you like, let it be granted for argument's sake, that you will live so many years, and will not sustain any reverse of fortune what is this compared with the endless ages, and those bitter and intolerable punishments? For here indeed both good and evil things have an end, and that very speedily: but there, both are coextensive with immortal ages, and in their quality differ unspeakably from the things which now are.

10. For when you hear of fire, do not suppose the fire in that world to be like this: for fire in this world burns up and makes away with anything which it takes hold of; but that fire is continually burning those who have once been seized by it, and never ceases: therefore also is it called unquenchable. For those also who have sinned must put on immortality, not for honour, but to have a constant supply of material for that punishment to work upon; and how terrible this is, speech could never depict, but from the experience of little things it is possible to form some slight notion of these great ones. For if you should ever be in a bath which has been heated more than it ought to be, think then, I pray you, on the fire of hell: or again if you are ever inflamed by some severe fever transfer your thoughts to that flame, and then you will be able clearly to discern the difference. For if a bath and a fever so afflict and distress us, what will our condtion be when we have fallen into that river of fire which winds in front of the terrible judg ...-seat. Then we shall gnash our teeth under the suffering of our labours and intolerable pains: but there will be no one to succour us: yea we shall groan mightily, as the flame is applied more severely to us, but we shall see no one save those who are being punished with us, and great desolation. And how should any one describe the terrors arising to our souls from the darkness? for just as that fire has no consuming power so neither has it any power of giving light: for otherwise there would not be darkness. The dismay produced in us then by this, and the trembling and the great astonishment can be sufficiently realized in that day only. For in that world many and various kinds of torment and torrents of punishment are poured in upon the soul from every side. And if any one should ask, "and how can the soul bear up against such a multitude of punishments and continue being chastised through interminable ages, let him consider what happens in this world, how many have often borne up against a long and severe disease. And if they have died, this has happened not because the soul was consumed but because the body was exhausted, so that had the latter not broken down, the soul would not have ceased being tormented. When then we have received an incorruptible and inconsumable body there is nothing to prevent the punishment being in-

definitely extended. For here indeed it is impossible that the two things should coexist. I mean severity of punishment and permanence of being, but the one contends with the other, because the nature of the body is perishable and cannot bear the concurrence of both: but when the imperishable state has supervened, there would be an end of this strife, and both these terrible things will keep their hold upon us for infinite time with much force. Let us not then so dispose ourselves now as if the excessive power of the tortures were destructive of the soul: for even the body will not be able to experience this at that time, but will abide together with the soul, in a state of eternal punishment, and there will not be any end to look to beyond this. How much luxury then, and how much time will you weigh in the balance against this punishment and vengeance? Do you propose a period of a hundred years or twice as long? and what is this compared with the endless ages? For what the dream of a single day is in the midst of a whole lifetime, that the enjoyment of things here is as contrasted with the state of things to come. Is there then any one who, for the sake of seeing a good dream, would elect to be perpetually punished? Who is so senseless as to have recourse to this kind of retribution? For I am not yet accusing luxury, nor revealing now the bitterness which lurks in it: for the present is not the proper time for these remarks, but when ye have been able to escape it. For now, entangled as you are by this passion, you will suspect me of talking nonsense, if I were to call pleasure bitter: but when by the grace of God you have been released from the malady then you will know its misery full well. Wherefore, reserving these topics for another season. what I will say now is just this: Be it so, that luxury is luxury, and pleasure, pleasure, and that they have nothing in them painful or disgraceful, what shall we say to the punishment which is in store for us? and what shall we do then if we have taken our pleasure now, as it were in a shadow and a figure, but undergo everlasting torment there in reality, when we might in a short space of time escape these tortures already mentioned, and enjoy the good things which are stored up for us? For this also is the work of the loving-kindness of God, that our struggles are not protracted to a great length, but that after struggling for a brief, and tiny twinkling of an eye (for such is present life compared with the other) we receive crowns of victory for endless ages. And it will be no small affliction to the souls of those who are being punished at that time, to reflect, that when they had it in their power in the few days of this life to make all good, they neglected their opportunity and surrendered themselves to everlasting evil. And lest we should suffer this let us rouse ourselves while it is the acepted time, while it is the day of salvation,[1] while the power of repentance is great. For not only the evils already mentioned, but others also far worse than these await us if we are indolent. These indeed, and some bitterer than these have their place in hell: but the loss of the good things involves so much pain, so much affliction and straitness, that even if no other kind of punishment were appointed for those who sin here, it would of itself be sufficient to vex us more bitterly than the torments in hell, and to confound our souls.

11. For consider I pray the condition of the other life, so far as it is possible to consider it; for no words will suffice for an adequate description: but from the things which are told us, as if by means of certain riddles, let us try and get some indistinct vision of it. "Pain and sorrow and sighing," we read "have fled away."[2] What then could be more blessed than this life? It is not possible there to fear poverty and disease: it is not possible to see any one injuring, or being injured, provoking, or being provoked, or angry, or envious, or burning with any outrageous lust, or anxious concerning the supply of the necessaries of life, or bemoaning himself over the loss of some dignity and power: for all the tempest of passion in us is quelled and brought to nought, and all will be in a condition of peace, and gladness and joy, all things serene and tranquil, all will be daylight and brightness, and light, not this present light, but one excelling this in splendour as much as this excels the brightness of a lamp. For things are not concealed in that world by night, or by a gathering of clouds: bodies there are not set on fire and burned: for there is neither night nor evening there, nor cold nor heat, nor any other variation of seasons: but the condition is of a different kind, such as they only will know who have been deemed worthy of it; there is no old age there, nor any of the evils of old age, but all things relating to decay are utterly removed, and incorruptible glory reigns in every part. But greater than all these things is the perpetual enjoyment of intercourse with Christ in the company of angels, and archangels, and the higher powers. Behold now the sky, and pass through it in thought to the region beyond the sky, and consider the transfiguration to take place in the whole creation; for it will not continue to be such as it is now, but will be far more brilliant and beautiful,

---

[1] 2 Cor. vi. 2. [2] Isa. xxxv. 10.

and just as gold glistens more brightly than lead, so will the future constitution of the universe be better than the present: even as the blessed Paul saith "Because the creation also itself shall be delivered from the bondage of corruption."[1] For now indeed, seeing that it partakes of corruption, it is subject to many things such as bodies of this kind naturally experience: but then, having divested itself of all these things, we shall see it display its beauty in an incorruptible form: for inasmuch as it is to receive incorruptible bodies, it will in future be itself also transfigured into the nobler condition. Nowhere in that world will there be sedition and strife: for great is the concord of the band of saints, all being ever in harmony with one another. It is not possible there to fear the devil, and the plots of demons, or the threatenings of hell, or death, either that death which now is, or the other death which is far worse than this, but every terror of this kind will have been done away. And just as some royal child, who has been brought up in mean guise, and subject to fear and threats, lest he should deteriorate by indulgence and become unworthy of his paternal inheritance, as soon as he has attained the royal dignity, immediately exchanges all his former raiment for the purple robe, and the diadem and the crowd of body-guards, and assumes his state with much confidence, having cast out of his soul thoughts of humility and subjection, and having taken others in their place; even so will it happen then to all the saints.

And to prove that these words are no empty vaunt let us journey in thought to the mountain where Christ was transfigured: let us behold him shining as He shone there; and yet even then He did not display to us all the splendour of the world to come. For that the vision was accommodated to human eyes, and not an exact manifestation of the reality is plain from the very words of the Evangelist. For what saith he? "He did shine as the Sun."[2] But the glory of incorruptible bodies does not emit the same kind of light as this body which is corruptible, nor is it of a kind to be tolerable to mortal eyes, but needs incorruptible and immortal eyes to contemplate it. But at that time on the mountain He disclosed to them as much as it was possible for them to see without injuring the sight of the beholders; and even so they could not endure it but fell upon their faces. Tell me, if any one led thee into some bright place, where all were sitting arrayed in vestures of gold, and in the midst of the multitude pointed out one other to thee who alone had garments wrought with precious stones, and a crown upon his head, and then promised to place thee in the ranks of this people, wouldst thou not do everything to obtain this promise? Open then even now in imagination thine eyes, and look on that assembly, composed not of men such as we are, but of those who are of more value than gold and precious stones, and the beams of the sun, and all visible radiance, and not consisting of men only but of beings of much more dignity than men,—angels, archangels, thrones, dominions, principalities, powers. For as concerning the king it is not even possible to say what he is like: so completely do his beauty, his grace, his splendour, his glory, his grandeur and magnificence elude speech and thought. Shall we then, I ask, deprive ourselves of such great blessings, in order to avoid suffering for a brief period? For if we had to endure countless deaths every day, or even hell itself, for the sake of seeing Christ coming in His glory, and being enrolled in the company of the saints, ought we not to undergo all those things? Hear what the blessed Peter says; "it is good for us to be here."[3] But if he, when he beheld some dim image of the things to come, immediately cast away all other things out of his soul, on account of the pleasure produced in it by that vision; what would any one say when the actual reality of the things is presented, when the palace is thrown open and it is permitted to gaze upon the King Himself, no longer darkly, or by means of a mirror,[4] but face to face; no longer by means of faith, but by sight?

12. The majority it is true of those who are not very sensibly minded propose to be content with escaping hell; but I say that a far more severe punishment than hell is exclusion from the glory of the other world, and I think that one who has failed to reach it ought not to sorrow so much over the miseries of hell, as over his rejection from heaven, for this alone is more dreadful than all other things in respect of punishment. But frequently now when we see a king, attended by a large body-guard, enter the palace, we count those happy who are near him, and have a share in his speech and mind, and partake of all the rest of his glory; and even if we have countless blessings, we have no perception of any of them, and deem ourselves miserable when we look at the glory of those who are round about him, although we know that such splendour is slippery and insecure, both on account of wars, and plots, and envy, and because apart from these things it is not in itself worthy of any

---

[1] Rom. viii. 21.   [2] Matt. xvii. 2.   [3] Matt. xvii. 4.   [4] 1 Cor. xiii. 12.

consideration. But where the king of all is concerned, he who holds not a portion of the earth but the whole circuit of it, or rather who comprehends it all in the hollow of his hand, and measures the Heavens with a span, who upholdeth all things by the word of His power,[1] by whom all the nations are counted as nought, and as a drop of spittle;—in the case of such a king I say shall we not reckon it the most extreme punishment to miss being enrolled in that company which is round about him, but be content if we merely escape hell? and what could be more pitiable than this condition of soul? For this king does not come to judge the earth, drawn by a pair of white mules, nor riding in a golden chariot, nor arrayed in a purple robe and diadem. How then does He come? Hear the prophets crying aloud and saying as much as it is possible to tell to men: for one saith " God shall come openly, even our God and shall not keep silence: a fire shall be kindled before Him, and a mighty tempest shall be round about Him: He shall call the Heaven from above and the earth that He may judge His people."[2] But Esaias depicts the actual punishment impending over us speaking thus: "Behold the day of the Lord cometh, inexorable, with wrath and anger; to lay the whole world desolate, and to destroy sinners out of it. For the stars of Heaven, and Orion, and the whole system of the heaven shall not give their light, and the sun shall be darkened in its going down,[3] and the moon shall not give her light; and I will ordain evils against the whole world, and visit their sins upon the ungodly, and I will destroy the insolence of the lawless, and humble the insolence of the proud, and they who are left shall be more precious than unsmelted gold, and a man shall be more precious than the sapphire stone. For the heaven shall be disturbed[4] and the earth shall be shaken from its foundations, by reason of the fury of the wrath of the Lord of Sabaoth, in the day when His wrath shall come upon us."[5] And again "windows" he saith "shall be opened from the Heaven, and the foundations of the earth shall be shaken: the earth shall be mightily confounded, the earth shall be bent low, it shall be perplexed with great perplexity, the earth shall stagger grievously like the drunkard and the reveller; the earth shall shake as a hut, it shall fall, and not be able to rise up again: for iniquity has waxed mighty therein. And God shall set His hand upon the host of the Heaven in the height in that day, and upon the kingdoms of the earth, and He shall gather together the congregation thereof into a prison, and shall shut them up in a stronghold."[6] And Malachi speaking concordantly with these said "Behold the Lord almighty cometh, and who shall abide the day of His coming or who shall stand when He appeareth? for He cometh like a refiner's fire, and like fuller's soap: and He shall sit refining and purifying as it were silver, and as it were gold."[7] And again, "Behold," he saith, "the day of the Lord cometh, burning like an oven, and it shall consume them, and all the aliens, and all who work iniquity shall be stubble, and the day which is coming shall set fire to them saith the Lord almighty; and there shall be left neither root nor branch."[8] And the man greatly beloved saith "I beheld until thrones were placed, and the Ancient of Days was seated, and his raiment was white as snow, and the hair of his head was pure as wool: His throne was a flame of fire, and the wheels thereof burning fire: a stream of fire wound its way in front of Him. Thousand thousands ministered unto Him, and ten thousand times ten thousand stood before Him. The judgment was set and the books were opened."[9] Then after a little space "I beheld," he says, "in a vision of the night and behold" with the clouds of Heaven, one came like the Son of Man, and reached unto the Ancient of Days, and was brought near before Him, and to Him was given rule, and honor, and the kingdom, and all the people, tribes and tongues serve Him. His dominion is an everlasting dominion, which shall not pass away, and His kingdom shall not be destroyed. As for me Daniel, my spirit shuddered within me, and the visions of my head troubled me."[10] Then all the gates of the heavenly vaults are opened, or rather the heaven itself is taken away out of the midst "for the heaven," we read "shall be rolled up like a scroll,"[11] wrapped up in the middle like the skin and covering of some tent so as to be transformed into some better shape. Then all things are full of amazement and horror and trembling: then even the angels themselves are holden by much fear, and not angels only but also archangels and thrones, and dominions, and principalities and authorities. " For the powers" we read " of the heavens shall be shaken," because their fellow-servants are required to give an account of their life in this world.[12] For if when a single city is being judged before rulers in this world, all men

---

[1] Heb. i. 3. The other expressions in this passage are most of them taken from Isaiah xl.
[2] Ps. iv. 4. [3] There is a variation from the LXX. here.
[4] The LXX. has θυμωθήσεται, " shall be made wroth."
[5] Isa. xiii. 9, 13.
[6] Isa. xxiv. 19–22, a very loose quotation from the LXX.
[7] Mal. iii. 2, 3. [8] Mal. iv. 1.
[9] Dan. vii. 9, 10. Slightly varied from the LXX.: for the designation of Daniel as " greatly beloved," see Dan. x. 11.
[10] Dan. vii. 13–15, a closer rendering of the Hebrew than the LXX.
[11] Isa. xxxiv. 4. [12] Matt. xxiv. 29.

shudder, even those who are outside the danger, when the whole world is arraigned before such a judge as this who needs no witnesses, or proofs, but independently of all these things brings forward deeds and words and thoughts, and exhibits them all as in some picture both to those who have committed the sins and to those who are ignorant of them, how is it not natural that every power should be confounded and shake? For if there were no river of fire winding by, nor any terrible angels standing by the side of the throne, but men were merely summoned some to be praised and admired, others to be dismissed with ignominy that they might not see the glory of God, ("For let the ungodly" we read "be taken away that he may not see the glory of the Lord"[1]) and if this were the only punishment would not the loss of such blessings sting the souls of those who were deprived of them more bitterly than all hell itself? For how great an evil this is cannot possibly be represented now in words; but then we shall know it clearly in the actual reality. But now I pray add the punishment also to the scene, and imagine men not only covered with shame, and veiling their heads, and bending them low, but also being dragged along the road to the fire, and haled away to the instruments of torture and delivered over to the cruel powers, and suffering these things just at the time when all they who have practised what is good, and wrought deeds worthy of eternal life, are being crowned, and proclaimed conquerors, and presented before the royal throne.

13. Now these are things which will happen in that day: but the things which will follow, after these, what language can describe to us —the pleasure, the profit, the joy of being in the company of Christ? For when the soul has returned to the proper condition of nobility, and is able henceforth with much boldness to behold its Master it is impossible to say what great pleasure it derives therefrom, what great gain, rejoicing not only in the good things actually in hand, but in the persuasion that these things will never come to an end. All that gladness then cannot be described in words, nor grasped by the understanding: but in a dim kind of way, as one indicates great things by means of small ones, I will endeavour to make it manifest. For let us scrutinize those who enjoy the good things of the world in this present life, I mean wealth and power, and glory, how, exulting with delight, they reckon themselves as no longer being upon the earth, and this although the things which they are enjoying are acknowledged not to be really good, and do not abide with them, but take to flight more quickly than a dream: and even if they should even last for a little time, their favour is displayed within the limits of this present life, and cannot accompany us further. Now if these things uplift those who possess them to such a pitch of joy, what do you suppose is the condition of those souls which are invited to enjoy the countless blessings in Heaven which are always securely fixed and stable? And not only this, but also in their quantity and quality they excel present things to such an extent as never entered even the heart of man.[2] For at the present time like an infant in the womb, even so do we dwell in this world confined in a narrow space, and unable to behold the splendour and the freedom of the world to come: but when the time of travail arrives and the present life is delivered at the day of judgment of all men whom it has contained, those who have been miscarried go from darkness into darkness, and from affliction into more grievous affliction: but those which are perfectly formed and have preserved the marks of the royal image will be presented to the king, and will take upon themselves that service which angels and archangels minister to the God of all. I pray thee then, O friend, do not finally efface these marks, but speedily restore them, and stamp them more perfectly on thy soul. For corporeal beauty indeed God has confined within the limits of nature, but grace of soul is released from the constraint and bondage arising from that cause inasmuch as it is far superior to any bodily symmetry: and it depends entirely upon ourselves and the grace of God. For our Master, being merciful, has in this special way honoured our race, that He has entrusted to the necessity of nature the inferior things which contribute nothing much to our advantage, and in their issue are matters of indifference, but of the things which are really noble He has caused us to be ourselves the artificers. For if He had placed corporeal beauty also under our control we should have been subjected to excessive anxiety, and should have wasted all our time upon things which are of no profit, and should have grievously neglected our soul.

For if, even as it is, when we have not this power in ourselves, we make violent efforts, and give ourselves up to shadow painting, and because we cannot in reality produce bodily beauty, cunningly devise imitations by means of paints, and dyes, and dressing of hair, and arrangement of garments, and pencilling of eyebrows, and many other contrivances: what leisure should we have set apart for the soul

---

[1] I have not succeeded in finding the source of this quotation. Comp. Ps. i. 5.

[2] Isa. lxiv. 4, quoted 1 Cor. ii. 9.

and serious matters, if we had it in our power to transfigure the body into a really symmetrical shape? For probably, if this were our business, we should not have any other, but should spend all our time upon it: decking the bondmaid with countless decorations, but letting her who is the mistress of this bondmaid lie perpetually in a state of deformity and neglect. For this reason God, having delivered us from this vain occupation, implanted in us the power of working upon the nobler element, and he who cannot turn an ugly body into a comely one, can raise the soul, even when it has been reduced to the extremity of ugliness, to the very acme of grace, and make it so amiable and desirable that not only are good men brought to long after it but even He who is the sovereign and God of all, even as the Psalmist also when discoursing concerning this beauty, said "And the king shall have desire of thy beauty."[1] Seest thou not also that in the houses of prostitutes the women who are ugly and shameless would hardly be accepted by prize-fighters, and runaway slaves, and gladiators: but should any comely, well-born and modest woman, owing to some mischance, have been reduced to this necessity, no man, even amongst those who are very illustrious and great, would be ashamed of marriage with her? Now if there is so much pity amongst men, and so much disdain of glory as to release from that bondage the women who have often been disgraced in the brothel, and to place them in the position of wives, much more is this the case with God, and those souls which, owing to the usurpation of the devil, have fallen from their original noble condition into the harlotry of this present life. And you will find the prophets filled with examples of this kind, when they address Jerusalem; for she fell into fornication, and a novel form of it, even as Ezekiel says: "To all harlots wages are given, but thou hast given wages to thy lovers, and there hath been perversion in thee beyond all other women,"[2] and again another saith "Thou didst sit waiting for them like a deserted bird."[3] This one then who hath committed fornication in this fashion God calls back again. For the captivity which took place was not so much by way of vengeance as for the purpose of conversion and amendment; since if God had wished to punish them outright, He would not again have brought them back to their home. He would not have established their city and their temple in greater splendour than before: "For the final glory of this house" He said "shall exceed the former."[4] Now if God did not exclude from repentance her who who had many times committed fornication, much more will He embrace thy soul, which has now fallen for the first time. For certainly there is no lover of corporeal beauty, even if he be very frantic, who is so inflamed with the love of his mistress as God longs after the salvation of our souls; and this we may perceive both from the things which happen every day and from the divine Scriptures. See at least, both in the introduction of Jeremiah, and many other places of the prophets, when He is despised and contemned, how He again hastens forward and pursues the friendship of those who turn away from him; which also He Himself made clear in the Gospels saying, "O Jerusalem! Jerusalem! thou that killest the prophets and stonest them that are sent unto thee, how often would I have gathered thy children together even as a hen gathereth her chickens under her wings, and ye would not?"[5] And Paul writing to the Corinthians said "that God was in Christ reconciling the world unto Himself, not reckoning their trespasses unto them, and having committed unto us the word of reconciliation. We are ambassadors therefore on behalf of Christ, as though God were entreating by us; we beseech you on behalf of Christ be ye reconciled to God."[6] Consider that this has now been said to us. For it is not merely want of faith, but also an unclean life which is sufficient to work this abominable enmity. "For the carnal mind" we read "is enmity against God."[7] Let us then break down the barrier, and hew it in pieces, and destroy it, that we may enjoy the blessed reconciliation, that we may become again the fondly beloved of God.

14. I know that thou art now admiring the grace of Hermione, and thou judgest that there is nothing in the world to be compared to her comeliness; but if you choose, O friend, you shall yourself exceed her in comeliness and gracefulness, as much as golden statues surpass those which are made of clay. For if beauty, when it occurs in the body, so fascinates and excites the minds of most men, when the soul is refulgent with it what can match beauty and grace of this kind? For the groundwork of this corporeal beauty is nothing else but phlegm, and blood, and humor, and bile, and the fluid of masticated food. For by these things both eyes and cheeks, and all the other features, are supplied with moisture; and if they do not receive that moisture, daily ascending from the stomach and the liver, the skin becoming unduly withered, and the eyes

---

[1] Ps. xlv. 12.
[2] Ezek. xvi. 33, an inexact quotation from LXX.
[3] Jer. iii. 2.
[4] Hagg. ii. 10.
[5] Matt. xxiii. 37.
[6] 2 Cor. v, 19, 20.
[7] Rom. viii. 7.

sunken, the whole grace of the countenance forthwith vanishes; so that if you consider what is stored up inside those beautiful eyes, and that straight nose, and the mouth and the cheeks, you will affirm the well-shaped body to be nothing else than a whited sepulchre; the parts within are full of so much uncleanness. Morever when you see a rag with any of these things on it, such as phlegm, or spittle you cannot bear to touch it with even the tips of your fingers, nay you cannot even endure looking at it; and yet are you in a flutter of excitement about the storehouses and depositories of these things? But thy beauty was not of this kind, but excelled it as heaven is superior to earth; or rather it was much better and more brilliant than this. For no one has anywhere seen a soul by itself stripped of the body; but yet even so I will endeavour to present to you the beauty of this soul from another source. I mean from the case of the greater powers. Hear at least how the beauty of these struck the man greatly beloved; for wishing to set forth their beauty and being unable to find a body of the same character, he had recourse to metallic substances, and he was not satisfied even with these, but took the brilliancy of lightning for his illustration.[1] Now if those powers, even when they did not disclose their essential nature pure and bare, but only in a very dim and shadowy way, nevertheless shone so brightly, what must naturally be their appearance, when set free from every veil? Now we ought to form some such image of the beauty of the soul. "For they shall be," we read "equal unto the angels."[2] Now in the case of bodies the lighter and finer kinds, and those which have retreated to the path which tend towards the incorporeal, are very much better and more wonderful than the others. The sky at least is more beautiful than the earth, and fire than water, and the stars than precious stones; and we admire the rainbow far more than violets and roses, and all other flowers which are upon the earth. And in short if it were possible with the bodily eyes to behold the beauty of the soul you would laugh to scorn these corporeal illustrations, so feebly have they presented to us the gracefulness of the soul. Let us not then neglect such a possession, nor such great happiness, and especially when the approach to that kind of beauty becomes easy to us by our hopes of the things to come. "For our light affliction," we read, "which is but for the moment, worketh for us more and more exceedingly an eternal weight of glory, while we look not at the things which are seen but at the things which are not seen; for the things which are seen are temporal, but the things which are not seen are eternal."[3] Now if the blessed Paul called such afflictions as thou wottest of light and easy, because he did not look at the things which are seen, much more tolerable is it merely to cease from wantonness. For we are not calling thee to those dangers which he underwent, nor to those deaths which he incurred daily,[4] the constant beatings and scourgings, the bonds, the enmity of the whole world, the hatred of his own people, the frequent vigils, the long journies, the shipwrecks, the attacks of robbers, the plots of his own kinsfolk, the distresses on account of his friends, the hunger, the cold, the nakedness, the burning, the despondency on account both of those who belonged to him, and those who did not belong to him. None of these things do we now demand of thee; all that we ask for is that you would release yourself from your accursed bondage, and return to your former freedom, having considered both the punishment arising from your wantonness, and the honor belonging to your former manner of life. For that unbelievers should be but languidly affected by the thought of the resurrection and never be in fear of this kind, is nothing wonderful; but that we who are more firmly persuaded concerning the things of the other world than those of the present, should spend our life in this miserable and deplorable way and be nowise affected by the memory of those things, but sink into a state of extreme insensibility—this is irrational in the highest degree. For when we who believe do the deeds of unbelievers, or rather are in a more miserable plight than they (for there are some among them who have been eminent for the virtue of their life), what consolation, what excuse will be left for us? And many merchants indeed who have incurred shipwreck have not given way, but have pursued the same journey, and this when the loss which has befallen them was not owing to their own carelessness, but to the force of the winds; and shall we who have reason to be confident concerning the end, and know certainly that if we do not wish it, neither shipwreck nor accident of any kind will bring us damage, not lay hold of the work again, and carry on our business as we did aforetime, but lie in idleness and keep our hands to ourselves? And would that we kept them merely *to* ourselves and did not use them *against* ourselves which is a token of stark madness. For if any pugilist, leaving his antagonist were to turn his hands against his own head, and deal blows to his own face, should

---

[1] Dan. x. 6.   [2] Luke xx. 36.   [3] 2 Cor. iv. 17.   [4] 1 Cor. xv. 31; also 2 Cor. xi 23-28.

we not, I ask, rank him among madmen? For the devil has upset us and cast us down; therefore we ought to get up, and not to be dragged down again and precipitate ourselves, and add blows dealt by ourselves to the blows dealt by him. For the blessed David also had a fall like that which has now happened to you; and not this only but another also which followed it. I mean that of murder. What then? did he remain prostrate? Did he not immediately rise up again with energy and place himself in position to fight the enemy? In fact he wrestled with him so bravely, that even after his death he was the protector of his offspring. For when Solomon had perpetrated great iniquity, and had deserved countless deaths, God said that He would leave him the kingdom intact, thus speaking "I will surely rend the kingdom out of thine hand and will give it to thy servant. Nevertheless I will not do this in thy days." Wherefore? "For David thy father's sake, I will take it out of the hand of thy son."[1] And again when Hezekiah was about to run the greatest possible risk, although he was a righteous man, God said that He would succour him for the sake of this saint. "For I will cast my shield," He saith, "over this city to save it for my own sake, and for my servant David's sake."[2] So great is the force of repentance. But if he had determined with himself, as you do now, that henceforth it was impossible to propitiate God, and if he had said within himself: "God has honoured me with great honour, and has given me a place among the prophets, and has entrusted me with the government of my countrymen, and rescued me out of countless perils, how then, when I have offended against Him after such great benefits, and have perpetrated the worst crimes, shall I be able to recover his favour?" If he had thought thus, not only would he not have done the things which he afterwards did, but he would have aggravated his former evils.

15. For not only the bodily wounds work death, if they are neglected, but also those of the soul; and yet we have arrived at such a pitch of folly as to take the greatest care of the former, and to overlook the latter; and although in the case of the body it naturally often happens that many wounds are incurable, yet we do not abandon hope, but even when we hear the physicians constantly declaring, that it is not possible to get rid of this suffering by medicines, we still persist in exhorting them to devise at least some slight alleviation; but in the case of souls, where there is no incurable malady; for it is not subject to the necessity of nature; here, as if the infirmities were strange we are negligent and despairing; and where the nature of the disorder might naturally plunge us into despair, we take as much pains as if there were great hope of restoration to health; but where there is no occasion to renounce hope, we desist from efforts, and become as heedless as if matters were desperate; so much more account do we take of the body than of the soul. And this is the reason why we are not able to save even the body. For he who neglects the leading element, and manifests all his zeal about inferior matters destroys and loses both; whereas he who observes the right order, and preserves and cherishes the more commanding element, even if he neglects the secondary element yet preserves it by means of saving the primary one. Which also Christ signified to us when He said, "Fear not them which kill the body, but are not able to kill the soul; but rather fear Him who is able to destroy both soul and body in Hell."[3]

Well, do I convince you, that one ought never to despair of the disorders of the soul as incurable? or must I again set other arguments in motion? For even if thou shouldst despair of thyself ten thousand times, I will never despair of thee, and I will never myself be guilty of that for which I reproach others; and yet it is not the same thing for a man to renounce hope of himself, as for another to renounce hope of him. For he who has this suspicion concerning another may readily obtain pardon; but he who has it of himself will not. Why so pray? Because the one has no controlling power over the zeal and repentance of the other, but over his own zeal and repentance a man has sole authority. Nevertheless even so I will not despair of you; though you should any number of times be affected in this way; for it may be, that there will be some return to virtue, and to restoration to thy former manner of life. And now hear what follows: The Ninevites when they heard the prophet vehemently declaring, and plainly threatening; "yet three days and Nineveh shall be overthrown,"[4] even then did not lose heart, but, although they had no confidence that they should be able to move the mind of God, or rather had reason to suspect the contrary from the divine message (for the utterance was not accompanied by any qualification, but was a simple declaration), even then they manifested repentance saying: "Who knoweth whether God will repent and be entreated, and turn from the fierceness of His wrath, and that we perish not? And God

---

[1] 1 Kings xi. 11.   [2] 2 Kings xix. 34.   [3] Matt. x. 28.   [4] Jonah iii. 4, LXX.

saw their works that they turned from their evil ways, and God repented of the evil which He said He would do unto them and He did it not."[1] Now if barbarian, and unreasoning men could perceive so much, much more ought we to do this who have been trained in the divine doctrines and have seen such a crowd of examples of this kind both in history and actual experience. "For my counsels" we read "are not as your counsels nor my ways as your ways; but far as is the Heaven from the earth, so far are my thoughts from your mind, and my counsels from your counsels."[2] Now if we admit to our favour household slaves when they have often offended against us, on their promising to become better, and place them again in their former position, and sometimes even grant them greater freedom of speech than before; much more does God act thus. For if God had made us in order to punish us, you might well have despaired, and questioned the possibility of your own salvation; but if He created us for no other reason than His own good will, and with a view to our enjoying everlasting blessings, and if He does and contrives everything for this end, from the first day until the present time, what is there which can ever cause you to doubt? Have we provoked Him severely, so as no other man ever did? this is just the reason why we ought specially to abstain from our present deeds and to repent for the past, and exhibit a great change. For the evils we have once perpetrated cannot provoke Him so much as our being unwilling to make any change in the future. For to sin may be a merely human failing, but to continue in the same sin ceases to be human, and becomes altogether devilish. For observe how God by the mouth of His prophet blames this more than the other. "For," we read, "I said unto her after she had done all these deeds of fornication, return unto me, and yet she returned not."[3] And again: from another quarter, when wishing to show the great longing which He has for our salvation, having heard how the people promised, after many transgressions, to tread the right way He said: "Who will grant unto them to have such an heart as to fear me, and to keep my commandments all their days, that it may be well with them and with their children forever?"[4] And Moses when reasoning with them said, "And now, O Israel, what doth the Lord thy God require of thee, but to fear the Lord thy God, and to walk in all His ways, and to love Him?"[5] He then who is so anxious to be loved by us, and does everything for this end, and did not spare even His only begotten Son on account of His love towards us, and who counts it a desirable thing if at any time we become reconciled to Himself, how shall He not welcome and love us when we repent? Hear at least what He says by the mouth of the prophet: "Declare thou first thy iniquities that thou mayest be justified."[6] Now this He demands from us in order to intensify our love towards Him. For when one who loves, after enduring many insults at the hands of those who are beloved, even then does not extinguish his fondness for them, the only reason why he takes pains to make those insults public, is that by displaying the strength of his affection he may induce them to feel a larger and warmer love. Now if the confession of sins brings so much consolation, much more does the endeavour to wash them away by means of our deeds. For if this was not the case, but those who had once swerved from the straight path were forbidden to return to it again, perhaps no one, except a few persons whose numbers would be easily reckoned, would ever enter the kingdom of Heaven; but as it is we shall find the most distinguished among those who have fallen. For those who have exhibited much vehemence in evil things, will also in turn exhibit the same in good things, being conscious what great debts they have incurred; which Christ also declared when He spoke to Simon concerning the woman: "For seest thou," saith He, "this woman? I entered into thine house, thou gavest me no water for my feet; but she hath washed my feet with her tears, and wiped them with the hairs of her head. Thou gavest me no kiss, but she since the time I came in hath not ceased to kiss my feet. Mine head with oil thou didst not anoint; but she hath anointed my feet with ointment. Wherefore I say unto thee: her sins which are many are forgiven; for she loved much; but to whom little is forgiven, the same loveth little. And He said unto her, thy sins are forgiven."[7]

16. For this reason also the devil, knowing that they who have committed great evils, when they have begun to repent, do this with much zeal, inasmuch as they are conscious of their offences, fears and trembles lest they should make a beginning of the work; for after they have made it they are no longer capable of being checked, and, kindling like fire under the influence of repentance, they render their souls purer than pure gold, being impelled by their conscience, and the memory of their former sins, as by some strong gale, towards the haven of virtue. And this is the point in

---

[1] Jonah iii. 9, 10. [2] Isa. lv. 8, 9, varied a little from the LXX. [3] Jer. iii. 7. [4] Deut. v. 29. [5] Deut. x. 12. [6] Isa. xliii. 26. [7] Luke vii. 44-48.

which they have an advantage over those who have never fallen, that they exercise more vehement energy; if only, as I said, they can lay hold of the beginning. For the task which is hard and difficult of accomplishment is to be able to set foot on the entrance, and to reach the vestibule of repentance, and to repulse and overthrow the enemy there when he is fiercely raging and assaulting us. But after this, he will not display so much fury when he has once been worsted, and has fallen where he was strong. and we shall receive greater energy, and shall run this good race with much ease. Let us then in future set about our return, let us hasten up to the city which is in Heaven, in which we have been enrolled, in which also we have been appointed to find our home as citizens. For to despair of ourselves not only has this evil that it shuts the gates of that city against us, and that it drives us into greater indolence and contempt, but also that it plunges us into Satanic recklessness. For the only cause why the devil became such as he is was that he first of all despaired, and afterwards from despair sank into recklessness. For the soul, when once it has abandoned its own salvation, will no longer perceive that it is plunging downwards, choosing to do and say everything which is adverse to its own salvation. And just as madmen, when once they have fallen out of a sound condition, are neither afraid nor ashamed of anything, but fearlessly dare all manner of things, even if they have to fall into fire, or deep water, or down a precipice; so they who have been seized by the frenzy of despair are henceforward unmanageable, rushing into vice in every direction, and if death does not come to put a stop to this madness, and vehemence, they do themselves infinite mischief. Therefore I entreat you, before you are deeply steeped in this drunkenness, recover your senses and rouse yourself up, and shake off this Satanic fit, doing it gently and gradually if it be not possible to effect it all at once. For to me indeed the easier course seems to be to wrench yourself once for all out of all the cords which hold you down, and transfer yourself to the school of epentance. But if this seems to you a difficult thing, that you should be willing to enter on the path which leads to better things, simply enter upon it, and lay hold on eternal life. Yea, I beseech and implore you by your former reputation, by that confidence which once was yours, let us see you once again standing on the pinnacle of virtue, and in the same condition of perseverance as before. Spare those who are made to stumble on thy account, those who are falling, who are becoming more indolent, who are despairing of the way of virtue. For dejection now holds possession of the band of brethren, while pleasure and cheerfulness prevail in the councils of the unbelieving, and of those young men who are disposed to indolence. But if thou return again to thy former strictness of life the result will be reversed, and all our shame will be transferred to them, while we shall enjoy much confidence, seeing thee again crowned and proclaimed victor with more splendour than before. For such victories bring greater renown and pleasure. For you will not only receive the reward of your own achievements, but also of the exhortation and consolation of others, being exhibited as a striking model, if ever any one should fall into the same condition, to encourage him to get up and recover himself. Do not neglect such an opportunity of gain, nor drag our souls down into Hades with sorrow, but let us breathe freely again, and shake off the cloud of despondency which oppresses us on thy account. For now, passing by the consideration of our own troubles, we mourn over thy calamities, but if thou art willing to come to thy senses, and see clearly, and to join the angelic host, you will release us from this sorrow, and will take away the greater part of sins. For that it is possible for those who have come back again after repentance to shine with much lustre, and oftentimes more than those who have never fallen at all, I have demonstrated from the divine writings. Thus at least both the publicans and the harlots inherit the kingdom of Heaven, thus many of the last are placed before the first.

17. But I will tell thee also of events which have happened in our own time, and of which thou mayest thyself have been witness. You know probably that young Phœnician, the son of Urbanus, who was untimely left an orphan, but possessed of much money, and many slaves and lands. This man, having in the first place bidden complete farewell to his studies in the schools, and having laid aside the gay clothing which he formerly wore, and all his worldly grandeur, suddenly arraying himself in a shabby cloak, and retreating to the solitude of the mountains, exhibited a high degree of Christian philosophy not merely in proportion to his age, but such as any great and wonderful man might have displayed. And after this, having been deemed worthy of initiation into the sacred mysteries, he made still greater advances in virtue. And all were rejoicing, and glorifying God, that one nurtured in wealth, and having illustrious ancestors, and being still a mere youth, should have suddenly trodden all the pomps of this life under foot, and have ascended to the true height. Now while he

was in this condition, and an object of admiration, certain corrupt men, who according to the law of kindred had the oversight of him dragged him back again into the former sea of worldliness. And so, having flung aside all his habits, he again descended from the mountains into the midst of the forum, and used to go all round the city, riding on horseback, and accompanied by a large retinue; and he was no longer willing to live even soberly; for being inflamed by much luxury, he was constrained to fall into foolish love intrigues, and there was no one of those conversant with him, who did not despair of his salvation; he was encompassed by such a swarm of flatterers, besides the snares of orphanhood, youth, and great wealth. And persons who readily find fault with everything, accused those who originally conducted him to this way of life,[1] saying that he had both missed his spiritual aims, and would no longer be of any use in the management of his own affairs, having prematurely abandoned the labours of study, and having been consequently unable to derive any benefit therefrom. Now while these things were being said, and great shame was felt, certain holy men who had often succeeded in this kind of chase, and had thoroughly learned by experience that those who are armed with hope in God ought not to despair at all of such characters, kept a continual watch upon him, and if ever they saw him appear in the marketplace they approached and saluted him. And at first he spoke to them from horseback, askance, as they followed by his side; so great was the shamelessness which had at first got possession of him. But they, being merciful and loving men, were not ashamed at all of this treatment, but continually looked to one thing only, how they might rescue the lamb from the wolves; which in fact they actually accomplished by means of their perseverance. For afterwards, as if he had been converted by some sudden stroke, and were put to shame by their great assiduity, if ever he saw them in the distance approaching, he would instantly dismount, and bending low would listen silently in that attitude to all which fell from their lips, and in time he displayed even greater reverence and respect towards them. And then, by the grace of God having gradually rescued him out of all those entanglements, they handed him over again to his former state of seclusion and devout contemplation. And now he became so illustrious, that his former life seemed to be nothing in comparison with that which he lived after his fall. For being well aware by experience of the snare, and having expended all his wealth upon the needy, and released himself from all care of that kind, he cut off every pretext for an attack from those who wished to make designs upon him; and now treading the path which leads to heaven, he has already arrived at the very goal of virtue.

This man indeed fell and rose again while he was still young; but another man, after enduring great toils during his sojourn in the deserts, with only a single companion, and leading an angelic life, and being now on the way to old age, afforded I know not how a little loophole to the evil one, through some Satanic condition of mind, and carelessness; and although he had never seen a woman since he transferred himself to the monastic life, he fell into a passionate desire for intercourse with women. And first of all he besought his companion to supply him with meat and wine, and threatened, if he did not receive it, that he would go down into the marketplace. And this he said, not so much out of a longing for meat, as because he wished to get some handle and pretext for returning into the city. The other being perplexed at these things, and fearing, that if he hindered this he might drive him into some great evil, suffered him to have his fill of this craving. But when his companion perceived that this was a stale device, he openly threw off shame, and unmasked his pretence, and said that he must positively himself go down to the city, and as the other had not power to prevent him, he desisted at last from his efforts, and following him at a distance, watched to see what the meaning of this return could possibly be. And having seen him enter a brothel, and knowing that he had intercourse with a harlot there, he waited until he had satiated that foul desire, and then, when he came out, he received him with uplifted hands, and having embraced and fervently kissed him, without uttering any rebuke on account of what had happened he only besought him, seeing that he had satiated his desire, to return again to his dwelling in the wilderness. And the other, put to shame by his great clemency, was immediately smitten at the heart, and being full of compunction for the deed which he had perpetrated, followed him to the mountain; and there he begged the man to shut him up in another hut, and, having closed the doors of the dwelling, to supply him with bread and water on certain days, and to inform those who enquired for him that he was laid to rest. And when he had said this, and persuaded him, he shut himself up, and was there continually, with fastings and prayers and tears, wiping off from his soul the defilement of his sin. And not long after when a drought had

---

[1] *i. e.*, the life of monastic seclusion.

settled on the neighbouring region, and all in that country were lamenting over it, a certain man was commanded by a vision to depart, and exhort this recluse to pray, and put an end to the drought. And when he had departed, taking companions with him, they found the man, who formerly dwelt with him, there alone; and on enquiring concerning the other they were informed that he was dead. But they, believing that they were deceived, betook themselves again to prayer, and again by means of the same vision heard the same things which they had heard before. And then, standing round the man who really had deceived them, they besought him to show the other to them; for they declared that he was not dead but living. When he heard this, and perceived that their compact was exposed, he brought them to that holy man; and they having broken through the wall (for he had even blocked up the entrance) and having all of them entered, prostrating themselves at his feet, and informing him of what had happened, besought him to succour them against the famine. But he at first resisted, saying that he was far from such confidence as that; for he ever had his sin before his eyes, as if it had only just taken place; but when they related all which had happened to them they then induced him to pray; and having prayed he put an end to the drought. And what happened to that young man who was at first a disciple of John the son of Zebedee, but afterwards for a long time became a robber chief, and then again, having been captured by the holy hands of the blessed Apostle returned from the robber dens and lairs to his former virtue, thou art not ignorant, but knowest it all as accurately as I do; and I have often heard thee admiring the great condescension of the saint, and how he first of all kissed the blood-stained hand of the young man, embracing him, and so brought him back to his former condition.[1]

18. Moreover also the blessed Paul not only welcomes Onesimus the unprofitable runaway thief, because he was converted, but also asks his master to treat him who had repented, on equal terms of honour with his teacher, thus saying: "I beseech thee for my son Onesimus, whom I have begotten in my bonds, who was aforetime unprofitable to thee, but now is profitable to thee and to me, whom I have sent back to thee; thou therefore receive him, that is my very heart, whom I would fain have kept with me, that in thy behalf he might minister unto me in the bonds of the Gospel; but without thy mind I would do nothing that thy goodness should not be as of necessity, but of free will. For perhaps he was therefore parted from thee for a season that thou shouldest have him back for ever; no longer as a servant, but above a servant, a brother beloved, specially unto me; but how much rather to thee both in the flesh and in the Lord? If then thou holdest me as a partner, receive him as myself."[2] And the same apostle, in writing to the Corinthians, said, "Lest when I come I should mourn over many of those who have sinned beforehand and have not repented;"[3] and again, "as I have said beforehand, so do I again declare beforehand, that if I come again I will not spare."[3] Seeest thou who they are whom he mourns, and whom he does not spare? Not those who have sinned, but those who have not repented, and not simply those who have not repented, but those who have been called once and again to this work, and would not be persuaded. For the expression "I have said beforehand and do now say beforehand, as if I were present the second time, and being absent I write," implies exactly that which we are afraid may take place now in our case. For although Paul is not present who then threatened the Corinthians, yet Christ is present, who was then speaking through his mouth; and if we continue obdurate, He will not spare us, but will smite us with a mighty blow, both in this world and the next. "Let us then anticipate His countenance by our confession,"[4] let us pour out our hearts before Him. For "thou hast sinned," we read, "do not add thereto any more, and pray on behalf of thy former deeds;"[5] and again "a righteous man is his own accuser in the first instance."[6] Let us not then tarry for the accuser, but let us seize his place beforehand, and so let us make our judge more merciful by means of our candour. Now I know indeed that you confess your sins, and call yourself miserable above measure; but this is not the only thing I wish, but I long for you to be persuaded that it can justify you. For as long as you make this confession unprofitable, even if you accuse yourself, you will not be able to desist from the sins which follow it. For no one will be able to do anything with zeal and the proper method, unless he has first of all persuaded himself that he does it to advantage. For even the sower, after he has scattered his seed, unless he expects the harvest, will never reap. For who would choose to fatigue himself in vain, if he was not to gain any good from his labor? So

---

[1] The story is told by Clement of Alexandria in his treatise entitled "Who is the rich man that is saved?" and has been inserted by Eusebius in his History, iii. 23.
[2] Philem. 10-18.
[3] 2 Cor. xii. 21; xiii. 2.
[4] Ps. xcv. 42, LXX.
[5] Ecclus. xxi. 1.
[6] Prov. xviii. 17; but a different meaning is given to the passage in our English Version [Revised].

then he also who sows words, and tears, and confession, unless he does this with a good hope, will not be able to desist from sinning, being still held down by the evil of despair; but just as that husbandman who despairs of any crop of fruit will not in future hinder any of those things which damage the seeds, so also he who sows his confession with tears, but does not expect any advantage for this, will not be able to overthrow those things which spoil repentance. And what does spoil repentance is being again entangled in the same evils. "For there is one" we read, "who builds, and one who pulls down, what have they gained more than toil? He who is dipped in water because of contact with a dead body, and then touches it again, what has he gained by his washing?"[1] Even so if a man fasts because of his sins, and goes his way again, and doeth the same things, who will hearken to his prayer? And again we read "if a man goes back from righteousness to sin the Lord will prepare him for the sword,"[2] and, "as a dog when he has returned to his vomit, and become odious, so is a fool who by his wickedness has returned to his sin."[3]

19. Do not then merely set forth thy sins being thy own accuser, but as one who ought to be justified by the method of repentance; for thus thou wilt be able to put thy soul, which makes its confession, to shame, so that it falls no more into the same sins. For to accuse ourselves vehemently and call ourselves sinners is common, so to say, to unbelievers also. Many at least of those who belong to the stage, both men and women, who habitually practise the greatest shamelessness, call themselves miserable, but not with the proper aim. Wherefore I would not even call this confession; for the publication of their sins is not accompanied with compunction of soul, nor with bitter tears, nor with conversion of life, but in fact some of them make it in quest of a reputation for the hearers for candor of speech. For offences do not seem so grievous when some other person announces them as when the perpetrator himself reports them. And they who under the influence of strong despair have lapsed into a state of insensibility, and treat the opinion of their fellowmen with contempt proclaim their own evil deeds with much effrontery, as if they were the doings of others. But I do not wish thee to be any of these, nor to be brought out of despair to confession, but with a good expectation, after cutting away the whole root of despair, to manifest zeal in the contrary direction. And what is the root and mother of this despair? it is indolence; or rather one would not call it the root only, but also the nurse and mother. For as in the case of wool decay breeds moths, and is in turn increased by them; so here also indolence breeds despair, and is itself nourished in turn by despair; and thus supplying each other with this accursed exchange, they acquire no small additional power. If any one then cuts one of these off, and hews it in pieces, he will easily be able to get the better of the remaining one. For on the one hand he who is not indolent will never fall into despair, and on the other he who is supported by good hopes, and does not despair of himself, will not be able to fall into indolence. Pray then, wrench this pair asunder, and break the yoke in pieces, by which I mean a variable and yet depressing habit of thought; for that which holds these two things together is not uniform, but manifold in shame and character. And what is this? It happens that one who has repented has done many great and good deeds, but meanwhile he has committed some sin equivalent to those good deeds, and this especially is sufficient to plunge him into despair, as if the buildings which had been set up were all pulled down, and all the labor which he had bestowed upon them had been vain and come to naught. But this must be taken into account, and such reasoning must be repelled, because, if we do not store up in good time a measure of good deeds equivalent to the sins which are committed after them, nothing can hinder us from sinking grievously and completely. But as it is, (right action[4]) like some stout breastplate does not suffer the sharp and bitter dart to accomplish its work, but even if it is itself cut through, it averts much danger from the body. For he who departs to the other world with many deeds both good and bad, will have some alleviation in respect of the punishment and the torment there; but if a man is destitute of these good works, and takes only the evil with him, it is impossible to say what great sufferings he will undergo, when he is conducted to everlasting punishment. For a balance will be struck there between the evil deeds and those which are not such; and should the latter weigh down the scale they will to no small extent have saved the doer of them, and the injury arising from the doing of evil deeds is not so strong as to drag the man down from the foremost place; but if the evil deeds exceed, they carry him off into hell fire, because the number of his good actions is not so great as to be able to make a stand against this violent impulse. And these things are not merely sug-

---

[1] Ecclus. xxxiv. 23, 25.   [2] Ecclus. xxvi. 28.   [3] Prov. xxvi. 11.   [4] These words seem to be understood, although they are not expressed in the original.

gested by our own reasoning, but declared also by the divine oracles; for He Himself saith, "He shall reward every man according to his works."[1] And not only in hell, but also in the kingdom one will find many differences; for He saith, "in my Father's house are many mansions;"[2] and, "there is one glory of the sun, and another glory of the moon."[3] And what wonder, if in dealing with such great matters he has spoken with such precision, seeing that He declares there is a difference in that world even between one star and another? Knowing then all these things let us never desist from doing good deeds, nor grow weary, nor, if we should be unable to reach the rank of the sun or of the moon, let us despise that of the stars. For if only we display thus much virtue at least, we shall be able to have a place in Heaven. And though we may not have become gold, or precious stone, yet if we only occupy the rank of silver we shall abide in the foundation; only let us not fall back again into that material which the fire readily devours, nor, when we are unable to accomplish great things, desist also from small ones, for this is the part of extreme folly, which I trust we may not experience. For just as material wealth increases if the lovers of it do not despise even the smallest gains, so is it also with the spiritual. For it is a strange thing that the judge should not overlook the reward of even a cup of cold water, but that we, if our achievements are not altogether great, should neglect the performance of little things. For he who does not despise the lesser things, will exercise much zeal concerning the greatest; but he who overlooks the former will also abstain from the latter; and to prevent this taking place Christ has defined great rewards even for these small things. For what is easier than to visit the sick? Yet even this He requites with a great recompense. Lay hold then on eternal life, delight in the Lord, and supplicate Him; take up again the easy yoke, bow thyself beneath the light burden, put a finish to thy life worthy of the beginning; do not suffer so great a stream of wealth to slip past thee. For if thou shouldst continue provoking God by thy deeds, thou wilt destroy thyself; but if before much damage has been done, and all thy husbandry has been overwhelmed with a flood, thou wilt dam up the channels of wickedness, thou wilt be able to recover again what has been spoiled and to add to it not a little further produce. Having considered all these things, shake off the dust, get up from the ground, and thou wilt be formidable to the adversary; for he himself indeed has overthrown thee, as if thou wouldst never rise again; but if he sees thee again lifting up thy hands against him, he will receive such an unexpected blow that he will be less forward in trying to upset thee again, and thou thyself wilt be more secure against receiving any wound of that kind in future. For if the calamities of others are sufficient to instruct us, much more those which we have ourselves undergone. And this is what I expect speedily to see in the case of thy own dear self, and that by the grace of God thou art again become more radiant than before, and displaying such great virtue, as even to be a protector of others in the world above. Only do not despair, do not fall back; for I will not cease repeating this in every form of speech, and wherever I see you, as well as by the lips of others; and if you listen to this you will no longer need other remedies.

LETTER II.

1. IF it were possible to express tears and groans by means of writing I would have filled the letter, which I now send to you, with them. Now I weep not because you are anxious concerning your patrimony, but because you have blotted out your name from the list of the brethren, because you have trampled upon the covenant which you had made with Christ. This is the reason why I shudder, this is the cause of my distress. On this account do I fear and tremble, knowing that the rejection of this covenant will bring great condemnation upon those who have enlisted for this noble warfare, and owing to indolence have deserted their proper rank. And that the punishment for such is heavier than for others is manifest for this reason. For no one would indite a private individual for shunning military service; but when once a man has become a soldier, if he be caught deserting the ranks, he runs a risk of suffering the most extreme penalty. There is nothing strange, beloved Theodore, in a wrestler falling, but in his remaining in a fallen condition; neither is it a grievous thing for the warrior to be wounded, but to despair after the blow has been struck, and to neglect the wound. No merchant, having once suffered shipwreck, and lost his freight, desists from sailing, but again crosses the sea and the billows, and the broad ocean, and recovers his former wealth. We see athletes also who after many falls have gained the wreath of victory; and often, before now, a soldier who has once ran away has turned out a champion, and prevailed over the enemy. Many also of those who have denied

---

[1] Rom. ii. 6.   [2] John xiv. 2.   [3] 1 Cor. xv. 41.

Christ owing to the pressure of torture, have fought again, and departed at last with the crown of martyrdom upon their brows. But if each of these had despaired after the first blow, he would not have reaped the subsequent benefits. Even so now, beloved Theodore, because the enemy has shaken thee a little from thy position, do not thou give thyself an additional thrust into the pit, but stand up bravely, and return speedily to the place from which thou hast departed, and deem not this blow, lasting but for a little while, any reproach. For if you saw a soldier returning wounded from war you would not reproach him; for it is a reproach to cast away one's arms, and to hold aloof from the enemy; but as long as a man stands fighting, even if he be wounded and retreat for a short time, no one is so unfeeling or inexperienced in matters of war, as to find any fault with him. Exemption from wounds is the lot of non-combatants; but those who advance with much spirit against the enemy may sometimes be wounded and fall; which is exactly what has now occurred in your case; for suddenly, while you attempted to destroy the serpent you were bitten. But take courage, you need a litle vigilance, and then not a trace of this wound will be left; or rather by the grace. of God thou wilt crush the head of the Evil One himself; nor let it trouble thee that thou art soon impeded, even at the outset. For the eye, the keen eye of the Evil One perceived the excellence of thy soul, and guessed from many tokens that a brave adversary would wax strong against him; for he expected that one who had promptly attacked him with such great vehemence would easily overcome him, if he persevered. Therefore he was diligent, and watchful, and mightily stirred up against thee, or rather against his own head, if thou wilt bravely stand thy ground. For who did not marvel at thy quick, sincere, and fervent change to good? For delicacy of food was disregarded, and costliness of raiment was despised, all manner of parade was put down, and all the zeal for the wisdom of this world was suddenly transferred to the divine oracles; whole days were spent in reading, and whole nights in prayer; no mention was made of thy family dignity, nor any thought taken of thy wealth; but to clasp the knees and hasten to the feet of the brethren thou didst recognize as something nobler than high birth. These things irritated the Evil One, these things stirred him up to more vehement strife; but yet he did not give a deadly blow. For if after a long time, and continual fastings, and sleeping on the bare ground and the rest of the discipline he overthrew you, even then there was no need to despair; nevertheless one would have said that the damage was great if defeat had taken place after many toils, and labours, and victories; but inasmuch as he upset you as soon as you had stripped for the contest with him, all that he accomplished was to render you more eager to do battle with him. For that fell pirate attacked thee just as thou wast sailing out of the harbor, not when thou hadst returned from thy trading voyage. bringing a full cargo. And as when one has attempted to stay a fierce lion, and has only grazed his skin, he has done him no injury but only stirred him up the more against himself, and rendered him more confident, and difficult to capture afterwards: even so the common enemy of all has attempted to strike a deep blow, but has missed it, and consequently made his antagonist more vigilant and wary for the future.

2. For human nature is a slippery thing, quick to be cheated, but quick also to recover from deceit, and as it speedily falls, so also does it readily rise. For even that blessed man, I mean David the chosen king and prophet, after he had accomplished many good deeds, betrayed himself to be a man, for once he fell in love with a strange woman, nor did he stop there but he committed adultery on account of his passion, and he committed murder on account of his adultery; but he did not try to inflict a third blow upon himself because he had already received two such heavy ones, but immediately hastened to the physician, and applied the remedies, fasting, tears, lamentation, constant prayer, frequent confession of the sin; and so by these means he propitiated God, insomuch that he was restored to his former position, insomuch that after adultery and murder the memory of the father was able to shield the idolatry of the son. For the son of this David, Solomon by name, was caught by the same snare as his father, and out of complaisance to women fell away from the God of his fathers.[1] Thou seest how great an evil it is not to master pleasure, not to upset the ruling principle in nature, and for a man to be the slave of women. This same Solomon then, who was formerly righteous and wise but who ran a risk of being deprived of all the kingdom on account of his sin, God permitted to keep the sixth part of the government on account of the renown of his father.[2]

Now if thy zeal had been concerned with worldly eloquence, and then thou hadst given it up in despair, I should have reminded thee of the law courts and the judgment seat and the victories achieved there and the former

---

[1] 1 Kings xi. 3, 4. [2] 1 Kings xi. 12, 13.

boldness of thy speech, and should have exhorted thee to return to your labours in that behalf: but inasmuch as our race is for heavenly things, and we take no account of the things which are on earth, I put thee in remembrance of another court of justice, and of that fearful and tremendous seat of judgment; "for we must all be made manifest before the judgment seat of Christ."[1] "And He will then sit as judge who is now disregarded by thee. What shall we say then, let me ask at that time? or what defence shall we make, if we continue to disregard Him? What shall we say then? Shall we plead the anxieties of business? Nay He has anticipated this by saying, "What shall it profit a man if he gain the whole world, and lose his own soul?"[2] Or that we have been deceived by others? But it did not help Adam in his defence to screen himself behind his wife, and say "the woman whom thou gavest me, she deceived me;"[3] even as the serpent was no excuse for the woman. Terrible, O beloved Theodore, is that tribunal, one which needs no accusers, and waits for no witnesses; for "all things are naked and laid open to Him"[4] who judges us, and we must submit to give an account not of deeds only but also of thoughts; for that judge is quick to discern the thoughts and intents of the heart.[5] But perhaps you will allege weakness of nature as the excuse, and inability to bear the yoke. And what kind of defence is this, that you have not strength to bear the easy yoke, that you are unable to carry the light burden? Is recovery from fatigue a grievous and oppressive thing? For it is to this that Christ calls us, saying, "Come unto me all ye that labour and are heavy laden, and I will give you rest; take my yoke upon you and learn of me, for I am meek and lowly in heart; for my yoke is easy and my burden is light."[6] For what can be lighter I ask, than to be released from anxieties, and business, and fears, and labors, and to stand outside the rough billows of life, and dwell in a tranquil haven?

3. Which of all things in the world seems to you most desirable and enviable? No doubt you will say government, and wealth, and public reputation. And yet what is more wretched than these things when they are compared with the liberty of Christians. For the ruler is subjected to the wrath of the populace and to the irrational impulses of the multitude, and to the fear of higher rulers, and to anxieties on behalf of those who are ruled, and the ruler of yesterday becomes a private citizen to-day; for this present life in no wise differs from a stage, but just as there, one man fills the position of a king, a second of a general, and a third of a soldier, but when evening has come on the king is no king, the ruler no ruler, and the general no general, even so also in that day each man will receive his due reward not according to the outward part which he has played, but according to his works. Well! is glory a precious thing which perishes like the power of grass? or wealth, the possessors of which are pronounced unhappy? "For woe" we read, "to the rich;"[7] and again, "Woe unto them who trust in their strength and boast themselves in the multitude of their riches!"[8] But the Christian never becomes a private person after being a ruler, or a poor man after being rich, or without honour after being held in honour; but he abides rich even when he is poor, and is exalted when he strives to humble himself; and from the rule which he exercises no human being can depose him, but only one of those rulers who are under the power of this world's potentate of darkness.

"Marriage is right," you say; I also assent to this. For "marriage," we read, "is honourable and the bed undefiled; but fornicators and adulterers God will judge;"[9] but it is no longer possible for thee to observe the right conditions of marriage. For if he who has been attached to a heavenly bridegroom deserts him, and joins himself to a wife the act is adultery, even if you call it marriage ten thousand times over; or rather it is worse than adultery in proportion as God is greater than man. Let no one deceive thee saying: "God hath not forbidden to marry;" I know this as well as you; He has not forbidden to marry, but He has forbidden to commit adultery, which is what thou art wishing to do; and may you be preserved from ever engaging thyself in marriage! And why dost thou marvel if marriage is judged as if it were adultery, when God is disregarded? Slaughter has brought about righteousness, and mercy has been a cause of condemnation more than slaughter; because the latter has been according to the mind of God, but the former has been forbidden. It was reckoned to Phinees for righteousness that he pierced to death the woman who committed fornication, together with the fornicator;[10] but Samuel, that saint of God, although he wept and mourned and entreated for whole nights, could not rescue Saul from the condemnation which God issued against him, because he saved, contrary to the design of God, the king of the alien tribes whom he ought to have slain.[11] If then mercy has been a cause of condemnation more than

---

[1] 2 Cor. v. 10.   [2] Matt. xvi. 26.   [3] Gen. iii. 12.   [7] Luke vi. 24.   [8] Ps. xlix. 6.   [9] Heb. xiii. 4.
[4] Heb. iv. 13.   [5] Heb. iv. 12.   [6] Matt. xi. 28.   [10] Num. xxv. 7-11.   [11] 1 Sam. xv.

slaughter because God was disobeyed, what wonder is it if marriage condemns more than adultery when it involves the rejection of Christ? For, as I said at the beginning, if you were a private person no one would indict you for shunning to serve as a soldier; but now thou art no longer thy own master, being engaged in the service of so great a king. For if the wife hath not power over her own body, but the husband,[1] much more they who live in Christ must be unable to have authority over their body. He who is now despised, the same will then be our judge; think ever on Him and the river of fire: "For a river of fire" we read, "winds before His face;"[2] for it is impossible for one who has been delivered over by Him to the fire to expect any end of his punishment. But the unseemly pleasures of this life no-wise differ from shadows and dreams; for before the deed of sin is completed, the conditions of pleasure are extinguished; and the punishments for these have no limit. And the sweetness lasts for a little while, but the pain is everlasting.

Tell me, what is there stable in this world? Wealth which often does not last even to the evening? Or glory? Hear what a certain righteous man says: "My life is swifter than a runner."[3] For as they dash away before they stand still, even so does this glory take to flight before it has fairly reached us. Nothing is more precious than the soul; and even they who have gone to the extremity of folly have not been ignorant of this; for "there is no equivalent of the soul" is the saying of a heathen poet.[4] I know that thou hast become much weaker for the struggle with the Evil One; I know that thou art standing in the very midst of the flame of pleasures; but if thou wilt say to the enemy "We do not serve thy pleasures, and we do not bow down to the root of all thy evils; if thou wilt bend thine eye upward, the Saviour will even now shake out the fire, and will burn up those who have flung thee into it, and will send to thee in the midst of the furnace a cloud, and dew, and a rustling breeze, so that the fire may not lay hold of thy thought or thy conscience. Only do not consume thyself with fire. For the arms and engines of besiegers have often been unable to destroy the fortification of cities, but the treachery of one or two of the citizens dwelling inside has betrayed them to the enemy without any trouble on his part. And now if none of thy thoughts within betray thee, should the Evil One bring countless engines against thee from without he will bring them in vain.

4. Thou hast by the grace of God many and great men who sympathize with thy trouble, who encourage you to the fight, who tremble for thy soul,—Valerius the holy man of God, Florentius who is in every respect his brother, Porphyrius who is wise with the wisdom of Christ, and many others. These are daily mourning, and praying for you without ceasing; and they would have obtained what they asked for, long ago, if only thou hadst been willing to withdraw thyself a little space out of the hands of the enemy. Now then is it not strange that, whilst others do not even now despair of thy salvation, but are continually praying that they may have their member restored to them, thou thyself, having once fallen, art unwilling to get up again, and remainest prostrate, all but crying aloud to the enemy: "Slay me, smite me, spare not?" "Does he who falls not rise up again?"[5] so speaks the divine oracle. But thou art striving against this and contradicting it; for if one who has fallen despairs it is as much as to say that he who falls does not rise up again I entreat thee do not so great a wrong to thyself; do not pour upon us such a flood of sorrow. I do not say at the present time, when thou hast not yet completed thy twentieth year, but even if, after achieving many things, and spending thy whole life in Christ thou hadst, in extreme old age, experienced this attack, even then it would not have been right to despair, but to call to mind the robber who was justified on the cross, the labourers who wrought about the eleventh hour, and received the wages of the whole day. But as it is not well that those who have fallen near the very extremity of life should abandon hope, if they be sober minded, so on the other hand it is not safe to feed upon this hope, and say, "Here for a while I will enjoy the sweets of life, but afterwards, when I have worked for a short time, I shall receive the wages of the whole working time. For I recollect hearing you often say, when many were exhorting you to frequent the schools;[6] "But what if I bring my life to a bad end in a short space of time, how shall I depart to Him who has said 'Delay not to turn to the Lord, nor put off day after day?'"[7] Recover this thought, and stand in fear of the thief; for by this name Christ calls our departure hence, because it comes upon us unawares. Consider the anxieties of life which befall us, both those which are personal to ourselves, and which are common to us with others, the fear of rulers, the envy of citizens, the danger which

---

[1] 1 Cor. vii. 4.
[2] Dan. vii. 10.
[3] Job ix. 25.
[4] Homer Il. ix. 401.
[5] Jer. viii. 4.
[6] *i. e.*, schools of Pagan philosophy: probably thos er w hich Libanius presided in Antioch.
[7] Ecclus. v. 8.

often hangs over us imperilling even life itself, the labours, the distresses, the servile flatteries, such as are unbecoming even to slaves if they be earnest minded men, the fruit of our labours coming to an end in this world, a fact which is the most distressing of all. It has been the lot indeed of many to miss the enjoyment of the things for which they have laboured, and after having consumed the prime of their manhood in labours and perils, just when they hoped that they should receive their reward they have departed taking nothing with them. For if, after undergoing many dangers, and completing many campaigns, one will scarcely look upon an earthly king with confidence, how will any one be able to behold the heavenly king, if he has lived and fought for another all his time.

5. Would you have me speak of the domestic cares of wife, and children and slaves? It is an evil thing to wed a very poor wife, or a very rich one; for the former is injurious to the husband's means, the latter to his authority and independence. It is a grievous thing to have children, still more grievous not to have any; for in the latter case marriage has been to no purpose, in the former a bitter bondage has to be undergone. If a child is sick, it is the occasion of no small fear; if he dies an untimely death, there is inconsolable grief; and at every stage of growth there are various anxieties on their account, and many fears and toils. And what is one to say to the rascalities of domestic slaves? Is this then life, Theodore, when one's soul is distracted in so many directions, when a man has to serve so many, to live for so many, and never for himself? Now amongst us, O friend, none of these things happen, I appeal to yourself as a witness. For during that short time when you were willing to lift your head above the waves of this world, you know what great cheerfulness and gladness you enjoyed. For there is no man free, save only he who lives for Christ. He stands superior to all troubles, and if he does not choose to injure himself no one else will be able to do this, but he is impregnable; he is not stung by the loss of wealth; for he has learned that we "brought nothing into this world, neither can we carry anything out;"[1] he is not caught by the longings of ambition or glory; for he has learned that our citizenship is in heaven;[2] no one annoys him by abuse, or provokes him by blows; there is only one calamity for a Christian which is, disobedience to God; but all the other things, such as loss of property, exile, peril of life, he does not even reckon to be a grievance at all. And that which all dread, departure hence to the other world,—this is to him sweeter than life itself. For as when one has climbed to the top of a cliff and gazes on the sea and those who are sailing upon it, he sees some being washed by the waves, others running upon hidden rocks, some hurrying in one direction, others being driven in another, like prisoners, by the force of the gale, many actually in the water, some of them using their hands only in the place of a boat and a rudder, and many drifting along upon a single plank, or some fragment of the vessel, others floating dead, a scene of manifold and various disaster; even so he who is engaged in the service of Christ drawing himself out of the turmoil and stormy billows of life takes his seat upon secure and lofty ground. For what position can be loftier or more secure than that in which a man has only one anxiety, "How he ought to please God?"[3] Hast thou seen the shipwrecks, Theodore, of those who sail upon this sea? Wherefore, I beseech thee, avoid the deep water, avoid the stormy billows, and seize some lofty spot where it is not possible to be captured. There is a resurrection, there is a judgment, there is a terrible tribunal which awaits us when we have gone out of this world; "we must all stand before the judgment-seat of Christ."[4] It is not in vain that we are threatened with hell fire, it is not without purpose that such great blessings have been prepared for us. The things of this life are a shadow, and more naught even than a shadow, being full of many fears, and many dangers, and extreme bondage. Do not then deprive thyself both of that world, and of this, when you may gain both, if you please. Now that they who live in Christ will gain the things of this world Paul teaches us when he says: "But I spare you;"[5] and again "But this I say for your profit."[6] Seest thou that even here he who cares for the things of the Lord is superior to the man who has married? It is not possible for one who has departed to the other world to repent; no athlete, when he has quitted the lists, and the spectators have dispersed, can contend again.

Be always thinking of these things, and break in pieces the sharp sword of the Evil One, by means of which he destroys many. And this is despair, which cuts off from hope those who have been overthrown. This is the strong weapon of the enemy, and the only way in which he holds down those who have been made captives is by binding them with this chain, which, if we choose, we shall speedily be able to break by the grace of God. I know that I have exceeded the due measure of a

---

[1] 1 Tim. vi. 7. [2] Phil. iii. 20. [3] 1 Thess. iv. 1. [4] Rom. xiv. 10.
[5] 1 Cor. vii. 28. [6] 1 Cor. vii. 35.

letter, but forgive me; for I am not willingly in this condition, but have been constrained by my love and sorrow, owing to which I forced myself to write this letter also,[1] although many would have prevented me. "Cease labouring in vain and sowing upon rock" many have been saying to me. But I hearkened to none of them. For there is hope I said to myself that, God willing, my letter will accomplish something; but if that which we deprecate should take place, we shall at least have the advantage of escaping self reproach for keeping silence, and we shall not be worse than sailors on the sea, who, when they behold men of their own craft drifting on a plank, because their ship has been broken to pieces by the winds and waves, take down their sails, and cast anchor, and get into a boat and try to rescue the men, although strangers, known to them only in consequence of their calamity. But if the others were unwilling to be rescued no one would accuse those of their destruction who attempted to save them. This is what we offer; but we trust that by the grace of God you also will do your part, and we shall again see you occupying an eminent place in the flock of Christ. In answer to the prayers of the saints may we speedily receive thee back, dear friend, sound in the true health. If thou hast any regard for us, and hast not utterly cast us out of thy memory, please vouchsafe a reply to our letter; for in so doing thou wilt give us much pleasure.

---

[1] This seems to imply a previous letter.

ST. CHRYSOSTOM:

LETTER TO A YOUNG WIDOW.

TRANSLATED WITH INTRODUCTION AND NOTES BY.

REV. W. R. W. STEPHENS, M.A.

PREBENDARY OF CHICHESTER CATHEDRAL, AND RECTOR OF WOOLBEDING, SUSSEX.

INTRODUCTION TO THE LETTER TO A YOUNG WIDOW.

THE date of the following letter can be determined within very narrow limits. It contains a reference (c. 5) to the defeat and death of the Emperor Valens in the battle with the Goths at Hadrianople, in A.D. 378, as a recent event. The Emperor who is described as having been incessantly engaged in war ever since his accession (c. 4) must be Theodosius, who succeeded Valens, and as the Goths are said to be still overrunning large regions with impunity, and insolently mocking the timidity of the imperial troops (ib.) the letter must have been written prior to the crushing defeat which Theodosius inflicted upon them in 382. The whole epistle is deeply tinged with that profound sense of the unhappiness and instability of human life which the moral corruption of society and recent calamities of the empire impressed with peculiar force on the minds of men; producing too often amongst Pagans either a cynical gloom or reckless indifference, but leading Christians to cling more closely and earnestly to the hopes and consolations of the Gospel.

LETTER TO A YOUNG WIDOW.

1. That you have sustained a severe blow, and that the weapon directed from above has been planted in a vital part all will readily admit, and none even of the most rigid moralists will deny it; but since they who are stricken with sorrow ought not to spend their whole time in mourning and tears, but to make good provision also for the healing of their wounds, lest, if they be neglected their tears should aggravate the wound, and the fire of their sorrow become inflamed, it is a good thing to listen to words of consolation, and restraining for a brief season at least the fountain of thy tears to surrender thyself to those who endeavour to console thee. On this account I abstained from troubling you when your sorrow was at its height, and the thunderbolt had only just fallen upon you; but having waited an interval and permitted you to take your fill of mourning, now that you are able to look out a little through the mist, and to open your ears to those who attempt to comfort you, I also would second the words of your handmaids by some contributions of my own. For whilst the tempest is still severe, and a full gale of sorrow is blowing, he who exhorts another to desist from grief would only provoke him to increased lamentations and having incurred his hatred would add fuel to the flame by such speeches besides being regarded himself as an unkind and foolish person. But when the troubled water has begun to subside, and God has allayed the fury of the waves, then we may freely spread the sails of our discourse. For in a moderate storm skill may perhaps play its part; but when the onslaught of the wind is irresistible experience is of no avail. For these reasons I have hitherto held my peace, and even now have only just ventured to break silence because I have heard from thy uncle that one may begin to take courage, as some of your more esteemed handmaids are now venturing to discourse at length upon these matters, women also outside your own household, who are your kinsfolk, or are otherwise qualified for this office. Now if you allow them to talk to you I have the greatest hope and confidence that you will not disdain my words but do your best to give them a calm and quiet hearing. Under any circumstances indeed the female sex is the more apt to be sensitive to suffering; but when in addition there is youth, and untimely widowhood, and inexperience in business, and a great crowd of cares, while the whole life previously has been nurtured in the midst of luxury, and cheerfulness and wealth, the evil is increased many fold, and if she who is subjected to it does not obtain help from on high even an accidental thought will be able to unhinge her. Now I hold this to be the foremost and greatest evidence of God's care concerning thee; for that thou hast not been overwhelmed by grief, nor driven out of thy natural condition of mind when such great troubles suddenly concurred to afflict thee was not due to any human assistance but to the almighty hand the understanding of which there is no measure, the wisdom which is past finding out, the "Father of mercies and the God of all comfort."[1] "For He Himself" it is said "hath smitten us, and He will heal us; He will strike, and He will dress the wound and make us whole."[2]

For as long as that blessed husband of thine was with thee, thou didst enjoy honour, and care and zealous attention; in fact you enjoyed such as you might expect to enjoy from a husband; but since God took him to Himself He has supplied his place to thee. And this is not my saying but that of the blessed prophet David for he says "He will take up the fatherless and the widow,"[3] and elsewhere

---

[1] 2 Cor. i. 3.   [2] Hosea vi. 2.   [3] Ps. cxlvi. 9.

he calls Him "father of the fatherless and judge of the widow;"[1] thus in many passages thou wilt see that He earnestly considereth the cause of this class of mankind.

2. But lest the continual repetition of this name of widow should upset thy soul, and disconcert thy reason, having been inflicted on thee in the very flower of thy age, I wish first of all to discourse on this point, and to prove to you that this name of widow is not a title of calamity but of honour, aye the greatest honour. For do not quote the erroneous opinion of the world as a testimony, but the admonition of the blessed Paul, or rather of Christ. For in his utterances Christ was speaking through him as he himself said "If ye seek a proof of Christ, who is speaking in me?"[2] What then does he say? "Let not a widow be enrolled under threescore years of age" and again "but the younger widows refuse"[3] intending by both these sayings to indicate to us the importance of the matter. And when he is making regulations about bishops he nowhere prescribes a standard of age, but in this case he is very particular on the point, and, pray, why so? not because widowhood is greater than priesthood, but because widows have greater labour to undergo than priests, being encompassed on many sides by a variety of business public and private. For as an unfortified city lies exposed to all who wish to plunder it, so a young woman living in widowhood has many who form designs upon her on every side not only those who aim at getting her money but also those who are bent upon corrupting her modesty. And besides these we shall find that she is subjected to other conditions also likely to occasion her fall. For the contempt of servants their negligence of business, the loss of that respect which was formerly paid, the sight of contemporaries in prosperity, and often the hankering after luxury, induce women to engage in a second marriage. Some there are who do not choose to unite themselves to men by the law of marriage, but do so secretly and clandestinely. And they act thus in order to enjoy the praise of widowhood; thus it is a state which seems to be not reproached, but admired and deemed worthy of honour among men, not only amongst us who believe, but even amongst unbelievers also. For once when I was still a young man I know that the sophist who taught me[4] (and he exceeded all men in his reverence for the gods) expressed admiration for my mother before a large company. For enquiring, as was his wont, of those who sat beside him who I was, and some one having said that I was the son of a woman who was a widow, he asked of me the age of my mother and the duration of her widowhood, and when I told him that she was forty years of age of which twenty had elapsed since she lost my father he was astonished and uttered a loud exclamation, and turning to those present "Heavens!" cried he "what women there are amongst the Christians." So great is the admiration and praise enjoyed by widowhood not only amongst ourselves, but also amongst those who are outside the Church. And being aware of all this the blessed Paul said "Let not a widow be enrolled under threescore years of age." And even after this great qualification of age he does not permit her to be ranked in this sacred society but mentions some additional requisites "well reported of for good works, if she have brought up children if she have lodged strangers if she have washed the saints feet if she have relieved the afflicted, if she have diligently followed every good work."[5] Heavens! what testing and scrutiny! how much virtue does he demand from the widow, and how precisely does he define it! which he would not have done, had he not intended to entrust to her a position of honour and dignity. And "the younger widows" he says "refuse; and then he adds the reason; "for when they have waxed wanton against Christ they will marry."[6] By this expression he gives us to understand that they who have lost their husbands are wedded to Christ in their stead. Observe how he asserts this by way of indicating the mild and easy nature of this union; I refer to the passage "when they have waxed wanton against Christ they will marry," as if He were some gentle husband who did not exercise authority over them, but suffered them to live in freedom. Neither did Paul confine his discourse on the subject to these remarks, but also in another place again he has manifested great anxiety about it where he says "Now she who liveth in pleasure is dead while she liveth; but she who is a widow indeed and desolate hath set her hope in God, and continueth in prayers and supplications day and night."[7] And writing to the Corinthians he says "But she is more blessed if she abide thus."[8] You see what great praise is bestowed upon widowhood, and this in the New Testament, when the beauty of virginity also was clearly brought to light. Nevertheless even the lustre of this state could not obscure the glories of widowhood, which shines on brightly all the same, keeping its own value. When then we make mention of widowhood from time to time, do not be cast down, nor consider the matter a reproach; for if this

---

[1] Ps. lxviii. 5.
[2] 2 Cor. xiii. 3.
[3] 1 Tim. v. 9, 11.
[4] Libanius.
[5] 1 Tim. v. 10.
[6] 1 Tim. v. 11.
[7] 1 Tim. v. 6, 5.
[8] 1 Cor. vii. 40.

be a matter of reproach, far more so is virginity. But this is not the case; no! God forbid. For inasmuch as we all admire and welcome women who live continently whilst their husbands are yet alive must we not be delighted with those who manifest the same good feeling concerning their husbands when they have departed this life, and praise them accordingly? As I was saying then, as long as you lived with the blessed Therasius you enjoyed honour and consideration such as is natural for a wife to receive from a husband; but now in his place you have God who is the Lord of all, who hath of old been thy protector and will be so now still more and with yet greater earnestness; and as I have already said He hath displayed no slight token of his providential care by having preserved thee whole and unharmed in the midst of such a furnace of anxiety and sorrow, and not suffering thee to undergo anything undesirable. Now if He has not permitted any shipwreck to take place in the midst of so much rough water, much more will He preserve thy soul in calm weather and lighten the burden of thy widowhood, and the consequences of it which seem to be so terrible.

3. Now if it is not the name of widow which distresses you, but the loss of such a husband I grant you that all the world over amongst men engaged in secular affairs there have been few like him, so affectionate, so gentle, so humble, so sincere, so understanding, so devout. And certainly if he had altogether perished, and utterly ceased to be, it would be right to be distressed, and sorrowful; but if he has only sailed into the tranquil haven, and taken his journey to Him who is really his king, one ought not to mourn but to rejoice on these accounts. For this death is not death, but only a kind of emigration and translation from the worse to the better, from earth to heaven, from men to angels, and archangels, and Him who is the Lord of angels and archangels. For here on earth whilst he was serving the emperor there were dangers to be expected and many plots arising from men who bore ill-will, for in proportion as his reputation increased did the designs also of enemies abound; but now that he has departed to the other world none of these things can be suspected. Wherefore in proportion as you grieve that God has taken away one who was so good and worthy you ought to rejoice that he has departed in much safety and honour, and being released from the trouble which besets this present season of danger, is in great peace and tranquillity. For is it not out of place to acknowledge that heaven is far better than earth, and yet to mourn those who are translated from this world to the other? For if that blessed husband of thine had been one of those who lived a shameful life contrary to what God approved it would have been right to bewail and lament for him not only when he had departed, but whilst he was still living; but inasmuch as he was one of those who are the friends of God we should take pleasure in him not only whilst living, but also when he has been laid to rest. And that we ought to act thus thou hast surely heard the words of the blessed Paul "to depart and to be with Christ which is far better."[1] But perhaps you long to hear your husband's words, and enjoy the affection which you bestowed upon him, and you yearn for his society, and the glory which you had on his account, and the splendour, and honour, and security, and all these things being gone distress and darken your life. Well! the affection which you bestowed on him you can keep now just as you formerly did.

For such is the power of love, it embraces, and unites, and fastens together not only those who are present, and near, and visible but also those who are far distant; and neither length of time, nor separation in space, nor anything else of that kind can break up and sunder in pieces the affection of the soul. But if you wish to behold him face to face (for this I know is what you specially long for) keep thy bed in his honour sacred from the touch of any other man, and do thy best to manifest a life like his, and then assuredly thou shalt depart one day to join the same company with him, not to dwell with him for five years as thou didst here, nor for 20, or 100, nor for a thousand or twice that number but for infinite and endless ages. For it is not any physical relation, but a correspondence in the way of living which qualifies for the inheritance of those regions of rest. For if it was identity of moral constitution which brought Lazarus although a stranger to Abraham into the same heavenly bosom with him, and qualifies many from east and west to sit down with him, the place of rest will receive thee also with the good Therasius, if thou wilt exhibit the same manner of life as his, and then thou shalt receive him back again no longer in that corporeal beauty which he had when he departed, but in lustre of another kind, and splendour outshining the rays of the sun. For this body, even if it reaches a very high standard of beauty is nevertheless perishable; but the bodies of those who have been well pleasing to God, will be invested with such glory as these eyes cannot even look upon. And God has furnished us with certain tokens, and obscure indications of these things both in the Old and in the New

---

[1] Phil. i. 33.

Dispensation. For in the former the face of Moses shone with such glory as to be intolerable to the eyes of the Israelites, and in the New the face of Christ shone far more brilliantly than his. For tell me if any one had promised to make your husband king of all the earth, and then had commanded you to withdraw for twenty years on his account, and had promised after that to restore him to you with the diadem and the purple, and to place you again in the same rank with him, would you not have meekly endured the separation with due self-control? Would you not have been well pleased with the gift, and deemed it a thing worth praying for? Well then submit to this now, not for the sake of a kingdom on earth, but of a kingdom in Heaven; not to receive him back clad in a vesture of gold but robed in immortality and glory such as is fitting for them to have who dwell in Heaven. And if you find the trial very unbearable owing to its long duration, it may be that he will visit you by means of visions and converse with you as he was wont to do, and show you the face for which you yearn: let this be thy consolation taking the place of letters, though indeed it is far more definite than letters. For in the latter case there are but lines traced with the pen to look upon, but in the former you see the form of his visage, and his gentle smile, his figure and his movements, you hear his speech and recognize the voice which you loved so well.

4. But since you mourn also over the loss of security which you formerly enjoyed on his account, and perhaps also for the sake of those great hopes of distinction which were dawning (for I used to hear that he would speedily arrive at the dignity of præfect, and this, I fancy, it is which more especially upsets and distresses thy soul) consider I pray the case of those who have been in a higher official position than his, and yet have brought their life to a very pitiable end. Let me recall them to your memory: you probably know Theodore of Sicily by reputation:[1] for he was one of the most distinguished men; he surpassed all in bodily stature and beauty as well as in the confidence which he enjoyed with the Emperor, and he had more power than any member of the royal household, but he did not bear this prosperity meekly, and having entered into a plot against the Emperor he was taken prisoner and miserably beheaded; and his wife who was not a whit inferior to thy noble self in education and birth and all other respects was suddenly stripped of all her possessions, deprived even of her freedom also, and enrolled amongst the household slaves, and compelled to lead a life more pitiable than any bondmaid, having this advantage only over the rest that owing to the extreme severity of her calamity she moved to tears all who beheld her. And it is said also that Artemisia who was the wife of a man of high reputation, since he also aimed at usurping the throne, was reduced to this same condition of poverty, and also to blindness; for the depth of her despondency, and the abundance of her tears destroyed her sight; and now she has need of persons to lead her by the hand, and to conduct her to the doors of others that she may obtain the necessary supply of food.[2] And I might mention many other families which have been brought down in this way did I not know thee to be too pious and prudent in disposition to wish to find consolation for thy own calamity out of the misfortunes of others. And the only reason why I mentioned those instances to which I referred just now was that you might learn that human things are nothingness but that truly as the prophet says "all the glory of man is as the flower of grass."[3] For in proportion to men's elevation and splendour is the ruin wrought for them, not only in the case of those who are under rule, but also of the rulers themselves. For it would be impossible to find any private family which has been immersed in such great calamities as the ills in which the imperial house has been steeped. For untimely loss of parents, and of husbands, and violent forms of death, more outrageous and painful than those which occur in tragedies, especially beset this kind of government.

Now passing over ancient times, of those who have reigned in our own generation, nine in all, only two have ended their life by a natural death; and of the others one was slain by a usurper,[4] one in battle,[5] one by a conspiracy of his household guards,[6] one by the very man who elected him, and invested him with the purple,[7] and of their wives some, as it is reported, perished by poison, others died of mere sorrow; while of those who still survive one, who has an orphan son, is trembling with alarm lest any of those who are in power dreading what may happen in the future should destroy him;[8] another has reluctantly yielded to much entreaty to return from the exile into

---

[1] According to Ammianus Marcellinus, B. xxxiv., this Theodore was a native of Gaul. He is probably called Theodore of Sicily by Chrysostom because he attempted to make himself a tyrant in that island. He was executed for treason in the year 371.

[2] I have not been able to discover any further information concerning Artemisia or her husband.
[3] Is. xl. 5.   [4] Constans by Magnentius.
[5] Constantine the younger.
[6] Jovian: there were several other versions of his death. See Gibbon, iv. 221 (Milman's edition). Chrysostom repeats this story in Homily XV., ad Philipp.
[7] Gallus Cæsar (who never became Augustus) by Constantius.
[8] Widow of Jovian, whose son Varronianus had been deprived of one eye (see Gibbon as above).

which she had been driven by him who held the chief power.[1] And of the wives of the present rulers the one who has recovered a little from her former calamities has much sorrow mingled with her joy because the possessor of power is still young and inexperienced and has many designing men on all sides of him;[2] and the other is ready to die of fear, and spends her time more miserably than criminals condemned to death because her husband ever since he assumed the crown up to the present day has been constantly engaged in warfare and fighting, and is more exhausted by the shame and the reproaches which assail him on all sides than by actual calamities.[3] For that which has never taken place has now come to pass, the barbarians leaving their own country have overrun an infinite space of our territory, and that many times over, and having set fire to the land, and captured the towns they are not minded to return home again, but after the manner of men who are keeping holiday rather than making war, they laugh us all to scorn;[4] and it is said that one of their kings declared that he was amazed at the impudence of our soldiers, who although slaughtered more easily than sheep still expect to conquer, and are not willing to quit their own country; for he said that he himself was satiated with the work of cutting them to pieces. Imagine what the feelings of the Emperor and his wife must be on hearing these words !

5. And since I have made mention of this war, a great crowd of widows has occurred to me, who in past times derived very great lustre from the honour enjoyed by their husbands, but now are all arrayed in a dark mourning robe and spend their whole time in lamentation. For they had not the advantage which was enjoyed by thy dear self. For thou, my excellent friend, didst see that goodly husband of thine lying on his bed, and didst hear his last words, and receive his instructions as to what should be done about the affairs of the family, and learn how by the provisions of his will they were guarded against every kind of encroachment on the part of rapacious and designing men. And not only this, but also when he was yet lying dead thou didst often fling thyself upon the body, and kiss his eyes, and embrace him, and wail over him, and thou didst see him conducted to burial with much honour, and didst everything necessary for his obsequies, as was fitting, and from frequent visits to his grave thou hast no slight consolation of thy sorrow. But these women have been deprived of all these things, having all sent out their husbands to war in the hope of receiving them back again, instead of which it has been their lot to receive the bitter tidings of their death. Neither has any one come back to them with the bodies of their slain, or bringing anything save a message describing the manner of their death. And some there are who have not even been vouchsafed this record, or been enabled to learn how their husbands fell, as they were buried beneath a heap of slain in the thick of battle.

And what wonder if most of the generals perished thus, when even the Emperor himself having been blockaded in a certain village with a few soldiers did not dare to go out and oppose the assailants, but remained inside and when the enemy had set fire to the building was burnt to death together with all that were therein, not men only, but horses, beams and walls, so that the whole was turned into a heap of ashes ? And this was the tale which they who departed to war with the Emperor brought back to his wife in place of the Emperor himself.[5] For the splendours of the world differ in no-wise whatever from the things which happen on the stage, and the beauty of spring flowers. For in the first place they flee away before they have been manifested; and then, even if they have strength to last a little while, they speedily become ready to decay. For what is more worthless than the honour and glory which is paid by the multitude ? what fruit has it ? what kind of profit ? what serviceable end does it meet ? And would that this only was the evil ! but in fact besides failing to get anything good from the possession, he who owns this most cruel mistress is continually forced to bear much which is painful and injurious; for mistress she is of those who own her, and in proportion as she is flattered by her slaves does she exalt herself against them, and ties them down by increasingly harsh commands; but she would never be able to revenge herself on those who despise and neglect her; so much fiercer is she than any tyrant and wild beast. For tyrants and wild animals are often mollified by humouring, but her fury is greatest when we are most complaisant to her, and if she finds any one who will listen to her, and yield to her in everything there is no kind of command from which in future she can be induced to abstain.

---

[1] Doubtful, possibly first wife of Valentinian I., divorced from him and sent into exile.
[2] Constantia, wife of Gratian.
[3] Flacilla, wife of Theodosius. The two emperors who died natural deaths were Constantine the Great, and his son Constantius. Compare this mournful list with the celebrated passage in Shakespeare's Richard II., act III. sc. 2.
"For Heaven's sake let's sit upon the ground
And tell sad stories of the death of kings," etc.
[4] See Introduction.

[5] The best account of the destruction of the Emperor Valens and his army in the battle of Hadrianople A.D. 378, is to be found in Hodgkin's "Italy and her Invaders," vol. i, pp. 120-6 (Clarendon Press, Oxford).

Moreover she has also another ally whom one would not do wrong to call her daughter. For after she herself has grown to maturity and fairly taken root amongst us, she then produces arrogance, a thing which is no less able than herself to drive the soul of those who possess it into headlong ruin.

6. Tell me then dost thou lament this that God hath reserved thee from such a cruel bondage, and that He has barred every avenue against these pestilential diseases? For whilst thy husband was living they ceased not continually assaulting the thoughts of thy heart, but since his death they have no starting point whence they can lay hold of thy understanding. This then is a discipline which ought to be practised in future—to abstain from lamenting the withdrawal of these evils, and from hankering after the bitter tyranny which they exercise. For where they blow a heavy blast they upset all things from the foundation and shatter them to pieces; and just as many prostitutes, although by nature ill favoured and ugly, do yet by means of enamels and pigments excite the feelings of the youthful whilst they are still tender, and when they have got them under their control treat them more insolently than any slave; so also do these passions, vainglory and arrogance, defile the souls of men more than any other kind of pollution. On this account also wealth has seemed to the majority of men to be a good thing; at least when it is stripped of this passion of vainglory it will no longer seem desirable. At any rate those who have been permitted to obtain in the midst of their poverty popular glory have no longer preferred wealth, but rather have despised much gold when it was bestowed upon them. And you have no need to learn from me who these men were, for you know them better than I do, Epaminondas, Socrates, Aristeides, Diogenes, Krates who turned his own land into a sheep walk.[1] The others indeed, inasmuch as it was not possible for them to get rich, saw glory brought to them in the midst of their poverty, and straightway devoted themselves to it, but this man threw away even what he possessed; so infatuated were they in the pursuit of this cruel monster. Let us not then weep because God has rescued us from this shameful thraldom which is an object of derision and of much reproach; for there is nothing splendid in it save the name it bears, and in reality it places those who possess it in a position which belies its appellation, and there is no one who does not laugh to scorn the man who does anything with a view to glory. For it is only he who has not an eye to this who will be enabled to win respect and glory; but he who sets a great value on popular glory, and does and endures everything for the sake of obtaining it is the very man who will fail to attain it, and be subjected to all the exact opposites of glory, ridicule, and accusation, scoffing, enmity and hatred. And this is wont to happen not only among men, but also among you women, and indeed more especially in your case. For the woman who is unaffected in mien, and gait, and dress, and seeks no honour from any one is admired by all women, and they are ecstatic in their praise and call her blessed, and invoke all manner of good things upon her; but a vain-glorious woman they behold with aversion and detestation, and avoid her like some wild beast and load her with infinite execrations and abuse. And not only do we escape these evils by refusing to accept popular glory, but we shall gain the highest advantages in addition to those which have been already mentioned, being trained gradually to loosen our hold of earth and move in the direction of heaven, and despise all worldly things. For he who feels no need of the honour which comes from men, will perform with security whatever good things he does, and neither in the troubles, nor in the prosperities of this life will he be very seriously affected; for neither can the former depress him, and cast him down, nor can the latter elate and puff him up, but in precarious and troubled circumstances he himself remains exempt from change of any kind. And this I expect will speedily be the case with your own soul, and having once for all torn yourself away from all worldly interests you will display amongst us a heavenly manner of life, and in a little while will laugh to scorn the glory which you now lament, and despise its hollow and vain mask. But if you long for the security which you formerly enjoyed owing to your husband, and the protection of your property, and immunity from the designs of any of those persons who trample upon the misfortunes of others "Cast thy care upon the Lord and He will nourish thee."[2] "For look," it is said, "to past generations and see, who ever placed his hope on the Lord and was put to shame, or who ever called upon Him, and was neglected, or who ever remained constant to His commandments and was forsaken?"[3] For He who has alleviated this intolerable calamity, and placed you even now in a state of tranquillity will also avert impending evils; for that you will never receive another blow more severe than this you would yourself admit.

---

[1] Krates was a cynic philosopher, a disciple of Diogenes. He flourished about 330 B.C. He was heir to a large fortune, but bestowed the whole of it upon his native city Thebes. Diogenes Laertius relates many curious stories about him.

[2] Ps. lv. 23.

[3] Ecclus. ii. 10.

Having then so bravely borne present troubles, and this when you were inexperienced, you will far more easily endure future events should any of the things contrary to our wishes, which God forbid, occur. Therefore seek Heaven, and all things which conduce to life in the other world, and none of the things here will be able to harm thee, not even the world-ruler of darkness himself, if only we do not injure ourselves. For if any one deprives us of our substance, or hews our body in pieces, none of these things concern us, if our soul abides in its integrity.

7. Now, once for all, if you wish your property to abide with you in security and yet further to increase I will show thee the plan, and the place where none of those who have designs upon it will be allowed to enter. What then is the place? It is Heaven. Send away thy possessions to that good husband of thine and neither thief, nor schemer, nor any other destructive thing will be able to pounce upon them. If you deposit these goods in the other world, you will find much profit arising from them. For all things which we plant in Heaven yield a large and abundant crop, such as might naturally be expected from things which have their roots in Heaven. And if you do this, see what blessings you will enjoy, in the first place eternal life and the things promised to those who love God, "which eye hath not seen, nor ear heard, neither have they entered into the heart of man," and in the second place perpetual intercourse with thy good husband; and you will relieve yourself from the cares and fears, and dangers, and designs, and enmity and hatred which beset you here. For as long as you are surrounded with this property there will probably be some to make attempts upon it; but if you transfer it to Heaven, you will lead a life of security and safety, and much tranquillity, enjoying independence combined with godliness. For it is very irrational, when one wishes to buy land, and is seeking for productive ground, if, Heaven being proposed to him instead of earth, and the possibility presented of obtaining an estate there he abides still on earth, and puts up with the toils that are connected with it; for it often disappoints our hopes.

But since thy soul is grievously upset and vexed on account of the expectation often entertained that thy husband would attain the rank of prefect, and the thought that he was untimely snatched away from that dignity consider first of all this fact, that even if this hope was a very well grounded one nevertheless it was only a human hope, which often falls to the ground; and we see many things of this kind happening in life, those which were confidently expected having remained unfulfilled, whereas those which never even entered the mind have frequently come to pass, and this we constantly see occurring everywhere in cases of governments and kingdoms, and inheritances, and marriages. Wherefore even if the opportunity were very near at hand, yet as the proverb says "between the cup and the lip there is many a slip" and the Scripture saith "from the morning until the evening the time is changed."[1]

So also a king who is here to-day is dead to-morrow; and again this same wise man illustrating the reversal of men's hopes says "many tyrants have sat down upon the ground, and one that was never thought of has worn the crown."[2] And it was not absolutely certain that if he lived he would arrive at this dignity; for that which belongs to the future is uncertain, and causes us to have various suspicions. For on what grounds was it evident that had he lived he would have attained that dignity and that things would not have turned out the other way, and that he would have lost the office he actually held either from falling a victim to disease, or from being exposed to the envy and ill will of those who wished to excel him in prosperity, or from suffering some other grievous misfortune. But let us suppose, if you please, that it was perfectly evident that in any case had he survived he would have obtained this high distinction; then in proportion to the magnitude of the dignity would have been the increased dangers, and anxieties, and intrigues which he must have encountered. Or put these even on one side, and let us suppose him to traverse that sea of difficulties safely, and in much tranquillity; then tell me what is the goal? not that which he has now reached; no, not that, but something different, probably unpleasant and undesirable. In the first place his sight of heaven, and heavenly things would have been delayed, which is no small loss to those who have put their trust in things to come; and in the next place, even had he lived a very pure life yet the length of his life and the exigencies of his high office would have prevented his departing in such a pure condition as has now been the case. In fact it is uncertain whether he might not have undergone many changes and given way to indolence before he breathed his last. For now we are confident that by the grace of God he has taken his flight to the region of rest, because he had not committed himself to any of those deeds which exclude from the kingdom of Heaven; but in that case after long contact with public busi-

---

[1] Ecclus. xviii. 26.   [2] Ecclus. xi. 5.

ness, he might probably have contracted great defilement. For it is an exceedingly rare thing for one who is moving in the midst of such great evils to hold a straight course, but to go astray, both wittingly and against his will, is a natural thing, and one which constantly occurs. But, as it is, we have been relieved from this apprehension, and we are firmly persuaded that in the great day he will appear in much radiance, shining forth near the King, and going with the angels in advance of Christ and clad with the robe of unutterable glory, and standing by the side of the King as he gives judgment, and acting as one of His chief ministers. Wherefore desisting from mourning and lamentation do thou hold on to the same way of life as his, yea even let it be more exact, that having speedily attained an equal standard of virtue with him, you may inhabit the same abode and be united to him again through the everlasting ages, not in this union of marriage but another far better. For this is only a bodily kind of intercourse, but then there will be a union of soul with soul more perfect, and of a far more delightful and far nobler kind.

ST. CHRYSOSTOM:

HOMILIES ON S. IGNATIUS AND S. BABYLAS.

TRANSLATED WITH INTRODUCTION AND NOTES BY

REV. W. R. W. STEPHENS, M.A.,

PREBENDARY OF CHICHESTER, AND RECTOR OF WOOLBEDING, SUSSEX.

ASSISTED BY

REV. T. P. BRANDRAM, M.A.,

RECTOR OF RUMBOLDSWHYKE, CHICHESTER.

INTRODUCTION TO THE HOMILIES ON S. IGNATIUS AND S. BABYLAS.

The following homilies have been selected out of a large number delivered by Chrysostom on the festivals of saints and martyrs, not only because they are good samples of his discourses on such occasions, but also on account of the celebrity of the two saints in whose honour they were spoken. There is really very little known about Ignatius beyond the fact that he was Bishop of Antioch, and suffered martyrdom at Rome in the reign of Trajan about the year 110 A.D.: being torn to death by wild beasts in the colossal amphitheatre erected for the display of such inhuman sports by the emperors of the Flavian dynasty. The tradition that he was a disciple of St. John does not rest on any trustworthy evidence, but on the other hand there is nothing inherently impossible or even improbable in the supposition.

According to a tradition which cannot be traced back earlier than the latter part of the fourth century the reliques were translated from Rome to Antioch and deposited in the Christian cemetery outside the gates called the Daphnitic gate, because it led from the city to the famous suburb of Daphne, on which we shall have more to say presently. It is clear from the following eulogy that Chrysostom accepted this tradition, and his repeated invitation to his hearers to "come hither" to enjoy the beneficent influence of the saint seems to imply that his discourse was delivered in the "martyry," that is the chapel erected to contain the martyr's remains, not in the "Great Church" of Antioch where he commonly preached. In the next generation the reliques of the saint were again translated by the Emperor, the younger Theodosius, to the building which had been the temple of the "Fortune of Antioch," and then the illustrious Christian martyr was substituted for the mythical goddess on the tutelary genius of the city.

The fame of S. Babylas rivalled and for a time almost threatened to overshadow that of S. Ignatius. He had been Bishop of Antioch from about 237 to 250. The heroic courage with which he had once repulsed the Emperor Philip from the church until he should have submitted to penance for some offence committed, and his martyrdom in the persecution under Decius were his original claims to popular veneration. But some later events shed a fresh lustre on his name. In the year 351 the Cæsar Gallus, brother of Julian, being resident in Antioch, transferred the reliques of Babylas from their resting place within the city to the beautiful suburb the garden or grove of Daphne. "In the history of this spot we have a singular instance of the way in which Grecian legend was transplanted into foreign soil. Daphne the daughter of the river-god Ladon were according to the Syrian version of the myth, overtaken by her lover Apollo near Antioch. Here it was, on the banks not of the Peneus but of the Oronete, that the maiden prayed to her mother earth to open her arms and shelter her from the pursuit of the amorous god, and that the laurel plant sprang out of the spot where she vanished from the eyes of her disappointed lover. The house of Seleucus Nicator, founder of the Syrian monarchy was said to have struck his hoof upon one of the arrows dropped by Apollo in the hurry of his pursuit; in consequence of which the king dedicated the place to the god. A temple was erected in his honour, ample in its proportions, sumptuous in its adornments; the internal walls were resplendent with polished marbles, the lofty ceiling was of cypress wood. The colossal image of the god, enriched with gold and gems, nearly reached the top of the roof. * * * With one hand the deity lightly touched the lyre which hung from his shoulders and in the other he held a golden dish, as if about to pour a libation on the earth "and supplicate the venerable mother to give to his arms the cold and beauteous Daphne."[1] The whole grove became consecrated to pleasure under the guise of festivity in honor of the god. * * * It contained everything which could gratify and charm the senses; the deep impenetrable shade of cypress trees, the delicious noise and coolness of falling waters, the fragrance of aromatic shrubs;" there were also baths, and grottos, porticoes, and colonnades. Such materials for voluptuous enjoyment told with fatal effect upon the morals of a people addicted at all times to an immoderate indulgence in luxurious pleasure."[2] Daphne became one of those places where gross and shameless vice was practised under the sanction of religion. The intention of Cæsar Gallus in translating the reliques of Babylas to Daphne was as Chrysostom expresses it to "bring a physician to the sick;" to introduce a pure and Christian association into a spot hitherto consecrated to Pagan and licentious rites. The bones of the saint were laid near the shrine of Apollo, and the Christian church standing hard by the heathen temple was a visible warning to any Christian who might visit the place to abstain from deeds abhorrent to the faith for which the bishop had died. But the remains of the martyr were not permitted to rest in peace. When the Emperor Julian visited Antioch 362, he consulted the oracle of Apollo at Daphne respecting the issue of the expedition which he was about to make into Persia. But the oracle was dumb. At length the god yielded to the importunity of prayers and sacrifices so far as to explain the cause of his silence. He was offended by the proximity of dead men. "Break open the sepulchres, take up the bones, and carry them hence." No name was mentioned, but the demand was interpreted as referring to the remains of Babylas, and the wishes of the affronted deity were complied with. The Christians were commanded by Julian to remove the bones of their saint from the neighbourhood of Apollo's sanctuary. They obeyed, but what was intended to be a humiliation was converted into a triumph. The reliques were conveyed to their resting place within the city as in a kind of festive procession, accompanied by crowds along the whole way, four or five miles, chanting the words of the Psalm, "Confounded be all they that worship carved images and delight in vain gods." In vain were some of the Christians seized and tortured. The popularity of the saint grew in proportion as Julian tried to put it down; and the insults done to him were speedily avenged. A fire, mysterious in its origin, broke out soon after the removal of the martyr's reliques in the shrine of Apollo, consuming the roof of the building, and the statue of the god. At the time when Chrysostom preached, about twenty years later, the columns and walls were still standing, the melancholy wreck serving as a memorial and witness of the judgment which had fallen upon the place.

The remains of Babylas were not brought back to Daphne, but removed from the city to a magnificent church built to receive them on the other side of the Orontes. Near the close of his discourse Chrysostom refers to the erection of this church and to the zeal of the Bishop Meletius in promoting it, who actually took part in the work with his own hands, as we are told that Hugh did in the building of the Minster at Lincoln. But although the body of the martyr rested elsewhere, his spirit and influence were supposed to inhabit in a special manner the spot where he had put the heathen deity to silence and shame, and to confer blessings on the pilgrims who resorted in crowds to his martyry in Daphne. The ruined and deserted temple indeed, and the well preserved Christian church thronged with worshippers, standing as they did side by side, formed a striking emblem of the two religions to which they were devoted—the one destined to crumble and vanish away, the other to endure and conquer.

---

[1] Gibbon, vol. iv. p. 111. Milman's ed.   [2] Life of St. John Chrysostom, by W. R. W. Stephens, pp. 101-3, 3d ed.

CONTENTS.

	PAGE
Eulogy on the Holy Martyr Saint Ignatius, Bishop of Antioch	137
Eulogy on the Holy Martyr Saint Babylas	143

HOMILIES ON S. IGNATIUS AND S. BABYLAS.

EULOGY.

On the holy martyr Saint Ignatius, the god-bearer,[1] arch-bishop of Antioch the great, who was carried off to Rome, and there suffered martyrdom, and thence was conveyed back again to Antioch.

1. SUMPTUOUS and splend identertainers give frequent and constant entertainments, alike to display their own wealth, and to show goodwill to their acquaintance. So also the grace of the Spirit, affording us a proof of his own power, and displaying much good-will towards the friends of God, sets before us successively and constantly the tables of the martyrs. Lately, for instance, a maiden quite young, and unmarried, the blessed martyr Pelagia, entertained us, with much joy. To-day again, this blessed and noble martyr Ignatius has succeeded to her feast. The persons are different: The table is one. The wrestlings are varied: The crown is one. The contests are manifold: The prize is the same. For in the case of the heathen contests, since the tasks are bodily, men alone are, with reason, admitted. But here, since the contest is wholly concerning the soul, the lists are open to each sex, for each kind the theatre is arranged. Neither do men alone disrobe, in order that the women may not take refuge in the weakness of their nature, and seem to have a plausible excuse, nor have women only quitted themselves like men, lest the race of men be put to shame; but on this side and on that many are proclaimed conquerors, and are crowned, in order that thou mayest learn by means of the exploits themselves that in Christ Jesus neither male nor female,[2] neither sex, nor weakness of body, nor age, nor any such thing could be a hindrance to those who run in the course of religion; if there be a noble readiness, and an eager mind, and a fear of God, fervent and kindling, be established in our souls. On this account both maidens and women, and men, both young and old, and slaves, and freemen, and every rank, and every age, and each sex, disrobe for those contests, and in no respect suffer harm, since they have brought a noble purpose to these wrestlings. The season then already calls us to discourse of the mighty works of this saint. But our reckoning is disturbed and confused, not knowing what to say first, what second, what third, so great a multitude of things calling for eulogy surrounds us, on every side; and we experience the same thing as if any one went into a meadow, and seeing many a rosebush and many a violet, and an abundance of lilies, and other spring flowers manifold and varied, should be in doubt what he should look at first, what second, since each of those he saw invites him to bestow his glances on itself. For we too, coming to this spiritual meadow of the mighty works of Ignatius, and beholding not the flowers of spring, but the manifold and varied fruit of the spirit in the soul of this man, are confused and in perplexity, not knowing to which we are first to give our consideration, as each of the things we see draws us away from its neighbours, and entices the eye of the soul to the sight of its own beauty. For see, he presided over the Church among us nobly, and with such carefulness as Christ desires. For that which Christ declared

---
[1] "Theophoros." This was probably only a second name assumed by Ignatius, perhaps at the time of his conversion or baptism. Legendary interpretations of it afterwards arose, which varied according as it was understood in an active or passive sense, the "god-bearer" or the "god-borne." See Bishop Lightfoot's Apostolic Fathers, vol. i., part ii., p. 25-28.
[2] Gal. iii. 28.

to be the highest standard and rule of the Episcopal office, did this man display by his deeds. For having heard Christ saying, the good shepherd layeth down his life for the sheep,[1] with all courage he did lay it down for the sheep.

He held true converse with the apostles and drank of spiritual fountains. What kind of person then is it likely that he was who had been reared, and who had everywhere held converse with them, and had shared with them truths both lawful and unlawful to utter, and who seemed to them worthy of so great a dignity? The time again came on, which demanded courage; and a soul which despised all things present, glowed with Divine love, and valued things unseen before the things which are seen; and he lay aside the flesh with as much ease as one would put off a garment. What then shall we speak of first? The teaching of the apostles which he gave proof of throughout, or his indifference to this present life, or the strictness of his virtue, with which he administered his rule over the Church; which shall we first call to mind? The martyr or the bishop or the apostle. For the grace of the spirit having woven a threefold crown, thus bound it on his holy head, yea rather a manifold crown. For if any one will consider them carefully, he will find each of the crowns, blossoming with other crowns for us.

2. And if you will, let us come first to the praise of his episcopate. Does this seem to be one crown alone? come, then, let us unfold it in speech, and you will see both two, and three, and more produced from it. For I do not wonder at the man alone that he seemed to be worthy of so great an office, but that he obtained this office from those saints, and that the hands of the blessed apostles touched his sacred head. For not even is this a slight thing to be said in his praise, nor because he won greater grace from above, nor only because they caused more abundant energy of the Spirit to come upon him, but because they bore witness that every virtue possessed by man was in him. Now how this is, I tell you. Paul writing to Titus once on a time—and when I say Paul, I do not speak of him alone, but also of Peter and James and John, and the whole band of them; for as in one lyre, the strings are different strings, but the harmony is one, so also in the band of the apostles the persons are different, but the teaching is one, since the artificer is one, I mean the Holy Spirit, who moves their souls, and Paul showing this said, "Whether therefore they, or I, so we preach."[2] This man, then, writing to Titus, and showing what kind of man the bishop ought to be, says, "For the bishop must be blameless as God's steward; not self-willed, not soon angry, no brawler, no striker, not greedy of filthy lucre; but given to hospitality, a lover of good, sober-minded, just, holy, temperate, holding to the faithful word, which is according to the teaching, that he may be able both to exhort in the sound doctrine, and to convict the gainsayers;"[3] and to Timothy again, when writing upon this subject, he says somewhat like this: "If a man seeketh the office of a bishop, he desireth a good work. The bishop, therefore, must be without reproach, the husband of one wife, temperate, sober-minded, orderly, given to hospitality, apt to teach, no brawler, no striker, but gentle, not contentious, no lover of money. Dost thou see what strictness of virtue he demands from the bishop? For as some most excellent painter from life, having mixed many colors, if he be about to furnish an original likeness of the royal form, works with all accuracy, so that all who are copying it, and painting from it, may have a likeness accurately drawn, so accordingly the blessed Paul, as though painting some royal likeness, and furnishing an original sketch of it, having mixed the different colors of virtue, has painted in the features of the office of bishop complete, in order that each of those who mount to that dignity, looking thereupon, may administer their own affairs with just such strictness.

Boldly, therefore, would I say that Ignatius took an accurate impression of the whole of this, in his own soul; and was blameless and without reproach, and neither self-willed, nor soon angry, nor given to wine, nor a striker, but gentle, not contentious, no lover of money, just, holy, temperate, holding to the faithful word which is according to the teaching, sober, sober-minded, orderly, and all the rest which Paul demanded. "And what is the proof of this?" says one. They who said these things ordained him, and they who suggest to others with so great strictness to make proof of those who are about to mount to the throne of this office, would not themselves have done this negligently. But had they not seen all this virtue planted in the soul of this martyr would not have entrusted him with this office. For they knew accurately how great danger besets those who bring about such ordinations, carelessly and hap-hazard. And Paul again, when showing this very thing to the same Timothy wrote and says, "Lay hands suddenly on no man, neither be partaker of other men's sins."[4] What dost thou say? Has an-

---

[1] John x. 11.   [2] 1 Cor. xv. 11.   [3] Titus i. 7–9.   [4] 1 Tim. v. 22.

other sinned, and do I share his blame and his punishment? Yes, says he, the man who authorizes evil; and just as in the case of any one entrusting into the hands of a raging and insane person a sharply pointed sword, with which the madman commits murder, that man who gave the sword incurs the blame; so any one who gives the authority which arises from this office to a man living in evil, draws down on his own head all the fire of that man's sins and audacity. For he who provides the root, this man is the cause of all that springs from it on every side. Dost thou see how in the meanwhile a double crown of the episcopate has appeared, and how the dignity of those who ordained him has made the office more illustrious, bearing witness to every exhibition of virtue in him?

3. Do you wish that I should also reveal to you another crown springing from this very matter? Let us consider the time at which he obtained this dignity. For it is not the same thing to administer the Church now as then, just as it is not the same thing to travel along a road well trodden, and prepared, after many wayfarers; and along one about to be cut for the first time, and containing ruts, and stones, and full of wild beasts, and which has never yet, received any traveller. For now, by the grace of God, there is no danger for bishops, but deep peace on all sides, and we all enjoy a calm, since the Word of piety has been extended to the ends of the world, and our rulers keep the faith with strictness. But then there was nothing of this, but wherever any one might look, precipices and pitfalls, and wars, and fightings, and dangers; both rulers, and kings, and people and cities and nations, and men at home and abroad, laid snares for the faithful. And this was not the only serious thing, but also the fact that many of the believers themselves, inasmuch as they tasted for the first time strange doctrines, stood in need of great indulgence, and were still in a somewhat feeble condition and were often upset. And this was a thing which used to grieve the teachers, no less than the fightings without, nay rather much more. For the fightings without, and the plottings, afforded much pleasure to them on account of the hope of the rewards awaiting them. On this account the apostles returned from the presence of the Sanhedrin rejoicing because they had been beaten;[1] and Paul cries out, saying: "I rejoice in my sufferings,"[2] and he glories in his afflictions everywhere. But the wounds of those at home, and the falls of the brethren, do not suffer them to breathe again, but always, like some most heavy yoke, continually oppress and afflict the neck of their soul. Hear at least how Paul, thus rejoicing in sufferings, is bitterly pained about these. "For who, saith he, is weak, and I am not weak? who is offended, and I burn not?"[3] and again, "I fear lest when I come I shall find you not such as I would, and I be found of you such as ye would not,"[4] and a little afterwards, "Lest when I come again to you, God humble me, and I shall mourn many of those who have sinned before, and have not repented of their uncleanness, and wantonness, and fornication which they have committed."[5] And throughout thou seest that he is in tears and lamentations on account of members of the household, and evermore fearing and trembling for the believers. Just as then we admire the pilot, not when he is able to bring those who are on board safe to shore when the sea is calm, and the ship is borne along by favourable winds, but when the deep is raging and the waves contending, and the passengers themselves within in revolt, and a great storm within and without besets those who are on board, and he is able to steer the ship with all security; so we ought to wonder at, and admire those who then had the Church committed to their hands, much more than those who now have the management of it; when there was a great war without and within, when the plant of the faith was more tender, and needed much care, when, as a newly-born babe, the multitude in the church required much forethought, and the greatest wisdom in any soul destined to nurse it; and in order that ye may more clearly learn, how great crowns they were worthy of, who then had the Church entrusted to them, and how great work and danger there was in undertaking the matter on the threshold and at the beginning, and in being the first to enter upon it, I bring forward for you the testimony of Christ, who pronounces a verdict on these things, and confirms the opinion which has been expressed by me. For when he saw many coming to him, and was wishing to show the apostles that the prophets toiled more than they, he says: "Others have laboured, and ye have entered into their labour."[6] And yet the apostles toiled much more than the prophets. But since they first sowed the word of piety, and won over the untaught souls of men to the truth, the greater part of the work is credited to them. For it is by no means the same thing for one to come and teach after many teachers, and himself to be the first to sow seeds. For that which has been already practised, and has become customary with many, would be easily

---

[1] Acts v. 41.   [2] Col. i. 24.   [3] 2 Cor. xi. 29.   [4] 2 Cor. xii. 20.   [5] 2 Cor. xii. 21.   [6] John iv. 38.

accepted; but that which is now for the first time heard, agitates the mind of the hearers, and gives the teacher a great deal to do. This at least it was which disturbed the audience at Athens, and on this account they turned away from Paul, reproaching him with, "Thou bringest certain strange things to our ears."[1] For if the oversight of the Church now furnishes much weariness and work to those who govern it, consider how double and treble and manifold was the work then, when there were dangers and fighting and snares, and fear continually. It is not possible to set forth in words the difficulty which those saints then encountered, but he alone will know it who comes to it by experience.

4. And I will speak of a fourth crown, arising for us out of this episcopate. What then is this? The fact that he was entrusted with our own native city. For it is a laborious thing indeed to have the oversight of a hundred men, and of fifty alone. But to have on one's hands so great a city, and a population extending to two hundred thousand, of how great virtue and wisdom dost thou think there is a proof? For as in the care of armies, the wiser of the generals have on their hands the more leading and more numerous regiments, so, accordingly, in the care of cities. The more able of the rulers are entrusted with the larger and more populous. And at any rate this city was of much account to God, as indeed He manifested by the very deeds which He did. At all events the master of the whole world, Peter, to whose hands He committed the keys of heaven, whom He commanded to do and to bear all, He bade tarry here for a long period. Thus in His sight our city was equivalent to the whole world. But since I have mentioned Peter, I have perceived a fifth crown woven from him, and this is that this man succeeded to the office after him. For just as any one taking a great stone from a foundation hastens by all means to introduce an equivalent to it, lest he should shake the whole building, and make it more unsound, so, accordingly, when Peter was about to depart from here, the grace of the Spirit introduced another teacher equivalent to Peter, so that the building already completed should not be made more unsound by the insignificance of the successor. We have reckoned up then five crowns, from the importance of the office, from the dignity of those who ordained to it, from the difficulty of the time, from the size of the city, from the virtue of him who transmitted the episcopate to him. Having woven all these, it was lawful to speak of a sixth, and seventh, and more than these; but in order that we may not, by spending the whole time on the consideration of the episcopate, miss the details about the martyr, come from this point, let us pass to that conflict. At one time a grievous warfare was rekindled against the Church, and as though a most grievous tyranny overspread the earth, all were carried off from the midst of the market-place. Not indeed charged with anything monstrous, but because being freed from error, they hastened to piety; because they abstained from the service of demons, because they recognized the true God, and worshipped his only begotten Son, and for things for which they ought to have been crowned, and admired and honoured, for these they were punished and encountered countless tortures, all who embraced the faith, and much more they who had the oversight of the churches. For the devil, being crafty, and apt to contrive plots of this kind, expected that if he took away the shepherds, he would easily be able to scatter the flocks. But He who takes the wise in their craftiness, wishing to show him that men do not govern His church, but that it is He himself who everywhere tends those who believe on Him, agreed that this should be, that he might see, when they were taken away, that the cause of piety was not defeated, nor the word of preaching quenched, but rather increased; that by these very works he might learn both himself, and all those who minister to him, that our affairs are not of men, but that the subject of our teaching has its root on high, from the heavens; and that it is God who everywhere leads the Church, and that it is not possible for him who fights against God, ever to win the day. But the Devil did not only work this evil, but another also not less than this. For not only in the cities over which they presided, did he suffer the Bishops to be slaughtered; but he took them into foreign territory and slew them; and he did this, in anxiety at once to take them when destitute of friends, and hoping to render them weaker with the toil of their journey, which accordingly he did with this saint. For he called him away from our city to Rome, making the course twice as long, expecting to depress his mind both by the length of the way and the number of the days, and not knowing that having Jesus with him, as a fellow traveller, and fellow exile on so long a journey, he rather became the stronger, and afforded more proof of the power that was with him, and to a greater degree knit the Churches together. For the cities which were on the road running together from all sides, encouraged the athlete, and sped him on his way with many supplies, sharing in his conflict

---

[1] Acts xvii. 20.

by their prayers, and intercessions. And they derived no little comfort when they saw the martyr hastening to death with so much readiness, as is consistent in one called to the realms which are in the heaven, and by means of the works themselves, by the readiness and by the joyousness of that noble man, that it was not death to which he was hastening, but a kind of long journey and migration from this world, and ascension to heaven; and he departed teaching these things in every city, both by his words, and by his deeds, and as happened in the case of the Jews, when they bound Paul, and sent him to Rome, and thought that they were sending him to death, they were sending a teacher to the Jews who dwelt there. This indeed accordingly happened in the case of Ignatius in larger measure. For not to those alone who dwell in Rome, but to all the cities lying in the intervening space, he went forth as a wonderful teacher, persuading them to despise the present life, and to think naught of the things which are seen, and to love those which are to come, to look towards heaven, and to pay no regard to any of the terrors of this present life. For on this and on more than this, by means of his works, he went on his way instructing them, as a sun rising from the east, and hastening to the west. But rather more brilliant than this, for this is wont to run on high, bringing material light, but Ignatius shone below, imparting to men's souls the intellectual light of doctrine. And that light on departing into the regions of the west, is hidden and straightway causes the night to come on. But this on departing to the regions of the west, shone there more brilliantly, conferring the greatest benefits to all along the road. And when he arrived at the city, even *that* he instructed in Christian wisdom. For on this account God permitted him there to end his life, so that this man's death might be instructive to all who dwell in Rome. For *we* by the grace of God need henceforward no evidence, being rooted in the faith. But they who dwelt in Rome, inasmuch as these was great impiety there, required more help. On this account both Peter and Paul, and this man after them, were all slain there, partly, indeed, in order that they might purify with their own blood, the city which had been defiled with blood of idols, and partly in order that they might by their works afford a proof of the resurrection of the crucified Christ, persuading those who dwell in Rome, that they would not with so much pleasure disdain this present life, did they not firmly persuade themselves that they were about to ascend to the crucified Jesus, and to see him in the heavens.

For in reality it is the greatest proof of the resurrection that the slain Christ should show forth so great power after death, as to persuade living men to despise both country and home and friends, and acquaintance and life itself, for the sake of confessing him, and to choose in place of present pleasures, both stripes and dangers and death. For these are not the achievements of any dead man, nor of one remaining in the tomb but of one risen and living,. Since how couldest thou account, when he was alive, for all the Apostles who companied with him becoming weaker through fear to betray their teachers and to flee and depart; but when he died, for not only Peter and Paul, but even Ignatius, who had not even seen him, nor enjoyed his companionship, showing such earnestness as to lay down life itself for his sake?

5. In order then that all who dwell in Rome might learn that these things are a reality, God allowed that there the saint should be perfected,[1] and that this was the reason I will guarantee from the very manner of his death. For not outside the walls, in a dungeon, nor even in a court of justice, nor in some corner, did he receive the sentence which condemned him, but in the midst of the theatre, while the whole city was seated above him, he underwent this form of martyrdom, wild beasts being let loose upon him, in order that he might plant his trophy against the Devil, beneath the eyes of all, and make all spectators emulous of his own conflicts. Not dying thus nobly only, but dying even with pleasure. For not as though about to be severed from life, but as called to a better and more spiritual life, so he beheld the wild beasts gladly. Whence is this manifest? From the words which he uttered when about to die, for when he heard that this manner of punishment awaited him, "may I have joy," said he, "of these wild beasts."[2] For such are the loving. For they receive with pleasure whatever they may suffer for the sake of those who are beloved, and they seem to have their desire satisfied when what happens to them is more than usually grievous. Which happened, therefore, in this man's case. For not by his death alone, but also by his readiness he studied to emulate the apostles, and hearing that they, after they had been scourged retired with joy, himself too wished to imitate his teachers, not only by his death, but by his joy. On this account he said, "may I have joy of thy wild beasts," and much milder than the tongue of the tyrant did he consider the mouths of these; and very reasonably. For while that invited

---
[1] Sc., suffer a martyr's death.
[2] Quoted from Epistle of Ignatius to the Romans, c. v.

him to Gehenna, their mouths escorted him to a kingdom. When, therefore, he made an end of life there, yea rather, when he ascended to heaven, he departed henceforward crowned. For this also happened through the dispensation of God, that he restored him again to us, and distributed the martyr to the cities. For that city received his blood as it dropped, but ye were honoured with his remains, ye enjoyed his episcopate, they enjoyed his martyrdom. They saw him in conflict, and victorious, and crowned, but ye have him continually. For a little time God removed him from you, and with greater glory granted him again to you. And as those who borrow money, return with interest what they receive, so also God, using this valued treasure of yours, for a little while, and having shown it to that city, with greater brilliancy gave it back to you. Ye sent forth a Bishop, and received a martyr; ye sent him forth with prayers, and ye received him with crowns; and not only ye, but 'all the cities which intervene. For how do ye think that they behaved when they saw his remains being brought back? What pleasure was produced! how they rejoiced! with what applause on all sides they beset the crowned one! For as with a noble athlete, who has wrestled down all his antagonists, and who comes forth with radiant glory from the arena, the spectators receive him, and do not suffer him to tread the earth, bringing him home on their shoulders, and besetting him with countless praises: so also the cities in order receiving this saint then from Rome, and bearing him upon their shoulders as far as this city, escorted the crowned one with praises, celebrating the champion, in song; laughing the Devil to scorn, because his artifice was turned against him, and what he thought to do against the martyr, this turned out for his behoof. Then, indeed, he profited, and encouraged all the cities; and from that time to this day he enriches this city, and as some perpetual treasure, drawn upon every day, yet not failing, makes all who partake of it more prosperous, so also this blessed Ignatius filleth those who come to him with blessings, with boldness, nobleness of spirit, and much courage, and so sendeth them home.

Not only to-day, therefore, but every day let us go forth to him, plucking spiritual fruits from him. For it is, it is possible for him who comes hither with faith to gather the fruit of many good things. For not the bodies only, but the very sepulchres of the saints have been filled with spiritual grace. For if in the case of Elisha this happened, and a corpse when it touched the sepulchre, burst the bands of death and returned to life again,[1] much rather now, when grace is more abundant, when the energy of the spirit is greater, is it possible that one touching a sepulchre, with faith, should win great power; thence on this account God allowed us the remains of the saints, wishing to lead by them us to the same emulation, and to afford us a kind of haven, and a secure consolation for the evils which are ever overtaking us. Wherefore I beseech you all, if any is in despondency, if in disease, if under insult, if in any other circumstance of this life, if in the depth of sins, let him come hither with faith, and he will lay aside all those things, and will return with much joy, having procured a lighter conscience from the sight alone. But more, it is not only necessary that those who are in affliction should come hither, but if any one be in cheerfulness, in glory, in power, in much assurance towards God, let not this man despise the benefit. For coming hither and beholding this saint, he will keep these noble possessions unmoved, persuading his own soul to be moderate by the recollection of this man's mighty deeds, and not suffering his conscience by the mighty deeds to be lifted up to any self conceit. And it is no slight thing for those in prosperity not to be puffed up at their good fortune, but to know how to bear their prosperity with moderation, so that the treasure is serviceable to all, the resting place is suitable, for the fallen, in order that they may escape from their temptations, for the fortunate, that their success may remain secure, for those in weakness indeed, that they may return to health, and for the healthy, that they may not fall into weakness. Considering all which things, let us prefer this way of spending our time, to all delight, all pleasure, in order that rejoicing at once, and profiting, we may be able to become partakers with these saints, both of their dwelling and of their home, through the prayers of the saints themselves, through the grace and lovingkindness of our Lord Jesus Christ, with whom be glory to the Father with the Holy Spirit, now and always forever and ever amen.

[1] 2 Kings xiii. 21.

ON THE HOLY MARTYR, S. BABYLAS.

1. I WAS anxious to-day to pay the debt which I promised you when I was lately here. But what am I to do? In the meanwhile, the blessed Babylas has appeared, and has called me to himself, uttering no voice, but attracting our attention by the brightness of his countenance. Be ye not, therefore, displeased at the delay in my payment; at all events, the longer the time is, the more the interest will increase. For we will deposit this money with interest.[1] Since thus did the master command who entrusted it to us. Being confident, therefore, about what is lent, that both the principal and the profit await you, let us not pass by the gain which falls in our way to-day, but revel in the noble actions of the blessed Babylas.

How, indeed, he presided over the Church which is among us, and saved that sacred ship, in storm, and in wave, and billow; and what a bold front he showed to the emperor, and how he lay down his life for the sheep and underwent that blessed slaughter; these things and such as these, we will leave to the elder among our teachers, and to our common father, to speak of. For the more remote matters, the aged can relate to you but as many things as happened lately, and within our lifetime, these, I a young man will relate to you, I mean those after death, those after the burial of the martyr, those which happened while he remained in the suburbs of the city. And I know indeed that the Greeks will laugh at my promise, if I promise to speak of the noble deeds after death and burial of one who was buried, and had crumbled to dust. We shall not assuredly on this account keep silence, but on this very account shall especially speak, in order that by showing this marvel truly, we may turn their laughter upon their own head. For of an ordinary man there would be no noble deeds after death. But of a martyr, many and great deeds, not in order that he might become more illustrious (for he has no need of glory from the multitude), but that thou, the unbeliever mayest learn that the death of the martyrs is not death, but the beginning of a better life, and the prelude of a more spiritual conversation, and a change from the worse to the better. Do not then look at the fact, that the mere body of the martyr lies destitute of energy of soul; but observe this, that a greater power takes its place by the side of it, different from the soul itself—I mean the grace of the Holy Spirit, which pleads to all on behalf of the resurrection, by means of the wonders which it works. For if God has granted greater power to bodies dead and crumbled to dust, than to all living, much more will he grant to them a better life than the former, and a longer, at the time of the bestowal of his crowns; what then are this saint's noble deeds? But be not disturbed, if we take our discourse a little further back. For they who wish to display their portraits to advantage, do not uncover them until they have placed the spectators a little way off from the picture, making the view clearer by the distance. Do you then also have patience with me while I direct my discourse into the past.

For when Julian who surpassed all in impiety, ascended the imperial throne, and grasped the despotic sceptre, straightway he lifted up his hands against the God who created him, and ignored his benefactor, and looking from the earth beneath to the heavens, howled after the manner of mad dogs, who alike bay at those who do not feed them and those who do feed them. But he rather was mad with a more savage madness than theirs. For they indeed turn from, and hate their friends and strangers alike. But this man used to fawn upon demons, strangers to his salvation, and used to worship them with every mode of worship. But his benefactor, and Saviour, and him who spared not the only Begotten, for his sake, he turned from and used to hate, and made havoc of the cross, the very thing which uplifted the whole world when it was lying prostrate, and drave away the darkness on all sides, and brought in light more brilliant than the sunbeams; nor yet even then did he desist from his frenzy, but promised that he would tear the nation of the Galilæans, out of the midst of the world; for thus he was wont to call us; and yet if he thought the names of the Christians an abomination, and Christianity itself to be full of much shame, for what reason did he not desire to put us to shame by that means, but with a strange name? Yea because he knew clearly, that to be called by what belongs to Christ, is a great ornament not only to men, but to angels, and to the powers above. On this account he set everything in motion, so as to strip us of this ornament, and put a stop to the preaching of it. But this was impossible, O wretched and miserable man! as it was impossible to destroy the heaven and to quench the sun, and to shake and cast down the foundations of the earth, and those things

---
[1] Luke xix. 23.

Christ foretold, thus saying: "Heaven and earth shall pass away, but my words shall not pass away."[1]

Well, thou dost not submit to Christ's words; accept therefore the utterance which thus his deeds give. For I indeed having been privileged to know what the declaration of God is, how strong, how invincible a thing, have believed that is more trustworthy than the order of nature, and than experience in all matters. But do thou still creeping on the ground, and agitated with the investigations of human reasoning, receive the witness of the deeds. I gainsay nothing. I strive not.

2. What then do the deeds say? Christ said that it was easier for heaven and earth to be destroyed, than for any of his words to fail.[2] The emperor contradicted these words, and threatened to destroy his decrees. Where then is the emperor who threatened these things? He is perished and is corrupted, and is now in Hades, awaiting the inevitable punishment. But where is Christ who uttered these decrees? In Heaven, on the right hand of the Father, occupying the highest throne of glory; where are the blasphemous words of the Emperor, and his unchastened tongue? They are become ashes, and dust and the food of worms. Where is the sentence of Christ? It shines forth by the very truth of the deed, receiving its lustre from the issue of the events, as from a golden column. And yet the emperor left nothing undone, when about to raise war against us, but used to call prophets together, and summon sorcerers, and everything was full of demons and evil spirits.

What then was the return for this worship? The overturning of cities, the bitterest famine of all famines. For ye know doubtless, and remember, how empty indeed the market place was of wares, and the workshops full of confusion, when everyone strove to snatch up what came first and to depart. And why do I speak of famine, when the very fountains of waters were failing, fountains which by the abundance of their stream, used to eclipse the rivers. But since I have mentioned the fountains, come, forthwith, let us go up to Daphne, and conduct our discourse to the noble deeds of the martyr. Although you desire me still to parade the indecencies of the Greeks, although I too desire this, let us abstain; for wherever the commemoration of a martyr is, there certainly also is the shame of the Greeks. This emperor then, going up to Daphne used to weary Apollo, praying, supplicating, entreating, so that the events of the future might be foretold to him. What then did the prophet, the great God of the Greeks? "The dead prevent me from uttering," saith he, "but break open the graves, dig up the bones, move the dead." What could be more impious than these commands? The Demon of grave-robbing, introduces strange laws and devises new methods of expelling strangers. Who ever heard of the dead being driven forth? who ever saw lifeless bodies ordered to be moved as he commanded, overturning from their foundations the common laws of nature. For the laws of nature are common to all men, that he who departs this life should be hidden in the earth, and delivered over for burial, and be covered up in the bosom of the earth the mother of all; and these laws, neither Greek, barbarian, Scythian, nor if there be any more savage than they, ever changed, but all reverence them, and keep them, and thus they are sacred and venerated by all. But the Demon raises his mask, and with bare head, resists the common laws of nature. For the dead, he says, are a pollution. The dead are not a pollution, a most wicked demon, but a wicked intention is an abomination. But if one must say something startling, the bodies of the living full of evil, are more polluting than those of the dead. For the one minister to the behests of the mind, but the other lie unmoved. Now that which is unmoved, and destitute of all perception would be free from all accusation. Not that I even would say that the bodies of the living are by nature polluting; but that everywhere a wicked and perverted intention is open to accusations from all.

The dead body then is not a pollution O Apollo, but to persecute a maiden who wishes to be modest, and to outrage the dignity of a virgin, and to lament at the failure of the shameless deed, this is worthy of accusation, and punishment. There were at all events, many wonderful and great prophets among ourselves, who spake also many things concerning the future, and they in no case used to bid those who asked them to dig up the bones of the departed. Yea Ezekiel standing near the bones themselves was not only not hindered by them, but added flesh, and nerves and skin to them, and brought them back to life again.[3] But the great Moses did not stand near the bones of the dead, but bearing off the whole dead body of Joseph, thus foretold things to come.[4] And very reasonably, for their words were the grace of the Holy Spirit. But the words of these, a deceit, and a lie which is no wise able to be concealed. For that these things were an excuse, and pretence and that he feared the blessed Babylas, is manifest from what the emperor did. For leaving all the other dead, he only moved that martyr. And

---

[1] Matt. xxiv. 35.   [2] Luke xvi. 17.   [3] Ez. xxxvii.   [4] Ex. xiii. 19.

yet if he did these things, in disgust at him, and not in fear, it were necessary that he should order the coffin to be broken, thrown into the sea, carried to the desert, be made to disappear by some other method of destruction; for this is the part of one who is disgusted. Thus God did when he spake to the Hebrews about the abominations of the Gentiles. He bade their statues to be broken, not to bring their abominations from the suburbs to the city.

3. The martyr then was moved, but the demon not even then enjoyed freedom from fear, but straightway learned that it is possible to move the bones of a martyr, but not to escape his hands. For as soon as the coffin was drawn into the city, a thunderbolt came from above upon the head of his image, and burnt it all up. And yet, if not before, then at least there was likelihood that the impious emperor would be angry, and that he would send forth his anger against the testimony of the martyr. But not even then did he dare, so great fear possessed him. But although he saw that the burning was intolerable, and knew the cause accurately; he kept quiet. And this is not only wonderful that he did not destroy the testimony, but that he not even dared to put the roof on to the temple again. For he knew, he knew, that the stroke was divinely sent, and he feared lest by forming any further plan, he should call down that fire upon his own head. On this account he endured to see the shrine of Apollo brought to so great desolation; For there was no other cause, on account of which he did not rectify that which had happened, but fear alone. For which reason he unwillingly kept quiet, and knowing this left as much reproach to the demon, as distinction to the martyr. For the walls are now standing, instead of trophies, uttering a voice clearer than a trumpet. To those in Daphne, to those in the city, to those who arrive from far off, to those who are with us, to those men which shall be hereafter, they declare everything by their appearance, the wrestling, the struggle, the victory of the martyr. For it is likely that he who dwells far off from the suburb, when he sees the chapel of the saint deprived of a shrine, and the temple of Apollo deprived of its roof would ask the reason of each of these things; and then after learning the whole history would depart hence. Such are the noble deeds of the martyr after death, wherefore I count your city blessed, that ye have shown much zeal about this holy man. For then, when he returned from Daphne, all our city poured forth into the road, and the market places were empty of men, and the houses were empty of women, and the bedchambers were destitute of maidens. Thus also every age and each sex passed forth from the city, as if to receive a father long absent who was returning from sojourn far away. And you indeed gave him back to the band of fellow enthusiasts. But the grace of God did not suffer him to remain there for good, but again removed him beyond the river,[1] so that many parts of the country were filled with the sweet savor of the martyr. Neither even when he came hither was he destined to be alone, but he quickly received, a neighbor, and a fellow-lodger, and one of similar life.[2] For he shared with him the same dignity, and for the sake of religion shewed forth equal boldness. Wherefore he obtained the same abode as he, this wonderful man being no vain imitator, as it seems, of the martyr. For for so long a time he laboured there, sending letters continually to the emperor, wearying the authorities, and bringing the ministry of the body to bear upon the martyr. For ye know, doubtless, and remember that when the midday summer sun possessed the heaven, he together with his acquaintances, used to walk thither everyday, not as spectator only, but also, as intending to be a sharer in what was going on. For he often handled stone, and dragged a rope, and listened, in advance of the workmen themselves, to one who wanted to erect any building, For he knew, he knew what rewards lie in store for him for these things. And on this account he continued doing service to the martyrs, not only by splendid buildings nor even by continual feasts, but by a better method than these. And what is this? He imitates their life, emulates their courage, throughout according to his ability he keeps the image of the martyrs alive, in himself. For see, they gave their bodies to the slaughter, he has mortified the members of his flesh which are upon the earth. They stopped the flame of fire, he quenched the flame of lust. They fought against the teeth of beasts, but this man bore off the most dangerous of our passions, anger. For all these things let us give thanks to God, because he hath thus granted us noble martyrs, and pastors worthy of martyrs, for the perfecting of the saints, for the edifying of the body of Christ[3] with whom be glory, honor, and might to the Father, with the Holy and lifegiving Spirit, now and always, for ever and ever. Amen.

---

[1] Viz., to the church built on the other side of the Orontes, where the reliques of the saint finally remained.
[2] Meletius, Bishop of Antioch, a man of very saintly life who died in 379 and was buried by the side of St. Babylas in the church which he had been active in erecting, mentioned in the preceding note.
[3] Eph. iv. 12.

ST. CHRYSOSTOM:

HOMILY

CONCERNING LOWLINESS OF MIND; AND COMMENTARY ON PHILIPPIANS I. 18

TRANSLATED BY

R. BLACKBURN, M.A.,

RECTOR OF SELHAM, SUSSEX, AND LATE FELLOW OF BRASENOSE COLLEGE, OXFORD.

CONTENTS.

		PAGE
1.	How much good there is in humility, and how much evil in arrogance	147
2.	The uselessness of other virtues without humility	148
3.	Misinterpretation of the passage in Philipp. i. 18	148
4.	The circumstances under which St. Paul wrote that Epistle	149
5.	His tender care for all his converts	150
6.	Examples of this	150
7.	Love knows no distinctions of rank and is insensible to fear	151
8.	St. Paul's captivity a source of encouragement to his disciples	151
9.	The true meaning of the passage in Philipp. i. 18	152
10.	How St. Paul turned evil to good account	152
11.	An exhortation to prayer	153
12.	The efficacy of persevering prayer	153
13.	A warning against despondency	154

CONCERNING LOWLINESS OF MIND.

HOMILY.

AGAINST THOSE WHO IMPROPERLY USE THE APOSTOLIC DECLARATION WHICH SAYS, "WHETHER IN PRETENCE, OR IN SINCERITY, CHRIST IS PREACHED:" (Phil. i. 18), AND ABOUT HUMBLENESS OF MIND.

INTRODUCTION.

THERE is an allusion at the beginning of this Homily to some remarks recently made on the parable of the Pharisee and the Publican. These occur in Chrysostom's fifth Homily against the Anomœans, one of a set of Homilies which, from internal evidence, may be assigned to the close of the year 386, or beginning of 387. The following homily therefore was delivered at Antioch, probably just before Christmas 386. There were some persons who explained the words of St. Paul cited in the title as signifying that provided Christ was preached it mattered not whether the actual doctrines taught were true or heretical. The main object of the homily is to vindicate the language of the Apostle from this erroneous and mischievous interpretation.

1. When lately we made mention of the Pharisee and the publican, and hypothetically yoked two chariots out of virtue and vice,[1] we pointed out each truth, how great is the gain of humbleness of mind, and how great the damage of pride. For this, even when conjoined with righteousness and fastings and tithes, fell behind; while that, even when yoked with sin, out-stripped the Pharisee's pair, even although the charioteer it had was a poor one. For what was worse than the publican? But all the same since he made his soul contrite, and called himself a sinner; which indeed he was; he surpassed the Pharisee, who had both fastings to tell of and tithes; and was removed from any vice. On account of what, and through what? Because even if he was removed from greed of gain and robbery, he had rooted over his soul[2] the mother of all evils—vain-glory and pride. On this account Paul also exhorts and says "Let each one prove his own work; and then he will have his ground of boasting for himself, and not for the other." Whereas he publicly came forward[3] as an accuser of the whole world;[4] and said that he himself was better than all living men. And yet even if he had set himself before ten only, or if five, or if two, or if one, not even was this endurable; but as it was, he not only set himself before the whole world, but also accused all men. On this account he fell behind in the running. And just as a ship, after having run through innumerable surges, and having escaped many storms, then in the very mouth of the harbour having been dashed against some rock, loses the whole treasure which is stowed away in her—so truly did this Pharisee, after having undergone the labours of the fasting, and of all the

---

[1] Chrysostom is referring to his Homily "on the incomprehensible: against the Anomœans," v. 6, 7. "Ἅρματα δύο ποίησον τῷ λόγῳ, κ.τ.λ., "the Pharisee's pair of horses being Righteousness and Pride; the publican's, Sin and Humility.
[2] Ἐπὶ τῆς ψυχῆς. The fibres spreading and entwining over it.
[3] Παρῆλθεν. The word used at Athens of orators rising to speak. Παρελθὼν δέ ἔλεξε τοιάδε. *Thucyd.* ii. 59.
[4] Fox said in parliament, "I cannot draw an indictment against humanity."

rest of his virtue, since he did not master his tongue, in the very harbour underwent shipwreck of his cargo.[1] For the going home from prayer, whence he ought to have derived gain, having rather been so greatly damaged, is nothing else than undergoing shipwreck in harbour.

2. Knowing therefore these things, beloved, even if we should have mounted to the very pinnacle of virtue, let us consider ourselves last of all; having learned that pride is able to cast down even from the heavens themselves him who takes not heed, and humbleness of mind to bear up on high from the very abyss of sins him who knows how to be sober. For this it was that placed the publican before the Pharisee; whereas that, pride I mean and an overweening spirit, surpassed even an incorporeal power, that of the devil; while humbleness of mind and the acknowledgment of his own sins committed brought the robber into Paradise before the Apostles. Now if the confidence which they who confess their own sins effect for themselves is so great, they who are conscious to themselves of many good qualities, yet humble their own souls, how great crowns will they not win.[2] For when sinfulness be put together with humbleness of mind it runs with such ease as to pass and out-strip righteousness combined with pride. If therefore thou have put it to with righteousness, whither will it not reach ? through how many heavens will it not pass ? By the throne of God itself surely it will stay its course;[3] in the midst of the angels, with much confidence. On the other hand if pride, having been yoked with righteousness, by the excess and weight of its own wickedness had strength enough to drag down *its* confidence; if it be put together with sinfulness, into how deep a hell will it not be able to precipitate him who has it? These things I say, not in order that we should be careless of righteousness, but that we should avoid pride; not that we should sin, but that we should be soberminded. For humbleness of mind is the foundation of the love of wisdom which pertains to us. Even if thou shouldest have built a superstructure of things innumerable; even if almsgiving, even if prayers, even if fastings, even if all virtue; unless this have first been laid as a foundation, all will be built upon it[4] to no purpose and in vain; and it will fall down easily, like that building which had been placed on the sand.[5] For there is no one, no one of our good deeds, which does not need this; there is no one which separate from this will be able to stand. But even if thou shouldest mention temperance, even if virginity, even if despising of money, even if anything whatever, all are unclean and accursed and loathsome, humbleness of mind being absent. Everywhere therefore let us take her with us,[6] in words, in deeds, in thoughts, and with this let us build these (graces).

3. But the things belonging to humbleness of mind have been sufficiently spoken of; not for the value of the virtue;[7] for no one will be able to celebrate it in accordance with its value; but for the intelligence of your love. For well do I know that even from the few things that have been said you will embrace it with much zeal. But since it is also necessary to make clear and manifest the apostolic saying which has been to-day read; seeming as it does to many to afford a pretext for indolence; so that some may not, providing for themselves hence a certain frigid defence, neglect their own salvation—to this let us direct our discourse. What then is this saying ? "Whether in pretence," it says, "or in sincerity,[8] Christ is preached."[9] This many wrest absolutely[10] and just as happens, without reading what precedes and what comes after it; but having cut it off from the sequence of the remaining members, to the destruction of their own soul they put it forward to the more indolent. For attempting to seduce them from the sound faith; then seeing them afraid and trembling; on the ground of its not being without danger to do this,[11] and desiring to relieve their fear, they bring forward this apostolic declaration, saying, Paul conceded this, by saying, "Whether in pretence or in sincerity, let Christ be proclaimed." But these things are not (true), they are not. For in the first place he did not say "let him be proclaimed," but "he is proclaimed," and the difference between this and that is wide. For the saying "let him be proclaimed" belongs to a lawgiver; but the saying "he is proclaimed" to one announcing the event. For that Paul does not ordain a law that there should be heresies, but draws away all who attended to him, hear what he says, "If any one preaches to you a gospel besides what ye have received, let him be ana-

---

[1] This must be the sense ; though there is some little difficulty in the original.
[2] ἐπιτεύξονται, Lit. light upon : as on the treasure of the parable, "hid in a field."
[3] Its race being ended ; the goal won.
[4] That is on whatever foundation, other than that which may have been laid.
[5] Οἰκοδομὴν τεθεῖσαν. "Οἱ περὶ Δωδώνην δυσχείμερον· οἰκί ἔθεντο." Iliad. B. 750.
[6] Παραλαμβάνωμεν. Take her to dwell with us. Comp. Chrysostom's expression, συζῆν ἀρετῇ.
[7] Κατόρθωμα. The highest form of duty ; Perfectum officium quod Græci, κατόρθωμα, Cic. De Off. i. 3.
[8] ἀλήθεια here is that of Aristotle's Ethics : sincerity.
[9] Philip. i. 18.
[10] Ἀπλῶς. without reference to circumstances.
[11] τοῦτο ποιεῖν, i. e., to be in that state. Ποιεῖν is not seldom used where παθεῖν might be expected.

thema, were it even I, were it even an angel from the heavens."[1] Now he would not have anathematized both himself and an angel, if he had known the act to be without danger. And again—"I am jealous of you with a jealousy of God," he says; "for I have betrothed you to one husband a chaste virgin: and fear lest at some time, as the serpent beguiled Eve by his wiliness, so your thoughts should be corrupted from the singleness that is towards Christ."[2] See, he both set down singleness, and granted no allowance. For if there were allowance, there was no danger; and if there was no danger Paul would not have feared: and Christ would not also have commanded that the tares should be burned up, if it were a thing indifferent to attend to this one or that or another; or to all indiscriminately.[3]

4. What ever then is what is meant? I wish to narrate to you the whole history from a point a little earlier;[4] for it is needful to know in what circumstances Paul was when he was writing these things by letter. In what circumstances therefore was he? In prison and chains and intolerable perils. Whence is this manifest? From the epistle itself. For earlier than this he says, "Now I wish you to know, brethren, that the circumstances in which I am have come rather to the furtherance[5] of the Gospel; so that my bonds have become manifest in Christ in the whole Court, and to all the others; and a good many[6] of the brethren, trusting to my bonds, the more exceedingly dare fearlessly to speak the word."[7] Now Nero had then cast him into prison. For just as some robber having set foot in the house, while all are sleeping, when stealing every thing,[8] if he see any one having lit a lamp, both extinguishes the light and slays him who holds the lamp, in order that he may be allowed in security to steal and rob the property of others; so truly also the Cæsar Nero then, just as any robber and burglar while all were sleeping a deep and unconscious slumber; robbing the property of all, breaking into marriage chambers,[9] subverting houses, displaying every form of wickedness; when he saw Paul having lighted a lamp throughout the world; (the word of his teaching;) and reproving his wickedness, exerted himself both to extinguish what was preached, and to put the teachers out of the way; in order that he might be allowed with authority to do anything he pleased; and after binding that holy man, cast him into prison. It was at that time then that the blessed Paul wrote these things. Who would not have been astounded? who would not have marvelled? or rather who could adequately have been astounded at and admired that noble and heaven-reaching soul; in that, while bound in Rome and imprisoned, at so great a distance as that, he wrote a letter to the Philippians? For you know how great is the distance between Macedonia and Rome. But neither did the length of the way, nor the amount of time (required), nor the press of business, nor the peril and the dangers coming one upon another, nor anything else, drive out his love for and remembrance of the disciples; but he retained them all in his mind; and not so strongly were his hands bound with the chains as his soul was bound together and rivetted by his longing for the disciples:[10] which very thing itself indeed also declaring, in the preface of the Epistle he said, "On account of my having you in my heart, both in my bonds, and in the defence and confirmation of the Gospel."[11] And just as a King, having ascended upon his throne at morningtide and taken his seat in the royal courts, immediately receives from all quarters innumerable letters; so truly he also, just as in royal courts, seated in the dungeon, both received and sent his letters in far greater number; the nations from all quarters referring to his wisdom every thing about[12] what had taken place among themselves; and he administered more business than the reigning monarch in proportion to his having had a larger dominion entrusted to him. For in truth God had brought and put into his hands not those who inhabited the country of the Romans only, but also all the barbarians, both land and sea. And by way of showing this he said to the Romans, "Now I would not that ye should be ignorant, brethren, that ofttimes I have purposed to come to you, and have been hindered until the present; in order that I might have some fruit also among you, as among the rest of the Gentiles too. Both to Greeks and barbarians, both to wise and those without understanding I am a debtor."[13] Every day therefore he was in anxious thought at one moment for Corinthians, at another for Macedonians; how Philippians, how Cappadocians, how Galatians, how Athenians, how they who inhabited Pon-

---

[1] Gal. i. 8, 9.
[2] 2 Cor. xi. 2, 3. Ἀπὸ τῆς ἁπλότητος τῆς εἰς Χριστόν. That is, from the singleness of affection and fidelity which must be maintained towards Him in that relation. Matt. vi. 22-24.
[3] Ἁπλῶς. Without reference to the truth of their doctrine.
[4] As from a fountain, lying higher, ἄνωθεν; *ab origine*.
[5] Προκοπήν, removal, clearing away, of obstacles to its advance.
[6] Τοὺς πλείονας. In the Greek of that day — πλείονας: like Lat., *plures*, a modified and weakened comparative.
[7] Philip. i. 12-14.
[8] Ὑφαιρούμενος, lit. secretly taking for himself. Lat. *surripio*. So, steal, stealth.
[9] Comp. Cic. in Verr. II, 1, 3, *non adulterum, sed expugnatorem pudicitiæ*.
[10] Πόθῳ, *desiderio*: absence being a test of love.
[11] Philip. i. 7.
[12] Ὑπέρ. As Lat. super. *Multa super Priamo rogitans, super Hectore multa*, Virg. Æn. i. 750.
[13] Rom. i. 13, 14.

tus, how all together were. But all the same, having had the whole world put into his hands, he continually cared not for entire nations only, but also for each single man; and now indeed he despatched a letter on behalf of Onesimus, and now on behalf of him who among the Corinthians had committed fornication. For neither used he to regard this—that it was the individual who had sinned and needed advocacy; but that it was a human being; a human being, the living thing most precious to God; and for whose sake the Father had not spared even the Only-begotten.

5. For do not tell me that this or that man is a runaway slave, or a robber or thief, or laden with countless faults, or that he is a mendicant and abject, or of low value and worthy of no account; but consider that for his sake the Christ died; and this sufficeth thee for a ground for all solicitude. Consider what sort of person *he* must be, whom Christ valued at so high a price as not to have spared even his own blood. For neither, if a king had chosen to sacrifice himself on any one's behalf, should we have sought out another demonstration of his being some one great and of deep interest to the King—*I* fancy not—for his death would suffice to show the love of him who had died towards him. But as it is not man, not angel, not archangel; but the Lord of the heavens himself, the only-begotten Son of God himself, having clothed himself with flesh, freely gave himself on our behalf. Shall we not do everything, and take every trouble, so that the men who have been thus valued may enjoy every solicitude at our hands? And what kind of defence shall we have? what allowance? This at least is the very thing by way of declaring which Paul also said, "Do not by thy meat destroy him for whose sake Christ died."[1] For desiring to shame, and to bring to solicitude, and to persuade to care for their neighbours, those who despise their brethren, and look down upon them as being weak, instead of all[2] else he set down the Master's death.

Sitting then in the prison he wrote the letter to the Philippians from that so great distance. For such as this is the love that is according to God:[3] it is interrupted by no one of human things, since it has its roots from above in the heavens[4] and its recompense. And what says he? "Now I desire that ye should know, brethren."[5] Seest thou solicitude for his scholars? seest thou a teacher's carefulness? Hear too of loving affection of scholars towards their teacher, that thou mayest know that this was what made them strong and unconquerable—the being bound together with one another. For if "Brother helped by brother is as a strong city;"[6] far more so many bound together by the bonds of love would have entirely repulsed the plotting of the wicked demon. That indeed then Paul was bound up with the disciples, requires not even any demonstration further nor argument for us, since in truth even when in bonds he anxiously cared for them, and each day he was also dying for them, burning with his longing.

6. And that the disciples too were bound up with Paul with all perfectness;[7] and that not men only, but women also, hear what he says about Phœbe. "Now I commend[8] to you Phœbe the sister, being a deaconess of the Church which is in Cenchreæ; that ye may receive her in the Lord worthily of the saints, and stand by her, in whatever matter she may require you, since[9] she has proved a helper[10] of many; and of me myself."[11] But in this instance he bore witness to her of her zeal so far as help went (only;)[12] but Priscilla and Aquila went as far even as death for Paul's sake; and about them he thus writes, saying, "Aquila and Priscilla salute you, who for my life's sake laid down their own neck;"[13] for death clearly. And about another again writing to these very persons he says, "Because he went as far as death; having counselled ill for his life, in order that he might supply your deficiency in your service towards me."[14] Seest thou how they loved their teacher? how they regarded his rest[15] before their own life? On this account no one surpassed them then. Now this I say, not that we may hear only, but that we may also imitate; and not to the ruled only, but also to those who rule is what we say addressed; in order that both scholars may display much solicitude about their teachers, and the teachers may have the same loving affection as Paul about those placed under them; not those present only, but also those who are far off. For also Paul, dwelling in the whole world just as in one house, thus

---

[1] Rom. xiv. 15.
[2] Ἀντὶ. It may mean, as an equivalent, in the balance; comprehending and out-weighing all other considerations.
[3] Ἡ κατὰ Θεὸν ἀγάπη, "ἡ γὰρ κατὰ Θεὸν λύπη μετάνοιαν εἰς σωτηρίαν ἐργάζεται." 2 Cor. vii. 10.
[4] Ἐκ τῶν οὐρανῶν. Chrysostom seems to use ἐκ and not ἐν, in reference to ἄνωθεν preceding. This is the Greek idiom; αὐτὸν ἐνὶ Τροίῃ, Il. B. 237, but αὐτόθεν ἐξ ἕδρης, T. 77.
[5] Philip. i. 12.
[6] Prov. xviii. 19. In our version it stands, "A brother offended is (harder to be won than) a strong city." Chrysostom quotes exactly from the LXX. On the other hand, Βοηθέω, as governing a dative, has no passive voice, at least in classical Greek. Βοηθούμενος may, as here, be used by the Alexandrians.
[7] Ἀκριβείας. As a chain accurately and closely linked; so as not to be severed asunder.
[8] Συνίστημι. Lit. establish, vouch for her.
[9] Ἥτις, answering to Lat. *quæ* with subjunctive, expressing the cause.
[10] Προστάτις, patroness: a relation well-known in Greece.
[11] Rom. xvi. 1, 2.
[12] *i. e.*, μόνον; a common ellipsis in Chrysostom.
[13] Rom. xvi. 3, 4. [14] Philip. ii. 30.
[15] From trouble, "ἄνεσιν." Comp. 2 Cor. vii. 5.

continually took thought for the salvation of all; and having dismissed every thing of his own; bonds and troubles and stripes and straits, watched over and inquired into each day, in what state the affairs of the disciples were; and often for this very purpose alone sent, now Timothy, and now Tychicus; and about him he says, "That he may know your circumstances, and encourage your hearts:"[1] and about Timothy; "I have sent him, being no longer able to contain myself; lest in some way the tempter have tempted you."[2] And Titus again elsewhere, and another to another place. For since he himself, by the compulsion of his bonds being often detained in one place, was unable to meet those who were his vitals, he met them through the disciples.

7. And then therefore being in bonds he writes to the Philippians, saying, "Now I desire that ye should know, brethren,"[3] calling the disciples brethren. For such a thing as this is love; it casts out all inequality, and knows not superiority and dignity; but even if one be higher than all, he descends to the lowlier position of all; just what Paul also used to do. But let us hear what it is that he desires they should know. "That the things which happened unto me," he says, "have fallen out rather to the furtherance of the gospel."[4] Tell me, how and in what way? Hast thou then been released from thy bonds? hast thou then put off thy chain? and dost thou with free permission preach in the city? hast thou then, having gone into an assembly, drawn out many long discourses about the faith, and departed after gaining many disciples? hast thou then raised the dead and been made an object of wonder? hast thou then cleansed lepers, and all were astounded? hast thou driven away demons, and been exalted? No one of these things, he says. How then did the furtherance of the gospel take place? tell me. "So that my bonds," he says, "have become openly known in the whole Court, and to all the rest."[5] What sayest thou? this then, this was the furtherance, this the advance, this the increase of the proclamation—that all knew that thou wast bound. Yes, he says: Hear at least what comes next, that thou mayest learn that the bonds not only proved no hindrance, but also a ground of greater freedom of speech. "So that several of the brethren in the Lord, in reliance on my bonds, more abundantly dare fearlessly to speak the word."[7] What sayest thou, O Paul? have thy bonds inspired not anxiety but confidence? not fear but earnest longing? The things mentioned have no consistency.[8] I too know it. For neither did these things take place according to the consistency of human affairs, he means,[9] but what came about was above nature, and the successes were of divine grace. On this account what used to cause anxiety to all others, that to him afforded confidence. For also if any one, having taken the leader of an army and confined him, have made this publicly known, he throws the whole camp into flight; and if any one have carried a shepherd away from the flock, the security with which he drives off the sheep is great. But not in Paul's case was it thus, but the contrary entirely. For the leader of the army was bound, and the soldiers became more forward in spirit; and the confidence with which they sprung upon their adversaries was greater: the shepherd was in confinement, and the sheep were not consumed, nor even scattered.

8. Who ever saw, who ever heard of, the scholars taking greater encouragement in the dangers of their teachers? How was it that they feared not? how was it that they were not terrified? how was it that they did not say to Paul, "Physician, heal thyself,"[10] deliver thyself from thy manifold perils, and then thou will be able to procure for us those countless good things? How was it they did not say these things? How! It was because they had been schooled, from the grace of the Spirit, that these things took place not out of weakness, but out of the permission of the Christ; in order that the truth might shine abroad more largely; through bonds and imprisonments and tribulations and straits increasing and rising, to a greater volume. Thus is the power of Christ in weakness perfected.[11] For indeed if his bonds had crippled Paul[12] and made him cowardly; either himself or those belonging to him; one could not but feel difficulty; but if rather they prepared him to feel confidence and brought him into greater renown, one must be astounded and marvel, how through a thing involving dishonour glory was procured for the disciple—through a thing inspiring cowardice confidence and encouragement resulted to them all. For who was not astounded at him then, seeing him encircled with a chain? Then demons took to flight all the more, when they saw him spending his

---

1 Ephes. vi. 22.   2 1 Thess. iii. 5.   3 Philip. i. 12.
4 Philip. i. 12.   5 Philip. i. 13.
6 Τοὺς πλείονας again, *plures, complures*, a good many.
7 Philip. i. 14.

8 Ἀκολουθίαν. Comp. Xen. *Exped. Cyri.* ii. iv. 19. ὡς οὐκ ἀκόλουθα εἴη; that the two things were incompatible.
9 Φησίν. This word, so constantly used by Chrysostom, is sometimes almost redundant; the nominative to it, if any, being uncertain. It may be redundant here; or it may be equivalent to λέγει; he means. He does not say it.
10 Luke iv. 23.
11 Διαλάμπῃ. In Attic Greek the optative would be used to express past time. But it may be noticed that Chrysostom nearly always has the subjunctive, a usage probably of the Alexandrian period of Greek literature. 2 Cor. xii. 9.
12 Ὑπεσκέλισε. Lit. tripped up, causing a fall.

time in a prison. For not so splendid does the diadem make a royal head, as the chain his hands; not owing to their proper nature, but owing to the grace that darted brightness on them.[1] On this account it was that great encouragement resulted to the disciples. For also they saw his body indeed bound, but his tongue not bound, his hands indeed tightly manacled,[2] but his voice unshackled, and traversing the whole world more swiftly than the solar ray. And this became to them an encouragement; learning as they did from the facts that no one of present things is to be dreaded. For when the soul has been genuinely imbued by divine longing and love, it pays regard to no one of things present; but just as those who are mad venture themselves against fire and sword and wild beasts and sea and all else, so these too, maddened with a most noble and most spiritual frenzy, a frenzy arising from sanity,[3] used to laugh at all things that are seen. On this account, seeing their teachers bound, they the more exulted, the more prided themselves; by facts giving to their adversaries a demonstration that on all sides they were impregnable and indomitable.

9. Then therefore, when matters were in this state, some of the enemies of Paul, desiring to fan up the war to greater vehemence, and to make the hatred of the tyrant, which was felt towards him greater, pretended that they themselves also preached; (and they did preach the right and sound faith,) for the sake of the doctrine advancing more rapidly: and this they did, not with the desire to disseminate the faith; but in order that Nero, having learnt that the preaching was increasing and the doctrine advancing, might the sooner have Paul led away to execution.[4] There were therefore two schools; that of Paul's scholars and that of Paul's enemies, the one preaching out of sincerity, and the others out of love of contention and the hatred they felt towards Paul. And by way of declaring this he said, "Some indeed through envy and strife are preaching Christ," (pointing out those his enemies) "but some also through good pleasure;"[5] saying this about his own scholars.[6] Then next about those; "Some indeed out of contentiousness," (his enemies,) not purely, not soundly, but, "thinking that they are thereby bringing pressure upon my bonds;[7] but the others out of love;" (this again about his own brethren;) "knowing that I am set[8] 'for the defence of the gospel.'" For what? Nevertheless, in any way; whether in pretence or in sincerity, Christ is being announced."[9] So that vainly and to no purpose is this saying taken in reference to heresies. For those who then were preaching were not preaching corrupt doctrine; but sound and right belief. For if they were preaching corrupt doctrine, and were teaching other things contrary to Paul, what they desired was certain not to succeed to them. Now what did they desire? That the faith having grown, and the disciples of Paul having become numerous, it should rouse Nero to greater hostility. And if they were preaching different doctrines, they would not have made the disciples of Paul numerous; and by not doing so,[10] they would not have exasperated the tyrant. He does not therefore say this—that they were bringing in corrupt doctrines—but that the motive from which they were preaching, *this* was corrupt. For it is one thing to state the pretext[11] of their preaching, and another that their preaching itself was not sound. For the preaching does not become sound when the doctrine is laden with deception; and the pretext does not become sound when the preaching indeed is sound, but they who preach do not preach for the sake of God, but either with a view of enmity, or with a view to the favour of others.

10. He therefore does not say this—that they were bringing in heresies; but that it was not from a right motive, nor through piety[12] that they were preaching what they did preach. For it was not that they might increase the gospel that they were doing this; but that they might wage war against him, and throw him into greater danger—on this account he accuses them. And see how with exactitude he laid it.[13] "Thinking," he says, "that they were putting pressure upon my bonds."[14] He did not say, putting, but "thinking they were putting upon," that is supposing, by way of pointing out that even if they so supposed,

---

[1] Ἀπανθοῦσαν. This properly is, dropping its flowers as a plant, withering, *defloresco*.' I strongly suspect that ἐπανθοῦσαν should be read ; which not only is just what is wanted, but gives a satisfactory government to αὐταῖς, which now it has not.
[2] Ἐσφιγμένας. Comp. the chaining of Prometheus ; "'Ἄρασσε μᾶλλον, σφίγγε." Lat. *stringo, constrictus*.
[3] Σωφροσύνης. Not in its ethical, but in its etymological sense, σώοι τὴν φρένα, sound in mind. The antithesis is doubtless intentional.
[4] Τὸ Βάραθρον. The Athenian place and mode of execution. It cannot be literally rendered. The Tarpeian rock may be meant. *Dejicere a saxo cives*, Hor. Serm. This sentence proves "ἀλήθεια" to be, not truth, but sincerity. They preached "'ὀρθὴν καὶ ὑγιῆ πίστιν."
[5] That is, heartily.
[6] Philip. i. 15.
[7] Philip. v. 17.
[8] Κεῖμαι. Perhaps lit. "I am lying"—here in prison.
[9] Philip. i. 16-18.
[10] μὴ ποιοῦντες δέ. Referring to ἐποίησαν, just used. But the Greeks (as Aristophanes) sometimes use ποιῶ in these cases, whatever word precedes ; as in English. They generally repeat the same word, *e. g.*, "μανθάνεις ; Οὐ μανθάνω," Aristoph. Here, then, taken in either way, it comes to the same. Μὴ, because hypothetical, "if they did not make."
[11] Πρόφασιν. But it was not their pretext, but their real motive: v. 17. Any one conversant with Greek authors cannot fail to notice that, with some mental process of their own, they at times use expressions naturally suggesting the very contrary to what they must mean.
[12] Εὐλάβειαν, Lit. carefulness in handling anything holy—reverence.
[13] Αὐτὸ, *i. e.*, the change : ἔγκλημα, involved in ἐγκαλεῖ.
[14] Philip. i. 17.

still he himself was not in such a position; but that he even rejoiced on account of the advance of the preaching. He added therefore, saying, "But in this I both rejoice and will rejoice:"[1] whereas if he held their doctrines deception, and they were bringing in heresies, Paul could not possibly rejoice. But since the doctrine was sound and of genuine parentage, on this account he says, "I rejoice and will rejoice." For what if they[2] are destroying themselves by doing this out of contentiousness? Still, even unwillingly, they are strengthening my cause. Seest thou how great is Paul's power? how he is caught by no one of the devil's machinations? And not only is he not caught; but also by these themselves he subdues him. For great indeed is both the devil's craftiness,[3] and the wickedness of those who minister to him; for under pretence of being of the same mind, they desired to extinguish the proclamation.[4] But "he who seizes the cunning in their craftiness"[5] did not permit that this should take place then. By way of declaring this very thing at least Paul said, "But the continuing in the flesh is the more necessary for your sake; and this I confidently know, that I shall continue and remain in company with you all."[6] For those men indeed set their mind on casting me out of the present life, and are ready to endure anything for this object; but God does not permit it on your account.

11. These things therefore, all of them, remember with exactness in order that you may be able with all wisdom to correct those who use the Scriptures without reference to circumstances[7] and at hap-hazard, and for the destruction of their neighbours. And we shall be able both to remember what has been said, and to correct others, if we always betake ourselves to prayers as a refuge, and beseech the God who gives the word of wisdom to grant both intelligence in hearing, and a careful and unconquerable guardianship of this spiritual deposit in our hands. For things which often we have not strength to perform successfully from our own exertions, these we shall have power to accomplish easily through prayers. I mean prayers which are persevering. For always and without intermission it is a duty to pray, both for him who is in affliction, and him who is in relief from it, and him who is in dangers, and him who is in prosperity—for him who is in relief and much prosperity, that these may remain unmoved and without vicissitude, and may never change; and for him who is in affliction and his many dangers, that he may see some favourable change brought about to him, and be transported into a calm of consolation. Art thou in a calm? Then beseech God that this calm may continue settled to thee. Hast thou seen a storm risen up against thee? Beseech God earnestly[8] to cause the billow to pass, and to make a calm out of the storm. Hast thou been heard? Be heartily thankful for this; because thou hast been heard. Hast thou not been heard? Persevere,[9] in order that thou mayest be heard. For even if God at any time delay the giving, it is not in hatred and aversion; [10] but from the desire by the deferring of the giving perpetually to retain thee with himself; just in the way also that affectionate fathers do; [11] for they also adroitly manage the perpetual and assiduous attendance of children who are rather indolent by the delay of the giving. There is to thee no need of mediators in audience with God; nor of that much canvassing; [12] nor of the fawning upon others; but even if thou be destitute, even if bereft of advocacy, alone, by thyself, having called on God for help, thou wilt in any case succeed.[13] He is not so wont to assent when entreated by others on our behalf, as by ourselves who are in need; even if we be laden with ten thousand evil deeds. For if in the case of men, even if we have come into countless collisions with them, when both at dawn and at mid-day and in the evening we show ourselves to those who are aggrieved against us, by the unbroken continuance and the persistent meeting and interview we easily demolish their enmity—far more in the case of God would this be effected.

12. But thou art unworthy. Become worthy by thy assiduity. For that it both is possible that the unworthy should become worthy from his assiduity; and that God assents more when called on by ourselves than by others; and

---

[1] Philip. v. 18. [2] Ἐκεῖνοι, Lat. *isti*, "the men."
[3] Κακουργία, "παρὰ τάυτας γὰρ κακουργεῖ," of the sophist Arist. *Rhet.* iii. 2, 7.
[4] Κήρυγμα. In its proper sense, the thing preached, the Gospel. But it more commonly is = κήρυξις, which word is scarcely used at all.
[5] 1 Cor. iii. 19. Δρασσόμενος, lit. clutches. Hence δραχμὴ, a handful of copper, σοφούς, falsely wise. "Σοφία; ἀρετὴ τεχνῆς." Arist. *Eth. Nich.* l. vi. Comp. Luke xvi. 8, of the dishonest steward.
[6] Philip. i. 24, 25. [7] Ἀπλῶς.
[8] Ἐκτενῶς. Like a racer, with every muscle "stretched out." Antilochus exclaims to his horses in the chariot race, Ἐμβήτον, κὰι σφώϊ τιταινετον. *Il.* xxiii. 403. Comp. Philip. iii. 13; τοῖς ἔμπροσθεν ἐπεκτεινόμενος διώκω : the same metaphor.
[9] Παράμεινον. Wait, as it were, at the door; παρά, until answered. Matt. vii. 7, τῷ κρουοντι (to him who continues knocking) ἀνοιγήσεται.
[10] Ἀποστρεφόμενος. The Pagans adopted the expression literally, *Diva solo fixos oculos aversa tenebat*, Virg. Æn. i. 482.
[11] Here we have ποιοῦσι, as in English, after κατέχειν. See previous note. It might be κατέχουσι, repeated.
[12] Περιδρομῆς, running about for votes and favour. Lat. *ambitio*. "*Non ego . . . Grammaticas ambire tribus et pulpita dignor*." Hor. *Epist.* i. 19, 40.
[13] To understand this description we have to bear in mind that, at Rome at least, legal advocates could claim no fees. They were forbidden, at least before the Imperial age, by the Cincian law. *Turpe reos emptâ miseros defendere linguâ*. Ov. *Amor.* i. 10, 39. Hence, the obtaining the services of an eminent lawyer required interest and entreaty. So the Sicilians begged Cicero to undertake the prosecution of Verres. Cic. *in Verr. Div.* c. 12.

that he often delays the giving, not from the wish that we should be utterly perplexed, nor to send us out[1] with empty hands; but in order that he may become the author of greater good things to us—these three points I will endeavour to make evident by the parable which has to-day been read to you. The woman of Chanaan had come to Christ praying on behalf of a daughter possessed by a demon, and crying out with much earnestness,[2] (it says,[3] " Have pity on me, Lord, my daughter is badly possessed by a demon." See, the woman of a strange nation, and a barbarian, and outside of the Jewish commonwealth. For indeed what else (was she) than a dog, and unworthy of the receiving her request? For "it is not," he says, "good to take the children's bread, and to give it to the dogs." But, all the same, from her assiduity, she became worthy. For not only did he admit her into the nobility of children, dog as she was; but also he sent her off with that high encomium saying, " O woman, great is thy faith; be it done to thee as thou wilt."[5] Now when the Christ says, "great is thy faith," seek thou no other demonstration of the greatness of soul which was in the woman. Seest thou how, from her assiduity the woman, being unworthy, became worthy? Desirest thou also to learn that we accomplish (our wish) by calling on him by ourselves more than by others? She cried out, and the disciples having come to him say, " Let her go away, for she is crying after us:"[6] and to them he says, " I am not sent, unless to the lost sheep of the house of Israel."[7] But when she had come to him by herself and continued crying, and saying, " Yes, Lord, for even the dogs eat from the table of their masters,"[8] then he granted the favour and says, " Be it done unto thee as thou wilt." Seest thou how, when they were entreating him, he repelled; but when she who needed the gift herself cried out, he assented? For to them he says, " I am not sent, unless to the lost sheep of the house of Israel;" but to her[9] he said, " Great is thy faith; be it done unto thee as thou wilt." Again, at the beginning and in the prelude of her request he answered nothing; but when both once and twice and thrice she had come to him, then he granted the boon; by the issue making us believe that he had delayed the giving, not that he might repel her[10] but that he might display to us all the woman's endurance. For if he had delayed in order that he might repel her, he would not have granted it even at the end; but since he was waiting to display to all her spiritual wisdom, on this account he was silent.[11] For if he had granted it immediately and at the beginning, we should not have known the woman's virtue.[12] " Let her go"[13] it says, "because she is clamouring behind us." But what (says) the Christ? "Ye hear a voice, but I see the mind: I know what she is going to say. I choose not to permit the treasure hidden in her mind to escape notice; but I am waiting and keeping silence; in order that having discovered it I may lay it down in publicity, and make it manifest to all.

13. Having therefore learned all these things, even if we be in sins, and unworthy of receiving, let us not despair; knowing, that by assiduity of soul we shall be able to become worthy of the request. Even if we be unaided by advocate and destitute, let us not faint; knowing that it is a strong advocacy—the coming to God one's self by one's self with much eagerness. Even if he delay and defer with respect to the giving, let us not be dispirited; having learned that the putting it off and delay is a sure proof of caring and love for mankind. If we have thus persuaded ourselves; and with a soul deeply pained and fervent, and thoroughly roused purpose; and such as that with which the woman of Chanaan approached, we too come to him, even if we be dogs; even if we have done anything whatever dreadful; we shall both rebut[14] our own crimes, and obtain so great liberty of speech[15] as also to be advocates for others; in the way in which also this woman of Chanaan not only herself enjoyed liberty of speech and ten thousand encomiums, but had power to snatch her dear daughter[16] out of her intolerable sufferings.

---

[1] Ἐκπέμψαι, *i. e.*, from the hall, as it were, of audience.
[2] Ἐκτενείας, as above.
[3] Φησίν, the parable says. An instance, however, of its redundancy before noticed. Ἐλέησον depends not on it, but on βοῶσα.
[4] Κυναρίοις. In Greek, as in Latin and German, the diminutive sometimes expresses contempt.
[5] Matt. xv. 22, 26, 28.   [6] Matt. v. 23.   [7] Matt. v. 24.
[8] Matt. v. 27. That is, the bread thrown to them, when it had been used to cleanse the fingers. Gr. ἀπομαγδαλία, *ab* ἀπομάσσομαι. Comp. the very apposite passage, in which Agaracritus, a low person, says that this had been his own fare; ἢ μάτην γὰρ Ἀπομαγδαλίας σιτούμενος τοσοῦτος ἐκτραφείην. Cleon rejoins, Ἀπομαγδαλίοις ὥσπερ κύων, ὦ παμπόνηρε; πῶς οὖν κυνὸς βορὰν σιτούμενος μάχει σύ, Aristoph. *Equ.*412. Κυνάρια. So " canicula," of the dog-star, *invisum sidus.*   [9] Ταύτῃ = αὐτῇ.

[10] Διακρούσηται, as with rude violence. Lit. knock to a distance from himself, as with a hard blow.
[11] Ἐσίγα. Not literally, for Christ had answered, "It is not meet to take the children's bread." But that was silence, as far as returning any favorable answer went.
[12] Τὴν ἀνδρείαν τῆς γυναικός. Lit. the woman's manliness; a courage above her sex. The antithesis is doubtless intentional. Ἐνάντια παράλληλα μᾶλλον γνώριμα, Arist. *Rhet.* Ἀνδρεία = Lat. *virtus.* Gibbon, using this in the general sense, has the expression, " manly virtue," in reference to ἀρετῆς Ἀνδρένα, Hom. *Odys.* xvii. 322.
[13] Φησὶν again : with no nominative. Certainly not Christ—the disciples said it. We might expect φάσιν; but this, I believe, Chrysostom never uses in these cases. " It says," *i. e.*, the history, or "he," the Evangelist. Sometimes τις is understood.
[14] Ἀποκρουσόμεθα. Rebut the charges brought against us. " Κακὰ," comp. the double sense of the Lat. *crimen.*
[15] Παρρησίαν. Here, liberty to address the Court. So King Agrippa says, " Paul, thou art permitted to speak for thyself." Acts xxvi. 1. Chrysostom throughout maintains the metaphor of the judicial process—ἀπροστάτευτος, κ.τ.λ
[16] Θυγατριον. Here a diminutive of endearment, "*filiola.*" ϭ Σωκρατίδιον φίλτατον, Arist. *Nub.* 736. As the Greeks said, ὑποκοριστικῶς.

For nothing—nothing is more powerful than prayer when fervent and genuine. This both disperses present dangers, and rescues from the penalties which take place at that hour.[1] That therefore we may both complete our passage through the present life with ease,[2] and depart thither[3] with confidence, with much zeal and eagerness let us perform this perpetually. For thus shall we be able both to attain the good things which are laid up, and to enjoy those excellent hopes; which God grant that we may all attain; by the grace and loving kindness and compassion of our Lord Jesus Christ—with whom to the Father together with the Holy Spirit be glory, honour, dominion, to the ages of the ages.[4] Amen.

---

[1] Καιρον, "μέρος χρονου," Aristotle, A critical moment.
[2] Εὐκολίας. Effect for cause; contentedness for that which creates it; ease. Comp. *O Melibæe, Deus nobis hæc otia fecit*," Virg. *Ecl*. i. 6.
[3] Ἐκεῖ. The Greek euphemism for the other world. Aristophanes speaks of the kindliness and contentedness of Sophocles in both states of being, 'Ο δ' εὔκολος μέν ἐνθάδ εὔκαλος δ' ἐκεῖ. *Ranæ*, 82. See last note.
[4] Perhaps this common phrase, "ages (consisting) of ages," is in contrast to ages of years. Comp. "*magnus annus-menses. Magnus ab integro sæclorum nascitur ordo.*" Vir. *Eccl*. IV. 5.

ST. CHRYSOSTOM:

INSTRUCTIONS TO CATECHUMENS.

TRANSLATED WITH INTRODUCTION, AND NOTES BY

REV. W. R. W. STEPHENS, M.A.,

PREBENDARY OF CHICHESTER, AND RECTOR OF WOOLBEDING, SUSSEX.

ASSISTED BY

REV. T. P. BRANDRAM, M.A.,

RECTOR OF RUMBOLDSWHYKE, CHICHESTER.

INSTRUCTIONS TO CATECHUMENS.

FIRST INSTRUCTION.

To those about to be illuminated;[1] and for what reason the laver is said to be of regeneration and not of remission of sins; and that it is a dangerous thing not only to forswear oneself, but also to take an oath, even though we swear truly.

1. How delightful and lovable is our band of young brethren! For brethren I call you, even now before you have been brought forth, and before your birth I welcome this relationship with you: For I know, I know clearly, to how great an honour you are about to be led, and to how great a dignity; and those who are about to receive dignity, all are wont to honor, even before the dignity is conferred, laying up for themselves beforehand by their attention good will for the future. And this also I myself now do. For ye are not about to be led to an empty dignity, but to an actual kingdom: and not simply to a kingdom, but to the kingdom of the Heavens itself. Wherefore I beseech and entreat you that you remember me when you come into that kingdom, and as Joseph said to the chief butler "Remember me when it shall be well with thee,"[2] this also I say now to you, do ye remember me when it is well with you. I do not ask this in return for interpreting your dreams, as he; for I have not come to interpret dreams for you, but to discourse of matters celestial, and to convey to you glad tidings of such good things as "eye hath not seen, and ear hath not heard and which have entered not into the heart of man, such are the things which God hath prepared for them that love him."[3] Now Joseph indeed said to that chief butler, "yet three days and Pharaoh will restore thee to thy chief butlership." But I do not say, yet three days and ye shall be set to pour out the wine of a tyrant, but yet thirty days, and not Pharaoh but the king of Heaven shall restore you to the country which is on high, Jerusalem, which is free—to the city which is in the heavens; and *he* said indeed, "Thou shalt give the cup into the hands of Pharaoh." But *I* say not that you shall give the cup into the hands of the king, but that the king shall give the cup into your hand—that dread cup, full of much power, and more precious than any created thing. The initiated know the virtue of this cup, and you yourselves shall know it a little while hence. Remember me, therefore, when you come into that kingdom, when you receive the royal robe, when you are girt with the purple dipped in the master's blood, when you will be

---

[1] *I.e.*, to be baptized. A common name for Baptism was "illumination," partly with reference to the instructions which preceded it, as Justin Martyr says; "The laver is called illumination because the minds of those who learn these things are enlightened:" partly also (perhaps rather) because baptism was regarded as a translation from the kingdom of darkness into the kingdom of light, the recipient becoming a child of God, and as such entitled to the grace of the illuminating Spirit. Catechumens were divided into four classes according to the stages of their preparation. It is to those who were in the final stage, the competentes or elect as they were called, that the following instructions are addressed.
[2] Gen. xl. 14.
[3] 1 Cor. ii. 9, 10.

crowned with the diadem, which has lustre leaping forth from it on all sides, more brilliant than the rays of the sun. Such are the gifts of the Bridegroom, greater indeed than your worth, but worthy of his lovingkindness.

Wherefore, I count you blessed already before those sacred nuptials, and I do not only count you blessed, but I praise your prudence in that you have not come to your illumination as the most slothful among men, at your last breath, but already, like prudent servants, prepared with much goodwill to obey your master, have brought the neck of your soul with much meekness and readiness beneath the bands of Christ, and have received His easy yoke, and have taken His light burden. For if the grace bestowed be the same both for you and for those who are initiated at their last hour, yet the matter of the intention is not the same, nor yet the matter of the preparation for the rite. For they indeed receive it on their bed, but you in the bosom of the Church, which is the common mother of us all; they indeed with lamentation and weeping, but you rejoicing, and exceeding glad: they sighing, you giving thanks; they indeed lethargic with much fever, you filled with much spiritual pleasure; wherefore in your case all things are in harmony with the gift, but in theirs all are adverse to it. For there is wailing and much lamentation on the part of the initiated, and children stand around crying, wife tearing her cheeks, and dejected friends and tearful servants; the whole aspect of the house resembles some wintry and gloomy day. And if thou shalt open the heart of him who is lying there, thou wilt find it more downcast than are these. For as winds meeting one another with many a contrary blast, break up the sea into many parts, so too the thought of the terrors preying upon him assail the soul of the sick man, and distract his mind with many anxieties. Whenever he sees his children, he thinks of their fatherless condition; whenever he looks from them to his wife, he considers her widowhood; when he sees the servants, he beholds the desolation of the whole house; when he comes back to himself, he calls to mind his own present life, and being about to be torn from it, experiences a great cloud of despondency. Of such a kind is the soul of him who is about to be initiated. Then in the midst of its tumult and confusion, the Priest enters, more formidable than the fever itself, and more distressing than death to the relatives of the sick man. For the entrance of the Presbyter is thought to be a greater reason for despair than the voice of the physician despairing of his life, and that which suggests eternal life seems to be a symbol of death. But I have not yet put the finishing stroke to these ills. For in the midst of relatives raising a tumult and making preparations, the soul has often taken its flight, leaving the body desolate; and in many cases, while it was present it was useless, for when it neither recognizes those who are present, nor hears their voice, nor is able to answer those words by which it will make that blessed covenant with the common master of us all, but is as a useless log, or a stone, and he who is about to be illuminated lies there differing nothing from a corpse, what is the profit of initiation in a case of such insensibility?

2. For he who is about to approach these holy and dread mysteries must be awake and alert, must be clean from all cares of this life, full of much self-restraint, much readiness; he must banish from his mind every thought foreign to the mysteries, and on all sides cleanse and prepare his home, as if about to receive the king himself. Such is the preparation of your mind: such are your thoughts; such the purpose of your soul. Await therefore a return worthy of this most excellent decision from God, who overpowers with His recompense those who show forth obedience to Him. But since it is necessary for his fellow servants to contribute of their own, then we will contribute of our own; yea rather not even are these things our own, but these too are our Master's. "For what hast thou," saith He, "that thou didst not receive? but if thou didst receive it, why dost thou glory, as if thou hadst not received it?"[1] I wished to say this first of all, why in the world our fathers, passing by the whole year, settled that the children of the Church should be initiated at this season; and for what reason, after the instruction from us, removing your shoes and raiment, unclad and unshod, with but one garment on, they conduct you to hear the words of the exorcisers. For it is not thoughtlessly and rashly that they have planned this dress and this season for us. But both these things have a certain mystic and secret reason. And I wished to say this to you. But I see that our discourse now constrains us to something more necessary. For it is necessary to say what baptism is, and for what reason it enters into our life, and what good things it conveys to us.

But, if you will, let us discourse about the name which this mystic cleansing bears: for its name is not one, but very many and various. For this purification is called the laver of regeneration. "He saved us," he saith, "through the laver of regeneration, and renewing of the

---

[1] 1 Cor. iv. 7.

Holy Ghost."[1] It is called also illumination, and this St. Paul again has called it, "For call to remembrance the former days in which after ye were illuminated ye endured a great conflict of sufferings;"[2] and again, "For it is impossible for those who were once illuminated, and have tasted of the heavenly gift, and then fell away, to renew them again unto repentance."[3] It is called also, baptism: "For as many of you as were baptized into Christ did put on Christ."[4] It is called also burial: "For we were buried" saith he, "with him, through baptism, into death."[5] It is called circumcision: "In whom ye were also circumcised, with a circumcision not made with hands, in the putting off of the body of the sins of the flesh."[6] It is called a cross: "Our old man was crucified with him that the body of sin might be done away."[7] 'It is also possible to speak of other names besides these, but in order that we should not spend our whole time over the names of this free gift, come, return to the first name, and let us finish our discourse by declaring its meaning; but in the meantime, let us extend our teaching a little further. There is that laver by means of the baths, common to all men, which is wont to wipe off bodily uncleanness; and there is the Jewish laver, more honorable than the other, but far inferior to that of grace; and it too wipes off bodily uncleanness, but not simply uncleanness of body, since it even reaches to the weak conscience. For there are many matters, which by nature indeed are not unclean, but which become unclean from the weakness of the conscience. And as in the case of little children, masks, and other bugbears are not in themselves alarming, but seem to little children to be alarming, by reason of the weakness of their nature, so it is in the case of those things of which I was speaking; just as to touch dead bodies is not naturally unclean, but when this comes into contact with a weak conscience, it makes him who touches them unclean. For that the thing in question is not unclean naturally, Moses himself who ordained this law showed, when he bore off the entire corpse of Joseph, and yet remained clean. On this account Paul also, discoursing to us about this uncleanness which does not come naturally but by reason of the weakness of the conscience, speaks somewhat in this way, "Nothing is common of itself save to him who accounteth anything to be common."[8] Dost thou not see that uncleanness does not arise from the nature of the thing, but from the weakness of the reasoning about it? And again: "All things indeed are clean, howbeit it is evil to that man who eateth with offense."[9] Dost thou see that it is not to eat, but to eat with offense, that is the cause of uncleanness?

3. Such is the defilement from which the laver of the Jews cleansed. But the laver of grace, not such, but the real uncleanness which has introduced defilement into the soul as well as into the body. For it does not make those who have touched dead bodies clean, but those who have set their hand to dead works: and if any man be effeminate, or a fornicator, or an idolator, or a doer of whatever ill you please, or if he be full of all the wickedness there is among men: should he fall into this pool of waters, he comes up again from the divine fountain purer than the sun's rays. And in order that thou mayest not think that what is said is mere vain boasting, hear Paul speaking of the power of the laver, "Be not deceived: neither idolators, nor fornicators, nor adulterers, nor effeminate, nor abusers of themselves with men, nor covetous, not drunkards, not revilers, not extortioners shall inherit the kingdom of God."[10] And what has this to do with what has been spoken? says one, "for prove the question whether the power of the laver thoroughly cleanses all these things." Hear therefore what follows: "And such were some of you, but ye were washed, but ye were sanctified, but ye were justified in the name of the Lord Jesus Christ, and in the spirit of our God." *We* promise to show you that they who approach the laver become clean from all fornication: but the word has shown more, that they have become not only clean, but both holy and just, for it does not say only "ye were washed," but also "ye were sanctified and were justified." What could be more strange than this, when without toil, and exertion, and good works, righteousness is produced? For such is the lovingkindness of the Divine gift that it makes men just without this exertion. For if a letter of the Emperor, a few words being added, sets free those who are liable to countless accusations, and brings others to the highest honors; much rather will the Holy Spirit of God, who is able to do all things, free us from all evil and grant us much righteousness, and fill us with much assurance, and as a spark falling into the wide sea would straightway be quenched, or would become invisible, being overwhelmed by the multitude of the waters, so also all human wickedness, when it falls into the pool of the divine fountain, is more swiftly and easily overwhelmed,

---

[1] Titus iii. 5. [2] Heb. x. 32. [3] Heb. vi. 4-6.
[4] Gal. iii. 27. [5] Rom. vi. 4. [6] Gal. ii. 11.
[7] Rom. vi. 6. [8] Rom. xiv. 14. [9] Rom. xiv. 20. [10] 1 Cor. vi. 9, 10.

and made invisible, than that spark. And for what reason, says one, if the laver take away all our sins, is it called, not a laver of remission of sins, nor a laver of cleansing, but a laver of regeneration? Because it does not simply take away our sins, nor simply cleanse us from our faults, but so as if we were born again. For it creates and fashions us anew, not forming us again out of earth, but creating us out of another element, namely, of the nature of water. For it does not simply wipe the vessel clean, but entirely remoulds it again. For that which is wiped clean, even if it be cleaned with care, has traces of its former condition, and bears the remains of its defilement, but that which falls into the new mould, and is renewed by means of the flames, laying aside all uncleanness, comes forth from the furnace, and sends forth the same brilliancy with things newly formed. As therefore any one who takes and recasts a golden statue which has been tarnished by time, smoke, dust, rust, restores it to us thoroughly cleansed and glistening: so too this nature of ours, rusted with the rust of sin, and having gathered much smoke from our faults, and having lost its beauty, which He had from the beginning bestowed upon it from himself, God has taken and cast anew, and throwing it into the waters as into a mould, and instead of fire sending forth the grace of the Spirit, then brings us forth with much brightness, renewed, and made afresh, to rival the beams of the sun, having crushed the old man, and having fashioned a new man, more brilliant than the former.

4. And speaking darkly of this crushing, and this mystic cleansing, the prophet of old said, "Thou shalt dash them in pieces like a potter's vessel."[1] For that the word is in reference to the faithful, what goes before sufficiently shows us, "For thou art my Son," he says, "to-day have I begotten thee, ask of me and I will give the heathen for thine inheritance, the utmost parts of the earth for thy possession."[2] Dost thou see how he has made mention of the church of the Gentiles, and has spoken of the kingdom of Christ extended on all sides? Then he says again, "Thou shalt rule them with a rod of iron;" not grievous, but strong: "thou shalt break them in pieces like a potter's vessel."[3] Behold then, the laver is more mystically brought forward. For he does not say earthen vessels: but vessels of the potter. But, give heed: For earthen vessels when crushed would not admit of refashioning, on account of the hardness which was gained by them from the fire. But the fact is that the vessels of the potter are not earthen, but of clay; wherefore, also, when they have been distorted, they can easily, by the skill of the artificer, be brought again to a second shape. When, therefore, God speaks of an irremediable calamity, he does not say vessels of the potter, but an earthen vessel; when, for instance, he wished to teach the prophet and the Jews that he delivered up the city to an irremediable calamity, he bade him take an earthen wine-vessel, and crush it before all the people, and say, "Thus shall this city be destroyed, be broken in pieces."[4] But when he wishes to hold out good hopes to them, he brings the prophet to a pottery, and does not show him an earthen vessel, but shows him a vessel of clay, which was in the hands of the potter, falling to the ground: and brings him to it saying, "If this potter has taken up and remodelled his vessel which has fallen, shall I not much rather be able to restore you when you have fallen?"[5] It is possible therefore for God not only to restore those who are made of clay, through the laver of regeneration, but to bring back again to their original state, on their careful repentance, those who have received the power of the Spirit, and have lapsed. But this is not the time for you to hear words about repentance, rather may the time never come for you to fall into the need of these remedies, but may you always remain in preservation of the beauty and the brightness which ye are now about to receive, unsullied. In order, then, that ye may ever remain thus, come and let us discourse to you a little about your manner of life. For in the wrestling schools falls of the athletes are devoid of danger. For the wrestling is with friends, and they practice all their exercises on the persons of their teachers. But when the time of the contest has come, when the lists are open, when the spectators are seated above, when the president has arrived, it necessarily follows that the combatants, if they become careless, fall and retire in great disgrace, or if they are in earnest, win the crowns and the prizes. So then, in your case these thirty days are like some wrestling school, both for exercise and practice: let us learn from thence already to get the better of that evil demon. For it is to contend with him that we have to strip ourselves, with him after baptism are we to box and fight. Let us learn from thence already his grip, on what side he is aggressive, on what side he can easily threaten us, in order that, when the contest comes on, we may not feel strange, nor become confused, as seeing new forms of wrestling; but having already prac-

---

[1] Ps. ii. 9. [2] Ps. ii. 7, 8. [3] Ps. ii. 9. [4] Jer. xix. 11. [5] Jer. xviii. 6.

ticed them amongst ourselves, and having learnt all his methods, may engage in these forms of wrestling against him with courage. In all ways, therefore, is he accustomed to threaten us, but especially by means of the tongue, and the mouth. For there is no organ so convenient for him for our deception and our destruction as an unchastened tongue and an unchecked utterance. Hence come many slips on our part: hence many serious accusations against us. And the ease of these falls through the tongue a certain one showed, when he said, "Many fell by the sword, but not so many as by the tongue."[1] Now the gravity of the fall the same person shows us again when he says: "To slip upon a pavement is better than to slip with the tongue."[2] And what he speaks of is of this kind. Better it is, says he, that the body should fall and be crushed, than that such a word should go forth as destroys the soul; and he does not speak of falls merely; he also admonishes us that much forethought should be exercised, so that we should not be tripped up, thus saying "Make a door and bars for thy mouth,"[3] not that we should prepare doors and bars, but that with much security, we should shut the tongue off from outrageous words; and again in another place, after showing that we need influence from above, both as accompanying and preceding our own effort so as to keep this wild beast within: stretching forth his hands to God, the prophet said, "Let the lifting up of my hands be an evening sacrifice, set a watch, O Lord, before my mouth, keep the door of my lips;" and he who before admonished, himself too[4] says again, "Who shall set a watch before my mouth, and a seal of wisdom upon my lips?"[5] Dost thou not see, each one fearing these falls and bewailing them, both giving advice, and praying that the tongue may have the benefit of much watchfulness? and for what reason, says one, if this organ brings us such ruin, did God originally place it within us? Because indeed, it is of great use, and if we are careful, it is of use only, and brings no ruin. Hear, for example, what he says who spoke the former words, "Death and life are in the power of the tongue."[6] And Christ points to the same thing when he says, "By thy words thou shalt be condemned, and by thy words thou shalt be justified."[7] For the tongue stands in the midst ready for use on either hand. Thou art its master. Thus indeed a sword lies in the midst, and if thou use it against thine enemies, this organ becomes a means of safety for thee. But if thou thrust its stroke against thyself, not the nature of the iron, but thine own transgression becomes the cause of thy slaughter. Let us then take this view of the tongue. It is a sword lying in the midst; sharpen it for the purpose of accusing thine own sins. Thrust not the stroke against thy brother. For this reason God surrounded it with a double fortification; with the fence of the teeth and the barrier of the lips, that it may not rashly and without circumspection utter words which are not convenient. Well, dost thou say it will not endure this? Bridle it therefore within. Restrain it by means of the teeth, as though giving over its body to these executioners and making them bite it. For it is better that when it sins now it should be bitten by the teeth, than one day when it seeks a drop of water and is parched with heat, to be unable to obtain this consolation. In many other ways indeed it is wont to sin, by raillery and blasphemy, by uttering foul words, by slander, swearing, and perjury.

5. But in order that we may not by saying everything at once to-day, confuse your minds, we put before you one custom, namely, about the avoidance of oaths, saying this much by way of preface, and speaking plainly—that if you do not avoid oaths, I say not perjury merely, but those too which happen in the cause of justice, we shall not further discourse upon any other subject. For it is monstrous that teachers of letters should not give a second lesson to their children until they see the former one fixed well in their memory, but that we, without being able to express our first lessons clearly, should inculcate others before the first are completed. For this is nothing else than to pour into a perforated jar. Give great care, then, that ye silence not our mouth. For this error is grave, and it is exceedingly grave because it does not seem to be grave, and on this account I fear it, because no one fears it. On this account the disease is incurable, because it does not seem to be a disease; but just as simple speech is not a crime, so neither does this seem to be a crime, but with much boldness this transgression is committed: and if any one call it in question, straightway laughter follows, and much ridicule, not of those who are called in question for their oaths, but of those who wish to rectify the disease. On this account I largely extend my discourse about these matters. For I wish to pull up a deep root, and to wipe out a long-standing evil: I speak not of perjury alone, but even of oaths in good faith. But so and so, says one, a forbearing man, consecrated to the priesthood, living in much self-control and piety, takes an oath. Do not speak to me of this forbearing person, this

---

[1] Ecclus. xxviii. 22. [2] Ecclus. xx. 18. [3] Ecclus. xx. 25.
[4] Ps. cxlii. 2, 3. [5] Ecclus. xxii. 27. [6] Prov. xviii. 21.
[7] Mark xii. 27.

self-controlled, pious man who is consecrated to the priesthood; but if thou wilt, add that this man is Peter, or Paul, or even an angel descended out of heaven. For not even in such a case do I regard the dignity of their persons. For the law which *I* read upon oaths, is not that of the servant, but of the King: and when the edicts of a king are read, let every claim of the servants be silent. But if thou art able to say that Christ bade us use oaths, or that Christ did not punish the doing of this, show me, and I am persuaded. But if he forbids it with so much care, and takes so much thought about the matter as to class him who takes an oath with the evil one (for whatsoever is more than these, namely, than yea and nay, saith he, is of the devil),[1] why dost thou bring this person and that person forward? For not because of the carelessness of thy fellow servants, but from the injunctions of his own laws, will God record his vote against thee. I have commanded, he says, thou oughtest to obey, not to shelter thyself behind such and such a person and concern thyself with other persons' evil. Since the great David sinned a grievous sin, is it then safe for us to sin? Tell me: on this account then we ought to make sure of this point, and only to emulate the good works of the saints; and if there is carelessness, and transgression of the law anywhere, we ought to flee from it with great care. For our reckoning is not with our fellow-servants, but with our Master, and to him we shall give account for all done in our life. Let us prepare ourselves therefore for this tribunal. For even if he who transgresses this law be beyond everything revered and great, he shall certainly pay the penalty attaching to the transgression. For God is no respecter of persons. How then and in what way is it possible to flee from this sin? For one ought to show not only that the crime is grievous, but to give counsel how we may escape from it. Hast thou a wife, hast thou a servant, children, friends, acquaintance, neighbors? To all these enjoin caution on these matters. Custom is a grievous thing, terrible to supplant, and hard to guard against, and it often attacks us unwilling and unknowing; therefore in so far as thou knowest the power of custom, to such an extent study to be freed from any evil custom, and transfer thyself to any other most useful one. For as that custom is often able to trip thee up, though thou art careful, and guardest thyself, and takest thought, and consideration, so if thou transferrest thyself to the good custom of abstaining from oaths, thou wilt not be able, either involuntarily or carelessly, to fall into the fault of oaths. For custom is really great and has the power of nature. In order then that we do not continually distress ourselves let us transfer ourselves to another custom, and ask thou each one of thy kindred and acquaintance this favor, that he advise thee and exhort thee to flee from oaths, and reprove thee, when detected in them. For the watch over thee which takes place on their part, is to them too counsel and a suggestion to what is right. For he who reproves another for oaths, will not himself easily fall into this pit. For much swearing is no ordinary pit, not only when it is about little matters but about the greatest. And we, whether buying vegetables, or quarrelling over two farthings, or in a rage with our servants and threatening them, always call upon God as our witness. But a freeman, possessed of some barren dignity, thou wouldest not dare to call upon as witness in the market to such things; but even if thou attemptedst it, thou wilt pay the penalty of thine insolence. But the King of Heaven, the Lord of Angels, when disputing both about purchases and money, and what not, thou draggest in for a testimony. And how can these things be borne? whence then should we escape from this evil custom? After setting those guards of which I spoke round us, let us fix on a specified time to ourselves for amendment, and adding thereto condemnation if, when the time has passed, we have not amended this. How long time will suffice for the purpose? I do not think that they who are very wary, and on the alert, and watchful about their own salvation, should need more than ten days, so as to be altogether free from the evil custom of oaths. But if after ten days we be detected swearing, let us add a penalty due to ourselves, and let us fix upon the greatest punishment and condemnation of the transgression; what then is this condemnation? This I do not fix upon, but will suffer you yourselves to determine the sentence. So we arrange matters in our own case, not only in respect of oaths but in respect of other defects, and fixing a time for ourselves, with most grievous punishments, if at any time we have fallen into them, shall come clean to our Master, and shall escape the fire of hell, and shall stand before the judgment seat of Christ with boldness, to which may we all attain, by the grace and lovingkindness of our Lord Jesus Christ, with whom be glory to the Father together with the Holy Spirit for ever and ever: Amen.

---

[1] Matt. v. 35.

SECOND INSTRUCTION.

To those about to be illuminated; and concerning women who adorn themselves with plaiting of hair, and gold, and concerning those who have used omens, and amulets, and incantations, all which are foreign to Christianity.

1. I HAVE come to ask first of all for some fruit in return for the words lately said out of brotherly love to you. For we do not speak in order that ye should hear simply, but in order that ye should remember what has been said, and may afford us evidence of this, by your works. Yea, rather, not us, but, God, who knows the secrets of the heart. On this account indeed instruction is so called, in order that even when we are absent, our discourse may instruct your hearts.[1] And be not surprised if, after an interval of ten days only, we have come asking for fruit from the seed sown. For in one day it is possible at once to let the seed fall, and to accomplish the harvest. For strengthened not by our own power alone, but by the influence which comes from God, we are summoned to the conflict. Let as many therefore as have received what has been spoken, and have fulfilled it by their works, remain reaching forth to the things which are before. But let as many as have not yet arrived at this good achievement, arrive at it straightway, that they may dispel the condemnation which arises out of their sloth by their diligence for the future. For it is possible, it is indeed possible for him who has been very slothful, by using diligence for the future to recover the whole loss of the time that is past. Wherefore, He says, "To-day if ye will hear his voice, harden not your hearts, as in the day of provocation."[2] And this, He says, exhorting and counselling us; that we should never despair, but so long as we are here, should have good hopes, and should lay hold on what is before us, and hasten towards the prize of our high calling of God. This then let us do, and let us inquire into the names of this great gift. For as ignorance of the greatness of this dignity makes those who are honored with it more slothful, so when it is known it renders them thankful, and makes them more earnest; and anyhow it would be disgraceful and ridiculous that they who enjoy such glory and honors from God, should not even know what the names of it are intended to show forth. And why do I speak about this gift, for if thou wilt consider the common name of our race, thou wilt receive the greatest instruction and incentive to virtue. For this name "Man," we do not define according as they who are without define it, but as the Divine Scripture has bidden us. For a man is not merely whosoever has hands and feet of a man, nor whosoever is rational only, but whosoever practices piety and virtue with boldness. Hear, at least, what he says concerning Job. For in saying that "there was a man in the land of Ausis,"[3] he does not describe him in those terms in which they who are without describe him, nor does he say this because he had two feet and broad nails, but he added the evidences of his piety and said, "just, true, fearing God, eschewing every evil deed,"[4] showing that this is a man; even as therefore another says, "Fear God, and keep his commandments, because this is the whole man."[5] But if the name man affords such a great incentive to virtue, much rather the term faithful. For thou art called faithful on this account, because thou hast faith in God, and thyself art entrusted from Him with righteousness, sanctification, cleansing of soul, adoption, the kingdom of heaven. He entrusted thee with these, and handed them over to thee. Thou in turn hast entrusted, and handed over other things to him, almsgiving, prayers, self-control and every other virtue. And why do I say almsgiving? If thou givest him even a cup of cold water, thou shalt not indeed lose this, but even this he keeps with care against that day, and will restore it with overflowing abundance. For this truly is wonderful, that he does not keep only that which has been entrusted to him, but in recompensing it increases it.

This too he has bidden thee do according to thy power, with what has been entrusted to thee, to extend the holiness which thou hast received, and to make the righteousness which comes from the laver brighter, and the gift of grace more radiant; even as therefore Paul did, increasing all the good things which he

---

[1] Catechism, or oral instruction, "Catechesis," in Greek, is called by that name. Chrysostom says, a word derived from ἠχή, a sound, in order that it may "resound" in your minds ἐνηχῇ. It is impossible to preserve the play upon words in the translation consistently with an exact rendering.
[2] Ps. xcv. 8.
[3] This is the Septuagint word for Uz, the situation of which is a matter of great uncertainty. A curious note at the end of the book of Job in the Septuagint states that it was on the borders of the Euphrates.
[4] Job i. 1.
[5] Eccles. xii. 13.

received by his subsequent labors, and his zeal, and his diligence. And look at the carefulness of God; neither did he give the whole to thee then, nor withhold the whole, but gave part, and promised part. And for what reason did he not give the whole then? In order that thou mightest show thy faith about Him, believing, on his promise alone, in what was not yet given. And for what reason again did he not there dispense the whole, but did give the grace of the Spirit, and righteousness and sanctification? In order that he might lighten thy labors for thee, and by what has been already given may also put thee in good hope for that which is to come. On this account, too, thou art about to be called newly-enlightened, because thy light is ever new, if thou wilt, and is never quenched. For this light of day, whether we will or no, the night succeeds, but darkness knows not that light's ray. "For the light shineth in the darkness, and the darkness apprehended it not."[1] Not so bright at least is the world, when the sunbeams come forth, as the soul shines and becomes brighter when it has received grace from the Spirit and learns more exactly the nature of the case. For when night prevails, and there is darkness, often a man has seen a coil of rope and has thought it was a serpent, and has fled from an approaching friend as from an enemy, and being aware of some noise, has become very much alarmed; but when the day has come, nothing of this sort could happen, but all appears just as it really is; which thing also occurs in the case of our soul. For when grace has come, and driven away the darkness of the understanding, we learn the exact nature of things, and what was before dreadful to us becomes contemptible. For we no longer fear death, after learning exactly, from this sacred initiation, that death is not death, but a sleep and a seasonable slumber; nor poverty nor disease, nor any other such thing, knowing that we are on our way to a better life, undefiled and incorruptible, and free from all such vicissitudes.

2. Let us not therefore remain craving after the things of this life, neither after the luxury of the table, or costliness of raiment. For thou hast the most excellent of raiment, thou hast a spiritual table thou hast the glory from on high, and Christ is become to thee all things, thy table, thy raiment, thy home, thy head, thy stem. "For as many of you as were baptized into Christ, did put on Christ."[2] See how he has become raiment for thee. Dost thou wish to learn how he becomes a table for thee? "He who eateth me," says He, "as I live because of the Father, he also shall live because of me;"[3] and that he becometh a home for thee, "he that eateth my flesh abideth in me, and I in him;[4] and that He is a stem He says again, "I am the vine, ye the branches,"[5] and that he is brother, and friend, and bridegroom, "I no longer call you servants: for ye are my friends;"[6] and Paul again, "I espoused you to one husband, that I might present you as a pure virgin to Christ;"[7] and again, "That he might be the first-born among many brethren;"[8] and we become not his brethren only, but also his children, "For behold," he says, "I and the children which God has given me"[9] and not this only, but His members, and His body. For as if what has been said were not enough to show forth the love and the good will which He has shown forth towards us, He has added another thing greater and nearer still, calling himself besides, our head. Knowing all these matters, beloved, requite thy benefactor by the best conversation, and considering the greatness of the sacrifice, adorn the members of thy body; consider what thou receivest in thine hand, and never suffer it to strike any one, nor shame what has been honored with so great a gift by the sin of a blow. Consider what thou receivest in thine hand, and keep it clean from all covetousness and extortion; think that thou dost not receive this in thy hand, but also puttest it to thy mouth, and guard thy tongue in purity from base and insolent words, blasphemy, perjury, and all other such things. For it is disastrous that what is ministered to by such most dread mysteries, and has been dyed red with such blood, and has become a golden sword, should be perverted to purposes of raillery, and insult, and buffoonery. Reverence the honor with which God has honoured it, and bring it not down to the vileness of sin, but having reflected again that after the hand and the tongue, the heart receives this dread mystery, do not ever weave a plot against thy neighbor, but keep thy thoughts pure from all evil. Thus thou shalt be able to keep thine eyes too, and thy hearing safe. For is it not monstrous, after this mystic voice is borne from heaven—I mean the voice of the Cherubim—to defile thy hearing with lewd songs,, and dissolute melodies? and does it not deserve the utmost punishment if, with the same eyes with which thou lookest upon the unspeakable and dread mysteries, thou lookest upon harlots, and dost commit adultery in thy heart. Thou art called to a marriage, beloved: enter not in clad in sordid raiment, but take a robe suitable to the

---

[1] John i. 5. οὐ κατέλαβεν, overcame it not.
[2] Gal. iii. 27.
[3] John vi. 57. The quotation is not exact.
[4] John vi. 56. [5] John xv. 5. [6] John xv. 15.
[7] 2 Cor. xi. 2. [8] Rom. viii. 29. [9] Is. viii. 18.

marriage. For if when men are called to a material marriage, though they be poorer than all others, they often possess themselves of or buy clean raiment, and so go to meet those who called them. Do thou too who hast been called to a spiritual marriage, and to a royal banquet, consider what kind of raiment it would be right for thee to buy, but rather there is not even need to purchase, yea he himself who calls thee gives it thee gratis, in order that thou mayest not be able to plead poverty in excuse. Keep, therefore, the raiment which thou receivedst. For if thou losest it, thou wilt not be able to use it henceforth, or to buy it. For this kind of raiment is nowhere sold. Hast thou heard how those who were initiated, in old time, groaned, and beat their breasts, their conscience thereupon exciting them? Beware then, beloved, that thou do not at any time suffer like this. But how wilt thou not suffer, if thou dost not cast off the wicked habit of evil men? For this reason I said before, and speak now and will not cease speaking, if any has not rectified the defects in his morals, nor furnished himself with easily acquired virtue, let him not be baptized. For the laver is able to remit former sins, but there is no little fear, and no ordinary danger lest we return to them, and our remedy become a wound. For by how much greater the grace is, by so much is the punishment more for those who sin after these things.

3. In order, therefore, that we return not to our former vomit, let us henceforward discipline ourselves. For that we must repent beforehand, and desist from our former evil, and so come forward for grace, hear what John says, and what the leader of the apostles says to those who are about to be baptized. For the one says, "Bring forth fruit worthy of repentance, and begin not to say within yourselves, we have Abraham to our Father;"[1] and the other says again to those who question him, "Repent ye and be baptized every one of you in the name of the Lord Jesus Christ."[2] Now he who repents, no longer touches the same matters of which he repented. On this account, also, we are bidden to say, "I renounce thee, Satan," in order that we may never more return to him.[3] As therefore happens in the case of painters from life, so let it happen in your case. For they, arranging their boards, and tracing white lines upon them, and sketching the royal likeness in outline, before they apply the actual colors, rub out some lines, and change some for others, rectifying mistakes, and altering what is amiss with all freedom. But when they put on the coloring for good, it is no longer in their power to rub out again, and to change one thing for another, since they injure the beauty of the portrait, and the result becomes an eyesore. Consider that thy soul is the portrait; before therefore the true coloring of the spirit comes, wipe out habits which have wrongly been implanted in thee, whether swearing, or falsehood, or insolence, or base talking, or jesting, or whatever else thou hast a habit of doing of things unlawful. Away with the habit, in order that thou mayest not return to it, after baptism. The laver causes the sins to disappear. Correct thy habits, so that when the colors are applied, and the royal likeness is brought out, thou mayest no more wipe them out in the future; and add damage and scars to the beauty which has been given thee by God.[4] Restrain therefore anger, extinguish passion. Be not thou vexed, be sympathizing, be not exasperated, nor say, "I have been injured in regard to my soul." No one is injured in regard to the soul if we do not injure ourselves in regard to the soul; and how this is, I now say. Has any one taken away thy substance? He has not injured thee in regard to thy soul, but thy money. But if thou cherish ill-will against him, thou hast injured thyself in regard to thy soul. For the money taken away has wrought thee no damage, nay has even been profitable, but thou by not dismissing thine anger wilt give account in the other world for this cherishing of ill-will. Has any one reviled thee and insulted thee. He has in no way injured thy soul, and not even thy body. Hast thou reviled in return and insulted? Thou hast injured thyself in regard to thy soul, for for the words which thou hast said thou art about to render account there; and this I wish you to know chiefly of all, that the Christian, and faithful man, no one is able to injure in regard to the soul, not even the devil himself; and not only is this wonderful, that God hath made us inaccessible to all his designs, but that he has constituted us fit for the practice of virtue, and there is no hinderance, if we will, even though we be poor, weak in body, outcast, nameless, bondservants. For neither poverty, nor infirmity, nor deformity of body, nor servitude, nor any other of such things could ever become a hinderance to virtue; and why do I say, poor, and a bondservant,

---

[1] Luke iii. 8.   [2] Acts ii. 38.
[3] Alluding to the vow of renunciation made by converts at baptism. A specimen of this vow may be read in the so-called Apostolic Constitutions, vii. c. 42. "I renounce Satan and his works, and his pomps, and his service, and his angels, and his inventions, and all things that belong or are subject to him." This vow of renunciation was uttered by the catechumens in the porch or ante-chamber of the baptistery with outstretched hands, and faces turned westwards. See below in Chapter V.

[4] The illustration is that of a portrait-painter making a likeness of the emperor, and there seems to be an allusion also to the divine image in which man was originally made.

and nameless? Even if thou art a prisoner, not even this would be ever any hinderance to thee as regards virtue. And how this is I proceed to say. Has any of thy household grieved thee and provoked thee? dismiss thy wrath against him. Have bonds, and poverty, and obscurity been any hinderance to thee in this respect? and why do I say hinderance? They have both helped and contributed to restrain pride. Hast thou seen another prospering? do not envy him. For not even in this case is poverty a bar. Again, whenever thou needest to pray, do so with a sober and watchful mind, and nothing shall be a bar even in that case. Show all meekness, forbearance, self-restraint, gravity. For these things need no external helps. And this especially is the chief point about virtue, that it has no necessity for wealth, power, glory, nor anything of that kind, but of a sanctified soul alone, and it seeks for nothing more. And behold, also, the same thing happening in respect of grace. For if any one be lame, if he has had his eyes put out, if he be maimed in body, if he has fallen into the last extremity of weakness, grace is not hindered from coming by any of these things. For it only seeks a soul receiving it with readiness, and all these external things it passes over. For in the case of worldly soldiers, those who are about to enlist them for the army seek for stature of body and healthy condition, and it is not only necessary that he who is about to become a soldier should have these alone, but he must also be free. For if anybody be a slave, he is rejected. But the King of Heaven seeks for nothing of this kind, but receives slaves into his army, and aged people, and the languid in limb, and is not ashamed. What is more merciful than this? What could be more kind? For he seeks for what is in our own power, but they seek for what is not in our power. For to be a slave or free is not our doing. To be tall, again, or short is not in our own power, or to be aged, or well grown, and such like. But to be forbearing and kind, and so forth, are matters of our own choice; and God demands of us only those things of which we have control. And quite reasonably. For He does not call us to grace because of his own need, but because of doing us kindness; but kings, because of services required by them; and they carry men off to an outward and material warfare, but He to a spiritual combat; and it is not only in the case of heathen wars, but in the case of the games also that one may see the same analogy. For they who are about to be brought into the theatre, do not descend to the contest until the herald himself takes them beneath the gaze of all, and leads them round, shouting out and saying, "Has any one a charge against this person?" although in that case the struggle is not concerned with the soul, but with the body. Wherefore then dost thou demand proofs of nobleness? But in this case there is nothing of the kind, but all is different, our contest not consisting of hand locked in hand, but in philosophy of soul, and excellence of mind. The president of our conflicts does the opposite. For he does not take us, and lead us round and say, "Has any one a charge against this man?" but cries out, "Though all men, though demons, stand up with the devil and accuse him of extreme and unspeakable crimes, I reject him not, nor abhor him, but removing him from his accusers, and freeing him from his wickedness, thus I bring him to the contest. And this is very reasonable. For there indeed the president contributes nothing towards the victory, in the case of the combatants, but stands still in the midst. But here, the President of the contests for holiness becomes a fellow-combatant, and helper, sharing with them the conflict against the devil.

4. And not only is this the wonderful thing that he remits our sins, but that he not even reveals them nor makes them manifest and patent, nor compels us to come forward into the midst, and to tell out our errors, but bids us make our defense to him alone, and to confess ourselves to him. And yet among secular judges, if any tell any of the robbers or grave-riflers, when they are arrested, to tell their errors and be quit of their punishment, they would accede to this with all readiness, despising the shame through desire of safety. But in this case there is nothing of this kind, but he both remits the sins, nor compels us to marshal them in array before any spectators. But one thing alone he seeks, that he who enjoys this remission should learn the greatness of the gift. How is it not, therefore, absurd that in case where he does us service, he should be content with our testimony only, but in those where we serve him we seek for others as witnesses, and do a thing for ostentation's sake? While we wonder then at his kindliness, let us show forth our doings, and before all others let us curb the vehemence of our tongue, and not always be giving utterance. "For in the multitude of words there wanteth not transgression."[1] If indeed then thou hast anything useful to say, open thy lips. But if there be nothing necessary for thee to say, be silent, for it is better. Art thou a handicraftsman? as thou sittest at work, sing psalms. Dost thou not wish to sing with thy mouth? do this in thine heart; a psalm is a great com-

[1] Prov. x. 19.

panion. In this case thou shalt undergo nothing serious, but shalt be able to sit in thy workshop as in a monastery. For not suitableness of place, but strictness of morals will afford us quiet. Paul, at least, pursuing his trade in a workshop suffered no injury to his own virtue.[1] Do not thou therefore say, How can I, being a handicraftsman and a poor man, be a philosopher? This is indeed the very reason why thou mayest be a philosopher. For poverty is far more conducive to piety for us than wealth, and work than idleness; since wealth is even a hinderance to those who do not take heed. For when it is needful to dismiss anger, to extinguish envy, to curb passion, to offer prayer, to exhibit forbearance and meekness, kindliness and charity, when would poverty be a bar? For it is not possible by spending money to accomplish these things, but by exhibiting a right disposition; almsgiving especially needs money, but even it shines forth in greater degree through poverty. For she who spent the two mites was poorer than all men, and yet surpassed all.[2] Let us not then consider wealth to be anything great, nor gold to be better than clay. For the value of material things is not owing to their nature, but to our estimate of them. For if any one would inquire carefully, iron is much more necessary than gold. For the one contributes to no need of our life, but the other has furnished us with the greater part of our needs, ministering to countless arts; and why do I speak of a comparison between gold and iron? For these stones[3] are more necessary than precious stones. For of those nothing serviceable could be made, but out of these, houses and walls and cities are erected. But do thou show me what gain could be derived from these pearls, rather what harm would not happen? For in order that thou mayest wear one pearl drop, countless poor people are pinched with hunger. What excuse wilt thou hit upon? what pardon?

Dost thou wish to adorn thy face? Do so not with pearls, but with modesty, and dignity. So thy countenance will be more full of grace in the eyes of thy husband. For the other kind of adorning is wont to plunge him into a suspicion of jealousy, and into enmity, quarrelsomeness and strife, for nothing is more annoying than a face which is suspected. But the ornament of compassion and modesty casts out all evil suspicion, and will draw thy partner to thee more strongly than any bond. For natural beauty does not impart such comeliness to the face as does the disposition of him who beholds it, and nothing is so wont to produce that disposition as modesty and dignity; so that if any woman be comely, and her husband be ill affected towards her, she appears to him the most worthless of all women; and if she do not happen to be fair of face, but her husband be well affected towards her, she appears more comely than all. For sentence is given not according to the nature of what is beheld, but according to the disposition of the beholders. Adorn thy face then with modesty, dignity, pity, lovingkindness, charity, affection for thy husband, forbearance, meekness, endurance of ill. These are the tints of virtue. By means of these thou wilt attract angels not human beings to be thy lovers. By means of these thou hast God to commend thee, and when God receives thee, he will certainly win over thy husband for thee. For if the wisdom of a man illuminates his countenance,[4] much more does the virtue of a woman illuminate her face; and if thou considerest this to be a great ornament, tell me what will be the advantage of the pearls in that day? But why is it necessary to speak of that day, since it is possible to show all this from what happens now. When, then, they who thought fit to revile the emperor were dragged to the judgment hall, and were in danger of extreme measures being taken, then the mothers, and the wives, laying aside their necklaces, and their golden ornaments, and pearls, and all adornment, and golden raiment, wearing a simple and mean dress, and besprinkled with ashes, prostrated themselves before the doors of the judgment hall and thus won over the judges; and if in the case of these earthly courts of justice, the golden ornaments, and the pearls, and the variegated dress would have been a snare and a betrayal, but forbearance, and meekness, and ashes, and tears, and mean garments persuaded the judge, much more would this take place in the case of that impartial and dread tribunal. For what reason wilt thou be able to state, what defense, when the Master lays these pearls to thy charge, and brings the poor who have perished with hunger into the midst? On this account Paul said, "not with braided hair, or gold, or pearls, or costly raiment."[5] For therein would be a snare. And if we were to enjoy them continually, yet we shall lay them aside with death. But arising out of virtue there is all security, and no vicissitude and changeableness, but here it makes us more secure, and also accompanies us there. Dost thou wish to possess pearls, and never to lay aside this wealth? Take off all ornament and place it in the hands

---

[1] Acts xviii. 3.   [2] Luke xxi. 2-4.
[3] Alluding probably to the stones of the building in which he was speaking.

[4] Eccles. viii. 1.   [5] 1 Tim. ii. 9.

of Christ through the poor. He will keep all thy wealth for thee, when He shall raise up thy body with much radiancy. Then He shall invest thee with better wealth and greater ornament, since this present is mean and absurd. Consider then whom thou wishest to please, and for whose sake thou puttest on this ornament, not in order that the ropemaker and the coppersmith and the huckster may admire. Then art thou not ashamed, nor blushest thou when thou showest thyself to them? doing all on their account whom thou dost not consider worthy of accosting.

How then wilt thou laugh this fancy to scorn? If thou wilt remember that word, which thou sentest forth when thou wert initiated, I renounce thee, Satan, and thy pomp, and thy service. For the frenzy about pearls is a pomp of Satan. For thou didst receive gold not in order that thou mightest bind it on to thy body, but in order that thou mightest release and nourish the poor. Say therefore constantly, I renounce thee, Satan. Nothing is more safe than this word if we shall prove it by our deeds.

5. This I think it right that you who are about to be initiated should learn. For this word is a covenant with the Master. And just as we, when we buy slaves, first ask those who are being sold if they are willing to be our servants: So also does Christ. When He is about to receive thee into service, He first asks if thou wishest to leave that cruel and relentless tyrant, and He receives covenants from thee. For his service is not forced upon thee. And see the lovingkindness of God. For we, before we put down the price, ask those who are being sold, and when we have learned that they are willing, then we put down the price. But Christ not so, but He even put down the price for us all; his precious blood. For, He says, ye were bought with a price.[1] Notwithstanding, not even then does He compel those who are unwilling, to serve him; but except thou hast grace, He says, and of thine own accord and will determinest to enroll thyself under my rule, I do not compel, nor force thee. And *we* should not have chosen to buy wicked slaves. But if we should at any time have so chosen, we buy them with a perverted choice, and put down a corresponding price for them. But Christ, buying ungrateful and lawless slaves, put down the price of a servant of first quality, nay rather much more, and so much greater that neither speech nor thought can set forth its greatness. For neither giving heaven, nor earth, nor sea, but giving up that which is more valuable than all these, his own blood, thus He bought us. And after all these things, he does not require of us witnesses, or registration, but is content with the single word, if thou sayest it from thy heart. "I renounce thee, Satan, and thy pomp," has included all. Let us then say this, "I renounce thee, Satan," as men who are about in that world at that day to have that word demanded of them, and let us keep it in order that we may then return this deposit safe. But Satan's pomps are theatres, and the circus, and all sin, and observance of days, and incantations and omens.

"And what are omens?" says one. Often when going forth from his own house he has seen a one-eyed or lame man, and has shunned him as an omen. This is a pomp of Satan. For meeting the man does not make the day turn out ill, but to live in sin. When thou goest forth, then, beware of one thing—that sin does not meet thee. For this it is which trips us up. And without this the devil will be able to do us no harm. What sayest thou? Thou seest a man, and shunnest him as an omen, and dost not see the snare of the devil, how he sets thee at war with him who has done thee no wrong, how he makes thee the enemy of thy brother on no just pretext; but God has bidden us love our enemies; but thou art turned away from him who did thee no wrong, having nothing to charge him with, and dost thou not consider how great is the absurdity, how great the shame, rather how great is the danger? Can I speak of anything more absurd? I am ashamed, indeed, and I blush: But for your salvation's sake, I am, I am compelled to speak of it. If a virgin meet him he says the day becomes unsuccessful; but if a harlot meet him, it is propitious, and profitable, and full of much business; are you ashamed? and do you smite your foreheads, and bend to the ground? But do not this on account of the words which I have spoken, but of the deeds which have been done. See then, in this case, how the devil hid his snare, in order that we might turn away from the modest, but salute and be friendly to the unchaste. For since he has heard Christ saying that "He who looketh on a woman to desire her, has already committed adultery with her,"[2] and has seen many get the better of unchastity, wishing by another wrong to cast them again into sin, by this superstitious observance he gladly persuades them to pay attention to whorish women.

And what is one to say about them who use charms and amulets, and encircle their heads and feet with golden coins of Alexander

---

[1] 1 Cor. vii. 25.

[2] Matt. v. 28.

of Macedon. Are these our hopes, tell me, that after the cross and death of our Master, we should place our hopes of salvation on an image of a Greek king? Dost thou not know what great result the cross has achieved? It has abolished death, has extinguished sin, has made Hades useless, has undone the power of the devil, and is it not worth trusting for the health of the body? It has raised up the whole world, and dost thou not take courage in it? And what wouldest thou be worthy to suffer, tell me? Thou dost not only have amulets always with thee, but incantations bringing drunken and half-witted old women into thine house, and art thou not ashamed, and dost thou not blush, after so great philosophy, to be terrified at such things? and there is a graver thing than this error. For when we deliver these exhortations, and lead them away, thinking that they defend themselves, they say, that the woman is a Christian who makes these incantations, and utters nothing else than the name of God. On this account I especially hate and turn away from her, because she makes use of the name of God, with a view to ribaldry. For even the demons uttered the name of God, but still they were demons, and thus they used to say to Christ, "We know thee who thou art, the Holy One of God,"[1] and notwithstanding, he rebuked them, and drave them away. On this account, then, I beseech you to cleanse yourselves from this error, and to keep hold of this word as a staff; and just as without sandals, and cloak, no one of you would choose to go down to the market-place, so without this word never enter the market-place, but when thou art about to pass over the threshold of the gateway, say this word first: I leave thy ranks, Satan, and thy pomp, and thy service, and I join the ranks of Christ. And never go forth without this word. This shall be a staff to thee, this thine armor, this an impregnable fortress, and accompany this word with the sign of the cross on thy forehead. For thus not only a man who meets you, but even the devil himself, will be unable to hurt you at all, when he sees thee everywhere appearing with these weapons; and discipline thyself by these means henceforth, in order that when thou receivest the seal[2] thou mayest be a well-equipped soldier, and planting thy trophy against the devil, may receive the crown of righteousness, which may it be the lot of us all to obtain, through the grace and lovingkindness of our Lord Jesus Christ, with whom be glory to the Father and to the Holy Spirit for ever and ever— Amen.

---

[1] Mark i. 24.

[2] *I. e.*, baptism. So called because of the covenant then made with God. So Tertullian calls it the *signaculum fidei*, the signature of the Christian faith as circumcision was of the Jewish faith.

ST. CHRYSOSTOM:

HOMILY I.

AGAINST THOSE WHO SAY THAT DEMONS GOVERN HUMAN AFFAIRS.

HOMILIES II AND III.

ON THE POWER OF MAN TO RESIST THE DEVIL.

TRANSLATED BY

T. P. BRANDRAM, M.A.,
RECTOR OF RUMBOLDSWHYKE, CHICHESTER.

CONTENTS.

HOMILY I.

	PAGE
Introduction	177
1. The insatiable zeal of St. Chrysostom's audience	178
2. The loving-kindness of God in spite of man's ingratitude.	179
3. This loving-kindness shown, not only in what He gives, but also in what He takes away	180
4. An instance of this in His "confusion of tongues," after the building of the tower of Babel	181
5. The various senses in which the word "evil" is used.	182
6. Instances of God's providential care, and of the malignity of Demons.	183
7. The prosperity of some bad men and the misfortunes of some good men no proof of disorder or injustice in the Divine government	184
8. The advantages of chastisement. An exhortation to reverence.	185

HOMILY II.

1. Praise of Bishop Flavian. Recapitulation of former discourse.	186
2. Man is not injured by the Devil, but by his own moral indolence	187
3. Things good in themselves become harmful through man's misuse of them.	188
4. The blessings of Christ's gospel a cause of condemnation to those who will not receive them	189
5. Exhortation to perseverance, and warning against despair	189
6. Five ways of repentance	190

HOMILY III.

1. Reproof of those who attended the theatre. Reasons why the bad and the good are permitted by God to be together in the world	191
2. Why the Devil is permitted to exist.	192
3. The Devil cannot compel any one to sin	193
4. The fall of Eve, and the victory of Job	194
5. The fortitude of Job an encouragement and consolation to the tempted.	195
6. The same argument continued	196
7. To resist temptation easier for the Christian than for Job	196

THREE HOMILIES CONCERNING THE POWER OF DEMONS.

INTRODUCTION BY REV. W. R. W. STEPHENS.

THE three following Homilies are closely connected in subject, and the opening sentence of the third clearly proves that it was delivered two days after the second; but it is impossible to say whether that which is placed first was really delivered before the other two. It must however have been spoken at Antioch, since Chrysostom refers at the beginning of it to his sermons "on the obscurity of prophecies" in which passages occur which clearly imply that he was not then a Bishop. The second of the three homilies here translated was delivered in the presence of a Bishop, as is clearly indicated by the commencement, and as the third was as already mentioned delivered two days after the second we may safely affirm that they were all spoken at Antioch when Chrysostom was a presbyter there under the Episcopate of Flavian.

They deal with errors against which Chrysostom throughout his life most strenuously contended. In an age of great depravity there seem to have been many who tried to excuse the weak resistance which they made to evil, both in themselves, and in others, by maintaining that the world was abandoned to the dominion of devils, or to the irresistible course of fate. To counteract the disastrous effects of such philosophy, which surrendered man to the current of his passions, it was necessary to insist very boldly and resolutely on the essential freedom of the will, on moral responsibility, and the duty of vigorous exertion in resisting temptation. And Chrysostom did this to an extent which some thought carried him perilously near the errors of the Pelagian heresy. No one however has described in more forcible language the powerful hold of sin upon human nature, and the insufficiency of man to shake it off without the assistance of divine grace. What he does most earnestly combat, both in the following homilies and very many others, is the doctrine that evil was an original integral part of our nature: he maintains that it is not a substantial inherent force ($\delta \acute{v} \nu a \mu \iota \varsigma$ $\dot{\epsilon} \nu v \pi \acute{o} \sigma \tau a \tau o \varsigma$). If evil was a part of our nature in this sense it would be no more reprehensible than natural appetites and affections. We do not try to alter that which is by nature ($\varphi \acute{v} \sigma \epsilon \iota$): sin therefore is not by nature, because by means of education, laws, and punishments we do seek to alter that. Sin comes through defect in the moral purpose ($\pi \rho o a \acute{\iota} \rho \epsilon \sigma \iota \varsigma$). Our first parents fell through indolence of moral purpose ($\dot{\rho} a \theta v \mu \acute{\iota} a$) and this is the principal cause of sin now. They marked out a path which has been trodden ever since: the force of will has been weakened in all their posterity: so that though evil is not an inherent part of man's nature yet he is readily inclined to it ($\dot{o} \xi v \rho \rho \epsilon \pi \grave{\eta} \varsigma$ $\pi \rho \grave{o} \varsigma$ $\kappa a \kappa \iota \acute{a} v$); and this tendency must be perpetually counteracted by vigorous exertion, and a bracing up of the moral purpose, with the aid of divine grace. Profoundly convinced therefore on the one hand of a strong and universal tendency to sin, but on the other of an essential freedom of the will, Chrysostom sounds alternately the note of warning and encouragement,—warning against that weakness, indolence, languor of moral purpose which occasions a fall,—encouragement to use to the full all the powers with which man is gifted, in reliance on God's forbearance and love, and on His willingness to help those who do not despair of themselves. Despair is the devil's most potent instrument for effecting the ruin of man; for it is that which prevents him from rising again after he has fallen. St. Paul repented, and, not despairing, became equal to angels: Judas repenting, but despairing, rushed into perdition.

HOMILY I.

AGAINST THOSE WHO SAY THAT DEMONS GOVERN HUMAN AFFAIRS, AND WHO ARE DISPLEASED AT THE CHASTISEMENT OF GOD, AND ARE OFFENDED AT THE PROSPERITY OF THE WICKED AND THE HARDSHIPS OF THE JUST.

I INDEED was hoping, that from the continuance of my discourse, you would have had a surfeit of my words: but I see that the contrary is happening: that no surfeit is taking place from this continuance, but that your desire is increased, that an addition is made not to your satiety but to your pleasure, that the same thing is happening which the winebibbers at heathen drinking-bouts experience; for they, the more they pour down unmixed wine, so much the rather they kindle their thirst, and in your case the more teaching we inculcate, so much the rather do we kindle your desire, we make your longing greater, your love for it the stronger. On this account, although I am conscious of extreme poverty, I do not cease to imitate the ostentatious among entertainers, both setting before you my table continuously, and placing on it the cup of my teaching, filled full: for I see that after having drunk it all, you retire again thirsting. And this indeed has become evident during the whole time, but especially since the last Lord's Day: For that ye partake of the divine oracles insatiably, that day particularly shewed: whereon I discoursed about the unlawfulness of speaking ill one of another, when I furnished you with a sure subject for self accusation, suggesting that you should speak ill of your own sins, but should not busy yourselves about those of other people: when I brought forward the Saints as accusing themselves indeed, but sparing others: Paul saying I am the chief of sinners, and that God had compassion on him who was a blasphemer, and a persecutor, and injurious,[1] and calling himself one born out of due time, and not even thinking himself worthy of the title of Apostle:[2] Peter saying "Depart from me because I am a sinful man:"[3] Matthew styling himself a publican even in the days of his Apostleship:[4] David crying out and saying "My iniquities have gone over my head, and as a heavy burden have been burdensome to me:"[5] and Isaiah lamenting and bewailing "I am unclean, and have unclean lips:"[6] The three children in the furnace of fire, confessing and saying that they have sinned and transgressed, and have not kept the commandments of God. Daniel again makes the same lamentation. When after the enumeration of these Saints, I called their accusers flies, and introduced the right reason for the comparison, saying, that just as they fasten themselves upon the wounds of others, so also the accusers bite at other people's sins, collecting disease therefrom for their acquaintance, and those who do the opposite, I designated bees, not gathering together diseases, but building honeycombs with the greatest devotion, and so flying to the meadow of the virtue of the Saint: Then accordingly—then ye shewed your insatiable longing. For when my discourse was extended to some length, yea to an interminable length, such as never was, many indeed expected that your eagerness would be quenched by the abundance of what was said. But the contrary happened. For your heart was the rather warmed, your desire was the rather kindled: and whence was this evident? The acclamations at least which took place at the end were greater, and the shouts more clear, and the same thing took place as at the forge. For as there at the beginning indeed the light of the fire is not very clear, but when the flame has caught the whole of the wood that is laid upon it, it is raised to a great height; so also accordingly this happened on the occasion of that day. At the beginning indeed, this assembly was not vehemently stirred by me. But when the discourse was extended to some length, and gradually took hold of all the subjects and the teaching spread more widely, then accordingly, then the desire

---

[1] 1 Tim. i. 13, 15.   [2] 1 Cor. xv. 8, 9.   [5] Ps. xxxvii. 5.   [6] Isa. vi. 5.
[3] Luke v. 8.   [4] Matt. x. 3.

of listening was kindled in you, and the applause broke forth, more vehemently. On this account, although I had been prepared to say less than was spoken, I then exceeded the measure, nay rather *I* never exceeded the measure. For I am wont to measure the amount of the teaching not by the multitude of the words spoken, but by the disposition of the audience. For he who meets with a disgusted audience, even if he abridge his teaching, seems to be vexatious, but he who meets with eager, and wide-awake, and attentive hearers, though he extend his discourse to some length, not even thus fulfils their desire.

But since it happens that there are in so great a congregation, certain weak ones, unable to follow the length of the discourse, I wish to suggest this to them, that they should hear and receive, as much as they can, and having received enough should retire: There is no one who forbids, or compels them to remain beyond their natural strength. Let them not however necessitate the abridgement of the discourse before the time and the proper hours. Thou art replete, but thy brother still hungers. Thou art drunk with the multitude of the things spoken, but thy brother is still thirsty. Let him then not distress thy weakness, compelling thee to receive more than thine own power allows: nor do thou vex his zeal by preventing him from receiving all that he can take in.

2. This also happens at secular feasts. Some indeed are more quickly satisfied, some more tardily, and neither do these blame those, nor do they condemn these. But there indeed to withdraw more quickly is praiseworthy, but here to withdraw more quickly is not praiseworthy, but excusable. There to leave off more slowly, is culpable and faulty, here to withdraw more tardily, brings the greatest commendation, and good report. Pray why is this? Because there indeed the tardiness arises from greediness, but here the endurance, and patience are made up of spiritual desire and divine longing.

But enough of preamble. And we will proceed hereupon to that business which remained over to us from that day. What then was that which was then spoken? that all men had one speech, just as also they had one nature, and no one was different in speech, or in tongue. Whence then comes so great a distinction in speech? From the carelessness of those who received the gift— of both of which matters we then spoke, shewing both the lovingkindness of the Master through this unity of speech, and the senselessness of the servants through their distinction of speech. For he indeed foreseeing that we should waste the gift nevertheless gave it: and they to whom it was entrusted, waxed evil over their charge This is then one way of explanation, not that God wrested the gift from us but that we wasted what had been given. Then next after that, that we received afterwards gifts greater than those lost. In place of temporal toil he honoured us with eternal life. In place of thorns and thistles he prepared the fruit of the Spirit to grow in our souls. Nothing was more insignificant than man, and nothing became more honoured than man. He was the last item of the reasonable creation. But the feet became the head, and by means of the first-fruits, were raised to the royal throne. For just as some generous and opulent man who has seen some one escape from shipwreck and only able to save his bare body from the waves, cradles him in his hands, and casts about him a bright garment, and conducts him to the highest honours; so also God has done in the case of our nature. Man cast aside all that he had, his right to speak freely, his communion with God, his sojourn in Paradise, his unclouded life, and as from a shipwreck, went forth bare. But God received him and straightway clothed him, and taking him by the hand gradually conducted him to heaven. And yet the shipwreck was quite unpardonable. For this tempest was due entirely not to the force of the winds, but to the carelessness of the sailor.

And yet God did not look at this, but had compassion for the magnitude of the calamity, and him who had suffered shipwreck in harbour, he received as lovingly as if he had undergone this in the midst of the open sea. For to fall in Paradise is to undergo shipwreck in harbour. Why so? Because when no sadness, or care, or labours, or toil, or countless waves of desire assaulted our nature, it was upset and it fell. And as the miscreants who sail the sea, often bore through the ship with a small iron tool, and let in the whole sea to the ship from below; so accordingly then, when the Devil saw the ship of Adam, that is his soul, full of many good things, he came and bored it through with his mere voice, as with some small iron tool, and emptied him of all his wealth and sank the ship itself. But God made the gain greater than the loss, and brought our nature to the royal throne. Wherefore Paul cries out and says, "He raised us up with him, and made us to sit with him, on his right hand in the heavenly places, that in the ages to come he might shew the exceeding riches of his grace in kindness towards us."[1] What dost thou say?

---

[1] Eph. ii. 6, 7.

the thing has already happened and has an end, and dost thou say "in order that he might shew to the ages to come?" Has he not shewn? He has already shewn, but not to all men, but to me who am faithful, but the unbelieving has not yet seen the wonder. But then, in that day the whole nature of man will come forward, and will wonder at that which has been done, but especially will it be more manifest to us. For we believe even now; but hearing and sight do not put a wonder before us in the same way, but just as in the case of kings when we hear of the purple robe, and the diadem, and the golden raiment, and the royal throne, we wonder indeed, but experience this in greater degree when the curtains are drawn aside and we see him seated on the lofty judgment seat. So also in the case of the Only-Begotten, when we see the curtains of heaven drawn aside, and the King of angels descending thence, and with his body-guard of the heavenly hosts, then we perceive the wonder to be greater from our sight of it. For consider with me what it is to see our nature borne upon the Cherubim, and the whole angelic force surrounding it.

3. But look, with me, too, at the wisdom of Paul, how many expressions he seeks for, so as to present to us the lovingkindness of God. For he did not speak merely the word grace, nor riches, but what did he say? "The exceeding riches of his grace in kindness."[1] But notwithstanding even so, he is below the mark; and even as the slippery bodies when grasped by countless hands, escape our hold, and slip through easily; so also are we unable to get hold of the lovingkindness of God in whatever expressions we may try to grasp it, but the exceeding magnitude of it baffles the feebleness of our utterances. And Paul therefore experiencing this, and seeing the force of words defeated by its magnitude, desists after saying one word: and what is this? "Thanks be to God for his unspeakable gift."[2] For neither speech, nor any mind is able to set forth the tender care of God. On this account he then says that it is past finding out, and elsewhere "The peace of God which passeth all understanding shall keep your hearts."[3]

But, as I was saying, these two ways of explanation are found in the meantime: one indeed that God has not wrested the gift that we have lost; and next, that the good things which have been given to us are even greater than those which we have lost. And I wish also to mention a third too. What then is the third? That even if he had not given the things after these, which were greater than those we had lost, but had only taken away what had been given to us, as we furnished the reason why, (for let this be added); even this is enough of itself to shew his tender care towards us. For not only to give, but also to take away what was given, is a mark of the greatest lovingkindness, and, if you will, let us lay bare the matter, in the case of Paradise. He gave Paradise. This of his own tender care. We were seen to be unworthy of the gift. This of our own senselessness. He took away the gift from those who became unworthy of it. This came of his own goodness. And what kind of goodness is it, says one, to take away the gift? Wait, and thou shalt fully hear. For think, what Cain would have been, dwelling in Paradise after his bloodguiltiness. For if, when he was expelled from that abode, if when condemned to toil and labour, and beholding the threat of death hanging over his head, if seeing the calamity of his father before his eyes, and holding the traces of the wrath of God still in his hands, and encompassed with so great horrors, he lashed out into such great wickedness, as to ignore nature, and to forget one born from the same birth pangs, and to slay him who had done him no wrong, to lay hold on his brother's person, and to dye his right hand with blood, and when God wanted him to be still, to refuse submission and to affront his maker, to dishonour his parents; if this man had continued to dwell in Paradise—look, into how great evil he would have rushed. For if when so many restraints were laid upon him, he leapt with fatal leaps; and if these walls were set at nought, whither would he not have precipitated himself?

Wouldest thou learn too from the mother of this man, what a good result the expulsion from the life of Paradise had, compare what Eve was before this, and what she became afterwards. Before this indeed, she considered that deceiving Devil, that wicked Demon to be more worth believing than the commandments of God, and at the mere sight of the tree, she trampled under foot the law which had been laid down by Him. But when the expulsion from Paradise came, consider how much better and wiser she grew. For when she bare a son, she says "I have gotten a man through the Lord."[4] She straightway flew to the master, who before this had despised the master, and she neither ascribes the matter to nature, nor puts the birth down to the laws of marriage, but she recognizes the Lord of Nature, and acknowledges thanks to Him for the birth of the little child. And she who before this deceived her husband, afterwards

---

[1] Eph. ii. 7.   [2] 2 Cor. ix. 15.   [3] Phil. iv. 7.   [4] Gen. iv. 1.

even trained the little child, and gave him a name which of itself was able to bring the gift of God to her remembrance: and again when she bare another, she says "God hath raised up seed to me in place of Abel whom Cain slew."[1] The woman remembers her calamity, and does not become impatient but she gives thanks to God, and calls the little child after his gift, furnishing it with constant material for instruction. Thus even in his very deprivation God conferred greater benefit. The woman suffered expulsion from Paradise, but by means of her ejection she was led to a knowledge of God, so that she found a greater thing than she lost. And if it were profitable, says one, to suffer expulsion from Paradise, for what cause did God give Paradise at the beginning? This turned out profitably to man, on account of our carelessness, since, if at least, they had taken heed to themselves, and had acknowledged their master, and had known how to be self-restrained, and to keep within bounds, they would have remained in honour. But when they treated the gifts which had been given them with insolence, then it became profitable, that they should be ejected. For what cause then did God give at first? In order that he might shew forth his own lovingkindness, and because He himself was prepared to bring us even to greater honour. But we were the cause of chastisement and punishment on all sides, ejecting ourselves through our indifference to goods which were given to us. Just as therefore an affectionate father, at first indeed, suffers his own son to dwell in his home, and to enjoy all his father's goods, but when he sees that he has become worthless of the honour, he leads him away from his table, and puts him far from his own sight, and often casts him forth from his paternal home, in order that he, suffering expulsion, and becoming better by this slight and this dishonour, may again shew himself worthy of restoration, and may succeed to his father's inheritance: So has God done. He gave Paradise to man. He cast him out when he appeared unworthy, in order that by his dwelling outside, and through his dishonour, he might become better, and more self-restrained, and might appear worthy again of restoration. Since after those things he did become better, he brings him back again and says "To-day shalt thou be with me in Paradise."[2] Dost thou see that not the gift of Paradise but even the ejection from Paradise was a token of the greatest tender care? For had he not suffered expulsion from Paradise, he would not again have appeared worthy of Paradise.

4. This argument therefore let us maintain throughout, and let us apply it to the case of the subject lying before us. God gave a speech common to all. This is part of his loving kindness to men. They did not use the gift rightly, but they lapsed to utter folly. He took away again that which had been given. For if when they had one speech, they fell into so great folly, as to wish to build a tower to heaven: had they not immediately been chastised would they not have desired to lay hold on the height of heaven itself? For why? If indeed that were impossible for them, yet notwithstanding their impious thoughts are made out from their plan. All which things God foresaw, and since they did not use their oneness of speech rightly, he rightly divided them by difference of speech. And see with me, his lovingkindness. "Behold," saith he "they all have one speech, and this they have begun to do."[3]

For what reason did he not at once proceed to the division of tongues, but first of all defend himself, as if about to be judged in a law-court? And yet at least no one can say to him why hast thou thus done? yea he is at liberty to do all things as he wills. But still as one about to give account, he thus sets up a defence, teaching us to be gentle and loving. For if the master defends himself to his servants, even when they have done him this wrong; much more ought we to defend ourselves to one another, even if we are wronged to the highest degree. See at least how he defends himself. "Behold they have all one mouth and one speech" saith he, "and this they have begun to do," as if he said let no one accuse me of this when he sees the division of tongues. Let no one consider that this difference of speech was made over to men from the beginning. "Behold they all have one mouth, and one speech." But they did not use the gift aright. And in order that thou mayest understand that he does not chastise for what has taken place so much as he provides for improvement in the future, hear the sequel "and now none of all the things will fail them, which they set on foot to do."[4] Now what he says, is of such a kind as this. If they do not pay the penalty now, and be restrained from the very root of their sins, they will never cease from wickedness. For this is what "none of the things will fail them which they set on foot to do" means, as if he said, and they will add other deeds yet more monstrous. For such a thing is wickedness; if when it has taken a start it be not hindered, as fire catching wood, so it rises to an un-

---

[1] Gen. iv. 25.   [2] Luke xxiii. 43.   [3] Gen. xi. 6.   [4] Gen. xi. 6.

speakable height. Dost thou see that the deprivation of oneness of speech was a work of much lovingkindness? He inflicted difference of speech upon them, in order that they might not fall into greater wickedness. Hold fast this argument then with me, and let it ever be fixed and immoveable in your minds, that not only when he confers benefits but even when he chastises God is good and loving. For even his chastisements and his punishments are the greatest part of his beneficence, the greatest form of his providence. Whenever therefore thou seest that famines have taken place, and pestilences, and drought and immoderate rains, and irregularities in the atmosphere, or any other of the things which chasten human nature, be not distressed, nor be despondent, but worship Him who caused them, marvel at Him for His tender care. For He who does these things is such that He even chastens the body that the soul may become sound. Then does God these things saith one? God does these things, and even if the whole city, nay even if the whole universe were here I will not shrink from saying this. Would that my voice were clearer than a trumpet, and that it were possible to stand in a lofty place, and to cry aloud to all men, and to testify that God does these things. I do not say these things in arrogance but I have the prophet standing at my side, crying and saying, "There is no evil in the city which the Lord hath not done"[1]—now evil is an ambiguous term; and I wish that you shall learn the exact meaning of each expression, in order that on account of ambiguity you may not confound the nature of the things, and fall into blasphemy.

5. There is then evil, which is really evil; fornication, adultery, covetousness, and the countless dreadful things, which are worthy of the utmost reproach and punishment. Again there is evil, which rather is not evil, but is called so, famine, pestilence, death, disease, and others of a like kind. For these would not be evils. On this account I said they are called so only. Why then? Because, were they evils, they would not have become the sources of good to us, chastening our pride, goading our sloth, and leading us on to zeal, making us more attentive. "For when," saith one, "he slew them, then they sought him, and they returned, and came early to God."[2] He *calls* this evil therefore which chastens them, which makes them purer, which renders them more zealous, which leads them on to love of wisdom; not that which comes under suspicion and is worthy of reproach; for that is not a work of God, but an invention of our own will, but this is for the destruction of the other. He calls then by the name of evil the affliction, which arises from our punishment; thus naming it not in regard to its own nature, but according to that view which men take of it. For since we are accustomed to call by the name of evil, not only thefts and adulteries, but also calamities; so he has called the matter, according to the estimate of mankind. This then is that which the prophet saith "There is no evil in the city which the Lord hath not done." This too by means of Isaiah God has made clear saying "I am God who maketh peace and createth evil,"[3] again naming calamities evils. This evil also Christ hints at, thus saying to the disciples, "sufficient for the day is the evil thereof,"[4] that is to say the affliction, the misery. It is manifest then on all sides, that he here calls punishment evil; and himself brings these upon us, affording us the greatest view of his providence. For the physician is not only to be commended when he leads forth the patient into gardens and meadows, nor even into baths and pools of water, nor yet when he sets before him a well furnished table, but when he orders him to remain without food, when he oppresses him with hunger and lays him low with thirst, confines him to his bed, both making his house a prison, and depriving him of the very light, and shadowing his room on all sides with curtains, and when he cuts, and when he cauterizes, and when he brings his bitter medicines, he is equally a physician. How is it not then preposterous to call him a physician who does so many evil things, but to blaspheme God, if at any time He doeth one of these things, if He bring on either famine or death, and to reject his providence over all? And yet He is the only true physician both of souls and bodies. On this account He often seizes this nature of ours wantoning in prosperity, and travailing with a fever of sins, and by want, and hunger, and death and other calamities and the rest of the medicines of which He knows, frees us from diseases. But the poor alone feel hunger, says one. But He does not chasten with hunger alone, but with countless other things. Him who is in poverty He has often corrected with hunger, but the rich and him who enjoys prosperity, with dangers, diseases, untimely deaths. For He is full of resources, and the medicines which He has for our salvation are manifold.

Thus too the judges do. They do not honour, or crown those only who dwell in cities, nor do they provide gifts alone, but they also

---

[1] Amos iii. 6.   [2] Ps. lxxviii. 34.   [3] Isa. xlv. 7.   [4] Matt. vi. 34.

often correct. On this account both the sword is sharpened by them, and tortures are prepared; both the wheel and the stocks, and the executioners, and countless other forms of chastisement. That which the executioner is to the judges, famine is to God—as an executioner correcting us and leading us away from vice. This too, it is possible to see in the case of the husbandmen: They do not then, only protect the root of the vine, nor hedge it round but prune it, and lop off many of the branches; on this account not only have they a hoe, but a sickle too, suitable for cutting: yet notwithstanding we do not find fault with them, but then above all we admire them, when we see them cutting off much that is unserviceable, so as through the rejection of what is superfluous to afford great security to that which remains. How is it not then preposterous, that we should thus approve of a father indeed and a physician and a judge, and a husbandman, and should neither blame nor censure him who casts his son out of his house nor the physician who puts his patient to torture nor the judge who corrects, nor the husbandman who prunes: but that we should blame and smite with countless accusations God, if he would at any time raise us up, when we are as it were, besotted through the great drunkenness which comes of wickedness? How great madness would it not be, not even to allow God a share of the same self-justification, of which we allow our fellow servants a share?

6. Fearing these things for them who reproach God, I speak now, in order that they may not kick against the pricks, and cover their own feet with blood, that they may not throw stones to heaven, and receive wounds on their own head. But I have somewhat else far beyond this to say. For omitting to ask (I say this by way of concession) if God took from us to our profit, I only say this; that if He took what had been given, not even thus, could anyone be able to reproach Him. For He was Lord of his own. Among men indeed, when they entrust us with money, and lend us silver, we give them our thanks for the time during which they lent it, we are not indignant at the time at which they take back their own. And shall we reproach God who wishes to take back his own? Indeed now is this not the extreme of folly? yea the great and noble Job did not act thus. For not only when he received, but even when he was deprived, he gives the greatest thanks to God saying "The Lord gave, the Lord hath taken away; may the name of the Lord be blessed for ever."[1] But if it is right to give thanks for both these even separately, and deprivation is not the less serviceable than bestowal; what excusableness should we have, tell me, in recompensing in a contrary spirit, and being impatient with Him when we ought to worship, who is so gentle, and loving and careful, who is wiser than every Physician, and more full of affection than any father, juster than any judge, and more anxious than any husbandman, in healing these souls of ours? What then could be more insane and senseless than they who in the midst of so great good order, say that we are deprived of the providence of God? For just as if some one were to contend that the soul was murky and cold, he would produce an example of extreme insanity, by his opinion; so if any one doubts about the providence of God, much rather is he liable to charges of madness.

Not so manifest is the Sun, as the providence of God is clear. But nevertheless some dare to say that Demons administer our affairs. What can I do? Thou hast a loving Master. He chooses rather to be blasphemed by thee through these words, than to commit thine affairs to the Demons and persuade thee by the reality how Demons administer. For then thou wouldest know their wickedness well by the experience of it. But rather indeed now it is possible to set it before you as it were by a certain small example. Certain men possessed of Demons coming forth out of the tombs met Christ, and the Demons kept beseeching him to suffer them to enter the herd of swine. And he suffered them, and they went away, and straightway precipitated them all headlong.[2] Thus do Demons govern; and yet to them the swine were of no particular account, but with thee there is ever a warfare without a truce, and an implacable fight, and undying hatred. And if in the case of those with whom they had nothing in common they did not even endure that they should be allowed a brief breathing space of time: if they had gotten unto their power us their enemies who are perpetually stinging them what would they not have done? and what incurable mischief would they not have accomplished? For for this reason God let them fall upon the herd of swine, in order that in the case of the bodies of irrational animals thou mayest learn their wickedness, and that they would have done to the possessed the things which they did to the swine, had not the demoniacs in their very madness experienced the providence of God, is evident to all: and now therefore when thou seest a man excited by a Demon, worship the Master. Learn the wickedness of the

[1] Job i. 21.
[2] Matt. viii. 28 sqq.

Demons. For it is possible to see both things in the case of these Demons, the lovingkindness of God, and the evil of the Demons. The evil of the Demons when they harass and disturb the soul of the demented: and the lovingkindness of God whenever he restrains and hinders so savage a Demon, who has taken up his abode within, and desires to hurl the man headlong, and does not allow him to use his own power to the full, but suffers him to exhibit just so much strength, as both to bring the man to his senses, and make his own wickedness apparent. Dost thou wish to form another example to see once more how a Demon arranges matters when God allows him to use his own power? Consider the herds, the flocks of Job, how in one instant of time he annihilated all, consider the pitiable death of the children, the blow that was dealt to his body: and thou shalt see the savage and inhuman and unsparing character of the wickedness of the Demons, and from these things thou shalt know clearly that if God had entrusted the whole of this world to their authority, they would have confused and disturbed everything, and would have assigned to us their treatment of the swine, and of those herds, since not even for a little breathing space of time could they have endured to spare us our salvation. If Demons were to arrange affairs, we should be in no better condition than possessed men, yea rather we should be worse than they. For God did not give them over entirely to the tyranny of the Demons, otherwise they would suffer far worse things than these which they now suffer. And I would ask this of those who say these things, what kind of disorder they behold in the present, that they set down all our affairs to the arrangement of Demons? And yet we behold the sun for so many years proceeding day by day in regular order, a manifold band of stars keeping their own order, the courses of the moon unimpeded, an invariable succession of night and day, all things, both above and below, as it were in a certain fitting harmony, yea rather even far more, and more accurately each keeping his own place, and not departing from the order which God who made them ordained from the beginning.

7. And what is the use of all this, says one, when the heaven indeed, and sun, and moon, and the band of stars, and all the rest keep much good order, but our affairs are full of confusion and disorder. What kind of confusion, O man, and disorder? A certain one, says he, is rich, and overbearing, He is rapacious and covetous, he drains the substance of the poor day by day, and suffers no terrible affliction. Another lives in forbearance, self-restraint, and uprightness, and is adorned with all other good qualities, and is chastened with poverty and disease, and extremely terrible afflictions. Are these then the matters which offend thee? Yes, these, says he. If then thou seest both of the rapacious, many chastened, and of those living virtuously, yea some even enjoying countless goods, why dost thou not abandon thine opinion, and be content with the Almighty? Because it is this very thing which offends me more. For why when there are two evil men, is one chastened, and another gets off, and escapes; and when there are two good men, one is honoured, and the other continues under punishment? And this very thing is a very great work of God's providence. For if he were to chasten all the evil men, here; and were to honour here all the good men, a day of judgment were superfluous. Again if he were to chasten no wicked man, nor were to honour any of the good, then the base would become baser and worse, as being more careless than the excellent, and they who were minded to blaspheme would accuse God all the more, and say that our affairs were altogether deprived of his providence. For if when certain evil men are chastened, and certain good men punished, they likewise say that human affairs are subject to no providence; if even this did not happen what would they not say? and what words would they not send forth? On this account some of the wicked he chastens, and some he does not chasten and some of the good he honours and some he does not honour. He does not chasten all, in order that he may persuade thee, that there is a Resurrection. But he chastens some in order that he may make the more careless, through fear by means of the punishment of the others, more in earnest. Again he honours certain of the good, in order that he may lead on others by his honours to emulate their virtue. But he does not honour all, in order that thou mayest learn that there is another season for rendering to all their recompense. For if indeed all were to receive their deserts here, they would disbelieve the account of the Resurrection. But if no one were to receive his desert here, the majority would become more careless. On this account some he chastens, and others he does not chasten, profiting both those who are chastened, and those who are not chastened. For he separates their wickedness from those, and he makes the others by their punishment, more self-restrained. And this is manifest from what Christ himself said. For when they announced to him that a tower had been brought to the ground, and had buried certain men, he saith to them "What think ye? that

these men were sinners only? I say to you nay, but if ye do not repent ye also shall suffer the same thing."[1]

Dost thou see how those perished on account of their sin, and the rest did not escape on account of their righteousness, but in order that they might become better by the punishment of the others? Were not then the chastened unjustly dealt with says one? For they could without being chastened themselves become better by the punishment of others. But if He had known that they would become better from penitence God would not have chastened them. For if when he foresaw that many would profit nothing from his longsuffering, he nevertheless bears with them, with much tolerance, fulfilling his own part, and affording them an opportunity of coming out of their own senselessness to their sober senses one day; how could he deprive those who were about to become better from the punishment of others, of the benefit of repentance? So that they are in no way unjustly treated, both their evil being cut off by their punishment, and their chastening is to be lighter there, because they suffered here beforehand. Again, they who were not chastened are in no way unjustly treated; for it was possible for them, had they wished, to have used the longsuffering of God, to accomplish a most excellent change, and wondering at his tolerance, to have become ashamed at his exceeding forbearance, and one day to have gone over to virtue, and to have gained their own salvation by the punishment of others. But if they remain in wickedness, God is not to blame, who on this account was longsuffering, that he might recover them, but they are unworthy of pardon, who did not rightly use the longsuffering of God: and it is not only possible to use this argument as a reason why all the wicked are not chastened here, but another also not less than this. Of what kind then is this? That if God brought upon all, the chastenings which their sins deserved, our race would have been carried off, and would have failed to come down to posterity. And in order that thou mayest learn that this is true, hear the prophet saying "If Thou observedst iniquity O Lord, who shall stand?"[2] And if it seems good to thee to investigate this saying, leaving the accurate enquiry into the life of each, alone: (For it is not possible even to know all that has been accomplished by each man) let us bring forward those sins which all, without contradiction, commit: and from these it will be plain and manifest to us, that if we were chastened for each of our sins, we should long ago have perished. He who has called his brother fool, "is liable to the hell of fire" saith He.[3] Is there then any one of us who has never sinned this sin? What then? ought he to be straightway carried off? Therefore we should have been all carried off and would have disappeared, long ago, indeed very long ago. Again he who swears, saith he, even if he fulfil his oath, doeth the works of the wicked one.[4] Who is there then, who has not sworn? Yea rather who is there who has never sworn falsely? He who looketh on a woman, saith he, with unchaste eyes,[5] is wholly an adulterer, and of this sin any one would find many guilty. When then these acknowledged sins are such and so insufferable, and each of these of itself brings upon us inevitable chastisement, if we were to reckon up the secret sins committed by us, then we shall see especially that the providence of God does not bring upon us punishment for each sin. So that when thou seest anyone rapacious, covetous, and not chastened, then do thou unfold thine own conscience; reckon up thine own life, go over the sins which have been committed and thou shalt learn rightly that in thine own case first, it is not expedient to be chastened for each of thy sins: for on this account the majority make reckless utterances, since they do not look on their own case before that of others, but we all leaving our own alone, examine that of the rest. But let us no longer do this, but the reverse, and if thou seest any righteous man chastened, remember Job: for if any one be righteous, he will not be more righteous than that man, nor within a small distance of approaching him. And if he suffer countless ills, he has not yet suffered so much, as that man.

8. Taking this then into thy mind, cease charging the master; learning that it is not by way of deserting him does God let such an one suffer ill, but through desire to crown him, and make him more distinguished. And if thou seest a sinner punished, remember the paralytic who passed thirty eight years on his bed. For that that man was delivered over then to that disease through sin, hear Christ saying "Behold thou art made whole; sin no more lest a worse thing happen to thee."[6] For either when we are chastened, we pay the penalty of our sins, or else we receive the occasion of crowning if, when we live in rectitude, we suffer ill. So that whether we live in righteousness, or in sins, chastening is a useful thing for us, sometimes making us more distinguished, sometimes rendering us more self-controlled, and lightening our punishment

---

[1] Luke xiii. 4. [2] Ps. cxxix. 3. [3] Matt. v. 22. [4] Matt. v. 37. [5] Matt. v. 28. [6] John v. 5, 14.

to come for us. For that it is possible that one chastened here, and bearing it thankfully should experience milder punishment there hear St. Paul saying "For this reason many are weak and sickly, and some sleep. For if we judged ourselves, we should not be judged. But when we are judged we are corrected by the Lord, that we should not be condemned with the world."[1] Knowing all these things therefore, Let us both moralize in this way on the providence of God, and stop the mouths of the gainsayers. And if any of the events which happen pass our understanding, let us not from this consider that our affairs are not governed by providence, but perceiving His providence in part, in things incomprehensible let us yield to the unsearchableness of His wisdom. For if it is not possible for one not conversant with it to understand a man's art, much rather is it impossible for the human understanding to comprehend the infinity of the providence of God. "For his judgments are unsearchable and his ways past finding out"[2] But nevertheless from small portions we gain a clear and manifest faith about the whole, we give thanks to him for all that happens. For there is even another consideration that cannot be contradicted, for those who wish to moralize about the providence of God For we would ask the gainsayers, is there then a God? and if they should say there is not, let us not answer them. For just as it is worthless to answer madmen, so too those who say there is no God. For if a ship having few sailors, and passengers, would not be conducted safely for one mile even, without the hand which guides it, much more, such a world as this, having so many persons in it, composed of different elements, would not have continued so long a time, were there not a certain providence presiding over it, both governing, and continually maintaining this whole fabric, and if in shame, through the common opinion of all men, and the experience of affairs, they confess that there is a God, let us say this to them. If there is a God, as indeed there is, it follows that He is just, for if He is not just neither is He God, and if He is just He recompenses to each according to their desert. But we do not see all here receiving according to their desert. Therefore it is necessary to hope for some other requital awaiting us, in order that by each one receiving according to his desert, the justice of God may be made manifest. For this consideration does not only contribute to our wisdom about providence alone, but about the Resurrection; and let us teach others, and let us do all diligence to shut the mouths of them who rave against the master, and let us ourselves glorify him in all things. For thus shall we win more of his care, and enjoy much of his influence, and thus shall we be able to escape from real evil, and obtain future good, through the grace and lovingkindness of our Lord Jesus Christ, By whom and with whom be glory to the Father, with the Holy Spirit, now and always, for ever and ever. Amen.

[1] 1 Cor. xi. 30-32.   [2] Rom. xi. 33.

HOMILY II.

AGAINST THOSE WHO OBJECT BECAUSE THE DEVIL HAS NOT BEEN PUT OUT OF THE WORLD: AND TO PROVE THAT HIS WICKEDNESS DOES NO HARM TO US—IF WE TAKE HEED: AND CONCERNING REPENTANCE.

1. WHEN Isaac, in old time, was desirous to eat a meal at the hands of his son, he sent his son forth from the house to the chace. But when this Isaac was desirous to accept a meal at my hands he did not send me forth from the house, but himself ran to our table. What could be more tenderly affectionate than he? What more humble? who thought fit to shew his warm love thus, and deigned to descend so far. On this account surely, we also having spent the tones of our voice, and the strength of our feet over the morning discourse, when we saw his fatherly face, forgot our weakness, lay aside our fatigue, were uplifted with pleasure; we saw his illustrious hoary head, and our soul was filled with light. On this account too, we set out our table with readiness, in order that he should eat and bless us. There is no fraud and guile, here, as there was then, there. One indeed was commanded to bring the meal—but another brought it. But *I* was commanded to bring it, and brought it too. Bless me then, O my father, with spiritual blessing, which we all also pray ever to receive, and

which is profitable not only to thee, but also to me, and to all these. Entreat the common master of us all, to prolong thy life to the old age of Isaac. For this is both for me, and for these, more valuable, and more needful than the dew of heaven, and the fatness of the earth.

But it is time to proceed to set out our table; what then is this? The remains of what was lately said with a view to our love of you. For still—still—we renew our discourse concerning the Devil, which we started two days ago, which we also addressed to the initiated, this morning when we discoursed to them about renunciation, and covenant. And we do this, not because our discourse about the Devil is sweet to us, but because the doctrine about him is full of security for you. For he is an enemy and a foe, and it is a great security to know clearly, the tactics of your enemies. We have said lately, that he does not overcome by force, nor by tyranny, nor through compulsion, nor through violence. Since were this so, he would have destroyed all men. And in testimony of this we brought forward the swine, against which the Demons were unable to venture anything, before the permission of the Master.[1] The herds and flocks of Job. For not even did the Devil venture to destroy these, until he received power from above. We learned therefore this one thing first, that he does not overcome us by force, or by compulsion; next after that, we added that even when he overcomes by deceitfulness, not thus does he get the better of all men, Then again we brought that athlete Job, himself into the midst, against whom he set countless schemes going, and not even thus got the better of him, but withdrew defeated. One question still remains. What then is this matter? That if he does not overcome says one, by force, yet by deceitfulness. And on this account it were better that he should be destroyed. For if Job got the better of him, yet Adam was deceived and overthrown. Now if once for all he had been removed from the world, Adam would never have been overthrown. But now he remains, and is defeated indeed by one, but gets the better of many. Ten overcame him, but he himself overcomes and wrestles down ten thousand and if God took him away from the world, these ten thousand would not have perished. What then shall we say to this? That first of all they who overcame are more valuable far than they who are defeated, even if the latter be more, and the former less. "For better is one," saith he "that doeth the will of God than ten thousand transgressors."[2] And next, that if the antagonist were taken away he who overcomes is thereby injured. For if thou lettest the adversary remain, the more slothful are injured, not on account of the more diligent, but by their own slothfulness; whereas if thou takest away the antagonist, the more diligent are betrayed on account of the slothful, and neither exhibit their own power, nor win crowns.

2. Perhaps ye have not yet understood what has been said. Therefore it is necessary that I should say it again more clearly. Let there be one antagonist. But let there be also two athletes about to wrestle gainst him, and of these two athletes let one be consumed with gluttony, unprepared, void of strength, nerveless; but the other diligent, of good habit, passing his time in the wrestling school, in many gymnastic exercises, and exhibiting all the practice which bears upon the contest. If then thou takest away the antagonist, which of these two hast thou injured? The slothful, pray, and unprepared, or the earnest one who has toiled so much? It is quite clear that it is the earnest one: For the one indeed is wronged by the slothful, after the antagonist has been taken away. But the slothful, while he remains, is no longer injured on account of the earnest. For he has fallen, owing to his own slothfulness.

I will state another solution of this question, in order that thou mayest learn, that the Devil does not injure, but their own slothfulness everywhere overthrows those who do not take heed. Let the Devil be allowed to be exceeding wicked, not by nature, but by choice and conviction. For that the Devil is not by nature wicked, learn from his very names. For the Devil, the slanderer that is, is called so from slandering; for he slandered man to God saying "Doth Job reverence thee for nought? but put out thine hand, and touch what he hath, see if he will not blaspheme thee to thy face."[3] He slandered God again to man saying "Fire fell from heaven and burnt up the sheep." For he was anxious to persuade him, that this warfare was stirred up from above, out of the heavens, and he set the servant at variance with the master, and the master with his servant; rather he did not set them at variance, but attempted to indeed, but was not able, in order that whenever thou mayest set another servant at variance with his master, Adam with God, and believing the Devil's slander, thou mayest learn that he gained strength, not owing to his own power but from that man's slothfulness and carelessness. He is called the Devil therefore on that

---

[1] Matt. viii. 31. [2] Ecclus. xvi. 3. [3] Job i. 9, 11. [4] Job i. 16.

account. But to slander, and to refrain from slander is not natural, but an action which takes place and which ceases to take place, occurring and ceasing to occur. Now such things do not reach the rank of the nature or of the essence of a thing. I know that this consideration about essence and accident is hard to be grasped by many. But there are they who are able to lend a finer ear, wherefore also we have spoken these things. Do you wish that I should come to another name? You shall see that that also is not a name which belongs to his essence or nature. He is called wicked. But his wickedness is not from his nature, but from his choice. For even this at one time is present, at another time is absent. Do not thou then say this to me that it always remains with him. For it was not indeed with him at the beginning, but afterwards came upon him; wherefore he is called apostate. Although many men are wicked, he alone is called wicked by pre-eminence. Why then is he thus called? Because though in no way wronged by us, having no grudge whether small or great, when he saw mankind had in honour, he straightway envied him his good. What therefore could be worse than this wickedness, except when hatred and war exist, without having any reasonable cause. Let the Devil then be let alone, and let us bring forward the creation, in order that thou mayest learn that the Devil is not the cause of ills to us, if we would only, take heed: in order that thou mayest learn that the weak in choice, and the unprepared, and slothful, even were there no Devil, falls, and casts himself into many a depth of evil. The Devil is evil. I know it myself and it is acknowledged by all, yet give heed strictly to the things which are now about to be said. For they are not ordinary matters, but those about which many words, many times, and in many places arise, about which there is many a fight and battle not only on the part of the faithful against unbelievers but also on the part of the faithful against the faithful. For this is that which is full of pain.

3. The Devil then is acknowledged, as I said, to be evil by all. What shall we say about this beautiful and wondrous creation? Pray is the creation too, wicked? and who is so corrupt, who so dull, and demented as to accuse the creation? what then shall we say about this? For it is not wicked, but is both beautiful and a token of the wisdom and power and lovingkindness of God. Hear at least how the prophet marvels at it, saying, "How are thy works magnified O Lord! in wisdom Thou hast made them all."[1] He did go through them one by one, but withdrew before the incomprehensible wisdom of God. And that he has made it thus beautiful and vast hear a certain one saying, "From the vastness and beauty of the creatures, the originator of them is proportionably seen."[2] Hear too Paul saying, "For the invisible things of Him, since the creation of the world, are clearly seen, being perceived through the things that are made."[3] For each of these by which he spake declared that the creation leads us to the knowledge of God, because it causes us to know the Master fully. What then? If we see this beautiful and wondrous creation itself becoming a cause of impiety to many, shall we blame it? In no wise, but them who were unable to use the medicine rightly. Whence then is this which leads us to the knowledge of God, a cause of impiety? "The wise" saith he "were darkened in their understandings, and worshipped and served the creature more than the creator"[4] The Devil is nowhere here, a Demon is nowhere here, but the creation alone is set before us, as the teacher of the knowledge of God. How then has it become the cause of impiety? Not owing to its own nature, but owing to the carelessness of those who do not take heed. What then? Shall we take away even the creation? tell me.

And why do I speak about the creation? Let us come to our own members. For even these we shall find to be a cause of destruction if we do not take heed, not because of their own nature, but because of our sloth. And look; an eye was given, in order that thou mayest behold the creation and glorify the Master. But if thou dost not use the eye well, it becomes to thee the minister of adultery. A tongue has been given, in order that thou mayest speak well, in order that thou mayest praise the Creator. But if thou givest not excellent heed, it becomes a cause of blasphemy to thee. And hands were given thee that thou mayest stretch them forth unto prayer. But if thou are not wary, thou stretchest them out unto covetousness. Feet were given in order that thou mayest run unto good works, but if thou art careless thou wilt cause wicked works by means of them: Dost thou see that all things hurt the weak man? Dost thou see that even the medicines of salvation inflict death upon the weak, not because of their own nature but because of his weakness? God made the heaven in order that thou mayest wonder at the work; and worship the master. But others leaving the creator alone, have worshipped the heaven; and this from their own carelessness and senselessness. But

---

[1] Ps. civ. 24.   [2] Wisd. xiii. 5.   [3] Rom. i. 20.   [4] Rom. i. 21, 25.

why do I speak of the creation? assuredly what could be more conducive to salvation than the Cross? But this Cross has become an offence to the weak. "For the word of the Cross is to them that are perishing, foolishness: but to those which are being saved, it is the power of God."[1] And again, "we preach Christ crucified, unto Jews a stumbling-block and unto Gentiles foolishness."[2] What could be more fit for teaching than Paul, and the apostles? But the Apostles became a savour of death to many. He says at least "to one a savour from death unto death: to the other a savour from life unto life."[3] Dost thou see that the weak is hurt even by Paul, but the strong is injured not even by the Devil?

4. Dost thou wish that we should exercise the argument in the case of Jesus Christ? What is equal to that salvation? what more profitable than that presence? But this very saving presence, so profitable, became an additional means of chastening to many. "For for judgment" saith he "came I into this world, that they which see not may see, and that they which see may become blind."[4] What dost thou say? The light became a cause of blindness? The light did not become a cause of blindness, but the weakness of the eyes of the soul was not able to entertain the light. Thou hast seen that a weak man is hurt on all sides, but the strong is benefited on all sides For in every case, the purpose is the cause, in every case the disposition is master. Since the Devil, if thou wouldest understand it, is even profitable to us, if we use him aright, and benefits us greatly, and we gain no ordinary advantages; and this, we shewed in a small degree from the case of Job. And it is possible also to learn this from Paul: for writing about the fornicator he thus speaks "Deliver such an one unto Satan for the destruction of the flesh, that the spirit may be saved."[5] Behold even the Devil has become a cause of salvation, but not because of his own disposition, but because of the skill of the Apostle. For as the physicians taking serpents and cutting off their destructive members, prepare medicines for antidotes; so also did Paul. He took whatever was profitable of the chastening that proceeds from the Devil, and left the rest alone; in order that thou mayest learn that the Devil is not the cause of salvation, but that he hasted to destroy and devour mankind. But that the Apostle through his own wisdom cut his throat: hear in the second epistle to the Corinthians, what he saith about this very fornicator, "confirm your love towards him," "lest by any means such an one should be swallowed up by over much sorrow." And, "we be taken advantage of by Satan."[6] We have snatched beforehand the man from the gullet of the wild beast, he saith. For the Apostle often used the Devil as an executioner. For the executioners punish those who have done wrong, not as they choose, but as the judges allow. For this is the rule for the executioner, to take vengeance, giving heed to the command of the judge. Dost thou see to what a dignity the Apostle mounted? He who was invested with a body, used the bodiless as an executioner; and that which their common master saith to the Devil, concerning Job: charging him thus, "Touch his flesh, but thou shalt not touch his life;"[7] giving him a limit, and measure of vengeance, in order that the wild beast might not be impetuous and leap upon him too shamelessly; this too the Apostle does. For delivering the fornicator over to him he says "For the destruction of the flesh,"[8] that is "thou shalt not touch his life." Dost thou see the authority of the servant? Fear not therefore the Devil, even if he be bodiless: for he has come in contact with him. And nothing is weaker than he who has come into such contact even though he be not invested with a body, as then nothing is stronger than he who has boldness even though he bear about a mortal body.

5. All these things have been now said by me, not in order that I may discharge the Devil from blame, but that I may free you from slothfulness. For he wishes extremely to attribute the cause of our sins to himself, in order that we being nourished by these hopes, and entering on all kinds of evil, may increase the chastening in our own case, and may meet with no pardon from having transferred the cause to him. Just as Eve met with none. But let us not do this. But let us know ourselves. Let us know our wounds. For thus shall we be able to apply the medicines. For he who does not know his disease, will give no care to his weakness. We have sinned much: I know this well. For we are all liable for penalties. But we are not deprived of pardon; nor shall we fall away from repentance for we still stand in the arena, and are in the struggles of repentance. Art thou old, and hast thou come to the last outlet of life? Do not consider even thus that thou hast fallen from repentance, nor despair of thine own salvation, but consider the robber who was freed on the cross. For what was briefer than that hour in which he was crowned? Yet notwithstanding even this was enough for him, for salvation. Art

---

[1] 1 Cor. i. 18.   [2] 1 Cor. i. 23.   [3] 2 Cor. ii. 16.
[4] John ix. 39.   [5] 1 Cor. v. 5.   [6] 2 Cor. ii. 8, 7, 11.   [7] Job ii. 5, 6.   [8] 1 Cor. v. 5.

thou young? Do not be confident in thy youth, nor think that thou hast a very fixed term of life, "For the day of the Lord so cometh as a thief in the night."[1] On this account he has made our end invisible, in order that we might make our diligence and our forethought plain. Dost thou not see men taken away prematurely day after day? On this account a certain one admonishes "make no tarrying to turn to the Lord and put not off from day to day,"[2] lest at any time, as thou delayest, thou art destroyed. Let the old man keep this admonition, let the young man take this advice. Yea, art thou in security, and art thou rich, and dost thou abound in wealth, and does no affliction happen to thee? Still hear what Paul says "when they say peace and safety, then sudden destruction cometh upon them."[3] Affairs are full of much change. We are not masters of our end. Let us be masters of virtue. Our Master Christ is loving.

6. Do you wish that I shall speak of the ways of repentance? They are many, and various, and different, and all lead to heaven. The first way of repentance is condemnation of sins. "Declare thou first thy sins that thou mayest be justified."[4] Wherefore also the prophet said "I said, I will speak out, my transgression to the Lord, and thou remittedst the iniquity of my heart."[5] Condemn thyself therefore for thy sins. This is enough for the Master by way of self-defence. For he who condemns his sins, is slower to fall into them again. Awake thy conscience, that inward accuser, in order that thou mayest have no accuser at the judgment seat of the Lord. This is one way of repentance, the best; and there is another not less than this, not to bear a grudge against thine enemies to overcome anger, to forgive the sins of our fellow-servants. For so will those which have been done against the master be forgiven us. See the second expiation of sins: "For if ye forgive" saith he, "your debtors, your Heavenly Father will also forgive you."[6] Dost thou wish to learn a third way of repentance? Fervent and diligent prayer, and to do this from the bottom of the heart. Hast thou not seen that widow, how she persuaded the shameless judge?[7] But thou hast a gentle Master, both tender, and kind. She asked, against her adversaries, but thou dost not ask against thine adversaries, but on behalf of thine own salvation. And if thou wouldest learn a fourth way, I will say almsgiving. For this has a great power and unspeakable. For Daniel saith to Nebuchadnezzar when he had come to all kinds of evil, and had entered upon all impiety, "O King let my counsel be acceptable unto thee, redeem thy sins by almsgiving and thine iniquities by compassion on the poor."[8] What could be compared with this lovingkindness? After countless sins, after so many transgressions, he is promised that he will be reconciled with him he has come into conflict with if he will show kindness to his own fellow-servants. And modesty, and humility, not less than all words spoken, exhaust the nature of sins. And the publican is proof, being unable to declare his good deeds, in sight of all, bringing forward his humility, and laying aside the heavy burden of his sins.[9] See we have shewn five ways of repentance: first the condemnation of sins, next the forgiveness of our neighbours' sins, thirdly that which comes of prayer, fourth that which comes of almsgiving, fifth that which comes of humility. Do not thou then be lazy; but walk in all these day by day. For the ways are easy, nor canst thou plead poverty. And even if thou livest poorer than all, thou art able to leave thine anger, and be humble, and to pray fervently, and to condemn sins, and thy poverty is in no way a hindrance. And why do I speak thus, when not even in that way of repentance in which it is possible to spend money (I speak of almsgiving), not even there is poverty any hindrance to us from obeying the command? The widow who spent the two mites is a proof.[10] Having learned then the healing of our wounds, let us constantly apply these medicines, in order that we may return to health and enjoy the sacred table with assurance; and with much glory, reach Christ the king of glory, and attain to everlasting good by the grace, and compassion, and lovingkindness of our Lord Jesus Christ, by whom and with whom be glory, power, honour, to the Father, together with the all holy, and good and quickening Spirit, now and always and for ever and ever. Amen.

---

[1] 1 Thess. v. 2. [2] Ecclus. v. 8. [3] 1 Thess. v. 3.
[4] Isa. xliii. 26. [5] Ps. xxxii. 5. [6] Matt. vi. 14.
[7] Luke xviii. 3.
[8] Dan. iv. 27. [9] Luke xviii. 13.
[10] Mark xii. 42.

HOMILY III.

THAT EVIL COMES OF SLOTH, AND VIRTUE FROM DILIGENCE, AND THAT NEITHER WICKED MEN, NOR THE DEVIL HIMSELF, ARE ABLE TO DO THE WARY MAN ANY HARM. THE PROOF OF THIS FROM MANY PASSAGES, AND AMONGST OTHERS FROM THOSE WHICH RELATE TO ADAM AND TO JOB.

1. THE day before yesterday we set on foot our sermon concerning the Devil, out of our love for you. But others, the day before yesterday while these matters were being set on foot here, took their places in the theatre, and were looking on at the Devil's show. They were taking part in lascivious songs; ye were having a share in spiritual music. They were eating of the Devil's garbage: ye were feeding on spiritual unguents. Who pray decoyed them? Who pray separated them from the sacred flock? Did the Devil pray deceive them? How did he not deceive you? you and they are men alike; I mean as regards your nature. You and they have the same soul, you have the same desires, so far as nature is concerned. How is it then that you and they were not in the same place? Because you and they have not the same purpose. On this account they indeed are under deception, but you beyond deception. I do not say these things again as discharging the Devil from accusation, but as desiring earnestly to free you from sins. The Devil is wicked; I grant this indeed, but he is wicked for himself not towards us if we are wary. For the nature of wickedness is of this kind. It is destructive to those alone who hold to it. Virtue is the contrary. It is not only able to profit those who hold to it, but those nearest at hand too. And in order that thou mayest learn that evil is evil in itself, but good is also good to others, I provide thee with proverbial evidence: "My son" saith he "if thou art become evil, thou shalt bear thine evils alone, but if wise, for thyself and thy neighbour."[1]

They were deceived in the theatre, but ye were not deceived. This is the greatest proof of things, a clear testimony, and unquestionable reasoning, that in every case, the purpose is master. Do thou accordingly use this method of proof, and if thou seest a man living in wickedness, and exhibiting all kinds of evil; then blaming the providence of God, and saying that by the necessity of fortune and fate and through tyranny of Demons He gave us our nature, and on all sides shifting the cause from himself indeed, and transferring it to the creator who provides for all; silence his speech not by word, but by deed, shewing him another fellow servant living in virtue and forbearance. There is no need of long speeches, no need of a complex plan, nor even of syllogisms. By means of deeds the proof is brought about. He said to him: thou art a servant, and he is a servant; thou art a man and he is a man. Thou livest in the same world: thou art nourished with the same nourishment under the same heaven: How is it that thou art living in wickedness, he in virtue? on this account God allowed the wicked to be mingled with the good; and did not give one law to the wicked indeed, and appointed another world as a colony for the good, but mixed these and those; conferring great benefit. For the good appear more thoroughly approved when they are in the midst of those who try to hinder them from living rightly, and who entice them to evil, and yet keep hold of virtue. "For there must" he saith "be also heresies among you that they which are approved may be made manifest among you."[2]

Therefore also on this account he has left the wicked to be in the world, in order that the good may shine the brighter. Dost thou see how great is the gain? But the gain is not owing to the wicked, but owing to the courage of the good. On this account also we admire Noe, not because he was righteous nor yet because he was perfect alone, but because in that perverse and wicked generation he preserved his virtue, when he had no pattern of virtue, when all men invited him to wickedness; and he went his whole way contrary to them, like some traveller, pursuing his way while the great multitude is being borne along vehemently. On this account he did not simply say "Noe was just, perfect," but added "in his generation"[3] in that perverse, that desperate generation, when there was no acquisition of virtue. To the good indeed then this was the gain from the wicked. Thus at all events, also trees tossed about by contrary winds, become stronger. And there is a gain to the wicked from their mixing with the good. They feel confusion, they are ashamed, they

---

[1] Prov. ix. 12.   [2] 1 Cor. xi. 19.   [3] Gen. vi. 9.

blush in their presence; and even if they do not abstain from evil, yet nevertheless they dare what they dare with secrecy. And this is no small thing not to have transgression publicly committed. For the life of the others becomes the accuser of the wickedness of these. Hear at least what they say about the righteous man. "He is grievous to us, even when beheld,"[1] and it is no small beginning of amendment to be tormented at his presence. For if the sight of the righteous man did not torment them, this word would not have been uttered. But to be stung, and pinched in conscience at his presence, would be no little hindrance to indulging in wickedness with pleasure, Dost thou see how great is the gain both to the good from the wicked, and to the wicked from the good? On this account God has not set them apart, but allowed them to be mingled together.

2. Let our argument also about the Devil be the same. For on this account He hath left him also to be here, in order that he might render thee the stronger, in order that he may make the athlete more illustrious, in order that the contests may be greater. When therefore any one says, why has God left the Devil here? say these words to him, because he not only does no harm to the wary and the heedful, but even profits them, not owing to his own purpose (for that is wicked), but owing to their courage who have used that wickedness aright. Since he even fixed upon Job not on this account that he might make him more illustrious, but in order that he might upset him. On this account he is wicked both because of such an opinion and such a purpose. But notwithstanding he did no harm to the righteous man, but he rather rejoiced in the conflict as we accordingly shewed. Both the Demon shewed his wickedness and the righteous man his courage. But he does upset many says one: owing to their weakness, not owing to his own strength: for this too has been already proved by many examples. Direct thine own intention aright then, and thou shalt never receive harm from any, but shall get the greatest gain, not only from the good but even from the wicked. For on this account, as I have before said, God has suffered men to be with one another, and especially the wicked with the good, in order that they may bring them over to their own virtue. Hear at least what Christ saith to his disciples, "The Kingdom of heaven is like unto a woman who took leaven and hid it in three measures of meal."[2] So that the righteous have the power of leaven, in order that they may transfer the wicked to their own manner of conduct. But the righteous are few, for the leaven is small. But the smallness in no way injures the lump, but that little quantity converts the whole of the meal to itself by means of the power inherent in it. So accordingly the power also of the righteous has its force not in the magnitude of their number, but in the grace of the Spirit. There were twelve Apostles. Dost thou see how little is the leaven? The whole world was in unbelief. Dost thou see how great is the lump? But those twelve turned the whole world to themselves. The leaven and the lump had the same nature but not the same manner of conduct. On this account he left the wicked in the midst of the good, that since they are of the same nature as the righteous they may also become of the same purpose.

Remember these things. With these stop the mouths of the indolent, the dissolute, the slothful, the indisposed towards the labours of virtue, those who accuse their common Master. "Thou hast sinned" he saith "be still."[3] "Do not add a second more grievous sin.[4] It is not so grievous to sin, as after the sin to accuse the Master. Take knowledge of the cause of the sin, and thou wilt find that it is none other than thyself who hast sinned. Everywhere there is a need of a good intention. I have shewn you this not from simple reasoning only, but from the case of fellow-servants living in the world itself. Do thou also use this proof. Thus too our common master will judge us. Learn this method of proof, and no one will be able to reason with you. Is any a fornicator? Shew him another who is self-restrained. Is any covetous and rapacious? Shew him one who gives alms. Does he live in jealousy and envy? Shew him one clean from passion. Is he overcome by anger? Bring into the midst one who is living in wisdom, for we must not only have recourse to ancient example, but take our models from present times. For even to-day by the grace of God, good deeds are done not less than of old. Is a man incredulous? and does he think that the scriptures are false? Does he not believe that Job was such as he was? Shew him another man, emulating the life of that righteous person. Thus will the Master also judge us: He places fellow servants with fellow-servants, nor does he give sentence according to his own judgment, in order that no one may begin to say again, as that servant said, who was entrusted with the talent, and who instead of a talent brought the accusation. "Thou art an austere man."[5] For he

---

[1] Wisd. ii. 15. [2] Matt. xiii. 33. [3] Gen. iv. 7. [4] Ecclus. xxi. 1. [5] Matt. xxv 24.

ought to mourn, because he did not double the talent, but rendered his sin the more grievous, by adding to his own idleness, his accusation against the Master. For what saith he? "I knew thee that thou art an austere man." O miserable, and wretched, ungrateful and lazy man! Thou oughtest to have accused thine own idleness, and to have taken away somewhat from thy former sin. But thou in bringing an account against the master hast doubled thy sin instead of doubling thy talent.

3. On this account God places together servants and servants in order that the one set may judge the other, and that some being judged by the others may not be able for the future to accuse the master. On this account, he saith "The Son of Man cometh in the glory of his Father."[1] See the equality of the glory: he does not say in glory like to the glory of the Father, but in the glory of the Father, and will gather together all the nations. Terrible is the tribunal: terrible to the sinful, and the accountable. Since to those who are conscious to themselves of good works, it is desirable and mild. "And he will place the sheep on his right hand, and the kids on his left."[2] Both these and those are men. For what reason then are those indeed sheep but these kids? Not that thou mayest learn a difference in their nature, but the difference in their purpose. But for what reason are they who did not show compassion kids? Because that animal is unfruitful and is not able to contribute services, either by its milk, or by progeny, or by its hair, to those who possess it, being on all sides destitute of such a contribution as this, on account of the immaturity of its age. On this account he has called those who bear no fruit, by comparison, kids, but those on the right hand sheep. For from these the offering is great, both of their natural wool, their progeny, and their milk. What then does he say to them? "Ye saw me hungering and ye fed me, naked and ye clothed me, a stranger and ye took me in." Again to those he says the contrary. And yet both these and those were alike men, both these and those received the same promises, the same rewards were assigned to both on doing right. The same person came both to these and to those, with the same nakedness: and to these and to those with the same hunger, and in the same way and a stranger. All things were alike to those and to these.

How then was the end not the same? Because the purpose did not permit it. For this alone made the difference. On this account the one set went to Gehenna, but the other to the Kingdom. But if the Devil were the cause to them of their sins, these would not be destined to be chastened, when another sinned and drove them on. Dost thou see here both those who sin, and those who do good works? Dost thou see how on seeing their fellow-servants they were silenced? Come and let us bring our discourse to another example for thy benefit. There were ten virgins he says.[3] Here again there are purposes which are upright, and purposes which are sinful, in order thou mayest see side by side, both the sins of the one and the good works of the others. For the comparison makes these things the plainer. And these and those were virgins; and these were five, and also those. All awaited the bridegroom. How then did some enter in, and others did not enter in? Because some indeed were churlish, and others were gentle and loving. Dost thou see again that the purpose determined the nature of the end, not the Devil? Dost thou see that the judgments were parallel, and that the verdict given proceeds from those who are like each other? Fellow-servants will judge fellow-servants. Dost thou wish that I should shew thee a comparison arising from contrasts? for there is one also from contrasts so that the condemnation may become the greater. "The men of Nineveh" he saith "shall rise up, and shall condemn this generation."[4] The judged are no longer alike, for the one are barbarians, the others are Jews. The one enjoyed prophetic teaching, the others were never partakers of a divine instruction. And this is not the only difference, but the fact that in that case a servant went to them, in this the master; and that man came and proclaimed an overthrow; but this man declared the glad tidings of a kingdom of heaven. Which of these was it the more likely, would believe? The barbarians, and ignorant, and they who had never partaken of divine teaching, or they who had from their earliest age been trained in prophetic books? To every one, it is plain, that the Jews would be more likely to believe. But the contrary took place. And these disbelieved the Master when he preached a kingdom of heaven, but those believed their fellow-servant when he threatened an overthrow: in order that their goodness, and these men's folly might be manifested to a greater degree. Is there a Demon? a Devil? chance? or Fate? has not each become the cause to himself both of evil, and of virtue? For if they themselves were not to be liable to account, he would not have said that they shall judge this generation. Nor would he have said that the Queen of the

---

[1] Matt. xvi. 27.   [2] Matt. xxv. 33.   [3] Matt. xxv.   [4] Matt. xii. 41.

South would condemn the Jews. For then indeed not only will one people condemn another people, but one man will often judge a whole people, when they who, it is allowed, might readily have been deceived, are found to remain undeceived, and they who ought in every way to have the advantage, turn out to be worsted. On this account, we made mention of Adam and of Job, for there is necessity to revert to that subject, so as to put the finish to our discourse. He attacked Adam indeed by means of mere words, but Job by means of deeds. For the one he denuded of all his wealth, and deprived of his children. But from this man he took not away anything, great or little of his possessions. But let us rather examine the very words and the method of the plot. "The serpent came" saith he "and said to the woman, What is it that God hath said, ye shall not eat of every tree which is in the garden?"[1] Here it is a serpent; there a woman, in the case of Job: mean while great is the difference between the counsellors. The one[2] is a servant, the other[3] a partner of the man's life. She is a helpmate, but the other is under subjection. Dost thou see how unpardonable this is? Eve indeed, the servant in subjection deceived: but him[4] not even his partner, and helpmate could overthrow. But let us see what he saith. "What is this that God hath said, thou shalt not eat of every tree?" Assuredly indeed God did not say this but the opposite. See the villany of the Devil. He said that which was not spoken, in order that he might learn what was spoken. What then did the woman? She ought to have silenced him, she ought not to have exchanged a word with him. In foolishness she declared the judgment of the Master. Thereby she afforded the Devil a powerful handle.

4. See what an evil it is to commit ourselves rashly to our enemies, and to conspirators against us. On this account Christ used to say, "Give not holy things to the dogs, neither cast ye your pearls before the swine, lest they turn and rend you."[5] And this happened in the case of Eve. She gave the holy things to the dog, to the swine. He trod under foot the words: and turned and rent the woman. And see how he works evil. "Ye shall not die the death" saith he.[6]

Give me your attention on this point, that the woman was able to understand the deceit. For he immediately announced his enmity, and his warfare against God, he immediately contradicted Him. Let it be so. Before this thou declaredst the judgment to one who wished to learn it. After this why didst thou follow one who said the opposite? God said ye shall die the death." The Devil made answer to this and said "ye shall not die the death." What could be clearer than this warfare? From what other quarter ought one to learn the enemy and the foe, than from his answer returned to God? She ought then immediately to have fled from the bait, she ought to have started back from the snare. "Ye shall not die the death," saith he "for God knoweth, that on the day on which ye eat, your eyes shall be opened, and ye shall be as Gods. In hope of a greater promise she cast away the goods in her hand. He promised that he would make them Gods, and cast them down into the tyranny of death. Whence then O woman didst thou believe the Devil? What good didst thou discern? Was not the trustworthiness of the lawgiver sufficient to prove that the one was God, both creator and framer of the world, and the other the Devil and an enemy? And I do not say the Devil. Thou thoughtest that he was a mere serpent. Ought a serpent to claim such equality that thou shouldest tell him the Master's judgment? Thou seest that it was possible to perceive the deceit, but she would not, and yet God gave many proofs of his own beneficence and shewed forth his care of his works. For he formed man, who had not existed before; and breathed a soul into him, and made him according to his image, making him ruler of all things upon the earth, and granted him a helpmate, planted Paradise, and having committed to him the use of the rest of the trees, refused him the taste of one only: and this very prohibition he made for man's advantage. But the Devil manifested no good things by his deed, whether little, or great: but exciting the woman with mere words and puffing her up with vain hopes, thus he deceived her. But nevertheless she considered the Devil to be more worthy of credit than God, although God shewed forth his good will by his works. The woman believed in one who professed mere words, and nothing else. Dost thou see how, from folly alone and sloth, and not from force, the deceit happened? and in order that thou mayest learn it more clearly hear how the scripture accuses the woman: For it does not say, being deceived, but "seeing the tree that it was fair, she ate." So that the blame belongs to her uncontrolled vision, not to the deceit alone which comes from the Devil. For she was defeated by yielding to her own desire, not by the wickedness of the Demon. On this account she did not have the benefit of pardon, but though she said, "the serpent deceived me," she paid the uttermost penalty. For it was in her power not to have fallen. And in

---

[1] Gen. iii. 1. [2] *i. e.*, the Devil. [3] *i. e.*, Job's wife.
[4] *i. e.*, Job. [5] Matt. vii. 6. [6] Gen. iii. 4.

order that thou mayest understand this more clearly, come, let us conduct our discourse to the case of Job; from the defeated to the vanquisher, from the conquered to the conqueror. For this man will give us greater zeal, so that we may raise our hands against the Devil. There he who deceived and conquered was a serpent; here the tempter was a woman, and she did not prevail: and yet at least she was far more persuasive than he. For to Job after the destruction of his wealth, after the loss of his children, after being stripped bare of all his goods, her wiles were added. But in the other case there was nothing of this kind. Adam did not suffer the destruction of his children, nor did he lose his wealth: he did not sit upon a dunghill, but inhabited a Paradise of luxury and enjoyed all manner of fruits, and fountains and rivers, and every other kind of security. Nowhere was there labour or pain, or despair and cares, or reproaches, and insults, or the countless ills which assailed Job: but nevertheless, when nothing of this kind existed, he fell and was overthrown. Is it not evident that it was on account of sloth? Even so therefore as the other, when all these things beset him, and weighed upon him, stood nobly and did not fall, is it not evident that his steadfastness was owing to his vigilance of soul?

5. On both sides, beloved, reap the utmost gain, and avoid the imitation of Adam knowing how many ills are begotten of indolence: and imitate the piety of Job, learning how many glorious things spring from earnestness. Consider him, the conqueror throughout, and thou shalt have much consolation in all pain and peril. For as it were in the common theatre of the world that blessed and noble man stands forth, and by means of the sufferings which happened to him discourses to all to bear all things which befal them nobly, and never give in to the troubles which come upon them. For verily, there is no human suffering which cannot receive consolation from thence. For the sufferings which are scattered over the whole world, these came together, and bore down upon one body, even his. What pardon then shall there be for him who is unable to bear with thankfulness his share of the troubles which are brought upon him? Since he appears not bearing a part only, but the entire ills of all men, and in order that thou mayest not condemn the extravagance of my words, come, and let us take in hand severally the ills that came upon him, and bring forward this fulfilment of them. And if thou wishest, let us first bring forward that which seems to be the most unendurable of all, I mean poverty, and the pain which arises from it. For everywhere all men bewail this. What was poorer then than Job, who was poorer than the outcasts at the baths, and those who sleep in the ashes of the furnace, poorer in fact than all men? For these indeed have one ragged garment, but he sat naked, and had only the garment which nature supplies, the clothing of the flesh, and this the Devil destroyed on all sides, with a distressing kind of decay. Again these poor folk are at least under the roof of the porches at the baths, and are covered with a shelter. But he continued always to pass his nights in the open air, not having even the consolation of a bare roof. And, what is still greater, the fact that these are conscious of many terrible evils within themselves, but he was conscious of nothing against himself. For this is to be noticed in each of the things which happened to him, a thing which caused him greater pain, and produced more perplexity; the ignorance of the reason of what took place. These persons then, as I said, would have many things with which to reproach themselves. And this contributes no little to consolation in calamity; to be conscious in oneself of being punished justly. But he was deprived of this consolation, and while exhibiting a conversation full of virtue, endured the fate of those who had dared to do extreme wickedness. And these folk who are with us, are poor from the outset, and from the beginning are versed in calamity. But he endured calamity in which he was unversed, experiencing the immense change from wealth. As then the knowledge of the cause of what takes place, is the greatest consolation; so it is not less than this, to have been versed in poverty from the beginning, and so to continue in it. Of both these consolations that man was deprived, and not even then, did he fall away. Dost thou see him indeed come to extreme poverty, even in comparison with which it is impossible to find a fellow? For what could be poorer than the naked who has not even a roof over him? Yea rather not even was it in his power to enjoy the bare ground, but he sat upon the dunghill. Therefore whenever thou seest thyself come to poverty, consider the suffering of the just one, and straightway thou shalt rise up, and shake off every thought of despondency. This one calamity therefore seems to men to be the groundwork of all sufferings together. And the second after it, yea rather before it, is the affliction of the body. Who then was even so disabled? Who endured such disease? Who received or saw any one else receive so great an affliction? No one. Little by little his body was wasted, and a stream of worms on every side issued from his limbs, the running was constant, and the evil smell which surrounded him was

strong, and the body being destroyed little by little, and decaying with such putrefaction, used to make food distasteful and hunger was to him strange and unusual. For not even was he able to enjoy the nourishment which was given to him. For saith he "I see my food to be loathsome."[1] Whenever then thou fallest into weakness, O man, remember that body and that saintly flesh. For it was saintly and pure, even when it had so many wounds. And if any one belong to the army, and then unjustly and without any reasonable pretext, be hanged upon the pillory, and has his sides rasped to pieces, let him not think the matter to be a reproach, nor let him give way to the pain when he thinks upon this saint. But this man, says one, has much comfort and consolation in knowing that God was bringing these sufferings upon him. This indeed especially troubled and disturbed him, to think that the just God who had in every way been served by him, was at war with him. And he was not able to find any reasonable pretext for what took place, since, when at least he afterwards learned the cause, see what piety he shewed, for when God said to him "Dost thou think that I have had dealings with thee in order that thou mightest appear righteous?"[2] conscious-stricken he says "I will lay my hand upon my mouth, once have I spoken but to a second word I will not proceed,"[3] and again "as far as the hearing of the ear I have heard thee before, but now mine eye hath seen thee, wherefore I have held myself to be vile, and am wasted away, and I consider myself to be earth and ashes."[4]

6. But if thou thinkest that this is sufficient for consolation, thou wilt thyself also be able to experience this comfort. And even if thou dost not suffer any of these misfortunes at the hands of God but owing to the insolence of men; and yet givest thanks and dost not blaspheme him who is able to prevent them indeed, but who permits them for the sake of testing thee: just as they who suffer at the hands of God are crowned, so also thou shalt obtain the same reward, because thou hast borne nobly the calamities which were brought upon thee from men, and didst give thanks to him who was able indeed to hinder them, but not willing.

Behold then! thou hast seen poverty and disease, and both in the extremest degree brought upon this just man. Dost thou wish that I should shew thee the warfare at nature's hands, in such excessive degree waged then against this noble man? He lost ten children, the ten at one fell swoop, the ten in the very bloom of youth, ten who displayed much virtue, and that not by the common law of nature, but by a violent and pitiable death. Who could be able to recount so great a calamity? No one. Whenever therefore thou losest son and daughter together, have recourse to this just man, and thou shalt find altogether much comfort for thyself. Were these then the only misfortunes which happened to him? The desertion and treachery of his friends, and the gibes, and raillery, and the mockery and derision, and the tearing in pieces by all, was something intolerable. For the character of calamities is not of such a kind, that they who reproach us about our calamities are wont to vex our soul. Not only was there no one to soothe him but many even on many sides beset him with taunts. And thou seest him lamenting this bitterly, and saying "but even you too fell upon me."[5] And he calls them pitiless, and says "My neighbours have rejected me, and my servants spake against me, and I called the sons of my concubines, and they turned away from me."[6] "And others" saith he "sport upon me, and I became the common talk of all.[7] And my very raiment" saith he "abhorred me"[8] These things at least are unbearable to hear, still more to endure in their reality, extreme poverty, and intolerable disease new and strange, the loss of children so many and so good, and in such a manner, reproaches and gibes, and insults from men. Some indeed mocked and some reproached and others despised; not only enemies, but even friends; not only friends, but even servants, and they not only mock and reproach, but even abhorred him, and this not for two or three, or ten days, but for many months; and (a circumstance which happened in that man's case alone) not even had he comfort by night, but the delusions of terrors by night were a greater aggravation of his misfortunes by day. For that he endured more grievous things in his sleep, hear what he says "why dost thou frighten me in sleep, and terrify me in visions?"[9] What man of iron, what heart of steel could have endured so many misfortunes? For if each of these was unbearable in itself, consider what a tumult their simultaneous approach excited. But nevertheless he bore all these, and in all that happened to him he sinned not, nor was there guile in his lips.

7. Let the sufferings of that man then be the medicines for our ills, and his grievous surging sea the harbour of our sufferings, and in each of the accidents which befal us, let us consider this saint, and seeing one person ex-

---

[1] Job vi. 7.   [2] Job xl. 8.   [5] Job xix. 5.   [6] Job xix. 14, 16.   [7] Job xix. 9, 10.
[3] Job xl. 4, 5.   [4] Job xlii. 5, 6.   [8] Job ix. 31.   [9] Job vii. 14.

hausting the misfortunes of the universe, we shall conduct ourselves bravely in those which fall to our share, and as to some affectionate mother, stretching forth her hands on all sides, and receiving and reviving her terrified children, so let us always flee to this book, and even if the pitiable troubles of all men assail us, let us take sufficient comfort for all and so depart. And if thou sayest, he was Job, and for this reason bore all this, but I am not like him; thou suppliest me with a greater accusation against thyself and fresh praise of him. For it is more likely that thou shouldest be able to bear all this than he. Why pray? Because he indeed was before the day of grace and of the law, when there was not much strictness of life, when the grace of the Spirit was not so great, when sin was hard to fight against, when the curse prevailed and when death was terrible. But now our wrestlings have become easier, all these things being removed after the coming of Christ; so that we have no excuse, when we are unable to reach the same standard as he, after so long a time, and such advantage, and so many gifts given to us by God. Considering therefore all these things, that misfortunes were greater for him, and that when the conflict was more grievous, then he stripped for the contest; let us bear all that comes upon us nobly, and with much thankfulness, in order that we may be able to obtain the same crown as he, by the grace and lovingkindness of Jesus Christ our Lord, with whom be glory to the Father together with the Holy Spirit, now and always and for ever and ever. Amen.

ST. CHRYSOSTOM:

HOMILY

ON THE PASSAGE (MATT. XXVI. 29), "FATHER IF IT BE POSSIBLE LET THIS CUP PASS FROM ME," ETC., AND AGAINST MARCIONISTS AND MANICHÆANS.

TRANSLATED BY

REV. W. R. W. STEPHENS, M.A.

PREBENDARY OF CHICHESTER CATHEDRAL, AND RECTOR OF WOOLBEDING, SUSSEX.

CONTENTS.

		PAGE
1.	The cross of Christ foretold and prefigured in the Old Testament.	201
2.	Christ voluntarily submitted to be crucified : the wonderful effects of the cross	202
3.	God the Father and the Son one in purpose and will. The mystery of the Incarnation.	204
4.	Christ prayed in order to prove the reality of His human nature, and to leave us an example	205

AGAINST MARCIONISTS AND MANICHÆANS.

ON THE PASSAGE "FATHER IF IT BE POSSIBLE LET THIS CUP PASS FROM ME, NEVERTHELESS NOT AS I WILL BUT AS THOU WILT:" AND AGAINST MARCIONISTS AND MANICHÆANS: ALSO, THAT WE OUGHT NOT TO RUSH INTO DANGER, BUT TO PREFER THE WILL OF GOD BEFORE EVERY OTHER WILL.

1. I LATELY inflicted a severe stroke upon those who are grasping and wish to overreach others;[1] I did this not in order to wound them but in order to correct them; not because I hate the men, but because I detest their wickedness. For so the physician also lances the abscess, not as making an attack upon the suffering body, but as a means of contending with the disorder and the wound. Well to-day let us grant them a little respite, that they may recover from their distress, and not recoil from the remedy by being perpetually afflicted. Physicians also act thus; after the use of the knife they apply plasters and drugs, and let a few days pass whilst they devise things to allay the pain. Following their example let me to-day, devising means for them to derive benefit from my discourse, start a question concerning doctrine, directing my speech to the words which have been read. For I imagine that many feel perplexed as to the reason why these words were uttered by Christ: and it is probable also that any heretics who are present may pounce upon the words, and thereby upset many of the more simple-minded brethren.

In order then to build a wall against their attack and to relieve those who are in perplexity from bewilderment and confusion, let us take in hand the words which have been cited, and dwell upon the passage, and dive into the depths of its meanings. For reading does not suffice unless knowledge also be added to it. Even as the eunuch of Candace read, but until one came who instructed him in the meaning of what he was reading he derived no great benefit from it. In order therefore that you may not be in the same condition attend to what is said, exert your understanding, let me have your mind disengaged from other thoughts, let your eye be quick-sighted, your intention earnest: let your soul be set free from worldly cares, that we may not sow our words upon the thorns, or upon the rock, or by the way side, but that we may till a deep and rich field, and so reap an abundant harvest. For if you thus attend to what is said you will render my labour lighter and facilitate the discovery of that which you are seeking.

What then is the meaning of the passage which has been read "Father if it be possible let this cup pass from me?" What does the saying mean? For we ought to unlock the passage by first giving a clear interpretation of the words. What then does the saying mean? "Father if it be possible take away the cross." How sayest thou? is he ignorant whether this be possible or impossible? Who would venture to say this? Yet the words are those of one who is ignorant: for the addition of the word "if," is indicative of doubt: but as I said we must not attend to the words merely, but turn our attention to the sense, and learn the aim of the speaker, and the cause and the occasion, and by putting all these things together turn out the hidden meaning. The unspeakable Wisdom then, who knoweth the Father even as the Father knoweth the Son, how should he have been ignorant of this?

---

[1] This was such a very common topic with Chrysostom that it affords no clue to the date of the Homily.

For this knowledge concerning His passion was not greater than the knowledge concerning His essential nature, which He alone accurately knew. "For as the Father knoweth me" He says "even so know I the Father."[1] And why do I speak of the only begotten Son of God? For even the prophets appear not to have been ignorant of this fact, but to have known it clearly, and to have declared beforehand with much assurance that so it must come to pass, and would certainly be.

Hear at least how variously all announce the cross. First of all the patriarch Jacob: for directing his discourse to Him he says "Out of a tender shoot didst thou spring up:"[2] by the word shoot signifying the Virgin and the undefiled nature of Mary. Then indicating the cross he said "Thou didst lie down and slumber as a lion, and as a lion's whelp; who shall raise him up?"[3] Here he called death a slumbering and a sleep, and with death he combined the resurrection when he said "who shall raise him up?" No one indeed save he himself—wherefore also Christ said "I have power to lay down my life, and I have power to take it again,"[4] and again "Destroy this temple and in three days I will raise it up."[5] And what is meant by the words "thou didst lie down and slumber as a lion?" For as the lion is terrible not only when he is awake but even when he is sleeping, so Christ also not only before the cross but also on the cross itself and in the very moment of death was terrible, and wrought at that time great miracles, turning back the light of the sun, cleaving the rocks, shaking the earth, rending the veil, alarming the wife of Pilate, convicting Judas of sin, for then he said "I have sinned in that I have betrayed the innocent blood;"[6] and the wife of Pilate declared "Have nothing to do with that just man, for I have suffered many things in a dream because of Him."[7] The darkness took possession of the earth, and night appeared at midday, then death was brought to nought, and his tyranny was destroyed: many bodies at least of the saints which slept arose. These things the patriarch declaring beforehand, and demonstrating that, even when crucified, Christ would be terrible, said "thou didst lie down and slumber as a lion." He did not say thou shalt slumber but thou didst slumbe, rbecause it would certainly come to pass. For it is the custom of the prophets in many places to predict things to come as if they were already past. For just as it is impossible that things which have happened should not have happened, so is it impossible that this should not happen, although it be future. On this account they predict things to come under the semblance of past time, indicating by this means the impossibility of their failure, the certainty of their coming to pass. So also spake David, signifying the cross; "They pierced my hands and my feet."[8] He did not say they "shall pierce" but "they pierced" "they counted all my bones."[9] And not only does he say this, but he also describes the things which were done by the soldiers. "They parted my garments among themselves, and upon my vesture did they cast lots."[10] And not only this but he also relates they gave Him gall to eat, and vinegar to drink. For he says "they gave me gall for my food, and for my thirst they gave me vinegar to drink."[11] And again another one says that they smote him with a spear, for "they shall look on Him whom they pierced."[12] Esaias again in another fashion predicting the cross said He was led as a sheep to the slaughter, and as a lamb before his shearer is dumb, so openeth he not his mouth." In his humiliation his judgment was taken away."[13]

2. Now observe I pray how each one of these writers speaks as if concerning things already past, signifying by the use of this tense the absolute inevitable certainty of the event. So also David, describing this tribunal, said, "Why did the heathen rage and the people imagine vain things? The Kings of the earth stood up, and the rulers were gathered together against the Lord and against his Christ."[14] And not only does he mention the trial, and the cross, and the incidents on the cross, but also him who betrayed him, declaring that he was his familiar companion and guest. "For," he saith, "he that eateth bread with me did magnify his heel against me."[15] Thus also does he foretell the voice which Christ was to utter on the cross saying "My God, My God why hast thou forsaken me?"[16] and the burial also does he describe: "They laid me in the lowest pit, in dark places, and in the shadow of death."[17] And the resurrection: "thou shalt not leave my soul in hell, neither shalt thou suffer thy Holy One to see corruption;"[18] and the ascension: "God has gone up with a merry noise, the Lord with the sound of the trump."[19] And the session on the right hand: "The Lord said to my Lord sit thou on my right hand until I make thy foes thy footstool."[20] But Esaias also declares the cause; saying, "for the transgressions of my

---

[1] John x. 15.   [2] Gen. xlix. 9. Septuagint rendering.
[3] Ibid.   [4] John x. 18.   [5] John ii. 19.
[6] Matt. xxvii. 4.   [7] Matt. xxvii. 19.
[8] Ps. xxii. 17.   [9] Ps. xxii. 18.   [10] Ps. xxii. 19.
[11] Ps. lxix. 22.   [12] Zach. xii. 10.   [13] Isa. liii. 7, 8.
[14] Ps. ii. 1, 2.   [15] Ps. xli. 9.   [16] Ps. xxii. 1.
[17] Ps. lxxxviii. 5.   [18] Ps. xvi. 11.   [19] Ps. xlvii. 5.
[20] Ps. cx. 1.

people is He brought to death,"[1] and because all have strayed like sheep, therefore is he sacrificed."[2] Then also he adds mention of the result, saying "by his stripes we have all been healed:"[3] and "he hath borne the sins of many."[4] The prophets then knew the cross, and the cause of the cross and that which was effected by it, and the burial and the resurrection, and the ascension, and the betrayal, and the trial, and described them all with accuracy: and is He who sent them and commanded them to speak these things ignorant of them Himself? What reasonable man would say that? Seest thou that we must not attend merely to the words? For this is not the only perplexing passage, but what follows is more perplexing. For what does He say? "Father if it be possible let this cup pass from me." Here he will be found to speak not only as if ignorant, but as if deprecating the cross: For this is what He says. "If it be permissible let me not be subjected to crucifixion and death." And yet when Peter, the leader of the apostles, said this to Him, "Be it far from thee Lord, this shall not happen unto Thee," He rebuked him so severely as to say; "get thee behind me Satan, thou art an offence unto me, for thou savourest not the things which be of God, but those which be of men:"[5] although a short time before he had pronounced him blessed. But to escape crucifixion seemed to Him so monstrous a thing, that him who had received the revelation from the Father, him whom He had pronounced blessed, him who had received the keys of Heaven, He called Satan, and an offence, and accused him of not savouring the things which be of God because he said to Him, "Be it far from thee Lord, this shall never be unto Thee"—namely crucifixion. He then who thus vituperated the disciple, and poured such an invective upon him as actually to call him Satan (after having bestowed such great praise on him), because he said "avoid crucifixion," how could He desire not to be crucified? and how after these things when drawing the picture of the good shepherd could He declare this to be the special proof of his virtue, that he should be sacrificed for the sake of the sheep, thus saying, "I am the good shepherd; the good shepherd layeth down his life for the sheep?"[6] Nor did He even stop there, but also added, "but he that is an hireling and not the shepherd seeth the wolf coming and leaveth the sheep, and fleeth."[7] If then it is the sign of the good shepherd to sacrifice himself, and of the hireling to be unwilling to undergo this, how can He who calls Himself the good shepherd beseech that he may not be sacrificed? And how could He say "I lay down my life of myself"? For if thou layest down thy life of thyself, how canst thou beseech another that thou mayest not lay it down? And how is it that Paul marvels at Him on account of this declaration, saying "Who being in the form of God counted it not a prize to be on an equality with God, but emptied Himself taking the form of a servant, being made in the likeness of men, and being found in fashion as a man he humbled himself, becoming obedient even unto death, yea, the death of the cross."[8] And He Himself again speaks in this wise, "For this cause doth my Father love me, because I lay down my life that I may take it again."[9] For if He does not desire to lay it down, but deprecates the act, and beseeches the Father, how is it that He is loved on this account? For love is of those who are like minded. And how does Paul say again "Love one another even as Christ also loved us and gave Himself for us?"[10] And Christ Himself when He was about to be crucified said "Father, the hour has come: glorify thy Son,"[11] speaking of the cross as glory: and how then does He deprecate it here when He urges it there? For that the cross is glory listen to what the evangelist says "the Holy Ghost was not yet given, because Jesus was not yet glorified."[12] Now the hearing of this expression is "grace was not yet given because the enmity towards men was not yet destroyed by reason that the cross had not yet done its work." For the cross destroyed the enmity of God towards man, brought about the reconciliation, made the earth Heaven, associated men with angels, pulled down the citadel of death, unstrung the force of the devil, extinguished the power of sin, delivered the world from error, brought back the truth, expelled the Demons, destroyed temples, overturned altars, suppressed the sacrificial offering, implanted virtue, founded the Churches. The cross is the will of the Father, the glory of the Son, the rejoicing of the Spirit, the boast of Paul, "for," he says, "God forbid that I should boast save in the cross of our Lord Jesus Christ."[13] The cross is that which is brighter than the sun, more brilliant than the sunbeam: for when the sun is darkened then the cross shines brightly: and the sun is darkened not because it is extinguished, but because it is overpowered by the brilliancy of the cross. The cross has broken our bond, it has made the prison of death ineffectual, it is the demonstration of the love of God. "For

---

[1] Isa. liii. 8. [2] Isa. liii. 6, 7. [3] Isa. liii. 5.
[4] Isa. liii. 12. [5] Matt. xvi. 22, 23. [6] John x. 11.
[7] John x. 12.
[8] Phil. ii. 6-8. [9] John x. 17. [10] Ephes. v. 2.
[11] John xvii. 1. [12] John vii. 39. [13] Gal. vi. 14.

God so loved the world that He gave His only-begotten Son, that every one who believes in Him should not perish."[1] And again Paul says "If being enemies we were reconciled to God by the death of His Son."[2] The cross is the impregnable wall, the invulnerable shield, the safeguard of the rich, the resource of the poor, the defence of those who are exposed to snares, the armour of those who are attacked, the means of suppressing passion, and of acquiring virtue, the wonderful and marvellous sign. "For this generation seeketh after a sign: and no sign shall be given it save the sign of Jonas";[3] and again Paul says, "for the Jews ask for a sign and the Greeks seek wisdom, but we preach Christ crucified."[4] The cross opened Paradise, it brought in the robber, it conducted into the kingdom of Heaven the race of man which was about to perish, and was not worthy even of earth. So great are the benefits which have sprung and do spring from the cross, and yet doth He not desire to be crucified I ask? Who would venture to say this? And if He did not desire it who compelled Him, who forced Him to it? and why did He send prophets beforehand announcing that He would be crucified, if He was not to be, and did not wish to undergo it? And for what reason does He call the cross a cup, if He did not desire to be crucified? For that is the word of one who signifies the desire which he has concerning the act. For as the cup is sweet to those who are thirsty so also was crucifixion to Him: wherefore also He said "With desire have I desired to eat this Passover with you,"[5] and this He meant not absolutely, but relatively, because after that evening the cross was awaiting Him.

3. He then who calls the thing glory, and rebukes the disciple because he was trying to hinder Him, and proves that what constitutes the good shepherd is his sacrificing himself on behalf of the sheep, and declares that he earnestly longs for this thing, and willingly goes to meet it, how is it that He beseeches it may not come to pass? And if He did not wish it what difficulty was there in hindering those who came for that purpose? But in fact you behold Him hastening towards the deed. At least when they came upon Him He said "Whom seek ye?" and they replied "Jesus." Then He saith to them "Lo! I am He: and they went backward and fell to the ground."[6] Thus having first crippled them and proved that He was able to escape their hands, He then surrendered Himself, that thou mightest learn that not by compulsion or force, or the tyrannical power of those who attacked Him, did He unwillingly submit to this, but willingly with purpose and desire, preparing for it a long time before. Therefore also were prophets sent beforehand, and patriarchs foretold the events, and by means of words and deeds the cross was prefigured. For the sacrifice of Isaac also signified the cross to us: wherefore also Christ said "Abraham your father rejoiced to see my glory and he saw it and was glad."[7] The patriarch then was glad beholding the image of the cross, and does He Himself deprecate it? Thus Moses also prevailed over Amalek when he displayed the figure of the cross: and one may observe countless things happening in the Old Testament descriptive by anticipation of the cross. For what reason then was this the case if He who was to be crucified did not wish it to come to pass? And the sentence which follows this is yet more perplexing. For having said "Let this cup pass from me He added "nevertheless not as I will but as Thou wilt."[8] For herein as far as the actual expression is concerned we find two wills opposed to one another: if at least the Father desires Him to be crucified, but He Himself does not desire it. And yet we everywhere behold Him desiring and purposing the same things as the Father. For when He says "grant to them, as I and Thou are one that they also may be one in us,"[9] it is equivalent to saying that the purpose of the Father and of the Son is one. And when He says "The words which I speak I speak not myself, but the Father which dwelleth in me, He doeth these works,"[10] He indicates the same thing. And when He says "I have not come of myself"[11] and "I can of my own self do nothing"[12] he does not say this as signifying that He has been deprived of authority, either to speak or to act (away with the thought!), but as desiring to prove the concord of his purpose, both in words and deeds, and in every kind of transaction, to be one and the same with the Father, as I have already frequently demonstrated. For the expression "I speak not of myself" is not an abrogation of authority but a demonstration of agreement. How then does He say here "Nevertheless not as I will but as Thou wilt"? Perhaps I have excited a great conflict in your mind, but be on the alert: for although many words have been uttered I know well that your zeal is still fresh: for the discourse is now hastening on to the solution. Why then has this form of speech been employed? Attend carefully. The doctrine of the incarnation was very hard to receive. For the exceeding measure of His lovingkindness and the magnitude of His con-

---

[1] John iii. 16. [2] Rom. v. 10. [3] Matt. xii. 39.
[4] 1 Cor. i. 22. [5] Luke xxii. 15. [6] John xviii. 6.
[7] John viii. 56. [8] Matt. xxvi. 39. [9] John xvii. 11.
[10] John xiv. 10. [11] John vii. 28. [12] John v. 30.

descension were full of awe, and needed much preparation to be accepted. For consider what a great thing it was to hear and to learn that God the ineffable, the incorruptible, the unintelligible, the invisible, the incomprehensible, in whose hand are the ends of the earth,[1] who looketh upon the earth, and causeth it to tremble, who toucheth the mountains, and maketh them smoke,[2] the weight of whose condescension not even the Cherubim were able to bear but veiled their faces by the shelter of their wings, that this God who surpasses all understanding, and baffles all calculation, having passed by angels, archangels, and all the spiritual powers above, deigned to become man, and to take flesh formed of earth and clay, and enter the womb of a virgin, and be borne there the space of nine months, and be nourished with milk, and suffer all things to which man is liable. Inasmuch then as that which was to happen was so strange as to be disbelieved by many even when it had taken place, He first of all sends prophets beforehand, announcing this very fact. For instance the patriarch predicted it saying "Thou didst spring from a tender shoot my son: thou didst lie down and slumber as a lion;"[3] and Esaias saying "Behold the Virgin shall conceive and bear a son and they shall call His name Emmanuel;"[4] and elsewhere again "We beheld Him as a young child, as a root in a dry ground;"[5] and by the dry ground he means the virgin's womb. And again "unto us a child is born, unto us a son is given;"[6] and again "there shall come forth a rod out of the root of Jesse, and a flower shall spring out of his root."[7] And Baruch in the book of Jeremiah says "this is our God: no other shall be reckoned by the side of Him: He found out every path of knowledge and gave it to Jacob His servant, and Israel his beloved. After these things also He appeared upon the earth, and held converse with men."[8] And David signifying His incarnate presence said "He shall come down like the rain into a fleece of wool, and like the drop which distills upon the earth"[9] because He noiselessly and gently entered into the Virgin's womb.

4. But these proofs alone did not suffice, but even when He had come, lest what had taken place should be deemed an illusion, He warranted the fact not only by the sight but by duration of time and by passing through all the phases incident to man. For He did not enter once for all into a man matured and completely developed, but into a virgin's womb, so as to undergo the process of gestation and birth and suckling and growth, and by the length of the time and the variety of the stages of growth to give assurance of what had come to pass. And not even here were the proofs concluded, but even when bearing about the body of flesh He suffered it to experience the infirmities of human nature and to be hungry, and thirsty, and to sleep and feel fatigue; finally also when He came to the cross He suffered it to undergo the pains of the flesh. For this reason also streams of sweat flowed down from it and an angel was discovered strengthening it, and He was sad and downcast: for before He uttered these words He said "my soul is troubled, and exceeding sorrowful even unto death."[10] If then after all these things have taken place the wicked mouth of the devil speaking through Marcion of Pontus, and Valentinus, and Manichæus of Persia and many more heretics, has attempted to overthrow the doctrine of the Incarnation and has vented a diabolical utterance declaring that He did not become flesh, nor was clothed with it, but that this was mere fancy, and illusion, a piece of acting and pretence, although the sufferings, the death, the burial, the thirst, cry aloud against this teaching; supposing that none of these things had happened would not the devil have sown these wicked doctrines of impiousness much more widely? For this reason, just as He hungered, as He slept, as He felt fatigue, as He ate and drank, so also did He deprecate death, thereby manifesting his humanity, and that infirmity of human nature which does not submit without pain to be torn from this present life. For had He not uttered any of these things, it might have been said that if He were a man He ought to have experienced human feelings. And what are these? in the case of one about to be crucified, fear and agony, and pain in being torn from present life: for a sense of the charm which surrounds present things is implanted in human nature: on this account wishing to prove the reality of the fleshly clothing, and to give assurance of the incarnation He manifests the actual feelings of man with full demonstration.

This is one consideration, but there is another no less important. And what is this? Christ having come to earth wished to instruct men in all virtue: now the instructor teaches not only by word, but also by deed: for this is the teacher's best method of teaching. A pilot for instance when he makes the apprentice sit by his side shows him how he handles the rudder, but he also joins speech to action, and does not depend upon words alone or example

---

[1] Ps. xcv. 4.   [2] Ps. civ. 32.   [3] Gen. xlix. 9.
[4] Isa. vii. 14.   [5] Isa. liii. 2.   [6] Isa. ix. 6.
[7] Isa. xi. 1.   [8] Bar. iii. 35-37.   [9] Ps. lxxii. 6.

[10] Matt. xxvi. 38.

alone: in like manner also an architect when he has placed by his side the man who is intended to learn from him how a wall is contructed, shows him the way by means of action as well as by means of oral teaching; so also with the weaver, and embroiderer, and gold refiner, and coppersmith;—and every kind of art has teachers who instruct both orally and practically. Inasmuch then as Christ Himself came to instruct us in all virtue, He both tells us what ought to be done, and does it. "For," he says, "he who does and teaches the same shall be called great in the kingdom of heaven."[1] Now observe; He commanded men to be lowly-minded, and meek, and He taught this by His words: but see how He also teaches it by His deeds. For having said "Blessed are the poor in spirit, blessed are the meek,"[2] He shows how these virtues ought to be practised. How then did He teach them? He took a towel and girded Himself and washed the disciples' feet.[3] What can match this lowliness of mind? for He teaches this virtue no longer by His words only but also by His deeds. Again He teaches meekness and forbearance by His acts. How so? He was struck on the face by the servant of the high priest, and said "If I have spoken evil bear witness of the evil: but if well why smitest thou me?"[4] He commanded men to pray for their enemies: this also again He teaches by means of His acts: for when He had ascended the cross He said "Father forgive them for they know not what they do."[5] As therefore He commanded men to pray so does He Himself pray, instructing thee to do so by his own unflagging utterances of prayer. Again He commanded us to do good to those who hate us, and to deal fairly with those who treat us despitefully:[6] and this He did by his own acts: for he cast devils out of the Jews, who said that He Himself was possessed by a devil, He bestowed benefits on His persecutors, He fed those who were forming designs against Him, He conducted into His kingdom those who were desiring to crucify Him. Again He said to His disciples "Get you no gold nor silver neither brass in your purses,"[7] thus training them for poverty: and this also He taught by His example, thus saying, "Foxes have holes, and the birds of the air have nests, but the Son of man hath not where to lay His head."[8] And He had neither table nor dwelling nor anything else of that kind: not because He was at a loss to obtain them, but because He was instructing men to go in that path. After the same manner then he taught them also to pray. They said to Him "Teach us to pray."[9] Therefore also He prays, in order that they may learn to pray. But it was necessary for them not merely to learn to pray but also how they ought to pray: for this reason He delivered to them a prayer in this form: "Our Father which art in Heaven hallowed be thy name, Thy kingdom come: Thy will be done, as in Heaven, so on earth. Give us this day our daily bread: and forgive us our debts as we also forgive our debtors: and lead us not into temptation:"[10] that is into danger, into snares. Since then He commanded them to pray "lead us not into temptation," He instructs them in this very precept by putting it in practice Himself, saying "Father if it be possible, let this cup pass away from me, thus teaching all the saints not to plunge into dangers, not to fling themselves into them but to wait for their approach, and to exhibit all possible courage, only not to rush forwards themselves, or to be the first to advance against terrors. Why so, pray? both to teach us lowliness of mind, and also to deliver us from the charge of vainglory. On this account it is said also in this passage that when He had spoken these words "He went away and prayed:" and after He had prayed He speaks thus to His disciples "Could ye not watch with me one hour? Watch and pray that ye enter not into temptation."[11] Seest thou He not only prays but also admonishes? "For the Spirit indeed is willing," He said, "but the flesh is weak."[12] Now this He said by way of emptying their soul of vanity, and delivering them from pride, teaching them self-restraint, training them to practice moderation. Therefore the prayer which He wished to teach them, He Himself also offered, speaking after the manner of men, not according to His Godhead (for the divine nature is impassable) but according to His manhood. And He prayed as instructing us to pray, and even to seek deliverance from distress; but, if this be not permitted, then to acquiesce in what seems good to God. Therefore He said "Nevertheless not as I will but as Thou wilt:" not because He had one will and the Father another; but in order that He might instruct men even if they were in distress and trembling, even if danger came upon them, and they were unwilling to be torn from present life, nevertheless to postpone their own will to the will of God: even as Paul also when he had been instructed practically exhibited both these principles; for he besought that temptations might be removed from him, thus saying "For this thing I besought the Lord thrice:"[13] and yet since it

---

[1] Matt. v. 19. [2] Matt. v. 3, 4. [3] John xiii. 4, 5.
[4] John xviii. 23. [5] Luke xxiii. 34. [6] Matt. v. 44.
[7] Matt. x. 9. [8] Matt. viii. 20.
[9] Luke xi. 1. [10] Luke xi. 2-4. [11] Matt. xxvi. 39-41.
[12] Matt. xxvi. 41. [13] 2 Cor. xii. 8.

did not please God to remove it, he says "Wherefore I take pleasure in infirmities, in insults, in persecutions."[1] But perhaps what I have said is not quite clear: therefore I will make it clearer. Paul incurred many dangers and prayed that he might not be exposed to them. Then he heard Christ saying "my grace is sufficient for thee, for my strength is made perfect in weakness."[2] As soon then as he saw what the will of God was, he in future submitted his will to God's will. By means of this prayer then Christ taught both these truths, that we should not plunge into dangers, but rather pray that we may not fall into them; but if they come upon us we should bear them bravely, and postpone our own will to the will of God. Knowing these things then let us pray that we may never enter into temptation: but if we do enter it let us beseech God to give us patience and courage, and let us honour His will in preference to every will of our own. For then we shall pass through this present life with safety, and shall obtain the blessings to come: which may we all receive by the favour and lovingkindness of our Lord Jesus Christ, with Whom be to the Father, together with the Holy Ghost, glory, might, honour, now and for ever world without end. Amen.

[1] 2 Cor. xii. 10.   [2] 2 Cor. xii. 9.

ST. CHRYSOSTOM:

HOMILY

ON THE PARALYTIC LET DOWN THROUGH THE ROOF: AND CONCERNING THE EQUALITY OF THE DIVINE FATHER AND THE SON.

TRANSLATED BY

REV. W. R. W. STEPHENS, M.A.,

PREBENDARY OF CHICHESTER CATHEDRAL, AND RECTOR OF WOOLBEDING, SUSSEX.

CONTENTS.

		PAGE
1.	A reference to the cure of the impotent man at the pool of Bethesda	211
2.	God deals with man as a physician with his patients, as a father with his children.	212
3.	Instances of Christ's tenderness in dealing with sinners. The accounts of the two paralytics cured by Christ recorded in St. Matt. ix. and St. John v. not to be confused	213
4.	Difference between the two cases, and our Lord's method of treating them.	214
5.	The faith of the paralytic let down through the roof	216
6.	Why Christ forgave his sins before he healed his infirmity: the equality of God the Father and the Son.	217
7.	Christ's power to heal the body a proof of His power to heal the soul.	219
8.	An exhortation to endure affliction with patience and fortitude	219

HOMILY ON THE PARALYTIC LET DOWN THROUGH THE ROOF.

1. HAVING lately come across the incident of the paralytic[1] who lay upon his bed beside the pool, we discovered a rich and large treasure, not by delving in the ground, but by diving into his heart: we found a treasure not containing silver and gold and precious stones, but endurance, and philosophy, and patience and much hope towards God, which is more valuable than any kind of jewel or source of wealth. For material riches are liable to the designs of robbers, and the tales of false accusers, and the violence of housebreakers, and the villany of servants, and when they have escaped all these things, they often bring the greatest ruin upon those who possess them by exciting the eyes of the envious, and consequently breeding countless storms of trouble. But the spiritual riches escape all these occasions of mischief and are superior to all abuse of this kind, laughing to scorn both robbers, and housebreakers, and slanderers, and false accusers and death itself. For they are not parted from the possessor by death, but on the contrary the possession becomes then more especially secured to the owners, and they accompany them on their journey to the other world, and are transplanted with them to the future life, and become marvellous advocates of those with whom they depart hence, and render the judge propitious to them.

This wealth we found in great abundance stored in the soul of the paralytic. And you are witnesses who with great zeal drew up draughts of this treasure yet without exhausting it. For such is the nature of spiritual wealth; it resembles fountains of water, or rather exceeds their plenteousness, being most abundant when it has many to draw upon it. For when it enters into any man's soul it is not divided, not diminished, but coming in its entireness to each remains continually unconsumed, being incapable of ever failing: which was just what took place at that time. For although so many have applied to the treasure, and all are drawing upon it as much as they can—but why do I speak of you, seeing that it has made countless persons rich from that time to the present day, and yet abides in its original perfection? Let us not then grow weary in having recourse to this source of spiritual wealth: but as far as possible let us now also draw forth draughts from it, and let us gaze upon our merciful Lord, gaze upon His patient servant. He had been thirty and eight years struggling with an incurable infirmity and was perpetually plagued by it, yet he did not repine, he did not utter a blasphemous word, he did not accuse his Maker, but endured his calamity bravely and with much meekness. And whence is this manifest? you say: for Scripture has not told us anything clearly concerning his former life, but only that he had been thirty-eight years in his infirmity; it has not added a word to prove that he did not show discontent, or anger or petulance. And yet it has made this plain also, if any one will pay careful attention to it, not looking at it curiously and carelessly. For when you hear that on the approach of Christ who was a stranger to him, and regarded merely as a man, he spoke to him with such great meekness, you may be able to perceive his former wisdom. For when Jesus said to him "Wilt thou be made whole?" he did not make the natural reply "thou seest me who have been this long time lying sick of the palsy, and dost thou ask

[1] The allusion is most probably to Homily XII. against the Anomœans, in which Chrysostom proves the equality of the Divine Son with God the Father by a reference to the cure of the paralytic by the pool of Bethesda. This Homily against the Anomœans was delivered at Constantinople, A. D. 398.

me if I wish to be made whole? hast thou come to insult my distress, to reproach me and laugh me to scorn and make a mock of my calamity? He did not say or conceive anything of this kind but meekly replied "Yea Lord."[1] Now if after thirty-eight years he was thus meek and gentle, when all the vigour and strength of his reasoning faculties was broken down, consider what he is likely to have been at the outset of his trouble. For be assured that invalids are not so hard to please at the beginning of their disorder, as they are after a long lapse of time: they become most intractable, most intolerable to all, when the malady is prolonged. But as he, after so many years, was so wise, and replied with so much forbearance, it is quite clear that during the previous time also he had been bearing that calamity with much thankfulness.

Considering these things then let us imitate the patience of our fellow-servant: for his paralysis is sufficient to brace up our souls: for no one can be so supine and indolent after having observed the magnitude of that calamity as not to endure bravely all evils which may befall him, even if they are more intolerable than all that were ever known. For not only his soundness but also his sickness has become a cause of the greatest benefit to us: for his cure has stimulated the souls of the hearers to speak the praise of the Lord, and his sickness and infirmity has encouraged you to patience, and urged you to match his zeal; or rather it has exhibited to you the lovingkindness of God. For the actual deliverance of the man to such a malady, and the protracted duration of his infirmity is a sign of the greatest care for his welfare. For as a gold refiner having cast a piece of gold into the furnace suffers it to be proved by the fire until such time as he sees it has become purer: even so God permits the souls of men to be tested by troubles until they become pure and transparent and have reaped much profit from this process of sifting: wherefore this is the greatest species of benefit.

2. Let us not then be disturbed, neither dismayed, when trials befall us. For if the gold refiner sees how long he ought to leave the piece of gold in the furnace, and when he ought to draw it out, and does not allow it to remain in the fire until it is destroyed and burnt up: much more does God understand this, and when He sees that we have become more pure, He releases us from our trials so that we may not be overthrown and cast down by the multiplication of our evils. Let us then not be repining, or faint-hearted, when some unexpected thing befalls us; but let us suffer Him who knows these things accurately, to prove our hearts by fire as long as He pleases: for He does this for a useful purpose and with a view to the profit of those who are tried.

On this account a certain wise man admonishes us saying "My Son, if thou come to serve the Lord prepare thy soul for temptation, set thy heart aright and constantly endure and make not haste in time of trouble";[2] "yield to Him" he says, "in all things," for He knoweth exactly when it is right to pluck us out of the furnace of evil. We ought therefore everywhere to yield to Him and always to give thanks, and to bear all things contentedly, whether He bestows benefits or chastisement upon us, for this also is a species of benefit. For the physician, not only when he bathes and nourishes the patient and conducts him into pleasant gardens, but also when he uses cautery and the knife, is a physician all the same: and a father not only when he caresses his son, but also when he expels him from his house, and when he chides and scourges him, is a father all the same, no less than when he praises him. Knowing therefore that God is more tenderly loving than all physicians, do not enquire too curiously concerning His treatment nor demand an account of it from Him, but whether He is pleased to let us go free or whether He punishes, let us offer ourselves for either alike; for He seeks by means of each to lead us back to health, and to communion with Himself, and He knows our several needs, and what is expedient for each one, and how and in what manner we ought to be saved, and along that path He leads us. Let us then follow whithersoever He bids us, and let us not too carefully consider whether He commands us to go by a smooth and easy path, or by a difficult and rugged one: as in the case of this paralytic. It was one species of benefit indeed that his soul should be purged by the long duration of his suffering, being delivered to the fiery trial of affliction as to a kind of furnace; but it was another benefit no less than this that God was present with him in the midst of the trials, and afforded him great consolation. He it was who strengthened him, and upheld him, and stretched forth a hand to him, and suffered him not to fall. But when you hear that it was God Himself do not deprive the paralytic of his meed of praise, neither him nor any other man who is tried and yet steadfastly endures. For even if we be infinitely wise, even if we are mightier and stronger than all men, yet in the absence of His grace we shall not

---

[1] We must suppose that Chrysostom considered such words to be implied in the answer actually given. They are not in the text of John v. 7, but it seems scarcely possible that Chrysostom should have forgotten the passage, or that the quotation should not have been subsequently corrected if he thought it misleading.

[2] Ecclus. i. 1, 2.

be able to withstand even the most ordinary temptation. And why do I speak of such insignificant and abject beings as we are? For even if one were a Paul, or a Peter, or a James, or a John, yet if he should be deprived of the divine help he would easily be put to shame, overthrown, and laid prostrate. And on behalf of these I will read you the words of Christ Himself: for He saith to Peter "Behold Satan hath asked to have you that he may sift you as wheat, but I have prayed for thee that thy faith fail not."[1] What is the meaning of "sift"? to turn and twist, and shake and stir and shatter, and worry, which is what takes place in the case of things which are winnowed: but I he says have restrained him, knowing that you are not able to endure the trial, for the expression "that thy faith fail not" is the utterance of one who signifies that if he had permitted it his faith would have failed. Now if Peter who was such a fervent lover of Christ and exposed his life for Him countless times and sprang into the foremost rank in the Apostolic band, and was pronounced blessed by his Master, and called Peter on this account because he kept a firm and inflexible hold of the faith, would have been carried away and fallen from profession if Christ had permitted the devil to try him as much as he desired, what other man will be able to stand, apart from His help? Therefore also Paul saith "But God is faithful, who will not suffer you to be tempted above that ye are able, but will with the temptation also make the way of escape that ye may be able to bear it."[2] For not only does He say that He does not suffer a trial to be inflicted beyond our strength, but even in that which is proportioned to our strength He is present carrying us through it, and bracing us up, if only we ourselves first of all contribute the means which are at our disposal, such as zeal, hope in Him, thanksgiving, endurance, patience. For not only in the dangers which are beyond our strength, but in those which are proportioned to it, we need the divine assistance, if we are to make a brave stand; for elsewhere also it is said "even as the sufferings of Christ abound to us, even so our comfort also aboundeth through Christ, that we may be able to comfort those who are in any trouble, by the comfort wherewith we ourselves are comforted of God."[3] So then he who comforted this man is the same who permitted the trial to be inflicted upon him. And now observe after the cure what tenderness He displays. For He did not leave him and depart, but having found him in the temple he saith "behold! thou art made whole; sin no more lest some worse thing happen unto thee."[4] For had He permitted the punishment because He hated him He would not have released him, He would not have provided for his future safety: but the expression "lest some worse thing happen unto thee" is the utterance of one who would check coming evils beforehand. He put an end to the disease, but did not put an end to the struggle: He expelled the infirmity but did not expel the dread of it, so that the benefit which had been wrought might remain unmoved. This is the part of a tender-hearted physician, not only to put an end to present pains, but to provide for future security, which also Christ did, bracing up his soul by the recollection of past events. For seeing that when the things which distress us have departed, the recollection of them oftentimes departs with them, He wishing it to abide continually, saith "sin no more lest some worse thing happen unto thee."

3. Moreover it is possible to discern His forethought and consideration not only from this, but also from that which seems to be a rebuke. For He did not make a public exposure of his sins, but yet He told him that he suffered what he did suffer on account of his sins, but what those sins were He did not disclose; nor did He say "thou hast sinned" or "thou hast transgressed," but He indicated the fact by one simple utterance "sin no more;" and having said so much as just to remind him of it He put him more on the alert against future events, and at the same time He made manifest to us all his patience and courage and wisdom, having reduced him to the necessity of publicly lamenting his calamity, and having displayed his own earnestness on the man's behalf, "for while I am coming," he says, "another steppeth down before me:"[5] yet he did not publicly expose his sins. For just as we ourselves desire to draw a veil over our sins even so does God much more than we: on this account He wrought the cure in the presence of all, but He gives the exhortation or the advice privately. For He never makes a public display of our sins, except at any time He sees men insensible to them. For when He says "ye saw me hungry, and fed me not: and thirsty and gave me no drink,"[6] He speaks thus at the present time in order that we may not hear these words in time to come. He threatens, He exposes us in this world, that He may not have to expose us in the other: even as He threatened to overthrow

---

[1] Luke xxii. 31, 32.   [2] 1 Cor. x. 13.
[3] Cor. i. 5, 4. Chrysostom transposes the clauses, and does not quote the exact words of the passage.

[4] John v. 14.   [5] John v. 7.   [6] Matt. xxv. 12.

the city of the Ninevites[1] for the very reason that He might not overthrow it. For if He wished to publish our sins He would not announce beforehand that He would publish them: but as it is He does make this announcement in order that being sobered by the fear of exposure, if not also by the fear of punishment we may purge ourselves from them all. This also is what takes place in the case of baptism: for He conducts the man to the pool of water without disclosing his sins to any one; yet He publicly presents the boon and makes it manifest to all, while the sins of the man are known to no one save God Himself and him who receives the forgiveness of them. This also was what took place in the case of this paralytic, He makes the reproof without the presence of witnesses, or rather the utterance is not merely a reproof but also a justification; He justifies Himself as it were for evil-entreating him so long, telling him and proving to him that it was not without cause and purpose that He had suffered him to be so long afflicted, for He reminded him of his sins, and declared the cause of his infirmity. "For having found him," we read, "in the temple, He said unto him, sin no more lest some worse thing happen unto thee."

And now since we have derived so much profit from the account of the former paralytic let us turn to the other who is presented to us in St. Matthew's Gospel. For in the case of mines where any one happens to find a piece of gold he makes a further excavation again in the same place: and I know that many of those who read without care imagine that one and the same paralytic is presented by the four evangelists: but it is not so. Therefore you must be on the alert, and pay careful attention to the matter. For the question is not concerned with ordinary matters, and this discourse when it has received its proper solution will be serviceable against both Greeks and Jews and many of the heretics. For thus all find fault with the evangelists as being at strife and variance: yet this is not the fact, Heaven forbid! but although the outward appearance is different, the grace of the Spirit which works upon the soul of each is one, and where the grace of the Spirit is, there is love, joy, and peace; and there war and disputation, strife and contention are not. How then shall we make it clear that this paralytic is not the same as the other, but a different man? By many tokens, both of place and time, and season, and day, and from the manner of the cure, and the coming of the physician and the loneliness of the man who was healed. And what of this? some one will say: for have not many of the evangelists given diverse accounts of other signs? Yes, but it is one thing to make statements which are diverse, and another, statements which are contradictory; for the former causes no discord or strife: but that which is now presented to us is a strong case of contradiction unless it be proved that the paralytic at the pool was a different man from him who is described by the other three evangelists. Now that you may understand what is the difference between statements which are diverse and contradictory, one of the evangelists has stated that Christ carried the cross,[2] another that Simon the Cyrenian carried it:[3] but this causes no contradiction or strife. "And how," you say, "is there no contradiction between the statements that he carried and did not carry?" Because both took place. When they went out of the Prætorium Christ was carrying it: but as they proceeded Simon took it from Him and bore it. Again in the case of the robbers, one says that the two blasphemed:[4] another that one of them checked him who was reviling the Lord.[5] Yet in this again there is no contradiction: because here also both things took place, and at the beginning both the men behaved ill: but afterwards when signs occurred, when the earth shook and the rocks were rent, and the sun was darkened, one of them was converted, and became more chastened, and recognized the crucified one and acknowledged his kingdom. For to prevent your supposing that this took place by some constraining force of one impelling him from within, and to remove your perplexity, he exhibits the man to you on the cross while he is still retaining his former wickedness in order that you may perceive that his conversion was effected from within and out of his own heart assisted by the grace of God and so he became a better man.

4. And it is possible to collect many other instances of this kind from the Gospels, which seem to have a suspicion of contradiction, where there is no real contradiction, the truth being that some incidents have been related by this writer, others by that; or if not occurring at the same hour one author has related the earlier event, another the later; but in the present case there is nothing of this kind, but the multitude of the evidences which I have mentioned proves to those who pay any attention whatever to the matter, that the paralytic was not the same man in both instances. And this would be no slight proof to demonstrate that the evangelists were in harmony with each

---

[1] Jonah i. 2.
[2] John xix. 17.
[3] Matt. xxvii. 32; Mark xxv. 31; Luke xiii. 26.
[4] Matt. xxvii. 44; Mark xv. 32.
[5] Luke xxiii. 40.

other and not at variance. For if it were the same man the discord is great between the two accounts: but if it be a different one all material for dispute has been destroyed.

Well then let me now state the actual reasons why I affirm that this man is not the same as that. What are they? The one is cured in Jerusalem, the other in Capernaum; the one by the pool of water, the other in some house; there is the evidence from place: the former during the festival: there is the evidence from the special season: the former had been thirty and eight years suffering from infirmity: concerning the other the evangelist relates nothing of that kind: there is the evidence from time: the former was cured on the Sabbath: there is the evidence from the day: for had this man also been cured on the Sabbath Matthew would not have passed by the fact in silence nor would the Jews who were present have held their peace: for they who found fault for some other reason even when a man was not cured on the Sabbath would have been yet more violent in their accusation against Christ if they had got an additional handle from the argument of the special day. Moreover this man was brought to Christ: to the other Christ Himself came, and there was no man to assist him. " Lord," said he," I have no man: " whereas this man had many who came to his aid, who also let him down through the roof. And He healed the body of the other man before his soul: for after he had cured the paralysis He then said "Behold thou art made whole, sin no more:" but not so in this case, but after He had healed his soul, for He said to him "Son be of good cheer thy sins be forgiven thee," He then cured his paralysis. That this man then is not the same as the other has been clearly demonstrated by these proofs, but it now remains for us to turn to the beginning of the narrative and see how Christ cured the one and the other, and why differently in each case: why the one on the Sabbath and the other not on the Sabbath, why He came Himself to the one but waited for the other to be brought to Him, why He healed the body of the one and the soul of the other first. For He does not these things without consideration and purpose seeing that He is wise and prudent. Let us then give our attention and observe Him as He performs the cure. For if in the case of physicians when they use the knife or cautery or operate in any other way upon a maimed and crippled patient, and cut off a limb, many persons crowd round the invalid and the physician who is doing these things, much more ought we to act thus in this case, in proportion as the physician is greater and the malady more severe, being one which cannot be corrected by human art, but only by divine grace. And in the former case we have to see the skin being cut, and matter discharging, and gore set in motion, and to endure much discomfort produced by the spectacle, and great pain and sorrow not merely from the sight of the wounds, but also from the suffering undergone by those who are subjected to this burning or cutting: for no one is so stony-hearted as to stand by those who are suffering these things, and hear them shrieking, without being himself overcome and agitated, and experiencing much depression of spirit; but yet we undergo all this owing to our desire to witness the operation. But in this case nothing of that kind has to be seen, no application of fire, no plunging in of an instrument, no flowing of blood, no pain or shrieking of the patient; and the reason of this is, the wisdom of the healer, which needs none of these external aids, but is absolutely self-sufficient. For it is enough that He merely utters a command and all distress ceases. And the wonder is not only that He effects the cure with so much ease, but also without pain, causing no trouble to those who are being healed.

Seeing then that the marvel is greater and the cure more important, and the pleasure afforded to the spectators unalloyed by any kind of sorrow, let us now carefully contemplate Christ in the act of healing. "And He entered into a boat and crossed over and came into His own city: and behold they brought to him a man sick of the palsy lying on a bed: and Jesus seeing their faith said unto the sick of the palsy "Son! be of good cheer: thy sins are forgiven." [1] Now they were inferior to the centurion in respect of their faith, but superior to the impotent man by the pool. For the former neither invited the physician nor brought the sick man to the physician; but approached Him as God and said "Speak the word only and my servant shall be healed." [2] Now these men did not invite the physician to the house, and so far they are on an equality with the centurion: but they brought the sick man to the physician and so far they are inferior, because they did not say "speak the word only." Yet they are far better than the man lying by the pool. For he said "Lord I have no man when the water is troubled to put me into the pool:" but these men knew that Christ had no need either of water, or pool, or anything else of that kind: nevertheless Christ not only released the servant of the centurion but the other two men also from their maladies, and did not say: "because thou hast proffered

---

[1] Matt. ix. 1, 2.   [2] Luke vii. 7.

a smaller degree of faith the cure which thou receivest shall be in proportion;" but He dismissed the man who displayed the greater faith with eulogy and honour, saying "I have not found so great faith, no, not in Israel."[1] On the man who exhibited less faith than this one he bestowed no praise yet He did not deprive him of a cure, no! not even him who displayed no faith at all. But just as physicians when curing the same disorder receive from some person a hundred gold pieces, from others half, from others less and from some nothing at all: even so Christ received from the centurion a large and unspeakable degree of faith, but from this man less and from the other not even an ordinary amount, and yet He healed them all. For what reason then did He deem the man who made no deposit of faith worthy of the benefit? Because his failure to exhibit faith was not owing to indolence, or to insensibility of soul, but to ignorance of Christ and having never heard any miracle in which He was concerned either small or great. On this account therefore the man obtained indulgence: which in fact the evangelist obscurely intimates when he says, "for he wist not who it was,"[2] but he only recognized Him by sight when he lighted upon Him the second time.

5. There are indeed some who say that this man was healed merely because they who brought him believed; but this is not the fact. For "when He saw their faith" refers not merely to those who brought the man but also to the man who was brought. Why so? "Is not one man healed," you say, "because another has believed?" For my part I do not think so unless owing to immaturity of age or excessive infirmity he is in some way incapable of believing. How then was it you say that in the case of the woman of Canaan the mother believed but the daughter was cured? and how was it that the servant of the centurion who believed rose from the bed of sickness and was preserved. Because the sick persons themselves were not able to believe. Hear then what the woman of Canaan says: "My daughter is grievously vexed with a devil[3] and sometimes she falleth into the water and sometimes into the fire:"[4] now how could she believe whose mind was darkened and possessed by a devil, and was never able to control herself, not in her sound senses? As then in the case of the woman of Canaan so also in the case of the centurion; his servant lay ill in the house, not knowing Christ, himself, nor who He was. How then was he to believe in one who was unknown to him, and of whom he had never yet obtained any experience? But in the case before us we cannot say this: for the paralytic believed. Whence is this manifest? From the very manner of his approach to Christ. For do not attend simply to the statement that they let the man down through the roof: but consider how great a matter it is for a sick man to have the fortitude to undergo this. For you are surely aware that invalids are so faint-hearted and difficult to please as often to decline the treatment administered to them on their sick bed, and to prefer bearing the pain which arises from their maladies to undergoing the annoyance caused by the remedies. But this man had the fortitude to go outside the house, and to be carried into the midst of the market place, and to exhibit himself in the presence of a crowd. And it is the habit of sick folk to die under their disorder rather than disclose their personal calamities. This sick man however did not act thus, but when he saw that the place of assembly was filled, the approaches blocked, the haven of refuge obstructed, he submitted to be let down through the roof. So ready in contrivance is desire, so rich in resource is love. "For he also that seeketh findeth, and to him that knocketh it shall be opened."[5] The man did not say to his friends "What is the meaning of this? why make this ado? why push on? Let us wait until the house is cleared and the assembly is dissolved: the crowds will withdraw, we shall then be able to approach him privately and confer about these matters. Why should you expose my misfortunes in the midst of all the spectators, and let me down from the roof-top, and behave in an unseemly manner?" That man said none of these things either to himself or to his bearers, but regarded it as an honour to have so many persons made witnesses of his cure. And not from this circumstance only was it possible to discern his faith but also from the actual words of Christ. For after he had been let down and presented Christ said to him, "Son! be of good cheer, thy sins are forgiven thee." And when he heard these words he was not indignant, he did not complain, he did not say to the physician "What mean you by this? I came to be healed of one thing and you heal another. This is an excuse and a pretence and a screen of incompetence. Do you forgive sins which are invisible?" He neither spoke nor thought any of these things, but waited, allowing the physician to adopt the method of healing which He desired. For this reason also Christ did not go to him, but

---

[1] Luke vii. 9. [2] John v. 13. [3] Matt. xv. 22.
[4] These words occur in the description of the lunatic lad in Matt. xvii. 15. Chrysostom, speaking from memory, confuses the two narratives.

[5] Luke xi. 10.

waited for him to come, that He might exhibit his faith to all. For could He not have made the entrance easy? But He did none of these things; in order that He might exhibit the man's zeal and fervent faith to all. For as He went to the man who had been suffering thirty and eight years because he had no one to aid him, so did He wait for this man to come to him because he had many friends that He might make his faith manifest by the man being brought to Him, and inform us of the other man's loneliness by going to him, and disclose the earnestness of the one and the patience of the other to all and especially to those who were present. For some envious and misanthropical Jews were accustomed to grudge the benefits done to their neighbours and to find fault with His miracles, sometimes on account of the special season, saying that He healed on the sabbath day; sometimes on account of the life of those to whom the benefit was done, saying "if this man were a prophet He would have known who the woman was who touched Him:"[1] not knowing that it is the special mark of a physician to associate with the infirm and to be constantly seen by the side of the sick, not to avoid them, 'or hurry from their presence—which in fact was what He expressly said to those murmurers; "They that are whole have no need of a physician but they that are sick."[2] Therefore in order to prevent their making the same accusations again He proves first of all that they who come to Him are deserving of a cure on account of the faith which they exhibit. For this reason He exhibited the loneliness of one man, and the fervent faith and zeal of the other: for this reason He healed the one on the Sabbath, the other not on the Sabbath: in order that when you see them accusing and rebuking Christ on another day you may understand that they accused him on the former occasion also not because of their respect for the law, but because they could not contain their own malice. But why did He not first address Himself to the cure of the paralytic, but said, "Son! be of good cheer, thy sins are forgiven thee?" He did this very wisely. For it is a habit with physicians to destroy the originating cause of the malady before they remove the malady itself. Often for example when the eyes are distressed by some evil humour and corrupt discharge, the physician, abandoning any treatment of the disordered vision, turns his attention to the head, where the root and origin of the infirmity is: even so did Christ act: He represses first of all the source of the evil. For the source and root and mother of all evil is the nature of sin. This it is which enervates our bodies: this it is which brings on disease: therefore also on this occasion He said, "Son! be of good cheer, thy sins are forgiven thee." And on the other He said, "Behold! thou art made whole, sin no more lest some worse thing happen unto thee," intimating to both that these maladies were the offspring of sin. And in the beginning and outset of the world disease as the consequence of sin attacked the body of Cain. For after the murder of his brother, after that act of wickedness, his body was subject to palsy.[3] For trembling is the same thing as palsy. For when the strength which regulates a living creature becomes weakened, being no longer able to support all the limbs, it deprives them of their natural power of direction, and then having become unstrung they tremble and turn giddy.

6. Paul also demonstrated this: for when he was reproaching the Corinthians with a certain sin he said, "For this cause many are weak and sickly among you." Therefore also Christ first removes the cause of the evil, and having said "Son! be of good cheer, thy sins are forgiven thee," He uplifts the spirit and rouses the downcast soul: for the speech became an efficient cause and having entered into the conscience it laid hold of the soul itself and cast out of it all distress. For nothing creates pleasure and affords confidence so much as freedom from self-reproach. For where remission of sins is there is sonship. Even so at least we are not able to call God Father until we have washed away our sins in the pool of the sacred water. It is when we have come up from thence, having put off that evil load, that we say "Our Father which art in Heaven." But in the case of the man who was infirm thirty and eight years why did He not act thus, but cured his body first of all? Because by that long period of time his sins had been exhausted: for the magnitude of a trial can lighten the load of sins; as indeed we read was the case with Lazarus, that he received his evil things in full, and thereupon was comforted: and again in another place we read, "Comfort ye my people, say ye to the heart of Jerusalem, that she hath received of the Lord's hand double for her sins."[4] And again the prophet says "O Lord give us peace, for thou hast requited all things to us,"[5] indicating that penalties and punishments work forgiveness of sins; and this we might prove

---

[1] Luke vii. 39.   [2] Matt. ix. 12.

[3] The allusion is to Gen. iv. 12, where the words rendered in the English translation "a fugitive and a vagabond shalt thou be" are in the LXX. rendered στένων καὶ τρέμων ἔσῃ, "groaning and trembling shalt thou be:" but our English version is the more correct.

[4] Isa. xl. 1, 2.   [5] Isa. xxvi. 12.

from many passages. It seems to me then that the reason why He said nothing to that man about remission of sins, but only secured him against the future, was because the penalty for his sins had been already worked out by the long duration of his sickness: or if this was not the reason, it was because he had not yet attained any high degree of belief concerning Christ that the Lord first addressed Himself to the lesser need, and one which was manifest and obvious, the health of the body; but in the case of the other man He did not act thus, but inasmuch as this man had more faith, and a loftier soul, He spoke to him first of all concerning the more dangerous disease: with the additional object of exhibiting his equality of rank with the Father. For just as in the former case He healed on the Sabbath day because He wished to lead men away from the Jewish mode of observing it, and to take occasion from their reproaches to prove Himself equal with the Father: even so in this instance also, knowing beforehand what they were going to say, He uttered these words that He might use them as a starting-point and a pretext for proving His equality of rank with the Father. For it is one thing when no one brings an accusation or charge to enter spontaneously upon a discourse about these things, and quite another when other persons give occasion for it, to set about the same work in the order and shape of a defence. For the nature of the former demonstration was a stumbling block to the hearers: but the other was less offensive, and more acceptable, and everywhere we see Him doing this, and manifesting His equality not so much by words as by deeds. This at any rate is what the Evangelist implied when he said that the Jews persecuted Jesus not only because He broke the Sabbath but also because He said that God was His Father, making Himself equal with God,[1] which is a far greater thing, for He effected this by the demonstration of His deeds. How then do the envious and wicked act, and those who repine at the good things of other people, and seek to find a handle in every direction? "Why does this man blaspheme?" they say for "no man can forgive sins save God alone."[2] As they persecuted Him there because He broke the Sabbath, and took occasion from their reproaches to declare His equality with the Father in the form of a defence, saying "my Father worketh hitherto and I work,"[3] so here also starting from the accusations which they make He proves from these His exact likeness to the Father. For what was it they said? "No man can forgive sins save God alone." Inasmuch then as they themselves laid down this definition, they themselves introduced the rule, they themselves declared the law, He proceeds to entangle them by means of their own words. "You have confessed," He says, "that forgiveness of sins is an attribute of God alone: my equality therefore is unquestionable." And it is not these men only who declare this but also the prophet thus saying: "who is God as thou?" and then, indicating His special attribute he adds "taking away iniquity and passing over unrighteousness."[4] If then any one else appears thus doing the same thing He also is God, God even as that one is God. But let us observe how Christ argues with them, how meekly and gently, and with all tenderness. "And behold some of the scribes said within themselves: this man blasphemeth." They did not utter the word, they did not proclaim it through the tongue, but reasoned in the secret recesses of their heart. How then did Christ act? He made public their secret thoughts before the demonstration which was concerned with the cure of the paralytic's body, wishing to prove to them the power of His Godhead. For that it is an attribute of God alone, a sign of His deity to shew the secrets of His mind, the Scripture saith "Thou alone knowest men's hearts."[5] Seest thou that this word "alone," is not used with a view of contrasting the Son with the Father. For if the Father alone knows the heart, how does the Son know the secrets of the mind? "For He Himself," it is said, "knew what was in man";[6] and Paul when proving that the knowledge of secret things is a special attribute of God says, "and He that searchest the heart,"[7] shewing that this expression is equivalent to the appellation "God." For just as when I say "He who causeth rain said," I signify none other than God by mentioning the deed, since it is one which belongs to Him alone: and when I say "He who maketh the sun to rise," without adding the word God, I yet signify Him by mentioning the deed: even so when Paul said "He who searcheth the hearts," he proved that to search the heart is an attribute of God alone. For if this expression had not been of equal force with the name "God" for pointing out Him who was signified, he would not have used it absolutely and by itself. For if the power were shared by Him in common with some created being, we should not have known who was signified, the community of power causing confusion in the mind of the hearers. Inasmuch then as this appears to be a special attribute of the Father, and yet is manifested of the Son whose equal-

---

[1] John v. 16. [2] Mark ii. 7. [3] John v. 17. [4] Micah vii. 18. [5] 1 Kings viii. 39. [6] John ii. 25. [7] Rom. viii. 27.

ity becomes thence unquestionable, therefore we read "why think ye evil in your hearts? for whether is easier: to say: Thy sins are forgiven thee or to say arise and walk?"

7. See moreover He makes a second proof of His power of forgiving sins. For to forgive sins is a very much greater act than to heal the body, greater in proportion as the soul is greater than the body. For as paralysis is a disease of the body, even so sin is a disease of the soul: but although this is the greater it is not palpable: whereas the other although it be less is manifest. Since then He is about to use the less for a demonstration of the greater proving that He acted thus on account of their weakness, and by way of condescension to their feeble condition He says "whether is easier? to say thy sins are forgiven thee or to say arise and walk?" For what reason then should He address Himself to the lesser act on their account? Because that which is manifest presents the proof in a more distinct form. Therefore He did not enable the man to rise until He had said to them "But that ye may know that the Son of man hath power on earth to forgive sins, (then saith He to the sick of the palsy) arise and walk:" as if He had said: forgiveness of sins is indeed a greater sign: but for your sakes I add the less also since this seems to you to be a proof of the other. For as in another case when He praised the centurion for saying "speak the word only and my servant shall be healed: for I also say to this man go and he goeth and to the other come and he cometh," He confirmed his opinion by the eulogy which He pronounced: and again when He reproved the Jews for finding fault with Him on the Sabbath day saying that He transgressed the law, He proved that He had authority to alter laws: even so in this instance also when some said "He maketh Himself equal with God by promising that which belongs only to the Father," He having upbraided and accused them and proved by His deeds that He did not blaspheme supplied us with indisputable evidence that He could do the same things as the Father who begat Him Observe at least the manner in which He pleases to establish the fact that what belongs to the Father only, belongs also to Himself: for He did not simply enable the paralytic to get up, but also said "but that ye may know that the Son of man hath power on earth to forgive sins:" thus it was his endeavour and earnest desire to prove above all things that He had the same authority as the Father.

8. Let us then carefully hold fast all these things, both those which were spoken yesterday and the day before that, and let us beseech God that they may abide immoveably in our heart, and let us contribute zeal on our side, and constantly meet in this place. For in this way we shall preserve the truths which have been formerly spoken, and we shall add others to our store; and if any of them slip from our memory through the lapse of time we shall easily be able to recover them by the aid of continual teaching. And not only will the doctrines abide sound and uncorrupt but our course of life will have the benefit of much diligent care and we shall be able to pass through this present state of existence with pleasure and cheerfulness. For whatever kind of suffering is oppressing our soul when we come here will easily be got rid of: seeing that now also Christ is present, and he who approaches Him with faith will readily receive healing from Him. Suppose some one is struggling with perpetual poverty, and at a loss for necessary food, and often goes to bed hungry, if he has come in here, and heard Paul saying that he passed his time in hunger and thirst and nakedness, and that he experienced this not on one or two or three days, but constantly (this at least is what he indicates when he says "up to the present hour we both hunger and thirst and are naked),"[1] he will receive ample consolation, learning by means of these words that God has not permitted him to be in poverty because He hated him or abandoned him: for if this were the effect of hatred, He would not have permitted it in the case of Paul who was of all men especially dear to Him: but He permitted it out of His tender love and providential care, and by way of conducting him to a higher degree of spiritual wisdom. Has some other man a body which is beset with disease and countless sufferings? The condition of these paralytics may be an ample source of consolation and besides these the blessed and brave disciple of Paul who was continually suffering from disorders, and never had any respite from prolonged infirmity, even as Paul also said "Use a little wine for thy stomach's sake and thine often infirmities,"[2] where he does not speak merely of infirmities as such. Or another having been subjected to false accusation has acquired a bad reputation with the public, and this is continually vexing and gnawing his soul: he enters this place and hears "Blessed are ye when men shall reproach you and say all manner of evil against you falsely: rejoice ye and be exceeding glad for great is your reward in Heaven:"[3] then he will lay aside all despondency and receive every kind of pleasure: for it is written "leap for joy, and

---

[1] 1 Cor. iv. 11.   [2] 1 Tim. v. 23.   [3] Matt. v. 11, 12.

be exceeding glad when men cast out your name as evil."[1] In this manner then God comforts those that are evil spoken of, and them that speak evil He puts in fear after another manner saying "every evil word which men shall speak they shall give an account thereof whether it be good or evil."[2]

Another perhaps has lost a little daughter or a son, or one of his kinsfolk, and he also having come here listens to Paul groaning over this present life and longing to see that which is to come, and oppressed by his sojourn in this world, and he will go away with a sufficient remedy for his grief when he has heard him say "Now concerning them that are asleep I would not have you ignorant brethren that ye sorrow not even as others who have no hope."[3] He did not say concerning the dying," but "concerning them that are asleep" proving that death is a sleep. As then if we see any one sleeping we are not disturbed or distressed, expecting that he will certainly get up: even so when we see any one dead, let us not be disturbed or dejected for this also is a sleep, a longer one indeed, but still a sleep. By giving it the name of slumber He comforted the mourners and overthrew the accusation of the unbelievers. If you mourn immoderately over him who has departed you will be like that unbeliever who has no hope of a resurrection. He indeed does well to mourn, inasmuch as he cannot exercise any spiritual wisdom concerning things to come: but thou who hast received such strong proofs concerning the future life, why dost thou sink into the same weakness with him? Therefore it is written "now concerning them that are asleep we would not have you ignorant that ye sorrow not even as others who have no hope."

And not only from the New Testament but from the Old also it is possible to receive abundant consolation. For when you hear of Job after the loss of his property, after the destruction of his herds, after the loss not of one, or two, or three, but of a whole troop of sons in the very flower of their age, after the great excellence of soul which he displayed, even if thou art the weakest of men, thou wilt easily be able to repent and regain thy courage. For thou, O man, hast constantly attended thy sick son, and hast seen him laid upon the bed, and hast heard him uttering his last words, and stood beside him whilst he was drawing his last breath and hast closed his eyes, and shut his mouth: but he was not present at the death struggle of his sons, he did not see them breathing their last gasp, but the house became the common grave of them all, and on the same table brains and blood were poured forth, and pieces of wood and tiles, and dust, and fragments of flesh, and all these things were mingled together in like manner. Nevertheless after such great calamities of this kind he was not petulant, but what does he say—" The Lord gave, the Lord hath taken away, as it seemed good unto the Lord even so has it come to pass, blessed be the name of the Lord for ever."[4] Let this speech be our utterance also over each event which befalls us; whether it be loss of property, or infirmity of body, or insult, or false accusation or any other form of evil incident to mankind, let us say these words "The Lord gave, the Lord hath taken away; as it seemed good to the Lord so has it come to pass; blessed be the name of the Lord for ever." If we practise this spiritual wisdom, we shall never experience any evil, even if we undergo countless sufferings, but the gain will be greater than the loss, the good will exceed the evil: by these words thou wilt cause God to be merciful unto thee, and wilt defend thyself against the tyranny of Satan. For as soon as thy tongue has uttered these words forthwith the Devil hastens from thee: and when he has hastened away, the cloud of dejection also is dispelled and the thoughts which afflict us take to flight, hurrying off in company with him, and in addition to all this thou wilt win all manner of blessings both here and in Heaven. And you have a convincing example in the case of Job, and of the Apostle, who having for God's sake despised the troubles of this world, obtained the everlasting blessings. Let us then be trustful and in all things which befall us let us rejoice and give thanks to the merciful God, that we may pass through this present life with serenity, and obtain the blessings to come, by the grace and lovingkindness of our Lord Jesus Christ to whom be glory, honour and might always, now and ever, world without end. Amen.

[1] Luke vi. 22, 23.　[2] Matt. xii. 36.　[3] 1 Thess. iv. 13.　[4] Job i. 21, LXX. version.

ST. CHRYSOSTOM:

HOMILY

TO THOSE WHO HAD NOT ATTENDED THE ASSEMBLY: AND ON THE APOSTOLIC SAYING, "IF THINE ENEMY HUNGER, FEED HIM," ETC. (ROM. XII. 20), AND CONCERNING RESENTMENT OF INJURIES.

TRANSLATED BY

REV. W. R. W. STEPHENS, M.A.

PREBENDARY OF CHICHESTER CATHEDRAL, AND RECTOR OF WOOLBEDING, SUSSEX.

CONTENTS.

		PAGE
1.	Chrysostom reproves the apathy of the congregation : he deprecates applause	223
2.	He combats various excuses for indolence.	224
3.	The indifference of Christians contrasted with the strictness of Jews in the observance of Holy Days	225
4.	The duty of Christians to bring others to Christ	226
5.	Explanation of St. Paul's words " by so doing thou shalt heap coals of fire on his head "	222
6.	How enemies are to be conquered by kindness. Examples of this	229
7.	Reconciliation with enemies in this world will save us from judgment in the world to come	231

TO THOSE WHO HAD NOT ATTENDED THE ASSEMBLY.

TO THOSE WHO HAD NOT ATTENDED THE ASSEMBLY; ON THE APOSTOLIC SAYING, "IF THY ENEMY HUNGER, FEED HIM," AND CONCERNING RESENTMENT OF INJURIES.

1. I DID no good as it seems by the prolonged discourse which I lately addressed to you with a view to kindling your zeal for the assemblies here:[1] for again our Church is destitute of her children. Wherefore also I am again compelled to seem vexatious and burdensome, reproving those who are present, and finding fault with those who have been left behind: with them because they have not put away their sloth, and with you because you have not given a helping hand to the salvation of your brethren. I am compelled to seem burdensome and vexatious, not on behalf of myself, or my own possessions, but on your behalf and for your salvation, which is more precious to me than anything else. Let him who pleases take it in bad part, and call me insolent and impudent, yet will I not cease continually annoying him for the same purpose; for nothing is better for me than this kind of impudence. For it may be, it may be, that this at least if nothing else, will put you to shame, and that to avoid being perpetually importuned concerning the same things, ye will take part in the tender care of your brethren. For what profit is there to me in praise when I do not see you making advances in virtue? and what harm is there from the silence of the hearers when I behold your piety increasing? For the praise of the speaker does not consist in applause, but in the zeal of the hearers for godliness: not in noise made just at the time of hearing, but in lasting earnestness. As soon as applause has issued from the lips it is dispersed in air and perishes; but the moral improvement of the hearers brings an imperishable and immortal reward both to him who speaks and to them who obey. The praise of your cheers makes the speaker illustrious here, but the piety of your soul affords the teacher much confidence before the judgment-seat of Christ. Wherefore if any one loves the speaker, let him not desire the applause but the profit of the hearers. To neglect our brethren is no ordinary wrong, but one which brings extreme punishment, and an inexorable penalty. And the case of the man who buried the talent proves this: he was not reproached at least on account of his own life: for as regarded the deposit itself he did not turn out a bad man, since he restored it intact: nevertheless he did turn out a bad man as regarded his management of the deposit. For he did not double that which was entrusted to him; and so was punished. Whence it is manifest that even if we are earnest and well trained, and have much zeal about hearing the holy scriptures this does not suffice for our salvation. For the deposit must be doubled, and it becomes doubled when together with our own salvation we undertake to make some provision for the good of others. For the man in the parable said "Lo! there thou hast that is thine:" but this did not serve him for a defence: for it was said to him "thou oughtest to have put the money to the exchangers."[2]

And observe I pray how easy the commands of the Master are: for men indeed make those who lend out capital sums at interest answera-

---

[1] The date of this Homily cannot be determined, but the allusions which it contains to the Imperial palace and guard, and some other points of internal evidence prove that it was delivered at Constantinople.

[2] Matt. xxv. 27.

ble for recalling them; "you have made the deposit," one says, "you must call it in: I have no concern with the man who has received it." But God does not act thus; He only commands us to make the deposit, and does not render us liable for the recall. For the speaker has the power of advising, not of persuading. Therefore he says: "I make thee answerable for depositing only, and not for the recall." What can be easier than this? And yet the servant called the master hard, who was thus gentle and merciful. For such is the wont of the ungrateful and indolent; they always try to shift the blame of their offences from themselves to their masters. And therefore the man was thrust out with torture and bonds into the outer darkness. And lest we should suffer this penalty let us deposit our teaching with the brethren, whether they be persuaded by it, or not. For if they be persuaded they will profit both themselves and us: and if they are not, they involve themselves indeed in inevitable punishment, but will not be able to do us the slightest injury. For we have done our part, by giving them advice: but if they do not listen to it no harm will result to us from that. For blame would attach to us not for failing to persuade, but for failing to advise: and after prolonged and continual exhortation and counsel they and not we, have to reckon henceforth with God.

I have been anxious at any rate to know clearly, whether you continue to exhort your brethren, and if they remain all the time in the same condition of indolence: otherwise I would never have given you any trouble: as it is, I have fears that they may remain uncorrected in consequence of your neglect and indifference. For it is impossible that a man who continually has the benefit of exhortation and instruction should not become better and more diligent. The proverb which I am about to cite is certainly a common one, nevertheless it confirms this very truth. For "a perpetual dropping of water," it says, "wears a rock," yet what is softer than water? and what is harder than a rock? Nevertheless perpetual action conquers nature: and if it conquers nature, much more will it be able to prevail over the human will. Christianity is no child's play, my beloved: no matter of secondary importance. I am continually saying these things, and yet I effect nothing.

2. How am I distressed, think you, when I call to mind that on the festival days the multitudes assembled resemble the broad expanse of the sea, but now not even the smallest part of that multitude is gathered together here? Where are they now who oppress us with their presence on the feast days? I look for them, and am grieved on their account when I mark what a multitude are perishing of those who are in the way of salvation,[1] how large a loss of brethren I sustain, how few are reached by the things which concern salvation, and how the greater part of the body of the Church is like a dead and motionless carcase. "And what concern is that to us?" you say. The greatest possible concern if you pay no attention to your brethren, if you do not exhort and advise, if you put no constraint on them, and do not forcibly drag them hither, and lead them away out of their deep indolence. For that one ought not to be useful to himself alone, but also to many others, Christ declared plainly, when He called us salt,[2] and leaven,[3] and light:[4] for these things are useful and profitable to others. For a lamp does not shine for itself, but for those who are sitting in darkness: and thou art a lamp not that thou mayest enjoy the light by thyself, but that thou mayest bring back yonder man who has gone astray. For what profit is a lamp if it does not give light to him who sits in darkness? and what profit is a Christian when he benefits no one, neither leads any one back to virtue? Again salt is not an astringent to itself but braces up those parts of the body which have decayed, and prevents them from falling to pieces and perishing. Even so do thou, since God has appointed thee to be spiritual salt, bind and brace up the decayed members, that is the indolent and sordid brethren, and having rescued them from their indolence as from some form of corruption, unite them to the rest of the body of the Church. And this is the reason why He called you leaven: for leaven also does not leaven itself, but, little though it is, it affects the whole lump however big it may be. So also do ye: although ye are few in number, yet be ye many and powerful in faith, and in zeal towards God. As then the leaven is not weak on account of its littleness, but prevails owing to its inherent heat, and the force of its natural quality, so ye also will be able to bring back a far larger number than yourselves, if you will, to the same degree of zeal as your own. Now if they make the summer season their excuse: for I hear of their saying things of this kind, "the present stifling heat is excessive, the scorching sun is intolerable, we cannot bear being trampled and crushed in the crowd, and to be steaming all over with perspiration and oppressed by the heat and confined space:" I am ashamed of them, believe me: for such excuses are

---

[1] τῶν σωζομένων, this signifies "members of the Church," merely, who, as such, are heirs of salvation, or as the English catechism expresses it, are in a "state of salvation," although they may forfeit their inheritance. Comp. Acts ii. 47.
[2] Matt. v. 13. [3] Implied in Matt. xiii. 33. [4] Matt. v. 14.

womanish: indeed even in their case who have softer bodies, and a weaker nature, such pretexts do not suffice for justification. Nevertheless, even if it seems a disgrace to make a reply to a defence of this kind, yet is it necessary. For if they put forward such excuses as these and do not blush, much more does it behove us not to be ashamed of replying to these things. What then am I to say to those who advance these pretexts? I would remind them of the three children in the furnace and the flame, who when they saw the fire encircling them on all sides, enveloping their mouth and their eyes and even their breath, did not cease singing that sacred and mystical hymn to God, in company with the universe, but standing in the midst of the pyre sent up their song of praise to the common Lord of all with greater cheerfulness than they who abide in some flowery field:[1] and together with these three children I should think it proper to remind them also of the lions which were in Babylon, and of Daniel and the den:[2] and not of this one only but also of another den, and the prophet Jeremiah, and the mire in which he was smothered up to the neck.[3] And emerging from these dens, I would conduct these persons who put forward heat as an excuse into the prison and exhibit Paul to them there, and Silas bound fast in the stocks, covered with bruises and wounds, lacerated all over their body with a mass of stripes, yet singing praises to God at midnight and celebrating their holy vigil. For is it not a monstrous thing that those holy men, both in the furnace and the fire, and the den, and amongst wild beasts, and mire, and in a prison and the stocks, and amidst stripes and gaolers, and intolerable sufferings, never complained of any of these things, but were continually uttering prayers and sacred songs with much energy and fervent zeal, whilst we who have not undergone any of their innumerable sufferings, small or great, neglect our own salvation on account of a scorching sun and a little short lived heat and toil, and forsaking the assembly wander away, depraving ourselves by going to meetings which are thoroughly unwholesome? When the dew of the divine oracles is so abundant dost thou make heat thy excuse? "The water which I will give him," saith Christ, "shall be in him a well of water springing up into everlasting life;"[4] and again; "He that believeth on me as the Scripture hath said, out of his belly shall flow rivers of living water."[5] Tell me; when thou hast spiritual wells and rivers, art thou afraid of material heat? Now in the market place where there is so much turmoil and crowding, and scorching wind, how is it that you do not make suffocation and heat an excuse for absenting yourself? For it is impossible for you to say that there you can enjoy a cooler temperature, and that all the heat is concentrated here with us:—the truth is exactly the reverse; here indeed owing to the pavement floor, and to the construction of the building in other respects (for it is carried up to a vast height), the air is lighter and cooler: whereas there the sun is strong in every direction, and there is much crowding, and vapour and dust, and other things which add to discomfort far more than these. Whence it is plain that these senseless excuses are the offspring of indolence and of a supine disposition, destitute of the fire of the Holy Spirit.

3. Now these remarks of mine are not so much directed to them, as to you who do not bring them forward, do not rouse them from their indolence, and draw them to this table of salvation. Household slaves indeed when they have to discharge some service in common, summon their fellow slaves, but you when you are going to meet for this spiritual ministry suffer your fellow servants to be deprived of the advantage by your neglect. "But what if they do not desire it?" you say. Make them desire it by your continual importunity: for if they see you insisting upon it they certainly will desire it. Nay these things are a mere excuse and pretence. How many fathers at any rate are there here who have not their sons standing with them? Was it so difficult for thee to bring hither some of thy children? Whence it is clear that the absence of all the others who remain outside is due not only to their own indolence, but also to your neglect. But now at least, if never before, rouse yourselves up, and let each person enter the Church accompanied by a member of his family: let them incite and urge one another to the assembly here, the father his son, the son his father, the husbands their wives, and the wives their husbands, the master his slave, brother his brother, friend his friend: or rather let us not summon friends only but also enemies to this common treasury of good things. If thy enemy sees thy care for his welfare, he will undoubtedly relinquish his hatred.

Say to him: "art thou not ashamed and dost thou not blush before the Jews who keep their sabbath with such great strictness, and from the evening of it abstain from all work? And if they see the sun verging towards setting on the day of the Preparation they break off business, and cut short their traffic: and if

---

[1] Song of the Three Children in the Apocryphal addition to Daniel iii.
[2] Dan. vi. 24.
[3] Jerem. xxxviii. 5.
[4] John iv. 14.
[5] John vii. 38.

any one who has been making a purchase from them, before the evening, comes in the evening bringing the price, they do not suffer themselves to take it, or to accept the money." And why do I speak of the price of market wares and transaction of business? Even if it were possible to receive a treasure they would rather lose the gain than trample on their law. Are the Jews then so strict, and this when they keep the law out of due season, and cling to an observance of it which does not profit them, but rather does them harm: and wilt thou, who art superior to the shadow, to whom it has been vouchsafed to see the Sun of Righteousness, who art ranked as a citizen of the Heavenly commonwealth, wilt thou not display the same zeal as those who unseasonably cleave to what is wrong, thou who hast been entrusted with the truth, but although thou art summoned here for only a short part of the day, canst thou not endure to spend even this upon the hearing of the divine oracles? and what kind of indulgence, pray, could you obtain? and what answer will you have to make which is reasonable and just? It is utterly impossible that one who is so indifferent and indolent should ever obtain indulgence, even if he should allege the necessities of wordly affairs ten thousand times over as an excuse. Do you not know that if you come and worship God and take part in the work which goes on here, the business you have on hand is made much easier for you? Have you worldly anxieties? Come here on that account that by the time you spend here you may win for yourself the favour of God, and so depart with a sense of security; that you may have Him for your ally, that you may become invincible to the dæmons because you are assisted by the heavenly hand. If you have the benefit of prayers uttered by the fathers, if you take part in common prayer, if you listen to the divine oracles, if you win for yourself the aid of God, if, armed with these weapons, you then go forth, not even the devil himself will be able henceforth to look you in the face, much less wicked men who are eager to insult and malign you. But if you go from your house to the market place, and are found destitute of these weapons, you will be easily mastered by all who insult you. This is the reason why, both in public and private affairs, many things occur contrary to our expectation, because we have not been diligent about spiritual things in the first place, and secondarily about the secular, but have inverted the order. For this reason also the proper sequence and right arrangement of things has been upset, and all our affairs are full of much confusion. Can you imagine what distress and grief I suffer when I observe, that if a public holy day and festival is at hand there is a concourse of all the inhabitants of the city, although there is no one to summon them; but when the holy day and festival are past, even if we should crack our voice by continuing to call you all day long there is no one who pays any heed? For often when turning these things over in my mind I have groaned heavily, and said to myself: What is the use of exhortation or advice, when you do everything merely by the force of habit, and do not become a whit more zealous in consequence of my teaching? For whereas in the festivals you need no exhortation from me, but, when they are past you profit nothing by my teaching, do you not show that my discourse, so far as you are concerned, is superfluous?

4. Perhaps many of those who hear these things are grieved. But such is not the sentiment of the indolent: else they would put away their carelessness, like ourselves, who are daily anxious about your affairs. And what gain do you make by your secular transactions in proportion to the damage you sustain? It is impossible to depart from any other assembly, or gathering, in the possession of so much gain as you receive from the time spent here, whether it be the law court, or council-chamber, or even the palace itself. For we do not commit the administration of nations or cities nor the command of armies to those who enter here, but another kind of government more dignified than that of the empire itself; or rather we do not ourselves commit it, but the grace of the spirit.

What then is the government, more dignified than that of the empire, which they who enter here receive? They are trained to master untoward passions, to rule wicked lusts, to command anger, to regulate ill-will, to subdue vainglory. The emperor, seated on the imperial throne, and wearing his diadem, is not so dignified as the man who has elevated his own inward right reason to the throne of government over base passions, and by his dominion over them has bound as it were a glorious diadem upon his brow. For what profit is there, pray, in purple, and raiment wrought with gold, and a jewelled crown, when the soul is in captivity to the passions? What gain is there in outward freedom when the ruling element within us is reduced to a state of disgraceful and pitiable servitude. For just as when a fever penetrates deep, and inflames all the inward parts, there is no benefit to be got from the outward surface of the body, although it is not affected in the same way: even so when our soul is violently carried away by the passion within, no outward government, not even the imperial throne, is of any profit, since reason is deposed from the throne of empire by the violent usurpation of the passions, and bows and trembles beneath their insurrectionary movements. Now to prevent this taking place prophets and apostles concur on all sides in helping us, repressing our passions, and expelling all the ferocity of the irrational element within us, and committing a mode of government to us far more dignified than the empire. This is why I said that they who deprive themselves of this care[1] receive a blow in the vital parts, sustaining greater damage than can be inflicted from any other quarter; inasmuch as they who come here get greater gain than they could derive from any other source: even as Scripture has declared. The law said "Thou shalt not appear before the Lord empty;"[2] that is, enter not into the temple without sacrifices. Now if it is not right to go into the house of God without sacrifices, much more ought we to enter the assembly accompanied by our brethren: for this sacrifice and offering is better than that, when thou bringest a soul with thee into the Church. Do you not see doves which have been trained, how they hunt for others when they are let out? Let us also do this. For what kind of excuse shall we have, if irrational creatures are able to hunt for an animal of their own species, while we who have been honoured with reason and so much wisdom neglect this kind of pursuit? I exhorted you in my former discourse with these words: "Go, each of you to the houses of your neighbours, wait for them to come out, lay hold of them, and conduct them to their common mother: and imitate those who are mad upon theatre going, who diligently arrange to meet each other and so wait at early dawn to see that iniquitous spectacle." Yet I have not effected anything by this exhortation. Therefore I speak again and shall not cease speaking, until I have persuaded you. Hearing profits nothing unless it is accompanied by practice. It makes our punishment heavier, if we continually hear the same things and do none of the things which are spoken. That the chastisement will be heavier, hear the statement of Christ. "If I had not come and spoken to them they had not had sin: but now they have no cloke for their sin."[3] And the Apostle says "for not the hearers of the law shall be justified."[4] These things He says to the hearers; but when He wishes to instruct the speaker also, that even he will not gain anything from his teaching unless his behaviour is in close correspondence with his doctrine, and his manner of life is in harmony with his speech, hear how the Apostle and the prophet address themselves to him: for the latter says "but to the sinner said God, why dost thou preach my laws and takest my covenant in thy mouth, whereas thou hast hated instruction?"[5] And the Apostle, addressing himself to these same again who thought great things of their teaching, speaks on this wise: "Thou art confident that thou thyself art a leader of the blind, a light of those who are in darkness, an instructor of the foolish, a teacher of babes: thou therefore that teachest another teachest thou not thyself?"[6] Inasmuch then as it could neither profit me the speaker to speak, nor you the hearers to hear, unless we comply with the things which are spoken, but rather would increase our condemnation, let us not limit the display of our zeal to hearing only, but let us observe what is said, in our deeds. For it is indeed a good thing to spend time continually in hearing the divine oracles: but this good thing becomes useless when the benefit to be derived from hearing is not linked with it.

Therefore that you may not assemble here in vain I shall not cease beseeching you with all earnestness, as I have often besought you before, "conduct your brethren to us, exhort the wanderers, counsel them not by word only but also by deed." This is the more powerful, teaching,—that which comes through our manners and behaviour—Even if you do not utter a word, but yet, after you have gone out of this assembly, by your mien, and your look, and your voice and all the rest of your demeanour you exhibit to the men who have been left behind the gain which you have brought away with you, this is sufficient for exhortation and advice. For we ought to go out from this place as it were from some sacred shrine, as men who have descended from heaven itself, who have become sedate, and philosophical, who do and say everything in proper measure: and when a wife sees her husband returning from the assembly, and a father his son, and a friend his friend, and an enemy his enemy, let them all receive an impression of the benefit which you have derived from coming here: and they will receive it, if they perceive that you have become milder, more philosophical, more devout. Consider what privileges you enjoy who hast been initiated into the mysteries,[7] with what company thou offerest up that mystic hymn, with what company thou criest aloud the "Ter sanctus."

---

[1] *i. e.*, the care of their brethren. That this is the meaning appears from what follows.
[2] Exod. xxiii. 15. [3] John xv. 22. [4] Rom. ii. 13.
[5] Ps. iv. 16, 17. [6] Rom. ii. 19-21.
[7] *i. e.*, admitted to Holy Communion, which catechumens were not permitted to witness.

Teach "them that are without" that thou hast joined the chorus of the Seraphim, that thou art ranked as a citizen of the commonwealth above, that thou hast been enrolled in the choir of Angels, that thou hast conversed with the Lord, that thou hast been in the company of Christ. If we regulate ourselves in this way we shall not need to say anything, when we go out to those who are left behind: but from our advantage they will perceive their own loss and will hasten hither, so as to enjoy the same benefits themselves. For when, merely by the use of their senses, they see the beauty of your soul shining forth, even if they are the most stupid of men, they will become enamoured of your goodly appearance. For if corporeal beauty excites those who behold it, much more will symmetry of soul be able to move the spectator, and stimulate him to equal zeal. Let us then adorn our inward man, and let us be mindful of the things which are said here, when we go out: for there especially is it a proper time to remember them; and just as an athlete displays in the lists the things which he has learned in the training school: even so ought we to display in our transactions in the world without the things which we have heard here.

5. Bear in mind then the things which are said here, that when you have gone out and the devil lays hold of you either by means of anger or vainglory, or any other passion, you may call to remembrance the teaching which you have received here and may be able easily to shake off the grasp of the evil one. Do you not see the wrestling-masters in the practising grounds, who, after countless contests having obtained exemption from wrestling on account of their age, sit outside the lines by the side of the dust and shout to those who are wrestling inside, telling one to grasp a hand, or drag a leg, or seize upon the back, and by many other directions of that kind, saying, "if you do so and so you will easily throw your antagonist," they are of the greatest service to their pupils? Even so do thou look to thy training master, the blessed Paul, who after countless victories is now sitting outside the boundary, I mean this present life, and cries aloud to us who are wrestling, shouting out by means of his Epistles, when he sees us overcome by wrath and resentment of injuries, and choked by passion; "if thy enemy hunger feed him, if he thirst give him drink;"[1]—a beautiful precept full of spiritual wisdom, and serviceable both to the doer and the receiver. But the remainder of the passage causes much perplexity, and does not seem to correspond to the sentiment of him who uttered the former words. And what is the nature of this? the saying that "by so doing thou shalt heap coals of fire on his head." For by these words he does a wrong both to the doer and the receiver: to the latter by setting his head on fire, and placing coals upon it; for what good will he get from receiving food and drink in proportion to the evil he will suffer from the heaping of coals on his head? Thus then the recipient of the benefit is wronged, having a greater vengeance inflicted on him, but the benefactor also is injured in another way. For what can he gain from doing good to his enemies when he acts in the hope of revenge? For he who gives meat and drink to his enemy for the purpose of heaping coals of fire on his head would not become merciful and kind, but cruel and harsh, having inflicted an enormous punishment by means of a small benefit. For what could be more unkind than to feed a person for the purpose of heaping coals of fire on his head? This then is the contradiction: and now it remains that the solution should be added, in order that by those very things which seem to do violence to the letter of the law you may clearly see all the wisdom of the lawgiver. What then is the solution?

That great and noble-minded man was well aware of the fact that to be reconciled quickly with an enemy is a grievous and difficult thing; grievous and difficult, not on account of its own nature, but of our moral indolence. But he commanded us not only to be reconciled with our enemy, but also to feed him; which was far more grievous than the former. For if some are infuriated by the mere sight of those who have annoyed them, how would they be willing to feed them when they were hungry? And why do I speak of the sight infuriating them? If any one makes mention of the persons, and merely introduces their name in society, it revives the wound in our imagination, and increases the heat of passion. Paul then being aware of all these things and wishing to make what was hard and difficult of correction smooth and easy, and to persuade one who could not endure to see his enemy, to be ready to confer that benefit already mentioned upon him, added the words about coals of fire, in order that a man prompted by the hope of vengeance might hasten to do this service to one who had annoyed him. And just as the fisherman surrounding the hook on all sides with the bait presents it to the fishes in order that one of them hastening to its accustomed food may be captured by means of it and easily held fast: even so Paul also wishing to lead on the man who has been wronged to bestow a benefit on the man who has

---

[1] Rom. xii. 20.

wronged him does not present to him the bare hook of spiritual wisdom, but having covered it as it were with a kind of bait, I mean the "coals of fire," invites the man who has been insulted, in the hope of inflicting punishment, to confer this benefit on the man who has annoyed him; but when he has come he holds him fast in future, and does not let him make off, the very nature of the deed attaching him to his enemy; and he all but says to him: "if thou art not willing to feed the man who has wronged thee for piety's sake: feed him at least from the hope of punishing him." For he knows that if the man once sets his hand to the work of conferring this benefit, a starting-point is made and a way of reconciliation is opened for him. For certainly no one would have the heart to regard a man continually as his enemy to whom he has given meat and drink, even if he originally does this in the hope of vengeance. For time as it goes on relaxes the tension of his anger. As then the fisherman, if he presented the bare hook would never allure the fish, but when he has covered it gets it unawares into the mouth of the creature who comes up to it: so also Paul if he had not advanced the expectation of inflicting punishment would never have persuaded those who were wronged to undertake to benefit those who had annoyed them. Wishing then to persuade those who recoiled in disgust, and were paralysed by the very sight of their enemies, to confer the greatest benefits upon them, he made mention of the coals of fire, not with a view of thrusting the persons in question into inexorable punishment, but in order that when he had persuaded those who were wronged to benefit their enemies in the expectation of punishing them, he might afterwards in time persuade them to abandon their anger altogether.

6. Thus then did he encourage the man who has been wronged; but observe also how he unites again the man who has done the wrong to him who has been provoked. First of all by the very manner of the benefit: (for there is no one so degraded and unfeeling as to be unwilling, when he receives meat and drink, to become the servant and friend of him who does this for him): and in the second place through the dread of vengeance. For the passage, "by so doing thou shalt heap coals of fire on his head" seems indeed to be addressed to the person who gives the food; but it more especially touches him who has caused the annoyance, in order that through fear of this punishment he may be deterred from remaining continually in a state of enmity, and being aware that the reception of food and drink might do him the greatest mischief if he constantly retains his animosity, may suppress his anger. For thus he will be able to quench the coals of fire. Wherefore the proposed punishment and vengeance both induces the one who has been wronged to benefit him who has annoyed him, and it deters and checks him who has given the provocation, and impels him to reconciliation with the man who gives him meat and drink. Paul therefore linked the two persons by a twofold bond, the one depending on a benefit, the other on an act of vengeance. For the difficulty is to make a beginning and to find an opening for the reconciliation: but when that has once been cleared in whatever way it may be, all which follows will be smooth and easy. For even if at first the man who has been annoyed feeds his enemy in the hope of punishing him, yet becoming his friend by the act of giving him food he will be able to expel the desire of vengeance. For when he has become a friend he will no longer feed the man who has been reconciled to him, with an expectation of this kind. Again he who has given the provocation, when he sees the man who has been wronged electing to give him meat and drink, casts out all his animosity, both on account of this deed, and also of his fear of the punishment which is in store for him, even if he be excessively hard and harsh and stony hearted, being put to shame by the benevolence of him who gives him food, and dreading the punishment reserved for him, if he continues to be an enemy after accepting the food.

For this reason Paul did not stop even here in his exhortation, but when he has emptied each side of wrath he proceeds to correct their disposition, saying, "be not overcome of evil." "For if," he says, "you continue to bear resentment and to seek revenge you seem indeed to conquer your enemy, but in reality you are being conquered by evil, that is, by wrath: so that if you wish to conquer, be reconciled, and do not make an attack upon your adversary;" for a brilliant victory is that in which by means of good, that is to say by forbearance, you overcome evil, expelling wrath and resentment. But the injured man, when inflamed with passion would not have borne these words. Therefore when he had satisfied his wrath he proceeded to conduct him to the best reason for reconciliation, and did not permit him to remain permanently animated by the wicked hope of vengeance. Dost thou perceive the wisdom of the lawgiver? And that you may learn that he introduced this law only on account of the weakness of those who would not otherwise be content to make terms amongst themselves, hear how Christ, when He ordained a law on this same subject did not propose the same reward, as the Apostle; but, having said "Love your enemies, do good to them that hate you," which means give them food and drink, He did not add "for in so doing ye shall heap coals of fire on their heads:" but what did He say? "that ye may become like your Father who is in Heaven."[1] Naturally so, for He was discoursing to Peter, James, and John and the rest of the apostolic band: therefore He proposed that reward. But if you say that even on this understanding the precept is onerous you improve once more the defence which I am making for Paul, but you deprive yourself of every plea of indulgence. For I can prove to you that this which seems to you onerous was accomplished under the Old Dispensation when the manifestation of spiritual wisdom was not so great as it is now. For this reason also Paul did not introduce the law in his own words, but used the very expressions which were employed by him who originally brought it in, that he might leave no room for excuse to those who do not observe it: for the precept "if thine enemy hunger feed him, if he thirst give him drink" is not the utterance of Paul in the first instance, but of Solomon.[2] For this reason he quoted the words that he might persuade the hearer that for one who has been advanced to such a high standard of wisdom to regard an old law as onerous and grievous which was often fulfilled by the men of old time, is one of the basest things possible. Which of the ancients, you ask, fulfilled it? There were many, but amongst others David especially did so more abundantly? He did not indeed merely give food or drink to his enemy, but also rescued him several times from death, when he was in jeopardy; and when he had it in his power to slay him he spared him once, twice, yea many times. As for Saul he hated and abhorred him so much after the countless good services which he had done, after his brilliant triumphs, and the salvation which he had wrought in the matter of Goliath, that he could not bear to mention him by his own name, but called him after his father. For once when a festival was at hand, and Saul, having devised some treachery against him, and contrived a cruel plot, did not see him arrive—"where," said he, "is the son of Jesse?"[3] He called him by his father's name, both because on account of his hatred he could not endure the recollection of his proper name, and also because he thought to damage the distinguished position of that righteous man by a reference to his low birth; —a miserable and despicable thought: for certainly, even if he had some accusation to bring against the father this could in no wise injure David. For each man is answerable for his own deeds, and by these he can be praised and accused. But, as it was, not having any evil deed to mention, he brought forward his low birth, expecting by this means to throw his glory into the shade, which in fact was the height of folly. For what kind of offence is it to be the child of insignificant and humble parents? Saul however did not understand true wisdom in these things. He called David then, "the son of Jesse," but when David found him sleeping inside the cave, he did not call him the "son of Kish," but by his title of honour: "for I will not lift up my hand," he said, "against the Lord's anointed."[4] So purely free was he from wrath and resentment of injuries: he calls him the Lord's anointed who had done him such great wrongs, who was thirsting for his blood, who after his countless good services had many times attempted to destroy him. For he did not consider how Saul deserved to be treated, but he considered what was becoming for himself both to do and to say, which is the greatest stretch of moral wisdom. How so? When thou hast got thy enemy in a prison, made fast by a twofold, or rather by a triple chain, confinement of space, dearth of assistance, and necessity of sleep, dost thou not demand a penalty and punishment of him? "No," he says; "for I am not now regarding what he deserves to suffer, but what it behoves me to do." He did not look to the facility for slaying, but to the accurate observance of the moral wisdom which was becoming to him. And yet which of the existing circumstances was not sufficient to prompt him to the act of slaughter? Was not the fact that his enemy was delivered bound into his hands a sufficient inducement? For you are aware I suppose that we hasten more eagerly to deeds for which facilities abound, and the hope of success increases our desire to act, which was just what happened then in his case.

Well! did the captain who then counselled and urged him to the deed,[5] did the memory of past events induce him to slay? no one of these things moved him: in fact the very facility for slaughter averted him from it: for he bethought him that God had put Saul in his hands for the purpose of furnishing ample ground and opportunity for the exercise of moral wisdom. You then perhaps admire him, because he did not cherish the memory of any of his past evils: but I am much more astonished at him for another reason. And what is this? that the fear of future events did not

---

[1] Matt. v. 44.   [2] Prov. xxv. 21, 22.   [3] 1 Sam. xx. 23.   [4] 1 Sam. xxvi. 11.   [5] Abishai. 1 Sam. xxvi. 8.

impel him to lay violent hands on his enemy. For he knew clearly that if Saul escaped his hands, he would again be his adversary; yet he preferred exposing himself to danger by letting go the man who had wronged him, to providing for his own security by laying violent hands upon his foe. What could equal then the great and generous spirit of this man, who, when the law commanded eye to be plucked out for eye, and tooth for tooth, and retaliation on equal terms,[1] not only abstained from doing this, but exhibited a far greater measure of moral wisdom? At least if he had slain Saul at that time he would have retained credit for moral wisdom unimpaired, not merely because he had acted on the defensive, not being himself the originator of violence, but also because by his great moderation he was superior to the precept "an eye for an eye." For he would not have inflicted one slaughter in return for one; but, in return for many deaths, which Saul endeavoured to bring on him, having attempted to slay him not once or twice but many times, he would have brought only one death on Saul; and not only this, but if he had proceeded to avenge himself out of fear of the future, even this, combined with the things already mentioned, would procure him the reward of forbearance without any deduction. For he who is angry on account of the things which have been done to him, and demands satisfaction, would not be able to obtain the praise of forbearance: but when a man dismisses the consideration of all past evils, although they are many and painful, but is compelled to take steps for self-defence from fear of the future, and by way of providing for his own security, no one would deprive him of the rewards of moderation.

7. Nevertheless David did not act even thus, but found a novel and strange form of moral wisdom: and neither the remembrance of things past, nor the fear of things to come, nor the instigation of the captain, nor the solitude of the place, nor the facility for slaying, nor anything else incited him to kill; but he spared the man who was his enemy, and had given him pain just as if he was some benefactor, and had done him much good. What kind of indulgence then shall we have, if we are mindful of past transgressions, and avenge ourselves on those who have given us pain, whereas that innocent man who had undergone such great sufferings and expected more and worse evils to befall him in consequence of saving his enemy, is seen to spare him, so as to prefer incurring danger himself and to live in fear and trembling, rather than put to a just death the man who would cause him endless troubles?

His moral wisdom then we may perceive, not only from the fact that he did not slay Saul, when there was so strong a compulsion, but also that he did not utter an irreverent word against him, although he who was insulted would not have heard him. Yet we often speak evil of friends when they are absent, he on the contrary not even of the enemy who had done him such great wrong. His moral wisdom then we may perceive from these things: but his lovingkindness and tender care from what he did after these things. For when he had cut off the fringe of Saul's garment, and had taken away the bottle of water he withdrew afar off and stood and shouted, and exhibited these things to him whose life he had preserved, doing so not with a view to display and ostentation, but desiring to convince him by his deeds that he suspected him without a cause as his enemy, and aiming therefore at winning him into friendship. Nevertheless when he had even thus failed to persuade him, and could have laid hands on him, he again chose rather to be an exile from his country and to sojourn in a strange land, and suffer distress every day, in procuring necessary food than to remain at home and vex his adversary. What spirit could be kinder than his? He was indeed justified in saying "Lord remember David and all his meekness."[2] Let us also imitate him, and let us neither say nor do evil to our enemies, but benefit them according to our power: for we shall do more good to ourselves than to them. "For if ye forgive your enemies," we are told, "ye shall be forgiven."[3] Forgive base offences that thou mayest receive a royal pardon for thy offences; but if any one has done thee great wrongs, the greater the wrongs you forgive, the greater will be the pardon which you will receive. Therefore we have been instructed to say "Forgive us, as we forgive," that we may learn that the measure of our forgiveness takes its beginning in the first place from ourselves. Wherefore in proportion to the severity of the evil which the enemy does to us is the greatness of the benefit which he bestows. Let us then be earnest and eager to be reconciled with those who have vexed us, whether their wrath be just or unjust. For if thou art reconciled here, thou art delivered from judgment in the other world; but if in the interval while the hatred is still going on, death interrupting steps in and carries the enmity away with it, it follows of necessity that the trial of the case should be

---

[1] Deut. xix. 21.
[2] Psalm cxxxii. 1, the LXX. translation has not very accurately rendered the original. "Trouble," or "anxiety," as in our English version, is the meaning of the word here rendered "meekness."
[3] Matt. vi. 14.

brought forward in the other world. As then many men when they have a dispute with one another, if they come to a friendly understanding together outside the law court save themselves loss, and alarm, and many risks, the issue of the case turning out in accordance with the sentiment of each party; but if they severally entrust the affair to the judge the only result to them will be loss of money, and in many cases a penalty, and the permanent endurance of their hatred; even so here if we come to terms during our present life we shall relieve ourselves from all punishment; but if while remaining enemies we depart to that terrible tribunal in the other world we shall certainly pay the utmost penalty at the sentence of the judge there, and shall both of us undergo inexorable punishment: he who is unjustly wroth because he is thus unjustly disposed, and he who is justly wroth, because he has, however justly, cherished resentment. For even if we have been unjustly ill-treated, we ought to grant pardon to those who have wronged us. And observe how he urges and incites those who have unjustly given pain to reconciliation with those whom they have wronged. "If thou offerest thy gift before the altar, and there rememberest that thy brother hath ought against thee, go thy way; first be reconciled to thy brother."[1] He did not say, "assemble, and offer thy sacrifice," but "be reconciled and then offer it." Let it lie there, he says, in order that the necessity of making the offering may constrain him who is justly wroth to come to terms even against his will. See how he again prompts us to go to the man who has provoked us when he says "Forgive your debtors in order that your Father may also forgive your trespasses." For He did not propose a small reward, but one which far exceeds the magnitude of the achievement. Considering all these things then, and counting the recompense which is given in this case and remembering that to wipe away sins does not entail much labour and zeal, let us pardon those who have wronged us. For that which others scarcely accomplish, I mean the blotting out of their own sins by means of fasting and lamentations, and prayers, and sackcloth, and ashes, this it is possible for us easily to effect without sackcloth and ashes and fasting if only we blot out anger from our heart, and with sincerity forgive those who have wronged us. May the God of peace and iove, having banished from our soul all wrath and bitterness, and anger, deign to grant that we being closely knit one to another according to the proper adjustment of the parts,[2] may with one accord, one mouth and one soul continually offer up our hymns of thanksgiving due to Him: for to Him be glory and power for ever and ever. Amen.

[1] Matt. v. 23, 24.
[2] Ephes. iv. 16.

ST. CHRYSOSTOM:

HOMILY

AGAINST PUBLISHING THE ERRORS OF THE BRETHREN, AND UTTERING IMPRECATIONS UPON ENEMIES.

TRANSLATED BY

R. BLACKBURN, M.A.,

RECTOR OF SELHAM, SUSSEX, AND LATE FELLOW OF BRASENOSE COLLEGE, OXFORD.

CONTENTS.

		PAGE
1.	The Church an unfailing source or medicine for the soul	235
2.	Some things are good or evil according to the use made of them	236
3.	The spiritual medicines of the Church are administered without publicity	236
4.	The advantage of not publicly exposing the sinner	236
5.	The devil assails men most of all when they pray	237
6.	Childlessness no retribution for sin	238
7.	Why Christ was born of a virgin	238
8.	The wisdom of God manifested in the nature of Christ's birth	239
9.	The birth of Esau and Jacob an answer to persevering prayer	240
10.	The devil persuades some men to be negligent of prayer, others to invoke curses on their enemies	240
11.	The wickedness of imprecating vengeance on enemies	241
12.	We must forgive if we would be forgiven	241

AGAINST PUBLISHING THE ERRORS OF THE BRETHREN.

HOMILY

UPON THE NOT PUBLISHING THE ERRORS OF THE BRETHREN, NOR UTTERING IMPRECATIONS UPON ENEMIES.

1. I ACCOUNT you happy for the zeal, beloved, with which you flock into the Father's house. For from this zeal I have ground for feeling confidence about your health also with respect to the soul; for indeed the school of the Church is an admirable surgery—a surgery, not for bodies, but for souls. For it is spiritual, and sets right, not fleshly wounds, but errors of the mind,[1] and of these errors and wounds the medicine is the word. This medicine is compounded, not from the herbs growing on the earth, but from the words proceeding from heaven—this no hands of physicians, but tongues of preachers have dispensed. On this account it lasts right through; and neither is its virtue impaired by length of time, nor defeated by any strength of diseases. For certainly the medicines of physicians have both these defects; for while they are fresh they display their proper strength, but when much time has passed; just as those bodies which have grown old; they become weaker; and often too the difficult character of maladies is wont to baffle them; since they are but human. Whereas the divine medicine is not such as this; but after much time has intervened, it still retains all its inherent virtue. Ever since at least Moses was born (for from thence dates the beginning of the Scripture) it has healed so many human beings; and not only has it not lost its proper power, but neither has any disease ever yet overcome it. This medicine it is not possible to get by payment of silver; but he who has displayed sincerity of purpose and disposition goes his way having it all. On account of this both rich and poor alike obtain the benefit of this healing process. For where there is a necessity to pay down money the man of large means indeed shares the benefit; but the poor man often has to go away deprived of the gain, since his income does not suffice him for the making up of the medicine. But in this case, since it is not possible to pay down silver coin, but it is needful to display faith and a good purpose, he who has paid down these with forwardness of mind, this is he who most reaps the advantage; since indeed these are the price paid for the medicinal treatment. And the rich and the poor man share the benefit alike; or rather it is not alike that they share the benefit, but often the poor man goes away in the enjoyment of more. What ever can be the reason? It is because the rich man, possessed beforehand by many thoughts, having the pride and puffed-up temper belonging to wealthiness; living with carelessness and lazy ease as companions, receives the medicine of the hearing of the Scriptures not with much attention, nor with much earnestness; but the poor man, far removed from delicate living and gluttony and indolence; spending all his time in handicraft and honest labours; and gathering hence much

[1] διανοίας. In Chrysostom equivalent to the νοῦς of St. Paul (Rom. xii. 2); the moral and spiritual mind. Ἁμαρτήματα. Lit. missings of the mark: errors of the moral will. Διάνοια is so used. 1 John v. 20.

love of wisdom for the soul; becomes thereby more attentive and free from slackness, and is wont to give his mind with more accurate care to all that is said: whence also, inasmuch as the price he has paid is higher, the benefit which he departs having reaped is greater.

2. It is not as absolutely bringing an accusation against those who are wealthy that I say all this; nor as praising the poor without reference to circumstances: for neither is wealth an evil, but the having made a bad use of wealth; nor is poverty a virtue, but the having made a virtuous use of poverty. That rich man who was in the time of Lazarus was punished,[1] not because he was rich, but because he was cruel and inhuman. And that poor man who rested in the bosom of Abraham was praised, not because he was poor, but because he had borne his poverty with thankfulness.

For of things—(now attend carefully to this saying; for it will avail to put into you sufficient religious knowledge, and to cast out all unsound reasoning, and to bring about your having your judgment right concerning the truth of things)—well, of things some are by nature morally good, and others the contrary; and others neither good nor evil, but they occupy the intermediate position. A good thing piety is by nature, impiety an evil thing; a good thing virtue, an evil thing wickedness; but wealth and poverty in themselves are neither the one nor the other; but from the will of those who use them they become either the one or the other. For if thou hast used thy wealth for purposes of philanthropy, the thing becomes to thee a foundation of good; but if for rapine and grasping and insolence, thou hast turned the use of it to the direct opposite; but for this wealth is not chargeable, but he who has used his wealth for insolence. So also we may say of poverty: if thou have borne it nobly by giving thanks to the Master, what has been done becomes to thee a cause and ground for receiving crowns; but if on account of this thou blaspheme thy Creator, and accuse Him for His providence, thou hast again used the thing to an evil purpose. But just as in that case it is not wealth that is responsible for the avarice, but the person who has made a bad use of wealth, so also here we are not to lay the blame of the blasphemy on poverty, but on him who did not choose to bear the thing in a sober spirit. For in every case both the praise and the blame belong to our own will and choice. Good is wealth, yet not absolutely, but to him only to whom it is not sin; and again poverty is wicked, but not absolutely, but only in the mouth of the impious, because he is discontented, because he blasphemes, because he is indignant, because he accuses Him who has made him.

3 Let us not therefore accuse riches, nor revile poverty absolutely, but those who do not will[2] to use these virtuously; for the things themselves lie in the middle. But as I was saying (for it is good to return to the former subject), both rich and poor enjoy the benefit of the medicines administered here with the same boldness and freedom; and often the poor with more earnestness. For the special excellence of the medicines is not this only, that they heal souls, that their virtue is not destroyed by length of time, that they are not worsted by any disease, that the benefit is publicly offered gratuitously, that the healing treatment is on a footing of equality both for rich and poor—but they have another quality also not inferior to these good points. Pray of what character is this? It is that we do not publicly expose those who come to this surgery. For they who go off to the surgeries of the outside world, have many who examine their wounds, and unless the physician have first uncovered the sore, he does not apply the dressing; but here not so, but seeing as we do innumerable patients, we go through the medical treatment of them in a latent manner. For not by dragging into publicity those who have sinned do we thus noise abroad the sins committed by them; but after putting forth our teaching, as common to all, we leave it entirely to the conscience of the hearers; so that each may draw to himself from what is said the suitable medicine for his own wound. For there proceeds the word of doctrine from the tongue of the speaker, containing accusation of wickedness, praise of virtue, blame of lewdness, commendation of chasteness, censure of pride, praise of gentleness, just as a medicine of varied and manifold ingredients, compounded from every kind; and to take what is applicable to himself and salutary is the part of each of the hearers. The word then issues openly, and settling into the conscience of each, secretly both affords the healing treatment which comes from it, and before the malady has been divulged, has often restored health.

4. You at all events heard yesterday how I extolled the power of prayer, how I reproached those who pray with listlessness; without having publicly exposed one of them. Those then who were conscious to themselves of earnestness, accepted that commendation of prayer,

---

[1] ἐκολάζετο. The imperfect denotes the continuous character of the punishment. So ἐπῃνεῖτο "had lasting praise." "ἡ ἀρετὴ ἕξις ἐπαινετή." Aristotle *Eth.*

[2] Ἐθέλοντας. In its theological sense. "Θέλημα σαρκός." Not a classical, but an ecclesiastical word (John i. 13). So our Lord, εἴ τις θέλει, has the will.

and became still more earnest by the praises, while those who were conscious to themselves of listlessness, accepted on the other hand the rebuking, and put off their carelessness. But neither these nor those do we know; and this ignorance is serviceable to both—how, I now tell you. He who has heard the commendations of prayer and is conscious to himself of earnestness, were he to have many witnesses of the commendations, would have lapsed towards pride; but, as it is, by having secretly accepted the praise, he is removed from all arrogance. On the other hand he who is conscious to himself of listlessness, having heard the accusation, has become better from the accusation, as having no one of men a witness of the rebuking; and this was of no ordinary profit to him. For on account of the being flurried at the opinion of the vulgar,[1] so long as we may think that we escape notice in our wickedness, we exert ourselves to become better; but when we have become notorious to all, and have lost the consolation derived from the escaping notice, we grow more shameless and remiss rather. And just as sores become more painful by being unbandaged and frequently exposed to cold air, so also the soul after having sinned, if in the presence of many it be rebuked for what it has done amiss, grows thereby more shameless. In order therefore that this might not take place, the word administered its medicine to you covertly. And that you may understand[2] that the gain which this covert treatment has is great, hear what the Christ says. "If thy brother have committed a fault against thee convince him of it," and he did not say "between him and the whole town," nor, "between thee and the whole people,"[3] but "only between thee and him." Let the accusation, he says, be unwitnessed to, in order that the change to amendment may be made easy of digestion. A great good surely, the making the advice unpublished. Sufficient is the conscience, sufficient that incorruptible judge. It is not so much thou who rebukest him who has done wrong as his own conscience (that accuser is the sharper), nor dost thou do it with the more exact knowledge of the faults committed. Add not therefore wound to wound by exposing him who has done wrong; but administer for thyself the counsel unwitnessed. This therefore we are doing now—the very thing that Paul also did, framing the indictment against him who among the Corinthians had sinned without citing of witnesses. And hear how. "On this account," he says, "brethren, I have applied these figures of speech to myself and Apollos." And yet not he himself nor Apollos were they who had rent the people in schism and divided the Church; but all the same he concealed the accusation, and just as by some masks, by hiding the countenances of the defendants by his own and Apollos' names, he afforded them power to amend of that wickedness. And again, "Lest in some way after I have come God humble me, and I may have to mourn many of those who have before sinned, and have not repented over the uncleanness and lasciviousness which they had committed."[4] See how here also he indefinitely mentions those who had sinned, in order that he might not, by openly bringing the accusation, render the soul of those who had sinned more shameless. Therefore, just as we administer our reproofs with so much sparing of your feelings, so do ye also with all seriousness receive the correction; and attend with carefulness to what is said.

5. We discoursed to you yesterday about the power which is in prayer. I pointed out[5] how the devil then lies in wait, deceiver that he is. For since he sees very great gain accruing to us from prayer, then most he assails us, in order that he may disable us from our defence;[6] that he may send us off home empty-handed. And just as before magistrates, when the officers of the court who are about the person of the magistrate have a hostile feeling toward those who come before him, they by their staves drive them away to a distance, preventing their coming near and resorting to lamentation and so obtaining compassion; so also the devil, when he has seen us coming to the judge, drives us away to a distance, not by any staff, but through our own slackness. For he knows, he knows clearly, that if they have come to him in a sober spirit, and have told the sins committed, and have mourned with their soul fervent, they will depart having received full forgiveness; for God loves mankind; and on this account he is beforehand with them, and debars them from access,[7] in order that they may obtain no one of the things which they need. But the soldiers of magistrates with violence scare away those who are coming to them; but he with no compulsion, but by deceiving us, and throwing us into security. On this account we are not deserving even of allowance, since we voluntarily deprive ourselves of the good things. Prayer with

---

[1] οἱ πολλοί, as opposed to οἱ χαρίεντες, those of culture and refinement. Arist. *Eth.*
[2] A common sense of μανθανω. "Μανθάνεις; οὐ μανθάνω." Aristophanes; who was a favorite author with Chrysostom.
[3] The article here has this universal force. Matt. xviii. 15.
[4] 1 Cor. iv. 6; 2 Cor. xii. 21.
[5] Ἔδειξα. Ἔνδειξις. Lat. index (*digitus*), the fore-finger.
[6] The idea seems to be that of making the accused entirely forget the defence, such as used to be written for him by some Attic orator.
[7] ἔντευξις, an Aristotelic term. "τῆς πρὸς τοὺς πολλοὺς ἐντεύξεως" Rhet., the way of addressing a large body.

earnestness is a light of the understanding and soul—a light unquenchable and perpetual. On this account he throws into our minds countless rubbish-heaps of imaginations; and things which we never had imagined, these collecting together at the very moment of prayer he pours down upon our souls. And just as winds often rushing from an opposite quarter by a violent gust extinguish a lamp's flame as it is being lighted, so also the devil, when he has seen the flame of our prayer being kindled, blowing it on every side with the blasts of countless thoughts, does not desist before and until he has quenched the light. But the very thing which they who are kindling those lamps do, this let us also do. And what do they do? When they see a violent wind coming, by laying their finger upon the opening of the lamp they bar the entrance against the wind. For so long as he assails from without we shall be able to stand against him; but when we have opened to him the doors of the mind, and have received the enemy inside; after that we are no longer able to withstand even a little; but, having on all sides completely extinguished the memory,[1] just as a smoking lamp, he allows our mouth to utter empty words. But just as they put their finger upon the opening of the lamp, so let us lay consideration upon our mind: let us close off from the wicked spirit the entrance, in order that he may not quench our light of prayer. Remember both those illustrations, both that of the soldiers and the magistrate, and that respecting the lamp. For with this purpose we adduce to you these illustrations; with which we are conversant, in which we live, in order that, after we have departed hence and have returned home, we may from things of familiar occurrence receive a reminder of what has been said.

6. Prayer is a strong piece of armour and a great security. You heard yesterday how the three children, fettered as they were, destroyed the power of the fire; how they trampled down the blaze; how they overcame the furnace, and conquered the operation of the element. Hear to-day again how the noble and great Isaac overcame the nature itself of bodies through prayer. They destroyed[2] the power of fire, this man to-day loosed the bonds of incapacitated nature. And learn how he effected this. "Isaac," it says, "prayed[3] concerning his wife, because she was barren." This has to-day been read to you; yesterday the sermon was about prayer; and to-day again there is a demonstration of the power of prayer. See how the grace of the Spirit has ordered that what has been read to-day harmonises with what was said yesterday. "Isaac," it says, "prayed concerning Rebecca his wife, because she was barren." This first is worth inquiring into, for what cause she was barren. She was of a life admirable and replete with much chastity—both herself and her husband. We cannot lay hold[4] of the life of those just ones, and say that the barrenness was the work of sin. And not only was she herself barren, but also his mother Sarah, who had borne him; not only was his mother barren and his wife, but also his daughter-in-law, the wife of Jacob, Rachel. What is the meaning of this band of barren ones? All were righteous, all living in virtue, all were witnessed to by God. For it was of them that He said, "I am the God of Abraham, and the God of Isaac, and the God of Jacob." Of the same persons Paul also thus speaks. "For which cause God is not ashamed to call himself their God."[5] Many are the commendations of them in the New, many the praises of them in the Old Testament. On all sides they were bright and illustrious, and yet they all had barren wives, and continued in childlessness until an advanced period. When therefore thou seest man and wife living with virtue; when thou seest them beloved of God, caring for piety, and yet suffering the malady of childlessness; do not suppose that the childlessness is at all a retribution for sins. For many are God's reasons for the dispensation, and to us inexplicable; and for all we must be heartily thankful, and think those only wretched who live in wickedness; not those who do not possess children. Often God does it expediently, though we know not the cause of events. On this account in every case it is our duty to admire His wisdom, and to glorify His unspeakable love of man.

7. Well,[6] this consideration indeed is able to school us in moral character, but it is necessary also to state the cause for which those women were barren. What then was the cause? It was in order that when thou hast seen the Virgin bringing forth our common Master, thou mightest not disbelieve. Wherefore exercise thy mind in the womb of the barren; in order that when thou hast seen the womb, disabled and bound as it is, being opened to the bearing of children from the grace of God, thou mightest not marvel at hearing that a virgin has brought forth. Or rather even marvel and be astounded; but do not disbelieve the marvel. When the Jew says to thee, "how did the virgin bear?" say to him "how did she bear who was barren and

---

[1] Still continuing the simile of a wind.
[2] κατέλυσαν, *de-struo*, to take to pieces, pull down, a building.
[3] ἐδέετο. Denotes continuance in prayer. Comp. Matt. vii. 7, 8.
[4] ἐπιλαβέσθαι, as in wrestling.   [5] Heb. xi. 16.
[6] Ἀλλά. This adverb is not always adversative. It is sometimes, as here, connective; denoting a transition in treating the subject. Comp. Aristophanes *Acharn.* 377-383.

enfeebled by old age?" There were then two hindrances, both the unseasonableness of her age and the unserviceableness of nature; but in the case of the Virgin there was one hindrance only, the not having shared in marriage. The barren one therefore prepares the way for the virgin. And that thou mayest learn that it was on this account that the barren ones had anticipated it, in order that the Virgin's child-birth might be believed, hear the words of Gabriel which were addressed to her—For when he had come and said to her, "thou shalt conceive in the womb and bear a son, and thou shalt call his name Jesus;" the Virgin was astonished and marvelled, and said, "how will this be to me, since I know not a man." What then said the Angel? "The Holy Ghost shall come upon thee." Seek not the sequence of nature, he says, when that which takes place is above nature; look not round for marriage and throes of child-birth, when the manner of the birth is too grand for marriage. "And how will this be," she says, "since I know not a husband." And verily on this account shall this be, since thou knowest no husband. For didst thou know a husband, thou wouldest not have been deemed worthy to serve this ministry. So that, for the reason why thou disbelievest, for this believe. And thou wouldest not have been deemed worthy to serve this ministry, not because marriage is an evil; but because virginity is superior; and right it was that the entry of the Master should be more august than ours; for it was royal, and the king enters through one more august. It was necessary that He should both share as to birth, and be diverse from ours. Wherefore both these things are managed.

For the being born from the womb is common in respect to us, but the being born without marriage is a thing greater than on a level with us. And the gestation and conception in the belly belongs to human nature; but that the pregnancy should take place without sexual intercourse is too august for human nature.[1] And for this purpose both these things took place, in order that thou mayest learn both the pre-eminence and the fellowship with thee of Him who was born.

8. And pray consider the wisdom of all that was done. Neither did the pre-eminence injure the likeness and kinship to us, nor did the kinship to us dim the pre-eminence; but both were displayed by all the circumstances; and the one had our condition in its entirety, and the other what was diverse compared with us. But just as I was saying, on this account the barren ones went before, in order that the Virgin's child-birth might be believed, that she[1] might be led by the hand to faith in that promise and undertaking which she heard from the angel, saying, "The Holy Ghost shall come upon thee, and the miraculous power[2] of the Most High shall overshadow thee"—thus, he says, thou art able to bear. Look not to the earth; it is from the heavens that the operation will come. That which takes place is a grace of the Spirit; pray inquire not about nature and laws of marriage. But since those words were too high for her, he wills to afford also another demonstration. But do thou, pray, observe how the barren one leads her on the way to the belief in this. For since that demonstration was too high for the Virgin's intelligence, hear how he brought down what he said to lower things also, leading her by the hand by sensible facts. For "behold," he says, "Elizabeth thy kinswoman—she also has conceived a son in her old age; and this month is the sixth to her who was called barren." Seest thou that the barren one was for the sake of the Virgin? since with what object did he adduce to her the child-bearing of her kinswoman? with what object did he say, "in her old age?" with what object did he add, "who was called barren?" It was by way of inducing her by all these things, manifestly, to the believing the glad annunciation. For this cause he spoke of both the age and the disabling effect of nature; for this cause he awaited the time also which had elapsed from the conception; for he did not tell to her the glad tidings immediately from the beginning,[3] but awaited for a six-months period to have passed to the barren one, in order that the puerperal swelling might, for the rest, be a pledge of the pregnancy, and an indisputable demonstration might arise of the conception. And pray again look at the intelligence of Gabriel. For he neither reminded her[4] of Sarah, nor of Rebecca, nor of Rachel; and yet they also were barren, and they had grown old, and that which took place was a marvel; but the stories were ancient. Now things new and recent and occurring in our generation are wont to induce us into the belief of marvels more than those which are old. On this account having let those women alone, that she should understand from her kinswoman Elizabeth herself what was coming upon her, he brought it forward; so as from her to lead her to her own—that most awful and august child-birth. For the child-birth of the barren one lay between ours and that of the Master less indeed than that of the Virgin, but greater

---

[1] Αὐτή. The use of αὐτός in the nominative in this sense; *ille*, not *ipse*, seems to have been introduced in the Alexandrian period of Greek literature. "Αὐτοὶ γὰρ οὐκ εἰσι θεοί," LXX.
[2] The constant signification of δύναμις in the Gospels.
[3] Προοιμίων, lit. the prelude, overture. Οἴμας Μοῦσ ἐδίδαξε φίλησε δὲ φῦλον ἀοιδῶν, Hom. *Od.* 481.
[4] Αὐτῆς, *lege* δὲ αὐτήν.

than ours. On this account it was by Elizabeth lying between, just as by some bridge, that he lifted up the mind of the Virgin from the travail which is according to nature, to that which is above nature.

9. I did desire to say more, and to teach you other reasons for which Rebecca, and Rachel, were barren; but the time does not permit; urging on the discourse to the power of prayer. For on this account indeed I have mooted all these points, that ye might understand how the prayer of Isaac unbound the barrenness of his wife; and that prayer for so long a time. "Isaac," it says, "continually prayed about Rebecca his wife, and God listened to him." For do not suppose that he invoked God and had immediately been listened to; for he had spent much time in praying to God. And if you desire to learn how much, I will tell you this too with exactness. He had spent the number of twenty years in praying to God. Whence is this manifest? from the sequence itself. For the Scripture, desiring to point out the faith and the endurance and the love of wisdom of that righteous man, did not break off and leave untold even the time, but made it also clear to us, covertly indeed, so as to rouse up our indolence; but nevertheless did not allow it to be uncertain. Hear then how it covertly indicated to us the time. "Now Isaac was forty years old when he took Rebecca, a daughter of Bethuel the Syrian." You hear how many years old he was when he brought home his wife: "Forty years old," it says, "he was when he took Rebecca." But since we have learnt how many years old he was when he married his wife, let us learn also when he after all became a father, and how many years old he was then, when he begat Jacob; and we shall be able to see how long a time his wife had remained barren; and that during all that time he continued to pray to God. How many years old then was he when he begat Jacob? "Jacob," it says, "came forth laying hold with his right hand of his brother's heel: on this account he called him Jacob, and him Esau. Now Isaac was sixty years old when he begat them." If therefore when he brought Rebecca home he was forty years old, and when he begat the sons sixty, it is very plain that his wife had remained barren for twenty years between, and during all this time Isaac continued to pray to God.

10. After this do we not feel shame, and hide our faces, at seeing that righteous man for twenty years persevering[1] and not desisting; we ourselves after a first or second petition often fainting and indignant? And yet he indeed had in large measure liberty of speech towards God,[2] and all the same he felt no discontent at the delay of the giving, but remained patient, whereas we, laden with countless sins, living with an evil conscience, displaying no good will towards the Master; if we are not heard before having spoken, are bewildered, impatiently recoil, desist from asking—on this account we always retire with empty hands. Who has for twenty years besought God for one thing, as this righteous man did? or rather who for twenty months only? Yesterday I was saying that they are many who pray with slackness, and yawning, and stretching themselves, and continually shifting their attitude, and indulging in every carelessness in their prayers—but to-day I have found also another damage attaching itself to their prayers more destructive than that one. For many, throwing themselves prostrate, and striking the ground with their forehead, and pouring forth hot tears, and groaning bitterly from the heart[3] and stretching out their hands, and displaying much earnestness, employ this warmth and forwardness against their own salvation. For it is not on behalf of their own sins that they beseech God; nor are they asking forgiveness of the offences committed by them; but they are exerting this earnestness against their enemies entirely, doing just the same thing as if one, after whetting his sword, were not to use the weapon against his enemies, but to thrust it through his own throat. So these also use their prayers not for the remission of their own sins, but about revenge on their enemies; which is to thrust the sword against themselves. This too the wicked one has devised, in order that on all sides we may destroy ourselves, both through slackness and through earnestness. For the one class by their carelessness in their prayers exasperate God, by displaying contempt through their slackness; and the others, when they display earnestness, display the earnestness on the other hand against their own salvation. "A certain person," he (the devil) says, "is slack: that is sufficient for me with a view to his obtaining nothing; this man is earnest and thoroughly aroused; what then must be done to accomplish the same result? I cannot slacken his earnestness, nor throw him into carelessness; I will contrive his de-

---

[1] παραμένοντα, waiting; as it were, like a beggar at the door.

[2] παρρησίαν, a phrase of courtly ceremonial; sometimes coupled with προσαγωγῇ, the antecedent ceremony of introduction to a king's presence. Xenphon *Cyrop.* vii. 5, 45. Both occur in Virg. *Æn.* i. 520. "*Postquam introgressi, et coram data copia fandi.*" The literal translation of παρρησία: *coram = παρά* "in the presence." Comp. Chrysost. Hom. II. in 2 Cor. of the catechumens standing outside the holy rails, and not allowed to take part in the Lord's Prayer. "οὐδέπω γὰρ παρρησίαν κέκτηνται."

[3] Literally "from below." Comp. Virgil *Æn.* i. 37; *imoqæ trahens de pectore vocem.*

struction in the other way. How so? I will manage that he use his earnestness for transgressing the law:" (for the praying against one's personal enemies is a transgression of law). "He shall depart therefore not only having gained nothing by his earnestness, but also having endured the hurt which is greater than that caused through slackness." Such as these are the injuries of the devil: the one sort he destroys through their remissness; and the other through their earnestness itself, when it is shown not according to God's laws.

11. But it is also worth hearing the very words of their prayer, and how the words are of a puerile mind; of how infantile a soul. I am ashamed in truth when about to repeat them; but it is absolutely necessary to repeat them, and to imitate that coarse tongue. What then are the words? "Avenge me of my enemies, show them that I too have God (on my side)." They do not then learn, man, that we have God, when we are indignant and angry and impatient; but when we are gentle and meek and subdued, and practise all love of wisdom. So also God said, "Let your light shine before men, that they may see your good works, and glorify your Father who is in the heavens."[1] Perceivest thou not that it is an insult to God, the making a request to God against thine enemies? And how is it an insult? one will say. Because He Himself said, "pray for your enemies;" and brought in this divine law. When therefore thou claimest that the legislator should relax his own laws; and callest upon him to legislate in opposition to himself; and supplicatest him who had forbidden thee to pray against thine enemies to hear thee praying against thine enemies; thou art not praying in doing this, nor calling upon him; but thou art insulting the lawgiver, and acting with drunken violence towards him, who is sure to give to thee the good things which result from prayer. And how is it possible to be heard when praying, tell me, when thou exasperatest him who is sure to hear? For by doing these things thou art pushing thine own salvation into a pit, and art rushing down a precipice, by striking thine enemy before the king's eyes.[2] For even if thou doest not this with the hands, with thy words thou strikest him, the thing which thou darest not do even in the case of thy fellow-slaves. At least dare to do this in a ruler's presence, and though thou hast done countless public services, thou wilt straightway surely be led away to execution. Then (I ask) in the presence of a ruler dost thou not dare to insult thine equal, but when doing this in God's presence, tell me, dost thou not shudder, nor fear when in the time of entreaty and prayer being so savage and turning thyself into a wild beast; and displaying greater want of feeling than he who demanded payment of the hundred pence?[3] For that thou art more insolent than he, listen to the story itself. A certain man owed ten thousand talents to his master; then, not having (wherewith) to pay, he entreated him to be longsuffering, in order that, his wife having been sold and his house and his children, he might settle his master's claim. And the master seeing him lamenting had compassion on him, and remitted the ten thousand talents. He having gone out and found another servant owing him a hundred pence, seizing his throat demanded them with great cruelty and inhumanity. The Master having heard this threw him into the prison, and laid on him again the debt of the ten thousand talents which he had before remitted; and he paid the penalty of the cruelty shown towards his fellow-servant.

12. Now do thou consider in how much more unfeeling and insensible in a way thou hast acted even than he, praying against thine enemies. He did not beg his master to demand, but he himself demanded, the hundred pence; whereas thou even callest on the Master for this shameless and forbidden demand. And he seized his fellow-servant's throat not before his lord's eyes, but outside; while thou in the very moment of prayer, standing in the King's presence, doest this. And if he, for doing this without either having urged his master to the demand, and after going forth, met with no forgiveness; thou, both stirring up the Master to (exacting) this forbidden payment, and doing this before his eyes, what sort of penalty will thou have to pay? tell me. But thy mind is inflamed by the memory of the enmity, and swells, and thy heart rises,[4] and when recurring in memory to him who has caused pain, thou art unable to reduce the swelling of thy thought. But set against this inflammation the memory resulting from thine own sins committed the fear resulting from the punishment to come. Recall to memory for how many things thou art accountable to thy master, and that for all those things thou owest Him satisfaction; and this fear will surely overcome that anger; since indeed this is far more powerful than that passion. Recall the memory of hell and punishment and vengeance during the time of thy prayer; and thou wilt not be able even to receive thine enemy into

---

[1] Matt. v. 16.
[2] To strike any one within "the precincts of the court" even has been made a capital offence.
[3] Matt. xviii. 28.
[4] Possibly "stomach." Comp. *Thuc.* ii. 49, ὁπότε ἐς τὴν καρδίαν στηρίξαι. Lat. *stomachor*. A medical sense, and the metaphor here is medical throughout. So "cardiacus." Juvenal.

thy mind.[1] Make thy mind contrite, humble thy soul by the memory of the offences committed by thee, and wrath will not be able even to trouble thee. But the cause of all these evils is this, that we scrutinise the sins of all others with great exactitude; while we let our own pass with great remissness. Whereas we ought to do the contrary—to keep our own faults unforgotten; but never even to admit a thought of those of others. If we do this we shall both have God propitious, and shall cease cherishing immortal anger against our neighbours, and we shall never have any one as an enemy; and even if we should have at any time we shall both quickly put an end to his enmity, and should obtain speedy pardon for our own sins. For just as he who treasures up the memory of wrong against his neighbour does not permit the punishment upon his own sins to be done away; so he who is clear of anger will speedily be clear of sins also. For if we, wicked as we are and enslaved to passion, on account of the commandment of God overlook all the faults committed against us, much more will He who is a lover of mankind, and good, and free from any passion, overlook our delinquencies, rendering to us the recompense of our kindly spirit towards our neighbour in the forgiveness of our own sins: which God grant that we may attain, by the grace and lovingkindness of our Lord Jesus Christ, to whom is the glory and the dominion, to the ages of the ages. Amen.

---

[1] Because it is filled with better thoughts. No room for him.

ST. CHRYSOSTOM:

TWO HOMILIES ON EUTROPIUS.

I. WHEN HE HAD TAKEN REFUGE IN THE CHURCH.

II. WHEN HE HAD QUITTED THE ASYLUM OF THE CHURCH, AND HAD BEEN TAKEN CAPTIVE.

TRANSLATED BY

REV. W. R. W. STEPHENS, M.A.

PREBENDARY OF CHICHESTER CATHEDRAL, AND RECTOR OF WOOLBEDING, SUSSEX.

CONTENTS.

HOMILY I.

	PAGE
Introduction	245
1. Contrast between the late prosperity and present misery of Eutropius	249
2. The same	250
3. The church has returned good for evil	250
4. Lessons to be learned from the spectacle of fallen greatness exhibited by Eutropius	251
5. An exhortation to mercy and forgiveness	252

HOMILY II.

1. The church an impregnable refuge	252
2. St. Chrysostom forcibly conducted to the Emperor's palace.	253
3. The uselessness of riches in the time of danger	254
4. The virtuous man is invulnerable	254
5. The shortness and insignificance of this present life	255
6. Lessons to be learned from seeing the calamities of others	255
7. Explanation of anthropomorphic expressions as applied to God in Holy Scripture	256
8. Explanation of symbolical names of God in Holy Scripture	257
9. Reasons why the acts and attributes of God are described in figurative language	257
10. The glory of the Transfiguration transcended the description of the Evangelists.	258
11. The Incarnation set forth under the image of a marriage	258
12. The spiritual dowry bestowed on human nature by the Incarnation	260
13. This dowry partly present, partly future	260
14. What the possession of spiritual gifts enabled St. Paul to do	261
15. The spiritual marriage and dowry illustrated by a reference to Psalm xlv.	262
16. The same	263
17. Corporeal and spiritual beauty contrasted	264

INTRODUCTION TO THE TWO HOMILIES ON EUTROPIUS.

THE interest of the two following discourses depends not only on their intrinsic value as specimens of Chrysostom's eloquence, but also on the singular and dramatic character of the incidents which gave occasion to them.

Arcadius the Emperor of the East like his brother Honorius the Emperor of the West was a man of feeble intellect. The history of the Empire under their reign is a melancholy record of imbecility on the part of the nominal rulers: of faithlessness and unscrupulous ambition on the part of their ministers. The chief administrator of affairs in the beginning of the reign of Arcadius was Rufinus, an Aquitanian Gaul; the very model of an accomplished adventurer. His intrigues, his arrogance, his rapacious avarice excited the indignation of the people, and he was at last assassinated by the troops to whom he was making an oration in the presence of the Emperor. His place in the favour and confidence of Arcadius was soon occupied by the eunuch Eutropius. The career of this person was a strange one. Born a slave, in the region of Mesopotamia, he had passed in boyhood and youth through the hands of many owners, performing the most menial offices incident to his position. At length Arnithus, an old military officer who had become his master, presented him to his daughter on her marriage; and in the words of the poet Claudian "the future consul of the East was made over as part of a marriage dowry."[1] But the young lady after a time grew tired of the slave who was becoming elderly and wrinkled, and without trying to sell him turned him out of her household. He picked up a precarious living in Constantinople and was often in great want until an officer about court took pity on him, and procured him a situation in the lower ranks of the imperial chamberlains. This was the beginning of his rise. By the diligence with which he discharged his humble duties, by occasional witty sayings, and the semblance of a fervent piety he attracted the notice of the great Emperor Theodosius (the father of Arcadius), and gradually won his confidence so as to be employed on difficult and delicate missions. On the death of Theodosius he became in the capacity of grand chamberlain the intimate adviser and constant attendant of Arcadius and the most subtle and determined rival of Rufinus. It was by his contrivance that the scheme of Rufinus for marrying his own daughter to the Emperor was defeated: and that Eudoxia the daughter of a Frankish general was substituted for her. After the murder of Rufinus the government was practically in his hands; but he exercised his power more craftily than the vain and boastful Gaul. He contrived at first to discharge all the duties which fell to his lot as chamberlain with humble assiduity, and sought no other title than he already possessed. Slowly but surely however he climbed to the summit of power by the simple process of putting out of the way on various pretexts all dangerous competitors. He deprived his victims of their last hope of escape by abolishing the right of the Church to afford shelter to fugitives. He sold the chief offices of the State, and the command of the provinces to the highest bidders. By surrounding the Emperor with a crowd of frivolous companions, by dissipating his mind with a perpetual round of amusements, by taking him every spring to Ancyra in Phrygia where he was subjected to the enervating influ-

---
[1] In Eutrop. i. 104, 105.

ence of a soft climate and luxurious style of living he made the naturally feeble intellect of Arcadius more feeble still and withdrew it from the power of every superior mind but his own. From the pettiest detail of domestic life to the most important affairs of state, the wily minister at length ruled supreme. Arcadius was little more than a magnificently dressed puppet, and the eunuch slave was the real master of half the Roman world. It was by his advice that on the death of Nectarius in 397 Chrysostom had been appointed, very much against his own will, to the vacant See of Constantinople. If Eutropius expected to find a complaisant courtier in the new Archbishop he certainly sustained a severe disappointment. Some little pretences which he made of assisting the work of the Church by patronising Chrysostom's missionary projects could not blind the Archbishop to the gross venality of his administration, or exempt him from the censure and warnings of one who was too honest and bold to be any respecter of persons. In fact when the Archbishop declaimed against the cupidity and oppressions of the rich it was obvious to all that Eutropius was the most signal example of those vices. At last the minister, not content to remain as he was—enjoying the reality of power without the name—prepared the way for his own ruin by inducing the Emperor to bestow on him the titles of Patrician and Consul. The acquisition of these venerable names by the eunuch slave caused a profound sensation of shame and indignation throughout the Empire, but especially in the Western capital, where they were bound up with all the noblest and most glorious memories in the history of the Roman people. The name of Eutropius was omitted from the Fasti or catalogue of consuls inscribed in the Capitol at Rome. Amidst the general decadence and degeneracy of public spirit in the Empire the West did not descend, could not have descended, to those depths of servile adulation to which the Byzantines stooped at the inauguration of Eutropius as Consul. The senate, and all the great officials military and civil, poured into the palace of the Cæsars to offer their homage, and emulated each other in the honor of kissing the hand and even the wrinkled visage of the eunuch. They saluted him as the bulwark of the laws, and the second father of the Emperor. Statues of bronze or marble were placed in various parts of the city representing him in the costume of warrior or judge, and the inscriptions on them styled him third founder of the city after Byzas, and Constantine. No wonder that Claudian declaimed with bitter sarcasm against "a Byzantine nobility and Greek divinities" and invokes Neptune by a stroke of his trident to unseat and submerge the degenerate city which had inflicted such a deep disgrace upon the Empire.[1] A blow indeed was about to fall upon the eastern capital, directed not by the hand of a mythic deity, but of a stout barbarian soldier. The consequences of it were averted from the city only by the sacrifice of the new consul upon whom it fell with crushing effect. He sank never to rise again. Tribigild, a distinguished gothic soldier who had been raised to the rank of Tribune in the Roman army, had demanded higher promotion for himself and higher pay for a body of military colonists in Phrygia of which he had the command. His petition had been coldly dismissed by Eutropius; Tribigild resented the affront and with the troops which he commanded broke into revolt. Eutropius entrusted the conduct of an expedition against him to one of his favorites, who suffered a most ignominious defeat in which he perished, and the greater part of his army was cut to pieces. Constantinople was convulsed with terror and indignation. Gäinas another Goth in command of the city troops declared that he could do nothing to check the progress of the revolt unless Eutropius was banished, the principal author of all the evils of the State. His demand was backed by the Empress Eudoxia, who had experienced much insolence from the minister. Eutropius was deprived of his official dignity, his property was declared confiscated, and he was commanded to quit the palace instantly under pain of death. Whither could the poor wretch fly who was thus in a moment hurled from the pinnacle of power into the lowest depths of degradation and destitu-

---

[1] In Eutrop. ii. 39, 136.

tion. There was but one place to which he could naturally turn in his distress—the sanctuary of the Church; but by the cruel irony of his fate, a law of his own devising here barred his entrance. Yet he knew that the law prohibiting asylum had been resented and resisted by the Church and it might be that the Archbishop would connive at the violation of the obnoxious measure by the very person who had passed it. He resolved to make the experiment. In the humblest guise of a suppliant, tears streaming down his puckered cheeks, his scant grey hairs smeared with dust, he crept into the Cathedral, drew aside the curtain in front of the altar and clung to one of the columns which supported it. Here he was found by Chrysostom in a state of pitiable and abject terror, for soldiers in search of him had entered the Church, and the clattering of their arms could be heard on the other side of the thin partition which concealed the fugitive. With quivering lips he craved the asylum of the church, and he was not repulsed as the destroyer of the refuge which he now sought.[1] Chrysostom rejoiced in the opportunity afforded to the church of taking a noble revenge on her adversary.[2] He concealed Eutropius in the sacristy, confronted his pursuers, and refused to surrender him. "None shall violate the sanctuary save over my body: the church is the bride of Christ who has entrusted her honor to me and I will never betray it." He desired to be conducted to the Emperor and taken like a prisoner between two rows of spearmen from the Cathedral to the palace[3] where he boldly vindicated the church's right of asylum in the presence of the Emperor. Arcadius promised to respect the retreat of the fallen minister, and with difficulty persuaded the angry troops to accept his decision. The next day was Sunday, and the Cathedral was thronged with a vast multitude eager to hear what the golden mouth of the Archbishop would utter who had dared in defence of the Church's right to defy the law, and confront the tide of popular feeling. But few probably were prepared to witness such a dramatic scene as was actually presented. The Archbishop had just taken his seat in the "Ambon" or high reading desk a little westward of the chancel from which he was wont to preach on account of his diminutive stature, and a sea of faces was upturned to him waiting for the stream of golden eloquence when the curtain of the sanctuary was drawn aside and disclosed the cowering form of the miserable Eutropius clinging to one of the columns of the Holy Table. Many a time had the Archbishop preached to unheeding ears on the vain and fleeting character of worldly honor, prosperity, luxury and wealth: now he would force attention, and drive home his lesson to the hearts of his vast congregation by pointing to a visible example of fallen grandeur in the poor wretch who lay grovelling behind him.

Eutropius remained for some days within the precincts of the Church and then suddenly departed. Whether he mistrusted the security of his shelter and hoped to make his escape in disguise, or whether he surrendered himself on the understanding that exile would be substituted for capital punishment cannot be certainly known. Chrysostom declared that if he had not abandoned the Church, the Church would never have given him up.[4] Anyhow he was captured and conveyed to Cyprus, but soon afterwards he was tried at Constantinople on various charges of high crimes and misdemeanors against the State, and condemned to suffer capital punishment. He was taken to Chalcedon and there beheaded.[5] The second of the two following discourses was delivered a few days after Eutropius had quitted the sanctuary of the Church.

---

[1] Hom. i. 2.   [2] Hom. i. 3.   [3] Hom. ii. 1.   [4] Hom. ii. 1.
[5] For a fuller account of all these events, see Life of St. John Chrysostom by W. R. W. Stephens (pp. 298-256, 3d edition).

EUTROPIUS, PATRICIAN AND CONSUL.

HOMILY I.

ON EUTROPIUS, THE EUNUCH, PATRICIAN AND CONSUL.

1. "VANITY of vanities, all is vanity"—it is always seasonable to utter this but more especially at the present time. Where are now the brilliant surroundings of thy consulship? where are the gleaming torches? Where is the dancing, and the noise of dancers' feet, and the banquets and the festivals? where are the garlands and the curtains of the theatre? where is the applause which greeted thee in the city, where the acclamation in the hippodrome and the flatteries of spectators? They are gone—all gone: a wind has blown upon the tree shattering down all its leaves, and showing it to us quite bare, and shaken from its very root; for so great has been the violence of the blast, that it has given a shock to all these fibres of the tree and threatens to tear it up from the roots. Where now are your feigned friends? where are your drinking parties, and your suppers? where is the swarm of parasites, and the wine which used to be poured forth all day long, and the manifold dainties invented by your cooks? where are they who courted your power and did and said everything to win your favour? They were all mere visions of the night, and dreams which have vanished with the dawn of day: they were spring flowers, and when the spring was over they all withered: they were a shadow which has passed away—they were a smoke which has dispersed, bubbles which have burst, cobwebs which have been rent in pieces. Therefore we chant continually this spiritual song—"Vanity of vanities, all is vanity." For this saying ought to be continually written on our walls, and garments, in the market place, and in the house, on the streets, and on the doors and entrances, and above all on the conscience of each one, and to be a perpetual theme for meditation. And inasmuch as deceitful things, and maskings and pretence seem to many to be realities it behoves each one every day both at supper and at breakfast, and in social assemblies to say to his neighbour and to hear his neighbour say in return "vanity of vanities, all is vanity." Was I not continually telling thee that wealth was a runaway? But you would not heed me. Did I not tell thee that it was an unthankful servant? But you would not be persuaded. Behold actual experience has now proved that it is not only a runaway, and ungrateful servant, but also a murderous one, for it is this which has caused thee now to fear and tremble. Did I not say to thee when you continually rebuked me for speaking the truth, "I love thee better than they do who flatter thee?" "I who reprove thee care more for thee than they who pay thee court?" Did I not add to these words by saying that the wounds of friends were more to be relied upon than the voluntary kisses of enemies.[1] If you had submitted to my wounds their kisses would not have wrought thee this destruction: for my wounds work health, but their kisses have produced an incurable disease. Where are now thy cup-bearers, where are they who cleared the way for thee in the market place, and sounded thy praises endlessly in the ears of all? They have fled, they have disowned thy friendship, they are providing for their own safety by means of thy distress. But I do not act thus, nay in thy misfortune I do not abandon thee, and now when thou art fallen I protect and tend thee. And the Church which

[1] Prov. xxvii. 6.

you treated as an enemy has opened her bosom and received thee into it; whereas the theatres which you courted, and about which you were oftentimes indignant with me have betrayed and ruined thee. And yet I never ceased saying to thee "why doest thou these things?" "thou art exasperating the Church, and casting thyself down headlong," yet thou didst hurry away from all my warnings. And now the hippodromes, having exhausted thy wealth, have whetted the sword against thee, but the Church which experienced thy untimely wrath is hurrying in every direction, in her desire to pluck thee out of the net.

2. And I say these things now not as trampling upon one who is prostrate, but from a desire to make those who are still standing more secure; not by way of irritating the sores of one who has been wounded, but rather to preserve those who have not yet been wounded in sound health; not by way of sinking one who is tossed by the waves, but as instructing those who are sailing with a favourable breeze, so that they may not become overwhelmed. And how may this be effected? by observing the vicissitudes of human affairs. For even this man had he stood in fear of vicissitude would not have experienced it; but whereas neither his own conscience, nor the counsels of others wrought any improvement in him, do ye at least who plume yourselves on your riches profit by his calamity: for nothing is weaker than human affairs. Whatever term therefore one may employ to express their insignificance it will fall short of the reality; whether he calls them smoke, or grass, or a dream or spring flowers, or by any other name; so perishable are they, and more naught than nonentities;[1] but that together with their nothingness they have also a very perilous element we have a proof before us. For who was more exalted than this man? Did he not surpass the whole world in wealth? had he not climbed to the very pinnacle of distinction? did not all tremble and fear before him? Yet lo! he has become more wretched than the prisoner, more pitiable than the menial slave, more indigent than the beggar wasting away with hunger, having every day a vision of sharpened swords and of the criminal's grave, and the public executioner leading him out to his death; and he does not even know if he once enjoyed past pleasure, nor is he sensible even of the sun's ray, but at mid day his sight is dimmed as if he were encompassed by the densest gloom. But even let me try my best I shall not be able to present to you in language the suffering which he must naturally undergo, in the hourly expectation of death. But indeed what need is there of any words from me, when he himself has clearly depicted this for us as in a visible image? For yesterday when they came to him from the royal court intending to drag him away by force, and he ran for refuge to the holy furniture,[2] his face was then, as it is now, no better than the countenance of one dead: and the chattering of his teeth, and the quaking and quivering of his whole body, and his faltering voice, and stammering tongue, and in fact his whole general appearance were suggestive of one whose soul was petrified.

3. Now I say these things not by way of reproaching him, or insulting his misfortune, but from a desire to soften your minds towards him, and to induce you to compassion, and to persuade you to be contented with the punishment which has already been inflicted. For since there are many inhuman persons amongst us who are inclined, perhaps, to find fault with me for having admitted him to the sanctuary, I parade his sufferings from a desire to soften their hardheartedness by my narrative.

For tell me, beloved brother, wherefore art thou indignant with me? You say it is because he who continually made war upon the Church has taken refuge within it. Yet surely we ought in the highest degree to glorify God, for permitting him to be placed in such a great strait as to experience both the power and the lovingkindness of the Church:—her power in that he has suffered this great vicissitude in consequence of the attacks which he made upon her: her lovingkindness in that she whom he attacked now casts her shield in front of him and has received him under her wings, and placed him in all security not resenting any of her former injuries, but most lovingly opening her bosom to him. For this is more glorious than any kind of trophy, this is a brilliant victory, this puts both Gentiles and Jews to shame, this displays the bright aspect of the Church: in that having received her enemy as a captive, she spares him, and when all have despised him in his desolation, she alone like an affectionate mother has concealed him under her cloak,[3] opposing both the wrath of the king, and the rage of the people, and their overwhelming hatred. This is an ornament for the altar. A strange kind of ornament, you say, when the accused sinner, the extortioner, the robber is permitted to lay hold of the altar. Nay! say not so: for even the harlot took hold of the feet of Jesus, she who was stained with the most accursed and unclean sin: yet her deed was no reproach to

---

[1] τῶν οὐδὲν ὄντων οὐδαμινώτερα.

[2] Holy *vessels* would be the literal rendering of the word (σκεύεσι), but it is clear from what follows that the altar is intended.
[3] Possibly an allusion to the curtain which, in Eastern Churches, was drawn in front of the altar.

Jesus, but rather redounded to His admiration and praise: for the impure woman did no injury to Him who was pure, but rather was the vile harlot rendered pure by the touch of Him who was the pure and spotless one. Grudge not then, O man. We are the servants of the crucified one who said "Forgive them for they know not what they do."[1] But, you say, he cut off the right of refuge here by his ordinances and divers kinds of laws. Yes! yet now he has learned by experience what it was he did, and he himself by his own deeds has been the first to break the law, and has become a spectacle to the whole world, and silent though he is, he utters from thence a warning voice to all, saying "do not such things as I have done, that ye suffer not such things as I suffer." He appears as a teacher by means of his calamity, and the altar emits great lustre, inspiring now the greatest awe from the fact that it holds the lion in bondage; for any figure of royalty might be very much set off if the king were not only to be seen seated on his throne arrayed in purple and wearing his crown, but if also prostrate at the feet of the king barbarians with their hands bound behind their backs were bending low their heads. And that no persuasive arguments have been used, ye yourselves are witnesses of the enthusiasm, and the concourse of the people. For brilliant indeed is the scene before us to day, and magnificent the assembly, and I see as large a gathering here to-day as at the Holy Paschal Feast. Thus the man has summoned you here without speaking and yet uttering a voice through his actions clearer than the sound of a trumpet: and ye have all thronged hither to-day, maidens deserting their boudoirs, and matrons the women's chambers, and men the market place that ye may see human nature convicted, and the instability of worldly affairs exposed, and the harlot-face which a few days ago was radiant (such is the prosperity derived from extortion) looking uglier than any wrinkled old woman, this face I say you may see denuded of its enamel and pigments by the action of adversity as by a sponge

4. Such is the force of this calamity: it has made one who was illustrious and conspicuous appear the most insignificant of men. And if a rich man should enter the assembly he derives much profit from the sight: for when he beholds the man who was shaking the whole world, now dragged down from so high a pinnacle of power, cowering with fright, more terrified than a hare or a frog, nailed fast to yonder pillar, without bonds, his fear serving instead of a chain, panic-stricken and trembling, he abates his haughtiness, he puts down his pride, and having acquired the kind of wisdom concerning human affairs which it concerns him to have he departs instructed by example in the lesson which Holy Scripture teaches by precept:—"All flesh is grass and all the glory of man as the flower of grass: the grass withereth and the flower faileth"[2] or "They shall wither away quickly as the grass, and as the green herb shall they quickly fail"[3] or "like smoke are his days,"[4] and all passages of that kind. Again the poor man when he has entered and gazed at this spectacle does not think meanly of himself, nor bewail himself on account of his poverty, but feels grateful to his poverty, because it is a place of refuge to him, and a calm haven, and secure bulwark; and when he sees these things he would many times rather remain where he is, than enjoy the possession of all men for a little time and afterwards be in jeopardy of his own life. Seest thou how the rich and poor, high and low, bond and free have derived no small profit from this man's taking refuge here? Seest thou how each man will depart hence with a remedy, being cured merely by this sight? Well! have I softened your passion, and expelled your wrath? have I extinguished your cruelty? have I induced you to be pitiful? Indeed I think I have; and your countenances and the streams of tears you shed are proofs of it. Since then your hard rock has turned into deep and fertile soil let us hasten to produce some fruit of mercy, and to display a luxuriant crop of pity by falling down before the Emperor or rather by imploring the merciful God so to soften the rage of the Emperor, and make his heart tender that he may grant the whole of the favour which we ask. For indeed already since that day when this man fled here for refuge no slight change has taken place; for as soon as the Emperor knew that he had hurried to this asylum, although the army was present, and incensed on account of his misdeeds, and demanded him to be given up for execution, the Emperor made a long speech endeavouring to allay the rage of the soldiers, maintaining that not only his offences, but any good deed which he might have done ought to be taken into account, declaring that he felt gratitude for the latter, and was prepared to forgive him as a fellow creature for deeds which were otherwise. And when they again urged him to avenge the insult done to the imperial majesty, shouting, leaping, and brandishing their spears, he shed streams of tears from his gentle eyes, and having reminded them of the Holy Table

---

[1] Luke xxiii. 34.   [2] Is. xl. 6, 7.   [3] Ps. xxxvii. 2.   [4] Ps. cii. 4.

to which the man had fled for refuge he succeeded at last in appeasing their wrath.

5. Moreover let me add some arguments which concern ourselves. For what pardon could you deserve, if the Emperor bears no resentment when he has been insulted, but ye who have experienced nothing of this kind display so much wrath? and how after this assembly has been dissolved will ye handle the holy mysteries, and repeat that prayer by which we are commanded to say "forgive us as we also forgive our debtors"[1] when ye are demanding vengeance upon your debtor? Has he inflicted great wrongs and insults on you? I will not deny it. Yet this is the season not for judgment but for mercy; not for requiring an account, but for showing loving kindness: not for investigating claims but for conceding them; not for verdicts and vengeance, but for mercy and favour. Let no one then be irritated or vexed, but let us rather beseech the merciful God to grant him a respite from death, and to rescue him from this impending destruction, so that he may put off his transgression, and let us unite to approach the merciful Emperor beseeching him for the sake of the Church, for the sake of the altar, to concede the life of one man as an offering to the Holy Table. If we do this the Emperor himself will accept us, and even before his praise we shall have the approval of God, who will bestow a large recompense upon us for our mercy. For as he rejects and hates the cruel and inhuman, so does He welcome and love the merciful and humane man; and if such a man be righteous, all the more glorious is the crown which is wreathed for him: and if he be a sinner, He passes over his sins granting this as the reward of compassion shown to his fellow-servant. "For" He saith "I will have mercy and not sacrifice,"[2] and throughout the Scriptures you find Him always enquiring after this, and declaring it to be the means of release from sin. Thus then we shall dispose Him to be propitious to us, thus we shall release ourselves from our sins, thus we shall adorn the Church, thus also our merciful Emperor, as I have already said, will commend us, and all the people will applaud us, and the ends of the earth will admire the humanity and gentleness of our city, and all who hear of these deeds throughout the world will extol us. That we then may enjoy these good things, let us fall down in prayer and supplication, let us rescue the captive, the fugitive, the suppliant from danger that we ourselves may obtain the future blessings by the favour and mercy of our Lord Jesus Christ, to whom be glory and power, now and for ever, world without end. Amen.

[1] Matt. vi. 12.

[2] Hosea vi. 6.

HOMILY II.

AFTER EUTROPIUS HAVING BEEN FOUND OUTSIDE THE CHURCH HAD BEEN TAKEN CAPTIVE.

1. DELECTABLE indeed are the meadow, and the garden, but far more delectable the study of the divine writings. For there indeed are flowers which fade, but here are thoughts which abide in full bloom; there is the breeze of the zephyr, but here the breath of the Spirit: there is the hedge of thorns, but here is the guarding providence of God; there is the song of cicadæ, but here the melody of the prophets: there is the pleasure which comes from sight, but here the profit which comes from study. The garden is confined to one place, but the Scriptures are in all parts of the world; the garden is subject to the necessities of the seasons, but the Scriptures are rich in foliage, and laden with fruit alike in winter and in summer. Let us then give diligent heed to the study of the Scriptures: for if thou doest this the Scripture will expel thy despondency, and engender pleasure, extirpate vice, and make virtue take root, and in the tumult of life it will save thee from suffering like those who are tossed by troubled waves. The sea rages but thou sailest on with calm weather; for thou hast the study of the Scriptures for thy pilot; for this is the cable which the trials of life do not break asunder. Now that I lie not events themselves bear witness. A few days ago the Church was besieged: an army came, and fire issued from their eyes, yet it did not scorch the olive tree; swords were unsheathed, yet no one received a wound; the imperial gates were in distress, but the Church was in security. And yet the tide of

war flowed hither; for here the refugee was sought, and we withstood them, not fearing their rage. And wherefore prithee? because we held as a sure pledge the saying "Thou art Peter, and upon this rock I will build my Church: and the gates of hell shall not prevail against it."[1] And when I say the Church I mean not only a place but also a plan of life:[2] I mean not the walls of the Church but the laws of the Church. When thou takest refuge in a Church, do not seek shelter merely in the place but in the spirit of the place. For the Church is not wall and roof but faith and life.

Do not tell me that the man having been surrendered was surrendered by the Church; if he had not abandoned the Church he would not have been surrendered. Do not say that he fled here for refuge and then was given up: the Church did not abandon him but he abandoned the Church. He was not surrendered from within the Church but outside its walls. Wherefore did he forsake the Church? Didst thou desire to save thyself? Thou shouldst have held fast to the altar. There were no walls here, but there was the guarding providence of God. Wast thou a sinner? God does not reject thee: for "He came not to call the righteous but sinners to repentance."[3] The harlot was saved when she clung to His feet. Have ye heard the passage read to-day? Now I say these things that thou mayest not hesitate to take refuge in the Church. Abide with the Church, and the Church does not hand thee over to the enemy: but if thou fliest from the Church, the Church is not the cause of thy capture. For if thou art inside the fold the wolf does not enter: but if thou goest outside, thou art liable to be the wild beast's prey: yet this is not the fault of the fold, but of thy own pusillanimity. The Church hath no feet. Talk not to me of walls and arms: for walls wax old with time, but the Church has no old age. Walls are shattered by barbarians, but over the Church even demons do not prevail. And that my words are no mere vaunt there is the evidence of facts. How many have assailed the Church, and yet the assailants have perished while the Church herself has soared beyond the sky? Such might hath the Church: when she is assailed she conquers: when snares are laid for her she prevails: when she is insulted her prosperity increases: she is wounded yet sinks not under her wounds; tossed by waves yet not submerged; vexed by storms yet suffers no shipwreck; she wrestles and is not worsted, fights but is not vanquished. Wherefore then did she suffer this war to be? That she might make more manifest the splendour of her triumph. Ye were present on that day, and ye saw what weapons were set in motion against her, and how the rage of the soldiers burned more fiercely than fire, and I was hurried away to the imperial palace.[4] But what of that? By the grace of God none of those things dismayed me.

2. Now I say these things in order that ye too may follow my example. But wherefore was I not dismayed? Because I do not fear any present terrors. For what is terrible? Death? nay this is not terrible: for we speedily reach the unruffled haven. Or spoliation of goods? "Naked came I out of my mother's womb, and naked shall I depart;"[5] or exile? "The earth is the Lord's and the fulness thereof;"[6] or false accusation? "Rejoice and be exceeding glad, when men shall say all manner of evil against you falsely, for great is your reward in Heaven."[7] I saw the swords and I meditated on Heaven; I expected death, and I bethought me of the resurrection; I beheld the sufferings of this lower world, and I took account of the heavenly prizes; I observed the devices of the enemy, and I meditated on the heavenly crown: for the occasion of the contest was sufficient for encouragement and consolation. True! I was being forcibly dragged away, but I suffered no insult from the act; for there is only one real insult, namely sin: and should the whole world insult thee, yet if thou dost not insult thyself thou art not insulted. The only real betrayal is the betrayal of the conscience: betray not thy own conscience, and no one can betray thee. I was being dragged away and I saw the events—or rather I saw my words turned into events, I saw my discourse which I had uttered in words being preached in the market-place through the medium of actual events. What kind of discourse? the same which I was always repeating. The wind has blown and the leaves have fallen "The grass has withered and the flower has faded."[8] The night has departed and the day has dawned; the shadow has been proved vain and the truth has appeared. They mounted up to the sky, and they came down to the level of earth: for the waves which were swelling high have been laid low by means of merely human events. How? The things which were taking place were a lesson. And I said to myself will posterity learn self-control? or before two days have passed by will these events have been abandoned to oblivion? The warnings were sounding in their ears. Again let me utter, yet again I will speak. What profit will there be? Certainly there will be profit. For

---

[1] Matt. xvi. 18.   [2] οὐ τόπον μόνον ἀλλὰ καὶ τρόπον.
[3] Matt. ix. 13.   [4] See Introduction.   [5] Job i. 21.   [6] Ps. xxiv. 1.
[7] Matt. v. 12.   [8] Is. xl. 8.

if all do not hearken, the half will hearken; and if not the half, the third part: and if not the third the fourth: and if not the fourth, perhaps ten: and if not ten, perhaps five: and if not five perhaps one: and if not one, I myself have the reward prepared for me. "The grass withereth and the flower fadeth; but the word of God abideth for ever."[1]

3. Have ye seen the insignificance of human affairs? have ye seen the frailty of power? Have ye seen the wealth which I always called a runaway and not a runaway only, but also a murderer. For it not only deserts those who possess it, but also slaughters them; for when any one pays court to it then most of all does it betray him. Why dost thou pay court to wealth which to-day is for thee, and to-morrow for another? Why dost thou court wealth which can never be held fast? Dost thou desire to court it? dost thou desire to hold it fast? Do not bury it but give it into the hands of the poor. For wealth is a wild beast: if it be tightly held it runs away: if it be let loose it remains where it is; "For," it is said, "he hath dispersed abroad and given to the poor; his righteousness remaineth forever."[2] Disperse it then that it may remain with thee; bury it not lest it run away. Where is wealth? I would gladly enquire of those who have departed. Now I say these things not by way of reproach, God forbid, nor by way of irritating old sores, but as endeavouring to secure a haven for you out of the shipwreck of others. When soldiers and swords were threatening, when the city was in a blaze of fury, when the imperial majesty was powerless, and the purple was insulted, when all places were full of frenzy, where was wealth then? where was your silver plate? where were your silver couches? where your household slaves? they had all betaken themselves to flight; where were the eunuchs? they all ran away; where were your friends? they changed their masks. Where were your houses? they were shut up. Where was your money? the owner of it fled: and the money itself, where was that? it was buried. Where was it all hidden? Am I oppressive and irksome to you in constantly declaring that wealth betrays those who use it badly? The occasion has now come which proves the truth of my words. Why dost thou hold it so tightly, when in the time of trial it profiteth thee nothing? If it has power when thou fallest into a strait, let it come to thy aid, but if it then runs away what need hast thou of it? events themselves bear witness. What profit was there in it? The sword was whetted, death was impending, an army raging: there was apprehension of imminent peril; and yet wealth was nowhere to be seen. Where did the runaway flee? It was itself the cause which brought about all these evils, and yet in the hours of necessity it runs away. Nevertheless many reproach me saying continually thou fasteneth upon the rich: while they on the other hand fasten upon the poor. Well I do fasten upon the rich: or rather not the rich, but those who make a bad use of their riches. For I am continually saying that I do not attack the character of the rich man, but of the rapacious. A rich man is one thing, a rapacious man is another: an affluent man is one thing, a covetous man is another. Make clear distinctions, and do not confuse things which are diverse. Art thou a rich man? I forbid thee not. Art thou a rapacious man? I denounce thee. Hast thou property of thy own? enjoy it. Dost thou take the property of others? I will not hold my peace. Wouldest thou stone me for this? I am ready to shed my blood: only I forbid thy sin. I heed not hatred, I heed not war: one thing only do I heed, the advancement of my hearers. The rich are my children, and the poor also are my children: the same womb has travailed with both, both are the offspring of the same travail-pangs. If then thou fastenest reproaches on the poor man, I denounce thee: for the poor man does not suffer so much loss as the rich. For no great wrong is inflicted on the poor man, seeing that in his case the injury is confined to money; but in thy case the injury touches the soul. Let him who wills cast me off, let him who wills stone me, let him who wills hate me: for the plots of enemies are the pledges to me of crowns of victory, and the number of my rewards will be as the number of my wounds.

4. So then I fear not an enemy's plots: one thing only do I fear, which is sin. If no one convicts me of sin, then let the whole world make war upon me. For this kind of war only renders me more prosperous. Thus also do I wish to teach you a lesson. Fear not the devices of a potentate, but fear the power of sin. No man will do thee harm, if thou dost not deal a blow to thyself. If thou hast not sin, ten thousand swords may threaten thee, but God will snatch thee away out of their reach: but if thou hast sin, even shouldest thou be in paradise thou wilt be cast out. Adam was in paradise yet he fell; Job was on a dung hill, yet he was crowned victorious. What profit was paradise to the one? or what injury was the dung hill to the other? No man laid snares for the one, yet was he overthrown: the devil laid snares for the other, and yet he was crowned. Did not the devil take

---

[1] Is. xl. 8.   [2] Ps. cxii. 9.

his property? Yes, but he did not rob him of his godliness. Did he not lay violent hands upon his sons? yes: but he did not shake his faith. Did he not tear his body to pieces? yes but he did not find his treasure. Did he not arm his wife against him? yes but he did not overthrow the soldier. Did he not hurl arrows and darts at him? yes but he received no wounds. He advanced his engines but could not shake the tower; he conducted his billows against him, but did not sink the ship. Observe this law I beseech you, yea I clasp your knees, if not with the bodily hand, yet in spirit, and pour forth tears of supplication. Observe this law I pray you, and no one can do you harm. Never call the rich man happy; never call any man miserable save him who is living in sin: and call him happy who lives in righteousness. For it is not the nature of their circumstances, but the disposition of the men which makes both the one and the other. Never be afraid of the sword if thy conscience does not accuse thee: never be afraid in war if thy conscience is clear. Where are they who have departed? tell me. Did not all men once bow down to them? did not those who were in authority tremble greatly before them? did they not pay court to them? But sin has come, and all things are manifested in their true lights; they who were attendants have become judges, the flatterers are turned into executioners; they who once kissed his hands, dragged him themselves from the church, and he who yesterday kissed his hand is to-day his enemy. Wherefore? Because neither did he yesterday love him with sincerity. For the opportunity came and the actors were unmasked. Didst thou not yesterday kiss his hands, and call him saviour, and guardian, and benefactor? Didst thou not compose panegyrics without end? wherefore to-day dost thou accuse him? Why yesterday a praiser, and to-day an accuser? why yesterday utter panegyrics, and to-day reproaches? What means this change? what means this revolution?

5. But I am not like this: I was the subject of his plots, yet I became his protector. I suffered countless troubles at his hands, yet I did not retaliate. For I copy the example of my Master, who said on the cross, "Forgive them, for they know not what they do." Now I say these things that you may not be perverted by the suspicion of wicked men. Now many changes have taken place, since I had the oversight of the city, and yet no one learns self-control? But when I say no one, I do not condemn all, God forbid. For it is impossible that this rich soil when it has received seed, should not produce one ear of corn: but I am insatiable, I do not wish many to be saved but all. And if but one be left in a perishing condition, I perish also, and deem that the Shepherd should be imitated who had ninety-nine sheep, and yet hastened after the one which had gone astray.[1] How long will money last? how long this silver and gold? how long these draughts of wine? how long the flatteries of slaves? how long these goblets wreathed with garlands? how long these satanic drinking feasts, full of diabolical activity?

Dost thou not know that the present life is a sojourn in a far country? for art thou a citizen? Nay thou art a wayfarer. Understandest thou what I say? Thou art not a citizen, but thou art a wayfarer, and a traveller. Say not: I have this city and that. No one has a city. The city is above. Present life is but a journey. We are journeying on every day, while nature is running its course. Some there are who store up goods on the way: some who bury jewellery on the road. Now when you enter an inn do you beautify the inn? not so, but you eat and drink and hasten to depart. The present life is an inn: we have entered it, and we bring present life to a close: let us be eager to depart with a good hope, let us leave nothing here, that we may not lose it there. When you enter the inn, what do you say to the servant? Take care where you put away our things, that you do not leave anything behind here, that nothing may be lost, not even what is small and trifling, in order that we may carry everything back to our home. Thou art a wayfarer and traveller, and indeed more insignificant than the wayfarer. How so? I will tell you. The wayfarer knows when he is going into the inn, and when he is going out; for the egress as well as the ingress is in his own power: but when I enter the inn, that is to say this present life, I know not when I shall go out: and it may be that I am providing myself with sustenance for a long time when the Master suddenly summons me saying "Thou fool, for whom shall those things be which thou hast prepared? for on this very night thy soul is being taken from thee."[2] The time of thy departure is uncertain, the tenure of thy possessions insecure, there are innumerable precipices, and billows on every side of thee. Why dost thou rave about shadows? why desert the reality and run after shadows?

6. I say these things, and shall not cease saying them, causing continual pain, and dressing the wounds; and this not for the sake of the fallen, but of those who are still standing. For they have departed, and their career is

---
[1] Luke xv. 4.
[2] Luke xii. 20, a free quotation. Chrysostom transposes the clauses and substitutes λαμβάνουσι "they are taking," for ἀπαιτοῦσιν ἀπὸ σοῦ, "they are demanding from thee."

ended, but those who are yet standing have gained a more secure position through their calamities. "What then," you say, "shall we do?" Do one thing only, hate riches, and love thy life—cast away thy goods; I do not say all of them, but cut off the superfluities. Be not covetous of other men's goods, strip not the widow, plunder not the orphan, seize not his house: I do not address myself to persons but to facts. But if any one's conscience attacks him, he himself is responsible for it, not my words. Why art thou grasping where thou bringest ill-will upon thyself? Grasp where there is a crown to be gained. Strive to lay hold not of earth but of heaven. "The kingdom of Heaven belongs to violent men and men of violence take it by force."[1] Why dost thou lay hold of the poor man who reproaches thee? Lay hold of Christ who praises thee for it. Dost thou see thy senselessness and madness? Dost thou lay hold of the poor man who has little? Christ says "lay hold of me; I thank thee for it, lay hold of my kingdom and take it by violence." If thou art minded to lay hold of an earthly kingdom, or rather if thou art minded to have designs upon it thou art punished; but in the case of the heavenly kingdom thou art punished if thou dost not lay hold of it. Where worldly things are concerned there is ill-will, but where spiritual there is love. Meditate daily on these things, and if two days hence thou seest another riding in a chariot, arrayed in raiment of silk, and elated with pride, be not again dismayed and troubled. Praise not a rich man, but only him who lives in righteousness. Revile not a poor man, but learn to have an upright and accurate judgment in all things.

Do not hold aloof from the Church; for nothing is stronger than the Church. The Church is thy hope, thy salvation, thy refuge. It is higher than the heaven, it is wider than the earth. It never waxes old, but is always in full vigour. Wherefore as significant of its solidity and stability Holy Scripture calls it a mountain: or of its purity a virgin, or of its magnificence a queen; or of its relationship to God a daughter; and to express its productiveness it calls her barren who has borne seven: in fact it employs countless names to represent its nobleness. For as the master of the Church has many names: being called the Father, and the way,[2] and the life,[3] and the light,[4] and the arm,[5] and the propitiation,[6] and the foundation,[7] and the door,[8] and the sinless one,[9] and the treasure,[10] and Lord, and God, and Son, and the only begotten, and the form of God,[11] and the image[12] of God so is it with the Church itself: does one name suffice to present the whole truth? by no means. But for this reason there are countless names, that we may learn something concerning God, though it be but a small part. Even so the Church also is called by many names. She is called a virgin, albeit formerly she was an harlot: for this is the miracle wrought by the Bridegroom, that He took her who was an harlot and hath made her a virgin. Oh! what a new and strange event? With us marriage destroys virginity, but with God marriage hath restored it. With us she who is a virgin, when married, is a virgin no longer: with Christ she who is an harlot, when married, becomes a virgin.

7. Let the heretic who inquires curiously into the nature of heavenly generation saying "how did the Father beget the Son?" interpret this single fact, ask him how did the Church, being an harlot, become a virgin? and how did she having brought forth children remain a virgin? "For I am jealous over you," saith Paul, "with a godly jealousy, for I espoused you to one husband that I might present you as a pure virgin to Christ."[13] What wisdom and understanding! "I am jealous over you with a godly jealousy." What means this? "I am jealous," he says: art thou jealous seeing thou art a spiritual man? I am jealous he says as God is. And hath God jealousy? yea the jealousy not of passion, but of love, and earnest zeal. I am jealous over you with the jealousy of God.

Shall I tell thee how He manifests His jealousy? He saw the world corrupted by devils, and He delivered His own Son to save it. For words spoken in reference to God have not the same force as when spoken in reference to ourselves: for instance we say God is jealous, God is wroth, God repents, God hates. These words are human, but they have a meaning which becomes the nature of God. How is God jealous? "I am jealous over you with the jealousy of God."[14] Is God wroth? "O Lord reproach me not in thine indignation."[15] Doth God slumber? "Awake, wherefore sleepest thou, O Lord?"[16] Doth God repent? "I repent that I have made man."[17] Doth God hate? "My soul hateth your feasts and your new moons."[18] Well do not consider the poverty of the expressions: but grasp their divine meaning. God is jealous,

---

[1] Matt. xi. 12, slightly altered by Chrysostom from the original ἡ βασιλεία τῶν οὐρανῶν βιάζεται, the kingdom of Heaven suffereth violence.
[2] John xiv. 6.   [3] Ibid.   [4] John i. 8, 9; viii. 12.
[5] Perhaps Ps. xcviii. 1; Is. xxxiii. 2; li. 9, and other passages of the same kind.
[6] 1 John ii. 2.   [7] 1 Cor. iii. 11.   [8] John x. 7.
[9] 1 John iii. 5; 1 Peter ii. 22.
[10] Perhaps Matt. vi. 21; viii. 44.   [11] Phil. ii. 6.
[12] Col. i. 15.   [13] 2 Cor. xi. 2.   [14] 2 Cor. xi. 2.
[15] Ps. vi. 2.   [16] Ps. xliv. 23.   [17] Gen. vi. 7.
[18] Is. i. 14.

for He loves, God is wroth, not as yielding to passion, but for the purpose of chastising, and punishing. God sleeps, not as really slumbering, but as being long-suffering. Choose out the expressions. Thus when thou hearest that God begets the Son, think not of division but of the unity of substance. For God has taken many of these words from us as we also have borrowed others from Him, that we may receive honour thereby.

8. Dost thou understand what I have said? Attend carefully my beloved. There are divine names, and there are human names. God has received from me, and He Himself hath given to me. Give me thine, and take mine He says. Thou hast need of mine: I have no need of thine, but thou hast of mine: inasmuch as my nature is unmixed, but thou art a human being, encompassed with a body, seeking also corporeal terms in order that, by borrowing expressions which are familiar to thee, thou who art thus encompassed with a body, mayest be able to think on thoughts which transcend thy understanding. What kind of names hath He received from me, and what kind hath He given to me? He Himself is God, and He hath called me God; with Him is the essential nature as an actual fact, with me only the honour of the name: "I have said ye are gods, and ye are all children of the most highest."[1] Here are words, but in the other case there is the actual reality. He hath called me god, for by that name I have received honour. He Himself was called man, he was called Son of man, he was called the Way, the Door, the Rock. These words He borrowed from me; the others He gave from Himself to me. Wherefore was He called the Way? That thou mightest understand that by Him we have access to the Father. Wherefore was He called the Rock? that thou mightest understand the secure and unshaken character of the faith. Wherefore was He called the Foundation? That thou mightest understand that He upholdeth all things. Wherefore was He called the Root? That thou mightest understand that in Him we have our power of growth. Wherefore was He called the Shepherd? Because He feeds us. Wherefore was He called a sheep? Because He was sacrificed for us and became a propitiatory offering. Wherefore was He called the Life? Because He raised us up when we were dead. Wherefore was He called the Light? Because He delivered us from darkness. Why was He called an Arm? Because He is of one substance with the Father. Why was He called the Word? Because He was begotten of the Father. For as my word is the offspring of my spirit, even so was the Son begotten of the Father. Wherefore is He called our raiment? Because I was clothed with Him when I was baptized. Why is He called a table? Because I feed upon Him when I partake of the mysteries. Why is He called a house? Because I dwell in Him. Why is He called an inmate of the house? Because we become His Temple. Wherefore is He called the Head? Because I have been made a member of His. Why is He called a Bridegroom? Because He hath taken me as His bride. Wherefore is He called undefiled? Because He took me as a virgin. Wherefore is He called Master? Because I am His bondmaid.

9. For observe the Church, how, as I was saying, she is sometimes a bride, sometimes a daughter, sometimes a virgin, sometimes a bondmaid, sometimes a queen, sometimes a barren woman, sometimes a mountain, sometimes a garden, sometimes fruitful in children, sometimes a lily, sometimes a fountain: She is all things. Therefore having heard these things, think not I pray you that they are corporeal; but stretch thy thought further: for such things cannot be corporeal. For example: the mountain is not the maid: the maid is not the bride: the queen is not the bondmaid: yet the Church is all these things. Wherefore? because the element in which they exist is not corporeal but spiritual. For in a corporeal sphere these things are confined within narrow limits: but in a spiritual sphere they have a wide field of operation. "The queen stood on thy right hand."[2] The queen? How did she who was down-trodden and poor become a queen? and where did she ascend? the queen herself stood on high by the side of the king. How? because the king became a servant; He was not that by nature, but He became so. Understand therefore the things which belong to the Godhead, and discern those which belong to the Dispensation. Understand what He *was*, and what He *became* for thy sake, and do not confuse things which are distinct, nor make the argument of his lovingkindness an occasion for blasphemy. He was lofty, and she was lowly: lofty not by position, but by nature. His essence was pure, and imperishable: His nature was incorruptible, unintelligible, invisible, incomprehensible, eternal, unchangeable, transcending the nature of angels, higher than the powers above, overpowering reason, surpassing thought, apprehended not by sight but by faith alone. Angels beheld Him and trembled, the Cheru-

---

[1] Ps. lxxxii. 6; comp. John x. 34.

[2] Ps. xlv. 10.

bim veiled themselves with their wings, in awe. He looked upon the earth, and caused it to tremble: He threatened the sea and dried it up:[1] he brought rivers out of the desert: He weighed the mountains in scales, and the valleys in a balance.[2] How shall I express myself? how shall I present the truth? His greatness hath no bounds, His wisdom is beyond reckoning, His judgments are untraceable, His ways unsearchable.[3] Such is His greatness and His power, if indeed it is safe even to use such expressions. But what am I to do? I am a human being and I speak in human language: my tongue is of earth and I crave forgiveness from my Lord. For I do not use these expressions in a spirit of presumption, but on account of the poverty of my resources arising from my feebleness and the nature of our human tongue. Be merciful to me, O Lord, for I utter these words not in presumption but because I have no others: nevertheless I do not rest content with the meanness of my speech, but soar upwards on the wings of my understanding. Such is His greatness and power. I say this, that without dwelling on the words, or on the poverty of the expressions, thou mayest also thyself learn to act in the same way. Why dost thou marvel if I do this, inasmuch as He also does the same, when He wishes to present something to our minds which transcends human powers? Since He addresses human beings He uses also human illustration, which are indeed insufficient to represent the thing spoken of, and cannot exhibit the full proportions of the matter, yet suffice for the infirmity of the hearers.

10. Make an effort, and do not grow weary of my prolonged discourse. For as when He manifests Himself, He is not manifested as He really is, nor is His bare essence manifested (for no man hath seen God in His real nature; for when He is but partially revealed the Cherubim tremble—the mountains smoke, the sea is dried up, the heaven is shaken, and if the revelation were not partial who could endure it?) as then, I say, He does not manifest Himself as He really is, but only as the beholder is able to see Him, therefore doth He appear sometimes in the form of old age, sometimes of youth, sometimes in fire, sometimes in air, sometimes in water, sometimes in armour, not altering his essential nature, but fashioning His appearance to suit the various condition of those who are affected by it. In like manner also when any one wishes to say anything concerning Him he employs human illustrations. For instance I say: He went up into the mountain and He was transfigured before them, and His countenance shone as the sun, and His raiment became white as snow."[4] He disclosed, it is said, a little of the Godhead, He manifested to them the God dwelling amongst them "and He was transfigured before them." Attend carefully to the statement. The writer says and He was transfigured before them, and His raiment shone as the light, and His countenance was as the sun. When I said "such is His greatness and power" and added "be merciful to me O Lord," (for I do not rest satisfied with the expression but am perplexed, having no other framed for the purpose) I wish you to understand, that I learned this lesson from Holy Scripture. The evangelist then wished to describe His splendour and he says "He shone." How did He shine? tell me. Exceedingly. And how do you express this? He shone "as the sun." As the sun sayest thou? Yea. Wherefore? Because I know not any other luminary more brilliant. And He was white sayest thou as snow? wherefore as snow? Because I know not any other substance which is whiter. For that He did not really shine thus is proved by what follows: the disciples fell to the ground. If he had shone as the sun the disciples would not have fallen; for they saw the sun every day, and did not fall: but inasmuch as he shone more brilliantly than the sun or snow, they, being unable to bear the splendour, fell to the earth.

11. Tell me then, O evangelist, did He shine more brightly than the sun, and yet dost thou say, "as the sun?" Yea: wishing to make that light known to thee, I know not any other greater luminary, I have no other comparison which holds a royal place amongst luminaries. I have said these things that thou mayest not rest contentedly in the poverty of the language used: I have pointed out to thee the fall of the disciples: they fell to the earth, and were stupified and overwhelmed with slumber. "Arise," He said, and lifted them up, and yet they were oppressed. For they could not endure the excessive brightness of that shining, but heavy sleep took possession of their eyes: so far did the light which was manifested exceed the light of the sun. Yet the evangelist said "as the sun," because that luminary is familiar to us and surpasses all the rest.

But as I was saying, He who was thus great and powerful desired an harlot. I speak of our human nature under that name. If a man indeed desire an harlot he is condemned, and doth God desire one? Yea verily. Again a

---

[1] Is. li. 10. [2] Is. xl. 12. Septuagint.
[3] Rom. xi. 33. Chrysostom has transposed the order of the adjectives.
[4] Matt. xvii. 2: Mark ix. 2. Chrysostom mixes up the accounts of the two Evangelists, and does not quote the exact words of either.

man desireth an harlot that he may become a fornicator: but God that He may convert the harlot into a virgin: so that the desire of the man is the destruction of her who is desired: but the desire of God is salvation to her who is desired. And why did He who is so great and powerful desire an harlot? that He might become the husband thereof. How doth He act? He doth not send to her any of His servants, He sendeth not angel, archangel, Cherubim, or Seraphim; but He himself draws nigh Who loves her. Again when thou hearest of love, deem it not sensuous. Cull out the thoughts which are contained in the words, even as an excellent bee settles on the flowers, and takes the honey comb, but leaves the herbs. God desired an harlot, and how doth He act? He does not conduct her on high; for He would not bring an harlot into Heaven, but He Himself comes down. Since she could not ascend on high, He descends to earth. He cometh to the harlot, and is not ashamed: He cometh to her secret dwelling place. He beholds her in her drunkenness. And how doth He come? not in the bare essence of His original nature, but He becomes that which the harlot was, not in intention but in reality does He become this, in order that she may not be scared when she sees Him, that she may not rush away, and escape. He cometh to the harlot, and becomes man. And how does He become this? He is conceived in the womb, he increases little by little and follows like me the course of human growth. Who is it who does this? the Deity as manifested, not the Godhead; the form of the servant not that of the Master; the flesh which belongs to me, not the essential nature which belongs to Him: He increases little by little, and has intercourse with mankind. Although He finds the harlot, human nature, full of sores, brutalised, and oppressed by devils, how does He act? He draws nigh to her. She sees Him and flees away. He calleth the wise men saying "Why are ye afraid? I am not a judge, but a physician. "I came not to judge the world, but to save the world."[1] Straightway He calleth the wise men. Oh! new and strange event. The immediate first-fruits of His coming are wise men. He who upholds the world lieth in a manger, and He who careth for all things is a nursling in swaddling bands. The temple is founded and the God dwelleth therein. And wise men come and straightway worship Him: the publican comes and is turned into an evangelist: the harlot comes and is turned into a maiden: the Canaanitish woman comes and partakes of his lovingkindness. This is the mark of one who loves, to forbear demanding an account of sins, and to forgive transgressions and offences. And how does He act? He takes the sinner and espouses her to himself. And what doth He give her? a signet ring. Of what nature? the Holy Spirit. Paul saith "now He who establisheth us with you is God who hath also sealed us, and given the earnest of the Spirit."[2] The Spirit then He giveth her. Next He saith "Did not I plant thee in a garden?" She saith "yea?" And how didst thou fall from thence? "The devil came and cast me out of the garden." Thou wast planted in the garden and he cast thee out: behold I plant thee in myself, I uphold thee. How? The devil dares not approach me. Neither do I take thee up into Heaven; but something greater than Heaven is here: I carry thee in myself who am the Lord of Heaven. The shepherd carries thee and the wolf no longer comes: or rather I permit him to approach. And so the Lord carrieth our nature: and the devil approaches and is worsted. "I have planted thee in myself:" therefore He saith "I am the root, ye are the branches:"[3] so He planted her in Himself. "But," she saith, "I am a sinner and unclean." "Let not this trouble thee, I am a physician. I know my vessel, I know how it was perverted. It was formerly a vessel of clay, and it was perverted. I remodel it by means of the laver of regeneration and I submit it to the action of fire." For observe: He took dust from the earth and made the man; He formed him. The devil came, and perverted him. Then the Lord came, took him again, and remoulded, and recast him in baptism, and He suffered not his body to be of clay, but made it of a harder ware. He subjected the soft clay to the fire of the Holy Spirit. "He shall baptize you with the Holy Ghost and with fire:"[4] He was baptized with water that he might be remodelled, with fire that he might be hardened. Therefore the Prophet speaking beforehand under divine guidance declared "Thou shalt dash them in pieces like vessels of the potter."[5] He did not say like vessels of earthenware which every one possesses: for by a potter's vessels are meant those which the potter is fashioning on the wheel: now the potter's vessels are of clay, but ours are of harder ware. Speaking beforehand therefore of the remoulding which is wrought by means of baptism he saith, "thou shalt dash them in pieces like vessels of a potter"—He means that He remodels and recasts them. I descend into the water

---

[1] John xii. 47.
[2] 2 Cor. i. 21, 22.
[3] John xv. 5. In the original, "I am the *vine*," etc.
[4] Matt. iii. 11.
[5] Ps. ii. 9.

of baptism, and the fashion of my nature is remoulded, and the fire of the Spirit recasts it, and it is turned into a harder ware. And that my words are no empty vaunt hear what Job says, "He hath made us as clay,"[1] and Paul, "but we have this treasure in earthen vessels."[2] But consider the strength of the earthen vessel: for it has been hardened not by fire, but by the Spirit. How was it proved to be an earthen vessel? "Five times received I forty stripes save one, thrice was I beaten with rods, once was I stoned,"[3] and yet the earthen vessel was not shattered. "A day and a night have I been in the deep." He hath been in the deep, and the earthen vessel was not dissolved: he suffered shipwreck and the treasure was not lost; the ship was submerged and yet the freight floated. "But we have this treasure" he says. What kind of treasure? a supply of the Spirit, righteousness, sanctification, redemption. Of what nature, tell me? "in the name of Jesus Christ rise up and walk."[4] "Æneas, Jesus Christ maketh thee whole,"[5] I say unto thee thou evil spirit, go out of him.[6]

12. Hast thou seen a treasure more brilliant than royal treasures? For what can the pearl of a king do like that which the words of an Apostle effected? Set crowns innumerable upon dead men, and they will not be raised: but one word went forth from an Apostle, and it brought back revolted nature, and restored it to its ancient condition. "But we have this treasure." O treasure which not only is preserved, but also preserves the house where it is stored up. Dost thou understand what I have said? The kings of the earth, and rulers when they have treasures, prepare large houses, having strong walls, bars, doors, guards, and bolts in order that the treasure may be preserved: but Christ did the contrary: He placed the treasure not in a stone vessel but in an earthen one. If the treasure is great wherefore is the vessel weak? But the reason why the vessel is weak is not because the treasure is great; for this is not preserved by the vessel, but itself preserves the vessel. I deposit the treasure: who is able henceforth to steal it? The devil has come, the world has come, multitudes have come, and yet they have not stolen the treasure: the vessel has been scourged, yet the treasure was not betrayed; it has been drowned in the sea, yet the treasure was not shipwrecked: it has died yet the treasure survives. He gave therefore the earnest of the Spirit. Where are they who blaspheme the Spirit's majesty? Give ye heed. "He that establisheth us with you in Christ is God who also hath given the earnest of the Spirit."[7] You all know that the earnest is a small part of the whole; let me tell you how. Some one goes to buy a house at a great price; and he says "give me an earnest that I may have confidence: or one goes to take a wife for himself, he arranges about dowry and property, and he says "give me an earnest." Observe: in the purchase of a slave and in all covenants there is an earnest. Since then Christ made a covenant with us (for He was about to take me as a bride) he also assigned a dowry to me not of money, but of blood. But this dowry which He assigns is the bestowal of good things "such as eye hath not seen, and ear hath not heard, neither hath entered into the heart of man."[8] He assigned them for the dowry:—immortality, praise with the angels, release from death, freedom from sin, the inheritance of a kingdom (so great are his riches), righteousness, sanctification, deliverance from present evils, discovery of future blessings. Great was my dowry. Now attend carefully: mark what He does. He came to take the harlot, for so I call her, unclean as she was, that thou mightest understand the love of the bridegroom. He came; He took me: He assigns me a dowry: He saith "I give thee my wealth." How? "Hast thou lost," He saith, "paradise?" take it back. Hast thou lost thy beauty? take it back; take all these things. But yet the dowry was not given to me here.

13. Observe, this is the reason why He speaks beforehand with reference to this dowry; He warranted to me in the dowry the resurrection of the body,—immortality. For immortality does not always follow resurrection, but the two are distinct. For many have risen, and been again laid low, like Lazarus and the bodies of the saints.[9] But in this case it is not so, but the promise is of resurrection, immortality, a place in the joyful company of angels, the meeting of the Son of Man in the clouds, and the fulfilment of the saying "so shall we ever be with the Lord,"[10] the release from death, the freedom from sin, the complete overthrow of destruction. Of what kind is that? "Eye hath not seen nor ear heard neither have entered into the heart of man the things which God hath prepared for them that love Him." Dost thou give me good things which I know not? He saith "yea; only be espoused to me here, love me in this world." "Wherefore dost thou not give me the dowry here?" "It will be given when thou hast come to my Father, when thou hast entered the royal palace. Didst thou come to me!

---

[1] Job x. 9. [2] 2 Cor. iv. 7. [3] 2 Cor. xi. 24, etc. [7] 2 Cor. i. 21, 22. [8] 1 Cor. ii. 9.
[4] Acts iii. 6. [5] Acts ix. 34. [6] Acts xvi. 18. [9] John xi.; Matt. xxvii. 52. [10] 1 Thess. iv. 17.

nay I came to thee. I came not that thou shouldst abide here but that I might take thee and return. Seek not the dowry here: all depends on hope, and faith. "And dost thou give me nothing in this world?" He answers. "Receive an earnest that thou mayest trust me concerning that which is to come: receive pledges and betrothal gifts." Therefore Paul saith "I have espoused you."[1] As gifts of betrothal God has given us present blessings: they are an earnest of the future; but the full dowry abides in the other world. How so? I will tell you. Here I grow old, there I grow not old; here I die, there I die not, here I sorrow, there I sorrow not; here is poverty, and disease, and intrigue, there nothing of that kind exists: here is darkness and light, there is light alone: here is intrigue, there is liberty; here is disease, there is health; here is life which has an end, there is life which hath no end; here is sin, there is righteousness, and sin is banished; here is envy, there nothing of the kind exists. "Give me these things" one says; "Nay! wait in order that thy fellow-servants also may be saved; wait I say. He who establisheth us and hath given us the earnest"—what kind of earnest? the Holy Spirit, the supply of the Spirit. Let me speak concerning the Spirit. He gave the signet ring to the Apostles, saying "take this and give it to all." Is the ring then portioned out, and yet not divided? It is so. Let me teach you the meaning of the supply of the Spirit: Peter received, and Paul also received the Holy Spirit. He went about the world, he released sinners from their sins, he restored the lame, he clothed the naked, he raised the dead, he cleansed the lepers, he bridled the devil, he strangled the demons, he held converse with God, he planted a Church, levelled temples to the earth, overturned altars, destroyed vice, established virtue, made angels of men.

14. All these things we were. But "the earnest" filled the whole world. And when I say the whole I mean all which the sun shines upon, sea, islands, mountains, valleys, and hills. Paul went hither and thither, like some winged creature, with one mouth only contending against the enemy, he the tentmaker, who handled the workman's knife and sewed skins together: and yet this his craft was no hindrance to his virtue, but the tentmaker was stronger than demons, the uneloquent man was wiser than the wise. Whence was this? He received the earnest, he bore the signet ring and carried it about. All men saw that the King had espoused our nature: the demon saw it and retreated, he saw the earnest, and trembled and withdrew: he saw but the Apostle's garments[2] and fled. O the power of the Holy Spirit. He bestowed authority not on the soul, nor on the body, but even on raiment; nor on raiment only but even on a shadow. Peter went about and his shadow put diseases to flight,[3] and expelled demons, and raised the dead to life. Paul went about the world, cutting away the thorns of ungodliness, sowing broadcast the seeds of godliness, like an excellent ploughman handling the ploughshare of doctrine. And to whom did he go? To Thracians, to Scythians, to Indians, to Maurians, to Sardinians, to Goths, to wild savages, and he changed them all. By what means? By means of "the earnest." How was he sufficient for these things? By the grace of the Spirit. Unskilled, ill-clothed, ill-shod he was upheld by Him "who also hath given the earnest of the Spirit." Therefore he saith "and who is sufficient for these things?[4] But our sufficiency is of God, who hath made us sufficient as ministers of the new Testament, not of the letter but of the Spirit."[5] Behold what the Spirit hath wrought: He found the earth filled with demons and He has made it heaven. For meditate not on present things but review the past in your thought. Formerly there was lamentation, there were altars everywhere, everywhere the smoke and fumes of sacrifice, everywhere unclean rites and mysteries, and sacrifices, everywhere demons holding their orgies, everywhere a citadel of the devil, everywhere fornication decked with wreaths of honour; and Paul stood alone. How did he escape being overwhelmed, or torn in pieces? How could he open his mouth? He entered the Thebaid,[6] and made captives of men, He entered the royal palace, and made a disciple of the king.[7] He entered the hall of judgment, and the judge saith to him "almost thou persuadest me to become a Christian,"[8] and the judge became a disciple. He entered the prison, and took the jailor captive.[9] He visited an island of barbarians, and made a viper the instrument of his teaching.[10] He visited the Romans, and attracted the senate to his doctrine. He visited rivers, and desert places in all parts of the world. There is no land or sea which has not shared in the benefits of his labours; for God has given human nature the earnest of His signet,

---

[1] 2 Cor. xi. 2.
[2] Acts xix. 11. [3] Acts v. 15.
[4] 2 Cor. ii. 16. [5] 2 Cor. iii. 5, 6.
[6] Strictly speaking, the name of the Egyptian desert in the neighborhood of Thebes; but here it must be used in a general sense, to denote any wild country. The whole passage is highly rhetorical.
[7] He probably means Sergius Paulus. Acts xiii. 12.
[8] Acts xxvi. 28. It is doubtful, however, whether this is the right interpretation of the words. See the revised translation.
[9] Acts xvi. 30, etc. [10] Acts xxviii. 3, etc.

and when He gives it He saith: some things I give thee now, and others I promise. Therefore the prophet saith concerning her "The queen did stand upon thy right hand in a vesture woven with gold." He does not mean a real vesture, but virtue. Therefore the Scripture elsewhere saith "How camest thou in hither not having a wedding garment?" so that here he does not mean a garment, but fornication, and foul and unclean living. As then foul raiment signifies sin, so does golden raiment signify virtue. But this raiment belonged to the king. He Himself bestowed the raiment upon her: for she was naked, naked and disfigured. "The queen stood on thy right hand in a vesture woven with gold."[1] He is speaking not of raiment but of virtue. Observe: the expression itself has great nobility of meaning. He does not say "in a vesture of gold" but "in a vesture woven with gold." Listen intelligently. A vesture of gold is one which is gold throughout: but a vesture woven with gold is one which is partly of gold, partly of silk. Why then did he say that the bride wore not a vesture of gold, but one woven with gold? Attend carefully. He means the consitution of the Church in its varied manifestations. For since we do not all belong to one condition of life, but one is a virgin, another a widow, a third lives a life of devotion—so the robe of the Church signifies the constitution of the Church.

15. Inasmuch then as our Master knew that if He carved out only one road for us, many must shrink from it, He carved out divers roads. Thou canst not enter the kingdom it may be by the way of virginity. Enter it then by the way of single marriage. Canst thou not enter it by one marriage? Perchance thou mayest by means of a second marriage. Thou canst not enter by the way of continence: enter then by the way of almsgiving: or thou canst not enter by the way of almsgiving? then try the way of fasting. If thou canst not use this way, take that—or if not that, then take this. Therefore the prophet spoke not of a garment of gold, but of one woven with gold. It is of silk, or purple, or gold. Thou canst not be a golden part? then be a silken one. I accept thee, if only thou art clothed in my raiment. Therefore also Paul saith "If any man builds upon this foundation, gold, silver, precious stones."[2] Thou canst not be the precious stone? then be the gold. Thou canst not be the gold? then be the silver, if only thou art resting upon the foundation. And again elsewhere, "there is one glory of the sun, and another glory of the moon, and another glory of the stars."[3] Thou canst not be a sun? then be a moon. Thou canst not be a moon? then be a star. Thou canst not be a large star? be content to be a little one if only thou art in the Heaven. Thou canst not be a virgin? then live continently in the married state, only abiding in the Church. Thou canst not be without possessions? then give alms, only abiding in the Church, only wearing the proper raiment, only submitting to the queen.[4] The raiment is woven with gold, it is manifold in texture. I do not bar the way against thee: for the abundance of virtues has rendered the dispensation of the king easy in operation. "Clothed in a vesture woven with gold, manifold in texture." Her vesture is manifold: unfold, if you please, the deep meaning of the expression here used, and fix your eyes upon this garment woven with gold. For here indeed some live celibate, others live in an honourable estate of matrimony, being not much inferior to them: some have married once, others are widows in the flower of their age. For what purpose is a paradise? and wherefore its variety? having divers flowers, and trees, and many pearls. There are many stars, but only one sun: there are many ways of living, but only one paradise; there are many temples, but only one mother of them all. There is the body, the eye, the finger, but all these make up but one man. There is the same distinction between the small, the great, and the less. The virgin hath need of the married woman; for the virgin also is the product of marriage, that marriage may not be despised by her. The virgin is the root of marriage: thus all things have been linked together, the small with the great, and the great with the small. "The queen did stand on thy right hand clothed in a vesture wrought with gold, manifold in texture." Then follows "Hearken! O daughter." The conductor of the bride says that thou art about to go forth from thy home to the home of the bridegroom who in his essential nature far surpasses thee. I am the conductor of the bride. "Hearken O daughter." Did she immediately become the wife? Yea: for here there is nothing corporeal. For He espoused her as a wife, He loves her as a daughter, He provides for her as a handmaid, He guards her as a virgin, He fences her round like a garden, and cherishes her like a member: as a head He provides for her, as a root he causes her to grow, as a shepherd He feeds her, as a bridegroom He weds her, as a propitiation He pardons her, as a sheep He is sacrificed, as a bridegroom He preserves her in beauty, as a

---

[1] Ps. xlv. 10.   [2] 1 Cor. iii. 12.   [3] 1 Cor. xv. 41.   [4] *i. e.*, the Church.

husband He provides for her support. Many are the meanings in order that we may enjoy a part if it be but a small part of the divine economy of grace. "Hearken O daughter" and behold, and look upon things which are bridal and yet spiritual. Hearken O daughter. She was at first a daughter of demons, a daughter of the earth, unworthy of the earth and now she has become a daughter of the king. And this He wished who loved her. For he who loves does not investigate character: love does not regard uncomeliness: on this account indeed is it called love because it oftentimes hath affection for an uncomely person.[1] Thus also did Christ. He saw one who was uncomely (for comely I could not call her) and He loved her, and He makes her young, not having spot or wrinkle. Oh what a bridegroom! adorning with grace the ungracefulness of his bride! Hearken O daughter! hearken and behold! Two things He saith "Hearken" and "Behold," two which depend on thyself, one on thy eyes, the other on thy hearing. Now since her dowry depended on hearing—(and although some of you have been acute enough to perceive this already, let them tarry for those who are feebler: I commend those who have anticipated the truth, and make allowances for those who only follow in their track) since the dowry then depended on hearing—(and what is meant by hearing? faith: for "faith cometh by hearing" faith as opposed to fruition, and actual experience) I said before that He divided the dowry into two, and gave some portion to the bride for an earnest, whilst He promised others in the future. What did He give her? He gave her forgiveness of sins, remission of punishment, righteousness, sanctification, redemption, the body of the Lord, the divine, spiritual Table, the resurrection of the dead. For all these things the Apostles had. Therefore He gave some parts and promised others. Of some there was experience and fruition, others depended upon hope and faith. Now listen. What did He bestow? Baptism and the Sacrifice. Of these there is experience. What did He promise? Resurrection, immortality of the body, union with angels, a place in the joyful company of archangels, and as a citizen in His kingdom, immaculate life, the good things "which eye hath not seen, nor ear heard nor have entered into the heart of man, things which God hath prepared for them that love Him."

16. Understand what is said, lest ye lose it: I am labouring to enable you to perceive it. The dowry of the bride then was divided into two portions consisting of things present and things to come; things seen and things heard, things given and things taken on trust, things experienced, and things to be enjoyed hereafter; things belonging to present life, and things to come after the resurrection. The former things you see, the latter you hear. Observe then what He says to her that you may not suppose that she received the former things only, though they be great and ineffable, and surpassing all understanding. "Hearken O daughter and behold;" hear the latter things and behold the former that thou mayest not say "am I again to depend on hope, again on faith, again on the future?" See now: I give some things, and I promise others: the latter indeed depend on hope, but do thou receive the others as pledges, as an earnest, as a proof of the remainder. I promise thee a kingdom: and let present things be the ground of thy trust, thy trust in me. Dost thou promise me a kingdom? Yea. I have given thee the greater part, even the Lord of the kingdom, for "he who spared not his own son, but gave him up for us all, how shall He not with Him also freely give us all things?"[2] Dost thou give me the resurrection of the body? Yea; I have given thee the greater part. What is the nature of it? Release from sins. How is that the greater part? Because sin brought forth death. I have destroyed the parent, and shall I not destroy the offspring? I have dried up the root, and shall I not destroy the produce. Hearken O daughter and behold." What am I to behold? Dead men raised to life, lepers cleansed, the sea restrained, the paralytic braced up into vigour, paradise opened, loaves poured forth in abundance, sins remitted, the lame man leaping, the robber made a citizen of paradise, the publican turned into an evangelist, the harlot become more modest than the maid. Hear and behold. Hear of the former things and behold these. Accept from present things a proof of the others; concerning those I have given thee pledges, things which are better than they are." "What is the meaning of this thy saying?" These things are mine. "Hearken O daughter and behold." These things are my dower to thee. And what doth the bride contribute? Let us see. What I pray thee dost thou bring that thou mayest not be portionless? What can I, she answers, bring to thee from heathen altars, and the steam of sacrifices and from devils? What have I to contribute? what? sayest thou? Thy will and thy faith. "Hearken O daughter and behold." And what wilt thou have me do? "Forget thy own

---

[1] The statement is grounded on a mistaken etymology. There is also an allusion to the proverbial blindness of love.

[2] Rom. viii. 32.

people." What kind of people? the devils, the idols, the sacrificial smoke, and steam, and blood. "Forget thy own people, and thy father's house." Leave thy father and come after me. I left my Father, and came to thee, and wilt thou not leave thy father? But when the word leave is used in reference to the Son do not understand by it an actual leaving. What He means is "I condescended, I accommodated myself to thee, I assumed human flesh." This is the duty of the bridegroom, and of the bride, that thou shouldest abandon thy parents, and that we should be wedded to one another. "Hearken O daughter and behold, and forget thy own people, and thy father's house." And what dost thou give me if I do forget them? "and the king shall desire thy beauty." Thou hast the Lord for thy lover. If thou hast Him for thy lover, thou hast also the things which are his. I trust ye may be able to understand what is said: for the thought is a subtle one, and I wish to stop the mouth of the Jews.

Now exert your minds I pray: for whether one hears, or forbears to hear I shall dig and till the soil. "Hearken O daughter, and behold, forget also thy own people, and thy father's house, and the king shall desire thy beauty." By beauty in this passage the Jew understands sensible beauty; not spiritual but corporeal.

17. Attend, and let us learn what corporeal, and what spiritual beauty are. There is soul and body: they are two substances: there is a beauty of body, and there is a beauty of soul. What is beauty of body? an extended eyebrow, a merry glance, a blushing cheek, ruddy lips, a straight neck, long wavy hair, tapering fingers, upright stature, a fair blooming complexion. Does this bodily beauty come from nature, or from choice? Confessedly it comes from nature. Attend that thou mayest learn the conception of philosophers. This beauty whether of the countenance, of the eye, of the hair, of the brow, does it come from nature, or from choice? It is obvious that it comes from nature. For the ungraceful woman, even if she cultivate beauty in countless ways, cannot become graceful in body: for natural conditions are fixed, and confined by limits which they cannot pass over. Therefore the beautiful woman is always beautiful, even if she has no taste for beauty: and the ungraceful cannot make herself graceful, nor the graceful ungraceful. Wherefore? because these things come from nature. Well! thou hast seen corporeal beauty. Now let us turn inwards to the soul: let the handmaid approach the mistress! let us turn I say to the soul. Look upon that beauty, or rather listen to it: for thou canst not see it since it is invisible—Listen to that beauty. What then is beauty of soul? Temperance, mildness, almsgiving, love, brotherly kindness, tender affection, obedience to God, the fulfilment of the law, righteousness, contrition of heart. These things are the beauty of the soul. These things then are not the results of nature, but of moral disposition. And he who does not possess these things is able to receive them, and he who has them, if he becomes careless, loses them. For as in the case of the body I was saying that she who is ungraceful cannot become graceful; so in the case of the soul I say the contrary that the graceless soul can become full of grace. For what was more graceless than the soul of Paul when he was a blasphemer and insulter: what more full of grace when he said "I have fought the good fight, I have finished the course, I have kept the faith."[1] What was more graceless than the soul of the robber? what more full of grace when he heard the words "Verily I say unto thee to-day shalt thou be with me in paradise?"[2] What was more graceless than the publican when he practised extortion? but what more full of grace when he declared his resolution.[3] Seest thou that thou canst not alter grace of body, for it is the result not of moral disposition, but of nature. But grace of soul is supplied out of our own moral choice. Thou hast now received the definition. Of what kind are they? that the beauty of the soul proceeds from obedience to God. For if the graceless soul obeys God it puts off its ungracefulness, and becomes full of grace. "Saul! Saul!" it was said, "why persecutest thou me?" and he replied "and who art Thou Lord?" "I am Jesus."[4] And he obeyed, and his obedience made the graceless soul full of grace. Again, He saith to the publican "come follow me"[5] and the publican rose up and became an apostle: and the graceless soul became full of grace. Whence? by obedience. Again He saith to the fishermen "Come ye after me and I will make you to become fishers of men:"[6] and by their obedience their minds became full of grace. Let us see then what kind of beauty He is speaking of here. "Hearken O daughter and behold, and forget thy own people and thy father's house, and the king shall desire thy beauty." What kind of beauty will he desire? the spiritual kind. How so? because she is to "*forget*" He saith "hearken and forget." These are acts of moral choice. "Hearken!" he said: "an ungraceful one hears and her ungracefulness being that of the

---

[1] 2 Tim. iv. 7.
[2] Luke xxiii. 43.
[3] Luke xix. 8.
[4] Acts ix. 4, 5.
[5] Matt. ix. 9.
[6] Matt. iv. 19.

body is not removed. To the sinful woman He has said "Hearken," and if she will obey she sees what manner of beauty is bestowed upon her. Since then the ungracefulness of the bride was not physical, but moral (for she did not obey God but transgressed) therefore he leads her to another remedy. Thou didst become ungraceful then, not by nature, but by moral choice: and thou didst become full of grace by obedience. "Hearken O daughter and behold and forget thy own people, and thy father's house, and the king shall desire thy beauty." Then that thou mayest learn that he does not mean anything visible to sense, when thou hearest the word beauty, think not of eye, or nose, or mouth, or neck, but of piety, faith, love, things which are within— "for all the glory of the king's daughter is from within." Now for all these things let us offer thanks to God, the giver, for to Him alone belongeth glory, honour, might, for ever and ever. Amen.

ST. CHRYSOSTOM:

A TREATISE

TO PROVE THAT NO ONE CAN HARM THE MAN WHO DOES NOT INJURE HIMSELF.

TRANSLATED BY

REV. W. R. W. STEPHENS, M.A.,
PREBENDARY OF CHICHESTER CATHEDRAL, AND RECTOR OF WOOLBEDING, SUSSEX.

CONTENTS.

		PAGE
Introduction		269
1. The theme seems paradoxical to ordinary men of the world		271
2. What kind of evil really injures human virtue		272
3. What constitutes virtue in man		272
4. The devil cannot really injure man		273
5. The assaults of the devil upon Job and St. Paul redounded to their glory		274
6. Deprivation of wealth no evil		275
7. Riches a source of manifold evils		276
8. The poor enjoy better health than the rich		277
9. Riches introduce evil passions into the soul		277
10. The blessedness of Lazarus		278
11. Adversities will not injure the good man, and advantages will not benefit the bad man		279
12. The houses built on the rock and the sand an illustration of this		279
13. Additional examples—the Israelites in the wilderness		280
14. The Ninevites		281
15. The "Three Children"		281
16. The same continued		282
17. Summary and conclusion		283

INTRODUCTION TO THE TREATISE THAT NO ONE CAN HARM THE MAN WHO DOES NOT INJURE HIMSELF.

This very beautiful treatise was composed when St. Chrysostom was in exile, probably not long before his death, and was sent with a letter to his great friend the deaconess Olympias in Constantinople.

Plato in the 10th book of his Dialogue called the "Republic" employs an argument to prove the immortality of the soul, so nearly resembling a portion of this treatise that I can scarcely doubt St. Chrysostom had it in his mind. The following is the passage in the Platonic dialogue as rendered in the excellent translation of Messrs. Davies & Vaughan. I omit a few sentences here and there.

"Have you not learned, I asked, that our soul is immortal and never dies?

He looked at me and said in amazement. No really I have not: but can you maintain this doctrine?

Yes as I am an honest man, I replied, and I think you could also. It is quite easy to do it.

Proceed by all means.

So you call one thing good and another evil?

I do.

And do we hold the same opinion as to the meaning of the two terms?

What opinion do you hold?

I hold that the term evil comprises everything that destroys and corrupts, and the term good everything that preserves and benefits.

So do I.

Again; do you maintain that everything has its evil and its good? Do you say for example that the eyes are liable to the evil of ophthalmia, the entire body to disease, corn to mildew, timber to rot, copper and iron to rust or in other words that almost everything is liable to some connatural evil and malady?

I do.

And is it not the case that, whenever an object is attacked by one of these maladies it is impaired; and in the end completely broken up and destroyed by it?

Doubtless it is so?

Hence everything is destroyed by its own connatural evil and vice: otherwise if it be not destroyed by this, there is nothing else that can corrupt it. For that which is good will never destroy anything, nor yet that which is neither good nor evil.

Of course not.

If then we can find among existing things one which is liable to a particular evil which can indeed mar it, but cannot break it up or destroy it, shall we not be at once certain that a thing so constituted can never perish?

That would be a reasonable conclusion.

Well then is not the soul liable to a malady which renders it evil?

Certainly it is: all those things which we were lately discussing—injustice, intemperance, cowardice, and ignorance—produce that result."

Then having proved that although these things injure the soul they do not actually destroy it he proceeds.

"Well, it is irrational to suppose that a thing can be destroyed by the depravity of another thing, though it cannot be destroyed by its own.

True it is irrational.

Yes it is: for you must remember that we do not imagine that a body is to be destroyed by the proper depravity of its food whatever that may be, whether mouldiness or rottenness or anything else. But if the depravity of the food itself produces in the body a disorder proper to the body, we shall assert that the body has been destroyed by its food remotely, but by its own proper vice or disease, immediately: and we shall always disclaim the notion that the body can be corrupted by the depravity of its food which is a different thing from the body—that is to say, the notion that the body can be corrupted by an alien evil without the introduction of its own native evil.

You are perfectly correct.

Then according to the same reasoning I continued, unless depravity of body introduces into the soul depravity of soul let us never suppose that the soul can be destroyed by an alien evil without the presence of its own peculiar disease: for that would be to suppose that one thing can be destroyed by the evil of another thing.

That is a reasonable statement.

Well then let us either refute this doctrine and point out our mistake or else, so long as it remains unrefuted, let us never assert that a fever or any other disease, or fatal violence, or even the act of cutting up the entire body into the smallest possible pieces can have any tendency to destroy the soul, until it has been demonstrated that in consequence of this treatment of the body the soul itself becomes more unjust and more unholy. For so long as a thing is exempt from its own proper evil, while an evil foreign to it appears in another subject, let us not allow it to be said that this thing whether it be a soul or anything else is in danger of being destroyed.

Well, certainly no one will ever prove that the souls of the dying become more unjust in consequence of death." Here follows a passage to prove that even injustice does not *destroy* the soul, after which he proceeds,

"Surely then when the soul cannot be killed and destroyed by its own depravity and its own evil, hardly will the evil which is charged with the destruction of another thing destroy a soul or anything else beyond its own appropriate object.

Hardly: at least that is the natural inference.

Hence, as it is destroyed by no evil at all, whether foreign to it or its own, it is clear that the soul must be always existing, and therefore immortal.

It must."

If any one will compare this extract with chapters 2 to 6 in the following treatise he cannot fail to be struck by the similarity of thought and language, although in the latter case it is more apparent in the original than it can be in a translation. The aim of the two writers is not indeed identical: Chrysostom's object is to prove that nothing can really injure a man except sin—depravity of soul—Plato begins by proving this, and proceeds to maintain that if even that which corrupts the soul cannot actually destroy it the soul must be imperishable. They employ the same argument, only Plato carries it a step further than Chrysostom.

A TREATISE

TO PROVE THAT NO ONE CAN HARM THE MAN WHO DOES NOT INJURE HIMSELF.

1. I KNOW well that to coarse-minded persons, who are greedy in the pursuit of present things, and are nailed to earth, and enslaved to physical pleasure, and have no strong hold upon spiritual ideas, this treatise will be of a strange and paradoxical kind: and they will laugh immoderately, and condemn me for uttering incredible things from the very outset of my theme. Nevertheless, I shall not on this account desist from my promise, but for this very reason shall proceed with great earnestness to the proof of what I have undertaken. For if those who take that view of my subject will please not to make a clamour and disturbance, but wait to the end of my discourse, I am sure that they will take my side, and condemn themselves, finding that they have been deceived hitherto, and will make a recantation, and apology, and crave pardon for the mistaken opinion which they held concerning these matters, and will express great gratitude to me, as patients do to physicians, when they have been relieved from the disorders which lay seige to their body. For do not tell me of the judgment which is prevailing in your mind at the present time, but wait to hear the contention of my arguments and then you will be able to record an impartial verdict without being hindered by ignorance from forming a true judgment. For even judges in secular causes, if they see the first orator pouring forth a mighty torrent of words and overwhelming everything with his speech do not venture to record their decision without having patiently listened to the other speaker who is opposed to him; and even if the remarks of the first speaker seem to be just to an unlimited extent, they reserve an unprejudiced hearing for the second. In fact the special merit of judges consists in ascertaining with all possible accuracy what each side has to allege and then bringing forward their own judgment.

Now in the place of an orator we have the common assumption of mankind which in the course of ages has taken deep root in the minds of the multitude, and declaims to the following effect throughout the world. "All things" it says "have been turned upside down, the human race is full of much confusion and many are they who every day are being wronged, insulted, subjected to violence and injury, the weak by the strong, the poor by the rich: and as it is impossible to number the waves of the sea, so is it impossible to reckon the multitude of those who are the victims of intrigue, insult, and suffering; and neither the correction of law, nor the fear of being brought to trial, nor anything else can arrest this pestilence and disorder, but the evil is increasing every day, and the groans, and lamentations, and weeping of the sufferers are universal; and the judges who are appointed to reform such evils, themselves intensify the tempest, and inflame the disorder, and hence many of the more senseless and despicable kind, seized with a new kind of frenzy, accuse the providence of God, when they see the forbearing man often violently seized, racked, and oppressed, and the audacious, impetuous, low and low-born man waxing rich, and invested with authority, and becoming formidable to many, and inflicting countless troubles upon the more moderate, and this perpetrated both in town and country, and desert, on sea and land. This discourse of ours of necessity comes in by way of direct opposition to what has been alleged, maintaining a contention which is new, as I said at the beginning, and contrary to opinion, yet useful and true, and profitable to those who will give heed to it and be persuaded by it; for what I undertake is to prove (only make no commotion) that no one of those who are wronged is wronged by another, but experiences this injury at his own hands.

2. But in order to make my argument plainer, let us first of all enquire what injustice is, and of what kind of things the material of it is wont to be composed; also what human virtue is, and what it is which ruins it; and further what it is which seems to ruin it but really does not. For instance (for I must complete my argument by means of examples) each thing is subject to one evil which ruins it; iron to rust, wool to moth, flocks of sheep to wolves. The virtue of wine is injured when it ferments and turns sour: of honey when it loses its natural sweetness, and is reduced to a bitter juice. Ears of corn are ruined by mildew and drought, and the fruit, and leaves, and branches of vines by the mischievous host of locusts, other trees by the caterpillar, and irrational creatures by diseases of various kinds: and not to lengthen the list by going through all possible examples, our own flesh is subject to fevers, and palsies, and a crowd of other maladies. As then each one of these things is liable to that which ruins its virtue, let us now consider what it is which injures the human race, and what it is which ruins the virtue of a human being. Most men think that there are divers things which have this effect; for I must mention the erroneous opinions on the subject, and, after confuting them, proceed to exhibit that which really does ruin our virtue: and to demonstrate clearly that no one could inflict this injury or bring this ruin upon us unless we betrayed ourselves. The multitude then having erroneous opinions imagine that there are many different things which ruin our virtue: some say it is poverty, others bodily disease, others loss of property, others calumny, others death, and they are perpetually bewailing and lamenting these things: and whilst they are commiserating the sufferers and shedding tears they excitedly exclaim to one another, "What a calamity has befallen such and such a man! he has been deprived of all his fortune at a blow." Of another again one will say: "such and such a man has been attacked by severe sickness and is despaired of by the physicians in attendance." Some bewail and lament the inmates of the prison, some those who have been expelled from their country and transported to the land of exile, others those who have been deprived of their freedom, others those who have been seized and made captives by enemies, others those who have been drowned, or burnt, or buried by the fall of a house, but no one mourns those who are living in wickedness: on the contrary, which is worse than all, they often congratulate them, a practice which is the cause of all manner of evils. Come then (only, as I exhorted you at the outset, do not make a commotion), let me prove that none of the things which have been mentioned injure the man who lives soberly, nor can ruin his virtue. For tell me if a man has lost his all either at the hands of calumniators or of robbers, or has been stripped of his goods by knavish servants, what harm has the loss done to the virtue of the man?

But if it seems well let me rather indicate in the first place what is the virtue of a man, beginning by dealing with the subject in the case of existences of another kind so as to make it more intelligible and plain to the majority of readers.

3. What then is the virtue of a horse? is it to have a bridle studded with gold and girths to match, and a band of silken threads to fasten the housing, and clothes wrought in divers colours and gold tissue, and head gear studded with jewels, and locks of hair plaited with gold cord? or is it to be swift and strong in its legs, and even in its paces, and to have hoofs suitable to a well bred horse, and courage fitted for long journeys and warfare, and to be able to behave with calmness in the battle field, and if a rout takes place to save its rider? Is it not manifest that these are the things which constitute the virtue of the horse, not the others? Again, what should you say was the virtue of asses and mules? is it not the power of carrying burdens with contentment, and accomplishing journeys with ease, and having hoofs like rock? Shall we say that their outside trappings contribute anything to their own proper virtue? By no means. And what kind of vine shall we admire? one which abounds in leaves and branches, or one which is laden with fruit? or what kind of virtue do we predicate of an olive? is it to have large boughs, and great luxuriance of leaves, or to exhibit an abundance of its proper fruit dispersed over all parts of the tree? Well, let us act in the same way in the case of human beings also: let us determine what is the virtue of man, and let us regard that alone as an injury, which is destructive to it. What then is the

virtue of man? not riches that thou shouldest fear poverty: nor health of body that thou shouldest dread sickness, nor the opinion of the public, that thou shouldest view an evil reputation with alarm, nor life simply for its own sake, that death should be terrible to thee: nor liberty that thou shouldest avoid servitude: but carefulness in holding true doctrine, and rectitude in life. Of these things not even the devil himself will be able to rob a man, if he who possesses them guards them with the needful carefulness: and that most malicious and ferocious demon is aware of this. For this cause also he robbed Job of his substance, not to make him poor, but that he might force him into uttering some blasphemous speech; and he tortured his body, not to subject him to infirmity, but to upset the virtue of his soul. But nevertheless when he had set all his devices in motion, and turned him from a rich man into a poor one (that calamity which seems to us the most terrible of all), and had made him childless who was once surrounded by many children, and had scarified his whole body more cruelly than the executioners do in the public tribunals (for their nails do not lacerate the sides of those who fall into their hands so severely as the gnawing of the worms lacerated his body), and when he had fastened a bad reputation upon him (for Job's friends who were present with him said "thou hast not received the chastisement which thy sins deserve," and directed many words of accusation against him), and after he had not merely expelled him from city and home and transferred him to another city, but had actually made the dunghill serve as his home and city; after all this, he not only did him no damage but rendered him more glorious by the designs which he formed against him. And he not only failed to rob him of any of his possessions although he had robbed him of so many things, but he even increased the wealth of his virtue. For after these things he enjoyed greater confidence inasmuch as he had contended in a more severe contest. Now if he who underwent such sufferings, and this not at the hand of man, but at the hand of the devil who is more wicked than all men, sustained no injury, which of those persons who say such and such a man injured and damaged me will have any defence to make in future? For if the devil who is full of such great malice, after having set all his instruments in motion, and discharged all his weapons, and poured out all the evils incident to man, in a superlative degree upon the family and the person of that righteous man nevertheless did him no injury, but as I was saying rather profited him: how shall certain be able to accuse such and such a man alleging that they have suffered injury at their hands, not at their own?

4. What then? some one will say, did he not inflict injury on Adam, and upset him, and cast him out of paradise? No: he did it not, but the cause was the listlessness of him who was injured, and his want of temperance and vigilance. For he who applied such powerful and manifold devices and yet was not able to subdue Job, how could he by inferior means have mastered Adam, had not Adam betrayed himself through his own listlessness? What then? Has not he been injured who has been exposed to slander, and suffered confiscation of his property, having been deprived of all his goods, and is thrown out of his patrimony, and struggles with extreme poverty? No! he has not been injured, but has even profited, if he be sober. For, tell me, what harm did this do the apostles? Were they not continually struggling with hunger, and thirst and nakedness? And this was the very reason why they were so illustrious, and distinguished, and won for themselves much help from God. Again what harm was done to Lazarus by his disease, and sores, and poverty and dearth of protectors? Were they not the reasons why garlands of victory were more abundantly woven for him? Or what harm was done to Joseph by his getting evil reported of, both in his own land, and in the land of strangers? for he was supposed to be both an adulterer and fornicator: or what harm did servitude do him or expatriation? Is it not specially on account of these things that we regard him with admiration and astonishment? And why do I speak of removal into a foreign land, and poverty, and evil report, and bondage? For what harm did death itself inflict on Abel, although it was a violent and untimely death, and perpetrated by a brother's hand? Is not this the reason why his praise is sounded throughout the whole world? Seest thou how the discourse has demonstrated even more than it promised? For not only has it disclosed the fact that no one is injured by anybody, but also that they who take heed to themselves derive the greater gain (from such assaults). What is the purpose then it will be said of penalties and punishments? What is the purpose of hell? What is the purpose of such great threatenings, if no one is either injured or injures? What is it thou sayest? Why dost thou confuse the argument? For I did not say that no one injures, but that no one is injured. And how is it possible, you will say, for no one to be injured when many

are committing injury? In the way which I indicated just now. For Joseph's brethren did indeed injure him, yet he himself was not injured: and Cain laid snares for Abel, yet he himself was not ensnared. This is the reason why there are penalties and punishments. For God does not abolish penalties on account of the virtue of those who suffer; but he ordains punishments on account of the malice of those who do wickedly. For although they who are evil entreated become more illustrious in consequence of the designs formed against them, this is not due to the intention of those who plan the designs, but to the courage of those who are the victims of them. Wherefore for the latter the rewards of philosophy are made ready and prepared, for the former the penalties of wickedness. Hast thou been deprived of thy money? Read the word "Naked came I out of my mother's womb, and naked shall I return thither."[1] And add to this the apostolic saying "for we brought nothing into this world; it is certain we can carry nothing out."[2] Art thou evil reported of, and have some men loaded thee with countless abuse? Remember that passage where it is said "Woe unto you when all men shall speak well of you"[3] and "rejoice ye and leap for joy when they shall cast upon you an evil name."[4] Hast thou been transported into the land of exile? Consider that thou hast not here a fatherland, but that if thou wilt be wise thou art bidden to regard the whole world as a strange country. Or hast thou been given over to a sore disease? quote the apostolic saying "the more our outward man decayeth, so much the more is the inward man renewed day by day."[5] Has any one suffered a violent death? consider the case of John, his head cut off in prison, carried in a charger, and made the reward of a harlot's dancing. Consider the recompense which is derived from these things: for all these sufferings when they are unjustly inflicted by any one on another, expiate sins, and work righteousness. So great is the advantage of them in the case of those who bear them bravely.

5. When then neither loss of money, nor slander, nor railing, nor banishment, nor diseases, nor tortures, nor that which seems more formidable than all, namely death, harms those who suffer them, but rather adds to their profit, whence can you prove to me that any one is injured when he is not injured at all from any of these things? For I will endeavour to prove the reverse, showing that they who are most injured and insulted, and suffer the most incurable evils are the persons who do these things. For what could be more miserable than the condition of Cain, who dealt with his brother in this fashion? what more pitiable than that of Phillip's wife who beheaded John? or the brethren of Joseph who sold him away, and transported him into the land of exile? or the devil who tortured Job with such great calamities? For not only on account of his other iniquities, but at the same time also for this assault he will pay no trifling penalty. Dost thou see how here the argument has proved even more than was proposed, shewing that those who are insulted not only sustain no harm from these assaults, but that the whole mischief recoils on the head of those who contrive them? For since neither wealth nor freedom, nor life in our native land nor the other things which I have mentioned, but only right actions of the soul, constitute the virtue of man, naturally when the harm is directed against these things, human virtue itself is no wise harmed. What then? supposing some one does harm the moral condition of the soul? Even then if a man suffers damage, the damage does not come from another but proceeds from within, and from the man himself. "How so," do you say? When any one having been beaten by another, or deprived of his goods, or having endured some other grievous insult, utters a blasphemous speech, he certainly sustains a damage thereby, and a very great one, nevertheless it does not proceed from him who has inflicted the insult, but from his own littleness of soul. For what I said before I will now repeat, no man if he be infinitely wicked could attack any one more wickedly or more bitterly than that revengeful demon who is implacably hostile to us, the devil: but yet this cruel demon had not power to upset or overthrow him who lived before the law, and before the time of grace, although he discharged so many and such bitter weapons against him from all quarters. Such is the force of nobility of soul. And what shall I say of Paul? Did he not suffer so many distresses that even to make a list of them is no easy matter? He was put in prison, loaded with chains, dragged hither and hither, scourged by the Jews, stoned, lacerated on the back not only by thongs, but also by rods, he was immersed in the sea, oftentimes beset by robbers, involved in strife with his own countrymen, continually assailed both by foes and by acquaintance, subjected to countless intrigues, struggling with hunger and

---

[1] Job. i. 21. [2] 1 Tim. vi. 7. [3] Luke vi. 26.
[4] There is a confusion in the quotation here between Matt. v. 11, and Luke vi. 22.
[5] 2 Cor. iv. 16.

nakedness, undergoing other frequent and lasting mischances and afflictions: and why need I mention the greater part of them? he was dying every day: but yet, although subjected to so many and such grievous sufferings, he not only uttered no blasphemous word, but rejoiced over these things and gloried in them: and one time he says "I rejoice in my sufferings,"[1] and then again "not only this but we also glory in afflictions."[2] If then he rejoiced and gloried when suffering such great troubles what excuse will you have, and what defence will you make if you blaspheme when you do not undergo the smallest fraction of them.

6. But I am injured in other ways, one will say, and even if I do not blaspheme, yet when I am robbed of my money I am disabled from giving alms. This is a mere pretext and pretence. For if you grieve on this account know certainly that poverty is no bar to almsgiving. For even if you are infinitely poor you are not poorer than the woman who possessed only a handful of meal,[3] and the one who had only two mites,[4] each of whom having spent all her substance upon those who were in need was an object of surpassing admiration: and such great poverty was no hindrance to such great lovingkindness, but the alms bestowed from the two mites was so abundant and generous as to eclipse all who had riches, and in wealth of intention and superabundance of zeal to surpass those who cast in much coin. Wherefore even in this matter thou art not injured but rather benefited, receiving by means of a small contribution rewards more glorious than they who put down large sums. But since, if I were to say these things for ever, sensuous characters which delight to grovel in worldly things, and revel in present things would not readily endure parting from the fading flowers (for such are the pleasant things of this life) or letting go its shadows: but the better sort of men indeed cling to both the one and the other, while the more pitiable and abject cling more strongly to the former than to the latter, come let us[5] strip off the pleasant and showy masks which hide the base and ugly countenance of these things, and let us expose the foul deformity of the harlot. For such is the character of a life of this kind which is devoted to luxury, and wealth and power: it is foul and ugly and full of much abomination, disagreeable and burdensome,

and charged with bitterness. For this indeed is the special feature in this life which deprives those who are captivated by it of every excuse, that although it is the aim of their longings and endeavours, yet is it filled with much annoyance and bitterness, and teems with innumerable evils, dangers, bloodshed, precipices, crags, murders, fears and tremblings, envy and ill-will, and intrigue, perpetual anxiety and care, and derives no profit, and produces no fruit from these great evils save punishment and revenge, and incessant torment. But although this is its character it seems to be to most men an object of ambition, and eager contention, which is a sign of the folly of those who are captivated by it, not of the blessedness of the thing itself. Little children indeed are eager and excited about toys and cannot take notice of the things which become full grown men. There is an excuse for them on account of their immaturity: but these others are debarred from the right of defence, because, although of full age they are childish in disposition, and more foolish than children in their manner of life.

Now tell me why is wealth an object of ambition? For it is necessary to start from this point, because to the majority of those who are afflicted with this grievous malady it seems to be more precious than health and life, and public reputation, and good opinion, and country, and household, and friends, and kindred and everything else. Moreover the flame has ascended to the very clouds: and this fierce heat has taken possession of land and sea. Nor is there any one to quench this fire: but all people are engaged in stirring it up, both those who have been already caught by it, and those who have not yet been caught, in order that they may be captured. And you may see every one, husband and wife, household slave, and freeman, rich and poor, each according to his ability carrying loads which supply much fuel to this fire by day and night: loads not of wood or faggots (for the fire is not of that kind), but loads of souls and bodies, of unrighteousness and iniquity. For such is the material of which a fire of this kind is wont to be kindled. For those who have riches place no limit anywhere to this monstrous passion, even if they compass the whole world: and the poor press on to get in advance of them, and a kind of incurable craze, and unrestrainable frenzy and irremediable disease possesses the souls of all. And this affection has conquered every other kind and thrust it away expelling it from the soul: neither friends nor kindred are taken into account: and why do I speak of friends and kindred? not even wife and children are

---

[1] Col. i. 24.   [2] Rom. v. 3.
[3] 1 Kings xvii. 12.   [4] Luke xxi. 2.
[5] The passage is obscure, but St. Chrysostom seems to divide the pleasures of this world into two classes : the more sensual he calls flowers, the rest he calls shadows: the grosser natures cling to the former more tenaciously than to any other kind. Comp. Homily LXXVI. on St. Matt., near the end.

regarded, and what can be dearer to man than these? but all things are dashed to the ground and trampled underfoot, when this savage and inhuman mistress has laid hold of the souls of all who are taken captive by her. For as an inhuman mistress, and harsh tyrant, and savage barbarian, and public and expensive prostitute she debases and exhausts and punishes with innumerable dangers and torments those who have chosen to be in bondage to her; and yet although she is terrible and harsh, and fierce and cruel, and has the face of a barbarian, or rather of a wild beast, fiercer than a wolf or a lion, she seems to those who have been taken captive by her gentle and loveable, and sweeter than honey. And although she forges swords and weapons against them every day, and digs pitfalls and leads them to precipices and crags and weaves endless snares of punishment for them, yet is she supposed to make these things objects of ambition to those who have been made captive, and those who are desiring to be captured. And just as a sow delights and revels in wallowing in the ditch and mire, and beetles delight in perpetually crawling over dung; even so they who are captivated by the love of money are more miserable than these creatures. For the abomination is greater in this case, and the mire more offensive: for they who are addicted to this passion imagine that much pleasure is derived from it: which does not arise from the nature of the thing, but of the understanding which is afflicted with such an irrational taste. And this taste is worse in their case than in that of brutes: for as with the mire and the dung the cause of pleasure is not in them, but in the irrational nature of the creatures who plunge into it; even so count it to be in the case of human beings.

7. And how might we cure those who are thus disposed? It would be possible if they would open their ears to us, and unfold their heart, and receive our words. For it is impossible to turn and divert the irrational animals from their unclean habit; for they are destitute of reason: but this the gentlest of all tribes, honoured by reason and speech, I mean human nature, might, if it chose, readily and easily be released from the mire and the stench, and the dung hill and its abomination. For wherefore, O man, do riches seem to thee worthy such diligent pursuit? Is it on account of the pleasure which no doubt is derived from the table? or on account of the honour and the escort of those who pay court to thee, because of thy wealth? is it because thou art able to defend thyself against those who annoy thee, and to be an object of fear to all? For you cannot name any other reasons, save pleasure and flattery, and fear, and the power of taking revenge; for wealth is not generally wont to make any one wiser, or more self-controlled, or more gentle, or more intelligent, or kind, or benevolent, or superior to anger, or gluttony or pleasure: it does not train any one to be moderate, or teach him how to be humble, nor introduce and implant any other piece of virtue in the soul. Neither could you say for which of these things it deserves to be so diligently sought and desired. For not only is it ignorant how to plant and cultivate any good thing, but even if it finds a store of them it mars and stunts and blights them; and some of them it even uproots, and introduces their opposites, unmeasured licentiousness, unseasonable wrath, unrighteous anger, pride, arrogance, foolishness. But let me not speak of these; for they who have been seized by this malady will not endure to hear about virtue and vice, being entirely abandoned to pleasure and therefore enslaved to it. Come then let us forego for the time being the consideration of these points, and let us bring forward the others which remain, and see whether wealth has any pleasure, or any honour: for in my eyes the case is quite the reverse. And first of all, if you please, let us investigate the meals of rich and poor, and ask the guests which they are who enjoy the purest and most genuine pleasure; is it they who recline for a full day on couches, and join breakfast and dinner together, and distend their stomach, and blunt their senses, and sink the vessel by an overladen cargo of food, and waterlog the ship, and drench it as in some shipwreck of the body, and devise fetters, and manacles, and gags, and bind their whole body with the band of drunkenness and surfeit more grievous than an iron chain, and enjoy no sound pure sleep undisturbed by frightful dreams, and are more miserable than madmen and introduce a kind of self-imposed demon into the soul and display themselves as a laughing stock to the gaze of their servants, or rather to the kinder sort amongst them as a tragical spectacle eliciting tears, and cannot recognize any of those who are present, and are incapable of speaking or hearing but have to be carried away from their couches to their bed;—or is it they who are sober and vigilant, and limit their eating by their need, and sail with a favourable breeze, and find hunger and thirst the best relish in their food and drink? For nothing is so conducive to enjoyment and health as to be hungry and thirsty when one attacks the viands, and to identify satiety with the sim-

ple necessity of food, never overstepping the limits of this, nor imposing a load upon the body too great for its strength.

8. But if you disbelieve my statement study the physical condition, and the soul of each class. Are not the bodies vigorous of those who live thus moderately (for do not tell me of that which rarely happens, although some may be weak from some other circumstance, but form your judgment from those instances which are of constant occurrence), I say are they not vigorous, and their senses clear, fulfilling their proper function with much ease? whereas the bodies of the others are flaccid and softer than wax, and beset with a crowd of maladies? For gout soon fastens upon them, and untimely palsy, and premature old age, and headache, and flatulence, and feebleness of digestion, and loss of appetite, and they require constant attendance of physicians, and perpetual doseing, and daily care. Are these things pleasurable? tell me. Who of those that know what pleasure really is would say so? For pleasure is produced when desire leads the way, and fruition follows: now if there is fruition, but desire is nowhere to be found, the conditions of pleasure fail and vanish. On this account also invalids, although the most charming food is set before them, partake of it with a feeling of disgust and sense of oppression: because there is no desire which gives a keen relish to the enjoyment of it. For it is not the nature of the food, or of the drink, but the appetite of the eaters which is wont to produce the desire, and is capable of causing pleasure. Therefore also a certain wise man who had an accurate knowledge of all that concerned pleasure, and understood how to moralize about these things said "the full soul mocketh at honeycombs:"[1] showing that the conditions of pleasure consist not in the nature of the meal, but in the disposition of the eaters. Therefore also the prophet recounting the wonders in Egypt and in the desert mentioned this in connexion with the others "He satisfied them with honey out of the rock."[2] And yet nowhere does it appear that honey actually sprang forth for them out of the rock: what then is the meaning of the expression? Because the people being exhausted by much toil and long travelling, and distressed by great thirst rushed to the cool spring, their craving for drink serving as a relish, the writer wishing to describe the pleasures which they received from those fountains called the water honey, not meaning that the element was converted into honey, but that the pleasure received from the water rivalled the sweetness of honey, inasmuch as those who partook of it rushed to it in their eagerness to drink.

Since then these things are so and no one can deny it, however stupid he may be: is it not perfectly plain that pure, undiluted, and lively pleasure is to be found at the tables of the poor? whereas at the tables of the rich there is discomfort, and disgust and defilement? as that wise man has said "even sweet things seem to be a vexation."[3]

9. But riches some one will say procure honour for those who possess them, and enable them to take vengeance on their enemies with ease. And is this a reason, pray, why riches seem to you desirable and worth contending for;—that they nourish the most dangerous passion in our nature, leading on anger into action, swelling the empty bubbles of ambition, and stimulating and urging men to arrogance? Why these are just the very reasons why we ought resolutely to turn our backs upon riches, because they introduce certain fierce and dangerous wild beasts into our heart depriving us of the real honour which we might receive from all, and introducing to deluded men another which is the opposite of this, only painted over with its colours, and persuading them to fancy that it is the same, when by nature it is not so, but only seems to be so to the eye. For as the beauty of courtesans, made up as it is of dyes and pigments, is destitute of real beauty, yet makes a foul and ugly face appear fair and beautiful to those who are deluded by it when it is not so in reality: even so also riches force flattery to look like honour. For I beg you not to consider the praises which are openly bestowed through fear and fawning: for these are only tints and pigments; but unfold the conscience of each of those who flatter you in this fashion, and inside it you will see countless accusers declaring against you, and loathing and detesting you more than your bitterest adversaries and foes. And if ever a change of circumstances should occur which would remove and expose this mask which fear has manufactured, just as the sun when it emits a hotter ray than usual discloses the real countenances of those women whom I mentioned, then you will see clearly that all through the former time you were held in the greatest contempt by those who paid court to you, and you fancied you were enjoying honour from those who thoroughly hated you, and in their heart poured infinite abuse upon you, and longed to see

---

[1] Prov. xxvii. 7. Septuagint.   [2] Ps. lxxxi. 16.   [3] Referring to Prov. xxvii. 7.

you involved in extreme calamities. For there is nothing like virtue to produce honour,—honour neither forced nor feigned, nor hidden under a mask of deceit, but real and genuine, and able to stand the test of hard times.

10. But do you wish to take vengeance on those who have annoyed you? This, as I was saying just now, is the very reason why wealth ought specially to be avoided. For it prepares thee to thrust the sword against thyself, and renders thee liable to a heavier account in the future day of reckoning, and makes thy punishment intolerable. For revenge is so great an evil that it actually revokes the mercy of God, and cancels the forgiveness of countless sins which has been already bestowed. For he who received remission of the debt of ten thousand talents, and after having obtained so great a boon by merely asking for it then made a demand of one hundred pence from his fellow servant, a demand, that is, for satisfaction for his transgression against himself, in his severity towards his fellow servant recorded his own condemnation; and for this reason and no other he was delivered to the tormentors, and racked, and required to pay back the ten thousand talents; and he was not allowed the benefit of any excuse or defence, but suffered the most extreme penalty, having been commanded to deposit the whole debt which the lovingkindness of God had formerly remitted.[1] Is this then the reason, pray, why wealth is so earnestly pursued by thee, because it so easily conducts thee into sin of this kind? Nay verily, this is why you ought to abhor it as a foe and an adversary teeming with countless murders. But poverty, some one will say, disposes men to be discontented and often also to utter profane words, and condescend to mean actions. It is not poverty which does this, but littleness of soul: for Lazarus also was poor, aye! very poor: and besides poverty he suffered from infirmity, a bitterer trial than any form of poverty, and one which makes poverty more severely felt; and in addition to infirmity there was a total absence of protectors, and difficulty in finding any to supply his wants, which increased the bitterness of poverty and infirmity. For each of these things is painful in itself, but when there are none to minister to the sufferer's wants, the suffering becomes greater, the flame more painful, the distress more bitter, the tempest fiercer, the billows stronger, the furnace hotter. And if one examines the case thoroughly there was yet a fourth trial besides these—the unconcern and luxury of the rich man who dwelt hard by. And if you would find a fifth thing, serving as fuel to the flame, you will see quite clearly that he was beset by it. For not only was that rich man living luxuriously, but twice, and thrice, or rather indeed several times in the day he saw the poor man: for he had been laid at his gate, being a grievous spectacle of pitiable distress, and the bare sight of him was sufficient to soften even a heart of stone: and yet even this did not induce that unmerciful man to assist this case of poverty: but he had his luxurious table spread, and goblets wreathed with flowers, and pure wine plentifully poured forth, and grand armies of cooks, and parasites, and flatterers from early dawn, and troops of singers, cupbearers, and jesters; and he spent all his time in devising every species of dissipation, and drunkenness, and surfeiting, and in revelling in dress and feasting and many other things. But although he saw that poor man every day distressed by grievous hunger and the bitterest infirmity, and the oppression of his many sores, and by destitution, and the ills which result from these things, he never even gave him a thought: yet the parasites and the flatterers were pampered even beyond their need; but the poor man, and he so very poor, and encompassed with so many miseries, was not even vouchsafed the crumbs which fell from that table, although he greatly desired them: and yet none of these things injured him, he did not give vent to a bitter word, he did not utter a profane speech; but like a piece of gold which shines all the more brilliantly when it is purified by excessive heat, even so he, although oppressed by these sufferings, was superior to all of them, and to the agitation which in many cases is produced by them. For if generally speaking poor men, when they see rich men, are consumed with envy and racked by malicious ill-will, and deem life not worth living, and this even when they are well supplied with necessary food, and have persons to minister to their wants; what would the condition of this poor man have been had he not been very wise and noble hearted, seeing that he was poor beyond all other poor men, and not only poor, but also infirm, and without any one to protect or cheer him, and lay in the midst of the city as if in a remote desert, and wasted away with bitter hunger, and saw all good things being poured upon the rich man as out of a fountain, and had not the benefit of any human consolation, but lay exposed as a perpetual meal for the tongues of the dogs, for he was so enfeebled and broken down in

---

[1] Matt. xviii. 23-35.

body that he could not scare them away? Dost thou perceive that he who does not injure himself suffers no evil? for I will again take up the same argument.

11. For what harm was done to this hero by his bodily infirmity? or by the absence of protectors? or by the coming of the dogs? or the evil proximity of the rich man? or by the great luxury, haughtiness and arrogance of the latter? Did it enervate him for the contest on behalf of virtue? Did it ruin his fortitude? Nowhere was he harmed at all, but that multitude of sufferings, and the cruelty of the rich man, rather increased his strength, and became the pledge for him of infinite crowns of victory, a means of adding to his rewards, an augmentation of his recompense, and a promise of an increased requital. For he was crowned not merely on account of his poverty, or of his hunger or of his sores, or of the dogs licking them: but because, having such a neighbour as the rich man, and being seen by him every day, and perpetually overlooked he endured this trial bravely and with much fortitude, a trial which added no small flame but in fact a very strong one to the fire of poverty, and infirmity and loneliness.

And, tell me, what was the case of the blessed Paul? for there is nothing to prevent my making mention of him again. Did he not experience innumerable storms of trial? And in what respect was he injured by them? Was he not crowned with victory all the more in consequence,—because he suffered hunger, because he was consumed with cold and nakedness, because he was often tortured with the scourge, because he was stoned, because he was cast into the sea? But then some one says he was Paul, and called by Christ. Yet Judas also was one of the twelve, and he too was called of Christ; but neither his being of the twelve nor his call profited him, because he had not a mind disposed to virtue. But Paul although struggling with hunger, and at a loss to procure necessary food, and daily undergoing such great sufferings, pursued with great zeal the road which leads to heaven: whereas Judas although he had been called before him, and enjoyed the same advantages as he did, and was initiated in the highest form of Christian life, and partook of the holy table and that most awful of sacred feasts, and received such grace as to be able to raise the dead, and cleanse the lepers, and cast out devils, and often heard discourses concerning poverty, and spent so long a time in the company of Christ Himself, and was entrusted with the money of the poor, so that his passion might be soothed thereby (for he was a thief) even then did not become any better, although he had been favoured with such great condescension. For since Christ knew that he was covetous, and destined to perish on account of his love of money he not only did not demand punishment of him for this at that time, but with a view to softening down his passion he was entrusted with the money of the poor, that having some means of appeasing his greed he might be saved from falling into that appalling gulf of sin, checking the greater evil beforehand by a lesser one.

12. Thus in no case will any one be able to injure a man who does not choose to injure himself: but if a man is not willing to be temperate, and to aid himself from his own resources no one will ever be able to profit him. Therefore also that wonderful history of the Holy Scriptures, as in some lofty, large, and broad picture, has portrayed the lives of the men of old time, extending the narrative from Adam to the coming of Christ: and it exhibits to you both those who are upset, and those who are crowned with victory in the contest, in order that it may instruct you by means of all examples that no one will be able to injure one who is not injured by himself, even if all the world were to kindle a fierce war against him. For it is not stress of circumstances, nor variation of seasons, nor insults of men in power, nor intrigues besetting thee like snow storms, nor a crowd of calamities, nor a promiscuous collection of all the ills to which mankind is subject, which can disturb even slightly the man who is brave, and temperate, and watchful; just as on the contrary the indolent and supine man who is his own betrayer cannot be made better, even with the aid of innumerable ministrations. This at least was made manifest to us by the parable of the two men, of whom the one built his house upon the rock, the other upon the sand:[1] not that we are to think of sand and rock, or of a building of stone, and a roof, or of rivers, and rain, and wild winds, beating against the buildings, but we are to extract virtue and vice as the meaning of these things, and to perceive from them that no one injures a man who does not injure himself. Therefore neither the rain although driven furiously along, nor the streams dashing against it with much vehemence, nor the wild winds beating against it with a mighty rush, shook the one house in any degree: but it remained undisturbed, unmoved: that thou mightest understand that no trial can agitate the man who does not betray himself. But the house of the other man

---

[1] Matt. vii. 24, etc.

was easily swept away, not on account of the force of the trials (for in that case the other would have experienced the same fate), but on account of his own folly; for it did not fall because the wind blew upon it, but because it was built upon the sand, that is to say upon indolence and iniquity. For before that tempest beat upon it, it was weak and ready to fall. For buildings of that kind, even if no one puts any pressure on them, fall to pieces of themselves, the foundation sinking and giving way in every direction. And just as cobwebs part asunder, although no strain is put upon them, but adamant remains unshaken even when it is struck: even so also they who do not injure themselves become stronger, even if they receive innumerable blows; but they who betray themselves, even if there is no one to harass them, fall of themselves, and collapse and perish. For even thus did Judas perish, not only having been unassailed by any trial of this kind, but having actually enjoyed the benefit of much assistance.

13. Would you like me to illustrate this argument in the case of whole nations? What great forethought was bestowed upon the Jewish nation! was not the whole visible creation arranged with a view to their service? was not a new and strange method of life introduced amongst them? For they had not to send down to a market, and so they had the benefit of things which are sold for money without paying any price for them: neither did they cleave furrows nor drag a plough, nor harrow the ground, nor cast in seed, nor had they need of rain and wind, and annual seasons, nor sunshine, nor phases of the moon, nor climate, nor anything of that kind; they prepared no threshing floor, they threshed no grain, they used no winnowing fan for separating the grain from the chaff, they turned no mill-stone, they built no oven, they brought neither wood nor fire into the house, they needed no baker's art, they handled no spade, they sharpened no sickle, they required no other art, I mean of weaving or building or supplying shoes: but the word of God was everything to them. And they had a table prepared off hand, free of all toil and labour. For such was the nature of the manna; it was new and fresh, nowhere costing them any trouble, nor straining them by labour. And their clothes, and shoes, and even their physical frame forgot their natural infirmity: for the former did not wear out in the course of so long a time nor did their feet swell although they made such long marches. Of physicians, and medicine, and all other concern about that kind of art, there was no mention at all amongst them; so completely banished was infirmity of every kind: for it is said "He brought them out with silver and gold; and there was not one feeble person among their tribes."[1] But like men who had quitted this world, and were transplanted to another and a better one, even so did they eat and drink, neither did the sun's ray when it waxed hot smite their heads; for the cloud parted them from the fiery beam, hovering all round them, and serving like a portable shelter for the whole body of the people. Neither at night did they need a torch to disperse the darkness, but they had the pillar of fire, a source of unspeakable light, supplying two wants, one by its shining, the other by directing the course of their journey; for it was not only luminous, but also conducted that countless host along the wilderness with more certainty than any human guide. And they journeyed not only upon land but also upon sea as if it had been dry land; and they made an audacious experiment upon the laws of nature by treading upon that angry sea, marching through it as if it had been the hard and resisting surface of a rock; and indeed when they placed their feet upon it the element became like solid earth, and gently sloping plains and fields; but when it received their enemies it wrought after the nature of sea; and to the Israelites indeed it served as a chariot, but to their enemies it became a grave; conveying the former across with ease, but drowning the latter with great violence. And the disorderly flood of water displayed the good order and subordination which marks reasonable and highly intelligent men, fulfilling the part at one time of a guardian, at another of an executioner, and exhibiting these opposites together on one day. What shall one say of the rocks which gave forth streams of water? what of the clouds of birds which covered the whole face of the earth by the number of their carcases? what of the wonders in Egypt? what of the marvels in the wilderness? what of the triumphs and bloodless victories? for they subdued those who opposed them like men keeping holiday rather than making war. And they vanquished their own masters without the use of arms; and overcame those who fought with them after they left Egypt by means of singing and music; and what they did was a festival rather than a campaign, a religious ceremony rather than a battle. For all these wonders took place not merely for the purpose of supplying their need, but also that the people might preserve more accurately

---

[1] Ps. cv. 37.

the doctrine which Moses inculcated of the knowledge of God; and voices proclaiming the presence of their Master were uttered on all sides of them. For the sea loudly declared this, by becoming a road for them to march upon, and then turning into sea again: and the waters of the Nile uttered this voice when they were converted into the nature of blood; and the frogs, and the great army of locusts, and the caterpillar and blight declared the same thing to all the people; and the wonders in the desert, the manna, the pillar of fire, the cloud, the quails, and all the other incidents served them as a book, and writing which could never be effaced, echoing daily in their memory and resounding in their mind. Nevertheless after such great and remarkable providence, after all those unspeakable benefits, after such mighty miracles, after care indescribable, after continual teaching, after instruction by means of speech, and admonition by means of deeds, after glorious victories, after extraordinary triumphs, after abundant supply of food, after the plentiful production of water, after the ineffable glory with which they were invested in the eyes of the human race, being ungrateful and senseless they worshipped a calf, and paid reverence to the head of a bull, even when the memorials of God's benefits in Egypt were fresh in their minds, and they were still in actual enjoyment of many more.

14. But the Ninevites, although a barbarous and foreign people who had never participated in any of these benefits, small or great, neither words, nor wonders, nor works, when they saw a man who had been saved from shipwreck, who had never associated with them before, but appeared then for the first time, enter their city and say "yet three days and Nineveh shall be overthrown,"[1] were so converted and reformed by the mere sound of these words, and putting away their former wickedness, advanced in the direction of virtue by the path of repentance, that they caused the sentence of God to be revoked, and arrested the threatened disturbance of their city, and averted the heaven-sent wrath, and were delivered from every kind of evil. "For," we read, "God saw that every man turned from his evil way, and was converted to the Lord."[2] How turned? I ask. Although their wickedness was great, their iniquity unspeakable, their moral sores difficult to heal, which was plainly shown by the prophet when he said "their wickedness ascended even unto the heaven:"[3] indicating by the distance of the place the magnitude of their wickedness; nevertheless such great iniquity which was piled up to such a height as to reach even to the heaven, all this in the course of three days in a brief moment of time through the effect of a few words which they heard from the mouth of one man and he an unknown shipwrecked stranger they so thoroughly abolished, removed out of sight, and put away, as to have the happiness of hearing the declaration "God saw that every one turned from his evil way, and He repented of the evil which God said He would do them." Seest thou that he who is temperate and watchful not only suffers no injury at the hands of man, but even turns back Heaven-sent wrath? whereas he who betrays himself and harms himself by his own doing, even if he receives countless benefits, reaps no great advantage. So, at least, the Jews were not profited by those great miracles, nor on the other hand were the Ninevites harmed by having no share in them; but inasmuch as they were inwardly well-disposed, having laid hold of a slight opportunity they became better, barbarians and foreigners though they were, ignorant of all divine revelation, and dwelling at a distance from Palestine.

15. Again, I ask, was the virtue of the "three children" corrupted by the troubles which beset them? Whilst they were still young, mere youths, of immature age, did they not undergo that grievous affliction of captivity? had they not to make a long journey from home, and when they had arrived in the foreign country were they not cut off from fatherland and home and temple, and altar and sacrifices, and offerings, and drink offerings, and even the singing of psalms? For not only were they debarred from their home, but as a consequence from many forms of worship also. Were they not given up into the hands of barbarians, wolves rather than men? and, most painful calamity of all, when they had been banished into so distant and barbarous a country, and were suffering such a grievous captivity were they not without teacher, without prophets, without ruler? "for," it is written, "there is no ruler, nor prophet, nor governor, nor place for offering before Thee and finding mercy."[4] Yea moreover they were cast into the royal palace, as upon some cliff and crag, and a sea full of rocks and reefs, being compelled to sail over that angry sea without a pilot, or signal man, or crew, or sails; and they were cooped up in the royal court as in a prison. For inasmuch as they knew spiritual wisdom, and were superior to worldly things, and despised all

---

[1] Jonah iii. 4.   [2] Jonah iii. 10.   [3] Jonah i. 2.   [4] Song of the Three Children, v. 15.

human pride and made the wings of their soul soar upwards, they counted their sojourn there as an aggravation of their trouble. For had they been outside the court, and dwelling in a private house they would have enjoyed more independence: but having been cast into that prison (for they deemed the splendour of the palace no better than a prison, no safer than a place of rocks and crags) they were straightway subjected to cruel embarrassment. For the king commanded them to be partakers of his own table, a luxurious, unclean and profane table, a thing which was forbidden them, and seemed more terrible than death; and they were lonely men hemmed in like lambs amongst so many wolves. And they were constrained to choose between being consumed by famine or rather led off to execution, and tasting of forbidden meats. What then did these youths do, forlorn as they were, captives, strangers, slaves of those who commanded these things. They did not consider that this strait or the absolute power of him who possessed the state sufficed to justify their compliance; but they employed every device and expedient to enable them to avoid the sin, although they were abandoned on every side. For they could not influence men by money: how should they, being captives? nor by friendship and social intercourse? how should they being strangers? nor could they get the better of them by any exertion of power: how was it possible being slaves? nor master them by force of numbers: how could they being only three? Therefore they approached the eunuch who possessed the necessary authority, and persuaded him by their arguments. For when they saw him fearful and trembling, and in an agony of alarm concerning his own safety, and the dread of death which agitated his soul was intolerable: "for I fear" said he "my lord the king, lest he should see your countenances sadder than the children which are of your sort and so shall ye endanger my head to the king,"[1] having released him from this fear they persuaded him to grant them the favour. And inasmuch as they brought to the work all the strength which they had, God also henceforth contributed his strength to it. For it was not God's doing only that they achieved those things for the sake of which they were to receive a reward, but the beginning and starting point was from their own purpose, and having manifested that to be noble and brave, they won for themselves the help of God, and so accomplished their aim.

16. Dost thou then perceive that if a man does not injure himself, no one else will be able to harm him? Behold at least youthfulness, and captivity and destitution, and removal into a foreign land, and loneliness, and dearth of protectors, and a stern command, and great fear of death assailing the mind of the eunuch, and poverty, and feebleness of numbers, and dwelling in the midst of barbarians, and having enemies for masters, and surrender into the hands of the king himself, and separation from all their kindred, and removal from priests and prophets, and from all others who cared for them, and the cessation of drink offerings and sacrifices, and loss of the temple and psalmody, and yet none of these things harmed them; but they had more renown then than when they enjoyed these things in their native land. And after they had accomplished this task first and had wreathed their brows with the glorious garland of victory, and had kept the law even in a foreign land, and trampled under foot the tyrant's command, and overcome fear of the avenger, and yet received no harm from any quarter, as if they had been quietly living at home and enjoying the benefit of all those things which I mentioned, after they had thus fearlessly accomplished their work they were again summoned to other contests. And again they were the same men; and they were subjected to a more severe trial than the former one, and a furnace was kindled, and they were confronted by the barbarian army in company with the king: and the whole Persian force was set in motion and everything was devised which tended to put deceit or constraint upon them: divers kinds of music, and various forms of punishment, and threats, and what they saw on every side of them was alarming, and the words which they heard were more alarming than what they saw; nevertheless inasmuch as they did not betray themselves, but made the most of their own strength, they never sustained any kind of damage: but even won for themselves more glorious crowns of victory than before. For Nabuchadonosor bound them and cast them into the furnace, yet he burnt them not, but rather benefited them, and rendered them more illustrious. And although they were deprived of temple (for I will repeat my former remarks) and altar, and fatherland, and priests and prophets, although they were in a foreign and barbarous country, in the very midst of the furnace, surrounded by all that mighty host, the king himself who wrought this looking on, they set up a glorious trophy, and won a notable victory, having sung that admirable and extraordinary hymn which from that day to this has been sung

---

[1] Dan. i. 10.

throughout the world and will continue to be sung to future generations.

Thus then when a man does not injure himself, he cannot possibly be hurt by another: for I will not cease harping constantly upon this saying. For if captivity, and bondage, and loneliness and loss of country and all kindred and death, and burning, and a great army and a savage tyrant could not do any damage to the innate virtue of the three children captives, bondmen, strangers though they were in a foreign land, but the enemy's assault became to them rather the occasion of greater confidence: what shall be able to harm the temperate man? There is nothing, even should he have the whole world in arms against him. But, some one may say, in their case God stood beside them, and plucked them out of the flame. Certainly He did; and if thou wilt play thy part to the best of thy power, the help which God supplies will assuredly follow.

17. Nevertheless the reason why I admire those youths, and pronounce them blessed, and enviable, is not because they trampled on the flame, and vanquished the force of the fire: but because they were bound, and cast into the furnace, and delivered to the fire for the sake of true doctrine. For this it was which constituted the completeness of their triumph, and the wreath of victory was placed on their brows as soon as they were cast into the furnace and before the issue of events it began to be weaved for them from the moment that they uttered those words which they spoke with much boldness and freedom of speech to the king when they were brought into his presence. "We have no need to answer thee concerning this thing: for our God in Heaven whom we serve is able to rescue us out of the burning fiery furnace: and He will deliver us out of thy hands, O King. But if not, be it known unto thee, O King, that we will not serve thy Gods nor worship the golden image which thou hast set up."[1] After the utterance of these words I proclaimed them conquerors; after these words having grasped the prize of victory, they hastened on to the glorious crown of martyrdom, following up the confession which they made through their words with the confession made through their deeds. But if when they had been cast into it, the fire had respect for their bodies, and undid their bonds, and suffered them to go down into it without fear, and forgot its natural force, so that the furnace of fire became as a fountain of cool water, this marvel was the effect of God's grace and of the divine wonder-working power. Yet the heroes themselves even before these things took place, as soon as they set foot in the flames had erected their trophy, and won their victory, and put on their crown, and had been proclaimed conquerors both in Heaven and on earth, and so far as they were concerned nothing was wanting for their renown. What then wouldst thou have to say to these things? Hast thou been driven into exile, and expelled from thy country? Behold so also were they. Hast thou suffered captivity, and become the servant of barbarian masters. Well! this also thou wilt find befell these men. But thou hast no one present there to regulate thy state nor to advise or instruct thee? Well! of attention of this kind these men were destitute. Or thou hast been bound, burned, put to death? for thou canst not tell me of anything more painful than these things. Yet lo! these men having gone through them all, were made more glorious by each one of them, yea more exceedingly illustrious, and increased the store of their treasures in Heaven. And the Jews indeed who had both temple, and altar, and ark and cherubim, and mercy-seat, and veil, and an infinite multitude of priests, and daily services, and morning and evening sacrifices, and continually heard the voices of the prophets, both living and departed, sounding in their ears, and carried about with them the recollection of the wonders which were done in Egypt, and in the wilderness, and all the rest, and turned the story of these things over in their hands, and had them inscribed upon their door posts and enjoyed the benefit at that time of much supernatural power and every other kind of help were yet no wise profited, but rather damaged, having set up idols in the temple itself, and having sacrificed their sons and daughters under trees, and in almost every part of the country in Palestine having offered those unlawful and accursed sacrifices, and perpetrated countless other deeds yet more monstrous. But these men although in the midst of a barbarous and hostile land, having their occupation in a tyrant's house, deprived of all that care of which I have been speaking, led away to execution, and subjected to burning, not only suffered no harm there from small or great, but became the more illustrious. Knowing then these things, and collecting instances of the like kind from the inspired divine Scriptures (for it is possible to find many such examples in the case of various other persons) we deem that neither a difficulty arising from seasons or events, nor compulsion and force, nor the arbitrary authority

---

[1] Dan. iii. 16-18.

of potentates furnish a sufficient excuse for us when we transgress. I will now conclude my discourse by repeating what I said at the beginning, that if any one be harmed and injured he certainly suffers this at his own hands, not at the hands of others even if there be countless multitudes injuring and insulting him: so that if he does not suffer this at his own hands, not all the creatures who inhabit the whole earth and sea if they combined to attack him would be able to hurt one who is vigilant and sober in the Lord. Let us then, I beseech you, be sober and vigilant at all times, and let us endure all painful things bravely that we may obtain those everlasting and pure blessings in Christ Jesus our Lord, to whom be glory and power, now and ever throughout all ages. Amen.

LETTERS OF ST. CHRYSOSTOM TO OLYMPIAS.

TRANSLATED WITH INTRODUCTION AND NOTES BY

REV. W. R. W. STEPHENS, M.A.

PREBENDARY OF CHICHESTER CATHEDRAL, AND RECTOR OF WOOLBEDING, SUSSEX.

INTRODUCTION TO THE LETTERS TO OLYMPIAS.

THE deaconess Olympias to whom seventeen of Chrysostom's extant letters are addressed was the most eminent of his female friends. She belonged to a Pagan family of high rank, and was born about 368. Her father Seleucus who was a count of the Empire died when she was a young girl, and she was brought up under the guardianship of an uncle Procopius, who was a devout Christian and a friend of Gregory of Nazianzus. Gregory took great interest in her, speaking of her in his letters as "his own Olympias" and delighting to be addressed by her as "father." Her governess Theodosia, sister of St. Amphilochius of Iconium, was a woman whom Gregory exhorted her to imitate as the very pattern of Christian goodness. The orphan girl had great personal beauty, and was the heiress of a large fortune. Naturally therefore she had many suitors, and in 384 at the age of sixteen she was wedded to Nebridius, a young man of high rank and irreproachable character. The marriage however does not seem to have been a happy one, and perhaps in this fact as well as in the death of her husband about two years after their union, Olympias saw a divine intimation that she should not entangle herself again in the worldly cares and anxieties incident to married life. The Emperor Theodosius wished to unite her to a young Spaniard, Elpidius, a kinsman of his own, and irritated by her refusal, ordered her property to be confiscated until she should have attained her thirtieth year, unless she consented to the proposed union. Olympias however remained inflexible and in a letter of dignified sarcasm thanked the Emperor for relieving her from a heavy burden. "He could not have conferred a greater blessing upon her unless he had ordered her wealth to be bestowed upon the Churches and the poor." Theodosius perceiving the uselessness, if not regretting the injustice, of his harsh decree, cancelled it, and left her in the undisturbed enjoyment of her property. Henceforward her time and wealth were devoted to the service of religion. She ministered to the necessities of the sick and poor, and supported the work of the Church in Greece, Asia Minor and Syria with such lavish donations, not only of her money but of her land, that even Chrysostom, who might be called the great preacher of almsgiving, warned her against indiscriminate liberality, reminding her that as her wealth was a trust committed to her by God she ought to be discreet in the management of it. This salutary advice gained him the ill-will of many avaricious bishops and clergy who had profited, or hoped to profit, by her gifts. She in her turn requited the Archbishop for his spiritual care by many little feminine attentions to his bodily wants, especially by seeing that he was supplied with wholesome food, and did not overstrain his feeble constitution by a too rigid abstinence. She herself however practised the most austere asceticism, renouncing the luxury of the bath, wearing none but old coarse clothing, and subjecting herself to severe restrictions in respect of food and sleep.

After the expulsion of Chrysostom from Constantinople 404, through the intrigues of his enemies, Olympias suffered much from the persecution to which all his followers were subjected. She was accused of having been concerned in causing the fire which broke out immediately after his departure, and destroyed the Cathedral Church and the Senate House.

Her intrepid demeanour before the præfect who tried in vain to frighten her into a confession of guilt, or induce her to acknowledge Arsacius who had been intruded into the See by an arbitrary exercise of imperial power, excited general admiration; and the tidings of her fortitude were a great consolation to the exiled archbishop in the midst of much bodily suffering, and mental distress. It is not quite certain whether she was driven from Constantinople or voluntarily retired from it; nor have we any definite information concerning the remainder of her life.

LETTERS TO OLYMPIAS.

TO MY LADY,

THE MOST REVEREND AND DIVINELY FAVORED DEACONESS OLYMPIAS, I JOHN, BISHOP, SEND GREETING IN THE LORD.

1. COME now let me relieve the wound of thy despondency, and disperse the thoughts which gather this cloud of care around thee. For what is it which upsets thy mind, and why art thou sorrowful and dejected? Is it because of the fierce black storm which has overtaken the Church, enveloping all things in darkness as of a night without a moon, and is growing to a head every day, travailing to bring forth disastrous shipwrecks, and increasing the ruin of the world? I know all this as well as you; none shall gainsay it, and if you like I will form an image of the things now taking place so as to present the tragedy yet more distinctly to thee. We behold a sea upheaved from the very lowest depths, some sailors floating dead upon the waves, others engulfed by them, the planks of the ships breaking up, the sails torn to tatters, the masts sprung, the oars dashed out of the sailors' hands, the pilots seated on the deck, clasping their knees with their hands instead of grasping the rudder, bewailing the hopelessness of their situation with sharp cries and bitter lamentations, neither sky nor sea clearly visible, but all one deep and impenetrable darkness, so that no one can see his neighbour, whilst mighty is the roaring of the billows, and monsters of the sea attack the crews on every side.

But how much further shall I pursue the unattainable? for whatever image of our present evils I may seek speech shrinks baffled from the attempt. Nevertheless even when I look at these calamities I do not abandon the hope of better things, considering as I do who the pilot is in all this—not one who gets the better of the storm by his art, but calms the raging waters by his rod. But if He does not effect this at the outset and speedily, such is His custom—He does not at the beginning put down these terrible evils, but when they have increased, and come to extremities, and most persons are reduced to despair, then He works wondrously, and beyond all expectation, thus manifesting his own power, and training the patience of those who undergo these calamities. Do not therefore be cast down. For there is only one thing, Olympias, which is really terrible, only one real trial, and that is sin; and I have never ceased continually harping upon this theme; but as for all other things, plots, enmities, frauds, calumnies, insults, accusations, confiscation, exile, the keen sword of the enemy, the peril of the deep, warfare of the whole world, or anything else you like to name, they are but idle tales. For whatever the nature of these things may be they are transitory and perishable, and operate in a mortal body without doing any injury to the vigilant soul. Therefore the blessed Paul, desiring to prove the insignificance both of the pleasures and sorrows relating to this life, declared the whole truth in one sentence when he said—"For the things which are seen are temporal."[1] Why then dost thou fear temporal things which pass away like the stream of a river. For such is the nature of present things whether they be pleasant or painful. And another prophet compared all human prosperity not to grass, but to another material even more flimsy, describing the whole of it "as the flower of grass." For he did not single out any one part of it, as wealth alone, or luxury alone, or power, or honour; but having comprised all the things which are esteemed splendid amongst men under the one designa-

---

[1] 2 Cor. iv. 18.

tion of glory he said "all the glory of man is as the flower of grass."[1]

2. Nevertheless, you will say, adversity is a terrible thing and grievous to be borne. Yet look at it again compared with another image and then also learn to despise it. For the railings, and insults, and reproaches, and gibes inflicted by enemies, and their plots are compared to a worn-out garment, and moth-eaten wool when God says "Fear ye not the reproach of men, neither be ye afraid of their revilings, for they shall wax old as doth a garment, and like moth-eaten wool so shall they be consumed."[2] Therefore let none of these things which are happening trouble thee, but ceasing to invoke the aid of this or that person, and to run after shadows (for such are human alliances), do thou persistently call upon Jesus, whom thou servest, merely to bow his head; and in a moment of time all these evils will be dissolved. But if thou hast already called upon Him, and yet they have not been dissolved, such is the manner of God's dealing (for I will resume my former argument); He does not put down evils at the outset, but when they have grown to a head, when scarcely any form of the enemy's malice remains ungratified, then He suddenly converts all things to a state of tranquillity and conducts them to an unexpected settlement. For He is not only able to turn as many things as we expect and hope, to good, but many more, yea infinitely more. Wherefore also Paul saith "now to Him who is able to do exceeding abundantly above all that we ask or think."[3] Could He not, for example, have prevented the three children at the outset from falling into trial? But He did not choose to do this, thereby conferring great pain upon them. Therefore He suffered them to be delivered into the hands of barbarians, and the furnace to be heated to an immeasurable height and the wrath of the king to blaze even more fiercely than the furnace, and hands and feet to be bound with great severity and they themselves to be cast into the fire; and then, when all they who beheld despaired of their rescue, suddenly, and beyond all hope, the wonder-working power of God, the supreme artificer, was displayed, and shone forth with exceeding splendour. For the fire was bound, and the bondmen were released; and the furnace became a temple of prayer, a place of fountains and dew, of higher dignity than a royal court, and the very hairs of their head prevailed over that all devouring element which gets the better even of iron and stone, and masters every kind of substance. And a solemn song of universal praise was instituted there by these holy men inviting every kind of created thing to join in the wondrous melody; and they uttered hymns of thanksgiving to God for that they had been bound, and also burnt, as far at least as the malice of their enemies had power; that they had been exiles from their country, captives deprived of their liberty, wandering outcasts from city and home, sojourners in a strange and barbarous land; for all this was the outpouring of a grateful heart. And when the malicious devices of their enemies were perfected (for what further could they attempt after their death?) and the labours of the heroes were completed, and the garland of victory was woven, and their rewards were prepared and nothing more was wanting for their renown; then at last their calamities were brought to an end, and he who caused the furnace to be kindled, and delivered them over to that great punishment, became himself the panegyrist of those holy heroes, and the herald of God's marvellous deed, and everywhere throughout the world issued letters full of reverent praise, recording what had taken place, and becoming the faithful herald of the miracles wrought by the wonder-working God. For inasmuch as he had been an enemy and adversary what he wrote was above suspicion even in the opinion of enemies.

3. Dost thou see the abundance of resource belonging to God? His wisdom, His extraordinary power, His loving-kindness and care? Be not therefore dismayed or troubled but continue to give thanks to God for all things, praising, and invoking Him; beseeching and supplicating; even if countless tumults and troubles come upon thee, even if tempests are stirred up before thy eyes let none of these things disturb thee. For our Master is not baffled by the difficulty, even if all things are reduced to the extremity of ruin. For it is possible for Him to raise those who have fallen, to convert those who are in error, to set straight those who have been ensnared, to release those who have been laden with countless sins, and make them righteous, to quicken those who are dead, to restore lustre to decayed things, and freshness to those which have waxen old. For if He makes things which are not, come into being, and bestows existence on things which are nowhere by any means manifest, how much more will He rectify things which already exist. But you will say there are many who perish, many who are caught by snares. Many such things have indeed often taken place, yet afterwards have all received their appropriate correction, save some few who have remained in an incurable condition, even after the change in their circumstances. Why are you troubled and distracted because such a person is cast out and

---

[1] Is. xl. 6.   [2] Is. l. 7, 8.   [3] Ephes. iii. 20.

such another is put into his place? Christ was crucified and the release of Barabbas the robber was demanded, and the depraved populace clamoured for the preservation of the murderer rather than of the Saviour and benefactor. How many think you then stumbled at these things? how many were destroyed? But I must carry my argument yet further back. Did not He who was crucified become immediately after his birth a wanderer and a fugitive? was He not from the very cradle removed with the whole household into a strange land, taking that long journey into a barbarous region? And this removal gave occasion to torrents of blood, and cruel murder and slaughter, and all the children of tender age were cut to pieces just as if they had been soldiers arrayed in battle, and infants torn from the breast were handed over to death, and even when the milk was in their throats, the sword was driven through their necks. What could be more distressing than this tragedy? And these things were done by him who sought to destroy Jesus, yet the long-suffering God endured this tragical cruelty, which caused so much bloodshed, and forbore to prevent it although He had the power, displaying his long-suffering for some inscrutably wise purpose. And when Jesus had returned from the foreign land and was grown up, war was rekindled against him on every side. First of all the disciples of John were envious of Him and tried to slander Him, although John himself behaved reverently to Him, and they said "He who was with thee beyond Jordan, behold the same baptizeth and all men come to Him."[1] For these were the words of men who were already irritated, and agitated by ill-will, and consumed by that passion. For the same reason also one of the disciples who said these things disputed with a certain Jew and raised a contentious argument about purifying, comparing one kind of baptism with another, the baptism of John with that of the disciples of Christ. "For there arose" it is said, "a questioning on the part of John's disciples with a certain Jew about purifying."[2] And when He began to work miracles how many calumniators He had! Some called Him a Samaritan and demoniac saying "Thou art a Samaritan and hast a Devil"[3] others "a deceiver," saying "This man is not of God but deceiveth the multitude"[4] others "a sorcerer" saying "He casteth out devils through Beelzebub the prince of the Devils"[5] and they continually said these things against Him and called Him an adversary of God, and a gluttonous, and greedy man, and a drunkard, and a friend of the wicked and depraved. "For" He said, "the Son of man came eating and drinking and they say behold a gluttonous man and a winebibber, a friend of publicans and sinners."[6] And when he was conversing with the harlot they called Him a false prophet; "For had He been a prophet," one said, "He would have known who this woman is which speaketh unto Him;"[7] in fact every day they sharpened their teeth against Him. And not only did the Jews thus oppose Him, but even those who were reputed to be his brethren were not sincerely attached to Him, but even out of his own family opposition was kindled against Him. See at least how they also themselves were perverted, from the evangelist adding the remark "for neither did His brethren believe on Him."[8]

4. But since you call to mind many who were offended and went astray, how many of the disciples do you suppose were offended at the time of the crucifixion? One betrayed Him, the others took to flight, one denied Him, and when all had abandoned Him He was led away bound without companions. How many then think you who had lately seen Him working His miracles, raising the dead, cleansing lepers, casting out devils, multiplying loaves, and doing all other kinds of wonderful deeds, were offended at that season, when they beheld Him led away and bound, surrounded by common soldiers, and followed by Jewish priests making a tumult and uproar; alone in the midst hemmed in by all his enemies, and the traitor standing by and exulting in his deed? And what was the effect think you when He was being scourged? and probably a vast multitude was present. For it was an illustrious festival which brought all together, and this drama of iniquity was enacted in the capital city, and in the very middle of the day. How many think you who were present then were offended when they saw Him bound, scourged, streaming with blood, examined before the governor's tribunal, and not one of His disciples standing by? What was the effect again when He was subjected to those manifold kinds of mockery, successively repeated, when they crowned Him with thorns, then arrayed Him in a gorgeous robe, then put a reed in His hand, then fell down and worshipped Him, setting in motion every species of ribaldry and derision? How many think you were offended, how many bewildered, how many perplexed when they smote Him on the cheek and said "prophesy unto us thou Christ who is He that smote thee?"[9] and when they led

---

[1] John iii. 26.
[2] John ii. 25. St. Chrysostom here follows the same reading which is found in the three oldest extant MSS. of the New Testament, the Sinaitic, Vatican and Alexandrian. The *textus receptus* has μετὰ Ἰουδαίων " with the Jews" instead of μετὰ Ἰουδαίου " with a Jew."
[3] John viii. 48. [4] John vii. 12. [5] Matt. ix. 34.
[6] Luke vii. 34. [7] Luke vii. 39.
[8] John vii. 5. [9] Matt. xxvi. 28.

Him hither and thither, and spent the whole day in scoffs and abuse, and ribaldry and derision in the midst of the Jewish assembly? and when the servant of the High-Priest dealt Him a blow; and when the soldiers parted His garments amongst them and when He was led up to the cross, having the marks of the scourge upon His back, and was fastened to the wood, how many think you were offended? For not even then were those savage beasts softened, but became more furious than before, and the tragedy became more intense, and the ribaldry increased. For some said "Ah! thou that destroyest the temple, and in three days buildest it up;"[1] and some, "He saved others, Himself He cannot save."[2]

And others said "If thou art the Son of God come down from the cross and we will believe thee."[3]

Again when they insulted Him by offering Him gall and vinegar on the sponge how many think you were offended? or when the robbers reviled Him? or when as I have already said, they made that dreadful and monstrous assertion that the robber and housebreaker, the man laden with the crime of murder deserved to be released rather than Jesus, and having received permission from the judge to make their choice preferred Barabbas, desiring not only to crucify Christ, but also to involve Him in infamy? For they thought that by these means they should be able to manufacture the belief that He was worse than the robber, and such a great transgressor that neither on the plea of mercy, nor of the privilege of the Festival was it possible to save Him. For they did everything with a view to slander His fame; which also was the reason why they crucified the two robbers with Him. Nevertheless the truth was not obscured, but shone forth all the more clearly. And they accused Him of usurping kingly power saying "Every one who maketh himself a king is not a friend of Cæsar"[4] bringing this charge of usurpation against one who had not where to lay his head. Moreover they brought a calumnious accusation of blasphemy against Him. For the High Priest rent his clothes saying "He hath spoken blasphemy; what further need have we of witnesses?"[5] And what was the nature of his death? was it not a violent one? was it not the death of capital offenders? of execrable criminals? was it not of the vilest kind? was it not the death of those who have perpetrated the worst offences, and are not worthy to draw even their last breath upon the earth? And then as to the manner of his burial, was it not accomplished as a matter of favour? For a certain one came and begged for his body. Thus not even he who buried Him belonged to his own friends, to those whom He had benefited, to his disciples, to those who had enjoyed such free and salutary intercourse with Him, for all had taken to flight, all had hurried away from Him. And that base suspicion which his enemies contrived in consequence of the resurrection when they said "His disciples came and stole Him"[6] how many think you were offended, how many for a time upset by that? For the story prevailed at that time, although it was a fabrication, and was bought for money; nevertheless it held its ground amongst some people, after the seals (of the sepulchre were broken)[7] after the manifest appearance of the truth. For the multitude did not know the prediction of the resurrection (and no wonder), inasmuch as even his disciples did not understand it; for we read "they did not know that He must rise again from the dead."[8] How many therefore think you were offended in those days? And yet the long-suffering God patiently endured, ordering all things according to His own inscrutable wisdom.

5. Then again after those days the disciples continued to live in hiding and secrecy, being fugitives full of fear and trembling, continually shifting from place to place, and even when they began to appear after fifty days, and to work miracles, they did not enjoy perfect security; but even after those events there were innumerable stumbling-blocks to offend the weaker brethren, when they were scourged, when the Church was distressed, when they themselves were driven away, and their enemies had the upper hand in many places, and raised tumults. For when they had acquired much confidence by means of the miracles which they wrought, then the death of Stephen again caused a severe persecution, and dispersed them all, and involved the Church in confusion; and the disciples were again alarmed, fugitive, and distressed. And yet the Church continually grew, when it flourished by means of the signs which were wrought and became illustrious from the manner of its introduction. One disciple for example was let down through a window, and so escaped the hands of the ruler; others were brought out of prison by an angel and so released from their fetters; others were received into the houses of common people and artisans when they were driven out by those in authority; they were courteously treated in every way, by female sellers of purple, by tentmakers, and

---

[1] Matt. xxvii. 40. [2] Matt. xxvii. 42. [3] Matt. xxvii. 40.
[4] John xix. 12. The latter part of the sentence, which is not correctly quoted, was probably suggested by the words immediately preceding, "if thou let this man go, thou art not Cæsar's friend." [5] Matt. xxvi. 65.

[6] Matt. xxviii. 13.
[7] These words in brackets are not in the original, but must be understood, to make sense of the passage. [8] John xx. 9.

tanners dwelling in the outskirts of the cities, and by the sea shore. Frequently moreover they did not dare to appear in the middle of the towns; and if they did venture there themselves their entertainers did not. And thus amidst alternate trials, and respites from trial, the fabric of the Church was wrought, and they who once stumbled were afterwards set upright, and they who wandered away were brought back, and the ruined places were built up more firmly than before. For this cause when Paul prayed that the preaching of the word might proceed by a smooth course only, God rich in wisdom and resource did not yield to His disciple; nay even when many times invoked he would not consent but said "my grace is sufficient for thee, for my strength is made perfect in weakness."[1] If then even now you will reckon up the good things with the painful, you will see that many events have occurred which if not positive signs and wonders do yet resemble signs, and are unspeakable proofs of the great providence and succour of God. But that you may not hear everything from me without any trouble, I leave this as thy task, that you may reckon up everything accurately and compare them with the misfortunes, and by occupying yourself with this good employment may divert your mind from despondency; for you will derive much consolation from this work.

Pray say many kind words from me to all your blessed household. May you continue in good health and good spirits, most reverend and divinely favoured lady.

If you wish me to write long letters inform me of this, and pray do not deceive me by saying that you have thrown off all despondency, and are enjoying a season of rest. For letters are a remedy of the proper kind to produce great cheerfulness in thee, and you will continually see letters from me. And when you write to me again do not say "I have much comfort from your letters, for this I know of myself, but tell me that you have as much as I wish you to have, that you are not confounded with sorrow, that you do not pass your time in weeping, but in serenity and cheerfulness.

TO OLYMPIAS.

Do not be anxious on my behalf, nor rack yourself with solicitude, on account of the severity of the winter, and the weakness of my digestion, and the incursions of the Isaurians. For the winter is only what it is wont to be in Armenia; nothing more need be said about it; and it does not very seriously injure me. For in anticipation of these things I have devised many plans for averting the mischief which might arise from them; keeping up a constant fire, setting screens about the chamber in which I live, using a large number of rugs, and staying always indoors. This indeed is irksome to me, if it were not for the benefit to be derived; for as long as I remain indoors I am not severely distressed by the cold; but if I am compelled to go out a little, and come in contact with the outer air, I suffer no small damage. Wherefore I beseech thee dear lady, and entreat thee as a very great favour to pay great attention to the restoration of thy bodily health. For dejection causes sickness; and when the body is exhausted and enfeebled, and remains in a neglected condition, deprived of the assistance of physicians, and of a wholesome climate, and an abundant supply of the necessaries of life, consider how great an aggravation of distress is occasioned thereby. Wherefore I beseech you, dear lady, to employ various and skilled physicians, and to take medicines which avail to correct these conditions. For a few days ago when I suffered from a tendency to vomiting, owing to the state of the atmosphere, I had recourse amongst other remedies to the drug which was sent me by my most discreet mistress Syncletion, and I found that no more than three days' application of it cured my infirmity. I beseech you therefore to make use of this remedy also yourself and to arrange that some more of it may be sent to me. For having again felt somewhat upset, I again had recourse to it, and completely cured my disorder; for it allays the deep internal inflammation, draws out moisture on the skin, causes a moderate degree of warmth, infuses no little vigor, and excites an appetite for food; and all these effects I experienced in the course of a few days. Let then my most honoured lord the Count Theophilus be exhorted to take means to send some of this to me again. And do not be distressed at my wintering here, for I am in a much more comfortable and sounder state of health than I was last year; so that if you also would take the requisite care of yourself, you would be in a far more satisfactory condition. Now if you say that your ailments have been produced by despondency how is it that you again ask for letters from me, seeing that you have not derived any benefit from them in the direction of cheerfulness, but have sunk so deeply under the tyranny of despondency as even to desire to depart out of this world. Are you ignorant how great a reward even of sickness awaits one who has a thankful spirit? Have I not often, both in person, and through letters, dis-

---

[1] 2 Cor. xii. 9.

coursed to you concerning this theme? But since the pressure of business perhaps, or the peculiar nature of your sickness, and the quick succession of changes in your condition do not permit you to retain what I have said constantly and clearly in your mind, listen once more whilst I try to heal the wounds of thy despondency by repeating the same incantations: "for to write the same things," it is said, "to me indeed is not grievous, and for you it is safe."[1]

2. What is it then which I say and write? Nothing, Olympias, redounds so much to the credit of any one as patient endurance in suffering. For this is indeed the queen of virtues, and the perfection of crowns; and as it excels all other forms of righteousness, so this particular species of it is more glorious than the rest. Perhaps what I have said seems obscure; I will therefore try to make it clearer. What then is it that I affirm? Not the spoliation of goods, even if one were to be stripped bare of all one's' possessions, not the loss of honours, nor expulsion from one's country, and transportation to a distant land, nor the strain of labour and toil, nor imprisonment, and bondage, nor reproaches, and abuse, and scoffings (not indeed that you are to think the courageous endurance of such things a slight kind of fortitude, as Jeremiah that great and eminent prophet proves who was not a little distressed by this kind of trial);[2] yet not even this, nor the loss of children, even should they be torn from us in one fell swoop, nor the perpetual assaults of enemies, nor anything else of that nature, no, nor even the head and crown of things accounted painful, namely death, terrible and loathsome though it be, is so oppressive as infirmity of body. And this is proved by the greatest hero of endurance,[3] who, when he was encompassed by bodily sickness, thought death would be a release from the calamities which were depressing him; and when he underwent all the other sufferings, was not sensible of them, although he received blow after blow, and at last a deadly one. For it was no slight matter, but rather an evidence of the most malignant cruelty on the part of his enemy in dealing with one who was no novice in suffering, nor entering the lists for the first time, but already exhausted with the frequent repetition of assaults, to inflict upon him that deadly blow, the destruction of his children, so cruelly inflicted moreover that all of either sex were destroyed at the same moment in early youth and by a violent end, and so instantaneous was their death that it involved their burial also. For their father neither saw them laid upon a bed, nor kissed their hands, nor heard their last words, nor touched their hands and knees, nor did he shut their mouths, or close their eyes when they were about to die, acts which tend not a little to console parents who are being parted from their children; neither did he follow some of them to burial, and find others on his return home to console him for those who had departed; but he heard that as they were reclining on their couches at a banquet, a banquet full of love, not of excess, a table of brotherly kindness, they were all overwhelmed; and blood, and wine, the cups and the ceiling, the table, and the dust, and the limbs of his children, were all mingled together. Nevertheless when he heard these things, and others before these which were also distressing; for they too had perished in a distressing way; flocks and whole herds had been destroyed, the latter having been consumed by fire sent down from heaven, (so said the evil messenger of this tragedy,) and the former having been all seized together by various enemies, and cut to pieces as well as the shepherds themselves; nevertheless I say when he saw this great storm stirred up in a brief moment of time affecting his lands, his house, his cattle, and his children, when he saw billow following billow, and long lines of rocks, and the darkness was profound, and the surging waves unbearable, even then he was not tortured by despondency, and scarcely seemed to feel the things which had happened, save so far as he was a man and a father. But when he was delivered over to sickness and sores, then did he also long for death, then did he also bewail himself and lament, so that you may understand how this kind of suffering is more severe than all others, and this form of patience the highest of all. Nor is the Devil himself unaware of this fact; for when after having set in motion all these trials he perceived that the hero remained untroubled and undismayed he rushed to this as the greatest contest of all, saying that all the other calamities were bearable, as loss of child, or property, or anything else (for this is what is meant by the expression "skin for skin"[4]) but the deadly blow was when pain was inflicted on a man's body. And therefore when he had been worsted after this contest, he had no longer a word to utter, although on former occasions he had made the most strenuous and shameless resistance. In this instance however he found that he could not invent any further shameless device, but hid his face and retreated.

3. Think not however that it is an excuse

---

[1] Phil iii. 1. [2] Jer. xv. [3] Sc. Job. [4] Job ii. 4.

to justify you in desiring death, that Job desired it, not being able to bear his sufferings. For consider the time when he desired it, and the disposition of his circumstances—the law was not given, the prophets had not appeared, grace had not been shed forth as it was afterwards, nor had he the advantage of any other kind of philosophy. For as a proof that more is demanded from us than from those who lived then, and that harder tasks are assigned to us, listen to Christ, when He says "Except your righteousness exceed the righteousness of the Scribes and Pharisees ye shall in no case enter into the kingdom of Heaven."[1] Do not think therefore that to pray for death now is exempt from blame, but hearken to the voice of St. Paul when he says "To depart and to be with Christ is far better, but to abide in the flesh is more necessary for your sake."[2] For in proportion as the strain of the affliction is increased are the garlands of victory multiplied; in proportion as the gold is heated does it become purified, the longer the merchant makes his voyage on the sea, the larger is the freight which he collects. Do not then think that the labour now allotted to you is a slight one, but rather that it is higher than all which you have undergone, I mean that which consists in infirmity of body. For in the case of Lazarus[3] (and although I may have often said this to you, it nowise hinders me from saying it now) this bodily infirmity availed for his salvation; and he departed to the bosom of the man who possessed a dwelling which he shared with all who passed by,[4] and was continually shifting his home on account of God's command, and sacrificed his own son, his only begotten, who had been given him in extreme old age; although Lazarus had done none of these things yet he obtained this blessing inasmuch as he cheerfully endured poverty, and infirmity, and friendlessness. For this is so great a good to those who bear anything bravely that it releases any one who may have committed the greatest sins from the heaviest burden of them; or if any one is an upright and just man it becomes an additional ground of the greatest confidence. For it is a bright wreath of victory for the just, shining far above the brightness of the sun, and it is the greatest means of purification for those who have sinned. On this account Paul delivers the man who had made the incestuous marriage to "destruction of the flesh," purifying him by this means. For as a proof that what was done did purify even from so great a stain hear his words "that his spirit may be saved in the day of the Lord."[5] And when he was accusing others of another very awful sin, that of partaking unworthily of the holy table and those secret mysteries, and had said that such a person will be "guilty of the body and blood of the Lord,"[6] observe how he says that they also are purified from that grievous stain—"therefore are many weak and sickly among you."[7] And then by way of proving that they will not be confined to this condition of punishment, but that some profit will be derived from it, namely release from the penalties to which the sin is liable, he added: "for if we would judge ourselves, we should not be judged. But now when we are judged, we are chastened of the Lord, that we should not be condemned with the world."[8] Moreover that they who have lived very righteously derive much benefit from such chastisement is plain from the case of Job, who was more illustrious after it than before, and from the case of Timothy, who although he was such a good man, and entrusted with such an important ministry, and made the circuit of the world with Paul passed not two or three days, nor ten or twenty, or a hundred, but many in succession in ill health, his body being very seriously enfeebled. Paul shows this where he said "Use a little wine for thy stomach's sake, and thine often infirmities."[9] And he who raised the dead did not cure this man's infirmity, but left him in the furnace of his sickness so that he might therefrom contract a very great abundance of confidence. For the lessons which Paul himself had enjoyed from his Master, and the training which he had received from Him, he imparted to his disciple. For although he was not subjected to bodily infirmity, yet he was buffeted by trials not less severe, which inflicted much physical pain. "For there was given unto me" he says "a thorn in the flesh, a messenger of Satan to buffet me"[10] meaning by this the blows, the bonds, the chains, the imprisonments, the being dragged about, and maltreated, and tortured by the scourges of public executioners. Wherefore also being unable to bear the pain occasioned to the body by these things "for this I besought the Lord thrice (thrice here meaning many times) that I might be delivered from this thorn." And then when he did not obtain his petition, having learned the benefit of the trial, he held his peace, and rejoiced at the things which happened unto him.

Therefore even if you remain at home, and are set fast in bed, do not consider your life

---

[1] Matt. v. 20.   [2] Phil. i. 23, 24.   [3] Luke xvi.
[4] Referring to the hospitality of Abraham as illustrated by his reception of the divine visitors, Gen. xviii.
[5] 1 Cor. v. 5.
[6] 1 Cor. xi. 27.   [7] 1 Cor. xi. 30.
[8] 1 Cor. xi. 31, 32.   [9] 1 Tim. v. 23.
[10] 2 Cor. xii. 7. The word rendered "thorn" more properly signifies a "stake;" and the expression, especially when compared with Gal. iv. 14, would rather seem to indicate some painful bodily infirmity, perhaps weakness of eyesight (see Gal. iv. 19) than the indignities to which he was subjected.

an idle one; for you undergo more severe pains than those who are dragged, and maltreated, and tortured by executioners, inasmuch as in this excessive infirmity of yours you have a perpetual executioner residing with you.

4. Do not then now desire death, nor neglect the means of cure; for indeed this would not be safe. On this account Paul also exhorts Timothy to take the greatest care of himself. As regards infirmity then enough has now been said. But if it is separation from me which causes your despondency expect release from this. And I have not said this now merely to encourage you, but I am sure that it really will be the case. For if it were not destined to happen, I should long ago, so at least I think, have departed from this world, considering the trials which have been inflicted on me. For to pass over all that occurred in Constantinople, after my departure thence, you may understand what sufferings I endured on that long and cruel journey, most of which were sufficient to produce death; what I endured after my arrival here, after my removal from Cucusus, and after my sojourn in Arabissus. Yet I have survived all these things, and now I am in sound health, and great security, so that all Armenians are astonished that with such a feeble and flimsy frame as mine I can support such an intolerable amount of cold, or that I can breathe at all, when those who are habituated to the winter are suffering from it in no common degree. Nevertheless I have remained uninjured up to the present day, having escaped the hands of robbers who have repeatedly attacked us, and yet in daily want of the necessaries of life, and deprived of the use of a bath; and although since my sojourn here I have been constantly without this luxury I am now so established in the habit that I do not even long for the comfort to be derived from it, but am in sounder health than before. And neither the inclemency of the climate, nor the desolation of the region, nor the scarcity of provisions, nor the lack of attendants, nor the unskillfulness of physicians, nor the deprivation of the bath, nor perpetual confinement in one chamber as in a prison, and the impossibility of moving about which I always used continually to need, nor perpetual contact with fire and smoke, nor fear of robbers, nor a constant state of siege, nor anything else of this kind has got the better of me; on the contrary I am in a sounder condition of health than I was elsewhere, although I then received great care and attention. Taking all these things then into consideration pray shake off the despondency which now oppresses you, and do not exact inordinate and cruel penances from yourself. I sent you the treatise which I have lately written, that "no one can harm the man who does not injure himself,"[1] and the letter which I now send your honour contends for the same position. I beg you therefore to go over it constantly, and if your health permits you, recite it aloud. For if you will, it may prove an effectual remedy for you. But if you are contentious with me, and do not try to cure yourself, and will not rouse yourself from these dismal swamps of despondency in spite of the unlimited amount of advice and exhortation which you enjoy I shall not on my part readily consent to send you frequent and long letters, if you are not to derive any benefit in the way of cheerfulness from them. How then shall I know this? not by your merely saying so, but by a practical proof, inasmuch as you lately affirmed that it was nothing but despondency which caused this sickness of yours. Since then you have yourself made this confession I shall not believe that you have got rid of your despondency unless you have got rid of your bodily infirmity. For if it is the former which causes your disorder, as you say in your letter, it is obvious that when that has been dispersed the other will be removed at the same time, and when the root has been plucked up, the branches perish with it;—and if the branches continue flowering and flourishing, and producing an unnatural amount of fruit I cannot believe that you have been set free from the root of your distress. Therefore do not show me words but facts, and, if you get well, you will see letters sent to you again exceeding the limits of former communications. Deem it then no small consolation that I am alive, and in good health, and that in the midst of such circumstances I have been set free from sickness and infirmity, which, as I know, is a great annoyance and vexation to my enemies. It follows therefore that you should deem this the greatest encouragement, and the crown of your consolation. Do not call your household desolate, which has now a higher place assigned to it in Heaven by reason of the sufferings which it endures. I was grievously distressed on account of Pelagius the monk.[2] Consider therefore what great rewards they deserve who bravely hold their ground, when men who pass their time in such a habit of discipline and endurance are found susceptible of degradation.

---

[1] Translated in this volume, see pages 270–284.
[2] If Pelagius the heresiarch were the person here alluded to, this would be the earliest historical notice of him. But as Pelagius was in Rome from 401 to 409, during which period he is mentioned with respect by his contemporaries, and this letter must have been written not later than 405 or 406, the identification is impossible.

TO OLYMPIAS.

Having risen from the very gates of death I address this letter to the discreet lady; and I am very glad that thy servants have met me just as I am anchoring at last in harbour. For had they met me when I was still tossing on the open sea, and experiencing the cruel waves of bodily sickness, it would not have been easy for me to deceive your cautious spirit, by sending good tidings instead of sorrowful. For the winter, which has become more than commonly severe, brought on a storm of internal disorder even more distressing, and during the last two months I have been no better than one dead, nay worse. For I had just enough life to be sensible of the horrors which encircled me, and day and dawn and noon were all one night to me as I spent all my time closely confined to my bed, and in spite of endless contrivances I could not shake off the pernicious effects of the cold; but although I kept a fire burning, and endured a most unpleasant amount of smoke, and remained cooped up in one chamber, covered with any quantity of wraps, and not daring to set a foot outside the threshold I underwent extreme sufferings, perpetual vomiting supervening on headache, loss of appetite, and constant sleeplessness. Thus restlessly did I pass through my long dark sea of troubles But not to distress thy mind by dwelling upon my miseries, from all of them I am now relieved. For as soon as spring approached, and a little change in the temperature took place, all my troubles spontaneously vanished. Nevertheless I still require great care as regards diet; therefore I put only a light load on my stomach, so that it may be able to digest it easily. But it has occasioned me no little concern to learn that my discreet mistress was brought to the verge of death. Nevertheless in consideraton of my great affection, and anxiety, and solicitude for your welfare I was relieved from this care, even before the arrival of your letters, many persons having come from thence who brought me tidings of your restoration to health.

And now I am exceedingly glad and delighted to hear, not only that you have been released from your infirmity, but above all that you bear the things which befall you so bravely, calling them all but an idle tale; and, which is indeed a greater matter, that you have applied this name even to your bodily infirmity, which is an evidence of a robust spirit, rich in the fruit of courage. For not only to bear misfortunes bravely but to be actually insensible to them, to overlook them, and with such little exertion to wreathe your brows with the garland prize of patience, neither labouring, nor toiling, neither feeling distress nor causing it to others, but as it were leaping and dancing for joy all the while, this is indeed a proof of the most finished philosophy.[1] Therefore I rejoice, and leap for joy, I am in a flutter of delight, I am insensible to my present loneliness, and the other troubles which surround me, being cheered, and brightened, and not a little proud on account of your greatness of soul, and the repeated victories which you have won, and this, not only for your own sake, but also for the sake of that large and populous city,[2] where you are like a tower, a haven, and a wall of defence, speaking in the eloquent voice of example, and through your sufferings instructing either sex to strip readily for these contests, and descend into the lists with all courage, and cheerfully bear the toils which such contests involve. And the wonder is that without thrusting yourself into the forum, or occupying the public centres of the city, but sitting all the while in a small house and confined chamber you serve and anoint the combatants for the contest, and whilst the sea is thus raging round you, and the billows are rising to a crest, and crags and reefs, and rocky ledges and fierce monsters appear on every side, and everything is shrouded in the most profound darkness you, setting the sails of patience, float on with great serenity, as if it was noonday, and calm weather, and a favourable breeze wafting you on, and so far from being overwhelmed by this grievous tempest are not even sprinkled by the spray; and very naturally so; such is the force of virtue as a rudder. Now merchants and pilots, and sailors and voyagers when they see clouds gathering up, or fierce winds rushing down upon them, or the breakers seething with an abundance of foam keep their vessels moored inside harbour; and if they chance to be tempest-tossed in the open sea they do their best, and devise every means to bring their ship to some anchorage, or island or shore. But you, although such innumerable winds, and fierce waves burst upon you together, and the sea is heaved up from its very depths owing to the severity of the storm, and some are submerged, others floating dead upon the water, others drifting naked upon planks, you plunging into the mid ocean of calamities call all these things an idle tale, sailing on with a favourable breeze in the midst of the tempest; and naturally so; for pilots, even if they are infinitely wise in that science, nevertheless have not skill sufficient to withstand every kind

---
[1] Here, as often elsewhere, St. Chrysostom uses the word φιλοσοφία in the sense of Christian training and moral discipline. The monastic form of life was commonly called ἡ φιλοσοφία, the "philosophy."
[2] Sc. Constantinople.

of storm; consequently they often shrink from doing battle with the waves. But the science which you have is superior to every kind of storm—the power of a philosophic soul—which is stronger than ten thousand armies, more powerful than arms, and more secure than towers and bulwarks. For the arms, and bulwarks, and towers which soldiers have, are serviceable for the security of the body only, and this not always, nor in every way; but there are times when all these resources are baffled, and leave those who fly to them for refuge destitute of protection. But thy powers do not repel the weapons of barbarians, nor the devices of hostile men, nor any assaults and stratagems of that kind, but they have trampled under foot the constraining forces of nature, put down their tyranny and levelled their citadel. And whilst ceaselessly contending with demons, you have won countless victories, yet have not received a single blow, but stand unwounded in the midst of a storm of darts and turn the spears which are hurled at you back upon those who discharge them. Such is the wisdom of your art; by the sufferings which you undergo you take vengeance on those who inflict them; by the plots of which you are the subject you put your enemies to pain, possessing in their malice the best foundation for the materials of fame. And you, knowing these things well yourself, and having gained perception by experience, naturally call them all an idle tale. For how, pray, should you not call them by that name, possessing as you do a mortal body, and yet despising death as if you were hastening to quit a foreign country, and return to your own land; a chronic sufferer from the most severe infirmity, and yet more cheerfully disposed than the thriving and robust, not depressed by insults, nor elated by honours and glory, the latter being a cause of infinite mischief to many who after an illustrious career in the priesthood, and after reaching extreme old age, and the most venerable hoar hairs, have fallen into disgrace on this account, and become a common spectacle of derision for those who wish to make merry. But you on the contrary, woman as you are, clothed with a fragile body, and subject to these severe attacks, have not only avoided falling into such a condition yourself, but have prevented many others from so doing. They indeed before they had advanced far in the contest, even at the very outset and starting point, have been overthrown; whereas you, after having gone countless times round the farther turning post, have won a prize in every course, after playing your part in manifold kinds of wrestling and combats. And very naturally so; for the wrestlings of virtue do not depend upon age, or bodily strength, but only on the spirit and the disposition. Thus women have been crowned victors, while men have been upset: so also boys have been proclaimed conquerors, while aged men have been put to shame. It is indeed always fitting to admire those who pursue virtue, but especially when some are found to cling to it at a time when many are deserting it. Therefore, my sweet lady, you deserve superlative admiration, inasmuch as after so many men, women, and aged persons who seemed to enjoy the greatest reputation have been turned to flight, all lying prostrate before the eyes of the world, and this not after a severe onslaught, nor any alarming muster of the enemy's force, but overthrown before the encounter and worsted before the struggle, you on the contrary after so many battles and such large muster of the enemy are so far from being unstrung, or dismayed by the number of your adversities, that you are all the more vigorous, and the increase of the contest gives you an increase of strength. For the recollection of what has been already achieved becomes the ground of cheerfulness, and joy, and greater zeal. Therefore I rejoice, and leap for joy; for I will not cease repeating this, and taking about with me everywhere the material of my joy; so that although my separation from you distresses you, yet you have this very great consolation arising from your successful exploits; for I also who am banished to so great a distance gain no small cheerfulness from this cause,—I mean your courage.

TO OLYMPIAS.

WHY do you lament? why do you belabour yourself, and demand of yourself a punishment which your enemies were not able to demand from you, having thus abandoned your soul to the tyranny of dejection? For the letters which you sent to me by the hands of Patricius have discovered to me the wounds which have been inflicted on your mind. Wherefore also I am very sorrowful and much distressed that when you ought to be using every exertion and making it your business to expel dejection from your soul, you go about collecting distressing thoughts, even inventing things (so you say) which do not exist, and tearing yourself to pieces for no purpose, and to your very great injury. For why are you grieved because you could not remove me from Cucusus? Yet indeed, as far as you were concerned, you did remove me, having made every exertion and endeavour for this purpose. And even if it has not been actually accomplished you ought not to be vexed on that account. For perhaps it seemed good to God that I should be set to run the longer double course,[1] in order that the garland of victory might be rendered more glorious. Why then are you vexed on account of these things, in consequence of which my fame is spread abroad, when you ought to leap and dance for joy and bind wreaths upon your brow, because I have been deemed worthy of so great an honour which far exceeds my merits? Is it the desolation of this place which grieves you? Yet what can be pleasanter than my sojourn here? I have quietness, and tranquillity, plenty of leisure and good bodily health. For although the town has neither market-place nor market that is nothing to me. For all things are poured abundantly upon me as out of a flowing spring. I find my lord the Bishop here and my lord Dioscorus are constantly employed in providing for my refreshment. And the good Patricius will tell you that as far as my sojourn here is concerned I pass my time cheerfully and gladly, surrounded by attention. But if you lament the events which occurred in Cæsarea, here again your conduct is unworthy of yourself. For there also bright garlands of victory were woven for me, inasmuch as all were proclaiming and publishing my praises, and expressing wonder and astonishment at the ill-treatment to which I had been subjected followed by expulsion. Meanwhile however do not let any one know these things, although they are the theme of much gossip. For my lord Pœanius has disclosed to me that the presbyters of Pharetrius himself[2] have arrived on the spot, who declare that they were in communion with me and had no communication or intercourse or partnership with my adversaries. Therefore to avoid upsetting them do not let any one know these things. For certainly the things which befell me were very grievous: and if I had not suffered any other distress the events which happened there would have sufficed to procure innumerable rewards for me: so extreme was the danger which I encountered. Now I beseech you to keep these matters secret, and so I will give you a short account of them, not in order to grieve you but rather to make you glad. For herein consists the material of my gain, herein consists my wealth, herein the means of getting rid of my sins—that my journey is continually encompassed by trials of this kind, and that they are inflicted upon me by persons from whom they were quite unexpected. For when I was about to enter the region of Cappadocia, having escaped from that man of Galatia, who nearly threatened me with death,[3] many persons met me on the way saying " the lord Pharetrius is awaiting you, and going about in all directions for fear of missing the pleasure of meeting you, and making every possible endeavour to see you, and embrace you, and show you all manner of affectionate regard; and he has set the monasteries of men and women in motion for this purpose. Now when I heard these things I did not expect that any of them would really take place, but formed an impression in my own mind precisely the reverse: but of this I said nothing to any of those who brought me this message.

2. Now when I arrived late one evening at Cæsarea, in an exhausted and worn-out condition, being in the very height of a burning fever, faint and suffering to the last degree, I lighted upon an inn situated just at the outskirts of the city, and took great pains to find some physicians and allay this fiery fever; for it was now the height of my tertian malady. And in addition to this there was the fatigue of the journey, the toil, the strain, the total absence of attendants, the difficulty of getting supplies, the want of a physician, the wasting effects of toil, and heat and sleeplessness; thus I was well nigh a dead man when I entered the city. Then indeed I was visited by the whole body of the clergy, and the people, monks, nuns, physicians, and I had the benefit of great attention, as all paid me every kind of ministration and assistance. Yet even thus, being oppressed by the lethargy arising from the feverish heat I was in an extremely distressed condition. At length by degrees the malady was coming to an end and abating. Pharetrius however nowhere appeared; but waited for my departure, I know not with what purpose in view. When then I saw that my disorder had slightly abated I began to form plans for my journey so as to reach Cucusus, and enjoy a little repose after the calamities of the way. And whilst I was thus situated it was suddenly announced that the Isaurians[4] in countless multitudes were overrunning the district of Cæsarea, and had burnt a large village, and were most violently disposed. The tribune, having heard this, took the soldiers which he had and went out. For they were afraid lest the enemy should make an assault also upon

---

[1] The single course in the Grecian games was the stadium, so called because it was a stade in length. In the double course the runner had to turn the post at the extremity of the stadium and run back again.
[2] Pharetrius was Bishop of Cæsarea, and, as the sequel shows, a malicious enemy of Chrysostom.
[3] Probably Leontius, Archbishop of Ancyra in Galatia, a bitter adversary of Chrysostom.
[4] A predatory race of barbarians who inhabited the fastnesses of Mount Taurus.

the city, and all were in terror, and in an agony of alarm the very soil of their country being in jeopardy, so that even the old men undertook the defence of the walls. While affairs were in this condition suddenly towards dawn a rabble[1] of monks (for so I must call them, indicating their frenzy by the expression) rushed up to the house where we were, threatening to set fire to it, and to treat us with the utmost violence unless we turned out of it. And neither the fear of the Isaurians, nor my own infirmity which was so grievously afflicting me, nor anything else made them more reasonable, but they pressed on, animated by such fierce rage that even the proconsular soldiers were terrified. For they kept threatening them with blows and boasted that they had shamefully beaten many of the proconsular soldiers. The soldiers having heard these things, sought refuge with me, and entreated and beseeched me, saying "even if we are to fall into the hands of the Isaurians deliver us from these wild beasts." When the governor heard this he hastened down to the house intending to succour me. But the monks would not pay any heed to his exhortations, and in fact he was powerless. Perceiving the great strait in which affairs were placed and not daring to advise me either to go out to certain death, or on the other hand to stay indoors, owing to the excessive fury of these men, he sent to Pharetrius beseeching him to grant a few days respite on account of my infirmity and the impending danger. But even then nothing was effected, and on the morrow the monks arrived even fiercer than before, and none of the presbyters dared to stand by me and help me, but covered with shame and blushes (for they said that these things were done by the instructions of Pharetrius) they concealed themselves and lay hid, not responding even when I called them. What need to make a long story? Although such great terrors were imminent, and death well nigh a certainty, and the fever was oppressing me (for I had not yet got relief from the troubles arising from that cause) I flung myself at high noon into the litter, and was carried out thence, all the people shrieking and howling, and imprecating curses on the perpetrator of these deeds, whilst every one wailed and lamented. But when I got outside the city, some of the clergy also gradually came out and escorted me, mourning as they went. And having heard some persons say "Where are you leading him away to manifest death?" one of those who was warmly attached to me said to me "Depart I entreat you; fall into the hands of the Isaurians, provided you get clear away from us. For wherever you may fall, you will fall into a place of security, if only you escape our hands." Having heard and seen these things the good Seleucia, the generous wife of my lord Ruffinus (a most attentive friend she was to me), exhorted and entreated me to lodge at her suburban house which was about five miles from the city and she sent some men to escort me, and so I departed thither.

3. But not even there was this plot against me to come to an end. For as soon as Pharetrius knew what she had done, he published, as she said, many threats against her. But when she received me into her suburban villa I knew nothing of these things; for when she came out to meet me she concealed these things from me, but disclosed them to her steward who was there, and ordered him to afford me every possible means of repose, and if any of the monks should make an assault, wishing to insult or maltreat me, he was to collect the labourers from her other farms, and thus marshal a force against them. Moreover she besought me to take refuge in her house, which had a fortress and was impregnable, that I might escape the hands of the bishop and monks. This however I could not be induced to do, but remained in the villa, knowing nothing of the plans which were devised after these things. For even then they were not content to desist from their fury against me but Pharetrius beset the lady as she says, straitly threatening her, constraining and forcing her to expel me even from the suburbs, so that at midnight, I knowing nothing of these things, the lady being unable to endure his annoyance, announced, without my knowledge, that the barbarians were at hand, for she was ashamed to mention the compulsion which she had undergone. So in the middle of the night Evethius the presbyter came to me, and having roused me from sleep, exclaimed with a loud voice "Get up, I pray you, the barbarians are upon us, they are close at hand." Imagine my condition on hearing this! Then, when I said to him what must we do? we cannot take refuge in the city lest we suffer worse things than what the Isaurians are going to do to us, he compelled me to go out. It was midnight, a dark, murky night without a moon—a circumstance which filled up the measure of our perplexity—we had no companion, no assistant, for all had deserted us. Nevertheless under the pressure of fear and in the expectation of immediate death, I got up, suffering as I was, having ordered

---

[1] There are many instances in the early history of the Eastern Church of similar fanatical fury on the part of monks.

torches to be lit. These however the presbyter ordered to be put out, for fear as he said lest the barbarians should be attracted by the light and attack us; so the torches were extinguished. Then the mule which carried my litter fell on its knees, the road being rugged, and steep and stony, and I who was inside was thrown down and narrowly escaped destruction, after which I dismounted, and was dragged along on foot, being held fast by Evethius the presbyter (for he also had alighted from his mule), and so I plodded on, led, or rather hauled by the hand, for to walk was impossible through such a difficult country, and amongst steep mountains in the middle of the night. Imagine what my sufferings must have been, encompassed as I was by such calamities, and oppressed by the fever, ignorant of the plans which had been made, but in terror of the barbarians and trembling with the expectation of falling into their hands. Do you not think that these sufferings alone, even if nothing else besides had befallen me, would avail to blot out many of my sins, and afford ample material for obtaining praise with God? Now the reason of all this, at least as I suppose, was, that as soon as I arrived in Cæsarea, those who were in official positions, the learned men who were ex-vicars, and ex-governors, the ex-tribunes and indeed the whole people visited me every day, paid me great attention, and treated me as the apple of their eye; I suppose these things irritated Pharetrius and that the envy which drove me from Constantinople did not refrain from pursuing me even here. This at least is what I suppose, for I do not positively declare it but only suspect it to be the fact.

And what is one to say about the other events which happened on the way, the fears and the perils? as I recall them day by day, and continually bear them in mind, I am elated with pleasure, I leap for joy as one who has a great treasure laid up in store for him; for such is my position and feeling about them. Wherefore also I beseech your Honour to rejoice at these things, to be glad, and leap for joy, and to glorify God who has counted me worthy to suffer such things. And I beseech you to keep these matters to yourself, and not to divulge them to any one, although for the most part the proconsular soldiers can fill all the city (with the story) as they themselves have undergone extreme danger.

4. Nevertheless do not let any one know this from your prudence, but rather put down those who talk about it. But if you are distressed lest the consequences of my ill-treatment should remain, know for certain that I have shaken myself entirely free from them, and that I am in better bodily health than when I was sojourning in Cæsarea. And why do you dread the cold? for a suitable dwelling has been prepared for me, and my lord Dioscorus does and arranges everything so as to prevent my having the least sensation of cold. And if I may form a conjecture from the outset of my experience, the climate now seems to me oriental in character, no less than that of Antioch. So great is the warmth, so pleasant is the temperature. But you have grieved me much by saying, "perhaps you are annoyed with me as having neglected you," yet I despatched a letter many days ago to your honour begging you not to move me from this place. Now I have had occasion to consider that you need a strong defence and much toil and labour to be able to make a satisfactory apology for this expression. But perhaps you have made a partial apology, by saying "I am generally occupied in thinking how to increase my affliction." But I in my turn reckon it as the greatest accusation that you should say "I take a pride in increasing my sorrow by thinking over it:" for when you ought to make every possible effort to dispel your affliction you do the devil's will, by increasing your despondency and sorrow. Are you not aware how great an evil despondency is?

As to the Isaurians, dismiss your fears in future concerning them: for they have returned into their own country: and the governor has done everything necessary in this respect; and I am in far greater security here than when I was in Cæsarea. For in future I have no one to fear so much as the bishops, with a few exceptions. On account of the Isaurians then fear nothing: for they have retreated, and when winter has set in they are confined to their own homes, although they may possibly come out after Whitsuntide. And what do you mean by saying that you have not the benefit of letters from me? I have already sent you three long letters, one by the proconsular soldiers, one by Antonius, and the third by Anatolius my servant; two of them were a salutary medicine capable of reviving any one who was desponding or stumbling, and conducting him into a healthy state of serenity. When you have received these letters then go over them constantly and thoroughly, and you will perceive their force and enjoy experience of their healing power, and benefit, and will inform me that you have derived much advantage therefrom. I have also a third letter ready, similar to these, which I do not choose to send at the present time having been exceedingly vexed at your saying "I accumulate sorrowful thoughts, even inventing things which do not exist," an utterance unworthy of yourself, which makes me hide my head for shame. But read those letters which I have sent, and you will no longer say these things, even if you are infinitely bent on being despondent.[1] I at least have not ceased, and will not cease saying that sin is the only thing which is really distressing; and that all other things are but dust and smoke. For what is there grievous in inhabiting a prison and wearing a chain? or in being ill-treated when it is the occasion of so much gain? or why should exile be grievous or confiscation of goods? These are mere words, destitute of any terrible reality, words void of sorrow. For if you speak of death you only mention that which is the debt of nature: a thing which must in any case be undergone even if no one hastens it: and if you speak of exile you mention that which only involves a change of country and the sight of many cities: or if you speak of confiscation of goods you mention what is only freedom and emancipation from care.

5. Do not cease to pay attention to Maruthas the Bishop, as far as it concerns you, so as to lift him up out of the pit.[2] For I have special need of him on account of the affairs in Persia. And ascertain from him, if you can, what has been accomplished there through his agency, and for what purpose he has come home, and let me know whether you have delivered the two epistles which I sent to him: and if he is willing to write to me, I will write again to him: but if he should not be willing let him at least signify to your prudence whether any thing more has taken place there, and whether he is likely to accomplish anything by going thither again. For on this account I was anxious to have an interview with him. Nevertheless let all things which depend on you be done, and take care to fulfill your own part, even if all men are rushing headlong to ruin. For your reward will thus be perfected. By all means therefore make friends with him as far as it is possible. I beseech you not to neglect what I am about to say, but to pay diligent heed to it. The Marsian and Gothic monks where the Bishop Serapion has constantly been concealed have informed me that Moduarius the deacon has come bringing word that Unilas, that excellent bishop whom I lately ordained and sent into Gothia, has been laid to rest, after achieving many great exploits: and the deacon was the bearer of a letter from the king of the Goths begging that a bishop might be sent to them. Since then I see no other means of meeting the threatened catastrophe with a view to its correction save delay and postponement (as it is impossible for them to sail into the Bosporus or into those parts at the present time), take measures to put them off for a time on account of the winter season: and do not by any means neglect this: for it is a matter of the greatest importance. For there are two things which would specially distress me if they were to happen, which God forbid: one is that a bishop should be appointed by these men who have wrought such great wickedness,[3] and who have no right to appoint, and the other is that any one should be made without consideration. For you know yourself that they are not anxious to create some worthy man bishop, and if this should take place, which heaven forbid, you are aware what will follow. Use all diligence therefore to prevent either of these things happening: but if it were possible for Moduarius quietly and secretly to hasten out to me it would be of the greatest advantage. But if this is not possible let what is practicable under the circumstances be done. For that which takes place in the case of money, and actually occurred in the case of the widow in the gospel, also holds good in the case of practical affairs. For as that poor woman when she had cast two mites into the treasury surpassed all those who had cast in more, because she used up her whole substance: even so they who devote themselves to the work in hand with all their might discharge it completely, so far as they are concerned, even if nothing results from it, and they have their reward perfected.

I am very grateful to Hilarius the bishop: for he wrote to me asking to be allowed to depart to his own country, and to set things in order there, and then to come back again. As his presence therefore is of great service (for he is a devout, inflexible, and zealous man) I have urged him to depart and to return speedily. Take care then that the letter is quickly and safely delivered to him and not cast on one side: for he eagerly and earnestly begged for letters from me, and his presence is a great benefit. By all means

---

[1] A short passage is omitted here in the translation. It refers to the transaction of some business between Olympias and an unknown bishop, Heracleides. The exact meaning is obscure, in the absence of any clue from historical knowledge of the incident.

[2] He means, "to detach him from the influence of the hostile party." Marutha was Bishop of Martyropolis in Persia. He had taken part in one of the synods at Constantinople which condemned Chrysostom; had returned to Persia, and after doing good work there had revisited Constantinople, and Chrysostom seems to have hopes of reclaiming him to his side.

[3] i. e., the party at Constantinople hostile to Chrysostom, and the Archbishop Atticus whom they had placed in the See after the death of Arsacius the first intruder.

therefore have a care of the letters; and if Helladius the presbyter be not on the spot see that they are delivered to my friends by the hands of some discreet man who has a head on his shoulders.

TO OLYMPIAS.

NOTHING strange or unnatural has befallen your Piety, but only what is quite natural and consonant to reason, that by a constant succession of trials the sinews of your soul should become more braced, and your zeal and energy for the struggle increased, and that you should therefrom derive much joy. For such is the nature of affliction;—when it lays hold of a brave and noble soul, this is what it is wont to effect. And as the fire makes the piece of gold, when it is applied to it, of better proof: so also affliction when it visits golden characters renders them purer and more proven. Wherefore also Paul said "affliction worketh patience, and patience probation."[1] For these reasons I also rejoice and leap for joy, and derive the greatest consolation of this my solitude from a consideration of thy fortitude. On this account, even though innumerable wolves encompass thee, and many crowds of wicked doers, I fear nothing; but I pray both that existing temptations may be suppressed, and that others may not occur, thus fulfilling the Lord's precept who bids us pray that we may not enter into temptation; but if it should be permitted to happen again I have good confidence concerning thy golden soul, which acquires therefrom the greatest riches for itself. For by what means will they be able to terrify you, who dare everything to their own destruction? Will it be by loss of goods? But I know well that these are counted by thee as dust and cheaper than dirt. Or shall it be by expulsion from country and home. But you know how to dwell in great and populous cities as if they were uninhabited, spending the whole of your time in quietness and rest, and treading worldly ambitions under foot. Or do they threaten death? This also you have constantly practiced by anticipation, and if they should drag you to slaughter, they will be dragging a body which is already dead. What need to speak more at length? No one will be able to do anything to thee of this kind which he will not find you have already abundantly made yourself undergo. For by always walking in the narrow and strait path, you have trained yourself in all these things. Wherefore having practised this most beautiful art in the course of your training, you now shine forth the more gloriously in the contest itself, not only being in no wise disturbed by the things which are happening, but rather elated, and leaping and dancing for joy. For the contests which you have anticipated in your training you now undertake with much ease, although it be in a woman's body, feebler than a cobweb, treading under foot with derisive scorn the fury of lusty men gnashing their teeth upon you; being ready to suffer even worse things than they prepare for you. Happy and thrice happy are you by reason of the crowns of victory to be won, but even more by reason of the contest itself. For such is the nature of these struggles, even before the prizes are given even in the midst of strife they have their recompense and reward;—the pleasure which you are now enjoying, the cheerfulness, the courage, the endurance, the patience, the power which is proof against capture and conquest and rises superior to all things; the perfect training which renders you insensible to any terror at the hands of any one, the power of standing on a rock in the midst of mighty billows of tribulation, and sailing in a calm with a favourable breeze when the sea is raging around you. These are the prizes of affliction even in this world before the kingdom of heaven is won. For I know very well that, even at this present time, being elated with joy, thou dost not consider thyself clothed with a body, but if an opportunity should summon thee to do it, thou wouldst divest thyself of it more readily than others do of the raiment which they wear. Rejoice therefore and be glad both for thyself, and for those who have died a blessed death, not in a bed, nor in a house, but in prison, and chains, and torment; and bewail those only who do these things, and grieve for them. But since you also wish to be informed concerning my bodily health, let me tell you that I have been relieved for the present from the infirmity which was lately oppressing me, and am now in a more comfortable condition: the only fear is lest the winter on its return should again make havoc of my feeble digestion; and as far as the Isaurians are concerned we now enjoy great security.

The following letter is added as a specimen, out of a very large number, of the natural, almost playful style, and tone of warm affection, in which Chrysostom wrote to his intimate friends. All his extant letters were written during his exile, and therefore there is much repetition in their contents, and great general similarity of character.

---

[1] Rom. v. 3, 4.

TO CASTUS, VALERIUS, DIOPHANTUS, CYRIACUS,

PRESBYTERS OF ANTIOCH.

I AM not surprised that you call my long letter a short one. For this is just the way with lovers; they do not recognize such a thing as satiety, they will not admit such a thing as satisfaction, but the more they receive from the objects of their love the more they seek. Therefore, even if the letter which you have received had been ten times as large as the former one, it would not have escaped the epithet of "brief;" in fact it would have been called a small letter, and not only would it have been so called, but it would have actually seemed such in your eyes. Hence I also in my turn am never satisfied with the measure of affection for me which you have attained, but am always seeking to make additions to your love-draught, and daily demanding the discharge of your love debt which is always being paid, and yet is always owing (for it is written, "owe no man anything but to love one another"[1]). I am indeed continually receiving what I ask in great abundance, yet never think that I have received the whole. Do not cease then to pay down this goodly debt, which has a twofold pleasure. For those who pay, and those who receive, derive equal enjoyment, inasmuch as they are both alike enriched by the payment; which in the case of money is an impossibility, for there the one who pays becomes poorer, and only the man who has received is richer. But this is not what commonly happens in the covenant of love. For he who pays it is not less bereft of it, as in the case of money when it is transferred to the receiver; but payment of love makes him who pays richer than before. Knowing these things then, O Sirs, most honoured and devout, cease not continually displaying this excellent disposition towards me. For although you need no exhortation for this purpose from me yet as I greatly long for your love I remind you, even when you need it not, both in order that you may constantly write to me, and also inform me of the state of your health. For even if you do not need any one to remind you on this account, I shall not desist from continually seeking this at your hands; as it is a matter which I have very much at heart. That it is a difficult task owing both to the season of the year, and the difficulty of the journey, and the scarcity of travellers who will do this service for you I am well aware: nevertheless as far as is possible and practicable in the midst of so much difficulty, we exhort you to write constantly, and crave this favour from your love.

---

[1] Rom. xiii. 8.

CORRESPONDENCE OF ST. CHRYSOSTOM WITH THE BISHOP OF ROME.

TRANSLATED WITH INTRODUCTION AND NOTES BY

REV. W. R. W. STEPHENS, M.A.

PREBENDARY OF CHICHESTER CATHEDRAL, AND RECTOR OF WOOLBEDING, SUSSEX.

INTRODUCTION TO THE CORRESPONDENCE OF ST. CHRYSOSTOM, AND THE CHURCH AT CONSTANTINOPLE, WITH INNOCENT, BISHOP OF ROME.

Of these four letters the last three were written during the final exile of St. Chrysostom from Constantinople. The first was written a few weeks before his departure. The complication of events which led to that exile cannot be unfolded here. The student will find a full account of them in most historians of this period of the Church, both ancient and modern, and in the Life of St. Chrysostom by the editor of this volume chapters XVI—XIX. It must suffice to say here that Theophilus Patriarch of Alexandria having been summoned by an imperial mandate to Constantinople to be tried on the charge of having cruelly ill-treated certain Egyptian monks, formed a cabal amongst the enemies of St. Chrysostom, and artfully contrived to change his own position from that of the accused into that of the accuser. His devices were in the end only too successful, and in the summer of the year 404 St. Chrysostom was driven from his see, never to return.

The first letter of St. Chrysostom seems to have been written soon after Easter 404 and refers to the events immediately preceding his expulsion.

The second was written, as we learn from the letter itself, after he had entered the third year of his exile, probably near the close of the year 406.

Copies of the first letter were addressed also to Venerius Bishop of Milan, and Chromatius Bishop of Aquileia. It is interesting therefore as indicating the relation between the Eastern and Western branches of the Church at the beginning of the fifth century. On the one hand it illustrates the growing tendency of Christendom to appeal to the authority of the Western Church, especially of the Bishop of Rome, on questions of ecclesiastical discipline. The law-making, law-protecting spirit of the West is invoked to restrain the turbulence and licentiousness of the East. No jealousy is entertained of the Patriarch of the old Rome by the Patriarch of the new. But on the other hand it is to be noted that the Bishop of Rome is in no sense addressed as a supreme arbitrator: aid and sympathy are solicited from him as from an elder brother, and two other prelates of Italy are joint recipients with him of the appeal.

To Chrysostom Innocent writes, as friend to friend and bishop to brother bishop, a letter of Christian consolation and encouragement, not entering into the legal questions of the case, and not pledging himself to decisive action of any kind. In his letter to the Church of Constantinople he denounces the illegality of the late proceedings of Theophilus and his accomplices, in the strongest terms; but insists upon the necessity of convoking an œcumenical council as the only means of allaying the tempest. And it must be allowed that he did his best to accomplish this object. He wrote a letter to Honorius, the Emperor of the Western Empire, who resided at Ravenna, describing the pitiable condition of the Church at Constantinople. The Emperor issued an order for the convention of an Italian synod, and the synod, swayed no doubt by Innocent, requested Honorius to write to his brother Arcadius the Eastern Emperor urging the convention of a general council to be held in Thessalonica which would be a convenient meeting-point for the prelates of East and West. Honorius complied, and the letter was despatched under the care of a deputation from the Italian Church, consisting of five bishops, two priests and a deacon. They were the bearers also of letters from Innocent, and the Bishops of Milan and Aquileia, and of a memorial from the Italian synod, recommending that Chrysostom should be reinstated in his see before he was required to take his trial before the Council. The party hostile to Chrysostom however had now such complete sway over the court at Constantinople that the deputation never succeeded in getting an audience with the Emperor, and after suffering many insults and indignities, returned to Italy without having accomplished anything.

The letters of Innocent were probably written in Latin, and afterwards translated into Greek. The Greek version is in several passages clumsy and obscure.

CORRESPONDENCE OF ST. CHRYSOSTOM WITH THE BISHOP OF ROME.

LETTER FROM ST. JOHN CHRYSOSTOM TO INNOCENT, BISHOP OF ROME.

TO MY LORD, THE MOST REVEREND AND DIVINELY BELOVED BISHOP INNOCENT, JOHN SENDS GREETING IN THE LORD.

1. I SUPPOSE that even before receiving our letter your Piety has heard of the iniquity which has been perpetrated here. For the magnitude of our distress has left scarcely a single portion of the world uninformed of this grievous tragedy: for report carrying the tidings of what has happened to the very extremities of the earth, has everywhere caused great mourning and lamentation. But inasmuch as we ought not to mourn, but to restore order, and to see by what means this most grievous storm of the Church may be stayed, we have deemed it necessary to persuade my lords, the most honoured and pious bishops Demetrius, Pansophius, Pappus and Eugenius to leave their own churches, and venture on this great sea voyage, and set out on a long journey from home, and hasten to your Charity, and, after informing you clearly of everything, to take measures for redressing the evils as speedily as possible. And with them we have sent the most honoured and beloved of our Deacons, Paulus and Cyriacus, but we also ourselves, in the form of a letter, will briefly instruct your Charity concerning the things which have come to pass. For Theophilus, who has been entrusted with the presidency of the Church in Alexandria, having been commanded to repair alone to Constantinople, certain men having brought an accusation against him to the most devout Emperor, arrived bringing with him no small multitude of Egyptian Bishops, as if wishing to show from the outset, that he came for war and antagonism; moreover when he set foot in the great and divinely beloved Constantinople he did not enter the Church according to the custom and the law which has prevailed from ancient time, he held no intercourse with us, and admitted us to no share in his conversation, his prayers, or his society: but as soon as he disembarked, having hurried past the vestibule of the Church, he departed and lodged somewhere outside the city, and although we earnestly entreated him, and those who had come with him, to be our guests (for everything had been made ready, and lodgings provided, and whatever was suitable) neither they, nor he consented. We seeing this, were in great perplexity, not being able to discover the cause of this unjust hostility; nevertheless we discharged our part, doing what became us, and continually beseeching him to meet us and to say for what cause he hazarded so great a contest at the outset, and threw the city into such confusion. But as he did not choose to state the reason, and those who accused him were urgent, our most devout Emperor summoned us and commanded us to go outside the walls to the place where Theophilus was sojourning, and hear the argument against him. For they accused him of assault, and slaughter and countless other crimes; but knowing as we did the laws of the fathers, and paying respect and deference to the man, and having also his own letters which prove that lawsuits ought not to be taken beyond the border, but that the affairs of the several provinces should be treated within the limits of the province, we would not accept the office of judge, but deprecated it with great earnestness. But he, as if striving to aggravate the former insults, having summoned my arch-

deacon, by a stretch of arbitrary power, as if the Church were already widowed, and had no bishop, by means of this man seduced all the clergy to his own side; and the Churches became destitute, as the clergy in each were gradually withdrawn, and instructed to hand in petitions against us, and trained to prepare accusations. And having done this he sent and summoned us to trial, although he had not yet cleared himself of the charges brought against him, a proceeding directly contrary to the canons and to all the laws.

2. But we being aware that we were not cited to a trial (for otherwise we would have presented ourselves any number of times) but to the presence of an enemy and an adversary, as was clearly proved by all which occurred both before and after, despatched certain bishops to him, Demetrius of Pesinus, Eulysius of Apamea, Lupicinus of Appiaria,[1] and the presbyters Germanus and Severus, who replied with the moderation which became us, and said, that we did not decline to be judged, but to appear before an open enemy, and manifest adversary. For how could one who had not yet received any bills of indictment against me, and had acted from the outset in the manner described, and severed himself from the Church, from communion, and from prayer, and was training accusers, and seducing the clergy, and desolating the Church, how, I say, could he with justice mount the throne of the judge which was not in any sense befitting him? For it is not suitable that one who belongs to Egypt should act as judge of those who are in Thrace, and this a man who is himself under an accusation, and an enemy and adversary. Nevertheless he, in no way abashed, but hurrying on to the completion of his design, although we had declared our readiness to clear ourselves of the charges in the presence of a hundred yea or a thousand bishops, and to prove ourselves innocent as indeed we are, would not consent: but in our absence, when we were appealing to a synod, and demanding a trial, and not shrinking from a hearing of our cause, but only from open enmity, he both received our accusers and absolved those who had been excommunicated by me, and from them, who had not yet cleared themselves of the offences laid to their charge, he received complaints[2] against me, and had minutes made of the proceedings, all which things are contrary to law, and the order of the canons. But what need is there of a long story? He did not cease doing and contriving everything until, with all possible display of arbitrary power and authority, he ejected us from the city and the church, when the evening was far advanced and all the people were streaming after us. Being drawn by the public informer[3] through the midst of the city, and dragged along by force I was taken down to the sea, and thrust on board ship, and made a night voyage, because I appealed to a synod for a just hearing of my cause. Who could hear these things without tears, even if he had a heart of stone?

But seeing, as I said before, that we ought not merely to lament the evils which have been done, but also to amend them, I beseech your Charity to rouse yourself and have compassion, and do everything so as to put a stop to the mischief at this point. For even after what I have mentioned he did not desist from his deeds of iniquity, but sought to renew the former attack. For when the most devout Emperor had turned out those who shamelessly rushed into the Church, and many of the Bishops present seeing their iniquity had retreated into their own dioceses, flying from the incursion of these men as from a fire devouring all things, we were again invited to the city, and to the Church, from which we had been unjustly expelled, more than thirty bishops introducing us, and our most pious Emperor sending a notary for this purpose, while Theophilus immediately took to flight. For what purpose, and from what cause? When we entered the city we besought our most pious Emperor to convene a synod for prosecuting the offenders in the late transactions. Being conscious therefore of what he had done, and dreading conviction, the imperial letters having been sent in every direction, convoking all men from all quarters, Theophilus secretly at midnight flung himself into a boat, and so made his escape, taking all his company with him.

3. But even then we did not desist, supported as we were by a clear conscience, from making the same supplication again to the most devout Emperor: and he, acting as became his piety, sent to Theophilus again, summoning him from Egypt, and his associates, in order to give an account of the late proceedings, and informing him that he was not to suppose that the one-sided deeds which he had so unjustly perpetrated in our absence, and in violation of so many canons, would suffice for his defence. He did not however submit to the royal mandate, but remained at home, alleging an insurrection of the people in excuse, and the unseasonable zeal of cer-

---

[1] Pesinus was in Galatia, Apamea in Bithynia, Appiaria I have not identified.
[2] *Libellos*, a technical word signifying a formal petition of complaint or accusation.
[3] *Curiosus*, an official whose duty it was to investigate charges, and inform the Emperor of offenders.

tain persons who were attached to him, as he pretended: and yet before the arrival of the imperial letters this same people had deluged him with abuse. But we do not make much of these matters now, but have said what we have said as wishing to prove the fact that he was arrested in his mischievous course. Yet even after these things we did not rest, but were urgent in our demand that a tribunal should be formed for the purpose of enquiry and defence: for we said that we were ready to prove that we ourselves were guiltless, but that they had flagrantly transgressed. For there were some Syrians amongst those present with him at that time, who were left behind here; and we accosted them expressing our readiness to plead our cause, and frequently importuned them on this behalf, demanding that the minutes (of the late transactions) should be given up to us, or that the formal bills of indictment, or the nature of the charges, or the accusers themselves, should be made known; and yet we did not obtain any of these things, but were again expelled from the Church. How am I to relate the events which followed, transcending as they do every kind of tragedy? What language will set forth these events? what kind of ear will receive them without shuddering? For when we were urging these things, as I said before, a dense troop of soldiers, on the great Sabbath itself,[1] as the day was hastening towards eventide, having broken into the Churches violently drove out all the clergy who were with us, and surrounded the sanctuary with arms. And women from the oratories[2] who had stripped themselves for baptism just at that time, fled unclothed, from terror at this grievous assault, not being permitted to put on the modest apparel which befits women; indeed many received wounds before they were expelled, and the baptismal pools were filled with blood, and the sacred water reddened by it. Nor did the distress cease even at this point; but the soldiers, some of whom as we understand were unbaptized, having entered the place where the sacred vessels were stored, saw all the things which were inside it, and the most holy blood of Christ, as might happen in the midst of such confusion, was spilt upon the garments of the soldiers aforesaid: and every kind of outrage was committed as in a barbarian siege. And the common people were driven to the wilderness, and all the people tarried outside the city, and the Churches became empty in the midst of this great Festival, and more than forty bishops who associated with us were vainly and causelessly expelled together with the people and clergy. And there were shrieks and lamentations, and torrents of tears were shed everywhere, in the market places, in the houses, in the desert places, and every part of the city was filled with these calamities; for owing to the immoderate extent of the outrage not only the sufferers, but also they who did not undergo anything of the kind sympathized with us, not only those who held the same opinions as ours, but also heretics, and Jews, and Greeks, and all places were in a state of tumult and confusion, and lamentation, as if the city had been captured by force. And these things were perpetrated contrary to the intention of our most pious Emperor, under cover of night, the Bishops contriving them, and in many places conducting the attack, nor were they ashamed to have sergeants[3] instead of deacons marching in front of them. And when day dawned all the city was migrating outside the walls under trees and groves, celebrating the festival, like scattered sheep.

4. All which happened afterwards I leave you to imagine; for as I said before it is not possible to describe each separate incident. The worst of it is that these evils, great and serious as they are, have not even now been suppressed nor is there any hope of their suppression; on the contrary the mischief is extending itself every day, and we have become a laughing stock to the multitude, or rather I should say, no one laughs even if he is infinitely lawless, but all men mourn, as I was saying, this new kind of lawlessness, the finishing stroke of all our ills.

What is one to say to the disorders in the other Churches? For the evil did not stop even here, but made its way to the east. For as when some evil humor is discharged from the head, all the other parts are corrupted, so now also these evils, having originated in this great city as from a fountain, confusion has spread in every direction, and clergy have everywhere made insurrection against bishops, there has been schism between bishop and bishop, people and people, and will be yet more; every place is suffering from the throes of calamity, and the subversion of the whole civilized world. Having been informed then of all these things, my lords, most honourable and devout, exhibit the courage and zeal which becomes you, so as to put a stop to this great assault of lawlessness which has been made upon the Churches. For if this

---

[1] *i. e.*, Easter Eve.
[2] οἶκοι εὐκτήριοι. Churches were sometimes so called, more often, however, private chapels as distinguished from parish churches. The meaning here is not very obvious; perhaps some chambers attached to the Church, where catechumens prayed before baptism, are referred to.
[3] Campiductores—their special business was to drill recruits.

custom were to prevail, and it became lawful for any persons who desired it to enter strange dioceses, so widely separated, and expel those whom one wished to remove, and do whatever they pleased according to their own arbitrary power, be assured that all things will go to ruin, and an implacable kind of war will overrun the whole world, all men attacking others, and being in turn attacked. Therefore to prevent such confusion overtaking the whole earth yield to our entreaties that ye will signify by writing that these lawless transactions executed in our absence, and after hearing one side only, although we did not decline a trial, are invalid, as indeed they are by the very nature of the case, and that those who are convicted of having committed such iniquities must be subjected to the penalty of the ecclesiastical laws; and for ourselves, who have not been detected or convicted, or proved liable to punishment may we continue to have the benefit of your correspondence, and your love, and all other things which we have enjoyed aforetime. But if even now those who have committed such lawless acts are willing to disclose the charges on the strength of which they have unjustly expelled us, neither memoranda, nor formal bills of indictment being given, nor the accusers having appeared: yet if an impartial tribunal is formed, we will submit to be tried, and will make our defence, and prove ourselves guiltless of the things laid to our charge, as indeed we are: for the things which they have done are outside the bounds of every kind of order, and every kind of ecclesiastical law and canon. And why do I say ecclesiastical canon? Not even in the heathen courts would such audacious deeds ever have been committed, or rather not even in a barbarian court, neither Scythians, nor Sarmatians would ever have judged a cause in this fashion, deciding it after hearing one side only, in the absence of the accused, who only deprecated enmity, not a trial of his case, who was ready to call any number of judges, asserting himself to be innocent and able to clear himself of the charges in the face of the world, and prove himself guiltless in every respect.

Having considered therefore all these things, and having been clearly informed of all particulars by my lords, our most devout brethren the bishops, may you be induced to exert your zeal on our behalf; for in so doing ye will confer a favour not upon ourselves alone but also upon the Church at large, and ye will receive your reward from God who does all things for the peace of the Churches. Fare thee well always, and pray for me, most honoured and holy master.

TO INNOCENT, BISHOP OF ROME, GREETING IN THE LORD.

OUR body it is true is settled in one place, but the pinion of love wings its way round every part of the world. Even so we also although we be separated by a journey of such great extent are nigh to your Piety, and in daily communion with you, beholding with the eyes of love the courage of your soul, the sterling nature of your disposition, your firmness and inflexibility, the great consolation, constant and abiding, which you bestow upon us. For in proportion as the billows mount higher, and concealed reefs increase, and the hurricanes are many does your vigilance wax stronger: and neither the great length of the journey between us, nor the large amount of time consumed, nor the difficulty in dealing with events has disposed you to become supine: but ye continue to imitate the best class of pilots who are on the alert at those times most especially when they see the waves crested, the sea swelling, the water dashing vehemently, and the deepest darkness in day-time. Therefore also we feel great gratitude towards you, and we long to send you showers of letters, thus affording ourselves the greatest gratification. But since we are deprived of this, owing to the desolation of the place; (for not only of those who arrive from your regions, but even of those who dwell in our part of the world no one could easily have intercourse with us, both on account of the distance, the spot in which we are confined being situated at the very extremity of the country, and also the terror of robbers acting as a bar to the whole journey:) we beseech you rather to pity us because of our long silence, than to condemn us for indolence on that account. For as a proof that our silence has not been due to negligence, we have now at last after a long time secured our most honoured and beloved John the presbyter, and Paul the deacon, and we send a letter through them, and continue to express our gratitude to you, that you have surpassed even affectionate parents in your good will and zeal concerning us. And indeed so far as your Piety is concerned all things would have been duly amended, and the accumulation of evils and offences have been swept away, and the Churches would have enjoyed peace and a glassy calm, and all things would have floated along with a smooth stream, and the despised laws and violated decrees of the fathers would have been vindicated. But since in reality none of these things has taken place, they who perpetrated the former deeds striving to aggravate their former iniquities, I omit any detailed narrative of their subsequent proceedings: for the narrative would exceed the limits not merely of a letter but even of a history; only this I beseech your vigilant soul, even if they who have filled everything with confusion be impenitently and incurably corrupt, let not those who have undertaken to cure them become faint-hearted or despondent, when they consider the magnitude of the thing to be accomplished. For the contest now before you has to be fought on behalf of nearly the whole world, on behalf of Churches humbled to the ground, of people dispersed, of clergy assaulted, of bishops sent into exile, of ancestral laws violated. Wherefore we beseech your Diligence, once, twice, yea many times, in proportion as the storm increases, to manifest still greater zeal. For we expect that something more will be done for the purpose of amending these wrongs. But even if this should not take place, ye at least have your crown made ready for you by the merciful God, and the resistance offered by your love will be no small consolation to those who are wronged: for now that we are passing the third year of our sojourn in exile exposed to famine, pestilence, wars, continual sieges, indescribable solitude, daily death, and Isaurian swords, we are not a little encouraged and comforted by the constant and abiding nature of your disposition and confidence, and by revelling in your abundant and genuine love. This is our wall of defence, this is our security, this our calm haven, this our treasure of infinite blessings, this our gladness, and ground of much joy. And even if we should be carried off again to some spot more desolate than this, we shall carry this love away with us as no small consolation of our sufferings.

TO THE BELOVED BROTHER JOHN, INNOCENT.

ALTHOUGH the innocent man ought to expect all good things, and to crave mercy from God, nevertheless we also, counselling resignation, have sent an appropriate letter by the hands of Cyriacus the deacon; so that insolence may not have more power in oppressing, than a good conscience has in retaining hope. For thou who art the teacher and pastor of so many people needest not to be taught that the best men are ever frequently put to the test whether they will persevere in the perfection of patience, and not succumb to any toil of distress: and certainly conscience is a strong defence against all things which unjustly befall us: and unless any one conquer these by patient endurance he supplies an argument for evil surmising. For he ought to endure all things who trusts first of all in God, and then in his own conscience; seeing that the noble and good man can be specially trained to endurance, inasmuch as the holy Scriptures guard his mind; and the sacred lessons which we deliver to the people abound in examples, testifying as they do that nearly all the saints have been continually oppressed in divers ways, and are tested as by a kind of scrutiny, and so attain to the crown of patience. Let conscience itself console thy love, most honoured brother, which in affliction supplies the consolation of virtue. For under the eye of the Master Christ, the conscience, having been purged, will find rest in the haven of peace.

INNOCENT, BISHOP, TO PRESBYTERS AND DEACONS, AND TO ALL THE CLERGY AND PEOPLE OF THE CHURCH OF CONSTANTINOPLE, THE BRETHREN BELOVED WHO ARE SUBJECT TO THE BISHOP JOHN, GREETING.

FROM the letters of your love which ye have sent by the hands of Germanus the presbyter, and Casianus the deacon, I have studied with anxious care the scene of calamity which ye have placed before my eyes, and by repeated perusal of your description I thoroughly perceived under what great distress and toil your faith is labouring: and this is a matter which can be cured only by the consolation of patience: for our God will speedily grant an end to such great afflictions, and He will aid you in your endurance of these things. Moreover whilst praising the statement of your case which contains many testimonies encouraging to patience I notice this necessary consolation placed at the beginning of the epistle of your love: for the consolation which we ought to have written to you, ye have anticipated by your letter. For this is the kind of patience which our Master is wont to supply to those who are in distress, in order that the servants of Christ when they are in affliction may console themselves by reflecting that the things which they themselves are suffering have happened to the saints also in former times. And we also from your letter shall be able to derive consolation: for we are not estranged from sympathy with you, inasmuch as we also are chastised in your persons. For who will be able to endure the offences committed by those men who ought to be specially zealous promoters of the tranquillity of the Church and of concord itself. At the present time, by a perversion of custom, guiltless priests are expelled from the presidency of their own

Churches. And this is what your chief brother, and fellow minister, John, your bishop has unjustly suffered, not having obtained any hearing: no crime is charged against him, none is heard. And what is the object of this iniquitous device? that no pretext for a trial may occur, or be sought, other men are introduced into the places of living priests, as if those who start from an offence of this description could be judged by any one to have anything good or to have done anything right.[1] For we understand that such deeds have never been perpetrated by our fathers; or rather that they were prevented by the fact that no one had authority given him to ordain another to take the place of one who was still living. For a spurious ordination cannot deprive the priest of his rank: seeing that neither can he be a bishop who is wrongfully substituted for another. And as regards the observance of the canons we lay it down that we ought to follow those, which were defined at Nicæa, to which alone the Catholic Church is bound to pay obedience and recognition. And if others are brought forward by certain men, which are at variance with the canons framed at Nicæa, and are proved to have been composed by heretics, let them be rejected by the Catholic bishops. For the inventions of heretics ought not to be appended to the Catholic canons; for by their adverse and unlawful decrees they are always intending to weaken the design of the canons of Nicæa. Not only therefore do we say that these ought not to be followed, but rather that they should be condemned amongst heretical and schismatic decrees, as was formerly done in the Council of Sardica by the bishops who were before us.[2] For it were more fitting, most honoured brethren, that good deeds should be condemned than that things done in direct opposition to the canons should have any validity. But what are we to do against such things at the present time? A synodical decision of them is necessary, and we have long declared that a synod ought to be convened, as it is the only means of allaying the agitation of such tempests as these: and if we obtain this it is expedient that the healing of these evils should be committed to the will of the great God, and His Christ our Lord. All the disturbances then which have been caused by the envy of the devil for the probation of the faithful will be mitigated; through the firmness of our faith we ought not to despair of anything from the Lord. For we ourselves also are considering much by what means the œcumenical synod may be brought together in order that by the will of God these disturbing movements may be brought to an end. Let us therefore endure for a while, and fortified by the wall of patience let us hope that all things may be restored to us by the assistance of our God. Moreover all things which ye say ye have undergone we have learned by accurate enquiry from our fellow bishops who have already taken refuge in Rome, although for the most part at different times, that is to say, Demetrius, Cyriacus, Eulysius and Palladius, who are here with us.

---

[1] I have followed the Latin here. The Greek version of the passage seems to me hopelessly confused.

[2] The Council of Sardica was convened A.D. 343, (or A.D. 344?) with a view of settling the Arian controversy. The Oriental bishops, however, of whom the majority belonged to the Arian faction, seceded from Sardica, and held a separate council at Philippopolis, where they drew up a creed which was condemned by the Western bishops as heretical.

ST. CHRYSOSTOM

THE HOMILIES ON THE STATUES.

TO THE PEOPLE OF ANTIOCH.

THE OXFORD TRANSLATION AND NOTES, REVISED BY

REV. W. R. W. STEPHENS, M.A.,

PREBENDARY OF CHICHESTER CATHEDRAL, AND RECTOR OF WOOLBEDING, SUSSEX.

PREFACE TO THE BENEDICTINE EDITION.

1. AMONG the events which occurred in the time of John Chrysostom,[1] there is none more memorable than that sedition of the inhabitants of Antioch, in which the Statues of the Emperor Theodosius and Flacilla his wife were thrown down and dragged about the city, at which Theodosius was so exasperated, as even to think of destroying the city entirely. This afforded ample matter for our Chrysostom to exercise his powers of preaching. For as the people of Antioch were fluctuating between hope and fear (sudden accidents offering of course daily some fresh cause for hope or alarm) Chrysostom, compelled as he was to adapt his style to circumstances as they arose, almost always without preparation, delivered on the spur of the occasion these Homilies, which are certainly well deserving of admiration. At one time his object here is to console a people struggling with present distress; at another, to strengthen minds that were sinking under the extremity of danger; and above all, by repeated admonition, to persuade the people of Antioch, on occasion of the threatened calamities, to correct the vices and to wipe away the crimes that had thus provoked God's wrath; which endeavour on the part of Chrysostom certainly ended in results agreeable to his desire, as he sometimes acknowledges.

2. But the cause of this great sedition was, according to the testimony of Zosimus, excess of taxation, which was daily inventing new imposts; an exaction required either for the celebration of the fifth year upon which Arcadius had entered, from the time he was proclaimed under the title of Augustus, and the tenth year of the Emperor Theodosius, commencing in the year 388, or for the expenses of the war against the tyrant Maximus,[2] or on account of both these events, as well as for other necessities of the state. The people of Antioch, that is to say, the superior class of the citizens, dismayed at the burden of this impost, first approached the prefect, and with tears lamented the excess of the tax that had been announced, and implored the Divine assistance. And next, a multitude of vagabonds and foreigners of the lowest class of the people,[3] in a state of excited feeling, broke out into deeds of violence. At first they turned every thing upside down in the public baths; hence they proceeded to the prefect's palace, and attacked the doors and windows, and were scarcely repelled, when they turned their rage in another direction, and attacked the painted tablets of the Emperors with stones, covered them with filth, and reduced them to a ruinous condition, while they loaded the Augusti themselves with curses and reproaches. At length they threw down the Statues of the Emperor Theodosius and Flacilla his deceased wife,[4] and dragged them through the streets of the city; and had already commenced further outrages, when they were put down by a band of archers, dispatched from the prefect. The sedition being thus extinguished, fear took the place of madness, and the expectation of impending punishment caused the burdensome tax that had been imposed to

---

[1] [That is events which occurred at *Antioch* during St. Chrysostom's sojourn in that city.—ED.]
[2] [And the Goths who were threatening the Danubian frontier.—ED.]
[3] [These low foreign adventurers were sometimes hired by actors to get up applause in the theatre, or by men of rank, not over-popular, to raise a cheer when they appeared in public.—ED.]
[4] See Hom. XXI., where St. Chrysostom speaks of him as especially pained at this.

be entirely forgotten. What followed afterwards will be narrated below in the review of the Homilies. Something must now be said as to the year of the sedition, in which these Homilies were delivered.

3. Dismissing the narrative of Sozomen and Theodoret, according to whose account, this sedition, and the delivery of these discourses, must have been after the war against Maximus, learned men, and Tillemont especially (at length in note 27 appended to his Life of the Emperor Theodosius) have proved from far more certain notes of time, that these events took place before the war against Maximus. In opposition to that former opinion, he produces a most convincing argument from Chrysostom's own words, who in the sixteenth Homily (No. 2.), testifies that this was the second year since he had begun to preach; but he began when he was first ordained presbyter at the end of the year 385, or at the beginning of 386. Wherefore these discourses ought to be attributed either to the year 388, or rather 387. For the former opinion Baronius contends, and after him, Petavius and Henry Valesius, who assign them to the year 388, for this reason, that the tenth year of the reign of Theodosius then commenced, for the celebration of which the tax before mentioned was imposed. But what is adduced from Libanius for the defence of this opinion is full of perplexity,[1] and is capable of being twisted to support either opinion. A still more certain indication than any of these is gathered from the circumstance, that the Emperor Theodosius was certainly at Constantinople during the winter and Lent of the year 387, in which year also the sedition must necessarily have occurred; for at the time of the sedition he was most certainly staying at Constantinople,[2] but on the other hand at the same season in the year immediately following, he was living at Thessalonica. But what is alleged to the contrary from the celebration of the tenth year of Theodosius, which commenced in the year 388, amounts, as I said, to nothing; since it is evident from the Fasti of Idatius and of Marcellinus, that he anticipated by one year the celebration of the tenth year of his reign, in order that he might celebrate his tenth together with his son Arcadius, who entered upon the fifth year of his reign in 387; just in the same manner as Maximianus Herculius did, when he celebrated the twentieth, though it was only the eighteenth, year of his reign, along with Diocletian, whose twentieth year of empire it was.[3]

4. But another and not a less difficulty arises, which has been already treated of in the Preface to the work, "Against the Jews;" viz. that in a certain discourse against the Jews, held in the month of September of the year 386, Chrysostom in reproving many of the Christians at Antioch who fasted and kept Easter[4] with the Jews, or at the time observed by the Jews, "Behold," saith he, "the first day of unleavened bread in this year falls on Sunday, and it is necessary that we should fast throughout the whole week, and after the Passion is past, and the Cross and the Resurrection arrived,[5] we should continue fasting; and very often the same thing occurs, that after the Passion has passed away, and the Cross and the Resurrection arrived, we are still keeping the fast, the week being not yet finished." From these words it is further evident, that those Christians, who acted as Jews in keeping

---

[1] *i. e.*, so far as the inference is concerned. His testimony is explicit to the fact that the tax was levied for that purpose, and he was on the spot.

[2] See the opening of the oration of Libanius, written *as if* to be delivered by him there, and Hom. XVII. 6, and Hom. XXI. (2).

[3] [See also *Life of St. John Chrysostom*, chapter xi. by Stephens, where the sedition at Antioch is described, and a summary of the Homilies on the Statues is given.—ED.]

[4] Pascha is either Passover or Easter. St. Thos. Aquinas, in the Hymn *Lauda Sion*, appropriates it to the Christian Festival, calling the Jewish *Phase vetus*.

[5] *i. e.*, the actual days of them on the Jewish computation. This appears the true answer to the difficulty. The Jews kept the Passover this year *earlier* than the Christians : viz. on the 14th day of the moon, or April 18. See *l'Art de Verifier les Dates* on the year. Thus the supposed difficulty becomes a confirmation of the date otherwise determined. Montfaucon understood it, "we must . . . if we follow the Judaizers." Tillemont is at a loss to explain the title of Homily III. against the Jews. *Against those who would fast the first Passover.* It may mean either the *original*, or that which then happened to be the earlier. The word *fast* is explained by taking it as their expression for *keep*. He thinks it necessary to tell them that the true Passover is not *fasting*, but the *Holy Communion*. Ben. t. i. p. 611, b. And this agrees with what he says is the common case, viz. that the Christian Easter is so much later, as is required to complete the week.

the fast and celebrating the Passover, must sometimes have fasted when other Christians were celebrating the Paschal feast, and at other times not so; for example, they fasted on the day of the Resurrection when the Jews celebrated the feast of the Passover later than the rest of the Christians did, but they did not fast when the Jews celebrated the same feast earlier than the Christians. But in the discourse of Chrysostom above mentioned, and held about the month of September of the year 386, he is doubtless treating of Lent and Easter of the year 387. But in that year, according to the Paschal tables, the feast fell on the 25th of April, that is to say, as late as it can possibly occur. How then could these judaizing Christians be fasting this year during the Paschal feast, and celebrate that feast too late, when this could not occur later than on the 25th of April, on which day the other non-judaizing Christians celebrated it this year, at least if the Paschal tables are to be relied upon? This is certainly a very great difficulty; but one which, as Tillemont himself confesses, is not sufficient to overturn the marks of the period by which we assign the Homily, "Against the Jews," to the month of September, in the year 386. For as we have said in the Preface to the Homilies against the Jews, it has not yet been made out to us so certainly, whether the people of Antioch always followed by an invariable rule the Alexandrian reckoning as to the Feast of the Lord's Passover, and if they had always followed it, can we affirm that they never fell into error in their reckoning? Certainly the persons best skilled in the Paschal reckonings, whom I have consulted, have admitted that an error of this sort sometimes does happen in such reckonings, and did happen not many years since; and that it is not always safe to prefer the Paschal indications to any other notes of time.

5. Tillemont, however, who notices this kind of difficulty, and discusses it in his notes to the Life of Chrysostom, where he treats of the Homilies against the Jews, has not mentioned it in the notes to the Life of the Emperor Theodosius, where he arranges these Homilies of Chrysostom to the people of Antioch as if the Feast of Easter had fallen on the 25th of April, as the Paschal tables have it. The first Homily therefore he places a little before the sedition; but the sedition on the 26th of February, ten days before Lent, which at Antioch began on the Monday of our Quinquagesima, falling that year on the 8th of March. The second Homily either on the Thursday, or the Saturday before Lent; viz. on the 6th of March, the eighth day after the sedition. The third on the following Sunday, the 7th of March, or thereabout. The fourth, on the Monday following, March 8. The fifth, on Tuesday, March 9. The sixth, about the next Wednesday, on March 10. The seventh, on Thursday, March 11. The eighth, on Friday, March 12. The ninth on the Monday of the second week in Lent, March 15. The tenth, after the lapse of a few days. The eleventh, (considering it transposed,) on the Monday of the fourth week in Lent, March 29. The twelfth, on the following Tuesday, March 30. The thirteenth, on the following Wednesday, March 31. The fourteenth, a little after that one which is numbered the eighteenth, which was delivered on the fifth Sunday in Lent, April 5. The fifteenth, on the Saturday of the second week in Lent, or March 20. The sixteenth, on the third Saturday in Lent, March 21. The seventeenth, about the end of the fourth week in Lent. The eighteenth, Sunday, April 5, or thereabout. The nineteenth, after the fourteenth, about April 11. The twentieth, on Easter Day, April 25. The twenty-first, about the same time as the twenty-second following it, which was delivered on the Friday after Passion Sunday, April 16.[1] Thus does Tillemont endeavour to restore with the utmost accuracy the deranged order of these Homilies. Whilst however we agree with him in many things, we are compelled to differ from him in others. The order of the Homilies, as he lays it down, we may here further represent in one tabular view.

---

[1] The second before Easter. It has lately become common to call the week immediately before Easter "Passion Week," but this name belongs to the week before it. The proper title of the last is the "Great" or "Holy" Week.

Tillemont's	1st	is placed in Edition of Fronto Ducæus	First
	2d		Second
	3d		Third
	4th		Fourth
	5th		Fifth
	6th		Sixth
	7th		Seventh
	8th		Eighth
	9th		Ninth
	10th		Tenth
	11th		Fifteenth
	12th		Sixteenth
	13th		Eleventh
	14th		Twelfth
	15th		Thirteenth
	16th		Seventeenth
	17th		Eighteenth
	18th		Fourteenth
	19th		Nineteenth
	20th		Twenty-second
	21st		Twenty-first
	22d		Twentieth

But before we discourse singly of the Homilies, and make a few observations as to the order as well as the argument of each, it may be worth while to remark, that from the title of the Homily which formerly was numbered the twenty-second, but now the twentieth, which title it has in the notes of Fronton, and in our Mss.; it must have been spoken ten days before Easter; and that from these words likewise, just before the end of the Homily, "Forty days have already passed away," Tillemont justly infers, that Lent among the people of Antioch began on the Monday after Quinquagesima; and that among them the whole Lent extended through seven weeks; and he rightly assigns this Homily to a Friday during Lent;[1] so that that day was both the fortieth from the beginning of the fast, and the tenth before Easter. Hence we hold it as a thing established, that Lent, which in divers Churches was defined by various limits, was observed at Antioch during seven[2] weeks.

Moreover, since for the causes before related, we may account the diurnal Paschal tables, which place the Easter of the year 387 upon the 25th of April, as of doubtful authority,[3] at least those for the use of the Church at Antioch; we have not discovered with certainty on what day the people of Antioch kept Easter in this year 387, we shall abstain from mentioning the day of the month in the review of the Homilies, and we shall account it sufficient to have indicated, when that may be safely done, on what day of the week the Homilies were spoken.

The first Homily, then, was delivered a few days before the sedition at Antioch, as is discoverable from these words in No. (3.) of the second Homily; "I lately protracted a long discourse to your charity . . . . and I have received[4] a reward for my labours. But what was the reward? To punish the blasphemers in the city, and to chastise those who treat God with contempt, and to restrain the violent." Without doubt these words have reference to the first Homily, one of great length, on the subject of the sorrows of the Saints, and the providence of God towards His Elect, who are tormented in this life, where

---

[1] "*Feriam sextam Quadragesima.*" This looks like a reprint, as he is more definite.
[2] As now in the Greek Church. The Latins do not count the week in which Ash-Wednesday is, as not being a whole one.
[3] It has been shewn, in a former note, that there is no reason for this doubt.
[4] "*accepi*," it should be, as in Text, "*exegi*," "I demanded."

at last he thus expresses himself in a manner certainly worthy of observation. "But since our discourse has now turned to the subject of blasphemy, I desire to ask one favour of you all in return for this address and speaking with you, which is, that you will correct on my behalf those who blaspheme in this city. And should you hear any one in the public thoroughfare, or in the midst of the forum, blaspheming God; go up to him, rebuke him; and should it be necessary to inflict blows, spare not to do so. Smite him on the face; strike his mouth; sanctify thy hand with the blow." Which truly would be a mode of correction not suited to modern usage.

The second Homily, Tillemont refers either to the Thursday or to the Saturday before Lent; but it may more safely be pronounced to have been spoken "about" that time, seven days having been completed as Chrysostom himself says, since the sedition, during which he declares that he had been silent, because the people of Antioch, being in consternation from the mighty calamity and from the immensity of the danger, were in no fit state for the hearing of Sermons; moreover, that this evil was one sent from God, on account of their having neglected the correction of their blaspheming brethren; and after he has drawn a beautiful picture of their state, he concludes the discourse, after having preached at length on riches, the use of riches, alms-giving, and poverty.

The third Homily follows close on the second. But we suppose with Tillemont, that it was delivered on Quinquagesima Sunday (to speak according to modern custom). Chrysostom treats here of the departure of Flavian the Bishop of Antioch to Constantinople for the purpose of appeasing the Emperor, and consoles the people with the hope of his succeeding. He then proves at length that there is no utility in fasting, unless there be an abstinence from vices. But after making a few remarks on avoiding slander, he deplores the present calamity, and relates some harsh severities. "Some," saith he, "have perished by the sword, some by fire; some given to wild beasts; and not men only but children. And neither this immaturity of age, nor the tumult of the people, nor the circumstance that they were infuriated by demons when they perpetrated such deeds, nor that the exaction was thought to be intolerable, nor poverty, nor having offended in company with all, nor promising that they would never hereafter dare to repeat such deeds, nor any thing else could at all rescue them; but they were led away to the pit without reprieve, armed soldiers conducting and guarding them on either side, lest any one should carry off the criminals; whilst mothers also followed afar off, seeing their children beheaded, but not daring to bewail their calamity; for terror conquered grief, and fear overcame nature."

All these evils were inflicted on the people of Antioch by the Prefects or Magistrates before Theodosius had heard any thing of the sedition, as Chrysostom says in the same place. But he concludes the address by admonishing that they should abstain from slander, from enmities, and from oaths.

The fourth Homily, delivered as it seems on the Monday, which was the beginning of Lent, describes the advantages gained from the calamity. He speaks of the people of Antioch as changed and brought back from their former habits. But at the close he again repeats the same admonition, which he reminds them that he had given in the foregoing Homily, that is to say, concerning slanders, enmities, and oaths. But in No. (6.), he says, that he should speak throughout this week concerning oaths.

The fifth Homily was pronounced on the day following, that is, on the Tuesday, as Chrysostom says at the beginning of it. In this Chrysostom consoles the people of Antioch as usual, under their sadness, and exhorts them to a contempt for death. In the end also he treats No. (7.) of the avoidance of oaths, and indicates somewhat of the order of the foregoing and following Homilies in these words. "Let us therefore persuade it (our soul) to make this first change for the better by the avoidance of oaths; for although I spake to you yesterday and the day before[1] on this same subject, yet neither to-day, nor to-morrow, nor the day after, will I desist from giving my counsel on this subject."

In the sixth Homily, delivered on the Wednesday of the first week, he imparts consolation to the afflicted, and urges them to hope for a prosperous turn of affairs. He speaks of the delays the messengers had met with, who were gone to announce to the Emperor the sedition at Antioch, as proceeding from God; and from thence deduces a favourable hope for his hearers, and bids them feel confidence of obtaining pardon by the petition of Flavian the Bishop; and after he had discoursed on the subject of not being afraid of death, he again speaks as usual against oaths.

The seventh Homily was delivered, as is evident from many indications, on the day following. "It is the fifth day," says Chrysostom, "we are engaged in speaking words of comfort to your charity." But this fifth day is reckoned by beginning from the Sunday, so that he must be speaking of the fifth day of the week. He here treats of the first words of Genesis, "In the beginning God made heaven and earth;" and he observes, that God is not only good when He chastises, but also when He confers favours;[2] and concludes by exhorting to avoid oaths.

The eighth Homily Tillemont supposes to have been spoken on the day following the seventh Homily, that is, on the Friday. But Chrysostom disclaims it, who testifies at the outset that he discoursed on the passage, "In the beginning God made heaven and earth, lately" ($\pi\rho\omega\eta\nu$) not yesterday ($\chi\theta\grave{\epsilon}\varsigma$), which without doubt belongs to the seventh Homily. Therefore the present Homily is to be assigned to the Saturday;[3] which these words just immediately after the beginning would also incline us to think. "The week hath nearly arrived at its close with us." The argument of the Homily he draws from these words, "God was walking in Paradise in the cool of the day." On this he observes the wicked are always timid and fearful, but the godly full of confidence. Finally, he treats according to his custom of the avoiding of oaths, and says, that it is now the sixth day since he had been admonishing as to the observance of this law.

The ninth Homily Tillemont with probability allots to the Monday of the second week in Lent. But as to this matter no indication presents itself by which we may lay down any thing certain or probable. This discourse was, however, delivered after a silence of one or more days, as Chrysostom expressly states[4] at the beginning; contrary to which is the opinion of Tillemont, who, whilst he allots the eighth Homily to the Friday of one week, and the ninth to the Monday of the week following, says in the Life of Chrysostom, Art. (15.), that the intervening Sabbaths and Lord's days were doubtless distinguished by discourses of Chrysostom, which discourses have been lost. Chrysostom, at the commencement of this, praises the people of Antioch, that yielding to his admonitions they were taking pains to expel the practice of oaths. On these words also, "The heavens declare the glory of God," he speaks at length, and sets forth God's providence in the order and harmony of the natural world, and at length he concludes the address by admonishing that oaths should be abstained from.

The tenth Homily was not delivered on the day following the ninth, although it follows up the same argument, as is shewn by the word, $\pi\rho\omega\eta\nu$ "lately." But Chrysostom here congratulates his auditors that they had yielded to his admonitions. He declares it is far better to hear the word of God than to fast. He then proves that the world could not pos-

---

[1] Lat. has only "the day before yesterday."

[2] This must be a slip of the pen. [The sentences have clearly got transposed, and we should read "not only good when He confers favours, but also when He chastises."—ED.]

[3] Both arguments may stand, as the common use of $\pi\rho\omega\eta\nu$ is undoubted.

[4] By using the word $\pi\rho\omega\eta\nu$. But this may be in anticipation of his reference to Hom. VII. But if this Homily were delivered on Monday, the first day of *strict* fasting, the scruples of the congregation would be accounted for. No difficulty remains but the use of $\pi\rho\omega\eta\nu$, in Hom. X., against which is $\epsilon\pi\iota o\tilde{\upsilon}\sigma\alpha\nu$. Placing the trials, and Hom. XI.-XVIII. a week later throughout, seems less consistent.

sibly subsist without a divine Providence, and he ends, at length, by an exhortation to abstain from oaths.

The eleventh Homily, Tillemont supposes to have been delivered after that which here has the inscription of the fifteenth, as well as after the sixteenth which follows it. The argument he employs is this; In this Homily he says, the subject is concerning certain dangers and distresses which the city of Antioch had already passed through, which events seem to have taken place after the arrival of Hellebichus and Cæsarius. But that arrival of Hellebichus and Cæsarius is mentioned in the Title of the seventeenth Homily,[1] long after the eleventh of which we are now treating.

Supported by this argument, Tillemont thinks that not only the fifteenth, but also the sixteenth ought to be placed before the eleventh. But besides that all the Manuscripts, without exception, preserve the very same order as the published Editions, we have not a sufficiently accurate knowledge of all the events, the dangers, terrors, and threats of the time, that for a reason of this sort we should deem there ought to be any change in the order. Chrysostom has spoken of many things, but was perhaps silent on many more. Wherefore, until something more certain be brought to light, we think the ancient order must be adhered to. In this Homily Chrysostom at the beginning gives thanks, because the city breathed again after the terror that had fallen on it, since multitudes had taken flight in consequence of suspicions that had been thrown out among them. For some days Chrysostom was silent (as he himself says) during this season of calamity and terror. But Tillemont assigns this Homily to the Monday of the fourth week in Lent, and indeed with the best reason, as we shall shew when we come to the thirteenth Homily. In the present Homily he treats principally of the wisdom of God in the constitution of man, and at the end concerning the avoiding of oaths.

The twelfth, as well as the thirteenth, for the same reason as above, Tillemont makes later than the fifteenth and sixteenth. But I know not in what way he understands that passage in this twelfth Homily, No. (2.) "On the three foregoing days, then, we have investigated one method of acquiring the knowledge of God, and have brought it to a conclusion, explaining how 'the' visible 'heavens declare the glory of God,' and what is the meaning of that which is said by Paul; 'The invisible things of Him from the creation of the world are clearly seen, being understood by the things that are made;' and we have shewed how from the creation of the world, and how by heaven, and earth, and sea, the Creator is glorified. But to-day," etc. Here Chrysostom clearly refers to a series of these Homilies in the order in which they were delivered before the twelfth, that is to say, the ninth, the tenth, and the eleventh. In the ninth (No. 2.) he places as the argument of his discourse the saying of Paul, "The invisible things of Him," etc. as well as that of the Psalms, "The heavens declare the glory of God." In the tenth (No. 2.) likewise he declares that he is pursuing this very argument. In the eleventh (No. 2.) also he testifies that he is insisting on the same argument. Is not Tillemont doing violence to the words of Chrysostom, when he wishes the tenth and the eleventh to be inserted between the fifteenth and sixteenth? This, however, he only proposes, half doubtingly, in note (29) on the Emperor Theodosius, No. 10, 11 seqq. and he confesses, that the order which we have laid down is clearly indicated by Chrysostom; but for what reason I know not, he afterwards departs from the same order. But when Chrysostom says, "on the three past days," it is not to be understood of three successive days, but of the three last days on which he had preached. In this twelfth Homily, likewise, which was delivered on the Tuesday of the fourth week, he dwells on the same subject of the wisdom of God in the creation of the

---

[1] See note at the beginning of that Homily and the preceding; it is almost certain from the whole character of Hom. XVII. that it was not delivered immediately after the events referred to. Probably many had returned, whom St. Chrysostom wished to inform of the events during their absence.

world. He afterwards treats of the natural law, the knowledge of which God hath implanted in man, and on the avoidance of oaths.

The thirteenth Homily was spoken the day after the twelfth. At the commencement he returns thanks to God that the face of affairs was changed, and the fear removed, which had been such that "the greater part of the city," as he says, "had taken refuge from the fear and danger of that occasion in secret places, in deserts, and hollows." Hence he proceeds to speak of many who were dragged to the tribunal; of the horrible inquisition that took place by means of the scourge; of others who were hurried away to punishment; of a mother and sister of a certain person, who, whilst he was undergoing his trial within, were rolling in the dust at the vestibule. Chrysostom describes pathetically these events which had been transacted a few days before, that is to say, before he delivered the eleventh discourse. But the words which Chrysostom uses in the beginning, οἵαν τὴν παρελθοῦσαν εἴδομεν τετράδα καὶ οἵαν τὴν παροῦσαν ὁρῶμεν νῦν, Bernard Brixianus thus renders, "Quale præteritum vidimus quatriduum et quale nunc videmus præsens:" I know not for what reason we have left this untouched. For although τετράς is sometimes taken to signify the fourth day, yet in ecclesiastical language, even from the time of Clemens Alexandrinus, τετράς is the fourth day of the week, so that the Translation should be corrected, and should stand, "Qualem feriam quartam præteritam vidimus," etc. In which it is declared, that the Homily was delivered on the fourth day of the week, and that indeed the fourth week in Lent, or perhaps the third, according to another mode of reckoning; since for many ages downwards the Greeks call that the first Sunday and week of the fast[1] which we call the first of Lent. But this is only a question as to a name. The Homily was however delivered on the fourth day of the week, and from the series of the Homilies, as well as from the silence of Chrysostom, there seems plainly to be an interval of some days between the tenth and eleventh Homilies. In this Homily, moreover, after much premised on that calamity of Antioch, he comes down to the former argument concerning man's creation, and concludes his discourse by an exhortation after his manner on avoiding oaths.

The fourteenth Tillemont thinks ought to be placed after the eighteenth; influenced by this reason, that Chrysostom says at the beginning, "Not a little did the devil yesterday disturb our city, but God hath also not a little comforted us again." These words, he observes, denote that the arrival of Hellebichus, and of news from Constantinople, had already occurred. But these are mere conjectures spoken at random.[2] How many suspicions and terrors think you were cast abroad among the people of Antioch, whilst they hung in doubt, and were ignorant to what result so unhappy an affair might lead? But how can we possibly argue respecting these terrors and reports, when we are doubtless ignorant of the greater part of them, and have so obscure a perception of what we do know, that we can scarcely gather from thence any indication of the time? This Homily is almost wholly on the subject of avoiding oaths.

The fifteenth Homily, Tillemont would have it, was delivered between the tenth and eleventh, both for the reasons above mentioned, and because Chrysostom has these words at the commencement. Ἔδει καὶ τήμερον καὶ τῷ προτέρῳ σαββάτῳ τὸν περὶ νηστείας κινῆσαι λόγον. "It had been right both to-day and on the former Sabbath, to let the discourse turn on the subject of fasting." Where he understands the expression, τῷ προτέρῳ, as though it were τῷ πρώτῳ,—the first Saturday in Lent, entertaining however some doubts on the point. But we, as well as Bernard Brixianus, understand it of the earlier or preceding one.[3] And we

---

[1] See Sir H. Nicolas, *Chron. of History*, p. 117. Gloss. of Dates, art. *Hebdomadæ Græcæ*, observes, that the Greeks named the weeks as beginning on Monday, and taking in Sunday at the end. Still they count Monday the second day, etc. Thus the first *Sunday* would be the same as with the Latins, but the first *week* earlier. It seems probable that this was a week earlier than here stated, see Hom. XVIII.

[2] And dependent on the erroneous notions, that Hom. XVII. was delivered immediately on the arrival of the commissioners.

[3] It may be that, or the first in Lent, considered as the last on which he had preached.

have already proved in a former paragraph, that no other Homily can be placed between the tenth and the eleventh. On the occasion of the dread with which the people of Antioch[1] were affected, he enlarges on the advantage of fear, and at the end he preaches against the custom of swearing, and of requiring an oath from others.

The sixteenth Homily was delivered when all were deliberating upon making their escape from the city, in consequence of a certain report, that a sack was to take place. Tillemont endeavours also to change the position of this Homily, and to place it between the tenth and eleventh, which, however, as we have said in our remarks upon the twelfth, it cannot admit of. Tillemont further supports his argument by these words: in No. 6, the holy Doctor says, "We have passed through the second week of the fast." He infers, therefore, that two weeks only of the fast had passed away, and Tillemont on that ground determines, that it ought to be moved out of its place. He supposes it was spoken on the third Sunday in Lent, reckoning for the first Sunday that which preceded the first day of the fast, which we call Quinquagesima Sunday. But what if at Antioch at that time, that was called the first Sunday of Lent, which according to modern custom occurs as the first within the fast?[2] For the fast did begin the Monday after Quinquagesima, and now it begins on the Wednesday, and the people of Antioch might not reckon that week for the first week of Lent, just as we do not reckon it as so, and in that way this Homily would have been delivered one week later, that is to say, taking the Sunday after the modern custom. But even then a great difficulty would remain, for this Homily would precede the thirteenth and following ones. Certainly all these points are full of perplexity, as Tillemont himself confesses, who is compelled to leave the question, without entirely coming to any conclusion upon it. Perhaps familarity, and longer handling, will add to our knowledge on so obscure a subject, which it is possible we may be able to determine, in drawing up the life of Chrysostom at the end of his works,[3] more clearly and accurately. For which reason we have purposely determined to leave the matter doubtful. That one point only we contend for, that this Homily cannot be placed between the tenth and eleventh, for the reasons above mentioned. Certain things being premised as to the timidity of the people of Antioch, and the avoiding of oaths, Chrysostom borrows the argument of the Homily from those words of Paul, "Paul, a prisoner of Jesus Christ, and Timothy our brother;" and shews that Paul was more glorious from bonds, than from the power of miracles.

The seventeenth was delivered after Ellebichus, or Hellebichus, (styled Magister Militum), and Cæsarius, (styled Magister), the persons sent by the Emperor for the purpose of instituting an inquiry into the sedition, had arrived at Antioch. This Hellebichus, Master of the Horse or[4] Foot, is found mentioned elsewhere, and was distinguished by a reputation for justice and clemency. Cæsarius, also styled elsewhere Master of the Offices, enjoyed a similar reputation for high character. But this Homily was pronounced when the people of Antioch were almost free from fear. "We expected," says Chrysostom (No. 1.), "innumerable horrors, that the property of all was to be plundered; the habitations consumed, together with their inmates; the city snatched away from the midst of the world; and all its relics obliterated, and its soil ploughed up: but, lo! all these things stood only in expectance, and came not actually to pass." Next he relates how the monks descended from the mountains to Antioch, that they might appease the judges, while at the same time all the Greek philosophers deserted the city; and in what way also the priests strenuously exerted

---

[1] Printed, Constantinople.

[2] He may exclude the τυροφάγος, or cheese-week, as not one of the strictest fasting. This appears to have been the case from Homily XVIII., which cannot well be placed anywhere but on the fourth Sunday, and which says that half the fast is over.

[3] This is chiefly a reprint of this preface. Here nothing better is suggested than the supposition of a mistake in transcribing. The difficulty arises from the mistaken notion, that it was before the trials, whereas it was probably delivered a little before the return of a messenger from Cæsarius. See Tabular View.

[4] In the Life "and Foot."

themselves on behalf of the people. He declares the penalties imposed by the Emperor to be light and easy, and no matter of grief or complaint, though the orchestra and public bath were closed, and the dignity of a metropolis taken away from the city of Antioch. The true dignity of Antioch was, that the disciples of Christ were first called Christians there; that the people of Antioch had brought assistance to the saints at Jerusalem, when struggling with famine; that not magnitude, but piety, is the ornament of cities. Finally, however, he says that some were yet remaining in prison; and that others were sent into exile. This Homily Tillemont assigns to the fourth week of Lent, after Wednesday, but only from conjecture.[1]

The eighteenth Homily was spoken after half the fast was over, as Chrysostom himself says at the beginning. But Tillemont thinks it may probably be assigned to the fifth Sunday of Lent. He treats moreover of the true reason for fasting; of contempt for riches; of godly sorrow, &c.

The nineteenth Homily was delivered as the title has it, τῇ κυριακῇ τῆς ἐπισωζομένης, or as Fronto Ducæus reads it, τῆς σωζομένης. Among the Cappadocians, ἐπισωζομένη is Ascension Day, as Allatius says in his book on the Sundays and Weeks of the Greeks, adding that the Sunday thus called is the fifth after Easter,[2] i. e. the one which precedes the Ascension of our Lord. But Savile says that it is [3] the first Sunday after Easter; from whence he got his information I know not. Yet there seems no doubt that it was some one of the last Sundays in Lent, or, as Tillemont supposes, Passion-Sunday, to which I rather incline. Chrysostom, who had been detained at home for some time by sickness, after he has prefaced his subject with some remarks on the Festival of the Martyrs, which had been just celebrated at Antioch, and on the arrival of the rustics, speaks according to his custom against oaths, and illustrates their pernicious effects by many examples.

Hitherto, in the number and order of the Homilies, we have followed the editions of Savile and Fronto Ducæus. But henceforth it is otherwise; for that which follows as the twentieth in former editions, is without doubt the twenty-first and last on the Statues. But the twenty-first is a Catechesis, which we have placed second after another Catechesis, which was inscribed as the first, as we remark in the Notice placed at the end of the Homilies on the Statues, and in front of the Catechetical Lectures; since this Catechesis ought to be placed entirely without the series of the Homilies on the Statues. But the Homily, which is in former editions the twenty-second, is without doubt the twentieth, which was delivered ten days before Easter. Therefore we proceed in this order.

The twentieth Homily has these words in the title, according to manuscripts mentioned by Fronto Ducæus, and likewise in some of ours, and particularly that in the Royal Library, numbered 1971. Ἐλέχθη δὲ πρὸ δέκα ἡμερῶν τῆς ἁγίας καὶ ζωοποιοῦ τοῦ Κυρίου ἡμῶν Ἰησοῦ Χριστοῦ ἐκ νεκρῶν ἀναστάσεως. "It was spoken ten days before the holy and life-giving Resurrection of our Lord Jesus Christ from the dead." This therefore is in perfect accordance with that saying of Chrysostom, a little before the end of the Homily, "Forty days have passed away." This sermon then was delivered on the Friday after the Sunday which we call Passion-Sunday. For this day was the fortieth, beginning from the Monday after Quinquagesima, which was the commencement of Lent. But it was likewise the tenth before Easter, reckoning Easter itself with it. The Homily is almost throughout against enmity and the remembrances of injuries, and at the close is, according to Chrysostom's accustomed manner, directed against oaths.

The twenty-first Homily, which is the last on the Statues, seems, from what he says just

---

[1] The Life adds, The rank of metropolis was transferred from Antioch to Laodicea, according to Theordoret, l. 5, c. 10.
[2] In the Life, and in Pref. to vol. 4, it is proved from Hom. I. *de Anna* (1), that this Homily was actually delivered on that day. This being so, Flavian would be the "Leader" of the Festival.
[3] *Dominica in albis.*

at the beginning, to have been delivered on the very day of the Lord's Resurrection, and after the return of Flavian the Bishop; whose journey to the Emperor, and address to the same on behalf of the city's preservation, as well as the Emperor's reply full of lenity in which he pardons the citizens, are all particularly related by Chrysostom, occupying the whole of this discourse. But even until the return of Flavian, the people of Antioch were terrified by every day's reports, and fluctuated between hope and fear, as Chrysostom observes a little after the beginning.

TABLE OF THE EVENTS CONNECTED WITH THE HOMILIES ON THE STATUES.

			Hom.	
Feb.	—.		1	
	26?			Sedition on the proclamation of a new impost.
March	6 Saturday		2	
	7 SUNDAY, QUINQUAGESIMA		3	Three precepts for this Lent.
	8 M		4	Plan for the week.
	9 T		5	
	10 W		6	
	11 T		7	
	12 F			
	13 S		8	($\pi\rho\psi\eta\nu$.)
	14 SUNDAY I. IN LENT			
	15 M		9	
	16 T		10	Arrival of Hellebichus and Cæsarius. Baths closed. Antioch deprived of its rank.
	17 W			Trial of prisoners. Intercession of monks. Senate kept in prison: sentence to be left to the Emperor.
	18 T			Departure of Cæsarius to Constantinople.
	21 SUNDAY II. IN LENT			
	22 M		11	
	23 T		12	Cæsarius arrives at Constantinople. (Sixth day, Lib.)
	24 W		13	(Trials referred to as on the preceding Wednesday.)
	25 T		14	
	26 F			
	27 S		15	(Ref. to former Saturday.)
	28 SUNDAY III. IN LENT		16	False alarm. (Second week of Fast past.)
	30? T?		17	News from Cæsarius. City to be spared. Senate still in prison.
April	4 SUNDAY IV. IN LENT		18	(Half Fast past, not twenty days from closing of Baths.)
	11 PASSION SUNDAY			
	16 F		20	
	18 PALM SUNDAY		—	
	25 EASTER		21	Return of Flavian, and full pardon, related.
June	—			Feast of the Martyrs. St. Chrysostom ill.
	28 SUNDAY BEFORE ASCENSION		19	Homily addressed to country people.

CONTENTS OF THE HOMILIES.

PAGE

HOMILY I.

This Homily was delivered in the Old Church of Antioch, while St. Chrysostom was yet a Presbyter, upon that saying of the Apostle, 1 Tim. v. 23: "Drink a little wine for thy stomach's sake, and thy often infirmities" 331

HOMILY II.

Spoken in Antioch in the Old Church, as it was called, while he was a presbyter, on the subject of the calamity that had befallen the city in consequence of the tumult connected with the overthrow of the Statues of the Emperor Theodosius, the Great and Pious. And on the saying of the Apostle, "Charge them that are rich that they be not high-minded," 1 Tim. vi. 17. And against covetousness . . . 344

HOMILY III.

On the departure of Flavian, Bishop of Antioch, who was gone on an embassy to the Emperor Theodosius, on behalf of the city. Of the dignity of the Priesthood. What is true fasting. Slander worse than devouring the human body. And finally of those who had been put to death on account of the sedition; and against those who complained that many innocent persons were apprehended 354

HOMILY IV.

An exhortation to the people respecting fortitude and patience, from the examples of Job and the Three Children in Babylon. The Homily concludes with an address on the subject of abstaining from oaths. 364

HOMILY V.

The exhortation of the last Homily is continued in this. The people are exhorted to bear with fortitude the impending wrath of the Emperor. The cases of Job and the Ninevites are referred to as examples. It is shewn that men ought not to fear death, but sin. What it is to die miserably is explained; and the Homily concludes with an earnest dissuasive against the use of oaths 371

HOMILY VI.

This Homily is intended to shew that the fear of Magistrates is beneficial. It also contains an account of what occurred, during their journey, to those who were conveying the tidings of the Sedition to the Emperor. The case of Jonah is further cited in illustration. The exhortation on the fear of death is here continued; and it is shewn, that he who suffers unjustly, and yet gives thanks to God, by whose permission it happens, is as one suffering for God's sake. Examples are again adduced from the history of the Three Children, and the Babylonian furnace. The Homily concludes with an address on the necessity of abstaining from oaths 381

HOMILY VII.

Recapitulation of former exhortations. Sin brought death and grief into the world, and they tend to its cure. Grief serviceable only for the destruction of sin. Remarks upon the passage, Gen. i. 1: "In the beginning God created the heaven and the earth." It is argued that God's forethought for man in the work of creation affords ground of comfort; and that mercy is shewn even in chastisement, as in the saying, "Adam, where art thou?" Concluding admonition on the avoidance of oaths . . . 390

HOMILY VIII.

An exhortation to virtue—and particularly upon the passage, "God was walking in Paradise in the cool of the day:"—and again on the subject of abstaining from oaths 395

HOMILY IX.

Commendation of those who had laid aside the practice of swearing. It is shewn that no one need scruple about hearing the divine oracles in the Church after a meal. Answer to the question, Why it was so long before the Holy Scriptures were given? Comment on the passage, "The heavens declare the glory of God," with a description of the natural world. And finally, an admonition against swearing. 399

HOMILY X.

Commendation of those who came to hear after taking a meal.—Observations on the physiology of the natural world; and against those who deify the creation; and on the duty of not swearing 406

HOMILY XI.

Thanksgiving to God for deliverance from the evils expected owing to the sedition; and recollection of the events which took place at the time. Also against those who find fault with the structure of the human body, and in general concerning the creation of man; and, in conclusion, on success in avoiding oaths. 412

HOMILY XII.

Thanksgiving to God for the pardon granted to the offenders against the Emperor. Physical discourse on the Creation. Proof that God, in creating man, implanted in him a natural law. Duty of avoiding oaths with the utmost diligence 418

HOMILY XIII.

A further thanksgiving to God for the change in the late melancholy aspect of affairs. Reminiscence of those who were dragged away, and punished because of the sedition. Exposition on the subject of the creation of man, and of his having received a natural law. Of the complete accomplishment of abstinence from oaths. 425

HOMILY XIV.

After the whole people had been freed from all distress, and had become assured of safety, certain persons again disturbed the city by fabricating false reports, and were convicted. Wherefore this Homily refers to that subject; and also to the admonition concerning oaths; for which reason also, the history of Jonathan, and Saul, and that of Jephthah, is brought forward; and it is shewn how many perjuries result from one oath 431

HOMILY XV.

Again on the calamity of the city of Antioch. That fear is every way profitable. That sorrow is more useful than laughter. And upon the saying, "Remember that thou walkest in the midst of snares." And that it is worse to exact an oath than to commit murder 438

HOMILY XVI.

This Homily was delivered on the occasion of the Prefect entering the Church, for the purpose of pacifying the minds of the people, in consequence of a rumour of an intended sack having been announced to him, when all were meditating flight. It treats also on the subject of avoiding oaths, and on the words of the Apostle, "Paul, a prisoner of Jesus Christ." 445

HOMILY XVII.

Of the Commissioners (Hellebichus, Commander of the Troops, and Cæsarius, Master of the Offices) sent by the Emperor Theodosius for the inquisition of the offenders, on account of the overturning of the Statues 452

HOMILY XVIII.

The former subject of the Sedition continued; also of fasting; and upon the Apostolic saying, "Rejoice in the Lord always" 458

HOMILY XIX.

On the Sunday called *Episozomenes*, to those who had come to Antioch from the country—also on the subject of avoiding oaths. 464

HOMILY XX.

That the fast of Lent is not sufficient to make us competent to partake of the Communion, but that holiness is the first thing required. How it is possible not to entertain resentment, and that God takes much account of this law; and that the entertaining of resentment punishes those who are guilty of it even before they reach the place of torment.—Also concerning abstinence from oaths, and those who have not succeeded in abstaining from swearing 471

HOMILY XXI.

On the return of Flavian the Bishop, and the reconciliation of the Emperor with the city, and with those who had offended in overthrowing the Statues. 482

HOMILIES OF ST. JOHN CHRYSOSTOM,

ARCHBISHOP OF CONSTANTINOPLE,

ADDRESSED TO THE PEOPLE OF ANTIOCH,

CONCERNING THE STATUES.

HOMILY I.

THE ARGUMENT.

This Homily was delivered in the Old Church[1] of Antioch, while St. Chrysostom was yet a Presbyter, upon that saying of the Apostle, 1 Tim. v. 23, "Drink a little wine for thy stomach's sake, and thy often infirmities."

1. YE have heard the Apostolic voice, that trumpet from heaven, that spiritual lyre! For even as a trumpet sounding a fearful and warlike note, it both dismays the enemy, and arouses the dejected spirits on its own side, and filling them with great boldness, renders those who attend to it invincible against the devil! And again, as a lyre, that gently soothes with soul-captivating melody, it puts to slumber the disquietudes of perverse thoughts; and thus, with pleasure, instils into us much profit. Ye have heard then to-day the Apostle discoursing to Timothy of divers necessary matters! for he wrote to him as to the laying on of hands, saying, "Lay hands suddenly on no man, neither be partaker of other men's sins."[2] And he explained the grievous danger of such a trangression, by showing that so men will undergo the punishment of the sins perpetrated by others, in common with them, because they confer the power on their wickedness by the laying on of hands. Presently again he says, "Use a little wine for thy stomach's sake, and thine often infirmities." To-day also he has discoursed to us concerning the subjection of servants, and the madness of misers, as well as on the arrogance of the rich, and on various other matters.

2. Since then it is impossible to go through every part, what part of the words rehearsed would you have us select for the subject of our address to your charity?[3] For as in a meadow, I perceive in what has been read a great diversity of flowers; a multiplicity of roses and violets, and of lilies not a few; and everywhere the various and copious fruit of the Spirit is scattered around, as well as an abundant fragrance. Yea, rather the reading of the divine Scriptures is not a meadow only, but a paradise; for the flowers here have not a mere fragrance only, but fruit too, capable of nourishing the soul. What part then of the things rehearsed do you desire that we bring before you this day? Do you wish what seems the more insignificant, and easy for any one to understand, to be that which we should handle at present? To me, indeed, this seems proper, and I doubt not you

---

[1] So called, because situated in the more ancient part of the city of Antioch, near the river Orontes. It was also called the Apostolic Church, as being that founded by the Apostles.

This Homily was spoken a little before the breaking out of the sedition. It has, however, always been classed with the rest because alluded to in the next Homily.

[2] 1 Tim. v. 22.

[3] Gr. "unto your love," a title by which St. Chrysostom addresses his hearers; as we say, "Your Grace," "Your Majesty."

will concur in this opinion. What then is this that might seem plainer than anything else? What but that, which seems so easy, and obvious for any one to say? Well! what is that? "Use a little wine for thy stomach's sake, and thine often infirmities." Well then, let us employ the whole of our discourse upon this subject; and this we would do, not for the love of praise, nor because we study to exhibit powers of oratory (for the things about to be spoken are not our own, but such as the grace of the Holy Spirit may inspire); but in order that we may stir up those hearers who are too listless, and may convince them of the greatness of the treasure of the holy Scriptures; and that it is neither safe, nor free from peril, to run through them hastily. For if indeed a text so simple and obvious as this one, which seems to the multitude to contain nothing that need be insisted on, should appear to afford us the means of abundant riches, and openings toward the highest wisdom, much rather will those others, which at once manifest their native wealth, satisfy those who attend to them with their infinite treasures. Assuredly then, we ought not hastily to pass by even those sentences of Scripture which are thought to be plain; for these also have proceeded from the grace of the Spirit; but this grace is never small, nor mean, but great and admirable, and worthy the munificence of the Giver.

3. Let us not therefore listen carelessly; since even they who roast the metallic earth, when they have thrown it into the furnace, not only take up the masses of gold, but also collect the small particles with the utmost care. Inasmuch, then, as we likewise have to roast[1] the gold drawn from the Apostolic mines, not by casting it into the furnace, but by depositing it in the thoughts of your souls; not lighting an earthly flame, but kindling the fire of the Spirit, let us collect the little particles with diligence.[2] For if the saying be brief, yet is its virtue great. For pearls too have their proper market, not owing to the size of the substance, but the beauty of their nature. Even so is it with the reading of the divine Scriptures; for worldly instruction rolls forth its trifles in abundance, and deluges its hearers with a torrent of vain babblings, but dismisses them empty-handed, and without having gathered any profit great or small. Not so however is it with the grace of the Spirit, but, on the contrary, by means of small sentences, it implants divine wisdom in all who give heed, and one sentence often times affords to those who receive it a sufficient source of provision for the whole journey of life.[3]

4. Since then its riches are so great, let us arouse ourselves, and receive that which is spoken with a watchful mind; for I am preparing to plunge our discussion to an extreme depth. The admonition itself hath no doubt seemed beside the purpose, and superfluous to many: and they are apt to talk much in this way, "Was Timothy of himself not able to judge what it was needful to make use of, and did he wait to learn this of his teacher.[4] And then did the teacher not only give directions, but also set them down in writing, graving it there as on a column of brass in his Epistle to him? and was he not ashamed to give directions about things of this nature, when writing in a public manner, to his disciple?" For this end then, that thou mayest learn that the admonition, so far from being beside the purpose, was a necessary and highly profitable one; and that the thing proceeded not from Paul, but from the grace of the Spirit, viz. that this should have been (I say) not a spoken precept, but one deposited in letters, and to be handed down to all future generations through the Epistle, I shall proceed at once to the proof.

5. For besides the subjects which have been mentioned, there is another, about which some are no less perplexed, enquiring within themselves on what account God permitted a man possessing such confidence towards Him,[5] whose bones and relics expelled demons,[6] to fall into such a state of infirmity; for it is not merely that he was sick, but constantly, and for a length of time; and by these recurring and prolonged infirmities he was not permitted to have even a brief respite. "How does this appear," it may be asked? From the very words of Paul, for he does not say, on account of the "infirmity," but on account of the "infirmities;" and not merely "infirmities," but he clearly speaks of these as being constant, when he says "thine often infirmities." Let those then attend to this, whoever they are, who being given over to a lingering[7] sickness are querulous and dejected under it.

---

[1] The operation of *roasting* the ore, in the Cornish mines, consists in placing it in a comminuted state in a furnace of a particular construction, where it is subjected to a strong heat, but not so strong as to *smelt* it; by which the arsenic, sulphur, and other impurities, are carried off in the form of vapor, leaving the heavier metallic substance behind.—Tr.
[2] See on Rom. xvi. 5, Hom. XXXI.
[3] Socr. H. E. iv. 23. Pambos was nineteen years in learning Ps. xxxix. 1. He excelled even St. Antony in exactness of speech. Pall. Hist. Laus. c. 10.
[4] Or, the teacher, as he is called emphatically, Doctor Gentium, see 1 Tim. ii. 7.
[5] Or, "claims," παῤῥησίαν. See 1 Tim. iii. 13. Suicer misinterprets the word as used by St. Chrysostom in Gen. Hom. IX, sec. 4, of what man lost in the fall; it means there not power, but confidence before God.
[6] See on Rom. xvi. 5, Hom. XXXI.
[7] An old translation has "slight," as if it were μικρᾷ.

6. But the subject of enquiry is not only, that being a holy man he was sick, and sick so continually, but that he was at the same time entrusted with the public affairs of the world. For if he had been one of those who have retreated to the tops of mountains; who have fixed their cells in solitude, and who have chosen that life which is free from all business, the matter now enquired into were no such difficulty; but that one thrust forward in the throng, and in whose hands the care of so many Churches was placed, and who superintended whole cities and nations; nay, the world at large,[1] with so much alacrity and diligence, should be subjected to the straitening of infirmities! This it is which may most of all bewilder one who does not duly consider it. Because, even if not for himself, yet for others at least, it was necessary he should have health. "He was the best general," says the objector. "The war was waged by him, not only against the unbeliever, but against demons, and against the devil himself. All the enemy contended with much vehemence, scattering the forces, and capturing prisoners;[2] but this man was able to bring back myriads to the truth, and yet he was sick! For if," he says, "no other injury to the cause had come of this sickness, yet this alone was sufficient to discourage and relax the faithful. If soldiers, when they see their general detained in bed, become discouraged and slack for the fight, much rather was it probable that the faithful should betray somewhat of human nature, when they saw that teacher, who had wrought so many signs, in continual sickness and suffering of body."

7. But this is not all. These sceptics propose yet a further enquiry, by asking for what reason Timothy neither healed himself, nor was healed by his instructor, when he was reduced to this state. Whilst the Apostles raised the dead, cast out devils, and conquered death with abundant ease, they could not even restore the body of one sick man! Although with respect to other bodies, both during their own lives and after death, they manifested such extraordinary power, they did not restore a stomach that had lost its vigour! And what is more than this, Paul is not ashamed, and does not blush, after the many and great signs which he had displayed even by a simple word; yet, in writing to Timothy, to bid him take refuge in the healing virtue of wine drinking. Not that to drink wine is shameful. God forbid! For such precepts belong to heretics; but the matter of astonishment is, that he accounted it no disgrace not to be able, without this kind of assistance, to set one member right when it was disordered. Nevertheless, he was so far from being ashamed of this, that he has made it manifest to all posterity.[3] You see then to what a depth we have brought down the subject, and how that which seemed to be little, is full of innumerable questions. Well then, let us proceed to the solution; for we have explored the question thus deep, in order that, having excited your attention, we might lay up the explanation in a safe storehouse.

8. But before I proceed to solve these questions, permit me to say something of the virtue of Timothy, and of the loving care of Paul. For what was ever more tender hearted than this man, who being so far distant, and encircled with so many cares, exercised so much consideration for the health of his disciple's stomach, and wrote with exact attention about the correction of his disorder? And what could equal the virtue of Timothy? He so despised luxury, and derided the sumptuous table, as to fall into sickness from excessive austerity, and intense fasting. For that he was not naturally so infirm a person, but had overthrown the strength of his stomach by fasting and water drinking; you may hear Paul himself carefully making this plain. For he does not simply say, "use a little wine;" but having said before, "drink no longer water," he then brings forward his counsel as to the drinking of wine. And this expression "no longer" was a manifest proof, that till then he had drunk water, and on that account was become infirm. Who then would not wonder at his divine wisdom and strictness? He laid hold on the very heavens, and sprang to the highest point of virtue. And his Teacher testifies this, when he thus speaks, "I have sent unto you Timothy, who is my beloved and faithful son in the Lord;"[4] and when Paul calls him "a son," and a "faithful and beloved son," these words are sufficient to show that he possessed every kind of virtue. For the judgments of the saints are not given according to favour or enmity, but are free from all prejudice. Timothy would not have been so enviable, if he had been Paul's son naturally, as he was now admirable, inasmuch as having no connection with him according to the flesh, he introduced himself by the relationship of piety into the Apostle's adoption;

---

[1] He appears to have acted beyond his local charge, as in joining in the address of several Epistles (see 2 Cor. i. 1, Phil. i. 1, Col. i. 1), and in various missions, as Phil. ii. 19, 22.
[2] 2 Tim. ii. 26.
[3] *i. e.*, by his precept to Timothy, ὁ (Paris reprint) seems a misprint for ὅτι. Hoogeveen questions whether ὅτι can be used as ὥστε. If that is not the sense here, the construction is imperfect.
[4] 1 Cor. iv. 17.

preserving the marks of his spiritual wisdom[1] with exactness in all things. For even as a young bullock[2] linked to a bull, so he drew the yoke along with him, to whatever part of the world he went: and did not draw it the less on account of his youth, but his ready will made him emulate the labours of his teacher. And of this, Paul himself was again a witness when he said, "Let no man despise him, for he worketh the work of the Lord as I also do."[3] See you how he bears witness, that the ardour of Timothy was the very counterpart of his own?

9. Furthermore, in order that he might not be thought to have said these things out of favour or kindness, he makes his hearers themselves to be witnesses of the virtue of his son, when he says, "But ye know the proof of him, that, as a son with a father, so he hath served with me in the Gospel;"[4] that is, "ye have had experience of his virtue, and of his approved soul." At the same time, however, that he had reached to this height of good works, he did not thereby grow confident; but was full of anxiety and fear, therefore also he fasted rigidly, and was not affected as many are, who, when they have kept themselves to it but ten, or perhaps twenty months,[5] straightway give up the matter altogether. He, I say, was in no wise thus affected, nor did he say anything like this to himself. "What further need have I of fasting? I have gotten the mastery of myself; I have overcome my lusts; I have mortified my body; I have affrighted demons: I have driven away the devil; I have raised the dead; I have cleansed lepers; I am become terrible to the adverse powers; what further need have I of fasting, or to seek safety from that quarter?" Anything like this he did not say, he did not think of; but, in proportion as he abounded with innumerable good works, so much the more did he fear and tremble.[6] And he learnt this spiritual wisdom from his preceptor; for even he, after he had been rapt into the third heaven, and transported to paradise; and had heard unutterable words; and taken part in such mysteries; and traversed the whole world, like some winged being, when he wrote to the Corinthians, said, I fear "lest by any means having preached to others, I myself should be a castaway."[7] And if Paul was afraid after so many signal good works; he who was able to say, "The world is crucified unto me, and I unto the world;"[8] much more does it become us to fear; and the rather in proportion as we have stored up[9] numerous good works. For then the devil becomes fiercer; then he is more savage, when he beholds us regulating our lives with carefulness! When he sees the cargo of virtue stowed together, and the lading become heavy, then he is in haste to accomplish a more grievous shipwreck! For the insignificant and abject man, although he may be supplanted and fall, brings not so great an injury to the common cause. But the man who has been standing most conspicuously as it were on some eminence of virtue, and who is one manifestly seen and known of all men, and admired of all; when he is assaulted and falls, causes great ruin and loss. Not only because he falls from this elevation but makes many of those who look up to him more negligent. And as it is in the body, some other limb may be destroyed without there being any great damage, but if the eyes be deprived of sight, or the head be seriously injured, the whole body is rendered useless; so also we must say of the saints, and of those who have performed the highest good works; when such are extinguished, when they contract any stain, they bring upon all the rest of the body a universal and, intolerable injury!

10. Timothy then, being aware of all these things, fortified himself on every side; for he knew that youth is an age of difficulty; that it is unstable; easily deceived; very apt to slip; and requires an exceedingly strong bridle. It is indeed a sort of combustible pile easily catching anything from without, and quickly kindled; and for that reason he took care to smother it on all sides; and strove to abate the flame in every way. The steed[10] that was unmanageable and restive he curbed with much vehemence, until he had tamed him of his wanton tricks; until he had made him docile; and delivered him under entire control, into the hands of that reason which is the charioteer.[11] "Let the body," saith he, "be infirm; but let not the soul be infirm; let the flesh be bridled; but let not the race of the spirit towards heaven be checked."

---

[1] Gr. philosophy, which is almost always used by St. Chrysostom in this practical sense. "Divine wisdom" has been sometimes put for it.
[2] μόσχος.   [3] 1 Cor. xvi. 10.   [4] Phil. ii. 22.
[5] A course of discipline was usual with those who intended to live a truly Christian life. St. Chrysostom spent four years in retirement. St. Augustin also practised self-discipline before his baptism (Conf. ix. 14, Tr. p. 165), and afterwards x. 47, p. 239; see the end of Hom. XXVI. on Rom. xvi. 2, 4. And of men's falling off soon after baptism, on Rom. vi. 3; Hom. X. p. 160, which passage favours the reading "days," adopted by Savile.
[6] St. Paul does not say, "I fear;" but he does say that he used means like these.
[7] 1 Cor. ix. 27.   [8] Gal. vi. 14.
[9] συνειληχότες. "Have shared," makes no sense here. Valckenaer, Opusc. i. p. 208, corrects the same word in Or. i. de Laud. St. Paul, fin. Read συνειλοχότες. Att. from συλλέγω.
[10] See on Rom. vii. 6; Hom. XII. p. 191.
[11] Or, "which guided himself." A less easy construction, but better suited to the context. Compare Plato's famous illustration (probably known to St. Chrysostom), Phædrus, 246, in which Reason is represented as a charioteer driving a chariot drawn by two horses, one of an aspiring, the other of a grovelling nature.

But moreover, one might especially wonder at the man for this, that being thus diseased, and struggling with such an infirmity, he did not become indifferent to God's business, but flew everywhere faster than those who have sound and vigourous constitutions; now to Ephesus; now to Corinth; often to Macedonia and Italy; appearing everywhere, by land and by sea, with the Teacher, sharing in everything his struggles and continuous dangers; while the spiritual wisdom of his soul was not put to shame by his bodily infirmity. Such a thing is zeal for God! such lightness of wing does it impart! For as with those who possess well-regulated and sound constitutions, strength is of no avail, if the soul is abject, slothful, and stupid; so with those who are reduced to extreme weakness, no hurt arises from their infirmity, if the soul be noble and well awake.

11. The admonition however, and the counsel, such as it is, appears to some to give authority for drinking wine too freely. But this is not so. If indeed we closely investigate this very saying, it rather amounts to a recommendation of abstinence. For just consider that Paul did not at first, nor at the outset give this counsel. But when he saw that all strength was overthrown, then he gave it; and even then not simply, but with a certain prior limitation. He does not say merely, "Use wine," but "a little" wine; not because Timothy needed this admonition and advice, but because we need it. On this account, in writing to him, he prescribes the measure and limit of wine-drinking for us; bidding him drink just so much as would correct disorder; as would bring health to the body, but not another disease. For the immoderate drinking of wine produces not fewer diseases of body and of soul, than much drinking of water, but many more, and more severe; bringing in as it does upon the mind the war of the passions, and a tempest of perverse thoughts, besides reducing the firmness of the body to a relaxed and flaccid condition. For the nature of land that is long disturbed by a superabundance of water, is not thereby so much dissolved, as the force of the human frame is enfeebled, relaxed, and reduced to a state of exhaustion, by the continual swilling of wine. Let us guard then against a want of moderation on either side, and let us take care of the health of the body, at the same time that we prune away its luxurious propensities. For wine was given us of God, not that we might be drunken, but that we might be sober; that we might be glad, not that we get ourselves pain. "Wine," it says, "maketh glad the heart of man,"[1] but thou makest it matter for sadness; since those who are inebriated are sullen beyond measure, and great darkness overspreads their thoughts. It is the best medicine, when it has the best moderation to direct it. The passage before us is useful also against heretics, who speak evil of God's creatures; for if it had been among the number of things forbidden, Paul would not have permitted it, nor would have said it was to be used. And not only against the heretics, but against the simple ones among our brethren, who when they see any persons disgracing themselves from drunkenness, instead of reproving such, blame the fruit given them by God, and say, "Let there be no wine." We should say then in answer to such, "Let there be no drunkenness; for wine is the work of God, but drunkenness is the work of the devil. Wine maketh not drunkenness; but intemperance produceth it. Do not accuse that which is the workmanship of God, but accuse the madness of a fellow mortal. But thou, while omitting to reprove and correct the sinner, treatest thy Benefactor with contempt!"

12. When, therefore, we hear men saying such things, we should stop their mouths; for it is not the use of wine, but the want of moderation which produces drunkenness, Drunkenness! that root of all evils. Wine was given to restore the body's weakness, not to overturn the soul's strength; to remove the sickness of the flesh, not to destroy the health of the spirit. Do not then, by using the gift of God immoderately, afford a handle to the foolish and the impudent. For what is a more wretched thing than drunkenness! The drunken man is a living corpse. Drunkenness is a demon self-chosen, a disease without excuse, an overthrow that admits of no apology; a common shame to our kind. The drunken man is not only useless in our assemblies; not only in public and private affairs; but the bare sight of him is the most disgusting of all things, his breath being stench. The belchings, and gapings, and speech of the intoxicated, are at once unpleasant and offensive, and are utterly abhorrent to those who see and converse with them; and the crown of these evils is, that this disease makes heaven inaccessible to drunkards, and does not suffer them to win eternal blessedness: for besides the shame attending those who labour under this disease here, a grievous punishment is also awaiting them there! Let us cut off then this evil habit, and let us hear Paul saying, "Use a little

---

5 Ps. ciii. 15.

wine." For even this little he permits him on account of his infirmity; so that if infirmity had not troubled him, he would not have forced his disciple to allow himself even a small quantity, since it is fitting that we should always mete out even the needful meat and drink, which are given us, by occasions and necessities; and by no means go beyond our need, nor do anything unmeaningly and to no purpose.

13. But since we have now learnt the tender care of Paul, and the virtue of Timothy, come and let us, in the next place, turn our discourse to the actual solution of those questions. What then are the questions? For it is necessary again to mention them, that the solution of them may be plainer. For what reason then did God permit that such a saint, and one entrusted with the management of so many matters, should fall into a state of disease; and that neither Timothy himself nor his teacher had strength to correct the disorder, but needed that assistance which was to be had by drinking wine? Such, indeed, were the questions proposed. But it is needful to bring forward a precise solution; so that if any should fall not only into the like sickness and disease, but into poverty, and hunger, and bonds, and torments, and discomfitures, and calumnies, and into all those evils which belong to the present life, although they were great and wonderful saints, you may still be able to find, even for their case, in the things which are to-day to be advanced, an exact and very clear reply to those who are disposed to find fault. For ye have heard many asking such questions, as, "Why ever is it that such an one, a moderate and meek man, comes to be dragged daily before the seat of judgment by another who is lawless and wicked, and to suffer evils without number, and God permits this? For what reason again was another man, upon false accusation, unjustly put to death?" "Such a man," says the objector, "was drowned; another was thrown down a precipice; and we might speak of many saints, as well in our own days as in the days of our forefathers, who have suffered divers and chequered tribulations." To the end, therefore, that we may see the reason of these things, and that we ourselves may not be disturbed, nor overlook the case of others who thus meet with a stumbling-block, we should attend with earnest heed to the reasons now about to be advanced.

14. For of the diversified and manifold affliction which befalls the saints, I have reasons eight in number to declare unto your love. Therefore let all direct themselves to me with the strictest attention, knowing that there will be no pardon nor excuse left us hereafter for stumbling at the things which happen, if after all, when there are so many reasons, we are just as much perplexed and disturbed as if there were not one to be found.

The first reason then is, that God permits them to suffer evil, that they may not too easily be exalted into presumption, by the greatness of their good works and miracles.

The second, that others may not have a greater opinion of them than belongs to human nature, and take them to be gods and not men.

The third, that the power of God may be made manifest, in prevailing, and overcoming, and advancing the word preached, through the efficacy of men who are infirm and in bonds.

The fourth, that the endurance of these themselves may become more striking, serving God, as they do, not for a reward; but showing even such right-mindedness as to give proof of their undiminished good will towards Him after so many evils.

The fifth, that our minds may be wise concerning the doctrine of a resurrection. For when thou seest a just man, and one abounding in virtue, suffering ten thousand evils, and thus departing the present life, thou art altogether compelled, though unwillingly, to think somewhat of the future judgment; for if men do not suffer those who have laboured for themselves, to depart without wages and recompense; much more cannot God design, that those who have so greatly laboured should be sent away uncrowned. But if He cannot intend to deprive those of the recompense of their labours eventually, there must needs be a time, after the end of the life here, in which they will receive the recompense of their present labours.

The sixth, that all who fall into adversity may have a sufficient consolation and alleviation, by looking at such persons, and remembering what sufferings have befallen them.

The seventh, that when we exhort you to the virtue of such persons, and we say to every one of you, "Imitate Paul, emulate Peter," ye may not, on account of the surpassing character of their good works, slothfully shrink from such an imitation of them, as deeming them to have been partakers of a different nature.

The eighth, that when it is necessary to call any blessed, or the reverse, we may learn whom we ought to account happy, and whom unhappy and wretched.

These then are the reasons; but it is necessary to establish them all from the Scriptures, and to show with exactness that all that has been said on this subject is not an invention of human reasoning, but the very sentence of the Scriptures. For thus will what we say be at once more deserving of credit, and sink the deeper into your minds.

15. That tribulation then is profitable to the saints, that they may exercise moderation and lowliness, and that they may not be puffed up by their miracles and good works, and that God permits it for this end; we may hear David the prophet, and Paul saying the same. The former says, "It is good for me, Lord, that I have been in trouble, that I might learn thy statutes:"[1] and the latter having said, "I was caught up into the third heaven, and" transported to Paradise, goes on to say, "And lest I should be exalted above measure through the abundance of the revelations, there was given me a thorn in the flesh, the messenger of Satan to buffet me."[2] What can be clearer than this? "That I might not be exalted above measure," for this reason, saith he, God permitted "the messengers of Satan to buffet me;" by messengers of Satan, indeed, he means not particular demons, but men[3] ministering for the devil, the unbelievers, the tyrants, the heathens, who perseveringly molested, and unceasingly worried him. And what he says is just this: "God was able to repress these persecutions and successive tribulations; but since I had been caught up into the third heaven, and transported to Paradise, lest through the abundance of these revelations I might be lifted up and think much of myself, he permitted these persecutions, and suffered these messengers of Satan to buffet me with persecutions and afflictions, that I might not be too much exalted." For although Paul and Peter, and all that are like them, be holy and wonderful men, as indeed they are, yet they are but men, and require much caution lest they should be too easily exalted; and as saints more than others. For nothing is so apt to exalt to presumption as a conscience full of good works, and a soul that lives in confidence. To the end, therefore, that these might suffer nothing of this kind, God permitted that there should be temptations and tribulations; these being powerful to keep them down, and to persuade to the exercise of moderation in all things.

16. That this very particular also contributes much to the showing forth of God's power, you may learn even from the same Apostle, who told us the former. In order that you may not say, (what indeed unbelievers think), that God in permitting this, is some infirm being, and suffers such persons to be continually afflicted, from not being able to deliver His own from dangers: this very thing, I say, observe how Paul has demonstrated by means of these events, showing not only that the events were far from accusing Him of weakness, but that they proved His power more strikingly to all. For having said, "There was given me a thorn in the flesh; a messenger of Satan to buffet me," and having thus signified his repeated trials, he goes on to add, "For this thing I besought the Lord thrice, that it might depart from me; and He said unto me, My grace is sufficient for thee, for My strength is perfected in weakness."[4] "My power," He means, "is seen then when ye are in weakness; and yet through you, who seem to grow weak, the word preached is magnified, and is sown in all quarters." When therefore he was led to the dungeon, after having received a great number of stripes, he took prisoner the keeper of the prison.[5] His feet were in the stocks, and his hands in the chain; and the prison shook at midnight while they were singing hymns. See you, how His power was perfected in weakness? If Paul had been at large, and had shaken that building, the thing would not have been so wonderful. "For this reason," He saith, "remain bound; and the walls shall be shaken on every side, and the prisoners shall be loosed; in order that My power may appear the greater, when through thee, confined and in fetters, all that are in bonds shall be loosed." This very circumstance then it was which at the time astounded the keeper of the prison, that being so forcibly confined, he, through prayer alone, prevailed to shake the foundations, and throw open the doors of the prison, and to unbind all the prisoners. Nor is this the only occasion. But with Peter too, and Paul himself, as well as the other disciples, one may see this occurring constantly; and in the midst of persecution, the grace of God ever flourishing, and appearing by the side of the tribulations, and thus proclaiming His power. Wherefore He saith, "My grace is sufficient for thee, for My strength is perfected in weakness."

17. But to show that many would be too often ready to imagine things of them above human nature, unless things saw them enduring such afflictions, hear how Paul was afraid on this very point; "For though I would desire to glory, I shall not be a fool, but now I forbear, lest any man should think of me above

---

[1] Ps. cxix. 71. [2] 2 Cor. xii. 2, 4, 7.
[3] So he explains it also on the passage, on 2 Cor., Hom. XXVI. See also on Rom. viii. 6, Trans. p. 251, and Bp. Bull, Serm. v.
[4] 2 Cor. xii. 8, 9. [5] Acts xvi. 24.

that which he seeth me to be, or that he heareth of me."[1] But what is it that he means? I am able, he declares, to speak of far greater miracles; but I am unwilling; lest the magnitude of the miracles should raise too high a notion of me among men. For this reason Peter also, when they[2] had restored the lame man, and all were wondering at them, in order to restrain the people, and persuade them that they had exhibited nothing of this power of themselves, or from their native strength, says, "Why look ye so earnestly on us, as though by our own power or holiness we had made this man to walk?"[3] And again at Lystra, the people were not only filled with astonishment, but led forth bulls, after crowning them with garlands, and were preparing to offer sacrifice to Paul and Barnabas. Observe the malice of the Devil. By those very same persons through whom the Lord was at work, to purge out ungodliness from the world, by the same did that enemy try to introduce it, again persuading them to take men for gods; which was what he had done in former times. And this is especially that which introduced the principle and root of idolatry. For many after having had success in wars, and set up trophies, and built cities, and done divers other benefits of this kind to the people of those times, came to be esteemed gods by the multitude, and were honoured with temples, and altars; and the whole catalogue of the Grecian gods is made up of such men. That this, therefore, may not be done towards the Saints,[4] God permitted them constantly to be banished,—to be scourged,—to fall into diseases; that the abundance of bodily infirmity, and the multiplicity of those temptations, might convince those who were then with them, both that they were men, who wrought such wonders, and that they contributed nothing of their own power; but that it was mere grace, that wrought through them all these miracles. For if they took men for gods, who had done but mean and vile things, much rather would they have thought these to be such, had they suffered nothing proper to humanity, when they performed miracles, such as no one had ever before seen or heard of. For if when they were scourged, thrown down precipices, imprisoned, banished, and placed in peril every day, there were, notwithstanding, some who fell into this impious opinion, how much rather would they have been thus regarded, had they endured nothing which belongs to human nature!

18. This then is the third cause of affliction; and the fourth is, that the saints might not be supposed to serve God from a hope of present prosperity. For many of those who live in debauchery, when blamed as they often are by many, and invited to the labours of virtue; and when they hear the saints commended for their cheerfulness under great hardships,[5] attack their character on this ground; and not men only, but the devil himself hath taken up this suspicion. For when Job was surrounded with great wealth, and enjoyed much opulence, that wicked demon,[6] being reproached by God on his account, and having nothing to say; when he could neither answer the accusations against himself, nor impugn the virtue of this just man; took refuge at once in this defence, speaking thus, "Doth Job fear thee for nought? Hast thou not made an hedge about him on all sides."[7] "For reward then," saith he, "that man is virtuous, enjoying thereby so much opulence." What then did God? Being desirous to show, that it was not for reward that his saints serve Him, He stripped him of all his opulence; gave him over to poverty; and permitted him to fall into grievous disease. Afterwards reproving him,[8] that he had suspected thus without cause, He saith, "He yet holdeth fast his integrity; to no purpose didst thou move me to destroy his substance." For it is a sufficient reward, and compensation to the saints, that they are serving God; since this indeed to the lover is reward enough, to love the object of his love;[9] and he seeks nothing besides, nor accounts anything greater than this. And if such be the case with regard to a man, much more in relation to God; which therefore that God might demonstrate, He gave more than the devil asked; for the latter said, "Put forth thine hand, and touch him;"[10] but God said

---

[1] 2 Cor. xii. 6.
[2] Or, "he," referring to οἱ περὶ; St. John, however, may be included.
[3] Acts iii. 12.
[4] The heathen altars, βωμοὶ, must not be confounded with the Christian θυσιαστήρια raised over the relics of saints *to God.* St. Aug. ser. 273, c. 7, in *Nat. Mart. Fructuosi &c. de Sanctis,* 1 (Ben. t. 5). "When didst thou ever hear me, or any of my brethren and colleagues, say at the memorial of St. Theogenes, 'I offer to thee, St. Theogenes;' or, 'I offer to thee, Peter;' or, 'I offer to thee, Paul?' and if it be said to you, 'Do you worship (colis) Peter?' Answer, . . . 'I do not worship Peter, but I worship God, whom Peter also worships.' Then doth Peter love thee." This passage of St. Chrysostom is, however, remarkable, as pointing out a tendency which has since been carried to excess.

[5] ἐπὶ τῇ τῶν δεινῶν εὐψυχίᾳ. One would have expected ἐν τοῖς δεινοῖς; but perhaps the true reading is δεινῶν, making the sense "for the noble spirit of such and such persons."
[6] See St. Greg. Mor. in B., Job l. 1, c. 8, 9, 23, &c. He comments on three senses, the Historical, the Allegorical, and the Moral. In the allegorical, Job represents Christ, in the moral, His Church. In the words, *whence comest thou,* he understands that Satan is called to account for his own ways. In *Hast thou considered,* &c., he sees a type of the Incarnation.
[7] Job i. 9, 10.   [8] Satan. Job ii. 3, LXX.
[9] ἐρώμενον. The Benedictine translator is mistaken in rendering this "to love one who loves him," see on Rom. ix. 6, Hom. XVI. Tr. p. 284. "For even being loved by Christ was not the only thing he cared for, but loving Him exceedingly. And this last he cared most for."
[10] Job ii. 5, 6.

not thus, but, "I deliver him unto thee." For just as in the contests[1] of the outer world, the combatants that are vigorous, and in high condition of body,[2] are not so well discerned, when they are enwrapt all around with the garment soaked in oil; but when casting this aside, they are brought forward unclothed into the arena; then above all they strike the spectators on every side with astonishment at the proportion of their limbs, there being no longer anything to conceal them; so also was it with Job. When he was enveloped in all that wealth, it was not visible to the many, what a man he was. But when, like the wrestler, that strips off his garment, he threw it aside, and came naked to the conflicts of piety, thus unclothed, he astonished all who saw him;[3] so that the very theatre of angels shouted at beholding his fortitude of soul, and applauded him as he won his crown! For, as I have already observed, he was not so well seen of men, when clad in all that wealth, as when, casting it away like a garment, he exhibited himself naked as it were in a theatre, in the midst of the world, and all admired his vigor of soul, evidenced as this was not only by his being stripped of all things, but by the conflict, and by his patience in respect of his infirmity. And as I said before, God Himself did not smite him; in order that the devil might not again say, "Thou hast spared him, and hast not inflicted so great a trial as was necessary:" but he gave to the adversary the destruction of his cattle, and power over his flesh. "I am sure," saith He, "of this wrestler; therefore I do not forbid thee to impose on him whatever struggles thou desirest." But as those who are well skilled in the sports of the palæstra, and have reason to rely on their art and bodily strength, often do not seize their antagonists upright, nor take an equal advantage, but suffer them to take them by the middle,[4] that they may make a more splendid conquest; so also God gave to the devil to take this saint by the waist, that when he had overcome, after an attack so greatly to his disadvantage, and stretched his adversary on the ground, his crown might be so much the more glorious!

19. It is tried gold! Try it as thou desirest; examine it as thou wishest, thou wilt not find in it any dross. This shows us not only the fortitude of others, but also brings much farther[5] consolation; for what saith Christ, "Blessed are ye when men shall revile you and persecute you, and shall say all manner of evil against you falsely for my sake. Rejoice and be exceeding glad, for great is your reward in heaven: for in like manner did their fathers unto the prophets."[6] Again, Paul writing to the Macedonians in his desire to console them, says, "For ye, brethren, became followers of the churches of God which are in Judea. For ye also have suffered like things of your own countrymen, even as they have of the Jews."[7] And again, he consoles the Hebrews in like manner, reckoning up all the just who had lived[8] in furnaces; in pits; in deserts; in mountains; in caves; in hunger; and in poverty.[9] For communion of suffering brings some consolation to the fallen.

20. But that this also introduces arguments for the resurrection, hear the same Paul again, saying, "If after the manner of men I have fought with beasts at Ephesus, what shall it profit me if the dead are not raised."[10] And further, "If in this life only we have hope, we are of all men the most miserable."[11] We suffer, he tells us, innumerable evils during the present life; if then there is no other life to be hoped for, what can be more wretched than our condition? Hence it is evident that our affairs are not bounded within the limits of this present state; and this becomes manifest from our trials. For God could never suffer those who have endured so many and so great evils, and who have spent all the present life in trials and dangers without number, to be without a recompense of far greater gifts; and if he could not suffer this, it is certain that he has prepared another, a better and brighter life, in which he will crown those who have wrestled in the cause of godliness, and proclaim their praises in the presence of the whole world. So that when you see a just man straitened and afflicted; and in sickness, and in poverty, as well as innumerable other woes, till he ends this present life; say to thyself, that if there were no resurrection and judgment, God would not have permitted one, who endured such great evils for His sake, to depart hence without enjoying any good thing; from whence it is evident, that for such He has prepared another life, and one which is sweeter and much more endurable. For if

---

[1] τῶν ἔξωθεν, as being Pagan.
[2] See St. Chrysostom on 1 Tim. iv. 8, where "bodily exercise" means training for these games, or similar exercise for health. On the "garment," see Hom. III. c. (3), and on 1 Tim. ii., Hom. VIII., Mor. *Fabr. Agon.* ii. 2, *Græv.* t. 8, he is mistaken in taking it to be a mere *subligaculum*.
[3] Job i. 21.
[4] See the wrestling match at Patroclus' funeral, Il. xxiii. 726, &c., where Ulysses, after an even trial, gives Ajax this advantage, and overthrows him by superior skill; and Ajax gives it in return, and gains an even fall by his greater weight and strength.
[5] ἑτέραν al. ἑτέροις "brings the rest much."
[6] Matt. v. 11, 12. The last clause of this passage seems quoted from the parallel passage, Luke vi. 23.
[7] 1 Thess. ii. 14.
[8] The word διάγοντας, in the Greek, comes last, and so separated from the "furnaces."
[9] Heb. xi. 34, 35. [10] 1 Cor. xv. 32. [11] 1 Cor. xvi. 19.

it were not so, then he would not suffer many of the wicked to luxuriate through the present life; and many of the just to remain in ten thousand ills: but since there is provided another life, in which he is about to recompense every man according to his deserts; one for his wickedness, another for his virtue; on that account he forbears, while he sees the former enduring evil, and the latter living in luxury.

21. And that other[1] reason too I will endeavor to bring forward from the Scriptures. But what was it? It was, that we might not say, when exhorted to the same virtue, that they were partakers of another nature, or were not men. On this account, a certain one speaking of the great Elias, says, "Elias was a man of like passions with us."[2] Do you perceive, that he shows from a communion of suffering,[3] that he was the same kind of man that we are? And again, "I too am a man of like passions with you."[4] And this guarantees a community of nature.

22. But that you may learn that this also teaches us to consider those blessed whom we ought to consider blessed, is evident from hence. For when you hear Paul saying, "Even unto this present hour we both hunger, and thirst, and are naked, and are buffetted, and have no certain dwelling place."[5] And again; "Whom the Lord loveth he chasteneth, and scourgeth every son whom he receiveth;"[6] it is certain that it is not those who are enjoying quietness, but those who are in affliction for God's sake, and who are in tribulation, whom we must applaud, emulating those who live virtuously, and cultivate piety. For so speaks the prophet: "Their right hand is a right hand of iniquity. Their daughters beautified, ornamented after the similitude of a temple. Their garners full, bursting from one into another; their sheep fruitful; abundant in their streets; their oxen fat. There is no breaking down of the fence, nor passage through; nor clamor in their streets. They call the people blessed whose affairs are in this state."[7] But what dost thou say, O prophet? "Blessed," saith he, "the people whose God is the Lord;" not the people affluent in wealth, but one adorned with godliness;[8] that people, saith he, I esteem happy, although they suffer innumerable hardships!

23. But if it were necessary to add a ninth[9] reason, we might say, that this tribulation maketh those who are troubled more approved; "For tribulation worketh patience; and patience, probation; and probation, hope; and hope maketh not ashamed."[10] Do you see that the probation, which comes of tribulation, fixes in us the hope of the good things to come, and that the abiding in trials causes us to have a good hope of the future? So that I did not say rashly, that these tribulations themselves mark out to us hopes of a resurrection, and make those who are tried the better; for, he saith, "as gold is tried in a furnace, so an acceptable man in the furnace of humiliation."[11]

24. There is besides a tenth reason to mention; and what is it, but the one I have before frequently referred to? viz. that if we have any spots, we thus put them away. And the patriarch, making this matter plain, said to the rich man, "Lazarus hath received[12] his evil things,"[13] hence "he is comforted." And besides this, we may find another reason, which is to this effect; that our crowns and rewards are thus increased. For in proportion as tribulations are more intense, so also are the rewards augmented; yea, even far more: "for the sufferings of the present time," it is said, "are not worthy to be compared to the glory that shall be revealed in us."[14] Thus many then being the reasons which we have to advance for the afflictions of the saints, let us not take our trials amiss, or be distressed, or disturbed on account of them; but both ourselves discipline our own souls, and teach others to do the same.

25. And if, O beloved, thou seest a man living in virtue, keeping fast hold of spiritual wisdom, pleasing God, yet suffering innumerable ills, do not stumble! And although thou seest any one devoting himself to spiritual affairs, and about to achieve something useful, yet presently supplanted, be not discouraged! For I know there are many who ofttimes propose a question to this effect: "Such a one," say they, "was performing a pilgrimage to some Martyr's shrine; and whilst conveying money to the poor, met with a shipwreck, and lost all. Another man, in doing the like, fell among robbers, and scarcely saved his life, leaving the place in a state of nudity." What then should we say? Why that in neither of these cases need one be sad. For if the one met with a shipwreck,

---

[1] τὴν ἐτέραν. [2] James v. 17. [3] πάθης.
[4] Wisd. vii. 1. [5] 1 Cor. iv. 11. [6] Heb. xii. 6.
[7] Ps. cxliv. 11-15.
[8] St. Chrysostom, it must be observed, in this quotation as elsewhere, follows the Septuagint Version. In the present instance that version is only supported by the Vulgate, Syriac, and Arabic. See Walton's Polyglott. But the Targum follows the Hebrew (*our sons*, v. 12), as do the English Translations. It is obvious that Job xxiv. or Ps. lxxiii. might have been alleged, but this doctrine is clearer and more frequent in the New Testament.

[9] St. Chrysostom has not exactly kept to his order of enumeration in these reasons, but considers the last three under one head, probably for the sake of brevity.
[10] Rom. v. 3-5. [11] Ecclus. ii. 3.
[12] "ἀπέλαβεν," which word he seems justified in applying to Lazarus too by the "*likewise*," the article bears out "*his* evil things." [13] Luke xvi. 25. [14] Rom. viii. 18.

yet he hath the fruit of his righteousness complete inasmuch as he fulfilled all his own part. He collected the money together, he stowed it away,[1] he took it with him, he departed on his pilgrimage; but the shipwreck that followed was not of his own will. "But why did God permit it?" In order that he might make the man approved. "But," says one, "the poor were deprived of the money." Thou dost not so care for the poor, as the God who made them? for if they were deprived of these things, He is able to provide a greater supply of wealth for them from another quarter.

26. Let us not then call Him to account for what He does; but let us give Him glory in all things. For it is not lightly and to no purpose that He often permits such events. But beside that He does not overlook those that would have enjoyed comfort from such wealth; and instead of it, affords them some other supply of sustenance; He also makes him who suffers the shipwreck more approved, and provides him a greater reward; inasmuch as the giving thanks to God, when one falls into such calamities, is a far greater matter than giving alms. For not what we give in alms only, but whatever we have been deprived of by others, and borne it with fortitude; this too brings us much fruit. And that you may learn, that the latter is indeed the greater thing, I will make it evident from what befell Job. He, when a possessor of wealth, opened his house to the poor, and whatever he had he bestowed; but he was not so illustrious when he opened his house to the poor, as when, upon hearing that his house had fallen down, he did not take it impatiently. He was not illustrious when he clad the naked with the fleece of his flock, as he was illustrious and renowned when he heard that the fire had fallen, and consumed all his flocks, and yet gave thanks. Before, he was a lover of man; now, he was a lover of Wisdom. Before, he had compassion on the poor; but now he gave thanks to the Lord! And he did not say to himself, "Why is it that this hath happened? The flocks are consumed from which thousands of the poor were supported; and if I was unworthy to enjoy such plenty, at least He should have spared me for the sake of the partakers."

27. Nothing of this sort did Job utter, no nor think, because he knew that God was dispensing all things for good. That you may learn, moreover, that he gave a heavier blow to the devil after this, when, being stripped of all things, he gave thanks, than when, being in possession of them, he gave alms; observe, that when he was in possession of them, the devil could utter a certain suspicion, and however false, he yet could utter it: "Doth Job serve thee for nought?" But when he had taken all, and stripped him of everything, and the man yet retained the same good will towards God, from that time his shameless mouth was stopped, and had nothing further to allege. For the just man was more illustrious than in his former state.[2] For to bear nobly and thankfully the privation of all things, is a far greater thing than it was to give alms whilst living in affluence; and it has been accordingly demonstrated in the case of this just man. Before, there was much benignity to his fellow-servants; now, there was exceeding love shown towards the Lord!

28. And I do not lengthen out this discourse without purpose; forasmuch as there are many, who, often whilst engaged in works of mercy, as supporting widows, have been spoiled of all their substance. Some again, by the accident of some fire, have lost their all; some have met with shipwreck; others, by false informations and injuries of that sort, though they have done many alms-deeds, have fallen into the extremes of poverty, sickness, and disease, and have obtained no help from any one. Lest we should say then, as many often do, "No man knoweth anything;"[3] what has just been said may suffice to remove all perplexity on this point. Suppose it is objected that "such an one, after having done many alms-deeds, has lost all?" And what if he had lost all? If he gives thanks for this loss, he will draw down much greater favour from God! And he will not receive twofold, as Job did, but a hundredfold in the life to come. But if here he does endure evil, the very circumstance of his sustaining all with fortitude will bring him a greater treasure; for God permits him to fall from plenty to poverty, for the purpose of calling him thus to the more frequent exercises, and greater conflicts. Hath it happened as is often the case, that the fire seizing upon thy house, hath burnt it up and devoured all thy substance? Remember

---

[1] Or, devoted it ἀπέθετο.

[2] So Ben. render λαμπρότερος γὰρ ἀπὸ τῶν προτέρων ὁ δίκαιος ἦν. No other sense seems possible, yet this is bad Greek: probably the right reading is γάρ ἢ ἀπὸ, and the sense, "he was more illustrious than from his former deeds."

[3] A proverbial expression, as it should seem, intended to deny that there is any evidence of a particular Providence. Comp. Iph. in Taur., 480.

Πάντα γὰρ τὰ τῶν θεῶν
Εἰς ἀφανὲς ἕρπει, κ'οὐδὲν οἶδ' οὐδεὶς κακόν.
'Η γὰρ τύχῃ παρήγορ' εἰς τὸ δυσμαθές.

"The Gods' decree
Moves all to unseen ends, and none can tell
What ill shall meet him; fortune blinds our way."

But the sentiment of Iphigenia will admit a pious interpretation.

what happened to Job; give thanks to the Lord, who though he was able to forbid, did not forbid it; and thou wilt receive as great a reward as if thou hadst deposited all thy wealth in the hands of the poor! But dost thou spend thy days in poverty and hunger, and in the midst of a thousand dangers? Remember Lazarus who had to buffet with disease, and poverty, and desolateness, and those other innumerable trials; and that after so high a degree of virtue![1] Remember the Apostles, who lived in hunger, and thirst, and nakedness; the prophets, the patriarchs, the just men, and you will find all these not among the rich or luxurious, but among the poor, the afflicted, and the distressed!

29. Saying these things to thyself, give thanks unto the Lord, that he hath made thee to be of this part, not hating thee, but loving thee greatly; since He would not have permitted those men either to suffer thus, if he had not exceedingly loved them, because He made them more illustrious by these evils. There is nothing so good as thanksgiving; even as there is nothing worse than blasphemy. We should not wonder, that when we become intent upon spiritual things, we suffer much that is grievous. For as thieves do not dig through and assiduously keep watch there, where there is hay, and chaff, and straw, but where there is gold and silver; so also the devil besets those especially who are engaged in spiritual matters. Where virtue is, there are many snares! where alms-giving is, there is envy! But we have one weapon which is the best, and sufficient to repel all such engines as these; in everything to give thanks to God. Tell me, did not Abel, when offering the first fruits to God, fall by the hand of his brother? But yet God permitted it, not hating one who had honoured him, but loving him greatly; and beside that which came of that excellent sacrifice, providing him another crown by martyrdom. Moses wished to protect a certain one who was injured, and he was put into the extremest peril, and banished his country.[2] This too God permitted, that thou mightest learn the patience of the saints. For if, foreknowing that we should suffer nothing of a grievous kind, we then put our hands to the work of religion, we should not seem to be doing anything great, as having such a pledge of safety. But as it is, those who do such things are the more to be wondered at, even for this; because, though they foresee dangers, and punishments, and deaths, and ten thousand evils, still they did not desist from those good works, nor become less zealous from the expectation of terrors.[3]

30. As, therefore, the Three Children said, "There is a God in heaven, who is able to deliver us; and if not, let it be known unto thee, O king, that we will not serve thy gods, and that we will not worship the golden image which thou hast set up."[4] Do thou also, when about to perform any duty to God, look forward to manifold dangers, manifold punishments, manifold deaths; and be not surprised, nor be disturbed, if such things happen. For it is said, "My Son, if thou come to serve the Lord, prepare thy soul for temptation."[5] For surely no one choosing to fight,[6] expects to carry off the crown without wounds! And thou, therefore, who hast undertaken to wage a complete combat[7] with the devil, think not to pursue a life without danger, and full of luxury! God hath not pledged to thee His recompense and His promise here; but everything that is splendid for thee is in the future life! Be glad and rejoice then, if when thou hast thyself done any good action, thou receive the contrary, or if thou see another suffering this; inasmuch as this becomes to thee the source of a higher recompense! Do not be downcast: nor give up thy zeal, nor become the more torpid; but rather press onward with more eagerness; since even the Apostles, when they preached, although scourged, stoned, and constant inmates of the prisons, did not only after deliverance from dangers, but also in those very dangers, announce with greater forwardness the message of Truth. Paul is to be seen in prison, yea, even in chains, instructing and initiating:[8] and moreover doing the very same in a court of justice, in shipwreck, in tempest, and in a thousand dangers. Do thou too imitate these saints, and cease not from good works, so long as thou art able; and although thou seest the devil thwarting thee ten thousand times, never fall back! Thou perchance, bearing with thee thy wealth, hast met with shipwreck; but Paul carrying the word, far more precious than all wealth, was going to Rome, and was wrecked; and sustained innumerable hardships. And this he himself signified, when he said, "Many times we desired to come unto you, but Satan hindered us."[9] And God permitted it; thus revealing the more abun-

---

[1] St. Chrysostom is frequent in his praises of the *patience* of Lazarus, as in his Disc. *Quod nemo læditur nisi a seipso*, sec. 10, Ben. iii. p. 455, and in his Homilies *de Lazaro*. Ben. i. p. 720, &c.
[2] Exod. ii.
[3] al. deaths. [4] Dan. iii. 17, 18. [5] Eccles. ii. 1. [6] πυκτεύειν.
[7] παγκρατιάζειν. The Pancration "consists of the two exercises of wrestling and boxing ; from the former it borrows the custom of throwing down ; from the latter, that of beating adversaries." Pott. Ant. c. 21.
[8] Baptizing, μυσταγωγοῦντα. Tr. [9] 1 Thess. ii. 18.

dantly His power, and showing that the multitude of things which the devil did, or prevented from being done, neither lessened nor interrupted the preaching of the Gospel. On this account Paul gave God thanks in all things; and knowing that he was himself thereby rendered more approved, he exhibited his exceeding forwardness on every occasion, letting none of these impediments prevent him!

31. As often then as we are frustrated in spiritual works, so often let us again take them in hand; and let us not say, "for what reason did God permit these impediments?" for He permitted them to this end, that He might show thy alacrity much more to others, and thy great love; this being the special mark of one that loves, never to desist from those things which are approved by him whom he loves. The man, indeed, who is flaccid and listless, will fall back from the first shock; but he who is energetic and alert, although he be hindered a thousand times, will devote himself so much the more to the things of God; fulfilling all as far as he is able; and in everything giving thanks. This then let us do! Thanksgiving is a great treasure; large wealth; a good that cannot be taken away; a powerful weapon! Even as blasphemy increases our present mishap; and makes us lose much more beside than we have lost already. Hast thou lost money? If thou hast been thankful, thou hast gained thy soul; and obtained greater wealth; having acquired a greater measure of the favour of God. But if thou blasphemest, thou hast, besides this, lost thine own safety; and hast not regained possession of thy wealth; yea and thy soul, which thou hadst, thou hast sacrificed!

32. But since our discourse has now turned to the subject of blasphemy, I desire to ask one favor of you all, in return for this my address, and speaking with you; which is, that you will correct on my behalf the blasphemers of this city. And should you hear any one in the public thoroughfare, or in the midst of the forum, blaspheming God; go up to him and rebuke him; and should it be necessary to inflict blows, spare not to do so. Smite him on the face; strike his mouth; sanctify thy hand with the blow, and if any should accuse thee, and drag thee to the place of justice, follow them thither; and when the judge on the bench calls thee to account, say boldly that the man blasphemed the King of angels! For if it be necessary to punish those who blaspheme an earthly king, much more so those who insult God. It is a common crime, a public injury; and it is lawful for every one who is willing, to bring forward an accusation. Let the Jews and Greeks learn, that the Christians are the saviours of the city; that they are its guardians, its patrons, and its teachers. Let the dissolute and the perverse also learn this; that they must fear the servants of God too; that if at any time they are inclined to utter such a thing, they may look round every way at each other, and tremble even at their own shadows, anxious lest perchance a Christian, having heard what they said, should spring upon them and sharply chastise them. Have you not heard what John did? He saw a man that was a tyrant overthrowing the laws of marriage; and with boldness, he proclaimed in the midst of the forum, "It is not lawful for thee to have thy brother Philip's wife."[1] But I urge thee on, not against a prince or a judge; nor against the marriage ordinance outraged; nor in behalf of fellow-servants insulted. But I require thee to castigate an equal, for insolence against the Lord. Truly, if I had said unto thee, punish and correct those kings or judges who transgress the laws, would you not say that I was mad? But John forsooth acted thus. So that even this is not too much for us. Now then, at least, correct a fellow-servant; an equal; and although it should be necessary to die, do not shrink from chastising[2] a brother. This is thy martyrdom, since John was also a martyr. And although he was not commanded to sacrifice, nor to worship an idol, yet for the sacred laws that were despised, he laid down his head. Do thou too then contend, even to the death, for the truth, and God will fight for thee! And make me not this cold reply. "What matters it to me? I have nothing in common with him."[3] With the devil alone we have nothing in common, but with all men we have many things in common; for they partake of the same nature with us; they inhabit the same earth, and they are nourished with the same food; they have the same Lord; they have received the same laws, and are invited to the same blessings with ourselves. Let us not say then, that we have nothing in common with them; for this is a satanic speech; a diabolical inhumanity. Therefore let us not give utterance to such words, but exhibit such a tender care as becomes brethren!

33. This indeed I, for my part, engage with the strictest certainty, and pledge myself to you all, that if all you who are present will but choose to take in hand the safety of

---

[1] Mark vi. 18.
[2] σωφρονίζειν, which implies a kind intention.
[3] *i. e.*, the blasphemer. Tr.

the inhabitants of this city, we shall speedily have it amended throughout. And this, even although but the least part of the city is here; the least as to multitude, but the chief part as it respects piety. Let us take in hand the safety of our brethren! One man inflamed with zeal is sufficient to reform a whole community! But when not merely one, or two, or three, but so great a multitude are able to take on them the care of the neglected, it is in no other way but by our own supineness, and not from our want of strength, that the majority perish and fall. Is it not indeed absurd? When we happen to see a fight taking place in the forum, we go into the midst of it, and reconcile the combatants! But why do I speak of a fight? If, perchance, we see an ass fallen down, we all make haste to stretch out a hand to raise him up. Yet we neglect our perishing brethren! The blasphemer is an ass; unable to bear the burden of his anger, he has fallen. Come forward and raise him up, both by words and by deeds; and both by meekness and by vehemence; let the medicine be various. And if we thus administer our own part, and take pains for the safety of our neighbours, we shall soon become objects of desire and affection to the very persons who have the benefit of our correction; and what is more than all, we shall enjoy those good things which are laid up in store. Which God grant that we may all obtain, by the grace and mercy of our Lord Jesus Christ; through whom and with whom, to the Father with the Holy Ghost, be glory and power and honor, both now and always, and forever and ever. Amen.

HOMILY II.

Spoken in Antioch in the Old Church, as it was called, while he was a presbyter, on the subject of the calamity that had befallen the city in consequence of the tumult connected with the overthrow of the Statues of the Emperor Theodosius, the Great and Pious. And on the saying of the Apostle, "Charge them that are rich that they be not high-minded," 1 Tim. vi. 17. And against covetousness.

1. WHAT shall I say, or what shall I speak of? The present season is one for tears, and not for words; for lamentation, not for discourse; for prayer, not for preaching. Such is the magnitude of the deeds daringly done; so incurable is the wound, so deep the blow, even beyond the power of all treatment, and craving assistance from above. Thus it was that Job, when he had lost all, sat himself down upon a dunghill; and his friends heard of it, and came, and seeing him, while yet afar off, they rent their garments, and sprinkled themselves with ashes, and made great lamentation.[1] The same thing now ought all the cities around to do, to come to our city and to lament with all sympathy what has befallen us. He then sat down on his dunghill; she is now seated in the midst of a great snare. For even as the devil then leaped violently the flocks, and herds, and all the substance of the just man, so now hath he raged against this whole city. But then, as well as now, God permitted it; then, indeed, that he might make the just man more illustrious by the greatness of his trials; and now, that he may make us more soberminded by the extremity of this tribulation. Suffer me to mourn over our present state. We have been silent seven days, even as the friends of Job were.[2] Suffer me to open my mouth to-day, and to bewail this common calamity.

2. Who, beloved, hath bewitched us? Who hath envied us? Whence hath all this change come over us? Nothing was more dignified than our city! Now, never was anything more pitiable! The populace so well ordered and quiet, yea, even like a tractable and well tamed steed, always submissive to the hands of its rulers, hath now so suddenly started off with us, as to have wrought such evils, as one can hardly dare to mention.

I mourn now and lament, not for the greatness of that wrath which is to be expected, but for the extravagance of the frenzy which has been manifested! For although the Emperor should not be provoked, or in anger, although he were neither to punish, nor take

---

[1] Job ii. 8, 12.   [2] Job ii. 13.

vengeance; how, I pray, are we to bear the shame of all that has been done? I find the word of instruction broken off by lamentation; scarcely am I able to open my mouth, to part my lips, to move my tongue, or to utter a syllable! So, even like a curb, the weight of grief checks my tongue, and keeps back what I would say.

3. Aforetime there was nothing happier than our city; nothing more melancholy than it is now become. As bees buzzing around their hive, so before this the inhabitants every day flitted about the forum, and all pronounced us happy in being so numerous. But behold now, this hive hath become solitary! For even as smoke does those bees, so fear hath driven away our swarms; and what the prophet says, bewailing Jerusalem, we may fitly say now, "Our city is become 'like a terebinth that hath lost its leaves,'[1] and as a garden that hath no water.'"[2] For in like manner as a garden when its irrigation fails, exhibits the trees stripped of their leaves, and bare of their fruits, so has it now fared with our city. For the help from above having forsaken her, she stands desolate stripped of almost all her inhabitants.

4. Nothing is sweeter than one's own country; but now, it has come to pass that nothing is more bitter! All flee from the place which brought them forth, as from a snare. They desert it as they would a dungeon; they leap out of it, as from a fire. And just as when a house is seized upon by the flames, not only those who dwell therein, but all who are near, take their flight from it with the utmost haste, eager to save but their bare bodies; even so now too, when the wrath of the Emperor is expected to come as a fire[3] from above, every one presses to go forth in time, and to save the bare body, before the fire in its progress reaches them. And now our calamity has become an enigma; a flight without enemies; an expulsion of inhabitants without a battle; a captivity without capture! We have not seen the fire of barbarians, nor beheld the face of enemies; and yet we experience the sufferings of captives. All men now hear of our calamities; for receiving our exiles, they learn from them the stroke which has fallen upon our city.

5. Yet I am not ashamed, nor blush at this. Let all men learn the sufferings of the city, that, sympathizing with their mother, they may lift up their united voice to God from the whole earth; and with one consent entreat the King of heaven for their universal nurse and parent.[4] Lately our city was shaken;[5] but now the very souls of the inhabitants totter! Then the foundations of the houses shook, but now the very foundations of every heart quiver; and we all see death daily before our eyes! We live in constant terror, and endure the penalty of Cain; a more pitiable one than that of those who were the former inmates of the prison; undergoing as we now do a new and strange kind of siege, far more terrible than the ordinary kind. For they who suffer this from enemies, are only shut up within the walls; but even the forum has become impassable to us, and every one is pent up within the walls of his own house! And as it is not safe for those who are besieged to go beyond the walls, while the enemy without is encamped around; so neither, to many of those who inhabit this city, is it safe to go out of doors, or to appear openly; on account of those who are everywhere hunting for the innocent as well as the guilty; and seizing them even in the midst of the forum, and dragging them to the court of justice, without ceremony, and just as chance directs.[6] For this reason, freemen sit in doors shackled up with their domestics; anxiously and minutely enquiring of those to whom they may safely put the question, "Who has been seized to-day;" who carried off;[7] or punished? How was it? and in what mannner?" They live a life more wretched than any kind of death; being compelled daily to mourn the calamities of others; while they tremble for their own safety, and are in no better case than the dead; inasmuch as they are already dead with fear.

6. But if any one who is devoid of this fear and anguish, chooses to enter the forum, he is presently driven back to his own dwelling, by the cheerless spectacle; finding hardly perchance one or two people, and those hanging their heads and creeping about with downcast looks, where but a few days before the multitude swept along more incessantly than[8] the streams of rivers. Yet all these have now been driven away from us! And, as when many trees in a thick wood of oak are cut down in all directions, the spectacle becomes a melancholy one, even like that of a head with many patches of baldness; even so the city itself, its inhabitants being dimin-

---

[1] E. V., *as an oak whose leaf fadeth*, Heb. אֵלָה which may be either tree.
[2] Isa. i. 30.
[3] Ben. πυρᾶς, "burning pile" (as of beams, &c.).
[4] St. Chrysostom alludes more than once in these Homilies to the distinction referred to in Acts xi. 26, as one that all must still recognize.
[5] Antioch suffered much from earthquakes before and after this period. It was almost demolished by this visitation, A.D. 340, and so again at several periods afterwards. More than 60,000 of its inhabitants perished from the same cause, A.D. 588.
[6] ἁπλῶς καὶ ὡς ἔτυχεν, *i. e.*, without regard to the ordinary forms of justice used in apprehending the guilty or suspected.
[7] Or executed, ἀπήχθη, see Hom. III. (6).
[8] Or "more than rivalled," ἀπέκρυπτεν.

ished and but few appearing here and there, is now become dreary, and sheds a heavy mist of sorrow over those who witness it. And not the ground only, but the very nature of the air, and even the circle of the sun's beams, seem now to me to look mournful, and to shine more dimly; not that the elements change their nature, but that our eyes being confused by the cloud of sadness, are unable to receive the light of the rays clearly, or with the same relish. This is what the prophet of old bewailed, when he said, "The sun shall go down at noon, and the day shall be darkened."[1] And this he said, not as though the Day Star[2] should be eclipsed, or the day should disappear, but because those who are in sorrow, are not able to perceive the light even of noon day on account of the darkness of their anguish; which indeed has been the case now. And wherever any one looks abroad, whether upon the ground or upon the walls; whether upon the columns of the city, or upon his neighbours, he seems to see night and deep gloom; so full is all of melancholy! There is a silence big with horror, and loneliness everywhere; and that dear hum of the multitude is stifled; and even as though all were gone beneath the earth, so speechlessness hath now taken possession of the city; and all men seem like stones, and being oppressed by the calamity like a gag on their tongues; they maintain the profoundest silence, yea, such a silence as if enemies had come on them, and had consumed them all at once by fire and sword!

7. Now is it a fit season to say, "Call for the mourning women, that they may come, and for the cunning women, and let them take up a wailing. Let your[3] eyes run down with water, and your eyelids gush out with tears."[4] Ye hills take up wailing, and ye mountains lamentation! Let us call the whole creation into sympathy with our evils. So great a city, and the head of those which lie under the eastern sky, is in danger of being torn away from the midst of the civilized world! She that had so many children, has now suddenly become childless, and there is no one who shall come to her aid! For he who has been insulted has not an equal in dignity upon earth; for he is a monarch; the summit and head of all here below! On this account then let us take refuge in the King that is above. Him let us call in to our aid. If we may not obtain the favour of heaven, there is no consolation left for what has befallen us!

8. Here I could wish to end this discourse; for the minds of those who are in anguish are indisposed to extend their discourses to a great length. And as when some dense cloud has formed, and flying under the solar rays, returns back to him all his splendour again, so indeed does the cloud of sadness, when it stands before our souls, refuse to admit an easy passage for the word, but chokes it and restrains it forcibly within. And this is the case not only with those who speak, but with those who hear; for as it does not suffer the word to burst forth freely from the soul of the speaker, so neither does it suffer it to sink into the mind of those who listen, with its natural power. Therefore also the Jews of old time, while slaving at the mud and bricks, had not the heart to listen to Moses, while he repeatedly told them great things respecting their future deliverance; despondency making their minds inaccessible to the address, and shutting up their sense of hearing. I could have wished then, as to myself, to have put an end here to my discourse; but thinking that it is not only the nature of a cloud to intercept the forward passage of the sun's rays, but that often just the opposite happens to the cloud; since the sun continually falling upon it with much warmth, wears it away, and frequently breaks through the midst of it; and shining forth all at once, meets cheerfully the gaze of the beholders. This also I myself expect to do this day; and the word being continually associated with your minds, and dwelling in them, I hope to burst the cloud of sadness, and to shine through your understandings again, with the customary instruction!

9. But afford me your attention! Lend me your ears awhile! Shake off this despondency! Let us return to our former custom;[5] and as we have been used always to meet here with gladness, so let us also do now, casting all upon God. And this will contribute towards our actual deliverance from calamity. For should the Lord see that His words are listened to carefully; and that our love of divine wisdom stands the trial of the difficulty of these times, He will quickly take us up again, and will make out of the present tempest a calm and happy change. For this too is a thing in which it behoves the Christian to differ from the unbelievers, the bearing all things nobly; and through hope of the future, soaring above the attack of human evils. The believer hath his stand on the Rock; for this reason he cannot be overthrown by the dashing of the billows. For should the waves of temptation rise, they

---

[1] Amos viii. 9. [2] τοῦ ἄστρου.
[3] E. V., that our eyes may. [4] Jer. ix. 17, 18. [5] ἦθος.

cannot reach to his feet. He stands too lofty for any such assault. Let us not then sink down, beloved! We do not care so much for our own safety, as God who made us. There is not so much solicitude on our part, lest we suffer any dreadful misfortune, as with Him who bestowed upon us a soul, and then gave us so many good things beside. Let us mount on the wings of these hopes, and hear the things about to be spoken with our accustomed readiness.

10. I made a prolonged discourse lately unto you beloved, and yet I saw all following it up, and no one turning back in the middle of the course.[1] I return thanks to you for that readiness, and have received the reward of my labours. But there was another reward, besides that attention, which I asked of you at that time; perchance you know and recollect it. And what was the reward? That you should punish and chastise the blasphemers that were in the city; that ye should restrain those who are violent and insolent against God! I do not think that I then spoke these things of myself; but that God, foreseeing what was coming, injected these words into my mind; for if we had punished those who dared to do such things, that which has now happened would never have happened. How much better would it have been, if necessity so required, to run into danger; yea, to suffer in castigating and correcting such persons (which would have brought us a martyr's crown), than now to fear, to tremble, and to expect death, from the insubordination of such persons! Behold, the crime was that of a few, but the blame comes on all! Behold, through these, we are all now placed in fear, and are ourselves suffering the punishment of what these men dared to do! But if we had taken them in time, and cast them out of the city, and chastised them, and corrected the sick member, we should not have been subjected to our present terror. I know that the manners of this city have been of a noble character from old times;[2] but that certain strangers, and men of mixed race,—accursed and pernicious characters,—hopeless of their own safety, have perpetrated what has been perpetrated. For this very reason I was always lifting up my voice, and unceasingly bearing my testimony, saying, Let us punish the madness of those blasphemers,—let us control their spirit, and provide for their salvation; —yea, though it be necessary to die in doing it, the deed would yet bring us great gain:— let us not overlook the insult done to our common Lord; overlooking such things will bring forth some great evil to our city!

11. These things I foretold, and they have now actually taken place;—and we are paying the penalty of that listlessness! You overlooked the insult that was done unto God!—Behold, he hath permitted the Emperor to be insulted, and peril to the utmost to hang over all, in order that we might pay by this fear the penalty of that listlessness; was it then vainly, and to no purpose I foretold these things, and assiduously urged your Charity? But nevertheless, nothing was done. Let it, however, be done now; and being chastened by our present calamity, let us now restrain the disorderly madness of these men. Let us shut up their mouths, even as we close up pestiferous fountains; and let us turn them to a contrary course, and the evils which have taken hold of the city shall undoubtedly be stayed. The Church is not a theatre, that we should listen for amusement. With profit ought we to depart hence, and some fresh and great gain should we acquire ere we leave this place. For it is but vainly and irrationally we meet together, if we have been but captivated for a time, and return home empty, and void of all improvement from the things spoken.

12. What need have I of these plaudits, these cheers and tumultuous signs of approval?[3] The praise I seek, is that ye show forth all I have said in your works. Then am I an enviable and happy man, not when ye approve, but when ye perform with all readiness, whatsoever ye hear from me? Let every one then correct his neighbour, for "edify ye one another,"[4] it is said, and if we do not this, the crimes of each one will bring some general and intolerable damage to the city. Behold, while we are unconscious of any part in this transaction, we are no less affrighted than those who were daringly engaged in it! We are dreading lest the wrath of the Emperor should descend upon all; and it is not sufficient for us to say in defence, "I was not present; I was not an accomplice, nor a participator in these acts." "For this reason," he may reply, "thou shalt be punished, and pay the extreme penalty, because thou wert not present; and didst not

---

[1] οὐδένα ἐκ μέσης ὑποστρέψαντα τῆς ὁδοῦ. He evidently alludes to the first Homily—a long one—and which it appears from what he has just said, was preached seven days before this, Tr. Montfaucon counts the seven days from the sedition. The order of reading the Epistles as *lessons* perhaps cannot be ascertained. The *Codex Ebneri* (Bodl. Auct. B. 123), has marks, but of later date than the text, for reading on the several days of thirty-four weeks: the passage presently mentioned and that in Hom. I. fall on Thursday and Friday in the 27th, but this does not seem to the purpose.
[2] See Hom. III. (i.) fin.
[3] Of public applause in the Church, see Bingham's *Christian Antiquities*, vol. 4, p. 593 sqq., New Ed.
[4] 1 Thess. v. 11.

check, nor restrain the rioters, and didst not run any risk for the honour of the Emperor! Hadst thou no part in these audacious deeds? I commend this, and take it well. But thou didst not check these things when being done. This is a cause of accusation!" Such words as these, we shall also hear from God, if we silently suffer the continuance of the injuries and insults committed against Him. For he also who had buried his talent in the earth, was called to account, not for crimes done by himself, for he had given back the whole of that which was entrusted to him, but because he had not increased it; because he had not instructed others; because he had not deposited it in the hands of the bankers; that is, he had not admonished, or counselled, or rebuked, or amended those unruly sinners who were his neighbours. On this account he was sent away without reprieve to those intolerable punishments! But I fully trust that though ye did not before, ye will now at least perform this work of correction, and not overlook insult committed against God. For the events which have taken place are sufficient, even if no one had given any warning, to convince men ever so disposed to be insensible, that they must exert themselves for their own safety.

13. But it is now time that we should proceed to lay out before you the customary table from St. Paul, by handling the subject of this day's reading, and placing it in view for you all. What then was the text read to-day?[1] "Charge them that are rich in this world that they be not high-minded."[2] When he says, "the rich in this world," he makes it manifest, that there are others who are rich, that is, in the world to come: such as was that Lazarus, poor as to the present life, but rich as to the future; not in gold and silver, and such like perishable and transitory store of wealth; but in those unutterable good things "which eye hath not seen, nor ear heard, nor hath it entered into the heart of man."[3] For this is true wealth and opulence, when there is good unmixed, and not subject to any change. Not such was the case of that rich man who despised him, but he became the poorest of mankind. Afterwards at least when he sought to obtain but a drop of water, he did not get possession even of that, to such extreme poverty was he come. For this reason he calls them rich "in the present world," to teach thee that along with the present life, worldly wealth is annihilated. It goes no further, neither does it change its place with its migrating possessors, but it often leaves them before their end; which therefore he shows by saying, "Neither trust in uncertain riches;" for nothing is so faithless as wealth; of which I have often said, and will not cease to say, that it is a runaway, thankless servant, having no fidelity; and should you throw over him ten thousand chains, he will make off dragging his chains after him. Frequently, indeed, have those who possessed him shut him up with bars and doors, placing their slaves round about for guards. But he has over-persuaded these very servants, and has fled away together with his guards; dragging his keepers after him like a chain, so little security was there in this custody. What then can be more faithless than this? what more wretched than men devoted to it? When men endeavour with all eagerness to collect so frail and fleeting a thing, they do not hear what the prophet saith: "Woe unto them who trust in their power, and boast themselves in the multitude of their riches."[4] Tell me why is this woe pronounced?—"He heapeth up treasure," saith he, "and knoweth not for whom he will gather it,"[5]—forasmuch as the labor is certain, but the enjoyment uncertain. Very often you toil and endure trouble for enemies. The inheritance of your wealth after your decease, coming as it does, in many instances, to those who have injured you, and plotted against you in a thousand ways, has assigned you the sins for your part, but the enjoyment to others!

14. But here, it is worthy of enquiry, for what reason he does not say, "Charge those who are rich in the present world, not to be rich; charge them to become poor; charge them to get rid of what they have;" but, "charge them, not to be high-minded." For he knew that the root and foundation of riches is pride; and that if any man understood how to be unassuming, he would not make much ado about the matter. Tell me, indeed, for what reason thou leadest about so many servants, parasites, and flatterers, and all the other forms of pomp? Not for necessity, but only for pride; to the end that by these thou mayest seem more dignified than other men! Besides, he knew that wealth is not forbidden if it be used for that which is necessary. For as I observed,[6] wine is not a bad thing, but drunkenness is so. A covetous man is one thing, and a rich man is another thing. The covetous man is not rich; he is in want of many things, and while he needs many things, he can never be rich.

---

[1] On the ancient usages of the Church as to the reading of select portions of the Old and New Testament at stated seasons, see Bingham's *Christian Antiquities*, b. 14, c. 3.
[2] 1 Tim. vi. 17.   [3] 1 Cor. ii. 9.   [4] Ps. xlix. 6.   [5] Ps. xxxix. 6.   [6] Hom. I.

The covetous man is a keeper, not a master, of wealth; a slave, not a lord. For he would sooner give any one a portion of his flesh, than his buried gold. And as though he were ordered and compelled of some one to touch nothing of these hidden treasures, so with all earnestness he watches and keeps them, abstaining from his own, as if it were another's. And certainly, they are not his own. For what he can neither determine to bestow upon others, nor to distribute to the necessitous, although he may sustain infinite punishments, how can he possibly account his own? How does he hold possession of those things, of which he has neither the free use, nor enjoyment? But besides this,—Paul is not accustomed to enjoin everything on every man, but accommodates himself to the weakness of his hearers, even, indeed, as Christ also did. For when that rich man came to him, and asked him concerning Life, he did not say at once, "Go, sell that thou hast,"[1] but omitting this, he spoke to him of other commandments. Nor afterwards, when he challenged[2] Him and said, "What lack I yet?" did He simply say, "Sell what thou hast;" but, "If thou wilt be perfect, go and sell that thou hast."[3] "I lay it down for your determination. I give you full power to choose. I do not lay upon you any necessity." For this reason also, Paul spoke nothing to the rich concerning poverty, but concerning humility; as well because of the weakness of his hearers, as because he perfectly knew, that could he bring them to exercise moderation, and to be free from pride, he should also quickly free them from eagerness about being rich.

15. And further, after giving this admonition, "not to be high-minded," he also taught the manner in which they would be able to avoid being so. And how was it? That they should consider the nature of wealth, how uncertain and faithless it is! therefore he goes on to say, "Neither trust in uncertain riches." The rich man is not one who is in possession of much, but one who gives much. Abraham was rich, but he was not covetous; for he turned not his thoughts to the house of this man, nor pryed into the wealth of that man; but going forth he looked around wherever there chanced to be a stranger, or a poor man, in order that he might succour poverty, and hospitably entertain the traveller. He covered not his roof with gold, but fixing his tent near the oak, he was contented with the shadow of its leaves. Yet so illustrious was his lodging, that angels were not ashamed to tarry with him; for they sought not splendour of abode, but virtue of soul. This man then let us imitate, beloved, and bestow what we have upon the needy. That lodging was rudely prepared, but it was more illustrious than the halls of kings. No king has ever entertained angels; but he, dwelling under that oak, and having but pitched a tent, was thought worthy of that honour: not receiving the honour on account of the meanness of his dwelling, but enjoying that benefit on account of the magnificence of his soul, and the wealth therein deposited.

16. Let us too, then, adorn not our houses, but our souls in preference to the house. For is it not disgraceful to clothe our walls with marble, vainly and to no end, and to neglect Christ going about naked? What does thy house profit thee, O man! For wilt thou take it with thee when thou departest? This thou canst not take with thee, when thou departest. But thy soul, when thou departest, thou shalt assuredly take with thee! Behold now this great danger has overtaken us! Let your houses stand by you! Let them deliver you from the threatened peril. but they cannot! And ye yourselves are witnesses, who are leaving them solitary, and hurrying forth to the wilderness; fearing them as ye would do snares and nets! Let riches now lend assistance! But it is no time for them to do so! If then the power of riches is found wanting before the wrath of man, much rather will this be the case, before the divine and inexorable tribunal! If it is but a man that is provoked and offended, and even now gold is of no avail, much more will the power of money be utterly impotent then, when God is angry, who has no need of wealth! We build houses that we may have a habitation; not that we may make an ambitious display. What is beyond our wants, is superfluous and useless. Put on a sandal which is larger than your foot! you will not endure it; for it is a hindrance to the step. Thus also a house larger than necessity requires, is an impediment to your progress towards heaven. Do you wish to build large and splendid houses? I forbid it not; but let it be not upon the earth! Build thyself tabernacles in heaven, and such that thou mayest be able to receive others;[4]—tabernacles which never fall to pieces. Why art thou mad about fleeting things; and things that must be left here? Nothing is more slippery

---

[1] Matt. xix. 16.
[2] Or "invited," as some read, προσεκαλέσατο. Ben. προεκαλέσατο.
[3] Matt. xix. 21.

[4] He may allude to Luke xvi. 9, but in Hom. *de Laz.* 3, he cautions men against thinking that friends could save them if they did not themselves do good works.

than wealth. To-day it is for thee; to-morrow it is against thee. It arms the eyes of the envious everywhere. It is a hostile comrade, a domestic enemy; and ye are witnesses of this, who possess it, and are in every way burying and concealing it from view; as even now too our very wealth makes the danger more insupportable to us! Thou seest indeed the poor ready for action, disengaged, and prepared for all things; but the wealthy in great perplexity, and wandering about, seeking where they may bury their gold, or seeking with whom they may deposit it! Why, O man, dost thou seek thy fellow slaves? Christ stands ready to receive, and to keep thy deposits for thee; and not to keep only, but also to augment them, and to pay them back with much interest. Out of His hand no man can forcibly take them away. And He not only keeps the deposit, but for this very thing He also frees thee from thy perils. For among men, they who receive treasures in trust think that they have done us a favour, in keeping that of which they took charge; but with Christ it is the contrary; for He does not say that He has conferred, but that He has received a favour, when He receives thy deposited treasures; and for the guardianship which He exercises over thy wealth, He does not demand a recompense of thee, but gives thee a recompense!

17. What defence then can we claim, or what excuse, when we pass by Him who is able to keep, and who is thankful for the trust giving in return great and unspeakable rewards, and in place of this guardianship commit our treasures to men who have not the power to keep them, and who think they grant us a favour, and pay us back at last only that which was given them. Thou art a stranger and a pilgrim with respect to the things here! Thou hast a country which is thine own in the heavens! There transfer all;—that before the actual enjoyment, thou mayest enjoy the recompense here. He who is nourished with good hopes, and is confident respecting things to come, hath here already tasted of the kingdom! For nothing ordinarily so repairs the soul, and makes a man better, as a good hope of things to come; so that if thou transfer thy wealth there, thou mayest then provide for thy soul with suitable leisure. For they who spend all their endeavours upon the decoration of their dwelling, rich as they are in outward things, are careless of that which is within, letting their soul abide desolate and squalid, and full of cobwebs. But if they would be indifferent to exterior things, and earnestly expend all their attention upon the mind, adorning this at all points; then the soul of such men would be a resting place for Christ. And having Christ for its inhabitant, what could ever be more blessed? Wouldest thou be rich? Have God for thy friend, and thou shalt be richer than all men!—Wouldest thou be rich? Be not high-minded!—This rule is suitable not only to things future, but to things present. For there is no such object of envy, as a man of wealth; but when pride is superadded, a two-fold precipice is formed; the war becomes fiercer on all sides. But if you know how to exercise moderation, you undermine the tyranny of envy by your humility; and you possess whatever you do possess with safety. For such is the nature of virtue, that it not only profits us, as it respects futurity, but it also here bestows a present reward.

18. Let us not then be high-minded in reference to riches, or indeed to any other thing; for if even in spiritual things the man who is high-minded is fallen, and undone, much more so as to carnal things. Let us be mindful of our nature. Let us recollect our sins. Let us understand what we are; and this will provide a sufficient groundwork for complete humility. Tell me not, "I have laid up the revenues of this or that number of years; myriads of talents of gold; gains that are increasing every day." Say as much as you will, you say all in vain, and to no purpose. Very often in one hour, yea, in one short moment, just as the light dust, when the wind rushes down upon it from above, are all these things swept out of the house by a blast. Our life is full of such examples, and the Scriptures abound with lessons of this sort. He who is rich to-day, is poor to-morrow. Wherefore, I have often smiled, when reading wills that said, let such a man have the ownership of these fields, or of this house, and another the use thereof. For we all have the use, but no man has the ownership.[1] For although riches may remain with us all our lifetime, undergoing no change, we must transfer them in the end, whether we will or no, into the hands of others; having enjoyed only the use of them, and departing to another life naked and destitute of this ownership! Whence it is plain, that they only have the ownership of property, who have despised its use, and derided its enjoyment. For the man that has cast his substance away from him, and bestowed it on the poor, he uses it as he ought; and takes with him the ownership of these things when he departs, not being stripped of the possession even in

---

[1] δεσποτεία, literally, the lordship.

death, but at that time receiving all back again; yea, and much more than these things, at that day of judgment, when he most needs their protection,[1] and when we shall all have to render up an account of the deeds we have done. So that if any one wishes to have the possession of his riches, and the use and the ownership entire, let him disencumber himself from them all; since, truly, he who doth not this must at all events be separated from them at death; and frequently before his death will lose them, in the midst of dangers and innumerable ills.

19. And this is not the only disaster, that the change comes suddenly; but that the rich man comes unpractised to the endurance of poverty. But not so the poor man; for he confides not in gold and silver, which are lifeless matter, but in "God, who giveth us all things richly to enjoy." So that the rich man stands in more uncertainty than the poor man, experiencing, as he does, frequent and diversified changes. What is the sense of this? "Who giveth to us all things richly to enjoy."[2] God giveth all those things with liberality, which are more necessary than riches; such, for example, as the air, the water, the fire, the sun; all things of this kind. The rich man is not able to say that he enjoys more of the sunbeams than the poor man; he is not able to say that he breathes more plenteous air: but all these are offered alike to all. And wherefore, one may say, is it the greater and more necessary blessings, and those which maintain our life, that God hath made common; but the smaller and less valuable (I speak of money) are not thus common. Why is this? In order that our life might be disciplined, and that we might have training ground for virtue. For if these necessaries were not common, perhaps they who are rich, practising their usual covetousness, would strangle those who were poor. For if they do this for the sake of money, much rather would they do so for the things referred to. Again, if money was also an universal possession, and were offered in the same manner to all, the occasion for almsgiving, and the opportunity for benevolence, would be taken away.

20. That we may live then securely, the sources of our existence have been made common. On the other hand, to the end that we may have an opportunity of gaining crowns and good report, property has not been made common; in order that hating covetousness, and following after righteousness, and freely bestowing our goods upon the poor, we may by this method obtain a certain kind of relief for our sins.[3] God hath made thee rich, why makest thou thyself poor? He hath made thee rich that thou mayest assist the needy; that thou mayest have release of thine own sins, by liberality to others. He hath given thee money, not that thou mayest shut it up for thy destruction, but that thou mayest pour it forth for thy salvation. For this reason also He hath made the possession of riches uncertain and unstable, that by this means he might slack the intensity of thy madness concerning it. For if its possessors, even now whilst they can have no confidence in regard to it, but behold a multitude of snares produced from this quarter, are so inflamed with the desire of these things; if the elements of security and stability were added to wealth, whom would they have spared? From whom would they have refrained? From what widows? From what orphans? From what poor?

21. Wherefore let us not consider riches to be a great good; for the great good is, not to possess money, but to possess the fear of God and all manner of piety. Behold, now if there were any righteous man here, having great boldness toward God,[4] notwithstanding he might be the poorest of mortals, he would be sufficient to liberate us from present evils! For he only needed to spread forth his hands towards heaven, and to call upon God, and this cloud would pass away! But now gold is treasured up in abundance; and yet it is more useless than mere clay for the purpose of deliverance from the impending calamities! Nor is it only in a peril of this kind; but should disease or death, or any such evil befall us, the impotency of wealth is fully proved, since it is at a loss, and has no consolation of its own to offer us amidst these events.

22. There is one thing in which wealth seems to have an advantage over poverty, viz. that it lives in a state of daily luxury, and is supplied with an abundance of pleasure in its banquets. This however may also be seen exemplified at the table of the poor; and these enjoy there a pleasure superior to that of the rich. And marvel not at this, nor think what I say a paradox; for I will make the matter clear to you from the evidence of facts. Ye know of course, and ye all confess

---

[1] προστασίας. Comp. Hom. *adv. Jud.* vii. v. fin., where he speaks of the intercession of those whose *souls* we may have benefitted as even of more avail; also in the Homilies on 2 Cor. iv. 13, no. 3, v. fin., he refers to Luke xvi. 9, and soon after calls the poor προστάται, in this sense. See *Cat. Aur.* on that passage.
[2] 1 Tim. vi. 17.
[3] Plato de Legg. x. (not xi.) uses παραμύθιον not, as Stephanus takes it, for "an expiation," but "a means of persuasion;" the word used here probably means relief.
[4] παρρησίαν, as is said of Timothy, Hom. I. 5. Comp. James v. 16.

that in feasts it is not the nature of the viands, but the disposition of those who feast upon them, which usually causes the pleasure; for instance, when any one comes to the table hungry, the food will taste sweeter than any delicacy, or condiment, or a thousand exquisite preparations for the palate, although it may be the most common article of diet. But he who without tarrying for necessity, or first waiting till he is hungry, (as the custom is with the wealthy), when he comes to the table, notwithstanding he finds the most refined dainties spread before him, has no sensation of pleasure, his appetite not being previously excited. And that you may learn that this is the actual state of the case, besides that you are all witnesses to it, let us hear the Scripture telling us the same truth; "The full soul," it is said, "loaths the honey comb, but to the hungry soul every bitter thing is sweet."[1] Yet what can be sweeter than honey, and the honey comb? Still he saith it is not sweet to the man that is not hungry. And what can be more disagreeable than bitter things? And yet to those who are poverty stricken they are sweet. But that the poor come to the meal with need and hunger, and that the rich do not wait for this is manifest, I suppose, to every one. Hence they do not reap the fruit of a genuine and unmixed pleasure. Nor is it only in the article of food, but any one may perceive that the same thing occurs with respect to drinks; and as in the one case hunger is the cause of pleasure, far more than the quality of the viands, so also in the other, thirst usually makes the draught sweetest, although what is drunk is only water. And this is that which the prophet intimated, when he said, "He satisfied them with honey out of the rock."[2] But we do not read in any part of Scripture that Moses brought honey out of the rock, but throughout the history we read of rivers, and waters, and cool streams. What then is it that was meant? For the Scripture by no means speaks falsely. Inasmuch, then, as they were thirsty and wearied with drought, and found these streams of water so cooling, in order to show the pleasure of such a draught, he calls the water honey, not as though its nature were changed into honey, but because the condition of the drinkers made these streams sweeter than honey. You see how the condition of the thirsty is wont to make the draught sweet? Yea oftentimes have many of the poor, when wearied, and distressed, and parched with thirst, partaken of such streams even with such pleasure as I have said. But the rich, whilst drinking wine that is sweet, and has the fragrance of flowers,[3] and every perfection that wine can have, experience no such enjoyment.

23. The same thing happens as every one may perceive with regard to sleep. For not a soft couch, nor a bedstead overlaid with silver, nor the quietness that exists throughout the house, nor anything else of this kind, are so generally wont to make sleep sweet and pleasant, as labour and fatigue, and the need of sleep, and drowsiness when one lies down. And to this particular the experience of facts, nay, before actual experience, the assertion of the Scriptures bears witness. For Solomon, who had passed his life in luxury, when he wished to make this matter evident, said, "The sleep of a labouring man is sweet, whether he eat little or much?"[4] Why does he add, "whether he eat little or much?" Both these things usually bring sleeplessness, viz. indigence, and excess of food; the one drying up the body, stiffening the eyelids and not suffering them to be closed; the other straitening and oppressing the breath, and inducing many pains. But at the same time so powerful a persuasive is labour, that though both these things should befall him, the servant is able to sleep. For since throughout the whole day, they are running about everywhere, ministering to their masters, being knocked about[5] and hard pressed, and having but little time to take breath, they receive a sufficient recompense for their toils and labours in the pleasure of sleeping. And thus it hath happened through the goodness of God toward man, that these pleasures are not to be purchased with gold and silver, but with labour, with hard toil, with necessity, and every kind of discipline. Not so the rich. On the contrary, whilst lying on their beds, they are frequently without sleep through the whole night; and though they devise many schemes, they do not obtain such pleasure. But the poor man when released from his daily labours, having his limbs completely tired, falls almost before he can lie down into a slumber that is sound, and sweet, and genuine, enjoying this reward, which is not a small one, of his fair day's toils. Since therefore the poor man sleeps, and drinks, and eats with more pleasure than the rich man, what further value is left to riches, now deprived of the one advantage they seemed to have over poverty? For this reason also, from the beginning, God tied the man to labour, not for the purpose of pun-

---

[1] Prov. xxvii. 7. [2] Ps. lxxx. 16, lxxxi. 16, LXX. [3] ἀνθοσμίαν, Plutus, 807. [4] Eccl. v. 12.
[5] κοπτόμενοι. Used thus Dem. Ol. 2, as we say "knocked about," not as Ben., *vapulantes*.

ishing or chastising, but for amendment and education. When Adam lived an unlabourious life, he fell from Paradise, but when the Apostle laboured abundantly, and toiled hard, and said, "In labour and travail, working night and day,"[1] then he was taken up into Paradise, and ascended to the third heaven!

24. Let us not then despise labour; let us not despise work; for before the kingdom of Heaven, we receive the greatest recompense from thence, deriving pleasure from that circumstance; and not pleasure only, but what is greater than pleasure, the purest health. For in addition to their want of relish, many diseases also attack the rich; but the poor are freed from the hands of physicians; and if at times they do fall into a sickness, they recover themselves quickly, being far removed from all effeminacy, and having robust constitutions. Poverty, to those who bear it wisely, is a great possession, a treasure that cannot be taken away; the stoutest of staves; a way of gain[2] that cannot be thwarted; a lodging that is safe from snares. The poor man, it may be objected, is oppressed. But then the rich man is still more subject to adverse designs. The poor man is looked down upon and insulted. But the rich man is the subject of envy. The poor man is not so easily assailed as the rich man, offering, as the latter does on every side, countless handles to the devil, and to his secret foes; and being the servant of all, on account of the great extent of his business. Standing in need of many things, he is compelled to flatter many persons, and to minister to them with much servility. But the poor man, if he knows how to be spiritually wise, is not assailable even by the devil himself. Job therefore, strong as he was before this, when he lost all, became still more powerful, and bore away an[3] illustrious victory from the devil!

25. But besides this, the poor man cannot possibly be injured, if he knows how to be spiritually wise. Now what I said of pleasure, that it consisted not in a costly provision of meats, but in the disposition of those who eat, this also I say respecting an insult; that the insult is either created or destroyed, not by the intention of those who insult, but by the disposition of those who bear it. For example. Some one hath insulted thee with much language, fit or unfit to repeat. If thou shalt laugh at the insults, if thou take not the words to heart, if thou showest thyself superior to the blow, thou art not insulted. And just as if we possessed an adamantine body, we should not be hurt, were we even attacked on all sides by a thousand darts, for darts beget wounds not from the hand of him who hurls them, but from the bodies of those who receive them, so too in this case, insults are constituted real and dishonourable ones, not from the folly of those who offer them, but from the weakness of the insulted. For if we know how to be truly wise, we are incapable of being insulted, or of suffering any serious evils. Some one it may be hath offered thee an insult, but thou hast not felt it? thou hast not been pained. Then thou art not insulted, but hast given rather than received a blow! For when the insulting person perceives that his blow did not reach the soul of those who were reviled, he is himself the more severely fretted; and whilst those who are reproached remain silent, the insulting blow is turned backwards, and recoils of its own accord upon him who aimed it.

26. In all things then, beloved, let us be spiritually wise, and poverty will be able to do us no harm, but will benefit us exceedingly, and render us more illustrious and wealthy than the richest. For tell me who was poorer than Elias? Yet for this reason he surpassed all the wealthy, in that he was so poor, and this very poverty of his was his own choice from an opulence of mind. For since he accounted the wealth of all riches to be beneath his magnanimity, and not worthy of his spiritual wisdom, therefore he welcomed this kind of poverty; so that if he had considered present things as of much worth, he would not have possessed only a mantle. But so did he contemn the vanity of the life that now is, and regard all gold as clay cast into the street,[4] that he possessed himself of nothing more than that covering. Therefore the king had need of the poor man, and he who had so much gold hung upon the words of him who had nothing more than a sheepskin. Thus was the sheepskin[5] more splendid than the purple, and the cave of the just man than the halls of kings. Therefore also when he went up to heaven, he left nothing to his disciple save the sheepskin. "By the help of this," said he, "I have wrestled with the devil, and taking this, be thou armed against him!" For indigence is a powerful weapon, an unassailable retreat, an unshaken fortress! Elisha received the sheepskin as the greatest inheritance; for it was truly such; a more precious one than all gold. And thenceforth[6] that Elias was a twofold person; an Elias above and an Elias below!

---

[1] 1 Thess. ii. 9.   [2] κτῆσις.   [3] Sav. a more.
[4] Comp. Ps. xviii. 42.
[5] μηλωτῇ, 2 Kings i. 2, LXX., lit. sheepskin, the Hebrew is אַדֶּרֶת which does not fix the material, they may have judged by 2 Kings i. 8.
[6] Sav. ἐκ τότε.

I know ye account that just person blessed, and ye would each desire to be that person. What then if I show you that all among us, who are initiated,[1] have received something far greater than he did? For Elias left a sheepskin to his disciple, but the Son of God ascending left to us His own flesh! Elias indeed, cast off his mantle, before he went up; but Christ left it behind for our sakes; and yet retained it when He ascended. Let us not then be cast down. Let us not lament, nor fear the difficulty of the times, for He who did not refuse to pour out His blood for all, and has suffered us to partake of His flesh and of His blood again,[2] what will He refuse to do for our safety? Confident then in these hopes, let us beseech Him continually; let us be earnest in prayers and supplications; and let us with all strictness give our attention to every other virtue; that so we may escape the danger that now threatens, and obtain the good things to come; which God grant we may all be worthy of, through the grace and lovingkindness of our Lord Jesus Christ, by Whom, and with Whom be glory to the Father together with the Holy Ghost, forever and ever. Amen.

---

[1] Or μεμυσταγωγημένοι. The baptized: those who were admitted to the mystic privileges of the faithful; a term adopted from St. Paul's μυστήριον, 1 Cor. iv. 1. It was also used in the ancient mysteries. See Bingham, b. i., c. iv., sec. 1, 2.

[2] This passage was quoted in favor of Transubstantiation against Bp. Ridley in the disputation at Oxford, A.D. 1554. See Foxe, *Acts and Mon.*, vol. vi. p. 468, New Ed. It is scarcely necessary to remark, that the words of St. Chrysostom here, and in many other passages, if examined in their whole bearing, do not of necessity imply any change of the material substance of the holy elements.

HOMILY III.

On the departure of Flavian,[1] Bishop of Antioch, who was gone on an embassy to the Emperor Theodosius, on behalf of the city. Of the dignity of the Priesthood. What is true fasting. Slander worse than devouring the human body. And finally of those who had been put to death on account of the sedition; and against those who complained that many innocent persons were apprehended.

1. WHEN I look on that throne, deserted and bereft of our teacher, I rejoice and weep at the same time. I weep, because I see not our father with us! but I rejoice that he hath set out on a journey for our preservation; that he is gone to snatch so great a multitude from the wrath of the Emperor! Here is both an ornament to you, and a crown to him! An ornament to you, that such a father hath been allotted to you; a crown to him, because he is so affectionate towards his children, and hath confirmed by actual deeds what Christ said. For having learnt that "the good shepherd layeth down his life for the sheep,"[2] he took his departure; venturing his own life for us all, notwithstanding there were many things to hinder his absence, and enforce his stay. And first, his time of life, extended as it is to the utmost limits of old age; next, his bodily infirmity, and the season of the year, as well as the necessity for his presence at the holy festival; and besides these reasons, his only sister even now at her last breath! He has disregarded, however, the ties of kindred, of old age, of infirmity, and the severity of the season, and the toils of the journey; and preferring you and your safety above all things, he has broken through all these restraints. And, even as a youth, the aged man is now hastening along, borne upon the wings of zeal! For if Christ (saith he) gave Himself for us, what excuse or pardon should we deserve, having undertaken the charge of so numerous a people, if we were not ready to do and to suffer anything for the security of those committed into our hands. For if (continues he) the patriarch Jacob, when in charge of flocks, and feeding brute sheep, and having to give account to man, passed sleepless nights, and bore heat and

---

[1] This Flavianus was one of those who maintained the true faith against the Arians, but allowed himself to be ordained Bishop of Antioch as successor to Meletius, who was placed there by the Arians, but afterwards became orthodox. Paulinus had been consecrated Bishop for the orthodox by Lucifer, and should have had full possession of the see at the death of Meletius, to whom many of the orthodox had adhered. Hence Flavianus was not acknowledged by the Roman and Alexandrian patriarchs till after the death of Paulinus, and of another who succeeded him, and the elevation of his friend St. John Chrysostom to the see of Constantinople. Socr. iii. 6, v. 9, 15. St. Chrysostom may allude to these circumstances in Rom. iii. 11; Hom. VII. Tr.

[2] John x. 11.

cold, and all the inclemency of the elements, to the end that not one of those animals might perish, much less doth it become us, who preside over those, who are not irrational, but spiritual sheep; who are about to give an account of this charge, not to man, but to God, to be slack in any respect, or shrink from anything which might benefit the flock. Besides, in proportion as the latter flock is superior to the former; men to brutes, and God to men; so it behoves us to manifest a greater and more intense anxiety and diligence. He knows well that his concern is now, not for one city only, but for the whole of the East. For our city is the head and mother of all that lie towards the East. For this reason he would encounter every danger, and nothing would avail to detain him here.

2. On this account I trust that there may be a good hope; for God will not disdain to look upon such earnestness and zeal, nor will He suffer his servant to return without success. I know that when he has barely seen our pious Emperor, and been seen by him, he will be able at once by his very countenance to allay his wrath. For not only the words of the saints, but their very countenances are full of grace. And he is a person too endowed with abundant wisdom; and being well skilled in the divine laws, he will say to him as Moses said to God, "Yet now, if thou wilt forgive their sin;—and if not, slay me together with them."[1] For such are the bowels of the saints, that they think death with their children sweeter than life without them. He will also make the special season his advocate and shelter himself behind the sacred festival of the Passover; and will remind the Emperor of the season when Christ remitted the sins of the whole world. He will exhort him to imitate his Lord. He will also remind him of that parable of the ten thousand talents, and the hundred pence. I know the boldness of our father, that he will not hesitate to alarm him from the parable, and to say, "Take heed lest thou also hear it said in that day, 'O thou wicked servant, I forgave thee all that debt, because thou desiredst me; you ought also to forgive thy fellow-servants!'[2] Thou dost to thyself a greater benefit than them, since by pardoning these few offences thou gainest an amnesty for greater." To this address he will add that prayer, which those who initiated him into the sacred mystery taught him to offer up, and say, "Forgive us our debts, as we forgive our debtors."[3]

3. He will moreover inform him, that the offence was not common to the whole city, but the deed of certain strangers and adventurers, men that act upon no deliberate plan, but with every sort of audacity and lawlessness; and that it would not be just for the disorderly conduct of a few to extirpate so great a city, and to punish those who had done no wrong; and that even though all had been transgressors, they had paid a sufficient punishment, being consumed by fear so many days, and expecting every day to be put to death, and being exiles and fugitives; thus living more wretchedly than condemned criminals, carrying their life in their hands, and having no confidence of escape! "Let this punishment (he will say) suffice. Carry not thy resentment further! Make the Judge above merciful to thyself, by humanity towards thy fellow-servants! Think of the greatness of the city, and that the question now is not concerning one, or two, or three, or ten souls, but of a vast multitude too numerous to be reckoned up! It is a question which affects the capital of the whole world. This is the city in which Christians were first called by that name.[4] Honor Christ. Reverence the city which first proclaimed that name, so lovely and sweet to all! This city hath been the tabernacle of Apostles; the dwelling place of the just! And now this is the first and only instance of insurrection against its rulers; and all past time will bear favourable witness to the manners of the city. For had the people been continually given to sedition, it might have been necessary to make an example of such iniquity; but if this hath happened only once in all time, it is plain that the offence has not arisen from the habit of the city, but that it was the transgression of those who had in an evil hour by mere random chance arrived there.

4. These things and more than these the priest will say with still greater boldness; and the Emperor will listen to them; and one is humane, and the other is faithful; so that on both sides we entertain favourable hopes. But much more do we rely upon the mercy of God, than upon the fidelity of our Teacher and the humanity of the Emperor. For whilst the Emperor is supplicated, and the priest is supplicating, He Himself will interpose, softening the heart of the Emperor, and exciting the tongue of the priest; facilitating

---

[1] Ex. xxxii. 31, 32.   [2] Matt. xviii. 32, 33.
[3] Matt. vi. 12. The use of the Lord's Prayer was at this period confined to those who were initiated or baptized. St. Chrysostom calls it the prayer of the faithful, and others of the Fathers speak in a similar manner. See Bingham, *Ant.* vol. I., p. 37, new ed.; St. Cyr. *Cat.* xxiii. 11; St. Cypr. *de Or. Tract.* vii. 6, p. 182; St. Chrys. *Hom. on Rom.* VII. 15.
[4] Acts xi. 26, probably in derision; the people of Antioch being notorious for the invention of scurrilous nick-names.

his utterance;—preparing the mind of the other to receive what is said and with much indulgence, to accede to the petitions. For our city is dearer to Christ than all others both because of the virtue of our ancestors, and of your own. And as Peter was the first among the apostles to preach Christ, so as I said before, this city was the first of cities that adorned itself by assuming the Christian appellation, as a sort of admirable diadem. But if where only ten just men were found, God promised to save all who dwelt therein, why should we not expect a favourable issue, and become assured of all our lives, when there are not only ten, twenty, or twice so many only, but far more; who are serving God with all strictness.

5. I have heard many saying, "The threats of a king are like the wrath of a lion;"[1] being full of dejection and lamentation. What then should we say to such? That He who said, "The wolves and the lambs shall feed together; and the leopard shall lie down with the kid, and the lion shall eat straw like the ox,"[2] will be able to convert the lion into a mild lamb. Let us therefore supplicate Him; let us send an embassy to Him; and He will doubtless allay the Emperor's wrath, and deliver us from the impending distress. Our Father hath gone thither on this embassy. Let us go on embassy from hence to the Majesty of heaven! Let us assist him by prayers! The community of the Church can do much, if with a sorrowful soul, and with a contrite spirit, we offer up our prayers! It is unnecessary to cross the ocean, or to undertake a long journey. Let every man and woman among us, whether meeting together at church, or remaining at home, call upon God with much earnestness, and He will doubtless accede to these petitions.

Whence does this appear evident? Because He is exceedingly desirous, that we should always take refuge in Him, and in everything make our requests unto Him; and do nothing and speak nothing without Him. For men, when we trouble them repeatedly concerning our affairs, become slothful and evasive, and conduct themselves unpleasantly towards us; but with God it is quite the reverse. Not when we apply to him continually respecting our affairs, but when we fail to do so, then is he especially displeased. Hear at least what He reproves the Jews for, when He says, "Ye have taken counsel, but not of Me, and made treaties,[3] but not by My Spirit."[4] For this is the custom of those who love; they desire that all the concerns of their beloved should be accomplished by means of themselves; and that they should neither do anything, nor say anything, without them. On this account did God not only on that occasion, but again elsewhere, uttering a reproof, speak the same language. "They[5] have reigned, but not by Me; they have ruled, and they made it not known to Me."[6] Let us not then be slow to take refuge in Him continually; and whatever be the evil, it will in any case find its appropriate solution.

6. Doth a man affright you? Hasten to the Lord above, and thou wilt suffer no evil. Thus the ancients had release from their calamities; and not men only, but also women. There was a certain Hebrew woman, Esther was her name. This Esther rescued the whole people of the Jews, when they were about to be delivered over to destruction, by this very method. For when the Persian king gave orders that all the Jews should be utterly destroyed, and there was no one who was able to stand in the way of his wrath,— this woman having divested herself of the splendid robe, and clothed herself with sackcloth and being besprinkled with ashes, supplicated the merciful God to go in with her to the king; and offering up her prayer to Him, these were the words she uttered, "O Lord, make my words acceptable,[7] and put eloquent speech in my mouth."[8] Let this be the prayer which we offer to God for our Teacher. For if a woman, supplicating on behalf of the Jews, prevailed to allay the wrath of a barbarian, much rather will our Teacher, entreating on behalf of so great a city, and in conjunction with so great a Church, be able to persuade this most mild and merciful Emperor. For if he hath received authority to loose sins committed against God, much more will he be able to take away and blot out those which have been committed against a man. He is also himself a ruler and a ruler of more dignity than the other. For the sacred laws take and place under his hands even the royal head. And when there is need of any good thing from above, the Emperor is accustomed to fly to the priest; but not the priest to the Emperor. He[9] too hath his breast-plate, that of right-

---

[1] Prov. xix. 12. [2] Isa. xi. 6, 7.
[3] So LXX. E. V., *cover with a covering*, if this be taken for protection, the sense is the same, and apposite here, as it refers to seeking help from Egypt. The Hebrew מסכה admits both by a double derivation, see סוך and סכך.
[4] Isa. xxx. 1.
[5] So LXX. E. V., *They have set up kings, but not by Me; they have made princes, and I knew it not;* which is more exact. Βασιλεύω, however, is used by the LXX. for "to make one king."
[6] Hos. viii. 4. [7] This clause is not in our text.
[8] From the additions to the Book of Esther, in the Apocrypha, ch. xiv. 2, 3, 13.
[9] Sav. and M. om. For.

eousness.[1] He too hath his girdle, that of truth, and sandals[2] of much greater dignity, those of the Gospel of peace. He too hath a sword, not of iron, but of the Spirit; he too hath a crown resting on his head. This panoply is the more splendid. The weapons are grander, the license of speech greater,[3] and mightier[4] the strength. So that from the weight of his authority, and from his own greatness of soul; and more than all the rest, from the hope which he has in God, he will address the Emperor with much freedom and much discretion.

7. Let us not then despair of our safety, but let us pray; let us make invocation; let us supplicate; let us go on embassy to the King that is above with many tears! We have this fast too as an ally, and as an assistant in this good intercession. Therefore, as when the winter is over and the summer is appearing, the sailor draws his vessel to the deep; and the soldier burnishes his arms, and makes ready his steed for the battle; and the husbandman sharpens his sickle; and the traveller boldly undertakes a long journey, and the wrestler strips and bares himself for the contest. So too, when the fast makes its appearance, like a kind of spiritual summer, let us as soldiers burnish our weapons; and as husbandmen let us sharpen our sickle; and as sailors let us order our thoughts against the waves of extravagant desires; and as travellers let us set out on the journey towards heaven; and as wrestlers let us strip for the contest. For the believer is at once a husbandman, and a sailor, and a soldier, a wrestler, and a traveller. Hence St. Paul saith, "We wrestle not against flesh and blood, but against principalities, against powers. Put on therefore the whole armour of God."[5] Hast thou observed the wrestler? Hast thou observed the soldier? If thou art a wrestler, it is necessary for thee to engage in the conflict naked. If a soldier, it behoves thee to stand in the battle line armed at all points. How then are both these things possible, to be naked, and yet not naked; to be clothed, and yet not clothed! How? I will tell thee. Divest thyself of worldly business, and thou hast become a wrestler. Put on the spiritual armour, and thou hast become a soldier. Strip thyself of worldly cares, for the season is one of wrestling. Clothe thyself with the spiritual armour, for we have a heavy warfare to wage with demons. Therefore also it is needful we should be naked, so as to offer nothing that the devil may take hold of, while he is wrestling with us; and to be fully armed at all points, so as on no side to receive a deadly blow. Cultivate thy soul. Cut away the thorns. Sow the word of godliness. Propagate and nurse with much care the fair plants of divine wisdom, and thou hast become a husbandman. And Paul will say to thee, "The husbandman that laboureth must be first partaker of the fruits."[6] He too himself practised this art. Therefore writing to the Corinthians, he said, "I have planted, Apollos watered, but God gave the increase."[7] Sharpen thy sickle, which thou hast blunted through gluttony—sharpen it by fasting. Lay hold of the pathway which leads towards heaven; rugged and narrow as it is, lay hold of it, and journey on. And how mayest thou be able to do these things? By subduing thy body, and bringing it into subjection. For when the way grows narrow, the corpulence that comes of gluttony is a great hindrance. Keep down the waves of inordinate desires. Repel the tempest of evil thoughts. Preserve the bark; display much skill, and thou hast become a pilot. But we shall have the fast for a groundwork and instructor in all these things.

8. I speak not, indeed, of such a fast as most persons keep, but of real fasting; not merely an abstinence from meats; but from sins too. For the nature of a fast is such, that it does not suffice to deliver those who practise it, unless it be done according to a suitable law.[8] "For the wrestler," it is said, "is not crowned unless he strive lawfully."[9] To the end then, that when we have gone through the labour of fasting, we forfeit not the crown of fasting, we should understand how, and after what manner, it is necessary to conduct this business; since that Pharisee also fasted,[10] but afterwards went down empty, and destitute of the fruit of fasting. The

---

[1] The imperial armature is here compared not with the Ecclesiastical dress, but with the spiritual armour, which the Church has somewhat differently, according to her discretion, represented by outward forms. What is applied by St. Paul to the individual Christian is here used specially of one who represents our Lord in authority as well as in person. Compare on the breastplate, Ex. xxvii. 15, Isa. lix. 7; on the girdle, Ex. xxviii. 40, Isa. xi. 5, Rev. i. 13, Eph. vi. 14; on the sandals, Isa. lii. 7, Eph. vi. 15; on the sword, Heb. iv. 12, Eph. vi. 17; on the crown, Ex. xxix. 6, Eph. vi. 17; see also Fabr. Ag. ii. 34 (Græv. Thes. viii. p. 2095) · Martene de Ant. Eccl. Rit. l. i. c. 4, art. 1, sec. 12; Durand. Rat. Div. Off. lib. 3.
[2] See on Rom. viii. 25; Hom. XIV. Mor., where the shoes are especially noticed as a part of imperial magnificence.
[3] μείζων ἡ παρρησία, lit. "greater the boldness of speech," but the context seems to give this meaning.
[4] i. e., than those belonging to an emperor. See Const. Ap. ii. 34, and note 11 of Cotelerius, p. 247.
[5] Eph. vi. 12.

[6] 2 Tim. ii. 6. St. Chrys. ad loc. Hom. IV. explains first, "before any other person." Hammond's interpretation "labouring first," requires a different order in the Greek.
[7] 1 Cor. iii. 6.
[8] See Fabr. Agon. iii. 1, where St. Chrysostom's interpretation on the passage (Hom. IV. in Ep. ad Tim.) is shown to be correct. Galen. Com. 1, ad Aph. xviii. fol. 45, is cited. "And they that contend by rule (or strive lawfully) eat only bread for breakfast and meat for dinner." There were other rules for the contest itself. See Hammond on 1 Cor. ix. notes f and g.
[9] 2 Tim. ii. 5.
[10] Luke xviii. 12.

Publican fasted not; and yet he was accepted in preference to him who had fasted; in order that thou mayest learn that fasting is unprofitable, except all other duties follow with it. The Ninevites fasted, and won the favour of God.[1] The Jews fasted too, and profited nothing, nay, they departed with blame.[2] Since then the danger in fasting is so great to those who do not know how they ought to fast, we should learn the laws of this exercise, in order that we may not "run uncertainly," nor "beat the air," nor while we are fighting contend with a shadow. Fasting is a medicine; but a medicine, though it be never so profitable, becomes frequently useless owing to the unskilfulness of him who employs it. For it is necessary to know, moreover, the time when it should be applied, and the requisite quantity of it; and the temperament of body that admits it; and the nature of the country, and the season of the year; and the corresponding diet; as well as various other particulars; any of which, if one overlooks, he will mar all the rest that have been named. Now if, when the body needs healing, such exactness is required on our part, much more ought we, when our care is about the soul, and we seek to heal the distempers of the mind, to look, and to search into every particular with the utmost accuracy.

9. Let us see then how the Ninevites fasted, and how they were delivered from that wrath—"Let neither man nor beast, herd nor flock, taste anything,"[3] saith (the prophet). What sayest thou? Tell me—must even the irrational things fast, and the horses and the mules be covered with sackcloth? "Even so," he replies. For as when, at the decease of some rich man, the relatives clothe not only the men servants and maid servants, but the horses also with sackcloth, and give orders that they should follow the procession to the sepulchre, led by their grooms; thus signifying the greatness of the calamity, and inviting all to pity; thus also, indeed, when that city was about to be destroyed, even the irrational nature was enveloped in sackcloth, and subjected to the yoke of fasting. "It is not possible," saith he, "that irrational creatures should learn the wrath of God by means of reason; let them be taught by means of fasting, that this stroke is of divine infliction. For if the city should be overturned, not only would it be one common sepulchre for us, the dwellers therein, but for these likewise. Inasmuch then as these would participate in the punishment, let them also do so in the fast. But there was yet another thing which they aimed at in this act, which the prophets also are wont to do. For these, when they see some dreadful chastisement proceeding from heaven, and those who are to be punished without anything to say for themselves; —laden with shame,—unworthy of the least pardon or excuse:—not knowing what to do, nor from whence they may procure an advocacy for the condemned, they have recourse to the things irrational; and describing their death in tragical fashion, they make intercession by them, putting forward as a plea their pitiable and mournful destruction. When therefore, aforetime, famine had seized upon the Jews, and a great drought oppressed their country, and all things were being consumed, one of the prophets spoke thus, "The young heifers leaped in their stalls; the herds of oxen wept, because there was no pasture; all the cattle of the field looked upward to Thee, because the streams of waters were dried up."[4] Another prophet bewailing the evils of drought again speaks to this effect: "The hinds calved in the fields and forsook it, because there was no grass. The wild asses did stand in the forests; they snuffed up the wind like a dragon; their eyes did fail, because there was no grass."[5] Moreover, ye have heard Joel saying to-day, "Let the bridegroom go forth of his chamber, and the bride out of her closet;—the infants that suck the breast."[6] For what reason, I ask, does he call so immature an age to supplication? Is it not plainly for the very same reason? For since all who have arrived at the age of manhood, have inflamed and provoked God's wrath, let the age, saith he, which is devoid of transgressions supplicate Him who is provoked.

10. But, as I said before, we may see what it was that dissolved such inexorable wrath. Was it, forsooth, fasting only and sackcloth? We say not so; but the change of their whole life. Whence does this appear? From the very language of the prophet. For he who hath discoursed of the wrath of God, and of their fasting,[7] himself too, when speaking of the reconciliation, and teaching us the cause of the reconciliation, speaks to this effect; "And God saw their works."[8] What kind of

---

[1] Jonah iii. 10.
[2] Isa. lviii. 3, 7; 1 Cor. ix. 26.   [3] Jonah iii. 7.
[4] Joel i. 17.   [5] Jer. xiv. 5.
[6] Joel ii. 16. This passage of scripture is read for the epistle in the service of our Church on Ash Wednesday as it also stands in the Roman Missal, it is read in the Greek Church on the same day. Ash Wednesday was not, however, constituted the first day of Lent till a later period, see Bingham, vol. vi. p. 456, b. xxi., c. 1, sec. 5. This Homily seems to have been preached on Quinquagesima Sunday, called by the Greeks, κυριακὴ τῆς ἀποκρέου [Lat. carnelevale, or in dimissione carnium, hence carnival] as the next is τῆς τυροφάγου (ἑβδ), denoting degrees of abstinence. See note near the end of the next Homily.
[7] διὰ τὴν νηστείαν, with the article it is "the Fast," or here Lent, without it "fasting."
[8] Jonah iii. 10.

works? That they had fasted? That they had put on sackcloth? Nothing of the sort: but passing all these points in silence, he adds, "That they turned every one from their evil ways, and the Lord repented of the evil that He had said He would do unto them." Seest thou, that fasting did not rescue from this danger, but it was the change of life, which rendered God propitious and kind to these barbarians?

11. I have said these things, not that we may disparage fasting, but that we may honour fasting; for the honour of fasting consists not in abstinence from food, but in withdrawing from sinful practices; since he who limits his fasting only to an abstinence from meats, is one who especially disparages it. Dost thou fast? Give me proof of it by thy works! Is it said by what kind of works? If thou seest a poor man, take pity on him! If thou seest an enemy, be reconciled to him! If thou seest a friend gaining honour, envy him not! If thou seest a handsome woman, pass her by! For let not the mouth only fast, but also the eye, and the ear, and the feet, and the hands, and all the members of our bodies. Let the hands fast, by being pure from rapine and avarice. Let the feet fast, by ceasing from running to the unlawful spectacles. Let the eyes fast, being taught never[1] to fix themselves rudely upon handsome countenances, or to busy themselves with strange beauties. For looking is the food of the eyes, but if this be such as is unlawful or forbidden, it mars the fast; and upsets the whole safety of the soul; but if it be lawful and safe, it adorns fasting. For it would be among things the most absurd to abstain from lawful food because of the fast, but with the eyes to touch even what is forbidden. Dost thou not eat flesh? Feed not upon lasciviousness by means of the eyes. Let the ear fast also. The fasting of the ear consists in refusing to receive evil speakings and calumnies. "Thou shalt not receive a false report,"[2] it says.

12. Let the mouth too fast from disgraceful speeches and railing. For what doth it profit if we abstain from birds and fishes;[3] and yet bite and devour our brethren? The evil speaker eateth the flesh of his brother, and biteth the body of his neighbour. Because of this Paul utters the fearful saying, "If ye bite and devour one another, take heed that ye be not consumed one of another."[4] Thou hast not fixed thy teeth in the flesh, but thou hast fixed the slander in the soul, and inflicted the wound of evil suspicion; thou hast harmed, in a thousand ways, thyself and him, and many others, for in slandering a neighbour thou hast made him who listens to the slander worse;[5] for should he be a wicked man, he becomes more careless when he finds a partner in his wickedness; and should he be a just man, he is lifted to arrogance, and puffed up; being led on by the sin of others to imagine great things concerning himself. Besides,[6] thou hast struck at the common welfare of the Church; for all those who hear not only accuse the supposed sinner, but the reproach is fastened on the Christian community; neither dost thou hear the unbelievers saying, "Such a person is a fornicator, or a libertine;" but instead of the individual who hath sinned, they accuse all Christians. In addition to this,[7] thou hast caused the glory of God to be blasphemed; for as His Name is glorified when we have good report, so when we sin, it is blasphemed and insulted!

13. A fourth reason is, that thou hast disgraced him who is ill reported; and hast thus rendered him more shameless than he was, by placing him in a state of enmity and hostility. Fifthly, thou hast made thyself liable to chastisement and vengeance; by involving[8] thyself in matters which in no way concerned thee. For let not any one tell me in reply, "Then I am an evil speaker when I speak falsely, but if I speak what is true, I cease to be so." Although it be with truth thou speakest evil, this also is a crime. For that Pharisee spake evil of the Publican with truth; but nevertheless this availed him not. For was not the latter, I ask, a publican and a sinner? It is manifest to every one that he was a publican. But at the same time inasmuch as the Pharisee spoke ill of him, he departed from the temple with the loss of every advantage. Dost thou wish to correct a brother? Weep; pray unto God; taking him apart, admonish, counsel, entreat him! So also Paul did, "Lest," saith he, "when I come again, my God will humble me among you, and I shall bewail many which have sinned already, and have not repented of the uncleanness and fornication and lasciviousness which they have committed."[9] Show thy charity towards the sinner. Persuade him that it is from care and anxiety for his welfare, and not from a wish to expose him, that thou puttest him in mind of his sin. Take hold of his feet; embrace him; be not

---

[1] μηδέποτε. This shows he did not mean only a temporary abstinence from *sin*, but a discipline to cure us of it for the future.
[2] E. V., *raise* Heb. תִשָּׂא. Exod. xxiii. 1, LXX.
[3] It would seem from this passage that not even the use of fish was then allowed during the season of Lent. On the strictness of the ancient fasts, consult Bingham, vol. 7, p. 208, new ed. Tr. (The like is now practiced in the Greek Church. Smith's Account of G. C., p. 35, and reports of recent travellers.)

[4] Gal. v. 15.   [5] 1st reason.   [6] 2d reason.
[7] 3d reason.   [8] πράγματα πλέξας.   [9] 2 Cor. xii. 21.

ashamed, if thou truly desirest to cure him. Physicians too do things of this sort, oftentimes, when their patients are hard to please;[1] by embraces and entreaties they at length persuade them to take a salutary medicine. Thus also do thou. Show the wound to the priest;[2] that is the part of one who cares for him, and provides for him, and is anxious on his behalf.

14. But not only do I now admonish the evil speakers; but those besides, who hear others ill spoken of, I exhort to stop up their ears, and to imitate the prophet who saith, "Whoso privily slandereth his neighbour, him will I punish."[3] Say to thy neighbour, "Hast thou any one to praise or highly to commend? I open my ears, to receive the fragrant oil; but if thou hast any evil to say, I block up the entrance to thy words,—for I am not to admit dung and dirt. What profit doth it afford me to learn that such a one is a bad man? The greatest injury indeed results from this, and the worst loss!" Say to him, "Let us be anxious about our own faults; how we may render up an account of our own transgressions; and exhibit this sort of curiosity and meddlesome activity respecting our own lives. What excuse or pardon shall we find; whilst we never even take into consideration our own affairs, but thus inquisitively pry into those of others!" And as it is mean and extremely disgraceful to peer into a house, and to observe what is within as one passes, so also to make inquisition into another man's life is the last degree of illiberality. But what is yet more ridiculous is, that those who lead this sort of life, and are neglectful of their own affairs, when they have mentioned any of these secret matters, beseech and adjure him who has heard it, not to mention it more to any other person; thus making it plain that they have done an action which deserves censure. For if thou beseechest him to tell this to no other person, much more did it not become thee to tell these things first to him. The matter was safe while in thy possession; now, after betraying it, thou art grown anxious for its safety. If thou art desirous that it be not carried abroad to another,[4] do not thyself tell it. But when thou hast betrayed the custody of the matter to another, thou doest what is superfluous and useless, in charging him, and putting him on oath for the safety of what has been spoken.

15. "But it is sweet to slander." Nay, it is sweet not to speak evil. For he that hath spoken evil is henceforth contentious; he is suspicious and he fears, repents, and gnaws his own tongue. Being timorous and trembling, lest at any time, what he said should be carried to others, and bring great peril, and useless and needless enmity, on the sayer. But he who keeps the matter to himself, will spend his days in safety, with much pleasantness. "Thou hast heard a word," we read, "let it die with thee; and be bold; it will[5] not burst thee."[6] What is the meaning of this? "let it die with thee?" Extinguish it; bury it; neither permit it to go forth, nor even to move at all; but, as the best course, be careful not to tolerate others in the practice of evil speaking. And should you perchance, at any time receive an impression from it, bury it, destroy what has been uttered, deliver it over to oblivion; in order that you may become like those who have not heard it; and spend the present life with much peace and security. Should the slanderers learn that we abhor them more than those do whom they accuse, they themselves will henceforth abandon this evil habit, and correct the sin; and will afterwards applaud, and proclaim us as those who were their saviours and benefactors. For, as to speak well, and to applaud, is the beginning of friendship, so to speak ill and to calumniate, has been the beginning and foundation of enmity, and hatred, and a thousand quarrels. From nothing else have our own affairs been more neglected, than from the habit of prying into and meddling with the concerns of others; for it is not possible for one who is given to evil speaking, and busying himself with other men's lives, ever to look after his own life. His whole study being expended upon meddling with other men's matters, all those which belong to himself must of necessity be left at hazard and neglected. For it is well if one who spends all his leisure on the anxious consideration of his own sins, and the judgment of them, can make any progress. But when thou art always busy about other men's matters, when wilt thou pay any heed to thy own evils?

16. Let us flee then, beloved, let us flee slander! knowing that it is the very gulph of Satan, and the place where he lurks with his snares. For in order that we may be careless of our own state, and may thus render

---

[1] δυσαρέστως ἔχοντας.
[2] This passage is erroneously quoted by Montfaucon, *Synops. Diatr.* l. t. 13, p. 179, as if it spoke of confessing one's own sins privately. St. Chrysostom certainly did not regard this as necessary. The original practice was a public confession of crimes. Private confession was at first subservient to this. See Bingham, b. xv. c. 8, sec. 6; xviii. c. 3, secs. 2, 7, 8; Socr. v. 19; Soz. vii. 16.
[3] Ps. ci. 5.   [4] Punct. Sav.
[5] οὐ μή is used thus with the future indicative at least in the third person. See Kühner, *Gr. Gram.* 779, 2 *Œd. Col.* 176.
[6] Ecclus. xix. 10.

our account heavier, the devil leads us into this custom. But more than this; it is not only a very serious matter, that we shall hereafter have to give account of what we have spoken, but that we shall make our own offences the heavier by these means; depriving ourselves of all excuse. For he who scans with bitterness the conduct of others, can never obtain pardon for the sins committed by himself. For God will determine the sentence, not only from the nature of our transgressions, but from the judgment which thou hast passed upon others. Therefore He gave the admonition, "Judge not, that ye be not judged."[1] For the sin, of whatever kind, will not there appear any more such as it was when committed, but will receive a great and unpardonable addition from the judgment passed by thee upon thy fellow servants. For as he who is humane, and merciful, and forgiving, cuts away the greater mass of his sins, so he who is bitter, and cruel, and implacable, greatly increases the magnitude of his own offences. Let us then expel from our mouth all slander, knowing that if we do not abstain from it, though we might feed upon ashes, this austerity would avail us nothing. "For not that which entereth into, but that which cometh out of the mouth defileth the man."[2] If any one were to stir up a cesspool, when you were passing, say, would you not reproach and rate the man who did it? This then also do with respect to the slanderer. For the stirred cesspool does not so grossly offend the sense of those who smell that ill savour, as the stirring up other men's sins, and the exposure of an impure life, offends and disturbs the soul of those who hear of it. Therefore let us abstain from evil speaking, from foul language, from blasphemy; and let us not speak ill of our neighbour, nor of God!

17. For many of our evil speakers have run into such madness, as to lift up their own tongue from their fellow servants against their Master. But how great an evil this is, you may learn from the affairs in which we are now involved. A man is insulted, and, lo! we are all fearing and trembling, both those who were guilty of the insult, and those who are conscious of nothing of the kind! But God is insulted every day! Why do I say every day?—every hour rather, by the rich, by the poor, by those who are at ease, by the afflicted, by those who calumniate, and those who are calumniated, and yet no one ever hears a word of this! Therefore He has permitted our fellow servant[3] to be insulted, in order that from the danger which has happened through this insult, thou mayest learn the benignity of the Lord! And notwithstanding that this is our first and only offence, we do not on that account expect to gain an excuse, or pardon. But we provoke God every day, and we show no signs of returning to Him, and yet He endures it with all long-suffering! Seest thou then how great the benignity of the Lord is? Yet, in this present outrage, those who had done amiss were taken and thrust into prison, and paid the penalty; nevertheless we are still in fear, for he who has been insulted has not as yet heard[4] what has taken place, nor pronounced sentence, and we are all trembling. But God every day hears of the insults offered Him, and no one heeds it, although God is thus merciful and loving toward man. With Him it suffices only to acknowledge the sin, and so to cancel the accusation. But with man it is altogether the reverse. When those who have sinned confess, then they are punished the more; which indeed has happened in the present instance. And some have perished by the sword, some by fire; some given to wild beasts, and not men only, but children. And neither this immaturity of age, nor the tumult of the people, nor the circumstance that they were infuriated by demons when they perpetrated these deeds;[5] nor that the exaction was thought to be intolerable;[6] nor poverty, nor having offended in company with all; nor promising that they would never hereafter dare to repeat such deeds; nor anything else, could at all rescue them; but they were led away to the pit,[7] without reprieve; armed soldiers conducting and guarding them on either side, lest any one should carry off the criminals; whilst mothers also followed afar off, seeing their children beheaded, but not daring to bewail their calamity; for terror conquered grief, and fear overcame nature! And just as when men beholding from the land those who are shipwrecked, are deeply distressed, but are not able to approach and to rescue the drowning, so too here, the mothers restrained through fear of the soldiers, as it were by so many waves, not only dared not go near to their children, and res-

---

[1] Matt. vii. 1.   [2] Matt. xv. 17, 18.   [3] The Emperor.

[4] The two capitals of Antioch and Constantinople were separated by the distance of 800 miles. See Gibbon, c. 27.
[5] He clearly means the same persons. See Soz. vii. 23. This might be pleaded as an excuse where demoniacal possession was a commonly acknowledged fact.
[6] He probably refers to a tax which had been imposed on the citizens to defray the expenses of celebrating the 10th year of Theodosius, whose treasury was exhausted by the late war with the Goths. (Sozomen and Theodoret mistake the date. See Pref. Ed.) See Gibbon, c. 27.
[7] τὸ βάραθρον. Xen. Hell. i. 7, 21, seems to imply that criminals at Athens were first put to death, and then thrown into the Barathrum. But they were sometimes thrown in alive, to be killed by the fall. The places so called may have differed both in nature and in use.

cue them from condemnation, but were afraid even to shed tears?

18. Assuredly ye gather from thence the mercy of God, how unspeakable, how boundless, how transcending all description! Here indeed the person who has been insulted is of the same nature;[1] and only once in all his lifetime has experienced this; and then it was not done to his face; nor while he was present to see or hear it; and nevertheless, none of those who perpetrated these deeds obtained pardon. But with regard to God nothing of the kind can be said; for the interval between man and God, is so great, as no language can at all express; and throughout every day He is insulted, although present, and seeing and hearing it: and yet He sends not forth the lightning, nor commands the sea to overflow the land, and submerge all men; nor does He bid the earth to cleave asunder and swallow up all the contumelious; but He forbears, and suffers long, and still offers to pardon those who have insulted Him, if they only repent and promise to do these things no more! Truly now is the season to proclaim, "Who can utter the mighty acts of the Lord? who can show forth all His praise?"[2] How many men have not only cast down, but also trodden under foot the images of God! For when thou throttlest a debtor, when thou strippest him, when thou draggest him away,[3] thou tramplest under foot God's image. Hear for a certainty Paul saying, that "a man ought not to cover his head, forasmuch as he is the image and glory of God."[4] And again, hear God Himself saying, "Let us make man in Our Image, after Our likeness."[5] But if thou sayest that man is not of the same substance as God,—what matters that? For neither was the brazen statue of the same substance as the Emperor; yet nevertheless, they who defied it paid the penalty. Thus also with regard to mankind, if men are not of the same substance as God, (as indeed they are not), still they have been called His image; and it were fitting they should receive honour on account of the appellation. But thou for the sake of a little gold dost trample them under foot, dost throttle them, and drag them away; and hast not to this day in any wise paid the penalty!

19. May there be then speedily some favourable and propitious change! This certainly I foretell and testify, that although this cloud should pass away, and we yet remain in the same condition of listlessness, we shall again have to suffer much heavier evils than those we are now dreading; for I do not so much fear the wrath of the Emperor, as your own listlessness. Surely it is not sufficient by way of apology that we supplicate[6] two or three days, but it is necessary that we should make a change in our whole life,[7] and that whilst abstaining from wickedness we should persevere continually in virtue. For as those who are sickly, unless they keep up a constant regimen, would find no advantage by their observing a two or three days' discipline; so those who are in sin, if they do not exercise sobriety at all times, will find no benefit in two or three days' amendment. For as it is said, that he who is washed, and is again afterwards polluted with the mire, hath gained nothing; so he who has repented for three days, and has again returned to his former state, has accomplished nothing. Let us not therefore, now act as we have always done hitherto. For many times, when we have been surprised by earthquakes, as well as famine and drought, after becoming more sober and gentle for three or four days, we did but return again to the former course. For this cause our present troubles have happened. But if we have not done so before; yet, now at least let us all persevere in the same piety; let us preserve the same meekness, that we may not again need another stroke. Was not God able to have prevented what has taken place? He did, however, permit it, that He might make those who despised Him more sober-minded, through dread of a fellow-servant!

20. But let not any one say, that many of the guilty escaped, and that many of the innocent incurred punishment. For I hear of numerous persons who frequently say this; not only in the case of the present sedition, but also in many other circumstances of this nature. What then should I reply to those who make such observations? Why, that if he who was captured was innocent of the present sedition, he had wrought some other transgression before this still more grievous, for which, not having afterwards repented, he has paid the penalty at the present time. For thus is the custom of God to deal with us. When we sin, He does not straightway visit the transgression, but lets it pass, giving us space[8] for repentance, in order that we may be amended and converted. But if, because we have not paid the penalty, we suppose that the offence too is blotted out, and make light of it; then somewhere, where

---

[1] οὐσίας. [2] Ps. cvi. 2.
[3] Some add ὅταν καταβάλλῃς, lit. "when thou throwest him down;" it may have some special meaning. See on Rom. ii. 18, Hom. XI. Comp. Ja. iii. 9.
[4] 1 Cor. xi. 7. [5] Gen. i. 26.
[6] λιτανεῦσαι.
[7] Sav. and M. "the change that of our whole life:" the Greek reads best so.
[8] προθεσμίαν.

we think not of it, we are sure afterwards to be punished. And this takes place in order that, when we sin and are not punished, we may not be free from fear, unless we amend, knowing that we shall certainly fall into punishment where we do not expect it. So that if thou sinnest, beloved, and art not punished, do not grow presumptuous, but for this very cause be the more alarmed, knowing that it is an easy matter with God to recompense again when he pleases. For this reason then he hath not punished thee, that thou mightest receive space for repentance. Let us not therefore say, that such a person whilst innocent incurred punishment; and another whilst guilty escaped, for he who incurred it, being guiltless, as I observed, paid the punishment of other transgressions; and he who now escapes it, if he repents not, will be captured in another snare. If our minds are thus disposed, we shall never forget our own sins, but, always fearful and trembling lest we should have to pay the penalty, we shall readily recollect them. For nothing is so apt to bring sin to remembrance as punishment and chastisement. And this is shown by Joseph's brethren. For when they had sold the just man, and thirteen years had passed away, suspecting they had fallen into punishment, and fearing for their lives, they remembered their sin, and said one to another, "We are verily guilty concerning our brother Joseph."[1] Seest thou, how fear brought their guilt to recollection? And yet when they were sinning they perceived it not, but when they were fearful of being punished, then they remembered it? Knowing, therefore, all these things, let us make a change and amendment of our lives; and let us think of religion and virtue, before we think of deliverance from the impending distress.

21. And in the meanwhile I desire to fix three precepts in your mind, to the end that you may accomplish me these during the fast,—viz. to speak ill of no one; to hold no one for an enemy; and to expel from the mouth altogether the evil custom of oaths. And as when we hear that some money tax is imposed, each one going within, and calling his wife and children and servants, considers and consults with them how he may pay this tribute, so also let us do with respect to these spiritual precepts. Let every one when he has returned home call together his wife and children, and let him say, that a spiritual tribute was imposed this day: a tribute by which there will be some deliverance and removal of these evils; a tribute which does not make those who pay it poor, but richer; that is to say, to have no enemy, to speak evil of no man, and to swear not at all. Let us consider; let us think; let us resolve how we may fulfill these precepts. Let us exert every endeavour. Let us admonish each other. Let us correct each other, that we may not go to the other world as debtors, and then, needing to borrow of others, suffer the fate of the foolish virgins, and fall from immortal salvation. If we thus set our lives in order, I warrant you and promise, that from this there will be deliverance from the present calamity, and a removal of these dreadful ills; and what is greater than all, there will be the enjoyment of the good things to come. For it were fitting that I should commit to you the whole body of virtue; but I think it the best method of correction, to take the laws by parts, and reduce them to practice, and then to proceed to others. For as in a given field, the husbandman, digging it all up piecemeal, gradually comes to the end of his task; so we too if we make this rule for ourselves, in any wise to reduce to a correct practice these three precepts during the present Lent, and to commit them to the safe custody of good habit, we shall proceed with greater ease to the rest; and by this means arriving at the summit of spiritual wisdom, we shall both reap the fruit of a favourable hope in the present life; and in the life to come we shall stand before Christ with great confidence, and enjoy those unspeakable blessings; which, God grant, we may all be found worthy of, through the grace and loving kindness of Jesus Christ our Lord, with Whom be glory to the Father and the Holy Spirit forever and ever. Amen.

---

[1] Gen. xlii. 21.

HOMILY IV.

An exhortation to the people respecting fortitude and patience, from the examples of Job and the Three Children in Babylon. The Homily concludes with an address on the subject of abstaining from oaths.

1. Blessed be God! who hath comforted your sorrowing souls, and stayed your agitated spirits! For that ye have received no small consolation is evident by the desire and readiness to listen which ye are now showing. For it is impossible that a soul in anguish, and oppressed with the cloud of despondency, should have power to hear with readiness anything that is spoken. But I see you are attending to us with much good will, and with an intense earnestness; and that you have shaken off gloomy thoughts, and put aside the sense of present distress, in your affectionate desire of listening. For this cause, I thank God heartily together with you, that the calamity has not overmatched your philosophy; nor fear relaxed your vigour; nor tribulation quenched your alacrity; nor danger dried up your zeal: nor the fear of men overcome the desire for God; nor the difficulty of the times overthrown your earnestness; nay, so far from overthrowing, it has strengthened it; so far from slackening, it has given it more intensity; so far from quenching, has kindled it the more. The forum is indeed empty, but the church is filled; the former supplies material for melancholy, the latter is an occasion of joy and spiritual gladness! When therefore, beloved, you betake yourself to the forum, and the sight of the solitude calls forth a groan, fly back to thy Mother, and straightway she will console thee with the multitude of her offspring and will show thee the chorus of the Brethren complete, and will drive away all thy despondency! For in the city we are as earnestly longing to see human beings, as those who inhabit the deserts; but when we take refuge in the church, we are straitened for room by the multitude. And as when the sea is in uproar, and rendered furious by the violent tempest, fear compels all to fly for refuge from without into the harbour; so also now, the waves of the forum, and the tempest of the city, drives together every one from all sides into the church, and by the bond of love knits the members close to one another.

2. Let us then give thanks to God even for these things, that we have reaped so much fruit from the tribulation; that we have received so great an advantage from the trial. If there were no trial, there would be no crown; if there were no wrestlings, there would be no prize; if there were no lists[1] marked out, there would be no honours; if there were no tribulation, there would be no rest; if there were no winter, there would be no summer. And this may be observed, not only amongst men, but even with the very seeds; for if, in that case, we expect the ear of corn to spring and flourish, there must be much rain, much gathering of the clouds, and much frost; and the time of sowing is also a rainy season. Since therefore the winter, a winter not of the elements, but of souls, has now set in, let us too sow in this winter that we may reap in the summer; let us sow tears, that we may reap gladness. This is not my word, it is a prophetic promise, "They who sow in tears, shall reap in joy."[2] The rain which cometh down, doth not so make the seeds to sprout and grow, as the shower of falling tears maketh the seed of godliness to spring up and flourish. This it is that cleanseth the soul; watereth the mind, and causeth the growing germ of doctrine to push rapidly forwards. For this reason also, it is needful to plough up a deep furrow. This the Prophet signified when he spoke thus, "Break up your fallow ground, and sow not among thorns."[3] Therefore, as when he who has set the plough on the field, turns up the earth from below, preparing beforehand a safe lodgment for the seeds, in order that they may not lie dispersed over the surface, but may be hidden in the very womb of the earth, and deposit their roots in safety: so also it is our business to act; and making use of the plough of tribulation to break up the depth of the heart. For another Prophet admonishes of this, when he says, "Rend your hearts and not your garments."[4] Let us then rend our hearts, that if any evil plant, any treacherous thought be present in

---

[1] σκάμματα, elsewhere translated "arena," see Fabr. *Ag.* ii. 7. Graev. viii. 1963, he quotes St. Ephraim *De Luctâ Spirituali. In luctaminibus hujus sæculi*, &c. Ed. Rom. Gr. Lat. iii. 577, Voss. p. 371. "The most perfect combatants are ever to be found fearless and active within the lines (scamma), but the timid and feeble fly this way and that before they begin to strive, and for their great softness and laziness will not exert themselves in the scamma. Now the scamma, beloved brethren, is the central place in which the wrestlers strive;" this may explain ἕλκωνται, p. 18; see also Voss's note, p. 123.
[2] Ps. cxxv. 5.   [3] Jer. iv. 3.   [4] Joel ii. 13.

us, we may tear it up by the roots, and provide a pure soil for the seeds of godliness. For if we do not now break up the fallow ground; if we do not now sow; if we do not now water it with tears, whilst it is a time of tribulation and fasting, when shall we ever be brought to compunction? Will it be when we are at ease, and in luxury? But this is impossible. For ease and luxury generally lead to indolence, just as tribulation leads back again to diligence; and restores to itself the mind that had wandered abroad, and been dreaming after a multitude of objects.

3. Let us not then grieve on account of this despondency, but even give thanks to God, for great is the gain that comes of tribulation. The husbandman, when he has sown the seed he had gathered with so much labour, prays that a shower may come; and the ignorant man, looking on, will be surprised at all that takes place; and perhaps say to himself, "what can this man be doing? He is scattering what he has collected; and not only scattering, but he is also mixing it up in the earth with much industry, so that it will be no easy matter for him to collect these together again; and besides mixing them with the earth, he is moreover desiring a heavy rain, so that all he has cast therein will rot, and become mire." Such a person is also terrified when he observes the thunders bursting through the clouds, and the lightnings striking downwards. But not so the farmer. He is glad and rejoices whilst beholding the heavy rain. For he does not regard what is present, but awaits the future. He does not attend to the thunderings, but is reckoning the number of his sheaves. He thinks not of the decaying seed, but of the flourishing ears of corn; not of the tedious rain, but of the delightful dust of the threshing floor. Thus indeed, also, should we regard, not our present tribulation, nor the pain of it, but the benefit that may arise from it—the fruit that it will bring forth. Let us wait for the sheaves of the threshing floor; for if we be sober, we shall be able to collect much fruit from the present time, and to fill the granaries of our minds. If we be sober, we shall not only be far from taking any harm from this trouble, but we shall also reap innumerable benefits. But should we be slothful, even tranquillity will destroy us! Either of these things is injurious to him who takes no heed; but they both profit him who lives with strictness. And even as gold if it be covered with water, still shows its own proper beauty, and although it should fall into the furnace, would again come forth brighter than before; but on the other hand, should clay or grass be mixed with water, the one dissolves and the other corrupts; and should they fall into the fire, the one is parched and the other is burnt up; so also in truth it is with the just man and the sinner! For should the former enjoy repose, he remains illustrious, even as gold is when immersed in water; and though he falls into trial, he becomes the more illustrious, like gold when subjected to the test of fire; but the sinner, if he obtains rest, is enervated and corrupted like the grass and the clay, when they come in contact with water; and should he undergo trial, he is burnt up and destroyed, in the same way as the grass and the clay are by the action of fire!

4. Let us not then be out of heart for the present evils; for if thou hast any sins[1] remaining, they will disappear, and easily be burnt up by the tribulation; but if thou possessest virtue, thou wilt become thereby more illustrious and distinguished; for if thou art continually vigilant and sober, thou wilt be superior to all injury. For it is not the nature of the trials, but the listlessness of those who are tried, that is apt to cause their overthrow. So that if thou desirest to rejoice, and to enjoy ease and pleasure, seek neither for pleasure nor ease, but seek for a soul full of patience, and one that is able to manifest fortitude; since if thou hast not this, not only will trial put thee to shame, but repose will destroy and overthrow thee yet more signally. For to prove that it is not the attack of evils, but the listlessness of the mind which subverts our salvation, hear what Christ saith: "Whosoever heareth these sayings of mine, and doeth them, I will liken him unto a wise man, which built his house upon a rock; and the rain descended, and the floods came, and the winds blew, and beat upon that house; and it fell not, for it was founded upon a rock." And again: "Every one who heareth these sayings of mine, and doeth them not, shall be likened unto a foolish man, which built his house upon the sand; and the rain descended, and the floods came, and the winds blew, and beat upon that house; and it fell, and great was the fall of it."[2] Do you perceive that it was not the attack of these trials that produced the overthrow, but the folly of the builders? For there was rain there, and there was rain here; there were floods there,

---

[1] ἁμαρτίας. This seems from the contrast to mean "sinful habits," which trouble affords facilities for amending. Had he meant removing *guilt*, he would probably have said ἁμαρτήματα, or κηλῖδας, as Hom. I. 22. See also Hom. III. 21, where he speaks of the removal of guilt as depending on the *use* made of chastisement. Also on Rom. v. 11; Hom. IX.; see also Hom. V. (5), Hom. VI. (5), and Hom. VII. (1).
[2] Matt. vii. 24–27.

and there were floods here; here the beating of winds, and there again the same. The one man built a house, and the other built a house. The building was the same; the trials were the same; but the end was not the same; because there was not the same foundation. For the folly of the builder, not the nature of the trials, caused the fall of the building; otherwise the house that was founded upon the rock should have fallen, whereas nothing of that kind befell it. But do not suppose that these things were spoken merely of a house; for the discourse relates to a soul, giving proof by its works that it hears the divine word, or rejects it. Thus Job builded up his soul. The rain descended;—for the fire fell from heaven and devoured all his flocks; the floods came;—the frequent,—the constant,—the successive messengers of his calamities, telling him of the destruction of his herds—of his camels—of his children. The winds blew,—the bitter words of his wife:—"Curse God," she said, "and die."[1] Yet the house fell not: the soul was not supplanted: the just man did not blaspheme; but even gave thanks thus, saying, "The Lord gave and the Lord hath taken away. As it pleased the Lord, so is it come to pass."[2] Seest thou that not the nature of the trials, but the negligence of the indolent, is wont to cause the overthrow? since tribulation makes the strong man stronger. Who saith this? It is the man who lived in tribulation, the blessed Paul; he speaks thus: "Tribulation worketh patience, and patience probation, and probation hope."[3] And even as the violence of the wind, when it rushes upon strong trees, and sways them in all directions, does not root them up, but renders them still firmer and stronger by these attacks; so the soul that is holy, and lives in a religious state, is not supplanted by the inroads of trial and tribulation, but stimulated thereby to more patience; even as the blessed Job, whom they made more illustrious and honourable.

5. At the present time then, a man is angry with us, a man of like passions, and of like soul, and we are afraid: but in the case of Job it was an evil and malignant demon who was angry; nay, he was not simply angry, but set in motion all sorts of machinations, and brought forward every stratagem; and yet even with all he could not conquer the fortitude of the just man. But here is a man, who is at one time angry, at another time is reconciled; and we are nevertheless dead with fear. On that occasion it was a devil that waged war, who is never reconciled to human nature, but has engaged in a war without treaty, and a battle without truce against our race; yet nevertheless, the just man laughed his darts to scorn. What apology then, or what pardon can be ours, if we cannot sustain a human trial; we who are taught such spiritual wisdom under grace; when this man before grace, and before the Old Testament, endured this most grievous war so nobly! These things, beloved, we should therefore always discourse of with one another; and by words of this kind encourage ourselves. For ye are witnesses, and your conscience is a witness how much gain we have already received from this trial! The dissolute man hath now become sober; the bold man meek; the slothful man active. They who never at any time saw a church, but constantly spent their time at the theatre, now remain in the church the whole day long. Tell me then, dost thou grieve on this account, that God hath made thee earnest through fear; that He hath led thee by tribulation to a sense of thine own safety? But is thy conscience pained? Yea, is thy mind pierced every day as with a dart, expecting death, and the greatest wrath? Nevertheless, from thence too we shall gain a great advance toward virtue, if our piety is made more earnest by means of the distress. For God is able to free you from all these evils this day. But not until He sees that you are purified; not until He sees that a conversion has taken place, and a repentance firm and unshaken, will He entirely remove the tribulation. The goldsmith, until he perceives the gold well refined, will not draw it out from the furnace; and even so God will not take away this cloud before He hath thoroughly amended us. For He Himself who hath permitted this trial, knows the time for removing it. So it is also with one who plays the harp; he neither overstrains the string, lest he break it, nor relaxes it too much, lest he mar the consonance of its harmony. Thus does God act. He neither places our souls in a state of constant repose, nor of lengthened tribulation; making use of both these at His discretion; for he neither suffers us to enjoy continual repose, lest we should grow listless, nor on the other hand does he permit us to be in constant tribulation, lest we sink under it, and become desperate.

6. Let us then leave to Him the time for the removal of our evils; let *us* only pray; let *us* live in piety: for this is our work, to turn to virtue; but to set us free from these evils is God's work! For indeed He is more desirous to quench this fire than thou who art

---

[1] Job ii. 9.   [2] Job i. 21.   [3] Rom. v. 3, 4.

tried by it: but He is waiting for thy salvation. As tribulation then came of rest, so also after tribulation, rest must be expected. For neither is it always winter, nor always summer; neither are there always waves, nor always a calm; neither always night, nor always day. Thus tribulation is not perpetual, but there will be also repose; only in our tribulation, let us give thanks to God always. For the three youths were cast into the furnace, and did not even for this forget their piety; neither did the flames affright them, but more earnestly than men sitting in a chamber, and suffering nothing to alarm them, did they, whilst encircled by the fire, send up to heaven those sacred prayers[1]—therefore the fire became a wall unto them, and the flame a robe; and the furnace was a fountain; and whereas it received them bound, it restored them free. It received bodies that were mortal, but abstained from them as if they had been immortal! It knew their nature, yet it reverenced their piety! The tyrant bound their feet, and their feet bound the operation of the fire! O marvellous thing! The flame loosed those who were bound, and was itself afterwards bound by those who had been in bonds; for the piety of the youths changed the nature of things; or rather it did not change the nature, but, what was far more wonderful, it stayed the operation of them, even whilst their nature remained. For it did not quench the fire, but though burning, made it powerless. And it was truly marvellous and unaccountable, that this not only happened with respect to the bodies of these saints, but also with respect to their garments, and their shoes. And as it was in the case of the Apostles, the garments of Paul expelled diseases and demons,[2] and the shadow[3] of Peter[4] put death to flight; so indeed also in this case, the shoes of these youths extinguished the power of the fire.

7. I know not how I should speak, for the wonder surpasses all description! The force of the fire was both quenched and not quenched: for whilst it came in contact with the bodies of these saints, it was quenched; but when it was needful to burst their bonds, it was not quenched; wherefore it broke their bonds, but touched not their ancles.[5] Do you see how very near it was? Yet the fire was not deceived, and dared not penetrate within the bonds. The tyrant bound, and the flame set loose; that thou mightest learn at once the fierceness of the barbarian, and the submissiveness of the element. For what reason did he bind, when he was about to cast into the fire? In order that the miracle might be the greater; that the sign might be the more unaccountable; that thou mayest not suppose that the things seen were an optical delusion. For if that fire had been no fire, it would not have consumed the bands; and what is much more, it would not have seized upon the soldiers who were placed without the furnace; but as the case was, it showed its power upon those without; but towards those within, its submissiveness. But observe, I pray, in everything, how the devil by the very same means with which he fights with the servants of God, pulls down his own power; not intentionally, but because the wisdom and abundant contrivance of God turns all his weapons and devices upon his own head; which assuredly happened on that occasion. For the devil at that time inspiring the tyrant, neither suffered the heads of the saints to be cut off with the sword, nor that they should be delivered to wild beasts, nor punished in any such manner; but that they should be thrown into the fire; to the end that not even any relics of these saints should remain, their bodies being altogether consumed, and their ashes being mingled with the ashes of the fagots. But God accordingly employed this very circumstance for the taking away of impiety.[6] And how? I will tell you. Fire is accounted by the Persians to be a god; and the barbarians, who inhabit that country even now honour it with much worship. God, therefore, being desirous to pull up by the roots the material of impiety, permitted the punishment to take this form, in order that He might give the victory to His servants before the eyes of all these fire-worshippers; persuading them by the plain fact, that the gods of the Gentiles are in dread not of God only, but even of the servants of God.

8. Consider, moreover, how the crown of this victory was woven by the adversaries, and the enemies themselves were made witnesses of this trophy. For "Nebuchadnezzar," it says, "sent to gather together the princes, the governors, and the captains, the judges, the sheriffs, and all the rulers of the provinces, to come to the dedication of the image, and they were all gathered together."[7]

---

[1] St. Chrysostom refers to the Benedicite, or "Song of the Three Children." In his book *Quod nemo læditur nisi a seipso*, he calls it " That admirable and marvellous song, which from that day to this hath been sung every where throughout the world, and shall yet be sung in future generations." Ben. t. iii. 464 ; E. quoted by Bingham, b. xiv. c. ii., sec. 6, New Ed., vol. iv., p. 461.
[2] Acts xix. 12.   [3] So Sav. and M. Ben. σκιαί.
[4] Acts v. 15.   [5] Dan. iii. 25.
[6] τῆς ἀσεβείας, used especially of Heathenism, as "ungodliness." Hom. I. 15, so εὐσεβεία perhaps ; Tit. i. 1, for *right* religion, but this use of the words belongs rather to the Fathers than to the New Testament.
[7] Dan. iii. 2.

The enemy prepares the theatre, and he himself collects together the spectators, and prepares the lists; a theatre too, not of chance persons, or of some private individuals, but of all those who were honourable and in authority, to the end that their testimony may be worthy of credit with the multitude. They had come summoned for one thing; but they all departed having beheld another thing. They came in order to worship the image; and they departed, having derided the image, and struck with wonder at the power of God, through the signs which had taken place with respect to these young men. And observe, where the field for this display was spread out. No city, nor select enclosure furnished room for this theatre of the whole world, but smooth and naked plains. For in the plain of Dura, outside the city, he set up the image, and the herald came and cried, " To you it is commanded, O people, nations, and languages, that at what time ye hear the sound of the cornet, flute, harp, sackbut, psaltery, dulcimer, and all kinds of music, ye fall down and worship the golden image;" (for a fall indeed it was to worship the idol); " and whoso falleth not down, and worshippeth, shall the same hour be cast into the midst of a burning fiery furnace."[1] Seest thou how difficult these struggles are made; how irresistible the snare; and how deep the gulph, and a precipice on either hand? But be not afraid. In whatever degree the enemy increases his machinations, so much the more does he display the courage of the young men. For this reason is there this symphony of so many musicians; for this reason the burning furnace; in order that both pleasure, and fear, may besiege the souls of those present. Is there any one of harsh and unyielding character among them? " Let the melody of every kind of music," saith he, " enchant and soften him." But is he superior to this artifice, " let the sight of the flame affright and astound him." Thus was fear as well as pleasure present; the one entering to assault the soul by the ears, the other by the eyes. But the noble character of these youths was not by any such means to be conquered; but even as, when they fell into the fire, they mastered the flames, even so they derided all desire and all fear. For it was for them the devil had prepared all these things beforehand. For he had no doubts of his own subjects, but was exceedingly confident that no one would resist the royal mandate. But when all fell down, and were subdued, then the youths alone are led into the midst; in order that from this too the conquest may become the more illustrious, they alone conquering and being proclaimed victors among so vast a multitude. For this would not have been so surprising if they had acted courageously at the first, when as yet no one had been overthrown. But the greatest, and most astonishing fact was, that the multitude of those who fell down, neither affrighted, nor enfeebled them. They did not say to themselves any such things as many are ofttimes wont to say; " If we were the first, and the only persons to worship the image, this would have been a sin: but if we do this with so many myriads, who will not make allowance? who will not think us worthy of defence?" nothing of that sort did they say or think, when they beheld the prostrate forms[2] of so many tyrants.[3] Consider thou also with me the wickedness of those who were their accusers, and how maliciously and bitterly they brought the accusation! " There are," say they, " certain Jews whom thou hast set up over the works of the province of Babylon."[4] They did not merely make mention of the nation, but they also bring to mind their honourable condition, that they may inflame the wrath of the king; almost as if they had said, " These slaves, these captives, who are without a city, thou hast made rulers over us. But they shew contempt for such honour, and treat insolently him who has given them this honour!" Therefore they say this; " The Jews whom thou hast set over the works of the province of Babylon, obey not thy decree, nor serve thy gods."[4] The accusation becomes their greatest praise; and the crimes imputed, their encomium; a testimony indeed that is indubitable, since their enemies bring it forward. What then does the king? He commands that they should be brought into the midst, so that he may affright them in every way. But nothing dismayed them, neither the wrath of the king, nor their being left alone in the midst of so many, nor the sight of the fire, nor the sound of the trumpet, nor the whole multitude looking fire at them; for deriding all these things, as if they were about to be cast into a cool fountain of water, they entered the furnace uttering that blessed sentence, " We will not serve thy gods, nor worship the golden image which thou hast set up."[5]

9. I have not referred to this history without reason, but that ye may learn that whether it be the wrath of a king, or the

---

[1] Dan. iii. 4, 6.
[2] πτώματα, usually of fallen carcases.
[3] Or princes, τυράννων.
[4] Dan. iii. 12.
[5] Dan. iii. 18.

violence of soldiers, or the envy of enemies, or captivity, or destitution, or fire, or furnace, or ten thousand terrors, nothing will avail to put to shame or terrify a righteous man. For if where the king was godless the youths were not dismayed at the tyrant's wrath, how much more ought we to be confident, having an emperor who is humane and merciful, and to express thankfulness to God for this tribulation, knowing from what has now been said, that tribulations render men more illustrious both in the presence of God and of man, if they know how to bear them with fortitude! For indeed if these had not been made slaves, we should not have known their freedom! If they had not been captives, we should not have learned their nobility of soul! If they had not been exiles from their country below, we should not have known the excellency of their citizenship above! If the earthly king had not been angry with them, we should not have known the favour with which they were regarded by the heavenly King!

10. Thou too then, if thou hast Him for thy Friend, be not despairing, although thou fallest into the furnace: and in like manner if He be angry, think not thou art safe though thou be in Paradise. For Adam indeed was in Paradise, yet, when he had provoked God, Paradise profited him nothing. These youths were in the furnace; yet, since they were approved, the furnace injured them not at all. Adam was in Paradise, but when he was supine, he was supplanted! Job sat down on the dunghill, yet, since he was vigilant he prevailed! Yet how much better was Paradise than a dunghill! still the excellency of the place benefitted in no degree the inhabitant; forasmuch as he had betrayed himself; as likewise indeed the vileness of the place did to one no injury, who was fortified on every side with virtue. As to ourselves then, let us fortify our souls; for if the loss of wealth should threaten us, or even death, and yet no one can rob us of our religion, we are the happiest of men, Christ commended this when he said, "Be ye wise as serpents."[1] For just as he exposes the whole body in order that he may save the head,[2] so also do thou. Although it should be necessary to expose wealth, or the body, or the present life, or all things, for the purpose of preserving thy religion; be not cast down! For if thou depart hence in possession of that, God will restore to thee all things with more abundant splendour, and will raise again thy body with greater glory; and instead of riches, there will be the good things that surpass all power of description. Did not Job sit naked on a dunghill, sustaining a life more grievous than ten thousand deaths? Yet since he did not cast away his piety, all his former things came back to him in greater abundance, soundness and beauty of body; his full band of children; his possessions; and what was greater than all, the splendid crown of his patience. For as it happens with trees, should any one pluck away the fruit and the leaves together; should he even cut off all the branches letting the root only remain; the tree will rise again entire, with greater beauty, so indeed is it also with us. If the root of piety remain, although wealth be taken away, although the body destroyed, all things again revert to us with greater glory than before. Casting away therefore all anxiety and superfluous care, let us return to ourselves; and let us adorn the body and the soul with the ornament of virtue; converting our bodily members into instruments of righteouness and not instruments of sin.

11. And first of all, let us discipline our tongue to be the minister of the grace of the Spirit, expelling from the mouth all virulence and malignity, and the practice of using disgraceful words. For it is in our power to make each one of our members an instrument of wickedness, or of righteousness. Hear then how men make the tongue an instrument, some of sin, others of righteousness! "Their tongue is a sharp sword."[3] But another speaks thus of his own tongue: "My tongue[4] is the pen of a ready writer."[5] The former wrought destruction; the latter wrote the divine law. Thus was one a sword, the other a pen, not according to its own nature, but according to the choice of those who employed it. For the nature of this tongue and of that was the same, but the operation was not the same. And again, as to the mouth likewise, we may see this same thing. For these had a mouth full of filth and of wickedness, therefore against such it is said by way of accusation, "Their mouth is full of cursing and bitterness;"[6] not such was his, but "My mouth shall speak of wisdom, and the meditation of my heart shall be of understanding."[7] Again, there were others who had their hands full of iniquity, and accusing these he said, "Iniquities are in their hands,

---

[1] Matt. x. 16.
[2] So St. Jerome, *Cat. Aur.*, St. Aug., *Doct. Christ.* II. xvi. (24); Comp. Gen. iii. 15. Luc. xvi. 8, 9; Origen on Prov. i. 2.
[3] Ps. lvii. 4.
[4] The references in the Psalms are made to the English version, which is divided as the Hebrew, except that it sometimes varies a verse or two. LXX. and Vulg. annex Ps. x. to ix., and call Ps. xi. Ps. x., and so on till Ps. cxlvii., which they divide, beginning their Ps. cxlvii. at v. 12.
[5] Ps. xlv. 1.   [6] Ps. xiv. 6.   [7] Ps. xlix. 3.

and their right hand is filled with gifts."[1] But he himself had hands practised in nothing but in being stretched out towards heaven. Therefore he said of these too, "The lifting up of my hands (let it be) an evening sacrifice."[2] The same may also be perceived with reference to the heart; for their heart indeed was foolish, but this man's was true; hence he speaks of them thus, "Their heart is vain;" but of his own, "My heart is inditing of a good matter."[3] And as to the ear, one may see that the case is the same; for some have a sense of hearing like that of beasts, which is not to be charmed or moved to pity; and reproaching such the Psalmist says, "They are like the deaf adder, that stoppeth her ears."[4] But his ear was the receptacle of the divine words, and this he again makes manifest, when he says, "I will incline mine ear to a parable, I will open my dark speech upon the harp."[5]

12. Knowing these things then, let us fortify ourselves with virtue on all sides, and thus we shall avert the wrath of God, and let us make the members of the body instruments of righteousness; and let us discipline eyes, and mouth, and hands, and feet, and heart, and tongue, and the[6] whole body, to be employed only in the service of virtue. And let us remember those three precepts, of which I discoursed[7] to your Charity, exhorting you to consider no one as an enemy, nor to speak evil of any one of those who have aggrieved you; and to expel from your mouth the evil custom of oaths. And with respect to the two former precepts, we will discourse to you on another occasion; but we shall speak to you during the whole of the present week respecting oaths; thus beginning with the easier precept. For it is no labour at all to overcome the habit of swearing, if we would but apply a little endeavour, by reminding each other; by advising; by observing; and by requiring those who thus forget themselves, to render an account, and to pay the penalty. For what advantage shall we gain by abstinence from meats, if we do not also expel the evil habits of the soul? Lo, we have spent the whole of this day fasting; and in the evening we shall spread a table, not such as we did on yester-eve, but one of an altered and more solemn kind.[8] Can any one of us then say that he has changed his life too this day; that he has altered his ill custom, as well as his food? Truly, I suppose not! Of what advantage then is our fasting? Wherefore I exhort,[9] and I will not cease to exhort, that undertaking each precept separately, you should spend two or three days in the attainment of it; and just as there are some who rival one another in fasting, and shew a marvellous emulation in it; (some indeed who spend two whole days without food; and others who, rejecting from their tables not only the use of wine, and of oil, but of every dish, and taking only bread and water, persevere in this practice during the whole of Lent); so, indeed, let us also contend mutually with one another in abolishing the frequency[10] of oaths. For this is more useful than any fasting; this is more profitable than any austerity. And this same care which we display in abstaining from food, let us exhibit with respect to abstinence from oaths; since we shall be chargeable with the reproach of extreme folly, while we regard not things that are forbidden, and expend all our care upon things indifferent; for to eat is not forbidden, but to swear is forbidden; we, however, abstaining from those things that are permitted, daringly venture upon those things that are forbidden! On this account I beseech your Charity to make some change, and to let the beginning of it be visible from this day. For if we spend the whole of the present fast with such zeal, having in this week attained the practice of not swearing at all; and in the following having extinguished wrath; and in that which succeeds it, having pulled up evil-speaking by the roots; and after that, having amended what yet remains; thus going forward in our course, we shall come by little and little to the very summit of virtue; and we shall escape the present danger; and shall make God propitious; and the multitude will come back again to our city; and we shall teach the fugitives that we are to place our hopes of safety neither in security of place, nor in flight and retirement; but in piety of soul, and in virtue of manners. And thus shall we obtain the good things of this and of the future life; which, God grant! we may all be found worthy of, by the grace and lovingkindness of our Lord Jesus Christ, through whom and with whom be glory to the Father, together with the Holy Ghost, now and for ever and ever. Amen.

---

[1] Ps. xxvi. 10. Or, more perspicuously, according to the usual sense of the Hebrew, *bribes*.
[2] Ps. cxli. 2.   [3] Ps. v. 9, LXX.; Ps. xlv. 1.
[4] Ps. lviii. 4.   [5] Ps. xlix. 4.   [6] Sav. our.
[7] *i. e.*, at the close of the last Homily.
[8] σεμνοτέραν. Tillemont supposes as well as Montfaucon, that the preceding Homily (the 3d) was delivered on Quinquagesima Sunday, and that this (the 4th) was preached on the Monday, which explains this allusion, Tr. The Lent fast began with that

Monday. During Lent the Greek Church allows the use of fish on Sundays.
[9] Or, beseech.
[10] νιφάδας, lit. snowflakes. Comp. *II.* iii. 222.

HOMILY V.

The exhortation of the last Homily is continued in this. The people are exhorted to bear with fortitude the impending wrath of the Emperor. The cases of Job and the Ninevites are referred to as examples. It is shewn that men ought not to fear death, but sin. What it is to die miserably is explained; and the Homily concludes with an earnest dissuasive against the use of oaths.

1. THE discourse concerning the three young men, and the Babylonian furnace, did, as it would seem, yesterday give no small comfort to your Charity; and still more the example in the case of Job, and that dunghill more to be venerated than any kingly throne. For from seeing a royal throne no advantage results to the spectators, but only a temporary pleasure, which has no profit; but from the sight of Job's dunghill, one may derive every kind of benefit, yea, much divine wisdom and consolation, in order to patience. Therefore to this day many undertake a long pilgrimage,[1] even across the sea, hastening from the extremities of the earth, as far as Arabia, that they may see that dunghill; and having beheld it, may kiss the land, which contained the wrestling-ground [2] of such a victor, and received the blood that was more precious than all gold! For the purple shines not so brilliantly, as did that body when dyed[3] not in another's blood, but in its own! Even those very wounds were more precious than all manner of jewels! For the nature of pearls is of no help to our life; nor do they satisfy any necessary want on the part of those who have them. But those wounds are a consolation for all sadness; and that thou mayest learn this to be the truth, suppose any one were to lose a beloved and only son. Shew him ten thousand pearls, and you will not console his grief, or lighten his anguish; but recall to his mind the wounds of Job, and thou wouldest easily be able to minister comfort by speaking thus: "Why sorrowest thou, O man? Thou hast lost one son; but that blessed man, after he had been bereaved of the whole family of his children, both received a plague in his own flesh, and sat down naked upon the dunghill, streaming with gore from every part, and his flesh gradually wasting away; even he who was just, and true, so devout a man, who abstained from every evil deed, and had even God for a witness to his virtue." By speaking thus thou wouldest extinguish all the sufferer's sadness, and remove all his distress. Thus the wounds of the just man become more useful than pearls!

2. Figure to yourselves then this wrestler; and imagine that you see that dunghill, and himself sitting in the midst of it! That golden statue! set with gems! I know not how to express it: for I am unable to find any material so precious as to compare it with that body stained with blood! So far above every substance, however costly, was the nature of that flesh, beyond all comparison more precious, and those wounds more splendid than the sun's beams; for these illumine the eyes of the body; but those enlighten the eyes of the mind! those struck the devil with utter blindness! Therefore it was, that after that blow, he started back and appeared no more. And do thou, O beloved, learn thence too what advantage there is in tribulation! For when the just man was rich, and enjoyed ease, he had the means of accusing him. However falsely, yet still he had it in his power to say, "Doth Job serve thee for nought?" But after he had stripped him and made him poor, he dared not even open his mouth any more. When he was wealthy, he prepared to wrestle with him, and threatened to overthrow him; but when he had made him poor, and taken away all he had, and thrown him into the deepest distress, then he started back. When indeed his body was sound, he lifted up his hands against him,[4] but when he had battered his flesh, then he fled,—defeated! Seest thou how to the vigilant, poverty is much better and more beneficial than riches; and infirmity and sickness, than health; and trial, than tranquillity; inasmuch as it makes the combatants more illustrious and vigorous?

3. Who hath seen or heard of such an astonishing contest? The fighters in worldly contests, when they have battered the heads of their adversaries, are then victorious, and are crowned! But this adversary, when he

---

[1] Comp. Hom. I. 23; Hom. XXXI. on Rom. xvi. 4.
[2] τὴν δεξαμένην τὰ σκάμματα, see Hom. IV., this word can only mean the prepared place, not the spectators.
[3] βαπτιζόμενον, perhaps rather "drenched," but the mention of the purple favors "dyed;" the present tense does not admit "baptized," though the allusion is well sustained in Ben. *tinctum.*

[4] Or buffetted with him, χεῖρας ἀντῆρεν.

had battered the body of the just man, perforating it with ulcers of every kind, and had reduced him to great weakness, was then conquered, and drew back. Even when he had pierced his ribs in every direction, he was no gainer thereby; for he spoiled him not of his hidden treasure, but he made him more conspicuous to us; and through that piercing he gave to all the privilege to look into his interior, and to discern completely the whole of his wealth! When he expected to prevail, then he withdrew with much ignominy, and never again uttered a syllable! What is the matter, O devil? For what cause withdrawest thou? Was not everything done that thou chosest? Hast thou not taken away his flocks, his herds, his droves of horses and of mules? Hast thou not also destroyed his troop of children? and battered his flesh to pieces. For what reason withdrawest thou? "Because," saith he, "every thing I chose[1] is come to pass, and yet that which I most desired should come to pass, and for which I did all those things, is not come to pass; he hath not blasphemed! For it was in order to this, continues he, that I was doing all those things; and as this is not come to pass, I am no gainer by having deprived him of his wealth; or by the destruction of his children; or by the plague inflicted upon his body; but the reverse of what I purposed hath come to pass; I have made my enemy more illustrious; I have added lustre to his reputation." Perceivest thou, O beloved, how great was the reward of tribulation? His body was fair and sound before, but it became more venerable, when pierced through and through by these wounds! And thus wool, fair as it is before the dyeing, when it becomes purple, takes an indescribable beauty, and an additional grace. But if he had not stripped him, we should not have known the good condition[2] of the victor; if he had not pierced the body with ulcers, the rays within would not have shone forth. If he had not made him sit down upon a dunghill, we should not have known his wealth. For a king sitting on a throne is not so illustrious, as this man was notable and conspicuous, whilst sitting upon his dunghill! For after the royal throne, comes death; but after that dunghill, the kingdom of heaven!

4. Collecting then all these reasons, let us raise ourselves from the dejection which oppresses us. For I have laid these histories before you, not that ye may applaud what is spoken, but that ye may imitate the virtue and the patience of such noble men; that ye may learn from the very facts, that there is nothing of human ills to be dreaded, save sin only; neither poverty, nor disease, nor insult, nor malicious treatment, nor ignominy, nor death, which is accounted the worst of all evils. To those who love spiritual wisdom, such things are only the names of calamities; names which have no substantial reality. But the true calamity consists in offending God, and in doing aught which is displeasing to Him. For tell me, what is there in death which is terrible? Is it because it transports thee more quickly to the peaceful haven, and to that life which is free from tumult? Although man should not put thee to death, will not the very law of nature, at length stealing upon thee, separate the body from the soul; and if this event which we fear does not happen now, it will happen shortly.

5. I speak thus, not anticipating any dread or melancholy event:[3] God forbid! But because I am ashamed for those who are afraid of death. Tell me, whilst expecting such good things as "eye hath not seen, nor ear heard, nor have entered the heart of man,"[4] dost thou demur about this enjoyment, and art negligent and slothful; and not only slothful, but fearful and trembling? And is it not shameful that thou art distressed on account of death, whereas Paul groaned on account of the present life, and writing to the Romans said, "The creation groaneth together, and ourselves also which have the first fruits of the Spirit do groan."[5] And he spoke thus, not as condemning the things present, but longing for the things to come. "I have tasted," saith he, "of the grace, and I do not willingly put up with the delay.[6] I have the first fruits of the Spirit, and I press on towards the whole. I have ascended to the third heaven; I have seen that glory which is unutterable; I have beheld the shining palaces; I have learnt what joys I am deprived of, while I linger here, and therefore do I groan." For suppose any one had conducted thee into princely halls, and shewn thee the gold everywhere glittering on the walls, and all the rest of the glorious show; if from thence he had led thee back afterward to a poor man's hut, and promised that in a short time he would bring thee back to those palaces, and would there give thee a perpetual mansion; tell me, wouldest thou not indeed languish with desire, and feel impatient, even at these few days? Thus think

---

[1] ἠθέλησα, desired is ἐβουλόμην. See Plat. Gorg. where Socrates argues that a tyrant has no great power, since, though he can do all he chooses, ἃ δοκεῖ αὐτῷ, he cannot attain what he wishes, ἃ βούλεται.
[2] εὐεξίαν. See Hom. I. 16.

[3] i. e., as connected with the present events.
[4] 1 Cor. ii. 9; Isa. lxiv. 4.   [5] Rom. viii. 22, 23.
[6] οὐ στέγω. Cf. 1 Thess. iii. 1.

then of heaven, and of earth, and groan with Paul, not because of death, but because of the present life!

6. But grant me, saith one, to be like Paul, and I shall never be afraid of death. Why, what is it that forbids thee, O man, to become like Paul? Was he not a poor man? Was he not a tent maker? Was he not a man of humble position? For if he had been rich and high born, the poor, when called upon to imitate his zeal, would have had their poverty to plead; but now thou canst say nothing of this sort. For this man was one who exercised a manual art, and supported himself too by his daily labours. And thou, indeed, from the first hast inherited true religion from thy fathers; and from thy earliest age hast been nourished in the study of the sacred writings; but he was "a blasphemer, and a persecutor, and injurious,"[1] and ravaged the Church! Nevertheless, he so changed all at once, as to surpass all in the vehemence of his zeal, and he cries out, saying, "Be ye imitators of me, even as I also am of Christ."[2] He imitated the Lord; and wilt not thou who hast been educated in piety from the first, imitate a fellow-servant; one who by conversion was brought to the faith at a later period of life? Knowest thou not, that they who are in sins are dead whilst they live; and that they who live[3] in righteousness, although they be dead, yet they live?[4] And this is not my word. It is the declaration of Christ speaking to Martha, "He that believeth in me though he were dead yet shall he live."[5] Is our doctrine, indeed, a fable? If thou art a Christian, believe in Christ; if thou believest in Christ, shew me thy faith by thy works.[6] But how mayest thou shew this? By thy contempt of death: for in this we differ from the unbelievers. They may well fear death; since they have no hope of a resurrection. But thou, who art travelling toward better things, and hast the opportunity of meditating on the hope of the future; what excuse hast thou, if whilst assured of a resurrection, thou are yet at the same time as fearful of death, as those who believe not the resurrection?

7. But I have no fear of death, says one, nor of the act of dying, but of a miserable death, of being beheaded. Did John then, I ask, die miserably? for he was beheaded. Or did Stephen die miserably? for he was stoned; and all the martyrs have thus died wretchedly, according to this objection: since some have ended their lives by fire; and others by the sword; and some cast into the ocean; others down a precipice; and others into the jaws of wild beasts, have so come by their death. To die basely, O man, is not to come to one's end by a violent death, but to die in sin! Hear, at least, the prophet moralising on this very matter, and saying, "The death of sinners is evil."[7] He does not say that a violent death is evil; but what then? "The death of sinners is evil."[8] And justly so; for after the departure from this life, there is an intolerable punishment; undying vengeance, the envenomed worm; the fire unquenchable, the outer darkness, the chains indissoluble; the gnashing of teeth, the tribulation, and the anguish, and the eternal justice.[9]

8. Since therefore such evils await sinners, what advantage can it be to them, though they should end their days at home, and in their bed? Even so, on the other hand, it can do no harm to the righteous to lay down the present life through sword, or steel, or fire, when they are to depart to the good things that are immortal. Truly "the death of sinners is evil." Such a death was that of the rich man, who despised Lazarus. He, when he had terminated his life by a natural end, at home and on his bed, and with his relatives about him, experienced after his departure to the other world a fiery torment; nor was he able to obtain there even a little comfort, out of all the pleasure he had enjoyed in the present life! But not so was it with Lazarus; for when lying upon the pavement, while the dogs came and licked his sores, he had suffered a violent death (for what could be more painful than hunger?), but on his departing hence he enjoyed eternal blessings, luxuriating in the bosom of Abraham! In what respect, then, did it injure him that he died a violent death? or what did it profit the rich man, that he died not with violence?

9. But, says some one, "We have no fear of dying by violence, but of dying unjustly; and of being punished in a similar way with the guilty,—we who have had nothing to do with the crimes of which we are suspected." What sayest thou, tell me? Art thou afraid

---

[1] 1 Tim. i. 13.
[2] 1 Cor. xi. 6.
[3] ζῶντες, but Ben. Mar. ὄντες, who are.
[4] 1 Tim. v. 6.
[5] John xi. 5.
[6] Jas. ii. 18.
[7] In this rendering of the Septuagint there is a coincidence with that of the Targum, and the Vulgate, Æthiopic, and Arabic versions. But the Syriac is conformable with the Hebrew. The discrepancy may be accounted for by a slight difference in the reading of the vowel points.
[8] Ps. xxxiv. 21. This passage is quoted by Bishop Latimer at the close of a sermon upon the epistle for the twenty-third Sunday after Trinity, preached A.D. 1552. His words are, *Mors peccatorum pessima.* "Death to sinners is the worst thing that can happen unto them." "What meaneth he by that? he signifieth unto us, that the wicked be not enough punished here, therefore it shall be worse with them after their death. So that it shall be a change: they that have their pleasure here, and live according to their desires, they shall come to afflictions in the other world."
[9] See Hom. III. on Rom. i. 18.

of dying unjustly, and wouldest thou wish to die justly. But who is there so wretched and miserable, that when he had the alternative of dying unjustly, would rather depart by an act of justice? For if it be necessary to fear death, it is necessary to fear it when it comes upon us justly; since he indeed who dies unjustly, is by this very means made a partaker with all the saints. For many of those who were approved and distinguished by God, have been subjected to an unjust end; and first of all Abel. For it was not that he had sinned against his brother, or done Cain any harm; but inasmuch as he had honoured God, therefore was he slaughtered. But God permitted it. Was it, think you, because He loved him, or because He hated him? Most clearly, because He loved him, and wished to make his crown the brighter, by that most unjust murder. Seest thou then, that it becomes us not to be afraid of dying by violence; nor yet of dying unjustly; but of dying in a state of sin? Abel died unjustly. Cain lived, groaning and trembling! Which then, I would ask, was the more blessed of the two; he who went to rest in righteousness, or he who lived in sin; he who died unjustly, or he who was justly punished? Would you have me declare unto your Charity, whence it is that we are afraid of death? The love of the kingdom hath not penetrated us, nor the desire of things to come inflamed us: otherwise we should despise all present things, even as the blessed Paul did. Add to this, on the other hand, that we do not stand in awe of hell; therefore death is terrible. We are not sensible of the unsufferable nature of the punishment there; therefore, instead of sin, we fear death; since if the fear of the one held possession of our souls, the fear of the other would not be able to enter.

10. And this I will endeavour to make manifest, not from anything of a remote nature, but from what is at our own doors; and from the events which have happened among us in these days. For when the Emperor's letter came, ordering that tribute to be imposed which was thought to be so intolerable, all were in a tumult; all quarrelled with it; thought it a sore grievance, resented it; and when they met one another said, "Our life is not worth living, the city is undone;—no one will be able to stand under this heavy burden;" and they were distressed as if placed in the extremest danger. After this, when the rebellion was actually perpetrated, and certain vile, yea, thoroughly vile persons, trampling under foot the laws, threw down the statues, and involved all in the utmost peril; and now that we are in fear for our very lives, through the indignation of the Emperor, this loss of money no longer stings us. But instead of such complaints, I hear from all a language of a different kind. "Let the Emperor take our substance, we will gladly be deprived of our fields and possessions, if any one will but ensure us safety for the bare body." As therefore, before the fear of death pressed upon us, the loss of our wealth tormented us; and after these lawless outrages had been perpetrated, the fear of death succeeding, expelled the grief for that loss; so if the fear of hell had held possession of our souls, the fear of death would not have possessed them. But even as it is with the body, when two kinds of pain seize upon us, the more powerful usually overshadows the weaker one, so also would it now happen; if the dread of future punishment remained in the soul, that would overshadow all human fear. So that if any one endeavours always to have the remembrance of hell, he will deride every kind of death; and this will not only deliver him from the present distress, but will even rescue him from the flame to come. For he who is always afraid of hell, will never fall into the fire of hell; being made sober by this continual fear!

11. Permit me, that I now say to you at a fitting time, "Brethren, be not children in understanding; howbeit in malice be ye children."[1] For this is a childish terror of ours, if we fear death, but are not fearful of sin. Little children too are afraid of masks, but fear not the fire. On the contrary, if they are carried by accident near a lighted candle, they stretch out the hand without any concern towards the candle and the flame; yet a mask which is so utterly contemptible terrifies them; whereas they have no dread of fire, which is really a thing to be afraid of. Just so we too have a fear of death, which is a mask that might well be despised; but have no fear of sin, which is truly dreadful; and, even as fire, devours the conscience! And this is wont to happen not on account of the nature of the things, but by reason of our own folly; so that if we were once to consider what death is, we should at no time be afraid of it. What then, I pray you, is death? Just what it is to put off a garment. For the body is about the soul as a garment; and after laying this aside for a short time by means of death, we shall resume it again with the more splendour. What is death at most? It is a journey for a season; a sleep longer than usual! So that if thou fearest

---

[1] 1 Cor. xiv. 20.

death, thou shouldest also fear sleep! If for those who are dying thou art pained, grieve for those too who are eating and drinking, for as this is natural, so is that! Let not natural things sadden thee; rather let things which arise from an evil choice make thee sorrowful. Sorrow not for the dying man; but sorrow for him who is living in sin!

12. Would you have me mention another reason on account of which we fear death? We do not live with strictness, nor keep a clear conscience; for if this were the case nothing would alarm us, neither death, nor famine, nor the loss of wealth, nor anything else of this kind. For he who lives virtuously, cannot be injured by any of these things, or be deprived of his inward pleasure. For being supported by favourable hopes, nothing will be able to throw him into dejection. What is there that any one can possibly effect, by which he can cause the noble-minded man to become sorrowful? Take away his riches? He has yet wealth that is in the heavens! Cast him out of his country? He will take his journey to[1] that city which is above! Load him with fetters? He has still his conscience free, and is insensible to the external chain! Put his body to death? Yet he shall rise again! And as he who fights with a shadow, and beaten the air, will be unable to hit any one; so he who is at war with the just man, is but striking at a shadow, and wasting his own strength, without being able to inflict any injury upon him. Grant me then to be sure of the kingdom of heaven; and, if thou wishest, slay me this day. I shall be thankful to thee for the slaughter; forasmuch as thou sendest me quickly to the possession of those good things! "This, however," says some one, "is what we especially lament, that hindered as we are by the multitude of our sins, we shall not attain to that kingdom." Such being the case then, leave off lamenting death, and lament thy sins, in order that thou mayest be freed from them! Grief, indeed, hath had its existence, not that we should sorrow for the loss of wealth, nor for death, nor for anything else of that kind, but that we may employ it for the taking away of our sins.[2] And I will make the truth of this evident by an example. Healing medicines[3] have been made for those diseases only which they are able to remove; not for those which are in no respect assisted by them. For instance (for I wish to make the matter still plainer), the medicine which is able to benefit a malady of the eyes only, and no other disease, one might justly say was made only for the sake of the eyes; not for the stomach, nor for the hands, nor any other member. Let us then transfer this argument to the subject of grief; and we shall find, that in none of those things which happen to us, is it of any advantage, except to correct sin; whence it is apparent that it hath had its existence only for the destruction of this. Let us now take a survey of each of those evils which befall us, and let us apply despondency as a remedy, and see what sort of advantage[4] results from it.

13. Some one is mulcted in property: he becomes sad, but this does not make good his loss. Some one hath lost a son: he grieves, but he cannot raise the dead, nor benefit the departed. Some one hath been scourged, beaten, and insulted; he becomes sorrowful. This does not recall the insult. Some one falls into sickness, and a most grievous disease; he is dejected. This does not remove his disease, but only makes it the more grievous. Do you see that in none of these cases does sadness answer any useful purpose? Suppose that any one hath sinned, and is sad. He blots out the sin; he gets free from the transgression. How is this shewn? By the declaration of the Lord; for, speaking of a certain one who had sinned, He said, "Because of his iniquity I made him sad for a while; and I saw that he was grieved, and he went on heavily; and I healed his ways."[5] Therefore also Paul saith, "Godly sorrow worketh repentance unto salvation not to be repented of."[6] Since then what I have said clearly shews, that neither the loss of riches, nor insult, nor abuse, nor stripes, nor sickness, nor death, nor any other thing of that kind can possibly be relieved by the interference of grief, but sin only can it blot out and do away, it is evident that this is the only reason why it hath its existence. Let us therefore no more grieve for the loss of wealth, but let us grieve only when we commit sin. For great in this case is the gain that comes of sorrow. Art thou amerced? Be not dejected, for thus thou wilt not be at all benefited. Hast thou sinned? Then be sorry: for it is profitable; and consider the skill and wisdom of God. Sin hath brought forth for us these two things, sorrow and death. For "in the day thou eatest," He saith, "thou shalt surely die;"

---

[1] στελεῖ εἰς, al. τελεῖ εἰς, is free of.
[2] ἁμαρτημάτων, see Hom. IV. 4.
[3] Thus in Plat. Gorg. 78. Socrates argues that it is best to be punished when one does wrong, comparing punishment to medicine.
[4] M. what is the advantage that.
[5] Isa. lvii. 17. The English version seems rather to give the sense of the Hebrew, and is less pointedly apposite, though it too implies that trouble is given for our good, and, as the context also implies, sorrow too.
[6] 2 Cor. vii. 10.

and to the woman, "In sorrow thou shalt bring forth children."[1] And by both of these things he took away sin, and provided that the mother should be destroyed by her offspring. For that death as well as grief takes away sin, is evident, in the first place, from the case of the martyrs;[2] and it is plain too from what Paul saith to those who had sinned, speaking on this wise, "For this cause many are weak and sickly among you, and many sleep."[3] Inasmuch, he observes, as ye have sinned, ye die, so that ye are freed from sin by death. Therefore he goes on to say, "For if we would judge ourselves, we should not be judged. But when we are judged, we are chastened of the Lord, that we should not be condemned with the world."[4] And even as the worm is brought forth from the wood, and devours the wood; and a moth consumes the wool, from whence it originates; so grief and death were born of sin, and devour sin.

14. Let us not then fear death, but let us only fear sin, and grieve on account of this. And these things I speak, not anticipating any thing fearful, God forbid! but wishing you when alarmed to be always thus affected, and to fulfil the law of Christ in very deed. For "he," saith Christ, "that taketh not his cross, and followeth after Me, is not worthy of Me."[5] This He said, not that we should bear the wood upon our shoulders, but that we should always have death before our eyes. Even so as Paul, that is, died daily, and laughed at death, and despised the present life. For indeed thou art a soldier, and standest continually at arms; but a soldier who is afraid of death, will never perform a noble action. Thus then neither will a Christian man, if fearful of dangers, perform anything great or admirable; nay, besides this, he will be apt to be easily vanquished. But not so is it with the man who is bold and lofty minded. He remains impregnable and unconquerable. As then the Three Children, when they feared not the fire, escaped from the fire, so also we, if we fear not death, shall entirely escape from death. They feared not the fire (for it is no crime to be burnt), but they feared sin, for it is a crime to commit impiety. Let us also imitate these and all such, and let us not be afraid of dangers, and then we shall pass safely through them.

15. As for me, "I am not a prophet nor the son of a prophet,"[6] yet I understand clearly thus much of the future, and I proclaim, both loudly and distinctly, that if we become changed, and bestow some care upon our souls, and desist from iniquity, nothing will be unpleasant or painful. And this I plainly know from the love of God toward man, as well as from those things which He hath done for men, and cities, and nations, and whole populations. For He threatened the city of Nineveh, and said, "There are yet three days,[7] and Nineveh shall be overthrown."[8] What then, I ask, Was Nineveh overthrown? Was the city destroyed? Nay, quite the contrary; it both arose, and became still more distinguished; and long as is the time which has elapsed, it has not effaced its glory, but we all still celebrate and admire it even to this day.[9] For from that time it hath been a sort of excellent haven for all who have sinned, not suffering them to sink into desperation, but calling all to repentance; and by what it did, and by what it obtained of God's favour, persuading men never to despair of their salvation, but exhibiting the best life they can,[10] and setting before them a[11] good hope, to be confident of the issue as destined in any wise to be favourable. For who would not be stirred up on hearing of such an example, even if he were the laziest of mortals?

16. For God even preferred that His own prediction should fall to the ground, so that the city should not fall. Or rather, the prophecy did not even so fall to the ground. For if indeed while the men continued in the same wickedness, the sentence had not taken effect, some one perhaps might have brought a charge against what was uttered. But if when they had changed, and desisted from their iniquity, God also desisted from His

---

[1] Gen. ii. 17.
[2] Martyrdom was held to be a kind of second baptism, or instead of baptism to those on whom it came before they could be baptized. St. Cyr. Cat. iii. (7); St. Cypr. Ex. to Mart.; Ep. 73, ad Jud., Ed. Ben. p. 136. Tertullian says, "This is a baptism which will either supply the place of water-baptism to one that has not received it, or will restore it to one that has lost (or defaced) it. De Bapt. c. xvi., quoted by Wall on Inf. Bapt. c. vi., t. ii., p. 190.
[3] So St. Aug. Serm. de Script. cxlviii. (al. 10, de Div.) on Acts v. 4, Origen, xv. 15, on Matt. xix. 21, Ed. Ben. iii. 673. C. thinks Ananias to have had this benefit, but he supposes his death not to have been an immediate judgment, but the effect of his feeling at the moment. Œcumenius speaks of 1 Cor. xi. 31, as not merely threatening death, but future punishment. Photius, Cat. Cramer, p. 223, speaks as St. Chrysostom.
[4] 1 Cor. xi. 31, 32.
[5] Matt. x. 38.
[6] Amos vii. 14.
[7] τρεῖς ἡμέραι. Thus it has always been read in the Septuagint, even from the first ages of the Church (note in Ed. Par. 1834). But this reading, it should be remarked, is not supported by the Targum, or the Vulgate, or Syriac, which all read forty days, as in the Hebrew copies. (St. Jerome on the passage corrects the error, and Theodoret says that the Syriac, and Hebrew, and the translations of Aquila, Symmachus, and Theodotion, read forty. Origen, Hom. XVI. on Num. xxiii. 19, Ed. Ben. ii. p. 330, d. corrects the LXX. from the Hebrew.)
[8] Jonah iii.
[9] Nineveh was entirely ruined in the reign of the Emperor Hadrian, and though it was afterwards rebuilt by the Persians, and not finally destroyed till about the seventh century, it seems probable that St. Chrysostom alludes here rather to its moral than to its actual glory at that time.
[10] βίον ἄριστον, "best life." The article is not used, and the words added seem nearly to express what is intended to be understood.
[11] Gr. The good hope, i. e., the hope of the better alternative.

wrath, who shall be able any longer to find fault with the prophecy, or to convict the things spoken of falsehood. The same law indeed which God had laid down from the beginning, publishing it to all men by the prophet, was on that occasion strictly observed. What then is this law? "I shall speak a sentence," saith He, "concerning a nation or a kingdom, to pluck up, and to pull down, and to destroy it; and it shall be, that if they repent of their evil, I will also repent of the wrath which I said I would do unto them."[1] Guarding then this law, he saved those who were converted and released from His wrath those who desisted from their wickedness. He knew the virtue of the barbarians; therefore He hastened the prophet thither. Thus was the city agitated at the time, when it heard the prophet's voice, but instead of being injured it was benefited by fear. For that fear was the cause of its safety. The threatening effected the deliverance from the peril. The sentence of overthrow put a stop to the overthrow. O strange and astonishing event! the sentence threatening death, brought forth life! The sentence after it was published became cancelled; the very opposite to that which takes place among temporal judges! for in their case the proclamation of the sentence causes it to become valid, is fully to ratify it; but on the contrary, with God, the publication of the sentence, caused it to be cancelled. For if it had not been published, the offenders would not have heard; and if they had not heard, they would not have repented, and if they had not repented,[2] they would not have warded off the punishment, nor would they have obtained that astonishing deliverance. For how is it less than astonishing, when the judge declares sentence, and the condemned discharge the sentence by their repentance! They, indeed, did not flee from the city as we are now doing, but remaining in it they caused it to stand. It was a snare, and they made it a fortification! It was a gulph, and a precipice, and they turned it into a tower of safety! They had heard that the buildings would fall, and yet they fled not from the buildings, but they fled from their sins! They did not depart each from his house as we do now, but each departed from his evil way; for, said they, "why should we think the walls have brought forth the wrath? we are the causes of the wound; we then should provide the medicine." Therefore they trusted for safety, not to a change of habitations,[3] but of habits.[4]

17. Thus did the barbarians! and are we not ashamed, and ought we not to hide our faces, whilst instead of changing our habits, as they did, we change only our habitations; privily removing our goods, and doing the deeds of men that are drunken? Our Master is angry with us; and we, neglecting to appease His wrath, carry about our household stuff from place to place, and run hither and thither, seeking where we may deposit our substance; while we ought rather to seek where we may deposit our soul in safety; or rather, it behoveth us not to seek, but to entrust its safety to virtue and uprightness of life. For when we were angry and displeased with a servant, if he, instead of defending himself against our displeasure, went down to his apartment, and collecting together his clothes, and binding up together all his movables, meditated a flight, we could not tamely put up with this contempt. Let us then desist from this unseasonable endeavour, and let us each say to God, "Whither shall I go from Thy Spirit, and whither shall I flee from Thy presence?"[5] Let us imitate the spiritual wisdom of the barbarians. They repented even on uncertain grounds! For the sentence had no such clause, "If ye turn and repent, I will set up the city;" but simply, "Yet three days, and Nineveh shall be overthrown."[6] What then said they? "Who knoweth whether God will repent of the evil He said He would do unto us?" Who knoweth? They know not the end of the event, and yet they do not neglect repentance! They are unacquainted with God's method of shewing mercy, and yet they change upon the strength of uncertainties! For neither was it in their power to look at other Ninevites who had repented and been saved; nor had they read prophets; nor had they heard patriarchs; nor had they enjoyed counsel, or partaken of admonition; nor had they persuaded themselves that they should certainly propitiate God by repentance. For the threatening did not imply this: but they were doubtful, and hesitating concerning it; and yet they repented with all diligence. What reason then shall we have to urge, when those, who had no ground for confidence as to the issue, are seen to have exhibited so great a change; but thou who hast ground of confidence in the mercy of God, and who hast frequently received many pledges of His care, and hast heard prophets, and apostles, and hast been instructed by actual events;

---

[1] Jer. xviii. 7, 8.
[2] The clause, "and if they had not repented," inserted from Savile. Both the general sense, and the parallel with Rom. x. 14, seem to require it.
[3] τόπων.
[4] τρόπων.
[5] Ps. cxxxix. 7.
[6] Jonah iii. 9.

hast yet no emulation to reach the same measure of virtue as these did! Great assuredly was their virtue! but greater by far was the mercy of God! and this may be seen from the very greatness of the threat. For this reason God did not add to the declaration, "But if ye repent, I will spare:" in order that by setting forth a sentence without limitation, He might increase the fear, and having increased the fear, He might constrain them more speedily to repentance.

18. The prophet is indeed ashamed, foreseeing what the issue would be, and conjecturing that what he had prophesied, would remain unaccomplished; God however is not ashamed, but is desirous of one thing only, viz. the salvation of men, and corrects His own servant. For when he had entered the ship, He straightway there raised a boisterous sea; in order that thou mightest know that where sin is, there is a tempest; where there is disobedience, there is the swelling of the waves.[1] The city was shaken because of the sins of the Ninevites; and the ship was shaken because of the disobedience of the prophet. The sailors therefore threw Jonah in the deep, and the ship was preserved. Let us then drown our sins, and our city will assuredly be safe! Flight will certainly be no advantage to us; for it did not profit him; on the contrary, it did him injury. He fled from the land indeed, but he fled not from the wrath of God; he fled from the land, but he brought the tempest after him on the sea; and so far was he from obtaining any benefit by his flight, that he plunged those also who received him into the extremest peril. And whilst he sat sailing in the ship, although the sailors, the pilots, and all the necessary apparatus of the ship were there present, he was placed in the utmost danger. After, however, having been thrown out into the deep, and having put away his sin by means of the punishment, he had been conveyed into that unstable[2] vessel, I mean, the whale's belly, he enjoyed great security. This was for the purpose of teaching thee, that as no ship can be of any use to him who is living in sin, so him who has put away his sin, the sea cannot drown, nor monsters destroy. Of a truth, the waves received, but they did not suffocate him. The whale received him, but did not destroy him; but both the animal and the element gave back to God unhurt that with which they were entrusted; and by all these things the prophet was taught to be humane and merciful; and not to be more cruel than wild beasts, or thoughtless sailors, or unruly waves. For even the sailors did not immediately at first give him up, but after much compulsion; and the sea and the monster guarded him with great kindness; all these things being under God's direction.

19. Therefore he came back again; he preached; he threatened; he persuaded; he preserved; he affrighted; he amended; he established; by one, and that the first preaching! Many days he needed not, nor continued counsel; but speaking these simple words only, he brought all to repentance! On this account God did not lead him directly from the ship into the city; but the sailors committed him to the sea; the sea to the whale; the whale to God; God to the Ninevites; and by this long circuit he brought back the fugitive, that he might instruct all, that it is impossible to fly from the hands of God; that whithersoever any one may roam, dragging his sin after him, he will have to undergo a thousand evils; and though no mortal were present, yet on every side the whole creation will rise up against him with the utmost vehemence! Let us not then provide for our safety by flight, but by a change of the moral character. Is it for remaining in the city that God is angry with thee, that thou shouldest fly? It is because thou hast sinned, that He is indignant. Lay aside therefore the sin, and where the cause of thy wound lies, thence remove[3] the fountain of the evil. For the physicians too give us directions to cure contraries by contraries. Is fever, for instance, produced by a full diet? They subject the disease to the regimen of abstinence. Does any one fall sick from sadness? They say that mirth is the suitable medicine for it. Thus also it befits us to act with respect to diseases of the soul. Hath listlessness excited the wrath? let us shake this off by zeal, and let us manifest in our conduct a great change. We have the fast, a very great auxiliary and ally in our warfare; and besides the fast, we have the impending distress, and the fear of danger. Now then, in season, let us be at work on the soul; for we shall easily be able to persuade it to whatever we choose; since he who is alarmed and trembling, and set free from all luxury, and who lives in terror, is able to practise moral wisdom without difficulty, and to receive the seeds of virtue with much alacrity.

20. Let us therefore persuade it to make

---

[1] κλυδώνιον.
[2] ἀτερμάτιστον, this word means "vast," "immeasurable," and does not suit the sense: ἀνερμάτιστον is undoubtedly the right reading, unless indeed St. Chrysostom used one for the other, as Suidas. Hesychius gives it "without ballast," and so Aristotle ἑρματίζειν, but Il. i. 486, ἕρματα are props used on shore.

[3] ἀνάστειλον, divert as a stream. The metaphor is explained by the sequel, the "wound" meaning an incision made for surgical purposes.

this first change for the better, by the avoidance of oaths; for although I spake to you yesterday, and the day before,[1] on this same subject; yet neither to-day, nor to-morrow, nor the day after, will I desist giving my counsel on this subject. And why do I say to-morrow and the day following? Until I see that you are amended, I will not abstain from doing so. If those, indeed, who transgress this law, are not ashamed, far less should we who bid them not transgress it, feel this frequency of the admonition to be a matter worthy of shame. For to be continually reminding men of the same topics is not the fault of the speaker, but of the hearers, needing as they do perpetual instruction, upon simple and easily-observed precepts. What indeed is easier than not to swear? It is only a good work of habit. It is neither labour of the body, nor expenditure of wealth. Art thou desirous to learn how it is possible to get the better of this infirmity, how it is possible to be set free from this evil habit? I will tell thee of a particular method by which if pursued thou wilt certainly master it. If thou seest either thyself or any other person, whether it be one of thy servants, or of thy children, or thy wife, ensnared in this vice; when thou hast continually reminded them of it, and they are not amended, order them to retire to rest supperless;[2] and impose this sentence upon thyself, as well as upon them, a sentence which will bring with it no injury, but a gain. For such is the nature of spiritual acts; they bring profit and a speedy reformation. The tongue when constantly punished, when straitened by thirst, and pained by hunger, receives a sufficient admonition, even whilst no one is its monitor; and though we were the most stupid of mortals, yet when we are thus reminded by the greatness of the punishment during a whole day, we shall need no other counsel and exhortation.

21. Ye have applauded what I have spoken. But still shew me your applause too by deeds. Else what is the advantage of our meeting here? Suppose a child were to go to school every day, yet if he learnt nothing the more for it, would the excuse satisfy us that he every day went there? Should we not esteem it the greatest fault, that going there daily, he did it to no purpose. Let us consider this with ourselves, and let us say to ourselves, For so long a time have we met together at church, having the benefit of a most solemn Communion,[3] which has in it much profit; and should we return back again just as we came, with none of our defects corrected, of what advantage is our coming here? For most actions are done, not for themselves, but for the effects which follow through their means; as, for example, the sower does not sow for the mere sake of sowing, but in order that he may reap too; since if this were not to follow, the sowing would be a loss, the seeds rotting without any kind of advantage. The merchant doth not take a voyage merely for sailing's sake, but that he may increase his substance by going abroad; since, if this be not attained beside, extreme mischief will result, and the voyage of merchants were but for loss. Let us indeed consider this in relation to ourselves. We also meet together in the church, not for the mere purpose of spending time here, but in order that we may return having gained a great and spiritual benefit. Should we then depart empty, and without having received any advantage, this our diligence becomes our condemnation! In order that this may not occur, and extreme mischief result, on departing from this place, let friends practise with one another; fathers with children; and masters with servants; and train yourselves to perform the task assigned you; so that when ye come back again, and hear us giving you counsel on the same subjects, ye may not be put to shame by an accusing conscience, but may rejoice and be glad, whilst ye perceive that ye have accomplished the greatest part of the admonition.

22. Let us not moralize on these things here only. For this temporary admonition does not suffice to extirpate the whole evil; but at home also, let the husband hear of these things from the wife, and the wife from the husband. And let there be a kind of rivalry among all in endeavouring to gain precedence in the fulfilment of this law; and let him who is in advance, and hath amended his conduct, reproach him who is still loitering behind; to the end that he may stir him up the more by these gibes. He who is deficient, and hath not yet amended his conduct, let him look at him who hath outstripped him, and strive with emulation to come up with him quickly. If we take advice on these points, and are anxiously concerned about:

---

[1] This passage will serve to shew, that during the season of Lent it was the practice to have sermons daily at Antioch. Bingham has given a variety of quotations to the same effect. B. xiv. c. iv., sec. 7, vol. iv. p. 536, New Ed.

[2] The supper, it should be remembered, was the chief meal of the day among the Greeks and Romans. And with those who observed the fast strictly the only meal: see Hom. VI. [6], and Hom. IV. 12.

[3] συνάξεως φρικωδεστάτης. The word σύναξις is of frequent occurrence in St. Chrysostom, but is of somewhat ambiguous signification, and means commonly the service of the Church; but here and in some other passages, it seems to mean the Communion service. See a passage in Homily IX. on Penitence, where the same expression receives a most striking commentary.

them, our other affairs will speedily be well adjusted. Be thou solicitous about God's business, and he will take care of thine! And do not say to me, "What if any one should impose upon us the necessity of taking oaths? What if he should not believe us?" For assuredly, where a law is transgressed, it is improper to make mention of necessity; forasmuch as there is but one necessity which cannot be dispensed with, viz. that of not offending God! This, however, I say further; cut off in the meantime superfluous oaths, those that are taken uselessly, and without any necessity; those to your own family, those to your friends, those to your servants; and should you take away these, you will have no further need of me for the others. For the very mouth that has been well disciplined to dread and to avoid the frequent oath, should any one constrain it a thousand times, would never consent to relapse again into the same habit. On the contrary, as now, with much labor and vast importunity, by alarming, threatening, exhorting, and counselling, we have scarcely been able to bring it over to a different habit, so in that case, although any one were to impose ever so great necessity, he could not possibly persuade to a transgression of this law. And as a person would never choose to take a particular poison, however urgent the necessity might be, so neither would he to utter an oath!

23. Should this amendment then take place, it will be an encouragement and inducement to the attainment of the remaining parts of virtue. For he who has not accomplished anything at all becomes listless, and quickly falls; but he who is conscious with himself that he has fulfilled at least one precept, coming by this to have a good hope, will go on with greater alacrity towards the rest; so that, after he has reached one, he will presently come to another; and will not halt until he has attained the crown of all. For if with regard to wealth, the more any one obtains of it, the more he desires, much rather may this be seen with reference to spiritual attainments. Therefore I hasten, and am urgent that this work may take its commencement, and that the foundation of virtue may be laid in your souls. We pray and beseech, that ye will remember these words, not only at the present time, but also at home, and in the market, and wheresoever ye pass your time. Oh! that it were possible for me familiarly to converse with you![1] then this long harangue of mine would have been unnecessary. But now since this may not be, instead of me, remember my words: and while you are sitting at table, suppose me to enter, and to be standing beside you, and dinning into you the things I now say to you in this place. And wheresoever there may be any discourse concerning me among you, above all things remember this precept, and render me this recompense for my love toward you. If I see that you have fulfilled it, I have received my full return, and have obtained a sufficient recompense for my labours. In order then that ye may both render us the more active, and that yourselves too may be in the enjoyment of a good hope; and may provide for the accomplishment of the remaining precepts with greater facility; treasure up this precept in your souls with much care, and ye will then understand the benefit of this admonition. And since a vestment broidered with gold is a beautiful and conspicuous object, but seems much more so to us when it is worn upon our own person; thus also the precepts of God are beautiful when being praised, but appear far more lovely when they are rightly practised. For now indeed ye commend what is spoken during a brief moment of time, but if ye reduce it to practice, you will alike commend both yourselves and us all day long, and all your lives long. And this is not the grand point, that we shall praise one another; but that God will accept us; and not only accept us, but will also reward us with those gifts that are great and unspeakable! Of which may we all be deemed worthy, through the grace and lovingkindness of our Lord Jesus Christ, through whom, and with whom, to the Father together with the Holy Ghost, be glory, now and always, for ever and ever. Amen.

---

[1] St. Chrysostom perhaps here refers to the interruption of his private pastoral duties, which were occasioned by the existing calamity. Possibly also to the numbers of his congregation. See the end of the next Homily. In Hom. LXXXV. on St. Matt. near the end, he estimates his congregation at 100,000. Ed. Ben. p. 810.

HOMILY VI.

This Homily is intended to shew that the fear of Magistrates is beneficial. It also contains an account of what occurred, during their journey, to those who were conveying the tidings of the sedition to the Emperor. The case of Jonah is further cited in illustration. The exhortation on the fear of death is here continued; and it is shewn, that he who suffers unjustly, and yet gives thanks to God, by whose permission it happens, is as one suffering for God's sake. Examples are again adduced from the history of the Three Children, and the Babylonian furnace. The Homily concludes with an address on the necessity of abstaining from oaths.

1. WE have spent many days addressing words of comfort to your Charity. We would not, however, on that account lay the subject aside; but as long as the sore of despondency remains, we will apply to it the medicine of consolation. For if in the case of bodily wounds, physicians do not give over their fomentations, until they perceive that the pain has subsided; much less ought this to be done in regard to the soul. Despondency is a sore of the soul; and we must therefore foment it continually with soothing words. For not so naturally is warm water efficacious to soften a hard tumour of the flesh, as words of comfort are powerful to allay the swelling passions of the soul.[1] Here, there is no need of the sponge as with physicians, but instead of this we employ the tongue. No need of fire here, that we may warm the water; but instead of fire, we make use of the grace of the Spirit. Suffer us then to do so to-day. For if we were not to comfort you, where else could ye obtain consolation? The judges affright; the priests therefore must console! The rulers threaten; therefore must the Church give comfort! Thus it happens with respect to little children. The teachers frighten them, and send them away weeping to their mothers; but the mothers receiving them back to their own bosoms, keep them there, embrace them, and kiss them, while they wipe away their tears, and relieve their sorrowing spirits; persuading them by what they say, that it is profitable for them to fear their teachers. Since therefore the rulers also make you afraid, and render you anxious, the Church, which is the common mother of us all, opening her bosom, and cradling us in her arms, administers daily consolation; telling us that the fear of rulers is profitable, and profitable too the consolation that comes from hence.[2] For the fear of the former does not permit us to be relaxed by listlessness, but the consolation of the latter does not allow us to sink under the weight of sadness; and by both these means God provides for our safety. He Himself hath armed magistrates with power; that they may strike terror into the licentious; and hath ordained His priests that they may administer consolation to those that are in sorrow.

2. And both these things are taught us by the Scripture, and by actual experience of recent events. For if, whilst there are magistrates and soldiers living under arms, the madness of a few individuals, a motley crew of adventurers, hath kindled such a fire among us, in so short a moment[3] of time, and raised such a tempest, and made us all to stand in fear of shipwreck, suppose the fear of magistrates to be wholly taken away? To what lengths would they not have gone in their madness? Would they not have overthrown the city from its foundations, turning all things upside down, and have taken our very lives? If you were to abolish the public tribunals, you would abolish all order from our life. And even as if you deprive the ship of its pilot, you sink the vessel; or as, if you remove the general from the army, you place the soldiers bound in the hands of the enemy; so if you deprive the city of its rulers, we must lead a life less rational than that of the brutes, biting and devouring one another; the rich man, the poorer; the stronger man, the weaker; and the bolder man, him who is more gentle. But now by the grace of God none of these things happen. For they who live in a state of piety, require no correction on the part of the magistrates; for "the law is not made for a righteous man,"[4] saith one. But the more numerous being viciously inclined, if they had no fear of these hanging over them, would fill the cities with innumerable evils; which Paul knowing, observed, "There is no power, but

---

[1] S. Ign. ad Pol. c. 2.   [2] *i. e.*, from the Church.   [3] ῥοπῇ.   [4] 1 Tim. i. 9.

of God, the powers that be are ordained of God."[1] For what the tie-beams[2] are in houses, that rulers are in cities; and in the same manner as if you were to take away the former, the walls, being disunited, would fall in upon one another of their own accord; so were you to deprive the world of magistrates, and of the fear that comes of them, houses at once, and cities, and nations, would fall on one another in unrestrained confusion, there being no one to repress, or repel, or persuade them to be peaceful, by the fear of punishment!

3. Let us not then be grieved, beloved, by the fear of our rulers, but let us give thanks to God that He hath removed our listlessness, and rendered us more diligent. For tell me, what harm hath arisen from this concern and anxiety? Is it that we are become more grave, and gentle; more diligent, and attentive? that we see no one intoxicated, and singing lascivious airs? Or is it that there are continual supplications,[3] and prayers, and tears? that unseasonable laughter, and impure words, and all dissoluteness is banished; and that the city is now in all respects, like the pattern of a modest and virtuous woman? Dost thou grieve, I ask, for any of these reasons? For these things, assuredly, it were right to rejoice, and to be thankful to God, that by the terror of a few days He hath put an end to such stupidity!

"Very true," saith some one, "if our danger did not go beyond fear, we should have reaped a sufficient benefit; but we are now in dread lest the mischief should proceed much farther, and we should be all placed in the extremest peril."

Nevertheless, I say, fear not. Paul comforteth you, saying, "God is faithful, who will not suffer you to be tempted above that ye are able, but will with the temptation also make the way of escape, that ye may be able to bear it."[4] He indeed Himself hath said, "I will never leave thee, nor forsake thee."[5] For had He resolved to punish us in deed, and in actual endurance, He would not have given us over to terror during so many days. For when He would not punish, He affrights; since if He were intending to punish, fear would be superfluous, and threatening superfluous. But now, we have sustained a life more grievous than countless deaths; fearing and trembling during so many days, and being suspicious of our very shadows; and paying the punishment of Cain; and in the midst of our sleep, starting up, through constant agony of mind. So that if we have kindled God's wrath, we have appeased Him in the endurance of such a punishment. For if we have not paid the satisfaction due to our sins, yet it hath been enough to satisfy the mercy of God.

4. But not this, but many other grounds for confidence ought we to have. For God hath already given us not a few pledges for favourable hopes. And first of all, those who carried the evil tidings departing hence with the speed of wings, supposing they should long ere this have reached the camp,[6] are yet delayed in the midst of their journey. So many hindrances and impediments have arisen; and they have left their horses, and are now proceeding in vehicles; whence their arrival must of necessity be retarded. For since God here stirred up our priest, and common father, and persuaded him to go forth, and undertake this embassy, he detained the messengers for a while, when they were but half way on their road, lest arriving before him they might kindle the fire, and make our teacher's efforts to mend matters useless, when the royal ears had become inflamed. For that this hindrance on the road, was not without God's interposition is evident from this. Men who had been familiar with such journeys all their lives, and whose constant business it was to ride on horseback, now broke down through the fatigue of this very riding; so that what hath now happened is the reverse of what took place in the case of Jonah. For God hastened him when unwilling, to go on his mission. But these, who were desirous to go, He hindered. O strange and wonderful event! He wished not to preach of an overthrow; and God forced him to go[7] against his will. These men with much haste set forward to be the bearers of a message of overthrow, and against their will again He has hindered them! For what reason think you? Why, because in this case the haste was an injury; but in the other case, haste brought gain. On this account, He hastened him forward by means of the whale; and detained these by means of their horses. Seest thou the wisdom of God? Through the very means by which each party hoped to accomplish their object, through these each received an hindrance. Jonah expected to

---

[1] Rom. xiii. 1.
[2] ἐν ταῖς οἰκίαις τῶν ξύλων αἱ ἱμαντώσεις, literally, "strappings of beams;" or "bondings of the timbers."
[3] λιταί.   [4] 1 Cor. x. 13.   [5] Heb. xiii. 5; Josh. i. 5.
[6] τὸ στρατόπεδον. The common Lexicons quote only Can. 7, of Sardica for the use of this word, to signify the court of an Emperor. Du Cange, Gloss. Med. Gr., shews it to be common, quoting St. Basil, Ep. 127, al. 59, &c.; St. Athanasius, Apol. ad Constantium, c. 4, St. Macar. Hom. XV. p. 213 (1st ed.) sec. 30, and other passages. The term is accounted for by the acknowledged dependence of the Emperors on the army, and their constantly having a strong guard about them. Compare our expression, "head-quarters" to denote the seat of government. Theodosius was now at Constantinople.
[7] ἀνέστησεν.

escape by the ship, and the ship became his chain. These couriers, by means of their horses, expected the more quickly to see the Emperor; and the horses became the obstacles; or rather, neither the horses in one case, nor the ship in the other, but the Providence of God everywhere directing all things according to its own wisdom!

5. Consider also His care over us, and how He both affrighted and consoled us. For after permitting them to set out on the very day when all these outrages were committed, as if they would report all that had taken place to the Emperor; He alarmed us all at their sudden departure. But when they were gone, and two or three days had elapsed, and we thought the journey of our Priest would now be useless, as he would arrive when it was too late, He delivered us from this fear, and comforted us by detaining them, as I observed, midway; and by providing persons coming to us from thence by the same road, to announce to us all the difficulties they had met with on their journey, that we might thus take a little breath, as indeed we did, and were relieved of a great part of our anxiety. Having heard of this, we adored God who had done it, who hath even now more tenderly than any father disposed all things for us, delaying by some invisible power those evil messengers, and all but saying to them, "Why do ye hasten? Why do ye press on, when ye are going to overwhelm so great a city? For are ye the bearers of a good message to the Emperor? Wait there till I have made ready my servant, as an excellent physician, to come up with you and anticipate you in your course." But if there was so much of providential care in the first breaking out of this wound of iniquity, much more shall we obtain a greater freedom from anxiety, after conversion, after repentance, after so much fear, after tears and prayers. For Jonah was very properly constrained, in order that he might be forcibly brought to repentance; but ye have already given striking evidences of repentance, and conversion. Therefore, it is necessary that you should receive consolation, instead of a threatening messenger. For this reason also hath He sent our common father hence, notwithstanding the many things to hinder it. But if He had not been tender of our safety, He would not have persuaded him to this, but would have hindered him, however disposed he might be to undertake the journey.

6. There is a third reason by which I may possibly persuade you to have confidence; I mean, the present sacred season,[1] which almost all, even unbelievers, respect; but to which this our divinely-favoured Emperor has shewn such reverence and honour, as to surpass all the Emperors who have reigned with a regard for religion before him. As a proof of this, by sending a letter on these days in honour of the feast, he liberated nearly all those who were lodged in prison; and this letter our Priest when he arrives will read to him; and remind him of his own laws, and will say to him, "Do thou exhort thyself, and remember thine own deeds! Thou hast an example for thy philanthropy at home! Thou didst choose to forbear from executing a justifiable slaughter, and wilt thou endure to perpetrate one that is unjust. Reverencing the feast, thou didst discharge those who had been convicted and condemned; and wilt thou, I ask, condemn the innocent, and those who have not committed any violence, and this when the sacred season is present? That be far from thee, O Emperor! Thou, speaking by this Epistle to all the cities, didst say, 'Would it were possible for me to raise even the dead.' This philanthropy and these words we now stand in need of. To conquer enemies, doth not render kings so illustrious, as to conquer wrath and anger; for in the former case, the success is due to arms and soldiers; but here the trophy is simply thine own, and thou hast no one to divide with thee the glory of thy moral wisdom. Thou hast overcome barbarian war, overcome also Imperial wrath! Let all unbelievers learn that the fear of Christ is able to bridle every kind of authority. Glorify thy Lord by forgiving the trespasses of thy fellow-servants; that He also may glorify thee the more; that at the Day of Judgment, He may bend on thee an Eye merciful and serene, being mindful of this thy lovingkindness!" This, and much more, he will say, and will assuredly rescue us from the Emperor's wrath. And not only will this fast be of the greatest assistance to us in influencing the Emperor in our favour, but also towards enduring what befalls us with fortitude; for we reap no small consolation from this season. For our very meeting together daily as we do, and having the benefit of hearing the divine Scriptures; and beholding each other; and weeping with each other; and praying, and receiving Benedictions,[2] and so

---

[1] Tillemont, *Theodos.* art. vi., mentions a law of his against holding criminal processes in Lent, and one deferring all executions thirty days. The massacre of Thessalonica, for which St. Ambrose caused him to do penance, occurred after the date of these Homilies, and that event forms a striking comment on Hom. III. 6. St. Ambrose then required him to renew the last-mentioned law.

[2] εὐλογίας. This word, rendered *benedictionem* by the Latin translator, meant according to Bingham the very same as the Eucharist in the more ancient writers, and is always so applied by Cyril of Alexandria, and Chrysostom. In after times, he further

departing home, takes off the chief part of our distress.

7. Let us, therefore, not despond, nor give ourselves up by reason of our distress; but let us wait, expecting a favourable issue; and let us give heed to the things that are now about to be spoken. For it is my purpose to discourse to you again to day respecting contempt for death. I said to you, yesterday, that we are afraid of death, not because he is really formidable; but because the love of the kingdom hath not kindled us, nor the fear of hell laid hold of us; and because besides this we have not a good conscience. Are you desirous that I should speak of a fourth reason for this unseasonable distress, one which is not less,[1] and truer than the rest? We do not live with the austerity that becometh Christians. On the contrary, we love to follow this voluptuous and dissolute and indolent life; therefore also it is but natural that we cleave to present things; since if we spent this life in fastings, vigils, and poverty of diet, cutting off all our extravagant desires; setting a restraint upon our pleasures; undergoing the toils of virtue; keeping the body under[2] like Paul, and bringing it into subjection; not "making provision for the lusts of the flesh;"[3] and pursuing the strait and narrow way, we should soon be earnestly desirous of future things, and eager to be delivered from our present labours. And to prove that what I say is not untrue, ascend to the tops of the mountains, and observe the monks who are there; some in sackcloth; some in bonds; some in fastings; some shut up[4] in darkness. Thou wilt then perceive, that all these are earnestly desiring death, and calling it rest. For even as the pugilist is eager to leave the stadium, in order that he may be freed from wounds; and the wrestler longs for the theatre to break up, that he may be released from his toils; so also he who by the aid of virtue leads a life of austerity, and mortification, earnestly longs for death in order that he may be freed from his present labours, and may be able to have full assurance in regard to the crowns laid up in store, by arriving in the still harbour, and migrating to the place where there is no further apprehension of shipwreck. Therefore, also, hath God provided for us a life that is naturally laborious and troublesome; to the end that being here urged by tribulation, we may conceive an eager longing for future blessings; for if now, whilst there are so many sorrows, and dangers, and fears, and anxieties, surrounding us on all sides, we thus cling to the present life; when should we ever be desirous of the life to come, if our present existence were altogether void of grief and misery?

8. Thus also God acted towards the Jews. For wishing to infuse into them a desire of returning (to Canaan), and to persuade them to hate Egypt, He permitted them to be distressed by working in clay, and brick-making, that being oppressed by that weight of toil and affliction, they might cry unto God respecting their return. For if, indeed when they departed after these things had happened, they did again remember Egypt, with their hard slavery, and were urgent to turn back to that former tyranny; what if they had received no such treatment from these barbarians? when would they have ever wished to leave that strange land?[5] To the end, therefore, that we may not be too closely attached to the earth, and grow wretched whilst gaping after present things, and become unmindful of futurity, God hath made our lives here full of labour. Let us not then cherish the love of the present life beyond what is necessary. For what doth it profit us? or what is the advantage of being closely rivetted to the desire of this present state? Art thou willing to learn in what respect this life is advantageous? It is so, inasmuch as it is the ground-work and starting point of the life to come; the wrestling-school and the arena for crowns of victory hereafter! so that if it does not provide these for us, it is worse than a thousand deaths. For if we do not wish to live so as to please God, it is better to die. For what is the gain? What have we the more? Do we not every day see the same sun, and the same moon, the same winter, the same summer, the same course of things? "The thing that hath been, shall be; and that which is done, is that which shall be done."[6] Let us not then at once pronounce those happy, who are alive, and

---

observes, that this term was applied to portions of bread blessed, but distinct from the Eucharist (being the residue of that brought for consecration), which was given to those who were not prepared to communicate, b. xv., c. iv., sec. 3, vol. v., p. 155, new Ed. The term was evidently derived from the Apostolic phraseology, τὸ ποτήριον τῆς εὐλογίας, 1 Cor. x. 16. It is used in the plural, for portions of the consecrated bread, both at communion, and when reserved to be sent to the sick, or to other churches.

[1] M. (and Ben. and Bas. Tr. apparently) read οὐκ ἔλαττον τῶν προτέρων ἀληθεστέραν; "not less the true one than those aforesaid." This use of the comparative, however, seems unusual.

[2] ὑπωπιάζων, the same word as used by St. Paul, 1 Cor. ix. 27, which alludes to the bruising of the face, or the parts under the eye, in the Greek games of boxing. Some read ὑποπιέζων, "pressing down," as indeed do some copies of the text and commentators, and among them St. Chrysostom ad loc., but this has less authority in its favor.

[3] Rom. xii. 14; Matt. vii. 14.

[4] This word may perhaps belong to the whole series of penances. St. Chrysostom is not recommending *such* austerities at all, but urging them to imitate in some measure a life which they already honored and esteemed holy. See on Rom. xiv. 23, Hom. XXVI. fin., where he accuses them of leaving religion to monks and hermits. Also on Rom. viii. 11, Hom. XIII. Mor. Tr. p. 229.

[5] Numb. xi. 5, xiv. 4, &c.   [6] Eccles. i. 9.

bewail the dead, but let us weep for those who are in their sins, whether they be dead or alive. And on the other hand, let us call those happy in whatsoever condition they be, who are in a state of righteousness. Thou, forsooth, fearest and lamentest "one" death; but Paul, who was dying daily,[1] was so far from shedding a tear on that account, that he rejoiced and exulted!

9. "O that I did endure the peril for God," saith some one, "then I should have no anxiety!" But do not even now sink into despondency; for not only indeed is he well approved, who suffers in the cause of God: but he who is suffering any thing unjustly,[2] and bearing it nobly, and giving thanks to God who permits it, is not inferior to him who sustains these trials for God's sake. The blessed Job is a proof of this, who received so many intolerable wounds through the devil's plotting against him uselessly, vainly, and without cause. Yet, nevertheless, because he bore them courageously, and gave thanks to God who permitted them, he was invested with a perfect[3] crown. Be not sad then on account of death; for it is natural to die: but grieve for sin; because it is a fault of the will. But if thou grievest for the dead, mourn also for those who are born into the world; for as the one thing is of nature, so is the other too of nature. Should any one, therefore, threaten thee with death, say to him, "I am instructed by Christ not to 'fear them which kill the body, but are not able to kill the soul.'"[4] Or should he threaten thee with the confiscation of thy goods, say to him, "Naked came I out of my mother's womb, and naked shall I return thither. We brought nothing into this world, and it is certain we can carry nothing out."[5] "And though thou take me not, death will come and take me; and though thou slay me not, yet the law of nature will presently interfere and bring the end." Therefore we should fear none of these things which are brought on us by the order of nature, but those which are engendered by our own evil will; for these bring forth our penalty. But let us continually consider this, that as regards the events which come upon us unexpectedly we shall not mend them by grieving, and so we shall cease to grieve.

10. And moreover we should think of this again, that if we suffer any evil unjustly, during the present life, we discharge a multitude of sins. Therefore it is a great advantage to have out the chastisement of our sins here, and not there; for the rich man received no evil here, and therefore he was scorched in the flames there; and that this was the reason why he did not enjoy any consolation,[6] hear in proof what Abraham saith, "Son, thou hast received thy good things; therefore thou art tormented." But that to the good things bestowed on Lazarus, not only his virtue, but his having here suffered a thousand ills, contributed, learn also from the patriarch's words. For having said to the rich man, "Thou hast received[7] thy good things," he goes on to say, "and Lazarus evil things, and for this reason he is comforted."[8] For as they who live virtuously, and are afflicted, receive a double reward from God, so he who liveth in wickedness, and fares sumptuously, shall have a double punishment. Again, I declare this not for the purpose of accusing those who have taken flight, for it is said, "Add not more trouble to a heart that is vexed;"[9] nor do I say it because I wish to rebuke; (for the sick man stands in need of consolation); but for the purpose of endeavouring to promote an amendment. Let us not entrust our safety to flight, but flee from sins, and depart from our evil way. If we escape from these things, although we be in the midst of ten thousand soldiers; not one of them will be able to smite us; but not flying from these, though we ascend to the very summit of the mountains, we shall there find innumerable enemies! Let us again call to mind those three children, who were in the midst of the furnace, yet suffered no evil, and those who cast them into it, how they that sat around were all consumed. What is more wonderful than this? The fire freed those it held possession of, and violently seized those whom it did not hold, to teach thee, that not the habitation, but the habit of life, bringeth safety or punishment. Those within the furnace escaped, but those without were consumed. To each alike were the same bodies, but not the same dispositions.[10] For this reason neither were the effects on them the same; for hay, although it lie without the flame, is quickly kindled; but gold, although it remain within, becomes the more resplendent!

11. Where now are those who said, "Let the Emperor take all, and grant us our bodies free?" Let such go and learn what is a free body. It is not immunity from

---

[1] 1 Cor. xv. 31.
[2] 1 Pet. xi. 19, 20: "*for it*" in this text is not in the original, as is marked by the italics in our version.
[3] ὁλόκληρον. He seems to mean a reward as full as if he had suffered for God. See on Rom. v. 11, Hom. IX.
[4] Matt. x. 28.   [5] Job i. 21; 1 Tim. vi. 7.
[6] παραμυθίας. See Hom. II. 19; also Hom. IV. (2).
[7] ἀπέλαβες. See Hom. I. 22.
[8] Luke xvi. 25.   [9] Ecclus. iv. 3.
[10] φρονήματα.

punishment that makes the body free, but perseverance in a life of righteousness. The bodies of these youths, for instance, were free, though they were given over to the furnace, because they had before put off the slavery of sin. For this alone is liberty; and not an immunity from punishment, or from suffering anything fearful. But having heard of the furnace, call thou to mind the "rivers of fire,"[1] which there shall be in that fearful day. For as on the above occasion, the fire seized upon some, but reverenced others, so also shall it be with those rivers. If any one should then have hay, wood, stubble, he increases[2] the fire; but if he has gold and silver, he[3] becomes the brighter. Let us therefore get together this kind of material, and let us bear the present state of things nobly; knowing that this tribulation will both bring us deliverance from that punishment if we understand how to practise true wisdom,[4] and will also make us better here; and not only us, but but often those too, who throw us into trouble, if we be vigilant; so abundant is the force of this spiritual wisdom; which was the case then even with the tyrant. For when he knew that they had suffered no harm, hear how he changed his language. "Ye servants of the most high God, come forth, and come hither."[5] Didst not thou say, a little before "Who is that God that shall deliver you out of my hands?"[6] What hath happened? Whence this change? Thou sawest those without destroyed, and dost thou call on those within? Whence hath it come to pass that thou art grown wise in such matters. Thou seest how great a change took place in the monarch! Whilst he had not yet exercised his power over them, he blasphemed, but as soon as he had cast them into fire, he began to shew moral wisdom. For this reason also God permitted all to take place, whatsoever the tyrant wished, in order that He might make it manifest, that none will be able to injure those who are kept by Him. And what He did towards Job, He performed here. For on that occasion also, He permitted the devil to manifest all his power; and not till he had exhausted all his darts, and no further mode of plotting against him remained, was the combatant led out of the field, that the victory might be brilliant and indubitable. So here too He did the very same thing. He willed to overthrow their city, and God stayed him not: he willed to carry them away captive, and He hindered him not: he willed to bind them, and He permitted; to cast them into the furnace, and He allowed it: to heat the flame beyond its measure, and this too He suffered; and when there was nothing further left for the tyrant to do, and he had exhausted all his strength, then God manifested His own power, and the patience of the youths. Seest thou how God permitted these tribulations even to the end, that He might shew the assailants the spiritual wisdom of those whom they assailed, as well as His own providence. Both of which circumstances also that man then discerned, and cried out, "Ye servants of the most high God, come forth, and come hither."

12. But consider thou with me the magnanimity of the youths; for they neither sprang out before the call, lest some should suppose they feared the fire; nor when they were called did they remain within, lest any one should think that they were ambitious and contentious. "As soon," say they, "as thou hast learnt whose servants we are, as soon as thou hast acknowledged our Lord, we come forth to be heralds to all who are present of the power of God." Or rather, not only they themselves, but even the enemy with his own voice, yea, both orally, and by his epistle, proclaimed to all men both the constancy of the combatants, and the strength of Him who presided over the contest. And even as the heralds, when they proclaim the names of the victorious combatants in the midst of the theatre, mention also the cities to which they belong; "such an one, of such a city!" So he too, instead of their city, proclaimed their Lord, by saying, "Shadrach, Meshach, and Abednego, ye servants of the most high God, come forth, and come hither." What is come to pass, that thou callest them the servants of God? Were they not thy servants? "Yea," saith he, "but they have overthrown[7] my sovereignty; they have trampled under foot my pride. They have shown by deeds, that He is their true Lord. If they were the servants of men, the fire would not have feared them; the flame would not have made way for them; for the creation knows nothing of reverencing or honoring the servants of men." Therefore again he saith, "Blessed be the God of Shadrach, Meshach, and Abednego."

---

[1] Dan. viii. 10. The *rivers* (or as some read *river*) *of fire*. This expression is taken from Dan. viii. 10, as appears by the coincidence of ἕλκεται, Hom. V. on Rom. ii. 16, and εἷλκεν in LXX. In Hom. *de Perf. Car.* near the end, Ben. vi. 298, E., he speaks of the fabled rivers of the heathen as a shadow of truth. So Greg. Naz. *in Jul.* inv. ii., *Or.* v. 38, Ben. (iv. 46, p. 132, Col.).
[2] See on 1 Cor. iii. 12, Hom. IX. (1).
[3] Or it.
[4] φιλοσοφεῖν, which is a favorite word of St. Chrysostom, and which he seems to use in a variety of passages to express the nobler emotions of the mind
[5] Dan. iii. 26.
[6] Dan. iii. 15.
[7] κατέλυσαν.

13. Contemplate with me also, how first he proclaims the Arbiter of the contest. "Blessed be God, who hath sent His angel and delivered His servants."[1] This of the power of God. He speaks also of the virtue of the combatants. "Because they trusted in Him, and have changed the king's word, and have yielded their bodies, that they might not worship any god except their own God." Could anything equal the virtue of this? Before this, when they said, "We will not serve thy gods," he was inflamed more fiercely than the very furnace; but now, when by their deeds they had taught him this, he was so far from being indignant, that he praised and admired them, for not having obeyed him! So good a thing is virtue, that it has even its enemies themselves to applaud and admire it! These had fought and conquered, but the vanquished party gave thanks, that the sight of the fire had not terrified them, but that the hope in their Lord had comforted them. And He names the God of the whole world after the three youths, not at all circumscribing His sovereignty, but inasmuch as these three youths were equivalent to the whole world.[2] For this reason he both applauds those who had despised him, and passing by so many governors, kings, and princes, those who had obeyed him, he stands in admiration of the three captives and slaves, who derided his tyranny! For they did these things, not for the sake of contention, but for the love of wisdom; not of defiance, but of devotion; not as being puffed up with pride, but fired with zeal. For great indeed is the blessing of a hope in God; which then also the barbarian learned, and making it manifest that it was from that source they had escaped the impending peril, he exclaimed aloud: "Because they trusted in Him!"[3]

14. But I say all this now, and select all the histories that contain trials and tribulations, and the wrath of kings, and their evil designs, in order that we may fear nothing, save only offending God. For then also was there a furnace burning; yet they derided it, but feared sin. For they knew that if they were consumed in the fire, they should suffer nothing that was to be dreaded; but that if they were guilty of impiety, they should undergo the extremes of misery. It is the greatest punishment to commit sin, though we may remain unpunished; as on the other hand, it is the greatest honour and repose to live virtuously, though we may be punished. For sins separate us from God; as He Himself speaks; "Have not your sins separated between you and Me?"[4] But punishments lead us back to God. As one saith, "Give peace; for Thou hast recompensed us for all things."[5] Suppose any one hath a wound; which is the most deserving of fear, gangrene, or the surgeon's knife? the steel, or the devouring progress of the ulcer? Sin is a gangrene, punishment is the surgeon's knife. As then, he who hath a gangrene, although he is not lanced, hath to sustain the malady, and is then in the worse condition, when he is not lanced; so also the sinner, though he be not punished, is the most wretched of men; and is then especially wretched, when he hath no punishment, and is suffering no distress. And as those who have a disease of the spleen, or a dropsy, when they enjoy a plentiful table, and cool drinks, and a variety of delicacies, and condiments, are then especially in a most pitiable state, increasing as they do their disease by luxury; but should they rigorously subject themselves to hunger and thirst, according to medical laws, they might have some hope of recovery; so also those who live in iniquity, if they are punished, may have favourable hopes; but if, together with their wickedness, they enjoy security and luxury, they become more wretched than those who cram their bellies, though they are in a state of dropsy; and so much the more, as the soul is better than the body. If then thou seest any who are in the same sins, and some of them struggling continually with hunger, and a thousand ills; while others are drinking their fill, and living sumptuously, and gormandizing; think those the better off, who endure sufferings. For not only is the flame of voluptuousness cut off by these misfortunes, but they also depart to the future Judgment, and that dread tribunal,[6] with no small relief; and go hence,

---

[1] Dan. iii. 28.
[2] Ecclus. xliv. 17, on Rom. i. 8, Hom. II.
[3] Dan. iii. 28.
[4] Isa. lix. 2.
[5] Isaiah xxvi. 12, LXX., the Eng. V. is, "*Thou hast wrought all our works in us.*" Compare, however, Isa. i. 5, xl. 2, liv. 8; Dan. ix. 12, 16; Lev. xxvi. 34; 2 Chron. xxxvi. 21.
[6] It was the common opinion of the Greek Fathers, that the fire of the day of judgment would cause severe suffering to some of those who would be finally saved, and that this might be mitigated by a severe repentance, and in some degree by suffering here, and by the prayers of others. St. Chrys. on Phil. i. 24; Hom. III. Mor. Orig. on Ps. xxxvi. (al. xxxvii.) v. 8; Ben. ii. 661, D.; St. Cyr. *Catech.* xv. (9); Greg. Nyss. *Or. de Mort.* ed. 1638, t. iii. 634, d. speaks of a cleansing fire. But in *Or. de fun. Pulcheriæ*, p. 460, he says, "such a soul, having nothing for which to be judged, fears not *Hell*, dreads not *Judgment*. It abides free from fear and astonishment, no evil conscience causing a fear of *Judgment*." However, St. Chrys. on 1 Cor. iii. 15, Hom. IX. explains the being *saved as by fire* of remaining undestroyed in eternal torment. This last exposition is attributed to "the Greeks" by Bellarmine, *de Purg.* lib. i. c. 5, having been defended by them in the discussion on Purgatory preliminary to the Council of Florence. Labbe, t. xiii. p. 26-30. It is also held by Photius, Œcum. *ad loc.* Theodoret, on 1 Cor. iii., takes the passage in general to refer to teachers and their work as such, but explains the words cited of a fiery trial of the teacher's own life. Euseb. (quoted as Emisen. really a Gall. Bp. of later date), *Bibl. Pat. Col.* iii. 549, speaks of rivers of fire (see p. 126); Hom. III. *de Epiph.*, Œcumenius on 1 Cor. iii. (doubtfully). Also the Commentary on Isaiah,

having discharged here the penalty of the greater part of their sins by the ills they have suffered.

15. But enough of consolation. It is time for us now, at last, to proceed to the exhortation on the subject of avoiding oaths, and to remove that seeming palliation on behalf of those who swear, which is but futile,[1] and useless. For when we bring an accusation against them, they allege the case of others who do the very same thing; and they say, "such and such persons swear." Let us then say to these, Nevertheless; such a man does not swear: and God will give His judgment concerning thee, from those who do good works; for sinners do not profit sinners by fellowship in transgressions; but they who perform what is right condemn sinners.[2] For they who gave not Christ food, or drink, were many; but they rendered no aid to each other.[3] Similar also was the case of the five virgins, who found no pardon from companionship,[4] but being condemned by a comparison with those who had acted wisely, both these and the former were alike punished.

16. Dismissing then this argument of frigid self-deception, let us not look at the case of those who fall, but at those who fashion their conduct rightly; and let us endeavour to carry along with us a memento of the present fast when it is over. And as it oftens happens when we have purchased a vestment, or a slave, or a precious vase, we recall again the time when we did so, and say to each other, "That slave I purchased at such a festival; that garment I bought at such a time;" so, in like manner, if we now reduce to practice this law, we shall say, I reformed the practice of swearing during that Lent; for till then I was a swearer; but from barely hearing an admonition, I have abstained from the sin.

But "the custom," it may be objected, "is a hard thing to be reformed." I know it is; and therefore am urgent to throw you into another custom, which is good and profitable. For when you say, it is difficult for me to abstain from what is habitual; for that very reason, I say, you should make haste to abstain, knowing for certain, that if you once[5] make another custom for yourself of not swearing, you will want no labour afterwards. Which is the more difficult thing; not to swear, or to remain the whole day without food; and to shrivel up[6] on water-drinking, and meagre diet? It is evident that the latter surpasses the former; yet, notwithstanding, custom has made this matter so possible and easy of execution, that when the fast comes round, although any one should exhort a thousand times, or as frequently constrain and compel one to partake of wine, or taste of any other of those things which are forbidden during fasts, yet a man would prefer to suffer anything, rather than touch the prohibited article of food;[7] and that not for want of relish for the table, nevertheless, we bear it all with fortitude, from the habit of our conscience. And the case will be the same in regard to oaths; and just as if now, any one were to impose ever so great necessity, you would remain immovable, holding fast the habit;[8] so also in that case, if any one should urge you ten thousand times, you would not depart from your custom.

18. When you go home, therefore, discourse of all these things with those who are in your house; and as many persons often do, when they come back from a meadow, having plucked there a rose, or a violet, or some flower of that kind, they return twisting[9] it about with their fingers; and as some, again, when they quit the gardens to go home, take with them branches of trees, with their fruit upon them; and as others, moreover, from sumptuous feasts, carry away leavings of the entertainment for their dependents; so indeed do thou, departing from hence, take an exhortation home to thy wife, thy children, and all thine household. For this admonition is more profitable than the meadow, the garden, or the banquetting table. These roses never wither; these fruits never drop off; these dainties never corrupt. The former yield a temporary delight; but the latter a lasting advantage, not only after this reformation has taken place, but in the very act of reforming. For think what a good practice this would be, having dismissed all other matters public or private, to discourse[10]

---

attributed to St. Basil, on c. ix. 19; Ben. t. i. p. 554 (cited as his by Photius), speak of a cleansing by the Judgment fire. Origen, on Ps. xxxvi. (37) 14, Hom. III. 1, says, "And, as I think, we must all come to that fire. Though one be Paul or Peter, yet he comes to that fire." So St. Ambr. on verse 15, sec. 26, of Ezekiel and Daniel, and St. Hil. on Ps. cxviii. (119) 20, of the Blessed Virgin herself, so applying Luc. ii. 35. See *Cat. Aur.* on St. Matt. iii. 11, 12, Tr. p. 104, note e. St. Greg. Naz. *Or.* xxxix. c. 19, speaks of Novatians, as "perhaps to be baptized in the fire of the other world, in that last Baptism, which is longer and more painful." There is no minutely defined and universal doctrine on the subject. See on Fleury, b. 19, c. 31.
[1] ψυχράν, somewhat as we say, "cold comfort." See Herod. v. i. 108, and note of Baehr., also Dem. *de Fals. Leg.* 207.
[2] Comp. Hom. IX. on 1 Cor. iii. and see Matt. xii. 41.
[3] Matt. xxv. 35. [4] Matt. xxv. 10.

[5] Implied in the aorist, ποιήσῃς.
[6] ταριχεύεσθαι, Dem. adv. Aristogit. i. 72, of the effect of long imprisonment, lit. "to be dried like a mummy."
[7] That this strictness was not quite universal appears from Hom. IX. 1. The feeling there referred to may have been partly occasioned by this passage.
[8] *i. e.*, of fasting.
[9] Sav. περιστρέφοντες. Ben. περιφέροντες. Thus St. Francis de Sales recommends "culling flowers" for the day from morning devotions.
[10] Deut. vi. 7.

only of the divine laws continually, at the table, in the forum, and in your other meetings. Would we give our attention to these things, we should say nothing of a dangerous or injurious nature, nor should we sin unwittingly. Giving our leisure to discourse respecting these things, we should be able to withdraw our soul even from this despondency that hangs over us, instead of looking with so much anxiety as we do, whilst we say one to another, "Hath the Emperor heard what hath happened? Is he incensed? What sentence hath he pronounced?[1] Hath any one petitioned him? What? Will he himself endure to destroy utterly a city so great and populous?" Casting these and all such cares upon God, let us be anxious only as to what He hath commanded! Thus shall we rid ourselves of all these sorrows; and although ten only among us should succeed, the ten would quickly become twenty; the twenty fifty; the fifty a hundred; the hundred a thousand; the thousand all the city. And just as when ten lamps are lighted, one may easily fill the whole house with light, so also with respect to right actions; should only ten act rightly, we shall light up a general flame throughout the city, to shine forth, and to procure us safety. For not so naturally does the fire, when it falls upon a forest, kindle the neighbouring trees successively, as will the emulation for virtue, when it seizes upon a few minds, be mighty in its progress to diffuse itself through the whole community.

19. Give me cause, then, to exult over you both in the present life, and at that future Day, when those to whom talents have been entrusted, shall be summoned! Your good reputation is a sufficient reward for my labours; and if I see you living in piety, I have all I wish. Do, then, what yesterday I recommended, and to-day will repeat, and will not cease to say it. Fix a penalty for those who swear; a penalty which is a gain, and not a loss; and prepare yourselves henceforth so as you may give us a proof of success. For I shall endeavour to hold a long conversation with each of you, when this assembly is dismissed; in order that in the continuance of discourse I may discover the persons who have been acting rightly, and those who have not.[2] And if I find any one still swearing, I shall make him manifest to all who are amended, that by reproving, rebuking, and correcting, we may quickly deliver him from this evil habit. For better it is that he should amend through being reproached here, than that he should be put to shame, and punished, in the presence of the whole assembled universe, on that Day, when our sins shall be revealed to the eyes of all men! But God forbid that any in this fair assembly should appear there suffering such things! but by the prayers of the holy fathers,[3] correcting all our offences, and hav-

[1] ἐψηφίσατο.   [2] Sav. adds, "and those who have not."

[3] εὐχαῖς τῶν ἁγίων πατέρων. See on Rom. xvi. 24, Hom. XXXII., where the translation perhaps ought to be, "These imitators of Paul. Only let us yield ourselves worthy of such intercession." This rendering is confirmed by its agreement with Hom. XLIV. on Gen. xix. 29; Ben. iv. 448, 449. But there is a difficulty in it owing to the reference to St. Paul's *departure*. This may be explained as a turn of rhetoric. The passage on Gen. xix. does not define whether saints on earth or above are spoken of; but from others it is probable he means the latter. The close of the Homily on St. Meletius, Ben. ii. 522, A. speaks of such intercession, and that of Hom. *in SS. Bernicen and Prosd.* Ben. ii. 645, D. of invoking it. The Homily quoted above, on the intercession of Abraham, warns men against trusting to prayers of saints so as to neglect their own life. An expression like that in the text occurs in a Homily *de Sp. Sancto*, attributed to St. Chrys. by Photius, Ben. iii. 799, C.; Origen on Cant. ii. 5; asserts the intercession of the saints, proving it from 2 Mac. xv. 14, and on Numb. xxxii., Hom. XXVI. 6, he asks, who doubts it? Hom. I. 7, on Ezekiel, he invokes an angel, as holding that angels are present, though in a rhetorical way. Lib. 2, in Job (fin.) sometimes cited as his, is spurious, and the Com. on Lament. doubtful, and the manner of invocation looks as if of later date. St. Cyprian, *Ep*. 57, *ad Cornel. fin.* desires that whoever dies first may pray for the other; and *de Hab. Virg. fin.* makes a similar request: and so Theodosia in *Euseb. de Mart. Pal.* c. 7.

In the fourth century, the invocation of departed saints, or prayer to God for their prayers, becomes common. So Eusebius, on Ps. lxxviii. (79) takes verse 11, *Preserve Thou the sons of the slain* (Heb. *of death*), *i. e.*, of the martyrs. At the close of his Com. on Isaiah, he prays just as St. Chrys. in the text. St. Athanas. *ad Marcellin.* 31. t. i. p. 1001, says we should sing the Psalms exactly, " that the inspired writers may know their own words, and pray with us, or rather, that the Holy Spirit who spoke in them, hearing the words He dictated to them, may take our part " (συναντιλάβηται, Comp. Rom. viii. 26). A direct address to the Blessed Virgin . . . . . " Queen, and Mother of God, intercede for us !" is quoted as his (*Serm. in Annunt.* t. ii. p. 401), but is spurious, as is there stated.

St. James, of Nisibis, Ser. 4, p. 72, seems to speak of an angel presenting our prayers, which his editor connects with Tertullian's *Angelus Orationis, de Or.* xii. and Tob. xii. 12. St. Hilary, on Ps. cxxiv. (125) 2, takes the *hills* (as others constantly elsewhere), for the saints and angels. On Matt. xxv. p. 736, he says, " none shall be helped by another's works and merits, because every one must buy oil for his own lamp." This seems to imply the existence of the same tendency which St. Chrysostom reproves, as quoted above on Gen. xix. The Martyr Justina, early in this century, is said by St. Greg. Naz. *Or.* xviii. p. 279 (Ben. Or. xxiv. 11, p. 443 d.), to have implored the aid of the Virgin Mary.

In the latter part of the century, instances are more frequent. St. Cyril of Jerusalem, *Cat. Myst.* v. (6), says, " Then we commemorate also those who have fallen asleep before us, first, patriarchs, prophets, apostles, martyrs, that at their prayers and intervention God would receive our petition." St. Basil, Hom. on the Forty Martyrs, c. 8, t. 2, p. 155, speaks strongly of the value of their intercession, and recommends asking it. " Here is found a pious woman praying for her children, the return of her husband, his recovery when sick: let your prayers be made with the martyrs !" To Julian the Apostate, Ep. 360, al. 205, Ben. iii. 462. " I also receive the holy apostles, prophets, and martyrs, and call on them to supplication unto God, that through them, that is, through their mediation, the merciful God may become propitious to me, and a ransom of my sins may be made and granted." To St. Ambrose, Ep. 197, al. 55, Ben. iii. 288, he speaks of the relics of a martyr as a protection to those who have them. St. Ephraim, in *Martyres*, t. iii. Gr. Lat. p. 251, has, " Victorious Martyrs, willing sufferers for the love of your God and Saviour, ye that have boldness of speech toward the Lord Himself ; intreat, holy as ye are, for us that are worthless, and sinners, and full of listlessness, that the grace of Christ may come upon us." Some prayers to the Blessed Virgin, calling her the only hope of sinners, and giving her the titles of our Lord, are ascribed to him. Such would stand alone in this age, and long after. But one which has been long known in Latin (ed. Voss, p. 543), has been generally thought spurious. The last Roman Edition contains more, but even the MSS. from which they are taken seem to ascribe them but doubtfully to him (" Prayers collected from Holy Scripture, but most of them from St. Ephraim," &c.), especially as others precede these. He, however, used invocation freely, though some allowance must be made for his rich imagination, and his fondness for apostrophe. Thus he apostrophises Faith, *adv. Scrut. Ser.* vi. Gr. Lat. iii. 160, 161. " O Faith! I pray Thee adapt Thy vastness to our littleness ! for while we may not see and measure thee, love can neither rest nor be silent !" " Come hither, O Faith, Gift of God to the Holy

ing shown forth the abundant fruit of virtue, may we depart hence with much confidence, through the grace and lovingkindness of our Lord Jesus Christ, through whom, and with whom, be glory to the Father together with the Holy Spirit, for ever and ever. Amen.

Church, and rest in this bosom!" Several spurious passages, as from the Christus Patiens attributed to St. Greg. Naz. l. 2582 (but rejected and objected to by the Ben. editor), are examined by Mr. Palmer, Letter v. to Dr. Wiseman. The real practice of St. Greg. Naz. appears in his funeral oration on St. Basil, *Or.* xx. fin. p. 373 (Ben. xliii. 82, p. 831). " But do thou, O divine and sacred head, look on us from above, and either remove by thy intercessions the thorn in the flesh that chastises us, or persuade us to bear it with fortitude," &c. *Or.* vi. *ad Greg. Nyss.* p. 140 (Ben. xi. 5, p. 245), he says, that martyrs are " Mediators for attaining a divine state (θέωσις). St. Chrysostom is of the same date. St. Greg. Nyss. on St. Theodorus, speaks repeatedly of asking his intercession. " To touch his relics, if any chance give one the opportunity. . . Then, shedding on them the tear of piety and affection, as though to the martyr, appearing in full presence, they present their entreaty for intercession; beseeching him, as an attendant* upon God, and invoking him as one who obtains favors at will," t. iii. p. 580, and so

* δορυφόρῳ, A term which shows that an allusion to an earthly court is intended.

in other parts of the oration; and in p. 586, he begs him, if need be, to call his brother-martyrs to his aid. And in the close of his life of St. Ephraim, he both invokes him, " Remember us all, asking remission for our sins;" and speaks of a person having invoked his help, in circumstances of danger, with success. St. Ambrose, *de Vid.* c. 9, says, " The angels are to be entreated for us, who are given us for our guard; the martyrs are to be entreated, whose patronage we may in a manner claim by the pledge of their bodies. They can pray for our sins, who have washed in their own blood their own sins, if such they had." These are most of the authors alleged down to the end of the fourth century, but in most of the later of them other passages of the same kind appear. Thus the practice of direct invocation seems to have come in by degrees, and that chiefly in the course of this century. Some passages relating merely to the intercession of the saints have been passed over, as they would rather confuse the view of the subject of *seeking* it. Bellarmine, *De Sanctis*, l. i. c. 19, and Coccius, *Thesaur.* l. v., art. 4, give collections of passages. See on Fleury, Book 19, c. 31, Tr. p. 202, note k.

HOMILY VII.

Recapitulation of former exhortations. Sin brought death and grief into the world, and they tend to its cure. Grief serviceable only for the destruction of sin. Remarks upon the passage, Gen. 1, 1. " In the beginning God created the heaven and the earth." It is argued that God's forethought for man in the work of creation affords grounds of comfort; and that mercy is shewn even in chastisement, as in the saying, "Adam, where art thou?" Concluding admonition on the avoidance of oaths.

1. YESTERDAY, I discoursed unto your Charity in many words, and upon many subjects; and if out of this variety, it be not possible for you to retain all, I wish more particularly to recall to memory the observation, that God hath implanted the affection grief in our natures for no other reason but because of sin, and He hath made this evident from actual experience. For whilst we are grieved and distressed through the loss of wealth; or by reason of sickness, and death, and the other evils that befall us, we not only reap no consolation from our sorrow, but we also increase the force of these calamities. But if we are in pain and sorrow[1] for our sins, we diminish the weight of sin; we make that little which is great; and very often we blot it all out entirely. Ye should continually remember this, I repeat, in order that ye may mourn for sin only, and for nothing besides; and the additional fact, that sin, though it brought death and sadness into our life, is again destroyed[2] by both these; which I have recently made evident. Therefore, let us fear nothing so much as sin and transgression. Let us not fear punishment, and then we shall escape[3] punishment. Even as the Three Children were not afraid of the furnace, and so escaped from the furnace. Such indeed it becomes the servants of God to be. For if those who were brought up under the Old dispensation, when death was not yet slain,[4] nor his " brazen gates broken down," nor his " iron bars smitten in sunder;"[5] so nobly encountered their end,[6] how destitute of all defence or excuse shall we be, if, after having had the benefit of such great grace, we attain not even to the same measure of virtue as they did, now when death is only a name, devoid of reality. For death is nothing more than a sleep, a journey, a migration, a rest, a tranquil haven; an escape from trouble, and a freedom from the cares of this present life!

2. But here let us dismiss the subject of consolation; it is the fifth day we are engaged in speaking words of comfort to your Charity, and we might now seem to be troublesome. For what hath been already said is sufficient

---

[1] St. Greg. Nyss. *de Beat.* iii. t. i. 781.
[2] Or. *in funere Pulcheriæ*, t. iii. 460.
[3] διαφευξόμεθα.
[4] Hos. xiii. 14, which, however, is less clear in LXX.
[5] Ps. cvii. 16; Isa. xlv. 2.
[6] Or, " defied death," κατετόλμησαν τῆς τελευτῆς.

for those who give heed; but to those who are pusillanimous it will be no gain, even though we were to add to what we have said. It is now time to direct our teaching to the exposition of the Scriptures. For as, if we had said nothing in reference to the present calamity, one might have condemned us for cruelty, and a want of humanity; so, were we always discoursing of this, we might justly be condemned for pusillanimity. Commending then your hearts to God, who is able to speak[1] into your minds, and to expel all grief from within, let us now take up our accustomed manner of instruction; and that especially since every exposition of Scripture is matter of comfort and relief. So that, although we may seem to be desisting from the topic of consolation, we shall again light upon the same subject by means of Scriptural exposition. For that all Scripture furnishes consolation to those who give attention to it, I will make manifest to you from its own evidence.[2] For I shall not go about among the Scripture narratives to search out certain arguments consolatory; but in order that I may make the proof of the matter which I have undertaken plainer, we will take in hand the book which has to-day been read to us; and bringing forward, if you will, the introduction and commencement of it, which may especially seem to present no trace of consolation, but to be altogether foreign to topics of comfort, I will make that which I affirm evident.

3. What then is this introduction? "In the beginning God made the heaven and the earth, and the earth was invisible, and unformed,[3] and darkness was upon the face of the abyss."[4] Do these words seem to some of you incapable of affording consolation under distress? Is it not an historical narrative, and an instruction about the creation?

Would you then that I show the consolation that is hidden in this saying? Arouse yourselves then, and attend with earnestness to the things which are about to be spoken. For when thou hearest that God made the heaven, the earth, the sea, the air, the waters, the multitude of stars, the two great lights, the plants, the quadrupeds, the swimming and the flying animals, and all things without exception which thou seest, for thee, and for thy safety and honour; dost thou not straightway take comfort and receive this as the strongest proof of the love of God, when thou thinkest that He produced such a world as this, so fair, so vast and wonderful, for such a puny being as thyself! When therefore thou hearest that, "In the beginning God made the heaven and the earth," run not hastily over the declaration; but traverse in thy mind the breadth of the earth; and reflect how He hath spread out[5] so sumptuous and exquisite a table for us, and provided us with such abundant gladness.[6] And this is, indeed, the most marvellous thing, that He gave us not such a world as this in payment for services done; or as a recompense for good works; but at the very time He formed us, He honoured our race with this kingdom. For He said, "Let us make man after our image, and after our likeness."[7] What is the sense of this, "after our image, and after our likeness?" The image of government[8] is that which is meant; and as there is no one in heaven superior to God, so let there be none upon earth superior to man. This then is one, and the first respect, in which He did him honour; by making him after His own image; and secondly, by providing us with this principality, not as a payment for services, but making it entirely the gift of His own love toward man; and thirdly, in that He conferred it upon us as a thing of nature. For of governments there are some natural, and others which are elective;—natural as of the lion over the quadrupeds, or as that of the eagle over the birds; elective, as that of an Emperor over us; for he doth not reign over his fellow-servants by any natural authority. Therefore it is that he oftentimes loses his sovereignty. For such are things which are not naturally inherent;[9] they readily admit of change and transposition. But not so with the lion; he rules by nature over the quadrupeds, as the eagle doth over birds. The character of sovereignty is, therefore, constantly allotted to his race; and no lion hath ever been seen deprived of it. Such a kind of sovereignty God bestowed upon us from the beginning, and set us over all things. And not only in this respect did He confer honour upon our nature,[10] but also, by the very eminence of the spot in which we

---

[1] See Isa. xl. 2, Heb. and LXX.   [2] αὐτόθεν.
[3] Or, *unfurnished*, E. V., *without form, and void*. This rendering came in with the Genevan Bible. All the previous translations had *void*, and *empty*. Perhaps by the term *void*, was meant just the same as the Septuagint ἀκατασκεύαστος. The word *Bohu*, which occurs Deut. xxxii. 10, and Ps. cvii. 40, is in both cases rendered a waste, or wilderness. See Dr. Buckland's Bridgewater Treatise, c. 2, and notes.
[4] Gen. i. 12, LXX.
[5] ἀνῆκεν, "sent up," *i. e.*, "caused to grow."
[6] εὐφροσύνην. Comp. Acts xiv. 17. *Filling our hearts with food and gladness.*
[7] Gen. i. 26.
[8] This of course does not exclude, but rather implies, an *intrinsic* resemblance. See St. Cyr. *Cat.* xii. (3), and xiv. (5); St. Aug. *De C. D.* xi. 26, xii. 23; *Conf.* xiii. 12; St. Greg. Nyss. on the text, t. ii. p. 22 sqq.
[9] So "nature" was usually understood. Arist. Eth. ii. 1. "Nothing that is by nature is made otherwise by habit; *e. g.*, a stone tends downwards by nature, and cannot be habituated to tend upwards."
[10] Or, kind.

were placed, fixing upon Paradise as our choice dwelling, and bestowing the gift of reason, and an immortal soul.

4. But I would not speak of these things: for I say that such was the abundance of God's care, that we may know His goodness, and His love towards man, not only from the way in which He hath honoured, but also from the way in which He hath punished us. And this, I especially exhort you to consider with attention, that God is alike good, not only whilst He is treating us with honour and beneficence, but also whilst He is punishing and chastising. And whether we should have to carry on our contest and combat against the heathen, or against the heretics, respecting the lovingkindness and goodness of God, we shall make His goodness evident, not only from the cases in which He bestows honour, but also from the cases in which He inflicts punishment. For if He is good only whilst honouring us, and not good whilst punishing us, He were but half good. But this is not the case. God forbid! Among men this may probably happen, when they inflict punishments in anger and passion; but God being free from passion, whether He exercise kindness, or whether He punish, He is alike good. Nor less does the threat of hell serve to show His goodness, than the promise of the kingdom.[1] But how? I answer. If He had not threatened hell, if He had not prepared punishment, there are not many who would have attained the kingdom.[2] For the promise of good things doth not so strongly induce the multitude to virtue; as doth the threat of evil things compel by fear, and arouse them to the care of the soul. So that, although hell be the opposite of the kingdom of heaven, yet each hath respect to the same end—the salvation of men; the one alluring to itself, the other driving them towards its opposite, and by the operation of fear correcting those who are carelessly disposed.

5. I do not enlarge upon this subject without reason; but because there are many who often, when famines, and droughts, and wars take place, or when the wrath of an Emperor overtakes them, or when any other unexpected events of this kind happen, deceive the simpler class by saying, that these things are unworthy of the Providence of God.

I am therefore compelled to dwell on this part of my discourse, that we may not be beguiled by words, but that we may plainly perceive, that whether He brings upon us a famine, or a war, or any calamity, whatsoever, He doth it out of His exceeding great care and kindness. For even those fathers, who especially love their offspring, will forbid them the table, and inflict stripes, and punish them by disgrace, and in endless other ways of this kind correct their children when they are disorderly; yet are they nevertheless fathers, not only while doing them honour, but when acting thus; yea, they are preeminently fathers when they act thus.[3] But if men, who are frequently carried away beyond what is meet by the force of angry feelings, are yet held to punish those whom they love, not from cruelty and inhumanity, but from a kind care and regard; much rather is it proper to be thus minded concerning God; who in the exceeding abundance of His goodness, far transcends every degree of paternal fondness. And that you may not suppose that what I say is a mere conjecture, let us, I pray you, direct our discourse to the Scripture itself. When man, then, had been deceived and beguiled by the wicked demon, let us observe how God treated him, after his committing so great a sin. Did He then altogether destroy him? Yet the reason of the thing in justice demanded this, that one who had displayed nothing that was good, but, after enjoying so much favour, had waxed wanton even from the very first, should be made away with, and utterly destroyed; yet God acted not so; neither did He regard with disgust and aversion him who had been so ungrateful towards his Benefactor, but He comes to him as a physician cometh to a sick man.

6. Do not, O beloved, pass over unthinkingly, what has just been said! but consider what an act it was, not to send an angel, or archangel, or any other of his fellow-servants, but that the Lord Himself should have descended to him who had fallen from the right way, and should have raised him when thus cast down; and should have approached him, One to one,[4] as a friend comes to a friend when he is unfortunate, and is plunged in great distress! For that He acted thus out of His great kindness, the very words too which He spake to him evidently show His ineffable affection. And why do I say, *all* the words? The first utterance signifies at once His tenderness. For He said not, what it was probable a person treated so contemptuously would say, "O wicked, yea most wicked man! When thou hadst enjoyed so great favour from Me, and hadst been honoured with such a sovereignty, being exalted above all the crea-

---

[1] Gal. iii. 24.
[2] 1 Tim. i. 9. St. Greg. Nyss. on the Beatitudes, *Or.* 3, t. i. p. 781, explains *Blessed are they that mourn*; first, of those whom the fear of hell causes to mourn for their sins; secondly, of those who mourn for their present exclusion from the good things they hope for hereafter. See on Rom. xiv. 13, Hom. XXV.
[3] Heb. xii. 9.
[4] μόνον πρὸς μόνον. There being no third party present.

tures upon the earth for no merit of thine own; and having received in actual deeds the pledges of My care, and a true manifestation of My Providence, didst thou esteem a wicked and pestiferous demon, the enemy of thy salvation, to be worthy of more credit than thy Lord and Benefactor? What proof did he give of regard for thee, like that which I have done? Did I not make for thee the heaven, the earth, the sea, the sun, the moon, and all the stars? For truly none of the angels needed this work of creation; but for thee, and for thy recreation, I made so great and excellent a world; and didst thou esteem mere words alone, a false engagement, and a promise full of deceit, as more worthy to be believed than the kindness and providence that was manifested by deeds; that thou gavest thyself over to him, and didst trample My laws under foot!" These words, and more of this kind, one who had been treated contemptuously would probably say. But God acted not so; but quite in the contrary manner. For by His first word He at once raised him up from his dejection, and gave the fearful and trembling man confidence, by being the first Himself to call him, or rather, not by merely calling him first, but by addressing him by his own familiar appellation, and saying, "Adam, where art thou?" Thus He shewed His tenderness, and the great regard He had for him. For ye must all know, that this is a mark of intimate friendship.[1] And thus those who call upon the dead are wont to do, continually repeating their names. And so, on the other hand, those who entertain hatred and enmity against any, cannot bear to mention the very names of those who have aggrieved them. Saul, for instance, though he had sustained no injury from David, but had wronged him exceedingly, since he abhorred and hated him, could not endure to mention his proper name; but when all were seated together, not seeing David to be present, what said he? He said not, "Where is David? but, 'Where is the son of Jesse?'"[2] calling him by his father's name. And again, the Jews did the same with respect to Christ, for since they abhorred and hated Him, they did not say, "Where is Christ?"[3] but, "Where is that man?"[4]

7. But God, willing to show even by this that sin had not quenched His tenderness, nor disobedience taken away His favor toward him, and that He still exercised His Providence and care for the fallen one, said, "Adam, where art thou?"[5] not being ignorant of the place where he was, but because the mouth of those who have sinned is closed up; sin turning the tongue backward, and conscience taking hold of it; so that such persons remain speechless, held fast in silence as by a kind of chain. And God wishing therefore to invite him to freedom of utterance, and to give him confidence, and to lead him to make an apology for his offences, in order that he might obtain some forgiveness, was Himself the first to call; cutting off much of Adam's distress by the familiar appellation, and dispelling his fear, and opening by this address the mouth that was shut. Hence also it was that he said, "Adam, where art thou?" "I left thee," saith he, "in one situation, and I find thee in another. I left thee in confidence and glory; and I now find thee in disgrace and silence!" And observe the care of God in this instance. He called not Eve;—He called not the serpent,—but him who had sinned in the lightest degree of all, he brings first to the tribunal, in order that beginning from him who was able to find some degree of excuse, He might pass a more merciful sentence, even against her who had sinned the most. And judges, indeed, do not deign to make inquiry in their own person of their fellow-servants, and those who are partakers of a common nature with them, but putting forward some one of their attendants to intervene, they instruct him to convey their own questions to the criminal; and through him they say and hear whatever they wish, when they examine the offenders.[6] But God had no need of a go-between in dealing with man; but Himself in His own person at once judges and consoles him. And not only this is wonderful, but also that he corrects the crimes that had been committed. For judges in general, when they find thieves and grave-robbers,[7] do not consider how they may make them better, but how they may make them pay the penalty of the offences committed. But God, quite on the contrary, when He finds a sinner, considers not how He may make him pay the penalty, but how He may amend him, and make him better, and invincible[8] for the

---

[1] Thus Thetis, *Il.* i. 361, and throughout Homer ἐκ τ' ὀνόμαζε expresses affection; the scholast, however, explains the word of merely speaking at length, which seems almost absurd.
[2] 1 Kings xx. 27.
[3] From this peculiar illustration it would seem, that St. Chrysostom supposed the term Christ to have been one of the familiar names by which our Saviour was known. But the term Jesus of Nazareth seems to have been His more general and distinctive appellation; though it by no means follows that He was not as familiarly known by the title of Christ among His followers, and addressed as such, especially after Peter's confession. (See John ix. 22; Matt. xxvii. 17, contrasted with verse 63.)
[4] John vii. 11.
[5] Gen. iii. 9, LXX.
[6] What it was to be brought to the bar in those days may be seen in Hom. XIII.
[7] A common crime then, probably from the richness of burials. See on Rom. vi. 18, Hom. XI.
[8] ἀχείρωτον, *i.e.*, to the adversary. See Hom. I., and εὐχείρωτον, Hom. VIII. (2).

future. So that God is at the same time a Judge, a Physician, and a Teacher; for as a Judge He examines, and as a Physician He amends, and as a Teacher He instructs those who have sinned, directing them unto all spiritual wisdom.

8. But if one short and simple speech thus demonstrates the care of God, what if we should read through this whole judgment, and unfold its entire records? Seest thou how all Scripture is consolation and comfort? But of these records we will speak at a befitting season; before that, however, it is necessary to state at what time this Book was given; for these things were not written in the beginning, nor at once when Adam was made,[1] but many generations afterwards; and it were worth while to enquire for what reason this delay took place, and why at length they were given to the Jews only, and not to all men; and why written in the Hebrew tongue; and why in the wilderness of Sinai? For the Apostle doth not mention the place merely in a cursory manner; but shews that in that circumstance too there was a great subject of contemplation for us, when he saith to us: "For these are two covenants, the one from Mount Sinai, which gendereth to bondage."[2]

9. Other things too besides these it were to our purpose to enquire into. But I see that the time doth not permit us to launch our discourse upon so wide a sea; wherefore prudently reserving these to a fit season, we would again address you on the subject of abstinence from oaths; and we would entreat your Charity to use much diligence respecting this matter. For what is it but an absurdity, that not even a servant dares to call his master by name, nor to mention him unceremoniously, and casually, but that he should everywhere bandy about the name of the Lord of Angels familiarly with much irreverence! And if it be necessary to take the book of the Gospel, thou receivest it with hands that have been first washed; and fearfully and tremblingly, with much reverence and devotion; and dost thou unceremoniously bandy about upon thy tongue the Lord of the Gospel? Dost thou desire to learn how the Powers above pronounce that Name; with what awe, with what terror, with what wonder? "I saw the Lord," saith the prophet, "sitting upon a throne, high, and lifted up; around Him stood the Seraphim; and one cried unto another, and said, Holy, Holy, Holy, Lord God of Sabaoth; the whole earth is full of His glory!"[3] Perceivest thou, with what dread, with what awe, they pronounce that Name, whilst glorifying and praising Him? But thou, in thy prayers and supplications, callest upon Him with much listlessness; when it would become thee to be full of awe, and to be watchful and sober! But in oaths, where it is wholly unsuitable that this wonderful Name should be introduced, there thou makest a long string of divers forms of imprecation! What pardon then, or what excuse shall we have, howsoever we may plead this "custom"? It is said, that a certain heathen orator, by a kind of foolish habit, was continually moving his right shoulder as he went along.[4] He conquered this habit, however, by fastening sharp knives on each side over his shoulders, so that the fear of being cut controlled the member in its unseasonable movement by fear of the wound! Do thou too, then, act thus with regard to thy tongue, and instead of the knife, suspend over it the fear of God's chastisement, and thou wilt assuredly get the better! For it seems impossible, utterly impossible, that those should ever be overcome, who are solicitous and earnest about this, and really make it their business.

10. Ye applaud what is now said, but when ye have amended, ye will applaud in a greater degree not only us, but also yourselves; and ye will hear with more pleasure what is spoken; and ye will call upon God with a pure conscience, who is so sparing of thee, O man! that He saith, "Neither shalt thou swear by[5] thy head."[6] But thou so despisest Him as to swear even by His glory. "But what shall I do," saith one, "with those who impose necessity on me?" What kind of necessity can there be, O man? Let all men understand that thou wilt choose to suffer anything rather than transgress the law of God; and they will abstain from compelling thee. For as a proof that it is not an oath which rendereth a man worthy of credit, but the testimony of his life, the uprightness of his conversation, and his good reputation, many have often split their throats with swearing, and yet have been able to convince no one; whereas others by a mere expression of assent, have been esteemed more deserving

---

[1] γενομένου. This seems the usual meaning, as Plut. *Mor.* p. 109 (cit. Steph.) ἀλλ' οἴει σὺ διαφορὰν εἶναι ἢ μὴ γένεσθαι ἢ γενόμενον ἀπογένεσθαι; but Luc. ix. 36, γένεσθαι seems to mean the completion of an event. He is speaking, however, of the whole Bible, or at least the Pentateuch, not merely of the history of the Fall, as appears from the sequel. Hom. VIII. 2, and the general argument of those which follow.
[2] Gal. iv. 24.
[3] Is. vi. 3.
[4] Demosthenes. Libanius says that it was in speaking he did this, and that he cured himself by hanging a sword before his shoulder in his private practice. Life of Dem. in *Orat. Att.* t. iv. and so Plutarch. St. Chrys. mentions him also on St. Matt. Hom. XVII. Ben. p. 232 a., βαδίζων may possibly be applied to the course of a speech.
[5] κατά, "against," and so on St. Matt. Hom. XVII., Ben. p. 228 e., but Griesbach gives no reading except ἐν.
[6] Matt. v. 36.

of belief than they who swore never so much. Knowing, therefore, all these things, and placing before our eyes the punishment that is in store for those who swear, as well as for those who swear falsely, let us abstain from this evil custom, that advancing from hence to the correction of what remains, we may enjoy the blessedness of the life to come, which God grant that we may all be found worthy to obtain, by the grace and love toward man of our Lord Jesus Christ, through Whom and with Whom to the Father with the Holy Ghost be glory, and power, and honour, now and ever, and world without end. Amen.

HOMILY VIII.

An exhortation to virtue—and particularly upon the passage, "God was walking in Paradise in the cool of the day:"—and again on the subject of abstaining from oaths.

YE have lately heard, how all Scripture bringeth consolation and comfort, although it be an historical narrative. For instance, "In the beginning, God created the heaven and the earth,"[1] was an historical declaration; but it was shewn in our discourse, that this sentence was one pregnant with comfort; as, for example, that God made us a twofold table,[2] by spreading out the sea and the land at the same time; by kindling above the twofold lights, the sun and moon; by determining the twofold seasons of their course, the day and night, the one for labour, and the other for rest. For the night ministers to us no less benefit than the day. But as I said with reference to trees, those which are barren, rival in their utility those which bear fruit; since we are thus not necessitated to touch those trees which are pleasant for food, for the purposes of building. The wild and untamed animals are also subservient to our need, in no less a degree than the tame animals; by driving us together, through the fear of them, into cities; making us more cautious, and binding us to one another; and by exercising the strength of some, and freeing others from their sicknesses; for the physicians concoct many medicines out of these;[3] and by reminding us of our ancient sin. For when I hear it said, "The fear of you, and the dread of you, shall be upon all the wild beasts of the earth:"[4] and then observe, that this honour was afterwards curtailed, I am reminded of sin, which hath dissipated the fear of us, and undermined our authority. Thus I become a better and a wiser[5] man, whilst I learn the harm that sin hath occasioned us. As then, what I said was, that the things alluded to, and others of a similar kind, which God, who is the Maker, knoweth of, contribute not a little to our present life; so now also I say, that the night no less than the day brings along with it its advantage, being a rest from labours, and a medicine for disease. Often, indeed, physicians, though exerting themselves in many ways, and preparing an endless variety of remedies, are not able to deliver the man who is labouring under infirmity. But sleep coming upon him of its own accord hath entirely removed the disease, and freed them[6] from an infinite deal of trouble. Night, again, is not only a medicine for bodily labours, but also for mental diseases, in giving rest to anguished souls. Ofttimes it happeneth that some one hath lost a son;[7] and comforters without number have been of no avail to withdraw him from tears and groans. But on the approach of night, conquered by the despotic power[8] of sleep, he hath closed his eyelids in slumber, and received some small relief from the miseries of the day time.

2. And now, I pray you, let us proceed to the subject which hath given rise to these observations. For well I know, that ye are all eagerly awaiting this matter; and that each one of you is in pain till he learn on what account this Book was not given from the beginning. But even now I do not see that the

---

[1] Gen. i. 1.
[2] τράπεζαν, *i. e.*, of refreshment, as "for thee and for thy recreation," Hom. VII. (3). What he says presently of the trees has not occurred in these Homilies.
[3] Viz. the wild animals: l. xxviii. of Pliny's Natural History is devoted to "medicines from animals."
[4] Gen. ix. 2.
[5] Or, more sober, σωφρονέστερος.   [6] The physicians.
[7] Comp. Apoll. *Rhod. Arg.* iii. 746,
"The traveller now,
And the tired porter, claimed the boon of sleep,
The mother's self, of children late bereaved,
Sunk in deep slumber lay."
and Virgil's imitation, *Æn.* iv. 522.
[8] τυραννίδι.

time is fit for a discourse on this subject. And why so? Because the week hath nearly arrived at its close with us, and I fear to touch upon a subject, the exposition of which I should presently afterwards be obliged to cut short. For the subject requires of us several days in succession, and a continuous effort of memory: wherefore we must again defer it.[1] But take it not amiss! we will assuredly pay you the debt with interest; for thus it is expedient both for you, and for us who are to discharge it. Meanwhile, however, let us now speak on that subject which we left out yesterday. And what was it we left out yesterday? "God was walking," it says, "in Paradise in the cool of the day."[2] What is here meant, I ask? "God was walking!" God was not walking; for how should He do this who is everywhere present, and filleth all things? But He caused a perception of this sort in Adam, in order that he might collect[3] himself; that he might not be careless; that in flying and in hiding himself, he might present beforehand some portion of the excuse, even before any words had passed. For even as those who are about to be led to the tribunal, to sustain the charges respecting the crimes they have committed, present themselves before those who are to try them with a squalid, begrimed, sad, and subdued visage, in order that from their appearance, they may incline them to lovingkindness, mercy, and forgiveness, so also did it happen in the case of Adam. For it was necessary that he should be led to this Tribunal in a subdued state. Therefore God took him beforehand, and humbled him. But that some one was walking there, he perceived; but whence came he to suppose that God was walking there? Such is the habitual custom of those who have committed sin. They are suspicious of all things; they tremble at shadows; they are in terror at every sound, and they imagine that every one is approaching them in a hostile manner. Often therefore the guilty, when they observe people running on another business, suppose that they are come against them; and when others are conversing one with another on quite a different subject, they that are conscious of sin suppose they are conversing about them.

3. For such is the nature of sin, that it betrays whilst no one finds fault; it condemns whilst no one accuses; it makes the sinner a timid being; one that trembles at a sound; even as righteousness has the contrary effect. Hear, at least, how the Scripture describes this cowardice of the former, and this boldness of the latter. "The wicked flee when no man pursueth."[4] How doth he flee when no man pursueth? He hath that within which drives him on—an accuser in his conscience; and this he carries about everywhere; and just as it would be impossible to flee from himself, so neither can he escape the persecutor within; but wherever he goeth,[5] he is scourged, and hath an incurable wound! But not such is the righteous man. Of what nature then is he? Hear: "The righteous is bold as a lion!" Such a man was Elias. He saw, for instance, the king coming towards him, and when he said, "Why is it that thou pervertest Israel?"[6] he answered, "I pervert not Israel, but thou and thy father's house."[7] Truly, the just man is bold as a lion; for he stood up against the king just as a lion doth against some vile cur. Although the one had the purple, the other had the sheepskin, which was the more venerable garment of the two; for that purple brought forth the grievous famine; but this sheepskin effected a liberation from that calamity! It divided the Jordan! It made Elisha a twofold[8] Elias! O how great is the virtue of the Saints! Not only their words; not only their bodies, but even their very garments are always esteemed venerable by the whole creation. The sheepskin of this man divided the Jordan! the sandals of the Three Children trampled down the fire! The word of Elisha changed the waters, so that it made them to bear the iron on their surface! The rod of Moses divided the Red Sea and cleft[9] the rock! The garments of Paul expelled diseases! The shadow of Peter put death to flight! The ashes of the holy Martyrs[10] drive away demons! For this reason they do all things with authority, even as Elias did. For he looked not on the diadem, nor the outward pomp[11] of the king, but he looked on the soul clad in rags, squalid, begrimed, and in a more wretched condition than that of any criminal; and seeing him the captive and slave of his passions, he despised his power. For he seemed to see a king but in a scene,

---

[1] Tillemont places this Homily on Friday, but the reference to the last is "lately," not "yesterday," so that it was probably delivered on Saturday, as Montfaucon supposes. The Ben. reading gives, "For a subject of several days in succession requires a continued recollection," &c.
[2] Gen. iii. 8.
[3] συστείλῃ. See Rom. xii. 1, Hom. XX., where it is used of reverence.

[4] Prov. xxviii. 1. [5] Sav. and M., ἀπίῃ.
[6] ἵνα τί διαστρέφεις. There is no authority for *why dost thou*, instead of *art thou he that*. The word *pervertest* is the LXX. rendering of עֹכֵר, *disturbest*, and seems to mean "turnest from right worship," or "from allegiance;" but the meaning of the Hebrew seems to be *troublest* (*i. e.*, with famine), as in E. V.: comp. Jos. vii. 25, where they render it "destroy."
[7] 1 Kings xviii. 17, 18. [8] See Hom. II. 25.
[9] Ps. lxxviii. 15.
[10] See Hom. I. 5. The like is said of the relics of St. Epiphanius, in the second part of the Homily against the Peril of Idolatry, quoted from Cassiodori *Hist. Eccl. Trip.* ix. 48 (Soz. vii. 27).
[11] φαντασία.

and not a real one. For what was the advantage of outward abundance, when the poverty within was so great? And what harm could outward poverty do, when there was such a treasure of wealth within? Such a lion also was the blessed Paul; for when he had entered into the prison, and only raised his voice, he shook all the foundations; he gnawed in pieces[1] the fetters, employing not his teeth, but words; on which account it were fitting to call such men not merely lions, but something more than lions; for a lion ofttimes, after he hath fallen into a net, is taken; but the Saints when they are bound, become still more powerful; just as this blessed man did then in the prison, having loosed the prisoners, shaken the walls, and bound the keeper, and overcome him by the word of godliness. The lion uttereth his voice, and putteth all the wild beasts to flight. The Saint uttereth his voice, and driveth away the demons on every side! The weapons of the lion are a hairy mane, pointed claws, and sharp teeth. The weapons of the righteous man are spiritual wisdom, temperance, patience, contempt of all present things. Whoever hath these weapons shall not only be able to deride wicked men, but even the adverse powers themselves.

4. Study then, O man, the life according to God, and no one shall conquer thee at any time; and although thou mayest be accounted the most insignificant of men, thou shalt be more powerful than all. On the other hand, if thou art indifferent about virtue of soul, though thou wert the most powerful of men, thou wilt easily be worsted by all that assail thee. And the examples already quoted proved this. But if thou art desirous, I will also endeavour to teach thee by actual facts[2] the unconquerableness of the righteous, and the vulnerable condition of sinners. Hear then how the prophet intimates both these particulars. "The ungodly," saith he, "are not so, but are like the chaff which the wind scattereth away from the face of the earth."[3] For even as chaff lies exposed to the gusts of wind, and is easily caught up and swept along, so is also the sinner driven about by every temptation; for whilst he is at war with himself, and bears the warfare about with him, what hope of safety does he possess; betrayed as he is at home, and carrying with him that conscience, which is a constant enemy? Such, however, is not the nature of the righteous man. But what manner of man is he? Hear the same prophet, saying, "They that trust in the Lord are as Mount Zion."[4] What means then, "As Mount Zion?" "He shall not be shaken," saith he, "for ever." For whatever engines thou bringest up, whatever darts thou hurlest, desiring to overturn a mountain, thou wilt never be able to prevail; for how canst thou? thou wilt break in pieces all thine engines, and exhaust thine own strength. Such also is the righteous man. Whatever blows he may receive, he suffereth no evil therefrom; but destroyeth the power of those who take counsel against him, and not of men only, but of demons. Thou hast heard often what engines the Devil brought up against Job; but not only did he fail to overthrow that mountain, but drew back exhausted, his darts broken to pieces, and his engines rendered useless, by that assault!

5. Knowing these things, let us take heed to our life; and let us not be earnest as to the goods that perish; neither as to the glory that goeth out; nor as to that body which groweth old; nor as to that beauty which is fading; nor as to that pleasure which is fleeting; but let us expend all our care about the soul; and let us provide for the welfare of this in every way. For to cure the body, when diseased, is not an easy matter to every one; but to cure a sick soul is easy to all; and the sickness of the body requires medicines, as well as money, for its healing; but the healing of the soul is a thing that is easy to procure, and devoid of expense. And the nature of the flesh is with much labour delivered from those wounds which are troublesome; for very often the knife must be applied, and medicines that are bitter; but with respect to the soul there is nothing of this kind. It suffices only to exercise the will, and the desire, and all things are accomplished. And this hath been the work of God's providence. For inasmuch as from bodily sickness no great injury could arise, (for though we were not diseased, yet death would in any case come, and destroy and dissolve the body); but everything depends upon the health of our souls; this being by far the more precious and necessary, He hath made the medicining of it easy, and void of expense or pain. What excuse therefore, or what pardon shall we obtain, if when the body is sick, and money must be expended on its behalf, and physicians called in, and much anguish endured, we make this so much a matter of our care (though what might result from that sickness could be no great

---

[1] κατέφαγεν.
[2] He seems to mean "by experience," *i. e.*, if they would follow his advice. The new Coll. MSS., and from it Harmar, however, read δἰ ἑτέρων, "through other (examples)," which removes the difficulty.
[3] Ps. i. 5.
[4] Ps. cxxiv. 1.

injury to us), and yet treat the soul with neglect? And this, when we are neither called upon to pay down money; nor to give others any trouble; nor to sustain any sufferings; but without any of all these things, by only choosing and willing, have it in our power to accomplish the entire amendment of it; and knowing assuredly that if we fail to do this, we shall sustain the extreme sentence, and punishments, and penalties, which are inexorable! For tell me, if any one promised to teach thee the healing art in a short space of time, without money or labour, wouldest thou not think him a benefactor? Wouldest thou not submit both to do and to suffer all things, whatsoever he who promised these things commanded? Behold, now, it is permitted thee without labour to find a medicine for wounds, not of the body, but of the soul, and to restore it to a state of health, without any suffering! Let us not be indifferent to the matter! For pray what is the pain of laying aside anger against one who hath aggrieved thee? It is a pain, indeed, to remember injuries, and not to be reconciled! What labour is it to pray, and to ask for a thousand good things from God, who is ready to give? What labour is it, not to speak evil of any one? What difficulty is there in being delivered from envy and ill-will? What trouble is it to love one's neighbour? What suffering is it not to utter shameful words, nor to revile, nor to insult another? What fatigue is it not to swear? for again I return to this same admonition. The labour of swearing is indeed exceedingly great. Oftentimes, whilst under the influence of anger or wrath, we have sworn, perhaps, that we would never be reconciled to those who have injured us. Yet afterwards, when our wrath was quenched, and our anger allayed, desiring to be reconciled, and restrained by the obligation of these oaths, we have suffered the same anguish, as if we were in a snare, and held fast by indissoluble bonds. Of which fact the Devil being aware, and understanding clearly that anger is a fire; that it is easily extinguished, and that when it is extinguished, then reconciliation and love follows; wishing this fire to remain unquenched, he often binds us by an oath; so that although the anger should cease, the obligation of the oath remaining may keep up the fire within us; and that one of these two things may take place, either that being reconciled we are forsworn, or that not being reconciled we subject ourselves to the penalties of cherishing malice.

6. Knowing these things then, let us avoid oaths; and let our mouth continually practise the saying, "Believe me;"[1] and this will be to us a foundation for all pious behaviour;[2] for the tongue, when it has been disciplined to use this one expression, is ashamed, and would blush to utter words that are disgraceful and ugly; and should it at any time be drawn away by habit, it will be checked again, by having many accusers. For when any one observes him who is not a swearer giving utterance to foul words, he will take his advantage over him, and ridicule, and exclaim tauntingly, "Thou who sayest in all affairs, 'Believe me,' and venturest not to utter an oath, dost thou disgrace thy tongue with these shameful expressions?" So that being forcibly urged by those who are with us, even if unwilling, we shall return again to a pious behaviour. "But what," says one, "if it be necessary to take an oath?" Where there is a transgression of the law, there is no such thing as necessity. "Is it possible then," it is replied, "not to swear at all?" What sayest thou? Hath God commanded, and darest thou to ask if it be possible for His law to be kept? Why, truly it is a thing impossible that His law should not be kept; and I am desirous to persuade you from present circumstances of this; that so far from its being impossible not to swear, it is impossible to swear.[3] For behold, the inhabitants of the city were commanded to bring in a payment of gold,[4] such as it might have seemed beyond the power of many to do; yet the greater part of the sum has been collected; and you may hear the tax gatherers saying, "Why delay, man? Why put us off from day to day? It is not possible to avoid it. It is the law of the Emperor, which admits of no delay." What sayest thou, I ask? The Emperor hath commanded thee to bring in thy money, and it is impossible not to bring it in! God hath commanded thee to avoid oaths! and how sayest thou, it is impossible to avoid them!

7. I am now for the sixth day admonishing you in respect of this precept. Henceforth, I am desirous to take leave[5] of you, meaning to abstain from the subject, that ye may be on your guard. There will no longer be any excuse or allowance for you; for of right, indeed, if nothing had been said on this matter, it ought to have been amended of yourselves, for it is not a thing of an intricate

---

[1] *i. e.*, instead of any stronger asseverations.
[2] εὐλαβείας.
[3] That is, assuming men to act as reasonably in their relations to God, as they do in their relations to man.
[4] The tax which was demanded previously to the sedition, and before alluded to, Hom. III. 18.
[5] συντάξασθαι, used as ἀποτάξασθαι (that word having passed rather to the sense of renouncing, see St. Cyr. *Hier. Cat.* xix.). See Du Cange, who quotes *Conc. Chalc.* act i., and many other passages.

nature, or that requires great preparation. But since ye have enjoyed the advantage of so much admonition and counsel, what excuse will ye have to offer, when ye stand accused before that dread tribunal, and are required to give account of this transgression. It is impossible to invent any excuse; but of necessity you must either go hence amended, or, if you have not amended, be punished, and abide the extremest penalty! Thinking, therefore, upon all these things, and departing hence with much anxiety about them, exhort ye one another, that the things spoken of during so many days may be kept with all watchfulness in your minds, so that whilst we are silent, ye instructing, edifying, exhorting one another, may exhibit great improvement; and having fulfilled all the other precepts, may enjoy eternal crowns; which God grant we may all obtain, through the grace and lovingkindness of our Lord Jesus Christ, by whom and with whom be glory, to the Father, together with the Holy Ghost, for ever and ever. Amen.

HOMILY IX.

Commendation of those who had laid aside the practice of swearing. It is shown that no one need scruple about hearing the divine oracles in the Church after a meal. Answer to the question, Why it was so long before the Holy Scriptures were given? Comment on the passage, "The heavens declare the glory of God," with a description of the natural world. And finally, an admonition against swearing.

1. It was but lately that I spoke to you as I do now to you again! And O that I could be always with you,—yea, rather am I always with you, though not by bodily presence, yet by the power of love! For I have no other life but[1] you, and the care of your salvation. As the husbandman hath no other anxiety, but about his seeds and his harvests; and the pilot about the waves and the harbours; so the preacher is anxious with respect to his auditors and their progress, even as I am at the present time! Wherefore I bear you all upon my mind, not only here, but also at home. For if the multitude be great, and the measure of my heart be narrow, yet love is wide; and "ye are not straitened in us." I will not add what follows next,[2] for neither are we straitened with you. Whence is this apparent? Because I have met with many who have said, "We have performed the precept, by making rules for each other, defining penalties for those who swear, and enforcing punishment upon those who transgress this law." A punishment which is indeed well becoming you,[3] and which is a sign of the greatest charity. For I am not ashamed of making myself busy in these matters, since this love of interference does not proceed from idle curiosity but from tender care.[4] For if it be no reproach to the physician to make enquiry concerning the patient, neither is it any fault in us to be ever asking about your salvation; since thus being informed what has been accomplished, and what has been left undone, we shall be able to apply the further remedies with the requisite knowledge.[5] These things we have ascertained by enquiry; and we give thanks to God that we have not sown our seed upon rocks, nor dropped it amidst thorns; and that we have neither needed much time, nor long delay, in order that we might reap the harvest. On this account I have you continually upon my heart. On this account I do not feel the labours of teaching, being eased of the burden by the profit of the hearer. This reward is, indeed, sufficient to recruit our strength, to give us wings, to elevate us, and to persuade us to undergo the utmost toil on your behalf.

2. Since therefore ye have manifested much generosity of feeling, suffer us to discharge the further debt of which we gave a promise the other day; although indeed I see not all present[6] who were here when I made the

---

[1] Comp. Phil. i. 24, Country Parson, c. 7.
[2] Alluding to the passage, 2 Cor. vi. 11, 12. *Ye are not straitened in us, but ye are straitened in your own bowels.*
[3] He seems to mean those who voluntarily submitted to it. He had recommended masters to punish themselves, as well as their dependents. See above.
[4] Country Parson, c. 32.   [5] Country Parson, c. 34.
[6] This Homily is placed by Montfaucon on the Monday after the last; it is difficult to find any especial reason for the circumstance here referred to; there was the same impediment when the following Homily was delivered. Perhaps the most probable account is, that some persons began the fast with a strictness from

promise. What, I would ask, can be the cause of this? What hath repelled them from our table? He that hath partaken of a bodily meal, it would seem, has thought it an indignity after receiving material food, to come to the hearing of the divine oracles. But not rightly do they think thus. For if this were improper, Christ would not have gone through His large and long discourses after that mystic supper; and if this had been unsuitable, He would not, when He had fed the multitude in the desert, have communicated His discourses to them after that meal. For (if one must say something startling on this point), the hearing of the divine oracles at that time is especially profitable. For when thou hast made up thy mind that after eating and drinking thou must repair also to the assembly, thou wilt assuredly be careful, though perchance with reluctance, of the duty of sobriety; and wilt neither be led away at any time into excess of wine, or gluttony. For the thought, and the expectation of entering the church, schools thee to partake of food and drink with becoming decency; lest, after thou hast entered there, and joined thy brethren, thou shouldest appear ridiculous to all present, by smelling of wine, and unmannerly eructation.[1] These things I now speak not to you who are now present, but to the absent; that they may learn them through your means. For it is not having eaten that hinders one's hearing, but listlessness. But thou whilst deeming it to be a condemnation not to fast, then addest another fault, which is far greater and heavier, in not being a partaker of this sacred food;[2] and having nourished the body, thou consumest the soul with famine. Yet what kind of apology hast thou for doing this? For in the matter of fasting thou hast, perhaps, bodily weakness to plead, but what hast thou to say with respect to hearing? For surely weakness of body is no impediment to thy partaking of the divine oracles! If I had said, "Let no one who has breakfasted[3] mix with us;" "let no one who has eaten be a hearer," thou wouldest have had some kind of excuse; but now, when we would fain drag, entice, and beseech you to come, what apology can ye have for turning away from us? The unfit hearer is not he that hath eaten and drunk; but he who gives no heed to what is said, who yawns, and is slack in attention, having his body here, but his mind wandering elsewhere, and such a one, though he may be fasting, is an unprofitable hearer. On the other hand, the man who is in earnest, who is watchful and keeps his mind in a state of attention, though he may have eaten and drunk, will be our most suitable hearer of all. For this rule, indeed, very properly prevails with relation to the secular tribunals and councils. Inasmuch as they know not how to be spiritually wise, therefore they eat not to nourishment, but to bursting; and they drink often to excess. For this reason, as they render themselves unfit for the management of their affairs, they shut up the court-houses and council-chambers in the evening and at midday.[4] But here there is nothing of this sort, —God forbid! But he who has eaten will rival him who fasts, as far as regards sobriety of soul; for he eats and drinks, not so as to distend the stomach, or to darken the reason, but in such a way as to recruit the strength of the body when it has become weakened.

3. But enough of this admonition. It is time now to deal with our subject; although our mind holds back and shrinks from giving this instruction, on account of those who are not come. And just as an affectionate mother when she is about to spread out her table, grieves and laments when all her children are not there, thus also do I now suffer; and when I think of the absence of our brethren, I am reluctant to discharge my debt. But ye have it in your power to rid me of this tardiness. For if ye promise me that ye will convey to them an exact report of all I say, we shall readily pay you down the whole;[5] for thus the instruction, charitably afforded on your part, will make up to them for their absence; and ye will hear me the more attentively, knowing that you must necessarily give an account of these things to others. In order then that our subject may be made the clearer, let us take it up and repeat it from the beginning. We were enquiring, then, the other day, "On what account the Scriptures were delivered after so many years. For this Book was delivered neither in the time of Adam, nor of Noah, nor of Abraham, but in that of Moses. And I hear many who say, that if the Book was profitable, it ought to

---

which they afterwards fell off. The meal spoken of was an early dinner. Eumæus takes his ἄριστον at daybreak, Od. xvi. 2. But Athenæus, l. i. c. 9 and 10, says that in his day such a meal was called ἀκράτισμα, and the δεῖπνον of the ancients, at mid-day, ἄριστον (quoted by Perizonius on Ælian. V. H. ix. 19).

[1] πολλάκις. But Sav. and M. πολλῆς, making the sense, "thou wilt assuredly, even if unwilling, observing great sobriety."

[2] i. e., the oracles of Scripture explained at church. (See Hom. II. 12.) The Holy Communion was always received fasting.

[3] ἠριστηκώς.

[4] A canon of Isaac Lingonensis (in the eighth century), Tit. viii. cap. 2, Labbe viii. 620, forbids any one to take an oath except fasting. The Athenian courts did not sit after sunset, and the great time for forensic business was the forenoon. Goeller on Thuc. viii. 92. Ælian, V. H. xii. 30, says that the luxurious Tarentines would be drunk even when the forum is fullest, περὶ πλήθουσαν ἀγοράν. v. Act. ii. 15; Perizonius on Ælian, cites Dio Chrys. Or. 67, de Glor. 2, who shews it was about that time.

[5] i. e., the promise of explaining that subject which had been proposed in the two foregoing Homilies; namely, the reason why the gift of Holy Scripture was so long delayed.

have been delivered from the very beginning; but if it was useless, it ought not to have been delivered afterwards. But this is an obsolete argument; for it is not quite true that anything which is profitable ought to have been delivered from the beginning, nor if anything was delivered from the beginning, is it quite necessary that the same should continue afterwards.[1] For example; Milk is useful, yet it is not always given; but it is given to us only when we are children; and solid food is useful; but no one ever gives it us in the beginning of our life, but when we have passed out of the age of childhood. Again, the summer season is useful; but it does not shew itself constantly; and the winter season is advantageous; yet this too makes room for others. What then? Do they say that the Scriptures are not useful? I reply; they are most useful and most necessary. And if so useful, for what reason then, say they, were they not delivered to us from the beginning? It was because God was desirous of instructing the nature of man, not by letters, but by things.[2] But what does the expression "by things" signify? By means of the Creation itself.

4. Observe then, how the Apostle, alighting upon this same topic, and directing himself to those very Greeks who said, that they had not from the beginning learnt the knowledge of God from the Scriptures, frames his answer. Having said that, "the wrath of God is revealed from heaven against all ungodliness and unrighteousness of men, who hold the truth in unrighteousness;"[3] when he saw that he was met by an objection; and that many would still enquire, from whence the Gentiles knew the truth of God, he goes on to add, "Because that which may be known of God is manifest in them." But how is it manifest in them? How were they able to know God, and who hath shewed? Declare this. "God," saith he, "hath shewed it unto them." In what manner? By the sending of what kind of prophet? what evangelist? what kind of teacher? if the holy Scriptures were not yet given. "The invisible things of Him," says he, "from the creation of the world are clearly seen, being understood by the things that are made, even His eternal Power and Godhead."[4] But what he means is just this, He hath placed His Creation in the midst, before the eyes of all men; in order that they may guess at the Creator from His works; which, indeed, another writer has referred to; "For from the greatness and beauty of the creatures, proportionably the Maker of them is seen."[5] Seest thou the greatness? Marvel at the power of Him that made it! Seest thou the beauty? be astonished at the wisdom which adorned it! This it was which the prophet signified when he said, "The heavens declare the glory of God."[6] How then, tell me, do they declare it? Voice they have none; mouth they possess not; no tongue is theirs! how then do they declare? By means of the spectacle itself. For when thou seest the beauty, the breadth, the height, the position, the form, the stability thereof during so long a period; hearing as it were a voice, and being instructed by the spectacle, thou adorest Him who created a body so fair and strange! The heavens may be silent, but the sight of them emits a voice, that is louder than a trumpet's sound; instructing us not by the ear, but through the medium of the eyes; for the latter is a sense which is more sure and more distinct than the former.

5. For if God had given instruction by means of books, and of letters, he who knew letters would have learnt what was written; but the illiterate man would have gone away without receiving any benefit from this source, unless some one else had introduced him to it; and the wealthy man would have purchased the Bible, but the poor man would not have been able to obtain it. Again, he who knew the language that was expressed by the letters, might have known what was therein contained; but the Scythian, and the Barbarian, and the Indian, and the Egyptian, and all those who were excluded from that language, would have gone away without receiving any instruction. This however cannot be said with respect to the heavens; but the Scythian, and Barbarian, and Indian, and Egyptian, and every man that walks upon the earth, shall hear this voice; for not by means of the ears, but through the sight, it reaches our understanding. And of the things that are seen, there is one uniform perception; and there is no difference, as is the case with respect to languages. Upon this volume the unlearned, as well as the wise man, shall be alike able to look; the poor man as well as the rich man; and wherever any one may chance to come, there looking upwards towards the heavens, he will receive a sufficient lesson from the view of them: and the

---

[1] See Butler's *Analogy*, p. ii. c. 6, where the somewhat similar objection, "that Christianity is not universal," is discussed.
[2] An enlarged view of this principle is given in Butler's *Analogy*, p. ii. c. 7, applying it further to the facts recorded in Holy Scripture. "The general design of Scripture, which contains in it this revelation, thus considered as historical, may be said to be, to give us an account of the world, in this one single view, *as God's world.*"
[3] Rom. i. 18. [4] Rom. i. 20. [5] Wisd. xiii. 5. [6] Ps. xix. 1.

prophet himself intimated and indicated this fact, that the creation utters this voice so as to be intelligible to barbarians, and to Greeks, and to all mankind without exception, when he spoke on this wise; "There is no speech, nor language, where there voice is not heard."[1] What he means is to this effect, that there is no nation or tongue which is unable to understand this language; but that such is their utterance, that it may be heard of all mankind. And that not merely of the heavens, but of the day and night. But how of the day and night? The heavens, indeed, by their beauty and magnitude, and by all the rest, astonish the beholder, and transport him to an admiration of the Creator; but as to the day and night, what can these show us of the same kind? Nothing certainly of the same kind, but other things which are not inferior to them; as for example; the harmony, and the order which they so accurately observe. For when thou considerest how they distribute between them the whole year, and mutually divide the length of the whole space, even as if it were by a beam and scales, thou wilt be astonished at Him who hath ordered them! For just as certain sisters dividing their father's inheritance among themselves with much affection, and not insulting one another in the smallest degree, even so too the day and the night distribute the year with such an equality of parts, with the utmost accuracy;[2] and keep to their own boundaries, and never push one another aside. Never hath the day been long in winter; and in like manner never hath the night been long in summer, whilst so many generations have passed away; but during so great an interval and length of time one hath not defrauded the other even in the smallest degree; not of half an hour's space, no, nor of the twinkling of an eye!

6. Therefore also the Psalmist,[3] struck with astonishment at the equality of this distribution, exclaimed, "Night unto night sheweth knowledge." If thou knowest how to meditate wisely on these matters, thou wilt admire the Being who fixed these immoveable boundaries even from the beginning. Let the avaricious hear these things; and those who are coveting the wealth of others; and let them imitate the equality of the day and night. Let those who are puffed up and high-minded also hear; and those who are unwilling to concede the first places to others!

The day gives place to the night, and does not invade the territory of others! But thou, whilst always enjoying honour, canst thou not bear to share it with thy brethren? Consider also with me the wisdom of the Lawgiver. In winter He hath ordered that the night should be long; when the germs[4] are tender, and require more coolness; and are unable to sustain the hotter rays of the sun; but when they are somewhat grown, the day again increases with them, and becomes then the longest, when the fruit has now attained ripeness. And this is a beneficial arrangement not only for seeds, but for our bodies. For since during winter, the sailor, and the pilot, and the traveller, and the soldier, and the farmer, sit down for the most part at home, fettered by the frost; and the season is one of idleness; God hath appointed that the greater part of this time should be consumed in night, in order that the length of the day might not be superfluous, when men were unable to do anything. Who can describe the perfect order of the seasons; and how these, like some virgins dancing in a circle, succeed one another with the happiest harmony; and how those who are in the middle cease not to pass over to the opposite ones with a gradual and noiseless transition? Therefore, neither are we overtaken by the summer immediately after winter; nor by the winter immediately after the summer; but mid-way the spring is interposed; that while we gently and gradually take up one season after the other, we may have our bodies hardened to encounter the summer heat without uneasiness. For since sudden changes to opposite extremes are productive of the worst injury and disease, God hath contrived that after winter we should take up the spring, and after the spring the summer; and after the summer the autumn; and thus transport us to winter, so that these changes from seasons which are opposite, should come upon us harmlessly and by degrees, through the aid of intermediate ones. Who then is so wretched and pitiable, that beholding the heavens; and beholding sea, and land; and beholding this exact adjustment of the seasons, and the unfailing order of day and night, he can think that these things happen of their own accord, instead of adoring Him who hath arranged them all with a corresponding wisdom!

7. But I have yet somewhat more to say on this head. For not only, indeed, does the magnitude and beauty of the creation, but

---

[1] Ps. xix. 3.
[2] The diurnal motion of the earth, or, as they called it, of the heavens, was taken by Plato for the very type of stability. The exactness of its rate is far greater than the ancients had means to appreciate, as is proved by constant observations, as well as by the oldest eclipses.
[3] ψαλμῳδὸς: St. Chrys. usually says "the prophet."
[4] σπέρματα. He seems to mean the young blade. These remarks are adapted to a climate in which the harvest is over before midsummer.

also the very manner of it, display a God who is the artificer of the universe. For since we were not present at the beginning, whilst he was engaged in the work of forming and creating all things; nor had we been present, could we have known how they came into being,[1] the power that disposed them being invisible; He hath made the mode of this creation to become our best teacher, by compounding all things in a manner which transcends the course of nature. Perhaps what I have said, is not sufficiently clear. Therefore it is necessary that I should again repeat it in a clearer manner. All men, then, must admit that it is the course of nature for water to be supported on the earth, and not the earth on the waters. For the earth being a certain dense, hard, unyielding, and solid substance, is easily able to support the nature of water; but the water, which is fluid, and rare, and soft, and diffusive, and giving way to all it meets with, must be unable to support any solid body, though it were of the lightest kind. Often indeed when a small pebble falls upon it, it yields, and makes way, and sends it down to the bottom. When therefore thou beholdest not a small pebble, but the whole earth borne upon the waters, and not submerged, admire the power of Him who wrought these marvellous things in a supernatural manner! And whence does this appear, that the earth is borne upon the waters? The prophet declares this when he says, "He hath founded it upon the seas, and prepared it upon the floods."[2] And again: "To him who hath founded the earth upon the waters."[3] What sayest thou? The water is not able to support a small pebble on its surface, and yet bears up the earth, great as it is; and mountains, and hills, and cities, and plants, and men, and brutes; and it is not submerged! What do I say? Is not submerged? How comes it to pass, that since the water has been in close contact with it below, during so long a period, it has not been dissolved, and the whole of it become mud? For the substance of wood, when soaked in water but a little time, is rotted and dissolved; and why do I say of wood? What can be firmer than iron? yet often this is softened, when it remains a long time in water; and well it may. For it derives its substance from the earth. Therefore many run-away servants, when they make their escape, dragging their shackles and chains along with them, go to brooks of water, and thrust their shackled feet therein, and after making the iron softer by this means, they easily break it by striking it with a stone. Iron, forsooth, is softened, and wood is rotted, and stones are worn away by the nature of water; yet so great a mass as the earth hath remained such a length of time lying upon the waters, without being either submerged, or dissolved, and destroyed![4]

8. And who is there that must not feel astonished and amazed at these things; and confidently pronounce that they are not the works of nature, but of that Providence which is above nature? Therefore one speaks thus: "Who hangeth the earth upon nothing."[5] And another observes, "In His hands are the corners of the earth."[6] And again: "He hath laid the foundation of it upon the seas."[7] And these declarations, though they seem contrary to one another, have yet an entire agreement. For he that said, "He hath laid the foundation of it upon the seas," meant the same thing as he did who declared, "He hath hung it upon nothing." For its standing upon the waters is just the same thing as hanging upon nothing. Where then is it suspended and placed? Hear the same one saying, "In His hands are the corners of the earth." Not that God hath hands, but that thou mayest know that His power it is, providing for all things which holds together[8] and supports the body of the earth! But if thou believest not what I now say, believe what thou beholdest! for even in another element it is possible to find this admirable workmanship. For it is the nature of fire to tend upwards,[9] and to be always mounting aloft; and although you force and constrain it never so much, it cannot submit to have its course directed downwards. For often, when we are carrying a lighted torch, although we incline its head downwards, we cannot compel the force of the flame to direct

---

[1] See Job xxxviii. 4. [2] Ps. xxiv. 2.
[3] Ps. cxxxvi. 6. Among the variety of opinions that anciently prevailed respecting the earth's form and situation, one of the principal was, that the heavens and earth above this ocean was the only visible universe ; and that all beneath the ocean was Hades, or the invisible world. Hence when the sun set, he was said, *tingere se oceano ;* and when any went to Hades, they must first pass the ocean. Of this opinion were not only the ancient poets, but some of the Christian Fathers, particularly Lactantius, and St. Augustin, and others, who thought their opinion was favoured by the Psalmist, in Ps. xxiv. 2, and cxxxvi. 6. Derham's *Physico-Theology*, p. 41. St. Chrysostom must evidently have adopted the same opinion. St. Greg. Nyss. *in Hexaem.* t. l., p. 22 e., speaks of the earth's conical shadow. See Plin. ii. 11. St. Bas. *in Hex.* i. c. 9, explains the "founding on the waters," of their being spread all round : ix. c. 1, he speaks of various opinions as to its shape, and some who thought it to be 180,000 stadia round. See St. Greg. Naz. *Or.* xxviii. al. xxxiv. c. 28, and Philoponus *de Mund. Cr.* iii. 6-13; Galland, xii. p. 525.

[4] This line of argument, from arrangements above the course of nature, is a dangerous one ; and it would be less difficult than invidious, to search out instances of fallacy in modern writers. It always brings men's *ignorance* into play.
[5] Job xxvi. 7. [6] Ps. xcv. 4. [7] Ps. xxiv. 2.
[8] συγκρατοῦσα, but Sav. συγκροτοῦσα. There is constant variation of reading wherever these words occur.
[9] See in Bacon's *Novum Organum*, his *Vindemiatio prima de forma calidi*, L. II. Aph. 20, Diff. 2, he says, "the motion of heat is at once expansive, and a tendency upwards."

itself to the ground; but still it turns upward, and passes from below toward that which is above. But with respect to the sun, God hath made it quite the contrary. For He hath turned his beams toward the earth, and made his light to direct itself downward, all but saying to him by the very shape (of the heavens), "Look downward.—Shine upon men, for thou wert made for them!" The light, indeed, of a candle cannot be made to submit to this; but this star, great and marvellous as it is, bends downward, and looks toward the earth, which is contrary to the nature of fire; owing to the power of Him who hath commanded it. Wouldest thou have me speak of another thing of the like kind? Waters embrace the back of the visible heaven[1] on all parts; and yet they neither flow down, nor are moved out of their place, although the nature of water is not of this kind. For it easily runs together into what is concave; but when the body is of a convex form, it glides away on all sides; and not even a small portion[2] is capable of standing upon such a figure.[3] But, lo! this wonder is found to exist in the heavens; and the prophet, again, to intimate this very circumstance, observes, "Praise the Lord, ye waters that are above the heavens."[4] Besides, the water hath not quenched the sun; nor hath the sun, which hath gone on his way beneath for so long a time, dried up the water that lies above.

9. Dost thou desire that we should lead thee down again to the earth, and point out the marvel? Seest thou not this sea abounding with waves, and fierce winds; yet this sea, spacious, and large, and furious as it is, is walled in with a feeble sand! Mark also the wisdom of God, He permitted it not to be at rest, nor tranquil, lest thou shouldest suppose its good order to be of mere natural regulation; but remaining within its limits, it lifts up its voice, and is in tumult, and roars aloud, and raises its waves to a prodigious height. But when it comes to the shores, and beholds the sand, it breaks up, and returns back again within itself; teaching thee, by both these things, that it is not the work of nature that it remains within its boundaries, but the work of Him whose power restrains it! For this cause accordingly He hath made the wall feeble; and hath not encompassed these shores with wood, or stone, or mountains, lest thou shouldest impute the regulation of the elements to such things. And, therefore, God Himself, upbraiding the Jews with this very circumstance, said, "Fear ye not Me, which have placed the sand for the bound of the sea that it cannot pass it."[5] But the marvellous thing is not this only, that He hath made a great and admirable world; and that He hath compacted it in a way above the usual course of nature; but that He hath also constituted it out of opposite things; such as hot and cold, dry and moist, fire and water, earth and air, and that these contrary elements, of which this whole universe consists, though continually at strife one with another, are not consumed of one another. The fire hath not overrun and burnt up all things; the water hath not overflowed and drowned the whole earth. With respect to our bodies, however, these effects really take place; and upon the increase of the bile, fever is generated; and the whole animal frame sustains an injury; and when there is a superabundance of phlegm, many diseases are produced which destroy the animal. But in the case of the universe, nothing of this kind happens; but each thing remains held as it were by a kind of bridle and band; preserving, by the will of the Creator, its own boundaries; and their strife becomes a source of peace to the whole. Are not these things evident even to a blind man? and are not even the simple easily able to comprehend, that they were made, and are upheld, by some Providence? For who is so silly and senseless, that beholding such a mass of substances, such beauty, such combination, the continual strife of such vast elements, their opposition, and yet durability, would not reason with himself and say, "If there were not some Providence to uphold the mass of these bodies, not permitting the universe to fall to pieces, it could not remain; it could not have been lasting. So perfect is the order of the seasons, such the harmony of the day and night, so many the kinds of brute animals, and plants, and seeds, and herbs, that preserve their course, and yet, to the present day, none has ever fallen into decay or sudden dissolution.

10. We might continue to speak not only of these things, but also of many others, which are even more profound; and might moralise even upon the Creation itself; but

---

[1] In accordance with the notions of his age, St. Chrysostom supposed that the firmament was something solid; and it seems to have been entirely a notion of modern times, that the visible heavens are formed of a subtle ether. Thus Homer terms them χάλκεον οὐρανὸν, and χαλκοβατῆ δώματα; and sometimes σιδήρειον οὐρανόν. The notion of St. Chrysostom seems to have been similar. He supposes a solid spherical arch, which he terms the visible heaven, which divided the waters above from those below it. See Gen. i. 7. A similar idea seems to have prevailed among those who translated the Bible into English, from the use of the word *firmament*, which was however a mere copying of the Vulgate, and the Greek στερεωμα. It is remarkable that this idea is defended by Drusius in his *Loca Difficiliora Pentateuchi*, and in Sylvester's translation of Du Bartas's *Weeks and Days*.

[2] Sav. and M., of it. [3] σχήματος. [4] Ps. cxlviii. 4. [5] Jer. v. 22.

reserving these subjects for the morrow,[1] let us earnestly endeavour to retain what has been said, and to convey it to the rest.[2] I know indeed, that the abstruseness of these speculations has seemed strange to your ears; but if we be a little vigilant, and accustom ourselves to them, we shall easily be able to teach others. Meanwhile, it is necessary farther to say this to your Charity. Even as God hath given us glory by means of this great creation, so let us also glorify Him by a pure conversation! "The heavens declare the glory of God," though only seen; and we therefore should declare God's glory[3] not only in speaking, but in silence, and in astonishing all men by the brightness of our life. For He saith, "Let your light so shine before men, that they may see your good works, and glorify your Father which is in heaven."[4] For when an unbeliever beholds thee, who art a believer, subdued, modest, and orderly in manners, he will wonder and say, "Truly great is the God of the Christians! What manner of men hath He formed? What, and from what hath He made them? Hath He turned them from men into angels? If any one treats them contemptuously, they revile not! If any one beats them, they are not enraged! If any one does them an injury, they pray for him who has put them in pain! They have no enemy! They know nothing of cherishing malice! They are guiltless of vain babbling! They have not learnt to utter a falsehood! They cannot endure a false oath, or rather, they swear not at all, but would prefer to have their tongue cut out, rather than to let an oath proceed out of their mouth!" Such are the things which we should give them cause to say of us; and we should exterminate our evil habit of oaths, and pay at least as much honour to God, as we do to our more valuable garments. For how truly absurd is it, that when we have one garment better than the rest, we do not suffer ourselves to be continually wearing it; and yet everywhere we draggle about the name of God without concern, or ceremony! Let us not, I earnestly pray and beseech you, let us not thus despise our own salvation; but the care which we have used respecting this precept from the beginning, let us carry on even to the end. For I thus continually exhort you on the subject of oaths, not as though condemning you of listlessness, but inasmuch as I have seen that ye are for the most part reformed, I press you, and am urgent, that the whole work should be finished off, and come to its perfection. Even so act the spectators of public games. They excite those who are near the prize, with the more vehemence. Let us, then, by no means become weary; for we have nearly reached the completion of this amendment; and the difficulty was at the beginning. But now that the greater part of the evil habit has been cut away, and less remains to correct, no labour is necessary, but we only need a moderate degree of watchfulness, and diligence for some short time, in order that we ourselves being amended, may also become instructors to others; and that we may behold the Holy Passover with much confidence, and that with much pleasure we may reap a double or treble measure of the customary gladness of the festival. For not so much does it delight us to be delivered from the toil and fatigue of fasting, as to meet that holy season with an illustrious and well-earned crown; a crown indeed that is never to fade!

11. But in order that the amendment may take place the more quickly, do this which I tell thee. Inscribe upon the wall of thy house, and upon the wall of thy heart, that "flying sickle;"[5] and think that it is flying forth on occasion of the curse, and constantly remember it. And if thou observest another person swearing, restrain, forbid, and be careful for him, and be careful for thine own domestics. For if we would look to this, that we might not merely correct ourselves, but also bring others to the same point, we shall ourselves quickly arrive at the goal; since while we undertake to instruct others, we shall be ashamed and blush, should we in our own case seem to leave those things unperformed, which we enjoin upon them. There is no need to say more; for much has been already spoken on these matters; and these things are now said only by way of remembrance. But may God, who is more sparing of our souls than we are, make us perfect in this, and every good work; that so having completed the whole fruit of righteousness, we may be found worthy of the kingdom of heaven, through the grace and lovingkindness of our Lord Jesus Christ, through Whom, and with Whom, to the Father, with the Holy Ghost, be glory, for ever and ever. Amen.

---

[1] Or the next day of preaching.
[2] See his request.
[3] See on Rom. xi. 6, Hom. XVIII.
[4] Matt. v. 16.
[5] Flying hook, or sickle. See Zech. v. 1-3. *A flying roll*, is the version given in the present translation of the Bible, which follows the Hebrew as well as the Vulgate, the Targum, and the Syriac. (See St. Jerome on the place, who adds Aquila, Theodotion, and Symmachus.) The Septuagint, which St. Chrysostom usually follows, instead of מְגִלָּה, probably read מַגָּל, which signifies a reap-hook, or sickle; in this, as in some other instances, the final letter having been dropped through the carelessness of transcribers. See Homily XV., conclusion.

HOMILY X.

Commendation of those who came to hear after taking a meal.—Observations on the physiology of the natural world; and against those who deify the creation; and on the duty of not swearing.

1. I JOY, and rejoice with you all, that ye have actually put in practice that admonition of ours, which we lately made with respect to those who were absent, for the reason that they were not fasting. For I think that many of those who have dined[1] are to-day present; and go to fill up this goodly assemblage; and that this is the fact, I conjecture from the more brilliant spectacle that I see around me, and the greater concourse of hearers. Not in vain, it seems, did I lately[2] spend so many words on their account, appealing to your Charity, to draw them to their Mother;[3] and to persuade them that it is lawful, even after bodily nourishment, to partake also of that which is spiritual. And in which case, beloved, I ask, did ye act for the better; at the time of the last assembly when after your meal ye turned to your slumbers; or now, when after the meal ye have presented yourselves at the hearing of the divine laws? Was it best when ye loitered about in the forum, and took part in meetings which were no wise profitable; or now, when ye stand with your own brethren, and hear the prophetic oracles? It is no disgrace, beloved, to have eaten, but after eating to remain at home, and so to be deprived of this sacred banquet. For whilst thou remainest at home, thou wilt be more slothful and supine; but coming here thou wilt shake off all slumber and listlessness; and laying aside not only listlessness,[4] but also all sadness, thou wilt be more at ease, and in better heart in all the events that may happen.

2. What need then is there to say more? Stand only nigh the man who fasts, and thou wilt straightway partake of his good odour; for fasting is a spiritual perfume; and through the eyes, the tongue, and every part, it manifests the good disposition of the soul. I have said this, not for the purpose of condemning those who have dined, but that I may shew the advantage of fasting. I do not, however, call mere abstinence from meats, fasting; but even before this, abstinence from sin; since he who, after he has taken a meal, has come hither with suitable sobriety, is not very far behind the man who fasts; even as he who continues fasting, if he does not give earnest and diligent heed to what is spoken, will derive no great benefit from his fast. He who eats, and yet takes a part in the sacred assembly with suitable earnestness, is in much better case than he who eats not at all, and remains absent. This abstinence will by no means be able to benefit us as much as the participation in spiritual instruction conveyeth to us benefit and advantage. Where indeed, besides, wilt thou hear the things upon which thou meditatest here? Wert thou to go to the bench of justice? quarrels and contentions are there! or into the council-chamber? there is anxious thought about political matters! or to thine home? solicitude on the subject of thy private affairs afflicts thee in every direction! or wert thou to go to the conferences and debates of the forum? every thing there is earthly and corruptible! For all the words that pass among those assembled there, are concerning merchandize, or taxes, or the sumptuous table, or the sale of lands, or other contracts, or wills, or inheritances, or some other things of that kind. And shouldest thou enter even into the royal halls, there again thou wouldest hear in the same way all discoursing of wealth, or power, or of the glory which is held in honour here, but of nothing that is spiritual. But here on the contrary everything relates to heaven, and heavenly things; to our soul, to our life, the purpose for which we were born, and why we spend an allotted time upon earth, and on what terms we migrate from hence, and into what condition we shall enter after these things, and why our body is of clay, what also is the nature of death, what, in short, the present life is, and what the future. The discourses that are here made by us contain nothing at all of an earthly kind, but are all in reference to spiritual things. Thus, then, it is that we shall have made great provision for our salvation, and shall depart hence with a good hope.

3. Since, therefore, we did not scatter the seed in vain, but ye hunted out all who were

---

[1] ἠριστηκότων. Suidas, however, places this meal about the third hour.
[2] πρώην. Montfaucon assumes that this word is never applied to the preceding day: if so, τὴν ἐπιοῦσαν, Hom. IX. sec. 10, cannot be the morrow, unless some accident delayed the delivery of this Homily. It may be the next *Synaxis*.
[3] See Hom. IV. 1.
[4] There is a play on the words ἀθυμία and ῥᾳθυμία which it seems impossible to preserve.

absent, as I exhorted you; suffer us now to return you a recompense; and having reminded you of a few things that were said before, to repay you again what remains. What then were those matters that were before treated of? We were enquiring how, and in what manner, before the giving of the Scriptures, God ordered His dispensation toward us; and we said, that by means of the creation He instructed our race, stretching out the heavens, and there openly unfolding a vast volume, useful alike to the simple and the wise, to the poor and to the rich, to Scythians and to barbarians, and to all in general who dwell upon the earth; a volume which is much larger than the multitude of those instructed by it. We discoursed also at length concerning the night, and the day, and the order of these, as well as of the harmony which is strictly preserved by them; and much was said respecting the measured dance of the seasons of the year, and of their equality. For just as the day defraudeth not the night even of half an hour throughout the whole year, so also do these distribute all the days among themselves equally. But, as I said before, not only does the greatness and beauty of the creation shew forth the Divine Architect, but the very manner likewise in which it is compacted together, and the method of operation, transcending as it does, the ordinary course of nature. For it would have been in accordance with nature for water to be borne upon the earth; but now we see, on the contrary, that the earth is supported by the waters. It would have been in accordance with nature that fire should tend upwards; but now on the contrary we see the beams of the sun directed towards the earth; and the waters to be above the heavens, yet not falling away;[1] and the sun running below them, yet not quenched by the waters, nor dispelling their moisture. Besides these things we said that this whole universe consists of four elements, these being adverse to and at strife with one another; yet one does not consume the other, although they are mutually destructive. Whence it is evident that some invisible power bridles them, and the will of God becomes their bond.

4. To-day, I wish to dwell a little more on this subject. Arouse yourselves, however, and give earnest heed unto us! And that the wonder may appear more clearly, I will draw the lesson concerning these things from our own bodies. This body of ours, so short, and small, consists of four elements; viz. of what is warm, that is, of blood; of what is dry, that is, of yellow bile; of what is moist, that is, of phlegm; of what is cold, that is, of black bile. And let no one think this subject foreign to that which we have in hand. "For He that is spiritual judgeth all things; yet He Himself is judged of no man."[2] Thus also Paul touched upon principles of agriculture, whilst discoursing to us of the Resurrection; and said, "Thou fool; that which thou sowest is not quickened, except it die."[3] But if that blessed man brought forward questions of agriculture, neither should any one blame us if we handle matters pertaining to medical science. For our discourse is now respecting the Creation of God; and this ground-work of ideas will be necessary for our purpose. As, therefore, I said before, this body of ours consists of four elements; and if either revolts against the whole, death is the result of this revolt. As for instance, by a superabundance "of bile" fever is produced; and should this proceed beyond a certain measure, it effects a rapid dissolution. Again, when there is an excess of the cold element, paralyses, agues, apoplexies, and an infinite number of other maladies are generated. And every form of disease is the effect of an excess of these elements; when either of them overpassing its own bounds, acts the part of a tyrant against the rest, and mars the symmetry of the whole. Interrogate then him who says, that all things are spontaneous and self-produced. If this little and diminutive body, having the advantage of medicines, and of medical skill, and of a soul within which regulates it, and of much moral wisdom, as well as innumerable other helps, be not always able to continue in a state of order, but often perishes, and is destroyed, when some disturbance takes place within it; how could a world like this, containing substances of such vast bulk and compounded of those same elements, remain during so long a time without any disturbance, unless it enjoyed the advantage of a manifold providence? Neither would it be reasonable to suppose that this body, which has the benefit of superintendence both without and within, should scarcely be sufficient for its own preservation; and that a world such as this is, enjoying no such superintendence, should during so many years suffer nothing of that sort which our body suffers. For how, I ask, is it that not one of these elements hath gone beyond its own boundaries, nor swallowed up all the rest? Who hath brought them together from the beginning? Who hath bound? Who hath bridled? Who

---

[1] οὐ διολισθαίνοντα.   [2] 1 Cor. ii. 15.   [3] 1 Cor. xv. 38.

hath held them together during so long a period? For if the body of the world were simple and uniform, what I speak of would not have been so impossible. But when there hath been such a strife between the elements, even from the beginning; who so senseless as to think that these things would have come together, and remained together when united, without One to effect this conjunction? For if we who are evil-affected towards one another not by nature, but by will, cannot come spontaneously to an agreement as long as we remain at variance, and hold ourselves ungraciously towards one another; if we have yet need of some one else to bring us into a state of conjunction; and after this conjunction further to clench us, and persuade us to abide by our reconciliation, and not again to be at variance; how could the elements, which neither partake of sense nor reason, and which are naturally adverse, and inimical to each other, have come together, and agreed and remained with one another, if there were not some ineffable Power which effected this conjunction; and after this conjunction, always restrained them by the same bond?

5. Dost thou not perceive how this body wastes away, withers, and perishes after the secession of the soul, and each of the elements thereof returns to its own appointed place?[1] This very same thing, indeed, would also happen to the world, if the Power which always governs it had left it devoid of Its own providence. For if a ship does not hold together without a pilot, but soon founders, how could the world have held together so long a time if there was no one governing its course? And that I may not enlarge, suppose the world to be a ship; the earth to be placed below as the keel; the sky to be the sail; men to be the passengers;[2] the subjacent abyss, the sea. How is it then that during so long a time, no shipwreck has taken place? Now let a ship go one day without a pilot and crew,[3] and thou wilt see it straightway foundering! But the world, though subsisting now five thousand years, and many more, hath suffered nothing of the kind. But why do I talk of a ship? Suppose one hath pitched a small hut in the vineyards; and when the fruit is gathered, leaves it vacant; it stands, however, scarce two or three days, but soon goes to pieces, and tumbles down! Could not a hut, forsooth, stand without superintendence? How then could the workmanship of a world, so fair and marvellous; the laws of the night and day; the interchanging dances of the seasons; the course of nature chequered and varied as it is in every way throughout the earth, the sea, the sky; in plants, and in animals that fly, swim, walk, creep; and in the race of men, far more dignified than any of these, continue yet unbroken, during so long a period, without some kind of providence? But in addition to what has been said, follow me whilst I enumerate the meadows, the gardens, the various tribes of flowers; all sorts of herbs, and their uses;[4] their odours, forms, disposition, yea, but their very names; the trees which are fruitful, and which are barren; the nature of metals,—and of animals,—in the sea, or on the land; of those that swim, and those that traverse the air; the mountains, the forests, the groves; the meadow below, and the meadow above; for there is a meadow on the earth, and a meadow too in the sky; the various flowers of the stars; the rose below, and the rainbow above! Would you have me point out also the meadow of birds? Consider the variegated body of the peacock, surpassing every dye, and the fowls of purple plumage.[5] Contemplate with me the beauty of the sky; how it has been preserved so long without being dimmed; and remains as bright and clear as if it had been only fabricated to-day; moreover, the power of the earth, how its womb has not become effete by bringing forth during so long a time! Contemplate with me the fountains; how they burst forth and fail not, since the time they were begotten, to flow forth continually throughout the day and night! Contemplate with me the sea, receiving so many rivers, yet never exceeding its measure! But how long shall we pursue things unattainable! It is fit, indeed, that over every one of these which has been spoken of, we should say, "O Lord, how hast Thou magnified Thy works; in wisdom hast Thou made them all."[6]

6. But what is the sapient argument of the unbelievers, when we go over all these particulars with them; the magnitude, the beauty of the creation, the prodigality, the munificence everywhere displayed? This very thing, say they, is the worst fault, that God hath made the world so beautiful and so vast. For if He had not made it beautiful and vast, we should not have made a god of it; but now being struck with its grandeur, and

---

[1] λῆξιν. See on Rom. iii. 11, Hom. VII.
[2] ἐπιβάτας. Usually soldiers on ship-board; here clearly distinguished from the *sailors*.
[3] Comp. Acts xxvii. 30, 31.
[4] χρείας: others read χροιάς, "colours."
[5] τοὺς πορφυρίζοντας στρουθούς. Ælian, *de Animalibus*, iii. 42, mentions a bird called Porphyrio, more esteemed even than the peacock, so that none ever killed it for the table. See also Plin. x. 46, but this expression may apply to various kinds.
[6] Ps. civ. 24.

marvelling at its beauty, we have thought it to be a deity.[1] But such an argument is good for nothing. For that neither the magnitude, nor beauty of the world is the cause of this impiety, but their own want of understanding, is what we are prepared to show, proved by the case of ourselves, who have never been so affected. Why then have "we" not made a deity of it? Do we not see it with the same eyes as themselves? Do we not enjoy the same advantage from the creation with themselves? Do we not possess the same soul? Have we not the same body? Do we not tread the same earth? How comes it that this beauty and magnitude hath not persuaded us to think the same as they do? But this will be evident not from this proof only, but from another besides. For as a proof that it is not for its beauty they have made a deity of it, but by reason of their own folly, why do they adore the ape, the crocodile, the dog, and the vilest of animals? Truly, "they became vain in their imaginations, and their foolish heart was darkened. Professing themselves to be wise, they became fools."[2]

7. Nevertheless, we will not frame our answer from these things only, but will also say something yet further. For God, foreseeing these things of old, destroyed, in His wisdom, this plea of theirs. On this account He made the world not only wonderful and vast, but also corruptible and perishable; and placed therein many evidences of its weakness; and what He did with respect to the Apostles,[3] He did with respect to the whole world. What then did He with respect to the Apostles? Since they used to perform many great and astonishing signs and wonders, He suffered them constantly to be scourged, to be expelled, to inhabit the dungeon, to encounter bodily infirmities, to be in continual tribulations, lest the greatness of their miracles should make them to be accounted as gods amongst mankind. Therefore when He had bestowed so great favour upon them, He suffered their bodies to be mortal, and in many cases obnoxious to disease; and did not remove their infirmity, that He might give full proof of their nature. And this is not merely my assertion, but that of Paul himself, who says, "For though I would desire to glory, I shall not be a fool; but now I forbear, lest any man should think of me above that which he seeth me to be, or that he heareth of me."[4] And again, "But we have this treasure in earthen vessels."[5] But what is meant by "earthen vessels?" In this body, he means, which is mortal and perishable. For just as the earthen vessel is formed from clay and fire, so also the body of these saints being clay, and receiving the energy of the spiritual fire, becomes an earthen vessel. But for what reason was it thus constituted, and so great a treasure, and such a plentitude of graces entrusted to a mortal and corruptible body? "That the excellency of the power may be of God, and not of us." For when thou seest the Apostles raising the dead, yet themselves sick, and unable to remove their own infirmities, thou mayest clearly perceive, that the resurrection of the dead man was not effected by the power of him who raised him, but by the energy of the Spirit. For in proof, that they were frequently sick, hear what Paul saith respecting Timothy, "Use a little wine for thy stomach's sake, and thine often infirmities."[6] And again, of another he saith, "But Trophimus I have left at Miletus sick."[7] And writing to the Philippians, he said, "Epaphroditus was sick nigh unto death."[8] For if, when this was the case, they accounted them to be gods, and prepared to do sacrifice unto them, saying, "The gods are come down to us in the likeness of men;"[9] had such infirmities not existed, to what extent of impiety might not men have proceeded, when they beheld their miracles? As then in this case, because of the greatness of these signs, He suffered their nature to remain in a state of infirmity, and permitted those repeated trials, in order that they might not be thought to be gods, thus likewise He did with respect to the creation, a thing nearly parallel to this. For He fashioned it beautiful and vast; but on the other hand corruptible.

8. And both of these points the Scriptures teach, for one in treating of the beauty of the heavens thus speaks "The heavens declare the glory of God."[10] And again, "Who hath placed the sky as a vault,"[11] and spread it out as a tent over the earth."[12] And again, "Who holdeth the circle of heaven."[13] But another writer, shewing that although the world be great and fair, it is yet corruptible, thus speaks; "Thou, Lord, in the beginning hast laid the foundation of the earth, and the

---

[1] See the argument of Balbus (the Stoic), Cic. *de Nat. Deor.* l. 2, c. 17, 34, &c. Seneca, *Nat. Quæst.* ii. 45, says, that God may likewise be called *Mundus*, or *Fatum*, or *Providentia*, or *Natura*.
[2] Rom. i. 21, 22.   [3] See Hom. I. 15.   [4] 2 Cor. xii. 6.
[5] 2 Cor. iv. 7.
[6] 1 Tim. v. 23.   The subject of the first of these Homilies.
[7] 2 Tim. iv. 20.   [8] Phil. ii. 25.   [9] Acts xiv. 11.
[10] Ps. xix. 1.
[11] The Hebrew דק means something *small* or *thin*, the Vulgate has *nihilum*. No ancient version has *curtain*. Perhaps the word is an emphatic allusion to the exquisitely minute consistence of the blue ether. The Hebrews say that by this word is signified *the finest dust*. In the revised version "gauze" is suggested in the margin.
[12] Isa. xl. 22.
[13] This seems a slip of memory for *earth* in the same verse; but see Ecclus. xliii. 12.

heavens are the works of Thine hands. They shall perish, but Thou remainest, and they all shall wax old as doth a garment, and as a vesture shalt Thou fold them up, and they shall be changed."[1] And again, David saith of the sun, that "he is as a bridegroom coming out of his chamber, and rejoiceth as a giant to run his course."[2] Seest thou how he places before thee the beauty of this star, and its greatness? For even as a bridegroom when he appears from some stately chamber,[3] so the sun sends forth his rays under the East; and adorning the heaven as it were with a saffron-coloured veil, and making the clouds like roses, and running unimpeded all the day; he meets no obstacle to interrupt his course. Beholdest thou, then, his beauty? Beholdest thou his greatness? Look also at the proof of his weakness! For a certain wise man, to make this plain, said, "What is brighter than the sun, yet the light thereof suffers eclipse."[4] Nor is it only from this circumstance that his infirmity is to be perceived, but also in the concourse of the clouds. Often, at least, when a cloud passes underneath him, though emitting his beams, and endeavouring to pierce through it, he has not strength to do so; the cloud being too dense, and not suffering him to penetrate through it. "He nourishes the seeds, however,"[5] replies some one—Yes—still he does not nourish them by himself, but requires the assistance of the earth, and of the dew, and of the rains, and of the winds, and the right distribution of the seasons. And unless all these things concur, the sun's aid is but superfluous. But this would not seem to be like a deity, to stand in need of the assistance of others, for that which he wishes to do; for it is a special attribute of God to want nothing; He Himself at least did not in this manner bring forth the seeds from the ground; He only commanded, and they all shot forth. And again, that thou mayest learn that it is not the nature of the elements, but His command which effects all things; He both brought into being these very elements which before were not; and without the need of any aid, He brought down the manna for the Jews. For it is said, "He gave them bread from heaven."[6] But why do I say, that in order to the perfection of fruits, the sun requires the aid of other elements for their sustenance; when he himself requires the assistance of many things for his sustenance, and would not himself be sufficient for himself. For in order that he may proceed on his way, he needs the heaven as a kind of pavement spread out underneath him; and that he may shine, he needs the clearness and rarity of the air; since if even this become unusually dense, he is not able to show his light; and, on the other hand, he requires coolness and moisture, lest his rays should be intolerable to all, and burn up everything. When, therefore, other elements overrule him, and correct his weakness (overrule as for example, clouds, and walls, and certain other bodies that intercept his light:—or correct his excess, as the dews, and fountains, and cool air), how can such a one be a Deity? For God must be independent, and not stand in need of assistance, be the source of all good things to all, and be hindered by nothing; even as Paul, as well as the prophet Isaiah, saith of God; the latter[7] thus making Him speak in His own Person, "I fill heaven and earth, saith the Lord."[8] And again, "Am I a God nigh at hand, and not a God afar off?"[9] And again, David says, "I have said unto the Lord, Thou art my Lord, for Thou hast no need of my good things."[10] But Paul, demonstrating this independence of help, and shewing that both these things especially belong to God; to stand in need of nothing, and of Himself to supply all things to all; speaks on this wise, "God that made the heaven, and the earth, and the sea, Himself needeth not any thing, giving to all life and all things."[11]

9. It would indeed be easy for us to take a survey of the other elements, the heaven, the air, the earth, the sea, and to shew the imbecility of these, and how each requires the assistance of his neighbour, and without this assistance, is lost and destroyed. For as it regards the earth, if the fountains fail it, and the moisture infused from the sea and the rivers, it quickly perishes by being parched. The remaining elements too stand in need of one another, the air of the sun, as well as the sun of the air. But not to protract this discourse; in what has been said, having given a sufficient supply of reasons to start from for those who are willing to receive them, we shall be content. For if the sun, which is the most surprising part of the whole creation, hath been proved to be so feeble and needy, how much more the other parts of the universe? What then I have advanced (offering these things for the consideration of the studious), I will myself again shew you in discourse from the Scriptures; and prove,

---

[1] Ps. cii. 25, 26. [2] Ps. xix. 6. [3] παστάδος.
[4] Ecclus. xvii. 31. [5] See Plin. ii. 6. [6] Ps. lxxviii. 24.
[7] St. Chrysostom here seems to have quoted from memory, and to have mentioned Isaiah in mistake for Jeremiah, where these passages occur, as above.
[8] Jer. xxiii. 24. [9] Jer. xxiii. 23. [10] Ps. xvi. 2.
[11] Acts xvii. 25. Here also St. Chrysostom quotes from memory, as the first clause shows.

that not only the sun, but also the whole universe is thus corruptible. For since the elements are mutually destructive, and when much cold intervenes, it chastens the force of the sun's rays; and on the other hand, the heat prevailing, consumes the cold; and since the elements are both the causes and subjects of contrary qualities, and dispositions, in one another; it is very evident that these things offer a proof of great corruptibility; and of the fact, that all these things which are visible, are a corporeal substance.

10. But since this subject is too lofty for our simplicity, permit me now to lead you to the sweet fountain of the Scriptures, that we may refresh your ears. For we will not discourse to you of the heaven and the earth separately, but will exhibit the Apostle declaring this very thing to us concerning the whole creation, in these plain terms, that the whole creation is now in bondage to corruption; and why it is thus in bondage, and at what time it shall be delivered from it, and unto what condition it shall be translated. For after he had said, "The sufferings of this present time are not worthy to be compared with the glory that shall be revealed in us;" he goes on to add; "For the earnest expectation of the creature waiteth for the manifestation of the sons of God. For the creature was made subject to vanity, not willingly, but by reason of Him who hath subjected the same in hope."[1] But what he intends is to this effect; "The creature," he says, "was made corruptible;" for this is implied in the expression, "being made subject to vanity." For it was made corruptible by the command of God. But God so commanded it for the sake of our race; for since it was to nurture a corruptible man, it was necessary itself should also be of the same character; for of course corruptible bodies were not to dwell in an incorruptible creation. But, nevertheless, he tells us, it will not remain so. "The creature[2] also itself shall be delivered from the bondage of corruption;" and afterwards, for the purpose of shewing when this event shall take place, and through whom, he adds, "Into the glorious liberty of the sons of God." For when we are raised, his meaning is, and assume incorruptible bodies; then also this body of the heaven, the earth, and the whole creation, shall be incorruptible, and imperishable. When, therefore, thou beholdest the sun arising, admire the Creator; when thou beholdest him hiding himself and disappearing, learn the weakness of his nature, that thou mayest not adore him as a Deity! For God hath not only implanted in the nature of the elements this proof of their weakness, but hath also bidden His servants, that were but men, command them; so that although thou shouldest not know their servitude from their aspect, thou mayest learn, from those who have commanded them, that they are all thy fellow-servants. Therefore it was, that Joshua, the son of Nave,[3] said, "Let the sun stand still in Gibeon, and the moon over against the valley of Ajalon." And again the prophet Isaiah made the sun to retrace his steps, under the reign of Hezekiah; and Moses gave orders to the air, and the sea, the earth, and the rocks. Elisha changed the nature of the waters; the Three Children triumphed over the fire. Thou seest how God hath provided for us on either hand; leading us by the beauty of the elements to the knowledge of His divinity; and, by their feebleness, not permitting us to lapse into the worship of them.

11. For the sake of all these things then, let us glorify Him, our Guardian; not only by words, but also by deeds; and let us shew forth an excellent conversation, not only in general, but in particular with regard to abstinence from oaths. For not every sin brings the same penalty; but those which are easiest to be amended, bring upon us the greatest punishment: which indeed Solomon intimated, when he said, "It is not wonderful if any one be taken stealing; for he stealeth that he may satisfy his soul that is hungry; but the adulterer, by the lack of understanding, destroyeth his own soul."[4] But what he means is to this effect. The thief is a grievous offender, but not so grievous a one as the adulterer: for the former, though it be a sorry reason for his conduct, yet at the same time has to plead the necessity arising from indigence; but the latter, when no necessity compels him, by his mere madness rushes into the gulph of iniquity. This also may be said with regard to those who swear. For they have not any pretext to allege, but merely their contempt.

12. I know, indeed, that I may seem to be too tedious and burdensome; and that I may be thought to give annoyance by continuing this admonition. But nevertheless, I do not desist, in order that ye may even be shamed by my shamelessness to abstain from the cus-

---

[1] Rom. viii. 21.
[2] κτίσις, rendered here *creature*, would be in modern English, *creation*. "Creature" is used by Wiclif even for the act of creating, Rom. i. 20. "Creation" properly means the act, "creature" an instance or effect of it, general or particular, but of late the latter only.
[3] Instead of Joshua, the son of *Nun*, the Greek Fathers, following the Septuagint, read *of Nave;* a mistake which originated evidently from the final n or ן of the Hebrew, so closely corresponding with the ך or ו.
[4] Prov. vi. 30, 32, LXX.

tom of oaths. For if that unmerciful and cruel judge, paying respect to the importunity of the widow, changed his custom, much more will ye do this; and especially when he who is exhorting you, doth it not for himself, but for your salvation. Or rather, indeed, I cannot deny that I do this for myself; for I consider your benefit as my own success. But I could wish that you, even as I labour, and weary myself for your safety, would in like manner make your own souls a matter of anxiety to yourselves; and then assuredly this work of reformation would be perfected. And what need is there to multiply words? For if there were no hell, neither punishment for the contumacious, nor reward for the obedient; and I had come to you, and asked this in the way of a favour, would ye not have consented? would ye not have granted my petition, when I asked so trifling a favour? But when it is God who asks this favour, and for the sake of yourselves, who are to grant it, and not for Himself, Who is to receive it; who is there so ungracious, who is there so miserable and wretched, that he will not grant this favour to God, when He asks it; and especially when he himself who grants it, is in future to enjoy the benefit of it? Considering these things then, repeat over to yourselves, when ye depart hence, all that has been said; and correct in every way those who take no heed to it; to the end that we may receive the recompense of other men's good actions, as well as our own, through the grace and lovingkindness of our Lord Jesus Christ, by Whom, and with Whom be glory to the Father, with the Holy Ghost, for ever and ever. Amen.

HOMILY XI.

Thanksgiving to God for deliverance from the evils expected owing to the sedition; and recollection of the events which took place at the time. Also against those who find fault with the structure of the human body, and in general concerning the creation of man; and, in conclusion, on success in avoiding oaths.

1. When I think of the past tempest, and of the present calm, I cease not saying, "Blessed be God, who maketh all things, and changeth them; who hath brought light out of darkness; who leadeth to the gates of hell, and bringeth back; who chastiseth, but killeth not."[1] And this I desire you too to repeat constantly, and never to desist. For if He hath benefitted us by deeds, what pardon shall we deserve, if we do not requite Him even by words. Therefore, I exhort that we never cease to give Him thanks; since if we are grateful for the former benefits, it is plain that we shall enjoy others also, which are greater. Let us say, then, continually, Blessed be God, who hath permitted us to spread before you in security the accustomed table, whilst He hath also granted you to hear our word with assurance of safety! Blessed be God, that we no longer run hither flying from the danger without, but only from desire to hear; that we no longer meet one another with agony, trembling, and anxious thoughts; but with much confidence, having shaken off all our fear. Our condition, indeed, on former days was nothing better than that of those who are tossed up and down in the midst of the deep; and expecting shipwreck every hour. We were scared all day long by innumerable rumours, and disturbed and agitated on every side; and were every day busy and curious to know who had come from the court?[2] what news he had brought? and whether what was reported was true or false? Our nights too we passed without sleep, and whilst we looked upon the city, we wept over it, as if it were on the eve of its destruction.

2. For this cause yourselves too kept silence on those former days, because the whole city was empty, and all had migrated to the deserts, and because those who were left behind were overshadowed[3] by the cloud of despondency. For the soul when once it is filled with despondency, is not apt to hear anything that may be said. For this cause, when the friends of Job came, and saw that tragedy of his house, and the just man sitting

---

[1] Amos v. 8; Job xxxvii. 15; 1 Sam. ii. 6; 2 Cor. vi. 19.
[2] Literally "camp," στρατοπέδου.
[3] Sav. ἐσκοτῶσθαι. Ben. κεκακῶσθαι, "were distressed."

down upon the dunghill, and covered with sores, they rent their garments, and groaned and sat down by him in silence; making it manifest that nothing is so suitable to the afflicted at first, as quiet and silence. For the calamity was too great for consolation. Therefore also the Jews, whilst they were in bondage to work in clay and the brickmaking, when they saw Moses come to them, were not able to give heed to his words, by reason of their failure of spirit, and their affliction. And what marvel is it that fainthearted men have felt this, when we find that the Disciples also fell into the same infirmity. For after that mystic Supper, when Christ took[1] them apart and discoursed with them, the disciples at first asked Him more than once, "Whither goest Thou?" But when He had told them what evils they should in a little while afterwards encounter, the wars, and the persecutions, and the universal enmity, the stripes, the prisons, the tribunals, the appearance before magistrates; then, their souls oppressed as by a heavy burthen with the dread of the things He had spoken, and with the sadness of these approaching events, remained henceforth in a state of stupor. Christ, therefore, perceiving their consternation, reproved it by saying, "I go to My Father, and no one among you asketh Me, Whither goest Thou? But because I have said these things unto you, sorrow hath filled your hearts." For this reason also we were silent for some time past, awaiting the present opportunity. For if a person who is about to ask a favour of any one, though the request be a reasonable one, waits a fitting occasion to propose it, that he may find him who is to grant the petition in a mild and well-disposed frame of mind; and that receiving assistance from the favourable opportunity, he may obtain the benefit; how much rather is it necessary that the speaker should seek a fit season, so that he may address his discourse to an auditor well affected, and free from all care and despondency; which accordingly we have done.

3. Inasmuch, then, as ye have now shaken off despondency, we are desirous to recall you to the recollection of former matters; so that our discourse may be rendered the clearer to you. For what we said of the creation, that God not only made it beautiful, and wonderful, and vast, but also weak and corruptible; and moreover that He hath established divers proofs of this; ordering both these circumstances for our advantage; leading us on by its beauty to admiration of Him who framed it; and by its weakness leading us away from the worship of the creature; this we may see, take place also in the case of the body. For with respect to this too there are many among the enemies to the truth, as well as among those who belong to our own ranks, who make it a subject of enquiry, why it was created corruptible and frail? Many also of the Greeks and heretics affirm, that it was not even created by God.[2] For they declare it to be unworthy of God's creative art, and enlarge upon its impurities, its sweat, its tears, its labours, and sufferings, and all the other incidents of the body. But, for my part, when such things are talked of, I would first make this reply. Tell me not of man, fallen, degraded and condemned. But if thou wouldest learn what manner of body God formed us with at the first, let us go to Paradise, and survey the Man that was created at the beginning. For that body was not thus corruptible and mortal; but like as some statue of gold just brought from the furnace, that shines splendidly, so that frame was free from all corruption. Labour did not trouble it, nor sweat deface it. Cares did not conspire against it; nor sorrows besiege it; nor was there any other affection of that kind to distress it. But when man did not bear his felicity with moderation, but threw contempt upon his Benefactor, and thought a deceiving demon more worthy of credit than God who cared for him, and who had raised him to honour, and when he expected to become himself a god, and conceived thoughts above his proper dignity, then,—then indeed it was that God, to humble him by decisive acts, made him mortal, as well as corruptible; and fettered him with such varied necessities; not from hatred or aversion, but in care for him, and to repress at the very outset that evil and destructive pride; and instead of permitting it to proceed any further, He admonished him by actual experience, that he was mortal and corruptible; thus to convince him that he must never again think or dream of such things as he had done. For the devil's suggestion, was, "Ye shall be as gods."[3] Desiring then utterly to eradicate this idea, God made the body subject to much suffering and disease; to instruct him by its very nature that he must never again entertain such a thought. And that

---

[1] Or, "had" (λαβών, which may refer to Judas' going out). John xiii. 31. For it is plain they did not go out until the end of the discourse. John xviii. 1.

[2] Plato, in his *Timæus*, 40, d. 42 e., makes the human *body* the work of (good) demons, or created gods, because it would have been of a more perfect nature if the Supreme God had made it. Of heretics who held such opinions as are here mentioned, see Rom. viii. 5-7, Hom. XIII. Valentinus, Marcion, Basilides, and other early heretics of the Gnostic school, held matter to be evil, and the world made by evil beings.

[3] Gen. iii. 5.

this is true, is really most evident from what befel him; for after such an expectation, he was condemned to this punishment. Consider also with me the wisdom [1] of God in this matter. He did not allow him to be the first to die, but permitted his son to suffer this death; in order that seeing before his eyes the body corrupting and decaying, he might receive a striking lesson of wisdom [2] from that spectacle; and learn what had come to pass, and be duly chastened before he departed hence.

4. Really then, as I said, this point is apparent from what has already taken place; but it will be made no less clear from what yet remains to be stated. For if whilst we are fettered with such necessities of the body; and whilst it is the lot of all men to die, to suffer corruption, to moulder in the sight of all, and to dissolve into dust, so that the Gentile philosophers made one and the same comprehensive definition of the human race (for when asked what man was, they answered, he is an animal, rational and mortal); if, forsooth, whilst all admitted this, there were some who dared in the opinion of the multitude to immortalize themselves; and notwithstanding that the very sense of sight bore witness to their mortality, were ambitious to be called gods, and were honoured as such; to what a length of impiety would not many men have proceeded, if death had not gone on teaching all men the mortality and corruptibility of our nature? Hear, for instance, what the prophet says of a barbarian king, when seized with this frenzy. "I will exalt," saith he, "my throne above the stars of heaven; and I will be like unto the Most High." [3] Afterwards, deriding him, and speaking of his death, he says, "Corruption is under thee, and the worm is thy covering;" [4] but his meaning is, "Dost thou dare, O man, whom such an end is awaiting, to entertain such imaginations?" Again, of another, I mean the king of the Tyrians, when he conceived the like aims, and was ambitious to be considered as a God, he says, "Thou art not a God, but a man, and they that pierce thee shall say so." [5] Thus God, in making this body of ours as it is, hath from the beginning utterly taken away all occasion of idolatry.

5. But why dost thou marvel if this hath happened in respect to the body, when even with respect to the soul it is plain, that a similar thing hath taken place. For God made it not mortal, but permitted it to be immortal; He constituted it however subject to forgetfulness, to ignorance, to sadness, and to care; and this, lest regarding its own nobility of birth, it might take up a conceit too high for its proper dignity. For if, even while the case stands thus, some have dared to aver, that it is of the Divine essence; to what a pitch of frenzy would they not have reached, if it had been devoid of these imperfections? What, however, I affirmed respecting the creation, I affirm also respecting the body, that both these things alike excite my admiration of God; that He hath made it corruptible; and that in its very corruptibility, He hath manifested His own power and wisdom. For that He could have made it of some better material, He hath evidenced from the celestial and the solar substance. For He that made those such as they are, could have made this also like them, had He thought proper to do so. But the cause of its imperfection is what I before adverted to. This circumstance by no means lowers the admiration due to the Creator's workmanship, but rather increases it; for the meanness of the substance, manifests the resource and adaptiveness of His art; since He hath introduced such a harmony of parts in clay and ashes, and senses so various and manifold and capable of such spiritual wisdom.

6. In proportion, therefore, as thou findest fault with the meanness of the substance, be so much the more astonished at the greatness of the art displayed. For this reason also, I do not so much admire the statuary who forms a beautiful figure out of gold, as him who, by the resources of art, is able, even in crumbling clay, to exhibit a marvellous and inimitable mould of beauty. In the former case, the material gives some aid to the artist, but in the latter, there is a naked display of his art. Wouldest thou learn then, how great the wisdom of the Creator is, consider what it is that is made out of clay? What else is there but brick and tile? Nevertheless, God, the Supreme Artist, from the same material of which only the brick and tile is formed, hath been able to make an eye so beautiful, as to astonish all who behold it, and to implant in it such power, that it can at once survey the high aerial expanse, and by the aid of a small pupil embrace the mountains, forests, hills, the ocean, yea, the heaven, by so small a thing! Tell me not then of tears and rheums, for these things are the fruit of thy sin; but consider its beauty, and visual power; and how it is that whilst it ranges over such an expanse of air, it experiences no weariness or distress! The feet indeed become tired and weakened even after going but a small distance; but the eye, in travers-

---

[1] σύνεσιν.
[2] φιλοσοφία.
[3] Isa. xiv. 13, 14.
[4] Isa. xiv. 11.
[5] Ezek. xxviii. 9.

ing a space so lofty and so wide, is not sensible of any infirmity. For since this is the most necessary to us of all our members, He has not suffered it to be oppressed with fatigue; in order that the service it renders us might be free and unfettered.

7. But rather, I should say, what language is fully adequate to set forth the whole excellency of this member? And why do I speak of the pupil and the visual faculty? for if you were to investigate that which seems the meanest of all the members, I mean the eyelashes, you would behold even in these the manifold wisdom of God the Creator! For as it is with respect to the ears of corn; the beards, standing forth as a sort of spears, repel the birds, and do not suffer them to settle upon the fruits, and to break the stalk, which is too tender to bear them; so also is it with regard to the eyes. The hairs of the eyelids are ranged in front, and answer the purpose of beards and spears; keeping dust and light substances at a distance from the eyes, and any thing that might incommode the sight; and not permitting the eyelids to be annoyed. Another instance of wisdom, no less remarkable, is to be observed in eyebrows. Who can help being struck by their position? For they do not project to an immoderate degree, so as to obscure the sight; nor do they retire farther back than is fitting; but in the same manner as the eaves of a house, they stand out above, receiving the perspiration as it descends from the forehead, and not permitting it to annoy the eyes. For this purpose too there is a growth of hair upon them, which serves by its roughness to stay what descends from above, and affords the exact protection that is needed, and contributes also much appearance of beauty to the eyes. Nor is this the only matter of wonder! There is another thing also which is equally so. How is it, I ask, that the hairs of the head increase, and are cut off; but those of the eyebrows, not so? For not even this has happened undesignedly, or by chance, but in order that they might not darken the sight too much by becoming very long; an inconvenience from which those suffer who have arrived at extreme old age.

8. And who could possibly trace out all the wisdom which is manifested by means of the brain! For, in the first place, He made it soft, since it serves as a fountain to all the senses. Next, in order that it might not suffer injury owing to its peculiar nature, He fortified it on every side with bones. Further; that it might not suffer from friction, by the hardness of the bones, He interposed a middle membrane; and not only a single one, but also a second; the former being spread out on the under side of the skull, but the latter enveloping the upper substance of the brain, and the first being the harder of the two. And this was done, both for the cause that has been mentioned, and in order that the brain might not be the first to receive the blows inflicted upon the head; but that these membranes first encountering them, might free it from all injury, and preserve it unwounded. Moreover, that the bone which covers the brain is not a single and continuous one, but has many sutures on every side, is a circumstance which contributes much to its security. For a ventilation of the vapours that surround it may easily take place outward through these sutures, so as to prevent it from being suffocated;[1] and if a blow should be inflicted upon it, on any particular point, the damage does not extend to the whole. For if the bone had been one and continuous, the stroke even when it fell upon one part, only, would have injured the whole; but now, by its being divided into many parts, this can never happen. For if one part should chance to be wounded, only the bone that is situated near that part receives injury, but all the rest remain unhurt; the continuity of the stroke being intercepted by the division of the bones, and being unable to extend itself to the adjacent parts. By reason of this God hath constructed a covering for the brain of many bones; and just as when one builds a house, he lays on a roof, and tiles upon the upper part, so God hath placed these bones above upon the head, and hath provided that the hairs should shoot forth, and serve as a kind of cap for it.

9. The very same thing also He hath done with regard to the heart. For inasmuch as the heart has preeminence over all the members in our body, and that the supreme power over our whole life is entrusted to it, and death happens when it receives but a slight blow; He hath fenced it about on every side with stiff and hard bones, surrounding it by the protection of the breast-bone[2] before, and the blade-bones[3] behind. And what He did with respect to the membranes of the brain, He hath done in this instance also. For in order that it might not be rubbed and pained in striking against the hard bones which encompass it, in the throbbing and quick pulsation to which it is subject in anger and similar affections, He both interposed many membranes there, and placed the lungs by

---

[1] This is an unfounded notion. What follows is true, since a fracture usually stops at a suture (or joining) of the skull, as a crack in glass does at a cross cut of the diamond. τὸ βρέγμα, above, is strictly the parietal bone. See also Hom. V. fin. on Ep. to Heb.
[2] θώρακος.
[3] ὠμοπλάταις.

the side of it to act the part of a soft bed to these pulsations, so that the heart may break its force on these without sustaining injury or distress.

But why do I speak of the heart, and of the brain, when if any one will investigate even the very nails, he will see the manifold wisdom of God displayed in these; as well by their form, as by their substance and position. I might also have mentioned why our fingers are not all equal, and many other particulars besides; but to those who are inclined to attend, the wisdom of God Who created us, will be sufficiently clear from what has been said. Wherefore, leaving this department to be investigated with diligence by those who are desirous of the task, I shall turn myself to another objection.

10. There are many forsooth, who, besides what has been already referred to, bring forward this objection. If man be the king of the brutes, why have many animals an advantage over him in strength, agility, and fleetness? For the horse is swifter, the ox is more enduring, the eagle is lighter, and the lion stronger, than man. What then have we to reply to this argument? Thus much; that from that circumstance we may especially discern the wisdom of God and the honour which He has put upon us. A horse, it is true, is swifter than man, but for making dispatch on a journey, the man is better fitted than the horse. For a horse, though the very swiftest and strongest that may be, can scarcely travel two hundred stadia in a day;[1] but a man, harnessing a number of horses in succession, will be able to accomplish a distance of two thousand stadia. Thus, the advantage which swiftness affords to the horse, intelligence and art afford to the man in a much greater excess. The man, it is true, has not feet so strong as the other, but then he has those of the other which serve him as well as his own. For not one of the brutes has ever been able to subjugate another to his own use; but man has the range of them all; and by that variety of skill which is given him of God, makes each of the animals subservient to the employment best suited to him. For if the feet of men had been as strong as those of horses, they would have been useless for other purposes, for difficult ground, for the summits of mountains, for climbing trees; for the hoof is usually an impediment to treading in such places. So that although the feet of men are softer than theirs, they are still adapted to more various uses, and are not the worse for their want of strength, while they have the power of the horse ministering to their aid, and at the same time they have the advantage over him in variety of tread. Again, the eagle has his light pinion; but I have reason and art, by which I am enabled to bring down and master all the winged animals. But if thou wouldest see my pinion too, I have one much lighter than he; one which can soar, not merely ten or twenty stadia, or even as high as heaven, but above heaven itself, and above the heaven of heavens; even to "where Christ sitteth at the right hand of God!"[2]

11. Again, the irrational animals have their weapons in their own body; thus, the ox has his horns; the wild boar his tusks; the lion his claws. But God hath not furnished the nature of my body with weapons, but hath made these to be extraneous to it, for the purpose of shewing that man is a gentle animal; and that I have not always occasion to use my weapons, for from time to time I lay these aside, and from time to time resume them. In order then that I might be free and unfettered in this matter, not being at all times compelled to carry my weapons, He hath made these to be separate from my nature. For it is not only in our possessing a rational nature that we surpass the brutes, but we also excel them in body. For God has made this to correspond with the soul's nobility, and fitted to excute its commands. He has not, indeed, made the body such as it is, without reason; but such as it ought to be, as having to minister to a rational soul; so that if it were not such as it is, the operations of the soul would be greatly impeded: and this is manifest from diseases. For if this nice adjustment of the body be diverted from its proper condition in ever so small a degree, many of the soul's energies are impeded; as, for instance, if the brain should become too hot, or too cold. So that from the body it is easy to see much of the Divine Providence, not only because He made it at first better than it is at present; nor because even now He hath changed it for a useful purpose, but also because He will raise it again to much greater glory.

12. But, if thou art desirous to learn in a different way what wisdom God hath shewn respecting the body, I will mention that by which Paul seems most especially to be constantly struck. But what is this? That He

---

[1] He must mean for a continuance, as the stadium was rather less than our furlong. The word harnessing, ὑποζεύξας, seems to imply a vehicle. It is very likely that the persons mentioned had not the advantage of relays of draught horses. Some read here "a thousand," for "two thousand;" see note of Ducæus.

[2] Col. iii. 1. So again Hom. XV. (3). Compare the lines in one of Wesley's hymns,
"And on the eagle wings of love,
To joys celestial rise."

hath made the members to excel one another, though not in the same things? Some He hath appointed to surpass the rest in beauty, and some in strength. Thus, the eye is beautiful, but the feet are stronger. The head is honourable, but it cannot say to the feet, "I have no need of you."[1] And this may be seen too with regard to irrational animals; and the same in all the relations of life. The king, for instance, has need of his subjects, and the subjects of the king; just as the head has need of the feet. And again, as to brutes; some are more powerful than the rest; and some more beautiful. Some there are that delight us; some that nourish; and some that clothe us. Thus the peacock delights; and fowls and swine nourish; sheep and goats provide us clothing; and the ox and ass share our labours. There are also others which provide us with none of these, but which call our powers into active exercise. Thus the wild animals increase the strength of the hunters; and instruct our race by the fear which they inspire, and render us more cautious; and for medical purposes, they supply no small contributions from their bodies.[2] So that if any one say to thee, "How art thou a lord of the brutes, whilst afraid of the lion?" Answer him, "Things were not ordered in this manner at the beginning, when I was in favour with God, when I dwelt in Paradise. But when I had offended my Master, I fell under the power of those who were my servants! Yet not even now entirely; since I possess an art by which I overcome the wild animals." So also it happens in great houses; the sons, while they are yet under age, are afraid of many of the servants; but when they have done amiss, their dread is greatly heightened. And this we may say also of serpents, and scorpions, and vipers; that they are formidable to us by reason of sin.

13. And not only as it regards our body, and the various states of life, is this diversity observable; nor is it confined to brutes; but it may be seen also in trees; and the meanest of them may be observed to have an excellence above those which are greater; so that all things are not alike in all, that all may be necessary to us; and that we may perceive the manifold wisdom of the Lord. Do not then lay blame on God on account of the body's corruptibleness, but for this the rather do Him homage, and admire Him for His wisdom and His tender care; His wisdom, that in so corruptible a body He hath been able to display such harmony; His tender care that for the benefit of the soul He hath made it corruptible, that He might repress her vanity, and subdue her pride! Why then did He not make it thus from the beginning, asks some one? It was, I reply, to justify Himself before thee by these very works; and as much as to say by the result itself, "I called thee to greater honour, but thou didst constitute thyself unworthy of the gift, banishing thyself from Paradise! Nevertheless, I will not even now despise thee, but I will correct thy sin, and bring thee back[3] to heaven. Therefore for thine own sake, I have permitted thee so long to decay and suffer corruption, that in the fulness of time the discipline of thy humility might be established; and that thou mightest never more resume thy former conceit."

14. For all these things then let us give thanks to God who loveth man; and for His tender care over us, render Him a recompense, that will also be profitable to ourselves; and as regards the commandment which I so frequently discourse of to you, let us use our utmost diligence! For I will not desist from the exhortation until ye are amended: seeing that what we aim at is not that we may address you seldom or frequently, but that we may continue speaking till we have persuaded you. To the Jews when God said by the prophet, "If ye fast for strife and debate, to what purpose do ye fast for me?"[4] And by us He saith to you, "If ye fast unto oaths and perjuries, to what purpose do ye fast? For how shall we behold the sacred Passover? How shall we receive the holy Sacrifice? How shall we be partakers of those wonderful mysteries by means of the same tongue with which we have trampled upon God's law, the same tongue with which we have contaminated the soul? For if no one would dare to receive the royal purple with filthy hands, how shall we receive the Lord's Body with a tongue that has become polluted! For the oath is of the wicked one, but the Sacrifice is of the Lord. "What communion then hath light with darkness, and what concord hath Christ with Belial?"[5]

15. That ye are desirous, indeed, to be rid of this impiety, I know well; but since each man may not be able easily to accomplish this by himself, let us enter into fraternities and partnerships in this matter; and as the poor do in their feasts,[6] when each one alone would not be able to furnish a complete banquet; when they all meet together, they each

---

[1] 1 Cor. xii. 21.   [2] See Hom. VIII. 1.
[3] Or, take thee up.   [4] Isa. lviii. 4, 5.
[5] 2 Cor. vi. 14, 15.
[6] See on Rom. xiii. 14, Hom. XXIV., where St. Chrysostom recommends sober conversation at such meetings.

bring their contribution to the feast; so also let us act. Inasmuch as we are of ourselves too listless, let us make partnerships with each other, and pledge ourselves to contribute counsel, and admonition, and exhortation, and rebuke and reminiscence, and threatening; in order that from the diligence of each we may all be amended. For seeing that we observe the affairs of our neighbour more sharply than we do our own, let us be watchful of the safety of others, and commit the guardianship of ourselves to them; and let us engage in this pious rivalry, to the end that thus becoming superior to such an evil habit, we may come with boldness to this holy feast; and be partakers of the holy Sacrifice, with a favourable hope and a good conscience; through the grace and lovingkindness of our Lord Jesus Christ, by whom and with whom, be glory to the Father, with the Holy Spirit, for ever and ever. Amen.

HOMILY XII.

Thanksgiving to God for the pardon granted to the offenders against the Emperor. Physical discourse on the Creation. Proof that God, in creating man, implanted in him a natural law. Duty of avoiding oaths with the utmost diligence.

1. YESTERDAY I said "Blessed be God!" and to-day again I say the very same thing. For although the evils we dreaded have passed away, we should not suffer the memory of them to disappear; not indeed that we may grieve, but that we may give thanks. For if the memory of these terrors abide with us, we shall never be overtaken by the actual experience of such terrors. For what need have we of the experience, whilst our memory acts the part of a monitor? Seeing then that God hath not permitted us to be overwhelmed in the flood of those troubles when upon us, let us not permit ourselves to become careless when these are passed away. Then, when we were sad, He consoled us, let us give thanks to Him now that we are joyful. In our agony He comforted us, and did not forsake us; therefore let us not betray ourselves in prosperity by declining into sloth. "Forget not," saith one, "the time of famine in the day of plenty."[1] Therefore let us be mindful of the time of temptation in the day of relief; and with respect to our sins let us also act in the same manner. If thou hast sinned, and God hath pardoned thy sin, receive thy pardon, and give thanks; but be not forgetful of the sin; not that thou shouldest fret thyself with the thought of it, but that thou mayest school thy soul, not to grow wanton, and relapse again into the same snares.[2]

2. Thus also Paul did; for having said, "He counted me faithful, putting me into the ministry," he goes on to add, "who was before a blasphemer, a persecutor, and injurious."[3] "Let the life of the servant," saith he, "be openly exposed, so that the lovingkindness of the Master be apparent. For although I have received the remission of sins, I do not reject the memory of those sins." And this not only manifested the lovingkindness of the Lord, but made the man himself the more illustrious. For when thou hast learnt who he was before, then thou wilt be the more astonished at him; and when thou seest out of what he came to be what he was, then thou wilt commend him the more; and if thou hast greatly sinned, yet upon being changed thou wilt conceive favourable hopes from this instance. For in addition to what has been said, such an example comforts those who are in despair, and causes them again to stand erect. The same thing also will be the case with regard to our city; for all the events that have happened serve to shew your virtue, who by means of repentance have prevailed to ward off such wrath, whilst at the same time they proclaim the lovingkindness of God, who has removed the cloud that was so threatening, in consequence of a small change of conduct, and so raises up again all those who are sunk in despair, when they learn, from our case, that

---

[1] Ecclus. xviii. 25. [2] See on Heb. vi. 4, Hom. IX. (4). [3] 1 Tim. i. 12, 13.

he who looks upward for the Divine help, is not to be overwhelmed, though innumerable waves should encompass him on all sides.

3. For who hath seen, who hath ever heard of sufferings such as were ours? We were every day in expectation that our city would be overturned from its foundations together with its inhabitants. But when the Devil was hoping to sink the vessel, then God produced a perfect calm. Let us not then be unmindful of the greatness of these terrors, in order that we may remember the magnitude of the benefits received from God. He who knows not the nature of the disease will not understand the physician's art. Let us tell these things also to our children; and transmit them to the remotest generations, that all may learn how the Devil had endeavoured to destroy the very foundation of the city; and how God was able visibly to raise it up again, when it was fallen and prostrate; and did not permit even the least injury to befall it, but took away the fear; and dispelled with much speed the peril it had been placed in. For even through the past week we were all expecting that our substance would be confiscated; and that soldiers would have been let loose upon us; and we were dreaming of a thousand other horrors. But lo! all these things have passed away, even like a cloud or a flitting shadow; and we have been punished only in the expectation of what is dreadful; or rather we have not been punished, but we have been disciplined, and have become better; God having softened the heart of the Emperor. Let us then always and every day say, "Blessed be God!" and with greater zeal let us give heed to our assembling, and let us hasten to the church, from whence we have reaped this benefit. For ye know whither ye fled at the first; whither ye flocked together; and from what quarter our safety came. Let us then hold fast by this sacred anchor; and as in the season of danger it did not betray us, so now let us not leave it in the season of relief; but let us await with exact attention the stated assemblies and prayers; and let us every day give a hearing to the divine oracles. And the leisure which we spent in busily running about after those who came from the court,[1] whilst we were labouring under anxiety in respect to the evils that threatened us; this let us consume wholly in hearing the divine laws, instead of unseasonable and senseless pastimes; lest we should again reduce ourselves to the necessity of that sort of occupation.[2]

4. On the three foregoing days, then, we have investigated one method of acquiring the knowledge of God, and have brought it to a conclusion; explaining how "the heavens declare the glory of God;"[3] and what the meaning of that is, which is said by Paul; viz. "That the invisible things of Him from the creation of the world are clearly seen, being understood by the things that are made."[4] And we shewed how from the creation of the world, and how by heaven, and earth, the sea, the Creator is glorified. But to-day, after briefly philosophising on that same subject, we will proceed to another topic. For He not only made it,[5] but provided also that when it was made, it should carry on its operations; not permitting it to be all immoveable, nor commanding it to be all in a state of motion. The heaven, for instance, hath remained immoveable, according as the prophet says, "He placed the heaven as a vault, and stretched it out as a tent over the earth."[6] But, on the other hand, the sun with the rest of the stars, runs on his course through every day.[7] And again, the earth is fixed, but the waters are continually in motion; and not the waters only, but the clouds, and the frequent and successive showers, which return at their proper season. The nature of the clouds is one, but the things which are produced out of them are different. For the rain, indeed, becomes wine in the grape, but oil in the olive. And in other plants is changed into their juices; and the womb of the earth is one, and yet bears different fruits. The heat, too, of the sun-beams is one, but it ripens all things differently; bringing some to maturity more slowly, and others more quickly. Who then but must feel astonishment and admiration at these things?

5. Nay, this is not the only wonder, that He hath formed it with this great variety and diversity; but farther, that He hath spread it before all in common; the rich and the poor, sinners as well as the righteous. Even as Christ also declared: "He maketh His sun to rise upon the evil and the good, and sendeth His rain upon the just and unjust."[8] Moreover, when He stocked the world with various animals, and implanted divers dispositions in the creatures, He commanded us to imitate some of these, and to avoid others. For example; the ant is industrious, and per-

---

[1] στρατοπέδον.
[2] That is, of being busy about the news from the court and the Emperor, upon which the fate of the city depended.

[3] Ps. xix. 1. [4] Rom. i. 20.
[5] αὐτήν, *i. e.*, τὴν κτίσιν, the Creation. [6] Isa. xl. 42.
[7] Hom. IX. (3) (4), and notes. St. Chrys. on Hebr viii. 1, Hom. XIV. (1), denies that the Heaven is either moveable or spherical. Plato, and most others, thought that the fixed stars moved with the whole solid firmament, but Philoponus argues that a sphere moving round its axis has motion of translation, and may be called fixed. See Mont. pref. to *Cosmas Ægypt.*, in Coll. *Nov. Patr.* t. ii.
[8] Matt. v. 45.

forms a laborious task. By giving heed then, thou wilt receive the strongest admonition from this animal not to indulge in sloth, nor to shun labour and toil. Therefore also the Scripture has sent the sluggard to the ant, saying, " Go to the ant, thou sluggard, emulate his ways, and be wiser than he." [1] Art thou unwilling, he means, to learn from the Scriptures, that it is good to labour, and that he who will not work, neither ought he to eat? [2] learn it from the irrationals! This also we do in our families, when those who are older, and who are considered superior, have done amiss, we bid them to attend to thoughtful children. We say, " Mark such an one, who is less than you, how earnest and watchful he is." Do thou then likewise receive from this animal the best exhortation to industry; and marvel at thy Lord, not only because He hath made heaven and the sun, but because He hath also made the ant. For although the animal be small, it affords much proof of the greatness of God's wisdom. Consider then how prudent the ant is, and consider how God hath implanted in so small a body, such an unceasing desire of working! But whilst from this animal thou learnest industry; take from the bee at once a lesson of neatness, industry, and social concord! For it is not more for herself [3] than for us, that the bee labours, and toils every day; which is indeed a thing especially proper for a Christian; not to seek his own things, but the things of others. As then she traverses all the meadows that she may prepare a banquet for another, so also, O man, do thou likewise; and if thou hast accumulated wealth, expend it upon others; if thou hast the faculty of teaching, [4] do not bury the talent, but bring it out publicly for the sake of those who need it! Or if thou hast any other advantage, become useful to those who require the benefit of thy labours! Seest thou not that for this reason, especially, the bee is more honoured than the other animals; not because she labours, but because she labours for others? For the spider also labours, and toils, and spreads out his fine textures over the walls, surpassing the utmost skill of woman; but the creature is without estimation, since his work is in no way profitable to us; such are they that labour and toil, but for themselves! Imitate too the simplicity of the dove! Imitate the ass in his love to his master, and the ox also! Imitate the birds in their freedom from anxiety! For great, great indeed is the advantage that may be gained from irrational creatures for the correction of manners.

6. From these animals Christ also instructs us, when He says, " Be ye wise as serpents, and harmless as doves." [5] And again; " Behold the fowls of the air, for they sow not, neither do they reap, nor gather into barns; yet your heavenly Father feedeth them." [6] The prophet also, to shame the ungrateful Jews, thus speaks; "The ox knoweth his owner, and the ass his master's crib; but Israel doth not know me." [7] And again; " The turtle and the swallow and the crane observe the time of their coming, but my people knoweth not the judgment of the Lord his God." [8] From these animals, and such as these, learn to achieve virtue, and be instructed to avoid wickedness by the contrary ones. For as the bee followeth good, so the asp is destructive. Therefore shun wickedness, lest thou hear it said, " The poison of asps is under their lips." [9] Again, the dog is devoid of shame. Hate, therefore, this kind of wickedness. The fox also is crafty, and fraudulent. Emulate not this vice; but as the bee, in flying over the meadows, does not choose every sort of flower; [10] but selecting that which is useful, leaves the rest; so also do thou; and whilst surveying the whole race of irrational animals, if any thing profitable may be drawn from these, accept it; the advantages which they have naturally, make it thy business to practise of thine own free choice. For in this respect also thou hast been honoured of God; that what they have as natural advantages He hath permitted thee to achieve of thy own free choice, in order that thou mayest also receive a reward. For good works with them spring not from free will, and reason, but from nature only. In other words, the bee makes honey, not because it has learnt this by reason and reflection, but because it is instructed by nature. Because if the work had not been natural, and allotted to the race, some of them assuredly would have been unskilled in their art; whereas from the time that the world was first made, even to the present day, no one hath observed bees resting from labour, and not making honey. For such natural characteristics are common to the whole race. But those things which depend on our free choice are not common; for labour is necessary that they may be accomplished.

7. Take then all the best things, and clothe thyself with them; for thou art indeed king of the irrationals; but kings, if there be any

---
[1] Prov. vi. 6.   [2] 2 Thess. iii. 10.
[3] See Wordsworth's *Vernal Ode, Poems*, vol. 3. He however only speaks of her as "a statist prudent to confer—upon the public weal."
[4] λόγους διδασκαλίας, v. 1 Tim. v. 17, Rom. xii. 7.

[5] Matt. x. 16.   [6] Matt. vi. 26.   [7] Isa. i. 3.
[8] Jer. vi i. 7.   [9] Ps. cxl. 3.   [10] πάντα.

thing excellent possessed by their subjects, be it gold or silver, or precious stones, or sumptuous vestments, usually possess the same in greater abundance. From the creation also, learn to admire thy Lord! And if any of the things thou seest exceed thy comprehension, and thou art not able to find the reason thereof, yet for this glorify the Creator, that the wisdom of these works surpasses thine understanding. Say not, wherefore is this? or, to what end? for everything is useful, even if we know not the reason of it. As therefore, if thou goest into a surgery, and seest many instruments lying before thee, thou wonderest at the variety of the implements though ignorant of their use; so also act with respect to the creation. Although thou seest many of the animals, and of the herbs, and plants, and other things, of which thou knowest not the use, admire the variety of these; and feel astonishment for this reason at the perfect workmanship of God; that He hath neither made all things manifest to thee, nor permitted all things to be unknown. For He hath not permitted all things to be unknown, lest thou shouldest say, that the things that exist are not of providence. He hath not permitted all things to be known to thee, lest the greatness of thy knowledge should excite thee to pride. Thus at least it was that the evil demon precipitated[1] the first man headlong and by means of the hope of greater knowledge, deprived him of that he already possessed. Therefore also, a certain wise man exhorts, saying, "Seek not out the things that are too hard for thee; neither search the things that are too deep for thee. But what is commanded thee, think thereupon with reverence; for the greater part of His works are done in secret."[2] And again; "More things are shewed unto thee than men understand." But this he speaks for the purpose of consoling the man who is sad and vexed, because he does not know all things; for even those things he observes, which thou art permitted to know, greatly surpass thine understanding; for thou couldest not have found them by thyself, but thou hast been taught them of God. Wherefore be content with the wealth given thee, and do not seek more; but for what thou hast received give thanks; and do not be angry on account of those things which thou hast not received. And, for what thou knowest, give glory, and do not stumble at those things of which thou art ignorant. For God hath made both alike profitably; and hath revealed some things, but hidden others, providing for thy safety.

8. One mode, then, of knowing God, is that by the creation, which I have spoken of, and which might occupy many days. For in order that we might go over the formation of man only with exactness, (and I speak of exactness such as is possible to us, not of real exactness; since many as are the reasons we have already given for the works of creation, many more of these there are, ineffable, which God who made them knoweth, for of course we do not know them all); in order then, I say, that we might take an exact survey of the whole modelling of man; and that we might discover the skill there is in every member; and examine the distribution and situation of the sinews, the veins, and the arteries, and the moulding of every other part; not even a whole year would suffice for such a disquisition.

9. For this reason, here dismissing this subject; and having given to the laborious and studious an opportunity, by what has been said, of going over likewise the other parts of Creation; we shall now direct our discourse to another point which is itself also demonstrative of God's providence. What then is this second point? It is, that when God formed man, he implanted within him from the beginning a natural law. And what then was this natural law? He gave utterance to conscience within us; and made the knowledge of good things, and of those which are the contrary, to be self-taught. For we have no need to learn that fornication is an evil thing, and that chastity is a good thing, but we know this from the first. And that you may learn that we know this from the first, the Lawgiver,[3] when He afterwards gave laws, and said, "Thou shalt not kill,"[4] did not add, "since murder is an evil thing," but simply said, "Thou shalt not kill;" for He merely prohibited the sin, without teaching. How was it then when He said, "Thou shalt not kill," that He did not add, "because murder is a wicked thing." The reason was, that conscience had taught this beforehand; and He speaks thus, as to those who know and understand the point. Wherefore when He speaks to us of another commandment, not known to us by the dictate of conscience, He not only prohibits, but adds the reason. When, for instance, He gave commandment

---

[1] ἐξετραχήλισεν (a word used of a horse who throws the rider over his head), lit. brake the neck of, but the word is generally used of overthrowing by treachery. St. Chrysostom also uses it of elevating with pride, which may be intended here. As Hom. XIII. in Heb. v. fin.
[2] Ecclus. iii. 21, 22, 23.
[3] He seems to mean the Divine Lawgiver. See Hom. *de Pœnit.* VI. (4), where he speaks of the "One Law-giver of the two Covenants," and so on Ps. xlvi. (al. xlvii.) (5), Ben. t. 5, p. 196; A. in Matt. Hom. XVI. Ben. t. 7, p. 213, B.
[4] Exod. xx. 13.

respecting the Sabbath; "On the seventh day thou shalt do no work;" He subjoined also the reason for this cessation. What was this? "Because on the seventh day God rested from all His works which He had begun to make."[1] And again; "Because thou wert a servant in the land of Egypt."[2] For what purpose then I ask did He add a reason respecting the Sabbath, but did no such thing in regard to murder? Because this commandment was not one of the leading ones. It was not one of those which were accurately defined of our conscience, but a kind of partial and temporary one; and for this reason it was abolished afterwards.[3] But those which are necessary and uphold our life, are the following; "Thou shalt not kill; Thou shalt not commit adultery; Thou shalt not steal." On this account then He adds no reason in this case, nor enters into any instruction on the matter, but is content with the bare prohibition.

10. And not only from thence, but from another consideration also, I will endeavour to shew you how man was self-taught with respect to the knowledge of virtue. Adam sinned the first sin; and after the sin straightway hid himself; but if he had not known he had been doing something wrong, why did he hide himself? For then there were neither letters, nor law, nor Moses. Whence then doth he recognise the sin, and hide himself? Yet not only does he so hide himself, but when called to account, he endeavours to lay the blame on another, saying, "The woman, whom Thou gavest me, she gave me of the tree, and I did eat." And that woman again transfers the accusation to another, viz. the serpent. Observe also the wisdom of God; for when Adam said, "I heard Thy voice, and I was afraid, for I was naked, and I hid myself,"[4] God does not at once convict him of what he had done, nor say, "Why hast thou eaten of the tree?" But how? "Who told thee," He asks, "that thou wast naked, unless thou hast eaten of that Tree of which alone I commanded thee not to eat?" He did not keep silence, nor did He openly convict him. He did not keep silence, that He might call him forth to the confession of his crime. He did not convict him openly, lest the whole might come from Himself, and the man should so be deprived of that pardon which is granted us from confession.[5] Therefore he did not declare openly the cause from whence this knowledge sprung, but he carried on the discourse in the form of interrogation, leaving the man himself to come to the confession.

11. Again, in the case of Cain and Abel, the same proceeding is observable. For, in the first place, they set apart the fruits of their own labours to God. For we would shew not from his sin only, but also from his virtue, that man was capable of knowing both these things. Wherefore that man knew sin to be an evil thing, Adam manifested; and that he knew that virtue was a good thing, Abel again made evident. For without having learnt it from any one, without having heard any law promulgated respecting the first fruits, but having been taught from within, and from his conscience, he presented that sacrifice. On this account I do not carry the argument down to a later period; but I bring it to bear upon the time of these earlier men, when there were as yet no letters, as yet no[6] law, nor as yet prophets and judges; but Adam only existed with his children; in order that thou mayest learn, that the knowledge of good and evil had been previously implanted in their natures. For from whence did Abel learn that to offer sacrifice was a good thing;[7] that it was good to honour God, and in all things to give thanks? "Why then?" replies some one, "did not Cain bring his offering?" This man also did offer sacrifice, but not in like manner. And from

---

[1] Exod. xx. 10.   [2] Deut. xxi. 18.
[3] κατελύθη μετὰ ταῦτα. See on Matt. v. 17, Hom. XVI. (1), St. Augustin, contr. Faust. vi. 4, speaks of it as allegorical, and now become superfluous in the letter. And Ep. lv. (al. cxix.), (*Ad inq.* Jan. i. 2), c. 22, he writes, "of all the Ten Commandments, only that of the Sabbath is enjoined to be observed figuratively, which figure we have received to be understood, not to be still celebrated by rest of the body." St. Chrys. on Gen. ii. 3, Hom. X. (7), has, "Now already from the beginning God offered us instruction typically (αἰνιγματωδῶς), teaching us to dedicate and separate the one day in the circle of the week wholly to employment in things spiritual;" thus making the Sabbath a *type* of the Lord's Day, and rest *from* secular, of rest *in* spiritual work.
[4] Gen. iii. 10, 11, 12.

[5] See Hom. VIII. 2. He does not mean that this of itself merits pardon; indeed the word is rather "allowance," or indulgence (συγγνώμη); but that it is a condition of pardon, and a great means of recovery. See on Heb. vi. 5, and Hooker, b. vi. c. iv. 16, where "Hom. *de Pæn. et conf.*" is an extract from one found in the Greek. Ben. t. ii. 663, a. Sav. viii. 97, 12.
[6] Sav. rep. as yet.
[7] See Davison's "Inquiry into the Origin and Intent of Primitive Sacrifice," reprinted in his Remains, where this view is maintained as at least probable, and freed from some objections. Archbishop Magee, in his work on the Atonement, vol. i. no. 41, vol. ii. no. 54, 58, &c., maintains the original, divine institution. It is difficult now to judge what may have been likely to seem reasonable and natural to our first parents, who had a stronger apprehension of natural things, as well as a more sensible communion with God, than we. It may be observed, that such a view does not interfere with the strictly typical character of the sacrifice, because man is made in the image of God, and many things which he does of mere nature, as well as moral actions not specially enjoined, are typical, and represented as typical in Holy Scripture. And again, sacrifice, if it originated in God's gift of reason, was certainly sanctioned, and endowed with an atoning power, by His special laws. The prevailing neglect of our Eucharistic oblation as such, and separating in thought our partaking of the sacrifice of our Lord from the sacrament of the altar, tend to obscure men's views on this subject. It is, however, difficult to conceive how the sacrifice of *animals* should have occurred to man, without some divine indication beyond the permission to use them for food. St. Chrys. on Gen. iv. Hom. XVIII. (5), speaks of nothing more than an offering "out of our possessions" as taught by natural conscience; and of Abel's offering being of the first-born, and of the best, as a proof of his devotion. On this view the *type* would arise from the divine permission of animal food.

thence again the knowledge of conscience is apparent. For when, envying him who had been honoured, he deliberated upon murder, he conceals his crafty determination. And what says he; "Come, let us go forth into the field."[1] The outward guise was one thing, the pretence of love; the thought another, the purpose of fratricide. But if he had not known the design to be a wicked one, why did he conceal it? And again, after the murder had been perpetrated, being asked of God, "Where is Abel thy brother?" he answers, "I know not; Am I my brother's keeper?" Wherefore does he deny the crime? Is it not evidently because he exceedingly condemns himself. For as his father had hid himself, so also this man denies his guilt, and after his conviction, again says, "My crime is too great to obtain pardon."[2]

12. But it may be objected, that the Gentile allows nothing of this sort. Come then, let us discuss this point, and as we have done with respect to the creation, having carried on the warfare against these objectors not only by the help of the Scriptures, but of reason, so also let us now do with respect to conscience. For Paul too, when he was engaged in controversy with such persons, entered upon this head. What then is it that they urge? They say, that there is no self-evident law seated in our consciences; and that God hath not implanted this in our nature. But if so, whence is it, I ask, that legislators have written those laws which are among them concerning marriages, concerning murders, concerning wills, concerning trusts, concerning abstinence from encroachments on one another, and a thousand other things. For the men now living may perchance have learned them from their elders;[3] and they from those who were before them, and these again from those beyond? But from whom did those learn who were the originators and first enactors of laws among them? Is it not evident that it was from conscience? For they cannot say, that they held communication with Moses; or that they heard the prophets. How could it be so when they were Gentiles? But it is evident that from the very law which God placed in man when He formed him from the beginning, laws were laid down, and arts discovered, and all other things. For the arts too were thus established, their originators having come to the knowledge of them in a self-taught manner.

13. So also came there to be courts of justice, and so were penalties defined, as Paul accordingly observes. For since many of the Gentiles were ready to controvert this, and to say, "How will God judge mankind who lived before Moses? He did not send a lawgiver; He did not introduce a law; He commissioned no prophet, nor apostle, nor evangelist; how then can He call these to account?" Since Paul therefore wished to prove that they possessed a self taught law; and that they knew clearly what they ought to do; hear how he speaks; "For when the Gentiles who have not the law, do by nature the things contained in the law, these having not the law, are a law unto themselves; which shew the work of the law written in their hearts."[4] But how without letters? "Their conscience also bearing witness, and their thoughts the meanwhile accusing, or else excusing one another. In the day when God shall judge the secrets of men by Jesus Christ according to my gospel."[5] And again; "As many as have sinned without law, shall perish without law; and as many as have sinned in the law, shall be judged by the law."[6] What means, "They shall perish without law?" The law not accusing them, but their thoughts, and their conscience; for if they had not a law of conscience, it were not necessary that they should perish through having done amiss. For how should it be so if they sinned without a law? but when he says, "without a law," he does not assert that they had no law, but that they had no written law, though they had the law of nature. And again; "But glory, honour, and peace, to every man that worketh good, to the Jew first, and also to the Gentile."[7]

14. But these things he spake in reference to the early times, before the coming of Christ; and the Gentile he names here is not an idolater, but one who worshipped God only; unfettered by the necessity of Judaical observances, (I mean Sabbaths, and circumcision, and divers purifications,) yet exhibiting all manner of wisdom and piety.[8] And

---

[1] Gen. iv. 9. This clause is added in the Vulgate as well as the Septuagint. The Hebrew seems to present an hiatus after וַיֹּאמֶר (*said* rather than *spake*). The Targum of Jerusalem and that called of Jonathan supply it, Tr. (The Samaritan and Syriac and Aquila also contain this clause. Origen did not find it in the Hebrew, and Onkelos omits it. Michælis quotes John xviii. 16, to meet the difficulty. Some render the word *told*, and refer it to what went before.)
[2] Gen. iv. 13, LXX.
[3] πρώτων, Lat. *majoribus natu*, which suggests πρὸ αὐτῶν, or πρεσβυτέρων, but 6 MSS. agree. See Hom. IX. in St. Matt. ed. Field.
[4] Rom. ii. 14, 15.   [5] Rom. ii. 16.   [6] Rom. ii. 12.
[7] Rom. ii. 10.
[8] The term Ἕλλην, "Gentile," or literally "Greek," usually at that time meant idolater. Thus we find many works of the Fathers "against the Greeks." But on the passage referred to, Hom. V. on Rom., he expressly includes Melchizedek and Job under the name as there used. These expressions, therefore, indicate what a man *might* be, though a Gentile, not what Gentiles usually were. Observe also that this description applies only to those spoken of in verse 10. But the being out of the Jewish Covenant applies also to the Gentiles in verses 8 and 9.

again, discoursing of such a worshipper, he observes, "Wrath and indignation, tribulation and anguish, upon every soul of man that doeth evil, of the Jew first, and also of the Gentile."[1] Again he here calls by the name of Greek one who was free from the observance of Judaic customs. If, then, he had not heard the law, nor conversed with the Jews, how could there be wrath, indignation and tribulation against him for working evil? The reason is, that he possessed a conscience inwardly admonishing him, and teaching him, and instructing him in all things. Whence is this manifest? From the way in which he[2] punished others when they did amiss; from the way in which he laid down laws; from the way in which he set up the tribunals of justice. With the view of making this more plain, Paul spoke of those who were living in wickedness. "Who, knowing the ordinance of God, that they which commit such things are worthy of death, not only do the same, but also consent with them that practise them."[3] "But from whence," says some one, "did they know, that it is the will of God, that those who live in iniquity should be punished with death?" From whence? Why, from the way in which they judged others who sinned. For if thou deemest not murder to be a wicked thing, when thou hast gotten a murderer at thy bar, thou shouldest not punish him. So if thou deemest it not an evil thing to commit adultery, when the adulterer has fallen into thy hands, release him from punishment! But if thou recordest laws, and prescribest punishments, and art a severe judge of the sins of others; what defence canst thou make, in matters wherein thou thyself doest amiss, by saying that thou art ignorant what things ought to be done? For suppose that thou and another person have alike been guilty of adultery. On what account dost thou punish him, and deem thyself worthy of forgiveness? Since if thou didst not know adultery to be wickedness, it were not right to punish it in another. But if thou punishest, and thinkest to escape the punishment thyself, how is it agreeable to reason that the same offences should not pay the same penalty?

15. This indeed is the very thing which Paul rebukes, when he says, "And thinkest thou this, O man, that judgest them which do such things, and doest the same, that thou shalt escape the judgment of God?"[4] It is not, it cannot be possible; for from the very sentence, he means, which thou pronouncest upon another, from this sentence God will then judge thee. For surely thou art not just, and God unjust! But if thou overlookest not another suffering wrong, how shall God overlook? And if thou correctest the sins of others, how will not God correct thee? And though He may not bring the punishment upon thee instantly, be not confident on that account, but fear the more. So also Paul bade thee, saying, "Despisest thou the riches of His goodness, and forbearance, and longsuffering, not knowing that the goodness of God leadeth thee to repentance?"[5] For therefore, saith he, doth he bear with thee, not that thou mayest become worse, but that thou mayest repent. But if thou wilt not, this longsuffering becomes a cause of thy greater punishment; continuing, as thou dost, impenitent. This, however, is the very thing he means, when he says, "But after thy hardness and impenitent heart treasurest up to thyself wrath against the day of wrath, and revelation of the righteous judgment of God. Who will render to every man according to his deeds."[6] Since, therefore, He rendereth to every man according to his works; for this reason He both implanted within us a natural law, and afterwards gave us a written one, in order that He might demand an account of sins, and that He might crown those who act rightly. Let us then order our conduct with the utmost care, and as those who have soon to encounter a fearful tribunal; knowing that we shall enjoy no pardon, if after a natural as well as written law, and so much teaching and continual admonition, we neglect our own salvation.

16. I desire then to address you again on the subject of oaths; but I feel ashamed. For to me, indeed, it is not wearisome both by day and by night to repeat the same things to you. But I am afraid, lest, having followed you up so many days, I should seem to condemn you of great listlessness, that you should require continual admonition respecting so easy a matter. And I am not only ashamed, but also in fear for you! for frequent instruction, to those who give heed, is salutary and profitable; but to those who are listless, it is injurious, and exceedingly perilous; for the oftener any one hears, the greater punishment does he draw upon himself, if he does not practise what is told him. With this accordingly God reproached the Jews, speaking thus: "I have sent my prophets, rising up early, and sending them; and even then ye did not hearken."[7] We therefore do this of our great care for you. But we fear, lest, on that tremendous Day, this ad-

---

[1] Rom. ii. 9. [2] al. they. [3] Rom. i. 32.
[4] Rom. ii. 3. [5] Rom. ii. 4. [6] Rom. ii. 5, 6. [7] Jer. xxix. 9.

monition and counsel should rise up against you all. For when the point to be attained is easy, and he whose office it is continually to admonish, desists not from his task, what defence shall we have to offer? or what argument will save us from punishment? Tell me, if a sum of money chance to be due to you, do you not always, when you meet the debtor, remind him of the loan? Do thou too[1] act thus; and let every one suppose that his neighbour owes him money, viz., the fulfilling of this precept; and upon meeting him, let him put him in mind of the payment, knowing that no small danger lies at our door, whilst we are unmindful of our brethren. For this cause I too cease not to make mention of these things. For I fear, lest by any means I should hear it said on that day, "O wicked and slothful servant, thou oughtest to have put my money to the exchangers."[2] Behold, however, I have laid it down,[3] not once, or twice, but oftentimes. It is left then for you to discharge the usury of it. Now the usury of hearing is the manifestation of it by deeds, for the deposit is the Lord's. Therefore let us not negligently receive that with which we are entrusted; but let us keep it with diligence, that we may restore it with much interest on That Day. For unless thou bring others to the performance of the same good works, thou shalt hear that voice, which he who buried the talent heard. But God forbid it should be this! but may you hear that different voice which Christ uttered, saying to him who had made profit, "Well done, good and faithful servant; thou hast been faithful over a few things, I will make thee ruler over many things."[4]

17. And this voice we shall hear, if we shew the same earnestness as he did. And we shall shew this earnestness, if we do this which I say. When you depart, whilst what you have heard is yet warm within you, exhort one another! And just as ye each salute at parting, so let every one go from hence with an admonition, and say to his neighbour, "Observe and remember that thou keep the commandment;" and thus shall we assuredly get the mastery. For when friends also dismiss one with such counsel; and on one's return home, one's wife again admonishes one to the same effect; and our word keeps its hold on you when alone; we shall soon shake off this evil habit. I know, indeed, that ye marvel why I am so earnest respecting this precept. But discharge the duty enjoined, and then I will tell you. Meanwhile, this I say; that this precept is a divine law; and it is not safe to transgress it. But if I shall see it rightly performed, I will speak of another reason,[5] which is not less than this, that ye may learn that it is with justice I make so much ado about this law. But it is now time to conclude this address in a prayer. Wherefore, let us all say in common, "O God, Who willest not the death of a sinner, but that he should be converted and live; grant that we, having discharged this and every other precept, may be found worthy so to stand at the tribunal of Thy Christ, that having enjoyed great boldness, we may attain the kingdom to Thy glory. For to Thee belongeth glory, together with Thine only begotten Son, and the Holy Ghost, now and ever, and world without end." Amen.

---

[1] *i. e.*, "as I am doing, and as thou wouldest in the case just mentioned."
[2] Matt. xxv. 26, 27.
[3] *i. e.*, considering them as the *exchangers*, to whom he was bound to deliver the truth entrusted to him, that its good effect might multiply. See his Commentary on the passage, Hom. LXXVIII., and another application on Rom. xvi. 6, Hom. XXXI.
[4] Matt. xxv. 21.
[5] See Hom. XIV. (6).

HOMILY XIII.

A further thanksgiving to God for the change in the late melancholy aspect of affairs. Reminiscence of those who were dragged away, and punished because of the sedition. Exposition on the subject of the creation of man, and of his having received a natural law. Of the complete accomplishment of abstinence from oaths.

1. WITH the same introduction and prelude that I began yesterday and the day before, I shall begin to-day. Now again I will say, "Blessed be God!" What a day did we see last Wednesday![1] and what in the present! On that day how heavy was the gloom! How bright the calm of the present! That was the day when that fearful tribunal was

---

[1] τετράδα. *Feriam quartam*, the fourth day of the week. The day referred to was probably one of the days of silence mentioned in the beginning of Hom. XI., where, first line of sec. 2, read "ourselves."

set in the city, and shook the hearts of all, and made the day to seem no better than night; not because the beams of the sun were extinguished, but because that despondency and fear darkened your eyes. Wherefore, that we may reap the more pleasure, I wish to relate a few of the circumstances which then occurred; for I perceive that a narrative of these things will be serviceable to you, and to all who shall come afterwards. Besides, to those who have been delivered from shipwreck, it is sweet to remember the waves, and the tempest, and the winds, when they are come into port. And to those who have fallen into sickness, it is an agreeable thing, when the sickness is over, to talk over with others the fevers by which they were nearly brought to the grave. When terrors have passed away, there is a pleasure in relating those terrors; the soul no longer fearing them, but deriving therefrom more cheerfulness. The remembrance of past evils always makes the present prosperity to appear more strikingly.

2. When the greater portion of the city had taken refuge from the fear and danger of that occasion, in secret places, in deserts, and in hollows;[1] terror besetting them in all directions; and the houses were empty of women, and the forum of men, and scarce two or three appeared walking together across it, and even these going about as if they had been animated corpses: at this period, I proceeded to the tribunal of justice, for the purpose of seeing the end of these transactions; and there, beholding the fragments of the city collected together, I marvelled most of all at this, that although a multitude was around the doors, there was the profoundest silence, as though there had been no man there, all looking upon one another; not one daring to enquire of his neighbour, nor to hear anything from him; for each regarded his neighbour with suspicion; since many already, having been dragged away, beyond all expectation, from the midst of the forum, were now confined within. Thus we all alike looked up to heaven, and stretched out our hands in silence, expecting help from above, and beseeching God to stand by those who were brought to judgment, to soften the hearts of the judges, and to make their sentence a merciful one. And just as when some persons on land, beholding others suffering shipwreck, cannot indeed go near to them, and reach out the hand, and relieve their distress, being kept back from them by the waves; yet away on the shore, with outstretched hands and tears, they supplicate God that He may help the drowning; so there in like manner, did all silently and mentally call upon God, pleading for those at the tribunal, as for men surrounded by the waves, that He would stretch out His hand, and not suffer the vessel to be overwhelmed, nor the judgment of those under trial to end in an utter wreck. Such was the state of things in front of the doors; but when I entered within the court, other sights I saw which were still more awful; soldiers armed with swords and clubs, and strictly keeping the peace for the judges within. For since all the relatives of those under trial, whether wives, or mothers, or daughters, or fathers, stood before the doors of the seat of justice; in order that if any one happened to be led away to execution, yet no one inflamed at the sight of the calamity might raise any tumult or disturbance; the soldiers drove them all afar off; thus preoccupying their mind with fear.

3. One sight there was, more pitiable than all; a mother, and a sister of a certain person, who was among those under trial within, sat at the very vestibule of the court of justice, rolling themselves on the pavement, and becoming a common spectacle to all the bystanders; veiling their faces, and shewing no sense of shame, but that which the urgency of the calamity permitted. No maid servant, nor neighbour, nor female friend, nor any other relative accompanied them. But hemmed in by a crowd of soldiers, alone, and meanly clad, and grovelling on the ground, about the very doors, they were in more pitiable case than those who were undergoing judgment within, and hearing as they did the voice of the executioners, the strokes of the scourge, the wailing of those who were being scourged, the fearful threats of the judges, they themselves endured, at every scourging, sharper pains than those who were beaten. For since, in the confessions of others, there was a danger of accusations being proved, if they heard any one scourged that he might mention those who were guilty, and uttering cries, they, looking up to heaven, besought God to give the sufferer some strength of endurance, lest the safety of their own relations should be betrayed by the weakness of others, while incapable of sustaining the sharp anguish of the strokes. And again, the same thing occurred as in the case of men who are struggling with a tempest. For just as when they perceive the violence of a wave lifting up its head from afar, and gradually increasing, and ready to overwhelm the vessel, they are

---

[1] φάραγγας, usually "ravines." There were, however, caves near Antioch.

almost dead with terror, before it comes near the ship; so also was it with these. If at any time they heard voices, and cries that reached them, they saw a thousand deaths before their eyes, being in terror, lest those who were urged to bear witness, giving way to their torments, should name some one of those who were their own relatives. And thus, one saw tortures both within and without. Those within the executioners were tormenting; these women, the despotic force of nature, and the sympathy of the affections. There was lamentation within, and without! inside, on the part of those who were found guilty, and outside on the part of their relatives. Yea, rather not these only, but their very judges inwardly lamented, and suffered more severely than all the rest; being compelled to take part in so bitter a tragedy.

4. As for me, while I sat and beheld all this, how matrons and virgins, wont to live in seclusion, were now made a common spectacle to all; and how those who were accustomed to lie on a soft couch, had now the pavement for their bed; and how they who had enjoyed so constant an attendance of female servants and eunuchs, and every sort of outward distinction, were now bereft of all these things; and grovelling at the feet of every one, beseeching him to lend help by any means in his power to those who were undergoing examination, and that there might be a kind of general contribution of mercy from all; I exclaimed, in those words of Solomon, "Vanity of vanities, all is vanity."[1] For I saw both this and another oracle fulfilled in every deed, which saith, "All the glory of man is as the flower of grass. The grass withereth, and the flower falleth away."[2] For then, indeed, wealth, and nobility, and notoriety, and the patronage of friends, and kinship and all worldly things, were found worthless; the sin, and transgression of the law which had taken place, having put all these succours to flight. And just as the mother of young birds, when the nestlings have been carried away, coming and finding her nest empty, is unable to rescue her captive brood; but by hovering around the hands of the fowler, in this way displays her grief; even so did these women then do, when their children were snatched away from their dwellings, and shut up within, as it were in a net, or a trap. They could not indeed come in and deliver the prisoners, but they manifested their anguish by wallowing on the ground near the very doors; by lamentation and groans; and by endeavouring to approach as near as possible to those who had captured them. These things then beholding, I cast in my mind That Dread Tribunal; and I said within myself, "If now, when men are the judges, neither mother, nor sister, nor father, nor any other person, though guiltless of the deeds which have been perpetrated, can avail to rescue the criminals; who will stand by us when we are judged at the dread Tribunal of Christ? Who will dare to raise his voice? Who will be able to rescue those who shall be led away to those unbearable punishments. Notwithstanding they were the first men of the city who were then brought to trial, and the very chief of the nobility, yet they would have been glad if it could be granted them to lose all their possessions, yea, if need were, their liberty itself, so that they might continue to enjoy this present life.

5. But to proceed. The day now hastening to its close, and late[3] evening arriving, and the final sentence of the court being expected, all were in still greater agony, and besought God that He would grant some delay and respite; and incline the soul of the judges to refer the facts that had been investigated to the decision of the Emperor; since perchance some advantage might arise from this reference.[4] Moreover, by the people general supplications[5] were sent up to the Merciful God; imploring that He would save the remnants of the city; and not suffer it entirely to be razed from its foundations. Nor could one see any one joining in this cry but with tears. Nevertheless, none of these things then moved the judges within, although they heard. One thing only they considered, that there might be a rigid enquiry into the deeds that had been perpetrated.

6. At last having loaded the culprits with chains, and bound them with iron, they sent them away to the prison through the midst of the forum. Men that had kept their studs of horses, who had been presidents of the games,[6] who could reckon up a thousand different offices of distinction which they had held, had their goods confiscated, and seals might be seen placed upon all their doors.

---

[1] Eccl. i. 2.   [2] Isa. xlii. 6, 7.

[3] βαθυτάτης, which seems to imply darkness. See Luc. xxiv. 1.
[4] Or. "delay." ὑπέρθεσις. But ὑπερτίθεμαι is "to refer" in Herodotus, as i. 8, and elsewhere.
[5] λιταί. The term was originally used of any kind of prayer, but about this time was beginning to be applied to a special kind of penitential prayer. St. Basil, A.D. 375, ep. 207 (al. 63), writes to the Neocaesareans in defence of λιτανεῖαι, to which they objected as newly introduced; and the prayers here mentioned seem to be something distinct from the common service. See Bingham, b. xiii. c. 1, sec. 10. The passage he quotes from St. Augustin, Hom. CLXXII. de Temp. is attributed by the Benedictine editor to Caesarius, after some MSS.
[6] ἀγωνοθέτας. Those who bore this office were men of distinction, and of wealth, as they usually furnished the spectacles at their own expense. Such were the Asiarchs, mentioned Acts xix. 31, and Mart. of St. Polycarp, c. 12. See note in ed. Jacobson.

Their wives also being ejected from their parents' home, each had literally to play the part of Job's wife. For they went "wandering[1] from house to house and from place to place, seeking a lodging."[2] And this it was not easy for them to find, every one fearing and trembling to receive, or to render assistance in any way to the relatives of those who were under impeachment. Nevertheless, though such events had happened, the sufferers were patient under all; since they were not deprived of the present life. And neither the loss of wealth, nor dishonour, nor so much public exposure, nor any other matter of that nature, caused them vexation. For the greatness of the calamity, and the circumstance of their having expected still worse things, when they suffered these, had prepared the soul for the exercise of a wise fortitude. And now they learnt, how simple a thing is virtue for us, how easy and expeditious of performance, and that from our neglect only it seems to be laborious. They who before this time could not bear the loss of a little money with meekness, now they were subject to a greater fear, although they had lost all their substance, felt as if they had found a treasure, because they had not lost their lives. So that if the sense of a future hell took possession of us, and we thought of those intolerable punishments, we should not grieve, even though for the sake of the law of God we were to give both our substance, and our bodies and lives too, knowing that we should gain greater things; deliverance from the terrors that are hereafter.

7. Perchance the tragedy of all I have told you, has greatly softened your hearts. Do not however take it amiss. For since I am about to venture upon some more subtle thoughts and require a more sensitive state of mind on your part, I have done this intentionally, in order that by the terror of the description your minds might have shaken off all listlessness, and withdrawn themselves from all worldly cares, and might with the more readiness convey the force of the things about to be spoken into the depths of your soul.

Sufficiently indeed, then, our discourse of late[3] evinced to you, that a natural law of good and evil is seated within us. But that our proof of it may be more abundantly evident, we will again to-day apply ourselves strenuously to the same subject of discourse. For that God from the beginning, when He formed man, made him capable of discriminating both these, all men make evident. Hence when we sin, we are all ashamed at the presence of our inferiors; and oftentimes a master, on his way to the house of a harlot, if he then perceives any one of his more respectable servants, turns back, reddening with shame, from this untoward path. Again, when others reproach us, fixing on us the names of particular vices, we call it an insult; and if we are aggrieved, we drag those who have done the wrong to the public tribunal. Thus we can understand what vice is, and what virtue is. Wherefore Christ, for the purpose of declaring this, and shewing that He was not introducing a strange law, or one which surpassed our nature, but that which He had of old deposited beforehand in our conscience, after pronouncing those numerous Beatitudes, thus speaks; "All things whatsoever ye would that men should do to you, do ye even so to them."[4] "Many words," saith He, "are not necessary, nor laws of great length, nor a diversity of instruction. Let thine own will be the law. Dost thou wish to receive kindness? Be kind to another. Dost thou wish to receive mercy? Show mercy to thy neighbour. Dost thou wish to be applauded? Applaud another. Dost thou wish to be beloved? Exercise love. Dost thou wish to enjoy the first rank? First concede that place to another. Become thyself the judge, thyself the lawgiver of thine own life. And again; "Do not to another what thou hatest."[5] By the latter precept, he would induce to a departure from iniquity; by the former, to the exercise of virtue. "Do not thou to another," he saith,[6] "what thou hatest." Dost thou hate to be insulted? Do not insult another. Dost thou hate to be envied? Envy not another. Dost thou hate to be deceived? Do not deceive another. And, in a word, in all things, if we hold fast these two precepts, we shall not need any other instruction. For the knowledge of virtue He hath implanted in our nature; but the practice of it and the correction He hath entrusted to our moral choice.[7]

8. Perhaps what is thus said, is obscure; wherefore I will again endeavour to make it more plain. In order to know that it is a good thing to exercise temperance, we need

---

[1] Chrysostom here alludes to the history of Job as given in the Septuagint. Job's wife is there made to address him in a long speech, of which the words, "wandering from house to house," &c., are a part.
[2] Job ii. 9, LXX.
[3] πρώην, which seems to refer to the last Homily, as also χθὲς at the beginning. This reference may, however, include also Hom. XI.

[4] Matt. vii. 12.   [5] Tobit iv. 16.   [6] So Sav.
[7] "The light of reason does not, any more than that of Revelation, force men to submit to its authority." Butler, *Analogy*, part ii. c. i. sec. 1, where the relation of Christianity to natural religion is investigated. See also his Sermons, II. and III. on Human Nature, for the sense in which the term nature is here used. See also Aristotle Eth. vi. 5, on φρόνησις.

no words, nor instruction; for we ourselves have the knowledge of it in our nature, and there is no necessity for labour or fatigue in going about and enquiring whether temperance is good and profitable; but we all acknowledge this with one consent, and no man is in doubt as to this virtue. So also we account adultery to be an evil thing, and neither is there here any need of trouble or learning, that the wickedness of this sin may be known; but we are all self-taught in such judgments; and we applaud virtue, though we do not follow it; as, on the other hand, we hate vice, though we practise it. And this hath been an exceeding good work of God; that He hath made our conscience, and our power of choice already, and before the action, claim kindred with virtue, and be at enmity with wickedness.

9. As I said then, the knowledge of each of these things resides within the conscience of all men, and we require no teacher to instruct us in these things; but the regulation of our conduct is left to our choice, and earnestness, and efforts. And why was this? but because if He had made everything to be of nature, we should have departed uncrowned and destitute of reward; and even as the brutes, who receive no reward nor praise for those advantages which they have naturally, so neither should we enjoy any of these things; for natural advantages are not the praise and commendation of those who have them, but of the Giver. For this reason, then, He did not commit all to nature; and again, He did not suffer our will to undertake the whole burden of knowledge, and of right regulation; lest it should despair at the labour of virtue. But conscience suggests to it what ought to be done; and it contributes its own exertions for the accomplishment. That it is a good thing to be temperate, we all understand without difficulty; for the knowledge is of nature: but we should not be able without difficulty, without bridling lust, and employing much exertion, to practise the rule of temperance; for this does not come to us by nature as the knowledge does, but requires also a willing mind and earnestness. And not only in this respect has He made the burden lighter for us, but also in another way again, by letting even some good dispositions exist naturally within us. For we are all naturally disposed to feel indignation along with those who are contemptuously treated, (whence it arises that we become the enemies of those who are insolent, though we ourselves may have suffered no part of the grievance,) and to sympathize in the pleasure of those who enjoy assistance and protection; and we are overcome by the calamities of others, as well as by mutual tenderness.[1] For although calamitous events may seem to induce a certain pusillanimity,[2] we entertain nevertheless a common fondness for each other. And to this effect a certain wise man speaks significantly; "Every animal loveth his like, and man his neighbour."[3]

10. But God hath provided many other instructors for us besides conscience; viz., fathers for children, masters for servants, husbands for wives, teachers for pupils, lawgivers and judges for those who are to be governed, and friends for friends. And frequently too we gain no less from enemies than friends; for when the former reproach us with our offences, they stir us up, even against our will, to the amendment of them. So many teachers hath He set over us, in order that the discovery of what is profitable, and the regulation of our conduct, might be easy to us, the multitude of those things which urge us on toward it not permitting us to fall away from what is expedient for us. For although we should despise parents, yet while we fear magistrates, we shall in any case be more submissive than otherwise. And though we may set them at nought[4] when we sin, we can never escape the rebuke of conscience: and if we dishonour and repel this, yet whilst fearing the opinion of the many, we shall be the better for it. And though we are destitute of shame with regard to this, the fear of the laws will press on us so as to restrain us, however reluctantly.

11. Thus fathers and teachers take the young in hand, and bring them into order;[5] and lawgivers and magistrates, those who are grown up. And servants, as being more inclined to listlessness, in addition to what has been previously mentioned, have their masters to constrain them to temperance; and wives have their husbands. And many are the walls which environ our race on all sides, lest it should too easily slide away, and fall into wickedness. Beside all these too, sicknesses and calamities instruct us. For poverty restrains, and losses sober us, and danger subdues us, and there are many other things of this sort. Doth neither father, nor teacher, nor prince, nor lawgiver, nor judge

---

[1] καὶ seems to be out of place. Without it the sense is, "are afflicted in the calamities of others through mutual tenderness." Or the true reading may be καὶ τὴν, "and we have a mutual tenderness," but six MSS. agree.
[2] That is, on the part of those who witness the calamity. In allusion to the disposition of many to forsake their friends in adversity.   [3] Eccles. xiii. 19.   [4] διαπτύσωμεν.
[5] Compare Herbert's Poems, No. xvii.
"Lord, with what care hast Thou begirt us round!
Parents first season us: then schoolmasters
Deliver us to laws;" &c.

make thee fear? Doth no friend move thee to shame, nor enemy sting thee? Doth no master chastise? Doth no husband instruct? Doth no conscience correct thee? Still, when bodily sickness comes, it often sets all right; and a loss has made the audacious man to become gentle. And what is more than this, heavy misfortunes, which befal not only ourselves but others too, are often of great advantage to us; and we who ourselves suffered nothing, yet beholding others enduring punishment, have been no less sobered by it than they.

12. And with respect to right deeds, any one may see that this happens; for as when the bad are punished others become better, so whenever the good achieve any thing right, many are urged onward to a similar zeal: a thing which hath also taken place with respect to the avoiding of oaths. For many persons, observing that others had laid aside the evil practice of oaths, took a pattern from their diligence, and got the better of the sin; wherefore we are the more disposed to touch again on the subject of this admonition. For let no one tell me that "many" have accomplished this; this is not what is desired, but that "all" should do so; and until I see this I cannot take breath.[1] That Shepherd had a hundred sheep, and yet when one of them had wandered away, he took no account of the safety of the ninety and nine, until he found the one that was lost, and restored it again to the flock.[2] Seest thou not that this also happens with respect to the body; for if by striking against any obstacle, we have only turned back a nail, the whole body sympathizes with the member. Say not this; that only a certain few have failed; but consider this point, that these few being unreformed, will corrupt many others. Although there was but one who had committed fornication among the Corinthians, yet Paul so groaned as if the whole city were lost. And very reasonably, for he knew that if that member were not chastened, the disease progressing onward would at length attack all the rest. I saw, but lately, in the court of justice, those distinguished men bound and conducted through the forum; and while some were wondering at this extraordinary degradation, others said there was nothing to wonder at; for that, where there is matter of treason,[3] rank must go for nothing. Is it not then much more true that rank must be of no avail where is impiety?

13. Thinking therefore of these things, let us arouse ourselves; for if ye bring not your own endeavours to the task, every thing on our part is to no purpose. And why so? Because it is not with the office of teaching, as it is with other arts. For the silversmith, when he has fabricated a vessel of any kind, and laid it aside, will find it on the morrow just as he left it. And the worker in brass, and the stone-cutter, and every other artificer, will each again take his own work in hand, whatever it is, just in the state he quitted it. But it is not so with us, but altogether the reverse; for we have not lifeless vessels to forge, but reasonable souls. Therefore we do not find you such as we leave you, but when we have taken you, and with manifold labour moulded, reformed you and increased your ardour on your departing from this place, the urgency of business, besetting you on every side, again perverts you, and causes us increased difficulty. Therefore, I supplicate and beseech you to put your own hand to the work; and when ye depart hence, to shew the same earnest regard for your own safety, that I have here shewn for your amendment.

14. Oh! that it were possible that I could perform good works as your substitute, and that you could receive the rewards of those works! Then I would not give you so much trouble. But how can I do this? The thing is impossible; for to every man will He render according to his own works. Wherefore as a mother, when she beholds her son in a fever, while she witnesses his sufferings[4] from choking and inflammation, frequently bewails him, and says to him, "O my son, would that I could sustain thy fever, and draw off its flame upon myself!" so now I say, Oh! that by labouring as your substitute, I could do good works for you all! But no, this is not to be done. But of his own doings must each man give the account, and one cannot see one person suffer punishment in the room of another. For this reason I am pained and mourn, that on That Day, when ye are called to judgment, I shall not be able to assist you, since, to say the truth, no such confidence of speech with God belongs to me. But even if I had much confidence, I am not holier than Moses, or more righteous than Samuel; of whom it is said, that though they had attained to so great virtue, they could not in any way avail to assist the Jews; inasmuch as that people had given themselves over to excessive negligence.[5] Since, then, from our own works we shall be

---

[1] *i. e.*, "to stop this exhortation;" an allusion to the exercise of running.
[2] Matt. xviii. 12, 13.
[3] καθοσίωσις, so called as being against the *sacred* person of the Emperor. See Ducange.

[4] Or, throttlings, ἀγχομένῳ. [5] Jer. xv. 1.

punished or saved; let us endeavour, I beseech you, in conjunction with all the other precepts, to fulfill this one; that, finally departing this life with a favourable hope, we may obtain those good things which are promised, through the grace and lovingkindness of our Lord Jesus Christ, through Whom and with Whom, to the Father, with the Holy Ghost, be glory both now and ever, world without end. Amen.

HOMILY XIV.

After the whole people had been freed from all distress, and had become assured of safety, certain persons again disturbed the city by fabricating false reports, and were convicted. Wherefore this Homily refers to that subject; and also to the admonition concerning oaths; for which reason also, the history of Jonathan, and Saul, and that of Jephthah, is brought forward; and it is shewn how many perjuries result from one oath.

1. Not a little did the devil yesterday disturb our city; but God also hath not a little comforted us again; so that each one of us may seasonably take up that prophetic saying, "In the multitude of the sorrows that I had in my heart, thy comforts have refreshed my soul."[1] And not only in consoling, but even in permitting us to be troubled, God hath manifested His tender care towards us. For to-day I shall repeat what I have never ceased to say, that not only our deliverance from evils, but also the permission of them arises from the benevolence of God. For when He sees us falling away into listlessness, and starting off from communion with Him, and making no account of spiritual things, He leaves us for a while; that thus brought to soberness, we may return to Him the more earnestly. And what marvel is it, if He does this towards us, listless as we are; since even Paul declares that with regard to himself and his disciples, this was the cause of their trials? For inditing his second Epistle to the Corinthians, he speaks thus: "We would not, brethren, have you ignorant of our trouble which came to us in Asia, that we were pressed out of measure, above strength, insomuch that we despaired even of life; but we had the sentence of death in ourselves."[2] As though he would say, "Dangers so great hung over us, that we gave up ourselves for lost; and no longer hoped that any favourable change would take place, but were altogether in expectation of death." For such is the sense of that clause, "We had the sentence of death in ourselves." But nevertheless, after such a state of desperation, God dispelled the tempest, and removed the cloud, and snatched us from the very gates of death. And afterwards, for the purpose of shewing that his being permitted to fall into this danger also was the result of much tender care for him, he mentions the advantage which resulted from the temptations, which was, that he might continually look to Him, and be neither highminded, nor confident. Therefore having said this, "We had the sentence of death in ourselves;"[3] he adds also the reason; "That we should not trust in ourselves, but in God which quickeneth the dead." For it is in the nature of trials to arouse us when we are dozing, or falling down, and to stir us up, and make us more religious. When, therefore, O beloved! thou seest a trial at one time extinguished, and at another time kindled again, be not cast down! Do not despond, but retain a favourable hope, reasoning thus with thyself, that God does not deliver us into the hands of our enemies either because He hates or abandons us, but because He is desirous to make us more in earnest, and more intimate with Himself.

2. Let us not then be desponding; nor let us despair of a change for the better; but let us hope that speedily there will be a calm; and, in short, casting the issue of all the tumults which beset us upon God, let us again handle the customary points; and again bring forward our usual topic of instruction. For I am desirous to discourse to you further concerning the same subject, to the end that we may radically extirpate from your souls the wicked practice of oaths. Wherefore it is necessary for me again to have recourse to the same entreaty that I made before. For

---

[1] Ps. xciv. 19.   [2] 2 Cor. i. 8, 9.   [3] 2 Cor. i. 9.

lately I besought you, that each one taking the head of John, just cut off, and the warm blood yet dripping from it, you would thus go home, and think that you saw it before your eyes, while it emitted a voice, and said, "Abhor my murderer, the oath!" What a rebuke did not effect, this an oath effected; what a tyrant's wrath was insufficient for, this the necessity of keeping an oath brought about! And when the tyrant was publicly rebuked in the hearing of all, he bore the censure nobly; but when he had thrown himself into the fatal necessity caused by oaths, then he cut off that blessed head. This same thing, therefore, I entreat; and cease not entreating, that wherever we go, we go bearing this head; and that we shew it to all, crying aloud, as it does, and denouncing oaths. For although we were never so listless and remiss, yet beholding the eyes of that head fearfully glaring upon us, and threatening us if we swear, we should be more powerfully kept in check by this terror, than by any curb; and be easily able to restrain and avert the tongue from its inclination toward oaths.

3. There is not only this great evil in an oath, that it punishes those who are guilty of it, both when violated, and when kept; a thing we do not see take place with any other sin; but there is another equally great evil attending it. And what is that? Why that ofttimes it is utterly impossible even for those who are desirous, and even make a point of it, to keep their oath. For, in the first place, he who is continually swearing, whether willingly or unwillingly; knowingly or unknowingly; in jest or in earnest; being frequently carried away by anger and by many other things, will most surely become perjured. And no one can gainsay this; so evident and generally allowed is the fact, that the man who swears frequently, must also be a perjurer. Secondly, I affirm, that although he were not carried away by passion, and did not become the victim of perjury [1] unwillingly and unwittingly, yet by the very nature of the case he will assuredly be necessitated both consciously and voluntarily to perjure himself. Thus, oftentimes when we are dining at home, and one of the servants happens to do amiss, the wife swears that he shall be flogged, and then the husband swears the contrary, resisting, and not permitting it. In this case, whatever they may do, perjury must in any case be the result; for however much they may wish and endeavour to keep their oaths, it is no longer possible; but whatever happens, one or other of these will be ensnared in perjury; or rather both in any case.

4. And how, I will explain; for this is the paradox. He who hath sworn that he would flog the man-servant or maid-servant, yet hath afterwards been prohibited from this, hath perjured himself, not having done what he hath sworn to do: and also, he hath involved in the crime of perjury the party forbidding and hindering the oath from being kept. For not only they who take a false oath, but they who impose that necessity on others, are liable to the same accusation. And not merely in houses, but also in the forum we may see that this takes place; and especially in fights, when those who box with one another swear things that are contrary. One swears that he will beat, the other that he will not be beaten. One swears that he will carry off the cloak, the other that he will not suffer this. One that he will exact the money, the other that he will not pay it. And many other such contradictory things, those who are contentious take an oath to do. So also in shops, and in schools, it may generally be observed that the same thing occurs. Thus the workman hath often sworn that he will not suffer his apprentice[2] to eat or drink, before he has finished all his assigned task. And so also the pedagogue has often acted towards a youth; and a mistress towards her maid-servant; and when the evening hath overtaken them, and the work hath remained unfinished, it is necessary either that those who have not executed their task should perish with hunger, or that those who have sworn should altogether forswear themselves. For that malignant demon, who is always lying in wait against our blessings, being present and hearing the obligation of the oaths, impels those who are answerable to indifference; or works some other difficulty; so that the task being unperformed, blows, insults, and perjuries, and a thousand other evils, may take place. And just as when children drag with all their might a long and rotten cord in directions opposite to each other; if the cord snaps in the middle, they all fall flat upon their backs, and some strike their heads, and some another part of the body; so also they who each engage with an oath to perform things that are contrary, when the oath is broken by the necessity of the case, both parties fall into the same gulf of perjury; these by actually perjuring themselves, and those by affording the occasion of perjury to the others.

5. That this also may be rendered evident,

---

[1] τοῦτο πάθῃ, al. ποιῇ, become guilty of. [2] τῷ μαθητῇ.

not only from what happens every day in private houses, and the places of public concourse, but from the Scriptures themselves, I will relate to you a piece of ancient history, which bears upon what has been said. Once, when the Jews had been invaded by their enemies, and Jonathan (now he was the son of Saul) had slaughtered some, and put the rest to flight; Saul, his father, being desirous to rouse the army more effectually against the remainder; and in order that they might not desist until he had subjugated them all, did that which was altogether opposite to what he desired, by swearing that no one should eat any food until evening, and until vengeance was taken of his enemies. What, I ask, could have been more senseless than this? For when it was needful that he should have refreshed those who were fatigued and exhausted, and have sent them forth with renewed vigour against their enemies, he treated them far worse than he had done their enemies, by the constraint of an oath, which delivered them over to excessive hunger. Dangerous, indeed, it is for any one to swear in a matter pertaining to himself; for we are forcibly impelled to do many things by the urgency of circumstances. But much more dangerous is it by the obligation of one's own oath, to bind the determination of others; and especially where any one swears, not concerning one, or two, or three, but an unlimited multitude, which Saul then inconsiderately did, without thinking that it was probable that, in so vast a number, one at least might transgress the oath; or that soldiers, and soldiers too on campaign, are very far removed from moral wisdom, and know nothing of ruling the belly; more especially when their fatigue is great. He, however, overlooking all these points, as if he were merely taking an oath about a single servant, whom he was easily able to restrain, counted equally on his whole army. In consequence of this he opened such a door for the devil, that in a short time he framed, not two, three, or four, but many more perjuries out of this oath. For as when we do not swear at all, we close the whole entrance against him, so if we utter but a single oath, we afford him great liberty for constructing endless perjuries. And just as those who twist skeins, if they have one to hold the end, work the whole string with nicety, but if there is no one to do this, cannot even undertake the commencement of it; in the same manner too the devil, when about to twist the skein of our sins, if he could not get the beginning from our tongues, would not be able to undertake the work; but should we only make a commencement, while we hold the oath on our tongue, as it were a hand, then with full liberty he manifests his malignant art in the rest of the work, constructing and weaving from a single oath a thousand perjuries.

6. And this was just what he did now in the case of Saul. Observe, however, what a snare is immediately framed for this oath: "The army passed through a wood, that contained a nest of bees, and the nest was in front of the people,[1] and the people came upon the nest, and went along talking."[2] Seest thou what a pit-fall was here? A table ready spread, that the easiness of access, the sweetness of the food, and the hope of concealment, might entice them to a transgression of the oath. For hunger at once, and fatigue, and the hour, (for "all the land," it is said, "was dining,")[3] then urged them to the transgression. Moreover, the sight of the combs invited them from without to relax the strain on their resolution. For the sweetness, as well as the present readiness of the table, and the difficulty of detecting the stealth, were sufficient to ensnare their utmost wisdom. If it had been flesh, which needed boiling or roasting, their minds would not have been so much bewitched; since while they were delaying in the cookery of these, and engaged in preparing them for food, they might expect to be discovered. But now there was nothing of this kind; there was honey only, for which no such labour was required, and for which the dipping of the tip of the finger sufficed to partake of the table, and that with secresy. Nevertheless, these persons restrained their appetite, and did not say within themselves, "What does it concern us? Hath any one of us sworn this? He may pay the penalty of his inconsiderate oath, for why did he swear?" Nothing of this sort did they think; but religiously passed on; and though there were so many enticements, they behaved themselves wisely. "The people went on talking."[4] What is the meaning of this word "talking?" Why, that for the purpose of soothing their pain with words, they held discourse with one another.

7. What then, did nothing more come of

---

[1] Some MSS. read τοῦ ἀγροῦ, *of the ground*, as LXX.
[2] 1 Sam. xiv. 26, LXX.
[3] So LXX., 1 Kings xiv. 24 (*i. e.*, 1 Samuel). The clause in the Hebrew, corresponding to the Greek words καὶ πᾶσα ἡ γῆ ἡρίστα, is בִּיעַר וְכָל־הָאָרֶץ בָּאוּ, E. V. "And all they of the land *came to a wood.*" It seems most likely that the word בָּאוּ was thus taken, *all the land went, i. e.*, "to dinner," as the word יַעַר stands in LXX. for the name of the wood.
[4] So LXX. Heb. וְהִנֵּה הֵלֶךְ דְּבַשׁ, E. V. *And behold the honey dropped.* This difference has arisen in all probability from their MSS. having read דָּבָר instead of דְּבָשׁ. This seems a probable conjecture: often, however, the variations of the LXX. can be accounted for as being paraphrastic.

this, when all the people had acted so wisely? Was the oath, forsooth, observed? Not even so was it observed. On the contrary, it was violated! How, and in what way? Ye shall hear forthwith, in order that ye may also thoroughly discern the whole art of the devil. For Jonathan, not having heard his father take the oath, "put forth the end of the rod that was in his hand, and dipped it in the honeycomb, and his eyes saw clearly."[1] Observe, who it was whom he impelled to break the oath; not one of the soldiers, but the very son of him who had sworn it. For he did not only desire to effect perjury, but was also plotting the slaughter of a son, and making provision for it beforehand; and was in haste to divide nature against her own self, and what he had done aforetime in the case of Jephthah, that he hoped now again to accomplish. For he likewise, when he had promised that the first thing that met him, after a victorious battle, he would sacrifice,[2] fell into the snare of child-murder; for his daughter first meeting him, he sacrificed her, and God did not forbid it. And I know, indeed, that many of the unbelievers impugn us of cruelty and inhumanity on account of this sacrifice; but I should say, that the concession[3] in the case of this sacrifice was a striking example of providence and clemency; and that it was in care for our race that He did not prevent that sacrifice. For if after that vow and promise He had forbidden the sacrifice, many also who were subsequent to Jephthah, in the expectation that God would not receive their vows, would have increased the number of such vows, and proceeding on their way would have fallen into child-murder. But now, by suffering this vow to be actually fulfilled,[4] He put a stop to all such cases in future. And to shew that this is true, after Jephthah's daughter had been slain, in order that the calamity might be always remembered, and that her fate might not be consigned to oblivion, it became a law among the Jews, that the virgins assembling at the same season should bewail during forty[5] days the sacrifice which had taken place; in order that renewing the memory of it by lamentation, they should make all men wiser for the future; and that they might learn that it was not after the mind of God that this should be done, for in that case He would not have permitted the virgins to bewail and lament her. And that what I have said is not conjectural, the event demonstrated; for after this sacrifice, no one vowed such a vow unto God. Therefore also He did not indeed forbid this; but what He had expressly enjoined in the case of Isaac, that He directly prohibited;[6] plainly shewing through both cases, that He doth not delight in such sacrifices.

8. But the malignant demon was labouring hard now again to produce such a tragedy. Therefore he impelled Jonathan to the trespass. For if any one of the soldiers had transgressed the law, it seemed to him no great evil that would have been done; but now being insatiate of human ills, and never able to get his fill of our calamities, he thought it would be no grand exploit if he effected only a simple murder. And if he could not also pollute the king's right hand with the murder of his child, he considered that he had achieved no great matter. And why do I speak of child-murder? For he, the wicked one, thought that by this means he should compass a slaughter even more accursed than that. For if he had sinned wittingly, and been sacrificed, this would only have been child-murder; but now sinning ignorantly, (for he had not heard of the oath), if he had been slain, he would have made the anguish of his father double; for he would have had both to sacrifice a son, and a son who had done no wrong. But now to proceed with the rest of the history; "When he had eaten," it is said, "His eyes saw clearly."[7] And here it condemns the king of great folly; shewing that hunger had almost blinded the whole army, and diffused much darkness over their eyes. Afterwards some one of the soldiers, perceiving the action, saith, "Thy father sware an oath upon all the people, saying, cursed be the man who eateth any food to-day. And the people were faint. And Jonathan said, My father hath made away[8] with the land."[9] What does he mean by the word, "made away with?" Why, that he had ruined, or destroyed them all. Hence, when the oath was transgressed, all kept silence, and no one dared to bring forth the criminal; and this became afterwards no small matter of blame, for not only are those who break an oath, but those also who are privy to it and conceal it, partakers of the crime.

9. But let us see what follows; "And Saul said, Let us go down after the strangers,[10] and spoil them. And the priest said, Let us

---

[1] 1 Sam. xiv. 27. [2] Jud. xi. 31.
[3] He means the absence of *interference*, for it was against the law of Moses. Deut. xii. 31.
[4] Jud. xi. 39.
[5] Some MSS. read *four*, as the text. Judg. xi. 40.
[6] Gen. xxii. 12.
[7] 1 Sam. xiv. 28. Or, "recovered their sight;" see Acts xxii. 13, where the same word occurs in reference to the restoration of St. Paul's sight.
[8] LXX., ἀπήλλαχεν. Heb. עָכַר, E. V., troubled.
[9] Used in this passage for the people.
[10] ἀλλοφύλων, usually put in LXX. for the Philistines.

draw near hither unto God."[1] For in old times God led forth the people to battle; and without His consent no one dared to engage in the fight, and war was with them a matter of religion. For not from weakness of body, but from their sins they were conquered, whenever they were conquered; and not by might and courage, but by favour from above they prevailed, whenever they did prevail. Victory and defeat were also to them a means of training, and a school of virtue. And not to them only, but to their adversaries; for this was made evident to them too, that the fate of battle with the Jews was decided not by the nature of their arms, but by the life and good works of the warriors. The Midianites at least perceiving this, and knowing that people to be invincible, and that to have attacked them with arms and engines of war would have been fruitless, and that it was only possible to conquer them by sin, having decked out handsome virgins, and set them in the array,[2] excited the soldiers to lasciviousness, endeavouring by means of fornication to deprive them of God's assistance; which accordingly happened. For when they had fallen into sin, they became an easy prey to all; and those whom weapons, and horses, and soldiers, and so many engines availed not to capture,[3] sin by its nature delivered over bound to their enemies. Shields, and spears, and darts were all alike found useless; but beauty of visage and wantonness of soul overpowered these brave men.

10. Therefore one gives this admonition; "Observe not the beauty of a strange woman, and meet not a woman addicted to fornication.[4] For honey distils from the lips of an harlot, which at the time may seem smooth to thy throat, but afterward thou wilt find it more bitter than gall, and sharper than a two-edged sword."[5] For the harlot knows not how to love, but only to ensnare; her kiss hath poison, and her mouth a pernicious drug. And if this does not immediately appear, it is the more necessary to avoid her on that account, because she veils that destruction, and keeps that death concealed, and suffers it not to become manifest at the first. So that if any one pursues pleasure, and a life full of gladness, let him avoid the society of fornicating women, for they fill the minds of their lovers with a thousand conflicts and tumults, setting in motion against them continual strifes and contentions, by means of their words, and all their actions. And just as it is with those who are the most virulent enemies, so the object of their actions and schemes is to plunge their lovers into shame and poverty, and the worst extremities. And in the same manner as hunters, when they have spread out their nets, endeavour to drive thither the wild animals, in order that they may put them to death, so also is it with these women. When they have spread out on every side the wings[6] of lasciviousness by means of the eyes, and dress, and language, they afterwards drive in their lovers, and bind them; nor do they give over until they have drunk up their blood, insulting them at last, and mocking their folly, and pouring over them a flood of ridicule. And indeed such a man is no longer worthy of compassion but deserves to be derided and jeered, since he is found more irrational than a woman, and a harlot besides. Therefore the Wise Man gives this word of exhortation again, "Drink waters from thine own cistern, and from the fountain of thine own well."[7] And again; "Let the hind of thy friendship, and the foal of thy favours, consort with thee."[8] These things he speaks of a wife associated with her husband by the law of marriage. Why leavest thou her who is a helpmate, to run to one who is a plotter against thee? Why dost thou turn away from her who is the partner of thy living, and court her who would subvert thy life? The one is thy member and body, the other is a sharp sword. Therefore, beloved, flee fornication; both for its present evils, and for its future punishment.

11. Perchance we may seem to have fallen aside from the subject; but to say thus much, is no departure from it. For we do not wish to read you histories merely for their own sake, but that you may correct each of the passions which trouble you: therefore also we make these frequent appeals,[9] preparing our discourse for you in all varieties of style; since it is probable that in so large an assembly, there is a great variety of distempers; and our task is to cure not one only, but many different wounds; and therefore it is necessary that the medicine of instruction should be various. Let us however return thither from whence we made this digression: "And the Priest said, Let us draw near unto God. And Saul asked counsel of God.

---

[1] 1 Sam. xiv. 36.
[2] ἐπὶ τῆς παρατάξεως. An expression so proper to *battle*, that it must be metaphorical, meaning "they adopted this method of warfare."
[3] This may perhaps be said with a tacit reference to Samson, as the Midianites did not gain any *victory*. See Numb. xxxi. 16; Jud. iii. 6.
[4] Eccles. ix. 8, 3.   [5] Prov. v. 3, 4.

[6] A word often used metaphorically, here probably of wide nets, spread out like wings.
[7] Prov. v. 15.
[8] Prov. v. 19, LXX. There is an ellipsis in the Hebrew text here which may account for the difference between it and the Septuagint.
[9] Or, "reproofs," ἐντροπὰς; [but Savile and Oxf. MSS. read ἐκτροπὰς, "digressions."]

Shall I go down after the strangers? Wilt Thou deliver them into my hands? But on that day the Lord answered him not."[1] Observe the benignity and mildness of God who loveth man. For He did not launch a thunderbolt, nor shake the earth; but what friends do to friends, when treated contemptuously, this the Lord did towards the servant. He only received him silently, speaking by His silence, and by it giving utterance to all His wrath. This Saul understood, and said, as it is recorded, "Bring near hither all the tribes of the people, and know and see in whom this sin hath been this day. For as the Lord liveth, Who hath saved Israel, though the answer be against Jonathan my son, he shall surely die."[2] Seest thou his rashness? Perceiving that his first oath had been transgressed, he does not even then learn self-control, but adds again a second. Consider also the malignity of the devil. For since he was aware that frequently the son when discovered, and publicly arraigned, is able by the very sight at once to make the father relent, and might soften the king's wrath, he anticipated his sentence by the obligation of a second oath; holding him by a kind of double bond, and not permitting him to be the master of his own determination, but forcing him on every side to that iniquitous murder. And even whilst the offender was not yet produced, he hath passed judgment, and whilst ignorant of the criminal, he gave sentence. The father became the executioner; and before the enquiry declared his verdict of condemnation! What could be more irrational than this proceeding?

12. Saul then having made this declaration, the people were more afraid than before, and all were in a state of great trembling and terror. But the devil rejoiced, at having rendered them all thus anxious. There was no one, we are told, of all the people, who answered. "And Saul said, Ye will be in bondage, and I, and Jonathan my son, will be in bondage."[3] But what he means is to this effect; "You are aiming at nothing else, than to deliver yourselves to your enemies, and to become slaves instead of free men; whilst you provoke God against you, in not delivering up the guilty person." Observe also another contradiction produced by the oath. It had been fitting, if he wished to find the author of this guilt, to have made no such threat, nor to have bound himself to vengeance by an oath; that becoming less afraid, they might more readily bring the offender to light.[4] But under the influence of anger, and great madness, and his former unreasonableness, he again does that which is directly contrary to what he desires. What need is there to enlarge? He commits the matter to a decision by lot; and the lot falleth upon Saul, and Jonathan; "And Saul said, Cast ye the lot between me and Jonathan; and they cast the lot, and Jonathan was taken. And Saul said to Jonathan, Tell me, what hast thou done? And Jonathan told him, saying, I only tasted a little honey on the top of the rod which is in my hand, and, lo! I must die."[5] Who is there that these words would not have moved and turned to pity? Consider what a tempest Saul then sustained, his bowels being torn with anguish, and the most profound precipice appearing on either hand! But nevertheless he did not learn self-control, for what does he say? "God do so to me, and more also; for thou shalt surely die this day."[6] Behold again the third oath, and not simply the third, but one with a very narrow limit as to time; for he does not merely say, "Thou shalt die;" but, "this day."[7] For the devil was hurrying, hurrying him on, constraining him and driving him to this impious murder. Wherefore he did not suffer him to assign any future day for the sentence, lest there should be any correction of the evil by delay. And the people said to Saul, "God do so to us, and more also, if he shall be put to death, who hath wrought this great salvation in Israel. As the Lord liveth, there shall not an hair of his head fall to the ground; because he hath wrought a merciful thing from God to-day."[8] Behold how, in the second place, the people also swore, and swore contrary to the king.

13. Now recollect, I pray, the cord pulled by the children, and breaking, and throwing on their backs those who pull it. Saul swore not once or twice, but several times. The people swore what was contrary, and strained in the opposite direction. Of necessity then it followed, that the oath must in any wise be broken through. For it were impossible that all these should keep their oaths. And now tell me not of the event of this transaction; but consider how many evils were springing from it; and how the devil from thence was preparing the tragedy and usurpation of Absalom. For if the king had chosen to resist, and to proceed to the execution of his oath, the people would have been

---

[1] 1 Sam. xiv. 36, 37.   [2] 1 Sam. xiv. 38.
[3] So LXX., as though there had stood לְעֵבֶר for לְעָבְר, *Be ye on one side, and I and Jonathan my son will be on the other side*, verse 40.
[4] εἰς μέσον.   [5] 1 Sam. xiv. 42, 43.   [6] 1 Sam. xiv. 44.
[7] The words *this day* are only found in the Septuagint.
[8] 1 Sam. xiv. 45.

in array against him; and a grievous rebellion[1] would have been set on foot. And again, if the son consulting his own safety had chosen to throw himself into the hands of the army, he would straightway have become a parricide. Seest thou not, that rebellion, as well as child-murder, and parricide, and battle, and civil war, and slaughter, and blood, and dead bodies without number, are the consequences of one oath. For if war had perchance broken out, Saul might have been slain, and Jonathan perchance too, and many of the soldiers would have been cut to pieces; and after all the keeping of the oath would not have been forwarded. So that it is not for thee to consider that these events did not occur, but to mark this point, that it was the nature of the case to necessitate the occurrence of such things. However, the people prevailed. Come then, let us reckon up the perjuries that were the consequence. The oath of Saul was first broken by his son; and again a second and a third, concerning the slaying of his son, by Saul himself. And the people seemed to have kept their oath. Yet if any one closely examines the matter, they too all became liable to the charge of perjury. For they compelled the father of Jonathan to perjure himself, by not surrendering the son to the father. Seest thou how many persons one oath made obnoxious to perjury,[2] willingly and unwillingly; how many evils it wrought, how many deaths it caused?

14. Now in the commencement of this discourse I promised to shew that perjury would in any case result from opposite oaths; but truly the course of the history has proved more than I was establishing. It has exhibited not one, two, or three individuals, but a whole people, and not one, two, or three oaths, but many more transgressed. I might also make mention of another instance, and shew from that, how one oath caused a still greater and more grievous calamity. For one oath[3] entailed upon all the Jews the capture of their cities, as well as of their wives and children; the ravages of fire, the invasion of barbarians, the pollution of sacred things, and ten thousand other evils yet more distressing. But I perceive that the discourse is running to a great length. Therefore, dismissing here the narration of this history, I beseech you, together with the beheading of John, to tell one another also of the murder of Jonathan, and the general destruction of a whole people (which did not indeed take place, but which was involved in the obligation of the oaths); and both at home, and in public, and with your wives, and friends, and with neighbours, and with all men in general, to make an earnest business of this matter, and not to think it a sufficient apology that we can plead custom.

15. For that this excuse is a mere pretext, and that the fault arises not from custom but from listlessness, I will endeavour to convince you from what has already occurred. The Emperor has shut up the baths of the city, and has given orders that no one shall bathe; and no one has dared to transgress the law, nor to find fault with what has taken place, nor to allege custom. But even though in weak health perchance, men and women, and children and old men; and many women but recently eased from the pangs of childbirth; though all requiring this as a necessary medicine; bear with the injunction, willingly or unwillingly; and neither plead infirmity of body, nor the tyranny of custom, nor that they are punished, whereas others were the offenders, nor any other thing of this kind, but contentedly put up with this punishment, because they were in expectation of greater evils; and pray daily that the wrath of the Emperor may go no further. Seest thou that where there is fear, the bond of custom is easily relaxed, although it be of exceedingly long standing, and great necessity? To be denied the use of the bath is certainly a grievous matter. For although we be never so philosophic, the nature of the body proves incapable of deriving any benefit for its own health, from the philosophy of the soul. But as to abstinence from swearing, this is exceedingly easy, and brings no injury at all; none to the body, none to the mind; but, on the contrary, great gain, much safety, and abundant wealth. How then is it any thing but absurd, to submit to the greatest hardships, when an Emperor enjoins it; but when God commands nothing grievous nor difficult, but what is very tolerable and easy, to despise or to deride it, and to advance custom as an excuse? Let us not, I entreat, so far despise our own safety, but let us fear God as we fear man. I know that ye shudder at hearing this, but what deserves to be shuddered at is that ye do not pay even so much respect to God; and that whilst ye diligently observe the Emperor's decrees, ye trample under foot those which are divine, and which have come down from heaven; and consider diligence concerning these a secondary object. For what apology will

---

[1] τυραννίς, here used for "rebellion" or "usurpation," as just above.
[2] It seems that all actually remained under this guilt. The only remedy would have been in Jonathan's confessing as soon as he knew his trespass, and an offering being made for him, according to Lev. v. 4-6, see also Lev. v. 1, iv. 22, and xxxvii. 2.
[3] See Hom. XIX.

there be left for us, and what pardon, if after so much admonition we persist in the same practices. For I began this admonition at the very commencement of the calamity which has taken hold of the city, and that is now on the point of coming to an end; but we have not as yet thoroughly put in practice even one precept. How then can we ask a removal of the evils which still beset us, when we have not been able to perform a single precept? How can we expect a change for the better? How shall we pray? With what tongue shall we call upon God? For if we perform the law, we shall enjoy much pleasure, when the Emperor is reconciled to the city. But if we remain in the transgression, shame and reproach will be ours on every hand, inasmuch as when God hath freed us from the danger we have continued in the same listlessness.

16. Oh! that it were possible for me to undress the souls of those who swear frequently, and to expose to view the wounds and the bruises which they receive daily from oaths! We should then need neither admonition nor counsel; for the sight of these wounds would avail more powerfully than all that could be said, to withdraw from their wickedness even those who are most addicted o this wicked practice. Nevertheless, if it be not possible to spread before the eyes the shameful state of their soul, it may be possible to expose it to the thoughts, and to display it in its rottenness and corruption. For as it saith, "As a servant that is continually beaten will not be clear of a bruise, so he that sweareth and nameth God continually will not be purified of his sin."[1] It is impossible, utterly impossible, that the mouth which is practised in swearing, should not frequently commit perjury. Therefore, I beseech you all, by laying aside this dreadful and wicked habit, to win another crown. And since it is every where sung of our city, that first of all the cities of the world, she bound on her brow[2] the name of Christians, so let all have to say, that Antioch alone, of all the cities throughout the wold, hath expelled all oaths from her own borders. Yea, rather, should this be done, she will not be herself crowned alone, but will also carry others along with her to the same pitch of zeal. And as the name of Christians having had its origin here, hath as it were from a kind of fountain overflown all the world, even so this good work, having taken its root and starting-point from hence, will make all men that inhabit the earth your disciples; so that a double and treble reward may arise to you, at once on account of your own good works, and of the instruction afforded to others. This will be to you the brightest of diadems! This will make your city a mother city, not on earth, but in the heavens! This will stand by us at That Day, and bring us the crown of righteousness; which God grant that we may all obtain, through the grace and lovingkindness of our Lord Jesus Christ, with Whom to the Father, together with the Holy Spirit, be glory, now and ever, and world without end. Amen.

[1] Ecclus. xxiii. 10.
[2] So Sav. and Oxf. MSS. ἀνεδήσατο, which is more spirited than Ben. ἐνεδύσατο, "put on." Lat. *induit* rather favours the latter, but Ducæus prefers the former, and quotes four MSS. for it.

HOMILY XV.

Again on the calamity of the city of Antioch. That fear is every way profitable. That sorrow is more useful than laughter. And upon the saying, "Remember that thou walkest in the midst of snares."[1] And that it is worse to exact an oath, than to commit murder

1. TO-DAY, and on the former Sabbath,[2] it had behoved us to enter on the subject of fasting; nor let any one suppose that what I said was unseasonable.[3] For on the days of the fast, counsel and admonition on that subject are indeed not at all necessary; the very presence of these days exciting even those who are the most remiss to the effort of fasting. But since many men, both when about to enter upon the fast, as if the belly were on the point of being delivered over to a sort of lengthened seige, lay in beforehand a stock of gluttony and drunkenness; and again, on being set at liberty, going forth as from a long famine and a grievous prison, run to the

[1] Ecclus. ix. 13. [2] *i. e.*, Saturday.
[3] As being at the close of the week, when the fast was just going to be intermitted, or at least relaxed.

table with unseemly greediness, just as if they were striving to undo again the advantage gained through the fast, by an excess of gluttony; it might have been needful, that then as well as now, we should agitate the subject of temperance. Nevertheless, we have neither lately said any thing of that kind, neither shall we now speak upon it. For the fear of the impending calamity suffices, instead of the strongest admonition and counsel, to sober the soul of every one. For who is there so miserable and degraded, as to be drunken in such a tempest? Who is there so insensible, when the city is thus agitated, and such a shipwreck is threatened, as not to become abstemious and watchful, and more thoroughly reformed by this distress than by any other sort of admonition and counsel? For discourse will not be able to effect as much as fear does. And this very thing it is now possible to shew from the events which have taken place. How many words then did we spend before this in exhorting many that were listless, and counselling them to abstain from the theatres, and the impurities of these places! And still they did not abstain; but always on this day they flocked together to the unlawful spectacles of the dancers; and they held their diabolical assembly in opposition[1] to the full congregation of God's Church; so that their vehement shouts, borne in the air from that place, resounded against the psalms which we were singing here. But behold, now whilst we were keeping silence, and saying nothing on the subject, they of themselves have shut up their orchestra; and the Hippodrome has been left deserted! Before this, many of our own people used to hasten to them; but now they are all fled hither from thence to the church, and all alike join in praising our God!

2. Seest thou what advantage is come of fear? If fear were not a good thing, fathers would not have set tutors[2] over their children; nor lawgivers magistrates for cities. What can be more grievous than hell? Yet nothing is more profitable than the fear of it; for the fear of hell will bring us the crown of the kingdom. Where fear is, there is no envy; where fear is, the love of money does not disturb; where fear is, wrath is quenched, evil concupiscence is repressed, and every unreasonable passion is exterminated. And even as in a house, where there is always a soldier under arms, no robber, nor housebreaker, nor any such evil doer will dare to make his appearance; so also while fear holds possession of our minds, none of the base passions will readily attack us, but all fly off and are banished, being driven away in every direction by the despotic power of fear. And not only this advantage do we gain from fear, but also another which is far greater. For not only, indeed, does it expel our evil passions, but it also introduces every kind of virtue with great facility. Where fear exists, there is zeal in alms-giving, and intensity of prayer, and tears warm and frequent, and groans fraught with compunction. For nothing so swallows up sin, and makes virtue to increase and flourish, as a perpetual state of dread. Therefore it is impossible for him who does not live in fear to act aright; as, on the other hand, it is impossible that the man who lives in fear can go wrong.

3. Let us not then grieve, beloved, let us not despond on account of the present tribulation, but let us admire the well-devised plan of God's wisdom. For by these very means through which the devil hoped to overturn our city, hath God restored and corrected it. The devil animated certain lawless men to treat the very statues of the Emperor contemptuously, in order that the very foundations of the city might be razed. But God employed this same circumstance for our greater correction; driving out all sloth by the dread of the expected wrath: and the thing has turned out directly opposite to what the devil wished, by the means which he had himself prepared. For our city is being purified every day; and the lanes and crossings, and places of public concourse, are freed from lascivious and voluptuous songs; and turn where we will there are supplications, and thanksgivings, and tears, instead of rude laughter; there are words of sound wisdom instead of obscene language, and our whole city has become a Church, the workshops being closed, and all being engaged throughout the day in these general prayers; and calling upon God in one united voice with much earnestness. What preaching, what admonition, what counsel, what length of time had ever availed to accomplish these things?

4. For this then let us be thankful, and let us not be petulant or discontented; for that fear is a good thing, what we have said hath made manifest. But hear Solomon thus uttering a lesson of wisdom concerning it; Solomon, who was nourished in every luxury,

---

[1] Or, "right opposite." ἀντικαθίστασαν. The word may be taken to imply that those spectacles were held in the immediate neighbourhood of the church. Stage plays, and players, and all who took part in the public games, were excluded from communion. The act, considered little short of idolatry, with which it was connected, was denounced in several Councils. See Bingham, b. xvi. c. 4, sec. 10.

[2] παιδαγωγούς. See Hom. vi. 1, p. 114, where the "teachers" are different from these. The paidagogos had the moral supervision of the child; part of his duty was to conduct him daily to school. See Galatians iii. 24, revised version.

and enjoyed much security. What then does he say? "It is better to go to the house of mourning than to the house of laughter."[1] What sayest thou, I ask? Is it better to go where there is weeping, lamentation, and groans, and anguish, and so much sadness, than where there is the dance, the cymbals, and laughter, and luxury, and full eating and drinking? Yes, verily, he replies. And tell me why is it so, and for what reason? Because, at the former place, insolence is bred, at the latter, sobriety. And when a person goes to the banquet of one more opulent, he will no longer behold his own house with the same pleasure, but he comes back to his wife in a discontented mood; and in discontent he partakes of his own table; and is peevish towards his own servants, and his own children, and every body in his house; perceiving his own poverty the more forcibly by the wealth of others. And this is not the only evil; but that he also often envies him who hath invited him to the feast, and returns home having received no benefit at all. But with regard to the house of mourning, nothing of this sort can be said. On the contrary, much spiritual wisdom is to be gained there, as well as sobriety. For when once a person hath passed the threshold of a house which contains a corpse, and hath seen the departed one lying speechless, and the wife tearing her hair, mangling her cheeks, and wounding her arms, he is subdued; his countenance becomes sad; and every one of those who sit down together can say to his neighbour but this, "We are nothing, and our wickedness is inexpressible!"[2] What can be more full of wisdom than these words, when we both acknowledge the insignificance of our nature, and accuse our own wickedness, and account present things as nothing? Giving utterance, though in different words, to that very sentiment of Solomon—that sentiment which is so marvellous and pregnant with Divine wisdom —"Vanity of vanities, all is vanity."[3] He who enters the house of mourning, weeps forthwith for the departed, even though he be an enemy. Seest thou how much better that house is than the other? for there, though he be a friend, he envies; but here, though he be an enemy, he weeps. This is a thing which God requires of us above all, that we should not insult over those who have occasioned us grief. And not only may we gather these advantages, but others also which are not less than these. For each one is also put in mind of his own sins, and of the fearful Tribunal; of the great Account, and of the Judgment; and although he may have been suffering a thousand evils from others, and have a cause for sadness at home, he will receive and take back with him the medicine for all these things. For reflecting that he himself, and all those who swell with pride, will in a little while suffer the same thing; and that all present things, whether pleasant or painful, are transitory; he thus returns to his house, disburdened of all sadness and envy, with a light and buoyant heart; and hence he will hereafter be more meek, and gentle, and benignant to all; as well as more wise; the fear of things to come having made its way into his soul, and consumed all the thorns.

6. All this Solomon perceived when he said, "It is better to go to the house of mourning than to the house of drinking."[4] From the one grows listlessness, from the other an earnest anxiety. From the one, contempt; from the other, fear; a fear which conducts us to the practice of every virtue. If fear were not a good thing, Christ would not have expended such long and frequent discourses on the subject of punishment, and vengeance to come. Fear is nothing less than a wall, and a defence, and an impregnable tower. For indeed we stand in need of much defence, seeing that there are many ambushments on every side. Even as this same Solomon again says admonishingly, "Perceive that thou goest in the midst of snares, and that thou walkest on the battlements of cities."[5] Oh with how many good things is this saying pregnant! Yea, not less than the former! Let us then, write it, each of us, upon our minds, and carry it about ever in our memories, and we shall not easily commit sin. Let us write it there, having first learnt it with the utmost exactness. For he does not say, "Observe"[6] that thou goest in the midst of snares; but, "Perceive!" And for what reason did he say, "Discern?"[7] He tells us that the snare is concealed; for this is indeed a snare, when the destruction does not appear openly, and the injury is not manifest, which lies hidden on all sides. Therefore he says, "Perceive!" Thou needest much reflection and diligent scrutiny. For even as boys conceal traps with earth, so the devil covers up our sins with the pleasures of this life.

7. But "perceive;" scrutinizing diligently;

---

[1] Eccles. vii. 3. This may be a proverbial misquotation; St. Chrysostom afterwards adopts the LXX., *house of drinking;* but his remarks are equally suitable to the E. V. *feasting.* Laughter is mentioned in verse 4.
[2] This seems to be a proverbial saying, from the next sentence.
[3] Eccles. i. 2.
[4] Eccles. vii. 3.
[5] Ecclus ix. 13.
[6] βλέπε, "see," as anything obvious.
[7] ἐπίγνωθι, "perceive," implies taking pains to discover.

and if any kind of gain falls in thy way, look not only at the gain, but inspect it carefully, lest somewhere death and sin lurk within the gain; and shouldest thou perceive this, fly from it. Again, when some delight or pleasure may chance to present itself, look not only at the pleasure; but lest somewhere in the depth of the pleasure some iniquity should lie enveloped, search closely, and if thou discoverest it, hasten away! And should any one counsel, or flatter, or cajole, or promise honours, or any other such thing whatever, let us make the closest investigation; and look at the matter on all sides, lest something pernicious, something perilous, should perchance befall us through this advice, or honour, or attention, and we run upon it hastily and unwittingly. For if there were only one or two snares, the precaution would be easy. But now, hear how Solomon speaks when he wishes to set forth the multitude of these; "Perceive that thou goest in the midst of snares;" he does not say, that thou "goest by" snares, but "in the midst" of snares. On either side are the pit-falls; on either side the deceits. One goes into the forum; one sees an enemy; one is inflamed by the bare sight of him! one sees a friend honoured; one is envious! One sees a poor man; one despises and takes no notice of him! One sees a rich man; one envies him! One sees some one injuriously treated; one recoils in disgust! One sees some one acting injuriously; one is indignant! One sees a handsome woman, and is caught! Seest thou, beloved, how many snares there are? Therefore it is said, "Remember that thou goest in the midst of snares." There are snares in the house, snares at the table, and snares in social intercourse. Very often a person unwittingly, in the confidence of friendship, gives utterance to some particular of those matters which ought not to be repeated again, and so great a peril is brought about, that the whole family is thereby ruined!

8. On every side then let us search closely into these matters. Often has a wife, often have children, often have friends, often have neighbours, proved a snare to the unheeding! And why, it is asked, are there so many snares? That we may not fly low, but seek the things that are above. For just as birds, as long as they cleave the upper air, are not easily caught; so also thou, as long as thou lookest to things above, wilt not be easily captured, whether by a snare, or by any other device. The devil is a fowler. Soar, then, too high for his arrows.[1] The man who hath mounted aloft will no longer admire any thing in the affairs of this life. But as when we have ascended to the top of the mountains, the city and its walls seem to us to be but small, and the men appear to us to be going along upon the earth like ants; so when thou hast ascended to the heights of spiritual wisdom, nothing upon the earth will be able to fascinate thee; but every thing, yea even riches, and glory, and honour, and whatever else there be of that kind, will appear insignificant when thou regardest heavenly things. According to Paul all the glories of the present life appeared trifling, and more unprofitable than dead things. Hence his exclamation, "The world is crucified unto me."[2] Hence also his admonition, "Set your affections on things above."[3] Above? What kinds of things do you speak of pray? Where the sun is, where the moon is? Nay, saith he. But where then? Where angels are? where archangels? where the cherubim? where the seraphim are? Nay, saith he. But where then? "Where Christ sitteth at the right hand of God."

9. Let us obey then, and let us think of this continually, that even as to the bird caught in the snare, wings are of no service, but he beats them about vainly, and to no purpose; so also to thee there is no utility in thy reasonings,[4] when once thou art powerfully captivated by wicked lust, but struggle as much as thou mayest, thou art captured! For this reason wings are given to birds; that they may avoid snares. For this reason men have the power of thinking; that they may avoid sin. What pardon then, or what excuse will be ours, when we become more senseless than the brutes? For the bird which has once been captured by the snare, yet afterwards escaped, and the deer which has fallen into the net, but has broken through it, are hard to be captured again with the like; since experience becomes a teacher of caution to every one. But we, though often snared in the same nets, fall into the same again; and though honoured with reason, we do not imitate the forethought and care of the irrational animals! Hence how often do we, from beholding a woman, suffer a thousand evils; returning home, and entertaining an inordinate desire, and experiencing anguish for many days; yet, nevertheless, we are not made discreet; but when we have scarcely cured one wound, we again fall into the same mischief, and are caught by the same means; and for the sake of the brief pleasure of a glance, we sustain a kind of lengthened and continual torment. But if we learn con-

---

[1] See on Rom. iii. 31, Hom. VIII. [2] Gal. vi. 14. [3] Col. iii. 2. [4] λογισμοί.

stantly to repeat to ourselves this saying,[1] we shall be kept from all these grievous evils.

10. The beauty of woman is the greatest snare. Or rather, not the beauty of woman, but unchastened gazing! For we should not accuse the objects, but ourselves, and our own carelessness. Nor should we say, Let there be no women, but Let there be no adulteries. We should not say, Let there be no beauty, but Let there be no fornication. We should not say, Let there be no belly, but let there be no gluttony; for the belly makes not the gluttony, but our negligence. We should not say, that it is because of eating and drinking that all these evils exist; for it is not because of this, but because of our carelessness and insatiableness. Thus the devil neither ate nor drank, and yet he fell! Paul ate and drank, and ascended up to heaven! How many do I hear say, Let there be no poverty! Therefore let us stop the mouths of those who murmur at such things. For it is blasphemy to utter such complaints. To such then, let us say, Let there be no meanness of spirit. For poverty brings innumerable good things into our state of life, and without poverty riches would be unprofitable. Hence we should accuse neither the one nor the other of these; for poverty and riches are both alike weapons which will tend to virtue, if we are willing. As then the courageous soldier, whichever weapon he takes, displays his own virtue, so the unmanly and cowardly one is encumbered by either. And that thou mayest learn that this is true, remember, I pray, the case of Job; who became both rich, and likewise poor, and handled both these weapons alike, and conquered in both. When he was rich, he said, "My door was open to every comer."[2] But when he had become poor, "The Lord gave, and the Lord hath taken away. As it seemed good unto the Lord, so hath it come to pass."[3] When he was rich, he shewed much hospitality; when he was poor, much patience. And thou, then,—art thou rich? Display much bountifulness! Hast thou become poor? Shew much endurance and patience! For neither is wealth an evil, nor poverty in itself; but these things, either of them, become so according to the free choice of those who make use of them. Let us school ourselves then to entertain no such opinions on these subjects; nor let us accuse the works of God, but the wicked choice of men. Riches are not able to profit the little-minded: nor is poverty able ever to injure the magnanimous.

11. Let us then discern the snares, and walk far off from them! Let us discern the precipices, and not even approach them! This will be the foundation of our greatest safety not only to avoid things sinful, but those things which seem indeed to be indifferent, and yet are apt to make us stumble towards sin. For example; to laugh, to speak jocosely, does not seem an acknowledged sin, but it leads to acknowledged sin. Thus laughter often gives birth to foul discourse, and foul discourse to actions still more foul. Often from words and laughter proceed railing and insult; and from railing and insult, blows and wounds; and from blows and wounds, slaughter and murder. If, then, thou wouldest take good counsel for thyself, avoid not merely foul words, and foul deeds, or blows, and wounds, and murders, but unseasonable laughter, itself, and the very language of banter; since these things have proved the root of subsequent evils. Therefore Paul saith, "Let no foolish talking nor jesting proceed out of thy mouth."[4] For although this seems to be a small thing in itself, it becomes, however, the cause of much mischief to us. Again, to live in luxury does not seem to be a manifest and admitted crime; but then it brings forth in us great evils,—drunkenness, violence, extortion, and rapine. For the prodigal and sumptuous liver, bestowing extravagant service upon the belly, is often compelled to steal, and to seize the property of others, and to use extortion and violence. If, then, thou avoidest luxurious living, thou removest the foundation of extortion, and rapine, and drunkenness, and a thousand other evils; cutting away the root of iniquity from its extremity. Hence Paul saith, that "she who liveth in pleasure is dead while she liveth."[5] Again, to go to the theatres, or to survey the horse-race, or to play at dice, does not seem, to most men, to be an admitted crime; but it introduces into our life an infinite host of miseries. For spending time in the theatres produces fornication, intemperance, and every kind of impurity. The spectacle of the horse-race also brings about fightings, railings, blows, insults, and lasting enmities. And a passion for dice-playing hath often caused blasphemies, injuries, anger, reproaches, and a thousand other things more fearful still.

12. Therefore, let us not only avoid sins, but those things too which seem to be indifferent, yet by degrees lead us into these misdeeds. He, indeed, who walks by the side of a precipice, even though he may not fall

---

[1] *i. e.*, Ecclus. ix. 20. [2] Job xxxi. 32.
[3] Job i. 21. This last clause is added in LXX. and Vulg.
[4] A quotation made up of two passages, in Ephes. iv. 29, and Ephes. v. 4.
[5] 1 Tim. v. 6.

over, trembles; and very often he is overset by this same trembling, and falls to the bottom. So also he who does not avoid sins from afar, but walks near them, will live in fear, and will often fall into them. Besides, he who eagerly looks at strange beauties, although he may not commit adultery, hath in so doing entertained lust; and hath become already an adulterer according to the declaration of Christ;[1] and often by this very lust he is carried on to the actual sin. Let us then withdraw ourselves far from sins. Dost thou wish to live soberly? Avoid not only adultery, but also the licentious glance! Dost thou wish to be far removed from foul words? Avoid not only foul words, but also inordinate laughter, and every kind of lust. Dost thou wish to keep far from committing murders? Avoid railing too. Dost thou wish to keep aloof from drunkenness? Avoid luxury and sumptuous tables, and pluck up the vice by the roots.

13. The licentiousness of the tongue is a great snare, and needs a strong bridle. Therefore also some one saith, "His own lips are a powerful snare to a man, and he is snared by the words of his own mouth."[2] Above all the other members, then, let us control this; let us bridle it; and let us expel from the mouth railings, and contumelies, and foul and slanderous language, and the evil habit of oaths. For again our discourse hath brought us to the same exhortation. But I had arranged with your charity, yesterday, that I would say no more concerning this precept, forasmuch as enough has been said upon it on all the foregoing days. But what is to become of me? I cannot bear to desist from this counsel, until I see that ye have put it in practice; since Paul also, when he saith to the Galatians, " Henceforth let no man trouble me,"[3] appears again to have met and addressed them.[4] Such are the paternal bowels; although they say they will depart, yet they depart not, until they see that their sons are chastened. Have ye heard to-day what the prophet speaks to us concerning oaths? "I lifted up mine eyes, and I saw," saith he, "and, behold, a flying sickle, the length thereof twenty cubits, and the breadth thereof ten cubits; and he said to me, What seest thou? and I said, I see a flying sickle, twenty cubits in length, and ten cubits in breadth. It shall also enter into the house," saith he, 'of every one that sweareth in my name, and shall remain[5] in the midst, and shall pull down the stones and the wood."[6] What, forsooth, is this which is here spoken? and for what reason is it in the form of a "sickle," and that a "flying sickle," that vengeance is seen to pursue the swearers? In order that thou mayest see that the judgment is inevitable, and the punishment not to be eluded. For from a flying sword some one might perchance be able to escape, but from a sickle, falling upon the neck, and acting in the place of a cord,[7] no one can escape. And when wings too are added, what further hope is there of safety? But on what account doth it pull down the stones and the wood of the swearer's house? In order that the ruin may be a correction to all. For since it is necessary that the earth must hide the swearer when dead; the very sight of his ruined house, now become a heap, will be an admonition to all who pass by and observe it, not to venture on the like, lest they suffer the like; and it will be a lasting witness against the sin of the departed. The sword is not so piercing as the nature of an oath! The sabre is not so destructive as the stroke of an oath! The swearer, although he seems to live, is already dead, and hath received the fatal blow. And as the man who hath received the halter,[8] before he hath gone out of the city and come to the pit,[9] and seen the executioner standing over him, is dead from the time he passed the doors of the hall of justice: so also the swearer.

14. All this let us consider, and let us not put our brethren on oath. What dost thou, O man? At the sacred table thou exactest an oath, and where Christ lies slain, there thou slayest thine own brother. Robbers, indeed, murder on the highways; but thou slayest the son in the presence of the mother: committing a murder more accursed than Cain himself; for he slew his brother in solitude and only with present death; but thou slayest thy brother in the midst of the church, and that with the deathless death that is to come! For think you that the church was made for this purpose, that we might swear? Yea, for this it was made, that we might pray! Is the Table placed there, that we may make adjurations? It is placed there to this end, that we may loose sins, not that we may bind them. But thou, if thou heedest nothing else, reverence at least that book, which thou reachest forth in putting the oath; and open the Gospel, which thou takest in hand when thou biddest swear; and when thou

---

[1] Matt. v. 28. [2] Prov. vi. 2. [3] Gal. vi. 17.
[4] He may mean Acts xviii. 23, but this seems to have been earlier. Or perhaps that he spoke afterwards to those who held the like error. See on Acts, Hom. XXXIX.
[5] καταλύσει in LXX. means this, though it is possible St. Chrys. may have taken it in the transitive sense, "shall destroy."
[6] Zech. v. 1, 4. St. Chrysostom, it should be observed, here only quotes a portion of these verses. See Hom. IX. fin.
[7] From its hooked shape: ξίφος is rather the pointed weapon for stabbing; μάχαιρα the edged weapon for cutting.
[8] σπαρτίον.
[9] βάραθρον. Into which his body would be thrown.

hearest what Christ there declares concerning oaths, shudder and desist! What then does He there say concerning oaths? "But I say unto you, Swear not at all."[1] And dost thou convert the Law[2] which forbids swearing into an oath. Oh, what contempt! Oh, what outrage! For thou doest just the same thing as if any one should bid the lawgiver, who prohibits murder, become himself a party to the murder. Not so much do I lament and weep, when I hear that some persons are slain[3] upon the highway, as I groan, and shed tears, and am horrified, when I see any one coming near this Table, placing his hands upon it, and touching the Gospels, and swearing! Art thou in doubt, I ask, concerning money, and wouldest thou slay a soul? What gainest thou to match the injury thou doest to thine own soul, and to thy neighbour? If thou believest that the man is true, do not impose the obligation of the oath; but if thou knowest him to be a liar, do not force him to commit perjury. "But that I may have a full assurance:" saith one. Verily, when thou hast not sworn him, then thou wilt receive a good and full assurance.[4]

15. For now, when thou hast returned home, thou wilt be continually the prey of conscience, whilst reasoning thus with thyself; "Was it to no purpose, then, that I put him upon his oath? Was he not really perjured? Have I not become the cause of the sin?" But if thou dost not put him upon his oath, thou wilt receive much consolation on returning home, rendering thanks to God, and saying, "Blessed be God, that I restrained myself, and did not compel him to swear vainly, and to no purpose. Away with gold! Perish the money!" for that which specially gives us assurance is, that we did not transgress the law, nor compel another to do it. Consider, for Whose sake thou didst not put any one on his oath; and this will suffice thee for refreshment and consolation. Often, indeed, when a fight takes place, we bear being insulted with fortitude, and we say to the insulter, "What shall I do with thee? Such an one hinders me, who is thy patron; he keeps back my hands." And this is sufficient to console us. So when thou art about to put any one on his oath, restrain thyself; and stop; and say to him who is about to swear, "What shall I do with thee? God hath forbidden me to put any one on oath. He now holds me back." This suffices both for the honour of the Lawgiver, and for thy safety, and for keeping him in fear who is ready to swear. For when he seeth that we are thus afraid to put others on oath, much more will he himself be afraid to swear rashly. Wouldest thou say thus, thy return to thine own home would be with much fulness of assurance. Hear God, therefore, in His Commandments, that He may Himself hear thee in thy prayers! This word shall be written in heaven, and shall stand by thee on the Day of Judgment, and shall discharge many sins.

16. This also let us consider not only with respect to an oath, but to every thing. And when we are about to do any good action for God's sake, and it is found to bring loss with it, let us look not merely at the loss connected with the matter, but at the gain which we shall reap by doing it for God. That is to say, Hath any one insulted thee? Bear it nobly! And thou wilt do so, if thou thinkest not of the insult merely, but of the dignity of Him who commands thee to bear it, and thou bearest it meekly. Hast thou given an alms? Think not of the outlay, but of the produce which arises from the outlay. Hast thou been mulcted of money? Give thanks, and regard not only the pain which is the result of the loss, but the gain which comes of thanksgiving. If we thus regulate ourselves, none of those heavy events which may befal us will give us pain; but from those things which may seem to be grievous, we shall be even gainers, and loss will be sweeter and more desired than wealth, pain than pleasure, and mirth and insult than honour. Thus all things adverse will turn to our gain. And here we shall enjoy much tranquillity, and there we shall attain the kingdom of heaven; which God grant that we may all be deemed worthy to obtain,[5] by the grace and

---

[1] Matt. v. 34.
[2] Upon oaths, see Bingham, b. xxi. c. vii. sec. 4, sqq., who however does not mention this use of the *altar*.
[3] σφαζομένους. The present participle is accounted for by the fact that robbers took advantage of those troubles. See Libanius, *Or. de Sedit. ad fin.*
[4] πληροφορία. This word occurs Heb. vi. 11, x. 22; and 1 Thess. i. 5; and Col. ii. 2. The elliptical sense of the word will be understood by a reference to these passages.

[5] Of remission of sins in the Holy Eucharist, see Theodorus in Cat. on 1 Cor. xii. 31. "He that practiseth the greatest and strongly forbidden sins, ought to abstain from the mysteries; for to such an one it is not good to partake of them, until he first abstain from his sins, through fear of the laws laid down. But of other things, such as must befall men .... if we fall into such, it is not well to deprive ourselves of the mysteries, but to come in the greater fear.... inasmuch as remission also comes to us from thence, when we abstain from what is in our power, and are found not neglectful of the rest; beside spiritual aid for the easier amendment of life. For all things that are added to us by the death of Christ, the same it is just should be accomplished by the symbols of His death." Ed. Cramer, p. 222. This is implied in our own service, in the prayer after communicating, and in the final answers of the catechism. So too in the Roman Canon of the Mass, "Deliver me, by this Thy Holy Body and Blood, from all my iniquities and all evils." Lit. of St. Basil, after the Gospel. ... "We pray and beseech Thy goodness, O Thou Lover of men, that this Mystery which Thou didst institute for our salvation, be not unto judgment to us, nor to Thy people, but to the wiping away of our sins, and the remission of our negligences." Renaudot, t. i. pp. 9, 58. Lit. of St. Cyril, in *Orat. Pacis.* ... "that we may offer Thee this holy, reasonable, spiritual, unbloody Sacrifice for the remission of our sins, and the pardon of the ignorances of Thy people." *Ib.* p. 30, and Goar, p. 164. So Lit. St. Greg. after the Invocation of the Holy Ghost, Ren. p. 106. Lit. St. Marc. pp.

lovingkindness of our Lord Jesus Christ, through Whom and with Whom, to the Father with the Holy Spirit, be glory, dominion, and honour, now and ever, and world without end. Amen.

143, 158; Canon *Univ. Ethiop.* p. 502; Lit. of St. Chrys., Prayer of Oblation, Goar, p. 74. See also the note on Tertullian referred to, p. 266, note z, and St. Irenæus, Fragm. ed. Pfaff, p. 27. "That they who partake of these pledges (ἀντιτύπων) may obtain remission of sins and eternal life."

HOMILY XVI.

This Homily was delivered on the occasion of the Prefect[1] entering the Church, for the purpose of pacifying the minds of the people, in consequence of a rumour of an intended sack[2] having been announced to him, when all were meditating flight. It treats also on the subject of avoiding oaths, and on the words of the Apostle, "Paul, a prisoner of Jesus Christ."[3]

1. I COMMEND the Prefect's consideration, that seeing the city agitated, and every one purposing a flight, he hath come here and afforded you consolation, and hath led you to entertain favourable hopes. But for you I blushed, and was ashamed, that after these long and frequent discourses ye should have needed consolation from without.[4] I longed that the earth would open and swallow me up, when I heard him discoursing with you, alternately administering comfort, or blaming such ill-timed[5] and senseless cowardice. For it was not becoming, that you should be instructed by him; but you ought yourselves to be teachers to all the unbelievers.[6] Paul did not permit even going to law before the unbelievers;[7] but thou, after so much admonition of our Fathers,[8] hast needed teachers from without; and certain vagabonds and miscreants have again unsettled this great city, and set it upon flight. With what eyes shall we hereafter look upon the unbelievers, we who were so timid and cowardly? With what tongue shall we speak to them, and persuade them to exercise courage as to approaching evils, when we became through this alarm more timid than any hare? "But what could we do," says some one, "we are but men!" This is indeed the very reason why we ought not to be terrified, because we are men, and not brutes. For these are scared by all manner of sounds and noises; because they have not reasoning power, which is adequate to dispel fear. But thou who hast been honoured with the gift of speech and reason, how is it that thou sinkest to their ignoble condition? Hath some one entered the city, and announced the march of soldiers against it? Be not terrified, but leaving him, bend the knee: call upon thy Lord: groan bitterly, and He will keep off the dreaded event.

2. Thou hadst heard indeed a false report of the march, and wert in danger of being severed from the present life.[9] But that blessed Job, when the messengers came one after another, and he had heard them announcing their dreadful news, and adding thereto the insupportable destruction of his children, neither cried nor groaned, but turned to prayer, and gave thanks to the Lord. Him do thou too imitate; and when any comer announces that soldiers have encircled the city, and are about to plunder its wealth, flee to thy Lord and say, "The Lord gave, the Lord hath taken away; as it seemeth good to the Lord, so is it done. Blessed be the name of the Lord for ever." The experience of the actual events did not terrify him; yet the mere report frightens thee. And how are we to be accounted of, who when we are commanded[10] boldly to encounter death itself, are thus affrighted by a false rumour! The man who is bewildered con-

---

[1] ἄρχοντος, some read κόμητος, which seems to imply that this officer was the Prætorian Præfect of the East. See note of Ducæus. Tillemont, art. xxxiv. calls him "le Gouverneur."
[2] πραίδας, from the Latin Præda. Ducæus takes it with πρὸς τὸν ἄρχοντα, making it only a confiscation. Montfaucon does not agree with Tillemont in dating the Homily, but it must have been delivered after the return of Cæsarius to the Emperor, and before any news from him. The Prefect may be Hellebichus, who was left at Antioch: but see Pref.
[3] Philem. i. 1.
[4] *i. e.*, from one outside the pale of the church.
[5] ἄκαιρον. This word favours the supposition, that all real ground of fear was at an end.
[6] It appears from this, and from what follows, that the Prefect was a Pagan.
[7] 1 Cor. vi. 1.   [8] See sec. 3.

[9] He seems to mean, "wert almost dead with fear." But this is harsh: the text may be in fault.
[10] He means that Job had no such command.

structs fear which is unreal; and trouble which is not visible; but he who abides in a settled and tranquil condition of soul, breaks in pieces even that which is real. Seest thou not pilots; when the sea is raging, and the clouds are rushing together, and the thunders are bursting forth, and all on board are in confusion, they seat themselves at the helm without tumult or disturbance; giving earnest heed to their own art, and considering how they may ward off the effects of the approaching storm. Be these thy example; and laying hold of the sacred anchor, the hope that is in God, remain unshaken and immoveable. "Whosoever heareth these sayings of mine, and doeth them not, shall be likened unto a foolish man, which built his house upon the sand; and the rain descended, and the floods came, and the winds blew, and beat upon that house; and it fell, and great was the fall of it."[1] Seest thou that it is the character of folly to fall down headlong, and to be overthrown? Or rather, we were not only reduced to the condition of that foolish man, but our fall was still more wretched. For the house of that man fell down after the rivers and rains had descended, and the winds had beaten upon it; but we, when there were no winds striking, nor floods invading, nor blasts assaulting, before the experience of disaster, were overturned by a mere rumour, and dropped at once all the philosophy we were meditating.

3. What think ye are now my thoughts? How should I conceal,—yea, bury myself? How must I blush with shame? If I had not been forcibly urged by our Fathers, I would not have arisen, I would not have spoken, whilst my mind was darkened with sadness because of your pusillanimity. But neither now have I been able to recover myself; since anger and sorrow have laid such seige to my soul. For who would not feel provoked and indignant, that after so much teaching ye should need the instructions of Gentiles, that ye might be comforted and persuaded to bear in a manly way the present alarm. Pray ye therefore that free utterance may be given us in opening our mouth; and that we may be able to shake off this sadness, and to hold up again a little; for indeed this shame on account of your pusillanimity hath greatly depressed our spirits.

4. Lately, I addressed to your Charity many things concerning the snares lying on all sides of us; and concerning fear and sadness, sorrow and pleasure; and also concerning the sickle that flieth down upon the houses of swearers. Now, out of all these many matters, I would have you especially to remember what I said respecting the "winged sickle," and its settling in the swearer's house; and pulling down the stones and the wood, and consuming the whole mass. And withal, take heed to this; that it is the extreme of folly to swear by taking the Gospels, and to turn the very Law which forbids swearing into an oath; and that it is better to suffer loss of property than to impose an oath on our neighbours; since this is a great honour to be done to God. For when thou sayest to God, "For thy sake I have not put such a one, who hath robbed and injured me, on his oath," God will pay thee back a great recompense on account of this honour, both here and hereafter. Say these things to others, and observe them also yourselves. I know that in this place we become more reverent, and lay aside every evil habit. But what is to be aimed at is, not that we be lovers of wisdom here only, but that when we depart, we may take this reverence out with us, where we especially need it. For those who carry water do not merely have their vessels full when near the fountain, and empty them when they reach home, but there they put them away with especial caution, that they may not be overturned, and their labours rendered useless. Let us all imitate these persons; and when we come home, let us strictly retain what has been spoken; since if ye here have gotten full, but return home empty, having the vessels of your understandings destitute of what ye have heard, there will be no advantage from your replenishment here. Shew me not the wrestler in the place of exercise, but of actual contest; and religion not at the season of hearing, but at the season of practice.

5. Thou applaudest what is said now. When thou art required to swear, then remember all these things. If ye quickly accomplish this law, we will advance our teaching to other and greater things. Lo! this is the second year that I am discoursing to your Charity; and I have not yet been able to explain a hundred lines[2] of the Scriptures. And the reason is, that ye need to learn of us what ye might reduce to practice at home, and of yourselves; and thus the greater part of our exhortation is consumed on ethical discourse. But this ought not to have been so; the regulation of manners you ought to

---

[1] Matt. vii. 26, 27.

[2] στίχοι. Lines, or sentences. The ancients had two kind of verses, one of which they called στίχοι, and the other ῥήματα. The stichoi were lines that contained a certain number of letters, and were not limited by the sense as our modern verses. The Codex Bezæ and Alex. are so divided into parts, shorter than verses.

have learnt at home, and of yourselves; but the sense of the Scriptures, and the speculations upon them, you might commit to us. If, however, it were necessary that you should hear such things of us, there was no need of more than one day: for what there is to be said is of no diversified or difficult character, or such as requires any elaboration. For when God declares His sentence, subtle arguments are unseasonable. God hath said, "Thou shalt not swear." Do not then demand of me the reasons of this. It is a royal law. He who established it, knows the reason of the law. If it had not been profitable, He would not have forbidden it. Kings bring in laws, and not all perchance profitable; for they are men, and cannot be competent to discover what is useful, like God. Nevertheless, we obey them. Whether we marry, or make wills, or are about to purchase servants, or houses, or fields, or to do any other act, we do these things not according to our own mind, but according to the laws which they ordain; and we are not entirely at liberty to dispose of the things which concern ourselves according to our own minds; but in many cases we are subject to their will; and should we do any thing that is contrary to their judgment, it becomes invalid and useless. So then tell me, are we to pay so much respect to the laws of men, and trample under foot the law of God? What defence, or what pardon can such conduct be worthy of? He hath said, "Thou shalt not swear." In order that thou mayest do and speak all things with safety, do not in practice lay down a law contrary to His.

6. But enough of these matters. Let us now proceed to lay before you one sentence of those which have been read to-day, and thus end this discourse. "Paul, a prisoner of Jesus Christ," saith he, "and Timothy the brother."[1] Great is the designation of Paul: no title of principality and power, but he speaks of bonds and chains! Truly great indeed! Although many other things made him illustrious; his being caught up into the third heaven, his being transported to Paradise, his hearing unutterable words; yet he sets down none of these, but mentions the chain instead of all, for this made him more conspicuous and illustrious than these. And why so? Because the one were the free gifts of the Lord's lovingkindness; and the other the marks of the constancy and patience of the servant. But it is customary with those who love, to glory more in the things which they suffer for those who are beloved, than in the benefits they receive from them. A king is not so proud of his diadem, as Paul gloried in his chains. And very justly. For a diadem affords but an ornament to the crowned head; but the chain is a much greater ornament as well as a security. The kingly crown often betrays the head it encircles, and allures innumerable traitors, and invites them to the lust of empire. And in battles this ornament is so dangerous, that it must be hidden and laid aside. Hence kings in battle, change the outward dress, and so mingle in the crowd of combatants; so much betrayal does there result from the crown; but the chain will bring nothing of this kind upon those who have it, but altogether the contrary; since if there be a war, and an engagement with demons, and the hostile powers; the man who is thus encompassed, by holding forth his chain, repels their assaults. And many of the secular magistrates not only bear the name of office while they are in authority, but when they have given up their authority. Such a one is called an ex-consul, such a one an ex-prætor. But he, instead of all such titles, says, "Paul the prisoner." And very rightly. For those magisterial offices are no complete evidences of virtue in respect to the soul; for they are to be purchased by money, and obtained by the solicitations of friends; but this distinction that is obtained by bonds is a proof of the soul's love of wisdom, and the strongest sign of a longing for Christ. And the former are soon gone, but this distinction has none to succeed to it. Behold at least from that time to the present day how long a time has passed, and yet the name of this Prisoner has become increasingly illustrious. As to all the consuls, whoever they were, of former times, they are passed into silence; and not even their names are known to the generality of mankind. But the name of this Prisoner, the blessed Paul, is still great here, great in the land of the barbarians, great also among the Scythians and Indians; and were you to go even to the very bounds of the habitable world, you would hear of this appellation, and whithersoever any one could come, he would perceive that the name of Paul was borne in the mouths of all men. And what marvel is it, if it be so by land and sea, when even in the heavens the name of Paul is great; with angels and archangels and the powers above, and with the King of these, even God! "But what were the chains," says some one, "that brought glory to him who was thus fettered? Were they not formed of iron?" Of iron, indeed, they were formed; but they contained the grace of the Spirit, abundantly flourish-

---

[1] Philem. i.

ing in them; since he wore them for Christ's sake. Oh, wonder! the servants were bound, the Master was crucified, and yet the preaching of the Gospel every day increases! And through the means by which it was supposed that it would be extinguished, by these very means it was kindled; and the Cross and bonds, which were thought to be an abomination, these are now become the symbols of salvation; and that iron was to us more precious than all gold, not by its intrinsic nature, but for this cause and ground!

7. But here I see an enquiry arising out of this point; and if you give me your attention, I will both state the question exactly, and will add the solution. What then is the subject of enquiry? This same Paul once having come before Festus, whilst discoursing to him, and defending himself concerning the charges which the Jews had alleged against him, and telling how he had seen Jesus, how he had heard that blessed voice; how he had been struck with blindness and recovered sight, and had fallen down and risen up again; how he had come a captive into Damascus, bound without chains; after speaking likewise of the Law and of the Prophets, and shewing that they had foretold all these things, he captured the judge, and almost persuaded him to come over to himself. For such are the souls of holy men: when they have fallen into dangers, they do not consider how they may be delivered from dangers, but strive every way how they may capture their persecutors. Just so did it then happen. He came in to defend himself, and he departed taking the judge with him![1] And to this the judge bore witness, saying, "Almost[2] thou persuadest me to be a Christian."[3] And this ought to have happened to-day; and this Prefect, on coming among you, ought to have admired your magnanimity, your fortitude, your perfect tranquillity; and to have gone away, taking with him a lesson from your good order, admiring your assembly, praising your congress, and learning from the actual fact, how great a difference there is between Gentiles and Christians!

8. But as I was saying:—When Paul had caught him, and he said, "Almost thou persuadest me to be a Christian," Paul answered thus, "I would to God that not only thou, but also all that hear me this day, were both almost and altogether such as I am, except these bonds."[4] What sayest thou, O Paul? When thou writest to the Ephesians, thou sayest, "I therefore, the prisoner of the Lord, beseech you, that ye walk worthy of the vocation wherewith ye are called."[5] And when thou speakest to Timothy, "Wherein I suffer trouble as an evil-doer, even unto bonds."[6] And again, when to Philemon, thus; "Paul, a prisoner of Jesus Christ."[7] And again, when debating with the Jews, thou sayest, "For the hope of Israel I am bound with this chain."[8] And writing to the Philippians, thou sayest, "Many of the brethren in the Lord, waxing confident by my bonds, are much more bold to speak the word without fear."[9] Every where thou bearest about the chain, everywhere thou puttest forward thy bonds, and boastest in the thing. But when thou comest to the tribunal, thou betrayest thy philosophy, where it were right to have spoken the most boldly, and sayest to the judge, "I would to God that thou mightest become a Christian 'without' these bonds!" Yet surely if the bonds were good, and so good, that they could be the means of making others to grow bold in the cause of true religion; (for this very thing thou didst declare before, when thou saidst, "Many of the brethren, waxing confident by my bonds, did speak the word without fear"); for what reason dost thou not glory in this thing in the presence of the judge, but doest even the reverse?

9. Does not what I say appear a question? The solution of it, however, I will bring forward at once. For Paul acted thus, not from distress or fear, but from an abundance of wisdom and spiritual understanding. And how this was, I proceed to explain. He was addressing a Gentile, and an unbeliever, who knew nothing of our matters. Hence he was unwilling to introduce him by way of disagreeable things, but as he said, "I became to them that are without law, as without law;"[10] so he acted in the present instance. His meaning is, "If the Gentile hear of bonds and tribulations, he will straightway be taking flight; since he knows not the power of bonds. First, let him become a believer; let him taste of the word preached, and then he will even of himself hasten towards these bonds. I have heard the Lord saying, "No man putteth a piece of new cloth into an old garment, for that which is put in to fill it up taketh from the garment, and the rent is made worse. Neither do men put new wine into old wine-skins; else the wine-skins

---

[1] *i. e.*, in conviction, though not in act. St. Chrysostom used the word *almost* a few lines back. Agrippa is named presently, but some there read Festus.
[2] ἐν ὀλίγῳ. St. Chrysostom clearly understood this as it is rendered in our English version of 1611. See above "almost persuaded him," σχεδὸν ἔπεισε. Modern scholars have attached a different sense to the expression. See Revised Version.
[3] Acts xxvi. 28.

[4] Acts xxvi. 29.   [5] Ephes. iv. 1.   [6] 2 Tim. ii. 9.
[7] Phil. i. 1.   [8] Acts xxviii. 20.   [9] Philip. i. 14.
[10] 1 Cor. ix. 21.

burst."[1] The soul of this man is an old garment: an old wine-skin. It is not renewed by the faith, nor renovated by the grace of the Spirit. It is yet weak and earthly. It affects the things of this life. It flutters eagerly after worldly show. It loves a glory that is present. Should he hear at once, even from the first, that if he becomes a Christian he will become immediately a prisoner, and will be encompassed with a chain; feeling ashamed and indignant, he will recoil from the word preached. Therefore, saith he, "Except these bonds."[2] Not as deprecating the bonds themselves, God forbid! But condescending to the other's infirmity; for he himself loved and welcomed his bonds, even as a woman fond of ornament doth her jewels of gold. Whence is this apparent? "I rejoice," saith he, "in my sufferings for you, and fill up that which is behind of the afflictions of Christ in my flesh."[3] And again; "Unto you it is given in the behalf of Christ, not only to believe on Him, but to suffer for His sake."[4] And again; "And not only so, but we also glory in tribulations."[5] Wherefore, if he rejoices and glories in this, and calls it a gift of grace, it is manifest that when he was addressing the judge, he spoke to him as he did, for the reason assigned. Moreover, also in a different passage, when he happened to find a necessity for glorying, he shews the very same by saying, "Most gladly, therefore, will I glory in my infirmities ..... in reproaches, in necessities, in persecutions, in distresses, that the power of Christ may rest upon me."[6] And again; "If I must needs glory, I will glory of the things which concern mine infirmities."[7] And elsewhere, comparing himself with others, and exhibiting to us his superiority in the comparison, he thus speaks; "Are they ministers of Christ? (I speak as a fool), I am more."[8] And wishing to shew this superiority, he did not say that he had raised the dead, nor that he had expelled demons, nor that he had cleansed lepers, nor that he had done any other thing of the sort, but that he had suffered those innumerable hardships. Hence when he said, "I am more," he presently cites the multitude of his trials; "In stripes, above measure, in deaths oft, in prisons more frequent .... of the Jews five times received I forty stripes save one, once was I stoned, thrice I suffered shipwreck, a night and a day I have been in the deep;"[9] and all the rest. Thus Paul everywhere glories in tribulations; and prides himself upon this circumstance exceedingly. And very justly. For this it is which especially shews the power of Christ, viz. that the Apostles conquered by such means; by bonds, by tribulations, by scourgings, and the worst of ills.

10. For these two things Christ had announced, tribulation and remission, labours and crowns, toils and rewards, things pleasant and sad. Nevertheless, to the present life he assigns the sorrowful things; but for the life to come, he has stored up those which are pleasant; at once shewing that He did not mean to deceive men, and wishing by this arrangement to diminish the burden of human woes. For the imposter first holds out the things which are pleasant, and afterwards brings forward those which are disagreeable. Thus for example:—Kidnappers, when they intend to steal and carry off little children, do not promise them blows and stripes, or any other thing of that kind, but offer them cakes, and sweetmeats, and such like, by which the age of childhood is usually gratified; in order that, enticed by these things, they may sell their liberty, and may fall into the utmost peril. Moreover, bird-catchers, and fishermen, thus entice the prey which they pursue, offering first their usual food, and such as is agreeable to them, and by this means concealing the snare. So that this is especially the work of imposters, first to hold out things which are agreeable, but afterwards to introduce the things which are disagreeable. But the case is altogether the reverse with those who are really careful and provident for others. Fathers at least act quite in a contrary manner to kidnappers. When they send their children to school, they set masters over them, threaten them with stripes, and encompass them with fear on all sides. But when they have thus spent the first portion of their lives, and their habits are formed, they then put them in possession of honour, and power, and luxury, and all the wealth that is theirs.

11. And thus God has acted. After the manner of provident fathers, and not after that of kidnappers, He has first involved us in things that are grievous; handing us over to present tribulation, as it were to schoolmasters and teachers; in order that being chastened and sobered by these things, after shewing forth all patience, and learning all right discipline, we may afterwards, when formed into due habits, inherit the kingdom of heaven. He first prepares and fits us for the management of the wealth He is to give, and then puts us into the actual possession of riches. For if He had not acted thus, the giving of riches would have been no boon.

---
[1] Matt. ix. 16, 17: Mark ii. 21; Luke v. 36.
[2] Acts xxvi. 28. [3] Coloss. i. 24. [4] Philip. i. 29.
[5] Rom. v. 3. [6] 2 Cor. xii. 9, 10. [7] 2 Cor. xi. 30.
[8] 2 Cor. xi. 23. [9] 2 Cor. xi. 23, 25.

but a punishment and a vengeance. For even as a son that is senseless and prodigal, when he has succeeded to a paternal inheritance, is precipitated headlong by this very thing, having none of the practical wisdom requisite for the economy of wealth; but if he be intelligent, and gentle, and sober, and moderate, managing his paternal estate as is befitting, he becomes by this means more illustrious and distinguished: so must it also necessarily happen in our case. When we have acquired spiritual understanding, when we have all attained to "perfect manhood," and the measure of full stature;" then He puts us in possession of all that He has promised: but now as little children He chastens us, together with consolation and soothing. And this is not the only advantage of receiving the tribulation beforehand, but there is also another, not less than this. For the man who first of all lives luxuriously, and then has to expect punishment after his luxurious living, has not even a sense of his present luxury, merely by reason of the expectation of impending woes; but he who is first in a sorrowful state, if he is anticipating the enjoyment of good things afterwards, overlooks present difficulties, in the hope of the good things which are to come. Not only, then, on account of our security, but also for our pleasure and consolation hath He ordained that the things which are grievous should be first; in order that being lightened with the hope of futurity, we should be rendered insensible to what is present. And this Paul would shew and make plain, when he said, "Our light affliction, which is but for a moment, worketh for us a far more exceeding and eternal weight of glory. While we look not at the things which are seen, but at the things which are not seen."[1] He calls tribulation light, not because of the intrinsic nature of things that are grievous, but because of the expectation of good things to come. For even as the merchant is indifferent to the labour that attends navigation, being buoyed up with the hope of a cargo; and as the boxer bravely sustains the blows on his head, looking to the crown beyond; so also indeed do we, earnestly gazing towards heaven, and the good things that are in the heavens, whatever evils come on us, sustain them all with fortitude, being nerved with the good hope of the things to come.

12. Therefore let us go home, taking with us this saying;[2] for though it be simple and short, it nevertheless contains much of the doctrine of spiritual wisdom. He who is in a state of grief and tribulation, hath a sufficient consolation; he who lives in luxury and abundance, hath that which may greatly sober him. For when as thou sittest at the table thou art reminded of this saying, thou wilt speedily shrink from drunkenness and gluttony; learning through this sentence, how needful it is for us to be striving; and thou wilt say with thyself, "Paul lived in bonds and in dungeons, but I in drunkenness and at a luxurious table! What pardon then shall I obtain?" This also is a fit saying for women; since those who are fond of ornament, and expensive dresses, and bind themselves about with gold on every side, when they remember this chain, will hate, I feel assured, and abominate that adorning of themselves; and will hasten to such bonds as these. For those ornaments have often been the cause of manifold evils, and introduced a thousand quarrels into a family, and have bred envy, and jealousy, and hatred. But these loosed the sins of the wide world, affrighted demons, and drove away the devil. With these, while tarrying in prison, he persuaded the jailor; with these he attracted Agrippa himself; with these he procured many disciples. Therefore he said, "Wherein I suffer trouble as an evil-doer unto bonds, but the word of God is not bound."[3] For just as it is not possible to bind a sunbeam, or to shut it up within the house, so neither the preaching of the word; and what was much more, the teacher was bound, and yet the word flew abroad; he inhabited the prison, and yet his doctrine rapidly winged its way every where throughout the world!

Knowing these things then, let us not be depressed, when adverse affairs meet us, but then let us be more strong, then more powerful; "for tribulation worketh patience."[4] Let us not grieve for the calamities which befall us, but let us in all things give thanks unto God!

13. We have completed the second week of the fast, but this we should not consider; for going through the fast does not consist in merely going through the time, but in going through it with amendment of manners. Let us consider this; whether we have become more diligent; whether we have corrected any of our defects; whether we have washed away our sins? It is common for every one to ask in Lent, how many weeks each has fasted; and some may be heard saying that they have fasted two, others three, and others that they have fasted the whole of the weeks. But what advantage is it, if we have gone through

---

[1] 2 Cor. iv. 17, 18.　[2] i. e., Paul, a prisoner of Jesus Christ.　[3] 2 Tim. ii. 9.　[4] Rom. v. 3.

the fast devoid of good works? If another says, "I have fasted the whole of Lent," do thou say, "I had an enemy, but I was reconciled; I had a custom of evil-speaking, but I put a stop to it; I had a custom of swearing, but I have broken through this evil practice." It is of no advantage to merchants, to have gone over a great extent of ocean, but to have sailed with a freight and much merchandise. The fast will profit us nothing, if we pass through it as a mere matter of course, without any result. If we practise a mere abstinence from meats, when the forty days are past, the fast is over too. But if we abstain from sins, this still remains, even when the fast has gone by, and will be from this time a continual advantage to us; and will here render us no small recompense, before we attain unto the kingdom of heaven. For as he who is living in iniquity, even before hell, hath punishment, being stung by his conscience; so the man who is rich in good works, even before the kingdom, will have the benefit of exceeding joy, in that he is nourished with blessed hopes.

14. Therefore Christ says, "I will see you again, and your heart shall rejoice, and your joy no man taketh from you."[1] A brief saying, but one that hath in it much consolation. What then is this, "your joy no man taketh?" If thou hast money, many are able to take away the joy that comes of thy wealth; as, for instance, a thief, by digging through the wall; a servant by carrying off what was entrusted to him; an emperor by confiscation; and the envious man by contumely. Should you possess power, there are many who are able to deprive you of the joy of it. For when the conditions of office are at an end, the conditions of pleasure will also be ended. And in the exercise of office itself too, there are many accidents occurring, which by bringing difficulty and care, strike at the root of thy satisfaction. If thou hast bodily strength, the assaults of disease put a stop to joy from that source. If thou hast beauty and bloom, the approach of old age withers it, and takes away that joy. Or if thou enjoyest a sumptuous table, when evening comes on the joy of the banquet is at an end; for every thing belonging to this life is liable to damage, and is unable to afford us a lasting pleasure; but piety and the virtue of the soul is altogether the reverse of this. If thou hast done an alms, no one is able to take away this good work. Though an army, or kings, or myriads of calumniators and conspirators, were to beset thee on all sides, they could not take away the possession, once deposited in heaven; but the joy thereof continually abideth; for it is said, "He hath dispersed, he hath given to the poor, his righteousness endureth for ever."[2] And very justly; for in the storehouses of heaven it is laid up, where no thief breaks in, nor robber seizes, nor moth devours.[3] If thou pourest out continued and fervent prayers, no man will be able to spoil thee of the fruit of them; for this fruit too is rooted in the heavens; it is out of the way of all injury, and remains beyond mortal reach. If when evil-treated thou has done a kind action; if thou hast borne with patience to hear thyself evil spoken of; if thou hast returned blessings for reproaches; these are good works that abide continually, and the joy of them no man taketh away; but as often as thou rememberest these, thou art glad and rejoicest, and reapest large fruits of pleasure. So also, indeed, if we succeed in avoiding oaths; and persuade our tongue to abstain from this pernicious practice, the good work will be finished in a short time, but the delight arising from it will be continuous and unfailing.

17. And now, it is time that you should be teachers and guides of others; that friends should undertake to instruct and lead on their neighbours; servants their fellow-servants; and youths those of their own age. What if any one had promised thee a single piece of gold for every man who was reformed, wouldest thou not then have used every exertion, and been all day long sitting by them, persuading and exhorting. Yet now God promises thee not one piece of gold, nor ten, or twenty, or a hundred, or a thousand; no, nor the whole earth, for thy labours, but He gives thee that which is greater than all the world, the kingdom of heaven; and not only this, but also another thing besides it. And what kind of thing is that? "He who taketh forth the precious from the vile,"[4] saith He, "shall be as my mouth."[5] What can be equal to this in point of honour or security? What kind of excuse or pardon can be left to those, who after so great a promise neglect their neighbour's safety? Now if you see a blind man falling into a pit, you stretch forth a hand, and think it a disgraceful thing to overlook one who is about to perish? But daily beholding all thy brethren precipitated into the wicked custom of oaths, dost thou not dare even to utter a word? Thou hast spoken once, perhaps, and he hath not heard. Speak there-

---

[1] John xvi. 22.
[2] Ps. cxii. 9.   [3] Matt. vi. 19; Luke xii. 33.
[4] *i.e.*, the soul of a man from the vile state of sin.   [5] Jer. xv. 19.

fore twice, and thrice, and as often as it may be, till thou hast persuaded him. Every day God is addressing us, and we do not hear; and yet He does not leave off speaking. Do thou, therefore, imitate this tender care towards thy neighbour. For this reason it is that we are placed with one another; that we inhabit cities, and that we meet together in churches, in order that we may bear one another's burdens, that we may correct one another's sins. And in the same manner as persons inhabiting the same shop, carry on a separate traffic, yet put all afterwards into the common fund, so also let us act. Whatever advantages each man is able to confer upon his neighbour, let him not grudge, nor shrink from doing it, but let there be some such kind of spiritual commerce, and reciprocity; in order that having deposited every thing in the common store, and obtained great riches, and procured a large treasure, we may be all together partakers of the kingdom of heaven; through the grace and lovingkindness of our Lord Jesus Christ, by Whom and with Whom, to the Father, with the Holy Ghost, be glory, both now and ever, and world without end. Amen.

HOMILY XVII.

Of the Commissioners (Hellebichus Commander of the Troops,[1] and Cæsarius Master of the Offices[2]) sent by the Emperor Theodosius for the inquisition of the offenders, on account of the overturning of the Statues.

1. MOST opportunely have we all this day sung together, "Blessed be the Lord God of Israel, who only doeth wondrous things."[3] For marvellous, and beyond all expectation, are the things which have happened? A whole city, and so great a population, when just about to be overwhelmed—to sink under the waves, and to be utterly and instantly destroyed—He hath entirely rescued from shipwreck in a single moment of time! Let us give thanks then, not only that God hath calmed the tempest, but that He suffered it to take place; not only that He rescued us from shipwreck, but that He allowed us to fall into such distress; and such an extreme peril to hang over us. Thus also Paul bids us "in every thing give thanks."[4] But when he says, "In every thing give thanks," he means not only in our deliverance from evils, but also at the time when we suffer those evils. "For all things work together for good to them that love God."[5] Let us be thankful to Him for this deliverance from trials; and let us never forget them. Let us devote ourselves to prayer, to continual supplications, and to much piety.

2. When the sad conflagration of these calamities was first kindled, I said, that it was a season not for doctrine, but for prayer.[6] The very same thing I now repeat, when the fire has been extinguished—that it is now especially, and more than before, a time for prayer; that now is the season especially for tears and compunction, for an anxious soul, for much diligence, and for much caution. For at that time the very nature of our tribulation restrained us, however unwillingly, and disposed us to sobriety; and led us to become more religious; but now when the bridle is removed, and the cloud has passed away, there is fear lest we should fall back again into sloth, or become relaxed by this respite; and lest one should have reason to say of us too, "When He slew them, then they sought Him, and returned, and enquired early after God."[7] Wherefore also Moses admonished the Jews, saying, "When thou shalt have eaten, and drunk, and art full, remember the Lord thy God."[8] The goodness of your disposition will now be rendered manifest, if you continue in the practice of the same piety. For at that time, many imputed your earnestness to fear, and the approach of calamity; but now, it will be purely your own achievement, if you still persevere in maintaining this earnestness. Since with a boy too, as long as he is guided

---

[1] στρατηλάτης. See Dufresne. This title was given to one who had the general command of the troops in a province, or division of the empire.
[2] Μάγιστρος. See Dufresne. Also Tillemont, *Hist. des Emp. Theod.* art. 33. Montfaucon has already called in question the judgment of Tillemont's note on these Homilies, placing this before XI. It does not appear that this was delivered immediately on the arrival of the Commissioners, but on occasion of some fresh news from the Emperor after the trials.
[3] Ps. lxxii. 18.   [4] 1 Thess. v. 18.   [5] Rom. viii. 28.   [6] Hom. II. 1.   [7] Ps. lxxviii. 34.   [8] Deut. vi. 11, 12.

by some tutor whom he fears, if he lives with sobriety and meekness, there is nothing to admire, for all persons ascribe the sobriety of the stripling to his fear of the tutor. But when he remains in the same seemly behaviour, after the restraint from that quarter is done away with, all persons give him credit too for the sobriety that was seen in his earlier age. Thus also let us act; let us continue in the same state of godly fear, in order that for our former diligence too we may gain much praise from God.

3. We had expected innumerable woes; that our property would be plundered, that the houses would have been burnt together with their inmates, that the city would have been plucked up from the midst of the world, that its very fragments would have been utterly destroyed, and that its soil would have been placed under the plough! But, lo! all these things existed only in expectation, and did not come into operation. And this is not the only wonder, that God hath removed so great a danger, but that He hath also greatly blessed us, and adorned our city; and by this trial and calamity hath made us more approved! But how, I will state. When those who were sent by the Emperor erected that fearful tribunal for making inquisition into the events which had taken place, and summoned every one to give account of the deeds which they had perpetrated, and various anticipations of death pervaded the minds of all, then the monks who dwelt on the mountain-tops shewed their own true philosophy. For although they had been shut up so many years in their cells, yet at no one's entreaty, by no one's counsel, when they beheld such a cloud overhanging the city, they left their caves and huts, and flocked together in every direction, as if they had been so many angels arriving from heaven. Then might one see the city likened to heaven, while these saints appeared everywhere; by their mere aspect consoling the mourners, and leading them to an utter disregard of the calamity. For who on beholding these would not deride death, would not despise life. And not only was this wonderful, but that when they drew nigh to the magistrates themselves, they spoke to them with boldness on behalf of the accused, and were all ready to shed their blood, and to lay down their heads, so that they might snatch the captured from the terrible events which they expected. They also declared that they would not depart until the judges should spare the population of the city, or send them themselves together with the accused to the Emperor. "He," said they, "who rules over our portion of the world is a godly man, a believer, one who lives in the practice of piety. We therefore shall assuredly reconcile him. We will not give you leave, nor permit you to embrue the sword, or take off a head. But if ye do not desist, we also are quite resolved to die with them. We confess that the crimes committed are very heinous; but the iniquity of those deeds does not surpass the humanity of the Emperor." One of them is also reported to have uttered another saying, full of wisdom, to this effect:[1] "The Statues which have been thrown down are again set up, and have resumed their proper appearance; and the mischief was speedily rectified; but if ye put to death the image of God, how will ye be again able to revoke the deed! or how to reanimate those who are deprived of life, and to restore their souls to their bodies?" Many things too they said to them of the Judgment.

4. Who could but be astonished? Who could but admire the moral wisdom of these men? When the mother of one of the accused, uncovering her head, and exposing her grey hairs, laid hold of the horse of the judge by the bridle, and running beside him through the forum, thus entered with him the place of justice, we were all struck with astonishment, we all admired that exceeding tenderness and magnanimity.[2] Ought we not, then, to have been much more impressed with wonder at the conduct of these men? For if she had even died for her son, it would have been nothing strange, since great is the tyranny of nature, and irresistible is the obligation arising from the maternal pangs! But these men so loved those whom they had not begotten, whom they had not brought up, yea rather, whom they had never seen, whom they had not heard of, whom they had never met, whom they knew only from their calamity, that if they had possessed a thousand lives, they would have chosen to deliver them all up for their safety. Tell me not that they were not slaughtered, that they did not pour forth their blood, but that they used as much boldness with their judges as it was likely that no other men would do, but such as had already renounced their own lives; and that with this sentiment they ran from the mountains to the tribunal. For, indeed, if they had not before prepared themselves against every sort of slaughter, they would not have been able to speak thus freely to the judges, or to have manifested such magnanimity. For they remained all day long sitting before

---

[1] The name of this monk was Macedonius (see Theodoret- *Hist. Relig.* No. xiii. where it is added that he spoke through an interpreter).
[2] See Lib. ad Helleb.

the doors of the place of justice, being prepared to snatch from the hands of the executioners those who were about to be led off to punishment!

5. Where now are those who are clad in threadbare cloaks, and display a long beard, and carry staves in the right hand; the philosophers of the world,[1] who are more abject in disposition than the dogs under the table; and do every thing for the sake of the belly? All these men then forsook the city, they all hasted away, and hid themselves in caves! But they only, who truly by works manifest the love of wisdom, appeared as fearlessly in the forum, as if no evil had overtaken the city. And the inhabitants of the city fled away to the mountains and to the deserts, but the citizens of the desert hastened into the city; demonstrating by deeds what, on the preceding days, I have not desisted from saying, that the very furnace will not be able to harm the man who leads a virtuous life. Such a thing is philosophy of soul, rising superior to all things, and to all prosperous or adverse events; for neither is it enfeebled by the former, nor beaten down and debased by the latter, but abides on the same level through the whole course of things, shewing its own native force and power! Who, indeed, was not convicted of weakness by the difficulty of the present crisis? Those who had held the first offices in our city, who were in places of power, who were surrounded with immense wealth, and who were in high favour with the Emperor, leaving their houses utterly deserted, all consulted their own safety, and all friendship and kindred were found worthless, and those whom they formerly knew, at this season of calamity, they desired not to know, and prayed to be unknown of them! But the monks, poor as they were, having nothing more than a mean garment, who had lived in the coarsest manner, who seemed formerly to be nobodies, men habituated to mountains and forests; as if they had been so many lions, with a great and lofty soul, whilst all were fearing and quaking, stood forth and relieved the danger, and that, not in the course of many days, but in a brief moment of time! And as distinguished warriors without coming into close conflict with their adversaries, but merely by making their appearance in the ranks, and shouting, put the foe to rout, so also these in one day descended, and said their say, and removed the calamity, and returned to their own tabernacles. So great is the moral wisdom that was brought among men by Christ.

6. And why do I speak of the rich, and of those in authority? When those very persons who had been invested with power to judge the criminals; who acted with the highest authority, were entreated by these selfsame monks to grant a sentence of pardon, they said, they had no power over the result; for that it was unsafe and dangerous, not only to insult the Emperor, but even to dismiss those who had insulted him, when taken, without punishment. But these men were too powerful for any one to resist; and besieging them by magnanimity and perseverance, they induced these officers by their importunity to exercise a power which they had not received from the Emperor; and even succeeded in persuading the judges, when men had been manifestly convicted of the guilt, not to declare the sentence of condemnation, but to defer the final result to the decision of the Emperor; and they promised certainly to persuade him to grant a pardon to those who had transgressed against him; and they were about to set out on a journey to him. But the judges, reverencing the moral wisdom of these men, and being struck with their loftiness of spirit, did not permit them to undertake this long journey, but promised that if they should only receive their words in writing, they would themselves depart and successfully importune[2] the Emperor to dismiss all anger (which, indeed, we are now expecting that he will). For when sentence should have been given, they, on being admitted into court, uttered words of the highest wisdom, and besought the Emperor by letters to shew mercy; and they reminded him of the Judgment, and said that they would lay down their own heads, if his mercy was not granted. And the judges took down these words in writing, and departed. This, more than the brightest crown, will adorn our city. And what has here taken place, the Emperor will now hear; yea, the great City will hear, and the whole world will hear, that the monks who dwell at the city of Antioch, are men who have displayed an apostolic boldness; and now when their letters are read at court, all men will admire their magnanimity; all men will call our city blessed; and we shall shake off our evil reputation; and it will be known every where, that what has happened was not the work of the inhabitants of the city, but of strangers and corrupt-minded men; and that this testimony of the monks will be a sufficient evidence of the character of the city.

---

[1] τῶν ἔξωθεν. "Of those without;" a common phrase with St. Chrysostom to denote those without the pale of the Church.

[2] δυσωπήσειν: same word as is rendered above "induced by importunity." Literally, "to put out of countenance;" to make another ashamed not to grant a request.

7. Therefore, beloved, let us not be distressed, but let us entertain favourable hopes; for if their boldness toward men has been able to prevent such a danger, then what will not their boldness toward God effect? These things also let us tell the Greeks, when they dare to dispute with us respecting their philosophers! From hence it is manifest that their stories of former days are false, but that the things of old reported among us are true; that is, the things concerning John, and Paul, and Peter, and all the rest. For inasmuch as these monks have succeeded to the piety of those men, they have consequently exhibited their boldness. Inasmuch as they were brought up in the same laws, they have consequently imitated their virtues. So that we stand in no need of writings for the purpose of shewing the apostolical virtues, whilst the very facts cry aloud, and the masters are shewn forth by the scholars. We have no need of disputation to display the trifling of the Greeks, and the little-mindedness of their philosophers, whilst their deeds now loudly proclaim, as they did aforetime, that all with them is a fable, a stage-play, a piece of acting.

8. And the same magnanimity was displayed by the priests too, as well as the monks, and they shared among them the charge of our safety. One[1] of them, indeed, proceeded to court, esteeming all things as secondary to the love of you; and being himself ready, if he could not persuade the Emperor, to lay down his own life. And these, who remained here, have displayed the same virtues as the monks themselves; and holding fast the judges with their own hands, they would not let them enter into the court, before they gave a promise respecting the result of the trial. And when they saw them making signs of refusal, they again exerted themselves with much boldness; and as soon as they saw that they did consent, embracing their feet and knees, and kissing their hands, they gave an exceeding proof of either virtue, of liberty and meekness. For that theirs was not the boldness of presumption, they plainly signified by their kissing the knees, and embracing the feet of the judges. Again, in proof that this was not flattery, nor a kind of fawning servility, nor the fruit of a slavish spirit, their former acts attested their boldness. And these are not the only good results we have reaped from the trial, but also an abundance of sobriety and meekness; and our city has become all at once a monastery.[2] Not thus would any one have adorned it, had he erected golden statues in the forum, as it has now been adorned and distinguished, in producing those beautiful images of virtue, and displaying its true riches!

9. But it may be that the things which the Emperor hath decreed are painful. No! not even these are really burdensome, but have brought much advantage with them. For what is there, I ask, which is oppressive in any of them? that the Emperor hath shut up the Orchestra, that he hath forbidden the Hippodrome, that he hath closed and stopped up these fountains of iniquity. May they never again be opened! From thence did the roots of wickedness shoot forth to the injury of the city![3] From thence sprung those who blast its character; men who sell their voices[4] to the dancers, and who for the sake of three obols prostitute their salvation to them, turning all things upside down! Art thou distressed, O beloved! for these things? Truly it were fitting that for these thou shouldest be glad, and rejoice, and express thy thanks to the Emperor, since his castigation hath proved a correction, his punishment a discipline, his wrath a means of instruction! But that the Baths are shut up? Neither is this an intolerable hardship, that those who lead a soft, effeminate, and dissolute life, should be brought back, though unwillingly, to the love of true wisdom.

10. But is it complained of, that the Emperor hath taken away the dignity of the city, and hath no more permitted it to be called a metropolis?[5] But what was he to do? Could he praise what had been done, and acknowledge it as a favour? Then who would not have blamed him, for not shewing even the outward form of indignation? Seest thou not that fathers do many things of a similar nature towards their children? They turn away from them, and forbid them the table. This also hath the Emperor done by imposing such punishments as have nothing in them hurtful, but carry with them much correction. Think what we expected, and what has taken place, and then we shall especially discern the favour of God! Dost thou grieve that the dignity of the city is taken away? Learn what the dignity of a city is; and then thou wilt know clearly, that if the inhabitants do not betray it, no one else will be able to take away the dignity of a city! Not the fact that it is a metropolis; nor that it contains large and beautiful buildings;[6] nor that

---

[1] The bishop, spoken of in the opening of Hom. III. and in Hom. XXI.
[2] The state of monasteries at that time may be gathered from Theodoret's *Historia Religiosa*; the Collations of Cassian; the ascetic works, and parts of the correspondence of St. Basil; the *Historia Lausiaca* of Palladius, and many parts of St. Macarius.
[3] Such was the case, too, with the tumults at Alexandria. See Libanius, *Or. de Sed.* [4] *i. e.*, their applause.
[5] It appears that the metropolitan dignity of Antioch was transferred to Laodicea.
[6] For such topics of praise, see the Antiochicus of Libanius, who however also extols the virtue of the citizens.

it has many columns, and spacious porticoes and walks, nor that it is named in proclamations before other cities, but the virtue and piety of its inhabitants; this is a city's dignity, and ornament, and defence; since if these things are not found in it, it is the most insignificant in the world, though it may enjoy unlimited honour from Emperors! Dost thou wish to learn the dignity of thy city? Dost thou wish to know its ancestry? I will tell it exactly; not only that thou mayest know, but that thou mayest also emulate. What then is after all the dignity of this city of ours? "It came to pass, that the disciples were first called Christians at Antioch."[1] This dignity, none of the cities throughout the world possesses, not even the city of Romulus herself! For this it can look the whole world in the face; on account of that love toward Christ, that boldness and virtue.[2] Dost thou wish farther to hear of a different dignity and commendation belonging to this city? A grievous famine was once approaching, and the inhabitants of Antioch determined, as far as each person had the means, to send relief to the Saints dwelling at Jerusalem.[3] Behold a second dignity, charity in a time of famine! The season did not make them niggardly, nor the expectation of the calamity backward in helping; but when all are apt to be scraping up what is not their own, then they distributed their own, not merely to those who were near, but also to those who were living afar off! Seest thou here the faith towards God, and the love towards their neighbour? Wouldest thou learn another dignity of this city? Certain men came down from Judæa to Antioch, defiling[4] the doctrine preached, and introducing Jewish observances.[5] The men of Antioch did not bear this novelty in silence. They did not hold their peace, but having come together, and made an assembly, they sent Paul and Barnabas to Jerusalem, and caused the Apostles to provide that pure doctrines, cleared from all Jewish imperfection, might be distributed throughout all parts of the world! This is the dignity of the city! this is its precedence! this makes it a metropolis, not in the earth, but in heaven; forasmuch as that all other honours are corruptible, and fleeting, and perish with the present life, and often come to their end before the close of it, as they have done in the present instance! To me, a city that hath not pious citizens is meaner than any village, and more ignoble than any cave.

11. And why do I speak of a city? For that thou mayest exactly understand that virtue alone is the ornament of the inhabitants, I will not speak to thee of a city, but I will endeavour to demonstrate this by bringing forward what is more venerable than any city —the Temple of God which was in Jerusalem. For this was the Temple in which were sacrifices and prayers and services; where was the Holy of Holies, and the Cherubim, the Covenant,[6] and the golden pot;[7] the great symbols of God's providence towards that people; where oracles from heaven were constantly being received, where prophets became inspired, where the fashioning was not the work of human art, but proceeded from the wisdom of God, where the walls were on every side resplendent with much gold, and where, in surpassing excellence, costliness of material and perfection of art met together, and demonstrated that there was no other temple like this upon earth! Yea rather, not only the perfection of art, but also the wisdom of God assisted in that building. For Solomon had learned all, not intuitively and from himself, but from God;[8] and having received the design of it from the heavens, he then marked it out and erected it. Nevertheless, this Temple, thus beautiful and marvellous and sacred, when those who used it were corrupted, was so dishonoured, despised, and profaned, that even before the captivity it was called "a den of robbers, a cave of hyænas;"[9] and afterwards it was delivered over to hands that were barbarous, polluted, and profane!

12. Wouldest thou learn the same truth respecting cities? What could be more illustrious than the cities of Sodom? For the houses and the buildings were splendid, and so were their walls; and the country was fat and fertile, and "like the Paradise of God."[10] But the tent of Abraham was mean and small, and had no fortification. Yet when a foreign war took place, the strangers broke down and took the walled cities, and departed, carrying away their inhabitants captives. Abraham, however, the citizen of the desert, they could not resist when he attacked them! And so it was likely to be. For he had true piety: a power much greater than numbers and the defence of walls. If thou art a Christian, no earthly city is thine. Of our City "the Builder and Maker is God."[11] Though we

---

[1] Acts xi. 26.
[2] These expressions imply that the name Christian was fastened on the disciples of Jesus by way of derision and reproach.
[3] Acts xi. 28, 29.
[4] Making turbid, *i. e.*, by additions, ἐπιθολοῦντες.
[5] See Acts. xv. 1.
[6] *i. e.*, the Tables, Ex. xxxiv. 28.
[7] That contained the manna. Ex. xvi. 33; Heb. ix. 4.
[8] 1 Kings iv. 29; 2 Chron. iii. 3.
[9] Jer. vii. 11.
[10] Gen. xiii. 10.
[11] Heb. xi. 10.

may gain possession of the whole world, we are withal but strangers and sojourners in it all! We are enrolled in heaven: our citizenship is there! Let us not, after the manner of little children, despise things that are great, and admire those which are little! Not our city's greatness, but virtue of soul is our ornament and defence. If you suppose dignity to belong to a city, think how many persons must partake in this dignity, who are whoremongers, effeminate, depraved and full of ten thousand evil things, and at last despise such honour! But that City above is not of this kind; for it is impossible that he can be a partaker of it, who has not exhibited every virtue.

13. Let us not therefore be senseless; but then let us grieve when any one deprives us of our dignity of soul, when we commit sin, when we have offended the common Lord of all; since as regards the things that have now befallen us, so far are they from injuring the city, that if we are watchful, they will greatly benefit us. For even already our city seems to be like a decorous, noble, sober-minded matron. Fear hath made her gentler and more dignified, and hath delivered her from those miscreants who were concerned in the late audacious deeds. Let us therefore not give way to womanish lamentations. For I have heard many about the forum saying, "Alas! for thee, Antioch! What hath befallen thee! How art thou dishonoured!" Truly when I heard, I smiled at the puerile mind which could give vent to these words! Such words were not becoming now; but when thou seest men dancing, drunken, singing, blaspheming, swearing, perjuring themselves, and lying, then apply such a saying as this: "Alas! for thee, O city, what hath befallen thee!" But if thou seest the forum containing a few meek, modest, and temperate persons, then pronounce the city, "Blessed!" For the fewness will never be able to injure it in any respect, if there be virtue withal; as on the other hand, numbers will never profit it at all, whilst iniquity is there. "If," saith the prophet, "the number of the sons of Israel be as the sand of the sea, the remnant shall be saved;"[1] that is to say, "Multitude will never prevail with Me." So also Christ spoke. He called cities wretched; not because of their littleness, nor because they were not of metropolitan rank.[2] And Jerusalem itself again, He calls wretched for the very same reason, speaking thus; "O Jerusalem, Jerusalem, thou that killest the prophets, and stonest them which are sent unto thee!"[3] For what advantage, I ask, does a multitude bring, if their system of living be vicious? Nay, on the contrary, even injury results from it. What else, indeed, hath wrought the evils which have lately sprung up? Was it not the sloth, the recklessness, and the depravity of the inhabitants? Did the dignity of the city, did the magnificence of its architecture, or the circumstance that it was a metropolis, do it any service? If with the king who is on earth, nothing could protect it when it had done thus amiss, but all these privileges are taken away; much more with the Lord of angels will its dignity fail to protect it? For at that Day, it will nought avail us, that we have dwelt in a metropolis, that has many spacious porticoes, and other dignities of this kind! And why do I say, at That Day? For as regards the present life, what can it benefit thee that this thy city is a metropolis? Pray, has any one restored a distressed family by means of this? or received any revenue from this dignity? or dispelled sadness? or got rid of any bodily infirmity? or put away a vice of the soul? Beloved! let us not trifle, nor regard the opinions of the multitude, but understand what is indeed the dignity of a city; what it is that makes a city truly a metropolis?

14. I say all this, though I expect that the city will again regain even this outward distinction, and appear in its own proper place of precedence. For the Emperor is both philanthropic and godly. But I am desirous that if it should be restored, ye may not think too much of this; nor be boastful of it; nor place the honour of our city to that account. When you wish to pronounce an encomium on the city, tell me not of the suburb of Daphne,[4] nor of the height and multitude of its cypresses, nor of its fountains of waters, nor of the great population who inhabit the city, nor of the great freedom with which its market-place is frequented even to midnight, nor of the abundance of its wares! All these are things of the outward sense, and remain only as long as the present life. But if you are able to mention virtue, meekness, almsgiving, nocturnal vigils, prayers, sobriety, true wisdom of soul; commend the city for these things! To those who inhabit the desert, the presence of these things makes it

---

[1] Isa. x. 22; Rom. ix. 27.
[2] It is possible that a clause may have been omitted here. If not, the next sentence refers back beyond this.
[3] Matt. xxiii. 37.
[4] See Hom. I. contr. Jud. (6). The same is to be said of the Synagogue. For though there be no idol there, yet devils inhabit the place. Which I say not only of the Synagogue that is here, but also of that in Daphne, where is that more abominable pit which they call Matrona's, &c. See also Macc. iv. 33, and Libanius Antioch. Reiske, t. i. pp. 302, 352. For some account of Daphne, see Introduction to the Homily on St. Babylas in this volume.

more illustrious than any city; and again the vilest of all places,[1] should these things not be found with its citizens. Let us make this estimate not in the case of cities only, but also of men. And if you see a big man, who has been brought into good condition, tall, and surpassing others in length of limb, do not admire him, until you have ascertained what the man's soul is. Not from the outward comeliness, but from the beauty that appertains to the soul, should we pronounce any persons blessed! David was little, and short of stature; nevertheless, one so short and little, and bare of all arms, brought down at one blow so large an army, and that tower of flesh; and this without hurling spear, or letting fly arrow, or unsheathing sword, but doing all with a small pebble! For this reason a certain one exhorts, saying, "Commend not a man for his beauty, neither abhor a man for his outward appearance. The bee is little among such as fly, but her fruit is the chief of sweet things."[2]

15. Thus also let us speak both of a city, and of men, and utter such wisdom one to another, and be continually thankful to God, as well for present as for past mercies; and call upon Him in common with all our might, that those who now dwell in prison[3] may be discharged, and that those who are about to be sent into exile may return back again. They too are our members. With us they have buffetted the waves, with us they have withstood the storm! Let us, then, beseech the merciful God, that with us they may enjoy the calm! Let no one say, "What farther concerns me? I am freed from danger; such an one may perish; such another may be destroyed!" Let us not provoke God by this indifference; but lament, as if we ourselves were in the same peril. So let us supplicate God with intense earnestness, fulfilling that saying of Paul, "Remember them that are in bonds, as bound with them; and them which suffer adversity, as being yourselves also in the body.[4] Weeping also with them that weep; condescending to men of low estate."[5] This will also be of the greatest advantage to ourselves; for nothing useth so much to delight God, as that we should be very ready to mourn for our own members. Him therefore let us supplicate in common, both for things present, and for things to come; in order that He may deliver us from punishment hereafter. For the things present, whatever they are, are endurable, and have an end; but the torments there are immortal, and interminable! And while we are consoled, let us also ourselves endeavour to fall no more into such sins, knowing that hereafter[6] we shall enjoy no pardon! Let us, then, all in common prostrate ourselves before God; and both while we are here, and when we are at home, let us say, "Thou, O Lord, art righteous in all things which Thou hast done towards us; for Thou hast brought upon us by a just judgment whatever Thou hast brought."[7] If "our sins rise up against us, undertake for us, for thy Name's sake;"[8] and do not permit us any more to experience such grievous troubles. "Lead us not into temptation, but deliver us from evil, for Thine is the kingdom, the Power, and the Glory, for ever and ever. Amen.

---

[1] Ben. καὶ πάλιν πάντων εὐτελεστέραν. Sav. πόλιν, "and a city the vilest." The former seems favoured by ἐκείνης following, and would be the more forcible, supposing the audience duly affected. The imperfect construction of the original is kept.
[2] Ecclus. xi. 2, 3.
[3] The whole Senate of Antioch were imprisoned till the Emperor's pleasure should be known. See Libanius' Or. to Hellebichus, whom he praises for providing them tolerable lodging.
[4] Heb. xiii. 3.
[5] Rom. xii. 15, 16.
[6] i. e., if not thus amended.
[7] Neh. ix. 33.
[8] Jer. xiv. 7.

HOMILY XVIII.

The former subject of the Sedition continued; also of fasting; and upon the Apostolic saying, "Rejoice in the Lord always."[1]

1. I HAVE observed many persons rejoicing, and saying one to another, "We have conquered; we have prevailed; the half of the fast is spent." But I exhort such persons not to rejoice on this account, that the half of the fast is gone, but to consider whether the half of their sins be gone; and if so, then to exult. For this is a fit subject of gratification. This is what is to be sought after, and for which all things are done, that we may correct our defects; and that we may not quit the fast the same persons as we entered upon it, but in a cleansed state; and

[1] Phil. iv. 4.

that having laid aside all that belongs to evil habits, we may thus keep the sacred feast, since if the case be otherwise, we shall be so far from obtaining any advantage, that the completion of the fast will be the greatest injury to us. Let us, therefore, not rejoice that we have gone through the length of the fast, for this is nothing great; but let us rejoice, if we have got through it with fresh attainments, so that when this is over, the fruit of it may shine forth. For the gain of winter is more especially manifested after the season is gone by. Then, the flourishing corn, and the trees teeming with leaves and fruit, proclaim, by their appearance, the benefit that has accrued to them from the winter! Let the same thing also take place with us. For during the winter, we have enjoyed divers and frequent showers, having been during the fast partakers of a continued course of instruction, and have received spiritual seeds, and cut away the thorns of luxury.

2. Wherefore let us persevere, retaining with all diligence what we have heard; that when the fast is over, the fruit of the fast may abound, and that by the good things we gathered from the fast, we may remember the fast itself.[1] If thus we fashion ourselves, we shall, when the fast returns, welcome it again with pleasure. For I see many who are so feeble-minded, that at the present season they are anxious about the following Lent; and I have heard many saying, that after their liberation from the fast, they are insensible to any pleasure from this remission, on account of their anxiety about the coming year. What can be more feeble-minded than this? I ask; and what is the cause of this? It is, that when the fast is arrived, we do not take pains that the concerns of the soul may be well ordered, but we limit the fast solely to an abstinence from food. Since, were we to reap the full benefit of it in a reformation of conduct, we should wish the fast to come round every day, receiving in very deed an experience of its good effects; and we should never cast away the desire of it, or be dejected and anxious whilst expecting it.

3. For there is nothing whatever that will be able to afflict one who is well ordered in mind, and careful about his own soul; but he will enjoy a pure and continued pleasure. And that this is true ye have to-day heard from Paul, who exhorts us, saying, "Rejoice in the Lord always, and again I say, rejoice."[2] I know indeed that to many this saying seems impossible. "For how is it possible," says some one, "that he who is but a man, can continually rejoice? To rejoice is no hard matter, but to rejoice continually, this seems to me to be impossible." For many are the causes of sadness, which surround us on all sides. A man has lost either a son, or a wife, or a beloved friend, more necessary to him than all kindred; or he has to sustain the loss of wealth; or he has fallen into sickness; or he has to bear some other change of fortune; or to grieve for contemptuous treatment which he did not deserve; or famine, or pestilence, or some intolerable exaction, or circumstances in his family trouble him;—nay, there is no saying how many circumstances of a public or private nature are accustomed to occasion us grief. How then, he may say, is it possible to "rejoice always?" Yea, O man! it is possible; and if it were not so, Paul would not have given the exhortation; nor would a man endowed with spiritual wisdom have offered such counsel; and for this reason I have constantly said to you, and will not cease to say, that what ye could no where have learnt from any other, that wisdom ye may here meditate. For mankind are universally desirous of pleasure,[3] and of rejoicing; and for this, they do all, say all, and undertake all things. Therefore it is, that the merchant goes on a voyage, in order that he may amass wealth; and he amasses wealth, to the end that he may rejoice over what he has treasured up. The soldier also for this reason exercises his warfare, and the husbandman his husbandry; for this each man plies his art. Those also who love dominion, love it for this end, that they may obtain glory; and they desire to obtain glory, that they may rejoice; and any one may perceive that each of our undertakings is directed to this point, and that every man looking to this makes haste to go towards it through a variety of means.

4. For as I said, all love gladness, but all are not able to attain it, since they know not the way which leads to it; but many suppose that the source of it is in being rich. But if this were its source, no one possessed of wealth would ever be sad. But in fact many of the rich think life not worth living, and would infinitely prefer death when they experience any hardship; and of all men these are the most liable to excessive sadness. For you should not look to their tables, or their flatterers, and parasites, but to the trou-

---

[1] See end of Hom. VI.   [2] Phil. iv. 4.

[3] See Arist. Eth. i, ch. 5, and Plat. Phileb., where the general aim of human action is discussed. Speaking popularly, St. Chrysostom does not enquire by what name it is most correct to call the real object of our desires. He is satisfied with shewing that the highest pleasure, satisfaction, joy, or whatever it may be called, is found in God. And this is a better beginning, for practical purposes, than a philosophical definition. But see Hooker, b. i. c. vii. and Butler, ser. xi. xii. xiii.

ble that comes of such things, the insults, the calumnies, the dangers, and the distresses, and what is far worse, that they meet these reverses unpractised, and know not how to take them philosophically, or to bear with fortitude what befalls them; whence it happens that calamities do not appear to them such as they are in their own nature, but even things which are really light come to seem intolerable; whereas, with regard to the poor, the contrary takes place; things that are irremediable seem easy to be borne, since they are familiar with many such. For it is not so much the nature of the events as the disposition of the sufferers, that makes the evils which come upon us seem great or small. And that I may not go a long way off for examples of both these facts, I will speak to you of what has lately befallen ourselves. Behold then how all the poor escaped, and the populace are delivered from the danger, and enjoy an entire freedom! but those who manage the affairs of the city, the men who keep their studs of horses, and preside over the public games, and such as have borne other public charges,[1] they are now the inmates of the prison, and fear the worst; and they alone pay the penalty of the deeds that have been perpetrated by all, and are in a state of constant terror; and they are now the most wretched of men, not because of the greatness of the danger, but on account of the luxury in which hitherto they have lived! Many, at least when exhorted by us, and counselled to sustain these adverse affairs with fortitude, said this, "We never practised any thing of the kind, and do not know how to exercise such philosophy; this is why we need so much consolation."

5. Others again suppose, that to enjoy good health is the source of pleasure. But it is not so. For many of those who enjoy good health have a thousand times wished themselves dead, not being able to bear the insults inflicted on them. Others again affirm, that to enjoy glory, and to have attained to power, and to administer the highest offices, and to be flattered by multitudes, is productive of continual gladness. But neither is this the case. And why do I speak of other offices of power? For although we were to mount up in thought to royalty itself, and to him who lives in that station, we should find it encompassed with a diversity of troubles, and having so many necessary causes the more of sadness, in proportion as it is surrounded with a greater weight of affairs. And what need is there to speak of wars, and battles, and the insurrections of barbarians? Oftentimes he has reason to fear those by whom he is surrounded at home. For many of those monarchs who have escaped from the hands of their enemies, have not escaped the conspiracies of their own body-guards. And kings have of necessity as many causes of sadness as there are waves on the ocean. But if monarchy is unable to render life devoid of grief, then what else can possibly achieve this? Nothing, indeed, of this life; but this saying of Paul alone, brief and simple as it is, will of itself open to us this treasure.

6. For many words are not needed, nor a long round of argument, but if we only consider his expression, we shall find the way that leads to it. He does not simply say, "Rejoice always;" but he adds the cause of the continual pleasure, saying, "Rejoice in the Lord always." He who rejoices "in the Lord," can not be deprived of the pleasure by any thing that may happen. For all other things in which we rejoice are mutable and changeable, and subject to variation. And not only does this grievous circumstance attend them, but moreover while they remain they do not afford us a pleasure sufficient to repel and veil the sadness that comes upon us from other quarters. But the fear of God contains both these requisites. It is steadfast and immoveable, and sheds so much gladness that we can admit no sense of other evils. For the man who fears God as he ought, and trusts in Him, gathers from the very root of pleasure, and has possession of the whole fountain of cheerfulness. And as a spark falling upon a wide ocean quickly disappears, so whatever events happen to the man who fears God, these, falling as it were upon an immense ocean of joy, are quenched and destroyed! This indeed is most to be wondered at, that whilst things which minister sadness are present, the man should remain joyful. For if there was nothing to produce grief, it would be no great matter to him that he was able continually to rejoice. But that at a time when he is urged to sadness by the pressure of many things, he is superior to all these, and is blithe in the midst of sorrow, this is truly a matter for astonishment! And as no one would have wondered that the three Children were not burnt, if they had remained far off from the furnace of Babylon! (for the circumstance that astonished all was, that having been so long in such close contact with the fire, they left it more free from hurt than those who had not been in contact with it); so also we are able to say of the saints, that if no temptation had fastened itself upon

---

[1] Proof of wealth.

them, we should not have wondered at their continual rejoicing. But the point worthy of admiration, and that which surpasses human nature, is this, that being encircled on all sides with innumerable waves, their condition is easier than that of those who enjoy an entire calm!

7. From what has been said, it is evident that amongst those who are outside the church it is impossible to find any situation in life, encircled with continual gladness from the things without. But that the believer cannot possibly be deprived of the enjoyment of a continued pleasure is what I will now proceed to prove, to the end that ye may not only learn, but also emulate this painless condition of life. For suppose a man having nothing for which to condemn himself, but cherishing a good conscience, and yearning after the future state, and the fulfilment of those good hopes; what, I ask, will be able to throw such a person into sadness? Does not death seem the most insupportable of all things? Yet the expectation of this is so far from grieving him, that it makes him the more joyful; for he knows that the arrival of death is a release from labour, and a speeding toward the crowns and rewards laid up for those who have contended in the race of piety and virtue. But is it the untimely end of his children? Nay, he will also bear this nobly, and will take up the words of Job, "The Lord gave, the Lord hath taken away; as it seemed good unto the Lord, so is it come to pass. Blessed be the name of the Lord for ever."[1] But if death and loss of children cannot grieve, much less can the loss of money, or dishonour, or reproaches, or false accusations, at any time affect a soul so great and noble; no, nor anguish of body, since the Apostles were scourged, yet they were not made sad. This, indeed, was a great thing; but what is much more, instead of being made sad, they considered their very scourgings, as a ground of additional pleasure. "And they departed from the presence of the council, rejoicing that they were counted worthy to suffer shame for the name of Christ."[2] Did any person insult and revile such a one? Well, he was taught by Christ to rejoice in these revilings. "Rejoice,"[3] saith He, "and be exceeding glad, when they shall say all manner of evil against you falsely for my sake; for great is your reward in heaven."[4] But suppose a man hath fallen into disease? Well, he hath heard another admonishing, and saying, "In disease and poverty trust thou in Him; for as gold is tried in the fire, so are acceptable men in the furnace of humiliation."[5] Since, therefore, neither death, nor loss of money, nor bodily disease, nor dishonour, nor reproach, nor any other thing of that nature, will be able to grieve him, but makes him even the more joyful, what foundation for sadness will he have at any time?

8. "What then," says some one, "used not the Saint to be in sadness? Do you not hear Paul saying, "I have great heaviness, and continual sorrow in my heart?"[6] This, indeed, is the thing to wonder at, that sorrow brought a gain, and a pleasure that resulted from the gain; for as the scourge did not procure them anguish, but gladness; so also again the sorrow procured them those great crowns. And this is the paradox; that not only the sadness of the world, but also its joy, contains extreme loss; but in the case of spiritual things, it is exactly the reverse; and not the joy only, but the sadness too contains a rich treasure of good things! But how, I proceed to explain. In the world, a person often rejoices, on beholding an enemy in trouble; and by this joy he draws on himself a great punishment. Again, another person mourns, on seeing a brother fall; and because of this sadness he will procure for himself much favour with God. Seest thou how godly sorrow is better and more profitable than the joy of the world? Thus also Paul sorrowed for sinners, and for those who disbelieved in God; and this sorrow was the means of laying up a great reward for him. But that I may make what I say more clear, and that ye may know that although what I assert is very strange, it is nevertheless true, viz. that grief is often capable of refreshing distressed souls, and of rendering a burdened conscience light: consider how often women, when they have lost their most beloved children, break their hearts, and perish, if they are forbidden to mourn, and to shed tears. But if they do all which those who are sad, are wont to do, they are relieved, and receive consolation. And what wonder that this should be the case with women, when you may even see a prophet affected in a similar manner? Therefore he was continually saying, "Suffer me—I will weep bitterly—labour not to comfort me, because of the spoiling of the daughter of my people."[7] So that, oftentimes, sadness is the bearer of consolation; and if it is so with regard to this world, much more with regard to spiritual things.

---

[1] Job i. 21.
[2] Acts v. 41.
[3] Sav. *Blessed are ye, &c.*, as in text.
[4] Matt. v. 11, 12.
[5] Ecclus. ii. 4, 5.   [6] Rom. ix. 2.   [7] Isa. xxii. 4.

Therefore he says, "Godly sorrow worketh repentance unto salvation, not to be repented of."[1] This indeed seems to be obscure; but what he says is to this effect: "If thou grievest over wealth, thou art nothing profited. If for sickness, thou hast gained nothing, but hast increased thy affliction."

9. And I have heard many, after such experience, blame themselves, and say, What advantage is it that I have grieved? I have not recovered my money, and I have injured myself. But if thou hast grieved on account of sin, thou hast blotted it out, and hast reaped the greatest pleasure. If thou hast grieved for thy brethren who have fallen, thou hast both encouraged and comforted thyself, and hast also restored them; and even if thou wert not to profit them, thou hast an abundant recompense. And that thou mayest learn that this grieving for those who have fallen, though we should not at all benefit them, still brings us a large reward, hear what Ezekiel says; or rather, what God Himself speaks through him. For when He had sent certain messengers to overturn the city, and to consume all the dwellings with sword and fire, along with their inhabitants, He thus charges one of them: "Set a mark upon the forehead of the men that groan, and are in anguish." And after charging the others, and saying, "Begin ye from mine holy ones," He goes on to add, "But upon whomsoever the sign is, touch them not."[2] For what reason, tell me? Because although they avail nothing, they nevertheless lament the things which are done, and deplore them. And again, He accuses others, saying, That in their luxury, and gluttony, and enjoyment of great security, when they beheld the Jews carried away into captivity, they did not grieve, nor partake of their sadness. And hear what He says, reproaching them: "They suffered nothing in the affliction of Joseph:"[3] meaning by Joseph the whole people. And again: "The inhabitants of Ænan went not forth to bewail the house next unto them."[4] For although they are justly punished, God willeth that we should condole with them, and not rejoice or insult. "For if I that punish," saith He, "do not this rejoicingly; nor take pleasure in their punishment; for "I do not at all will the death of the sinner;"[5] it is right that thou shouldest imitate thy Lord; and shouldest mourn for this very thing, that the sinner hath provided matter and occasion for a just punishment." So that if any one entertains a godly sorrow, he will thence reap a great advantage.

10. Since therefore those who are scourged are more blessed than the scourgers, and those in tribulation among us than those who are free from it outside the Christian pale; and those who are sad are more blessed than those in pleasure; what further source of tribulation shall we have? On this account we should call no man happy, save him only who lives according to God. These only the Scripture terms blessed. For "blessed," it is said, "is the man who hath not walked in the counsel of the ungodly. Blessed is he whom Thou chastenest, and teachest him out of Thy law. Blessed are the undefiled in the way. Blessed are all they who trust in Him. Blessed is the people whose God is the Lord. Blessed is he whom his soul condemneth not. Blessed is the man that feareth the Lord."[6] And again, Christ speaks thus: "Blessed are they that mourn; blessed are the humble; blessed are the meek; blessed are the peacemakers; blessed are they who are persecuted for righteousness' sake."[7] Seest thou how the divine laws everywhere pronounce blessed none of the rich, or of the well-born, or of the possessors of glory, but the man who has gotten hold of virtue. For what is required of us is, that in every thing we do or suffer, the fear of God should be the foundation; and if you implant this as the root, not merely will ease, and honour, and glory, and attention, produce fruits that shall be pleasurable to thee; but hostilities also, and calumnies, and contempt, and disgrace, and torments, and all things without exception. And just as the roots of trees are bitter in themselves, and yet produce our sweetest fruits, so, verily, godly sorrow will bring us an abundant pleasure. They know, who have often prayed with anguish, and shed tears, what gladness they have reaped; how they purged the conscience; how they rose up with favourable hopes! For as I am always saying, it is not the nature of the things, but our disposition, which is wont to make us sad or joyful. If then we can render the latter such as it ought to be, we shall have a pledge for all gladness. And just as, with the body, it is not so much the nature of the air, or the things it meets from without, as its own internal condition, that either injures or assists it, so also it is in the case of the soul; and much more so; for in the one case, there is the necessity of nature; in the other, the whole is seated in the power of choice. Therefore Paul, when he had endured innumerable evils—shipwrecks, wars, persecutions, plots, the assaults of robbers, and things too numerous to be

---

[1] 2 Cor. vii. 10. [2] Ezek. ix. 4. [3] Amos vi. 6.
[4] Mich. i. 4. [5] Ezek. xviii. 32.
[6] Ps. i. 1, xciv. 12, cxix. 1, ii. 13, xxxiii. 12; Ecclus. xiv. 2; Ps. cxii. 1.
[7] Matt. v. 3–10.

recounted, dying also daily deaths—was so far from grieving or being discontented, that he gloried, and rejoiced, and said, "I now rejoice in my sufferings, and fill up that which is behind of the afflictions of Christ in my flesh."[1] And again: "And not only so, but we glory in tribulations."[2] Now, glorying signifies an extension of pleasure.

11. If then thou desirest joy, seek not after riches, nor bodily health, nor glory, nor power, nor luxury, nor sumptuous tables, nor vestures of silk, nor costly lands, nor houses splendid and conspicuous, nor any thing else of that kind; but pursue that spiritual wisdom which is according to God, and take hold of virtue; and then nought of the things which are present, or which are expected, will be able to sadden thee. Why do I say to sadden? Verily, the things that make others sad, will prove to thee an accession of pleasure. For scourges, and death, and losses, and slanders, and the being evil entreated, and all such things, when they are brought upon us for God's sake, and spring from this root, will bring into our souls much pleasure. For no one will be able to make us miserable, if we do not make ourselves such; nor, on the other hand, blessed, if we do not make ourselves such, following up the grace of God.

12. And that ye may learn that he only is blessed, who feareth the Lord, I will now demonstrate this to you, not by what has happened in past times, but by what has befallen ourselves. Our city was in danger of being utterly effaced; and no man among the rich, or eminent, or illustrious, dared to appear in public, but all fled, and hurried out of the way. But they who feared God, the men who passed their time in monasteries, hastened down with much boldness, and set all free from this terror; and the terrible events that had taken place, and the threats which had been expected to be put into execution, were so far from causing them to fear, or from throwing them into anxiety, that although they were placed far off from the calamity, and had no share in it, they cast themselves willingly into the midst of the fire, and rescued all; and as for death, which seems universally terrible and awful, they awaited it with the utmost readiness, and ran to meet it with more pleasure than others do towards principalities and honours. And why, but because they knew, that this is the greatest principality and honour? And they shewed in very deed that he only is blessed who lays hold of the wisdom which is from above, that he undergoes no change and sustains no adversity, but enjoys a continued tranquillity, and laughs to scorn all things which seem to be sorrowful. At the present time at least, those who were once in power are oppressed by much sadness, inhabiting the prison, and loaded with chains, and daily expecting to be put to death. But these men on the contrary enjoy the purest pleasure; and if it be their lot to suffer anything terrible, this, and the very things which seem formidable to others, are welcome to them, for they know well towards what point they are running, and what lot will await them when they depart hence. But whilst they live with so much exactness, and smile at death, they nevertheless grieve for others, and reap therefrom, in turn, the greatest advantage. Let us then be in earnest to take care of our souls, and nothing which may come unlooked for can make us sad. And on behalf of those who are in prison, let us beseech God that He will deliver them from their present calamity. For it was in God's power at once to release us from this dire evil, and not to suffer even the smallest part of it to remain; but in order that we may not again go back to our former negligence, He hath provided that the torrent of these evils should subside gently and by little and little, holding us fast to the same pious resolutions.

13. And that this is true, and that many would have gone back to their former supineness, if we had been released from the whole difficulty at once, is manifest from this circumstance; that whilst yet the remnants of the calamity are left, whilst the sentence of the Emperor is yet doubtful, and those who conducted the affairs of the city are all in prison,[3] many of our fellow inhabitants, through their inordinate desire of bathing, run to the river, there making endless merriment, behaving wantonly, leaping, dancing, and dragging women after them. What pardon can such be worthy of? What kind of excuse can they offer? Or rather, what kind of punishment and vengeance do they not deserve? The head of the city is in the public prison; our members are in exile; the sentence concerning them is doubtful; and dost thou, I ask, dance, sport, and laugh? "Why, we could not endure," says some one, "to remain without the bath?" O shameless disposition, sordid and perverted! How many months, I ask, how many years, have past? Thou hast not been as yet shut out from the bath for twenty days; and thou art as much distressed and discontented, as if thou hadst continued without washing for a

---

[1] Coloss. i. 24.   [2] Rom. v. 3.   [3] See Libanius ad Helleb.

whole year! Tell me, was this thy state, when thou wert expecting an attack from the military, when thou wert daily anticipating bring put to death, when thou fleddest to the deserts, and wast hurrying to the mountain tops? If any one had then proposed to thee to remain "a year" without the bath, so that thou mightest be rescued from the impending distress, wouldest thou not readily have accepted the proposal, and submitted to it? When, therefore, it were becoming that thou shouldest give thanks to God, Who hath freed thee from all these things without any loss, dost thou again grow wanton and contemptuous; and when the fear has passed away, turn back afresh to a worse state of negligence? Have these dire events really touched thee, and yet art thou so desirous of the baths? Why, if the bath had been permitted, would not the calamity of those who are yet in confinement have been sufficient to persuade those who are not in the same grievous condition to be forgetful of every luxury? Life itself is at stake, and dost thou remember the baths, and desire to be luxurious? Dost thou despise the danger because thou hast now escaped it? Take heed lest thou entangle thyself in the necessity of a greater punishment, and call back in larger measure the wrath which is removed, and experience the very thing which Christ declared concerning the devils. For He says, that "when the unclean spirit is gone out, and afterwards findeth the house void and swept, he taketh seven other spirits more wicked than himself, and entereth into the soul, and the last state of that man is worse than the first."[1] Therefore let us also fear, lest now we are liberated from our former evils, we afterwards by our listlessness draw upon us those which are greater! I know that ye yourselves[2] are free from this folly; but ye should restrain, punish, and sober those who walk disorderly, that ye may always rejoice even as Paul commanded, that both for our own good works, and for our forethought for others, we may enjoy both here and in the life to come an abundant recompense; through the grace and lovingkindness of our Lord Jesus Christ, by Whom, and with Whom, to the Father, with the Holy Ghost, be glory, honour, and adoration, now and ever, and world without end. Amen.

[1] Luke xi, 24, 26.   [2] That is, those present.

HOMILY XIX.

On the Sunday called "Episozomenes,"[1] to those who had come to Antioch from the country—also on the subject of avoiding oaths.

1. YE have revelled during the last few days in the Holy Martyrs! Ye have taken your fill of the spiritual feast! Ye have all exulted with honest exultation! Ye have beheld their ribs laid bare, and their loins lacerated; the blood flowing forth all around; ten thousand forms of torture! Ye have seen human nature exhibiting that which is above nature, and crowns woven with blood! Ye have danced a goodly dance throughout the whole city; this, your noble captain[2] leading you on; but sickness compelled me to remain at home, although against my will. But if I did not take a part in the festival, I partook of the pleasure of it. If I could not have the enjoyment of your public assembly, yet did I share in your gladness. For such is the power of love, that it makes those who are not actually in the enjoyment to rejoice equally with those who are; persuading them to think the good things of their neighbour common to themselves. Therefore even whilst I sat at home, I was rejoicing with you; and now whilst I am not yet entirely freed from my sickness, I have risen up, and run to meet you, that I may see your much desired faces, and take a part in the present festival.

2. For I think the present day to be a very great festival indeed on account of our brethren, who by their presence beautify our city, and adorn the Church; a people foreign to us in language,[3] but in harmony with us concerning the faith, a people passing their

[1] Τῆς Ἐπισωζομένης. The Sunday *before* Ascension Day, which, according to Allatius, was called Episozomene by the Cappadocians; but little seems to be certainly known on the subject. The Homily is placed here on account of the argument continued in it. See Montf. Pref. The philosophers may not have returned, or he may refer to the superiority of the ancients.
[2] Flavian, who had returned before Easter.

[3] It seems that they spoke not the Greek, but the Syriac language.

time in tranquillity, and leading an honest and sober life. For among these men there are no spectacles of iniquity—no horse racings, nor harlots, nor any of that riot which pertains to a city, but every kind of licentiousness is banished, and great sobriety flourishes every where. And the reason is, that their life is a laborious one; and they have, in the culture of the soil, a school of virtue and sobriety, and follow that art which God introduced before all others into our life. For before the sin of Adam, when he enjoyed much freedom, a certain tillage of the ground was enjoined upon him; not indeed a laborious or a troublesome one, but one which afforded him much good discipline, for he was appointed, it is said, "to till the garden, and to keep it." Each of these men you may see at one time employed in yoking the labouring oxen, and guiding the plough, and cutting the deep furrow; and at another acsending the sacred pulpit,[1] and cultivating the souls of those under their authority; at one time cutting away the thorns from the soil with a bill-hook, at another purging out the sins of the soul by the Word. For they are not ashamed of work like the inhabitants of our city, but they are ashamed of idleness, knowing that this has taught every kind of wickedness; and that to those who love it, it has proved a teacher of iniquity from the beginning.

3. These are our philosophers, and theirs the best philosophy, exhibiting their virtue not by their outward appearance, but by their mind. The pagan philosophers are in character no wise better than those who are engaged on the stage, and in the sports of actors; and they have nothing to shew beyond the threadbare cloak, the beard, and the long robe! But these, quite on the contrary, bidding farewell to staff and beard, and the other accoutrements, have their souls adorned with the doctrines of the true philosophy, and not only with the doctrines, but also with the real practice. And were you to question any one of these, who live a rustic life at the spade and plough, as to the dogmas respecting which the pagan philosophers have discoursed an infinite deal, and have expended a multitude of words, without being able to say any thing sound; one of these would give you an accurate reply from his store of wisdom. And not only is this to be wondered at, but that they confirm the credibility of these doctrines by their actions. For of the fact that we have an immortal soul, and that we shall hereafter render an account of what we have done here, and stand before a fearful Tribunal, their minds are at once thoroughly persuaded, and they have also regulated their whole course of life by such hopes as these; and have become superior to all worldly show, instructed as they have been by the sacred Scriptures, that "all is vanity, yea, vanity of vanities,"[2] and they do not greedily long for any of those things which seem to be so splendid.

4. These too know how to philosophize concerning God, even as God hath determined; and if, taking one of them, you were now to bring forward some pagan philosopher;—or rather, now you could not find one![3]—But if you were to take one of these, and then open the books of their ancient philosophers, and go through them, and institute an enquiry by way of parallel as to what these now answer, and the others in their day philosophically advanced; you would see how much wisdom belonged to the former, and how much folly to the latter. For whilst some of those would aver, that the things existing were destitute of a providence, and that the creation had not its origin from God; that virtue was not sufficient for itself, but stood in need of wealth, and nobility, and external splendour, and other things still more ridiculous; and whilst these, on the other hand, would discourse wisely respecting Providence, respecting the future Tribunals of judgment, respecting the creative power of God, bringing forth all things out of nothing, as well as respecting all other points, although at the same time they were entirely destitute of worldly schooling; who could but learn from hence the power of Christ, which hath proved these unlearned and simple persons to be as much wiser than those, who make so much boast of their wisdom, as men of discretion are seen to be in comparison of little children? For what harm can result to them from their simplicity in regard to learning, when their thoughts are full of much wisdom? And what advantage have those philosophers from this learning, when the understanding is devoid of right thoughts? It were just as if one should have a sword that had its hilt of silver, whilst the blade was weaker than the vilest lead. For truly these philosophers have their tongue decked out with words and names, but their understanding is full of mere weakness and good for nothing. Not so with these philosophers, but quite the reverse. Their understanding is full of spiritual wis-

---

[1] τὸ ἱερὸν βῆμα. The whole of the raised part of the Church, entered by none but the clergy, was so called. On the cases in which secular occupations were allowed to the clergy, see Bingham, b. vi. c. iv. sec. 13.

[2] Eccl. i. 2.
[3] St. Chrysostom here satirically alludes to the flight of the philosophers from the city during the panic succeeding the sedition. See Homily XVII.

dom[1] and their mode of life is a transcript of their doctrines. Amongst these there are no luxurious women; there are no ornaments of dress, nor colours, nor paints; but all such corruption of manners is discountenanced. Hence the population under their charge are the more readily trained to sobriety, and the law which Paul gave, when he directed that food and covering should be had, and nothing more be sought after, they most rigidly observe.[2] Amongst them, there are no perfumed unguents to fascinate the senses;[3] but the earth bringing forth herbs, prepares for them a varied fragrance of flowers, above all the skill of perfumers. For this reason, their bodies as well as souls enjoy a sound state of health, inasmuch as they have banished all luxury of diet, and driven off all the evil floods of drunkenness; and they eat just as much as suffices for subsistence. Let us then not despise them because of their outward appearance, but let us admire their mind. For of what advantage is the external habit, when the soul is more wretchedly clad than any beggar! The man ought to be praised and admired, not for dress, nay more, not even for his bodily form, but for his soul. Lay bare the soul of these men, and you will see its beauty, and the wealth it possesses, in their words, in their doctrines, and in the whole system of their manners!

5. Let the Gentiles then be ashamed, let them hide their heads, and slink away on account of their philosophers, and their wisdom, wretched as it is beyond all folly! For the philosophers that have been amongst them in their lifetime have hardly been able to teach their doctrines to a very few, who can easily be numbered; and when any trifling peril overtook them, they lost even these. But the disciples of Christ, the fishermen, the publicans, and the tent-makers, in a few years brought over the whole world to the truth; and when from that time, ten thousand perils have been constantly arising, the preaching of the Gospel was so far from being put down, that it still flourishes and increases; and they taught simple people, tillers of the ground, and occupied with cattle, to be lovers of wisdom. Such are the persons, who beside all the rest having deeply rooted in them that love which is the source of all good things,[4] have hastened to us, undertaking so long a journey, that they might come and embrace their fellow-members.

6. Come then, and in return for these favours, (I speak of their love and kind feeling), let us give them a provision, and so send them home; and let us again raise the question concerning oaths; that from the minds of all we may pluck up by the roots this evil custom. But first, I desire to put you a little in mind to-day of the things we spoke of lately.[5]

When the Jews, having been released from Persia, and set free from that tyranny, were returned back to their own country, "I saw," saith one, "a flying sickle, twenty cubits in length, and ten cubits broad."[6] They heard also the Prophet giving them this instruction, "This is the curse, that goeth forth over the face of the whole land, and entereth into the house of him that sweareth falsely; and it shall rest in the midst thereof, and throw down the timber and all the stones." When we had read this passage, we also enquired then why it was, that it should destroy not the swearer only, but also his house, and we stated this to be the reason; that God will have the punishments of the most grievous sins to remain continually visible; that all may afterwards learn prudence. Inasmuch then as it was necessary that the perjurer when dead should be buried, and committed to the bosom of the earth; in order that his wickedness might not be buried along with him, his house was made a heap, so that all who passed by, beholding it, and learning the reason of the overthrow, might avoid imitating the sin.

7. This also happened at Sodom. For when they burned in their lust one towards another, then too the very earth itself was burned up, being kindled by the fire from above. For He designed, that the vengeance of this sin should permanently remain.

And observe the mercy of God! Those who had sinned, He caused not to continue burning to the present day, but when they had been for once in flames, He buried them; and burning up the face of the ground, He placed it visibly before all who after should desire to look at these things; and now the sight of the land, through all the generations since, hath given an admonition beyond all powers of speech, crying out, as it were, and saying, "Dare not to do the deeds of Sodom, lest ye suffer the lot of Sodom!" For precept commonly makes not so deep an impression upon the mind as a fearful spectacle does, which bears upon it the vestiges of calamity through all time. And persons that have visited these places bear witness, who

---

[1] From the marg. reading, al. "philosophy."
[2] 1 Tim. vi. 8. [3] Comp. *Georg.* ii. 466. [4] Eph. iii. 17.
[5] Bingham asserts, that this Homily and Homily XV. appear to have been preached on the same day, *Antiquities*, b. 14, c. 4, sec. 8, vol. 4. The opening of the Homily disproves this. Bingham's mistake is easily accounted for, by the wording of this passage in the Greek.
[6] Zech. v. 1, 2.

often, when they hear the Scripture discoursing of these things, are not much terrified; but when they have gone and stood upon the site, and see the whole surface of it disfigured, and have witnessed the effects of the fire, with soil no where visible, but every thing dust and ashes, they come away astonished with the sight, and taking with them a strong lesson of chastity. For truly, the very nature of the punishment was a pattern of the nature of the sin! Even as they devised a barren intercourse, not having for its end the procreation of children, so did God bring on them such a punishment, as made the womb of the land ever barren, and destitute of all fruits! For this reason also He threatened to destroy the dwellings of the swearers, in order that by their punishments, they may make others to be more self-controlled.

8. But I am ready to shew to-day, not the destruction of one, two, or three houses in consequence of oaths, but that of a whole city and of a people beloved of God; of a nation that had always enjoyed much of the divine care; and of a race that had escaped many dangers.[1] For Jerusalem herself, the city of God, which had the holy ark, and all that divine service;—where there were once prophets, and the grace of the Spirit, and the ark; and the tables of the covenant, and the golden pot;—where angels were frequent visitors;—this city, I say, when a multitude of wars took place, and many foreign nations made attacks upon it, as if girt by a wall of adamant, ever laughed them all to scorn, and whilst the land was utterly destroyed, sustained no injury! And not only is this to be wondered at, but that frequently in driving out its enemies, it inflicted upon them a heavy blow, and enjoyed so much of the providential care of God, that God Himself said, "I found Israel as a bunch of grapes in the desert; and I beheld your fathers as the earliest fruit on the fig tree."[2] And again, of the city itself: "As olive berries on the extremity of the highest bough, and they shall say, Do them no harm."[3] Nevertheless, the city beloved of God; that had escaped so many perils; that had been favoured with pardon, amidst the multitude of its sins; that alone had been able to avoid captivity, whilst all the rest were carried away, not once or twice, but very often; was ruined solely by an oath. But how, I proceed to state.

9. One of their kings was Zedekiah. This Zedekiah took an oath to Nebuchadnezzar, king of the barbarians, that he would remain in alliance with him. Afterwards he revolted, and went over to the king of Egypt, disdaining the obligation of his oath, and suffered the things of which ye shall hear presently. But first, it is necessary to mention the parable of the prophet, in which he enigmatically represented all these matters: "The word of the Lord," saith he, "came to me, saying, Son of man, put forth a riddle, and speak a parable, and say, Thus saith the Lord God: A great eagle, with great wings, and long extended, full of claws."[4] Here he calls the king of the Babylonians an eagle, and speaks of him as being "great, and long-winged;" and he calls him long-extended and "full of claws," on account of the multitude of his army, and the greatness of his power, and the swiftness of his invasion. For just as the wings and claws of the eagle are his armour, so are horses and soldiers to kings. This eagle, he goes on to say, "hath the leading[5] to enter into Lebanon." What is meant by the "leading?" Counsel—design. And Judæa is called Lebanon, because of its situation near that mountain. Afterwards, intending to speak of the oaths and treaties, "He took," saith he, "of the seed of the land, and planted it in a fruitful field, that it might take root by great waters. He placed it to be looked upon; and it grew, and became a weak vine, and of small stature, and it stretched out its branches towards him, and its roots were under him."[6] Here he calls the city of Jerusalem[7] a vine; but in saying that it stretched out its branches towards the eagle, and that its roots were under him, he refers to the treaties and alliances made with him; and that it cast itself upon him. Next, purposing to declare the iniquity of this, he saith, "And there was another great eagle," (speaking of the Egyptian king), "with great wings, and having many claws;[8] and the vine did bend itself toward him, and its tendril toward him, and shot out its branches, that it might be watered. Therefore, I said, Thus saith the Lord God: Shall it prosper?"[9] That is to say, "after having broken the oath, and the treaties, shall it be able to remain, or to be safe, or to avoid falling?" Presently, for the purpose of shewing that this is not to happen, but that it is certainly to be destroyed on account of the oath, he discourses concerning its punishment, and alleges the cause. "For its tender roots and

---

[1] St. Chrysostom here carries on the argument against the use of oaths, which he had broken off in Homily XIV., after ending the history of Saul and Jonathan.
[2] Hosea ix. 10.　　[3] Isa. lxv. 8, not exactly as LXX.
[4] Ezek. xvii. 2, 3.
[5] τὸ ἥγημα, literally *the generalship*, as that of an army.
[6] Ezek. xvii. 5, 6.
[7] Rather the king, who was of the seed (royal) of the land, but made king by Nebuchadnezzar, 2 Kings xxiv. 17.
[8] In this expression of *many claws*, and in some others, the LXX. differs from the Hebrew.　　[9] Ezek. vii. 7, 8.

its fruits shall become corrupt, and all which springs therefrom shall be withered."[1] And for the purpose of shewing that it will not be destroyed by human strength, but because it hath made God its enemy by means of these oaths, he subjoins, "Not by a mighty arm, nor by much people, to pluck it up by its roots." Such indeed is the parable, but the prophet again explains it, when he says, "Behold, the king of Babylon cometh against Jerusalem."[2] And then, after saying some other things between, he mentions the oaths and the treaties. "For," saith he, "he shall make a covenant with him;"[3] and presently, speaking of the departure from it, he goes on to say, "And he will depart from him, by sending messengers into Egypt, that they might give him horses and much people." And then he proceeds to shew that it is on account of the oath that all this destruction is to take place. "Surely in the place where the king dwelleth that made him king, he who hath despised My curse, and hath transgressed My covenant, in the midst of Babylon he shall die; and not by great power nor by multitude, because he despised the oath in transgressing this My covenant; I will surely recompense upon his own head this My oath which he hath dishonoured, and My covenant which he hath broken; and I will spread My net upon him."[4] Seest thou, that not once, or twice, but repeatedly, it is said that because of the oath he was to suffer all these things. For God is inexorable when oaths are treated contemptuously. Nor merely from the punishment which was brought upon the city by the oath, but also from the delay, and the postponement, may it be seen how much God is concerned for the inviolability of oaths. "For it came to pass," we are told, "in the ninth year of the reign of Zedekiah, on the tenth day of the month, that Nebuchadnezzar the king of Babylon came, and all his host, against Jerusalem, and pitched against it, and built a wall against it round about, and the city was besieged until the eleventh year of king Zedekiah, and the ninth day of the month,[5] and there was no bread for the people to eat, and the city was broken up."[6] He might indeed, at once from the first day, have delivered them up, and have given them into the hands of their enemies; but He permitted that they should first be wasted for the space of three years, and experience a most distressing siege; to the end that during this interval, being humbled by the terror of the forces without, or the famine that oppressed the city within, they might compel the king, however unwillingly, to submit to the barbarian; and some alleviation might be obtained for the sin committed. And to prove that this is true, and no conjecture of my own, hear what He saith to him by the prophet: "If thou shalt go forth to the king of Babylon's princes, then thy soul shall live, and this city shall not be burned with fire; and thou shalt live, and thine house. But if thou wilt not go forth to the king of Babylon's princes, then shall this city be given into the hand of the Chaldeans; and they shall burn it with fire, and thou shalt not escape out of their hand. And the king said, I am afraid of the Jews that are fallen to the Chaldeans, lest they deliver me into their hands and they mock me. But Jeremiah said, They shall not deliver thee. Obey, I beseech thee, the word of the Lord, which I speak unto thee; so shall it be better for thee, and thy soul shall live. But if thou refuse to go forth, this is the word that the Lord hath shewed me. All the women that are left in the king of Judah's house, shall be brought forth to the king of Babylon's princes; and those shall say, The men who are at peace with thee have deceived thee, and have prevailed over thee; they shall prevail when thy feet slip; they are turned away from thee, and they shall bring out all thy wives, and thy children to the Chaldeans, and thou shalt not escape out of their hand, for thou shalt be taken by the hand of the king of Babylon, and this city shall be burned with fire."[7]

10. But when He did not prevail with him by this address, but he remained in his sin and transgression, after three years, God delivered up the city, displaying at once His own clemency and the ingratitude of that king. And entering in with the utmost ease, they "burnt the house of the Lord, and the king's house, and the houses of Jerusalem, and every great house, the captain of the guard[8] burnt, and overthrew the wall of Jerusalem;"[9] and everywhere there was the fire of the barbarian, the oath being the conductor of the conflagration, and carrying about the flame in all directions. "And the captain of the guard carried away the rest of the people that were left in the city, and the fugitives that fell away to the king of Babylon.[10] And the pillars of brass that were in the house of the Lord the Chaldeans brake up, and the bases, and the brazen sea that was in the house of the Lord, did the Chaldees break in

---

[1] Ezek. xvii. 9.　[2] Ezek. xvii. 12.　[3] Ezek. xvii. 14.
[4] Ezek. xvii. 16-20.
[5] The *fourth*, Jer. xxxix. 2; lii. 6.　[6] 2 Kings xxv. 1-4.
[7] Jer. xxxviii. 17-23.
[8] LXX., ἀρχιμάγειρος, *chief of the cooks*, the Hebrew is literally *of the slaughterers*.
[9] 2 Kings xxv. 9; Jer. xxxix. 8.　[10] Jer. xxxix. 9.

pieces. And the pots, and the flesh-hooks, and the bowls, and the censers, and all the vessels of brass wherewith they ministered, took they away. And the firepans, and all the golden and silver bowls they took away. Moreover, Nebuzaradan, the captain of the guard, took away the two pillars, and the bases, and the sea which Solomon had made in the house of the Lord. And they took away Seraiah the chief priest, and Zephaniah the second priest, and the three keepers of the door; and out of the city one eunuch that was set over the men of war; and five men that were in the king's presence; and Shaphan the chief captain, and the principal scribe, and threescore men. And he took these, and brought them to the king of Babylon, and the king smote them, and slew them."[1]

11. Be mindful therefore, I pray, now of the "flying sickle," that "resteth in the swearer's house;" and "destroyeth the walls and the timber and the stones." Be mindful, I pray, how this oath entered into the city, and overturned houses, and temple, and walls, and splendid buildings, and made the city an heap; and that neither the Holy of Holies, nor the sacred vessels, nor any thing else could ward off that punishment and vengeance, for that the oath had been transgressed! The city, indeed, was thus miserably destroyed. But the king endured what was still more wretched and deplorable.[2] And as the flying sickle overthrew the buildings, so did it also cut him down in his flight. For "the king," it says, "went forth by night, by way of the gate, and the Chaldeans encompassed the city, and the army of the Chaldeans pursued after the king and overtook him, and they took the king, and brought him to the king of Babylon, and the king of Babylon gave judgment[3] upon Zedekiah, and slew his sons before his face, and put out the eyes of Zedekiah, and bound him with fetters, and carried him to Babylon." What is meant by the expression, "he spake judgment with him?" He demanded of him an account of his conduct, he pleaded against him; and first he slew his two sons, that he might be a spectator of the calamity of his house, and might behold[4] that deplorable tragedy; and then he put out his own eyes. For what reason, I ask again, did this occur? In order that he might go as a teacher to the barbarians, and to the Jews who dwelt among them; and that they who had eyes might discern by him who was bereft of sight, how great an evil is an oath! Nor only these; but all who dwelt by the way, beholding the man fettered and blinded, might learn by his calamity the greatness of his sin. Therefore one of the prophets declares, "He shall not see Babylon."[5] And another, "He shall be carried away to Babylon."[6] And the prophecy seems, indeed, to be contradictory. But it is not so; for both of these are true. For he saw not Babylon, though he was carried away to Babylon. How then did he not see Babylon? Because it was in Judæa he had his eyes put out; for where the oath had been set at nought, there also was it vindicated, and he himself subjected to punishment. And how was he carried away to Babylon? In a state of captivity. For since the punishment was twofold, deprivation of sight and captivity, the prophets took them severally. The one saith, "He shall not see Babylon," speaking of the loss of his eyes; the other saith, "He shall be carried away to Babylon," signifying his captivity.

12. Knowing these things, then, brethren, and gathering up what has been now advanced, as well as what has been said before; let us at last desist from this evil custom, yea, I pray and beseech you all! For if in the old dispensation, when the Jews had not the strictest moral wisdom required of them, but much condescension was extended to them, such wrath was the effect of one oath; such capture and captivity; what punishment is it likely that those who swear should now be subjected to, after an express law forbidding the practice, and so large an addition of precepts. Is it, indeed, all that is required, that we come to the assembly, and hear what is spoken? Why truly it is a reason for greater condemnation, and for more inevitable punishment, that we are continually hearing, and yet do not what is bidden! What excuse shall we have, or what pardon, if assembling here from earliest youth to latest old age, and enjoying the advantage of so much instruction, we remain just like them, and do not take pains to correct a single defect. Let no one henceforth allege custom. For this is the very thing at which I am indignant and provoked, that we are not able to get the better of custom. And, pray, if we do not get the better of custom, how can we get the better of concupiscence, which hath its root even in the principles of our nature; for it is natural to feel desire; but to desire wickedly, comes after of choice. But this practice of swearing takes not even its first

---

[1] 2 Kings xxv. 13-20.
[2] 2 Kings xxv. 4-7.
[3] Lit. *spake judgment with him*, as E. V. mar.
[4] The last Par. Ed. adopts ἴδῃ from Savile, and so M. and three MSS. at Venice. Ben. ἴδε, N. R. and Lat. εἴδε.

[5] Ezek. xii. 13. [6] Jer. xxxii. 5.

principle from nature,[1] but from mere negligence.

13. And that thou mayest learn that not from the difficulty of the thing, but through our inattention, this sin has advanced to such a pitch, let us call to mind how many things far more difficult than these, men accomplish; and that too without expecting any recompense therefrom. Let us think what services the Devil imposes; how laborious, how troublesome they are; and yet, the difficulty has not become an obstacle to these services. For what can be more difficult, I ask, than when any young person delivering himself up to those, who undertake to make his limbs supple and pliant, uses his most strenuous exertion to bend his whole body into the exact shape of a wheel, and to turn over upon the pavement; his powers being tasked at the same time through the eyes, and through the movement of the hands, as well as other convolutions for the purpose of being transformed into the likeness of woman-kind.[2] Yet neither the difficulty of these feats, nor the degradation arising from them, are thought of. And again, those who are dragged upon the dancing-stage, and use the members of the body as though they were wings, who that beholds them can help being struck with wonder? So too they who toss knives aloft in the air one after another, and catch them all by the handle, whom might they not put to shame of those who refuse to undergo any labour for the sake of virtue? And what can any one say of those men, who balancing a pole on the forehead, keep it just as steady as a tree rooted in the ground? And this is not the only marvellous part of the affair; but that they set little children to wrestle with one another on the top of the tree; and neither the hands, nor any other part of the body assisting, the forehead alone sustains the pole unshaken, and with more steadiness than any kind of fastening. Again: another walks on the slenderest rope, with the same fearlessness as men do when they run over level plains. Nevertheless these things, which even in thought seem impracticable, have become possible by art. What like this have we, I ask, to allege concerning oaths? What kind of difficulty? what toil? what art? what danger? There is only needed on our part a little earnestness, and the whole of our task will be quickly performed.

14. And do not tell me, "I have accomplished the greater part of it;" but if thou hast not accomplished the whole, consider that thou hast not as yet done any thing; for this little, if neglected, is destruction to all the rest. Often indeed when men have built a house, and put on the roof, they have destroyed the whole fabric, by not making any concern of a single tile that has been shaken off from it. And one may see the same thing occur with respect to garments; for there too if a small hole is made, and not repaired, a large rent is the consequence. And this also is frequently the case in regard to floods; for these, if they find but a small entrance, let in the whole torrent. Thou also, then, even if thou hast fortified thyself all around, and but a small part be left still unfortified, yet block up this also against the devil, that thou mayest be made strong on all sides! Thou hast seen the sickle! Thou hast seen the head of John! Thou hast heard the history pertaining to Saul! Thou hast heard the manner of the Jewish captivity! And beside all these, thou hast heard the sentence of Christ declaring, that not only to commit perjury, but to swear in any way, is a diabolical thing, and the whole a device of the evil one.[3] Thou hast heard that every where perjuries follow oaths. Putting all these things then together, write them upon thy understanding. Dost thou not see how women and little children suspend Gospels[4] from their necks as a powerful amulet, and carry them about in all places wherever they go. Thus do thou write the commands of the Gospel and its laws upon thy mind. Here there is no need of gold or property, or of buying a book; but of the will only, and the affections of the soul awakened, and the Gospel will be thy surer guardian, carrying it as thou wilt then do, not outside, but treasured up within; yea, in the soul's secret chambers. When thou risest up then from thy bed, and

---

[1] This is the reading in some MSS. adopted by Savile, but the Benedictine reads ἐκ τῆς προαιρέσεως "from moral choice," or "purpose," *i. e.*, aiming at something supposed to be good.

[2] Xenophon, in his Symposium, describes a dancing girl as performing tricks of this kind, "turning over backwards, bent into the form of a wheel," and "reading and writing while whirled on a potter's wheel," &c. (on which Socrates takes occasion to say how much women might learn). Wilkinson observes, that this bears some resemblance to a feat indicated in Egyptian paintings, not less than 1300 years before the age of Socrates. See Manners and Customs of the Ancient Egyptians, vol. ii. p. 415. Of the degradation attached to such feats, see Herodotus, b. vi. c. 129.

[3] So *cometh of evil* may be understood. St. Chrysostom scarcely allows an oath in any case, unless perhaps as quoted on Eph. i. 14. His words are sometimes marked as *caute legenda*. Other Fathers, and the usual practice, allowed them on *just occasions*. See Bingham, xvi. c. vii. sec. 4. Where, however, St. Athanasius uses a qualified form of putting an oath. See also his Comment on Ps. lxiii. 11, he speaks almost as strongly as St. Chrysostom, as does also St. Basil, still using himself an affirmation before God, and discussing questions of obligation by oath.

[4] Texts or extracts from the Gospels. On 1 Cor. xvi. 9, Hom. XLIII., he notices a like practice. Bingham says, b. xvi. c. v. sec. 6, that he, and St. Basil, and St. Epiphanius, *complain* of it, but the passages he quotes do not do so. St. Chrys. tolerates this, seemingly, but expressly denies its efficacy as a mere charm. On the use of charms he is severe, though used by Christians, and containing nothing of decidedly heathenish import. He considers making the sign of the cross as *opposed* to these, and an act of faith. See on Ep. to Col. Hom. VIII. Suicer in Εὐαγγέλιον, and St. Chrys. in Matt. Hom. LXXII.

when thou goest out of thine house, repeat this law: "I say unto you, Swear not at all."[1] And the saying will be to thee a discipline; for there is no need of much labour, but only of a moderate degree of attention. And that this is true, may thus be proved. Call thy son, and frighten him, and threaten to lay a few stripes upon him, if he does not duly observe this law; and thou wilt see, how he will forthwith abstain from this custom. Is it not therefore truly absurd, that little children, out of the fear we inspire, should perform this commandment, and that we should not fear God as our sons fear us?

15. What then I said before this, I now again repeat. Let us lay down a law for ourselves in this matter; not to meddle either with public or private affairs until we have fulfilled this law; and then surely under the pressure of this obligation we shall easily conquer, and we shall at once adorn ourselves, and decorate our city. For consider what a thing it would be to have it said every where throughout the world, "A practice becoming Christians is established at Antioch, and you will hear no one giving utterance to an oath, even though the greatest nceessity is laid upon him!" This is what the neighbouring cities will certainly hear; nay, not the neighbouring cities only, but even to the ends of the earth will the report be conveyed. For it is indeed probable that both the merchants who mix with you, and others who arrive from this place, will report all these matters. When, therefore, many persons in the way of encomium mention the harbours of other cities, or the markets, or the abundance of wares, enable those who come from hence to say, that there is that at Antioch, which is to be seen in no other city; for that the men who dwell there would sooner have their tongues cut out, than suffer an oath to proceed from their mouths! This will be your ornament and defence, and not only so, but it will bring an abundant reward. For others also will certainly emulate, and imitate you. But if, when a person has gained but one or two,[2] he shall receive so great a reward from God; what recompense shall ye not receive when ye are the instructors of the whole world. It is your duty then to bestir yourselves, to be watchful, and to be sober; knowing that not only from our own personal good works, but from those we have also wrought in others, shall we receive the best recompense, and enjoy much favour with God, which may He grant us all continually to enjoy, and hereafter to obtain the kingdom of heaven, in Christ Jesus our Lord; to Whom with the Father, and the Holy Ghost, be glory and power both now and ever, and world without end. Amen.

[1] Matt. v. 34.

[2] Jas. v. 20.

HOMILY XX.[1]

That the fast of Lent is not sufficient to make us competent to partake of the Communion, but that holiness is the first thing required. How it is possible not to entertain resentment, and that God takes much account of this law; and that the entertaining of resentment punishes those who are guilty of it even before they reach the place of torment.—Also concerning abstinence from oaths, and those who have not succeeded in abstaining from swearing.

1. AT length the season is verging towards the end of the Fast, and therefore we ought the more earnestly to devote ourselves to holiness. For as in the case of those who run a race, all their circuits will be of no avail if they miss the prize; so neither will any advantage result from these manifold labours and toils with regard to the fast, if we are not able to enjoy the sacred Table with a good conscience. For this end are fasting and Lent appointed, and so many days of solemn assemblies, auditories, prayers, and teachings, in order that by this earnestness[2] being cleansed in every possible way from

[1] Savile places this Homily after those on the Statues, putting here the first Catechesis, as do most MSS. In the new Coll. MS. this is the 19th; its title has been cut out of the list of those on the Statues, and reinserted by another hand. A New College MS. consisting of select passages, quotes from it as one of them. It is not in any of the Bodleian MSS., but in that at Sion College it is placed as in Savile. Montfaucon placed it here as considering the Catechesis evidently out of place.

[2] Ben. adds "for the commands of God," but it seems to be a gloss; 2 MSS. at Venice omit it.

the sins which we had contracted during the whole year, we may with spiritual boldness religiously partake of that unbloody Sacrifice; so that should this not be the result, we shall have sustained so much labour entirely in vain, and without any profit. Let every one, therefore, consider with himself what defect he hath corrected, what good work he hath attained to; what sin he hath cast off, what stain he hath purged away; in what respect he has become better. And should he discover that in this good traffic he has made any gain by the fast, and be conscious in himself of much care taken of his wounds, let him draw near! But if he hath remained negligent, having nothing to shew but mere fasting, and hath done nothing which is right besides, let his remain outside;[1] and then let him enter, when he hath purged out all these offences. Let no one rest on the fast merely; whilst continuing unreformed in evil practices. For it is probable, that he who omits fasting may obtain pardon, having infirmity of body to plead; but it is impossible that he can have an excuse who hath not amended his faults. Thou hast not fasted, it may be, on account of bodily weakness. Tell me for what reason thou art not reconciled to thine enemies? Hast thou, indeed, here to allege bodily infirmity? Again; if thou retainest envy and hatred, what apology hast thou then I ask? For no one in offences of this kind is able to take refuge in the plea of bodily infirmity. And this was a work of Christ's[2] love toward man, viz. that the chief of the precepts, and those which maintain our life, should not be impaired in any degree through the weakness of the body.

2. But since we need to practise all the divine laws alike, and more especially that which bids us consider no man as an enemy, nor retain resentment long, but forthwith to be reconciled; suffer us to-day to discourse to you concerning this commandment. For as it is not to be imagined that the fornicator and the blasphemer can partake of the sacred Table, so it is impossible that he who hath an enemy, and bears malice, can enjoy the holy Communion. And this with good reason. For a man when he has committed fornication, or adultery, at the same time that he hath accomplished his lust, hath also completed the sin; and should he be willing by watchful living to recover from that fall, he may afterwards, by manifesting great penitence, obtain some relief. But he who is resentful worketh the same iniquity every day, and never brings it to an end. In the former case the deed is over, and the sin completed; but here the sin is perpetrated every day. What excuse can we then have, I ask, for delivering ourselves willingly to such an evil monster? How canst thou ask thy Lord to be mild and merciful to thee, when thou hast been so hard and unforgiving to thy fellow-servant?

3. But thy fellow-servant hath treated thee with contempt perhaps? Yes! and thou hast treated God with contempt oftentimes. And what comparison is there between a fellow-servant and the Lord? As to the former, when he was perchance in some way injured, he insulted thee, and thou wert exasperated. But thou insultest the Lord, when thou art neither treated with injustice nor ill-will by Him, but receiving blessing of Him day by day. Consider, then, that if God chose to search out rigorously what is done against Him, we should not live a single day. For the prophet saith, "If Thou wilt be extreme to mark iniquity, O Lord, O Lord, who shall stand?"[3] And, to pass by all those other things, of which the conscience of every sinner is aware, and of which he no has no human witness, but God only; were we to be called to account for those which are open and admitted, what allowance could we expect for such sins? What if He were to scrutinize our listlessness and negligence in our prayers; and how, whilst standing before God and supplicating Him, we do not exhibit even so much fear and reverence for Him as servants do toward their masters, as soldiers do toward their officers, as friends do toward friends?[4] When thou discoursest with a friend, thou givest heed to what thou art doing, but when waiting on God on account of thy sins, and asking pardon for so many offences, and thinking that thou shalt obtain forgiveness, thou art often listless; and whilst thy knees are lying on the ground, thou sufferest thy mind to wander every where, in the market, or in the house, babbling the while with thy mouth vainly and to no purpose! And this we experience, not once or twice, but frequently! Did God then choose to scrutinize this alone, do you think that we could obtain pardon, or be able to find any excuse? Truly, I think not!

4. But what if the evil-speakings which we unkindly utter every day one against another, were brought forward against us; as well as the rash judgments with which we condemn our neighbour; and that for no reason, but

---

[1] This alludes to the penitential discipline of the primitive Church, which confined penitents of the lowest order to the church porch. Consult Bingham in Antiq. viii. c. 3, and xviii. c. 1.
[2] Sav. God's.
[3] Ps. cxxx. 3.
[4] Herbert's Poems, No. lxviii.,
"I would not use a friend as I use Thee."

because we are fond of blaming, and given to find fault; what, I say, should we be able to allege in defence? Again, should He scrutinize those roving glances of ours, and those evil desires which we carry in the mind, so frequently admitting disgraceful and impure thoughts from the unlicensed wandering of the eyes, what punishment must we not sustain? And should He demand a reason for our revilings, (for He saith, "Whosoever shall say to his brother, Thou fool, shall be in danger of hell fire,") how could we, forsooth, open our mouths, or move our lips at all, or say any thing great or small in reply? Moreover, as to the vainglorious feelings we allow in our prayers, our fastings, our almsgiving, were we to scrutinize them,—I do not say, were God, but were we ourselves, who are the sinners, to do this,—should we be able to lift up our eyes toward heaven? Then, as to the deceits which we devise one against another,—praising a brother now, whilst he is present, and discoursing as with a friend; and when he is absent, reviling him; can we endure the punishments of all these? Then what of the oaths? or what of the lying? what of the perjuries? what of the unjust anger, and of the envy with which we too often regard men when honoured, not enemies only, but also friends? Furthermore, what of the fact, that we are pleased when others suffer evil, and account the misfortunes of others a consolation for our own distress?

5. But suppose the penalty were exacted for our listlessness in our solemn assemblies what would our condition be? For this ye cannot but know, that often whilst God Himself is addressing us all by His prophet, we are holding frequent and long conversations with those near us, about matters which in no way concern us. Passing by, then, all the rest, should He choose to exact of us the penalty due for this sin only, what hope of salvation will there be? For do not suppose that this offence is a small one, but if thou wouldest be aware of its magnitude, examine how this very thing is regarded among men, and then thou wilt perceive the enormity of the sin. Just venture, when some magistrate is talking to thee, or rather some friend who is of somewhat superior dignity, to turn from him, and enter into conversation with thy servant; and thou wilt then perceive, what thou venturest on in dealing thus with God! For if he be any one of the more distinguished classes, he will even demand reparation of thee for such an insult. Yet God, whilst He is treated with as great, and still greater contempt than this, every day; and that not by one, or two, or three persons, but by almost all of us; is still forbearing and longsuffering, not in regard to this alone, but to other things which are far more grievous. For these things are what must be admitted, and what are obvious to all, and by almost all men they are daringly practised. But there are yet others, which the conscience of those who commit them is privy to. Surely, if we were to think of all this; if we were to reason with ourselves, supposing even that we were the cruelest and harshest of men, yet upon taking a survey of the multitude of our sins, we should for very fear and agony be unable to remember the injury done by others towards ourselves. Bear in mind the river of fire; the envenomed worm; the fearful Judgment, where all things shall be naked and open! Reflect, that what are now hidden things, are then to be brought to light! But shouldest thou pardon thy neighbour, all these sins which till then await their disclosure are done away with here; and when thou shalt depart this life, thou wilt not drag after thee any of that chain of transgressions; so that thou receivest greater things than thou givest. For many such transgressions, indeed, we have often committed, which no other person knoweth; and when we think, that on That Day these our sins shall lie exposed to the eyes of all, upon the public theatre of the universe, we are in pain beyond any punishment, being choked and strangled by our conscience. Yet this shame, great as it is; these sins, these punishments, great as they are; there is a possibility of purging away through forgiveness exercised toward our neighbour.

6. For indeed there is nothing equal to this virtue.[1] Wouldest thou learn the power of this virtue? "Though Moses and Samuel stood before Me," saith God, "my soul would not regard them."[2] Nevertheless, those whom Moses and Samuel were not able to snatch away from God's wrath, this precept when observed was able to snatch away. Hence it is, that He continually exhorts those to whom He had spoken these things, saying, "Let none of you revengefully imagine evil against his brother in your heart," and "let none of you think of his neighbour's malice."[3] It is not said merely, forego wrath; but retain it not in thy mind; think not of it; part with all thy resentment; do away the sore. For thou supposest that thou art paying him back the injury; but thou art first tormenting thyself, and setting up thy rage as an execu-

---

[1] St. Chrys. seems to mean, that there is none so remarkably connected with promises of remission of sin, as Matt. v. 7, vi. 14; Luke vi. 37.
[2] Jer. xv. 1.
[3] Zech. viii. 17, vii. 10, LXX.

tioner within thee in every part, and tearing up thine own bowels. For what can be more wretched than a man perpetually angry? And just as maniacs, who never enjoy tranquility, so also he who is resentful, and retains an enemy, will never have the enjoyment of any peace; incessantly raging, as he does, and daily increasing the tempest of his thoughts calling to mind his words and acts, and detesting the very name of him who has aggrieved him. Do you but mention his enemy, he becomes furious at once, and sustains much inward anguish; and should he chance to get only a bare sight of him, he fears and trembles, as if encountering the worst evils. Yea, if he perceives any of his relations, if but his garment, or his dwelling, or street, he is tormented by the sight of them. For as in the case of those who are beloved, their faces, their garments, their sandals, their houses, or streets, excite us, the instant we behold them; so also should we observe a servant, or friend, or house, or street, or any thing else belonging to those we hate and hold our enemies, we are stung by all these things; and the strokes we endure from the sight of each one of them are frequent and continual.

7. What is the need then of sustaining such a siege, such torment and such punishment? For if hell did not threaten the resentful; yet for the very torment resulting from the thing itself we ought to forgive the offences of those who have aggrieved us. But when deathless punishments remain behind, what can be more senseless than the man, who both here and there brings punishment upon himself, while he thinks to be revenged upon his enemy! For suppose that we see him still prosperous, then we are ready to die of chagrin; but if in an adverse condition, we are in fear, lest some propitious turn of events should take place. But for both of these there is stored up for us an inevitable punishment. For, "Rejoice not," he saith, "when thine enemy stumbleth."[1] And tell me not of the greatness of the injuries received; for it is not this which maketh thy wrath to be retained; but this, that thou art unmindful of thine own offences; that thou hast not before thine eyes either hell or the fear of God! To convince thee that this is true, I will endeavour to make it manifest from the events which have happened in this city. For when the persons impeached of those flagrant crimes were dragged to the tribunal of justice;—when the fire was kindled within, and the executioners stood around, and were lacerating their ribs,[2] if any one standing beside them had proclaimed, "If ye have any enemies, dismiss your resentment, and we shall be able to set you free from this punishment;"—would they not have kissed their very feet?[3] And why do I say their feet? If one had bidden them take them for their masters, they would not then have refused. But if punishment that is human, and hath its bounds, would have triumphed over all anger, much more would the punishment to come, if it had continual possession of our thoughts, expel from the soul not only resentment, but every evil imagination? For what is easier, I ask, than to get rid of resentment against the injurer? Is there any long journey to be undertaken? Is there any expenditure of money? Is the aid of others to be invoked? It suffices only to resolve, and the good deed at once reaches the goal. What punishment, then, must we not deserve, if on account of worldly affairs we stoop to slavish occupations; and shew a servility unworthy of ourselves; and expend money; and enter into conversation with porters, that we may flatter[4] impious men; and do and say all manner of things, so that we may perfectly attain the end we have in view; and yet cannot endure, for the sake of God's laws, to entreat a brother who hath injured us, but consider it a disgrace to be the first to make advances. Art thou ashamed, tell me, when thou art going to be the first to make gain? Rather, on the contrary, you ought to be ashamed of persisting in this passion; and waiting until the person who has committed the injury comes to you to be reconciled; for this is a disgrace, and a reproach, and the greatest loss.

8. For he who comes the first it is, who reaps all the fruit; and when at the entreaty of another thou layest aside thine anger, the good work is to be accounted his; for thou hast discharged the law as doing a favour to him, not as obeying God. But if, when no one entreats, when not even the man who has done the injury approaches, or solicits thee, thou thyself dismissing from thy thoughts all shame, and all delay, runnest forward freely to the injurer, and dost quell anger entirely, the good deed becomes wholly thine own, and thou shalt receive all the reward. If I say, "Practise fasting," thy plea, perchance, is

---

[1] Prov. xxiv. 17.

[2] From Hom. XIII. 3, we know that the torture was chiefly by scourging, but fire (if *literally* used, as it had often been in torturing Christians) might be applied in various ways. The allusion favours the insertion of the Homily in this place. A passage towards the end of the Homily places it unquestionably in this Lent.

[3] *i. e.*, the feet of their enemies.

[4] κολακεύσωμεν. The aorist implies that the object intended is to get an audience. For a striking picture of such servility, see Tac. Ann. iv. 77.

bodily weakness. If I say, "Give to the poor," it is poverty, and bringing up children. If I say, "Make time for the assemblies of the Church," it is worldly cares. If I say, "Give heed to what is spoken, and consider the power of what is taught," it is want of learning. If I say, "Correct another," you say, "When counsel is given him, he takes no heed, for I have often spoken, and been scorned." Frigid, as such pretences are, yet you have some pretences to allege. But suppose I say, "Dismiss thine anger," which of these wilt thou then allege?" For neither infirmity of body, nor poverty, nor lack of culture, nor want of leisure, nor any other thing of that kind hast thou to advance; but this sin is above all other the most inexcusable. How wilt thou be able to stretch thine hands toward heaven, or how to move thy tongue, or to ask pardon? For although God be desirous to pardon thy sins, thou thyself dost not suffer Him, while thou retainest that of thy fellow-servant! But suppose that he is cruel, fierce, and savage, and greedy of revenge and retaliation? Why for this reason thou oughtest especially to grant forgiveness.[1] Hast thou been wronged much, and robbed, and slandered, and injured in matters of the first importance; and dost thou wish to see thine enemy punished? Yet even for this, it will be of use to thee to pardon him. For suppose that thou thyself takest vengeance, and prosecutest it, either by words, by deeds, or imprecation against the adversary; then God will not afterwards prosecute it too, inasmuch as thou hast taken thy revenge; and not only will He not prosecute the matter for thee, but will also demand a penalty of thee as a despiser of Himself. For if this same thing takes place amongst mankind, viz. that if we beat the servant of another, the master is indignant, and calls the act an insult (for although we be treated injuriously, whether by slaves, or by freemen, it is fitting that we should await the legal decisions of magistrates or masters); if then even amongst men, to avenge ourselves would not be safe, how much more so when God is the avenger!

9. Hath thy neighbour wronged and grieved thee, and involved thee in a thousand ills? Be it so, yet do not prosecute vengeance on thine own part, lest thou do despite to the Lord! Yield the matter to God, and He will dispose of it much better than thou canst desire. To thee He has given charge simply to pray for the injurer; but how to deal with him, He hath ordered thee to leave to Himself. Never canst thou so avenge thyself, as He is prepared to avenge thee, if thou givest place to Him alone, and dost not utter imprecations on him who has aggrieved thee; but sufferest God to be sole arbiter of the sentence. For although we may pardon those who have aggrieved us; although we may be reconciled; although we may pray for them; yet God does not pardon, unless they themselves are converted, and become better. And He withholds pardon, with a view to their own advantage. For He praises thee, and approves thee for thy spiritual wisdom; but visits him, in order that he may not grow worse by thy wisdom. So that the common saying on this subject is not to the point. For many there are, who when I reproach them because after being exhorted to be reconciled to their enemies, they will not be persuaded to it, think fit to proffer this apology, which is nothing less than a cloak for their iniquity. "I am unwilling," says one, "to be reconciled, lest I shoud make the man worse, more ill-tempered, and more disposed to treat me contemptuously hereafter." Besides this, they also make this plea: "Many people," say they, "think it is weakness in me to come first to a reconciliation, and to entreat my enemy." All these things are foolish; for the Eye that slumbers not has seen thy good intention; wherefore, it behoveth thee to make no account of the opinion of thy fellow-servants, when thou hast gained the opinion of the Judge, Who is about to try thy cause.

10. But if thy concern be, lest thine enemy should become worse by thy clemency learn this,—that it is not thus he is made worse; but far rather if thou art unreconciled. For although he were the vilest of men; although he might neither confess nor publish it openly; yet he will silently approve thy Christian wisdom, and in his own conscience will respect thy gentleness. Should he, however, persist in the same iniquity, whilst thou art endeavouring to soften and conciliate, he will have to abide the heaviest punishment from God. And that ye may know, that although we should pray for our enemies, and for those who have injured us, God does not pardon, if they are, likely to become worse by our forbearance, I will mention to you an ancient piece of history. Miriam once spake against Moses. What then did God do? He sent a leprosy upon her, and made her unclean; notwithstanding that in other respects she had been meek and modest. Afterwards, when Moses himself, the party injured, besought that the wrath might be removed, God consented not: but what did

---

[1] See on Rom. xii. 21, Hom. XXII.

He say? "If her father had but spit in her face, should she not be ashamed? Let her remain," saith He, "without the camp seven days."[1] But what He means is to this effect. "If," saith He, "she had a father, and he had put her away from his presence, would she not have undergone the rebuke? I approve thee indeed for thy fraternal piety, and thy meekness and clemency; but I know when is the due time to remit her punishment." Do thou then shew all humanity towards thy brother; and do not pardon his offences in the desire of a greater punishment for him, but of thy tenderness and good will; yet understand this very plainly, that the more he shall slight thee, whilst thou art labouring to conciliate, so much the greater punishment will he draw down upon himself.

11. What sayest thou? tell me, Is he the worse for thy attentions? This is blame to him, but thy praise. Thy praise, that, whilst seeing him thus behave himself, thou didst not desist from doing God's will in conciliating him. But to him it is blame, because he has not been made better by thy clemency. But[2] "it is far more desirable that others should be blamed because of us, than we because of them." Make me not this frigid reply, of saying, "I am afraid of its being thought that I made an overture to him out of fear; and that he will therefore despise me the more." Such a reply indicates a childish and foolish mind, agitated about human approbation. Let him suppose, that it was out of fear you made the first advance to him; your reward will be so much the greater; since, being aware of this beforehand, you still consented to endure all for the fear of God. For he who is in chase of human approbation, and seeks reconciliation for that end, curtails the recompense of reward; but he who is quite sure of the fact, that many will vilify and ridicule him, and even then does not desist, from the attempt at reconciliation, will have a twofold, yea, a threefold crown. And this is indeed the man who does it for the sake of God. Nor tell me, that the man has wronged thee in this, or in that particular; for if he hath displayed, in his conduct towards thee, every kind of iniquity that is in man, yet even so God hath enjoined thee to forgive him all!

12. Lo! I forewarn, and testify, and proclaim this with a voice that all may hear! "Let no one who hath an enemy draw near the sacred Table, or receive the Lord's Body! Let no one who draws near have an enemy! Hast thou an enemy? Draw not near! Wilt thou draw near? Be reconciled, and then draw near, and touch the Holy Thing!" Nor, indeed, is this my declaration. Rather it is that of the Lord Himself, Who was crucified for us. That He might reconcile thee to the Father, He refused not to be sacrificed, and to shed His blood! And art thou unwilling to utter a word, or to make the first advance, that thou mayest be reconciled to thy fellow-servant? Hear what the Lord saith, concerning those who are in this disposition; "If thou bring thy gift to the altar, and there rememberest that thy brother hath aught against thee"—He does not say, "wait for him to come to thee," nor "speak with another as mediator," nor "entreat some other," but "do thou thyself make the advance towards him." For the exhortation is, "Go thy way, first be reconciled to thy brother."[3] O transcendent wonder! Does He Himself account it no dishonour, that the gift should be left unoffered, and dost thou think it a mark of disgrace to go first and be reconciled? And how can such a case, I ask, be deemed worthy of pardon? Were you to see a member of yours cut off, would you not use every exertion so that it might be reunited to the body? This do with regard to thy brethren; when thou seest them cut off from thy friendship, make all haste to recover them! Do not wait for them to make the first advance, but press onward, that thou mayest be foremost to receive the prize.

13. We are commanded to have only one enemy, the devil. With him be thou never reconciled! But with a brother, never be at enmity in thy heart. And if there should be any narrowness of soul, let it be only an ephemeral thing, and never last beyond a day's space. For, "let not the sun," he saith, "go down upon your wrath."[4] For if, before evening, you are reconciled, you will obtain some pardon from God. But if you remain longer at enmity, that enmity is no longer the result of your being suddenly carried away by anger and resentment, but of wickedness, and of a foul spirit, and one which makes a practice of malice! And this is not the only terrible thing, that you deprive yourself of pardon, but that the right course becomes still more difficult. For when one day is past, the shame becomes greater; and when the second has arrived, it is still further increased; and if it reach a third, and a fourth day, it will add a fifth. Thus the five become ten; the ten, twenty; the twenty an hundred; and thenceforth the wound will

---

[1] Numb. xii. 14.
[2] Benedictine "Paul saith," but this is not in Savile nor in the Latin, and is omitted in a Venice MS. and some at Paris; it is accounted for by πολὺ, but Ducæus suggests 1 Peter iii. 17.
[3] Matt. v. 23, 24.
[4] Ephes. iv. 26.

become incurable; for as time goes on, the breach becomes wider. But do thou, O man, give way to none of these irrational passions; nor be ashamed, nor blush, nor say within yourself, "A short time ago we called each other such names, and said a vast number of things fit or not fit to be spoken; and shall I now hurry at once to a reconciliation? Who then will not blame my excessive easiness?" I answer, no one who has sense will blame thy easiness; but when thou remainest implacable, then, all persons will deride thee. Then thou wilt give to the devil the advantage of this wide breach. For the enmity becomes then more difficult to be got rid of, not by mere lapse of time, but from the circumstances too that take place in the meanwhile. For as "charity covereth a multitude of sins,"[1] so enmity gives a being to sins that do not exist, and all persons henceforth, are deemed worthy of credit who turn accusers; who rejoice in the ills of others, and blaze abroad what is disgraceful in their conduct.

14. Knowing all these things then, make the first advance to a brother; lay hold of him before he has entirely shrunk away from thee; and should it be necessary to run through all the city on the same day; should it be necessary to go beyond the walls, or to take a long journey; still leaving all other things that may be in hand, attend only to this one work of reconciling thy brother. For if the work be laborious, reflect that it is for God's sake thou undergoest all this, and thou shalt receive sufficient consolation. Stir up thy soul also when it is shrinking, and backward, and bashful, and ashamed, by perpetually harping on this theme and saying, Why art thou delaying? Why art thou shrinking and holding back? our concern is not for money, nor for any other of these fleeting things, but for our salvation. God bids us do all these things, and all things should be secondary to His commands. This matter is a sort of spiritual merchandise. Let us not neglect it, let us not be slothful. Let our enemy too understand that we have taken much pains, in order to do what is well-pleasing unto God. And though he may again insult, or strike us, or do any other such thing of a still more grievous kind, let us sustain all things courageously, since we are not so much benefitting him thereby, as ourselves. Of all good works, this shall most especially befriend us on That Day. We have sinned and offended in many and great matters, and have provoked our Lord. Through His lovingkindness He hath given us this way of reconciliation. Let us, then, not betray this good treasure. For had He not power to charge us simply to make reconciliation, and not have any reward assigned to it? for whom hath He to gainsay or rectify His appointment? Nevertheless, through His great lovingkindness, He hath promised us a large and unspeakable reward, and one which we must be especially desirous to obtain, the pardon of our sins; thus also making this our obedience more easy of performance.

15. What allowance then can be made for us, if even when we might receive so great a reward we still do not obey the Lawgiver, but persist in our contempt; for that this is a contempt is plain from hence. If the Emperor had laid down a law, that all those who were enemies should be reconciled to one another, or have their heads cut off, should we not every one make haste to a reconciliation with his neighbour? Yes! truly, I think so! What excuse then have we, in not ascribing the same honour to the Lord, that we should do to those who are our fellow-servants? For this reason we are commanded to say, "Forgive us our debts, as we forgive our debtors."[2] What can be more mild, what more merciful, than this precept! He hath made thee a judge of the pardon of thine own offences! If thou forgivest few things, He forgives thee few! If thou forgivest many things, He forgives thee many! If thou pardonest from the heart, and sincerely, God in like manner also pardons thee! If besides pardoning him thou accountest him a friend, God will also thus deal with thee; so that the more he has sinned, so much the more is it necessary that we should hasten to a reconciliation; since it becomes a cause of greater offences being forgiven us.[3] Art thou willing to learn[4] that there is no pardon for us, if we are mindful of injuries, and that there is no one who can deliver us? I will make what I assert plain by an example. Suppose that a neighbour has done you a certain injury, that he has seized your goods; has confiscated or embezzled them; and not to confine myself to such a case, let me add to it more things and worse beside, and whatever you will; he has longed to destroy you; he has exposed you to a thousand perils; he has manifested every sort of malice towards you; and left nothing undone that human wickedness can do? For not to go

---

[1] 1 Pet. iv. 8.
[2] Matt. vi. 12.
[3] This and similar language of the Fathers, is startling to many, but is hardly more than a transcript of the passages of Holy Scripture they refer to. A general acknowledgment and explanation of them occurs in the "Homily of Alms-deeds."
[4] Or wouldest thou have proof.

over every thing separately, suppose that he has injured you to such an extent as no one ever injured any before;—why, even in this case, if you are resentful, you will not be worthy of pardon. And I will explain how it is so.

16. If one of your servants owed you an hundred pieces of gold; and some one again was indebted to him in a few pieces of silver; and if the servants' debtor were to come, and entreat and supplicate you that he might obtain indulgence, and you were to call in your own servant, and charge him, saying, " Forgive this man the debt, and from the sum thou owest me I will deduct this debt;" should that servant afterwards be wicked and shameless enough to seize on his debtor, could any one then rescue him out of your hands? Would you not most assuredly inflict a thousand stripes upon him, as having been insulted to the last extremity? And very justly too. This also God will do: for He will say to thee on That Day, " O wicked and villainous servant, yea, was it of thine own thou forgavest him? Out of what thou wert indebted to Me, thou wert ordered to account to him. For "Remit," He saith, "and I will remit unto thee! although, to speak truly,[1] if I had not added this condition, it would have been even then thy duty to have remitted at the instance of thy Lord. But in this case, I did not command thee as a master, but I asked it as a favour from a friend; and I asked it out of My own property; and I promised to give greater things in return; and yet with all this, thou wert not made a better man." Moreover men, when they act in this manner, put down as much to their own servants' accounts, as the measure of the debt is. Thus, for example, suppose the servant owes his master a hundred pieces of gold; and the debtor of the servant owes ten pieces, should the latter remit his debt, the master does not remit him his hundred pieces, but these ten only; and all the rest he still demands. But it is not so with God; if you remit a[2] few things to your fellow-servant, He remits all your debt.

17. Whence does this appear? From the very Prayer[3] itself. "For if," saith He, " ye forgive men their debts, your heavenly Father will forgive your debts."[4] And as much as the difference is between "a hundred pence" and "ten thousand talents,"[5] so great is it between the debts on the one side, and those on the other!

What punishment then must he not deserve, who when he would receive ten thousand talents, in the room of a hundred pence,[6] yet will not even so remit this small sum, but offers up the Prayer against himself. For when thou sayest, " Forgive us, as we forgive," and afterwards dost not forgive, thou art supplicating of God nothing else than that He would entirely deprive thee of all excuse or indulgence. " But I do not presume to say," replies some one, " Forgive me as I forgive," but only, " Forgive me." But what matters this? For if thou say it not thyself, yet God so doeth; as thou forgivest, He forgives. And this He hath made quite evident from what follows; for there it is said, " If ye forgive not men, neither doth your heavenly Father forgive you." Think not, therefore, that it is a pious caution, not to repeat the whole sentence; nor offer up the Prayer by halves, but as He bade thee so pray thou, in order that the very obligation of that expression, putting thee daily in fear, may compel thee to the exercise of forgiveness towards thy neighbours.

18. Do not tell me, " I have besought him many times, I have intreated, I have supplicated, but I have not effected a reconciliation." Never desist till you have reconciled him. For He said not, " Leave thy gift, and go thy way." Entreat thy brother. But, " Go thy way. Be reconciled."[7] So that, although you may have made many entreaties, yet you must not desist until you have persuaded. God entreats us every day, and we do not hear; and yet He does not cease entreating. And dost thou then disdain to entreat thy fellow-servant. How is it then possible for thee ever to be saved? Suppose that thou hast often pleaded and been repulsed; for this, however, thou wilt obtain a larger reward. For in proportion as he is contentious, and thou perseverest in entreating, so much the more is thy recompense increased. In proportion as the good work is accomplished with greater difficulty, and the reconciliation is one of much labour, so much the greater will be the judgment on him, and so much the brighter will be the crowns of victory for thy forbearance. Let us not merely applaud all this, but exemplify it too in our deeds; and never recede from the work, until we are restored to our former state of friendship. For it is not enough merely to avoid grieving an enemy, or doing him an injury, or being in our minds unkindly disposed towards him; but it is necessary that we should prepare him to be kindly

---

[1] Ven. adds, the things remitted are not equal.
[2] Sav. mar. those.
[3] Often called emphatically, " The Prayer," as constantly in the title of Comments on it. Tertullian *de Oratione*, and the like.
[4] Matt. vi. 14.   [5] Matt. xviii. 24, 28.   [6] Denarii.   [7] Matt. v. 24.

affected towards ourselves. For I hear many saying, "I have no hostility; I am not annoyed; neither have I any thing to do with him."[1] But this is not what God commands, that thou shouldest have nothing to do with him; but that thou shouldest have much to do with him. For this reason he is thy "brother."[2] For this reason He said not, "Forgive thy brother what thou hast against him. But what then? "Go thy way. First be reconciled to him;" and should he have "any thing against thee," yet desist not, before thou hast reunited the member in friendly concord." But thou, who in order that thou mayest obtain a useful servant, tellest out the gold, and discoursest with many merchants, and often undertakest long journeys, tell me, art thou not up and doing to the utmost, in order that thou mayest convert an enemy into a friend? And how then wilt thou be able to call upon God, whilst thou art thus neglecting His laws? Assuredly, the possession of a servant will be of no great profit to us; but the making an enemy a friend, will render God propitious and favourable toward us; and will easily set us free from our sins; and gain us praise with men, as well as great security in our life; for nothing can be more unsafe than he who has even only a single enemy. For our earthly reputation is injured, whilst such a man is saying a thousand evil things of us to every body. Our minds are also in a state of fermentation, and our conscience disturbed; and we are exposed to a continual tempest of anxious thoughts.

19. Now since we are conscious of the truth of all this, let us set ourselves free from chastisement and vengeance; and let us shew our reverence for the present feast, by doing all that has been said; and those same favours which we think to obtain from the Emperor on account of the feast, let us ourselves enable others to enjoy. For I hear, indeed, many saying, that the Emperor, out of his reverence for the Holy Passover, will be reconciled to the city, and will pardon all its offences. How absurd then is it, that when we have to depend for our safety upon others, we bring forward the feast, and its claims; but that when we are commanded to be reconciled one with another, we treat this same feast with disdain, and think nothing of it. No one, truly, so pollutes this holy feast, as he does, who, whilst he is keeping it, cherishes malignity. Or rather, I might say, that such a person cannot possibly keep it, though he should remain without food ten days successively. For where there is enmity and strife, there can be neither fast nor festival. Thou wouldest not dare to touch the holy Sacrifice with unwashed hands,[3] however pressing the necessity might be. Approach not then with an unwashed soul! For this is far worse than the other, and brings a heavier punishment. For[4] nothing so fills the mind with impurity, as anger remaining constantly within it. The spirit of meekness settles not where wrath or passion exists; and when a man is destitute of the Holy Spirit, what hope of salvation shall he have, and how shall he walk aright? Do not then, O beloved, whilst thou art desirous to be revenged of thine enemy, cast thyself down headlong; nor cause thyself to be left alone without the guardianship of God! For, in truth, if the duty were a difficult one, yet the greatness of the punishment, which results from this action of disobedience, were sufficient to arouse the most slothful and supine, and to persuade them to undergo every degree of labour. But now our argument has shewn that the duty is most easy, if we are willing.

20. Let us not then be negligent of what is our life, but let us be in earnest; and do every thing, in order that we may be without an enemy, and so present ourselves at the sacred Table. For nothing,—nothing, I repeat, of what God commands will be difficult, if we give heed: and this is evident from the case of those who are already reformed. How many used to be cheated by the habit of using oaths, and to fancy this practice extremely difficult of reformation. Nevertheless, through the grace of God, when ye put forth but a little effort, ye for the most part washed yourselves clean of this vice. For this reason I beseech you to lay aside also what remains, and to become teachers of others. And to those who have not yet achieved it, but allege to us the length of time during which they were before swearers, and say that it is impossible for them to pluck up in a short time that which has been rooted for many years; I would make this answer, that where any precept among those commanded by God requires to be put in due practice, there is no need of length of time, nor of a multitude of days, nor an interval of years; but of fear only, and reverence of

---

[1] Literally anything common with him, οὐδὲ ἔχω τι κοινὸν πρὸς αὐτὸν: see end of Hom. I.
[2] i. e., is called so in this passage.
[3] If such rules are found fault with because they do not necessarily involve holy living, it should be remembered that where strictly kept, they are grounds for such an appeal as this; and why not, in better men, for holy recollections? They are not truly parallel to those censured by our Lord, which did not relate to the treatment of holy things, and here they are treated quite as subservient to duties of a higher order. The word here rendered "necessity" may be "compulsion."
[4] i. e., "and if thou bearest malice thy soul is unwashed; for," &c.

soul; and then we shall be sure to accomplish it, and that in a short time. But lest you should suppose that I speak these things at random, take a man whom you think much addicted to swearing; one that swears more times than he speaks;[1] hand this man over to me for only ten days, and if I do not rid him of all his habit in these few days, pass the severest sentence on me.

21. And that these words are not a vain boast, shall be made manifest to you from things that have already happened. What could be more stupid than the Ninevites? What more devoid of understanding? Yet, nevertheless, these barbarian, foolish people, who had never yet heard any one teaching them wisdom, who had never received such precepts from others, when they heard the prophet saying, "Yet three days, and Nineveh shall be overthrown,"[2] laid aside, within three days, the whole of their evil customs. The fornicator became chaste; the bold man meek; the grasping and extortionate moderate and kind; the slothful industrious. They did not, indeed, reform one, or two, or three, or four vices by way of remedy, but the whole of their iniquity. But whence does this appear, says some one? From the words of the prophet; for the same who had been their accuser, and who had said, that "the cry of their wickedness hath ascended up even to heaven:"[3] himself again bears testimony of an opposite kind, by saying, "God saw that every one departed from their own evil ways."[4] He does not say, from fornication, or adultery, or theft, but from their "own evil ways." And how did they depart? As God knew, not as man judged of the matter. After this are we not ashamed, must we not blush, if it turns out that in three days only the barbarians laid aside all their wickedness, but that we, who have been urged and taught during so many days,[5] have not got the better of one bad habit? These men had, moreover, gone to the extreme of wickedness before; for when you hear it said, "The cry of their wickedness is come up before me;" you can understand nothing else than the excess of their wickedness. Nevertheless, within three days they were capable of being transformed to a state of complete[6] virtue. For where the fear of God is, there is no need of days, or of an interval of time; as likewise, on the contrary, days are of no service where there is a want of this fear. For just as in the case of rusted[7] implements, he that rubs them only with water, though he spend a long time on them, will not rid them of all that foulness; but he that puts them in a furnace, will make them presently brighter than even those newly fabricated: so too a soul, stained with the rust of sin, if it cleanse itself slightly, and in a negligent way, and be every day repenting, will gain no further advantage. But if it cast itself into the furnace, as it were, of the fear of God, it will in a very short time purge all away.

22. Let us not then be procrastinating till to-morrow. For we "know not what the next day may bring forth;"[8] nor let us say, "we shall conquer this habit by little and little;" since this little and little will never come to an end. Wherefore, dismissing that excuse, we should say, "If we do not reform the practice of swearing to-day, we will not leave off till we do,[9] though ten thousand things were to press us; though it were necessary to die, or to be punished, or to lose all we have; we will not give the devil the advantage of slackness, nor the pretext of delay." Should God perceive thy soul inflamed, and thy diligence quickened, then He also Himself will lend His assistance to thy reformation! Yea, I pray and beseech you, let us be in earnest, lest we also hear it said of us, "The men of Nineveh shall rise up, and shall condemn this generation;"[10] for these, when they had once heard, reformed themselves; but we are not converted after frequent hearing. These were proficients in every part of virtue, but we in no part. They when they heard that their city would be overthrown were affrighted; but we, though we have heard of Hell, are not affrighted: these, men who did not partake of the instructions of the prophets; we, enjoying the advantage of perpetual teaching, and of much grace.

23. These things I now speak to you, not as if reproving you for your own sins, but for the sake of others; for I know full well that by you (as I have already observed), this law concerning swearing has been accomplished. But this does not suffice for our safety, unless by teaching we amend others, since he who produced the one talent, restoring as he did the whole portion committed to him, was

---

[1] *i. e.*, more words than he can articulate. St. Chrysostom supposes here a man who in his wrath loses the power of distinct utterance. (Such may be the meaning, or, that he never speaks without several oaths, or oftener speaks with an oath than without one, πλείονα ὀμνύοντα μᾶλλον ἢ φθεγγόμενον.)
[2] Jonah ii. 4. [3] Jonah i. 5.
[4] Jonah iii 10. St. Chrysostom here of course supposes Jonah to be the *author* of the book which bears his name.
[5] He refers to his own instructions during Lent: see the close of this Homily.
[6] ὁλόκληρον, wanting no constituent part.
[7] Or vessels, τὰ ἰωθέντα τῶν σκευῶν. Ἰὸς also means "venom," and stains are taken out of rough earthenware in the same manner.
[8] Prov. xxvii. 1.
[9] οὐκ ἀποστησόμεθα πρότερον. *i. e.*, will not leave off the plan proposed above, of attending to nothing else till this was accomplished.
[10] Luke xi. 32.

punished, because he had not enriched that with which he was entrusted. Wherefore, let us not regard this point, that we ourselves have been set free from this sin; but until we have delivered others from it, let us not desist; and let every one offer to God ten friends whom he has corrected; whether thou hast servants, or apprentices:[1] or if you have neither servants, nor apprentices, you have friends; these do thou reform. Further, do not make me this reply; "We have banished oaths for the most part, and we are rarely caught in that snare;" but let even this rarity of offending be got rid of. If you had lost one piece of gold, would you not go about to all persons, searching and making enquiry, in order to find it? This do also with regard to oaths. If you perceive that you have been cheated out of one oath, weep, lament, as though your whole substance were lost. Again I say what I did before. Shut up thyself at home; make it a subject of practice and exercise along with thy wife, thy children, and domestics. Say to thyself in the first instance, " I must not put a finger to private or public matters until I have rectified this soul of mine." If you will thus school your own sons, they too will instruct their children in turn, and thus this discipline, reaching even to the consummation and appearing of Christ, will bring all that great reward to those who go to the root of the matter. If your son has learnt to say, "Believe me;"[2] he will not be able to go up to the theatre, or to enter a tavern, or to spend his time at dice; for that word, lying upon his mouth instead of a bridle, will make him however unwilling feel shame and blush. But if at any time he should appear in these places, it will quickly compel him to retreat.[3] Suppose some persons laugh. Do thou on the other hand weep for their transgression! Many also once laughed at Noah whilst he was preparing the ark; but when the flood came, he laughed at them; or rather, the just man never laughed at them at all, but wept and bewailed! When therefore thou seest persons laughing, reflect that those teeth, that grin now, will one day have to sustain that most dreadful wailing and gnashing, and that they will remember this same laugh on That Day whilst they are grinding and gnashing! Then thou too shalt remember this laugh! How did the rich man laugh at Lazarus! But afterwards, when he beheld him in Abraham's bosom, he had nothing left to do but to bewail himself!

24. Being mindful then of all these things, be urgent with all, for the speedy fulfilment of this precept. And tell me not, that you will do this by little and little; nor put it off till the morrow, for this to-morrow never finds an end. Forty days[4] have already passed away. Should the Holy Easter pass away, I will thenceforward pardon no one, nor employ further admonition, but a commanding authority, and severity not to be despised. For this apology drawn from custom is of no force. Why may not the thief as well plead custom, and get free from punishment? Why may not the murderer and adulterer? Therefore I protest, and give warning to all, that if, when I have met you in private, and put the matter to the proof (and I will certainly put it to the proof), I detect any who have not corrected this vice, I will inflict punishment upon them, by ordering them to be excluded from the Holy Mysteries;[5] not that they may remain always shut out, but that having reformed themselves, they may thus enter in, and with a pure conscience enjoy the Holy Table; for this is to be a partaker of the Communion! God grant that through the prayers of those who preside over us,[6] as well as of all the saints, having corrected these and all other deficiencies, we may obtain the kingdom of heaven through the grace and lovingkindness of our Lord Jesus Christ, with Whom to the Father, together with the Holy Spirit, be glory, honour, and adoration, now and ever, world without end. Amen.

---

[1] μαθητὰς. [2] πίστευσον.
[3] As one who could not talk like others.
[4] Forty days from Quinquagesima, leaving ten till Easter; see Pref.
[5] St. Ambrose (Life by Paulinus, sec. 34), forbade Theodosius to enter the church at all, after the massacre of Thessalonica. St. Basil refused *Communion* to Valens, who had joined the Arians, but did not attempt to prevent his entering the church, See St. Greg. Naz. Or. 20 (Ben. 43). He even allowed him to present an offering; but this was an indulgence. Offenders would be liable of course to Ecclesiastical censure, if they took a nearer place than was allowed them.
[6] τῶν προέδρων, a title of bishops. See Bingham, b. 2, c. 2, sec. 5. Flavian was probably not yet returned, but would be always supposed to pray for the people. The plural is sometimes used of a single person, especially one of dignity. Some other persons are called πατέρες in Hom. XVI., and in Hom. VI. probably departed saints, where see of the intercession of saints in general.

HOMILY XXI.

On the return of Flavian the Bishop, and the reconciliation of the Emperor with the city, and with[1] those who had offended in overthrowing the Statues.

1. TO-DAY, I shall begin with that very same saying with which I have ever been used to open my address to you during the season of danger, and shall say together with you, "Blessed be God," Who hath granted us this day to celebrate this holy Feast with much joy and gladness; and hath restored the head to the body, the shepherd to the sheep, the master to the disciples, the general to the soldiers, the High Priest to the Priests! Blessed be God, "Who doeth exceeding abundantly above what we ask or think!"[2] For to us it would have seemed sufficient, had we been but delivered from the hitherto impending evil; and for this we made all our supplication. But the God who loveth man, and ever in His giving surpasseth our prayers by an excess of bounty, hath brought back our Father too, sooner than we could at all have expected. Who would, indeed, have thought that in so few days, he would have gone, and have had audience with the Emperor, and set us free from the calamity, and again come back to us so quickly, as to be able to anticipate the Holy Passover, and to celebrate it with ourselves? Behold, however, this event, which was so contrary to expectation, hath been realized! We have received back our Father; and we enjoy so much the greater pleasure, inasmuch as we have received him back now beyond our hopes. For all these things, let us give thanks to the merciful God, and be amazed at the power, the lovingkindness, the wisdom, and the tender care which has been manifested on behalf of the city. For the devil had attempted its entire subversion through the daring crimes committed; but God, by means of this same calamity, hath adorned the city, the Priest, and the Emperor; and hath made them all more illustrious.

2. The city hath won renown, because when such a danger had overtaken her, passing by at once all those who were in power, those who were surrounded with much wealth, those who possessed great influence with the Emperor, it fled for refuge to the Church, and to the Priest of God, and with much faith, rested itself entirely upon the hope which is from above! Many indeed, after the departure of the common Father, were ready to terrify those who lay in prison, by saying, "The Emperor does not lay aside[3] his wrath, but is still more provoked, and is thinking of the utter ruin of the city." But whilst they were whispering all this, and much more, they who were then in bonds were not the least intimidated, but upon our saying, "These things are false, and they are a device of the devil, who desires to fill you with consternation;" they replied to us, "We need no consolation to be addressed to us; for we know where we have taken refuge from the first; and upon what hope we have rested ourselves. We have fixed our safety upon the sacred anchor! We have not entrusted this to man, but to the Almighty God; therefore we are most assuredly confident, that the result will be favourable; for it is impossible, truly impossible, that this hope can ever be confounded!" To how many crowns, how many encomiums, is this equivalent for our city? How much of God's favour will it draw down upon us too in our other affairs! For it is not, indeed it is not a thing belonging to a soul of mean order to be watchful against the attack of temptations, and to look to God; and scorning all that is human, to yearn after that Divine aid.

3. The city then hath thus won renown; and the Priest again not less than the city, for he exposed his life for all; and while there were many things to hinder him, as the winter, his age, the feast, and not less than these, his sister, then at her last breath, he raised himself above all these obstacles, and did not say to himself, "What a thing is this? Our only remaining sister, she who hath drawn the yoke of Christ along with me, and who hath been my domestic companion so long, is now at her last breath; and shall we desert her, and go hence, and not behold her expiring, and uttering her parting words? But she indeed was praying daily, that we might close her eyes,[4] and shut and compose her mouth, and attend to all other things

---
[1] Benedictine πρὸς, Savile εἰς, which rather implies a full stop after "city," and that the Homily contained an invective "against" the offenders. It does contain a very strong one obliquely.
[2] Eph. iii. 20.
[3] Sav. relax.
[4] Ducæus quotes *Il.* xi. 453, *Æn.* ix. 486, *Stat. Theb.* l. 2. *Alternâ clauserunt lumina dextrâ.* Plin. 22, 37; *Varro apud Nonium;* Sigil. as illustrating the custom of doing these offices for the dead among heathens.

pertaining to the burial; but now in this case, as one deserted, and deprived of a protector, she will obtain none of these offices from her brother; of him whom she especially desired to obtain them; but when she gives up the ghost, she will not see him whom she loved more to have with her than all others? And will not this be heavier to her than dying many times over? Yes, although I were far away, would it not be right to come with speed, and do, and suffer any thing, for the purpose of shewing her this kindness? And now when I am near, shall I leave her, and taking my departure abandon her? And how then will she sustain the remainder of her days?"

4. Yet, so far was he from saying any of these things, that he did not even think of them; but esteeming the fear of God above all the ties of kindred, he recognized the fact, that as tempests display the pilot, and dangers the general, so also a time of trial makes the Priest to become manifest. "All men," saith he, "are eagerly looking on us; the Jews as well as the Greeks; let us not confound the expectations which these have of us; let us not overlook so great a shipwreck; but having committed to God all things that pertain to ourselves, let us venture our life itself too!" Consider, moreover, the magnanimity of the Priest, and the lovingkindness of God! All those things which he disregarded, all those he enjoyed; in order that he might both receive the reward of his readiness, and that he might obtain a greater pleasure by enjoying them contrary to expectation! He preferred to celebrate the festival in a foreign place, and far from his own people, for the sake of the city's safety. But God restored him to us before the Paschal feast, so as to take a common part with us in the conduct of the festival; in order that he might have the reward of his choice, and enjoy the greater gladness! He feared not the season of the year; and there was summer during the whole period he was travelling. He took not his age into account; and he dispatched this long journey with just as much ease as if he had been young and sprightly! He thought not of his sister's decease nor was enervated by it, and when he returned he found her still alive, and all things which were disregarded by him, were all obtained!

5. Thus, the priest hath indeed won renown both with God and man! This transaction hath also adorned the Emperor with a splendour beyond the diadem! First, in that it was then made apparent that he would grant that to the priests which he would not to any other; secondly, that he granted the favour without delay, and quelled his resentment. But that you may more clearly understand the magnanimity of the Emperor, and the wisdom of the priest, and more than both these, the lovingkindness of God; allow me to relate to you a few particulars of the conference which took place. But what I am now about to relate I learnt from one of those who were within the palace; for the Father has told us neither much nor little on the affair; but ever imitating the magnanimity of Paul, he hides his own good deeds; and to those who on all sides were asking him questions as to what he said to the Emperor; and how he prevailed upon him; and how he turned away his wrath entirely, he replied, "We contributed nothing to the matter, but the Emperor himself (God having softened his heart), even before we had spoken, dismissed his anger, and quelled his resentment; and discoursing of the events that had taken place as if some other person had been insulted, he thus went over all the events that had happened without anger." But those things which he concealed from humility, God hath brought to light.

6. And what were these? I will proceed to relate them to you by going a little farther back in the story. When he went forth from the city, leaving all in such great despondency, he endured what was far more grievous than we ourselves suffered, who were in the midst of these calamities. For, in the first place, meeting in the midst of his journey with those who had been sent by the Emperor to make inquisition upon the events which had happened; and learning from them, on what terms they were sent; and reflecting upon the dreadful events that were in store for the city, the tumults, the confusion, the flight, the terror, the agony, the perils, he wept a flood of tears, and his bowels were rent with compassion; for with fathers, it is usual to grieve much more, when they are not able to be present with their suffering children; which was just what this most tender-hearted man now endured; not only lamenting the calamities which were in reserve for us, but that he was far away from us, whilst we were enduring them. But this was, however, for our safety. For as soon as he had learned these things from them; more warmly did the fountain of his tears then gush forth, and he betook himself to God with more fervent supplication; and spent his nights without sleep, beseeching Him that He would succour the city, while enduring these things, and make the mind of the Emperor more placable. And as soon as he came to that great city,

and had entered the royal palace, he stood before the Emperor at a distance,—speechless,—weeping,—with downcast eyes,—covering his face as if he himself had been the doer of all the mischief; and this he did, wishing first to incline him to mercy by his posture, and aspect, and tears; and then to begin an apology on our behalf; since there is but one hope of pardon for those who have offended, which is to be silent, and to utter nothing in defence of what has been done. For he was desirous that one feeling should be got rid of, and that another should take its place; that anger should be expelled, and sadness introduced,[1] in order that he might thus prepare the way for the words of his apology; which indeed actually took place. And just as Moses going up to the mount, when the people had offended, stood speechless himself, until God called him, saying, "Let me alone, and I will blot out this people;"[2] so also did he now act. The Emperor therefore, when he saw him shedding tears, and bending toward the ground, himself drew near; and what he really felt on seeing the tears of the priest, he made evident by the words he addressed to him; for they were not those of a person provoked or inflamed, but of one in sorrow; not of one enraged, but rather dejected, and under constraint of extreme pain.

7. And that this is true, ye will understand when ye hear what were his words. For he did not say, "What does this mean? Hast thou come heading an embassy on behalf of impious and abominable men, such as ought not even to live; on behalf of rebels,[3] of revolutionists, who deserve the utmost punishment?" But dismissing all words of that sort, he composed a defence of himself full of respectfulness and dignity; and he enumerated the benefits, which during the whole time of his reign he had conferred upon the city; and at each of these he said, "Was it thus I should have been treated in return for these things? What injuries had I done, that they should take such revenge? What complaint had they, great or small, that they must not insult me only, but the deceased also?[4] Was it not sufficient to wreak their resentment against the living? Yet they thought they were doing nothing grand, unless they insulted those now in their graves. Granting that I had injured them, as they suppose; surely it would have been becoming to spare the dead, who had done them no wrong; for they could not have the same complaint against them. Did I not ever esteem this city above every thing, and account it as dearer than my native place? And was it not a matter of my continual prayers to visit this city; and did I not make this my oath[5] to all men?"

8. Upon this, the priest sobbing bitterly, and shedding warmer tears, no longer kept silence: for he saw that the defence of the Emperor was raising our crime to a still higher amount; but heaving from the bottom of his heart[6] a deep and bitter sigh, he said, "We must confess, O Emperor, this love which you have shewn towards our country! We cannot deny it! On this account, especially, we mourn, that a city thus beloved has been bewitched by demons; and that we should have appeared ungrateful towards her benefactor, and have provoked her ardent lover. And although you were to overthrow; although you were to burn; although you were to put to death; or whatever else you might do, you would never yet have taken on us the revenge we deserve. We ourselves have, by anticipation, inflicted on ourselves what is worse than a thousand deaths! For what can be more bitter, than when we are found to have unjustly provoked our benefactor, and one who loved us so much, and the whole world knows it, and condemns us for the most monstrous ingratitude! If Barbarians had made an incursion on our city,[7] and razed its walls, and burnt its houses, and had taken and carried us away captive, the evil had been less. And why so? but because, whilst you live, and continue such a generous kindness towards us, there might be a hope that all these evils would be got rid of; and that we might again be brought back to our former condition, and regain a more illustrious liberty. But now, having been deprived of your favour, and having quenched your love, which was a greater security to us than any wall, whom have we left to fly to? Where else shall we have to look, when we have provoked so benign a lord, so indulgent a father? So that while they seem to have committed offences of the most intolerable kind, they have on the other hand suffered the most terrible evils; not daring to look any man in the face; nor being able to look upon the sun with free eyes; shame everywhere weighing down their eyelids, and compelling them to hide their heads! Deprived of their confidence, they are now in a more

---

[1] ἀθυμίαν here opposed to θυμὸν, and meaning especially such sadness as represses violent emotion.
[2] Exod. xxxii. 10.   [3] τυράννων.
[4] St. Chrysostom here alludes to the pulling down the statues of his wife and mother, which, together with his own and those of his two sons, were dragged about the streets of Antioch during the riot.
[5] He seems to mean some such expression as "so may I live to see Antioch."
[6] κάτωθεν.
[7] A kind of event then becoming familiar to the Roman world.

miserable condition than any captives, and undergo the umost dishonour; and whilst thinking of the magnitude of their evils, and the height of insolence to which they have rushed, they can scarce draw breath; inasmuch as they have drawn on their own heads severer reproaches from all the inhabitants of the world, than even from him who is seen to have been insulted.

9. But yet, O Emperor, if you are willing, there is a remedy for the wound, and a medicine for these evils, mighty as they are! Often, indeed, has it occurred amongst private individuals, that great and insufferable offences have become a foundation for great affection. Thus also did it happen in the case of our human race. For when God made man, and placed him in Paradise, and held him in much honour; the devil could not bear this his great prosperity, and envied him, and cast him out from that dignity which had been granted. But God was so far from forsaking him, that He even opened Heaven to us instead of Paradise; and in so doing, both shewed His own lovingkindness, and punished the devil the more severely. So do thou too now! The demons have lately used all their efforts, that they may effectually rend from your favour that city which was dearest of all to you. Knowing this then, demand what penalty you will, but let us not become outcasts from your former love! Nay, though it is a strange thing, I must say, display towards us now still greater kindness than ever; and again write this city's name among the foremost in your love;—if you are indeed desirous of being revenged upon the demons who were the instigators of these crimes! For if you pull down, and overturn, and raze the city, you will be doing those very things which they have long been desiring. But if you dismiss your anger, and again avow that you love it even as you did before, you have given them a deadly blow. You have taken the most perfect revenge upon them by shewing, not only that nothing whatever has come for them of their evil designs; but that all hath proved the very opposite of what they wished. And you would be just in acting thus, and in shewing mercy to a city, which the demons envied on account of your affection; for if you had not so exceedingly loved her, they would not have envied her to such a degree! So that even if what I have asserted is extraordinary, it is nevertheless, true, that what the city hath suffered, hath been owing to thee, and thy love! What burning, what devastation, so bitter as those words, which you uttered in your own defence?

10. You say now, that you have been insulted, and sustained wrongs such as no Emperor ever yet did. But if you will, O most gracious, most wise, and most religious Sovereign, this contempt will procure you a crown, more honourable and splendid than the diadem you wear! For this diadem is a display of your princely virtue, but it is also a token of the munificence of him who gave it; but the crown woven from this your humanity will be entirely your own good work, and that of your own love of wisdom; and all men will admire you less for the sake of these precious stones,[1] than they will applaud you for your superiority over this wrath. Were your Statues thrown down? You have it in your power again to set up others yet more splendid. For if you remit the offences of those who have done you injury, and take no revenge upon them, they will erect a statue to you, not one in the forum of brass, nor of gold, nor inlaid with gems; but one arrayed in that robe which is more precious than any material, that of humanity and tender mercy! Every man will thus set you up in his own soul; and you will have as many statues, as there are men who now inhabit, or shall hereafter inhabit, the whole world! For not only we, but all those who come after us, and their successors, will hear of these things, and will admire and love you, just as if they themselves had experienced this kindness!

11. And to shew that I do not speak this in a way of flattery, but that it will certainly be so, I will relate to you an ancient piece of history, that you may understand that no armies, nor warlike weapons, nor money, nor multitude of subjects, nor any other such things are wont to make sovereigns so illustrious, as wisdom of soul and gentleness. It is related of the blessed Constantine, that on one occasion, when a statue of himself had been pelted with stones, and many were instigating him to proceed against the perpetrators of the outrage; saying, that they had disfigured his whole face by battering it with stones, he stroked his face with his hand, and smiling gently, said, "I am quite unable to perceive any wound inflicted upon my face. The head appears sound, and the face also quite sound." Thus these persons, overwhelmed with shame, desisted from their unrighteous counsel.

This saying, even to the present day, all repeat; and length of time hath neither

---

[1] It is here evidently supposed that the Emperor appeared with the crown actually upon his head. The magnificence of the Emperor's appearance is dwelt upon at length by Chrysostom in other Homilies, though with different feelings from what Gibbon would insinuate. See c. xxxii. where he quotes the Homily on Perfect Charity (6). Also on Eph. iv. 1, Hom. IX.

weakened nor extinguished the memory of such exalted wisdom. How much more illustrious is such an action, than any number of warlike trophies! Many and great cities did he build, and many barbarous tribes did he conquer; not one of which we now remember; but this saying is repeated over and over again, to the present day; and those who follow us, as well as those who come after them, will all hear of it. Nor indeed is this the only admirable thing; that they will hear of it; but that when men speak of it, they do so with approbation and applause; and those who hear of it, receive it with the like; and there is no one who, when he has heard it, is able to remain silent, but each at once cries out, and applauds the man who uttered it, and prays that innumerable blessings may be his lot even now deceased. But if amongst men, this saying has gained him so much honour, how many crowns will he obtain with the merciful God!

12. And why need I speak of Constantine, and other men's examples, when it were fitting that I should exhort you by considerations nearer home, and drawn from your own praiseworthy actions. You remember how but lately, when this feast was near at hand, you sent an epistle to every part of the world; giving orders that the inmates of the prisons should be set free, and their crimes be pardoned. And as if this were not sufficient to give proof of your generosity, you said in your letters, "O that it were possible for me to recal and to restore those who are dead, and to bring them back to their former state of life!" Remember now these words. Behold the season of recalling and restoring the deceased, and bringing them back to former life! For these are indeed already dead, even before the sentence hath been pronounced; and the city hath now taken up its tabernacle at the very gates of Hades! Therefore raise it up again, which you can do without money, without expense, without loss of time or labour! It is sufficient merely for you to open your lips, and you will restore to life the city which at present lieth in darkness. Grant now, that henceforth it may bear an appellation derived from your philanthropy; for it will not be so much indebted to the kindness of him who first founded it, as it will be to your sentence. And this is exceedingly reasonable; for he but gave it its beginning, and departed; but you, when it had grown up and become great; and when it was fallen, after all that great prosperity; will have been its restorer. There would have been nothing so wonderful in your having delivered it from danger, when enemies had captured, and barbarians overrun it, as in your now sparing it. That, many of the Emperors have frequently done; but should you alone accomplish this, you will be first in doing it, and that beyond all expectation. And the former of these good deeds, the protection of your subjects, is not at all wonderful or extraordinary; but is one of those events which are of continual occurrence; but the latter, the dismissal of wrath after the endurance of such provocations, is something which surpasses human nature.

13. Reflect, that the matter now for your consideration is not respecting this city only, but is one that concerns your own glory; or rather, one that affects the cause of Christianity in general. Even now the Gentiles, and Jews, and the whole empire as well as the barbarians, (for these last have also heard of these events,) are eagerly looking to you, and waiting to see what sentence you will pronounce with regard to these transactions. And should you decree a humane and merciful one; all will applaud the decision, and glorify God, and say one to another, "Heavens! how great is the power of Christianity, that it restrains and bridles a man who has no equal upon earth; a sovereign, powerful enough to destroy and devastate all things; and teaches him to practice such philosophy as one in a private station had not been likely to display! Great indeed must be the God of the Christians, who makes angels out of men, and renders them superior to all the constraining force of our nature!"

14. Nor ought you, assuredly, to entertain that idle fear; nor to bear with those who say that other cities will become worse, and grow more contemptuous of authority, if this city goes unpunished. For if you were unable to take vengeance; and they, after doing these things, had forcibly defied you; and the power on each side was equally matched; then reasonably enough might such suspicions be entertained. But if, terrified and half dead with fear, they run to cast themselves at your feet, through me; and expect daily nothing else but the pit of slaughter, and are engaged in common supplications; looking up to heaven and calling upon God to come to their aid, and to favour this our embassy; and have each given charge about his private affairs, as if they were at their last gasp; how can such a fear be otherwise than superfluous? If they had been ordered to be put to death, they would not have suffered as much as they do now, living as they have done so many days in fear and trembling; and when the evening approaches, not expecting to behold the morning; nor when the day arrives, hop-

ing to reach the evening! Many too have fallen in with wild beasts, while pursuing their way through desert places, and removing to untrodden spots; and not men only, but also little children and women; free born, and of good condition; hiding themselves many days and nights in caves, and ravines, and holes of the desert! A new mode of captivity hath indeed befallen the city. Whilst the buildings and walls are standing, they suffer heavier calamities than when cities have been set on fire! Whilst no barbarian foe is present, whilst no enemy appears, they are more wretchedly situated than if actually taken; and the rustling only of a leaf scares them all every day! And these are matters which are universally known; so that if all men had seen the city razed to the ground, they would not have been taught such a lesson of sobriety, as by hearing of the calamities which have now befallen it. Suppose not, therefore, that other cities will be made worse in future! Not even if you had overturned other cities, would you have so effectually corrected them, as now, by this suspense concerning their fate, having chastised[1] them more severely than by any punishment!

15. Do not, then, carry this calamity any farther; but allow them henceforth to take breath again. For to punish the guilty, and to exact the penalty for these deeds, were easy and open to any one; but to spare those who have insulted you, and to pardon those who have committed offences undeserving of pardon, is an act of which only some one or two are capable; and especially so, where the person treated with indignity is the Emperor. It is an easy matter to place the city under the subjection of fear; but to dispose all to be loving subjects; and to persuade them to hold themselves well affected towards your government; and to offer not only their common, but individual prayers for your empire; is a work of difficulty. A monarch might expend his treasures, or put innumerable troops in motion, or do what else he pleased, but still he would not be able to draw the affections of so many men towards himself as may now very easily be done. For they who have been kindly dealt with, and those who hear of it too, will be well affected towards you, even as the recipients of the benefit. How much money, how many labours would you not have expended to win over to yourself the whole world in a short space of time; and to be able to persuade all those men who are now in existence, as well as all future generations, to invoke upon your head the same blessings which they pray for on behalf of their own children! And if you will receive such a reward from then, how much greater will you have from God! And this, not merely from the events which are now taking place, but from those good deeds which shall be performed by others in time to come. For if ever it should be that an event similar to what has now occurred should take place, (which God forbid!) and any of those who have been treated with indignity, should then be consulting about prosecuting measures against the rioters; your gentleness and moral wisdom will serve them instead of all other teaching and admonition; and they will blush and be ashamed, having such an example of wisdom, to appear inferior. So that in this way you will be an instructor to all posterity; and you will obtain the palm amongst them, even although they should attain to the highest point of moral wisdom! For it is not the same thing for a person to set the first example of such meekness himself, and by looking at others, to imitate the good actions they have performed. On this account, whatever philanthropy, or meekness, those who come after you may display, you will enjoy the reward along with them; for he who provides the root, must be considered the source of the fruits. For this reason, no one can possibly now share with you the reward that will follow your generosity, since the good deed hath been entirely your own. But you will share the reward of all those who shall come after, if any such persons should make their appearance; and it will be in your power to have an equal share in the merit of the good work along with them, and to carry off a portion as great as teachers have with scholars. And supposing that no such person should come into being, the tribute of commendation and applause will be accumulating to you throughout every age.

16. For consider, what it is for all posterity to hear it reported, that when so great a city had become obnoxious to punishment and vengeance, that when all were terrified, when its generals, its magistrates and judges, were all in horror and alarm, and did not dare to utter a word on behalf of the wretched people; a single old man, invested with the priesthood of God, came and moved the heart of the Monarch by his mere aspect and intercourse; and that the favour which he bestowed upon no other of his subjects, he granted to this one old man, being actuated by a reverence for God's laws! For in this very thing, O Emperor, that I have been sent hither on this embassy, the city hath done you no small honour; for they have thus

---

[1] αὐτούς, "the Antiochenes." Some read αὐτάς, "the cities," which does not make so good sense.

pronounced the best and the most honourable judgment on you, which is, that you respect the priests of God, however insignificant they may be, more than any office placed under your authority!

17. But at the present time I have come not from these only, but rather from One who is the common Lord of angels and men, to address these words to your most merciful and most gentle soul, "If ye forgive men their debts, your heavenly Father will forgive you your trespasses."[1] Remember then that Day when we shall all give an account of our actions! Consider that if you have sinned in any respect, you will be able to wipe away all offences by this sentence[2] and by this determination, and that without difficulty and without toil. Some when they go on an embassy, bring gold, and silver, and other gifts of that kind. But I am come into your royal presence with the sacred laws; and instead of all other gifts, I present these; and I exhort you to imitate your Lord, who whilst He is daily insulted by us, unceasingly ministers His blessings to all! And do not confound our hopes, nor defeat our promises.[3] For I wish you withal to understand, that if it be your resolution to be reconciled, and to restore your former kindness to the city, and to remit this just displeasure, I shall go back with great confidence. But if you determine to cast off the city, I shall not only never return to it, nor see its soil again, but I shall in future utterly disown it, and enrol myself a member of some other city; for God forbid that I should ever belong to that country, which you, the most mild and merciful of all men, refuse to admit to peace and reconciliation!

18. Having said this, and much more to the same effect, he so overcame the Emperor, that the same thing occurred which once happened to Joseph. For just as he, when he beheld his brethren, longed to shed tears, but restrained his feeling, in order that he might not spoil the part which he was playing;[4] even so did the Emperor mentally weep, but did not let it be seen, for the sake of those who were present. He was not, however, able to conceal the feeling at the close of the conference; but betrayed himself, though against his will. For after this speech was finished, no further words were necessary, but he gave utterance to one only sentiment, which did him much more honour than the diadem. And what was that? "How, said he, "can it be any thing wonderful or great, that we should remit our anger against those who have treated us with indignity; we, who ourselves are but men; when the Lord of the universe, having come as He did on earth, and having been made a servant for us, and crucified by those who had experienced His kindness, besought the Father on behalf of His crucifiers, saying, "Forgive them, for they know not what they do?"[5] What marvel, then, if we also should forgive our fellow-servants! And that these words were not a pretence was proved by all that followed. And not the least, that particular circumstance which I am now about to mention; for this our priest, when he would have remained there, and celebrated the feast together with himself, he urged, though contrary to what he would have wished,—to use all speed, and diligence, to present himself to his fellow-citizens. "I know," said he, "that their souls are still agitated; and that there are many relics of the calamity left. Go, give them consolation! If they see the helmsman, they will no longer remember the storm that has passed away; but all recollection of these sorrowful events will be effaced!" And when the Priest was urgent, entreating him to send his own son, he, wishing to give the most satisfactory proof of his having entirely blotted out from his soul every wrathful feeling, answered; "Pray that these hindrances may be taken out of the way; that these wars may be put an end to;[6] and then I will certainly come myself."

19. What could be gentler than such a soul? Let the Gentiles henceforward be ashamed; or rather, instead of being ashamed, let them be instructed; and leaving their native error, let them come back[7] to the strength of Christianity, having learned what our philosophy is, from the example of the Emperor and of the Priest! For our most pious Emperor stayed not at this point; but when the Bishop had left the city, and come over the sea, he dispatched thither also certain persons, being most solicitous and painstaking to prevent any waste of time lest the city should be thus deprived of half its pleasure, whilst the bishop was celebrating the feast beyond its walls. Where is the gracious father that would have so busied himself on behalf of those who had insulted him? But I must mention another circum-

---

[1] Matt. vi. 12.
[2] No one who knows St. Chrysostom will suppose that he means by this to exclude the other conditions of a sincere repentance, as of course our Lord did not, in the saying just before quoted, which is equally unqualified.
[3] Perhaps referring to promises the bishop had made to his flock, of what they might expect from his intercession.
[4] τὴν ὑπόκρισιν, i.e., his counterfeited ignorance of his brethren.
[5] Luke xxiii. 34.
[6] The allusion is to the war with Maximus, who had been acknowledged Emperor of Spain, Gaul and Britain, but was now trying to wrest Italy from the rule of Valentinian II.
[7] As being God's creatures, and having departed from Him.

stance that redounds to the praise of the just man.[1] For when he had accomplished this, he did not make it his endeavour, as any one else might have done, who was fond of glory, to deliver those letters himself, which were to set us free from the state of dejection in which we were; but since he was journeying at too slow a rate for this, he thought proper to send forward another person in his stead; one among those who were skilled in horsemanship, to be the bearer of the good news to the city;[2] lest its sadness should be prolonged by the tardiness of his arrival. For the only thing he earnestly coveted was this; not that he might come himself, bringing these favourable tidings, so full of all that is delightful, but that our country might as soon as possible breathe freely again.

20. What therefore ye then did, in decking the forum with garlands; lighting lamps, spreading couches[3] of green leaves before the shops, and keeping high festival, as if the city had just come into being, this do ye, although in another manner, throughout all time;—being crowned, not with flowers, but with virtue;—kindling in your souls the light which comes from good works; rejoicing with a spiritual gladness. And let us never fail to give God thanks continually for all these things, not only that he hath freed us from these calamities, but that he also permitted them to happen; and let us acknowledge his abundant goodness! for by both these has He adorned our city.[4] Now all these things according to the prophetic saying, "Declare ye to your children; and let your children tell their children; and their children again another generation."[5] So that all who shall be hereafter, even to the consummation, learning this act of God's lovingkindness towards the city, may call us blessed, in having enjoyed such a favour;—may marvel at our Sovereign, who raised up the city when it was so grievously falling;—and may themselves be profited, being stimulated to piety by means of all which has happened! For the history of what has lately happened to us, will have power to profit not only ourselves, if we constantly remember it, but also those who shall come after us. All these things then being considered, let us always give thanks to God who loveth man; not merely for our deliverance from these fearful evils, but for their being permitted to overtake us,—learning this from the divine Scriptures, as well as from the late events that have befallen us; that He ever disposes all things for our advantage, with that lovingkindness which is His attribute, which God grant, that we may continually enjoy, and so may obtain the kingdom of heaven, in Christ Jesus our Lord; to whom be glory and dominion for ever and ever. Amen.

---

[1] The bishop.
[2] Comp. what is said of Cæsarius, Lib. Reiske. t. i. p. 691. This may relate to a different occasion, as it seems likely that there were two rescripts, the second of which conveyed the *full* pardon.
[3] στιβάδας. Cave, in his life of St. Chrysostom, has rendered it, "the doors and shop windows set off with flowers and green branches;" but this seems purely fanciful; the word *stibadium* among the Romans meant a couch of particular construction, which allowed seven or eight to recline upon it at supper. These were probably temporary couches, made of, or strewed with, green leaves, for a public feast. (Libanius mentions this feasting, and praises the sympathy and good nature of Hellebichus on the occasion. His mention of a *fish* may be connected with the fast. *Or. ad Helleb. fin.*)
[4] *i. e.*, both by sending the calamity and by delivering from it.
[5] Joel i. 3.

INDEXES.

INDEX OF SUBJECTS.

For Pages 1 to 317.

(EXCLUSIVE OF HOMILIES ON THE STATUES.)

AARON, his office no palliation of his sin, 61.
Abel, unharmed by death, 273.
Adam, fall of, due to his slothfulness, 181, 195, 273.
Advent, the second, 180.
Adversity not really terrible, 290.
Afflictions, part of God's providential dealings, 182.
Ahab, God's mercy in dealing with, 95.
Angels, guard the dying Communicant's soul, 76; present at the Liturgy, 76; their character, 73.
Anger, ill effects of in a priest, 51.
Anomœans, heresy of, referred to, 147.
Apostles, unity of their doctrine, 136.
Applause in church deprecated by Chrysostom, 223.
Aquila, friend of St. Paul, referred to, 150.
Arcadius, Eastern Emperor referred to, 245, 251, 252; embassy on behalf of Chrysostom, 308.
Aristides, referred to, 126.
Arius, his heresy, 66, n.
Armenia, severity of winter in, 293.
Arsacius, usurper of the See of Constantinople, 288.
Attendance at church, neglect of, rebuked by Chrysostom, 224, 225.
Atticus, usurper of the See of Constantinople, 302.
Ausis, Uz so called in the Septuagint, 165, n.

BABYLAS, ST., removal of his bones ordered by Julian, 142; effect of this on shrine of Apollo, 143.
Baptism, clerical described, 165; called a "seal," 171, n.; requirements for right reception of, 167; sins hidden in, 168; different names given to, 160, 161.
Basil, his friendship with Chrysostom, 33, 34; entrapped by Chrysostom into ordination, 35; his remonstrances, 36-44.
Beauty, corporeal and spiritual contrasted, 102-104, 264.

Bishops, unsatisfactory mode of electing, 50, 53, 54, n.; difficult duties of, 58, 59; share the punishment of those on whom they lay hands suddenly, 63.
Bishopric, age at which men were eligible for a, 36, n.
Burial of the dead, a human instinct, 142.

CÆSAREA and Cappadocia, Chrysostom's visit to, 299.
Cain more unhappy than Abel, 274.
Canaan, the woman of, referred to, 154, 216.
Childlessness not to be regarded as retribution for sin, 238.
Chrysostom, St., his friendship with Basil, 33, 34; his purpose to enter monastic retreat, 34; remonstrances of his mother, 34; entraps Basil into ordination, but avoids it himself, 35, justifies his conduct in so doing, 37, 38, 42-46, 49, 53; his conflict with the passions of the soul, 80; his despondency and alarm at the prospect of ordination, 81, 82; his reasons for adopting a secluded life, 81; protects Eutropius, 247 maintains the Church's right of asylum, 250, 251; his condition in exile, 293, 296, 297, 299, 300; appeals to Innocent Bishop of Rome, 307; his letters to Innocent, 309-313.
Chromatius, Bishop of Aquileia, Chrysostom writes to, 307.
Church (as a building) duty of bringing men to the, 225-227; a surgery for souls, 235, 236; (as the Christian body) various names of the, 256.
Circumcision, a name given to baptism, 161.
Communion, holy, the obligations which it lays on the recipient, 166.
Constans, Emperor, 124, n.
Constantia, wife of Gratian, 125, n.
Constantine, the younger, 124, n.
Contradictions, some supposed in the Gospels, how to be explained, 214.
Cross, signing oneself with the sign of, 171; the power of, 171; an offence and a blessing, 189; of Christ, prefigured and predicted, 202; in what sense desired by Him, 203, 204; why deprecated by Him, 205.
Custom, the power of, 164.
Cyriacus, deacon, emissary from Chrysostom to Innocent, 309.

DANIEL, in the lion's den referred to, 225.
Daphne, a suburb of Antioch containing shrine of Apollo, 142.
David, his fall and repentance, 112; his treatment of Saul, 230, 231.
Deceit, when justifiable, 37, 38.
Demetrius, Bishop of Pesinus, emissary from Chrysostom to Innocent, 309, 310.
Demons, conduct of, at Gadara, and in the case of Job, specimens what their government of the world would be, 183, 184; powerless without God's permission, 197.
Departed, prayers for the, 76, n.
Despair, the devil's instrument to work man's ruin, 92, 93, 97, 106, 107.
Devil, the, evil by choice and not by nature, 197; existence of the, permitted for the sake of the Christian athlete, 197; only mischievous to the slothful, 198; used by St. Paul as an executioner, 189; why called "apostate," 188; why called "the Devil," 188; why called "the wicked one," 188.
Dignity, offices of, in God's kingdom entail responsibility, 62.
Diodorus of Tarsus, instructor of Chrysostom, 87.
Diogenes, referred to, 126.
Domestic cares described, 115.

EARNEST of the Spirit, meaning of the, 261.

Eli, his inherited office no palliation of his sin, 61.
Elisha, his wonder-working sepulchre, 140.
Enemies, St. Paul's advice how to treat, 228; vengeance on, not to be invoked, 241.
Epaminondas, referred to, 126.
Eucharist, the Holy, teaching of Chrysostom concerning, 46, 47, n.
Eutropius, sketch of his life, 245–247; quits the asylum of the Church, 253.
Eve, her fall, her own fault, 194; the better for her expulsion from Paradise, 180, 181.
Evil, two senses in which the word is to be understood, 188; a form of, peculiar to each thing, 272.
Evils, inward not outward the ruin of man, 279; why permitted by God to come to extremity, 290.
Exile, no injury, 274.

Faith, different degrees of, 215, 216.
Festival days, large attendance at Church on, 226.
Flacilla, Empress, wife of Theodosius, 125, n.
Forgiveness of injuries, duty of, 229–232.

Gainas, Gothic general, demands surrender of Eutropius, 246.
Gallus Cæsar, reference to, 124, n.
God, not chargeable with our sins, 61; the patience and lovingkindness of, 93; His merciful dealings with Nebuchadnezzar, 94; Ahab, 95; Hezekiah, 105; the Ninevites, 105; His moral government of the world indicated, 184, 185; His ways past finding out, 186; language descriptive of, accommodated to human mind, 256–258.
Good, a greater power than evil, 191.
Goths, incursions of, 119, 125.
Gratian, Emperor, 125, n.
Gregory, of Nazianzus, his friendship for Olympias, 287.

Hadrianople, battle of, referred to, 119, 125.
Heaven, the joys of, 99, 100, 102; degrees of glory in, 111.
Hell, not made for man, 97; nature of sufferings in, 98, 99; degrees of punishment in, 111.
Hermione, a young lady beloved by Theodore, 87, 103.
Hezekiah, God's merciful dealing with, 105.
Holy Scripture, consolations of the, under all forms of trial, 219, 220; advantages of studying, 252.
Holy Spirit, invocation of, in the Liturgy, 76, n.; His enlightenment of the soul, 166.
Honorius, Emperor, Innocent appeals to on behalf of Chrysostom, 307; writes to Arcadius on behalf of Chrysostom, 308.
Hope never to be abandoned in this world, 97.
Houses, comparison of the, on a rock and sand referred to, 279.
Humility, the benefits of, 148.
Hunger, the best sauce, 276.

Ignatius, St., difficulties and dangers of his Episcopate, 137; personifies St. Paul's ideal of the Christian bishop, 136; his last journey to Rome, 139; his martyrdom, 139; miracles wrought at his sepulchre, 140; removal of his bones to Antioch, 140 meaning of his name Theophorus, 135, n.
Illumination, a name for baptism, 159, n., 161.
Incarnation, the, predicted, 205; reality of, how proved, 205; figurative descriptions of in Holy Scripture, 258–265.
Indolence, the mother of despair, 106.
Innocent, Bishop of Rome, Chrysostom appeals to, 307; appeal of, to Honorius, 307; Chrysostom's letters to, 309–313; his letters to Chrysostom and the Church of Constantinople, 313, 314.
Isaac, perseverance of in prayer, 240.
Isaurians, a predatory tribe, incursions of, 293, 299.

Jesus Christ, desired the Cross, 203; rebuked St. Peter, 203; His will identical with God the Father's, 204; His power equal, 218; the incidents of His passion recounted, 291; His sufferings a stumbling-block to many, 290, 292.
Jews, not saved by reason of their privileges, 280, 283.
Job, his thanksgiving amidst affliction, 183; consideration of his case a consolation in pain and peril, 195, 196; his ignorance of the reason of his afflictions, 195; his saintliness not to be urged as impossible for us, 197; his sufferings in mind, body and estate, 195, 196; his temptation contrasted with that of Adam, 194; the devil unable to injure, 255; unharmed by the devil, 273; his sufferings unmitigated, 294.
John, St., story of his meeting the robber-chief, 109.
John the Baptist, unharmed by death, 274.
Joseph, the removal of his bones, 142, 161; unharmed by afflictions, 294.
Jovian, Emperor, his death referred to, 124, n.
Judas Iscariot, his apostleship no palliation of his sin, 61; ruined by despair, 97; not benefited by privileges, 279.
Judgment, why all do not receive it here, 184; the last, observations on, 101, 102.
Julian, Emperor, referred to, 141, 142.

Kingdom, the heavenly, various ways of entering, 262.
Krates, Cynic philosopher referred to, 126, n.

Lazarus, parable of Dives and, 98, 236; not injured by poverty, 273, 278; his reward proportioned to his sufferings, 295.
Love, supreme, importance of in a pastor, 39, 40.
Lovingkindness of God, instances of, 94–96; inexpressible, 180.
Lupicinus, Bishop of Appiaria, emissary from Chrysostom to Theophilus, 310.

Man, his expulsion from Paradise more than redressed by God, 185.
Manasses, his repentance accepted, 95.
Manichæans, their heresy, 65, 205.
Marcion, his heresy, 65, 205.
Marriage, honourable, 113.
Maruthas, Bishop of Martyropolis in Persia, 302.
Meletius, Bishop of Antioch, his zeal for the sepulchre of St. Babylas, 143.
Modesty, the true female adornment, 169.
Mopsuestia, Theodore, Bishop of, 87.
Moses, held responsible though he had deprecated his office, 61; referred to, 106.
Mother, of Chrysostom, referred to, 122.

Nebuchadnezzar, God's merciful dealings with, 94, 95.
Nero, Emperor, referred to, 149, 152.
Nicæa, Canons of, 314.
Nineveh, men of, at the Judgment, 193.
Ninevites, their repentance accepted, 95, 105, 281.

Olympias, deaconess, treatise addressed to her, 269; sketch of her life, 287, 288; letters to and from Chrysostom, 289–303.
Omens, the folly of, 170.
Ordinations, compulsory, 35, n.

Pansophius, a Bishop, emissary from Chrysostom to Innocent, 309.
Pappus, a Bishop, emissary from Chrysostom to Innocent, 309.
Parables, lessons of, 96, 98; of the leaven, 192; of the sheep and the kids, 193; of the Ten Vir-

gins, 193; of the unprofitable servant, 192, 193.
Paradise, the expulsion from, a mark of Divine love, 180; the loss of, compensated by greater blessings, 180.
Paralytic, the (a) by the pool of Bethesda, 211, 212; the (b) let down through the roof, 214; the latter not to be confused with the former, 215; faith of the latter, 216; reasons why Christ absolved him before healing him, 217.
Paul, St., his zeal and humility, 48; knowledge of the word of God essential to his work, 64; panegyric on his life and labours, 66, 67; what is meant by his being "rude in speech," 67; the power of his epistles, 68; his deference to popular suspicion, 79; his dealings with the Corinthian sinner, 96; his imprisonment at Rome, 149; his care for the Churches, 149; Epistle to the Hebrews quoted as his, 161; on the power of baptism, 161, 162; his imprisonment at Philippi, 225; compared to a training master of wrestlers, 228; his advice concerning treatment of enemies, 229; not injured by afflictions, 279; learned to rejoice in hardship, 295.
Paul of Samosata, his heresy, 66, n.
Paulus, a deacon, emissary from Chrysostom to Innocent, 309.
Peter, St., pastoral charge of Christ to, 39, 40; Bishop of Antioch, 138; his martyrdom at Rome, 139; "the leader of the Apostles," 167; rebuked by Christ, 203.
Pharetrius, Bishop of Cæsarea, an enemy to Chrysostom, 299.
Pharisee and Publican, parable of referred to, 147.
Phineas, referred to, 113.
Phœnician, story of a young, 107, 108.
Plato, his argument to prove immortality of the soul, 269, 270.
Poor, the, relish food more than the rich, 276, 277.
Poverty, no bar to piety, 168; good or evil according to the use made of it, 236; unable to injure the good, 274.
Prayer, perseverance in necessary, 153, 154; the power of, 237; slackness in reproved, 240; for vengeance on enemies rebuked, 241.
Preacher, the, his need of fluency, and constant study, 71; of indifference to praise, 70, 73; of indifference to slander and envy, 71, 72; the proper aim of his sermons to please God, 73.
Pride, the evils of, 148.
Priest, the Christian, greater than the Jewish, 48; power of the, greater than that of parents, 48; moral dangers which beset the, 49, 50; sobriety and self-control needful in, 51; his life contrasted with that of the recluses, 75-77; his need of purity, 76; his relations towards God, and his flock, 75; his social intercourse with the women of his flock, 78, 79.
Priesthood, supreme importance of the, 40; difficulties of the, 41; careful scrutiny of character needed for the, 42; sanctity of the, 46, 47; knowledge of the word of God essential for the, 64; not to be undertaken rashly or merely on solicitation, 62, 63; penalties when the office is ill-discharged, 64; enemies of the, 65, 66.
Priscilla, wife of Aquilla, referred to, 150.
Prodigal Son, parable of the, 96.
Punishment, the remedial discipline of temporal, 186.

RACHEL, wife of Jacob, 238.
Readers, their lives contrasted with that of the priest, 75-77.
Rebecca, wife of Isaac, 238.
Redemption, our, by the blood of Jesus Christ, 170.
Regeneration, laver of, 161, 162.
Repentance, instances of, accepted, 94-96, 103-106, 108; ruined by despair, 92, 93, 97, 106, 107; five different ways of: almsgiving; forgiveness; humility; prayer; self-condemnation, 190.
Resurrection of Jesus Christ, evidence for, in the life of St. Ignatius, 139.
Rich, the, often pay less heed than the poor to Holy Scripture, 235.
Riches, good or evil according to the use made of them, 236; of no use in time of danger, 254; the evils of, 275-277.
Rufinus, chief minister at the court of Constantinople, 245.

SABELLIUS, his heresy, 66, n.
Saints, their presence wholesome for the wicked, 192.
Salvation, not profitable to the careless, 189.
Sarah, wife of Abraham, 238, 239.
Sardica, the Council of, 314.
Satan, his methods of warfare, 82; "I renounce thee" a Christian watchword, 170, 171.
Saul, accountable for his acts as king, though he had deprecated the throne, 61; king of Israel referred to, 113; his treatment of David, 230.
Seal, a name for baptism, 171.
Severus, a presbyter, emissary from Chrysostom to Theophilus, 310.
Sheep, parable of the lost, 96.
Sin, the only real object of fear, 254; the only real source of misery, 255; the only thing really injurious, 289.
Sinners, not rewarded according to their iniquity and why, 185; why they are left in the world, 191, 192.
Soldiers, secular compared with soldiers of Christ, 168.
Spirit, earnest of the Holy, meaning of, 261.
Stoics, the, referred to, 65, n.
Swearing: custom, sin, and danger of: conquest of habit of, 163, 164.

THEODORE, of Mopsuestia, friend of Chrysostom, 87; letters to, 91-116.
Theodore, of Sicily, a usurper, 124, n.
Theodosius, Emperor, referred to, 119, 125; tries to force Olympia to marry, 287.
Theophilus, Patriarch of Alexandria, his intrigues against Chrysostom, 307, 309-311.
Therasius, Chrysostom consoles the widow of, 121-128.
Three Children, the, unharmed by trials, 281-283, 290.
Timothy, St., infirmities of, 295.
Tongues, confusion of, at Babel, 183; a mark of God's lovingkindness, 182.
Transfiguration, the, of Christ, described, 100.
Trials, benefits of, 212; Divine help under, 212, 213.
Tribigild, revolt of, 246.

UNMERCIFUL servant, parable of the, 241, 278.

VAINGLORY, danger of in priests, 49.
Valens, Emperor, his defeat of the Goths, 119, 125.
Valentinus, his heresy, 205.
Venerius, Bishop of Milan, Chrysostom writes to, 307.
Virgin Mary, the, 239.
Virgins, of the Church, difficulties in the care of, 56-58.
Virtue, the, of anything, what is meant by, 272; of man, what it is, 273.

WEALTH, the snares of, 126.
Widows, of the Church, difficulties in the care of, 55; St. Paul's instructions respecting, 122.
Women, intrusion of, into ecclesiastical affairs, 49.
World, only mischievous to the careless, 188; order in the natural, forbids our ascribing its government to Demons, 184.
Worldly honours, precarious nature of, 127.
Wrestling, illustration from the practice of trainers in, 228.
Wrongs, they who inflict them more injured than they who receive them, 274.

INDEX OF TEXTS.

For Pages 1 to 317.

(EXCLUSIVE OF HOMILIES ON THE STATUES.)

	PAGE		PAGE		PAGE		PAGE
Gen. iii. 1, 4	194	2 Kings ix. 12.	38	Ps. xcv. 8.	165	Isa. xl. 6, 7	251
iii. 12	113	xiii. 21	140	xcv. 9.	95	xl. 8	253
iv. 1.	180	xix. 34	105	xcviii. 1	256	xl. 12	258
iv. 7.	192	xxvii. 19.	38	cii. 4	251	xliii. 26	106, 190
iv. 25	181	2 Chron. xxxiii. 10-19	95	civ. 24.	188	xlv. 7	182
iv. 12	217	Job i. 1.	165	civ. 32.	205	l. 7, 8.	290
vi. 7.	256	i. 9, 11, 16	187	cv. 37.	280	li. 9.	256
vi. 9.	191	i. 21, 183, 220, 253, 274		cvii. 42	44	li. 10	258
xi. 6.	181	ii. 4	294	cx. 1	202	liii. 2.	205
xviii. 1-8	295	ii. 5, 6.	189	cxii. 9.	254	liii. 5-8, 12	203
xxii. 3	38	vi. 7, 8	196	cxiii. 7-9.	91	liii. 7, 8	202
xl. 14	159	vii. 14.	196	cxxiii. 2, 3	92	lv. 8	106
xlix. 9	202, 205	ix. 25.	114	cxxix. 3	185	lvii. 17	95
Ex. iv. 13	61	ix. 31.	196	cxxxi. 1	231	lix. 2.	96
xi. 2.	38	x. 9.	260	cxlii. 2, 3.	163	lxiv. 4.	102
xiii. 19	142	xix. 5, 9, 10, 14, 16	196	cxlvi. 9	121	lxv. 24	64
xxiii. 10, 11	61	xl. 4, 5, 8	196	Prov. ix. 12	191	Jer. iii. 2	103
xxiii. 15	227	xlii. 5, 6	196	x. 19.	168	iii. 3	41
xxviii. 4	46	Ps. ii. 1, 2.	202	xv. 1.	51	iii. 7	106
xxxiii. 11	62	ii. 7, 8, 9.	162	xviii. 17.	109	viii. 4.	96, 114
Lev. iv. 3, 14.	80	ii. 9	259	xviii. 19.	150	ix. 1	91
xxi. 9.	80	iv. 4	101	xviii. 21.	163	xv.	294
Num. xi. 15	61	iv. 16, 17.	227	xxv. 21, 22.	230	xix. 11.	162
xii. 3	62	vi. 2	259	xxvi. 11.	110	xxiii. 23	96
xx. 12	61	vi. 5	93	xxvii. 6.	249	xxxviii. 6.	225
xxv. 7	38	xvi. 11.	202	xxvii. 7.	276	Ezek. xvi. 33	103
xxv. 7, 11	113	xxiv. 1	212	Eccles. viii. 1.	169	xxxiv. 17	80
Deut. v 29	106	xxxii. 5	190	xii. 13.	165	xxxvii.	142
x. 12	106	xxxvi. 6	66	Isa. i. 14	256	Dan. i. 10	282
xix. 21.	231	xxxvii. 2.	251	vi. 5	178	ii.	94
1 Sam. ix. 21	61	xxxvii. 5.	178	vii. 14.	205	iii. 16-18	283
x. 33	40	xli. 9.	202	viii. 18	166	iv. 27.	94, 190
xv.	113	xliv. 23	256	ix. 6	205	vi. 24.	225
xix. 12-18	37	xlv. 10	257	xi. 1	205	vii. 9, 10	101
xx. 11	37	xlv. 12	103	xiii. 9, 13.	101	vii. 10	114
xx. 23.	230	xlvii. 5	202	xviii. 6	162	vii. 13-15	101
xxvi. 8	230	xlix. 6.	113	xxiv. 19-22	101	x. 6	104
xxvi. 11	230	lxviii. 5	122	xxvi. 12	217	Hos. vi. 2	121
1 Kings viii. 39	218	lxxii. 6	205	xxxii. 4	92	vi. 6.	252
xi. 3, 4	112	lxxviii. 34.	182	xxxiii. 2	256	Amos ii. 11	80
xi. 11.	105	lxxxi. 16	276	xxxiv. 4	101	iii. 2.	80
xi. 12, 13	112	lxxxii. 6	257	xxxv. 10	99	iii. 6.	182
xvii. 12	275	lxxxiii. 5	202	xl. 1, 2	217	Jonah i. 2	214, 281
xviii. 34.	38	xcv. 2.	109	xl. 5	124	iii. 4	105
xxi. 29	95	xcv. 4.	205	xl. 6	290	iii. 4, 10	281

> # INDEX OF TEXTS FOR PAGES 1 TO 317.

	PAGE		PAGE		PAGE		PAGE
Jonah iii. 9, 10	106	Matt. xv. 22, 26, 28.	154	Luke xxiii. 43.	181, 264	Rom. ii. 6	111
Micah vii. 18	218	xvi. 18	253	John i. 5	166	ii. 13, 19, 21	227
Haggai ii. 10	103	xvi. 22, 23.	203	i. 8, 9	256	v. 3.	275
Zech. xii. 10	202	xvi. 26.	113	ii. 19	202	v. 3, 4	303
Mal. iii. 2, 3	101	xvi. 27.	193	ii. 25.	218, 291	v. 10.	204
Wisd. ii. 15	192	xvii. 2	258	iii. 16	39, 214	vi. 4, 6	161
xiii. 5	185	xvii. 2, 4	100	iii. 26	291	viii. 7	103
Ecclus. i. 1, 2.	212	xvii. 15.	216	iv. 14	225	viii. 21	100
ii. 10	126	xviii. 6.	75	iv. 38	137	viii. 24	92
iv. 8	56	xviii. 18	47	v. 5, 14	185	viii. 27	218
v. 8	114, 190	xviii. 23–35	278	v. 7, 14	213	viii. 29	166
xi. 5	127	xviii. 28	241	v. 13.	216	viii. 32.	40, 263
xvi. 3.	187	xxii. 13	76	v. 16, 17	218	ix. 3.	48, 67
xviii.15–17	56	xxiii. 37	103	v. 20.	235	xi. 33	186, 258
xviii. 26	127	xxiii. 52	260	v. 22.	47	xii. 2.	235
xx. 18, 25	163	xxiv. 15	42	v. 30.	214	xii. 17	79
xxi. 1.	109, 192	xxiv. 35	142	vi. 56, 57	166	xii. 20	228
xxii. 27	163	xxiv. 45	39	vii. 12	291	xiii. 8	304
xxvi. 28	110	xxiv. 47	40	vii. 28	214	xiv. 10	115
xxviii. 22.	163	xxiv. 51	61, 64	vii. 38	225	xiv. 14, 20.	161
xxxiv. 23, 25.	110	xxv.	193	vii. 39	203	xiv. 15	150
xlii. 9.	56	xxv. 12.	213	viii. 12	256	xvii. 10	43
Baruch iii. 35–37.	205	xxv. 24.	79, 192	viii. 48	291	1 Cor. i. 18, 23	189
Song of the Three Children 15	225, 281	xxv. 27.	223	viii. 56	214	i. 22.	204
		xxv. 30.	61	ix. 39	189	ii. 3.	48
Matt. i. 13.	236	xxv. 33.	193	x. 7.	256	ii. 9.	102, 260
iii. 10	56	xxv. 34.	97	x. 11.	136	ii. 9, 10	159
iii. 11	259	xxvi. 28	291	x. 11, 12, 17	203	ii. 11	41, 256
iv. 19	264	xxvi. 38	205	x. 15, 18.	202	iii. 12	262
v. 1.	50	xxvi. 39	204	xii. 6.	62	iv. 6	237
v. 3, 4, 19, 44.	206	xxvi. 39–41	206	xii. 47	259	iv. 7.	160
v. 11	274	xxvi. 65	292	xiii. 4, 5.	206	iv. 11	219
v. 11, 12	219	xxvii. 4, 19	202	xiii. 35	43	v. 5	96, 189, 295
v. 12	253	xxvii. 32, 44	214	xiv. 2	111	vi. 9, 10	161
v. 13	76	xxvii. 40, 42	292	xiv. 6	256	vii. 4	114
v. 13, 14	224	xxviii. 13	292	xiv. 10	214	vii. 25	170
v. 16	241	Mark i. 24.	171	xv. 5.	259	vii. 28, 35.	115
v. 20	295	ii. 7.	218	xv. 5, 15	166	vii. 40	122
v. 22	51	ix. 2.	258	xv. 22	227	viii. 12.	74
v. 22, 28, 37	185	xii. 27	163	xv. 22, 24	62	x. 13	213
v. 23	154	xii. 42	190	xvii. 11	214	xi. 19	191
v. 23, 24	232	xv. 31, 32.	214	xviii. 6.	214	xi. 27, 30–32.	295
v. 24	154	Luke iii. 8.	167	xviii. 23.	206	xi. 30, 32	186
v. 27	154	iv. 23	151	xix. 17	214	xii. 26	53
v. 28	170	v. 8	178	xx. 9.	292	xiii. 12	100
v. 35	164	vi. 22, 23	220	xx. 23	47	xv. 8, 9	178
v. 44	230	vi. 36	274	xxi. 15–17	39	xv. 11	136
vi. 12	252	vii. 7.	215	Acts ii. 38	167	xv. 31	111, 262
vi. 14	190, 231	vii. 9, 39	216	iii. 6.	260	xv. 41	104
vi. 21	256	vii. 34, 39	291	v. 15	261	2 Cor. i. 3	121
vi. 34	182	vii. 44–48	106	v. 41	137	i. 5, 4	213
vii. 6	194	xi. 1, 2–4	206	vi. 4	65	i. 22.	259
vii. 7	153	xi. 10	216	ix. 4, 5	264	i. 24	41
vii. 24	279	xii. 20	255	ix. 22, 29	67	ii. 6.	96
viii. 20	206	xii. 46	61	ix. 34.	260	ii. 7.	58
viii. 28	183	xiii. 4	185	xiii. 12	261	ii. 7, 8, 11, 16.	189
viii. 31	187	xiii. 26	214	xiv. 11	67, 68	ii. 16	261
viii. 44	256	xiv. 28, 29.	64	xvi. 18	260	iii. 5, 6.	261
ix. 1, 2.	215	xv. 4.	255	xvi. 30	261	iii. 10	46
ix. 9.	264	xv. 4, 5, 29, 30.	96	xvii. 10	68	iv. 7.	260
ix. 13	253	xvi. 17	142	xvii. 20	138	iv. 16	274
ix. 22	217	xvi. 26	97	xvii. 34	67	iv. 17	104
ix. 34	291	xviii. 3, 13.	190	xviii. 3	169	iv. 18	289
x. 3.	178	xix. 8	264	xix. 11	261	v. 10	113
x. 9.	206	xix. 23	141	xx. 9.	67	v. 19, 20	103
x. 28	105	xx. 36	104	xx. 10	67	vi. 2.	99
xi. 12	256	xxi. 2–4.	169	xx. 31	69	vii. 5, 10	150
xii. 36	220	xxi. 11	275	xxi. 26	38	viii. 20, 21	79
xii. 39	204	xxii. 15	204	xxvi. 28	261	ix. 15	180
xii. 41	193	xxii. 31, 32.	213	xxviii. 3.	261	x. 5.	68
xiii. 33	192, 224	xxiii. 34.	206, 251	Rom. i. 13, 14	149	x. 10	68
xv. 22	216	xxiii. 40.	214	i. 20, 21, 25	188	xi. 2	68, 166

INDEX OF TEXTS FOR PAGES 1 TO 317.

Reference	PAGE	Reference	PAGE	Reference	PAGE	Reference	PAGE
2 Cor. xi. 2, 3.	149	Gal. iii. 28 .	135	Phil. iii. 7 .	38	1 Tim. v. 5, 6, 9–11.	122
xi. 3 .	48	iv. 19 .	97	iii. 20.	115	v. 17 .	68
xi. 6 .	66, 67	v. 2 .	38	iv. 7 .	180	v. 22 .	63, 136
xi. 9 .	48	v. 2, 4.	97	v. 17 .	152	v. 23 .	219, 295
xi. 23–28 .	104	v. 19–21 .	40	v. 18 .	153	vi. 7 .	115, 274
xi. 24 .	260	vi. 14 .	203	Col. i. 15 .	260	2 Tim. ii. 24 .	68
xi. 29 .	137	Ephes. ii. 6, 7 .	179	i. 18–24 .	64	ii. 25 .	42
xii. 2, 21 .	109	iii. 20 .	290	i. 24 .	137, 275	iii. 14–17 .	68
xii. 2–4 .	67	iv. 12 .	143	iii. 16.	.65–68	iv. 16 .	68
xii. 7 .	295	v. 2 .	203	iv. 6 .	68, 71	v. 17 .	68
xii. 8 .	206	v. 27 .	64	1 Thess. ii. 9 .	48	Titus i. 7–9 .	136
xii. 9 .	151	vi. 12 .	40	iii. 5.	151	iii. 5.	161
xii. 9, 10 .	207	vi. 16, 17 .	64	iv. 1 .	115	Philem. 10–18.	109
xii. 9, 27 .	293	vi. 22 .	151	iv. 13 .	220	Heb. i. 3 .	101
xii. 20 .	40	Phil. i. 7 .	149	iv. 17 .	260	iv. 12, 13 .	113
xii. 20, 21 .	137	i. 12–14 .	149	v. 11.	68	vi. 4–6 .	161
xii. 21 .	237	i. 13, 14.	151	v. 23.	190	x. 32 .	161
xiii. 3 .	122	i. 15, 17 .	152	1 Tim. i. 13, 15 .	178	xi. 16 .	238
xiv. 34 .	49	i. 18 .	148	ii. 9 .	169	xiii. 4 .	113
Gal. i. 8, 9.	149	i. 23, 24 .	295	ii. 12 .	49	xiii. 17 .	59, 75
ii. 11 .	161	i. 33 .	123	iii. 1 .	50	James v. 14, 15 .	48
ii. 20 .	75	ii. 1 .	83	iii. 7 .	42	1 Pet. ii. 22 .	256
iii. 4 .	97	ii. 6, 8 .	203, 262	iv. 7 .	264	iii. 15 .	64, 68
iii. 5 .	96	ii. 30 .	150	iv. 13 .	68	1 John ii. 2 .	256
iii. 27 .	161, 166	iii. 1 .	294	iv. 16 .	68	iii. 5 .	256

HOMILIES ON THE STATUES.

INDEX OF SUBJECTS.

ABEL, beloved of God, yet slain, 342; more blessed in his death than Cain, 374; died the first to instruct Adam, 414; his sacrifice good, 422.
Abraham, rich but not covetous: entertaining angels, 349; tent of, stronger than Sodom, 456.
Absolution, 356; at the altar, 443.
Accused at Antioch, tortured, 474.
Acrobats, 470.
Actions, few, for their own sake, 379; end of, 459, n.; the proof of philosophy, 465.
Adam, fell when idle, 353, 369; wretchedness of his fall, 393; what he merited, 392; fitted, by humiliation, to appear before God, 396; pride of, cast down, 413; his hiding was due to his sense of guilt, 422; his being made to confess, a mercy, 422.
Admonition, repeated, a shame, 379; obligation and advantage of, 425, 437; to be repeated, 452; not like seeing, 467; of others a duty, 481.
Adultery, self-condemned, 429; in desire, 443.
Advantages of nature and art not the dignity of a city, 457.
Alms, given at martyrs' shrines, 340; of less worth than thankfulness, 341; recompensed at the Judgment, 350; riches given for, 351; means of pardon, 351.
Altars, raised by the heathen to men, 338; by Christians only to God, though in memory of men, 338, n.; Christian, for remission of sin, 443.
Ambrose, St., obliged Theodosius to do penance, 383, n.; on invocation of Saints and Angels, 390.
Angels, applauded Job's victory, 339; invocation of, 390, n.; visited Jerusalem, 467.
Animals, wild, uses of, 395, 417; their fear of man lessened at the fall, 395; the vilest worshipped, 409; man dreads from sin, 417; their excellences not of free-will, and invariable, 420; sacrifice of, discussed, 422, n.; refugees of Antioch, destroyed by, 487.
Art, a pattern of industry, 420.
Antioch, old church of, 331, n.; blasphemy prevailing in, 343; hopes of reforming, 344; state of after sedition, 344, 425, 453; compared to Job, 344; disgraced and deserted, 345, 364, 454, 463; a mother of cities, 345, 355; shaken as with an earthquake, 345; fears of the inhabitants, 346, 412, 419, 453; character of, 347, 355; schism at 354, n.; Christians first so named there, 345, n., 355, 438; amended by danger, 382, 383, 418, 439, 455; dealt with tenderly, 383, 419; deliverance from danger, 412, 452; spared on repentance, 418; inhabitants had recourse to God, 427, 439, 482; confiscation and disruption at, 427; again disturbed, 431; submission of the people to the Emperor, 437; cowardice in, 445; distinguished in virtue, 456; exhortation before calamities, 463; accused tortured, 474; prisoners at, their trust in God, 482; the dead insulted, 484; reproached for the sedition, 484; wretched state from terror, 486; public rejoicings at, 389.
Apostles, powerful both living and departed, 333; example of, 342; dwelt in Antioch, 355; words of, like music, 331; would have been too magnified, but for sufferings and infirmities, 337; persecutions of, why permitted, 409; despondent, were dull, 413; victorious by suffering, 449; few natural advantages of, 466.
Applause, in church, 347, 379, 394.

Armour, spiritual of the Bishop, 357, n.; of all Christians, 357.
Arms, of the righteous, 396; of brutes and men compared, 416.
Army, of Saul, wisely abstemious, 433; excessive hunger of, 434.
Art, great in the temple at Jerusalem, 456.
Artificer, finds his work as he left it, 430.
Ascension Day, Sunday before, how styled, 464.
Ash Wednesday, epistle for, 358, n.
Asiarchs, 427, n.
Ass, fondness to its master, 420.
Assurance, greater from not exacting oaths, 444.
Athanasius, St., strong against oaths, 470, n.
Athenian courts, 400, n.
Audience, of the powerful, artifices to obtain, 474.
Augustin, St., on the Sabbath, 422, n.
Avengers, 475.

BAPTISM, called initiation, 342, 354, 355; Lord's Prayer taught with, 355.
Barathrum, 361, n.
Basil, St., strong terms on the invocation of saints, 389, n., 390; strong against oaths, 470, n.; kept Valens from communion, 481, n.
Basilides, 413, n.
Baths, closed, 455; highly prized, 464.
Battle, kings lay aside their crowns in, 447.
Beatitudes, 392, n., 428.
Beauty of person not to be cherished, 397, 466; of woman a snare, 442; no criterion of merit, 458.
Bee, labouring for others, 420.
Beginning, a small, great results from, 405, 470.
"Believe me," a phrase instead of

swearing, 398, n.; as a bridle, 481.
Bema occupied by clergy alone, 465, n.
Benefits of God at the creation twofold, 395; doing, for others a duty, 451; never to be desisted from, 452; from reminding one another of duty, 399.
Birds, 408; finding nests robbed, 427; flying high escape snares, 441; caught, cannot use wings, 441.
Bishop, how regarded, 354, 356, 383; duty of, 355; a Priest, 355; a High Priest, 482; a Ruler and above emperors, 356; armour of, 357.
Blasphemy, evil of, 342, 361, 437; adds to trouble, 343; to be sharply corrected in others, 343, 347; a public wrong, 343; Job's wife tempts him to, 366.
Blessed bread given to those who do not communicate, 384, n.; the righteous alone to be held, 385; who called, in Scripture, 462.
Blessedness, real, what, 340.
Blessings, the chief, common, 351.
Blind, fallen into a pit, 451.
Body, human, frailer than matter, 404; elementary parts of, 407; becomes an earthen vessel, 409; by whom framed, 413; feebleness of, why, 413; as it was framed at first, 413, 417; might have been created better, 414; fineness of, 415; excellent as joined with the soul, 416; sustains injury in spite of prudence, 437; effects upon, of externals, 462.
Boldness of monks, 453, 454.
Bones of the skull, a defence, 415; around the heart, 415.
Brain, construction of, 415.
Bread, consecrated, reservation of for sick, 384, n.
Brutes, fasted with the Ninevites, 358.
Burdens, duty of bearing another's, 452.
Burial, pomp of, 358.
Business, worldly, the clergy engaged in, 465.
Butler, Bishop, on "Law of Nature," 428, n.

CAIN, misery of, 345; consciousness of his sin and denial, 423.
Camp, place so called, 382, n.
Careless, Christian ready to fast, 431.
Carnival, 358, n.
Catechism, Church of England on Real Presence, 354 n.; on remission of sin in the Eucharist, 444, n.
Chains, how got rid of, 403; of St. Paul, 447; a security, 447; efficacy of St. Paul's, 450.
Charms, texts of Scripture as, 470; those used by Christians condemned, 470, n.

Chastity learnt from Sodom, 466.
Children, unreasonable in their fears, 374; little ones by whom frightened and quieted, 381; to be taught public deliverances, 419, 489; under instruction from fathers and teachers, 429; pulling at a rotten cord, 432; murder of, prevented by not vowing, 434; fond of sweets, severe training for, 449; virtue of, proved, 453; wrestling at the top of a pole, 470; fear their fathers more than we fear God, 471.
Christ, teaching of, 348; scorned in the poor, 349; keeps for us what we give them, 350; left us His flesh and blood, 354; instructed after feeding, 400; instructs from irrational creatures, 420; taught the law of conscience, 428; instructs us to fear, 440; forbids oaths, 444; set against Himself by swearing on the Gospel, 444, 446; gave warning of sorrow before reward, 449; judgment of, on cities, 457; teaches reconciliation by His Sacrifice, 470.
Christianity, not universal, 401, n.; a stricter law than the Mosaic, 469.
Christians, the saviors of Antioch, 343; bear trials cheerfully, 346; soldiers and wrestlers, 357; all reproached for sins of any, 359; should admonish each other, 425, 451; name diffused worldwide, 438; instructors and comforters of unbelievers, 445; under training like heirs: with heaven in view like the merchant, 450; are citizens of heaven, 456.
Chrysostom, St., requests the people to check blasphemy, 343; silent for seven days: as Job's friends, 344; bewails Antioch, 345; hopes to cheer the people, 346; speaks at length, and warns, 347; applauded, 347, 379; made bishop, 354, n.; proposes three precepts for memory, 363; blesses God for comforting, 364; love and anxiety for his people, 380, 399, 443; like a mother for a sick child, 430; watchfulness over his flock, 399; regrets the absence of some, 400; repeats admonitions, 424, 443; rewarded through their obedience, 380, 389, 399; confidence for Antioch's rescue, 382; interpretation of 1 Cor. iii. 15, 387, n.; intercourse with his people, 389, 481; mode of dealing with the unreformed, 389; success of special preaching, 438; testimony of, as to relics, 396; opinion concerning the earth, 403; shape and motion of the heavens, 419; on the Sab-

bath, 422; notions about sacrifice, 422; admonitions about theatres ineffectual, 439; on remission in Eucharist, 443, n., 444; indignation over the people's irreverence, 445, 446; teaching, practical not doctrinal, 447; welcome to the country clergy, 465; forbids all oaths, 470, n.; offers to cure the swearer, 480; threatens, 481; gives thanks for Flavian's return, 482; his praises of city, Bishop, Emperor, etc., 482.
Church (building), old at Antioch, 331; not a place of amusement, 347; full in time of distress, 364; then resorted to by the wicked, 366; to be absent from sinful, disgraceful, 400, 406; no other place so good, 406; the fittest place for thanksgiving after deliverance, 419; a place of prayer, 443; feelings in, are not religious attainments, 446; part of, reserved for clergy, 465, n.; common talk in, 473; exclusion from, 481.
Church (community), prayers of, 356; injured by evil speaking, 359; Greek, its lenten observances, 359, n.; mother of the afflicted, 364, 386; influences all ranks, 481; censure of, for familiarity, 481.
Citizens of heaven, none without virtue, 457.
City, strength of, in virtue, 457; by virtue a pattern to the world, 471; contemptuous, infects others, 486.
Clouds, cause different productions, 419.
Commander of troops, 452, n.
Common cause, most injured by fall of the most eminent, 334.
Communication with others during self-discipline, 379, 481; to the absent, of religious instructions, 400; of the Pastor to all his flock, 389; object of, 401; with the wicked in guilt, 331; in sufferings marks affiliation, 340; in many things with all men, 343; of good with the disorderly, 464.
Confession, private to a Priest, 360; of sins overcome, 418; an encouragement to others to repent, 419; a condition of pardon, 422.
Confusion, prevented by fear of Rulers, 381.
Congregation, number of St. Chrysostom's, 380, n., 406; eager for instruction, 395; obedient to his counsels, 399, 406, 430; one bad member corrupts many, 430.
Conjurer's tricks shame our endeavours at virtue, 470.
Conscience, roused by fear, 363; a bad makes us suspicious: a scourge, 396; a good makes bold, 396; a natural law, 421;

shewn from the case of Adam, 422; adds obligations to the enlightened, 424; proved from sense of shame and reproach, 428; facilitates virtue, 429; disturbed by having enemies, 479.
Consolation in adversity as witnessed by the Saints, 336; effects of, 346; is for the sad, 381; derived from religious communion with others, 383; derived from every part of the Bible, 391; from God's chastising in mercy, 431, 434; mode of, 444; in temporal distress to be sought from God's ministers, 445.
Constantine, instance of mildness, 486.
Constantinople, distance from Antioch, 361.
Contemplation of heavenly things like a view from an height, 441.
Conversation, on religious subjects how good, 388; cheering effects of, 489; reverted to by Saul's army, 433; in divine service wrong, 473.
Corn, ears of, 415.
Correction of others a means of self-correction, 405.
Corruptibility of creation, 409, 411.
Covetousness, 348; is poverty, 349; cured by considering the equality of day and night, 402.
Councils, secular, customs of, 400.
Country, one's, how to be advanced, 471.
Courage from a good conscience, 396.
Cowards realize groundless fear, 445.
Cowardice unbecoming men, 446.
Creation, not to be disparaged, 335; dishonors fawners, 386; a proof of God's love for us, 391; when written of, in Scripture, 394; testifies to God, 401, 407; mode of above the power of Nature, 403; consists of contraries harmonized, 404; decay of, without Providence, 408; deified, 408; why subject to decay, 409, 411; like the Apostles under persecution, 409; mutual dependence of parts, 411; neither all at rest nor all in motion, 419; the parts not understood ought to amaze, 421.
Creature, use of word, 411, n.
Criminals, wretched appearance of at the bar, 396.
Cross, the, a symbol of salvation, 448; sign of, not a charm, 470, n.
Crown, given for overcoming sin, 438; inferior to chains, 447; humanity gained by Theodosius, 485.
Custom, no match for fear, 437; easier overcome than concupiscence, 469.
Cyprian, St., on intercession of Saints, 389, n.

DANCING, feats in, 470, n.
Danger of arguing about nature, 403, n.; unconcern of Saints for, 448; of relapsing under prosperity, 452.
Daphne, a suburb of Antioch, 457, n.
David, though small, a victor, 458.
Davison vindicates the idea of sacrifice, 422, n.
Day, unvarying and equal with night, 402.
Death, proves vanity of riches, 351; no subject of alarm, 372; eagerness of St. Paul for, 372; base if in sin, but not so from violence, 373; evil to sinners only, 373; an unjust brings into special communion with the Saints, 374; unjust permitted by God, 374; what is, 374, 390; having it before our eyes, 376; soldier fearing, ignoble, 376; dreaded for want of self-mortification, 384; full of joy to the godly, 461; courted by the monks of Antioch, 463.
Debtors, treatment of, 362.
Debts, God's remission of to men, and a creditor's compared, 478.
Deer, escaped from a snare, 441.
Degradation, attaching to athletics, 470.
Demosthenes, bad habit of: how cured, 394.
Desertion of the Philosophers in distress, 454.
Dice-playing to be shunned, 442.
Differences, seeming, reconciled, 403, 469.
Difficulties for God's sake, 477; none can stand against the fear of God, 480.
Dignity of a city is its virtue, 456; of no avail at the Judgment, 457.
Discipline, course of usual, 334, n; under Christianity a preparation for trials, 366; moral from war, 435.
Discontent from going to feasts, 440.
Discourse, subjects of, at conventions, 406.
Diseases, their origin, 407.
Disposition, makes sad or cheerful, 460, 463.
Dog, shameless, 420.
Doubt, Ninevites doubted the consequences of their repentance, 377.
Dove, an example of simplicity, 420.
Dress, finery in, how cured, 450; not to be despised or admired, 466.
Drunkenness, 335.

EAGLE, under man's dominion, 416; a king so styled, 467.
Ear, fasting of the, 359; to be closed against slander, 360.
Earth, diurnal motion of a type, 402, n.; supported on water, 403; productiveness of, 404.
Earthquake, alluded to, 345, n.; 362.
Easter, mercy suited to, 355; act of human mercy at, 383, n.
Eating a meal no reason for staying away from church, 400, 406;
moderation favors attendance, 400.
Edification, mutual of members of a household in religious practice, 379, 480.
Elements, harmony and opposition of, 404; weakness and dependence of, 410.
Elijah, of like passions with us, 340; his poverty, 353; twofold, 353, 396.
Elisha, his inheritance, 353; changed the water, 396, 411.
Emotions, high term for, 386.
Emperor, see Theodosius, vengeance expected from, 345; has no equal on earth, 346; inferior to a Bishop, 356; a fellow-servant, 361.
Emulation, in religious practice, 370, 379; in reforming the community advantageous, 389; spirit of, promotes self-restraint, 430.
Enemies, none to be held, 363, 370; not reconciled without a third person, 408; Jews knew righteousness prevailed in Israel, 435; misfortunes of, rejoiced in, 461; the sight of possessions of, disturbs, 473; good and bad fortune alike annoys, 474; the worse, the more reason for forgiving, 475; implacable, how treated by God, 475; the worst softened by gentleness, 475; like a limb cut off, 476; duty of making friends of, 478; are alone enough to cause insecurity, 479.
Ephraim, St., quotations from, 389, n.
Episozomenes, title of a Sunday, 464.
Equanimity from true wisdom, 454.
Esther, prayer of, saved the Jews, 356.
Ether, consistence of, 409, n.
Eucharist, a greater gift than Elisha's, 354; doctrine of, 354, n.; fasting or sufficiency at, 400; an oblation distinct, 422, n.; efficacy for remitting sin, 444, n.; the prize of fasting during Lent, 471; not to be approached unless healed of sins, 472; prohibited the resentful, 472; and the swearer, 481; hands washed before receiving, 479; object of exclusion from, 481.
Evils, temporal, of little moment, 372; the worse make the less unfelt, 374, 428; warded off by repentance, 376; cannot touch the righteous, 385; God merciful amidst, 393; past, remembrance of, 426; a source of pain, 444, 457; must run to God under, 448; an occasion of thanksgiving, 452; felt according to the disposition, 459; comfort from, 463.
Evil speaking, mischief of, 359, 370; pleasure of, 360; causes quarrels, 361; hinders pardon: spoils

fasting, 361; breaking away from, 363.
Examination of our path necessary, 440.
Example, partakes of our own nature, 340; the irrational animals are, 420; the old referred to the young for, 420; effects of, 405, 429; of pilots in a storm, 446; of one city upon the whole world, 438; the giver of, precedes, 487.
Excellences, natural, liable to fail, 448.
Excuses for not seeking reconciliation, 474, 475, 478; concerning inveterate swearing, 479.
Eye, government of the, 359; a surer organ than the ear, 401; beauty and power of, 414; eyebrows like eaves, 415; of God, 475.

FAITH, shewn by works, 373; like an eagle's wing, 416.
Fall, sin of, 393; the human body changed after, 413, 417; of another bewailed is pleasing to God, 461.
Fame, injured by enemies, 479.
Famine, relieved by the people of Antioch, 456.
Fasting of Timothy, 33; easily misjudged, 334; moderation urged, 335; a help to prayer: bodily, not enough, 357, 370, 406, 459; of Ninevites accepted, 358; due honor of, 359; of the eye, ear, and tongue, 359, 406; general practice, 370, 388, 450, n.; together with danger facilitates repentance, 378; made easy by custom, 388; from sin, 406, 472; indulgence before and after, 438; without fresh gains a loss, 459; well used welcomed, 459; omission of, may be excused, 472.
Fathers, the view of, about the earth 403, n.; upon oaths, 470, n.; strong statements of, as in the Bible, 477, n.; most such, in punishing their children, 392; first severe then indulgent, 449; grieve more when absent, 483.
Favour, the overcoming bad habits accounted by God a, 412; Divine, bestowed on Jerusalem, 467; the forgiving others a, asked by God, 478.
Fear, needful to holy men, 334; a chastisement for carelessness, 347; of the Lord true riches, 351; a punishment, 355; awakens conscience, 363; of harm from man ignoble, 366; a good man firm against, 369; without the fear of hell death terrible, 374; of hell profitable, 374, 439; prevents magnanimity, 376; of Rulers promotes order, 381; effect of, on public morals, 382, 439; a most powerful motive, 392, 437; God's wrath a cure of bad habits, 394; of scorpions from sin, 417; prevents bad passions, like a soldier on guard, 439; breeds virtue, 439; why Christ broadly taught, 440; groundless made real, 446; an ocean of joy, 460; of God overcomes quickly, masters, 479; purifies like a furnace, 480.
Feasts, evil of frequenting, 440; beget envy, 440.
Festival, of Easter an argument for mercy, 355; in celebration of martyrs, 464.
Festus, how approached by St. Paul, 448.
Fingers, unequal, 416.
Fire worshipped by the Persians: then worshipped, 367; rivers of, 386; purgatorial, 387, n.; in a forest, 389; its property of rising, 404; used in torture, 474.
Firmament, use of word, 404.
Fish, 408; caught with baits, 449.
Flavian, Bishop of Antioch, 354, n.; leaves his sister almost dying, 354, 482; his boldness, 355; prayers of, for his people, 482; return from Constantinople, 482; obstacles to his journey, 483; magnanimity of, 483; absent, grieved for Antioch, 484; silent like Moses, 484; will quit Antioch if unpardoned, 488; proofs of forethought for the people, 488.
Flattery of the great, 474.
Flesh, an unruly steed, 334.
Floods, 470.
Flowers, 408; yield a sweeter, than artificial smells, 466.
Folly of laboring for worldly things, and not to be reconciled, 479.
Food, carried away by guests, 38.
Forgiveness of sin by forgiving others, 473; brings our minds into peace, 474.
Fountains, 408.
Fowler, a zealous, 441; enticements of, 449.
Fox, cunning of, 420.
Frailty of the body a cure for pride, 413.
Fraternities for mutual religious help, 417.
Freedom, in righteousness, not immunity from punishment, 386.
Friend, a, shews dissatisfaction by silence, 436.
Fruits of fasting, remain, 459; from bitter roots, 462.
Fund, common, 452.

GAIN, whatever promises, to be suspected, 441; from evils, 444.
Games, alluded to, 339, 405; presidents of, 427, n.; participants of, excluded from the Communion, 439, n.
Garment, oiled of wrestlers, 339, n.; miraculous virtue of, 396; a rich, how used, 405.
Gazing at the beauty of a woman a snare, 442.

Gentiles, see Heathen, signifying a worshipper of God, 423.
Gifts, Divine, on the temple, 456.
Glory of suffering for Christ, 447; not happiness, 460; in shewing mercy, 485.
Gluttony, 357: inexcusable before prayer: incapacitates, 400; cured by considering St. Paul, 450.
God, His work good, 335; power of shewn in weakness, 337, 409; love of Him, its own reward, 338; challenged Satan to try Job, 339; cares more than we for the poor, 341; not to be called in question, 341, 362; afflicts those He loves, 342; His honour to be vindicated, 343, 347; cares for us more than ourselves, 347; never weary of our prayers, 356; blasphemed for our sins, 359; His mighty longsuffering, 361, 362; tempers prosperity and adversity for our good, 366; overrules Satan's worst efforts to his loss, 367; if our friend, nothing matters, 369; cares less for His repute than our salvation, 378; does not punish when the threats affect, 382; overrules the designs of men, 383, 447; judges sinners by the standard of the good, 388; His love shewn in our punishment, 392, 413, 431; otherwise only half good, 392; deals with fallen man as a father, 392, 449; tenderness of in addressing Adam, 393; His walking was in Adam's perception, 396; His providence shewn in making the cure of the soul easy, 397; instructs by the creation, 401; His ordering of the seasons and the day, 402; uses weak instruments to shew His power, 404; glorified man in the works of creation, 405; needs nothing, 410; the source of all things, 410; skill of in human frame, 414; known by His works, 421; mercy and wisdom of bringing Adam to confession, 422; why He delays punishment, 424; His goodness shewn in man's natural love of virtue, 429; the leader of the Jews in war, 435; silence toward Saul from gentleness, 436; turns causes of evil to good, 448; to believers is the whole fountain of cheerfulness, 460; ordains suffering first, 450; unceasingly gracious, 452; reproaches for insensibility to the ills of others, 462; fear of, the foundation of peace, 463; insulted worse than man ever is, 473; our Avenger, and despised when we avenge, 475; like a friend in requiring forgiveness of others, 478; never ceases to entreat us, 478; assists earnest endeavours, 480; exceeds hopes, 482; takes occasion

HOMILIES ON THE STATUES: INDEX OF SUBJECTS.

of offences to shew love, 485; overrules all for good, 489.
Gods, heathen, who, 339; the vilest animals made, 409; the Apostles held to be, 409; ambition of some men to be held, 413.
Good, what is, at one time is not always, 401; temporal, yields pleasure to the reverent, 463; temporal, is mutable and insufficient, 460.
Gospel, the book of the, oaths taken on, 443; preaching of promoted by conflicts, 448; like a sunbeam, not bound, 450; portions of worn by women and children, 470.
Government, two sorts of, natural and elective, 391.
Grave, robbing, 393, n.
Greek Church, usage in fasting, 370, n.; Fathers of, opinions of on Purgatory, 387, n.
Gregory, St. Naz. on invocation of the Saints, 390, n.; on Beatitudes, 392, n.
Grief, a medicine only profitable when felt for sin, 375, 390; this the end of it, 375, 390; temporal ills, not cured by, 375; produced by sin, 419.
Grief, a wound, how to be treated, 381; for infants as reasonable as for the dead, 385; makes men inattentive to instruction, 413; spreads darkness over every thing, 426; for the ills of others pleasing to God, 458; a refreshment, 461; fruits of, sweet, 463.
Guilt shared by those who give power to the sinner, 331.

Habits, good to be formed, 363; difficult to be overcome, 388; easy, the subject being hard, 388; mastered in a given time, 370; almost mastered require less pains, 405; in man acquired by free-will, 420; easily conquered by fear, 437; under severe training, 449; easier to be overcome than nature, 469.
Hades, where, according to the heathen, 403, n.
Hair of eyebrows and head, 415.
Hands of God, His power, 403.
Happiness in God alone, 460.
Harlot, bad influences of, 435.
Harm, none to God's people, 378; limited to the sutures of the bones, 415.
Hares, timidity of, 445.
Hatred, to be forsaken, 363; mark of, to avoid naming the person, 393; disquiets, 473; is unbecoming brothers: increases with time, 476; to cease from is not all enough, 478; cherished corrupts fast or feast, 479; pollutes the mind, 479.
Health, won by labour, 352; bad to be borne with patiently, 332; St. Timothy's, no hindrance to

his labours, 334; not happiness, 460; by sobriety, 466; ill, an excuse for not fasting, 472, 475.
Hearing without doing of no avail, 379.
Heart, the chief member, well defended, 415.
Heat, properties of, 403, n.
Heathenism, designation of, in Scripture, 367, n.
Heathen, the alleged reason for deifying the universe, 408; by their own folly make idols, 409; philosophers were actors, 465; instructed by the example of Theodosius, 488; the laws of, from the conscience, 423; not responsible without a natural law, 423; not fit instructors for Christians, 445.
Heaven, hope of, 350; not won without labour, 449.
Heavens, sight of, proclaims God: effects of, 401; matter and form of, 404; beauty of, 408; fixed, 419, n.
Hell, fear of, is profitable, 439.
Heralds in the games, 386.
Heretics, found fault with creation, 335; opinions of about the human body, 413.
Hippodrome, 439.
History, design of Scripture viewed as, 410, n.
Honey, water so called, 352; as a feast to Saul's army, resisted, 433.
Honour, bestowed on man in three ways, 391; done to God is rewarded, 446; worldly has no real dignity, 456.
Hope, in God an anchor, 446; makes present ill light, 450.
Horse, inferior to man in the foot, 416.
Hospitality, of Abraham, 349; of Job, 442.
House not to be extravagantly adorned, 349; built on a rock, 365; guarded is not robbed, 439; of mourning and feasting, 440; of the sinner overthrown a witness to all, 259, 466; brought to ruin by neglect of small repairs, 470.
Humility, produced by adversity, 337; scope for in the human frame, 417.
Hunger, gives relish to food, 351.
Hunters, 435.
Husbandry, spiritual, 357, 365; the first art, a school of virtue, 465.
Hut, in the vineyards, 408.

Idolatry, origin of, 337.
Ignorance of men brought out in arguing about nature, 403, n., 421.
Ignorant, the, taught by the creation, 402.
Illuminations, at Antioch, 489.
Image of God, 362; consists of sovereignty, 391.

Implacability, in an enemy, punished by God, 475.
Inattention, at prayers, 394; leaves us without excuse, 473.
Incarnation, alluded to in Job, 339, n.
Indifferent things, to be avoided, 442.
Indignation at the wrongs of others, of nature, 429.
Inferiority of material calls for greater skill, 414.
Inferiors, men are ashamed to sin before, 428.
Inheritance, needs previous training, 450.
Insensibility to the sins of others, 462.
Instincts, 420.
Instruction, spiritual, stored in the mind, 388; like picking a flower, 399; increases obligations, 424; conveyed formerly by *things*, 401; given in church, 406; to be obeyed on trust, 425; in virtue by temporal ills, 429; requires personal ardor and promptness, 430, 480; like water from a well, for use afterwards, 446; in morals precedes that in revealed truth, 446; inattention to, excused by dullness, 475.
Instruments, weakness of, shews God's power, 409.
Insult, effect of, our own fault: recoils when slighted, 353; towards aggressors an offence to God, 440; from one under high patronage, 444.
Intemperance, before and after fasting, 439.
Intentions, provided by God are rewarded, 341; known to God, 475.
Intercession to be made for Antioch, 346; arguments used in, 383; of the poor, 351, n.; bold, of monks, 453, 454; of saints departed, 389, n.
Invocation of saints and angels, 389, n.
Iron softened by water, 403.
Isaiah commands the sun, 411.

Jacob, his care of Laban's sheep, 354.
Jailor at Philippi, 450.
Jephthah's vow allowed by God, 434.
Jerusalem, temple at, 456; wretchedness of, 457; favours of God bestowed on, 467; a vine, 467.
Jesus of Nazareth, the common name of our Lord, 393, n.
Jews in distress could not listen, 346; reproved for not looking to God, 356; saved by Esther's prayer, 356; oppressed in Egypt to increase their desire of Canaan, 384; would not name Christ from hatred, 393; gave no heed to Moses, 413.
Jewels, the pride of some women, 449.

HOMILIES ON THE STATUES: INDEX OF SUBJECTS.

Job, his character shewn by affliction, 338, 341; his wrestling with Satan: tried as gold, 339; Antioch compared to him, 344; safest when poor, 353; his trust in God, 366; loved before grace, or the old covenant, 366; rewarded for retaining godliness, 369; dunghill of, in Arabia, 371; consolation to be derived from, 371; his body, preciousness of, 371, 372; an instance of the merit of suffering, 385; silence of his friends, 412; a Gentile, 423, n.; his virtue lofty in prosperity and adversity, 442; losses of, led him to God, 445, 461.

John, St., Baptist, to be followed in reproving sin, 343; his martyrdom a warning against oaths, 432, 470.

Jonah's flight of no avail, 378; how taught mercy, 378; forced by God, 382; author of the book of, 480, n.

Jonathan's eating the honey, 434; if slain, a double misery to Saul, 434

Joseph sold, 363; wept, 488.

Joshua commands the sun's motion, 411.

Joy, from temporal good soon ends, 451; continual under misfortune possible, 459; aim of all, 459; aim of all, 459; in God, 460; of the world brings loss, 461.

Judge, unjust, parable of, 412; man made, of his own pardon, 477; does not question or correct the culprit, 393; sympathy of the judges at Antioch, 427; rigour of human, 427; shewed mercy upon the intercession of the monks, 453.

Judgment, the last, proved by the afflictions of the saints, 339; riches of no avail in, 349; alms help us in, 351; and mercy, 355; without benefit of others' intercession, 427; rulers threatened with, 453; harsh over others visited on ourselves, 361; rash on others without excuse, 472: temporal, effectual, 481.

Justice, courts of, originated in the natural moral law, 423.

Kidnappers entice by pleasant things, 449.

Kings excel their subjects in wealth, 421; make unreasonable laws, 447; doff their crowns in battle, 447; have more cause for sadness than any, 460; armour of, 467; made glorious by mercy, 485; may easily conquer, but not win, 487.

Knives, feats performed with, 470.

Knowledge of the creation from God, 421; withheld to remove occasion of pride, 421; of God by His works, 421; of good and evil by nature, 428; not for its own sake, 435.

Labour brings sleep, 352; our safest state, 353; spiritual reward of, 357; of life ordained by whom, 384.

Laughter often leads to sin, 442; how to be met, 481.

Law, of Nature (see Conscience) the ground of Christ's teaching, 428; against criminal suits in Lent, 383, n.; of God takes precedence of human laws, 398; civil, of the heathen, from conscience, 423; of kings not to be questioned, 447.

Lazarus gained a reward, 340, 385; example of, 342, 373; truly rich, 348.

Learning, how long Pambos was learning one verse, 332, n.; without wisdom avails nothing, 465.

Lebanon for Judæa, 467.

Legerdemain, feats of, 470.

Lent, Christian's working time, 357; commencement of, 358, n., 370 n.; precepts to learn in, 363; celebrated with daily sermons, 379, n.; covers sins of the past year, 472.

Leprosy of Miriam, 475.

Lessons, Scripture, in worship, order of, 347, n.; from Jonah's history, 378; from the irrational animals, 420.

Letter of the monks to Theodosius, 454.

Libanius, 394, n.

Life, a burden, a cottage here, in heaven a palace, 372; why made laborious, 384; without religion dull and wearisome, 385; a good, honours God, 405; bordering on sin like walking along a precipice, 443; in the country favourable to virtue, 465.

Litanies, 362, n.

Longsuffering of God, 424.

Loss, by doing one's duty versus the gain, 444; of children no grief to the good, 461.

Love, its own reward, 338, n.; shewn in patient endurance, 341, 342; in perseverance, 342; takes interest in everything, 356; of God absent, causes fear of death, 374; glories in suffering, 448; maternal, 453; delights in all that belongs to the object of it, 474; exercised in great offences, 485; delights in the good of others, 464.

Lucifer, consecrates Paulinus, Bishop of Antioch, 354, n.

Lungs, position of, 415.

Lust, by looking, 443.

Luxury, tendencies of, 442; unfit for trials, 459; untimely in public troubles, 464.

Madmen, never at rest, 474.

Magee, Archbishop, on Sacrifice, 422, n.

Magistrates, out of office bear the same titles, 447.

Magnanimity of monks at Antioch, 453.

Manichees, alluded to, 335.

Manners, purity of, 466.

Marcion, 413, n.

Martyrs, shrines of, places of almsgiving, 340; become mediators, 389, n.

Martyrdom, of Abel, 342; of St. John Baptist, 343; crown of, how to win, 343, 347; has efficacy of Baptism, 376, n.

Masters, approved by their scholars, 455; insulted by injuries done to their servants, 475.

Matter, heretical opinions about, 413, n.

Meal, 399, n.; principal among the Romans was supper, 379, n.

Means effecting opposite ends, 448; all to be adopted to win an enemy, 477.

Mediator, the Bishop so employed with the Emperor, 354.

Medicine, skill required to apply it, 358; the end of, 375; natural, 395; from animals, 395, n.

Meekness of the monks, 455; does not anger an enemy, 475.

Melchisideck a Gentile, 423, n.

Members, the instruments of good and evil according to our choice, 369; each its excellence, 417; one cut off to be reunited, 476.

Membranes, covering the brain, 415.

Memorial, perpetual, of sin, 466.

Men, all have much in common, 343; a spiritual flock, 355; soon tire of other's affairs, 356; images of God, 362; the race after the fall deserved destruction, 392; command over the creation, 411; gentler than brutes, 416; to be measured by virtue, not natural gifts, 457; self-taught in good and evil, 422, 428; in the Arts and Sciences, 423; naturally at enmity with vice, 429; disinterested in love and hatred, 429; of well regulated minds not distracted by events, 459; pleasure the aim of all, 459.

Merchandise, spiritual, in doing God's bidding, 477.

Merchants, labour in hope, 450; cargo not distance their care, 451; labour for enjoyment afterwards, 459.

Mercy, shewn to others, procures mercy for ourselves, 355; of judges at Antioch, 454; makes kings glorious, 485.

Merit, not proved by titles of honour, 477.

Metropolis, avails naught for salvation, 457.

Milk, for children a simile, 401.

Minister, his people's conduct his glory, 347.

Miracles, by relics, 332, 333, 367; power of, limited, 333; does not dispense with fasting, 334; tempt the ignorant to worship

men, 338; an extraordinary, 367; of the Apostles, not by their own power, 409.
Miriam's punishment not remitted, 475.
Misfortunes of others open men's hearts, 429, n.; subdue our vanity, 429; light, felt by the rich, 460; without excuse before God, 472.
Monasteries, 455, n.
Monks, services of, 453; effects of their intercession, 454; account of one, 455; undismayed, 463.
Moral and Positive to Laws, difference between, 421; moral teaching, 447.
Mortality, human, for overthrowing pride, 413.
Mortification, spiritual acts of, 379; incumbent on all, 384.
Moses, suffered for doing good, 342; disregarded by the people in extreme distress, 346; wherein he brought honey from the rock, 352; his intercession, 355; rod of, 396; command over created things, 411; his righteousness availed not the Jews, 430.
Mothers miss their children at table, 400; case of a mother at Antioch, 453; grief often relieves, 461.
Mourning, sight of, sobers: reminds of Judgment, 440; calls forth sympathy from enemies, 440.
Mourner, to others like a cloud parted by the sun's rays, 346.
Multitude, the, influenced by fear and threats, 392; of inhabitants avails nothing, 457.
Murder, why not reasoned about, where forbidden, 421; by exacting oaths, 443.
Mutability of earthly good, 460.

NAILS, construction of, 416.
Name, calling by, a mark of affection, 393, n.; common to our Lord, 393, n.; of God how pronounced in heaven, 394.
National calamities ought to direct us to God, 346; work national amendments, 366.
Nature, overruled by the piety of Saints, 367; what exists by, comforts, 391; gifts of, commend the Giver, 429; course of, not to be maligned, 442; ties of, are a great obligation, 453.
Nebuchadnezzar, change wrought in him, 386; herald of his own defeat, 386.
Neighbours, spiritual good of, to be furthered, 452; afflictions of, to be shared, 458; good of, an enjoyment, 464.
Night, as good as day, 395; succeeds day without change, 402.
Ninevites, their fasting accepted, 358; why, 359; teach repentance and hope, 376; forsook their sins, the city saved, 377; their disadvantages in comparison with Jews and Christians, 377, 480; *complete* repentance of, from fear, 480.
Noah, laughed at, 481.
Noise from "spectacles" disturbed divine service, 439.
Number, the, of fellows in sin no profit, 388.

OATHS, testimony of the life instead, 394; how Satan works amidst, 398; only to be taken fasting, 400; have caused the worst evils, 432; binding others more dangerous, 433; at the altar, 443; either superfluous or perjury, 444; caused the ruin of Jerusalem many times, 467; signified in Ezekiel's parable, 467; occasions of admitted by the Fathers, 470, n.
Observances, formal, in religion use of, to good and bad Christians, 479, n.
Occasions, passing, used for instructing, 374, 381, 398, 427, 437, 460, 463, 474.
Occurrences, incidental, often are of God, 382.
Ocean, earth upon the, 403, n.
Offences, of every man against God greater than towards other men, 472; great, an occasion of shewing mercy, 485.
Openness of Christ's declaration to His followers, 449.
Order, in nature and human fellowship proclaims God, 401, 402.
Orders, holy, sin of giving to the unworthy, 331.
Origen, on intercession of Saints, 389, n.
Ownership, unreal and real, 350, 351.

PAMBOS, how he learned Scripture, 332, n.
Paradise, St. Paul transported to, 447.
Pardon, of others gains our own, 355, 477, 488.
Partners in a shop, 452.
Passion, God free from, 392.
Passover, a time of mercy, 355; reverenced by pardon of offences, 479.
Pastor, bound to suffer for his people, 354; efficacy to his intercessions, 356; how to be regarded by his people, 380; intercourse with each severally, 389; like a husbandman and a pilot, 399; invigorated by success, 399; good of his flock, his good, 412; to be followed trustfully, 425; concern of, for all, 430; living by husbandry: true philosophers, 465.
Patience, 341; of Lazarus, praised by St. Chrysostom, 342, n.; punishes insolence, 353.
Paul, St., teacher of the Gentiles, 332, n.; care for Timothy, 333; distrusted himself, 334; kept humble by affliction, 337; strong though in bonds, 337; his example 342; hindered by Satan, 342; adapts himself to hearers, 349; his labours and reward, 353; reproved sin, 359, eagerness to die, 373, 385; advantages of Christians over St. Paul, 373; his garments, virtue of, 396; more than a lion, 397; his illustrations from nature, 407; recollection of his sins, 419; proves a natural law, 423; concern about one incestuous person, 430; dangers of, for his mending, 431; counted all things loss, 441; feels paternal anxiety, 443; glories in his sufferings for Christ, 447, 462; attempts to convert his judges, 448; recommends continual joy, 459; greatness of, in hiding good deeds, 483.
Paulinus, Bishop of Antioch, 354, n.
Peacock, 408.
Penalty for swearing, 389, 399.
Penitential acts of use, 378.
Penitents, discipline of, 472, n.
Pentateuch, 394, n.
Perfection, precepts of, 348, 349; how attained, 370; St. Paul's height within the reach of every one, 373; of art in the temple, 456.
Perfume, spiritual, 406; of flowers the best, 466.
Perjury from the habit of swearing, in two ways, 432, 438; of both persons swearing the contrary, 432; who forces another to, is guilty himself, 432, 439; the object of Satan, 433; guilt of, shared by those privy to it, 434; manifold from one oath, 436.
Persecutors, benefitted by the virtue of their victims, 387.
Perseverance in prosperity a test of virtue, 452.
Peter, St., the first to preach Christ, 356.
Pharisee, fasted in vain, 357; his evil speaking, 359.
Philoponus on the heavens, 419, n.
Philosophers, cowardice of the heathen, 454; the simple made, 466.
Philosophy of this world shrinks from danger, 454; worldly, falsified by deeds, 455; pagan, is but in the garb, 465; like a sword with a silver hilt and leaden blade, 465; heathen, taught a few only, 466.
Physician, spiritual, 360, 394; cures. by contraries, 378.
Piety, the chief good, 369; abides, 451.
Pilgrimages, 340; to the dunghill of Job, 371; use of, 467.
Pilot, 408; his chief concern, 399; in storms, 446, 483.
Place, importance of, for the delivery of the law, 394.

Plato, 402, n.; on the human body, 413, n.; on the motions of heavenly bodies, 419, n.
Players, deprived of the holy Communion, 439, n.
Pleasure depends on relish, 352; present diminished, pain in view, 450.
Plural number, use of, 481, n.
Pole, balancing, 470.
Poor, God's care for, 341; represent Christ for us, 349; trust in God, 351; relish food and sleep, 352.
Porch, of church for penitents, 472, n.
Porphyrio, a bird greatly esteemed, 408, n.
Porters, cajoled for favours, 474.
Pot, the golden, of the temple, 467.
Poverty, a benefit and protection, 342, 353, 372; of Elijah, 353; of Job, 442; alleged to excuse almsgiving, 475.
Power, of injuring the just, why granted, 386; taken away easily, 451; of judges, 454.
Practice, laxity of, causes death to be feared, 375; a matter of choice and endeavours, 428; right, impossible without *fear* of God, 439; the season of, is the test of religion, 446; without questioning, 447; of Saints proves Scripture, 455.
Praise, of one another beside the purpose, 380; to be suspected, 441; of men from reconciliation, 479.
Prayer, the only resource in trouble, 346; power of, 351; recommended, 354, 356; united powerful, 356; of women, 356; to be persevered in, 362; inattention at, 394, 472; natural as a way of assisting the distressed, 426; penitential, a special kind, 427, n.; fruit of, never lost, 451; most needful after deliverance, 452; for fellows in affliction, 458; *the Lord's*, taught in Baptism, 355, n.; how entitled, 478, n.; not to be used by halves, 478.
Preaching, suits not extreme distress, 346; may solace the suffering, 346; to be heard for improvement, 347; of the Gospel not bound as the preacher, 450.
Precepts, three proposed to be learnt, 363; moral without the reason, 421; of the Gospel better carried in heart than on paper, 470.
Preservation of the world by God, 403.
Pride, 348; how to check, in the rich, 349; evil of, 350; spiritual, on account of good works, 337; remedied by considering the weakness of the body, 413, 417; preceded by ignorance, 421.
Priest, our wound to be shewn to, 360, n.; consoles the afflicted in adversity, 483.

Prison, likeness to, 345; emptied at Easter, 383, 486; senate of Antioch confined in, 458, n.
"Prisoner," more glorious than any title to St. Paul, 447.
Prodigal, the, unfit to manage an inheritance, 450.
Promises, of God infinitely excellent, 451.
Prophecy, not false because not accomplished, 376.
Prosperity, no ground for security, 369, 450; present, heightened by contrast, 425; transient, 427.
Proverbial sayings against Providence, 341, n.; of contempt for others, 343.
Providence, denied by some, 341; shewn in apparently accidental cases, 382, 383; in the deliverance of His children, 386; in the use of weak means, 404; proved from the human body, 407; in Flavian's journey, 483.
Publican, accepted without fasting, 358.
Punishment, a medicine, 375; of the prosperous twofold, 384; inflicted by parents, 392; severest for sins easily avoided, 411; delayed for repentance, 424; inflicted on Antioch beneficial, 455; of an inexorable enemy, 475.
Purgatory, doctrine of, 387, n.
Pusillanimity, to be always dwelling on miseries, 391; to look to man for comfort, 445.

QUESTIONS, raised to win attention, 333; on the permission of suffering, 336, 340; on brute animals fasting, 358.
Quinquagesima, 358, n.

RACING, ill effects of, 442.
Rank not to be regarded in rebuking vice, 430.
Reason, appropriates the superior powers of brutes, 416; does not constrain, 428, n.; given to avoid sin, 441.
Reasons, of God's works, a few revealed, 421; of God's laws not to be required, 447.
Recollection of past evils useful, 418.
Reconciliation, the one seeking has the whole merit, 474; endeavours after, always acceptable to God, 475; imputed to wrong motives, 476; to God by the Crucifixion, 476; every day makes, more difficult, 476; only to please God, 477; a cause of forgiveness, 477; repulses must not quell, 478; very easy, 479.
Reflection on words of Scripture, 391; from the sight of grief, 440; on being laughed at for doing right, 481.
Reformation, spiritual, of the community, rapid when begun, 389; at Antioch, 455.
Relics of Timothy expelled demons,

332; of the Apostles, 333; of Job in great repute, 371; virtue of, 389, n.; of martyrs expelled demons, 396.
Relief from grieving, 462.
Religion, how designated in Scripture, 367, n.; training in, increases obligation, 373; not to left to the clergy, 384.
Reminding one another of duties, 399.
Remission from God, according to our excusing, 477; full, by full, 478.
Repairs, small, neglected, bring ruin, 470.
Repentance, pardon offered to, 362; time given for, 363; procures the removal of evils, 376; speedy, from fear of God, 480; duty of bringing others to, 481.
Reproach felt as a wrong, 428; a spur to amendment, 429.
Reproof to be administered in love, 343, 359; calls forth love, 344; an improvement of our talent, 348.
Repulse, no excuse for not being reconciled, 472, 478.
Resentment is a practice of malice, 476; excludes from the holy Communion, 476; precluded by considering our sins, 472, 473; continually forbidden, 473; madness: punished here and hereafter, 474; merits the worst punishment, 474; the most inexcusable of all sins, 475; gives advantage to Satan: is contempt of God, 477; unjust toward our worst foes, 473.
Reserve, practised by St. Paul and our Lord, 349.
Responsibility from religious instruction, 398, 424.
Rest, must be preceded by tribulation, 366.
Restraint upon vice provided by God, 429; human on our freedom submitted to, 447; tribulation is, 452.
Resurrection, proved by afflictions of the Saints, 339; hope of, removes fear of death, 373.
Revelation by letters would have availed the learned and the rich only, 401; by things is understood by all men, 401.
Reward bestowed for pains, not natural gifts, 429; temporal and spiritual contrasted, 451; of grieving over the sins of others, 462.
Rich, the, more miserable than the poor, 460.
Riches, the true, 348, 351, 353; earthly, vanity of, 348; wherein not forbidden, 348; an encumbrance, 349; where to deposit, 349, 350; the use of, only ours, 350; why not given equally, 351; drive men to mean arts, 353; a means of virtue, 442; liability

to loss of, 451; not happiness, 460.
Ridicule, for well-doing, how to be met, 481.
Righteous, arms of, 397; overthrow demons, 397; never sad, 461; alone happy, 462.
Robes, rich, look best on ourselves, 380.
Roman Catholic Church on Eucharist, 444, n.
Roots, bitter, sweet fruits from, 462.
Rope walking, 470.
Ruin of Jerusalem by breaking oaths, 469.
Rule self-imposed for the cure of faults, 471.
Rulers, God arms, 381; fear of, proper, 381; like the supports of a building, 382.

SABBATH, why enjoined in Decalogue, 422; made a type of the Lord's Day, 422, n.
Sacrament, more than Elisha had, 353.
Sacrifice, a dictate of the natural law, 422, n.; unbloody, 472.
Sadness, darkens the sight, 346; of the rich, 459.
Saints, especially assailed, 334, 342; eight reasons why afflicted, 336; their power from God, 338; motives of, for serving Him, 338; not to be worshipped, 338, n.; ninth and tenth reason why afflicted, 340; their countenance, 355; a few save their country, 356; effects of their sanctity on nature, 367; daunted by nothing, 368; surmount all natural ills, 375; the more tried, the more glorious, 386; meekness of, when magnified by men, 386; departed, intercession of, 389, n.; unconcern for their own safety, 448; the living, proclaim the virtues of their teachers, 455; joy of, under trouble wonderful, 461.
Salvation, obtained by few without threats, 392; precepts of, not hindered by the body, 472.
Sand, the boundary of the sea, 404; house built on, 446.
Satan aims most at the advanced, 334, 342; messengers of, 337; would have men reckoned gods, 338; called to account by Jehovah, 338; accuses Job, 339; assails him, 339; foiled by Job's patience, 341; man has nothing in common with, 343; his rage against Antioch, 344; how he resisted, 357; his spite at Job, 366; greatest efforts abortive, 367, 386; most defeated by the righteous in adversity, 371; arts of, to keep alive anger, 398; attempts of, thwarted by God, 419, 439; specially flourishes amidst oaths, 433; agency of, in the case of Saul and the honey, 434, 436; reason of, urging Jonathan to eat, 434; a fowler, 441; service of, often hard, 469; author of swearing, 470; our sole enemy, 476; disappointed at the Emperor's clemency, 485.
Saul, would not from hatred name David, 393; his prohibition to eat defeated, 433, 436; rashness of, 433, 436; grief over Jonathan's confession, 436; likely consequences of his oath, 437.
Scene of remarkable events affects us, 467.
School, severity of, 381, 449.
Sciences, application to spiritual subjects, 407.
Scripture Holy, as a lyre and a trumpet, 331; flowery meadow, 331; a mine of wisdom, 332; to be alleged in teaching, 336, 337; allegorical sense of, 338, n.; course of reading, 347, 348, 358, ns.; food from, 348; consolation from every part of, 391, 394; an instance, 391; not needed in the first ages, 400; entirely agrees, 403; slowness in explaining, 446; sense of, with the clergy, 447; accounts of the faithful verified in living Saints, 455.
Seal, set on confiscated houses, 427.
Seasons, order and harmony of, 402.
Secrecy, a sign of guilt, 360.
Sedition, state of Antioch after, 344, sqq.; raised by a few strangers, 347, 355, 381; offenders in, punished, 362; what befel messengers of, 382; how punished, 455; turned to the honour of the city, Bishop and Emperor, 482.
Self-possession, the best defence against dangers, 446.
Septuagint, followed by St. Chrysostom, 340, n.
Sermons, daily during Lent, 379, n.
Servants, sitting with, 345; consulting with, 363; dare not name their masters, 394; runaway, how they break their chains, 403; their spiritual good, needs attention, 405; have masters to overcome sloth, 429; flogging of, 432; not remitting debts at their master's bidding, 478.
Servility to the powerful, 474, n.
Severity before indulgence, 449.
Shame, of sinning before inferiors, 428; of not serving God better after great mercies, 438; to wait for advances to reconciliation, 474.
Sheep, parable of, 430.
Ship without pilot and crew, 408.
Shipwreck in retrospect, 426; spectators of, help by their prayers, 426; of the state, 452.
Sick, the, glutton a pitiable object, 387.
Sickle, flying, seen by the Prophet, 443.
Sickness, borne cheerfully, 332; no bar to zeal, 334; proves wealth vain, 351; no great evil, 397; past is pleasant to remember, 420; an instructor, 429; of St. Chrysostom, 464.
Silence, from suspicion, 426.
Significant, 480; the only hope of offenders, 484.
Simplicity of the country clergy, 465; of the Apostles, 466.
Sin, most hurtful in good men, 334; comes not of God's work, 335; pardon of, through affliction, 340, 387; shared by indifference, 348; how focused in pride, 348; pardon of, through alms, 351; through forgiving others, 355; by Priests, 356; on repentance, 362; to be reproved, 360; our own to be examined, 360; sure to find us out, 363, 378; removed through tribulation, 365, 385; alone to be dreaded, 372, 374, 387; blotted out by grief, 376, 461; by death, 376, 390; here punished better, 385; is misery punishment aside, 387; strikes dumb, 393; consciousness of makes cowards, 396; makes vulnerable, 397; to abstain from, no labour, 398; those easily avoided most punished, 411; forgiven, not to be forgotten, 418; the skein of our, 433; increased by frequent instruction, 438; remitted in the Eucharist, 444, n.; is dishonour, 456; great witness against, perpetuated, 466; excludes from holy Communion, 472; *all*, exposed at the Judgment, 430.
Sinner, the, like chaff, 397.
Sisters dividing an inheritance in peace, 402.
Slander, to be buried, 360; a snare of Satan, 360.
Sleep, sweet to the weary, 352; a medicine, 395.
Sloth, requires chastisement, 431; banished by fear, 439; danger of, under prosperity, 452, 463.
Snares, beset us on all sides, 440; wife, children, etc., may become, 441; same, catch men again, 441.
Sobriety, needful before going to church, 400; of country people, 466.
Socrates, on the faculty of women for learning, 470, n.; opinions on punishment, 375, n.
Sodom, its greatness no defense, 456; a perpetual witness, 466.
Soldiers, Christians are, 357; Christian, incapacitated by dread, 376; employed at the trials at Antioch, 426; intemperate particularly in battle, 433; on guard prevent robbers, 439; alert for conquest, 459; reverence their officers, 472.
Solomon, made trial of luxury, 352;

his thoughts on mirth, 440; learned in Art and Science by God, 456.
Sores, treatment of, 387.
Sorrow, an occasion of joy to Saints, 461.
Soul, the, to be adorned for Christ's dwelling, 350; medicine for, 358; the only proper object of concern, 397; subject to infirmity to prevent pride, 414; wounded by swearing, 438; stedfast, is proof against danger, 446; of unconverted, an old wine-skin, 449; philosophy of the even, in all events, 454; dignity of, in virtue, 457; like the body as affected from without, 462; the seat of philosophy, 465; beauty of, to be admired, 466; under the fear of God like a rusty tool in the furnace, 480; sign of greatness of, looking to God, 482.
Spark, falling on the ocean, 460.
Speculations, on the Universe above us, 411; folly of, 421; improper on Divine commands, 447.
Speech, how precious, is certain, 332; how restrained, 397.
Spider, not esteemed because he toils for himself, 420.
Spirit Holy, gives matter for discourse, 332, 347; all His gifts munificent, 332; His gold needs His flame, 332; enters not where wrath is, 479.
Stability, type of, 402.
Stadium, 416, n.
Stars, like flowers, 408.
State, without Rulers, illustrated, 381; dependence of members on each other in, 417; not saved by multitude, 457.
Statuary's skill on rude materials, 414.
Statues, of the Emperor demolished, 344; a device of Satan, 439; Theodosius's mother and wife, dishonoured, 484, n.; for humaneness, 485; of Constantine, dishonoured, 485.
Stibadium, 489, n.
Storm, approaching, 446.
Striving, lawful, what, 357, n.
Substance, 362.
Suffering, for Christ, our glory, 447; fellowship in, soothes, 339.
Sun, transcends nature, 404; a bridegroom: not a god, 410; in constant motion, 419.
Superfluous, what seems, may be full of Divine wisdom, 332.
Surfeit, breaks sleep, 352.
Suspiciousness from guilt, 396.
Swearer, ought to reflect on martyrdom of St. John B., 432; house of, ruined, 443.
Swearing, 363, 370, 379, 394, 417, 424, 443; easily overcome, 370, 379, 388, 398, 437; methods of overcoming, 370, 379; the excuse answered when imposed by another, 380, 398; no excuse that others swear, 388; insult to God shewn by, 304; substitute for, 398, 481; mode adopted to overcome, 399; the easier the worse, 411; abstaining from a Divine precept, 425; of contraries common in many relations, 432; Satan lies in wait for, 432, 433; doubling of Saul in, 437; to abstain from easier than to obey the Emperor, 437; forbidden by Christ, 444; worse in Christians than in Jews, 469; comes of negligence, 470; all, from Satan, 470; difficulty of curing, imaginary, 479; not to be cured little by little, 480.
Sympathy in the joy of others, 429.
Synagogue at Daphne, 457, n.

TABLE of spiritual food from Holy Writ, 348; of the rich not relished, 351.
Talents, parable of, 348; ten thousand, parable of, 355, 478.
Tarentines, drunkenness and luxury of, 400, n.
Taxes, 363, 398; indignation caused by, 374.
Teacher, the, a title of St. Paul, 332; to take fit seasons, 413; number of natural, 430; differs from the artificer as to consequences, shares in the merit of his scholars, 487.
Temperance, naturally approves itself, 428; practice of severe, 429.
Temple, the, honoured by God, dishonoured by sinners, 456.
Thankfulness, in trouble rewarded, 341.
Thanksgiving, contrasted with blasphemy, 342, 343; equals crossbearing, 385; for favours procures others, 412; repeated, 412, 425, 450; in distress, 452; for evils, 489.
Theatres, forbidden, 359; one opposite the church, 439; cause many evils, 442, 455,
Theodosius, statues of, thrown down, 344, 362; embassy to, 354; hopes from his piety and clemency, 355, 356, 453, 457; baptized, 355; compared to Ahasuerus, 356; tax levied by 361, n.; not present when insulted, 362; his religious character, 383, 487; opposite acts from, 383, n.; closing of the baths, 437; stopped public amusements as a punishment, 455; like a father in demeaning Antioch, 455; reverence of, for Priests, 483; reception of Flavian, 484; his upbraiding, restitution produced, 485; greater in pardoning than in succouring Antioch, 486; by pardoning shews the power of Christianity, 486; reasons for his expecting a reward from God, 487; an example to posterity, 487; bidden to consider the Judgment, 488; pardons Antioch, imitating Jesus, 488; proofs of his entire forgiveness, 488.
Thessalonica, massacre at, 383, n.
Thirst gives relish to drink, 352.
Thoughts, bad, how dispelled, 331; government of, 357.
Three Children, delivered by prayer, 367; song of, in use every where and always, 367, n.; a surpassing miracle variously tried upon, 367; the reverse of the idolaters, 368; example of, 376, 385; they and their executioners like gold and hay, 385; freedom and wisdom of, 386; motives in disobeying the king, 387.
Times, stated, proper for contending with particular bad habits, 370, 388; different things for different times, 401.
Timothy, St., power of, with God, 332; his labours, 333, 335; his abstinence, 333; spiritual son and yokefellow to St. Paul, 334; resolution in self-discipline, 335.
Title, the most illustrious of St. Paul's, 447; of worldly dignity soon perishes, 447; of metropolis taken from Antioch, 455.
Tongue, a snare, 443.
Torture, by scourging, 426, 474, n.
Translation of Scriptures, source of error in, 405, n.
Transubstantiation, 354, n.
Treason, a subject of fear to kings, 460.
Trees, each kind has its excellence, 417; roots of, bitter, 462.
Trials at Antioch, terrors of, 426, 453; painful instance at, 426.
Tribulation of Saints a means of pardon, 340; increased reward, 340, 342; a sign of God's love, 342; temptation by, 342; permitted for good, 344, 365; a seed time; 364; a rain, 365; strengthens the good, 366; not removed until amendment, 366; exalts men, 369; suffering unjustly like to, 385; comes before joy, 449; present, subdued by bright prospect, 450; to the godly like a spark on the ocean, 460.
Tribunals, secular, closed at midday, why, 160; at Antioch, 426.
Truth, shadows of, attained by the heathen, 386, n.; to be applied variously, 435.
Tutors compel to good conduct, 453.

UNBELIEVERS, how affected by the example of Christians, 405, 486.
Union of men for various purposes, 452.

VALENS excommunicated, 481, n.
Valentinus on matter, 413, n.
Vanity, being subject to, 411.
Vengeance on our enemies defeats

its own end, 475; God the Judge for, 475.
Venture, by heathens acting upon Prophecy, 377; its lessons, 401.
Verses, division of, in Bible among the ancients, 446, n.
Vessels, earthen, 409.
Vice, hatred of, while followed, 429.
View, from the top of mountains, 441.
Vine, Jerusalem so called, 467.
Virgin, the, Mary, invocation of, 389, n.
Virgins, the ten, parable of, 388; dancing, 402; God's disapproval manifested through, 434.
Virtue, like a fine dress, looks best on the person, 380; applauded by its opponents, 387; a blessing, reward aside, 387; some, natural, 429; promoted by teachers, 429; school of, war, 435; bred by fear, 439; fruit of, rooted above, 451; test by perseverance in prosperity, 452; the defence of a people, 456; easier in country life, 465.
Void, meaning in Gen. i., 391, n.
Voyage, length of, no help to the merchant, 451.
Vow, of Jephthah, what resulted, 454.

WAR, a religious matter with the Jews, 435; defeat in from sin, 435.
arriors, great, by their presence secure victory, 454.

Washing of hands before taking the Bible, 394; before receiving the sacred elements, 479.
Watchfulness over those in our charge, 354; needed especially after deliverances, 453.
Water, honey to the thirsty, 352; bearing the earth a marvel, 403; fixed in the heavens unnatural, 404; in constant motion, 419; drawing of, 446.
Wicked, often prosper here, 340.
Wilkinson on the dancing represented in hieroglyphics, 470, n.
Will, rests with, to cure the soul, 397; in man effects what nature does in brutes, 420.
Wings of zeal, 335; of birds, use of, 441; of the flying sickle, 443.
Wine, use of, lawful, 333, 348; to be used for health, 335; perfumed, 352.
Wine-skin, 449.
Winter, good of, felt afterwards, 459.
Wisdom, force of, upon the wicked, 386; to be alone sought, 463; among the humble, 465.
Wives have husbands as instructors, 430; keeping to, 435.
Women, their prayers heard, 356; at Antioch, wretchedness during disorder, 427; case of two, 426; delight in their jewels, 449; cured of finery by the thoughts of St. Paul, 450; dancing, 470.
Woods, rot from immersion, 403.

Word of God never fails, 377; sufficient to effect any thing, 410.
Words, exact use of, 332; not necessary for instruction, 402.
Wordsworth's Vernal Ode, 420, n.
Works, good, may breed presumption, 337; to be persevered in, 343; needful with fasting, 359; each man's, the measure of his moral nature, 430; bring joy, 451; laid up in heaven, 451.
Workshops closed, 439.
World, its wisdom vain, 332; Christians in, are strangers, 457; converted by simple men, 466.
Worm, undying, 473.
Wounds of the soul, 438.
Wrath of God pacified by our forgiveness, 473.
Wrestlers, stripped for contest, 339, 357; give advantage to shew their skill, 339, n.; rules for, 357, n.; must strive, 364, n.; tried in the lists, 446.

XENOPHON, on dancing, 470, n.

YOUTH requires discipline, 334.

ZEAL overcomes infirmity, 335; and difficulties, 342; of one reforms many, 344; of inhabitants of Antioch for the faith, 456.
Zedekiah's oath brought ruin, 468; a witness against breaking oaths, 469.

HOMILIES ON THE STATUES.

INDEX OF TEXTS.

	PAGE		PAGE		PAGE		PAGE
Gen. i. 1	390, 395	2 Kings xxv. 1–4.	468	Ps. ci. 5	360	Isa. xl. 22	409
i. 12, LXX.	391	xxv. 4–7.	469	cii. 25, 26	410	xl. 42	419
i. 26	362, 391	xxv. 9	468	ciii. 15.	335	xlii. 6, 7	427
ii. 17.	76	xxv. 13–20.	469	civ. 24.	408	xlv. 2	390
iii. 8	396	2 Chron. iii. 3.	456	cvi. 2	362	lvii. 17	375
iii. 5	413	Neh. ix. 33	458	cvii. 16	390	lviii. 3, 7	358
iii. 9, LXX.	393	Job i. 9, 10	338	cxii. 1	462	lviii. 4, 5	417
iii. 10–12	422	i. 21	339, 366, 385, 442, 461	cxii. 9	451	lix. 2	387
iv. 9	423	ii. 3, LXX.	388	cxix. 1.	462	lxiv. 4.	372
iv. 13, LXX.	423	ii. 5, 6.	338	cxix. 71	337	lxv. 8	467
ix. 2	395	ii. 8, 12	344, 366	cxxiv. 1	397	Jer. iv. 3	364
xiii. 13	456	ii. 9, LXX.	428	cxxv. 5	364	v. 22	404
xxii. 12	434	ii. 13	344	cxxx. 3	472	vii. 11	456
xlii. 21	363	xxvi. 7	403	cxxxvi. 6.	403	viii. 7.	420
Ex. ii.	342	xxxi. 32	442	cxxxix. 7.	377	ix. 17, 18.	346
xvi. 33.	456	xxxvii. 15.	412	cxl. 3	420	xiv. 5	358
xx. 10.	422	xxxviii. 4.	403	cxli. 2.	370	xiv. 7	458
xx. 13.	421	Ps. i. 1.	462	cxliv. 11–15.	340	xv. 1	430, 473
xxiii. 1, LXX.	359	i. 5.	397	cxlviii. 4.	404	xv. 19.	451
xxxii. 10.	484	ii. 13	462	Prov. v. 3, 4	435	xviii. 7, 8.	377
xxxii. 31, 32.	355	v. 9, LXX.	370	v. 15.	435	xxiii. 23	410
xxxiv. 28.	456	xiv. 6	369	v. 19, LXX.	435	xxiii. 24	410
Num. xi. 5	384	xvi. 1	410	vi. 2	443	xxviii. 9	414
xii. 14	476	xviii. 42	353	vi. 6.	420	xxix. 9.	424
xiv. 4, etc.	384	xix. 1	401, 409, 419	vi. 30, 32, LXX.	411	xxxii. 5	469
Deut. vi. 7.	388	xix. 3.	402	xix. 12	356	xxxviii. 17–23	468
vi. 11, 12.	452	xix. 6.	410	xxiv. 17.	474	xxxix. 2.	468
xii. 31.	434	xxiv. 2	403	xxvii. 1.	480	xxxix. 8.	468
xxi. 18.	422	xxvi. 10	370	xxvii. 7.	352	xxxix. 9.	468
Josh. i. 5	382	xxxiii. 12.	462	xxviii. 1.	396	lii. 6	468
Judges xi. 31	434	xxxiv. 21.	373	xix. 12	356	Ezek. ix. 4	462
xi. 39, 40.	434	xxxix. 6	348	Eccles. i. 2.	427, 440, 465	xii. 13	469
1 Sam. ii. 2	412	xlv. 1	369, 370	i. 9.	364	xvii. 2, 3	467
xiv. 26, LXX.	433	xlix. 3.	369	ii. 1	342	xvii. 5, 6	467
xiv. 27.	434	xlix. 4.	370	v. 12	352	xvii. 7, 8	467
xiv. 28.	434	xlix. 6.	348	vii. 9.	440	xvii. 9.	468
xiv. 36.	435	lvii. 4.	369	ix. 8, 3	435	xvii. 12.	468
xiv. 36, 37	436	lviii. 4.	370	Isa. i. 3.	420	xvii. 14.	468
xiv. 38.	436	lxxii. 18	452	i. 30	345	xvii. 16–20.	468
xiv. 40, LXX.	436	lxxviii. 15	396	vi. 3	394	xviii. 32	462
xiv. 42, 43	436	lxxviii. 24	410	x. 22	457	xxviii. 9	414
xiv. 44	436	lxxviii. 34	452	xi. 6, 7	356	Dan. iii. 2.	367
xiv. 45	436	lxxx. 16, LXX.	352	xiv. 11	414	iii. 4, 6	368
1 Kings iv. 29	456	lxxxi. 16, LXX.	352	xiv. 13, 14	414	iii. 12	368
xiv. 24, LXX.	433	xciv. 12	462	xxii. 4.	461	iii. 15	386
xviii. 17, 18.	396	xciv. 19	431	xxvi. 12, LXX.	387	iii. 17	342
xx. 27	393	xcv. 4.	403	xxx. 1.	356	iii. 18	368
2 Kings i. 2	353			xl. 2	391	iii. 25	367

HOMILIES ON THE STATUES: INDEX OF TEXTS.

Reference	PAGE
Dan. iii. 26	386
iii. 28	387
viii. 10	386
Hos. viii. 4	356
ix. 10	467
xiii. 14	390
Joel i. 3	489
i. 17	358
ii. 13	364
ii. 16	358
Amos v. 8	412
vi. 6	462
vii. 14	376
viii. 9	346
Jonah i. 5	480
ii. 4	480
iii.	376
iii. 7	358
ii. 9	377
iii. 10	358, 480
Micah i. 4	462
Zech. v. 1, 2	466
v. 1, 4	443
vii. 10, LXX.	473
viii. 17	473
Tobit iv. 16	428
Wisd. vii. 1	340
xiii. 5	401
Ecclus. ii. 3	340
ii. 4, 5	461
iii. 21–23	421
iv. 3	385
ix. 3, 8	435
iv. 13	438, 440
ix. 20	442
xi. 2, 3	458
xiii. 15	429
xiv. 2	462
xvii. 31	410
xviii. 25	418
xix. 10	360
xxiii. 10	438
xliv. 17	387
Matt. v. 3–10	462
v. 11, 12	339, 461
v. 16	405
v. 23, 24	476, 478
v. 28	443
v. 34	444, 471
v. 36	394
v. 45	419
vi. 12	355, 477, 488
vi. 14	478
vi. 19	451
vi. 26	420

Reference	PAGE
Matt. vii. 1	361
vii. 12	428
vii. 14	384
vii. 24–27	365
vii. 26, 27	446
ix. 16, 17	449
x. 16	369, 420
x. 28	385
x. 38	376
xv. 17, 18	361
xviii. 12, 13	430
xviii. 24, 28	478
xviii. 32, 33	355
xix. 16	349
xix. 21	349
xxiii. 37	457
xxv. 10	388
xxv. 21	425
xxv. 26, 27	425
xxv. 35	388
Mark ii. 21	449
vi. 18	343
Luke v. 36	441
vi. 23	339
xi. 24, 26	464
xi. 32	480
xii. 33	451
xvi. 25	340, 385
xviii. 12	357
xxiii. 34	488
John vii. 11	393
x. 11	354
xi. 5	373
xvi. 22	451
xviii. 1	413
Acts iii. 12	338
v. 15	367
v. 41	461
xi. 26	355, 456
xi. 28, 29	456
xiv. 11	409
xvi. 22	451
xvi. 24	337
xvii. 25	410
xix. 12	367
xxvi. 28	448, 449
xxvi. 29	448
xxviii. 20	448
Rom. i. 18	401
i. 20	401, 411, 419
i. 21, 22	409
i. 32	424
ii. 3	424
ii. 4	424
ii. 5, 6	424

Reference	PAGE
Rom. ii. 9	424
ii. 10	423
ii. 12	423
ii. 14, 15	423
ii. 16	423
v. 3	449, 450, 463
v. 3, 4	366
v. 3–5	340
viii. 18	340
viii. 21	411
viii. 22, 23	372
viii. 28	452
ix. 2	461
ix. 27	457
xii. 7	420
xii. 14	384
xii. 15, 16	458
xiii. 1	382
1 Cor. ii. 9	348, 372
ii. 15	407
iii. 6	357
iv. 11	340
iv. 17	333
vi. 1	445
ix. 21	448
ix. 26	358
ix. 27	334
x. 13	382
xi. 6	373
xi. 7	362
xi. 31, 32	376
xii. 21	417
xiv. 20	374
xv. 31	385
xv. 32	339
xv. 38	407
xvi. 10	334
xvi. 19	339
2 Cor. i. 1	333
i. 8, 9	431
iv. 7	409
iv. 17, 18	450
vi. 14, 15	417
vi. 19	412
vii. 10	375, 462
xi. 30	449
xi. 23, 25	449
xii. 2, 4	337
xii. 6	338, 409
xii. 7	337
xii. 8, 9	337
xii. 9, 10	449
xii. 21	359
Gal. iii. 24	392
iv. 24	394

Reference	PAGE
Gal. v. 15	359
vi. 14	334, 441
vi. 17	443
Ephes. iii. 17	466
iii. 20	482
iv. 1	448
iv. 26	476
iv. 29	442
v. 4	442
vi. 12	357
Phil. i. 1	333, 448
i. 14	448
i. 29	449
ii. 19	333
ii. 22	334
ii. 25	409
iv. 4	458, 459
Col. i. 1	333
i. 24	449, 463
iii. 1	416
iii. 2	441
1 Thess. ii. 9	353
ii. 14	339
ii. 18	342
v. 11	347
v. 18	452
2 Thess. iii. 10	420
1 Tim. i. 9	381, 392
i. 12, 13	418
i. 13	373
ii. 7	332
v. 6	373, 442
v. 22	331
v. 23	331, 409
vi. 7	385
vi. 8	460
vi. 17	344, 348, 351
2 Tim. ii. 5, 6	357
ii. 9	448, 450
ii. 26	333
iv. 20	409
Philem. i.	445, 447
Heb. ix. 4	456
xi. 10	456
xii. 6	340
xii. 9	392
xiii. 3	458
xiii. 5	382
Jas. ii. 18	373
v. 17	340
v. 20	471
1 Pet. ii. 19, 20	385
iv. 8	477